Putnam's Contemporary Dictionaries

French-English
Anglais-Français

Putnam's
Contemporary Dictionaries

French-English
Anglais-Français

**GUSTAVE RUDLER, Agr. des Let.,
Doct. ès Let., M.A.**
Formerly Professor of French Literature,
University of Oxford

NORMAN C. ANDERSON, L-ès-L., M.A.
Formerly Senior Lecturer in French,
University of Glasgow

Revised by:
ANTHONY C. BRENCH, M.A.
CHRISTOPHER D. BETTINSON, B.A.
W. MARY BILLINGTON, M.A.
FRANÇOISE SALGUES, L.ès L.
Lecturers in French, University of Glasgow

CHARLES BERLITZ
MARY SOLAK
Special Editors to the American Edition

G. P. PUTNAM'S SONS New York

General Editor: J. B. Foreman, M.A.
Executive Editor: Iseabail C. Macleod, M.A.

Contents

Table des Matières

Introduction

In order to economize space we have not given the feminine form of those French adjectives which regularly form their feminine by adding *e* to the masculine form, e.g., *crue, grivoise, guindée,* will be found under the masculine form only, *cru, grivois, guindé.* The feminine form has been indicated in the case of all other adjectives, e.g., *audacieux, -euse, bon, bonne, décisif, -ive; moyen, -enne, premier, -ière, rêveur, -euse.* We have also on occasion omitted the adverb (often formed by adding *-ment* to the feminine singular of the adjective) and the verbal nouns in *-ment* and *-age,* where the presence of the adjective and the verb should enable the reader to recognize a family of words from one main entry.

In the case of adjectives of nationality, the French translation has been written beginning with a small letter. When used as a noun, however, such words begin with a capital letter.

Abbreviations used in the Dictionary

ABRÉVIATIONS		ABBREVIATIONS
adjectif	a	adjective
adverbe	ad	adverb
adjectif et nom	an	adjective and noun
architecture	archit	architecture
automobile	aut	automobile
aviation	av	aviation
botanique	bot	botany
chimie	chem	chemistry
conjonction	cj	conjunction
colonial	col	colonial
commerce	com	commerce
comparatif	comp	comparative
cuisine	cook	cooking
datif	dat	dative
article défini	def art	definite article
disjonctif	disj	disjunctive
ecclésiastique	eccl	ecclesiastical
électricité	el	electricity
exclamation	excl	exclamation
féminin	f	feminine
familier	fam	familiar
figuré	fig	figuratively
finances	fin	finance
gouvernement	govt	government
article indéfini	indef art	indefinite article
interrogatif	inter	interrogative
invariable	inv	invariable
juridique	jur	juridical
masculin	m	masculine
médecine	med	medicine

vi

militaire	**mil**	military
mines	**min**	mining
musique	**mus**	music
nom	**n**	noun
nautique, marine	**naut**	nautical
nom féminin	**nf**	noun feminine
nom masculin	**nm**	noun masculine
numéral	**num**	numeral
	o.s.	oneself
péjoratif	**pej**	pejorative
personne	**pers**	person
pluriel	**pl**	plural
pronom	**pn**	pronoun
politique	**pol**	politics
participe passé	**pp**	past participle
préposition	**prep**	preposition
passé	**pt**	past tense
quelque chose	**qch**	
quelqu'un	**qn**	
relatif	**rel**	relative
chemins de fer	**rl**	railroad
singulier	**s**	singular
écossais	**Scot**	Scottish
argot, populaire	**sl.**	slang
	s.o.	someone
	sth	something
superlatif	**sup**	superlative
technique	**tec**	technical
télévision	**TV**	television
généralement	**usu**	usually
verbe	**v**	verb
verbe intransitif	**vi**	verb intransitive
verbe impersonnel	**v imp**	verb impersonal
verbe intransitif, réfléchi	**vir**	verb intransitive, reflexive
verbe réfléchi	**vr**	verb reflexive
verbe transitif	**vt**	verb transitive
verbe transitif, intransitif	**vti**	verb transitive, intransitive
verbe transitif, intransitif, réfléchi	**vtir**	verb transitive, intransitive, reflexive
verbe transitif, réfléchi	**vtr**	verb transitive, reflexive
vulgaire	**vul**	vulgar

English and French Numerals

CARDINAL NUMBERS—NOMBRES CARDINAUX

1	one—un, une	11	eleven—onze
2	two—deux	12	twelve—douze
3	three—trois	13	thirteen—treize
4	four—quatre	14	fourteen—quatorze
5	five—cinq	15	fifteen—quinze
6	six—six	16	sixteen—seize
7	seven—sept	17	seventeen—dix-sept
8	eight—huit	18	eighteen—dix-huit
9	nine—neuf	19	nineteen—dix-neuf
10	ten--dix	20	twenty—vingt

vii

21 twenty-one—vingt et un
22 twenty-two—vingt-deux
30 thirty—trente
40 forty—quarante
50 fifty—cinquante
60 sixty—soixante
70 seventy—soixante-dix
71 seventy-one—soixante-et-onze
72 seventy-two—soixante-douze
80 eighty—quatre-vingts
81 eighty-one—quatre-vingt-un

90 ninety—quatre-vingt-dix
91 ninety-one—quatre-vingt-onze
100 a hundred—cent
101 one hundred and one—cent un
300 three hundred—trois cents
301 three hundred and one—trois cent un
1000 a thousand—mille
5000 five thousand—cinq mille
1,000,000 a million—un million

ORDINAL NUMBERS—NOMBRES ORDINAUX

First—premier, -ère
Second—deuxième; second, -e
Third—troisième
Fourth—quatrième
Fifth—cinquième
Sixth—sixième
Seventh—septième
Eighth—huitième
Ninth—neuvième
Tenth—dixième
Eleventh—onzième
Twelfth—douzième
Thirteenth—treizième
Fourteenth—quatorzième
Fifteenth—quinzième
Sixteenth—seizième
Seventeenth—dix-septième
Eighteenth—dix-huitième
Nineteenth—dix-neuvième
Twentieth—vingtième
Twenty-first—vingt-et-unième
Twenty-second—vingt-deuxième
Thirtieth—trentième
Fortieth—quarantième

Fiftieth—cinquantième
Sixtieth—soixantième
Seventieth—soixante-dixième
Seventy-first—soixante-et-onzième
Seventy-second—soixante-douzième
Eightieth—quatre-vingtième
Eighty-first—quatre-vingt-unième
Ninetieth—quatre-vingt-dixième
Ninety-first—quatre-vingt-onzième
Hundredth—centième
Hundred-and-first—cent-unième
Two hundredth—deux-centième
Two hundred-and-first—deux-cent-unième
Thousandth—millième
Thousand-and-first—mille-et-unième
Thousand-and-second—mille-deuxième
Millionth—millionième

viii

Pronunciation

A simple and accurate transcription of pronunciation is given by the phonetic system of the International Phonetic Association. Although it is not as widely used in the United States as it is in other countries, we thought that its use in this dictionary would help readers to feel at ease with the spoken language. The phonetic transcription of English words is that of Received Pronunciation. It does not mention regional variations. The same convention has been applied to the transcription of French words, Standard French being roughly the pronunciation of educated people from the north of France. The readers will find below a comparative presentation of phonetic symbols (IPA) both French and English.

Length of vowels is noted thus: short—no symbol
    long—[ː] after the vowel
In English, stress is shown by the symbol ['] before the stressed syllable and also secondary stress by the symbol [ˌ].

Pour la transcription phonétique nous avons employé le système de l'Association internationale de phonétique, système qui, nous semble-t-il, permettra aux lecteurs de ce dictionnaire de se sentir à l'aise avec la langue parlée. La transcription des mots anglais est celle de la prononciation reçue, et ne tient pas compte des variations régionales. Pour le français, la même convention a été suivie. La prononciation donnée ne tient également pas compte des différences locales.

Les lecteurs trouveront en bas une présentation comparative de symboles phonétiques pour les deux langues.

La longueur des voyelles est indiquée de la façon suivante:
    courte—pas de symbole
    longue—[ː] après la voyelle
En anglais l'accentuation d'une voyelle est donnée par le symbole ['] placé devant le syllabe accentué, et l'accentuation secondaire par le symbole [ˌ].

CONSONNES CONSONANTS

p	poupée	p	puppy	(in French [p, t, k] are not aspirated)
t	tente	t	tent	(en français [p, t, k] ne sont pas aspirés)
k	coq	k	cork	
b	bombe	b	bomb	

d	dinde	*d*	daddy
g	gringalet	*g*	gag
f	ferme	*f*	farm
v	vite	*v*	very
s	souci	*s*	so
z	cousin	*z*	cousin
		θ	thorn
		ð	that
ʃ	chose	ʃ	sheep
		tʃ	church
ʒ	juge	ʒ	pleasure
		dʒ	judge
w	oui	*w*	wall
y	huit		
j	hier	*j*	yet
		h	hat
		x	loch (*Scots*)
r	rentrer	*r*	rat

(English *r* is pronounced with the tip of the tongue against the front of the palate, French *r* with the back of the tongue against the back of the palate, not unlike, though, softer, than the Scots [*x*] of loch)

(le *r* anglais se prononce avec le bout de la langue contre le palais)

m	maman	*m*	mummy
n	non	*n*	no
ɲ	campagne		
		ŋ	singing
l	lait	*l*	little

(in English the pronunciation of the two [*l*] of little is not the same. There is no such difference in French [*l*] as in lot)

(en anglais la prononciation des deux [*l*] de little n'est pas semblable)

VOYELLES VOWELS

i	ici	*i*	heel
		i	hit
e	est, été	*e*	said
ɛ	mère	ɛə	there
a	patte	æ	bat
a	pâte	*a:*	car
ɔ	donne	ɔ	lot
o	côte	ɔ:	all
u	cou	*u*	put
u:	cour	*u:*	shoe
		ʌ	but
œ:	beurre	ə:	bird
ə	le	ə	rodent
ø	feu	(mouth set as for [ə:] of bird, lips rounded as for [*u:*] of shoe
y	rue	(mouth set as for [*i:*], lips rounded as for [*u:*]

(these equivalents are obviously only approximate because French vowels and English vowels are produced differently)

(ces équivalents ne sont pas absolument semblables, les voyelles françaises et anglaises se prononcent différemment)

nasales (nasals); these French vowels are produced by pronouncing the corresponding oral vowel through the nose
ɑ̃ sang ɛ̃ vin œ̃ lundi ɔ̃ long

diphthongs (diphthongs)
iə beer ei date ai life au fowl ɔi boil ou low uə poor

French — English

A

à [ɑ] *prep* to, at, in, on, according to, by, of, with *etc*.

abaissement [abɛsmɑ̃] *nm* lowering, falling, degradation, derogation, humiliation.

abaisser [abɛse] *vt* to lower, bring down; *vr* to fall away, stoop, droop, demean oneself.

abandon [abɑ̃dɔ̃] *nm* surrender, relinquishing, withdrawal, desertion, neglect, abandon; **à l'—** neglected, at random.

abandonné [abɑ̃dɔne] *a* forsaken, forlorn, stray, desolate, derelict, shameless.

abandonnement [abɑ̃dɔnmɑ̃] *nm* surrender, desertion, abandon, degradation, profligacy.

abandonner [abɑ̃dɔne] *vt* to surrender, give up, relinquish, make over (to **à**), desert; *vr* to give oneself up (to), indulge (in).

abasourdir [abazurdiːr] *vt* to astound, take aback, bewilder, stun.

abat-jour [abaʒuːr] *nm* lampshade, awning.

abats [aba] *nm pl* offal.

abattage [abataːʒ] *nm* felling, slaughtering.

abattement [abatmɑ̃] *nm* dejection, prostration.

abattoir [abatwaːr] *nm* slaughterhouse, shambles.

abattre [abatr] *vt* to knock down, overthrow, bring (pull, blow) down, fell, slaughter, depress, lower, lay; *vr* to fall (swoop) down, crash, abate, become downhearted.

abattu [abaty] *a* depressed, despondent, downcast.

abbaye [abɛ(j)i] *nf* abbey.

abbé [abe] *nm* abbot, priest.

abbesse [abɛs] *nf* abbess.

abcès [apsɛ] *nm* abscess, gathering, fester.

abdiquer [abdike] *vt* to abdicate, (*post*) resign.

abeille [abɛːj] *nf* bee.

aberration [abɛr(r)asjɔ̃] *nf* aberration, derangement, (*mental*) lapse.

abhorrer [abɔr(r)e] *vt* to abhor, detest, loathe.

abîme [abiːm] *nm* abyss, chasm, deep.

abîmer [abime] *vt* to injure, damage, spoil; *vr* to be swallowed up, be sunk, get damaged.

abject [abʒɛkt] *a* despicable, vile.

abjurer [abʒyre] *vt* to abjure, recant.

ablation [ablasjɔ̃] *nf* ablation, removal, excision.

ablution [ablysjɔ̃] *nf* ablution.

abnégation [abnegasjɔ̃] *nf* sacrifice, selflessness.

aboiement [abwamɑ̃] *nm* bark(ing), baying.

abois [abwa] *nm pl* **aux —** at bay, hard pressed.

abolir [abɔliːr] *vt* to abolish.

abolition [abɔlisjɔ̃] *nf* abolition.

abominable [abɔminabl] *a* abominable, loathsome, wretched.

abomination [abɔminasjɔ̃] *nf* abomination; **avoir en —** to detest.

abondamment [abɔ̃damɑ̃] *ad* abundantly.

abondance [abɔ̃daːs] *nf* abundance, plenty; **en —** galore.

abondant [abɔ̃dɑ̃] *a* abundant, plentiful, copious.

abonder [abɔ̃de] *vi* to abound, be plentiful.

abonnement [abɔnmɑ̃] *nm* subscription, installment; **carte d'—** season-ticket.

abonné [abɔne] *n* subscriber, season-ticket holder.

s'abonner [sabɔne] *vr* to subscribe (to **à**), take a season-ticket.

abord [abɔːr] *nm* access, approach, landing; **d'—** first, to begin with; **de prime —, au premier —** at first sight; **dès l'—** from the start.

abordable [abɔrdabl] *a* approachable, accessible.

abordage [abɔrdaːʒ] *nm* landing, boarding, collision.

aborder [abɔrde] *vi* to land; *vt* to approach, accost, board, tackle, collide.

aboutir [abutiːr] *vi* to lead (to **à**), end (in), result (in), succeed, come off.

aboyer [abwaje] *vi* to bark, bay.

abrasif [abrazif] *a* abrasive.

abrégé [abreʒe] *nm* abridgment, epitome.

abréger [abreʒe] *vt* to shorten, abbreviate, abridge; *vr* to grow shorter.

abreuver [abrœve] *vt* to water, soak; *vr* to drink, quench one's thirst.

abreuvoir [abrœvwaːr] *nm* wateringplace, drinking-trough.

abréviation [abrevjasjɔ̃] *nf* abbreviation, contraction.

abri [abri] *nm* shelter, cover; **à l'—** sheltered, immune.

abricot [abriko] *nm* apricot.

abricotier [abrikɔtje] *nm* apricot-tree.

abriter [abrite] *vt* to shelter, protect, house, shade; *vr* to take shelter.

abroger [abrɔʒe] *vt* to abrogate, repeal; *vr* to lapse.

abrupt [abrypt] *a* abrupt, sheer.

abrut [abryti] *a* besotted, sodden, stupefied, dazed; *nm* sot, idiot.

abrutir [abryti:r] *vt* to stupefy, besot.

abrutissant [abrytisã] *a* stupefying, degrading, killing.

absence [apsã:s] *nf* non-appearance.

absent [apsã] *a* not at home, vacant.

s'absenter [sapsãte] *vr* to absent oneself, stay away.

absinthe [apsɛ̃:t] *nf* absinthe, worm-wood.

absolu [apsɔly] *a* absolute, utter, unqualified.

absolument [apsɔlymã] *ad* absolute-ly, utterly; —! quite so, just so!

absolution [apsɔlysjɔ̃] *nf* absolution.

absorber [apsɔrbe] *vt* to absorb, engross; *vr* to become absorbed (in), pore (over **dans**).

absoudre [apsudr] *vt* to absolve, condone, exonerate.

s'abstenir [sapstəni:r] *vr* to abstain, eschew, refrain.

abstinence [apstinã:s] *nf* abstinence.

abstinent [apstinã] *a* abstinent; *n* teetotaller.

abstraction [apstraksjɔ̃] *nf* abstrac-tion; — **faite de** apart from, dis-regarding, setting aside

abstraire [apstrɛ:r] *vt* to abstract.

abstrait [apstrɛ] *a nm* abstract, absent-minded.

abstrus [apstry] *a* abstruse.

absurde [apsyrd] *a* ludicrous; *nm* absurd.

absurdité [apsyrdite] *nf* absurdity, nonsense.

abus [aby] *nm* abuse, misuse, error; — **de confiance** breach of faith.

abuser [abyze] *vi* to misuse, take advantage of; *vt* to delude; *vr* to delude oneself.

abusif, -ive [abysif, i:v] *a* contrary to usage, wrong, excessive.

acabit [akabi] *nm* (*of people*) nature, stamp.

académicien [akademisjɛ̃] *nm* aca-demician, member of the French Academy.

académie [akademi] *nf* academy, school, regional education unit, learn-ed society, riding-school.

académique [akademik] *a* academic (al), choice, distinguished.

acajou [akaʒu] *nm* mahogany.

acariâtre [akarjɑ:tr] *a* shrewish, bad-tempered, cantankerous.

accablant [akablã] *a* overwhelming, crushing, oppressive.

accablé [akable] *a* overwhelmed, overcome, prostrate.

accablement [akabləmã] *nm* dejec-tion, despondency, prostration.

accabler [akable] *vt* to overwhelm, overload, weigh down, snow under.

accalmie [akalmi] *nf* lull, respite.

accaparement [akaparmã] *nm* cor-nering, securing, monopoly.

accaparer [akapare] *vt* to corner, monopolize, hoard.

accéder [aksede] *vi* to accede, agree, have access.

accélération [akselerasjɔ̃] *nf* acceler-ation.

accélérateur [akseleratœ:r] *nm* accelerator.

accélérer [aks’elere] *vtr* to accelerate, quicken.

accent [aksã] *nm* accent, emphasis, stress; *pl* strains.

accentuation [aksãtɥasjɔ̃] *nf* ac-centuation.

accentuer [aksãtɥe] *vt* to accentuate, stress, emphasize, intensify; *vr* to become more marked.

acceptable [aksɛptabl] *a* reasonable.

acceptation [aksɛptasjɔ̃] *nf* accept-ance.

accepter [aksɛpte] *vt* to accept.

acception [aksɛpsjɔ̃] *nf* acceptation, meaning.

accès [aksɛ] *nm* access, approach, attack, fit, bout.

accessible [aksɛsibl] *a* available, open (to **à**).

accession [aksɛsjɔ̃] *nf* accession.

accessoire [aksɛswɑ:r] *a* adjunct, accessory, incidental; *nm* accessory; *pl* theatrical properties.

accident [aksidã] *nm* accident, mishap; (*of ground*) fold; **par** — accidentally, casually.

accidenté [aksidãte] *a* uneven, eventful; *n* victim (of accident).

accidentel, -elle [aksidãtɛl] *a* ac-cidental.

acclamation [aklamasjɔ̃] *nf* accla-mation; *pl* cheers.

acclamer [aklame] *vt* to acclaim, cheer.

acclimatation [aklimatasjɔ̃] *nf* ac-climatization.

acclimater [aklimate] *vt* to acclimat-ize.

s'accointer [sakwɛ̃te] *vr* to take up (with **avec**).

accolade [akɔlad] *nf* embrace, ac-colade, bracket.

accoler [akɔle] *vt* to couple, bracket.

accommodant [akɔmɔdã] *a* ac-commodating, easy-going.

accommodation [akɔmɔdasjɔ̃] *nf* adaptation.

accommodement [akɔmɔdmã] *nm* compromise.

accommoder [akɔmɔde] *vt* to suit, adapt, settle, prepare, cook; *vr* to settle down, make the best (of), adapt oneself (to **de**), come to an agreement (with **avec**).

accompagnateur, -trice [akɔ̃paɲa-tœ:r, tris] *n* accompanist.

accompagnement [akɔ̃paɲmɑ̃] *nm* accompaniment.

accompagner [akɔ̃paɲe] *vt* to accompany, escort.

accompli [akɔ̃pli] *a* accomplished, finished, perfect.

accomplir [akɔ̃pliːr] *vt* to accomplish, achieve, fulfill, complete; *vr* to be fulfilled.

accomplissement [akɔ̃plismɑ̃] *nm* accomplishment, fulfillment, completion.

accord [akɔːr] *nm* agreement, harmony, tune, chord; **d'—** agreed, (all) right; **être d'—** to concur, be at one (with **avec**), be in tune.

accorder [akɔrde] *vt* to reconcile, square, grant, award, concede, extend, tune, key; *vr* to agree, accord, harmonize.

accordeur [akɔrdœːr] *nm* tuner.

accort [akɔːr] *a* trim, pleasing.

accoster [akɔste] *vt* to accost, come alongside.

accoter [akɔte] *vt* to shore up; *vr* to lean (against **contre**).

accouchement [akuʃmɑ̃] *nm* confinement, labor, delivery.

accoucher [akuʃe] *vi* to be confined, give birth (to **de**).

s'accouder [sakude] *vr* to lean on one's elbow.

accoupler [akuple] *vt* to couple, mate, connect.

accourcir [akursiːr] *vt* to shorten.

accourir [akuriːr] *vi* to hasten, come running, rush.

accoutrement [akutrəmɑ̃] *nm* rig (-out), kit.

accoutrer [akutre] *vt* to rig out; *vr* to get oneself up.

accoutumé [akutyme] *a* accustomed, used, customary.

accoutumer [akutyme] *vt* to accustom; *vr* to get used (to **à**).

accréditer [akredite] *vt* to accredit.

accroc [akro] *nm* hitch, rip, infraction.

accrochage [akrɔʃaːʒ] *nm* grazing, hanging up, picking up, altercation, set-to, (*aut*) accident.

accroche-cœur [akrɔʃkœːr] *nm* kiss-curl.

accrocher [akrɔʃe] *vt* to hook, catch, collide with, hang up, pick up, tune in; *vr* to cling, hang on, get caught, clinch, have a set-to.

accroire [akrwaːr] *vt* **en faire — à qn** to delude s.o.

accroissement [akrwasmɑ̃] *nm* growth, increase.

accroître [akrwaːtr] *vt* to increase, enlarge, enhance.

s'accroupir [akrupiːr] *vr* to squat, crouch (down), cower.

accueil [akœːj] *nm* welcome, reception.

accueillir [akœjiːr] *vt* to welcome, greet, receive.

acculer [akyle] *vt* to drive back, corner.

accumulateur, -trice [akymylatœːr tris] *n* hoarder; *nm* accumulator, storage battery.

accumulation [akymylasjɔ̃] *nf* accumulation.

accumuler [akymyle] *vt* to accumulate, amass, heap up.

accusateur, -trice [akyzatœːr, tris] *a* accusatory, incriminating; *n* accuser, indicter, plaintiff.

accusation [akyzasjɔ̃] *nf* charge, indictment; **mettre en —** to impeach, arraign.

accusé [akyze] *a* prominent; *n* accused; *nm* acknowledgment.

accuser [akyze] *vt* to accuse, indict, tax (with **de**), accentuate; **— réception de** to acknowledge receipt of.

acerbe [asɛrb] *a* bitter, harsh, sharp, sour.

acerbité [asɛrbite] *nf* bitterness, harshness, sharpness.

acéré [asere] *a* sharp-pointed, cutting.

acharné [aʃarne] *a* eager, keen, desperate, inveterate, fierce, relentless, strenuous.

acharnement [aʃarnəmɑ̃] *nm* eagerness, keenness, desperation, relentlessness.

s'acharner [saʃarne] *vr* to be dead set (against **à**), persist (in), be bent (on).

achat [aʃa] *nm* purchase; **faire des —s** to go shopping.

acheminer [aʃmine] *vt* to direct, dispatch, convey; *vr* to make one's way, proceed.

acheter [aʃte] *vt* to buy, purchase, bribe.

acheteur, -euse [aʃtœːr, øːz] *n* buyer, purchaser.

achevé [aʃve] *a* accomplished, perfect, thorough.

achèvement [aʃɛvmɑ̃] *nm* completion.

achever [aʃve] *vt* to complete, end, finish off; *vr* to draw to a close, end, culminate.

achoppement [aʃɔpmɑ̃] *nm* obstacle; **pierre d'—** stumbling-block.

acide [asid] *a* acid, tart; *nm* acid.

acidité [asidite] *nf* acidity.

acier [asje] *nm* steel.

aciérie [asjeri] *nf* steelworks.

acompte [akɔ̃t] *nm* installment.

acoquiner [akɔkine] *vr* to be thick with.

à-côté [akote] *nm* aside; *pl* side-issues, extras.

à-coup [aku] *nm* jerk, sudden stop, snatch; **par —s** by fits and starts, in spasms.

acoustique [akustik] *nf* acoustics.

acquérir [akeriːr] *vt* to acquire, get.

acquiescer [akjese] *vt* to acquiesce, assent.

acquis [aki] *a* acquired, established, vested; **mal —** ill-got(ten); **— d'avance** foregone; *nm* attainments, acquired knowledge.

acquisition [akizisjɔ̃] *nf* acquisition.
acquit [aki] *nm* acquittance, receipt; **pour — received, paid (with thanks); par — de conscience** for conscience' sake.
acquittement [akitmã] *nm* discharge, acquittal.
acquitter [akite] *vt* to discharge, acquit, clear, fulfill, receipt; *vr* to acquit o.s.; **— de** carry out, discharge.
âcre [ɑːkr] *a* acrid, pungent.
âcreté [ɑkrəte] *nf* acridity, pungency.
acrimonie [akrimɔni] *nf* acrimony.
acrimonieux, -euse [akrimɔnjø, jøːz] *a* acrimonious.
acrobate [akrɔbat] *n* acrobat.
acrobatie [akrɔbasi] *nf* acrobatics.
acte [akt] *nm* act, deed, record; **— de naissance, de décès, de mariage** birth, death, marriage certificate.
acteur, -trice [aktœːr, tris] *n* actor, actress.
actif, -ive [aktif, iːv] *a* active, busy, brisk, live, industrious; *nm* credit, assets.
action [aksjɔ̃] *nf* action, effect, shares, lawsuit.
actionnaire [aksjɔnɛːr] *n* shareholder.
actionner [aksjɔne] *vt* to sue, set in motion, drive.
activer [aktive] *vt* to push on, stir up, whip up.
activité [aktivite] *nf* activity, industry.
actuaire [aktɥɛːr -tyɛːr] *nm* actuary.
actualité [aktɥalite -tya-] *nf* reality, topical question; *pl* current events, newsreel.
actuel, -elle [aktɥɛl -tyɛl] *a* real, current, topical, of the present.
actuellement [aktɥɛlmã -tyɛl] *ad* at present.
acuité [akɥite] *nf* keenness, sharpness.
adage [adaːʒ] *nm* adage.
adaptable [adaptabl] *a* adaptable.
adaptation [adaptasjɔ̃] *nf* adaptation.
adapter [adapte] *vt* to adapt, adjust, accommodate.
addition [adisjɔ̃] *nf* addition, appendage, bill.
additionner [ad(d)isjɔ̃ne] *vt* to add (up).
adepte [adɛpt] *a* adept.
adhérence [aderãːs] *nf* adhesion.
adhérent [aderã] *a* adherent, adhesive; *n* adherent, member, follower.
adhérer [adere] *vi* to adhere, stick, hold, join.
adhésif, -ive [adezif, iːv] *a nm* adhesive.
adhésion [adezjɔ̃] *nf* adhesion.
adieu [adjø] *ad* good-bye; *nm* farewell, leave-taking; **faire ses —x à** to say farewell to, take leave of.

adjacent [adʒasã] *a* adjacent.
adjectif, -ive [adʒektif, iːv] *a* adjectival; *nm* adjective.
adjoindre [adʒwɛ̃ːdr] *vt* to unite, associate, add; *vr* to join in (with à).
adjoint [adʒwɛ̃] *an* assistant; **— au maire** deputy mayor, alderman.
adjudant [adʒydã] *nm* company sergeant-major, adjutant, warrant-officer.
adjudication [adʒydikasjɔ̃] *nf* adjudication; **mettre en — to invite bids for, put up for sale by auction.
adjuger [adʒyʒe] *vt* to adjudge, award, knock down; *vr* to appropriate.
adjurer [adʒyre] *vt* to adjure, beseech, conjure.
admettre [admɛtr] *vt* to admit, assume, allow, concede, pass.
administrateur, -trice [administratœːr, tris] *n* administrator, director, trustee.
administration [administrasjɔ̃] *nf* administration, government, civil service, trusteeship.
administrer [administre] *vt* to administer, govern, manage, dispense.
admirable [admirabl] *a* admirable, wonderful.
admirateur, -trice [admiratœːr, tris] *n* admirer, fan.
admiratif, -ive [admiratif, iːv] *a* admiring.
admiration [admirasjɔ̃] *nf* admiration, wonderment.
admirer [admire] *vt* to admire, wonder at, marvel at.
admissible [admisibl] *a* admissible, eligible, qualified for oral examination.
admission [admisjɔ̃] *nf* admission.
admonestation [admɔnɛstasjɔ̃] *nf* reprimand.
admonester [admɔnɛste] *vt* to admonish.
adolescence [adɔlɛssãːs] *nf* adolescence, youth.
adolescent [adɔlɛssã] *n* adolescent, youth, girl.
s'adonner [sadɔne] *vr* to give oneself up (to à), take (to).
adopter [adɔpte] *vt* to adopt.
adoptif, -ive [adɔptif, iːv] *a* adopted, adoptive.
adoption [adɔpsjɔ̃] *nf* adoption.
adorable [adɔrabl] *a* adorable, charming, lovely.
adorateur, -trice [adɔratœːr, tris] *n* adorer, worshipper; *a* adoring.
adorer [adɔre] *vt* to adore, worship.
adosser [adɔse] *vt* to place back to back, lean back (against à); *vr* to lean one's back (against à).
adoucir [adusiːr] *vt* to soften, subdue, alleviate, mitigate, mollify; *vr* to grow softer, milder.
adoucissement [adusismã] *nm* soft-

ening, toning down, alleviation, mitigation.

adresse [adrɛs] *nf* address, destination, skill, deftness, sleight, adroitness, craftiness.

adresser [adrɛse] *vt* to address, direct; *vr* to address, apply, ask.

adroit [adrwa] *a* skillful, deft, clever, handy. shrewd.

adulation [adylasjɔ̃] *nf* adulation.

adulte [adylt] *an* adult, grown-up, full-grown.

adultère [adyltɛːr] *a* adulterous; *n* adulterer, adulteress; *nm* adultery.

advenir [advəniːr] *v imp* to happen, occur, come to pass, become of; **advienne que pourra** come what may.

adverbe [advɛrb] *nm* adverb.

adversaire [advɛrsɛːr] *nm* adversary, opponent.

adverse [advɛrs] *a* adverse.

adversité [advɛrsite] *nf* adversity, misfortune.

aération [aɛrasjɔ̃] *nf* aeration, airing, ventilation.

aérer [aere] *vt* to air, aerate, ventilate.

aérien, -ienne [aerjɛ̃, jɛn] *a* airy, aerial, ethereal; **raid** — long-distance flight, air-raid; **forces** **—nes** air-force.

aéro-club [aerɔklyb, -klœb] *nm* flying-club.

aérodrome [aerɔdroːm] *nm* airdrome.

aérodynamique [aerɔdinamik] *a* stream-lined.

aéronaute [aerɔnoːt] *nm* aeronaut.

aéronautique [aerɔnotik] *a* aeronautical; *nf* aeronautics.

aéroport [aerɔpɔːr] *nm* airport.

aéroporté [aerɔpɔrte] *a* airborne.

aérostat [aerɔsta] *nm* airship, balloon.

aérostatique [aerɔstatik] *a* **barrage** — balloon barrage; *nf* aerostatics.

affabilité [afabilite] *nf* affability, graciousness.

affable [afaːbl] *a* affable.

affadir [afadiːr] *vt* to make insipid; *vr* to become insipid.

affaiblir [afɛbliːr] *vt* to weaken, enfeeble, impair, lower, water down; *vr* to become weaker, flag, abate.

affaiblissement [afɛblismɑ̃] *nm* weakening, enfeeblement, impairment.

affaire [afɛːr] *nf* affair, thing, matter, concern, case; *pl* business, dealings, belongings; **— de cœur** love affair; **son — est faite** it's all up with him; **la belle —!** is that all!; **avoir — à, avec** — to deal with; **le Ministère des — étrangères** Foreign Office.

affairé [afɛre] *a* busy.

affaissement [afɛsmɑ̃] *nm* subsidence, collapse.

s'affaisser [safɛse] *vr* to subside, collapse.

affamé [afame] *a* hungry, starving, famished.

affectation [afɛktasjɔ̃] *nf* affectation, primness, assignment, (mil) posting.

affecté [afɛkte] *a* affected, conceited, prim, (mil) posted.

affecter [afɛkte] *vt* to affect, assign (to à), post (to).

affection [afɛksjɔ̃] *nf* affection, liking, trouble.

affectionner [afɛksjɔne] *vt* to have a liking for.

affectueux, -euse [afɛktɥø, øːz] *a* affectionate, fond.

affermir [afɛrmiːr] *vt* to strengthen; *vr* to grow stronger, harden.

afféterie [afetri] *nf* affectation, primness, gewgaws.

affichage [afiʃaːʒ] *nm* bill-posting.

affiche [afiʃ] *nf* bill, poster, placard; **panneau à —s** billboard; **tenir l'—** (of a play) to run.

afficher [afiʃe] *vt* to stick up, post up, make a display of; **défense d'—** no bills; *vr* to show off.

afficheur [afiʃœːr] *nm* bill-poster.

affilée [afile] *nf* **d'—** at a stretch.

affiler [afile] *vt* to sharpen, grind, whet, strop.

affiliation [afiljasjɔ̃] *nf* affiliation, branch.

affilier [afilje] *vt* to affiliate.

affinité [afinite] *nf* affinity, connection.

affirmatif, -ive [afirmatif, iːv] *a* affirmative.

affirmation [afirmasjɔ̃] *nf* affirmation, assertion.

affirmative [afirmatiːv] *nf* affirmative.

affirmer [afirme] *vt* to affirm, assert, aver, avouch.

affleurer [aflœre] *vt* to make flush; *vi* to be level.

affliction [afliksjɔ̃] *nf* affliction, grief.

affligé [afliʒe] *a* afflicted, aggrieved, sorrowful.

affligeant [afliʒɑ̃] *a* distressing, sad, grievous.

affliger [afliʒe] *vt* to afflict, distress; *vr* to grieve.

affluence [aflyɑ̃ːs] *nf* flow, influx, affluence, concourse, crowd; **heures d'—** rush hours.

affluent [aflyɑ̃] *nm* tributary.

affluer [aflye] *vi* to flow, flock, abound, throng.

affolé [afɔle] *a* crazy, distracted, panicky.

affolement [afɔlmɑ̃] *nm* distraction, panic.

affoler [afɔle] *vt* to distract, drive crazy; *vr* to become panicky, become infatuated (with **de**).

affranchi [afrɑ̃ʃi] *a* freed, stamped, unscrupulous; **colis —** prepaid

parcel; *n* emancipated man, woman.
affranchir [afrɑ̃ʃiːr] *vt* to set free, emancipate, stamp, enfranchise; *vr* to become free, shake off (**de**).
affranchissement [afrɑ̃ʃismɑ̃] *nm* freeing, setting free, stamping, postage.
affréter [afrete] *vt* to charter, freight.
affreux, -euse [afrø, øːz] *a* horrible, awful, dreadful.
affront [afrɔ̃] *nm* affront, insult, disgrace, public shame.
affronter [afrɔ̃te] *vt* to affront, face.
affût [afy] *nm* hiding-place, gun-carriage; à l'— on the watch.
affûter [afyte] *vt* to sharpen, whet.
afin [afɛ̃] *ad* — de in order to; *cj* — que so that.
africain [afrikɛ̃] *an* African.
Afrique [afrik] *nf* Africa.
agaçant [agasɑ̃] *a* annoying, irritating, grating.
agacer [agase] *vt* to annoy, irritate, set teeth on edge.
âge [ɑːʒ] *nm* age, period; **d'un certain** — elderly; **prendre de l'**— to be getting on in years; **quel** — **avez-vous?** how old are you?
âgé [ɑʒe] *a* old, aged.
agence [aʒɑ̃ːs] *nf* agency, office.
agencer [aʒɑ̃se] *vt* to arrange, fit together, set.
agenda [aʒɛ̃da] *nm* agenda, diary.
agenouillé [aʒnuje] *a* kneeling.
s'agenouiller [saʒnuje] *vr* to kneel (down).
agent [aʒɑ̃] *nm* agent; — de police policeman; — de change stockbroker; — voyer road surveyor.
agglomération [aglɔmerasjɔ̃] *nf* agglomeration, built-up area.
aggloméré [aglɔmere] *nm* conglomerate, compressed fuel, coal-dust, briquette.
agglomérer [aglɔmere] *vt* to agglomerate, cluster, bind.
aggraver [agrave] *vt* to aggravate, worsen, increase.
agile [aʒil] *a* agile, nimble.
agilité [aʒilite] *nf* agility, nimbleness.
agioteur [aʒjɔtœːr] *nm* speculator, stockbroker.
agir [aʒiːr] *vi* to act; *v imp* s'— to be in question, concern; **il s'agit de** it is a question of; **de quoi s'agit-il?** what is the matter?
agissements [aʒismɑ̃] *nm pl* dealings, doings.
agitateur, -trice [aʒitatœːr, tris] *n* agitator.
agitation [aʒitasjɔ̃] *nf* agitation, restlessness, bustle; **faire de l'**— to agitate.
agité [aʒite] *a* agitated, restless, excited, agog, rough.
agiter [aʒite] *vt* to agitate, stir up, wave, flap, dangle; *vr* to become agitated, bustle, fidget, toss.

agneau [aɲo] *nm* lamb.
agonie [agɔni] *nf* death agony; à l'— dying.
agonisant [agɔnizɑ̃] *a* dying; *n* dying person.
agoniser [agɔnize] *vi* to be dying.
agouti [aguti] *nm* agouti.
agrafe [agraf] *nf* hook, clasp, clip, fastener; —s et portes hooks and eyes.
agrafer [agrafe] *vt* to fasten, clip.
agrandir [agrɑ̃diːr] *vt* to enlarge, magnify; *vr* to grow larger, become more powerful.
agrandissement [agrɑ̃dismɑ̃] *nm* aggrandizement, enlargement.
agréable [agreabl] *a* pleasant, congenial, acceptable.
agréer [agree] *vt* to accept; **veuillez** — **l'expression de mes sentiments distingués** yours faithfully, yours truly.
agrégation [agregasjɔ̃] *nf* aggregation, aggregate, State competitive examination for recruitment of secondary school teachers.
agrégé [agreʒe] *an* teacher who has passed the aggregation.
s'agréger [sagreʒe] *vr* to aggregate, join together.
agrément [agremɑ̃] *nm* pleasure, charm, approbation.
agrès [agrɛ] *nm pl* rigging, tackle.
agresseur [agrɛsœːr] *nm* aggressor.
agressif, -ive [agrɛsif, iːv] *a* aggressive.
agression [agresjɔ̃] *nf* aggression, assault.
agreste [agrɛst] *a* rustic, rural, uncouth.
agricole [agrikɔl] *a* agricultural.
agriculteur [agrikyltœːr] *nm* farmer.
agriculture [agrikyltyːr] *nf* agriculture.
agripper [agripe] *vt* to clutch, grip; *vr* to cling, come to grips (with à).
aguerri [agɛri] *a* seasoned.
aguerrir [agɛriːr] *vt* to harden, train, season.
aguets [agɛ] *nm pl* être aux — to lie in wait, be on the look-out, on the lurk.
aguicher [agiʃe] *vt* to allure, inflame.
ahuri [ayri] *a* bewildered, dumbfounded, dazed.
ahurir [ayriːr] *vt* to bewilder, flabbergast, daze.
ahurissement [ayrismɑ̃] *nm* bewilderment.
aide [ɛ(ː)d] *nf* aid, help, assistance; à l'—! help!, **venir en** — à to help, benefit; *n* assistant, helper, mate.
aide-mémoire [ɛdmemwaːr] *nm* memorandum.
aider [ɛde] *vt* to aid, help, assist, avail.
aïeul [ajœl] *n* ancestor, ancestress, grandfather, grandmother.
aigle [ɛgl] *nm* eagle, lectern.
aiglefin [ɛgləfɛ̃] *nm* haddock.

aiglon [ɛglɔ̃] *nm* eaglet.

aigre [ɛːgr] *a* sour, tart, bitter, crabbed, shrill, sharp.

aigre-doux, -douce [ɛgrədu, dus] *a* bittersweet.

aigrefin [ɛgrəfɛ̃] *nm* sharper, swindler, haddock.

aigrette [ɛgrɛt] *nf* aigrette, tuft, plume.

aigreur [ɛgrœːr] *nf* sourness, tartness, embitterment, crabbedness; *pl* heartburn.

aigrir [ɛgriːr] *vt* to sour, turn sour, embitter.

aigu, -uë [egy] *a* pointed, sharp, shrill, high-pitched.

aiguière [egjɛːr] *nf* ewer.

aiguille [egɥiːj] *nf* needle, hand, pointer, spire, cock, switch; *pl* points.

aiguiller [egɥije] *vt* to switch, shunt, divert.

aiguilleur [egɥijœːr] *nm* switchman.

aiguillon [egɥijɔ̃] *nm* goad, spur, prickle, sting.

aiguillonner [egɥijɔne] *vt* to goad, spur on, stimulate.

aiguisé [eg(ɥ)ize] *a* sharp.

aiguiser [eg(ɥ)ize] *vt* to sharpen, point, stimulate; **pierre à —** hone, whetstone.

ail [aːj] *nm* garlic.

aile [ɛl] *nf* wing, fender, aisle.

ailé [ɛle] *a* winged.

aileron [ɛlrɔ̃] *nm* pinion, fin, aileron, wing-flap.

ailette [ɛlɛt] *nf* fin, blade.

ailier [ɛlje] *nm* wing-player, winger.

ailleurs [ajœːr] *ad* elsewhere; **d'—** moreover, besides; **par —** in other respects, from another source.

aimable [ɛmabl] *a* amiable, pleasant, bland, kind.

aimablement [ɛmabləmɑ̃] *ad* amiably, agreeably.

aimant [ɛmɑ̃] *a* affectionate; *nm* magnet, lodestone.

aimanter [ɛmɑ̃te] *vt* to magnetize.

aimer [ɛme] *vt* to love, like, be fond of, care for, enjoy.

aine [ɛn] *nf* groin.

aîné [ɛne] *a* elder, eldest, senior.

ainsi [ɛ̃si] *ad* thus, so; **et — de suite** and so on; **— soit-il** amen, so be it; **pour — dire** so to speak; **— que** as, like, as well as.

air [ɛːr] *nm* air, wind, appearance, look, tune, melody; **avoir l'—** to look, seem; **en plein —** in the open air; **qui tient l'—** airworthy.

airain [ɛrɛ̃] *nm* bronze, brass.

aire [ɛːr] *nf* threshing-floor, area, surface, eyrie, point of the compass.

aisance [ɛzɑ̃ːs] *nf* ease, comfort, affluence.

aise [ɛːz] *nf* ease, comfort; **à l'—** comfortable, well-off; **à votre —** just as you like; **mal à l'—** uncomfortable, uneasy; **bien —** very glad.

aisé [ɛze] *a* easy, well-to-do.

aisément [ɛzemɑ̃] *ad* easily.

aisselle [ɛsɛl] *nf* armpit.

ajonc [aʒɔ̃] *nm* furze, gorse.

ajournement [aʒurnəmɑ̃] *nm* postponement.

ajourner [aʒurne] *vt* to postpone; *vr* to adjourn.

ajouter [aʒute] *vt* to add, supplement.

ajustage [aʒystaːʒ] *nm* adjustment, fitting.

ajustement [aʒystəmɑ̃] *nm* adjusting, settlement, fit.

ajuster [aʒyste] *vt* to adjust, fit, settle.

ajusteur [aʒystœːr] *nm* fitter.

alacrité [alakrite] *nf* alacrity.

alanguir [alɑ̃giːr] *vt* to enfeeble; *vr* to grow languid.

alanguissement [alɑ̃gismɑ̃] *nm* languor.

alarmant [alarmɑ̃] *a* alarming.

alarme [alarm] *nf* alarm.

alarmer [alarme] *vt* to alarm; *vr* to take fright.

alarmiste [alarmist] *a* alarmist, panicky; *n* scaremonger.

album [albɔm] *nm* album.

alchimie [alʃimi] *nf* alchemy.

alchimiste [alʃimist] *nm* alchemist.

alcool [alkɔl] *nm* alcohol, spirit(s); **— à brûler** methylated spirit.

alcoolique [alkɔlik] *a* alcoholic.

alcoolisme [alkɔlism] *nm* alcoholism.

alcôve [alkoːv] *nf* alcove, recess.

aléatoire [aleatwaːr] *a* risky, chancy.

alène [alɛn] *nf* awl.

alentour [alɑ̃tuːr] *ad* around; *nm pl* surroundings.

alerte [alɛrt] *a* alert, quick; *nf* alarm, alert, air-raid warning; **fin d'—** all clear.

alerter [alɛrte] *vt* to give the alarm to, warn.

alésage [alezaːʒ] *nm* (*tec*) boring, bore.

alèse [alɛːz] *nf* draw-sheet, rubber sheet.

algèbre [alʒɛbr] *nf* algebra.

Algérie [alʒeri] *nf* Algeria.

algérien, -ienne [alʒerjɛ̃, jɛn] *an* Algerian.

algue [alg] *nf* alga, seaweed.

alibi [alibi] *nm* alibi.

aliénation [aljenasjɔ̃] *nf* alienation, estrangement.

aliéné [aljene] *a* insane; *n* lunatic.

aliéner [aljene] *vt* to alienate, estrange.

aliéniste [aljenist] *nm* mental specialist.

alignement [aliɲmɑ̃] *nm* alignment, line, row, putting in lines.

aligner [aliɲe] *vt* to align, line up, draw up; *vr* to fall into line.

aliment [alimɑ̃] *nm* aliment, food.

alimentation [alimɑ̃tasjɔ̃] *nf* alimentation, feeding, nourishment.

alimenter [alimɑ̃te] *vt* to feed, nourish.
alinéa [alinea] *nm* paragraph, break.
s'aliter [salite] *vr* to take to one's bed.
allaiter [alɛte] *vt* to suckle.
allant [alɑ̃] *nm* dash, go.
allécher [al(l)eʃe] *vt* to entice, allure.
allée [ale] *nf* avenue, drive, path, lane, passage.
allégation [al(l)egasjɔ̃] *nf* allegation.
alléger [al(l)eʒe] *vt* to lighten, alleviate.
allégorie [allegɔri] *nf* allegory.
allègre [allɛgr] *a* lively.
alléguer [al(l)ege] *vt* to allege, urge, plead.
Allemagne [almaɲ] *nf* Germany.
allemand [almɑ̃] *an* German.
aller [ale] *vi* to go, suit, fit; — **chercher** to fetch; **comment allez-vous?** how do you do?; **allez-y!** fire away!; **cela va de soi** that is a matter of course; **y — de qch.** to be at stake; **allons donc!** come along! nonsense!; *vr* **s'en — ** to go away, clear off, depart; *nm* one-way ticket, one-way; **billet d'— et retour** round trip; **au pis —** if the worst comes to the worst.
alliage [aljaːʒ] *nm* alloy.
alliance [aljɑ̃ːs] *nf* alliance, blending, wedding ring.
allier [alje] *vt* to ally.
allocation [allɔkasjɔ̃] *nf* allocation, allowance, grant.
allonger [alɔ̃ʒe] *vt* to lengthen, stretch out, strike, eke out; *vr* to lengthen, stretch.
allumage [alymaːʒ] *nm* lighting, putting on, ignition.
allumer [alyme] *vt* to light, put on, set alight, arouse.
allumette [alymɛt] *nf* match.
allure [alyːr] *nf* carriage, gait, walk, speed, turn, style.
aloi [alwa] *nm* quality, standard; **de bon —** genuine.
alors [alɔːr] *ad* then, at that time, so, in that case.
alouette [alwɛt] *nf* lark.
alpinisme [alpinism] *nm* mountaineering.
altercation [altɛrkasjɔ̃] *nf* altercation, dispute.
altérer [altere] *vt* to change, spoil, impair, falsify, make thirsty; *vr* to change, be spoiled, become thirsty.
alternatif, -ive [altɛrnatif, iːv] *a* alternative, alternate, alternating.
alterner [altɛrne] *vt* to alternate, to take turns.
altier [altje] *a* haughty, lofty.
amabilité [amabilite] *nf* amiability, civility.
amadouer [amadwe] *vt* to wheedle, coax, win over.
amaigrir [amɛgriːr] *vt* to make thin, reduce.
amande [amɑ̃ːd] *nf* almond.

amant [amɑ̃] *n* lover.
amarre [amaːr] *nf* hawser; *pl* moorings.
amarrer [amare] *vtr* to moor, tie up.
amas [ama] *nm* pile, heap.
amasser [amase] *vt* to amass, pile up; *vr* to mass.
amateur, -trice [amatœːr, tris] *n* amateur, lover.
ambages [ɑ̃baːʒ] *nf pl* **sans —** bluntly, plainly.
ambassade [ɑ̃basad] *nf* embassy.
ambiance [ɑ̃bjɑ̃ːs] *nf* surroundings, atmosphere.
ambigu, -uë [ɑ̃bigy] *a* ambiguous.
ambition [ɑ̃bisjɔ̃] *nf* ambition.
ambre [ɑ̃ːbr] *nm* amber.
ambulant [ɑ̃bylɑ̃] *a* traveling, itinerant, strolling.
âme [ɑːm] *nf* soul, spirit, core, heart, life; (*of gun*) bore.
améliorer [ameljɔre] *vtr* to improve, mend.
aménager [amenaʒe] *vt* to fit up (out), lay out.
amende [amɑ̃ːd] *nf* fine.
amender [amɑ̃de] *vtr* to improve.
amener [amne] *vt* to lead, bring, induce.
amer, -ère [ameːr] *a* bitter.
américain [amerikɛ̃] *an* American.
Amérique [amerik] *nf* America.
amertume [amɛrtym] *nf* bitterness.
ameublement [amœbləmɑ̃] *nm* furnishing, furniture.
ameuter [amøte] *vt* to rouse; *vr* to mutiny.
ami [ami] *n* friend, boy-, girl-friend.
amical [amikal] *a* friendly.
amidon [amidɔ̃] *nm* starch.
amincir [amɛ̃siːr] *vt* to make thinner, thin down; *vr* to grow thinner.
amiral [amiral] *nm* admiral.
amirauté [amirote] *nf* admiralty.
amitié [amitje] *nf* friendship, favor; *pl* kind regards.
amoindrir [amwɛ̃driːr] *vtr* to lessen, decrease.
amollir [amɔliːr] *vt* to soften; *vr* to grow weak.
amonceler [amɔ̃sle] *vtr* to pile up; *vr* to gather.
amont [amɔ̃] *nm* upper reaches; **en —** upstream.
amorce [amɔrs] *nf* bait, beginning, detonator.
amortir [amɔrtiːr] *vt* to deaden, allay, muffle, slacken, pay off, sink, redeem.
amortissement [amɔrtismɑ̃] *nm* deadening, redemption; **fonds d'—** sinking-fund.
amortisseur [amɔrtisœːr] *nm* shock-absorber.
amour [amuːr] *nm* (*pl usually f*) love; **pour l'— de** for love of, for the sake of.
s'amouracher [samuraʃe] *vr* to fall head over heels in love (with **de**).

amourette [amurɛt] *nf* passing love affair.

amoureux, -euse [amurø, øːz] *a* loving, amorous; **être — de** to be in love with, enamored of; *n* lover.

amour-propre [amurprɔpr] *nm* self-esteem, -respect, vanity, egotism.

amovible [amɔvibl] *a* removable, detachable.

amphibie [ãfibi] *a* amphibious; *nm* amphibian.

ample [ãːpl] *a* ample, roomy; **plus — further, fuller.**

ampleur [ãplœːr] *nf* fullness, copiousness, magnitude.

amplificateur, -trice [ãplifikatœːr, tris] *a* amplifying; *nm* amplifier.

amplification [ãplifikasjɔ̃] *nf* amplification.

amplifier [ãplifje] *vt* to amplify.

ampoule [ãpul] *nf* blister, phial, (electric light) bulb.

ampoulé [ãpule] *a* bombastic, high-flown, stilted.

amputation [ãpytasjɔ̃] *nf* amputation.

amputer [ãpyte] *vt* to amputate, reduce.

amusant [amyzã] *a* amusing, entertaining.

amusement [amyzmã] *nm* amusement, entertainment, fun.

amuser [amyze] *vt* to amuse, entertain, interest; *vr* to enjoy oneself, take pleasure (in à), have fun.

amusette [amyzɛt] *nf* toy.

amygdale [ami(g)dal] *nf* tonsil.

amygdalite [ami(g)dalit] *nf* tonsillitis.

an [ã] *nm* year; **le jour de l'— New Year's Day.**

analogie [analɔʒi] *nf* analogy.

analogue [analɔg] *a* analogous, kindred.

analyse [analiːz] *nf* analysis, abstract.

analyser [analize] *vt* to analyze, parse.

analyste [analist] *nm* analyst.

analytique [analitik] *a* analytical.

ananas [ananɑ(ːs)] *nm* pineapple.

anarchie [anarʃi] *nf* anarchy.

anarchiste [anarʃist] *an* anarchist.

anathème [anatɛm] *nm* anathema, curse.

anatomie [anatɔmi] *nf* anatomy.

anatomiste [anatɔmist] *nm* anatomist.

ancestral [ãsɛstral] *a* ancestral.

ancêtre [ãsɛːtr] *n* ancestor, ancestress, forefather.

anchois [ãʃwa] *nm* anchovy.

ancien, -ienne [ãsjɛ̃, jɛn] *a* ancient, old, long-standing, former, past, senior; **— combattant** ex-serviceman.

anciennement [ãsjɛnmã] *ad* formerly.

ancienneté [ãsjɛnte] *nf* antiquity, seniority.

ancre [ãːkr] *nf* anchor; **lever l'— to weigh anchor.**

andouille [ãduːj] *nf* (*chitterling*) sausage, duffer, fool.

âne [ɑːn] *nm* ass, donkey, fool; **en dos d'—** hog-backed.

anéantir [aneãtiːr] *vt* to destroy, wipe out; *vr* to come to nothing.

anéantissement [aneãtismã] *nm* destruction, annihilation.

anecdote [anekdɔt] *nf* anecdote.

anémie [anemi] *nf* anemia.

anémique [anemik] *a* anemic.

anesthésie [anɛstezi] *nf* anesthesia.

anesthésier [anɛstezje] *vt* to anesthetize.

anesthésique [anɛstezik] *a nm* anesthetic.

anesthésiste [anɛstezist] *nm* anesthetist.

ange [ãːʒ] *nm* angel.

angélique [ãʒelik] *a* angelic.

angélus [ãʒelyːs] *nm* angelus.

angine [ãʒin] *nf* sore throat, quinsy, tonsillitis; **— de poitrine** angina (pectoris).

anglais [ãglɛ] *a nm* English; *n* Englishman, -woman.

angle [ãːgl] *nm* angle.

Angleterre [ãglətɛːr] *nf* England.

anglican [ãglikã] *an* Anglican.

angoissant [ãgwasã] *a* distressing.

angoisse [ãgwas] *nf* anguish, anxiety, distress.

anguille [ãgiːj] *nf* eel; **— sous roche** something in the wind, something brewing; **— de mer** conger-eel.

angulaire [ãgylɛːr] *a* angular; **pierre — corner-stone.**

anguleux [ãgylø] *a* angular, gaunt.

animal [animal] *a nm* animal.

animateur, -trice [animatœːr, tris] *n* animator, moving spirit, organizer.

animation [animasjɔ̃] *nf* animation.

animé [anime] *a* animated, lively, spirited, heated.

animer [anime] *vt* to animate, enliven, vivify, brighten, actuate; *vr* to become animated, brighten up.

animosité [animɔzite] *nf* animosity.

anis [ani] *nm* aniseed.

annales [annal] *nf pl* annals.

anneau [ano] *nm* ring, link, ringlet, quoit.

année [ane] *nf* year, vintage; **bonne—!** a Happy New Year!

annexe [an(n)ɛks] *nm* annex.

annexer [an(n)ɛkse] *vt* to annex.

annexion [an(n)ɛksjɔ̃] *nf* annexation.

annihiler [an(n)iile] *vt* to annihilate.

anniversaire [anivɛrsɛːr] *a* anniversary; *nm* anniversary, birthday.

annonce [anɔ̃ːs] *nf* announcement, advertisement.

annoncer [anɔ̃se] *vt* to announce, herald, usher in, advertise, betoken, denote.

annonciation [anɔ̃sjasjɔ̃] *nf* Annunciation, Lady Day.

annotation [an(n)ɔtasjɔ̃] *nf* annotation.
annoter [an(n)ɔte] *vt* to annotate, note.
annuaire [an(n)ɥɛːr] *nm* annual, telephone directory.
annuel [an(n)ɥɛl] *a* annual.
annuité [an(n)ɥite] *nf* annuity.
annulaire [an(n)ylɛːr] *a* annular; *nm* third finger.
annulation [an(n)ylasjɔ̃] *nf* annulment, nullification, revocation, cancellation.
annuler [an(n)yle] *vt* to annul.
anoblir [anɔbliːr] *vt* to ennoble.
anoblissement [anɔblismɑ̃] *nm* ennoblement.
anodin [anɔdɛ̃] *a* anodyne, harmless; *nm* palliative.
anomalie [anɔmali] *nf* anomaly.
ânonner [ɑnɔne] *vt* to mumble, stammer through.
anonymat [anɔnima] *nm* anonymity.
anonyme [anɔnim] *a* anonymous; **société** — limited company; *nm* anonymity.
anormal [anɔrmal] *a* abnormal, anomalous.
anse [ɑ̃ːs] *nf* handle, cove.
antagonisme [ɑ̃tagɔnism] *nm* antagonism.
antécédent [ɑ̃tesedɑ̃] *a nm* antecedent.
antenne [ɑ̃tɛn] *nf* antenna, feeler, aerial.
antérieur [ɑ̃terjœːr] *a* anterior, former, prior.
antériorité [ɑ̃terjɔrite] *nf* anteriority.
anthrax [ɑ̃traks] *nm* carbuncle.
anthropophage [ɑ̃trɔpɔfaːʒ] *a nm* cannibalistic, cannibal.
antiaérien, -ienne [ɑ̃tiaerjɛ̃, jɛn] *a* anti-aircraft.
antibiotique [ɑ̃tibiɔtik] *nm* antibiotic.
antichambre [ɑ̃tiʃɑ̃ːbr] *nf* anteroom, hall, waiting-room.
antichar [ɑ̃tiʃar] *a* anti-tank.
anticipation [ɑ̃tisipasjɔ̃] *nf* anticipation.
anticiper [ɑ̃tisipe] *vt* to anticipate, forestall; *vi* to anticipate, encroach (upon **sur**).
anticorps [ɑ̃tikɔr] *nm* antibody.
antidater [ɑ̃tidate] *vt* to antedate.
antidérapant [ɑ̃tiderapɑ̃] *a* non-skid.
antidote [ɑ̃tidɔt] *nm* antidote.
antipathie [ɑ̃tipati] *nf* antipathy, repugnance.
antipathique [ɑ̃tipatik] *a* antipathetic, uncongenial.
antipodes [ɑ̃tipɔd] *nm pl* antipodes.
antiquaille [ɑ̃tikɑːj] *nf* lumber, junk.
antiquaire [ɑ̃tikɛːr] *nm* antiquarian.
antique [ɑ̃tik] *a* antique, ancient, old-fashioned.
antiquité [ɑ̃tikite] *nf* antiquity.

antiseptique [ɑ̃tisɛptik] *a nm* antiseptic.
antithèse [ɑ̃titɛːz] *nf* antithesis.
antithétique [ɑ̃titetik] *a* antithetical.
antre [ɑ̃ːtr] *nm* den, lair, sinus.
anxiété [ɑ̃ksjete] *nf* anxiety, solicitude.
anxieux, -euse [ɑ̃ksjø, øːz] *a* anxious, solicitous.
aorte [aɔrt] *nf* aorta.
août [u] *nm* August.
apache [apaʃ] *nm* hooligan.
apaiser [apɛze] *vt* to appease, alleviate, mollify, mitigate; *vr* to calm down.
aparté [aparte] *nm* aside, stage whisper.
apathie [apati] *nf* apathy, listlessness.
apathique [apatik] *a* apathetic, listless.
apercevoir [apɛrsəvwaːr] *vt* to perceive, catch sight of; *vr* to notice, realize.
aperçu [apɛrsy] *nm* glimpse, sidelight, outline, summary.
apéritif [aperitif] *nm* appetizer.
aphone [afɔn] *a* voiceless.
aphteux, -euse [aftø, øz] *a* aphthous; **la fièvre aphteuse** foot-and-mouth disease.
apiculteur [apikyltœːr] *nm* beekeeper.
apitoyer [apitwaje] *vt* to move to pity; *vr* to commiserate (with **sur**).
aplanir [aplaniːr] *vt* to smooth (away), plane, level.
aplanissement [aplanismɑ̃] *nm* smoothing, leveling.
aplatir [aplatiːr] *vt* to flatten, iron out; *vr* to grovel, collapse, fall flat.
aplatissement [aplatismɑ̃] *nm* flattening.
aplomb [aplɔ̃] *nm* perpendicularity, level, self-possession, nerve; **d'**— upright, firm on one's feet, four-square.
apogée [apɔʒe] *nm* apogee, acme, zenith, peak.
apologie [apɔlɔʒi] *nf* vindication, justification.
apologiste [apɔlɔʒist] *nm* apologist.
apoplectique [apɔplɛktik] *a* apoplectic.
apoplexie [apɔplɛksi] *nf* apoplexy.
apostat [apɔsta] *nm* apostate.
apostolat [apɔstɔla] *nm* apostleship.
apostolique [apɔstɔlik] *a* apostolic.
apothicaire [apɔtikɛːr] *nm* apothecary.
apôtre [apoːtr] *nm* apostle.
apparaître [aparɛːtr] *vi* to appear, become apparent.
apparat [apara] *nm* pomp, show, state.
appareil [aparɛːj] *nm* apparatus, mechanism, plant, set, airplane; — **photographique** camera.
appareillage [aparɛjaːʒ] *nm* fitting

up, getting under way, equipment.
appareiller [apaʀɛje] *vt* to fit out;
vi get under way.
apparemment [aparamᾶ] *ad*
apparently, evidently, seemingly.
apparence [aparᾶːs] *nf* appearance,
look, show, guise.
apparent [aparᾶ] *a* apparent, seeming, obvious.
apparenté [aparᾶte] *a* related.
apparier [aparje] *vt* to match, pair,
mate.
apparition [aparisjɔ̃] *nf* appearance,
apparition.
appartement [apartəmᾶ] *nm* flat,
apartment, suite, rooms.
appartenir [apartəniːr] *vi* to belong;
v imp to appertain (to **à**), rest
(with **à**).
appas [apɑ] *nm pl* charms.
appât [apɑ] *nm* bait, lure.
appâter [apɑte] *vt* to lure, bait.
appauvrir [apovriːr] *vt* to impoverish; *vr* to become poor(er).
appeau [apo] *nm* bird-call, decoy.
appel [apɛl] *nm* appeal, call, cry,
call-up, roll-call, muster; **aller**,
**renvoyer en — to appeal; —
d'incendie** fire-alarm.
appeler [aple] *vt* to call (for, in, to,
up); **en — à** to appeal to; **faire —**
to send for; *vr* to be called, named.
appendice [ap(p)ɛ̃dis] *nm* appendix.
appendicite [ap(p)ɛ̃disit] *nf* appendicitis.
appentis [apᾶti] *nm* outhouse,
lean-to shed.
appesantir [apəzᾶtiːr] *vt* to make
heavy, dull; *vr* to become heavy,
dwell (upon **sur**).
appétissant [apetisᾶ] *a* appetizing.
appétit [apeti] *nm* appetite; **de bon
—** hearty appetite.
applaudir [aplodiːr] *vt* to applaud.
applaudissements [aplodismᾶ] *nm
pl* applause.
applicable [aplikabl] *a* applicable.
application [aplikasjɔ̃] *nf* application, enforcement, diligence, concentration.
applique [aplik] *nf* bracket.
appliqué [aplike] *a* diligent, assiduous, applied.
appliquer [aplike] *vt* to apply, carry
out; *vr* to apply oneself (to **à**).
appoint [apwɛ̃] *nm* balance, odd
money, contribution; **faire l'—** to
tender exact amount, ' no change
given '.
appointements [apwɛ̃tmᾶ] *nm pl*
salary.
appontement [apɔ̃tmᾶ] *nm* landing-
stage, pier.
apport [apɔːr] *nm* contribution,
share.
apporter [apɔrte] *vt* to bring (in,
forward, forth).
apposer [apoze] *vt* to affix.
apposition [apozisjɔ̃] *nf* apposition,
affixing.

appréciation [apresjasjɔ̃] *nf* appreciation, estimate, valuation.
apprécier [apresje] *vt* to appreciate,
estimate, value.
appréhender [apreᾶde] *vt* to apprehend.
appréhension [apreᾶsjɔ̃] *nf* apprehension.
apprendre [aprᾶːdr] *vt* to learn,
teach, inform, tell.
apprenti [aprᾶti] *n* apprentice.
apprentissage [aprᾶtisaːʒ] *nm*
apprenticeship.
apprêté [aprɛte] *a* affected.
apprêter [aprɛte] *vt* to prepare,
dress; *vr* to get ready.
apprivoiser [aprivwaze] *vt* to tame,
domesticate.
approbateur, -trice [aprɔbatœːr,
tris] *a* approving; *n* approver.
approbatif, -ive [aprɔbatif, iːv] *a*
approving.
approbation [aprɔbasjɔ̃] *nf* approbation, approval, sanction.
approche [aprɔʃ] *nf* approach.
approcher [aprɔʃe] *vt* to approach,
draw near; *vi* to approach, draw
near, border (on); *vr* to come near.
approfondi [aprɔfɔ̃di] *a* deep,
thorough, exhaustive.
approfondir [aprɔfɔ̃diːr] *vt* to
deepen, go deeply into, fathom.
approfondissement [aprɔfɔ̃dismᾶ]
nm deepening, investigation.
approprié [aprɔprie] *a* appropriate,
suitable, proper.
approprier [aprɔprie] *vt* to appropriate, adapt.
approuver [apruve] *vt* to approve
of, favor, consent to.
approvisionnement [aprɔvizjɔnmᾶ]
nm provisioning, victualing, supply,
stores, provisions.
approvisionner [aprɔvizjɔne] *vt* to
stock, supply; *vr* to lay in supplies,
get supplies.
approximatif, -ive [aprɔksimatif,
iːv] *a* approximate, rough.
approximation [aprɔksimasjɔ̃] *nf*
approximation.
appui [apɥi] *nm* support, prop,
stress, rest; **point d'—** strong point,
defended locality.
appuyer [apɥije] *vt* to support, prop,
favor, further; *vi* **sur** dwell on,
stress, emphasize, press; *vr* to lean,
rest (on, against **sur, contre**),
depend, rely (on).
âpre [ɑːpr] *a* rough, harsh, bitter,
stern, grim, keen.
après [aprɛ] *prep* after; **d'—** according to, from; *ad* afterward; *cj*
— que after.
après-demain [aprɛdmɛ̃] *ad* the day
after tomorrow.
après-guerre [aprɛgɛːr] *nm* post-
war period.
après-midi [apremidi] *nm or f*
afternoon.
âpreté [ɑprəte] *nf* roughness, harsh-

ness, bitterness, sternness, keenness, greed.

à-propos [aprɔpo] *nm* aptness, opportuneness.

apte [apt] *a* apt, qualified.

aptitude [aptityd] *nf* aptitude, proficiency.

apurement [apyrmɑ̃] *nm* — de **comptes** audit(ing).

apurer [apyre] *vt* to audit.

aquarelle [akwarel] *nf* water-color.

aqueduc [ak(ə)dyk] *nm* aqueduct.

aqueux, -euse [akø, øːz] *a* aqueous, watery.

aquilin [akilɛ̃] *a* aquiline.

arabe [arab] *a* Arab, Arabian, Arabic; *n* Arab, Arabic.

arable [arabl] *a* arable.

arachide [araʃid] *nf* peanut.

araignée [arɛɲe] *nf* spider; — dans **le plafond** bee in the bonnet.

arbitrage [arbitraːʒ] *nm* arbitration, umpiring, refereeing.

arbitraire [arbitrɛːr] *a* arbitrary, high-handed.

arbitre [arbiːtr] *nm* arbitrator, umpire, referee; **libre** — free will.

arbitrer [arbitre] *vt* to arbitrate, umpire, referee.

arborer [arbɔre] *vt* to hoist, raise, sport.

arbre [arbr] *nm* tree, shaft.

arbrisseau [arbriso] *nm* shrub.

arbuste [arbyst] *nm* bush.

arc [ark] *nm* bow, arch, arc; **tir à l'**— archery.

arcade [arkad] *nf* arcade.

arc-boutant [ar(k)butɑ̃] *nm* flying-buttress, stay.

arceau [arso] *nm* arch, hoop.

arc-en-ciel [arkɑ̃sjɛl] *nm* rainbow.

archaïsme [arkaism] *nm* archaism.

archange [arkɑ̃ːʒ] *nm* archangel.

arche [arʃ] *nf* ark, arch, span.

archéologie [arkeɔlɔʒi] *nf* archaeology.

archéologue [arkeɔlɔg] *nm* archaeologist.

archer [arʃe] *nm* archer.

archet [arʃɛ] *nm* bow.

archevêché [arʃəvɛʃe] *nm* archbishopric, archbishop's palace.

archevêque [arʃəvɛːk] *nm* archbishop.

archicomble [arʃikɔ̃bl] *a* packed.

archipel [arʃipɛl] *nm* archipelago.

architecte [arʃitɛkt] *nm* architect.

architecture [arʃitɛktyːr] *nf* architecture.

archives [arʃiːv] *nf pl* archives, records, Record Office.

arctique [arktik] *a* arctic.

ardemment [ardamɑ̃] *ad* ardently, eagerly.

ardent [ardɑ̃] *a* ardent, glowing, keen, eager, live.

ardeur [ardœːr] *nf* ardor, heat, glow, eagerness, zeal, enthusiasm, spirit.

ardoise [ardwaːz] *nf* slate.

ardu [ardy] *a* arduous, tough.

arène [arɛn] *nf* arena.

arête [arɛt] *nf* fishbone, ridge, edge.

argent [arʒɑ̃] *nm* silver, money; — **comptant** ready money, cash down.

argenté [arʒɑ̃te] *a* silver, silver-plated.

argenterie [arʒɑ̃tri] *nf* silver-plate.

argentin [arʒɑ̃tɛ̃] *a* silvery, silver-toned.

argile [arʒil] *nf* clay.

argot [argo] *nm* slang.

argument [argymɑ̃] *nm* argument, plea, summary.

argumentation [argymɑ̃tasjɔ̃] *nf* argumentation.

argumenter [argymɑ̃te] *vi* to argue.

argutie [argysi] *nf* quibble.

aride [arid] *a* arid, dry, barren.

aridité [aridite] *nf* aridity.

aristocrate [aristɔkrat] *n* aristocrat.

aristocratie [aristɔkrasi] *nf* aristocracy.

arithmétique [aritmetik] *a* arithmetical; *nf* arithmetic.

armateur [armatœːr] *nm* shipwright, shipowner.

armature [armatyːr] *nf* framework, mainstay, reinforcement, armature.

arme [arm] *nf* arm, weapon, branch of the army; **maître d'**—s fencing master; **prise d'**—s parade.

armée [arme] *nf* army, host; — de **métier** professional army; — de **l'air** Air Force; **aux** —s on active service.

armement [armɑ̃mɑ̃] *nm* arming, fitting out, loading, equipment, crew; *pl* armaments.

armer [arme] *vt* to arm, strengthen, fit out, equip, load, commission, man.

armistice [armistis] *nm* armistice.

armoire [armwaːr] *nf* wardrobe, cupboard, press, closet.

armoiries [armwari] *nf pl* coat of arms, crest.

armure [armyːr] *nf* armor.

armurerie [armyr(ə)ri] *nf* armory, arms factory.

armurier [armyrje] *nm* armorer, gunsmith.

arôme [aroːm] *nm* aroma.

arpenter [arpɑ̃te] *vt* to measure, survey, pace.

arqué [arke] *a* arched, curved, bow.

arquer [arke] *vt* to arch, bend.

arrache-pied [araʃpje] *ad* **d'**— steadily.

arracher [araʃe] *vt* to tear away (off, out, up), pull away (out, up), snatch.

arraisonner [arɛzɔne] *vt* to hail, stop and examine a ship.

arrangement [arɑ̃ʒmɑ̃] *nm* arrangement, order.

arranger [arɑ̃ʒe] *vt* to arrange, compose, settle; *vr* to manage, come to terms.

arrérages [arɛraːʒ] *nm pl* arrears.
arrestation [arɛstasjɔ̃] *nf* arrest, detention.
arrêt [arɛ] *nm* stop(ping), stoppage, detention, arrest, seizure, decree, judgment; — **facultatif** ' stop here if required '; **mandat d'**— warrant; **maison d'**— jail.
arrêté [arɛte] *a* fixed; *nm* decision, decree, bylaw.
arrêter [arɛte] *vt* to stop, stem, check, clog, detain, arrest, decide; *vi* to halt, stop, draw up; *vr* to dwell (on **sur**), stop.
arrière [arjɛːr] *a* back, rear; *ad* backward; **en** — behind, in arrears, back; **en** — **de** behind; **faire marche** — to reverse; *nm* rear, back part, full back; **à l'**— in the rear, at the back, behind, astern.
arrière-boutique [arjɛrbutik] *nf* shopyard.
arrière-bras [arjɛrbra] *nm* upper arm.
arrière-cour [arjɛrkuːr] *nf* backyard.
arrière-garde [arjɛrgard] *nf* rearguard.
arrière-goût [arjɛrgu] *nm* aftertaste, smack.
arrière-grand-père, -grand'mère [arjɛrgrɑ̃pɛːr, grɑ̃mɛːr] *n* greatgrandfather, -grandmother.
arrière-pensée [arjɛrpɑ̃se] *nf* ulterior motive, mental reservation.
arrière-plan [arjɛrplɑ̃] *nm* background.
arrière-saison [arjɛrsɛzɔ̃] *nf* late autumn, fall.
arrière-train [arjɛrtrɛ̃] *nm* hindquarters, hind-carriage.
arriéré [arjere] *a* in arrears, backward, old-fashioned.
arrimer [arime] *vt* to stow, trim.
arrivage [arivaːʒ] *nm* arrival, consignment.
arrivée [arive] *nf* arrival, coming, winning-post.
arriver [arive] *vi* to arrive, reach, get, succeed, happen, occur, come about.
arriviste [arivist] *n* careerist, gogetter.
arrogance [arɔgɑ̃ːs] *nf* arrogance, bumptiousness.
arrogant [arɔgɑ̃] *a* arrogant, bumptious, assuming.
s'arroger [sarɔʒe] *vr* to arrogate, assume as a right.
arrondir [arɔ̃diːr] *vt* to round (off), make round.
arrondissement [arɔ̃dismɑ̃] *nm* rounding (off), subdivision of a French department, municipal ward.
arrosage [arozaːʒ] *nm* watering, spraying.
arroser [aroze] *vt* to water, spray, sprinkle, baste.

arrosoir [arozwaːr] *nm* wateringcan, -cart, sprinkler.
arsenal [arsənal] *nm* arsenal, naval dockyard.
arsenic [arsənik] *nm* arsenic
art [aːr] *nm* art, skill.
artère [artɛːr] *nf* artery, thoroughfare.
artériel, -elle [arterjɛl] *a* arterial.
artichaut [artiʃo] *nm* globe artichoke.
article [artikl] *nm* article, implement, paper; *pl* wares; —**s de Paris** fancy goods; **à l'**— **de la mort** at the point of death.
articulation [artikylasjɔ̃] *nf* articulation, joint.
articuler [artikyle] *vt* to articulate.
artifice [artifis] *nm* artifice, art, expedient, scheming; **feu d'**— fireworks.
artificiel, -elle [artifisjɛl] *a* artificial, imitation.
artillerie [artijri] *nf* artillery.
artimon [artimɔ̃] *nm* **mât d'**— mizzen-mast.
artisan [artizɑ̃] *nm* artisan, workman, maker.
artisanat [artizana] *nm* working classes.
artiste [artist] *a* artistic; *n* artist, performer.
artistique [artistik] *a* artistic.
aryen, -yenne [arjɛ̃, jɛn] *an* Aryan.
as [ɑːs] *nm* ace, crack, swell.
asbeste [azbɛst] *nm* asbestos.
ascendance [as(s)ɑ̃dɑ̃ːs] *nf* ancestry.
ascendant [as(s)ɑ̃dɑ̃] *a* ascending, climbing; *nm* ascendancy; *pl* ancestry.
ascenseur [asɑ̃sœːr] *nm* elevator.
ascension [asɑ̃sjɔ̃] *nf* ascent, ascension.
ascète [asɛt] *n* ascetic.
ascétique [asetik] *a* ascetic(al).
ascétisme [asetism] *nm* asceticism.
asepsie [asɛpsi] *nf* asepsis.
aseptique [asɛptik] *a* aseptic.
asiatique [azjatik] *a* Asiatic, Oriental.
Asie [azi] *nf* Asia.
asile [azil] *nm* shelter, refuge, sanctuary, home, almshouse; — **des pauvres** workhouse; — **d'aliénés** lunatic asylum.
aspect [aspɛ] *nm* aspect, appearance, look, sight.
asperge [aspɛrʒ] *nf* asparagus.
asperger [aspɛrʒe] *vt* to sprinkle, splash, spray.
aspérité [asperite] *nf* asperity, roughness, harshness.
asphalte [asfalt] *nm* asphalt, bitumen, pitch.
asphyxiant [asfiksjɑ̃] *a* asphyxiating, poison.
asphyxie [asfiksi] *nf* asphyxia.
asphyxier [asfiksje] *vt* to asphyxiate.
aspirant [aspirɑ̃] *a* sucking; *n* candidate, aspirant; *nm* midshipman.
aspirateur, -trice [aspiratœːr, tris]

a aspiratory; *nm* aspirator, vacuum cleaner.
aspiration [aspirasjɔ̃] *nf* aspiration, longing (for à), inhaling, suction, gasp.
aspirer [aspire] *vt* to aspire, long (for à), hanker (after à), inhale, suck up ,aspirate.
aspirine [aspirin] *nf* aspirin.
assaillant [as(s)ajɑ̃] *nm* assailant.
assaillir [as(s)ajiːr] *vt* to assail.
assainir [asɛniːr] *vt* to make healthier, cleanse.
assaisonnement [asɛzɔnmɑ̃] *nm* seasoning, flavoring, dressing, relish, sauce.
assaisonner [asɛzɔne] *vt* to season, flavor, dress.
assassin [asasɛ̃] *n* assassin, murderer.
assassinat [asasina] *nm* assassination, murder.
assassiner [asasine] *vt* to assassinate, murder.
assaut [aso] *nm* assault, onslaught, attack, bout; **emporter d'—** to storm; **troupes d'—** shock troops.
assécher [aseʃe] *vt* to drain, dry; *vir* to dry up.
assemblage [asɑ̃blaːʒ] *nm* collating, gathering, assembly, joining up.
assemblée [asɑ̃ble] *nf* assembly, meeting, gathering, convocation; **Assemblée Nationale** Lower Chamber of French Parliament.
assembler [asɑ̃ble] *vt* to assemble, gather, connect; *vr* to meet, assemble, flock.
assener [asəne] *vt* to deliver, deal, land (a blow).
assentiment [asɑ̃timɑ̃] *nm* assent.
asseoir [aswaːr] *vt* to set, lay, found; *vr* to sit down.
assermenter [asɛrmɑ̃te] *vt* to swear in.
asservir [asɛrviːr] *vt* to enslave.
asservissement [asɛrvismɑ̃] *nm* enslavement.
assesseur [asɛsœːr] *nm* assessor.
assez [ase] *ad* enough, rather, fairly.
assidu [asidy] *a* assiduous, sedulous, constant, regular.
assiduité [asidɥite] *nf* assiduity, application, regularity.
assiégeant [asjeʒɑ̃] *a* besieging; *nm* besieger.
assiéger [asjeʒe] *vt* to besiege, beleaguer.
assiette [asjɛt] *nf* position, situation, set, foundation, plate; **n'être pas dans son —** to be out of sorts.
assignation [asiɲasjɔ̃] *nf* assignment, writ, subpoena.
assigner [asiɲe] *vt* to assign, allot, allocate, summon, serve a writ on.
assimiler [as(s)imile] *vt* to assimilate, digest.
assimilation [as(s)imilasjɔ̃] *nf* assimilation.
assis [asi] *a* seated, sitting, established, situated.

assise [asiːz] *nf* foundation, base, seating, course; *pl* assizes, sittings, sessions.
assistance [asistɑ̃ːs] *nf* assistance, relief, presence, audience.
assistant [asistɑ̃] *n* assistant, onlooker; **—e sociale** welfare worker; *pl* audience, those present.
assister [asiste] *vt* to assist, help; *vi* to be present, witness, attend.
association [asɔsjasjɔ̃] *nf* association, society, partnership.
associé [asɔsje] *n* partner, associate.
associer [asɔsje] *vt* to associate, band, club, connect; *vr* to participate (in à), enter into a partnership (with à).
assoiffé [aswafe] *a* thirsty.
assombrir [asɔ̃briːr] *vt* to darken, dim, cast a gloom over; *vr* to become dark, cloud (over), become sad.
assommant [asɔmɑ̃] *a* overwhelming, tiresome, deadly dull, humdrum, boring.
assommer [asɔme] *vt* to knock senseless, bludgeon, tire out, wear out, bore.
assommeur [asɔmœːr] *nm* slaughterer.
assommoir [asɔmwaːr] *nm* pole-ax, bludgeon, low tavern.
assomption [asɔ̃psjɔ̃] *nf* assumption.
assortiment [asɔrtimɑ̃] *nm* matching, sorting. assortment, set.
assortir [asɔrtiːr] *vt* to match, sort, assort, stock.
assoupi [asupi] *a* dozing.
assoupir [asupiːr] *vt* to send to sleep, allay; *vr* to doze (off), die away.
assoupissement [asupismɑ̃] *nm* drowsiness, allaying.
assourdir [asurdiːr] *vt* to deafen, stun, muffle, subdue, mute; *vr* to die away.
assourdissant [asurdisɑ̃] *a* deafening, stunning.
assouvir [asuviːr] *vt* to satisfy, slake, wreak; *vr* to become sated.
assujetti [asyʒeti] *a* subject (to), tied (to).
assujettir [asyʒetiːr] *vt* to subdue, govern.
assujettissant [asyʒetisɑ̃] *a* tying.
assumer [asyme] *vt* to assume.
assurance [asyrɑ̃ːs] *nf* assurance, confidence, insurance.
assurément [asyremɑ̃] *ad* certainly.
assuré [asyre] *a* sure, confident, certain, safe, steady; *n* policyholder.
assurer [asyre] *vt* to assure, ensure, make secure, insure; *vr* to make sure.
assureur [asyrœːr] *nm* underwriter.
astérisque [asterisk] *nm* asterisk.
asthmatique [asmatik] *a* asthmatic, wheezy.
asthme [asm] *nm* asthma.

asticot [astiko] *nm* maggot.
astiquer [astike] *vt* to polish.
astral [astral] *a* astral.
astre [astr] *nm* star.
astreindre [astrɛ̃:dr] *vt* to compel; *vr* to keep (to à).
astrologie [astrɔlɔʒi] *nf* astrology.
astrologue [astrɔlɔg] *nm* astrologer.
astronaute [astrɔnot] *nm* astronaut.
astronef [astrɔnɛf] *nm* space-ship.
astronome [astrɔnɔm] *nm* astronomer.
astronomie [astrɔnɔmi] *nf* astronomy.
astuce [astys] *nf* wile, astuteness, guile, gimmick.
astucieux, -euse [astysjø, ø:z] *a* wily, astute.
atelier [atəlje] *nm* workshop, studio.
atermoyer [atɛrmwaje] *vti* to put off, delay.
athée [ate] *a* atheistic, godless; *n* atheist.
athéisme [ateism] *nm* atheism.
athlète [atlɛt] *nm* athlete.
athlétique [atletik] *a* athletic.
athlétisme [atletism] *nm* athleticism, athletics.
atmosphère [atmɔsfɛ:r] *nf* atmosphere, environment.
atmosphérique [atmɔsferik] *a* atmospheric.
atome [ato:m] *nm* atom.
atomique [atɔmik] *a* atomic.
atomiser [atɔmize] *vt* to atomize, spray.
atomiseur [atɔmizœ:r] *nm* atomizer, spray.
atours [atu:r] *nm pl* finery, attire.
atout [atu] *nm* trump.
âtre [a:tr] *nm* hearth.
atroce [atrɔs] *a* atrocious, outrageous, heinous, terrible, excruciating, woeful.
atrocité [atrɔsite] *nf* atrocity.
s'attabler [satable] *vr* to sit down to table.
attachant [ataʃɑ̃] *a* interesting, attractive, winning.
attache [ataʃ] *nf* tie, fastening, connection, brace, leash, fastener, paper-clip, joint; **port d'—** home port.
attaché [ataʃe] *nm* attaché.
attachement [ataʃmɑ̃] *nm* attachment, adherence, fondness.
attacher [ataʃe] *vt* to attach, fasten, tie (up), connect, lash, strap, brace; *vr* to cling, stick, become attached, apply oneself.
attaquable [atakabl] *a* assailable.
attaque [atak] *nf* attack, thrust, fit, stroke, seizure.
attaquer [atake] *vt* to attack, assault, tackle, attempt, (*cards*) lead; *vr* to attack, grapple (with à).
s'attarder [satarde] *vr* to linger, tarry.
atteindre [atɛ̃:dr] *vt* to reach, attain, hit, affect.
atteint [atɛ̃] *a* affected, attacked, hit.

atteinte [atɛ̃:t] *nf* reach, blow, attack; **porter — à** to hurt, damage.
attelage [atla:ʒ] *nm* harnessing, team, yoke, coupling.
atteler [atle] *vt* to harness, yoke, couple, team; *vr* to buckle to.
attelle [atɛl] *nf* splint.
attenant [atnɑ̃] *a* adjacent, adjoining.
attendant [atɑ̃dɑ̃] *ad* **en —** meanwhile, pending; *cj* **en — que** until.
attendre [atɑ̃:dr] *vt* to await, wait for, expect, look for; *vr* to expect.
attendri [atɑ̃dri] *a* fond, compassionate.
attendrir [atɑ̃dri:r] *vt* to soften, move, touch; *vr* to become tender, be moved.
attendrissant [atɑ̃drisɑ̃] *a* touching, affecting.
attendrissement [atɑ̃drismɑ̃] *nm* tender emotion, pity.
attendu [atɑ̃dy] *prep* considering, owing to, on account of; **— que** seeing that, whereas.
attentat [atɑ̃ta] *nm* attempt, outrage, murder attempt.
attente [atɑ̃:t] *nf* wait, expectation, hope; **salle d'—** waiting-room; **être dans l'— de** to be awaiting.
attenter [atɑ̃te] *vt* make an attempt (on, against à).
attentif, -ive [atɑ̃tif, i:v] *a* attentive, careful, heedful, considerate.
attention [atɑ̃sjɔ̃] *nf* attention, care, regard, mindfulness; **—!** look out! **faire — à** to pay attention to, heed.
attentionné [atɑ̃sjɔne] *a* thoughtful.
atténuant [atenɥɑ̃] *a* extenuating.
atténuation [atenɥasjɔ̃] *nf* extenuation, qualification, understatement.
atténuer [atenɥe] *vt* to attenuate, extenuate, mitigate, qualify, understate, subdue, dim; *vr* to lessen, diminish.
atterrer [atɛre] *v* to overwhelm, fell, stun.
atterrir [atɛri:r] *vi* to ground, alight, land; *vt* to run ashore, beach.
atterrissage [atɛrisa:ʒ] *nm* grounding, landing.
attestation [atɛstasjɔ̃] *nf* attestation, voucher.
attester [atɛste] *vt* to attest, testify, vouch.
attiédir [atjedi:r] *vt* to make tepid, lukewarm.
attifer [atife] *vtr* to dress up.
attirail [atira:j] *nm* outfit, tackle, gear, show.
attirance [atirɑ̃:s] *nf* attraction, lure.
attirant [atirɑ̃] *a* attractive, engaging.
attirer [atire] *vt* to attract, draw, entice, inveigle.
attiser [atize] *vt* to stir (up), poke (up).
attitude [atityd] *nf* attitude.

attouchement [atuʃmã] *nm* touch (ing), contact.
attraction [atraksjɔ̃] *nf* attraction, attractiveness; *pl* variety show.
attrait [atrɛ] *nm* attraction, allurement, enticement, charm.
attrape [atrap] *nf* trap, snare, trick, catch.
attrape-mouches [atrapmuʃ] *nm* fly-paper.
attrape-nigaud [atrapnigo] *nm* booby-trap.
attraper [atrape] *vt* to catch, trick, get, seize, scold.
attrayant [atrɛjã] *a* attractive.
attribuer [atribɥe] *vt* to attribute, ascribe, assign, put down (to à); *vr* to assume.
attribut [atriby] *nm* attribute.
attribution [atribysjɔ̃] *nf* attribution, allocation, award, conferment; *pl* powers, functions.
attristé [atriste] *a* saddened, sorrowful.
attrister [atriste] *vt* to sadden; *vr* to grow sad.
attrition [atrisjɔ̃] *nf* attrition.
attroupement [atrupmã] *nm* mob.
attrouper [atrupe] *vt* to gather, collect; *vr* to flock, form into a mob, crowd.
au [o] = à + le.
aubaine [obɛn] *nf* windfall, godsend.
aube [oːb] *nf* early dawn, paddle, blade.
aubépine [obepin] *nf* hawthorn, may.
auberge [oberʒ] *nf* inn; — **de la jeunesse** youth hostel.
aubergine [oberʒin] *nf* egg-plant, aubergine.
aubergiste [oberʒist] *n* innkeeper.
aucun [okœ̃] *pn* anyone, no one, nobody; *pl* some people; *a* any, not any.
aucunement [okynmã] *ad* not at all, in no way.
audace [odas] *nf* audacity, boldness, daring, hardihood.
audacieux, -euse [odasjø, øːz] *a* audacious, bold, daring, dashing, impudent.
au-delà [od(ə)la] *ad* beyond; *nm* the after-life.
au-dessous [odsu] *ad* underneath, below; *prep* — de below, under.
au-dessus [odsy] *ad* above, over (head); *prep* — de above, over, beyond.
au-devant [odvã] *ad* **aller** — **de** to go to meet.
audience [odjãːs] *nf* audience, hearing; **lever l'**— to close the session, sitting.
auditeur, -trice [oditœːr, tris] *n* listener.
audition [odisjɔ̃] *nf* audition, hearing.
auditoire [oditwaːr] *nm* audience.
auge [oːʒ] *nf* trough.

augmentation [ɔgmãtasjɔ̃] *nf* increase, rise.
augmenter [ɔgmãte] *vt* to augment, increase, add, raise; *vr* to increase, rise.
augure [ɔgyːr] *nm* augury, omen; **de mauvais** — unpropitious, inauspicious.
augurer [ɔgyre] *vt* to augur, promise.
auguste [ɔgyst] *a* august, majestic.
aujourd'hui [oʒurdɥi] *ad* today; **d'**— **en huit** a week from today.
aumône [omoːn] *nf* alms, charity.
aumônier [omonje] *nm* almoner, chaplain.
aune [oːn] *nf* alder.
auparavant [oparavã] *ad* before, first.
auprès [oprɛ] *ad* hard by, close at hand; *prep* — de close (to, by), near, beside, at, with, in comparison with.
auquel [okɛl] = à + lequel.
auréole [ɔreɔl] *nf* halo.
auriculaire [ɔrikylɛːr] *nm* little finger.
aurore [ɔrɔːr] *nf* dawn.
ausculter [ɔskylte] *vt* to sound.
auspice [ospis] *nm* auspice, omen.
aussi [osi] *ad* as, so, also, too; *cj* therefore, so.
aussitôt [osito] *ad* at once, immediately; *cj* — **que** as soon as; — **dit,** — **fait** no sooner said than done.
austère [ostɛːr] *a* austere, severe, stern.
austérité [osterite] *nf* austerity, severity, sternness.
Australie [ostrali] *nf* Australia.
australien, -ienne [ostraljɛ̃, jɛn] *an* Australian.
autant [otã] *ad* as much, so much, as many, so many; — **que** as much as, as many as, as far as; **d'**— **que,** **d'** — **plus que** more especially as, all the more . . . as.
autel [otɛl] *nm* altar.
auteur [otœːr] *nm* author, writer, promoter, originator, perpetrator; **femme** — authoress; **droits d'**— royalties.
authenticité [otãtisite] *nf* authenticity.
authentique [otãtik] *a* authentic, genuine.
auto [oto] *nf* motor car, car, auto.
auto b graphie [otɔbjɔgrafi] *nf* autobiography.
autobus [otɔbyːs] *nm* omnibus, bus.
autocar [otɔkaːr] *nm* motor coach, excursion bus.
autochtone [otɔktoːn, -tɔn] *a* native, indigenous.
autocrate [otɔkrat] *n* autocrat; *a* autocratic.
autocratie [otɔkrasi] *nf* autocracy.
autocratique [otɔkratik] *a* autocratic.

autodémarreur [otɔdemarœ:r] *nm* self-starter.

autodétermination [otɔdetɛrminasjɔ̃] *nf* (*govt*) self-determination.

autodidacte [otɔdidakt] *a* self-taught, -educated; *nm* autodidact.

autodrome [otɔdrɔm, -dro:m] *nm* motor-racing track, speedway.

autographe [otɔgraf] *nm* autograph.

autographier [otɔgrafje] *vt* to autograph.

automate [otɔmat] *nm* automaton, robot.

automatique [otɔmatik] *a* automatic, automaton-like.

automnal [otɔmnal] *a* autumnal.

automne [otɔn] *nm* autumn, fall; *a* d'—autumnal.

automobile [otɔmɔbil] *a* automotive; *nf* automobile, motor car; **salon de l'**— automobile show.

automobilisme [otɔmɔbilism] *nm* motoring.

automobiliste [otɔmɔbilist] *n* motorist.

automoteur [otɔmɔtœ:r] *a* self-propelling.

autonome [otɔnɔm] *a* autonomous, self-governing.

autonomie [otɔnɔmi] *nf* autonomy, home-rule.

autopsie [otɔpsi] *nf* autopsy, post-mortem examination.

autorail [otɔra:j] *nm* rail-car.

autorisation [otɔrizasjɔ̃, ɔt-] *nf* authorization, permit, license.

autorisé [otɔrize, ɔt-] *a* authorized, authoritative.

autoriser [otɔrize, ɔt-] *vt* to authorize, empower, sanction, license.

autoritaire [otɔritɛ:r, ɔt-] *a* authoritative, domineering.

autorité [otɔrite, ɔt-] *nf* authority, warrant; **faire** — to be an authority; **qui fait** — authoritative.

autoroute [otɔrut] *nf* highway.

auto-stop [otɔstɔp] *nm* hitch-hiking.

autour [otu:r] *ad* around, about; *prep* — **de** around.

autre [o:tr] *a pn* other; *a* further, different; **d'un moment à l'**— any moment; **de temps à** — now and again; **nous** —**s Français** we French; **l'un et l'**— both; **les uns . . . les** —**s** some . . . others; — **chose** something else; **quelqu'un d'**— someone else; **j'en ai vu bien d'**—**s** that's nothing;— **part** elsewhere.

autrefois [otrəfwɑ] *ad* formerly, in the past.

autrement [otrəmɑ̃] *ad* otherwise, else, in a different way.

Autriche [otriʃ] *nf* Austria.

autrichien, -ienne [otriʃjɛ̃, jɛn] *an* Austrian.

autruche [otryʃ] *nf* ostrich.

autrui [otrɥi] *pn indef* others, other people.

aux [o] = **à** + **les.**

auxiliare [ɔksiljɛ:r, o-] *a* auxiliary, sub-; *nm* auxiliary.

auxquels [okel] = **à** + **lesquels.**

aval [aval] *nm* lower part of river; **ad en** — downstream; *prep* **en** — **de** below.

avalanche [avalɑ̃:ʃ] *nf* avalanche.

avaler [avale] *vt* to swallow, drink up, gulp down, stomach; — **une insulte** to pocket an insult, affront.

avance [avɑ̃:s] *nf* advance, start, lead, drive, dash; loan; **à l', d', par** — beforehand, in advance; **être en** — to be fast, before time, ahead.

avancé [avɑ̃se] *a* advanced, forward, onward, well on, high; **vous voilà bien** — much good that has done you.

avancement [avɑ̃smɑ̃] *nm* advancing, putting forward, furtherance, rise, promotion, advancement.

avancer [avɑ̃se] *vt* to advance, put (forward, on), carry on, promote; *vi* to move forward, advance, get on, be fast, be ahead of time; *vr* to advance, make one's way, progress, jut out.

avant [avɑ̃] *prep* before; — **peu** presently; *ad* before, far (into), deep, further (in, back); **en** — before, forward, in front, ahead, onward; *cj* — **que** before; *a* fore-; *nm* bow, forward, front.

avantage [avɑ̃ta:ʒ] *nm* advantage; **tirer** — **de** to turn to account.

avantager [avɑ̃taʒe] *vt* to favor, improve.

avantageux, -euse [avɑ̃taʒø, ø:z] *a* advantageous, beneficial, favorable, becoming, self-satisfied.

avant-bras [avɑ̃bra] *nm* forearm.

avant-corps [avɑ̃kɔ:r] *nm* fore-part.

avant-cour [avɑ̃ku:r] *nf* forecourt.

avant-coureur [avɑ̃kurœ:r] *a* precursory; *nm* forerunner.

avant-dernier, -ière [avɑ̃dɛrnje, jɛ:r] *a* next to the last.

avant-garde [avɑ̃gard] *nf* van (guard), advanced guard, avant-garde.

avant-goût [avɑ̃gu] *nm* foretaste, earnest.

avant-guerre [avɑ̃gɛ:r] *nm* pre-war period.

avant-hier [avɑ̃tjɛ:r] *ad* day before yesterday.

avant-plan [avɑ̃plɑ̃] *nm* foreground.

avant-port [avɑ̃pɔ:r] *nm* outer harbor.

avant-poste [avɑ̃pɔst] *nm* outpost.

avant-première [avɑ̃prəmjɛ:r] *nf* dress rehearsal.

avant-propos [avɑ̃prɔpo] *nm* preface.

avare [ava:r] *a* miserly, tight-fisted, chary; *nm* miser.

avarice [avaris] *nf* avarice, miserliness, closeness.

avaricieux, -euse [avarisjø, jø:z] *a* avaricious, mean.

avarie [avari] *nf* damage.

avarier [avarje] *vt* to damage; *vr* to deteriorate.
avatar [avataːr] *nm* avatar; *pl* ups and downs.
avec [avɛk] *prep* with; — ça! nonsense; **et** — **ça Monsieur?** do you require anything else? **d'**— from; *ad* with it, with them.
avenant [avnã] *a* comely, prepossessing, buxom; **à l'**— in keeping, to match.
avènement [avɛnmã] *nm* advent, accession.
avenir [avniːr] *nm* future; **à l'**— henceforth, hereafter.
aventure [avãtyːr] *nf* adventure, luck, love-affair; **à l'**— at random, aimlessly; **d'**— by chance; **dire, tirer la bonne** — to tell fortunes.
aventurer [avãtyre] *vtr* to venture, risk.
aventureux, -euse [avãtyrø, øːz] *a* adventurous, venturesome, reckless, risky.
aventurier, -ière [avãtyrje, jɛːr] *n* adventurer, adventuress.
avenu [avny] *a* **non** — cancelled, void.
avenue [avny] *nf* avenue, drive, walk.
avéré [avere] *a* established, proved, authenticated.
averse [avɛrs] *nf* shower of rain, downpour.
aversion [avɛrsjɔ̃] *nf* aversion, dislike, repulsion.
averti [avɛrti] *a* experienced, well-informed, knowing.
avertir [avɛrtiːr] *vt* to warn, caution, give notice (of).
avertissement [avɛrtismã] *nm* warning, notice, caution; **sans** — **préalable** at a moment's notice.
avertisseur [avɛrtisœːr] *nm* alarm, warning, automobile horn.
aveu [avø] *nm* confession, avowal, admission, consent.
aveugle [avœgl] *a* blind, sightless; **à l'**— blindly, wildly; *nm* blind person.
aveuglement [avœgləmã] *nm* blindness.
aveuglément [avœglemã] *ad* blindly.
aveugler [avœgle] *vt* to blind, dazzle, hoodwink.
aveuglette [avœglɛt] *ad* **à l'**— blind(ly).
aviateur, -trice [avjatœr, tris] *n* aviator, flyer.
aviation [avjasjɔ̃] *nf* aviation, air force.
avide [avid] *a* avid, greedy, grasping, eager (for **de**).
avidité [avidite] *nf* avidity, greed, eagerness.
avilir [aviliːr] *vt* to debase, depreciate; *vr* to lower oneself, stoop, lose value.
avilissement [avilismã] *nm* abase-

ment, degradation, depreciation.
avion [avjɔ̃] *nm* airplane, aircraft; — **de bombardment** bomber; — **de chasse, de combat** fighter; — **de ligne** airliner; — **en remorque** glider; — **à réaction** jet plane; **par** — by airmail.
aviron [avirɔ̃] *nm* oar, rowing.
avis [avi] *nm* opinion, advice, judgment, notice, warning; **à mon** — to my mind; **changer d'**— to change one's mind.
avisé [avize] *a* far-seeing, wary, canny, shrewd, advised.
aviser [avize] *vt* to warn, perceive; *vi* to see about (**à**); *vr* to take it into one's head.
avocat [avɔka] *nm* lawyer, counsel, advocate.
avoine [avwan] *nf* oats; **folle** — wild oats.
avoir [avwaːr] *vt* to have, possess, get, obtain; — **vingt ans** to be twenty years old; **qu'avez-vous?** what is the matter with you? **en** — **à, contre qn.** to bear s.o. a grudge; **y** — *v imp* to be; **qu'est-ce qu'il y a?** what's up, what's the matter?; **il y a sept ans** seven years ago; *nm* property, possessions, balance in hand; **doit et** — debit and credit.
avoisinant [avwazinã] *a* neighboring.
avoisiner [avwazine] *vt* to be near, border on.
avorter [avɔrte] *vi* to abort, miscarry.
avortement [avɔrtmã] *nm* abortion, miscarriage.
avorton [avɔrtɔ̃] *nm* undersized, stunted creature, aborted infant.
avoué [avwe] *a* professed; *nm* solicitor, attorney.
avouer [avwe] *vt* to avow, confess, acknowledge.
avril [avril] *nm* April; **un poisson d'**— an April fool.
axe [aks] *nm* axis, spindle.
axiome [aksjoːm] *nm* axiom.
azimut [azimyt] *nm* azimuth, bearing, (*sl*) direction.
azote [azɔt] *nm* nitrogen.
azotique [azɔtik] *a* nitric.
azur [azyːr] *nm* azure, blue.
azyme [azim] *a* unleavened; *nm* unleavened bread.

B

baba [baba] *nm* sponge-cake; *a* dumbfounded.
babeurre [babœːr] *nm* buttermilk.
babil [babi(l)] *nm* prattling, twittering.
babillard [babijaːr] *a* talkative, babbling; *n* chatterbox.
babiller [babije] *vi* to chatter, babble, prattle.
babines [babin] *nf pl* chops, drooping lips.

babiole [babjɔl] nf bauble, curio, trinket, frippery.

bábord [babɔːr] nm port (side).

babouin [babwɛ̃] nm baboon.

bac [bak] nm ferryboat, tub.

bâche [baːʃ] nf tarpaulin, awning, cistern; **— de campement** ground-sheet.

bachelier, -ière [baʃəlje, jɛːr] n pre-university student.

bâcher [baʃe] vt to cover with a tarpaulin.

bachot [baʃo] nm baccalaureate, punt.

bacille [basil] nm bacillus, germ.

bâcler [bakle] vt to bolt, bar, block, scamp, dash off.

bactériologie [bakterjɔlɔʒi] nf bacteriology.

badaud [bado] a idle; n stroller, idler.

badauder [badode] vi to saunter, idle about.

badigeon [badiʒɔ̃] nm distemper, whitewash brush.

badigeonner [badiʒɔne] vt to distemper, color-wash, paint.

badin [badɛ̃] a playful, jocular, waggish; n joker, wag.

badinage [badinaːʒ] nm bantering, joking.

badine [badin] nf switch, cane.

badiner [badine] vt to tease, banter; vi to joke, trifle, banter.

bafoué [bafwe] a scorned, discomfited.

bafouer [bafwe] vt to scoff, jeer at, sneer at.

bafouiller [bafuje] vti to stammer, splutter, gabble.

bâfrer [bafre] vt to gobble, guzzle; vi to gormandize; vr to stuff.

bagage [bagaːʒ] nm baggage; pl luggage; **plier —** to pack up, clear out.

bagarre [bagaːr] nf brawl, disturbance, affray, scrap.

bagatelle [bagatɛl] nf trifle.

bagnard [baɲaːr] n convict.

bagne [baɲ] nm prison.

bagnole [baɲɔl] nf worn-out car, car.

bagout [bagu] nm **avoir du —** to have the gift of gab.

bague [bag] nf ring, cigar-band.

baguenauder [bagnode] vi to waste time, trifle.

baguette [bagɛt] nf wand, rod, stick, pointer, beading, long loaf.

bahut [bay] nm (fam) cupboard, trunk, chest; school.

bai [bɛ] a (color) bay.

baie [bɛ] nf bay, bight, berry, bay-window.

baignade [bɛɲad] nf bathe, bathing-place.

baigner [bɛɲe] vt to bathe, bath, wash; vi to soak, steep; vr to take a bath, bathe, welter.

baigneur, -euse [bɛɲœːr, øːz] n bather, bathing attendant.

baignoire [bɛɲwaːr] nf bath, (theatre) pit-box.

bail [baːj] nm lease.

bâillement [bajmɑ̃] nm yawn(ing), gaping.

bâiller [baje] vi to yawn, gape, be ajar.

bailleur [bajœːr] nm lessor; **— de fonds** money-lender, sleeping-partner.

bâillon [bajɔ̃] nm gag.

bâillonner [bajɔne] vt to gag, muzzle.

bain [bɛ̃] nm bath, bathe, dip; **—s de mer** sea-bathing.; **—(s) de soleil** sunbath(ing).

bain-marie [bɛ̃mari] nm double boiler, water-bottle.

baïonnette [bajɔnɛt] nf bayonet.

baiser [bɛze] vt to kiss; nm kiss.

baisse [bɛs] nf fall, drop, ebb, abatement.

baisser [bɛse] vt to lower, let down, turn down; vi to fall, go down, sink, droop, slump; vr to stoop.

baissier [bɛsje] nm (Stock Exchange) bear.

bajoue [baʒu] nf cheek, chap, chop.

bal [bal] nm ball, dance.

balade [balad] nf amble, drive, stroll.

balader [balade] vir to go for a stroll, a drive.

baladeuse [baladøːz] nf handcart, trailer, inspection-lamp.

baladin [baladɛ̃] nm buffoon.

balafre [balafr] nf gash, cut, scar.

balafrer [balafre] vt to gash, scar, slash.

balai [balɛ] nm brush, broom.

balance [balɑ̃ːs] nf balance, scale(s), suspense; **faire la —** to strike a balance.

balancer [balɑ̃se] vt to balance, swing, rock; vi to swing, dangle, waver, hesitate; vr to sway, swing, rock.

balancier [balɑ̃sje] nm pendulum, balance-wheel, beam, balancing-pole.

balançoire [balɑ̃swaːr] nf swing, seesaw.

balayage [balɛjaːʒ] nm sweeping, (radar) scanning.

balayer [balɛje] vt to sweep (out, away, up), scour, throw out.

balayeur, -euse [balɛjœːr, øːz] nmf sweeper, cleaner, scavenger; nf carpet-sweeper.

balayures [balɛjyːr] nf pl sweepings.

balbutier [balbysje] vti to stammer, stutter, falter.

balcon [balkɔ̃] nm balcony, dress-circle.

baldaquin [baldakɛ̃] nm canopy.

baleine [balɛn] nf whale, whalebone, rib.

baleinière [balɛnjɛːr] nf whaleboat.

balise [baliːz] nf beacon, seamark, groundlight, radiosignal.

balistique [balistik] *a* ballistic; *nf* ballistics.
baliverne [balivɛrn] *nf* idle story; *pl* balderdash, rubbish.
ballade [balad] *nf* ballad.
ballant [balɑ̃] *a* dangling.
ballast [balast] *nm* ballast, bottom.
balle [bal] *nf* ball, bullet, franc, bale, pack, chaff, husk; **avoir la — belle** to have the ball at one's feet; **c'est un enfant de la —** he has been brought up in the trade.
ballet [balɛ] *nm* ballet (dancing).
ballon [balɔ̃] *nm* balloon, football; **lancer un — d'essai** to fly a kite.
balloner [balɔne] *vir* to swell, balloon out, distend, bulge.
ballot [balo] *nm* bundle, bale, kitbag.
ballotage [balɔtaːʒ] *nm* shaking, tossing, second ballot.
balloter [balɔte] *vt* to shake, toss about, buffet; *vi* to toss, shake, rattle, swing.
balnéaire [balneɛːr] *a* **station —** seaside resort.
balourd [baluːr] *a* uncouth, clumsy, awkward; *n* awkward person, yokel, dullard.
balourdise [balurdiːz] *nf* clumsiness, stupid mistake.
baluchon [balyʃɔ̃] *nm* bundle, kit.
balustrade [balystrad] *nf* balustrade, rail.
balustre [balystr] *nm* baluster; *pl* banisters.
bambin [bɑ̃bɛ̃] *n* little child, urchin, baby.
bamboche [bɑ̃bɔʃ] *nf* puppet, undersized person, carousal, spree.
bambou [bɑ̃bu] *nm* bamboo.
ban [bɑ̃] *nm* ban, proclamation, round of cheers, banishment; *pl* banns; **mettre au —** to banish, ostracize.
banal [banal] *a* commonplace, hackneyed, trite, casual.
banalité [banalite] *nf* triteness, commonplace remark.
banane [banan] *nf* banana.
bananier [bananje] *nm* banana-tree.
banc [bɑ̃] *nm* bench, form, seat, bed, pew, layer, shoal; **— des accusés** dock; **— de sable** sandbank.
bancal [bɑ̃kal] *a* bow-legged, rickety.
banco [bɑ̃ko] *nm* swish, baked mud, (for building) clay.
bandage [bɑ̃daːʒ] *nm* bandaging, bandage, binder, truss, binding.
bande [bɑ̃ːd] *nf* band, group, gang, flock, shoal, stripe, belt, shaft, wrapper, cushion, reel, film; **donner de la —** (of ship) to list.
bandeau [bɑ̃do] *nm* headband, bandeau, bandage.
bander [bɑ̃de] *vt* to bind up, bandage, stretch, bend; *vr* to band together; **— les yeux à** to blindfold.
banderole [bɑ̃drɔl] *nf* streamer, shoulder-belt, sling.

bandit [bɑ̃di] *nm* bandit, gangster, rascal.
bandoulière [bɑ̃duljɛːr] *nf* bandolier, shoulder-belt.
banlieue [bɑ̃ljø] *nf* suburb.
banne [ban] *nf* hamper, awning, coal-cart.
banneau [bano] *nm* fruit-basket, hamper.
bannière [banjɛːr] *nf* banner.
banni [bani] *a* outlawed, exiled; *n* outlaw, exile.
bannir [baniːr] *vt* to outlaw, banish.
bannissement [banismɑ̃] *nm* exile, banishment.
banque [bɑ̃ːk] *nf* bank, banking.
banqueroute [bɑ̃krut] *nf* bankruptcy; **faire —** to go bankrupt.
banquet [bɑ̃kɛ] *nm* banquet, feast.
banquette [bɑ̃kɛt] *nf* seat, bench.
banquier, -ière [bɑ̃kje, jɛːr] *a* banking; *n* banker.
banquise [bɑ̃kiːz] *nf* ice-field, -pack, -flow.
baptême [batɛːm] *nm* baptism, christening; *a* **de —** baptismal, maiden.
baptiser [batize] *vt* to baptize, christen.
baquet [bakɛ] *nm* tub, bucket.
bar [baːr] *nm* bar, pub; bass.
baragouiner [baragwine] *vti* to jabber, gibber.
baraque [barak] *nf* hut, booth, stall.
baraquement [barakmɑ̃] *nm* hut, lodging in huts; *pl* hutments.
baratte [barat] *nf* churn.
baratter [barate] *vt* to churn.
barbare [barbaːr] *a* barbarous, cruel, barbaric; *n* barbarian.
barbarie [barbari] *nf* barbarity, barbarousness, barbarism.
barbe [barb] *nf* beard, whiskers; **se faire la —** to shave; **rire dans sa —** to laugh up one's sleeve.
barbelé [barbəle] *a* barbed.
barbiche [barbiʃ] *nf* goatee beard.
barboter [barbɔte] *vt* to splash up and down; *vi* to paddle, flounder, splash about.
barbouillage [barbujaːʒ] *nm* smearing, scrawl, daubing, scribble, scribbling.
barbouiller [barbuje] *vt* to smear, smudge, dirty.
barbu [barby] *a* bearded.
barbue [barby] *nf* brill.
bard [baːr] *nm* hand truck.
barde [bard] *nf* pack-saddle, slice of bacon.
barder [barde] *vt* to carry on a hand-barrow, bard; *vi* to rage; **ça va —** there will be ructions.
barème [barɛːm] *nm* ready-reckoner, scale.
baril [bari] *nm* barrel, cask.
barillet [barijɛ] *nm* keg, drum, cylinder.
bariolé [barjɔle] *a* multicolored, motley, gaudy.

baromètre [barɔmɛtr] nm weather glass, barometer.

baroque [barɔk] a odd, quaint; nm baroque style.

barque [bark] nf boat, fishing-smack.

barrage [bɑrɑːʒ] nm road-block, barrier, dam, weir, (sport) replay.

barre [bɑːr] nf iron bar, wooden batten, rod, tiller, helm, stroke, (law courts) bar, rail, rung, surf, undertow; — des témoins witness-box; homme de — coxswain, helmsman.

barreau [baro] nm (law courts) bar, rail, rung; pl (prison) bars.

barrer [bare] vt to bar, block, dam, obstruct, cross out, steer; — un chèque to cancel a check; rue barrée no thoroughfare.

barrette [barɛt] nf biretta, barette.

barreur [barœːr] nm helmsman, coxswain.

barricade [barikad] nf barricade.

barricader [barikade] vt to barricade.

barrière [barjɛːr] nf gate, toll-gate, bar, rail.

barrique [barik] nf large barrel, cask, hogshead.

baryton [baritɔ̃] nm baritone.

bas, -se [bɑ, bɑːs] a low, base, deep, mean, lower; ad low, quietly; nm lower part, end, bottom, stocking; pl hose; en — downstairs, below; en — de at the foot of; à — down (with); mettre — to lay down, bring forth.

basalte [bazalt] nm basalt.

basaner [bazane] vt to tan; vr to become tanned.

bas-bout [babu] nm bottom, lower end.

bas-côté [bakote] nm aisle, lay-by.

bascule [baskyl] nf seesaw, platform scale, rocker; chaise à — rocking-chair; wagon à — tipcart.

basculer [baskyle] vt to rock, swing; vti to dip, tip.

base [bɑːz] nf foundation, basis, foot, root; de — basic; sans — unfounded.

baser [baze] vt to base, found; vr to be founded.

bas-fond [bafɔ̃] nm low ground, swamp, shoal, deep pool; pl riffraff, dregs.

basilique [bazilik] nf basilica.

basque [bask] nf tail.

basse [bɑːs] nf bass.

basse-cour [baskuːr] nf farmyard.

bassesse [basɛs] nf lowness, vileness, baseness.

basse-fosse [basfoːs] nf dungeon.

bassin [basɛ̃] nm basin, pond, ornamental lake, dock; — houiller coalfield.

bassine [basin] nf pan.

bât [bɑ] nm pack-saddle; cheval de — pack-horse.

bataille [batɑːj] nf battle, contest.

batailleur, -euse [batajœːr, øːz] a pugnacious, cantankerous, quarrelsome.

bataillon [batajɔ̃] nm battalion.

bâtard [bɑtɑːr] an bastard, mongrel.

bateau [bato] nm boat, vessel; — -école training ship; — -feu light ship; — pétrolier tanker.

bateleur, -euse [batlœːr, øːz] n juggler, mountebank.

batelier, -ière [batəlje, jɛːr] n boatman, -woman, ferryman, -woman, bargee.

bâter [bate] vt to put a pack-saddle on.

bath [bat] a (fam) great, swell.

batifoler [batifole] vi to frolic, lark.

bâtiment [batimɑ̃] nm building (trade), edifice, ship.

bâtir [batiːr] vt to build, erect.

bâtisse [batis] nf ramshackle building, masonry.

batiste [batist] nf cambric.

bâton [batɔ̃] nm stick, staff, baton, pole, truncheon; à —s rompus desultory, by fits and starts.

bâtonner [batɔne] vt to beat, whip, cane.

battage [batɑːʒ] nm beating, threshing, churning, boosting.

battant [batɑ̃] a beating, driving, pelting, banging; porte —e swing-door; nm bell-clapper, table, counter top.

batte [bat] nf beetle, mallet.

battement [batmɑ̃] nm beating, stamping, flapping, banging, fluttering, tapping, throbbing, margin (of time), interval.

batterie [batri] nf beat of drums, roll of drums, artillery battery; set; — de cuisine set of kitchen utensils.

batteur -euse [batœːr, øːz] nf threshing machine, egg whisk; nm beater, thresher.

battre [batr] vt to beat, thrash, thresh, batter, defeat, churn, whisk, (flag) fly, shuffle; vi to beat, throb, belt, flap, bang; — la campagne to scour the countryside, to be delirious; — des mains to clap one's hands; vr to fight.

battu [baty] a beaten, wrought; avoir les yeux —s to have circles under one's eyes.

battue [baty] nf beat, round-up.

baudet [bodɛ] nm donkey.

baudrier [bodrije] nm shoulder-belt, cross-belt.

bauge [boːʒ] nf lair, hole, squirrel's nest, pigsty.

baume [boːm] nm balm, balsam.

bauxite [boksit] nf bauxite.

bavard [bavaːr] a talkative, garrulous; n chatterbox, gossip.

bavardage [bavardaːʒ] nm chattering, gossip.

bavarder [bavarde] vi to gossip, chatter.

bave [baːv] *nf* froth, foam, slaver, slime.

baver [bave] *vi* to slaver, dribble, foam, run.

bavette [bavɛt] *nf* bib.

baveur, -euse [bavœːr, øːz] *a* slavering, driveling; *nm* slobberer.

baveux, -euse [bavø, øːz] *a* slobbery, juicy.

bavure [bavyːr] *nf* burr, blot, smudge.

bayer [baje] *vi* — **aux corneilles** to gape at the moon.

bazar [bazaːr] *nm* bazaar, cheap stores; **tout le** — the whole caboodle.

béant [beɑ̃] *a* gaping, yawning.

béat [bea] *a* smug, complacent.

béatitude [beatityd] *nf* bliss, complacency.

beau, belle [bo, bɛl] *a* lovely, beautiful, fair, fine, handsome, noble; **il en a fait de belles** he has been up to some nice things; **bel et bien** well and truly, fairly; **bel et bon** all very well; **l'échapper belle** to have a narrow escape; **il avait beau faire** in spite of all he did.

beaucoup [boku] *ad* (very) much, a lot, a good deal, (very) many, lots.

beau-fils [bofis] *nm* son-in-law, stepson.

beau-frère [bofrɛːr] *nm* brother-in-law, stepbrother.

beau-père [bopɛːr] *nm* father-in-law, stepfather.

beaupré [bopre] *nm* bowsprit.

beauté [bote] *nf* beauty, loveliness, handsomeness, belle, beautiful woman; **salon de** — beauty parlor; **soins de** — beauty treatment; **se faire une** — to do oneself up; **finir en** — to finish in grand style.

beaux-arts [bozaːr] *nm pl* fine arts.

bébé [bebe] *nm* baby.

bébête [bebɛːt] *a* silly.

bec [bɛk] *nm* beak, bill, spout, mouthpiece, nose, nozzle; — **de gaz** gas burner, jet, lamp-post; — **de plume** pen-nib; **coup de** — peck; **fin** — gourmet; **prise de** — row, altercation; **clouer le** — **à qn.** to shut someone up.

bécane [bekan] *nf* bike.

bécasse [bekas] *nf* woodcock.

bécassine [bekasin] *nf* snipe.

bec-de-cane [bɛkdəkan] *nm* lever, (*of door*) handle, pliers.

bec-de-lièvre [bɛkdəljɛːvr] *nm* harelip.

bêche [bɛʃ] *nf* spade.

bêcher [beʃe] *vt* to dig, run down.

bécot [beko] *nm* kiss, peck.

becquée [beke] *nf* beakful; **donner la** — **à** to feed.

becqueter [bɛkte] *vt* to peck at, pick up, kiss.

bedaine [bədɛn] *nf* paunch.

bedeau [bədo] *nm* verger.

bedon [bədɔ̃] *nm* paunch.

bedonner [bədɔne] *vi* to get stout.

bée [be] *af* gaping; **regarder qn bouche** — to gape at someone.

beffroi [bɛfrwa] *nm* belfry.

bégaiement [begɛmɑ̃] *nm* stammering, stuttering.

bégayer [begeje] *vt* to stammer out, through; *vi* to stutter, splutter, stammer.

bègue [bɛg] *a* stammering; *n* stammerer.

bégueule [begœl] *a* priggish, prudish; *nf* prude.

béguin [begɛ̃] *nm* hood, bonnet; **avoir le** — **pour qn.** to fall for s.o.

beige [bɛːʒ] *nm* beige.

beignet [bɛɲɛ] *nm* fritter.

béjaune [beʒoːn] *nm* nestling, freshman, greenhorn.

bêler [bɛle] *vi* to bleat.

bel-esprit [bɛlɛspri] *nm* wit.

belette [bəlɛt] *nf* weasel.

belge [bɛlʒ] *an* Belgian.

Belgique [bɛlʒik] *nf* Belgium.

bélier [belje] *nm* ram, battering-ram.

bellâtre [belɑːtr] *a* foppish; *nm* fop.

belle [bɛl] *nf* beauty; **jouer la** — to play the deciding game.

belle-fille [bɛlfiːj] *nf* daughter-in-law, stepdaughter.

belle-mère [bɛlmɛːr] *nf* mother-in-law, stepmother.

belles-lettres [bɛlɛtr] *nf* humanities.

belle-sœur [bɛlsœːr] *nf* sister-in-law, stepsister.

belligérance [bɛlliʒerɑ̃ːs] *nf* belligerence.

belligérant [bɛlliʒerɑ̃] *a* belligerent.

belliqueux, -euse [bɛllikø, øːz] *a* bellicose, warlike.

belvédère [bɛlvedeːr] *nm* viewpoint, summer-house.

bémol [bemɔl] *nm* (*music*) flat.

bénédicité [benedisite] *nm* grace, blessing.

bénédictin [benediktɛ̃] *an* Benedictine.

bénédiction [benediksjɔ̃] *nf* blessing.

bénéfice [benefis] *nm* profit, benefit, (*eccl*) living; *pl* profits, drawings.

bénéficiaire [benefisjɛːr] *an* beneficiary.

bénéficier [benefisje] *vi* to benefit, (make a) profit.

benêt [bənɛ] *a* stupid, silly; *nm* ninny, simpleton.

bénévole [benevɔl] *a* benevolent, gentle, voluntary.

bénin, -igne [benɛ̃, iɲ] *a* benign, mild, kindly.

bénir [beniːr] *vt* to bless, consecrate.

bénit [beni] *a* blessed, holy, consecrated; **eau** —**e** holy water.

bénitier [benitje] *nm* holy-water font.

benne [bɛn] *nf* hamper, basket, hutch, bucket; **camion à** — **basculante** dump truck.

benzine [bɛ̃zin] *nf* benzine.

benzol [bɛ̃zol] *nm* benzol.

béquille [bekiːj] *nf* crutch, prop, stand.
bercail [bɛrkaːj] *nm* sheep fold.
berceau [bɛrso] *nm* cradle, cot, arbor.
bercer [bɛrse] *vt* to rock, lull, beguile, soothe; *vr* to rock, sway.
berceuse [bɛrsøːz] *nf* cradle, lullaby.
bergamote [bɛrgamɔt] *nf* bergamot.
berge [bɛrʒ] *nf* bank, parapet.
berger [bɛrʒe] *nm* shepherd.
bergère [bɛrʒɛːr] *nf* shepherdess, easy-chair, wagtail.
bergerie [bɛrʒəri] *nf* sheepfold, pen.
bergeronnette [bɛrʒərɔnɛt] *nf* wagtail.
berline [bɛrlin] *nf* berline, limousine, truck.
berlingot [bɛrlɛ̃go] *nm* caramel, toffee.
berlue [bɛrly] *nf* avoir la — to have a wrong view of things.
berne [bɛrn] *nf* en — at half-mast.
berner [bɛrne] *vt* to toss in a blanket, take in, deceive.
bernique [bɛrnik] *int* nothing doing.
besicles [bəzikl] *nf* spectacles, goggles.
besogne [bəzɔɲ] *nf* work, job, task, bit of work.
besogneux, -euse [bəzɔɲø, øːz] *a* needy, poor.
besoin [bəzwɛ̃] *nm* need, want, necessity, poverty, urge, craving, addiction; **au** — if need be, in a pinch; **avoir** — **de** to need, require.
bestial [bɛstjal] *a* brutish, beastly.
bestialité [bɛstjalite] *nf* bestiality, beastliness.
bestiaux [bɛstjo] *nm pl* livestock, cattle.
bestiole [bɛstjɔl] *nf* little beast, insect.
bêta [bɛta] *nm* nincompoop, wiseacre, nitwit.
bétail [betaːj] *nm* livestock, cattle.
bête [bɛːt] *nf* animal, beast, blockhead, fool; **faire la** — to act the fool; — **à bon Dieu** ladybird, harmless creature; — **noire** pet aversion; **chercher la petite** — to quibble, be overcritical.
bêtise [betiːz] *nf* stupidity, foolishness, silly thing.
béton [betɔ̃] *nm* concrete; — **armé** reinforced concrete, ferro-concrete.
bétonner [betɔne] *vt* to concrete.
bétonnière [betɔnjɛːr] *nf* concrete mixer.
bette [bɛt] *nf* beet.
betterave [bɛtraːv] *nf* beetroot, mangel; — **sucrière** sugar-beet.
beuglement [bøgləmɑ̃] *nm* bellowing, lowing.
beugler [bøgle] *vt* to bellow, bawl out; *vi* to bellow, low.
beurre [bœːr] *nm* butter; **cuit au** — noir cooked in brown butter; **œil au** — **noir** black eye.

beurrer [bœre] *vt* to butter.
bévue [bevy] *nf* blunder.
biais [bjɛ] *a* sloping, slanting, oblique, askew; *nm* slant, slope, bias, expedient; **de** — sideways; **en** — on the slant.
bibelot [biblo] *nm* trinket, curio, knick-knack.
biberon [bibrɔ̃] *nm* feeding-bottle, feeder, tippler.
bible [bibl] *nf* Bible.
bibliographe [bibliɔgraf] *nm* bibliographer.
bibliographie [bibliɔgrafi] *nf* bibliography.
bibliomane [bibliɔman] *nm* book collector.
bibliophile [bibliɔfil] *nm* booklover.
bibliothécaire [bibliɔtekɛːr] *nm* librarian.
bibliothèque [bibliɔtɛk] *nf* library, bookcase.
biblique [biblik] *a* biblical.
bicarbonate [bikarbɔnat] *nm* bicarbonate.
biche [biʃ] *nf* hind, doe, darling.
bichon [biʃɔ̃] *n* lapdog, darling.
bicoque [bikɔk] *nf* jerry-built house, shanty.
bicyclette [bisiklɛt] *nf* bicycle; **aller à** — à to cycle to; **faire de la** — to cycle.
bidet [bidɛ] *nm* nag, bidet, trestle.
bidon [bidɔ̃] *nm* can, tin, drum, water-bottle; **du** — rubbishy; **bidonville** — shanty town.
bief [bjɛf] *nm* mill-race, -course, -lade, (of river) reach.
bielle [bjɛl] *nf* rod, crank-arm.
bien [bjɛ̃] *ad* well, good, right, proper, really, very, quite, indeed, much, many; *nm* property, wealth, blessing; *pl* belongings, chattels, assets; **elle est** — she is nicelooking; **être** — **avec** to be on good terms with; — **que** *cj* although.
bien-aimé [bjɛ̃nɛme] *an* beloved.
bien-être [bjɛ̃nɛːtr] *nm* comfort, well-being, welfare.
bienfaisance [bjɛ̃fəzɑ̃ːs] *nf* beneficence, generosity, charity; **œuvre de** — charitable society, work.
bienfaisant [bjɛ̃fəzɑ̃] *a* charitable, kind, beneficial.
bienfait [bjɛ̃fɛ] *nm* benefit, favor, boon, kindness.
bienfaiteur, -trice [bjɛ̃fɛtœːr, tris] *n* benefactor, -tress.
bien-fondé [bjɛ̃fɔ̃de] *nm* merits, justice, soundness.
bien-fonds [bjɛ̃fɔ̃] *nm* real estate.
bienheureux, -euse [bjɛ̃nœrø, øːz] *a* happy, blessed.
biennal [biɛnnal] *a* biennial.
bienséance [bjɛ̃seɑ̃ːs] *nf* decorum, propriety.
bienséant [bjɛ̃seɑ̃] *a* decorous, seemly, proper.
bientôt [bjɛ̃to] *ad* soon, before long; **à** — good-bye.

bienveillance [bjɛ̃vɛjɑ̃:s] nf benevolence, goodwill, kindness.
bienveillant [bjɛ̃vɛjɑ̃] a benevolent, kindly.
bienvenu [bjɛ̃vny] an welcome.
bienvenue [bjɛ̃vny] nf welcome.
bière [bjɛːr] nf beer, ale; bier, coffin.
biffer [bife] vt to delete.
biffin [bifɛ̃] nm ragman, junkman, foot-soldier, footslogger.
bifteck [biftek] nm beefsteak.
bifurcation [bifyrkasjɔ̃] nf fork, branch line.
bifurquer [bifyrke] vi to fork, branch off.
bigame [bigam] a bigamous; n bigamist.
bigamie [bigami] nf bigamy.
bigarré [bigare] a variegated, mottled, motley.
bigorneau [bigɔrne] nm periwinkle, whelk.
bigot [bigo] a sanctimonious, overdevout; n bigot.
bigoudi [bigudi] nm hair-curler.
bijou [biʒu] nm jewel.
bijouterie [biʒutri] nf jewelry, jeweler's shop, jeweler's trade.
bijoutier, -ière [biʒutje, jɛːr] n jeweler.
bilan [bilɑ̃] nm balance-sheet, schedule; dresser le — to strike a balance.
bile [bil] nf spleen, anger; se faire de la — to worry, fret.
bilieux, -euse [biljø, øːz] a bilious, liverish.
billard [bijaːr] nm billiards, billiard-table, billiard room; — japonais bagatelle table.
bille [biːj] nf billiard ball, marble, log; (rl) sleeper; rolling pin; roulement à —s ball-bearing.
billet [bijɛ] nm (bank-)note, letter, ticket, bill, permit; — simple one-way ticket; — d'aller et retour return ticket; — à ordre promissory note.
billot [bijo] nm (of wood) block.
bimensuel, -elle [bimɑ̃sɥel] a fortnightly, every two weeks.
bimestriel [bimestriel] a every other month, bimonthly.
binaire [binɛːr] a binary.
bine [bin] nf hoe.
biner [bine] vt to hoe.
binette [binɛt] nf hoe.
binocle [binɔkl] nm eye-glasses, pince-nez.
binoculaire [binɔkylɛːr] a two-eyed, binocular.
biographe [biɔgraf] nm biographer.
biographie [biɔgrafi] nf biography.
biographique [biɔgrafik] a biographical.
biologie [biɔlɔʒi] nf biology.
biplan [biplɑ̃] nm biplane.
birman [birmɑ̃] an Burmese.
Birmanie [birmani] nf Burma.

bis [bis, bi] a grayish-brown; ad twice, encore, repeat; pain — whole-wheat bread.
bisannuel, -elle [bizanɥel] a biennial.
bisbille [bisbiːj] nf bickering, squabble.
biscornu [biskɔrny] a distorted, misshapen, irregular, weird, inconsistent.
biscotte [biskɔt] nf rusk.
biscuit [biskɥi] nm biscuit, plain cake.
bise [biːz] nf north wind, cold blast; kiss.
biseau [bizo] nm bevel, chamfer.
biseauter [bizote] vt to bevel, chamfer.
bison [bizɔ̃] nm bison.
bisque [bisk] nf shellfish soup; ill humor; donner une — to give odds.
bissecter [bisɛkte] vt to bisect.
bisser [bise] vt to encore.
bissextile [bisɛkstil] a année — leap year.
bistouri [bisturi] nm lancet.
bistré [bistre] a darkened, swarthy, browned.
bistro(t) [bistro] nm café, pub, tavern.
bitte [bit] nf bollard.
bitume [bitym] nm bitumen, asphalt, pitch.
bivouaquer [bivwake] vi to bivouac.
bizarre [bizaːr] a odd, peculiar, queer, weird, strange.
blackbouler [blakbule] vt to blackball, reject.
blafard [blafaːr] a wan, pale, livid, pallid.
blague [blag] nf tobacco-pouch; joke, banter; sans — you don't say! really!
blaguer [blage] vt to chaff, pull someone's leg; vi to joke.
blagueur, -euse [blagœːr] a scoffing, ironical; n cynical scoffer, cynic.
blaireau [blɛro] nm badger, shaving-brush.
blâmable [blɑmabl] a blameworthy.
blâme [blɑːm] nm blame, reproof
blâmer [blame] vt to blame, reprove, rebuke
blanc, -che [blɑ̃, blɑ̃ːʃ] a white, pale, pure, clean, blank; nm white, blank; nuit blanche sleepless night.
blanc-bec [blɑ̃bek] nm tyro, greenhorn, raw youth.
blanchâtre [blɑ̃ʃɑːtr] a whitish.
blanche [blɑ̃ːʃ] nf minim, white ball.
blancheur [blɑ̃ʃœːr] nf whiteness, purity, paleness.
blanchir [blɑ̃ʃiːr] vt to whiten, bleach, wash, whitewash; vi to turn white, pale.
blanchissage [blɑ̃ʃisaːʒ] nm laundering, whitewashing, sugar refining.
blanchisserie [blɑ̃ʃisri] nf laundry, wash-house.

blanchisseur, -euse [blɑ̃ʃisœːr, øːz] n laundryman, laundress, bleacher, washer-woman.

blanc-seing [blɑ̃sɛ̃] nm (signature to a) blank document; **donner —** à to give a free hand to.

blandices [blɑ̃dis] nf pl blandishment.

blanquette [blɑ̃kɛt] nf veal stew.

blaser [blaze] vt to blunt, satiate, cloy; vr to become blasé, tired (of de).

blason [blazɔ̃] nm coat of arms, escutcheon, heraldry.

blasphémateur, -trice [blasfɛmatœːr, tris] a blasphemous; n blasphemer.

blasphématoire [blasfɛmatwaːr] a blasphemous.

blasphème [blasfɛːm] nm blasphemy, curse.

blasphémer [blasfeme] vti to blaspheme, curse.

blatte [blat] nf cockroach.

blé [ble] nm wheat; **— noir** buckwheat; **— d'Inde** maize, corn.

bled [blɛd] nm (pej) wilds, countryside.

blême [blɛːm] a pale, wan.

blêmir [blemiːr] vi to turn pale, blanch, grow dim.

blessé [blɛse] a wounded, hurt; n wounded man, casualty.

blesser [blɛse] vt to wound, hurt, offend, injure; vr to be wounded, be hurt, hurt oneself.

blessure [blɛsyːr] nf wound, injury, hurt, sore.

blet, -te [blɛ, blɛt] a over-ripe, soft.

bleu [blø] a blue; nm recruit, rookie, greenhorn, bruise; pl dungarees; **avoir des —s** to be black and blue; **n'y voir que du —** to be all at sea.

bleuâtre [bløaːtr] a bluish.

bleuir [bløiːr] vt to make blue; vi to turn blue.

blindé [blɛ̃de] a armor-plated, timbered; nm pl **les —s** the armor.

blinder [blɛ̃de] vt to armor plate, line with timber.

bloc [blɔk] nm block, mass, lump, pad, coalition, clink, prison; **en —** all together, in one piece; **à —** thoroughly.

blocage [blɔkaːʒ] nm blocking up, clamping, seizing.

bloc-notes [blɔknɔt] nm writing, scribbling pad, scratch pad.

blocus [blɔkyːs] nm blockade; **braver le —** to run the blockade.

blond [blɔ̃] a fair-haired, light, blond.

blondir [blɔ̃diːr] vt to dye blond, bleach; v to turn yellow.

bloquer [blɔke] vt to block up, obstruct, blockade, jam, dam; vr to stick, jam.

se blottir [səblɔtiːr] vr to crouch, cower, huddle, nestle, snuggle.

blouse [bluːz] nf smock, blouse.

blouson [bluzɔ̃] nm battle-dress jacket, skiing jacket; **—s noirs** n pl young ruffians.

bluet [blye] nm cornflower, bluebottle.

bluffer [blœfe] vti to bluff.

bobard [bɔbaːr] nm tall tale, fib.

bobèche [bɔbɛʃ] nf socket, sconce.

bobine [bɔbin] nf bobbin, reel, spool, coil, dial.

bocage [bɔkaːʒ] nm copse.

bocal [bɔkal] nm jar, bottle.

bock [bɔk] nm glass of beer, beerglass.

bœuf [bœf] nm ox, bullock, beef; **— de conserve** corned beef; **— à la mode** stewed beef.

bohème [bɔɛːm] a unconventional, Bohemian; n Bohemian; nf Bohemia, art-world.

bohémien, -ienne [bɔɛmjɛ̃, jɛn] an gipsy, Bohemian.

boire [bwaːr] vt to drink (in, up), imbibe, absorb, soak in, up; nm drink(ing); **— un coup en vitesse** to have a quick one.

bois [bwa] nm wood, forest, timber; pl antlers, woodwind instruments.

boisage [bwazaːʒ] nm timbering, scaffold(ing), woodwork, afforestation.

boisé [bwaze] a wooded, woody, wainscoted.

boiser [bwaze] vt to timber, put under timber, wainscot.

boiserie [bwazri] nf woodwork, wainscoting, joinery.

boisseau [bwaso] nm bushel, drain, flue-tile.

boisselier [bwasəlje] nm cooper.

boisson [bwasɔ̃] nf drink, beverage; **pris de —** under the influence.

boîte [bwaːt] nf box, case, tin, casket, jail; **— aux lettres** mailbox; **— à ordures** garbage can; **— à thé** tea-caddy; **— de nuit** night-club; **— de vitesses** gear-box.

boiter [bwate] vi to limp, hobble, be lame.

boiteux, -euse [bwatø, øːz] a lame, shaky, lop-sided.

boîtier [bwatje] nm case.

bol [bɔl] nm bowl, basin.

bolchevisme [bɔlʃevism] nm Bolshevism.

bolchevique [bɔlʃevik] an bolshevik.

bolide [bɔlid] nm meteor, fast car.

bombance [bɔ̃bɑ̃ːs] nf feast(ing); **faire —** to carouse, have a blow-out.

bombardement [bɔ̃bardəmɑ̃] nm bombardment, bombing, shelling; **— en piqué** dive-bombing.

bombarder [bɔ̃barde] vt to bombard, bomb, shell.

bombardier [bɔ̃bardje] nm bombardier, bomb-aimer, bomber plane.

bombe [bɔ̃b] nf bomb, spree; **— à retardement** time-bomb; **faire la — to go on a binge.**

bombé [bɔ̃be] *a* bulging, convex, cambered.

bomber [bɔ̃be] *vt* to stick out, arch, bend, camber; *vi* bulge, belly.

bon, -ne [bɔ̃, bɔn] *a* good, nice, right, correct, sound, righteous, kind, fitting, profitable; *nm* voucher, warrant, bond, draft, bill; **pour de** — for good, in earnest; **bon! right!**; — **à rien** good-for-nothing.

bonasse [bɔnas] *a* simple, silly.

bonbon [bɔ̃bɔ̃] *nm* candy, sweet-(meat), drop; *pl* confections.

bonbonne [bɔ̃bɔn] *nf* carboy.

bonbonnière [bɔ̃bɔnjɛːr] *nf* candy box, well-furnished little house.

bond [bɔ̃] *nm* jump, leap, spring, bounce; **faire faux** — to break.

bonde [bɔ̃ːd] *nf* bung, plug, bung-hole.

bondé [bɔ̃de] *a* packed, crowded, crammed.

bondir [bɔ̃diːr] *vi* to jump, leap, spring, bound, bounce, skip about.

bonheur [bɔnœːr] *nm* happiness, bliss, welfare, success; **par** — fortunately; **au petit** — indiscriminately, haphazardly.

bonhomie [bɔnɔmi] *nf* good nature, humor.

bonhomme [bɔnɔm] *a* good-natured; *nm* (good-natured) man, figure.

boni [bɔni] *nm* surplus, premium, bonus.

bonification [bɔnifikasjɔ̃] *nf* bonus, rebate, improvement.

bonifier [bɔnifje] *vti* to improve.

boniment [bɔnimɑ̃] *nm* patter, moonshine.

bonjour [bɔ̃ʒuːr] *nm* good-day, -morning, -afternoon.

bonne [bɔn] *nf* maid, servant; — **d'enfants** nursemaid.

bonnet [bɔnɛ] *nm* cap, bonnet; **gros** — bigwig; **avoir la tête près du** — to be hot tempered; **opiner du** — to agree, have no opinion of one's own.

bonneterie [bɔntri] *nf* hosiery, knitted ware.

bonneteur [bɔntœːr] *nm* card-sharper, confidence man.

bonnetier, -ière [bɔntje, jɛːr] *n* hosier.

bon(n)iche [bɔniʃ] *nf* maidservant, slavey.

bon-papa [bɔ̃papa] *nm* grandpa, grand-dad.

bonsoir [bɔ̃swaːr] *nm* good-evening, -night.

bonté [bɔ̃te] *nf* kindness, goodness, good nature.

bonze [bɔ̃ːz] *nm* bonze, Buddhist priest, **vieux** — old fossil.

bord [bɔːr] *nm* edge, brink, brim, rim, bank, verge, side, flap, tack; **livre de** — log book; **à** — **de** aboard; **à pleins** —**s** brim-full.

bordage [bɔrdaːʒ] *nm* border(ing), curb, edging, planking.

bordeaux [bɔrdo] *nm* Bordeaux wine; — **rouge** claret.

bordée [bɔrde] *nf* broadside, watch, tack, volley; **tirer des** —**s** to tack; **être en** — to be on a spree.

bordel [bɔrdel] *nm* brothel.

border [bɔrde] *vt* to border, edge, run along, fringe, braid, plank; — **qn. dans son lit** to tuck s.o. in.

bordereau [bɔrdəro] *nm* statement, account, memorandum, docket, file.

bordure [bɔrdyːr] *nf* edge, fringe, binding, curb, rim.

borgne [bɔrɲ] *a* one-eyed, blind in one eye, shady.

borne [bɔrn] *nf* limit, boundary mark, guard-stone, terminal; — **kilométrique** milestone; **cela passe les** —**s** that is going too far.

borné [bɔrne] *a* limited, narrow, restricted.

borner [bɔrne] *vt* to bound, limit, restrict, stake, mark out the limits of; *vr* to confine, restrict oneself.

bosquet [bɔskɛ] *nm* thicket, grove, arbor.

bosse [bɔs] *nf* hump, lump, bump, dent, bruise; **rouler sa** — to knock about.

bosseler [bɔsle] *vt* to emboss, dent, bash.

bosselure [bɔslyːr] *nf* dent, bruise.

bossoir [bɔswaːr] *nm* davit, cathead, (*of ship*) bow.

bossu [bɔsy] *a* hunch-backed, humped; *n* hunchback.

bot [bo] **à pied** — club-foot, club-footed person.

botanique [bɔtanik] *a* botanical; *nf* botany.

botaniste [bɔtanist] *n* botanist.

botte [bɔt] *nf* boot, field-boot, bunch, truss, bundle, lunge, thrust, slip; —**s retroussées** top boots; —**s à l'écuyère** riding-boots.

botteler [bɔtle] *vt* to truss, bundle, bunch, tie up.

botter [bɔte] *vt* to put boots on, kick.

bottier [bɔtje] *nm* bootmaker.

bottin [bɔtɛ̃] *nm* directory.

bottine [bɔtin] *nf* ankle-boot.

bouc [buk] *nm* he-, billy-goat; — **émissaire**, scapegoat.

boucan [bukɑ̃] *nm* din, shindy, row, smoked meat.

boucaner [bukane] *vt* (*meat*) to cure, to stink.

boucanier [bukanje] *nm* buccaneer, pirate.

bouche [buʃ] *nf* mouth, muzzle, slot, opening; — **d'eau** hydrant; **garder qch. pour la bonne** — to keep something as a titbit; **fine** — gourmet; **être porté sur la** — to think of nothing but one's belly; **faire la petite** — to pick at one's food, be difficult.

bouché [buʃe] *a* plugged, stopped up, dense.

bouchée [buʃe] nf mouthful, bite, morsel; — à la reine vol-au-vent of chicken; **mettre les —s doubles** to gobble one's food, put a spurt on.

boucher [buʃe] nm butcher; vt to plug, stop (up), cork, bung, obstruct.

boucherie [buʃri] nf butcher's shop, -trade; slaughter, shambles.

bouchon [buʃɔ̃] nm cork, stopper, plug, fishing float.

boucle [bukl] nf buckle, loop, bow, ringlet, curl; — **d'oreille** earring.

bouclé [bukle] a curly.

boucler [bukle] vt to buckle on, knot, fasten, settle, clinch, curl, lock up; vi to buckle, be curly.

bouclier [bukli(j)e] nm shield, buckler.

bouder [bude] vt to be in the sulks with; vi to sulk.

bouderie [budri] nf sulkiness.

boudeur, -euse [budœːr, øːz] a sulky; nf double settee.

boudin [budɛ̃] nm black-pudding, inner tube, twist, roll, flange, beading.

boudoir [budwaːr] nm boudoir.

boue [bu] nf mud, dirt, deposit.

bouée [bwe, bue] nf buoy; — **de sauvetage** lifebuoy.

boueux, -euse [buø, øːz] a muddy, miry, dirty; nm scavenger, garbage man.

bouffant [bufɑ̃] a puffed, baggy.

bouffe [buf] a **opéra** — comic opera.

bouffée [bufe] nf whiff, puff, waft, gust, breath; **tirer des —s de sa pipe** to puff at one's pipe.

bouffer [bufe] vt to puff out, gobble; vi to balloon out, bag, swell.

bouffi [bufi] a puffed up, puffy, bloated, swollen, turgid.

bouffir [bufiːr] vt to bloat, inflate; vi to become swollen, puffed up.

bouffon, -onne [bufɔ̃, ɔn] a farcical; nm clown, jester.

bouge [buːʒ] nm hovel, slum, den, pigsty, (of ship) bilge.

bougeoir [buʒwaːr] nm candlestick.

bougeotte [buʒɔt] nf **avoir la —** to be fidgety.

bouger [buʒe] vt to move; vi to budge, stir.

bougie [buʒi] nf candle, taper, spark plug.

bougon, -onne [bugɔ̃, ɔn] a testy, grumpy; n grumbler.

bougonner [bugɔne] vi to grumble, grouse.

bougran [bugrɑ̃] nm buckram.

bouillabaisse [bujabɛs] nf fish-soup.

bouillant [bujɑ̃] a boiling, ebullient, impetuous.

bouillie [buji] nf gruel, pap.

bouilloire [bujwaːr] nf kettle.

bouillon [bujɔ̃] nm bubble, soup, stock, beeftea, cheap restaurant, unsold copies.

bouillonnement [bujɔnmɑ̃] nm boiling, seething.

bouillonner [bujɔne] vt to gather material into puffs; vi to boil up, seethe, bubble.

bouillotte [bujɔt] nf hot-water bottle.

boulanger, -ère [bulɑ̃ʒe, ɛːr] n baker, baker's wife; vti to bake.

boulangerie [bulɑ̃ʒri] nf bread-baking, baker's shop.

boule [bul] nf bowl, ball, globe, bulb, lump, head, face; **joueur de —s** bowler; **jeu de —s** bowls, bowling-green.

bouleau [bulo] nm birch-tree.

bouledogue [buldɔg] nm bulldog.

boulet [bule] nm cannonball, fet-lock-joint.

boulette [bulɛt] nf pellet, meatball.

boulevard [bulvaːr] nm avenue, boulevard.

boulevardier, -ière [bulvardje, ɛːr] a of the boulevards; nm man-about-town.

bouleversement [bulvɛrsəmɑ̃] nm upheaval, overthrow, disturbance, confusion.

bouleverser [bulvɛrse] vt to upset, overturn, perturb, bowl over, astound, stagger.

boulon [bulɔ̃] nm bolt, pin.

boulot, -otte [bulo, ɔt] a chubby, plump, dumpy; nm work, food.

boulotter [bulɔte] vt to eat; vi to jog along. on.

bouquet [bukɛ] nm bunch, posy, bouquet, nosegay, clump, cluster, aroma, crowning-piece, highlight; **c'est le —** that crowns it; **pour le —** . . . last but not least. . .

bouquetier [buktje] nm flower vase.

bouquetière [buktjɛːr] nf flower-girl.

bouquin [bukɛ̃] nm old book, book, buck-rabbit, hare.

bouquiner [bukine] vi to collect old books, read.

bouquiniste [bukinist] nm second-hand bookseller.

bourbe [burb] nf mud, mire.

bourbeux, -euse [burbø, øːz] a muddy, miry.

bourbier [burbje] nm bog, mire.

bourde [burd] nf bloomer, fib.

bourdon [burdɔ̃] nm drone, great bell, bumble-bee.

bourdonnement [burdɔnmɑ̃] nm buzzing, humming, drumming, whirr.

bourdonner [burdɔne] vt to hum; vi to buzz, hum, drone, whirr.

bourg [buːr] nm market town.

bourgeois [burʒwa] a middle-class, plain, common; n citizen, towns-man, commoner.

bourgeoisie [burʒwazi] nf middle class; **la haute (petite) —** the upper (lower) middle class.

bourgeon [burʒɔ̃] nm bud, pimple.

bourgeonner [burʒɔne] vi to bud, break out in pimples.

bourgeron [burʒərɔ̃] nm workman's overall.

Bourgogne [burgɔɲ] nf Burgundy; m Burgundy wine.

bourguignon [burgiɲɔ̃] a nmf Burgundian, of Burgundy.

bourlinguer [burlɛ̃ge] vi to labor, make heavy weather, knock about.

bourrade [burad] nf blow, thrust, thump, rough word.

bourrage [buraːʒ] nm stuffing, padding, cramming; — de crâne bunkum, eyewash, dope.

bourrasque [burask] nf squall.

bourre [buːr] nf flock, floss, wad, waste.

bourreau [buro] nm hangman, executioner, tormentor.

bourrée [bure] nf bundle of firewood, faggot.

bourreler [burle] vt to torment, rack, goad.

bourrelet [burlɛ] nm pad, cushion, fold, roll, rim, bead.

bourrelier [burəlje] nm saddler.

bourrer [bure] vt to pad, stuff, pack, cram, fill, thrash, trounce; — le crâne à qn. to fill someone's head with stuff and nonsense.

bourriche [buriʃ] nf basket, hamper.

bourrique [burik] nf she-ass, donkey, duffer.

bourru [bury] a churlish, surly, rude, gruff.

bourse [burs] nf purse, pouch, bag, grant, bursary, scholarship, stock exchange; jouer à la — to speculate.

boursier, -ière [bursje, jɛːr] n scholar, paymaster, speculator.

boursouflé [bursufle] a swollen, bloated, turgid.

boursouflement [bursufləmɑ̃] nm swelling, blistering.

boursoufler [bursufle] vt to swell, blister, bloat; vi to swell, blister.

boursouflure [bursuflyːr] nf swelling, blister, turgidity.

bousculade [buskylad] nf scuffle, scurry, hustle, rush.

bousculer [buskyle] vt to jostle, hustle, upset.

bouse [buːz] nf dung.

bousiller [buzije] vt to bungle, botch, crash (plane).

boussole [busɔl] nf compass.

boustifaille [bustifaːj] nf grub, food.

bout [bu] nm end, extremity, tip, bit, tag, scrap; bas (haut) bout foot (head); à — de forces exhausted, worn out, spent; au — de at the end of, after; jusqu'au — right to the end, to the bitter end, through; de — en — through and through; venir à — de to overcome, manage, cope with; à — portant point-blank.

boutade [butad] nf whim, outburst, sally, quip.

boute-en-train [butɑ̃trɛ̃] nm bright and cheery companion, life and soul.

boutefeu [butfø] nm firebrand.

bouteille [buteːj] nf bottle.

bouteroue [butru] nf curbstone, fender.

boutique [butik] nf shop, caboodle.

boutiquier, -ière [butikje, jɛːr] n shopkeeper.

bouton [butɔ̃] nm button, bud, pimple, handle, knot; — de col stud; — de manchettes cuff-link; — d'or buttercup; tourner le — to switch on, off.

boutonner [butɔne] vt to button up; vi to bud.

boutonneux, -euse [butɔnø, øːz] a pimply.

boutonnière [butɔnjɛːr] nf buttonhole, rosette.

bouture [butyːr] nf cutting.

bouvier [buvje] nm cowherd, drover.

bouvreuil [buvrœːj] nm bullfinch.

bovin [bɔvɛ̃] a bovine.

box [bɔks] nm loose box, lock-up garage, cubicle, dock.

boxe [bɔks] nf boxing.

boxer [bɔkse] vt to box with; vi to box, spar.

boxeur [bɔksœːr] nm boxer.

boy [bɔj] nmf steward.

boyau [bwajo] nm bowel, gut, inner tube, hosepipe, communication trench.

boycotter [bɔjkɔte] vt to boycott.

bracelet [braslɛ] nm bracelet, bangle, armband.

braconnage [brakɔnaːʒ] nm poaching.

braconner [brakɔne] vti to poach.

braconnier, -ière [brakɔnje, jɛːr] a poaching; nm poacher.

braguette [bragɛt] nf (of trousers) fly.

braillard [brajaːr] a noisy, bawling, rowdy; n brawler.

brailler [braje] vti to bawl out, shout.

braire [brɛːr] vi to bray.

braise [brɛːz] nf embers.

braiser [brɛze] vt to braise.

bramer [brame] vi (of stag) to bell.

brancard [brɑ̃kaːr] nm shaft, stretcher.

brancardier [brɑ̃kardje] nm stretcher-bearer.

branche [brɑ̃ːʃ] nf branch, bough, prong, leg, (of family) line.

branchement [brɑ̃ʃmɑ̃] nm branching, forking, junction, lead.

brancher [brɑ̃ʃe] vt to connect, branch, plug in; on m'a mal branché I was given the wrong number.

brandir [brɑ̃diːr] vt to brandish, flourish, wave.

brandon [brɑ̃dɔ̃] nm firebrand.

branlant [brɑ̃lɑ̃] a shaky, loose, ramshackle.

branle [brɑ̃ːl] nm swing, impetus, oscillation, motion; mettre qch. en — to set something going.

branle-bas [brɑ̃ləba] nm stir, bustle,

commotion; **faire le —** to clear decks for action.

branler [brăle] *vt* to swing, wag, shake; *vi* to shake, rock, be loose.

braquage [braka:ʒ] *nm* levelling, aiming, pointing; **angle de —** lock (of car).

braquer [brake] *vt* to aim, level, point, fix, direct.

bras [bra, brɑ] *nm* arm, limb, bracket; **— droit** right-hand man, *pl* workmen, hands, henchmen; **— dessus — dessous** arm in arm; **— de mer** arm of the sea, (*Scot*) sea loch; **en — de chemise** in one's shirt sleeves; **à — le corps** round the waist; **— de rivière** backwater; **manquer de —** to be short-handed.

brasero [brazero] *nm* brazier.

brasier [brazje] *nm* fire, inferno, furnace.

brasiller [brazije] *vt* to grill, broil; *vi* to sizzle.

brassard [brasa:r] *nm* armlet, arm-band.

brasse [brɑ:s] *nf* arm-span, fathom, stroke; **nager à la —** to swim the breast stroke.

brassée [brase] *nf* armful.

brasser [brase] *vt* to mix, stir, brew, brace; **— de grosses affaires** to do big business.

brasserie [brasri] *nf* brewery, ale-house, restaurant.

brasseur, -euse [brasœ:r, ø:z] *n* brewer, puddler, mixer; **— d'affaires** big businessman.

brassière [brasje:r] *nf* baby's vest; *pl* slings, leading strings; **— de sauvetage** life-jacket.

bravache [bravaʃ] *a* blustering, swaggering; *nm* braggadocio, bully.

bravade [bravad] *nf* bluster.

brave [bra:v] *a* brave, gallant, decent, worthy, good.

braver [brave] *vt* to brave, dare, defy, face, run (blockade).

bravoure [bravu:r] *nf* bravery, valor.

brebis [brəbi] *nf* ewe, sheep; **— galeuse** black sheep.

brèche [breʃ] *nf* breach, hole, gap; **battre en —** to breach.

bréchet [breʃɛ] *nm* breastbone.

bredouille [brədu:j] *a inv* empty-handed.

bredouiller [brəduje] *vt* to stammer out, mumble; *vi* to stutter, splutter, gabble.

bref, brève [brɛf, brɛ:v] *a* brief, short, curt; *ad* curtly, in short.

breloque [brəlɔk] *nf* trinket, charm.

Brésil [brezil] *nm* Brazil.

brésilien, -ienne [breziljɛ̃, jɛn] *a* Brazilian.

Bretagne [brətaɲ] *nf* Brittany.

bretelle [brətɛl] *nf* strap, sling; *pl* braces.

breton, -onne [brətɔ̃, ɔn] *an* Breton.

bretteur [brɛtœ:r] *nm* duelist, swashbuckler.

breuvage [brœva:ʒ] *nm* drink, beverage, draught.

brevet [brəvɛ] *nm* patent, certificate.

breveté [brəvte] *a* certificated, by special appointment; *n* patentee.

breveter [brəvte] *vt* to grant a patent to, patent.

bréviaire [brevjɛ:r] *nm* breviary.

brévité [brevite] *nf* shortness.

bribe [brib] *nf* scrap, fragment.

bric-à-brac [brikabrak] *nm* curios, bits and pieces.

bricole [brikɔl] *nf* strap, breast harness strap, ricochet; *pl* trifles, odd jobs.

bricoler [brikɔle] *vt* to arrange; *vi* to do odd jobs, potter about.

bricoleur [brikɔlœ:r] *nm* handyman, jobber, jack of all trades.

bride [brid] *nf* bridle, string, flange, strap; **à — abattue** full tilt, at full speed; **lâcher la — à** to give free rein to, full scope to.

brider [bride] *vt* to bridle, curb, restrain, truss, flange, fasten.

bridge [bridʒ] *nm* (*game*) bridge.

bridgeur, -euse [bridʒœ:r, ø:z] *n* bridge player.

brièvement [briɛvmɑ̃] *ad* briefly, curtly, succinctly.

brièveté [briɛvte] *nf* brevity, shortness, conciseness.

brigade [brigad] *nf* brigade, squad, shift, gang.

brigadier [brigadje] *nm* corporal, bombardier, sergeant (*police*).

brigand [brigɑ̃] *nm* robber, brigand, highwayman.

brigandage [brigɑ̃da:ʒ] *nm* brigandage, highway robbery.

brigue [brig] *nf* canvassing, intrigue, plot.

briguer [brige] *vt* to canvass for, solicit.

brillament [brijamɑ̃] *ad* brilliantly.

brillant [brijɑ̃] *a* brilliant, shining, glossy; *nm* brilliancy, gloss(iness), shine, polish.

briller [brije] *vi* to shine, sparkle, glitter.

brimade [brimad] *nf* rough joke.

brimbaler [brɛ̃bale] *vt* to lug about; *vi* to swing, wobble.

brimborion [brɛ̃bɔrjɔ̃] *nm* bauble, trifle.

brimer [brime] *vt* to haze, persecute.

brin [brɛ̃] *nm* blade, sprig, stalk, shoot, strand, bit, crumb, jot, touch, shred, chit.

brindille [brɛ̃di:j] *nf* twig, tiny branch.

bringue [brɛ̃:g] *nf* bit, piece; **faire la —** to go on a spree.

brio [bri(j)o] *nm* vigor, dash, gusto, brilliance.

brioche [briɔʃ] *nf* bun.

brique [brik] *nf* brick.

briquet [brikɛ] *nm* flint, tinderbox, cigarette lighter.

brisant [brizɑ̃] *a* shattering; *nm* breaker, reef.

brise [briːz] *nf* breeze.

brise-bise [brizbiːz] *nm* weather stripping, short window curtain.

brisées [brize] *nf pl* tracks; **aller sur les — de qn.** to compete with someone; **suivre les — de qn.** to follow in someone's footsteps.

brise-lames [brizlam] *nm* breakwater, mole.

briser [brize] *vt* to break (up, down, off), shatter, smash; *vr* to break.

brisure [brizyːr] *nf* break, flaw, crack.

britannique [britanik] *an* British; *n* Briton.

broc [bro] *nm* jug, pitcher.

brocanter [brɔkɑ̃te] *vt* to sell, barter; *vi* to deal in second-hand goods.

brocanteur, -euse [brɔkɑ̃tœːr, øːz] *n* second-hand dealer.

brocard [brɔkaːr] *nm* taunt, lampoon.

brocart [brɔkaːr] *nm* brocade.

broche [brɔʃ] *nf* spit, skewer, peg, brooch, spindle, pin, spigot.

brocher [brɔʃe] *vt* to stitch, sew, brocade; **livre broché** paper-bound book.

brochet [brɔʃɛ] *nm* pike.

brochette [brɔʃɛt] *nf* skewer, stick; **élevé à la — fed** by hand, brought up with tender care.

brochure [brɔʃyːr] *nf* booklet, pamphlet.

brodequin [brɔdkɛ̃] *nm* sock, ankle-boot; *pl* marching boots.

broder [brɔde] *vt* to embroider, embellish, amplify.

broderie [brɔdri] *nf* (piece of) embroidery, embellishment.

bromure [brɔmyːr] *nm* bromide.

broncher [brɔ̃ʃe] *vi* to stumble, falter, flinch, shy.

bronches [brɔ̃ʃ] *nf pl* bronchial tubes.

bronchite [brɔ̃ʃit] *nf* bronchitis.

bronze [brɔ̃ːz] *nm* bronze (statue).

bronzer [brɔ̃ze] *vt* to bronze, brown, tan.

brosse [brɔs] *nf* brush; **cheveux en — crewcut.**

brosser [brɔse] *vt* to brush, thrash.

brouet [bruɛ] *nm* gruel, skilly.

brouette [bruɛt] *nf* wheelbarrow.

brouhaha [bruaa] *nm* uproar, din, clatter, hubbub.

brouillage [brujaːʒ] *nm* interference, jamming, mixing.

brouillard [brujaːr] *nm* fog, mist, daybook; **il fait du — it is foggy.**

brouille [bruːj] *nf* quarrel, dispute wrangle, broil; **être en — avec qn.** to have fallen out with s.o.

brouiller [bruje] *vt* to confuse, mix (up), fuddle, scramble, perplex, jam; *vr* to get confused, mixed, blurred, quarrel, fall out.

brouillon, -onne [brujɔ̃, ɔn] *a* muddleheaded; *nm* rough copy, draft.

broussailles [brusaːj] *nf pl* undergrowth, brushwood, scrub.

broussailleux, -euse [brusajø, øːz] *a* bushy, shaggy.

brousse [brus] *nf* bush, scrub, wilds.

brouter [brute] *vt* to graze, crop, browse.

broyer [brwaje] *vt* to crush, grind, pound; **— du noir** to have the blues.

bru [bry] *nf* daughter-in-law.

brugnon [brynɔ̃] *nm* nectarine.

bruine [brɥin] *nf* drizzle.

bruiner [brɥine] *vi* to drizzle, spit.

bruire [brɥiːr] *vi* to rustle, murmur, hum.

bruissement [brɥismɑ̃] *nm* rustling, whisper, humming.

bruit [brɥi] *nm* noise, clatter, din, rumor, sound, fuss, ado.

brûlant [brylɑ̃] *a* burning, blazing, scorching, fervent.

brûlé [bryle] *a* burnt, scorched; **odeur de — smell** of burning.

brûle-gueule [brylɡœl] *nm* clay pipe, nose warmer.

brûle-pourpoint [brylpurpwɛ̃] *ad* **à — point-blank.**

brûler [bryle] *vt* to burn (up, down, out, away), singe, nip, scorch; *vi* to burn, be on fire, be aflame, singe, scorch, be eager (to); **— une gare** to run through a station without stopping; **— les feux** to jump the lights; **— la cervelle à qn.** to blow s.o.'s brains out.

brûleur, -euse [brylœːr, øːz] *n* burner, distiller; *nm* gas jet, Bunsen burner.

brûlot [brylo] *nm* fireship.

brûlure [brylyːr] *nf* burn, scald, blight; *pl* heartburn.

brume [brym] *nf* fog, mist, haze.

brumeux, -euse [brymø, øːz] *a* foggy, misty, hazy.

brun [brœ̃] *a* brown, dark, dusky; *nm* brown; *n* dark person.

brunâtre [brynaːtr] *a* brownish.

brunir [bryniːr] *vt* to brown, darken, tan, burnish; *vi* to become dark, tan.

brusque [brysk] *a* abrupt, hasty, sudden.

brusquer [bryske] *vt* to hurry, rush, be sharp with.

brusquerie [brysk(ə)ri] *nf* bluntness, abruptness, bluffness, roughness.

brut [bryt] *a* rough, crude, unrefined, raw, unpolished, uncut, gross, extra dry.

brutal [brytal] *a* coarse, callous, rough, blunt.

brutaliser [brytalize] *vt* to bully, ill-treat.

brutalité [brytalite] *nf* (act of) brutality, brutishness, callousness.

brute [bryt] *nf* beast, bully.
bruyant [bryjɑ̃] *a* noisy, boisterous, loud, blatant.
bruyère [bryjɛːr] *nf* heather, heath (land), briar; **coq de —** grouse.
buanderie [bɥɑ̃dri] *nf* wash-house.
bucarde [bykard] *nf* cockle.
bûche [by(ː)ʃ] *nf* log, fall, spill, duffer.
bûcher [byʃe] *vt* to work at, cram; *vi* to work, roughhew; *nm* woodshed, woodpile, pyre, stake.
bûcheron [byʃrɔ̃] *nm* woodcutter, woodman, lumberjack.
bûcheur, -euse [byʃœːr, øːz] *n* hard worker, plodder.
bucolique [bykɔlik] *a* bucolic, pastoral.
budget [bydʒɛ] *nm* estimates; **boucler le —** to balance the budget.
budgétaire [bydʒetɛːr] *a* fiscal, financial.
buée [bye] *nf* vapor, steam.
buffet [byfɛ] *nm* sideboard, refreshment room.
buffle [byfl] *nm* buffalo, hide.
buffleterie [byflətri] *nf* leather equipment.
buis [bɥi] *nm* boxwood.
buisson [bɥisɔ̃] *nm* bush, thicket, brake.
buissonnier, -ière [bɥisɔnje, jɛːr] *a* which lives in the woods; **faire l'école buissonnière** to play truant.
bulgare [bylgaːr] *an* Bulgarian.
Bulgarie [bylgari] *nf* Bulgaria.
bulbe [bylb] *nm* bulb.
bulle [byl] *nf* bubble, (*eccl*) bull.
bulletin [byltɛ̃] *nm* report, ticket; **— de vote** voting paper; **— de bagages** baggage check.
buraliste [byralist] *n* clerk, collector of taxes, tobacconist.
bure [byːr] *nf* frieze, homespun.
bureau [byro] *nm* desk, office, board, committee, orderly room; **— de placement** Labor Exchange, registry; **— de poste** post office; **— de tabac** tobacconist's shop.
bureaucrate [byrokrat] *nm* bureaucrat.
bureaucratie [byrokrasi] *nf* bureaucracy, officialdom, red tape.
burette [byrɛt] *nf* burette, oilcan, flagon.
burin [byrɛ̃] *nm* graving tool, etcher's pen.
buriner [byrine] *vt* to engrave.
burlesque [byrlɛsk] *a* comical.
buse [byːz] *nf* buzzard, tube, nozzle.
busqué [byske] *a* aquiline, hooked.
buste [byst] *nm* bust; **en —** half-length.
but [by(t)] *nm* aim, goal, purpose, object(ive), target, mark; **sans —** aimless(ly); **marquer un —** to score a goal; **de — en blanc** point blank.
buté [byte] *a* obstinate, set.
butée [byte] *nf* buttress, stop.

buter [byte] *vi* to knock, stumble, strike, abut; *vr* to knock, prop oneself up.
butin [bytɛ̃] *nm* booty, loot, spoils, plunder.
butoir [bytwaːr] *nm* buffer, check.
butor [bytɔːr] *nm* bittern, lout, bully.
butte [byt] *nf* hillock, mound, butte; **être en — à** to be exposed to.
buvable [byvabl] *a* drinkable.
buvard [byvaːr] *a* **papier —** blotting paper; *nm* blotter, blotting pad.
buvette [byvɛt] *nf* refreshment bar, stand; soda fountain.
buveur, -euse [byvœːr, øːz] *n* drinker, toper.

C

c' see **ce**
ça [sa] see **cela.**
çà [sa] *ad* here, hither; **— et là** here and there; **ah —!** now then!
caban [kabɑ̃] *nm* pea-jacket, pilot-coat.
cabane [kaban] *nf* hut, shanty, hutch.
cabanon [kabanɔ̃] *nm* padded cell, small hut.
cabaret [kabarɛ] *nm* tavern, public house, restaurant.
cabaretier, -ière [kabartje, jɛːr] *n* publican, tavern-keeper.
cabas [kaba] *nm* shopping basket, satchel, tool-bag.
cabestan [kabɛstɑ̃] *nm* capstan, windlass, winch.
cabillaud [kabijo] *nm* cod.
cabine [kabin] *nf* cabin, saloon, box, telephone booth, hut.
cabinet [kabinɛ] *nm* closet, small room, office, consulting room, cabinet, government, collection; *pl* toilet, lavatory; **— de travail** study; **— de toilette** dressing room.
câble [kɑːbl] *nm* cable, rope, line, wire.
câbler [kɑble] *vt* to cable.
caboche [kabɔʃ] *nf* pate, head.
cabosse [kabɔs] *nm* pod.
cabot [kabo] *nm* mongrel.
cabotage [kabɔtaːʒ] *nm* coasting-trade.
caboteur [kabɔtœːr] *nm* coaster.
cabotin [kabɔtɛ̃] *n* ham actor.
cabrer [kabre] *vt* (*plane*) to elevate; *vr* to rear, buck, jib (at).
cabriole [kabriɔl] *nf* leap, caper, somersault.
cabriolet [kabriɔlɛ] *nm* gig, cabriolet, coupé.
cacahuète [kakawɛt] *nf* peanut.
cacao [kakao] *nm* cacao, cocoa.
cacaotière [kakaotjɛːr] *nf* cocoa plantation.
cacaoyer [kakaɔje] *nm* cocoa-tree.
cacatoès [kakatɔɛːs] *nm* cockatoo.
cache [kaʃ] *nf* hiding-place.

cache-cache [kaʃkaʃ] nm hide-and-seek.
cache-col [kaʃkɔl] nm man's scarf.
cachemire [kaʃmiːr] nm cashmere.
cache-nez [kaʃne] nm muffler.
cacher [kaʃe] vt to hide, conceal, keep secret; vr to lie in hiding, hide (from à).
cachet [kaʃɛ] nm seal, mark, stamp, fee, cachet.
cacheter [kaʃte] vt to seal (up).
cachette [kaʃɛt] nf hiding-place; **en — on the quiet.**
cachot [kaʃo] nm dungeon.
cachotterie [kaʃɔtri] nf mystery.
cachottier, -ière [kaʃɔtje, jɛːr] a secretive, reticent.
cadastre [kadastr] nm cadastral survey.
cadavéreux, -euse [kadaverø, øːz] a cadaverous.
cadavre [kadɑːvr] nm corpse, dead body, carcass.
cadeau [kado] nm present, gift.
cadenas [kadnɑ] nm padlock, clasp.
cadenasser [kadnase] vt to padlock, clasp.
cadence [kadɑ̃ːs] nf cadence, rhythm, time, tune.
cadencé [kadɑ̃se] a measured, rhythmical.
cadet, -ette [kadɛ, ɛt] a younger, junior; n youngest; nm caddie.
cadran [kadrɑ̃] nm dial, face.
cadre [kɑːdr] nm frame(work), limits, bounds, outline, plan, cadre, list, strength, management staff.
cadrer [kadre] vi to agree, square, tally, fit in.
caduc, -uque [kadyk] a declining, decrepit, weak, lapsed, null and void.
cafard [kafaːr] a sanctimonious; nm cockroach, telltale; **avoir le — to have the blues.**
cafarder [kafarde] vi to tell tales, sneak.
café [kafe] nm coffee, café; **— nature** black coffee; **— crême** white coffee; **— complet** coffee with milk, roll and butter.
caféier(e) [kafeje] n coffee plant, plantation.
cafetier, -ière [kaftje, jɛːr] n owner of a café.
cafetière [kaftjɛːr] nf coffee-pot.
cafouiller [kafuje] vi to splutter, (car) misfire.
cage [kaːʒ] nf cage, coop, casing, well, shaft, stairway.
cagneux, -euse [kaɲø, øːz] a knock-kneed, crooked.
cagnotte [kaɲɔt] nf pool, kitty.
cagot [kago] a hypocritical; n hypocrite.
cagoule [kagul] nf cowl, hood.
cahier [kaje] nm exercise book, copy-book.
cahin-caha [kaɛ̃kaa] ad middling, so-so, limping.

cahot [kao] nm jolt, bump.
cahoter [kaɔte] vti to jolt, bump, shake, toss about.
cahoteux, -euse [kaɔtø, øːz] a bumpy, rough.
caille [kɑːj] nf quail.
caillebotte [kajbɔt] nf curds.
cailler [kaje] vtir to clot, curdle; **lait caillé** curds.
caillot [kajo] nm clot.
caillou [kaju] nm pebble.
caillouter [kajute] vt to metal, pave with pebbles.
caillouteux, -euse [kajutø, øːz] a stony, pebbly.
caiman [kaimɑ̃] nm crocodile.
caisse [kɛs] nf case, chest, casing, tub, body, cashbox, till, pay-desk, counting-house, fund, bank, drum; **tenir la — to be in charge of the money; — d'épargne** savings bank.
caissier, ière [kɛsje, jɛːr] n cashier.
caisson [kɛsɔ̃] nm box, trunk, ammunition wagon, locker, caisson.
cajoler [kaʒɔle] vt to cajole, coax.
cajolerie [kaʒɔlri] nf cajolery, coaxing.
calamité [kalamite] nf calamity.
calamiteux, -euse [kalamitø, øːz] a calamitous, broken-down, seedy.
calao [kalao] nm hornbill.
calcaire [kalkɛːr] a calcareous, chalky; nm limestone.
calcul [kalkyl] nm calculation, reckoning, arithmetic, calculus, (in bladder) stone.
calculé [kalkyle] a calculated, studied, deliberate.
calculer [kalkyle] vt to calculate, reckon.
cale [kal] nf hold, slipway, stocks, wedge, chock, prop; **— sèche** dry dock; **— de radoub** graving dock; **mettre sur — to lay down.**
calé [kale] a wedged, jammed, good (at en).
calebasse [kalbɑːs] nf calabash, gourd.
caleçon [kalsɔ̃] nm drawers, pants.
calembour [kalɑ̃buːr] nm pun.
calendrier [kalɑ̃dri(j)e] nm calendar.
calepin [kalpɛ̃] nm notebook.
caler [kale] vt to wedge, chock (up), prop up, adjust, stall; vi to stall, draw water, funk.
calfat [kalfa] nm caulker.
calfater [kalfate] vt to caulk.
calfeutrer [kalføtre] vt to stop (up), block (up), make draft-proof; vr to shut oneself up, make oneself cosy, comfortable.
calibre [kalibr] nm caliber, bore, gauge, pattern.
calice [kalis] nm calyx, chalice, cup.
calicot [kaliko] nm calico, draper's shop assistant.
califourchon [kalifurʃɔ̃] ad **à — astride.**
câlin [kɑlɛ̃] a caressing, winning, wheedling.

câliner [kaline] vt to caress, fondle, pet, wheedle.

câlinerie [kalinri] nf caress(ing), petting, wheedling.

calleux, -euse [kalø, øːz] a horny, callous.

calligraphie [kalligrafi] nf penmanship, handwriting.

callosité [kallɔzite] nf callosity.

calme [kalm] a calm, still, quiet, composed, collected; nm calm(ness), stillness.

calmer [kalme] vt to calm, quiet, soothe; vr to calm down, abate.

calomniateur, -trice [kalɔmnjatœːr, tris] n slanderer.

calomnie [kalɔmni] nf calumny, slander, libel.

calomnier [kalɔmnje] vt to slander.

calomnieux, -euse [kalɔmnjø, øːz] a slanderous.

calorie [kalɔri] nf calory.

calorifère [kalɔrifɛːr] nm central-heating apparatus, hot-air stove.

calorifuge [kalɔrifyːʒ] a heat-insulating, heat-proof.

calorique [kalɔrik] a caloric, heat.

calot [kalo] nm forage cap, rough slate, stone.

calotte [kalɔt] nf skull cap, box on the ears.

calotter [kalɔte] vt to cuff.

calque [kalk] nm tracing, traced copy.

calquer [kalke] vt to trace.

calvitie [kalvisi] nf baldness.

camarade [kamarad] n comrade, chum, friend, mate.

camaraderie [kamaradri] nf comradeship, fellowship.

camard [kamaːr] a flat-, snub-, pug-nosed.

Cambodge [kãbodʒ] nm Cambodia.

cambouis [kãbwi] nm dirty oil, grease.

cambré [kãbre] a cambered, arched, curved, bent.

cambrer [kãbre] vt to arch, bend, camber, curve; vr to brace oneself.

cambriolage [kãbriɔlaːʒ] nm burglary.

cambrioler [kãbriɔle] vt to burgle, break into.

cambrioleur, -euse [kãbriɔlœːr, øːz] n burglar.

cambrure [kãbryːr] nf camber, curve, arch, instep.

cambuse [kãbyːz] nf steward's room, glory hole, hovel.

came [kam] nf cam.

camée [kame] nm cameo.

caméléon [kameleõ] nm chameleon.

camélia [kamelja] nm camellia.

camelot [kamlo] nm street hawker, newsvender.

camelote [kamlɔt] nf rubbish, trash, shoddy goods.

caméra [kamɛra] nf movie camera.

camion [kamjõ] nm wagon, dray, truck.

camionnage [kamjɔnaːʒ] nm cartage, haulage.

camionnette [kamjɔnɛt] nf light truck, van.

camionneur [kamjɔnœːr] nm carrier.

camisole [kamizɔl] nf woman's vest, dressing-jacket; — de force straitjacket.

camouflage [kamuflaːʒ] n camouflage.

camoufler [kamufle] vt to disguise, fake, camouflage.

camouflet [kamuflɛ] nm insult, snub.

camp [kã] nm camp, side.

campagnard [kãpaɲaːr] a country, rustic; n countryman, -woman.

campagne [kãpaɲ] nf country(side), field, campaign; partie de — picnic.

campé [kãpe] a bien — well set-up, strapping.

campement [kãpmã] nm encampment, camping.

camper [kãpe] vi to (en)camp; vt to put under canvas, place, put, stick; — là to leave in the lurch; vr to pitch one's camp, plant oneself.

camphre [kãːfr] nm camphor.

camphrer [kãfre] vt to camphorate.

camus [kamy] a snub-, flat-, pug-nosed.

canaille [kanaːj] nf rabble, mob, blackguard, rascal.

canal [kanal] nm canal, channel, pipe, duct.

canalisation [kanalizasjõ] nf canalization, draining, piping, pipes, wiring, mains.

canaliser [kanalize] vt to canalize, pipe, lay down pipes in, wire.

canapé [kanape] nm sofa; canapé.

canard [kanaːr] nm duck, drake, false report, hoax, lump of sugar dipped in coffee.

canari [kanari] nm canary, earthenware pot.

cancan [kãkã] nm cancan dance, scandal.

cancanier, -ière [kãkanje, jɛːr] a addicted to tittle-tattle; n scandalmonger.

cancer [kãsɛːr] nm cancer.

cancéreux, -euse [kãserø, øːz] a cancerous.

cancrelat [kãkrəla] nm cockroach.

candélabre [kãdɛlaːbr] nm candelabrum, branched lamp-post.

candeur [kãdœːr] nf ingenuousness, artlessness.

candidat [kãdida] nm candidate.

candide [kãdid] a ingenuous, artless, guileless.

cane [kan] nf duck.

caneton [kantõ] nm duckling.

canette [kanɛt] nf beer-bottle, spool.

canevas [kanva] nm canvas, outline, sketch.

caniche [kaniʃ] n poodle.

canicule [kanikyl] *nf* dog-days.
canif [kanif] *nm* penknife.
caniveau [kanivo] *nm* gutter, conduit.
canne [kan] *nf* cane, walking-stick, fishing-rod; — **à sucre** sugar cane.
cannelle [kanɛl] *nf* cinnamon, spigot, tap.
cannelure [kanlyːr] *nf* groove, fluting.
canner [kane] *vt* to cane-bottom.
cannibale [kanibal] *nm* cannibal, man-eater.
cannibalisme [kanibalism] *nm* cannibalism.
canon [kanɔ̃] *nm* cannon, gun, barrel, pipe, tube, canon.
cañon [kaɲɔ̃] *nm* canyon.
canonique [kanɔnik] *a* canonical.
canoniser [kanɔnize] *vt* to canonize.
canonnade [kanɔnad] *nf* cannonade.
canonnier [kanɔnje] *nm* gunner.
canonnière [kanɔnjɛːr] *nf* gunboat.
canot [kano] *nm* boat, dinghy, cutter.
canotage [kanɔtaːʒ] *nm* boating, rowing.
canoter [kanɔte] *vi* to go rowing, boating.
canotier [kanɔtje] *nm* rower, oarsman, boatman, straw hat, boater.
cantatrice [kɑ̃tatris] *nf* singer, vocalist.
cantine [kɑ̃tin] *nf* canteen.
cantinier, -ière *n* canteen-keeper.
cantique [kɑ̃tik] *nm* canticle, hymn.
canton [kɑ̃tɔ̃] *nm* canton, district.
cantonade [kɑ̃tɔnad] *nf* **à la** — in the wings, ' off '.
cantonal [kɑ̃tɔnal] *a* cantonal, district.
cantonner [kɑ̃tɔne] *vt* to divide into cantons, quarter, billet, confine, limit.
cantonnement [kɑ̃tɔnmɑ̃] *nm* cantonment, quarters, billet.
cantonnier [kɑ̃tɔnje] *nm* roadman, road-mender.
canulant [kanylɑ̃] *a* boring.
canule [kanyl] *nf* nozzle.
caoutchouc [kautʃu] *nm* (india) rubber, waterproof coat; *pl* galoshes, overshoes, rubbers.
caoutchouter [kautʃute] *vt* to rubberize, treat with rubber.
cap [kap] *nm* cape, headland.
capable [kapabl] *a* capable, fit, able.
capacité [kapasite] *nf* capacity, ability, capability.
cape [kap] *nf* cape, cloak; **rire sous** — to laugh up one's sleeve.
capillaire [kapillɛːr] *a* capillary.
capitaine [kapitɛn] *nm* captain, master, head; — **de vaisseau** captain; — **de frégate** commander; — **de corvette** lieutenant-commander; — **de port** harbor-master.
capital [kapital] *a* capital, chief, principal; *nm* capital, assets, principal.

capitale [kapital] *nf* capital, chief town.
capitaliser [kapitalize] *vt* to capitalize.
capitalisme [kapitalism] *nm* capitalism.
capitaliste [kapitalist] *n* capitalist.
capiteux, -euse [kapitø, øːz] *a* heady, strong.
capitonner [kapitɔne] *vt* to upholster, quilt.
capituler [kapityle] *vi* to capitulate.
caporal [kapɔral] *nm* corporal, (ordinary quality) tobacco.
capot [kapo] *nm* cover, hood, bonnet, cowl.
capotage [kapɔtaːʒ] *nm* capsizing, overturning.
capote [kapɔt] *nf* greatcoat, bonnet, hood, cowl, contraceptive.
capoter [kapɔte] *vt* to capsize, overturn.
câpre [kɑːpr] *nm* caper.
caprice [kapris] *nm* caprice, whim, impulse.
capricieux, -euse [kaprisjø, jøːz] *a* capricious, wayward.
capsule [kapsyl] *nf* capsule, seal, firing-cap.
captage [kaptaːʒ] *nm* catching, collecting.
captation [kaptasjɔ̃] *nf* catching, tapping, picking up.
capter [kapte] *vt* to catch, collect, obtain, pick up.
captieux, -euse [kapsjø, øːz] *a* captious, specious.
captif, -ive [kaptif, iːv] *an* captive.
captiver [kaptive] *vt* to captivate, charm.
captivité [kaptivite] *nf* captivity.
capture [kaptyːr] *nf* capture, seizure, booty.
capturer [kaptyre] *vt* to capture, catch, collect.
capuchon [kapyʃɔ̃] *nm* hood, cowl, cap.
capucine [kapysin] *nf* nasturtium.
caque [kak] *nf* keg, herring barrel.
caquet [kakɛ] *nm* cackle, chattering.
caqueter [kakte] *vi* to cackle, chatter.
car [kaːr] *cj* for, because; *nm* motor coach.
carabin [karabɛ̃] *nm* medical student.
carabine [karabin] *nf* carbine, rifle.
carabiné [karabine] *a* stiff, violent, strong.
carabinier [karabinje] *nm* rifleman.
caractère [karaktɛːr] *nm* character, temper, personality, characteristic, nature.
caractériser [karakterize] *vt* to characterize; *vr* to assume the character (of **par**), be distinguished (by **par**).
caractéristique [karakteristik] *a* characteristic, typical; *nf* trait, feature.

carafe [karaf] *nf* decanter, carafe.
caravane [karavan] *nf* desert caravan, trailer.
carbone [karbɔn] *nm* carbon.
carbonisé [karbɔnize] *a* carbonized, charred, burnt to death.
carburant [karbyrᾶ] *nm* motor fuel.
carburateur [karbyratœ:r] *nm* carburetor.
carbure [karby:r] *nf* carbide.
carcasse [karkas] *nf* carcass, frame.
cardiaque [kardjak] *a* cardiac; **crise** — heart attack.
cardinal [kardinal] *anm* cardinal.
carême [karɛm] *nm* Lent.
carence [karᾶ:s] *nf* insolvency, default, deficiency.
carène [karɛn] *nf* hull, bottom.
caresse [karɛs] *nf* caress.
caresser [karɛse] *vt* to caress, stroke, fondle, cherish.
cargaison [kargɛzɔ̃] *nf* cargo.
cargo [kargo] *nm* cargo boat, tramp steamer.
caricature [karikaty:r] *nf* caricature.
carie [kari] *nf* caries, decay.
carié [karje] *a* decayed.
carillon [karijɔ̃] *nm* chime, peal of bells.
carillonner [karijɔne] *vi* to chime, ring a peal of bells.
carillonneur [karijɔnœ:r] *nm* bellringer.
carlingue [karlɛ̃:g] *nf* fuselage, cockpit.
carnage [karna:ʒ] *nm* slaughter, bloodshed.
carnassier, -ière [karnasje, jɛ:r] *a* carnivorous.
carnassière [karnasjɛ:r] *nf* gamebag.
carnaval [karnaval] *nm* carnival.
carnet [karnɛ] *nm* notebook; — **de banque** pass-book; — **de chèques** checkbook; — **de bal** dance program.
carnier [karnje] *nm* game-bag.
carnivore [karnivɔ:r] *a* carnivorous.
carotte [karɔt] *nf* carrot; (*of tobacco*) plug; fraud, trick, catch.
carpe [karp] *nf* carp.
carpette [karpɛt] *nf* rug.
carquois [karkwa] *nm* quiver.
carré [kare] *a* square (-shouldered), straightforward; *nm* square, lodgings.
carreau [karo] *nm* tile, floor, small square, window-pane, diamonds.
carrefour [karfu:r] *nm* crossroads, square.
carrelage [karla:ʒ] *nm* tiling, tileflooring.
carreler [karle] *vt* to pave, lay with tiles.
carrelet [karlɛ] *nm* plaice.
carrément [karemᾶ] *ad* squarely, firmly, bluntly.
carrer [kare] *vt* to square; *vr* to swagger, settle oneself.

carrier [karje] *nm* quarryman.
carrière [karjɛ:r] *nf* career, quarry; **donner libre** — à to give free play, scope, vent to.
carriole [karjɔl] *nf* light cart.
carrossable [karɔsabl] *a* **route** — carriageway.
carrosse [karɔs] *nm* coach.
carrosserie [karɔsri] *nf* coachbuilding, body(work).
carrousel [karuzɛl] *nm* tournament, merry-go-round.
carrure [kary:r] *nf* build, stature.
cartable [kartabl] *nm* satchel, portfolio.
carte [kart] *nf* map, chart, card, bill, list, menu; — **blanche** free hand, carte blanche.
cartel [kartɛl] *nm* trust, combine, coalition.
carter [kartɛ:r] *nm* gearcase, sump, spool-box.
cartographe [kartɔgraf] *nm* mapmaker, cartographer.
cartographie [kartɔgrafi] *nf* mapmaking.
cartomancie [kartɔmᾶsi] *nf* fortunetelling by cards.
cartomancien, -ienne [kartɔmᾶsjɛ̃, jɛn] *n* fortune-teller by cards.
carton [kartɔ̃] *nm* cardboard box, carton, cartoon.
cartonné [kartɔne] *a* (*books*) bound in boards.
cartouche [kartuʃ] *nf* cartridge.
cartouchière [kartuʃjɛ:r] *nf* cartridge-pouch.
cas [ka] *nm* case, matter, affair, instance, circumstance; **le** — **échéant** should the occasion arise; **au, dans le** — **où** in the event of; **en tout** — in any case; **faire (grand)** — **de** to value highly.
casanier, -ière [kazanje, jɛ:r] *a* stay-at-home, sedentary.
cascade [kaskad] *nf* waterfall, cascade.
case [ka:z] *nf* hut, cabin, pigeonhole, compartment, space, division, square.
casemate [kazmat] *nf* casemate.
caser [kaze] *vt* to put away, stow, file, find a place for, settle; *vr* to settle down.
caserne [kazɛrn] *nf* barracks.
casier [kazje] *nm* set of pigeonholes, rack, cabinet; — **judiciaire** police record.
casque [kask] *nm* helmet.
casquette [kaskɛt] *nf* cap.
cassant [kasᾶ] *a* brittle, crisp, short, blunt, abrupt.
cassation [kasasjɔ̃] *nf* cassation, quashing, reduction to the ranks.
casse [ka:s] *nf* breakage, ructions, damage.
casse-cou [kasku] *nm* dare-devil, death-trap.
casse-croûte [kaskrut] *nm* snack, quick lunch.

casse-noisettes [kɑsnwazɛt] *nm* nut-crackers.

casser [kɑse] *vt* to break, crack, cashier, degrade, annul, quash; *vr* to break, give way, snap; **se — la tête** to puzzle, rack one's brains.

casserole [kasrɔl] *nf* saucepan, stewpan, casserole.

casse-tête [kɑstɛt] *nm* club, loaded stick, teaser, din.

cassette [kasɛt] *nf* casket, money-box.

cassis [kɑsi(s)] *nm* blackcurrant (liqueur); open gutter across road.

cassonade [kasɔnad] *nf* brown sugar.

cassure [kasyːr] *nf* break, fracture, crack.

castor [kastɔːr] *nm* beaver.

casuel [kɑzɥɛl] *nm* perquisites, casual profits, fees.

cataclysme [kataklism] *nm* cata-clysm.

catacombes [katakɔ̃ːb] *nf pl* cata-combs.

catalepsie [katalɛpsi] *nf* catalepsy.

catalogue [katalɔg] *nm* catalogue.

cataloguer [katalɔge] *vt* to catalogue, list.

catalyseur [katalizœːr] *nm* catalyst.

cataplasme [kataplasm] *nm* poultice; **— sinapisé** mustard poul-tice.

cataracte [katarakt] *nf* cataract.

catarrhe [kataːr] *nm* catarrh.

catastrophe [katastrɔf] *nf* cata-strophe, disaster.

catch [katʃ] *nm* all-in wrestling.

catéchiser [kateʃize] *vt* to catechize, lecture, reason with, try to persuade.

catéchisme [kateʃism] *nm* cate-chism.

catégorie [kategɔri] *nf* category.

catégorique [kategɔrik] *a* categoric-al, positive.

cathédrale [katedral] *nf* cathedral.

catholicisme [katɔlisism] *nm* Catholicism.

catholique [katɔlik] *a* catholic, orthodox; universal; *an* Roman Catholic; **ce n'est pas — that is fishy.

catimini [katimini] *ad* **en — on the sly, stealthily.

cauchemar [koʃmaːr, ko-] *nm* night-mare.

cauri [kɔri] *nm* cowrie shell.

cause [koːz] *nf* cause, grounds, suit, action, brief; **et pour — for a very good reason, very properly; pour — de for reasons of; à — de on account of, owing to, through; — célèbre famous case, trial; mettre en — to implicate, bring into question; en connaissance de — with full knowledge of the case.

causer [koze] *vt* to cause; *vi* to talk, converse, chat.

causerie [kozri] *nf* talk, chat.

causeur, -euse [kozœːr, øːz] *a* talkative, chatty; *n* talker.

caustique [kostik] *a* caustic, burn-ing, cutting, biting.

cauteleux, -euse [kotlø, øːz] *a* cunning, sly, wary.

cautériser [koterize] *vt* to cauterize.

caution [kosjɔ̃] *nf* security, surety, bail, guarantee; **sujet à — un-confirmed.

cautionnement [kosjɔnmɑ̃] *nm* sure-ty, deposit, security, guarantee.

cavalerie [kavalri] *nf* cavalry.

cavalier, -ière [kavalje, jɛːr] *a* off-hand, free and easy, jaunty, riding; *n* horseman, horsewoman, rider; *nm* trooper, escort, cavalier, partner, knight.

cave [kaːv] *a* hollow, sunken, deep-set; *nf* cellar, stake.

caveau [kavo] *nm* vault.

caverne [kavɛrn] *nf* cave, cavern, den, cavity.

caverneux, -euse [kavɛrnø, øːz] *a* cavernous, hollow, sepulchral.

caviarder [kavjarde] *vt* to suppress, block-out.

cavité [kavite] *nf* cavity, hollow, pit.

ce [s(ə)] *pn* it, he, she; **— qui, — que** what, which; **sur — thereupon; pour — qui est de as regards; *a* **ce, cet, cette, ces** this, that, such; *pl* **these, those, such; **— soir** this evening, tonight; **cette nuit** last night.

ceci [səsi] *pn* this.

cécité [sesite] *nf* blindness.

céder [sede] *vt* to give up, surrender, assign; *vi* to yield, give way, sag; **le — à qn.** to be inferior to s.o.

cèdre [sɛːdr] *nm* cedar.

ceindre [sɛ̃ːdr] *vt* to gird (on), encircle, encompass.

ceinture [sɛ̃tyːr] *nf* girdle, belt, sash, waist, circle.

ceinturon [sɛ̃tyrɔ̃] *nm* waistbelt, sword-belt.

cela [səla, sla] *pn* that, it, so; **comme ci, comme ça** so so; **c'est ça** that's right, that's it.

célèbre [selɛbr] *a* famous.

célébrer [selebre] *vt* to celebrate, observe, hold, solemnize, sing the praises of.

célébrité [selebrite] *nf* celebrity.

céleri [selri] *nm* celery.

célérité [selerite] *nf* celerity, speed, swiftness.

céleste [selɛst] *a* celestial, heavenly.

célibat [seliba] *nm* celibacy.

célibataire [selibatɛːr] *a* celibate, unmarried, single; *n* bachelor, spinster.

celle see **celui.**

cellulaire [selylɛːr] *a* cellular; **voiture — police van.

cellule [selyl] *nf* cell.

celluloïd [selylɔid] *nm* celluloid.

cellulose [selyloːz] *nf* cellulose.

celte [sɛlt] *n* Celt.

celtique [sɛltik] *a* Celtic.

celui, celle, ceux, celles [səlɥi] *pn* he,

she, the one, those; —-ci the latter, this one; —-là the former, that one.
cendre [sã:dr] *nf* ash(es), cinders, embers.
cendré [sãdre] *a* ashy, ash-gray.
cendrier [sãdrie] *nm* ashbin, -pan, -pit, -tray.
cène [sɛn] *nf* the Last Supper.
censé [sãse] *a* supposed.
censeur [sãsœ:r] *nm* censor, critic, disciplinary head of French school.
censure [sãsy:r] *nf* censorship, blame.
censurer [sãsyre] *vt* to censor, criticize.
cent [sã] *a* one hundred; *nm* a hundred; **faire les — pas** to walk up and down.
centaine [sãtɛn] *nf* (about) a hundred.
centenaire [sãtnɛ:r] *an* centenarian; *nm* centenary.
centième [sãtjɛm] *anm* hundredth.
centigrade [sãtigrad] *a* centigrade.
centigramme [sãtigram] *nm* centigram.
centilitre [sãtilitr] *nm* centiliter.
centime [sãtim] *nm* centime.
centimètre [sãtimɛtr] *nm* centimeter, tape-measure.
central [sãtral] *a* central, middle; *nm* telephone exchange.
centrale [sãtral] *nf* power-house, electricity works.
centraliser [sãtralize] *vt* to centralize.
centre [sã:tr] *nm* center, middle.
centrifuge [sãtrify:ʒ] *a* centrifugal.
centuple [sãtypl] *a* centuple, hundredfold.
cep [sɛ(p)] *nm* vine-plant.
cependant [s(ə)pãdã] *ad* meanwhile, meantime; *cj* still, yet, nevertheless.
cerceau [sɛrso] *nm* hoop.
cercle [sɛrkl] *nm* circle, set, club, hoop, ring, dial.
cercler [sɛrkle] *vt* to encircle, ring, hoop.
cercueil [sɛrkœ:j] *nm* coffin.
céréale [sereal] *anf* cereal.
cérébral [serebral] *a* cerebral, of the brain.
cérémonie [seremɔni] *nf* ceremony; **tenue de — full dress; sans —** informally.
cérémonieux, -euse [seremɔnjø, ø:z] ceremonious, formal.
cerf [sɛ:r, sɛrf] *nm* stag.
cerfeuil [sɛrfœ:j] *nm* chervil.
cerf-volant [sɛrvɔlã] *nm* kite.
cerise [səri:z] *nf* cherry.
cerisier [s(ə)rizje] *nm* cherry-tree.
cerné [sɛrne] *a* **les yeux —s** with rings under the eyes.
cerner [sɛrne] *vt* to encircle, surround, hem in.
certain [sɛrtɛ̃] *a* certain, sure, fixed, stated; *pn pl* some, certain.
certainement [sɛrtɛnmã] *ad* certainly, by all means.
certes [sɛrt] *ad* yes indeed, most certainly, to be sure.

certificat [sɛrtifika] *nm* certificate, script.
certifier [sɛrtifje] *vt* to attest, authenticate.
certitude [sɛrtityd] *nf* certainty.
cerveau [sɛrvo] *nm* brain, mind; **— brûlé** hot-head
cervelas [sɛrvəla] *nm* saveloy.
cervelle [sɛrvɛl] *nf* brain(s), mind; **se creuser la — to rack one's brains.**
ces see **ce.**
cessation [sɛsasjɔ̃] *nf* cessation, suspension.
cesse [sɛs] *nf* cease, ceasing.
cesser [sɛse] *vit* to cease, leave off, stop.
cet see **ce.**
cette see **ce.**
ceux see **celui.**
chacal [ʃakal] *nm* jackal.
chacun [ʃakœ̃] *pn* each, each one, every one, everybody, everyone.
chagrin [ʃagrɛ̃] *a* sad, glum, peevish, fretful; *nm* grief, annoyance, worry.
chagriner [ʃagrine] *vt* to grieve, afflict, vex, annoy.
chahut [ʃay] *nm* noise, uproar, rowdyism.
chahuter [ʃayte] *vi* to kick up a row, boo; *vt* to banter.
chahuteur, -euse [ʃaytœ:r, ø:z] *an* rowdy.
chaîne [ʃɛn] *nf* chain, cable, range, warp; *pl* bonds, fetters; **travail à la —** assembly-line production.
chaînon [ʃɛnɔ̃] *nm* link.
chair [ʃɛ:r] *nf* flesh, meat, pulp; **en — et en os** in the flesh; **— de poule** gooseflesh, creeps; **— à canon** cannon fodder.
chaire [ʃɛ:r] *nf* pulpit, desk, rostrum, chair, professorship.
chaise [ʃɛ:z] *nf* chair, seat.
chaise-longue [ʃɛzlɔ̃:g] *nf* couch.
chaland [ʃalã] *nm* customer, lighter, barge.
châle [ʃɑ:l] *nm* shawl, wrap.
chalet [ʃɑlɛ, ʃa-] *nm* chalet.
chaleur [ʃalœ:r] *nf* warmth, heat, ardor, zeal; **craint la —** keep in a cool place.
chaleureux, -euse [ʃalœrø, ø:z] *a* warm, cordial.
chaloupe [ʃalup] *nf* launch.
chalumeau [ʃalymo] *nm* straw, pipe, blowpipe.
chalutier [ʃalytje] *nm* drifter, trawler.
se chamailler [səʃamaje] *vr* to quarrel, squabble, row.
chambarder [ʃãbarde] *vt* to smash up, upset, sack.
chambellan [ʃãbɛlã] *nm* chamberlain.
chambranle [ʃãbrã:l] *nm* frame, mantelpiece.
chambre [ʃã:br] *nf* (bed)room, chamber, House (parliament); **— à air** inner tube; **— d'ami** spare room.

chambrée [ʃɑ̃bre] *nf* roomful, barrack room.

chambrer [ʃɑ̃bre] *vt* to lock up in a room; (*wine*) take the chill off.

chameau [ʃamo] *nm* camel, scoundrel, beast, swine.

chamois [ʃamwa] *nm* chamois.

champ [ʃɑ̃] *nm* field, ground, course, range, scope; **à tout bout de —** at every turn.

champagne [ʃɑ̃paɲ] *nm* champagne; **fine — liqueur** brandy.

champêtre [ʃɑ̃pɛːtr] *a* rustic, rural.

champignon [ʃɑ̃piɲɔ̃] *nm* mushroom.

champion, -ionne [ʃɑ̃pjɔ̃, jɔn] *n* champion.

championnat [ʃɑ̃pjɔna] *nm* championship.

chance [ʃɑ̃ːs] *nf* chance, luck.

chancelant [ʃɑ̃slɑ̃] *a* staggering, shaky, delicate.

chanceler [ʃɑ̃sle] *vi* to stagger, totter.

chancelier [ʃɑ̃səlje] *nm* chancellor.

chancellerie [ʃɑ̃sɛlri] *nf* chancellery, secretaryship.

chanceux, -euse [ʃɑ̃sø, øːz] *a* hazardous, lucky.

chancre [ʃɑ̃ːkr] *nm* canker, ulcer.

chandail [ʃɑ̃daːj] *nm* sweater, pullover.

Chandeleur [ʃɑ̃dlœːr] *nf* Candlemas.

chandelier [ʃɑ̃dəlje] *nm* candlestick.

chandelle [ʃɑ̃dɛl] *nf* candle, prop, shore; **voir trente-six —s** to see stars; **économies de bouts de —** cheese-paring.

change [ʃɑ̃ːʒ] *nm* exchange; **lettre de — bill** of exchange.

changeable [ʃɑ̃ʒabl] *a* changeable, exchangeable.

changeant [ʃɑ̃ʒɑ̃] *a* changing, changeable, fickle.

changement [ʃɑ̃ʒmɑ̃] *nm* change, alteration, variation, variety; **— de vitesse** gear, change of gear; **— de voie** points.

changer [ʃɑ̃ʒe] *vt* to change, exchange, alter; *vi* to change; *vr* to alter, change one's clothes.

changeur [ʃɑ̃ʒœːr] *nm* money-changer.

chanoine [ʃanwan] *nm* canon.

chanson [ʃɑ̃sɔ̃] *nf* song; **—s!** nonsense!

chansonnier, -ière [ʃɑ̃sɔnje, jɛːr] *n* songwriter; *nm* songbook.

chant [ʃɑ̃] *nm* song, singing, crow (ing), chant, canto.

chantage [ʃɑ̃taːʒ] *nm* blackmail.

chantant [ʃɑ̃tɑ̃] *a* singing, musical, sing-song.

chanter [ʃɑ̃te] *vt* to sing, crow, chirp, suit; **faire —** to blackmail.

chanteur, -euse [ʃɑ̃tœːr, øːz] *n* singer, vocalist; **maître —** master-singer, blackmailer.

chantier [ʃɑ̃tje] *nm* stand, ship (building) yard, dockyard; **sur le —** in hand.

chantonner [ʃɑ̃tɔne] *vt* to hum.

chanvre [ʃɑ̃ːvr] *nm* hemp.

chaos [kao] *nm* chaos.

chaotique [kaotik] *a* chaotic.

chape [ʃap] *nf* cope, coping.

chapeau [ʃapo] *nm* hat, cover, cap, cowl, heading; **donner un coup de — à** to raise one's hat to; **— melon** bowler; **— haut-de-forme, à, de haute forme** top hat.

chapelet [ʃaplɛ] *nm* rosary, string.

chapelier [ʃapəlje] *nm* hatter.

chapelle [ʃapɛl] *nf* chapel, coterie, clique.

chapelure [ʃaplyːr] *nf* breadcrumbs.

chaperon [ʃaprɔ̃] *nm* hood, chaperon.

chapitre [ʃapitr] *nm* chapter, heading, item, point; **avoir voix au —** to have a say in the matter.

chapitrer [ʃapitre] *vt* to lecture, reprimand.

chaque [ʃak] *a* each, every.

char [ʃaːr] *nm* chariot, car, wagon; **— d'assaut** tank.

charbon [ʃarbɔ̃] *nm* coal, carbon; **— de bois** charcoal.

charbonnage [ʃarbɔnaːʒ] *nm* pl collieries, coal-mining; (*naut*) bunkering.

charbonner [ʃarbɔne] *vt* to carbonize, blacken with charcoal.

charbonnier [ʃarbɔnje, jɛːr] *nm* collier, charcoal-burner, coal merchant, coalman.

charcuterie [ʃarkytri] *nf* pork-butcher's shop, pork-butcher's meat, pork.

charcutier, -ière [ʃarkytje, jɛːr] *n* pork-butcher.

chardon [ʃardɔ̃] *nm* thistle.

chardonneret [ʃardɔnrɛ] *nm* goldfinch.

charge [ʃarʒ] *nf* load, burden, charge, onus, care, trust, expense, office, duty, exaggeration, skit, indictment; **à la — de** chargeable to, dependent on, assigned to; **en — (el)** live; **à — de** on condition that, provided that; **témoin à —** witness for the prosecution.

chargé [ʃarʒe] *a* loaded, live, furred, coated, full, busy, overcast; **lettre —e** registered letter; *nm* **— de cours** lecturer, reader.

chargement [ʃarʒəmɑ̃] *nm* lading, loading (up), charging, registration, freight.

charger [ʃarʒe] *vt* to load, charge, fill, instruct, caricature, exaggerate, saddle; *vr* to undertake, shoulder.

chariot [ʃarjo] *nm* wagon, go-cart, truck, trolley.

charité [ʃarite] *nf* charity, alms.

charme [ʃarm] *nm* charm, spell.

charmer [ʃarme] *vt* to charm, bewitch, delight, please.

charnel, -elle [ʃarnɛl] *a* carnal, sensual.

charnier [ʃarnje] *nm* charnel-house, ossuary.

charnière [ʃarnjɛːr] nf hinge.
charnu [ʃarny] a fleshy, plump.
charognard [ʃarɔɲar] nm vulture.
charogne [ʃarɔɲ] nf carrion, decaying carcass.
charpente [ʃarpɑ̃ːt] nf frame(work).
charpenter [ʃarpɑ̃te] vt to frame, build, construct.
charpenterie [ʃarpɑ̃tri] nf carpentry, carpenter's shop.
charpentier [ʃarpɑ̃tje] nm carpenter.
charpie [ʃarpi] nf lint; **en —** in shreds.
charretier [ʃartje] nm carter, carrier.
charrette [ʃarɛt] nf cart; **— à bras** barrow; **— anglaise** trap, dogcart.
charrier [ʃarje] vt to cart, carry.
charron [ʃarɔ̃] nm cartwright, wheelwright.
charrue [ʃary] nf plow.
charte [ʃart] nf charter.
chartreux [ʃartrø] nm Carthusian monk.
chasse [ʃas] nf chase, hunting, shooting, shoot; **— à courre** riding to hounds; **— à l'affût** stalking; **— d'eau** flush.
châsse [ʃaːs] nf reliquary, shrine, frame.
chasser [ʃase] vt to chase, hunt, shoot, drive (away, out), dismiss, expel; vi to hunt, go hunting, shooting, drive.
chasseur, -euse [ʃasœːr, øːz] n huntsman, sportsman, shooter; nm pageboy, messenger, rifleman, fighter-plane; **— de fauves** big-game hunter.
chassieux, -euse [ʃasjø, øːz] a blear-eyed.
chassis [ʃasi] nm frame, sash, chassis, under carriage.
chaste [ʃast] a chaste, pure.
chasteté [ʃastəte] nf chastity, purity.
chat, -atte [ʃa, -at] n cat; **— de gouttières** stray cat.
châtaigne [ʃatɛɲ] nf chestnut.
châtaignier [ʃatɛɲe] nm chestnut tree.
châtain [ʃatɛ̃] a chestnut-brown, auburn.
château [ʃato] nm castle, country-residence, manor, palace; **—x en Espagne** castles in the air; **— d'eau** water tower.
châteaubriand [ʃatobriɑ̃] nm grilled steak.
chat-huant [ʃayɑ̃] nm tawny, brown owl.
châtier [ʃatje] vt to punish, chastise, (style) polish.
châtiment [ʃatimɑ̃] nm punishment, chastisement.
chatoiement [ʃatwamɑ̃] nm shimmer, sheen.
chaton [ʃatɔ̃] nm kitten, catkin, stone in its setting.
chatouiller [ʃatuje] vt to tickle.
chatouilleux, -euse [ʃatujø, øːz] a ticklish, touchy, sensitive, delicate.

chatoyer [ʃatwaje] vi to shimmer, sparkle.
châtrer [ʃatre] vt to castrate, geld.
chatterton [ʃatɛrtɔ̃] nm insulating tape.
chaud [ʃo] a warm, hot; **pleurer à —es larmes** to weep bitterly; **il fait —** it is warm; **tenir au —** to keep in a warm place; **avoir —** to be warm.
chaudière [ʃodjɛːr] nf boiler.
chaudron [ʃodrɔ̃] nm caldron.
chaudronnerie [ʃodrɔnri] nf copper-smith's work; boiler-making, boiler-works.
chaudronnier [ʃodrɔnje] nm copper-smith, brazier, boiler-smith, boiler-maker.
chauffage [ʃofaːʒ] nm heating, firing, stoking; **— central** central heating.
chauffard [ʃofaːr] nm roadhog.
chauffe [ʃoːf] nf heating, stoking, firing.
chauffer [ʃofe] vt to warm, heat, stoke up, fire up, nurse, cram; vi to get hot, warm (up), get up steam.
chauffeur, -euse [ʃofœːr, øːz] n stoker, fireman, driver.
chaume [ʃoːm] nm thatch, stubble (-field).
chaumière [ʃomjɛːr] nf (thatched) cottage.
chaussée [ʃose] nf causeway, road-way, carriageway.
chausse-pied [ʃospje] nm shoehorn.
chausser [ʃose] vt to put on (shoes, stockings), make footwear for, supply with footwear; vr to put on one's shoes, stockings.
chausse-trape [ʃostrap] nf trap, ruse.
chaussette [ʃosɛt] nf sock.
chausson [ʃosɔ̃] nm slipper, dancing sandal, gymnasium shoe, bootee, bed-sock, footlet; **— aux pommes** apple turnover.
chaussure [ʃosyːr] nf footwear, boot, shoe.
chauve [ʃoːv] a bald.
chauve-souris [ʃovsuri] nf bat.
chauvin [ʃovɛ̃] an chauvinist(ic).
chaux [ʃo] nf lime; **— vive** quick-lime; **blanchir à la —** to whitewash.
chavirer [ʃavire] vi to capsize; vt to upset, tip (up).
chéchia [ʃeʃja] nm fez.
chef [ʃɛf] nm head, chief, leader, principal, foreman, master, authority, right; **— de cuisine** head cook, chef; **— d'orchestre** conductor; **— de train** guard.
chef-d'œuvre [ʃedœːvr] nm master-piece.
chef-lieu [ʃɛfljø] nm county seat.
chelem [ʃlɛm] nm (cards) slam.
chemin [ʃmɛ̃] nm way, road, track, path, headway; **— de fer** railroad; **— des écoliers** roundabout road; **— faisant** on the way; **se mettre en —** to set out; **— de traverse**

crossroad; **ne pas y aller par quatre —s** to go straight to the point.

chemineau [ʃmino] *nm* tramp.

cheminée [ʃmine] *nf* fireplace, mantelpiece, chimney, funnel.

cheminer [ʃmine] *vi* to tramp, proceed, walk, trudge.

chemise [ʃmiːz] *nf* shirt, chemise, jacket, folder, casing, dust jacket; **— de nuit** nightshirt (man), nightdress, nightgown (woman); **en bras de —** in one's shirt sleeves.

chenal [ʃ(ə)nal] *nm* channel.

chenapan [ʃnapɑ̃] *nm* rogue, rascal.

chêne [ʃɛn] *nm* oak (tree).

chenet [ʃ(ə)nɛ] *nm* fire-dog, andiron.

chenil [ʃ(ə)ni] *nm* kennel.

chenille [ʃ(ə)niːj] *nf* caterpillar, chenille, caterpillar tracks.

cheptel [ʃətɛl, ʃɛptɛl] *nm* livestock.

chèque [ʃɛk] *nm* check.

chéquier [ʃekje] *nm* checkbook.

cher, -ère [ʃɛːr] *a* dear, beloved, expensive, costly, precious; *ad* dearly, at a high price; **cela ne vaut pas —** it is not worth much.

chercher [ʃɛrʃe] *vt* to look (for, up), seek, search for, endeavor, try (to); **envoyer —** to send for.

chère [ʃɛːr] *nf* countenance, food.

chéri [ʃeri] *a* dear, beloved; *n* darling.

chérir [ʃeriːr] *vt* to love dearly, cherish.

cherté [ʃɛrte] *nf* dearness, high price.

chérubin [ʃerybɛ̃] *nm* cherub.

chétif, -ive [ʃetif, iːv] *a* puny, weak, sickly, poor.

cheval [ʃəval, ʃfal] *nm* horse, horse-power; **— à bascule** rocking-horse; **— de bois** wooden horse; *pl* merry-go-round, roundabout; **— de trait** draft horse; **à —** on horseback; **être à — sur** to be astride, straddle, be a stickler for; **remède de —** drastic remedy.

chevaleresque [ʃ(ə)valrɛsk, ʃfal-] *a* chivalrous, knightly.

chevalerie [ʃ(ə)valri, ʃfal-] *nf* chivalry, knighthood.

chevalet [ʃ(ə)valɛ, ʃfalɛ] *nm* support, trestle, stand, easel, clothes-horse.

chevalier [ʃ(ə)valje, ʃfal-] *nm* knight; **— d'industrie** swindler, adventurer.

chevalière [ʃ(ə)valjɛːr, ʃfal-] *nf* signet-, seal-ring.

chevalin [ʃəvalɛ̃, ʃfalɛ̃] *a* equine; **boucherie —e** horse-meat butcher's shop.

cheval-vapeur [ʃəvalvapœːr] *nm* horsepower.

chevaucher [ʃ(ə)voʃe] *vti* to ride; *vt* to span, overlap.

chevelu [ʃəvly] *a* hairy.

chevelure [ʃəvlyːr] *nf* (head) of hair, locks.

chevet [ʃ(ə)vɛ] *nm* headboard, bedside, bolster.

cheveu [ʃ(ə)vø] *nm* hair; **couper un — en quatre** to split hairs; **argu-**ment tiré par les **—x** a far-fetched argument.

cheville [ʃ(ə)viːj] *nf* pin, peg, bolt, expletive, padding, ankle; **— ouvrière** king-pin.

chèvre [ʃɛːvr] *nf* goat.

chevreau [ʃəvro] *nm* kid.

chèvrefeuille [ʃɛvrəfœːj] *nm* honeysuckle.

chevreuil [ʃəvrœːj] *nm* roe-deer, roebuck.

chevron [ʃəvrɔ̃] *nm* rafter, chevron, stripe.

chevrotant [ʃəvrɔtɑ̃] *a* quavering.

chez [ʃe] *prep* at, in the house of, care of, with, among, in; **— lui** at his home; **— mon frère** at my brother's.

chic [ʃik] *a* stylish, smart, posh, swell, decent.

chicane [ʃikan] *nf* quibbling, wrangling, pettifoggery.

chicaner [ʃikane] *vt* to wrangle with; *vi* to quibble, haggle over, cavil (at **sur**).

chiche [ʃiʃ] *a* scanty, poor, stingy, sparing of; *excl* go on!, I dare you!; **pois —** chick pea.

chichis [ʃiʃi] *nm pl* affected manners, airs.

chicorée [ʃikɔre] *nf* chicory; **— (frisée)** endive.

chien, chienne [ʃjɛ̃, ʃjɛn] *n* dog, bitch; *nm* (of *gun*) hammer; **faire le — couchant** to cringe, toady; **un temps de —** filthy weather; **entre — et loup** at dusk, in the gloaming; **— loup** Alsatian dog, police dog.

chiffon [ʃifɔ̃] *nm* rag, duster, piece of lace, ribbon, material, scrap, chiffon; **parler —s** to talk dress.

chiffonner [ʃifɔne] *vt* to crumple, rumple, annoy.

chiffonnier, -ière [ʃifɔnje, jɛːr] *n* ragman, rag-picker; *nm* small chest of drawers.

chiffre [ʃifr] *nm* figure, number, cipher, account, monogram; **— d'affaires** turnover.

chiffrer [ʃifre] *vt* to number, work out, cipher, mark; *vi* to calculate, reckon.

chignole [ʃiɲɔl] *nf* (hand-)drill.

chimère [ʃimɛːr] *nf* chimera, illusion.

chimérique [ʃimerik] *a* fanciful, unpractical.

chimie [ʃimi] *nf* chemistry.

chimique [ʃimik] *a* chemical.

chimiste [ʃimist] *nm* chemist (scientist).

Chine [ʃin] *nf* China.

chinois [ʃinwa] *an* Chinese.

chinoiserie [ʃinwazri] *nf* Chinese curio; *pl* red tape, irksome complications.

chiper [ʃipe] *vt* to pinch, pilfer, sneak, scrounge, bag.

chipie [ʃipi] *nf* shrew, ill-natured woman.

chique [ʃik] *nf* quid (tobacco), roundworm.

chiqué [ʃike] *nm* sham, pretense, make-believe.

chiquenaude [ʃikno:d] *nf* fillip, flick (of fingers).

chiquer [ʃike] *vt* to chew tobacco.

chiromancie [kirɔmãsi] *nf* palmistry.

chiromancien, -ienne [kirɔmãsjɛ̃, jɛn] *n* palmist.

chirurgical [ʃiryrʒikal] *a* surgical.

chirurgie [ʃiryrʒi] *nf* surgery; — **esthétique du visage** face-lifting.

chirurgien, -ienne [ʃiryrʒjɛ̃, jɛn] *n* surgeon.

chloroforme [klɔrɔfɔrm] *nm* chloroform.

choc [ʃɔk] *nm* shock, clash, impact, knock.

chocolat [ʃɔkɔla] *nm* chocolate.

chœur [kœ:r] *nm* chorus, choir, chancel.

choisi [ʃwazi] *a* choice, select, picked.

choisir [ʃwazi:r] *vt* to choose, select, pick.

choix [ʃwa] *nm* choice, choosing, selection, pick; **de** — choice, best, first-class; **au** — all at the same price.

choléra [kɔlɛra] *nm* cholera.

chômage [ʃoma:ʒ] *nm* unemployment, idleness, closing down.

chômer [ʃome] *vi* to stop work, close, shut down, be idle, be unemployed.

chômeur [ʃomœ:r] *nm* unemployed person.

chope [ʃɔp] *nf* tankard.

chopine [ʃɔpin] *nf* pint mug.

choquer [ʃɔke] *vt* to shock, offend, strike, bump, clink; *vr* to come into collision, be shocked.

chose [ʃo:z] *nf* thing, case, matter; **bien des —s de ma part** à remember me to; **monsieur** — Mr. Thingummy, Mr. What's-his-name; **être tout** — to feel queer, look queer.

chou [ʃu] *nm* cabbage, rosette, cream-cake; — **de Bruxelles** Brussels sprouts; **feuille de** — rag (newspaper); **mon** — my darling, pet.

choucas [ʃuka] *nm* jackdaw.

choucroute [ʃukrut] *nf* sauerkraut.

chouette [ʃwɛt] *nf* owl; *a* great, posh, swell.

chou-fleur [ʃuflœ:r] *nm* cauliflower.

choyer [ʃwaje] *vt* to pet, pamper, cherish.

chrétien, -ienne [kretjɛ̃, jɛn] *an* Christian.

chretienté [kretjɛ̃te] *nf* Christendom.

Christ [krist] *nm* **le** — Christ.

christianisme [kristjanism] *nm* Christianity.

chromatique [krɔmatik] *a* chromatic.

chrome [kro:m] *nm* chromium, chrome.

chromo [krɔmo] *nm* color-print.

chronique [krɔnik] *a* chronic; *nf* chronicle, news, notes, reports.

chroniqueur [krɔnikœ:r] *nm* chronicler, reporter.

chronologie [krɔnɔlɔʒi] *nf* chronology.

chronologique [krɔnɔlɔʒik] *a* chronological.

chronomètre [krɔnɔmɛtr] *nm* chronometer.

chronométrer [krɔnɔmetre] *vt* to time.

chronométreur [krɔnɔmetrœ:r] *nm* time-keeper.

chrysalide [krizalid] *nf* chrysalis.

chrysanthème [krizãtɛ(:)m] *nm* chrysanthemum.

chuchotement [ʃyʃɔtmã] *nm* whispering.

chuchoter [ʃyʃɔte] *vti* to whisper.

chuchoterie [ʃyʃɔtri] *nf* whispered conversation.

chut [ʃyt, ʃt] *excl* hush!

chute [ʃyt] *nf* fall, drop, downfall, collapse, chute; **la** — **des reins** small of the back.

Chypre [ʃipr] *nm* Cyprus.

ci [si] *ad* **par-ci, par-là** here and there; **de-ci de-là** on all sides; **dem þn** *neuter* **comme ci, comme ça** so-so.

ci-après [siaprɛ] *ad* hereafter, farther on, below.

cible [sibl] *nf* target.

ciboire [sibwa:r] *nm* ciborium, pyx.

ciboulette [sibulɛt] *nf* chives.

cicatrice [sikatris] *nf* scar.

ci-contre [sikɔ̃:tr] *ad* opposite, annexed, on the other side, per contra.

ci-dessous [sidsu] *ad* undermentioned, below.

ci-dessus [sidsy] *ad* above (mentioned).

ci-devant [sidvã] *ad* previously, formerly, late.

cidre [si(:)dr] *nm* cider.

ciel [sjɛl] *pl* **cieux** [sjø] *nm* sky, heaven, air, climate, canopy.

cierge [sjɛrʒ] *nm* wax candle, taper.

cigale [sigal] *nf* cicada.

cigare [siga:r] *nm* cigar.

cigarette [sigarɛt] *nf* cigarette.

ci-gît [siʒi] here lies.

cigogne [sigɔɲ] *nf* stork.

ci-inclus [siɛ̃kly] *a* herewith, enclosed.

ci-joint [siʒwɛ̃] *a* herewith, attached, subjoined.

cil [sil] *nm* eyelash.

cime [sim] *nf* summit, top.

ciment [simã] *nm* cement; — **armé** reinforced concrete.

cimenter [simãte] *vt* to cement, consolidate.

cimetière [simtjɛ:r] *nm* cemetery, graveyard.

cinéaste [sineast] *nm* film technician, producer.

cinéma [sinɛmɑ] *nm* cinema, movie theater.

cinématographier [sinɛmatɔgrafje] *vt* to cinematograph, film.

cinématographique [sinɛmatɔgrafik] *a* cinematographic, film.

cinéprojecteur [sineprɔʒɛktœːr] *nm* movie projector.

cinglant [sɛ̃glɑ̃] *a* biting, cutting, scathing.

cingler [sɛ̃gle] *vt* to lash, cut with a lash, whip, sting; *vi* to sail, scud along.

cinq [sɛ̃(ː)k] *num a* five; **moins —** a near thing.

cinquantaine [sɛ̃kɑ̃tɛn] *nf* (about) fifty.

cinquante [sɛ̃kɑ̃ːt] *num a* fifty.

cinquantenaire [sɛ̃kɑ̃tnɛːr] *nm* fiftieth anniversary, jubilee; *n* a man, woman of fifty.

cinquantième [sɛ̃kɑ̃tjɛm] *num an* fiftieth.

cintre [sɛ̃ːtr] *nm* curve, bend, arch.

cintrer [sɛ̃tre] *vt* to curve, arch, take in at the waist.

cirage [siraːʒ] *nm* polishing, wax(ing), polish.

circoncire [sirkɔ̃siːr] *vt* to circumcise.

circonférence [sirkɔ̃ferɑ̃ːs] *nf* circumference, perimeter, girth.

circonflexe [sirkɔ̃fleks] *a* circumflex.

circonscription [sirkɔ̃skripsjɔ̃] *nf* circumscription, division, constituency.

circonscrire [sirkɔ̃skriːr] *vt* to circumscribe, encircle, limit.

circonspect [sirkɔ̃spɛ, -spɛk, -spɛkt] *a* circumspect, cautious.

circonspection [sirkɔ̃speksjɔ̃] *n* circumspection, prudence, caution.

circonstance [sirkɔ̃stɑ̃ːs] *n* circumstance, occasion, event.

circuit [sirkɥi] *nm* circuit, round; **établir le —** to switch on; **couper le —** to switch off, cut out.

circulaire [sirkylɛːr] *anf* circular.

circulation [sirkylasjɔ̃] *nf* circulation, traffic; **— interdite** no thoroughfare.

circuler [sirkyle] *vi* to circulate, move (on, about).

cire [siːr] *nf* wax.

ciré [sire] *a* waxed, polished; **toile —e** oilcloth; *nm* oilskins.

cirer [sire] *vt* to wax, polish.

cireur, -euse [sirœːr, øːz] *n* polisher, bootblack.

cirque [sirk] *nm* circus.

cisaille(s) [sizaːj] *nf* shears, clippers.

ciseau [sizo] *nm* chisel; *pl* scissors, shears.

ciseler [sizle] *vt* to chisel, carve, chase, cut.

citadelle [sitadɛl] *nf* citadel, stronghold.

citadin [sitadɛ̃] *nm* townsman.

citation [sitasjɔ̃] *nf* quotation, summons, (*in dispatches*) mention.

cité [site] *nf* town, (old) city,

housing scheme, students' hostel(s).

citer [site] *vt* to quote, cite, summon, mention.

citerne [sitɛrn] *nf* cistern, tank.

citoyen, -enne [sitwajɛ̃, jɛn] *n* citizen.

citron [sitrɔ̃] *nm* lemon, lime; *a inv* lemon-colored; **— pressé** lemonade.

citronnade [sitrɔnad] *nf* lemonade, lime-juice cordial.

citronnier [sitrɔnje] *nm* lemon tree, lime-tree.

citrouille [sitruːj] *nf* pumpkin.

civil [sivil] *a* civil, civic, lay, civilian, polite; **en —** in mufti, in plain clothes.

civilisation [sivilisasjɔ̃] *nf* civilization, culture.

civiliser [sivilize] *vt* to civilize.

civilité [sivilite] *nf* civility, courtesy; *pl* regards.

clabauder [klabode] *vi* to babble, chatter; **— contre** to run down.

claie [klɛ] *nf* wattle, hurdle, screen, fence.

clair [klɛːr] *a* clear, obvious, plain, bright, light, pale; *ad* clearly, plainly; *nm* light, clearing; **tirer au —** to clear up.

claire-voie [klɛrvwa] *nf* lattice, openwork, grating.

clairière [klɛrjɛːr] *nf* clearing, glade.

clairon [klɛrɔ̃] *nm* bugle, bugler.

clairsemé [klɛrsəme] *a* scattered, thin.

clairvoyance [klɛrvwajɑ̃ːs] *nf* perspicacity.

clairvoyant [klɛrvwajɑ̃] *a* perspicacious, shrewd; *n* clairvoyant.

clameur [klamœːr] *nf* outcry, clamor, howl.

clandestin [klɑ̃dɛstɛ̃] *a* clandestine, secret, surreptitious, underground.

clapier [klapje] *nm* rabbit-hutch.

claque [klak] *nf* smack, slap, hired applauders; *nm* opera hat.

claqué [klake] *a* dog-tired.

claquer [klake] *vi* to clap, bang, clatter, slap, snap, die; *vt* to smack.

claquettes [klakɛt] *nf pl* tap-dance.

clarifier [klarifje] *vt* to clarify.

clarinette [klarinɛt] *nf* clarinet.

clarté [klarte] *nf* clearness, brightness, light, perspicacity.

classe [klɑːs] *nf* class, order, form, standard, classroom, contingent, school.

classement [klɑsmɑ̃] *nm* classification, grading, filing.

classer [klɑse] *vt* to class, classify, sort out, grade, file.

classeur [klɑsœːr] *nm* file, filing-cabinet, sorter.

classification [klasifikasjɔ̃] *nf* classification.

classifier [klasifje] *vt* to classify.

classique [klasik] *a* classic, classical, standard; *nm pl* classics, classicists.

clavicule [klavikyl] *nf* collarbone.

clavier [klavje] *nm* keyboard.

clé, clef [kle] *nf* key, clue, clef; — **anglaise** monkey wrench; — **de voûte** keystone; **sous** — under lock and key.

clémence [klɛmɑːs] *nf* clemency, mercy, mildness.

clément [klɛmɑ̃] *a* clement, merciful, lenient, mild.

clerc [klɛːr] *nm* clerk, cleric, scholar, learned man.

clergé [klɛrʒe] *nm* clergy.

clérical [klerikal] *a* clerical.

cliché [kliʃe] *nm* stereotype, block, negative, hackneyed expression, tag.

client [kliɑ̃] *n* client, customer, patient.

clientèle [kliɑ̃tɛl] *nf* clientele, practice, custom, customers, public, connection.

clignement [kliɲmɑ̃] *nm* blink(ing), wink(ing).

cligner [kliɲe] *vti* to blink, wink, flicker the eyelids.

clignoter [kliɲɔte] *vi* to blink, twinkle, twitch, flicker.

climat [klima, -mɑ] *nm* climate.

climatique [klimatik] *a* climatic.

climatisé [klimatize] *a* air-conditioned.

clin d'œil [klɛ̃dœːj] *nm* wink, twinkling of an eye.

clinique [klinik] *a* clinical; *nf* nursing home, clinic.

clinquant [klɛ̃kɑ̃] *nm* foil, tinsel, tawdriness.

clique [klik] *nf* gang, set, clique, bugle-band.

cliqueter [klikte] *vi* to rattle, click, clink, (*of car*) knock.

cliquetis [klikti] *nm* rattling, click, clink(ing), jingle.

cloaque [klɔak] *nf* cesspool.

clochard [klɔʃaːr] *nm* tramp; hobo.

cloche [klɔʃ] *nf* bell, blister.

cloche-pied [klɔʃpje] *ad* à — on one foot.

clocher [klɔʃe] *nm* belfry, steeple; *vi* to limp, go wrong.

cloison [klwazɔ̃] *nf* partition, bulkhead.

cloître [klwaːtr] *nm* cloister(s), monastery, convent.

clopin-clopant [klɔpɛ̃klɔpɑ̃] *ad* hobbling about, limping along.

cloque [klɔk] *nf* lump, blister.

clos [klo] *a* closed, shut up; **maison** —e brothel; *nm* enclosure.

clôture [klotyːr] *nf* enclosure, fence, closing, closure, end.

clou [klu] *nm* nail, staple, (*pedestrian crossing*) stud, boil, star turn.

clouer [klue] *vt* to nail (up, down), pin, tie to, root to.

clouté [klute] *a* studded; **passage** — pedestrian crossing.

coaguler [koagyle] *vt* to coagulate, congeal, curdle.

coasser [koase] *vi* to croak.

coassement [koasmɑ̃] *nm* croaking.

cobaye [kɔbaːj] *nm* guinea-pig.

cobra [kɔbra] *nm* cobra.

cocaïne [kɔkain] *nf* cocaine.

cocaïnomane [kɔkainɔman] *n* cocaine addict.

cocarde [kɔkard] *nf* cockade, rosette.

cocasse [kɔkas] *a* comical.

coccinelle [kɔksinɛl] *nf* ladybird.

coche [kɔʃ] *nf* notch, nick; *nm* stage-coach.

cocher [kɔʃe] *nm* coachman, cabman, driver.

cochon, -onne [kɔʃɔ̃, ɔn] *a* beastly, obscene, swinish; *nm* pig; — **d'Inde** guinea-pig.

cochonnerie [kɔʃɔnri] *nf* beastliness, rubbish, trash, obscenity, dirty trick.

coco [kɔko] *nm* **noix de** — coconut.

cocoteraie [kɔkɔtrɛ] *nf* coconut plantation.

cocotier [kɔkɔtje] *nm* coconut tree.

cocotte [kɔkɔt] *nf* darling, pet, woman of easy virtue, stew-pan.

code [kɔd] *nm* code, law, statute-book; **mettre en** — to dim, dip motor lights.

codicille [kɔdisil] *nm* codicil.

coefficient [koefisjɑ̃] *nm* coefficient.

coercition [kɔɛrsisjɔ̃] *nf* coercion.

cœur [kœːr] *nm* heart, soul, mind, courage, core, depth, height, hearts; **avoir mal au** — to feel sick; **avoir le** — **gros** to be sad at heart; **de bon** — heartily, ungrudgingly; **de mauvais** — reluctantly.

coffre [kɔfr] *nm* box, chest, bin, trunk.

coffre-fort [kɔfrfɔːr] *nm* safe.

cognac [kɔɲak] *nm* brandy.

cognée [kɔɲe] *nf* ax, hatchet.

cogner [kɔɲe] *vt* to drive in, hit; *vti* to knock, hit, bump.

cohérent [kɔerɑ̃] *a* coherent.

cohésion [kɔezjɔ̃] *nf* cohesion

cohue [kɔy] *nf* crowd, mob, crush.

coiffe [kwaf] *nf* head-dress, cap, lining.

coiffer [kwafe] *vt* to cap, cover, put on hat, dress the hair; *vr* to put on one's hat, do one's hair, take a fancy (to de); **du combien coiffez-vous?** what is your size in hats?

coiffeur, -euse [kwafœːr, øːz] *n* hairdresser; *nf* dressing-table.

coiffure [kwafyːr] *nf* head-dress, style of hairdressing.

coin [kwɛ̃] *nm* corner, spot, plot, patch, wedge, hallmark.

coincer [kwɛ̃se] *vt* to wedge (up); *vr* to jam, stick.

coïncidence [kɔɛ̃sidɑːs] *nf* coincidence.

coïncider [kɔɛ̃side] *vi* to coincide.

coing [kwɛ̃] *nm* quince.

col [kɔl] *nm* collar, neck, mountain pass; **faux** — detachable collar, (*beer*) froth.

coléoptère [kɔleɔptɛːr] *nm* beetle.

colère [kɔlɛːr] *a* angry, irascible; *nf* anger, rage, temper.
colérique [kɔlerik] *a* quick-tempered, choleric, fiery.
colifichet [kɔlifiʃɛ] *nm* trinket, knick-knack.
colimaçon [kɔlimasɔ̃] *nm* snail; **en — spiral.**
colin-maillard [kɔlɛ̃majaːr] *nm* blindman's buff.
colique [kɔlik] *a* colic; *nf* colic, gripes.
colis [kɔli] *nm* parcel, package, packet, piece of luggage; **par — postal** by parcel post.
collaborateur, -trice [kɔlabɔratœːr, tris] *n* collaborator, contributor.
collaboration [kɔlabɔrasjɔ̃] *nf* collaboration.
collaborer [kɔlabɔre] *vi* to collaborate, contribute (to à).
collant [kɔlɑ̃] *a* sticky, clinging, close-fitting; *nm* tights.
collatéral [kɔlateral] *a* collateral, side.
collation [kɔl(l)asjɔ̃] *nf* collation, conferment, snack.
collationner [kɔl(l)asjɔne] *vt* to collate, read over, repeat; *vi* to have a snack.
colle [kɔl] *nf* paste, glue, size, oral test, poser.
collecte [kɔllɛkt] *nf* collection, collect.
collecteur, -trice [kɔlɛktœːr, tris] *n* collector.
collectif, -ive [kɔlɛktif, iːv] *a* collective, joint.
collection [kɔlɛksjɔ̃] *nf* collecting, collection, file.
collectionner [kɔlɛksjɔne] *vt* to collect.
collectionneur, -euse [kɔlɛksjɔnœːr, øːz] *n* collector.
collectivité [kɔlɛktivite] *nf* collectivity.
collège [kɔlɛːʒ] *nm* college, secondary school, electoral body.
collégien, ienne [kɔleʒjɛ̃, jɛn] *n* schoolboy, -girl.
collègue [kɔllɛg] *n* colleague.
coller [kɔle] *vt* to paste, stick, glue, fail, stump; *vi* to adhere, fail, stump; *vi* to adhere, cling, stick (to); *vr* to stick, cling close (to).
collet [kɔlɛ] *nm* collar, scruff of the neck, snare; **— monté** strait-laced, prim.
colleter [kɔlte] *vt* to collar, grapple with.
collier [kɔlje] *nm* necklace, necklet, collar, band; **un coup de — tug,** great effort.
colline [kɔlin] *nf* hill.
collision [kɔllizjɔ̃] *nf* collision, clash.
colloque [kɔlɔk] *nm* colloquy, conversation.
colombe [kɔlɔ̃ːb] *nf* dove.
colombier [kɔlɔ̃bje] *nm* dovecote, pigeon-house.

colon [kɔlɔ̃] *nm* colonist, settler.
colonel [kɔlɔnɛl] *nm* colonel.
colonial [kɔlɔnjal] *a nm* colonial.
colonie [kɔlɔni] *nf* colony, settlement; **— de vacances** holiday camp.
colonisation [kɔlɔnizasjɔ̃] *nf* colonization.
coloniser [kɔlɔnize] *vt* to colonize, settle.
colonne [kɔlɔn] *nf* column, pillar; **— vertébrale** spine.
colorer [kɔlɔre] *vt* to color, stain, tint; *vr* to take on a color, grow ruddy.
coloris [kɔlɔri] *nm* color(ing), hue.
colossal [kɔlɔsal] *a* colossal, huge, gigantic.
colporter [kɔlpɔrte] *vt* to hawk, peddle.
colporteur, -euse [kɔlpɔrtœːr, øːz] *n* peddler.
combat [kɔ̃ba] *nm* combat, fight, battle, action, conflict, struggle, match.
combatif, -ive [kɔ̃batif, iːv] *a* combative, pugnacious.
combattant [kɔ̃batɑ̃] *nm* combatant, fighting-man; **anciens —s** ex-servicemen.
combattre [kɔ̃batr] *vt* to combat, fight, battle with; *vi* to strive, struggle, fight.
combien [kɔ̃bjɛ̃] *ad* how much, how many, how far; **le — sommes-nous?** what day of the month is this?
combinaison [kɔ̃binɛzɔ̃] *nf* arrangement, combine, plan, underslip, overalls, flying suit.
combine [kɔ̃bin] *nf* scheme, racket.
combiner [kɔ̃bine] *vt* to combine, arrange, contrive.
comble [kɔ̃ːbl] *nm* heap, summit, top, acme, roof(ing); **pour — de malheur** as a crowning misfortune; **ca, c'est le —** that's the limit; *a* heaped up, crowded; **faire salle —** to play to a full house.
combler [kɔ̃ble] *vt* to fill (up, in), make good, crowd, fill to overflowing, gratify.
combustible [kɔ̃bystibl] *a* combustible; *nm* fuel.
combustion [kɔ̃bystjɔ̃] *nf* combustion.
comédie [kɔmedi] *nf* comedy, play, drama; **jouer la —** to act a part.
comédien, -ienne [kɔmedjɛ̃, jɛn] *n* actor, actress.
comestible [kɔmɛstibl] *a* edible, eatable; *nm pl* food, provisions.
comète [kɔmɛt] *nf* comet.
comique [kɔmik] *a* comic, funny; *nm* comedy, comedian, humorist, joke.
comité [kɔmite] *nm* committee, board.
commandant [kɔmɑ̃dɑ̃] *nm* commanding officer, major (army), squadron leader.
commande [kɔmɑ̃ːd] *nf* order,

control, lever, driving-gear; **de** — essential, forced, feigned; **sur** — made to order, bespoke.

commandement [kɔmãdmã] *nm* command, order, commandment.

commander [kɔmãde] *vt* to order, govern, be in command of, compel, control.

commanditaire [kɔmãditɛːr] *nm* (**associé**) — silent partner (*in business*).

comme [kɔm] *ad* as, like, such as, in the way of, how; **c'est tout** — it amounts to the same thing; *cj* as, since.

commémorer [kɔmmemɔre] *vt* to commemorate.

commençant [kɔmãsã] *nm* beginner, learner; *a* budding, beginning, early.

commencement [kɔmãsmã] *nm* beginning.

commencer [kɔmãse] *vti* to commence, begin, start.

comment [kɔmã] *ad* how? what? *excl* why! what!

commentaire [kɔmãtɛːr] *nm* commentary, comment.

commentateur, -trice [kɔmãtatœːr, tris] *n* commentator.

commenter [kɔmãte] *vti* to comment (on), annotate.

commérage [kɔmɛraːʒ] *nm* gossip, tittle-tattle.

commerçant [kɔmɛrsã] *nm* merchant, tradesman; *a* commercial, mercantile.

commerce [kɔmɛrs] *nm* commerce, trade, business, intercourse, dealings.

commercial [kɔmɛrsjal] *a* commercial, trading.

commettre [kɔmɛtr] *vt* to commit, perpetrate, entrust.

commis [kɔmi] *nm* clerk, bookkeeper, shop-assistant; — **voyageur** traveling salesman.

commissaire [kɔmisɛːr] *nm* commissioner, steward, purser, police superintendent, commissar.

commissaire-priseur [kɔmisɛrprizœːr] *nm* auctioneer.

commissariat [kɔmisarja] *nm* commissionership, police station.

commission [kɔmisjɔ̃] *nf* commission, message, errand, board, committee.

commissionnaire [kɔmisjɔnɛːr] *nm* (commission) agent, porter, messenger.

commode [kɔmɔd] *a* convenient, handy, commodious, easy-going; *nf* chest of drawers.

commodité [kɔmɔdite] *nf* convenience, comfort, commodiousness.

commotion [kɔm(m)osjɔ̃] *nf* commotion, shock, upheaval, concussion.

commun [kɔmœ̃] *a* common, usual, ordinary, vulgar; **d'un** — **accord**

with one accord; **peu** — out-of-the-way, uncommon; *nm* common run, generality, common fund; *pl* offices, outhouses.

communauté [kɔmynote] *nf* community, commonwealth, society, religious order.

commune [kɔmyn] *nf* commune, parish.

communément [kɔmynemã] *ad* commonly.

communicatif, -ive [kɔmynikatif, iːv] *a* communicative, talkative, infectious.

communication [kɔmynikasjɔ̃] *nf* communication, connection, telephone call, message.

communion [kɔmynjɔ̃] *nf* communion.

communiqué [kɔmynike] *nm* communiqué, official statement, bulletin.

communiquer [kɔmynike] *vt* to communicate, transmit, convey, connect; *vr* to be communicated.

communisant [kɔmynizã] *n* fellow-traveler.

communisme [kɔmynism] *nm* communism.

communiste [kɔmynist] *n* communist.

commutateur [kɔmytatœːr] *nm* commutator, switch.

compagne [kɔ̃paɲ] *nf* companion, partner, wife.

compagnie [kɔ̃paɲi] *nf* company, party, firm; **de bonne, de mauvaise** — well-, ill-bred.

compagnon [kɔ̃paɲɔ̃] *nm* companion, fellow, mate.

comparable [kɔ̃parabl] *a* comparable.

comparaison [kɔ̃parɛzɔ̃] *nf* comparison, simile.

comparatif, -ive [kɔ̃paratif, iːv] *a nm* comparative.

comparé [kɔ̃pare] *a* comparative.

comparer [kɔ̃pare] *vt* to compare.

compartiment [kɔ̃partimã] *nm* compartment.

compas [kɔ̃pɑ] *nm* compass(es), scale, standard.

compassé [kɔ̃pɑse] *a* stiff, formal, set, prim.

compassion [kɔ̃pasjɔ̃] *nf* compassion, pity.

compatible [kɔ̃patibl] *a* compatible.

compatir [kɔ̃patiːr] *vi* to sympathize (with à), feel (for).

compatissant [kɔ̃patisã] *a* compassionate.

compatriote [kɔ̃patriɔt] *nm* compatriot.

compensation [kɔ̃pãsasjɔ̃] *nf* compensation, offset, balancing, adjustment.

compensé [kɔ̃pãse] *a* **semelles** —**es** wedge heels.

compenser [kɔ̃pãse] *vt* to compensate, make good, set off, balance, adjust.

compétence [kɔ̃petãːs] *nf* jurisdic-

tion, competence, proficiency, skill.
complaisance [kɔ̃plɛzɑ̃:s] *nf* complaisance, obligingness, kindness, complacency, accommodation.
complaisant [kɔ̃plɛzɑ̃] *a* complaisant, obliging, kind, complacent.
complémentaire [kɔ̃plemɑ̃tɛ:r] *a* complementary, fuller.
complet, -ète [kɔ̃plɛ, ɛt] *a* complete, total, entire, full; *nm* suit of clothes; **au — complete**, at full strength.
compléter [kɔ̃plete] *vt* to complete, finish off.
complexe [kɔ̃plɛks] *a* complex, complicated, compound; *nm* complex.
complexion [kɔ̃plɛksjɔ̃] *nf* constitution, temperament.
complexité [kɔ̃plɛksite] *nf* complexity.
complication [kɔ̃plikasjɔ̃] *nf* complication, intricacy.
complice [kɔ̃plis] *a nm* accessory, accomplice.
complicité [kɔ̃plisite] *nf* complicity, aiding and abetting.
compliment [kɔ̃plimɑ̃] *nm* compliment; *pl* greetings, regards, congratulations.
complimenter [kɔ̃plimɑ̃te] *vt* to compliment, congratulate.
compliqué [kɔ̃plike] *a* complicated, intricate, difficult.
complot [kɔ̃plo] *nm* plot.
comploter [kɔ̃plɔte] *vt* to plot, scheme.
componction [kɔ̃pɔ̃ksjɔ̃] *nf* compunction.
comporter [kɔ̃pɔrte] *vt* to admit of, require, comprise, involve; *vr* to behave.
composé [kɔ̃poze] *a* composed, impassive, composite; *a nm* compound.
composer [kɔ̃poze] *vt* to compose, form, make up, set, arrange; *vi* to come to terms; *vr* to consist.
compositeur, -trice [kɔ̃pozitœ:r, tris] *n* composer, compositor.
composition [kɔ̃pozisjɔ̃] *nf* composing, composition, making-up, setting, essay, test, arrangement.
compote [kɔ̃pɔt] *nf* compote, stewed fruit.
compréhensible [kɔ̃preɑ̃sibl] *a* comprehensible.
compréhensif, -ive [kɔ̃preɑ̃sif, i:v] *a* comprehensive, inclusive, understanding.
compréhension [kɔ̃preɑ̃sjɔ̃] *nf* understanding.
comprendre [kɔ̃prɑ̃:dr] *vt* to include, comprise, understand, comprehend.
compression [kɔ̃prɛsjɔ̃] *nf* compression, crushing, repression.
comprimé [kɔ̃prime] *nm* tablet.
comprimer [kɔ̃prime] *vt* to compress, repress, restrain.
compris [kɔ̃pri] *a* **y — including**; **non — exclusive of.**

compromettre [kɔ̃prɔmɛtr] *vt* to compromise, implicate, endanger.
compromis [kɔ̃prɔmi] *nm* compromise.
comptabilité [kɔ̃tabilite] *nf* book-keeping, accountancy, accounting dept.
comptable [kɔ̃tabl] *a* accounting, book-keeping, accountable, responsible; *nm* accountant, book-keeper; **expert — chartered accountant.**
comptant [kɔ̃tɑ̃] *a* **argent — ready money**; *ad* **(in) cash**; **au — cash down.**
compte [kɔ̃:t] *nm* account, reckoning, calculation, count; **à bon — cheap**; **tout — fait all things considered**; **versement à — payment on account**; **pour mon — for my part**; **— rendu report, review**; **se rendre — de** to realize.
compte-gouttes [kɔ̃tgut] *nm* dropping-tube, dropper.
compter [kɔ̃te] *vt* to count, reckon, charge, expect; *vi* rely, reckon, depend, count.
compteur [kɔ̃tœ:r] *nm* (taxi)meter, counting-machine.
comptoir [kɔ̃twa:r] *nm* counter; **— d'escompte**, discount bank.
compulser [kɔ̃pylse] *vt* to go through, examine.
comte [kɔ̃:t] *nm* count.
comté [kɔ̃te] *nm* county.
comtesse [kɔ̃tɛs] *nf* countess.
concéder [kɔ̃sede] *vt* to concede, grant, allow.
concentrer [kɔ̃sɑ̃tre] *vt* to concentrate, focus, repress; *vr* to concentrate, center (in, on, around).
concentrique [kɔ̃sɑ̃trik] *a* concentric.
conception [kɔ̃sɛpsjɔ̃] *nf* conception.
concerner [kɔ̃sɛrne] *vt* to concern, affect.
concert [kɔ̃sɛ:r] *nm* concert, agreement.
concerter [kɔ̃sɛrte] *vt* to concert, plan; *vr* to act in concert.
concession [kɔ̃sɛsjɔ̃] *nf* concession, grant, compound.
concessionnaire [kɔ̃sɛsjɔnɛ:r] *nm* concessionary, grantee, licenseholder.
concevable [kɔ̃s(ə)vabl] *a* conceivable.
concevoir [kɔ̃səvwa:r] *vt* to conceive, imagine, understand, word.
concierge [kɔ̃sjɛrʒ] *n* hall porter, doorkeeper, caretaker.
concilier [kɔ̃silje] *vt* to conciliate, reconcile, win over.
concis [kɔ̃si] *a* concise, terse, brief, crisp.
concision [kɔ̃sizjɔ̃] *nf* concision, terseness.
concluant [kɔ̃klyɑ̃] *a* conclusive, decisive.
conclure [kɔ̃kly:r] *vt* to conclude, end, clinch, infer.

conclusion [kɔklyzjɔ̃] *nf* conclusion, end, settlement, inference, decision.
concombre [kɔkɔ̃:br] *nm* cucumber.
concorde [kɔkɔrd] *nf* concord.
concourir [kɔkuri:r] *vi* to coincide, combine, compete.
concours [kɔku:r] *nm* concourse, concurrence, coincidence, cooperation, assistance, competition, contest, show.
concret, -ète [kɔkrɛ, -ɛt] *a nm* concrete.
concurrence [kɔkyrɑ̃:s] *nf* concurrence, competition.
concurrent [kɔkyrɑ̃] *a* competitive, rival; *nm* competitor, rival, candidate.
condamnable [kɔdɑnabl] *a* blameworthy.
condamnation [kɔdɑnasjɔ̃] *nf* condemnation, judgment, sentence, censure.
condamné [kɔdɑne] *n* convict, condemned person.
condamner [kɔdɑne] *vt* to condemn, sentence, convict, censure, block up.
condensateur [kɔdɑ̃satœ:r] *nm* condenser.
condensation [kɔdɑ̃sasjɔ̃] *nf* condensation.
condenser [kɔdɑ̃se] *vt* to condense.
condenseur [kɔdɑ̃sœ:r] *nm* condenser.
condescendance [kɔdɛsɑ̃dɑ̃:s] *nf* condescension.
condescendre [kɔdɛsɑ̃:dr] *vt* to condescend.
condition [kɔdisjɔ̃] *nf* condition, state, position, rank; *pl* conditions, circumstances, terms; **à — on** approval; **à — que** on condition that; **être en — to** be in domestic service.
conditionnel, -elle [kɔdisjɔnɛl, ɛl] *a nm* conditional.
conditionner [kɔdisjɔne] *vt* to condition.
condoléance [kɔdɔleɑ̃:s] *nf* condolence; *pl* sympathy.
conducteur, -trice [kɔdyktœ:r, tris] *a* conducting, guiding; *n* leader, guide, driver; *nm* conductor, main.
conduire [kɔdɥi:r] *vt* to conduct, lead, guide, conduce (to), drive, convey, manage; *vr* to behave, conduct oneself.
conduit [kɔdɥi] *nm* passage, pipe, conduit, duct.
conduite [kɔdɥit] *nf* behavior, driving, pipe, management, conducting, leading.
cône [ko:n] *nm* cone.
confection [kɔfɛksjɔ̃] *nf* confection, putting together, manufacture, making up, ready-made clothes.
confectionner [kɔfɛksjɔne] *vt* to make up, manufacture.
confectionneur, -euse [kɔfɛksjɔnœ:r, ø:z] *n* ready-made outfitter, clothier.

confédération [kɔfederasjɔ̃] *nf* federation, confederacy.
confédérer [kɔfedere] *vtr* to confederate, unite.
conférence [kɔferɑ̃:s] *nf* conference, lecture.
conférencier, -ière [kɔferɑ̃sje, jɛ:r] *n* lecturer.
conférer [kɔfere] *vt* to confer, award, bestow, compare; *vi* to confer (with **avec**).
confesser [kɔfɛse] *vt* to confess, own; *vr* to confess.
confesseur [kɔfɛsœ:r] *nm* confessor.
confession [kɔfɛsjɔ̃] *nf* confession, religion, denomination.
confessional [kɔfɛsjɔnal] *nm* confessional(-box).
confiance [kɔfjɑ̃:s] *nf* confidence, trust, reliance; **de — on** trust, reliable.
confiant [kɔfjɑ̃] *a* confiding, (self-)confident, assured.
confidence [kɔfidɑ̃:s] *nf* confidence, secret; **en — in** confidence, confidentially.
confidentiel, -elle [kɔfidɑ̃sjɛl, ɛl] *a* confidential.
confier [kɔfje] *vt* to confide, disclose, entrust, commit; *vr* to rely (on **à**), take into one's confidence.
confiner [kɔfine] *vt* to confine, shut up; *vi* to be contiguous, border upon.
confins [kɔfɛ̃] *nm pl* confines, borders.
confirmatif, -ive [kɔfirmatif, i:v] *a* confirmative, corroborative.
confirmation [kɔfirmasjɔ̃] *nf* confirmation, corroboration.
confirmer [kɔfirme] *vt* to confirm, corroborate.
confiscation [kɔfiskasjɔ̃] *nf* confiscation.
confiserie [kɔfizri] *nf* confectionery, confectioner's shop.
confiseur, -euse [kɔfizœ:r, ø:z] *n* confectioner.
confisquer [kɔfiske] *vt* to confiscate.
confit [kɔfi] *a* preserved, steeped in; **un air — sanctimonious air; *nm pl* confections, comfits, sweets.
confiture [kɔfity:r] *nf* preserves, jam; **— d'orange** marmalade.
conflagration [kɔflagrasjɔ̃] *nf* conflagration, blaze, fire.
conflit [kɔfli] *nm* conflict, clash, strife; **être en — to** conflict, clash.
confluent [kɔflyɑ̃] *nm* confluence, junction, meeting.
confondre [kɔfɔ̃:dr] *vt* to confound, mingle, blend, mistake, disconcert, put to confusion; *vr* to blend, intermingle, be identical; **se — en excuses** to apologize profusely.
confondu [kɔfɔ̃dy] *a* overwhelmed, disconcerted.
conforme [kɔfɔrm] *a* conformable, according (to **à**), in keeping (with **à**).
conformément [kɔfɔrmemɑ̃] *ad*

according (to à), in keeping (with à).
conformer [kɔ̃fɔrme] *vt* to form,
conform; *vr* to conform (to),
comply (with à).
conformité [kɔ̃fɔrmite] *nf* conformity, agreement.
confort [kɔ̃fɔːr] *nm* comfort.
confortable [kɔ̃fɔrtabl] *a* comfortable.
confrère [kɔ̃frɛːr] *nm* colleague, fellow-member, brother.
confrérie [kɔ̃freri] *nf* brotherhood, confraternity.
confrontation [kɔ̃frɔ̃tasjɔ̃] *nf* confrontation, comparison.
confronter [kɔ̃frɔ̃te] *vt* to confront, compare.
confus [kɔ̃fy] *a* confused, jumbled, indistinct, embarrassed, abashed, ashamed.
confusion [kɔ̃fyzjɔ̃] *nf* confusion, welter, mistake, embarrassment.
congé [kɔ̃ʒe] *nm* leave, holiday, furlough, dismissal, discharge, notice to quit.
congédier [kɔ̃ʒedje] *vt* to dismiss, discharge.
congélation [kɔ̃ʒelasjɔ̃] *nf* congelation, freezing.
congeler [kɔ̃ʒle] *vtr* to congeal, freeze (up).
congénital [kɔ̃ʒenital] *a* congenital.
congestion [kɔ̃ʒɛstjɔ̃] *nf* congestion; — cérébrale stroke; — pulmonaire pneumonia.
congestionné [kɔ̃ʒɛstjɔne] *a* congested, apoplectic, red in the face.
congestionner [kɔ̃ʒɛstjɔne] *vt* to congest; *vr* to become congested.
congrégation [kɔ̃gregasjɔ̃] *nf* congregation.
congrès [kɔ̃grɛ] *nm* congress.
conique [kɔnik] *a* conic(al), cone-shaped, tapering.
conjecture [kɔ̃ʒɛktyːr] *nf* conjecture, surmise, guess.
conjecturer [kɔ̃ʒɛktyre] *vt* to conjecture, surmise.
conjoint [kɔ̃ʒwɛ̃] *a* conjoined, united, married; *nm pl* husband and wife.
conjonction [kɔ̃ʒɔ̃ksjɔ̃] *nf* union, conjunction.
conjoncture [kɔ̃ʒɔ̃ktyːr] *nf* conjuncture.
conjugaison [kɔ̃ʒygɛzɔ̃] *nf* conjugation.
conjugal [kɔ̃ʒygal] *a* conjugal, married, wedded.
conjugué [kɔ̃ʒyge] *a* conjugated, interconnected, coupled, twin.
conjuration [kɔ̃ʒyrasjɔ̃] *nf* plot, conspiracy; incantation.
conjuré [kɔ̃ʒyre] *nm* conspirator.
connaissance [kɔnɛsɑ̃ːs] *nf* knowledge, understanding, acquaintance, consciousness, senses; *pl* learning, attainments; **en pays de** — on familiar ground, among familiar faces; **sans** — unconscious, insensible.

connaisseur, -euse [kɔnɛsœːr, øːz] *n* expert, connoisseur, judge.
connaître [kɔnɛːtr] *vt* to know, be acquainted with, take cognizance, distinguish, have a thorough knowledge of; *vr* to be a good judge (of **en**), know all (about **en**).
connexe [kɔn(n)ɛks] *a* connected, allied, like.
connexion [kon(n)ɛksjɔ̃] *nf* connection, connector.
connivence [kɔnivɑ̃ːs] *nf* connivance, collusion.
conquérant [kɔ̃kerɑ̃] *a* conquering; *n* conqueror.
conquérir [kɔ̃keriːr] *vt* to conquer.
conquête [kɔ̃kɛːt] *nf* conquest.
consacré [kɔ̃sakre] *a* consecrated, hallowed, established, time-honored, accepted, stock.
consacrer [kɔ̃sakre] *vt* to devote, ordain, consecrate.
conscience [kɔ̃sjɑ̃ːs] *nf* conscience, consciousness.
consciencieux, -euse [kɔ̃sjɑ̃sjø, jøːz] *a* conscientious.
conscient [kɔ̃sjɑ̃] *a* conscious, aware, sentient.
conscription [kɔ̃skripsjɔ̃] *nf* conscription, draft.
conscrit [kɔ̃skri] *nm* conscript, draftee.
consécration [kɔ̃sekrasjɔ̃] *nf* consecration, dedication.
consécutif, -ive [kɔ̃sekytif, iːv] *a* consecutive.
conseil [kɔ̃sɛːj] *nm* advice, decision, council, counsel, board, court; — **des ministres** cabinet; — **de guerre** council of war, court martial.
conseiller, -ère [kɔ̃sɛje, ɛːr] *n* adviser, councilor, judge.
conseiller [kɔ̃sɛje] *vt* to advise, counsel.
consentement [kɔ̃sɑ̃tmɑ̃] *nm* consent, assent.
consentir [kɔ̃sɑ̃tiːr] *vi* to consent, agree.
conséquemment [kɔ̃sekamɑ̃] *ad* consequently.
conséquence [kɔ̃sekɑ̃ːs] *nf* consequence, outcome, sequel, inference, importance.
conséquent [kɔ̃sekɑ̃] *a* consistent, following, important; **par** — accordingly.
conservateur, -trice [kɔ̃sɛrvatœːr, tris] *a* preserving, conservative; *n* keeper, guardian, curator, conservative.
conservation [kɔ̃sɛrvasjɔ̃] *nf* preservation, keeping, care.
conservatoire [kɔ̃sɛrvatwaːr] *nm* school, academy (of music).
conserve [kɔ̃sɛrv] *nf* preserved canned food; *pl* dark glasses; — **au vinaigre** pickles; **de** — together.
conserver [kɔ̃sɛrve] *vt* to preserve, keep.
considérable [kɔ̃siderabl] *a* con-

siderable, large, eminent, important.
considération [kɔ̃siderasjɔ̃] *nf* consideration, regard, respect.
considérer [kɔ̃sidere] *vt* to consider, contemplate, regard, respect, esteem.
consigne [kɔ̃siɲ] *nf* order(s), duty, countersign, detention, cloakroom, checkroom.
consigner [kɔ̃siɲe] *vt* to deposit, consign, confine to barracks, keep in, put out of bounds, hold up.
consistance [kɔ̃sistã:s] *nf* consistence, consistency, firmness, standing.
consistant [kɔ̃sistã] *a* firm, set, solid.
consister [kɔ̃siste] *vi* to consist, be composed (of **en**).
consolateur, -trice [kɔ̃solatœ:r, tris] *a* consoling; *n* consoler, comforter.
consolation [kɔ̃sɔlasjɔ̃] *nf* consolation, comfort.
console [kɔ̃sɔl] *nf* bracket, console (table).
consoler [kɔ̃sɔle] *vt* to console, solace, comfort, cheer.
consolider [kɔ̃sɔlide] *vt* to consolidate, fund (debt).
consommateur, -trice [kɔ̃sɔmatœ:r, tris] *n* consumer, customer.
consommation [kɔ̃sɔmasjɔ̃] *nf* consummation, consumption, drink.
consommé [kɔ̃sɔme] *a* consummate; *nm* stock, clear soup.
consommer [kɔ̃sɔme] *vt* to consummate, consume.
consomption [kɔ̃sɔ̃psjɔ̃] *nf* consuming, consumption.
consonne [kɔ̃sɔn] *nf* consonant.
conspirateur, -trice [kɔ̃spiratœ:r, tris] *n* conspirer, conspirator, plotter.
conspiration [kɔ̃spirasjɔ̃] *nf* conspiracy, plot.
conspirer [kɔ̃spire] *vti* to conspire, plot.
conspuer [kɔ̃spɥe] *vt* to decry, boo, hoot.
constamment [kɔ̃stamã] *ad* constantly.
constance [kɔ̃stã:s] *nf* constancy, steadfastness, perseverance, stability.
constant [kɔ̃stã] *a* constant, steadfast, firm.
constatation [kɔ̃statasjɔ̃] *nf* ascertainment, verification, record, statement.
constater [kɔ̃state] *vt* to establish, ascertain, state, record.
constellation [kɔ̃stɛllasjɔ̃] *nf* constellation, galaxy.
consternation [kɔ̃stɛrnasjɔ̃] *nf* consternation, dismay.
consterner [kɔ̃stɛrne] *vt* to dismay, stagger.
constipation [kɔ̃stipasjɔ̃] *nf* constipation.
constipé [kɔ̃stipe] *a* constipated, costive.

constituer [kɔ̃stitɥe] *vt* to constitute, form, set up, incorporate, settle (on); **se — prisonnier** to give oneself up.
constitution [kɔ̃stitysjɔ̃] *nf* constitution, composition, settlement.
constitutionnel, -elle [kɔ̃stitysjɔnɛl, ɛl] *a* constitutional.
constructeur [kɔ̃stryktœ:r] *nm* constructor, builder, maker.
construction [kɔ̃stryksjɔ̃] *nf* construction, making, building, structure.
construire [kɔ̃strɥi:r] *vt* to construct, build, make.
consul [kɔ̃syl] *nm* consul.
consulaire [kɔ̃sylɛ:r] *a* consular.
consulat [kɔ̃syla] *nm* consulate.
consultant [kɔ̃syltã] *a* consulting; *nm* consultant.
consultation [kɔ̃syltasjɔ̃] *nf* consultation, opinion, advice; **cabinet de —** consulting-room, doctor's office.
consulter [kɔ̃sylte] *vt* to consult.
consumer [kɔ̃syme] *vt* to consume, destroy, wear away, use up; *vr* to waste away, burn away.
contact [kɔ̃takt] *nm* contact, touch, connection, switch.
contagieux, -euse [kɔ̃taʒjø, jø:z] *a* contagious, infectious, catching.
contagion [kɔ̃taʒjɔ̃] *nf* contagion, contagiousness.
contamination [kɔ̃taminasjɔ̃] *n* contamination, infection.
contaminer [kɔ̃tamine] *vt* to contaminate, infect.
conte [kɔ̃:t] *nm* story, tale, yarn, short story; **— bleu** fairy tale; **— à dormir debout** cock-and-bull story.
contemplation [kɔ̃tãplasjɔ̃] *nf* contemplation, meditation, gazing.
contempler [kɔ̃tãple] *vt* to contemplate, meditate upon, gaze at, upon.
contemporain [kɔ̃tãpɔrɛ̃] *n* contemporary; *a* contemporaneous.
contenance [kɔ̃tnã:s] *nf* capacity, content, countenance, bearing.
contenir [kɔ̃tni:r] *vt* to contain, hold, restrain; *vr* to contain oneself, keep one's temper.
content [kɔ̃tã] *a* content, satisfied, pleased, glad; *nm* **manger tout son—** to eat one's fill.
contentement [kɔ̃tãtmã] *nm* satisfaction.
contenter [kɔ̃tãte] *vt* to content, satisfy, gratify; *vr* to be satisfied (with **de**).
contenu [kɔ̃tny] *a* restrained, reserved; *nm* contents.
conter [kɔ̃te] *vt* to tell.
contestable [kɔ̃testabl] *a* questionable, debatable.
contestation [kɔ̃testasjɔ̃] *nf* contestation, dispute.
conteste [kɔ̃test] *nf* **sans —** unquestionably.
contester [kɔ̃teste] *vt* to contest, dispute, challenge.

conteur, -euse [kɔ̃tœːr, øːz] *n* narrator, story-teller.

contexte [kɔ̃tɛkst] *nm* context.

contigu, -uë [kɔ̃tigy] *a* contiguous, adjoining.

continent [kɔ̃tinɑ̃] *a* continent, chaste; *nm* continent, mainland.

contingent [kɔ̃tɛ̃ʒɑ̃] *a* contingent; *nm* contingent, quota, share.

continu [kɔ̃tiny] *a* continuous, sustained.

continuation [kɔ̃tinɥasjɔ̃] *nf* continuation.

continuel, -elle [kɔ̃tinɥɛl, el] *a* continual.

continuer [kɔ̃tinɥe] *vt* to continue, proceed with, go on with; *vi* to carry on, continue, go on.

continuité [kɔ̃tinɥite] *nf* continuity.

contour [kɔ̃tuːr] *nm* outline, contour.

contournement [kɔ̃turnəmɑ̃] *nm* route de — by-pass.

contourner [kɔ̃turne] *vt* to shape, get round, by-pass, twist, distort.

contracter [kɔ̃trakte] *vt* to contract, incur, draw together; *vr* to shrink, contract.

contraction [kɔ̃traksjɔ̃] *nf* contraction, shrinking.

contradiction [kɔ̃tradiksjɔ̃] *nf* contradiction, discrepancy, inconsistency.

contradictoire [kɔ̃tradiktwaːr] *a* contradictory.

contraindre [kɔ̃trɛ̃ːdr] *vt* to constrain, compel, force, restrain.

contraint [kɔ̃trɛ̃] *a* constrained, cramped, forced.

contrainte [kɔ̃trɛ̃ːt] *nf* constraint, compulsion, restraint.

contraire [kɔ̃trɛːr] *a* contrary, opposite, opposed, adverse, bad; **jusqu'à avis** — until further notice; *nm* contrary, opposite.

contrarier [kɔ̃trarje] *vt* to thwart, oppose, annoy, vex, provoke, interfere with.

contrariété [kɔ̃trarjete] *nf* contrariety, annoyance, nuisance.

contraste [kɔ̃trast] *nm* contrast.

contraster [kɔ̃traste] *vti* to contrast.

contrat [kɔ̃tra] *nm* contract, agreement, deed, policy.

contravention [kɔ̃travɑ̃sjɔ̃] *nf* contravention, breach, infringement, offense; **dresser une** — à to take the name and address of, prosecute.

contre [kɔ̃ːtr] *prep* against, contrary to, for, to, versus; *ad* against, hard by; **le pour et le** — pros and cons.

contre-amiral [kɔ̃tramiral] *nm* rear-admiral.

contre-attaque [kɔ̃tratak] *nf* counter-attack.

contre-avion(s) [kɔ̃travjɔ̃] *a* anti-aircraft.

contre-avis [kɔ̃travi] *nm* contrary opinion.

contre-balancer [kɔ̃trəbalɑ̃se] *vt* to counterbalance, offset.

contrebande [kɔ̃trəbɑ̃ːd] *nf* contraband, smuggling.

contrebandier [kɔ̃trəbɑ̃dje] *nm* smuggler.

contrecarrer [kɔ̃trəkɑre] *vt* to thwart, cross.

contrecœur [kɔ̃trəkœːr] *ad* à — reluctantly.

contre-coup [kɔ̃trəku] *nm* rebound, recoil, reaction, repercussion.

contredire [kɔ̃trədiːr] *vt* to contradict, gainsay; *vr* to contradict oneself, be inconsistent.

contredit [kɔ̃trədi] *ad* sans — unquestionably.

contrée [kɔ̃tre] *nf* region, district, country.

contre-espionnage [kɔ̃trɛspjɔnaːʒ] *nm* counter-espionage.

contrefaçon [kɔ̃trəfasɔ̃] *nf* counterfeit, forgery.

contrefaire [kɔ̃trəfɛːr] *vt* to imitate, feign, forge.

contrefait [kɔ̃trəfɛ] *a* disguised, feigned, sham, counterfeit, forged.

contrefort [kɔ̃trəfɔːr] *nm* buttress, spur.

contre-jour [kɔ̃trəʒùːr] *nm* unfavorable light; à — against the light, in one's own light.

contremaître, -tresse [kɔ̃trəmɛːtr, tres] *n* foreman, -woman, overseer.

contremander [kɔ̃trəmɑ̃de] *vt* to countermand, cancel, call off.

contre-ordre [kɔ̃trɔrdr] *nm* counter-order, countermand; **sauf** — unless we hear to the contrary.

contre-partie [kɔ̃trəparti] *nf* opposite view, other side, counterpart, contra.

contre-pied [kɔ̃trəpje] *nm* opposite, contrary view.

contrepoids [kɔ̃trəpwa] *nm* counterweight, counterbalance, counterpoise.

contre-poil [kɔ̃trəpwal] *ad* à — the wrong way.

contrer [kɔ̃tre] *vt* to counter; *vi* to double.

contre-sens [kɔ̃trəsɑ̃ːs] *nm* misconstruction, mistranslation, wrong way; à — in the wrong direction.

contresigner [kɔ̃trəsiɲe] *vt* to countersign.

contretemps [kɔ̃trətɑ̃] *nm* mishap, hitch, inconvenience; à — inopportunely.

contre-torpilleur [kɔ̃trətɔrpijœːr] *nm* destroyer.

contrevent [kɔ̃trəvɑ̃] *nm* outside shutter.

contre-voie [kɔ̃trəvwa] *ad* à — in the wrong direction, on the wrong side.

contribuable [kɔ̃tribɥabl] *a* tax-paying; *nm* taxpayer.

contribuer [kɔ̃tribɥe] *vi* to contribute.

contribution [kɔ̃tribysjɔ̃] *nf* contribution, share, tax, rate.

contrit [kɔ̃tri] *a* contrite, penitent.
contrition [kɔ̃trisjɔ̃] *nf* contrition, penitence.
contrôle [kɔ̃troːl] *nm* checking, inspection, roll, roster, hallmark, ticket office.
contrôler [kɔ̃trole] *vt* inspect, control, verify.
contrôleur, -euse [kɔ̃trolœːr, øːz] *n* inspector, inspectress, assessor, controller, ticket-collector, time-keeper.
controuvé [kɔ̃truve] *a* fabricated, invented.
controverse [kɔ̃trɔvɛrs] *nf* controversy, dispute.
contumace [kɔ̃tymas] *nf* contumacy.
contusion [kɔ̃tyzjɔ̃] *nf* bruise.
contusionner [kɔ̃tyzjone] *vt* to contuse, bruise.
conurbation [kɔ̃nyrbasjɔ̃] *nf* conurbation.
convaincre [kɔ̃vɛ̃ːkr] *vt* to convince, convict.
convalescence [kɔ̃valɛssɑ̃ːs] *nf* convalescence.
convalescent [kɔ̃valɛssɑ̃] *an* convalescent.
convenable [kɔ̃vnabl] *a* suitable, proper, fit(ting), decent, decorous, well-behaved.
convenance [kɔ̃vnɑ̃ːs] *nf* agreement, suitability, convenience, propriety, decorum; *pl* convention.
convenir [kɔ̃vniːr] *vi* to suit, fit, agree, own, admit, be advisable, befitting.
convention [kɔ̃vɑ̃sjɔ̃] *nf* covenant, agreement, convention.
conventionnel, -elle [kɔ̃vɑ̃sjɔnɛl, ɛl] *a* conventional.
convenu [kɔ̃vny] *a* agreed, stipulated, settled.
conversation [kɔ̃vɛrsasjɔ̃] *nf* conversation, talk.
converser [kɔ̃vɛrse] *vi* to converse, talk.
conversion [kɔ̃vɛrsjɔ̃] *nf* conversion, change.
converti [kɔ̃vɛrti] *n* convert.
convertir [kɔ̃vɛrtiːr] *vt* to convert, change, win over; *vr* to become converted, turn.
convertisseur [kɔ̃vɛrtisœːr] *nm* converter, transformer.
convexe [kɔ̃vɛks] *a* convex.
conviction [kɔ̃viksjɔ̃] *nf* conviction.
convier [kɔ̃vje] *vt* to invite, urge.
convive [kɔ̃viːv] *n* table-companion, guest.
convocation [kɔ̃vɔkasjɔ̃] *nf* convocation, summons, convening, calling-up.
convoi [kɔ̃vwa] *nm* convoy, column, procession.
convoiter [kɔ̃vwate] *vt* to covet, desire.
convoitise [kɔ̃vwatiːz] *nf* covetousness, desire, lust.
convoquer [kɔ̃vɔke] *vt* to convoke, summon, convene, call up.

convulsif, -ive [kɔ̃vylsif, iːv] *a* convulsive.
convulsion [kɔ̃vylsjɔ̃] *nf* convulsion, upheaval.
coopérative [kɔɔperatːv] *nf* cooperative stores.
coopérer [kɔɔpere] *vi* to cooperate.
coordination [kɔɔrdinasjɔ̃] *nf* coordination.
coordonner [kɔɔrdɔne] *vt* to coordinate, arrange.
copain [kɔpɛ̃] *nm* chum, pal.
copeau [kɔpo] *nm* shaving, chip.
copie [kɔpi] *nf* copy, (examination-) paper, reproduction, imitation.
copier [kɔpje] *vt* to copy, reproduce, imitate.
copieux, -euse [kɔpjø, jøːz] *a* copious, full, hearty.
copiste [kɔpist] *nm* transcriber, imitator.
coq [kɔk] *nm* cock, weathercock, ship's cook; **poids — bantam** weight; **vivre comme un — en pâte** to live in clover.
coq-à-l'âne [kɔkalɑːn] *nm* cock-and-bull story.
coque [kɔk] *nf* shell, husk, hull, bottom, loop; **œuf à la — boiled egg.**
coquelicot [kɔkliko] *nm* poppy.
coqueluche [kɔklyʃ] *nf* whooping-cough; darling.
coquerico [kɔkriko] *nm* cock-a-doodle-doo.
coquet, -ette [kɔkɛ, ɛt] *a* coquettish, smart, stylish, trim, interested in dress.
coquetier [kɔktje] *nm* egg-cup, egg merchant.
coquette [kɔkɛt] *nf* flirt.
coquetterie [kɔkɛtri] *nf* coquetry, affectation, love of finery, smartness.
coquillage [kɔkijaːʒ] *nm* shellfish, shell.
coquille [kɔkiːj] *nf* shell, case; misprint, printer's error.
coquin, -e [kɔkɛ̃, in] *nm* rogue, rascal, scamp; *nf* hussy, minx.
cor [kɔːr] *nm* horn, (*of stag*) tine, corn; **réclamer à — et à cri** to clamor for.
corail [kɔraːj] *nm* coral.
coran [kɔrɑ̃] *nm* Koran.
corbeau [kɔrbo] *nm* crow, raven; corbel, bracket.
corbeille [kɔrbɛːj] *nf* basket, round flowerbed; **— de noces** bridegroom's wedding present(s) to bride.
corbillard [kɔrbijaːr] *nm* hearse.
cordage [kɔrdaːʒ] *nm* rope, cordage.
corde [kɔrd] *nf* rope, cord, line, string, wire, thread.
cordeau [kɔrdo] *nm* tracing-line, string, fuse.
cordelière [kɔrdəljɛr] *nf* girdle, cord.
corder [kɔrde] *vt* to twist, cord, rope, string.
cordial [kɔrdjal] *a* hearty, cordial; *nm* cordial.

cordialité [kɔrdjalite] nf cordiality, heartiness.

cordon [kɔrdɔ̃] nm cordon, row, cord, ribbon, rope, string.

cordonnerie [kɔrdonri] nf shoemaking, boot and shoe trade, shoemaker's shop.

cordonnier [kɔrdɔnje] nm shoemaker, bootmaker.

coriace [kɔrjas] a tough, leathery; hard, grasping.

corne [kɔrn] nf (animal) horn; coup de — butt, gore; — du sabot horse's hoof; — d'un livre (book) dog-ear; — à souliers shoehorn; — de brume foghorn.

cornée [kɔrne] nf cornea.

corneille [kɔrnɛːj] nf crow, rook.

cornemuse [kɔrnəmyːz] nf bagpipes.

corner [kɔrne] vt to trumpet, din, dog-ear, turn down; vi to sound the horn, ring.

cornet [kɔrnɛ] nm horn, trumpet, cornet; — à dés dice-box.

corniche [kɔrniʃ] nf cornice, ledge.

cornichon [kɔrniʃɔ̃] nm gherkin, simpleton.

cornu [kɔrny] a horned.

cornue [kɔrny] nf retort.

corollaire [kɔrollɛːr] nm corollary.

corporation [kɔrpɔrasjɔ̃] nf corporation, guild.

corporel, -elle [kɔrpɔrɛl, ɛl] a corporeal, corporal, bodily.

corps [kɔːr] nm body, substance, corpse, corps, frame, main part; — à — hand to hand, clinch; prendre— to take shape; perdu — et biens lost with all hands; à — perdu recklessly.

corpulence [kɔrpylɑ̃ːs] nf stoutness, corpulence.

corpulent [kɔrpylɑ̃] a stout, corpulent, fat.

corpuscule [kɔrpyskyl] nm corpuscle.

correct [kɔr(r)ɛkt] a correct, proper, accurate, polite, well-behaved.

correcteur, -trice [kɔr(r)ɛktœːr, tris] n corrector, proof-reader.

correction [kɔr(r)ɛksjɔ̃] nf correcting, proof-reading, correctness, accuracy, propriety, punishment.

correctionnel, -elle [kɔr(r)ɛksjɔnɛl, ɛl] a tribunal de police —le police court; délit — minor offense.

correspondance [kɔrɛspɔ̃dɑ̃ːs] nf correspondence, letters, communication, connection, intercourse.

correspondant [kɔrɛspɔ̃dɑ̃] a corresponding, connecting; nm correspondent, friend acting for parent.

correspondre [kɔrɛspɔ̃ːdr] vi to correspond, tally, agree, comunicate.

corridor [kɔridɔːr] nm corridor, passage.

corrigé [kɔriʒe] nm fair copy, correct version.

corriger [kɔriʒe] vt to correct, rectify, (proofs) read, cure, chastize.

corroboration [kɔrrɔbɔrasjɔ̃] nf corroboration, confirmation.

corroborer [kɔrrɔbɔre] vt to corroborate.

corroder [kɔrrɔde] vt to corrode, eat away.

corrompre [kɔr(r)ɔ̃ːpr] vt to corrupt, spoil, bribe, taint.

corrompu [kɔr(r)ɔ̃py] a corrupt, depraved, tainted.

corrosif, -ive [kɔrrozif, iːv] a nm corrosive.

corrosion [kɔrrozjɔ̃] nf corrosion.

corroyer [kɔrwaje] vt to curry, weld, trim, puddle.

corrupteur, -trice [kɔr(r)yptœːr, tris] a corrupt(ing); n corrupter.

corruptible [kɔr(r)yptibl] a corruptible, bribable.

corruption [kɔr(r)ypsjɔ̃] nf corruption, bribery, bribing.

corsage [kɔrsaːʒ] nm bodice, blouse.

Corse [kɔrs] nf Corsica.

corse [kɔrs] an Corsican.

corsé [kɔrse] a full-bodied, strong, broad, meaty.

corser [kɔrse] vt to give body to, fortify, intensify; vr to get serious, thicken.

corset [kɔrsɛ] nm corset; — de sauvetage life-jacket.

corsetier, -ière [kɔrsətje, jɛːr] n corset-maker.

cortège [kɔrtɛːʒ] nm procession, train, retinue.

corvée [kɔrve] nf fatigue duty, task, (piece of) drudgery.

cosmétique [kɔsmetik] a nm cosmetic.

cosmopolite [kɔsmɔpolit] an cosmopolitan.

cosse [kɔs] nf pod, husk.

cossu [kɔsy] a wealthy.

costaud [kɔsto] a nm strong, burly, brawny (man).

costume [kɔstym] nm costume, dress, suit.

costumé [kɔstyme] a bal — fancydress ball.

cote [kɔt] nf share, proportion, assessment, mark, number, classification, quotation, list of prices, odds.

côte [koːt] nf rib, hill, slope, coast, shore; — à — side by side.

côté [kote] nm side, way, direction, aspect, broadside, beam-ends; à — near, to one side; à — de beside, by the side of, next to; de — on one side, sideways, aside, by; de mon — for my part.

coteau [kɔto] nm hill, hillside, slope.

côtelé [kotle] a ribbed, corded, corduroy (velvet).

côtelette [kotlɛt] nf cutlet, chop.

coter [kɔte] vt to assess, quote, classify, number, award marks for, back.

coterie [kɔtri] *nf* set, clique, circle.
côtier, -ière [kotje, jɛːr] *a* coast, coastal, inshore; *nm* coaster.
cotisation [kɔtizasjɔ̃] *nf* share, contribution, subscription, fee.
se cotiser [səkɔtize] *vr* to club together, get up a subscription.
coton [kɔtɔ̃] *nm* cotton; **filer un mauvais** — to be in a poor way, go to the dogs.
cotonnerie [kɔtɔnri] *nf* cotton plantation.
cotonnier [kɔtɔnje] *nm* cotton plant.
côtoyer [kotwaje] *vt* to keep close to, hug, run along, skirt.
cou [ku] *nm* neck.
couardise [kwardiːz] *nf* cowardice, cowardliness.
couchage [kuʃaːʒ] *nm* bedding, bedclothes; **sac de** — sleeping-bag.
couchant [kuʃɑ̃] *a* setting; *nm* west, setting sun; **chien** — setter.
couche [kuʃ] *nf* bed, couch, layer, stratum, coat(ing), baby's diaper; *pl* confinement.
couché [kuʃe] *a* lying, recumbent, in bed.
coucher [kuʃe] *vt* to put to bed, lay down, set down; — **en joue** to aim (at); *vi* to sleep, spend the night; *vr* to go to bed, lie down, set, go down; *nm* night's lodging, setting.
couchette [kuʃɛt] *nf* crib, cot, berth, bunk, sleeper.
coucou [kuku] *nm* cuckoo.
coude [kud] *nm* elbow, bend, crank; **jouer des** —s to elbow one's way.
coudée [kude] *nf pl* elbow room, scope.
cou-de-pied [kudpje] *nm* instep.
coudoyer [kudwaje] *vt* to elbow, jostle, rub shoulders with.
coudre [kudr] *vt* to sew (up), stitch (on).
coudrier [kudrie] *nm* hazel tree.
couenne [kwan] *nf* thick skin, rind, membrane.
coulage [kulaːʒ] *nm* pouring, casting, running, sinking.
coulant [kulɑ̃] *a* running, flowing, easy, accommodating; **nœud** — slip-knot, noose.
coulé [kule] *a* cast, sunk, done for; *nm* slide, slur.
coulée [kule] *nf* running, flow, streak, casting.
couler [kule] *vt* to run, pour, cast, sink, slip, slur; *vi* to flow, run, leak, sink, slip, slur; *vr* to slip, glide, slide; **se la** — **douce** to take it easy, sit back.
couleur [kulœːr] *nf* color, complexion, coloring, paint, suit, flag.
couleuvre [kulœːvr] *nf* grass snake; **avaler une** — to pocket an insult.
coulisse [kulis] *nf* groove, slot, slide, unofficial stock-market; *pl* wings, slips; **à** — sliding; **en** — sidelong.
couloir [kulwaːr] *nm* corridor,

passage, lobby, channel, gully, lane.
coup [ku] *nm* blow, stroke, knock, hit, attempt, deed, attack, poke, stab, shot, blast, gust, move, ring, peal, influence, threat; **manquer son** — to miss the mark; — **de froid** cold snap, chill; **boire à petits** —s to sip; — **d'envoi** kick-off; **tout d'un** — all at once; **du** — now at last, this time; **sur le** — on the spot; **tout à** — suddenly.
coupable [kupabl] *a* guilty, culpable, sinful; *n* culprit.
coupe [kup] *nf* cup, glass, bowl, cut(ting), section, stroke.
coupé [kupe] *a* cut (up), sliced, broken, jerky, diluted; *nm* brougham, coupé.
coupe-coupe [kupkup] *nm* cutlass, long knife.
coupe-jarret [kupʒarɛ] *nm* cutthroat, ruffian.
coupe-papier [kuppapje] *nm* paperknife.
couper [kupe] *vt* to cut (out, up, down, off, in), intersect, cross, turn off, switch off, interrupt, stump, dilute; *vr* to cut oneself, cut, intersect, contradict oneself.
couperet [kuprɛ] *nm* chopper, cleaver, knife, blade (of guillotine).
couperosé [kuproze] *a* blotchy.
couple [kupl] *nm* couple, pair; *nf* two, brace, yoke, couple.
coupler [kuple] *vt* to couple, connect, join up.
couplet [kuplɛ] *nm* verse.
coupole [kupɔl] *nf* cupola, dome.
coupon [kupɔ̃] *nm* coupon, warrant, ticket, cut(ting), remnant, (short) length.
coupure [kupyːr] *nf* cut, gash, cutting, note.
cour [kuːr] *nf* court, courtship, courtyard, square, playground; **faire la** — **à** to make love to.
courage [kuraːʒ] *nm* courage, fortitude, spirit, heart.
courageux, -euse [kuraʒø, øːz] *a* brave, courageous.
couramment [kuramɑ̃] *ad* fluently, easily, generally.
courant [kurɑ̃] *a* running, current, present, standard, rife; *nm* current, stream, course; — **d'air** draft.
courbature [kurbatyr] *nf* stiffness, tiredness, ache.
courbaturé [kurbatyre] *a* aching, stiff.
courbe [kurb] *nf* curve, bend, sweep.
courber [kurbe] *vtir* to curve, bend; *vr* to stoop.
coureur, -euse [kurœːr, øːz] *n* runner, racer, sprinter, gadabout, adventurer, rake; — **de dots** fortune-hunter.
courge [kurʒ] *nf* pumpkin.
courgette [kurʒɛt] *nf* courgette, small marrow.
courir [kuriːr] *vi* to run, race, go,

be current, circulate; *vt* run (after), pursue, roam, gad about, haunt, frequent; **le bruit court** it is rumored; **par le temps qui court** nowadays, as things are.

courlis [kurli] *nm* curlew.

couronne [kurɔn] *nf* crown, coronet, wreath, corona, ring, rim.

couronnement [kurɔnmɑ̃] *nm* crowning, coronation, coping.

couronner [kurɔne] *vt* to crown, cap, reward, award a prize to, cope.

courrier [kurje] *nm* courier, messenger, mail, letters, post, newspaper paragraph.

courroie [kurwa] *nf* strap, transmission, belt, band.

courroux [kuru] *nm* anger, wrath.

cours [kuːr] *nm* course, flow, run, path, circulation, currency, quotation, price, course of lectures; *pl* classes; **en —** in progress, on hand, present, current.

course [kurs] *nf* run, race, excursion, outing, errand, course, path, flight.

court [kuːr] *a* short, brief, limited; *ad* short; **à — de** short of; **tout —** simply, merely; *nm* tennis court.

courtage [kurtaːʒ] *nm* broking, brokerage.

courtaud [kurto] *a* thickset, dumpy.

court-circuit [kursirkɥi] *nm* short-circuit.

courtier [kurtje] *nm* broker.

courtisan [kurtizɑ̃] *nm* courtier.

courtisane [kurtizan] *nf* courtesan prostitute.

courtiser [kurtize] *vt* to court, curry favor with.

courtois [kurtwa] *a* courteous, polite, courtly.

courtoisie [kurtwazi] *nf* courtesy, courteousness.

couru [kury] *a* run after, sought after, popular.

cousin [kuzɛ̃] *n* cousin; *nm* gnat, midge; **— germain** first cousin; **à la mode de Bretagne** distant relation.

coussin [kusɛ̃] *nm* cushion.

coussinet [kusinɛ] *nm* pads, small cushion, bearing; **—s à billes** ball-bearings.

cousu [kuzy] *a* sewn, stitched; **— d'or** rolling in money.

coût [ku] *nm* cost; **— de la vie** cost of living.

couteau [kuto] *nm* knife, blade; **à —x tirés** at daggers drawn.

coutelas [kutlɑ] *nm* cutlass, large knife.

coutelier [kutəlje] *nm* cutler.

coutellerie [kutɛlri] *nf* cutlery, cutler's shop or trade.

coûter [kute] *vi* to cost, pain, cause an effort; **coûte que coûte** at all costs.

coûteux, -euse [kutø, øːz] *a* costly, expensive.

coutil [kuti] *nm* drill, twill, ticking.

coutume [kutym] *nf* custom, habit; **de —** usual.

couture [kutyːr] *nf* needlework, seam, scar; **battre à plate(s) —(s)** to trounce.

couturier, -ière [kutyrje, jɛːr] *n* dressmaker.

couvée [kuve] *nf* brood, hatch, clutch.

couvent [kuvɑ̃] *nm* convent, monastery.

couver [kuve] *vt* to sit (on eggs), hatch (out), brood (over); *vi* to smolder, brew, hatch; **— des yeux** to look fondly or longingly at.

couvercle [kuvɛrkl] *nm* lid, cover, cap.

couvert [kuvɛːr] *a* covered, clad, wearing one's hat, shady, wooded, overcast, covert, overgrown; *nm* cover(ing), shelter, place, knife and fork and spoon, cover charge.

couverture [kuvɛrtyːr] *nf* cover(ing), rug, blanket, cloth, bedspread, wrapper, roofing.

couvre-feu [kuvrfø] *nm* curfew, lights out.

couvre-lit [kuvrli] *nm* bedspread.

couvre-pied [kuvrpje] *nm* quilt.

couvreur [kuvrœːr] *nm* roofer, slater, tiler.

couvrir [kuvriːr] *vt* to cover (with, up), clothe, conceal, roof, drown (sound); *vr* to clothe oneself, put on one's hat, become overcast.

crabe [krɑːb] *nm* crab.

crachat [kraʃa] *nm* spittle, spit.

craché [kraʃe] *a* **tout —** the dead spit of, to a tee.

cracher [kraʃe] *vt* to spit (out), splutter; *vi* to spit.

crachoir [kraʃwaːr] *nm* spittoon.

craie [krɛ] *nf* chalk.

craindre [krɛ̃ːdr] *vt* to fear, dread, be afraid of; **il n'y rien à —** there's no need to worry, nothing to worry about.

crainte [krɛ̃t] *nf* fear, dread.

craintif, -ive [krɛ̃tif, iːv] *a* timid, afraid, fearful.

cramoisi [kramwazi] *a* crimson.

crampe [krɑ̃ːp] *nf* cramp.

crampon [krɑ̃pɔ̃] *nm* clamp, fastener, crampon, stud, limpet, pest.

cramponner [krɑ̃pɔne] *vt* to cramp, clamp together, fasten, pester, stick to; *vr* to hold on, hang on (to **à**).

cran [krɑ̃] *nm* safety catch, notch, hole, pluck, spirit.

crâne [krɑːn] *nm* skull; *a* plucky, jaunty, swaggering.

crâner [krɑne] *vi* to swagger, assume a jaunty air, brazen it out.

crâneur [krɑnœːr] *n* braggart, swaggerer.

crapaud [krapo] *nm* toad.

crapule [krapyl] *nf* debauchery, blackguard.

crapuleux, -euse [krapylø, øːz] *a* debauched, dissolute, lewd, filthy.

craquelure [kraklyːr] nf crack.
craquer [krake] vi to crack, crackle, crunch, creak.
crasse [kras] af gross; nf dirt, squalor, dross, slag, meanness, dirty trick.
crasseux, -euse [krasø, øːz] a dirty, grimy, squalid.
cratère [krateːr] nm crater.
cravache [kravaʃ] nf riding-whip, horsewhip.
cravate [kravat] nf (neck)tie.
crayeux, -euse [krɛjø, øːz] a chalky.
crayon [krɛjɔ̃] nm pencil, pencil-drawing, crayon.
crayonner [krɛjɔne] vt to pencil, sketch, jot down.
créance [kreɑ̃ːs] nf credence, belief, credit, trust, debt, claim; lettre(s) de — letter of credit, credentials.
créancier, -ière [kreɑ̃sje, jɛːr] n creditor.
créateur, -trice [kreatœːr, tris] a creative; n creator, maker, inventor, founder.
création [kreasjɔ̃] nf creation, creating, founding.
créature [kreatyːr] nf creature, person.
crèche [krɛʃ] nf crib, manger, day-nursery.
crédence [kredɑ̃ːs] nf sideboard.
crédibilité [kredibilite] nf credibility.
crédit [kredi] nm credit, loan, bank, repute, influence.
créditeur, -trice [kreditœːr, tris] a credit; n creditor.
credo [kredo] nm creed.
crédule [kredyl] a credulous.
crédulité [kredylite] nf credulity, credulousness.
créer [kree] vt to create, make, found, build up.
crémaillère [kremajɛːr] nf pot hook; pendre la — to give a house-warming.
crématoire [krematwaːr] a four — crematorium.
crème [krɛm] nf cream, custard.
crémerie [kremri] nf creamery, dairy, milk-shop, small restaurant.
crémeux, -euse [kremø, øːz] a creamy.
crémier, -ière [kremje, jɛːr] n dairyman, dairywoman.
crémière [kremjɛːr] nf cream-jug.
créneau [kreno] nm loophole; pl battlements.
crénelé [krɛnle] a crenellated, loop-holed, notched, toothed.
créosote [kreozot] nf creosote.
crêpe [krɛːp] nf pancake; nm crape, crêpe.
crêper [krɛpe] vt to crimp, crisp, frizz, backcomb.
crépi [krepi] nm rough-cast.
crépir [krepiːr] vt to rough-cast, grain.
crépiter [krepite] vi to crackle, sputter, patter.

crépu [krepy] a crimped, crisp, frizzy, fuzzy.
crépuscule [krepyskyl] nm dusk, twilight, gloaming.
cresson [krəsɔ̃] nm cress.
crête [krɛːt] nf comb, crest, ridge.
crétin [kretɛ̃] nm cretin, idiot, half-wit.
cretonne [krətɔn] nf cretonne.
creuser [krøze] vt to hollow (out), excavate, dig (out), go deeply into.
creuset [krøze] nm crucible, melting-pot.
creux, -euse [krø, øːz] a hollow, sunk(en), empty, slack, futile; nm hollow, hole, pit, cavity.
crevaison [krəvɛzɔ̃] nf puncture, bursting, death.
crevant [krəvɑ̃] a funny, killing, exhausting.
crevasse [krəvas] nf crevice, crevasse, crack, split.
crève-cœur [krɛvkœːr] nm heart-break, disappointment.
crever [krəve] vi to burst, split, die; vt to puncture, burst, put out.
crevette [krəvɛt] nf shrimp, prawn.
cri [kri] nm cry, shout, call, squeal; le dernier — the latest fashion, the last word.
criailler [kriɑje] vi to shout, bawl, whine, squeal.
criant [kriɑ̃] a crying, flagrant glaring.
criard [kriaːr] a crying, squealing, shrill, garish.
crible [kribl] nm sieve, riddle, screen.
cribler [krible] vt to sift, riddle, screen.
cric [krik] nm jack.
cricri [krikri] nm chirping, cricket.
criée [krie] nf auction.
crier [krie] vti to cry, shout; vi scream, squeak.
crime [krim] nm crime.
criminel, -elle [kriminɛl] an criminal.
crin [krɛ̃] nm horsehair.
crinière [krinjɛːr] nf mane.
crique [krik] nf creek, cove.
crise [kriːz] nf crisis, problem, shortage, slump, attack.
crispation [krispasjɔ̃] nf twitching, clenching, wincing, shriveling up.
crisper [krispe] vt to clench, contract, contort, screw up; vr to contract, shrivel up.
crisser [krise] vi to grate.
cristal [kristal] nm crystal.
cristallin [kristalɛ̃] a crystalline, crystal-clear.
cristalliser [kristalize] vti to crystal-lize.
critère [kritɛːr] nm criterion.
critiquable [kritikabl] a open to criticism.
critique [kritik] a critical, crucial, ticklish, decisive; nf criticism, censure; nm critic.

critiquer [kritike] *vt* to criticize, censure.
croasser [krɔase] *vi* to caw. croak.
croc [kro] *nm* hook, fang, tusk.
croc-en-jambe [krɔkɑ̃ʒɑ̃:b] *nm* **faire donner un — à qn** to trip.
croche [krɔʃ] *nf* quaver.
crochet [krɔʃe] *nm* hook, crochet, skeleton key, swerve, sudden turn; *pl* square brackets.
crochu [krɔʃy] *a* hooked, crooked.
crocodile [krɔkɔdil] *nm* crocodile.
croire [krwa:r] *vt* to believe, think; *vi* believe (in **à, en**).
croisade [krwazad] *nf* crusade.
croisé [krwaze] *a* crossed, cross, double-breasted; *nm* crusader.
croisée [krwaze] *nf* crossing, cross-roads, casement window.
croisement [krwazmɑ̃] *nm* crossing, meeting, intersection, interbreeding.
croiser [krwaze] *vt* to cross, fold, pass, meet; *vi* to fold over, cruise; *vr* to intersect, cross, meet and pass.
croiseur [krwazœ:r] *nm* cruiser.
croisière [krwazjɛ:r] *nf* cruise.
croissance [krwasɑ̃:s] *nf* growth.
croissant [krwasɑ̃] *nm* crescent, crescent roll.
croître [krwa:tr] *vi* to grow, increase, rise, wax, lengthen
croix [krwa] *nf* cross.
croque-mitaine [krɔkmitɛn] *nm* bogy(man).
croquer [krɔke] *vt* to crunch, munch, sketch.
croquis [krɔki] *nm* sketch.
crosse [krɔs] *nf* crook, crosier, stick, club, butt.
crotte [krɔt] *nf* mud, dirt, dung, chocolate sweet.
crotté [krɔte] *a* dirty, muddy, bespattered.
crottin [krɔtɛ̃] *nm* dung, droppings.
croulant [krulɑ̃] *a* crumbling, tottering.
croulement [krulmɑ̃] *nm* collapse, crumbling, falling in.
crouler [krule] *vi* to collapse, totter, crumble.
croupe [krup] *nf* croup, crupper, rump.
croupion [krupjɔ̃] *nm* rump, parson's nose.
croupir [krupi:r] *vi* to wallow, stagnate.
croustillant [krustijɑ̃] *a* crisp, crusty, spicy, smutty.
croûte [krut] *nf* crust, rind, scab, daub; **casser la —** to have a snack.
croûton [krutɔ̃] *nm* crust, crusty end, crouton.
croyable [krwajabl] *a* credible, believable, trustworthy.
croyance [krwajɑ̃:s] *nf* belief.
croyant [krwajɑ̃] *a* believing; *n* believer; *pl* the faithful.
cru [kry] *a* raw, crude, broad, coarse, blunt, garish; *nm* vintage, growth, vineyard, invention; **vin du**

— local wine; **les meilleurs —s** the best vineyards; **un bon —** a good vintage.
cruauté [kryote] *nf* cruelty.
cruche [kryʃ] *nf* pitcher, jug, blockhead, dolt.
crucifier [krysifje] *vt* to crucify.
crucifix [krysifi] *nm* crucifix.
crucifixion [krysifiksjɔ̃] *nf* crucifixion.
crudité [krydite] *nf* crudity, rawness, coarseness; *pl* raw fruit or vegetables.
crue [kry] *nf* rising, flood spate.
cruel, -elle [kryɛl] *a* cruel.
crûment [krymɑ̃] *ad* crudely, bluntly, roughly.
crustacés [krystase] *nm* *pl* crustaceans.
crypte [kript] *nf* crypt.
cube [kyb] *a* cubic; *nm* cube.
cubique [kybik] *a* cubic(al), cube.
cubisme [kybism] *nm* cubism.
cueillaison [kœjezɔ̃] *nf* gathering, picking, gathering season.
cueillette [kœjɛt] *nf* gathering, picking, crop.
cueillir [kœji:r] *vt* to gather, pick, pluck.
cuiller, -ère [kyjɛ:r, kɥijɛ:r] *nf* spoon.
cuillerée [kyjre, kɥijre] *nf* spoonful.
cuir [kɥi:r] *nm* leather, hide, skin, strop; **— chevelu** scalp.
cuirasse [kɥiras] *nf* breastplate, armor.
cuirassé [kɥirase] *a* armor-plated, armored; *nm* ironclad, battleship.
cuire [kɥi:r] *vt* to cook, roast, bake, fire, burn; *vi* to cook, stew, burn, smart.
cuisant [kɥizɑ̃] *a* burning, smarting, biting, bitter.
cuisine [kɥizin] *nf* kitchen, cooking, cookery, food.
cuisiner [kɥizine] *vt* to cook; **— les comptes** manipulate the books, pull strings, (*a suspect*) interrogate.
cuisinier, -ière [kɥizinje, jɛ:r] *n* cook.
cuisinière [kɥizinjɛ:r] *nf* stove, cooker.
cuisse [kɥis] *nf* thigh, leg.
cuisson [kɥisɔ̃] *nf* cooking, baking, firing, burning, smarting.
cuistre [kɥistr] *nm* pedant, ill-mannered man.
cuit [kɥi] *a* cooked, baked, drunk; **— à point** done to a turn; **trop —** overdone; **pas assez —** underdone.
cuite [kɥit] *nf* baking, firing, burning, batch; **prendre une —** to get tight (drunk).
cuivre [kɥi:vr] *nm* copper, copper-plate; **— jaune** brass; **les —s** the brass(es).
cuivré [kɥivre] *a* coppered, copper-colored, bronzed, metallic, brassy.
cul [ky] *nm* (*fam*) bottom, behind, rump, tail, stern.
culasse [kylas] *nf* breech.

culbute [kylbyt] *n* somersault, tumble, fall.

culbuter [kylbyte] *vi* to turn a somersault, tumble; *vt* to knock over, dump, trip.

cul-de-sac [kydsak] *nm* blind alley, dead end.

culinaire [kyline:r] *a* culinary.

culminant [kylminã] *a* culminating, highest.

culot [kylo] *nm* bottom, base, dottle, cheek, sauce.

culotte [kylɔt] *nf* breeches knickerbockers, shorts.

culotter [kylɔte] *vt* to breech, color, season.

culpabilité [kylpabilite] *nf* culpability, guilt.

culte [kylt] *nm* worship, cult.

cultivateur [kyltivatœ:r] *nm* farmer, cultivator, grower.

cultivé [kyltive] *a* cultivated, cultured.

cultiver [kyltive] *vt* to farm, till, cultivate.

culture [kylty:r] *nf* cultivation, farming, culture; *pl* fields, land under cultivation.

cumul [kymyl] *nm* plurality of offices.

cumuler [kymyle] *vt* to occupy several posts.

cupide [kypid] *a* covetous, greedy, grasping.

cupidité [kypidite] *nf* covetousness, greed.

Cupidon [kypidɔ̃] *nm* Cupid.

curatif, -ive [kyratif, i:v] *a* curative.

cure [ky:r] *nf* care, heed, presbytery, vicarage, rectory, cure.

curé [kyre] *nm* parish priest.

cure-dents [kyrdã] *nm* toothpick.

curer [kyre] *vt* to pick, clean (out), cleanse, clear.

curieux, -euse [kyrjø, ø:z] *a* interested, curious, odd, quaint.

curiosité [kyrjɔzite] *nf* interestedness, inquisitiveness, curiosity, oddness, peculiarity, curio; *pl* sights.

curviligne [kyrviliɲ] *a* curvilinear, rounded.

cuticule [kytikyl] *nf* cuticle.

cuve [ky:v] *nf* vat, tun, tank.

cuver [kyve] *vti* to ferment; — **son vin** to sleep off one's drink.

cuvette [kyvɛt] *nf* wash-basin, dish, pan, basin.

cyanure [sjany:r] *nm* cyanide.

cycle [sikl] *nm* cycle.

cyclisme [siklism] *nm* cycling.

cyclone [siklon] *nm* cyclone.

cygne [siɲ] *nm* swan.

cylindre [silɛ̃:dr] *nm* cylinder, drum, roller.

cylindrer [silɛ̃dre] *vt* to roll, calender, mangle.

cylindrique [silɛ̃drik] *a* cylindrical.

cymbale [sɛ̃bal] *nf* cymbal.

cynique [sinik] *a* cynic(al), brazen, barefaced; *nm* cynic.

cynisme [sinism] *nm* cynicism, effrontery.

cynocéphale [sinɔsefal] *nm* baboon.

cyprès [siprɛ] *nm* cypress-tree.

cytise [siti:z] *nm* laburnum.

D

daba [daba] *nf* hoe.

dactylo(graphe) [daktilɔgraf] *n* typist.

dactylographier [daktilɔgrafje] *vt* to type.

dada [dada] *nm* hobby (-horse).

dadais [dadɛ] *nm* ninny.

dague [dag] *nf* dagger.

daigner [dɛɲe] *vi* to condescend, deign.

daim [dɛ̃] *nm* deer, buck.

dais [dɛ] *nm* canopy, dais.

dallage [dala:ʒ] *nm* paving, tiled floor.

dalle [dal] *nf* flagstone, slice, slab.

daller [dale] *vt* to pave, tile.

daltonisme [daltɔnism] *nm* colorblindness.

damas [damɑ(:s)] *nm* damask, damson.

dame [dam] *nf* lady, queen, king (checkers), beetle; *pl* checkers.

damer [dame] *vt* to crown a piece (at checkers).

damier [damje] *nm* checkerboard.

damner [dane] *vt* to damn, condemn.

dancing [dãsɛ̃:g] *nm* dance hall.

dandiner [dãdine] *vt* to dandle, dance; *vr* to waddle.

Danemark [danmark] *nm* Denmark.

danger [dãʒe] *nm* danger, peril, jeopardy, risk.

dangereux, -euse [dãʒrø, ø:z] *a* dangerous, perilous, risky.

danois [danwa, wa:z] *a nm* Danish; *n* Dane.

dans [dã] *prep* in, into, within, out of, from.

danse [dã:s] *nf* dance, dancing.

danser [dãse] *vti* to dance; *vi* to prance, bob.

danseur, -euse [dãsœ:r, ø:z] *n* dancer, partner.

dard [da:r] *nm* dart, javelin, harpoon, sting, tongue.

darder [darde] *vt* to dart, hurl, shoot out.

darse [dars] *nf* floating dock.

date [dat] *nf* date.

dater [date] *vti* to date; **à — de** as from.

datte [dat] *nf* date.

dattier [datje] *nm* date palm.

dauphin [dofɛ̃] *nm* dolphin, dauphin.

davantage [davãta:ʒ] *ad* more, any more, any further.

de [də] *prep* from, of, by, with, in.

dé [de] *nm* thimble, dice, die, tee.

débâcle [debɑ:kl] *nf* collapse, break-up, downfall, rout.

déballer [debale] *vt* to unpack.

débandade [debãdad] *nf* rout, stampede; **à la —** in disorder, helterskelter.

débander [debãde] *vt* to loosen, relax, unbend.

débarbouiller [debarbuje] *vt* to clean, wash; *vr* wash one's face.

débarcadère [debarkadɛːr] *nm* landing-stage, wharf.

débarder [debarde] *vt* to unload, discharge.

débardeur [debardœːr] *nm* stevedore, docker.

débarquement [debarkəmã] *nm* disembarking, landing, unloading, detraining.

débarquer [debarke] *vti* to land, disembark, detrain; *vt* to unload, set down.

débarras [debarɑ] *nm* storeroom; **bon —!** good riddance!

débarrasser [debarase] *vt* to rid, free, relieve; *vr* to get rid (of **de**).

débarrer [debare] *vt* to unbar.

débat [deba] *nm* debate, argument, discussion.

débattre [debatr] *vt* to discuss, debate; *vr* to struggle.

débauche [deboːʃ] *nf* debauchery, dissipation.

débaucher [deboʃe] *vt* to corrupt, lead astray; *vr* go to the bad.

débile [debil] *a* feeble, weak, sickly.

débilité [debilite] *nf* feebleness, debility.

débit [debi] *nm* sale, shop, flow, delivery, debit.

débiter [debite] *vt* to sell, retail, deliver, spin, debit.

débiteur, -trice [debitœːr, tris] *n* debtor.

déblai [deblɛ] *nm* clearing, excavation; **voie en —** railway cutting.

déblatérer [deblatere] *vi* to rail (against **contre**).

déblayage [deblɛjaʒ] *nm* clearance, clearing.

déblayer [deblɛje] *vt* to clear away.

déboire [debwaːr] *nm* nasty aftertaste, disappointment.

déboisement [debwazmã] *nm* deforestation.

déboîter [debwate] *vt* to dislocate, disjoint, disconnect.

débonder [debɔ̃de] *vt* to unbung.

débonnaire [debɔnɛːr] *a* goodnatured, easy-tempered.

débordement [debɔrdəmã] *nm* overflowing, depravation, dissoluteness.

déborder [debɔrde] *vti* to overflow, boil over, brim over; *vt* to overlap, extend beyond, to outflank.

débouché [debuʃe] *nm* outlet, opening, market.

déboucher [debuʃe] *vt* to uncork, open, clear; *vi* to emerge, debouch.

déboucler [debukle] *vt* to unbuckle; *vr* (*hair*) to lose its curl.

déboulonner [debulɔne] *vt* to unbolt, unrivet.

débourber [deburbe] *vt* to clean out, sluice, dredge.

débours [debuːr] *nm pl* out of pocket expenses.

débourser [deburse] *vt* to spend, disburse.

debout [dəbu] *ad* erect, upright, standing, on end, up.

déboutonner [debutɔne] *vt* to unbutton.

débraillé [debrɑje] *a* untidy, disheveled, improper.

débrayer [debrɛje] *vt* to disconnect, throw out of gear, declutch.

débrider [debride] *vt* to unbridle; **sans —** without a stop.

débris [debri] *nm pl* fragments, bits, remains, ruins.

débrouillard [debrujaːr] *a* ingenious, resourceful, smart.

débrouiller [debruje] *vt* to unravel, disentangle; *vr* to find a way out, not to be stuck.

débrousser [debruse] *vt* to clear forest, bush.

débusquer [debyske] *vt* to dislodge, ferret out.

début [deby] *nm* beginning, start, first appearance.

débutant [debytã] *n* beginner.

débuter [debyte] *vi* to lead, begin, come out.

deçà [dəsa] *ad* on this side.

décacheter [dekaʃte] *vt* to unseal, break open.

décadence [dekadãːs] *nf* decay, decline, downfall.

décaler [dekale] *vt* to remove wedge from, alter.

décamper [dekãpe] *vi* to decamp, scuttle off.

décapiter [dekapite] *vt* to behead.

décati [dekati] *a* worn out, senile.

décatir [dekatiːr] *vt* to sponge, steam, finish.

décéder [desede] *vt* to die, decease.

déceler [desle] *vt* to reveal, disclose, divulge.

décembre [desãːbr] *nm* December.

décence [desãːs] *nf* decency, propriety, decorum.

décent [desã] *a* decent, proper, modest.

décentraliser [desãtralize] *vt* to decentralize.

déception [desɛpsjɔ̃] *nf* deception, disappointment.

décerner [desɛrne] *vt* to confer, award, decree.

décès [desɛ] *nm* decease.

décevant [des(ə)vã] *a* deceptive, disappointing.

décevoir [desəvwaːr] *vt* to disappoint, deceive, dash.

déchaîner [deʃene] *vt* to unchain, let loose, unfetter; *vr* to break loose, break (out).

décharge [deʃarʒ] *nf* unloading, volley, discharge, acquittal, rebate; **témoin à —** witness for defense.

déchargement [deʃarʒəmɑ̃] *nm* unloading, discharging.

décharger [deʃarʒe] *vt* to dump, exonerate, unload, discharge, let off; *vr* to go off, run down, get rid (of de).

décharné [deʃarne] *a* gaunt, emaciated, skinny.

déchausser [deʃose] *vt* to take off s.o.'s shoes; *vr* take off one's shoes.

déchéance [deʃeɑ̃:s] *nf* fall, downfall, forfeiture.

déchet [deʃɛ] *nm* loss, decrease; *pl* refuse, scraps, failures.

déchiffrer [deʃifre] *vt* to decipher, decode, read.

déchiqueté [deʃikte] *a* torn, slashed, jagged.

déchirant [deʃirɑ̃] *a* heart-rending, ear-splitting, excruciating, harrowing.

déchirer [deʃire] *vtr* to tear, rend.

déchirure [deʃiry:r] *nf* tear, slit, rent.

déchoir [deʃwa:r] *vi* to fall.

décidément [desidemɑ̃] *ad* decidedly, resolutely.

décider [deside] *vt* to decide, settle, induce; *vir* to make up one's mind, decide.

décimale [desimal] *nf* decimal.

décimer [desime] *vt* to decimate.

décisif, -ive [desizif, i:v] *a* decisive, crucial, conclusive.

décision [desizjɔ̃] *nf* decision, resolution.

déclamation [deklamasjɔ̃] *nf* declamation, oratory, elocution.

déclamatoire [deklamatwa:r] *a* declamatory.

déclamer [deklame] *vti* to declaim, spout.

déclarable [deklarabl] *a* liable to customs' duty.

déclaration [deklarasjɔ̃] *nf* announcement, declaration; — assermentée affidavit.

déclarer [deklare] *vt* to declare, state; *vr* declare oneself, break out, avow one's love, own up.

déclassé [deklase] *a* degraded, ostracized; *n* outcast, pariah.

déclasser [deklase] *vt* to transfer from one class to another, degrade.

déclencher [deklɑ̃ʃe] *vt* to loosen, release, launch.

déclic [deklik] *nm* latch, trigger, click, snap.

déclin [deklɛ̃] *nm* decline, close, end, deterioration.

déclinaison [deklinɛzɔ̃] *nf* declension, variation.

décliner [dekline] *vt* to decline, refuse; *vi* to decline, deteriorate, decay, fall; — son nom to give one's name.

déclivité [deklivite] *nf* declivity, slope, incline.

décocher [dekɔʃe] *vt* to shoot, discharge, let fly, fire.

décoiffer [dekwafe] *vt* to remove s.o.'s hat, undo s.o.'s hair; *vr* take one's hat off.

décollage [dekɔla:ʒ] *nm* unsticking, removal of gum, take-off (plane); piste de — runway.

décoller [dekɔle] *vt* to unstick, loosen, remove gum from; *vi* to take off; *vr* to come unstuck, work loose.

décolleté [dekɔlte] *a* low-necked.

décolorant [dekɔlɔrɑ̃] *anm* bleaching (agent).

décolorer [dekɔlɔre] *vt* to discolor, take color out of.

décombres [dekɔ̃:br] *nm pl* rubbish, debris.

décommander [dekɔmɑ̃de] *vt* to cancel, countermand, call off.

décomposer [dekɔ̃poze] *vt* to decompose, alter, distort; *vr* to decompose, become distorted.

décompte [dekɔ̃:t] *nm* discount, deduction.

déconcerter [dekɔ̃sɛrte] *vt* to confound, take aback.

déconfiture [dekɔ̃fity:r] *nf* defeat, discomfiture.

déconseiller [dekɔ̃sɛje] *vt* to dissuade, advise against.

déconsidération [dekɔ̃siderasjɔ̃] *nf* discredit, disrepute.

déconsidéré [dekɔ̃sidere] *a* disreputable.

déconsidérer [dekɔ̃sidere] *vt* to bring into disrepute.

décontenancer [dekɔ̃tnɑ̃se] *vt* to abash.

déconvenue [dekɔ̃vny] *nf* mishap, misfortune.

décor [dekɔr] *nm* decoration, scenery, set(ting).

décorateur, -trice [dekɔratœ:r, tris] *n* decorator, scene-painter.

décoration [dekɔrasjɔ̃] *nf* decoration, scene-painting.

décorer [dekɔre] *vt* to decorate.

décortiquer [dekɔrtike] *vt* to remove bark from, shell, peel, husk.

découcher [dekuʃe] *vi* to sleep out.

découdre [dekudr] *vt* to unstitch, unpick; *vr* to come unstitched.

découler [dekule] *vi* to flow, run down, fall.

découpage [dekupa:ʒ] *nm* cutting out, fretwork.

découper [dekupe] *vt* to cut out, cut up, carve; *vr* to stand out.

découplé [dekuple] *a* bien — well-built.

découpure [dekupy:r] *nf* cutting out, cutting.

découragé [dekuraʒe] *a* downhearted, despondent.

décourageant [dekuraʒɑ̃] *a* disheartening.

découragement [dekuraʒmɑ̃] *nm* despondency, discouragement.

décousu [dekuzy] *a* disconnected, incoherent, rambling; *nm* incoherency.

découvert [dekuvɛːr] *a* uncovered, open, exposed; **à —** openly.

découverte [dekuvɛrt] *nf* discovery.

découvrir [dekuvriːr] *vt* to uncover, discover, reveal, detect, expose; *vr* to doff one's hat, be discovered.

décrasser [dekrase] *vt* to scour, clean.

décrépitude [dekrepityd] *nf* decay, senility.

décret [dekrɛ] *nm* decree.

décréter [dekrete] *vt* to decree, enact.

décrier [dekrie] *vt* to decry, run down, disparage.

décrire [dekriːr] *vt* to describe.

décrocher [dekrɔʃe] *vt* to unhook, take down, undo.

décroissance [dekrwasɑ̃ːs] *nf* decrease, decline.

décroître [dekrwaːtr] *vi* to decrease, grow shorter.

décrotter [dekrɔte] *vt* to clean, brush, scrape.

décrottoir [dekrɔtwaːr] *nm* scraper.

déçu [desy] *a* disappointed.

dédaigner [dedɛɲe] *vt* to disdain, scorn.

dédaigneux, -euse [dedɛɲø, øːz] *a* disdainful, supercilious.

dédain [dedɛ̃] *nm* disdain.

dédale [dedal] *nm* maze.

dedans [dədɑ̃] *ad* inside, within, in it; *nm* interior, inside.

dédicace [dedikas] *nf* dedication.

dédier [dedje] *vt* to dedicate, inscribe.

se dédire [sədediːr] *vr* to retract, take back one's words.

dédommagement [dedɔmaʒmɑ̃] *nm* compensation, damages, amends.

dédommager [dedɔmaʒe] *vt* to compensate, make amends to; *vr* to make up one's loss.

déduction [dedyksjɔ̃] *nf* deduction, inference.

déduire [dedɥiːr] *vt* to deduce, deduct.

déesse [deɛs] *nf* goddess.

défaillance [defajɑ̃ːs] *nf* weakness, lapse, falling-off, swoon; **tomber en — to faint.**

défaillant [defajɑ̃] *a* failing, sinking; *n* defaulter.

défaillir [defajiːr] *vi* to grow weak, fail, faint.

défaire [defɛːr] *vt* to undo, untie, defeat; *vr* to come undone, rid oneself, get rid (of).

défait [defɛ] *a* haggard, drawn, worn, undone.

défaite [defɛt] *nf* defeat.

défaitiste [defetist] *an* defeatist.

défalquer [defalke] *vt* to deduct, write off.

défaut [defo] *nm* defect, fault, lack, blemish, flaw; **à — de** for lack of; **prendre qn en —** to catch someone out.

défaveur [defavœːr] *nf* disgrace, disfavor.

défavorable [defavɔrabl] *a* unfavorable, disadvantageous.

défection [defɛksjɔ̃] *nf* disloyalty, defection.

défectueux, -euse [defɛktɥø, øːz] *a* faulty, defective.

défendable [defɑ̃dabl] *a* defensible.

défendeur, -eresse [defɑ̃dœːr, ərɛs] *n* defendant.

défendre [defɑ̃ːdr] *vt* to defend, uphold, protect, forbid.

défense [defɑ̃ːs] *nf* defense, support, interdiction; *pl* tusks; **—de fumer** no smoking; **— passive** anti-aircraft defense, civil defense.

défenseur [defɑ̃sœːr] *nm* defender, protector, upholder, counsel for defense.

défensif, -ive [defɑ̃sif, iːv] *a* defensive.

défensive [defɑ̃siːv] *nf* defensive.

déférence [deferɑ̃ːs] *nf* respect, deference, compliance.

déférer [defere] *vt* to refer, hand over, administer; *vi* to assent, defer, comply.

déferler [defɛrle] *vt* to unfurl; *vi* to break.

déferrer [defɛre] *vt* to unshoe, remove the iron from; *vr* to cast a shoe.

défi [defi] *nm* defiance, challenge.

défiance [defjɑ̃ːs] *nf* distrust, suspicion, diffidence.

défiant [defjɑ̃] *a* distrustful, suspicious, wary.

déficeler [defisle] *vt* to untie.

déficit [defisit] *nm* deficit.

déficitaire [defisitɛːr] *a* deficient, unbalanced.

défier [defje] *vt* to defy, dare, challenge, beggar; *vr* to distrust.

défigurer [defigyre] *vt* to disfigure, distort, deface.

défilade [defilad] *nf* filing past.

défilé [defile] *nm* pass, defile, parade, march past.

défiler [defile] *vi* to march past, parade, flash past.

définir [definiːr] *vt* to determine, define.

définitif, -ive [definitif, iːv] *a* final, definitive.

définition [definisjɔ̃] *nf* definition.

déflation [deflasjɔ̃] *nf* deflation.

déflorer [deflɔre] *vt* to take the bloom off, take the novelty off, deflower.

défoncer [defɔ̃se] *vt* to break in, burst in, knock the bottom out of.

déformer [defɔrme] *vt* to disfigure, distort, put out of shape; *vr* to lose its shape.

défraîchi [defrɛʃi] *a* faded, soiled.

défrayer [defrɛje] *vt* to defray, pay s.o.'s expenses.

défricher [defriʃe] *vt* to clear, prepare, break.

défroncer [defrɔ̃se] *vt* to unplait, smooth.

défroque [defrɔk] *nf pl* cast-off clothing, wardrobe.

défroquer [defrɔke] *vt* to unfrock.

défunt [defœ̃] *a* deceased, dead, defunct.

dégagé [degaʒe] *a* free, easy, offhand, airy.

dégagement [degaʒmɑ̃] *nm* disengagement, release, slackening, redemption.

dégager [degaʒe] *vt* to disengage, release, to redeem.

dégainer [degɛne] *vt* to unsheathe, draw.

dégarnir [degarniːr] *vt* to strip, deplete, dismantle; *vr* to be stripped, grow bare, empty.

dégâts [degɑ] *nm pl* damage, havoc.

dégauchir [degoʃiːr] *vt* to smooth, straighten, take the rough edges off.

dégel [deʒɛl] *nm* thaw.

dégeler [deʒle] *vti* to melt, thaw.

dégénération [deʒenɛrasjɔ̃] *nf* degeneration, degeneracy.

dégénérer [deʒenere] *vi* to degenerate.

dégingandé [deʒɛ̃gɑ̃de] *a* ungainly, gawky.

dégivreur [deʒivrœr] *nm* de-icer.

dégoiser [degwaze] *vt* to say hurriedly, race through; *vi* to chatter.

dégonfler [degɔ̃fle] *vt* to deflate, reduce, debunk, explode; *vr* to go flat, subside, climb down.

dégorger [degɔrʒe] *vt* to disgorge, clear; *vi* to flow out, overflow.

dégouliner [deguline] *vi* to drip, trickle.

dégourdi [degurdi] *a* smart, knowing, wide-awake.

dégourdir [degurdiːr] *vt* to revive, restore circulation to; *vr* to loosen one's muscles, stretch one's limbs.

dégoût [degu] *nm* disgust, aversion, distaste, annoyance.

dégoûtant [degutɑ̃] *a* disgusting, sickening.

dégoûté [degute] *a* disgusted, sick, fastidious, fed up.

dégoûter [degute] *vt* to disgust, sicken.

dégoutter [degute] *vi* to trickle, drip, drop.

dégradation [degradasjɔ̃] *nf* abasement, degeneracy, reduction to the ranks, shading off.

dégrader [degrade] *vt* to degrade, reduce to ranks, shade off, graduate.

dégrafer [degrafe] *vt* to unclasp, unhook, undo.

dégraisser [degrɛse] *vt* to scour, clean.

degré [dəgre] *nm* degree, stage, grade, step.

dégringolade [degrɛ̃gɔlad] *nf* fall, tumble, collapse, slump, bathos.

dégringoler [degrɛ̃gɔle] *vti* to rush, tumble down.

dégriser [degrize] *vt* to sober, bring

s.o. to his senses; *vr* to come back to earth.

dégrossir [degrosiːr] *vt* to rough plane, rough hew, take the rough edges off.

déguenillé [degnije] *a* ragged, tattered.

déguisement [degizmɑ̃] *nm* disguise, fancy dress.

déguiser [degize] *vt* to disguise; *vr* to dress in fancy costume, disguise oneself.

déguster [degyste] *vt* to taste, sample, sip.

dehors [dəɔːr] *ad* out(side); *nm* exterior, outside.

déjà [deʒa] *ad* already, before, by this time, as it is.

déjeuner [deʒœne] *vi* to breakfast, have lunch; *nm* lunch; **petit —** breakfast.

déjouer [deʒwe] *vt* to baffle, outwit, foil, thwart.

délabrement [delabrəmɑ̃] *nm* dilapidation, disrepair, ruin, decay.

délabrer [delabre] *vt* to pull to pieces, wreck; *vr* to fall into ruins, disrepair.

délacer [delase] *vt* to unlace; *vr* to come unlaced.

délai [delɛ] *nm* delay, notice, extension.

délaissement [delɛsmɑ̃] *nm* desertion, neglect, relinquishment.

délaisser [delɛse] *vt* to desert, forsake, relinquish.

délassement [delasmɑ̃] *nm* pastime, relaxation.

délasser [delase] *vt* to refresh; *vr* to take some relaxation.

délateur, -trice [delatœːr, tris] *n* informer.

délayer [delɛje] *vt* to dilute, water down, spin out.

délégation [delegasjɔ̃] *nf* delegation, assignment.

déléguer [delege] *vt* to depute, assign, delegate.

délester [delɛste] *vt* to unballast, relieve.

délibération [delibɛrasjɔ̃] *nf* deliberation, discussion, thought, resolution.

délibéré [delibere] *a* deliberate, purposeful.

délibérer [delibere] *vt* to discuss, think over; *vi* to deliberate, ponder.

délicat [delika] *a* delicate, dainty, fastidious, ticklish.

délicatesse [delikatɛs] *nf* delicacy, frailty, daintiness.

délice [delis] *nm* (*usu pl f*) delight, pleasure.

délicieux, -euse [delisjø, øːz] *a* delightful, delicious.

délié [delje] *a* slender, slim, shrewd.

délier [delje] *vt* to untie, unbind; *vr* to come loose.

délimiter [delimite] *vt* to mark the limits of, define.

délinquant [delɛ̃kɑ̃] *n* offender, delinquent.
délirant [delirɑ̃] *a* raving, frenzied, delirious.
délire [deli:r] *nm* frenzy, delirium.
délirer [delire] *vi* to rave, be delirious.
délit [deli] *nm* offense, misdemeanor.
délivrance [delivrɑ̃:s] *nf* deliverance.
délivrer [delivre] *vt* free, release; *vr* to rid oneself (of **de**).
déloger [delɔʒe] *vt* to dislodge, eject; *vi* to remove.
déloyal [delwajal] *a* unfaithful, false, unfair, unequal.
déloyauté [delwajote] *nf* unfaithfulness, treachery, dishonesty, disloyalty.
déluge [dely:ʒ] *nm* flood, deluge, downpour.
déluré [delyre] *a* wide-awake, cute, sly.
demain [dəmɛ̃] *ad* tomorrow; — **en huit** a week from tomorrow.
démailler [demɑje] *vr* to run (stocking).
demande [d(ə)mɑ̃:d] *nf* request, question, inquiry, application, indent.
demander [d(ə)mɑ̃de] *vt* to ask, ask for, apply for, request, sue; *vr* to wonder.
demandeur, -eresse [d(ə)mɑ̃dœ:r, ərɛs] *n* claimant, petitioner.
démanger [demɑ̃ʒe] *vi* to itch.
démanteler [demɑ̃tle] *vt* to dismantle.
démarcation [demarkasjɔ̃] *nf* demarcation.
démarche [demarʃ] *nf* walk, bearing, step, approach.
démarrage [demara:ʒ] *nm* unmooring, start-off.
démarrer [demare] *vt* to unmoor; *vi* to leave moorings, start off.
démarreur [demarœ:r] *nm* self-starter.
démasquer [demaske] *vt* to unmask, expose; *vr* to show one's true colors.
démêlé [demele] *nm* quarrel, tussle.
démêler [demele] *vt* to unravel, disentangle.
démembrer [demɑ̃bre] *vt* to dismember, partition.
déménagement [demenaʒmɑ̃] *nm* removal.
déménager [demenaʒe] *vi* to remove.
démence [demɑ̃:s] *nf* madness, insanity.
démener [demne] *vr* to struggle, make violent efforts.
démenti [demɑ̃ti] *nm* contradiction, denial, lie.
démentir [demɑ̃ti:r] *vt* to contradict, belie; *vr* to go back on one's word.
démesuré [demzyre] *a* huge, immoderate.
démettre [demɛtr] *vt* to dislocate; *vr* to resign.

demeurant [dəmœrɑ̃] *ad* **au** — after all, moreover.
demeure [dəmœ:r] *nf* abode dwelling.
demeurer [dəmœre] *vi* to dwell, live remain, stay
demi [dəmi] *a ad* half; *nm* half, half-back.
demi-finale [dəmifinal] *nf* semi-final.
demi-pensionnaire [dəmipɑ̃sjɔnɛ:r] *n* day-boarder.
demi-place [dəmiplas] *nf* half-fare, half-price.
demi-saison [dəmisɛzɔ̃] *nf* between-season.
démission [demisjɔ̃] *nf* resignation.
démissionner [demisjɔne] *vi* to resign.
demi-tour [dəmitu:r] *nm* **faire** — to turn back.
démobilisation [demɔbilizasjɔ̃] *nf* demobilization.
démobiliser [demɔbilize] *vt* to demobilize.
démocrate [demɔkrat] *a* democratic; *n* democrat.
démocratie [demɔkrasi] *nf* democracy.
démocratique [demɔkratik] *a* democratic.
démodé [demɔde] *a* old-fashioned, out-of-date.
démographie [demɔgrafi] *nf* demography.
demoiselle [dəmwazɛl] *nf* young lady, maiden, spinster; dragonfly, beetle; — **d'honneur** bridesmaid; — **de compagnie** lady companion.
démolir [demɔli:r] *vt* to pull down, demolish.
démon [demɔ̃] *nm* demon, fiend, devil, imp.
démonstration [demɔ̃strasjɔ̃] *nf* demonstration, proof.
démonté [demɔ̃te] *a* dismounted, stormy, flustered.
démonter [demɔ̃te] *vt* to unseat, take to pieces.
démontrer [demɔ̃tre] *vt* to demonstrate, prove.
démoralisateur, -trice [demɔralizatœ:r, tris] *a* demoralizing.
démoraliser [demɔralize] *vt* to demoralize, dishearten; *vr* to lose heart, be demoralized.
démordre [demɔrdr] *vi* to let go, give up; **en** — to climb down.
démuni [demyni] *a* short (of), without, out (of **de**).
dénaturé [denatyre] *a* unnatural, perverted.
dénaturer [denatyre] *vt* to falsify, pervert.
dénégation [denɛgasjɔ̃] *nf* denial.
dénicher [deniʃe] *vt* to remove from the nest, find, unearth; *vi* to forsake the nest.
dénigrement [denigrəmɑ̃] *nm* disparagement

dénigrer [denigre] *vt* to run down, disparage.

dénombrement [denɔ̃brəmɑ̃] *nm* enumeration, numbering, census.

dénommer [denɔme] *vt* to name.

dénoncer [denɔ̃se] *vt* to denounce, declare, inform against, squeal on.

dénonciateur, -trice [denɔ̃sjatœːr, tris] *a* tell-tale; *n* informer.

dénonciation [denɔ̃sjasjɔ̃] *nf* denunciation.

dénoter [denɔte] *vt* to denote, betoken.

dénouement [denumɑ̃] *nm* issue, end(ing), outcome.

dénouer [denwe] *vt* to untie, undo, unravel; *vr* to come loose, be unraveled.

denrée [dɑ̃re] *nf* commodity, foodstuff.

dense [dɑ̃ːs] *a* dense, thick.

densité [dɑ̃site] *nf* density, denseness.

dent [dɑ̃] *nf* tooth, prong, cog; **avoir une — contre qn** to bear s.o. a grudge; **à belles —s** with relish.

dentaire [dɑ̃tɛːr] *a* dental.

denté [dɑ̃te] *a* cogged.

denteler [dɑ̃tle] *vt* to indent, notch, serrate.

dentelle [dɑ̃tɛl] *nf* lace.

dentellerie [dɑ̃tɛlri] *nf* lace manufacture.

dentelure [dɑ̃tlyːr] *nf* indentation, serration.

dentier [dɑ̃tje] *nm* denture, set of false teeth.

dentifrice [dɑ̃tifris] *nm* toothpaste, -powder; **pâte —** toothpaste.

dentiste [dɑ̃tist] *nm* dentist.

dentition [dɑ̃tisjɔ̃] *nf* dentition, teething.

denture [dɑ̃tyːr] *nf* (set of) teeth (natural).

dénudation [denydasjɔ̃] *nf* laying bare, stripping.

dénudé [denyde] *a* bare, bleak.

dénuder [denyde] *vt* to lay bare, denude.

dénué [denɥe] *a* devoid (of **de**).

dénuement [denɥmɑ̃] *nm* destitution, distress, want.

dénuer [denɥe] *vt* to strip, divest; *vr* to part (with).

dépannage [depanaːʒ] *nm* running or emergency repairs; **équipe de —** wrecking crew.

dépanner [depane] *vt* to repair, help out.

dépaqueter [depakte] *vt* to unpack.

dépareillé [depareje] *a* odd, unmatched.

déparer [depare] *vt* to mar, spoil, disfigure.

départ [depaːr] *nm* departure, start (ing), difference.

départager [departaʒe] *vt* to decide between; **— les suffrages** to give the deciding vote.

département [departəmɑ̃] *nm* department, administrative subdivision.

départir [departiːr] *vt* to share out, divide, dispense; *vr* to depart (from **de**), part (with **de**).

dépasser [depase] *vt* to pass, surpass, exceed.

dépaysé [depe(j)ize] *a* out of one's element, strange.

dépayser [depe(j)ize] *vt* to bewilder, disconcert.

dépecer [depəse] *vt* to cut up, carve.

dépêche [depɛ(ː)ʃ] *nf* dispatch, telegram, wire.

dépêcher [depɛʃe] *vt* to dispatch; *vr* to hurry, hasten.

dépeigner [depɛɲe] *vt* to disarrange, ruffle s.o.'s hair.

dépeindre [depɛ̃ːdr] *vt* to depict, describe.

dépendance [depɑ̃dɑ̃ːs] *nf* dependence, appurtenance; *pl* outbuildings.

dépendant [depɑ̃dɑ̃] *a* dependent.

dépendre [depɑ̃ːdr] *vt* to take down; *vi* to depend, be answerable, hinge.

dépens [depɑ̃] *nm pl* cost, expense.

dépense [depɑ̃ːs] *nf* expenditure, outlay, expense, consumption, pantry.

dépenser [depɑ̃se] *vt* to spend, expend, consume, use up; *vr* to expend one's energies.

dépensier, -ière [depɑ̃sje, jɛːr] *a* extravagant.

dépérir [deperiːr] *vi* to pine away, decline, wilt.

dépérissement [deperismɑ̃] *nm* decline, decay.

dépêtrer [depɛtre] *vt* to extricate; *vr* to extricate oneself.

dépeupler [depœple] *vt* to depopulate, thin, empty.

dépiécer [depjese] *vt* to cut up, carve.

dépiècement [depjɛsmɑ̃] *nm* carving, dismemberment.

dépister [depiste] *vt* to run to earth, throw off the scent.

dépit [depi] *nm* spite, annoyance, vexation; **en — de** in spite of.

dépiter [depite] *vt* to annoy, spite.

déplacé [deplase] *a* out of place, incongruous, misplaced, uncalled for.

déplacement [deplasmɑ̃] *nm* displacing, moving, transfer; *pl* movements, journey.

déplacer [deplase] *vt* to displace, move, shift, transfer; *vr* to remove, move about, travel, shift.

déplaire [deplɛːr] *vt* to displease, offend; **ne vous en déplaise** with all due respect.

déplaisant [deplɛzɑ̃] *a* disagreeable, unpleasant.

déplaisir [deplɛziːr] *nm* displeasure, vexation, sorrow.

déplanter [deplɑ̃te] *vt* to lift (plant), transplant.

déplantoir [deplɑ̃twaːr] *nm* trowel.

déplier [deplie] *vtr* to unfold, open.
déplisser [deplise] *vt* to take out of its folds.
déploiement [deplwamã] *nm* unfolding, display, deployment.
déplorable [deplɔrabl] *a* lamentable.
déplorer [deplɔre] *vt* to deplore, bewail, mourn.
déployer [deplwaje] *vt* to unfold, spread out, display, deploy; *vr* to spread, deploy.
déplumer [deplyme] *vt* to pluck; *vr* to molt.
dépolir [depɔliːr] *vt* to take gloss off, frost (glass).
dépopulation [depɔpylasjɔ̃] *nf* depopulation.
déportements [depɔrtəmã] *nm pl* misconduct, excesses.
déporter [depɔrte] *vt* to deport.
déposant [depozã] *n* witness, depositor.
déposer [depoze] *vt* to lay down, deposit, lodge, drop; *vi* to testify, attest.
dépositaire [depɔziteːr] *n* trustee, sole agent.
déposition [depɔzisjɔ̃] *nf* testimony, evidence, attestation.
déposséder [depɔsede] *vt* to dispossess, strip.
dépossession [depɔsesjɔ̃] *nf* dispossessing.
dépôt [depo] *nm* deposit(ing), store, depot, warehouse, dump, coating.
dépouille [depuːj] *nf* skin, (earthly) remains, spoils, relics.
dépouiller [depuje] *vt* to skin, strip, plunder, rob; *vr* to cast its skin, rid oneself, shed; — **son courrier** to go through one's mail.
dépourvu [depurvy] *a* devoid, bereft; **pris au** — caught unawares.
dépravation [depravasjɔ̃] *nf* depravity,
dépraver [deprave] *vt* to deprave.
dépréciation [depresjasjɔ̃] *nf* depreciation, wear and tear, disparagement.
déprécier [depresje] *vt* to underrate, depreciate, disparage, cheapen.
déprédation [depredasjɔ̃] *nf* depredation, embezzlement.
dépression [depresjɔ̃] *nf* depression, fall, hollow, gloom, dejection.
déprimer [deprime] *vt* to depress; *vr* to become depressed.
depuis [dəpɥi] *prep* since, for, from; *ad* afterward, since then.
députation [depytasjɔ̃] *nf* deputation, deputing, membership in Parliament; **se présenter à la** — to stand for Parliament.
député [depyte] *n* deputy, Member of Parliament; **chambre des** —s parliament house.
députer [depyte] *vt* to depute, appoint as deputy.
déraciner [derasine] *vt* to uproot, root out, extirpate.

dérailler [deraje] *vi* to be derailed, run off rails; *vt* **faire** — to derail.
déraison [derɛzɔ̃] *nf* unreasonableness, folly.
déraisonnable [derɛzɔnabl] *a* unreasonable.
déraisonner [derɛzɔne] *vi* to talk nonsense.
dérangement [derãʒmã] *nm* disarrangement, disorder, derangement.
déranger [derãʒe] *vt* to disarrange, disturb, upset, derange; *vr* to move, inconvenience oneself, trouble.
dérapage [derapaːʒ] *nm* dragging anchor, skid.
déraper [derape] *vi* to drag its anchor, to skid.
dératé [derate] *a* spleened; **courir comme un** — to run like a hare.
derechef [dərəʃɛf] *ad* once again.
déréglé [deregle] *a* out of order, dissolute, inordinate.
dérèglement [derɛgləmã] *nm* disorder, irregularity, profligacy.
dérégler [deregle] *vt* to upset, disarrange, put out of order, unsettle; *vr* to get out of order, go wrong.
dérider [deride] *vt* to smoothe, remove wrinkles from, brighten up; *vr* to unbend.
dérision [derizjɔ̃] *nf* mockery, derision.
dérisoire [derizwaːr] *a* absurd, derisive, ridiculous.
dérivation [derivasjɔ̃] *nf* derivation, diversion, deflection, drift.
dérive [deriːv] *nf* drift, leeway; **à la** — adrift.
dériver [derive] *vt* to divert; *vi* to drift, be derived.
dernier, -ière [dɛrnje, jɛːr] *a* last, latter, latest, hindmost, utmost, extreme.
dernièrement [dɛrnjɛrmã] *ad* recently, lately.
dérobé [derɔbe] *a* secret; **à la** —e secretly, stealthily.
dérober [derɔbe] *vt* to steal, hide; *vr* to escape, hide, avoid, give way.
dérogatoire [derɔgatwaːr] *a* derogatory.
déroger [derɔʒe] *vi* to derogate, depart (from à), lose dignity.
dérouiller [deruje] *vt* to remove rust from, polish, brush up.
dérouler [derule] *vt* to unroll, uncoil, unfold; *vr* to unfold, stretch, spread, happen.
déroute [derut] *nf* rout, flight, downfall.
dérouter [derute] *vt* to lead astray, baffle, put off.
derrière [dɛrjeːr] *prep* behind, beyond; *ad* behind, astern, at the back, in the rear; *nm* back, rear, bottom.
des [de, dɛ] = **de** + **les**.
dès [dɛ] *prep* since, from; — **lors** from then; — **que** as soon as.

désabuser [dezabyze] *vt* to disillusion, undeceive.

désaccord [dezakɔ:r] *nm* disagreement, variance, clash.

désaccoutumer [dezakutyme] *vt* to break (s.o.) of a habit; *vr* to get out of the habit.

désaffecter [dezafɛkte] *vt* to put to another use, convert.

désaffection [dezafɛksjɔ̃] *nf* disaffection.

désagréable [dezagreabl] *a* unpleasant, offensive.

désagrégation [dezagregasjɔ̃] *nf* disintegration, breaking-up.

désagrément [dezagremɑ̃] *nm* source of irritation, vexatious incident.

désaltérer [dezaltere] *vt* to quench s.o.'s thirst; *vr* to quench one's thirst.

désappointer [dezapwɛte] *vt* to disappoint.

désapprendre [dezaprɑ̃:dr] *vt* to unlearn.

désapprobateur, -trice [dezaprɔbatœ:r, tris] *a* disapproving.

désapprobation [dezaprɔbasjɔ̃] *nf* disapprobation, disapproval.

désapprouver [dezapruve] *vt* to disapprove, frown upon.

désarçonner [dezarsɔne] *vt* to unseat, unsaddle.

désarmement [dezarməmɑ̃] *nm* disarming, disarmament, laying up.

désarmer [dezarme] *vt* to disarm, dismantle, lay up; *vi* to disarm, be disbanded.

désarroi [dezarwa] *nm* confusion, disorder.

désassocier [dezasɔsje] *vt* to dissociate; *vr* to dissociate o.s. (from de).

désassorti [dezasɔrti] *a* made up of odd bits.

désastre [dezastr] *nm* disaster, calamity, catastrophe.

désastreux, -euse [dezastrø, ø:z] *a* disastrous.

désavantage [dezavɑ̃ta:ʒ] *nm* handicap.

désavantager [dezavɑ̃taʒe] *vt* to mar, handicap, put at a disadvantage.

désavantageux, -euse [dezavɑ̃taʒø, ø:z] *a* detrimental, disadvantageous.

désaveu [dezavø] *nm* denial, disavowal.

désavouer [dezavwe] *vt* to repudiate, disown, disclaim.

désceller [desɛle] *vt* to unseal, open, loosen.

descendant [dɛsɑ̃dɑ̃] *a* descending, downward; *n* descendant, offspring.

descendre [dɛsɑ̃:dr] *vt* to go down, carry down, bring down; *vi* to descend, go down, alight, dismount; **— en panne** to come down with engine trouble; **— à un hôtel** to put up at a hotel.

descente [dɛsɑ̃:t] *nf* descent,

declivity, swoop, raid; **— de lit** rug.

descriptible [deskriptibl] *a* describable.

descriptif, -ive [deskriptif, i:v] *a* descriptive.

description [deskripsjɔ̃] *nf* description.

désemballer [dezɑ̃bale] *vt* to unpack.

désemparé [dezɑ̃pare] *a* helpless, crippled, in distress.

désemparer [dezɑ̃pare] *vt* to disable, disjoint; **sans —** without stopping.

désencombrer [dezɑ̃kɔ̃bre] *vt* to clear, free.

désenfler [dezɑ̃fle] *vt* to reduce the swelling of; *vi* to become less swollen, go down.

désengager [dezɑ̃gaʒe] *vt* to release, free, take out of pawn.

désengrener [dezɑ̃grəne] *vt* to put out of gear, disengage.

désenivrer [dezɑ̃nivre] *vt* to sober; *vr* to come to one's senses.

désenterrer [dezɑ̃tɛre] *vt* to disinter, dig up.

déséquilibrer [dezekilibre] *vt* to throw off balance, unbalance.

désert [dezɛ:r] *a* lonely, empty, deserted, bleak; *nm* desert, wilderness

déserter [dezɛrte] *vt* to desert, abandon; *vi* to desert.

déserteur [dezɛrtœ:r] *nm* deserter.

désertion [dezɛrsjɔ̃] *nf* desertion, running away.

désespérance [dezɛsperɑ̃:s] *nf* despair.

désespérant [dezɛsperɑ̃] *a* hopeless, heartbreaking.

désespéré [dezɛspere] *a* desperate, hopeless.

désespérer [dezɛspere] *vt* to drive to despair; *vi* to despair; *vr* to be in despair.

désespoir [dezɛspwa:r] *nm* despair, despondency.

déshabillé [dezabije] *nm* negligee.

déshabiller [dezabije] *vtr* to undress.

déshabituer [dezabitɥe] *vt* to break s.o. of the habit; *vr* to get out of the habit.

déshériter [dezerite] *vt* to disinherit.

déshonnête [dezɔnɛ:t] *a* immodest, improper, indecent.

déshonnêteté [dezɔnɛtəte] *nf* impropriety.

déshonneur [dezɔnœ:r] *nm* dishonor, disgrace.

déshonorer [dezɔnɔre] *vt* to dishonor, disgrace.

déshydrater [dezidrate] *vt* dehydrate.

désignation [deziɲasjɔ̃] *nf* designation, appointment, choice, description.

désigner [deziɲe] *vt* to appoint, designate, show, fix, detail, post, draft.

désillusion [dezillyzjɔ̃] *nf* disillusion.

désillusionner [dezillyzjɔne] *vt* to disillusion.
désinfectant [dezɛ̃fɛktɑ̃] *nm* disinfectant.
désinfection [dezɛ̃fɛksjɔ̃] *nf* disinfection, decontamination.
désinfecter [dezɛ̃fɛkte] *vt* to disinfect, decontaminate.
désintégrer [dezɛ̃tegre] *vt* to disintegrate, split.
désintéressé [dezɛ̃terɛse] *a* disinterested, unselfish, selfless.
désintéressement [dezɛ̃terɛsmɑ̃] *nm* disinterestedness, unselfishness.
désintéresser [dezɛ̃terɛse] *vr* to lose interest, take no interest (**de** in).
désinvolte [dezɛ̃vɔlt] *a* free, offhand, flippant.
désinvolture [dezɛ̃vɔltyːr] *nf* unselfconsciousness, ease, airy manner, flippancy; **avec —** airily, flippantly.
désir [deziːr] *nm* desire, wish, longing.
désirable [dezirabl] *a* desirable.
désirer [dezire] *vt* to desire, want, long for.
désireux, -euse [dezirø, øːz] *a* desirous, anxious.
désobéir [dezɔbeiːr] *vti* to disobey.
désobéissance [dezɔbeisɑ̃s] *nf* disobedience.
désobligeance [dezɔbliʒɑ̃s] *nf* ungraciousness, disagreeableness.
désobliger [dezɔbliʒe] *vt* to disoblige, offend.
désobstruer [dezɔpstrye] *vt* to clear, free.
désœuvré [dezœvre] *a* idle, at loose ends.
désœuvrement [dezœvrəmɑ̃] *nm* idleness; **par —** for want of something to do.
désolant [dezɔlɑ̃] *a* distressing, grievous.
désolation [dezɔlasjɔ̃] *nf* desolation, grief.
désolé [dezɔle] *a* desolate, dreary, grieved; **je suis —** I am very sorry.
désoler [dezɔle] *vt* to ravage, grieve, distress.
désopilant [dezɔpilɑ̃] *a* screamingly funny.
désordonné [dezɔrdɔne] *a* disordered, untidy, dissolute.
désordre [dezɔrdr] *nm* confusion, disorder, untidiness, disturbance.
désorganisation [dezɔrganizasjɔ̃] *nf* disorganization, disarrangement.
désorganiser [dezɔrganize] *vt* to disorganize.
désorienter [dezɔrjɑ̃te] *vt* to put s.o. off his bearings, bewilder; *vr* to lose one's bearings, get lost.
désormais [dezɔrmɛ] *ad* henceforward, from now on.
désosser [dezose] *vt* to bone.
despote [despɔt] *nm* despot.
despotisme [despɔtism] *nm* despotism.
dessaisir [desɛziːr] *vt* to dispossess;

se **— de** to give up, relinquish.
dessaler [desale] *vt* to remove salt from, teach s.o. a thing or two.
se **dessécher** [sədeseʃe] *vr* to dry, wither; *vt* parch.
dessein [desɛ̃] *nm* plan, design, purpose, intention; **à —** intentionally.
desseller [desele] *vt* to unsaddle.
desserrer [desɛre] *vt* to loosen, slacken, release; *vr* to come loose, slacken, relax.
dessert [desɛːr] *nm* dessert.
desservant [desɛrvɑ̃] *nm* officiating priest.
desservir [desɛrviːr] *vt* to clear (away), serve, connect.
dessin [desɛ̃] *nm* drawing, sketch, cartoon, design.
dessinateur, -trice [desinatœːr, tris] *n* designer, draftsman, black and white artist.
dessiner [desine] *vt* to draw, design, plan, outline; *vr* to stand out, be outlined.
dessouler [desule] *vt* to sober; *vi* to become sober.
dessous [dəsu] *ad* below, underneath, under it, them; **regarder qn en —** to look furtively at s.o.; **avoir le —** to get the worst of it; *nm* bottom, underside; *pl* seamy side.
dessus [dəsy] *ad* above, over, on it, them, above it, them; *nm* top, upper side, advantage; **avoir le —** to have the best of it; **— d'assiette** doily; **— de lit** bedspread; **— du panier** the pick of the crop.
destin [dɛstɛ̃] *nm* destiny, fate.
destinataire [dɛstinatɛːr] *n* addressee, payee.
destination [dɛstinasjɔ̃] *nf* destination; **à — de** bound for.
destinée [dɛstine] *nf* fate, destiny, fortune.
destiner [dɛstine] *vt* to destine, intend, mean; *vr* to aim, intend to be; **être destiné à** to be fated to.
destituer [dɛstitɥe] *vt* to dismiss, remove.
destitution [dɛstitysjɔ̃] *nf* dismissal.
destructeur, -trice [dɛstryktœːr, tris] *a* destructive; *n* destroyer.
destructif, -ive [dɛstryktif, iːv] *a* destructive.
destruction [dɛstryksjɔ̃] *nf* destruction.
désuet, -uète [desɥɛ, ɛt] *a* obsolete, out-of-date.
désuétude [desɥetyd] *nf* disuse, abeyance.
désunion [dezynjɔ̃] *nf* disunion, separation, breach.
désunir [dezyniːr] *vtr* to disunite.
détaché [detaʃe] *a* loose, detached, unconcerned.
détachement [detaʃmɑ̃] *nm* detaching, detachment, indifference, contingent, draft.

détacher [detaʃe] *vt* to detach, unfasten, untie, disaffect, detail, draft, remove stains from; *vr* to come loose, come off, stand out.

détail [detaːj] *nm* detail, retail; **vente au — retail selling.**

détailler [detaje] *vt* to retail, detail, divide up, look over, appraise.

détaler [detale] *vi* to clear out, scamper off, bolt.

détartrer [detartre] *vt* to scale, fur.

détection [deteksjɔ̃] *nf* detection.

détective [detektiːv] *nm* detective.

déteindre [detɛ̃ːdr] *vt* to take the color out of; *vir* to fade, run; *vi* to influence.

dételer [detle] *vt* to unyoke, unharness.

détendre [detɑ̃ːdr] *vtr* to slacken, loosen, relax.

détenir [detniːr] *vt* to hold, detain, withhold.

détente [detɑ̃ːt] *nf* slackening, relaxation, trigger.

détenteur, -trice [detɑ̃tœːr, tris] *n* holder.

détention [detɑ̃sjɔ̃] *nf* detention.

détérioration [deterjɔrasjɔ̃] *nf* damage, wear and tear.

détériorer [deterjɔre] *vt* to damage, spoil; *vr* to deteriorate.

détermination [determinasjɔ̃] *nf* determination.

déterminé [determine] *a* determined, definite.

déterminer [determine] *vt* to determine, fix, bring about, decide; *vr* to make up one's mind.

déterrer [detere] *vt* to dig up, unearth, find out.

détestable [detɛstabl] *a* wretched, hateful.

détester [detɛste] *vt* to hate, loathe, dislike.

détonateur [detɔnatœːr] *nm* detonator, fog-signal.

détonation [detɔnasjɔ̃] *nf* detonation, report.

détoner [detɔne] *vi* to detonate, bang.

détonner [detɔne] *vi* to be out of tune, jar.

détour [detuːr] *nm* turning, winding, curve, bend, roundabout way.

détourné [deturne] *a* circuitous, devious.

détournement [deturnəmɑ̃] *nm* diversion, embezzlement, abduction.

détourner [deturne] *vt* to divert, avert, ward off, abduct, alienate, embezzle; *vr* to turn aside.

détracteur, -trice [detraktœːr, tris] *n* detractor.

détraquement [detrakmɑ̃] *nm* breakdown.

détraquer [detrake] *vt* to put out of order; *vr* to break down.

détrempe [detrɑ̃ːp] *nf* distemper, wash.

détremper [detrɑ̃pe] *vt* to soak, soften.

détresse [detrɛs] *nf* distress, misery,

détriment [detrimɑ̃] *nm* detriment, prejudice, loss.

détritus [detrityːs] *nm* detritus, refuse.

détroit [detrwa] *nm* strait(s), channel, pass.

détromper [detrɔ̃pe] *vt* put right, enlighten, *vr* **détrompez-vous!** get that out of your head!

détrôner [detrone] *vt* to dethrone.

détrousser [detruse] *vt* to let down, rob.

détruire [detrɥiːr] *vt* to destroy, overthrow, demolish.

dette [dɛt] *nf* debt, indebtedness, duty.

deuil [dœːj] *nm* mourning, grief, bereavement.

deux [dø] *a* two, second; *nm* two, deuce.

deuxième [døzjɛm] *an* second.

dévaler [devale] *vti* to rush down; *vi* to slope, descend, rush down.

dévaliser [devalize] *vt* to rob, rifle, plunder.

dévaluer [devalɥe] *vt* to devaluate.

devancer [d(ə)vɑ̃se] *vt* to go before, precede, forestall.

devancier, -ière [d(ə)vɑ̃sje, jɛːr] *n* predecessor.

devant [d(ə)vɑ̃] *prep* before, in front of, in face of; *ad* ahead, in front; *nm* front; **prendre les —s sur** to steal a march on.

devanture [d(ə)vɑ̃tyːr] *nf* front, shop window.

dévastateur, -trice [devastatœːr, tris] *a* damaging, devastating; *n* ravager.

dévastation [devastasjɔ̃] *nf* devastation, havoc.

dévaster [devaste] *vt* to lay waste, devastate, gut.

déveine [devɛn] *nf* bad luck.

développement [devlɔpmɑ̃] *nm* development, growth, expansion.

développer [devlɔpe] *vt* to develop, expand, enlarge (upon); *vr* to develop, expand.

devenir [dəvniːr] *vi* to become, get, grow; **qu'est-il devenu?** what has become of him?

dévergondage [devɛrgɔ̃daːʒ] *nm* shamelessness.

dévergondé [devɛrgɔ̃de] *a* shameless, profligate.

déverrouiller [devɛruje] *vt* to unbolt.

dévers [devɛr] *a* leaning, warped, out of plumb; *nm* slope, warp, banking.

déversement [devɛrs(ə)mɑ̃] *nm* overflow, tipping.

déverser [devɛrse] *vt* to slant, incline, pour, dump; *vi* to lean, get out of true line.

dévêtir [devɛtiːr] *vt* to strip, undress, take off; *vr* to undress, divest oneself.

déviation [devjasjɔ̃] *nf* deviation,

deflexion, departure, (*road*) detour.
dévider [devide] *vt* to unwind, reel, pay out.
dévidoir [devidwaːr] *nm* reel, drum, winder.
dévier [devje] *vt* to turn aside, deflect; *vi* to swerve, deviate.
deviner [dəvine] *vt* to guess, foretell, make out.
devinette [dəvinɛt] *nf* conundrum, riddle.
devis [dəvi] *nm* estimate.
dévisager [devisaʒe] *vt* to stare at.
devise [dəviːz] *nf* device, slogan, currency, bill.
dévisser [devise] *vt* to unscrew.
dévoiler [devwale] *vt* to unveil, disclose, reveal.
devoir [dəvwaːr] *vt* to owe, be indebted, have to, be obliged to, must, ought, should; *nm* duty, task, exercise.
dévolu [devɔly] *a* devolving, devolved; *nm* **jeter son — sur** to choose.
dévorer [devɔre] *vt* to devour, eat up, consume.
dévot [devo] *an* devout, religious (person).
dévotion [devosjɔ̃] *nf* piety, devotion.
dévoué [devwe] *a* devoted, sincere, loyal.
dévouement [devumɑ̃] *nm* devotion, devotedness, self-sacrifice.
dévouer [devwe] *vt* to devote, dedicate; *vr* to devote oneself, sacrifice oneself.
dévoyer [devwaje] *vtr* to lead astray, go off the rails.
dextérité [dɛksterite] *nf* dexterity, skill.
diabète [djabɛt] *nm* diabetes.
diabétique [djabetik] *an* diabetic.
diable [djɑːbl] *nm* devil; **allez au —!** go to hell!
diablerie [djɑbləri] *nf* deviltry, witchcraft, mischievousness, turbulence.
diablotin [djɑblɔtɛ̃] *nm* imp, cracker.
diabolique [djabɔlik] *a* diabolical, fiendish.
diaconesse [djakɔnɛs] *nf* deaconess.
diacre [djakr] *nm* deacon.
diadème [djadɛm] *nm* diadem.
diagnostic [djagnɔstik] *nm* diagnosis.
diagnostiquer [djagnɔstike] *vt* to diagnose.
diagonal [djagɔnal] *a* diagonal.
dialecte [djalɛkt] *nm* dialect.
dialogue [djalɔg] *nm* dialogue.
diamant [djamɑ̃] *nm* diamond.
diamètre [djamɛtr] *nm* diameter.
diane [djan] *nf* reveille.
diantre [djɑ̃ːtr] *excl* well!
diapason [djapazɔ̃] *nm* tuning fork, diapason, range.
diaphane [djafan] *a* diaphanous, transparent.
diaphragme [djafragm] *nm* diaphragm, sound-box.

diapré [djapre] *a* mottled, speckled, variegated.
dictateur [diktatœːr] *nm* dictator.
dictature [diktatyːr] *nf* dictatorship.
dictée [dikte] *nf* dictation.
dicter [dikte] *vt* to dictate.
diction [diksjɔ̃] *nf* diction, elocution.
dictionnaire [diksjɔnɛːr] *nm* dictionary.
dicton [diktɔ̃] *nm* saying, proverb, maxim.
dièse [djɛːz] *nm* (*mus*) sharp.
diète [djɛt] *nf* diet, regimen.
dieu [djø] *nm* god; *excl* goodness!
diffamation [diffamasjɔ̃] *nf* slander, libel.
diffamatoire [diffamatwaːr] *a* slanderous, defamatory, libelous.
diffamer [diffame] *vt* to defame, slander.
différence [difɛrɑ̃ːs] *nf* difference, distinction, discrepancy, gap.
différend [difɛrɑ̃] *nm* difference, dispute.
différent [difɛrɑ̃] *a* different, unlike, various.
différentiel, -ielle [difɛrɑ̃sjɛl] *a nm* differential.
différer [difere] *vt* to put off, postpone; *vi* to differ, put off.
difficile [difisil] *a* difficult, hard, hard to please.
difficilement [difisilmɑ̃] *ad* with difficulty.
difficulté [difikylte] *nf* difficulty; **faire des —s** to be fussy, raise difficulties.
difforme [difɔrm] *a* deformed, shapeless.
difformité [difɔrmite] *nf* deformity.
diffus [dify] *a* diffuse, wordy, diffused.
diffuser [difyze] *vt* to diffuse.
diffusion [difyzjɔ̃] *nf* spreading, broadcasting.
digérer [diʒere] *vt* to digest, assimilate.
digestible [diʒestibl] *a* digestible.
digestif, -ive [diʒestif] *a* digestive.
digestion [diʒestjɔ̃] *nf* digestion, assimilation.
digital, -ale, -aux [diʒital, al, o] *a* **empreinte —** fingerprint; *nf* foxglove, digitalis.
digne [diɲ] *a* worthy, stately, dignified, deserving.
dignitaire [diɲitɛːr] *nm* dignitary.
dignité [diɲite] *nf* dignity, nobility, greatness.
digression [digrɛsjɔ̃] *nf* digression.
digue [dig] *nf* dike, sea-wall, embankment, dam.
dilapider [dilapide] *vt* to waste, squander, embezzle.
dilater [dilate] *vtr* to dilate, expand, distend.
dilemme [dilɛm] *nm* dilemma.
diligence [diliʒɑ̃ːs] *nf* application, industry, haste; stage-coach.
diligent [diliʒɑ̃] *a* busy.

diluer [dilɥe] *vt* to dilute, water down.

dimanche [dimɑ̃:ʃ] *nm* Sunday.

dimension [dimɑ̃sjɔ̃] *nf* size; *pl* measurements.

diminuer [diminɥe] *vt* to diminish, lessen, reduce; *vi* to decrease, abate.

diminution [diminysjɔ̃] *nf* decrease, reduction.

dinde [dɛ̃:d] *nf* turkey-hen.

dindon [dɛ̃dɔ̃] *nm* turkey-cock.

dîner [dine] *vi* to dine; *nm* dinner (party).

dîneur, -euse [dinœ:r, ø:z] *n* diner.

diocèse [djɔsɛ:z] *nm* diocese.

dioula [diula] *nm* itinerant peddler.

diphtérie [difteri] *nf* diphtheria.

diplomate [diplɔmat] *nm* diplomat (ist).

diplomatie [diplɔmasi] *nf* diplomacy, diplomatic service.

diplomatique [diplɔmatik] *a* diplomatic.

diplôme [diplo:m] *nm* diploma, certificate.

diplômé [diplome] *a* certificated.

dire [di:r] *vt* to say, tell, speak; *nm* statement, words; **dites donc!** look here!; **ce vin ne me dit rien** I don't care for this wine; **et — que** and to think that; **que dites-vous de cela?** what do you think of that?

direct [dirɛkt] *a* direct, straight, pointed, flat.

directeur, -trice [dirɛktœ:r, tris] *a* guiding, controlling; *n* chief, leader, manager, manageress, headmaster, headmistress, superintendent.

direction [dirɛksjɔ̃] *nf* direction, management, guidance, leadership, steering.

directives [dirɛkti:v] *nf pl* guidelines.

dirigeant [diriʒɑ̃] *a* directing, guiding, governing.

dirigeable [diriʒabl] *nm* airship.

diriger [diriʒe] *vt* to direct, manage, conduct, guide, steer, point; *vr* to make one's way, proceed.

discernement [disɛrnəmɑ̃] *nm* discernment, discrimination.

discerner [disɛrne] *vt* to discern, descry, distinguish.

disciple [disipl] *nm* disciple, follower.

discipline [disiplin] *nf* discipline, order.

discipliner [disipline] *vt* to discipline.

discontinuer [diskɔ̃tinɥe] *vt* to discontinue, leave off, break off.

disconvenance [diskɔ̃vnɑ̃:s] *nf* disparity, unsuitableness.

disconvenir [diskɔ̃vni:r] *vi* to be unsuitable, deny.

discordance [diskɔrdɑ̃:s] *nf* disagreement, clash.

discordant [diskɔrdɑ̃] *a* harsh, grating, clashing.

discorde [diskɔrd] *nf* strife, lack of unity.

discourir [diskuri:r] *vi* to talk

volubly, hold forth, discourse.

discours [disku:r] *nm* discourse, speech, talk.

discourtois [diskurtwa] *a* impolite, discourteous.

discrédit [diskredi] *nm* disrepute.

discréditer [diskredite] *vt* to discredit, disparage, bring into disrepute.

discret, -ète [diskrɛ, ɛt] *a* discreet, unobtrusive.

discrétion [diskresjɔ̃] *nf* restraint.

discriminer [diskrimine] *vt* to discriminate.

disculper [diskylpe] *vt* to exonerate, clear.

discussion [diskysjɔ̃] *nf* argument, debate.

discutable [diskytabl] *a* debatable, disputable.

discuter [diskyte] *vt* to discuss, talk over, question.

disette [dizɛt] *nf* want, scarcity, dearth.

diseur, -euse [dizœ:r, ø:z] *n* **— de bonne aventure** fortune-teller.

disgrâce [disgrɑ:s] *nf* disfavor, misfortune.

disgracieux, -euse [disgrasjø, ø:z] *a* ungraceful, awkward, ungracious.

disjoindre [disʒwɛ̃:dr] *vt* to sever, disjoin.

dislocation [dislɔkasjɔ̃] *nf* dislocation, dismemberment.

disloquer [dislɔke] *vt* to dislocate, dismember; *vr* to fall apart, break up.

disparaître [dispare:tr] *vi* to disappear, vanish.

disparate [disparat] *a* unlike, illassorted.

disparition [disparisjɔ̃] *nf* disappearance.

dispendieux, -euse [dispɑ̃djø, ø:z] *a* expensive.

dispensaire [dispɑ̃sɛ:r] *nm* dispensary, out-patients' department.

dispensation [dispɑ̃sasjɔ̃] *nf* dispensing.

dispense [dispɑ̃:s] *nf* dispensation, exemption.

dispenser [dispɑ̃se] *vt* to dispense, distribute, excuse, exempt; *vr* to get exempted (from **de**), get out (of **de**).

disperser [dispɛrse] *vtr* to scatter, disperse.

dispersion [dispɛrsjɔ̃] *nf* scattering, dispersal.

disponibilité [dispɔnibilite] *nf* availability; *pl* available funds; **être en — to** be on half-pay.

disponible [dispɔnibl] *a* available.

dispos [dispo] *a* fit, bright, well.

disposé [dispoze] *a* disposed, agreeable, ready; **être bien (mal) — to** be in a good (bad) temper.

disposer [dispoze] *vt* to arrange, array, set out, incline; *vr* to get ready; **— de** to have at one's disposal.

dispositif [dispɔzitif] *nm* apparatus, gadget.

disposition [dispɔzisjɔ̃] *nf* disposition, disposal, arrangement, tendency; *pl* natural gift, provisions.

disproportion [disprɔpɔrsjɔ̃] *nf* lack of proportion.

disproportionné [disprɔpɔrsjɔne] *a* disproportionate, out of proportion.

disputailler [dispytaje] *vi* to cavil, bicker.

dispute [dispyt] *nf* dispute, squabble.

disputer [dispyte] *vt* to discuss, argue about, dispute, challenge; *vi* to quarrel; *vr* to argue, wrangle, contend for.

disqualifier [diskalifje] *vt* to disqualify.

disque [disk] *nm* discus, disc, phonograph record.

dissemblable [di(s)sãblabl] *a* unlike, dissimilar.

dissemblance [dis(s)ãblã:s] *nf* unlikeness, dissimilarity.

disséminer [dis(s)emine] *vt* to scatter, spread.

dissension [dis(s)ãsjɔ̃] *nf* dissension, discord.

dissentiment [dis(s)ãtimã] *nm* dissent, disagreement.

disséquer [dis(s)eke] *vt* to dissect.

dissertation [disɛrtasjɔ̃] *nf* essay, composition.

disserter [disɛrte] *vi* to dissert, expatiate.

dissident [dis(s)idã] *a* dissentient, dissident.

dissimulateur, -trice [dis(s)imylatœ:r, tris] *n* dissembler; *a* deceitful.

dissimulation [dis(s)imylasjɔ̃] *nf* deceit, dissimulation, hiding.

dissimuler [dis(s)imyle] *vt* to dissimulate, conceal, disguise; *vr* to hide.

dissipation [disipasjɔ̃] *nf* dissipation, dispersion, wasting, dissolute conduct, inattentiveness.

dissipé [disipe] *a* dissipated, giddy, inattentive.

dissiper [disipe] *vt* to dissipate, dispel, waste, divert; *vr* to disappear, be dispelled, clear, become dissolute.

dissolu [dis(s)ɔly] *a* profligate, abandoned, dissolute.

dissolution [dis(s)ɔlysjɔ̃] *nf* disintegration, dissolving, breaking-up, solution.

dissoudre [dis(s)udr] *vtr* to dissolve, break up.

dissuader [dis(s)ɥade] *vt* to dissuade, talk out of.

distance [distã:s] *nf* distance, range.

distancer [distãse] *vt* to outdistance, outstrip.

distant [distã] *a* distant, aloof.

distillateur [distilatœ:r] *nm* distiller.

distillation [distilasjɔ̃] *nf* distillation, distilling.

distiller [distile] *vt* to distil, drop.

distillerie [distilri] *nf* distillery.

distinct [distɛ̃(:kt)] *a* distinct, clear audible.

distinctif, -ive [distɛ̃ktif, i:v] *a* distinctive.

distinction [distɛ̃ksjɔ̃] *nf* distinction, honor, distinguished air.

distingué [distɛ̃ge] *a* eminent, distinguished.

distinguer [distɛ̃ge] *vt* to distinguish, discriminate, characterize, perceive, bring to notice; *vr* to distinguish oneself, be distinguishable.

distraction [distraksjɔ̃] *nf* separation, distraction, absent-mindedness, entertainment.

distraire [distrɛ:r] *vt* to separate, distract, take one's mind off, amuse, entertain; *vr* to amuse oneself.

distrait [distrɛ] *a* absent-minded, listless.

distribuer [distribɥe] *vt* to distribute, apportion, share out, hand out, deliver; **— les rôles** to cast a play.

distributeur, -trice [distribytœ:r, tris] *n* dispenser, distributor; **— automatique** slot-machine.

distribution [distribysjɔ̃] *nf* distribution, issue, allotting, delivery; **— des prix** prize-giving; **— des rôles** cast(ing).

dit [di] *a* called, named; **autrement —** alias, in other words.

divagation [divagasjɔ̃] *nf* deviation, wandering.

divaguer [divage] *vi* to deviate, wander, rave.

divan [divã] *nm* couch.

divergence [divɛrʒã:s] *nf* divergence, spread.

diverger [divɛrʒe] *vi* to diverge.

divers [divɛ:r] *a* various, sundry, divers, different, diverse; *nm pl* sundries.

diversion [divɛrsjɔ̃] *nf* diversion, change.

diversité [divɛrsite] *nf* variety, diversity.

divertir [divɛrti:r] *vt* to entertain, divert; *vr* to amuse oneself.

divertissement [divɛrtismã] *nm* recreation, entertainment, diversion.

dividende [dividã:d] *nm* dividend.

divin [divɛ̃] *a* divine, sacred, heavenly, sublime.

divinateur, -trice [divinatœ:r, tris] *n* soothsayer.

divinité [divinite] *nf* divinity, deity.

diviser [divize] *vt* to divide; *vr* to divide, break up.

diviseur [divizœ:r] *nm* divisor.

divisible [divizibl] *a* divisible.

division [divizjɔ̃] *nf* division, section, dissension.

divorce [divɔrs] *nm* divorce.

divorcer [divɔrse] *vti* to divorce.

divulgation [divylgasjɔ̃] *nf* disclosure.

divulguer [divylge] *vt* to divulge, disclose, reveal.

dix [dis] *a nm* ten, tenth.

dixième [dizjɛm] *a nm* tenth.

dizaine [dizɛn] *nf* (about) ten.

docile [dɔsil] *a* compliant, manageable.

docilité [dɔsilite] *nf* docility.

dock [dɔk] dock(s), warehouse.

docte [dɔkt] *a* learned.

docteur [dɔktœːr] *nm* doctor.

doctoral [dɔktɔral] *a* doctoral, pompous.

doctorat [dɔktɔra] *nm* doctorate.

doctrine [dɔktrin] *nf* doctrine, belief, teaching.

document [dɔkymɑ̃] *nm* document.

documentaire [dɔkymɑ̃tɛːr] *a* documentary.

documentation [dɔkymɑ̃tasjɔ̃] *nf* gathering of facts.

documenter [dɔkymɑ̃te] *vt* to document, give information to; *vr* to collect material, information.

dodeliner [dɔdline] *vti* to dandle, nod, shake.

dodo [dɔdo] *nm* sleep; **faire — to** go to sleep, to go bye-bye.

dodu [dɔdy] *a* plump.

dogme [dɔgm] *nm* dogma.

dogue [dɔg] *nm* mastiff.

doigt [dwa] *nm* finger; **— de pied** toe.

doigté [dwate] *nm* tact, (*mus*) fingering.

doigtier [dwatje] *nm* finger-stall.

doit [dwa] *nm* debit.

doléances [dɔleɑ̃ːs] *nf pl* grievances, sorrows.

dolent [dɔlɑ̃] *a* doleful.

domaine [dɔmɛn] *nm* domain, estate, province, field.

dôme [doːm] *nm* dome.

domesticité [dɔmɛstisite] *nf* domesticity, staff of servants.

domestique [dɔmɛstik] *a* domestic; *n* servant.

domicile [dɔmisil] *nm* abode, residence.

domicilié [dɔmisilje] *a* residing, resident.

domicilier [dɔmisilje] *vr* to settle, take up residence.

dominance [dɔminɑ̃ːs] *nf* dominion, predominance.

dominant [dɔminɑ̃] *a* ruling, (pre) dominant.

dominateur, -trice [dɔminatœːr, tris] *a* domineering.

domination [dɔminasjɔ̃] *nf* rule, sway.

dominer [dɔmine] *vt* to dominate, rule, master, control, overlook; *vi* to rule.

domino [dɔmino] *nm* hood, domino.

dommage [dɔmaːʒ] *nm* harm, injury, pity; *pl* damage, destruction; **dommages et intérêts** damages (*in law*).

dompter [dɔ̃te] *vt* to tame, break in, master.

dompteur, -euse [dɔ̃tœːr, øːz] *n* tamer, trainer.

don [dɔ̃] *nm* donation, giving, gift, present, talent.

donateur, -trice [dɔnatœːr, tris] *n* donor, giver.

donc [dɔ̃ːk] *cj* so, therefore, then; *ad* well, just, ever.

donjon [dɔ̃ʒɔ̃] *nm* (*of castle*) keep.

donne [dɔn] *nf* (*card games*) deal.

donnée [dɔne] *nf* fundamental idea; *pl* data.

donner [dɔne] *vt* to give, furnish, yield, ascribe, deal; *vi* to look out (sur on to); **— dans** to have a taste for, fall into; **s'en — à cœur joie** to have a high old time; **c'est donné** it's dirt cheap.

dont [dɔ̃] *pr* of (by, from, with, about) whom or which, whose.

doré [dɔre] *a* gilt, golden.

dorénavant [dɔrenavɑ̃] *ad* henceforth.

dorer [dɔre] *vt* to gild, brown.

dorloter [dɔrlɔte] *vt* to cuddle, pet, coddle, pamper.

dormant [dɔrmɑ̃] *a* dormant, sleeping, stagnant.

dormeur, -euse [dɔrmœːr, øːz] *n* sleeper, sleepy-head.

dormir [dɔrmiːr] *vi* to sleep, be asleep, be stagnant, lie dormant.

dortoir [dɔrtwaːr] *nm* dormitory.

dorure [dɔryːr] *nf* gilt, gilding.

dos [do] *nm* back, bridge.

dose [doːz] *nf* dose, amount.

doser [doze] *vt* to dose, decide the amount of.

dossier [dɔsje] *nm* (*of chair*) back; record, documents, brief.

dot [dɔt] *nf* dowry.

doter [dɔte] *vt* to give a dowry to, endow.

douaire [dwɛːr] *nm* marriage settlement, dower.

douane [dwan] *nf* customs, custom-house, duty; **en — in** bond.

douanier, -ière [dwanje, jɛːr] *a* customs; *n* customs-officer.

double [dubl] *a* double, twofold; *nm* double, duplicate.

doubler [duble] *vt* to double, fold in two, line, overtake, quicken; **— une classe** to repeat a class; **— un rôle** to understudy a part; **— le cap** to get out of a scrape.

doublure [dublyːr] *nf* lining, understudy.

doucement [dusmɑ̃] *ad* gently, quietly, smoothly.

doucereux, -euse [dusrø, øːz] *a* sweetish, cloying, glib, sugary.

douceur [dusœːr] *nf* sweetness, smoothness, gentleness, softness, mildness; *pl* comforts, sweets.

douche [duʃ] *nf* shower-bath, douche.

doué [dwe] *a* gifted, endowed.

douer [dwe] *vt* to endow.

douille [duːj] *nf* case, casing, socket, sleeve.

douillet, -ette [dujɛ, ɛt] *a* soft, cosy, delicate, tender.

douleur [dulœːr] *nf* suffering, pain, grief, sorrow.

douloureux, -euse [dulurø, øːz] *a* painful, aching, sad, sorrowful, grievous.

doute [dut] *nm* doubt. misgiving, scruple; **mettre en —** to call in question; **sans —** probably.

douter [dute] *vi* to doubt, suspect; *vr* to suspect, surmise; **je m'en doutais bien** I thought as much.

douteux, -euse [dutø, øːz] *a* doubtful, questionable.

douve [duːv] *nf* ditch, moat.

doux, douce [du, dus] *a* sweet, gentle, smooth, soft, mild, pleasant; **eau douce** fresh water.

douzaine [duzɛn] *nf* dozen.

douze [duːz] *nm* twelve, twelfth.

doyen, -enne [dwajɛ̃, ɛn] *n* dean, doyen, senior.

dragage [dragaːʒ] *nm* dredging, dragging, mine-sweeping.

dragée [draʒe] *nf* sugared almond, comfit.

dragon [dragɔ̃] *nm* dragon, dragoon.

draguer [drage] *vt* to dredge, drag, sweep.

dragueur [dragœːr] *nm* dredger; **— de mines** mine-sweeper.

drainer [drɛne] *vt* to drain.

dramatique [dramatik] *a* dramatic; **auteur —** playwright.

dramatiser [dramatize] *vt* to dramatize.

dramaturge [dramatyrʒ] *nm* dramatist.

drame [dram] *nm* drama, play, sensational event.

drap [dra] *nm* cloth; **— de lit** bedsheet; **être dans de beaux —s** to be in a mess.

drapeau [drapo] *nm* flag, colors.

draper [drape] *vt* to drape, hang.

draperie [drapri] *nf* cloth-trade, drapery.

drapier, -ière [drapje, jɛːr] *n* draper, clothier.

dresser [drɛse] *vt* to raise, set up, draw up, make out, train, break in; *vr* to rise, sit up, straighten up; **— les oreilles** to cock one's ears; **faire — les cheveux à qn** to make s.o.'s hair stand on end.

dresseur, -euse [drɛsœːr, øːz] *n* trainer, trimmer, adjuster.

dressoir [drɛswaːr] *nm* dresser, sideboard.

drogue [drɔg] *nf* drug.

droguer [drɔge] *vt* to give medicine to, drug, dope.

droguiste [drɔgist] *nm* druggist.

droit [drwa] *a* straight, direct, upright, right (hand), honest; *ad* straight (on); *nm* right, due, fee, law; **veston —** single-breasted jacket; **— d'auteur** copyright; **—s acquis** vested interests **à bon —**

with good reason; **— d'aînesse** birthright.

droite [drwat] *nf* right (-hand, side).

droitier, -ière [drwatje, jɛːr] *a* right-handed.

droiture [drwatyːr] *nf* integrity, uprightness.

drôle [droːl] *a* funny, odd, queer; *n* rogue, rascal.

dromadaire [drɔmadɛːr] *nm* dromedary.

dru [dry] *a* thick, dense, strong; *ad* thickly, heavily.

du [dy] = **de + le.**

duc [dyk] *nm* duke.

duché [dyʃe] *nm* duchy, dukedom.

duchesse [dyʃɛs] *nf* duchess.

duelliste [dɥɛlist] *nm* duelist.

dûment [dymɑ̃] *ad* duly, in due form.

dune [dyn] *nf* dune, sand-hill.

dunette [dynɛt] *nf* (*deck*) poop.

duo [dyo] *nm* duet.

dupe [dyp] *nf* dupe, catspaw.

duper [dype] *vt* to dupe, trick, take in.

duperie [dypri] *nf* trickery, sell, a piece of double-dealing.

duplicité [dyplisite] *nf* duplicity, falseness, deceit, double-dealing.

dur [dyːr] *a* hard, harsh, difficult, tough, inured; *ad* hard; **avoir l'oreille —e** to be hard of hearing; **avoir la tête —e** to be slow-witted; **œufs —s** hard-boiled eggs; **c'est un — à cuire** he is a tough nut.

durabilité [dyrabilite] *nf* durability, lasting quality.

durable [dyrabl] *a* hard-wearing, lasting, enduring.

durant [dyrɑ̃] *prep* during, for.

durcir [dyrsiːr] *vt* to harden, make hard; *vi* to grow hard.

durcissement [dyrsismɑ̃] *nm* hardening.

durée [dyre] *nf* duration, continuance, wear, life.

durement [dyrmɑ̃] *ad* hard(ly), roughly, harshly.

durer [dyre] *vi* to last, endure, wear well.

dureté [dyrte] *nf* hardness, harshness, callousness.

durillon [dyrijɔ̃] *nm* callosity.

duvet [dyvɛ] *nm* down, fluff.

duveté [dyvte] *a* downy, fluffy.

dynamique [dinamik] *a* dynamic; *nf* dynamics.

dynamite [dinamit] *nf* dynamite.

dynastie [dinasti] *nf* dynasty.

dysenterie [disɑ̃tri] *nf* dysentery.

dyspepsie [dispɛpsi] *nf* dyspepsia.

dyssymétrie [dis(s)imetri] *nf* asymmetry.

E

eau [o] *nf* water; **— oxygénée** hydrogen peroxide; **mortes —x** neap

tides; **vives —·x** spring tides; **faire
— to leak,** bilge; **faire venir l'—** à
la bouche to make one's mouth
water; **laver à grande —** to swill.
eau-de-vie [odvi] *nf* brandy, spirits.
eau-forte [ofɔrt] *nf* aqua fortis,
etching.
ébahir [ebaiːr] *vt* to amaze, dumb-
found; *vr* to be dumbfounded,
abashed.
ébahissement [ebaismɑ̃] *nm* amazement, wonder.
ébats [eba] *nm pl* frolic, sport,
gambols, revels.
s'ébattre [sebatr] *vr* to frolic, gambol,
frisk about.
s'ébaubir [sebobiːr] *vr* to be
astounded, flabbergasted.
ébauche [eboːʃ] *nf* sketch, outline.
ébaucher [eboʃe] *vt* to sketch,
rough draw, outline.
ébène [ebɛn] *nf* ebony.
ébéniste [ebenist] *nm* cabinet-maker.
ébénisterie [ebenistri] *nf* cabinet-
making.
éberlué [eberlɥe] *a* dumbfounded.
éblouir [ebluiːr] *vt* to dazzle.
éblouissement [ebluismɑ̃] *nm*
dazzling, dazzle, dizziness.
ébonite [ebɔnit] *nf* vulcanite.
éborgner [ebɔrɲe] *vt* to put s.o.'s
eye out.
ébouillanter [ebujɑ̃te] *vt* to scald.
éboulement [ebulmɑ̃] *nm* falling-in,
landslide.
s'ébouler [sebule] *vr* to fall in, cave
in, slip.
éboulis [ebuli] *nm* mass of fallen rock
and earth.
ébouriffer [eburife] *vt* to dishevel,
ruffle, take aback.
ébrancher [ebrɑ̃ʃe] *vt* to lop the
branches off.
ébranlement [ebrɑ̃lmɑ̃] *nm* shaking,
tottering, shock, commotion.
ébranler [ebrɑ̃le] *vt* to shake,
loosen, set in motion; *vr* to totter,
start, move off.
ébrécher [ebreʃe] *vt* to notch, chip,
make inroads into.
ébriété [ebriete] *nf* intoxication.
s'ébrouer [sebrue] *vr* to snort; (*birds*)
take a dust bath.
ébruiter [ebrɥite] *vt* to noise abroad,
spread, make known; *vr* to be
noised abroad, spread.
ébullition [ebylisjɔ̃] *nf* boiling, fever,
ferment.
écaille [ekaːj] *nf* scale, shell, flake,
chip.
écailler [ekaje] *vt* to scale, open; *vr*
to peel, flake off.
écailleux, -euse [ekajø. øːz] *a* scaly,
flaky.
écale [ekal] *nf* shell, pod.
écaler [ekale] *vt* to shell, husk.
écarlate [ekarlat] *a* scarlet.
écarquiller [ekarkije] *vtr* to open
wide, spread wide apart.
écart [ekaːr] *nm* step aside, swerve,

deflection, straying, divergence,
difference, error, variation, discard-
ing; **à l'—** aside; **faire un —** to shy,
step aside; **faire le grand —** to do
the splits.
écarté [ekarte] *a* lonely, remote,
out-of-the-way.
écarteler [ekartəle] *vt* to quarter;
être écartelé to be torn between.
écartement [ekartəmɑ̃] *nm* separation, spacing, gap, gauge.
écarter [ekarte] *vt* to separate, space,
spread, pull aside, fend off, brush
aside, discard; *vr* to diverge, stray,
step aside.
ecclésiastique [eklezjastik] *a*
ecclesiastical, clerical; *nm* clergyman.
écervelé [esɛrvəle] *a* hare-brained,
giddy, rash.
échafaud [eʃafo] *nm* scaffold.
échafaudage [eʃafodaːʒ] *nm* scaffolding.
échafauder [eʃafode] *vt* to construct,
build up.
échalas [eʃalɑ] *nm* vine-pole, hop-
pole, spindle-shanks.
échalis [eʃali] *nm* stile.
échancrer [eʃɑ̃kre] *vt* to cut out,
scallop, indent.
échancrure [eʃɑ̃kryːr] *nf* cut-out
piece, opening.
échange [eʃɑ̃ːʒ] *nm* exchange, barter.
échangeable [eʃɑ̃ʒabl] *a* exchangeable.
échanger [eʃɑ̃ʒe] *vt* to exchange,
barter, bandy.
échantillon [eʃɑ̃tijɔ̃] *nm* sample,
pattern.
échappatoire [eʃapatwaːr] *nf* loophole, way out.
échappement [eʃapmɑ̃] *nm* escape,
leakage, exhaust-pipe.
échapper [eʃape] *vi* to escape; *vr* to
run away, escape, leak; **il l'a
échappé belle** he had a narrow
escape; **— à qn** to elude s.o.
échappée [eʃape] *nf* vista; turning
space; (*racing*) spurt; (*cattle*) straying.
écharde [eʃard] *nf* splinter.
écharpe [eʃarp] *nf* scarf, sash, sling.
échasse [eʃɑːs] *nf* stilt.
échauder [eʃode] *vt* to scald.
échauffant [eʃofɑ̃] *a* heating,
exciting.
échauffement [eʃofmɑ̃] *nm* heating,
over-heating, over-excitement.
échauffer [eʃofe] *vt* to overheat,
heat, warm; *vt* to get overheated,
warm up.
échauffourée [eʃofure] *nf* scuffle,
skirmish.
échéance [eʃeɑ̃ːs] *nf* date, expiration, falling due.
échec [eʃɛk] *nm* check, set-back,
failure; *pl* chess, chessmen; **échec et
mat** checkmate.
échelle [eʃɛl] *nf* ladder, scale; **après
lui il faut tirer l'—** he always goes

one better than anyone else; **faire la courte —** à to give a leg up to; **— de sauvetage** fire-escape.

échelon [eʃlɔ̃] *nm* rung, step, degree, echelon.

échelonner [eʃlɔne] *vt* to space out, stagger.

écheveau [eʃvo] *nm* skein, hank.

échevelé [eʃəvle] *a* disheveled, wild, frenzied.

échine [eʃin] *nf* spine.

échiner [eʃine] *vt* to work to death; *vr* to slave, wear o.s. out.

échiquier [eʃikje] *nm* chessboard, exchequer.

écho [eko] *nm* echo.

échoir [eʃwaːr] *vi* to fall (due), expire, devolve.

échoppe [eʃɔp] *nf* stall, booth.

échouage [eʃwaːʒ] *nm* stranding, grounding.

échouer [eʃwe] *vt* to beach; *vi* to run aground, ground, fail, miscarry.

éclabousser [eklabuse] *vt* to splash, spatter.

éclaboussure [eklabusyːr] *nf* splash, spatter.

éclair [eklɛːr] *nm* lightning, flash; eclair.

éclairage [eklɛraːʒ] *nm* lighting (up); **— par projecteurs** floodlighting.

éclaircie [eklɛrsi] *nf* break, bright interval, clearing.

éclaircir [eklɛrsiːr] *vt* to clarify, clear up, solve, enlighten, thin out; *vr* to clear, grow thin, be cleared up.

éclaircissement [eklɛrsismɑ̃] *nm* clearing-up, enlightenment, elucidation.

éclairer [eklɛre] *vt* to light, brighten, enlighten, reconnoiter; *vr* to light up, brighten up, clear.

éclaireur, -euse [eklɛrœːr, øːz] *n* scout, Boy Scout, Girl Scout.

éclat [ekla] *nm* splinter, chip, flash, brilliancy, glamor, burst; **rire aux --s** to laugh uproariously.

éclatant [eklatɑ̃] *a* bursting, loud, brilliant, resounding, flagrant.

éclater [eklate] *vt* to burst, split; *vi* to burst, explode, break out; **— en colère** to fly into a rage; **— de rire** to burst out laughing.

éclectique [eklɛktik] *a* eclectic, catholic.

éclipse [eklips] *nf* eclipse.

éclipser [eklipse] *vt* to eclipse, put in the shade, surpass; *vr* to vanish.

éclisse [eklis] *nf* splint; fish-plate.

éclopé [eklɔpe] *a* lame, limping; *nm* cripple, lame person.

éclore [eklɔːr] *vt* to hatch (out), open out, burst.

éclosion [eklozjɔ̃] *nf* hatching, blossoming, opening out.

écluse [eklyːz] *nf* lock, sluice-gate.

écœurant [ekœrɑ̃] *a* sickening, fulsome.

écœurement [ekœrmɑ̃] *nm* disgust, loathing.

écœurer [ekœre] *vt* to sicken, disgust.

école [ekɔl] *nf* school; **— polytechnique** military academy; **— normale** teachers college.

écolier, -ière [ekɔlje, jɛːr] *n* schoolboy, -girl.

éconduire [ekɔ̃dɥiːr] *vt* to show out, put out.

économe [ekɔnɔm] *a* economical, thrifty; *nm* steward, housekeeper, bursar.

économie [ekɔnɔmi] *nf* economy, thrift; *pl* savings; **faire des —s** to save, retrench.

économique [ekɔnɔmik] *a* economic (al).

économiser [ekɔnɔmize] *vt* to economize, save.

économiste [ekɔnɔmist] *nm* economist.

écope [ekɔp] *nf* scoop, ladle, bailer.

écoper [ekɔpe] *vt* to bail out; *vi* to catch it.

écorce [ekɔrs] *nf* bark, peel, rind, crust.

écorcer [ekɔrse] *vt* to bark, peel, husk.

écorcher [ekɔrʃe] *vt* to skin, flay, graze, scratch.

écorchure [ekɔrʃyːr] *nf* abrasion, scratch.

écorner [ekɔrne] *vt* to take the horns off, break the corners of, dog-ear, make inroads in.

écornifler [ekɔrnifle] *vt* to scrounge, cadge.

Écosse [ekɔs] *nf* Scotland.

écossais [ekɔsɛ] *a* Scottish, Scotch, Scots; **étoffe —e** tartan; *n* Scot, Scotsman, Scotswoman.

écosser [ekɔse] *vt* to shell, pod, husk.

écot [eko] *nm* share, quota.

écoulement [ekulmɑ̃] *nm* flow, discharge, waste-pipe, sale.

écouler [ekule] *vt* to sell, dispose of; *vr* to flow, run out, to pass, elapse.

écourter [ekurte] *vt* to shorten, curtail, cut short.

écoute [ekut] *nf* listening post, listening-in; **être aux —s** to be on the look-out; **faire, rester à l'—** to listen in.

écouter [ekute] *vt* to listen to; *vi* to listen; **— à la porte** to eavesdrop.

écouteur, -euse [ekutœːr, øːz] *n* listener; *nm* earphone, receiver.

écoutille [ekutiːj] *nf* hatchway.

écran [ekrɑ̃] *nm* screen.

écrasement [ekrazmɑ̃] *nm* crushing, crashing, defeat.

écraser [ekraze] *vt* to crush, run over, overburden, dwarf; *vr* to collapse, crash.

écrémer [ekreme] *vt* to skim, cream.

écrevisse [ekrəvis] *nf* crayfish.

s'écrier [sekrie] *vr* to exclaim, cry out.

écrin [ekrɛ̃] *nm* case, casket.

écrire [ekriːr] *vt* to write, note down, spell; **machine à —** typewriter.

écrit [ekri] *a* written; *nm* writing, paper with writing on it.

écriteau [ekrito] *nm* placard, notice.

écritoire [ekritwaːr] *nf* inkwell.

écriture [ekrityːr] *nf* handwriting; *pl* accounts, Scripture.

écrivain [ekrivɛ̃] *nm* writer, author.

écrou [ekru] *nm* screw-nut.

écrouer [ekrue] *vt* to send to prison, lock up.

écroulement [ekrulmɑ̃] *nm* collapse, falling in, crash.

s'écrouler [sekrule] *vr* to collapse, crumble, tumble down.

écru [ekry] *a* unbleached, raw, natural-colored.

écu [eky] *nm* shield, escutcheon, crown.

écueil [ekœːj] *nm* reef, stumbling block.

écuelle [ekɥɛl] *nf* bowl, basin.

éculer [ekyle] *vt* to wear away the heels of (shoes).

écume [ekym] *nf* foam, froth, scum; **— de mer** meerschaum.

écumer [ekyme] *vt* to skim; *vi* to foam, froth; **— les mers** to scour the seas.

écumeux, -euse [ekymø, øːz] *a* foamy, frothy, scummy.

écumoire [ekymwaːr] *nf* skimming ladle.

écurer [ekyre] *vt* to scour.

écureuil [ekyrœːj] *nm* squirrel.

écurie [ekyri] *nf* stable.

écusson [ekysɔ̃] *nm* escutcheon, coat-of-arms, shield.

écuyer, -ère [ekɥije, ɛːr] *n* rider, horseman, -woman; *nm* equerry, squire; **bottes à l'écuyère** riding-boots.

édenté [edɑ̃te] *a* toothless.

édenter [edɑ̃te] *vt* to break the teeth of.

édicter [edikte] *vt* to decree, enact.

édification [edifikasjɔ̃] *nf* building, erection; edification.

édifice [edifis] *nm* edifice, building, structure.

édifier [edifje] *vt* to build, erect, edify.

édit [edi] *nm* edict.

éditer [edite] *vt* to edit, publish.

éditeur, -trice [editœːr, tris] *n* editor, editress, publisher.

édition [edisjɔ̃] *nf* edition, publishing trade; **maison d'—** publishing house.

éditorial [editɔrjal] *a* editorial; *nm* editorial.

édredon [edrədɔ̃] *nm* eiderdown, quilt.

éducation [edykasjɔ̃] *nf* training, rearing, breeding, upbringing.

éduquer [edyke] *vt* to educate, bring up.

effacé [ɛfase] *a* unobtrusive, unassuming, retiring.

effacement [ɛfasmɑ̃] *nm* obliteration, wearing out, unobtrusiveness.

effacer [ɛfase] *vt* to efface, blot out, delete; *vr* to wear away, fade, remain in the background.

effarement [ɛfarmɑ̃] *nm* alarm, fright.

effarer [ɛfare] *vt* to scare, alarm; *vr* to be scared, take fright.

effaroucher [ɛfaruʃe] *vt* to scare away; *vr* to be startled.

effectif, -ive [efɛktif, iːv] *a* effective, actual, real; *nm* total strength, manpower.

effectivement [efɛktivmɑ̃] *ad* actually, as a matter of fact, exactly.

effectuer [efɛktɥe] *vt* to bring about, carry out, execute.

efféminé [efemine] *a* effeminate.

effervescence [efɛrvɛssɑ̃ːs] *nf* excitement, ebullience, turmoil.

effet [efɛ] *nm* effect, result, impression, operation; *pl* effects, possessions, stocks; **à cet —** for this purpose; **en —** indeed, as a matter of fact; **manquer son —** to fall flat; **faire de l'—** to be effective; **mettre à l'—** to put into operation.

effeuiller [efœje] *vt* to remove the leaves from; *vr* to shed its leaves.

efficace [efikas] *a* effective, efficacious, effectual.

efficacité [efikasite] *nf* efficacy, effectiveness, efficiency.

effigie [efiʒi] *nf* image, likeness.

effilé [efile] *a* fringed, slender, slim, tapering.

effiler [efile] *vt* to unravel, taper; *vr* to fray, taper.

effilocher [efilɔʃe] *vt* to unravel; *vr* to fray.

efflanqué [eflɑ̃ke] *a* lean.

effleurer [eflœre] *vt* to graze, brush, skim, touch upon.

effondrement [efɔ̃drəmɑ̃] *nm* collapse, falling in, subsidence, slump, breakdown.

effondrer [efɔ̃dre] *vt* to break down, smash in; *vr* to collapse, fall in, slump.

s'efforcer [sefɔrse] *vr* to strive, endeavor.

effort [efɔːr] *nm* endeavor, exertion, strain.

effraction [efraksjɔ̃] *nf* housebreaking.

effrayer [efrɛje] *vt* to frighten, terrify, scare, daunt; *vr* to get a fright, be frightened.

effréné [efrene] *a* unbridled, frantic, frenzied.

effriter [efrite] *vt* to wear away; *vr* to crumble.

effroi [efrwa] *nm* fright, dread, terror.

effronté [efrɔ̃te] *a* shameless, impudent, cheeky, saucy.

effronterie [efrɔ̃tri] *nf* effrontery, impudence.

effroyable [efrwajabl] *a* frightful, dreadful, appalling.

effusion [efyzjɔ̃] *nf* effusion, outpouring, effusiveness; — **de sang** bloodshed.

égailler [egaje] *vt* to flush, scatter; *vr* to scatter.

égal [egal] *a* equal, level, even; **cela lui est** — it is all the same to him.

également [egalmã] *ad* equally, likewise, as well.

égaler [egale] *vt* to be equal to, compare with.

égaliser [egalize] *vt* to equalize, regulate, level.

égalitaire [egalitɛːr] *an* equalitarian.

égalité [egalite] *nf* equality, evenness, smoothness; **être à** — to be all square, equal.

égard [egaːr] *nm* regard, respect, consideration; *pl* esteem, attentions, consideration; **avoir** — **à** to take into account; **à cet** — in this respect; **à tous les** —**s** in every respect; **à l'**— **de** with regard to, toward.

égaré [egare] *a* lost, stray, distracted.

égarement [egarmã] *nm* loss, mislaying; aberration, frenzy; *pl* disorderly conduct.

égarer [egare] *vt* to lead astray, mislead, mislay; *vr* to go astray, lose one's way.

égayer [egɛje] *vt* to cheer up, brighten (up).

égide [eʒid] *nf* shield, aegis.

églantier [eglãtje] *nm* wild rose, sweet brier.

églantine [eglãtin] *nf* wild rose (flower).

église [egliːz] *nf* church.

égoïsme [egɔism] *nm* selfishness, egoism.

égoïste [egɔist] *a* selfish; *n* egoist, egotist.

égorger [egɔrʒe] *vt* to cut the throat of, butcher.

s'égosiller [segozije] *vr* to shout oneself hoarse.

égout [egu] *nm* drain, sewer, gutter; **eaux d'**— sewage.

égoutter [egute] *vt* to drain; *vr* drip, drop, drain.

égratigner [egratiɲe] *vt* to scratch, graze.

égratignure [egratiɲyːr] *nf* scratch, graze.

égrener [egrəne] *vt* to pick out, pick off; *vr* to drop (one by one); — **son chapelet** to tell one's beads.

égrillard [egrijaːr] *a* ribald, daring, spicy.

Égypte [eʒipt] *nf* Egypt.

égyptien, -enne [eʒipsjɛ̃, jɛn] *an* Egyptian.

éhonté [eɔ̃te] *a* shameless, brazenfaced.

éjaculer [eʒakyle] *vt* to ejaculate.

élaborer [elabɔre] *vt* to elaborate, draw up, labor.

élaguer [elage] *vt* to lop off, prune, cut down.

élan [elã] *nm* spring, bound, dash,

impetus, abandon, (out)burst; moose.

élancé [elãse] *a* slender, slim, tapering.

élancement [elãsmã] *nm* twinge, stabbing pain.

s'élancer [selãse] *vr* to dash forward, rush, spring.

élargir [elarʒiːr] *vt* to widen, enlarge, broaden, release, discharge; *vr* to broaden out, extend.

élargissement [elarʒismã] *nm* broadening, extension, release, discharge.

élasticité [elastisite] *nf* elasticity, resilience, spring.

élastique [elastik] *a* elastic, springy, resilient; *nm* elastic, rubber band.

électeur, -trice [elɛktœːr, tris] *n* voter, constituent.

électif, -ive [elɛktif, iːv] *a* elective.

élection [elɛksjɔ̃] *nf* election, choice; **se présenter aux** —**s** to run in an election.

électoral [elɛktɔral] *a* electoral; **collège** — constituency; **campagne** —**e** electioneering; **corps** — electorate.

électorat [elɛktɔra] *nm* electorate.

électricien [elɛktrisjɛ̃] *nm* electrician.

électricité [elɛktrisite] *nf* electricity.

électrique [elɛktrik] *a* electric.

électriser [elɛktrize] *vt* to electrify.

électrocuter [elɛktrɔkyte] *vt* to electrocute.

électronique [elɛktrɔnik] *a* electronic; *nf* electronics.

élégance [elegãːs] *nf* stylishness, smartness.

élégant [elegã] *a* well-dressed, fashionable.

élégiaque [eleʒjak] *a* elegiac.

élégie [eleʒi] *nf* elegy.

élément [elemã] *nm* component, element, ingredient; *pl* rudiments.

élémentaire [elemãtɛːr] *a* elementary, rudimentary.

éléphant [elefã] *nm* elephant.

élevage [ɛlvaːʒ] *nm* raising, rearing, breeding.

élévation [elevasjɔ̃] *nf* elevation, raising, rise, height, grandeur.

élève [elɛːv] *n* pupil, boy, girl.

élevé [elve] *a* elevated, high, lofty, exalted; **bien (mal)** — well- (ill-) bred, well (badly) behaved.

élever [elve] *vt* to elevate, erect, raise; *vr* to rise up, arise.

éleveur, -euse [elvœːr, øːz] *n* stockbreeder, grower, keeper.

élider [elide] *vt* to elide.

éligibilité [eliʒibilite] *nf* eligibility.

éligible [eliʒibl] *a* eligible.

élimer [elime] *vt* to wear threadbare; *vr* to wear, be worn threadbare.

éliminatoire [eliminatwaːr] *a* eliminatory, preliminary.

éliminer [elimine] *vt* to eliminate, weed out.

élire [eliːr] *vt* to elect, choose, appoint, return.

élision [elizjɔ̃] *nf* elision.

élite [elit] *nf* élite, pick, flower; a d'— crack.

ellipse [elips] *nf* ellipse, ellipsis.

élocution [elɔkysjɔ̃] *nf* elocution.

éloge [elɔʒ] *nm* eulogy, commendation, praise.

élogieux, -euse [elɔʒjø, jøːz] *a* laudatory, glowing.

éloigné [elwaɲe] *a* distant, far (away, off).

éloignement [elwaɲmɑ̃] *nm* absence, removal, isolation, postponement, distance.

éloigner [elwaɲe] *vt* to remove, get out of the way, alienate, postpone; *vr* to withdraw, stand farther away.

éloquence [elɔkɑ̃ːs] *nf* eloquence.

éloquent [elɔkɑ̃] *a* eloquent.

élu [ely] *a* chosen; *nm pl* the elect, the elected members.

élucider [elyside] *vt* to elucidate.

éluder [elyde] *vt* to elude, evade.

émacié [emasje] *a* emaciated.

émail [emaːj] *nm* enamel, glaze.

émailler [emaje] *vt* to enamel, glaze, fleck, besprinkle.

émancipé [emɑ̃sipe] *a* full-fledged, having advanced ideas, emancipated.

émanciper [emɑ̃sipe] *vt* to emancipate; *vr* to become emancipated, kick over the traces.

émaner [emane] *vi* to emanate, come, originate (from).

émasculer [emaskyle] *vt* to emasculate, weaken.

emballage [ɑ̃balaːʒ] *nm* packing, wrapping.

emballement [ɑ̃balmɑ̃] *nm* (*of machine*) racing, enthusiasm, boom, craze.

emballer [ɑ̃bale] *vt* to pack, wrap up, (*car engine*) race, fill with enthusiasm; *vr* (*horse*) to bolt, be carried away, rave (with enthusiasm), fly into a temper.

emballeur [ɑ̃balœːr] *nm* packer.

embarcadère [ɑ̃barkadɛːr] *nm* landing-stage, wharf, platform.

embarcation [ɑ̃barkasjɔ̃] *nf* boat, craft.

embardée [ɑ̃barde] *nf* lurch, swerve, skid.

embargo [ɑ̃bargo] *nm* embargo.

embarquement [ɑ̃barkəmɑ̃] *nm* loading, embarking, shipping, entrainment.

embarquer [ɑ̃barke] *vt* to embark, take aboard, entrain; *vir* to go abroad, entrain.

embarras [ɑ̃barɑ] *nm* embarrassment, difficulty, quandary, superfluity; *pl* fuss.

embarrassé [ɑ̃barase] *a* embarrassed, involved.

embarrasser [ɑ̃barase] *vt* to embarrass, perplex, confound, hamper, obstruct.

embaucher [ɑ̃boʃe] *vt* to engage, take on, employ.

embauchoir [ɑ̃boʃwaːr] *nm* shoetree.

embaumer [ɑ̃bome] *vt* to embalm, perfume; *vi* to have a lovely perfume, smell of.

embellir [ɑ̃bɛliːr] *vt* to embellish, improve, beautify.

embellissement [ɑ̃bɛlismɑ̃] *nm* embellishment.

embêtant [ɑ̃bɛtɑ̃] *a* (*fam*) annoying.

embêter [ɑ̃bete] *vt* to annoy.

emblée [ɑ̃ble] *ad* d'— right away.

emblème [ɑ̃blɛːm] *nm* emblem, badge, sign.

embobeliner [ɑ̃bɔbline] *vt* to coax, get round.

emboîtement [ɑ̃bwatmɑ̃] *nm* joint, fitting, encasing.

emboîter [ɑ̃bwate] *vt* to joint, fit together, dovetail, encase; — le pas à to fall into step with.

embolie [ɑ̃bɔli] *nf* embolism, stroke.

embonpoint [ɑ̃bɔ̃pwɛ̃] *nm* corpulence, stoutness.

embouché [ɑ̃buʃe] *a* mal — coarsetongued.

emboucher [ɑ̃buʃe] *vt* to put to one's mouth, blow.

embouchure [ɑ̃buʃyːr] *nf* mouthpiece. (*river, volcano*) mouth.

embourber [ɑ̃burbe] *vt* to bog; *vr* to be bogged, stuck in the mud.

embout [ɑ̃bu] *nm* ferrule, tip.

embouteillage [ɑ̃butɛjaːʒ] *nm* bottling (up), bottleneck, trafficjam.

embouteiller [ɑ̃butɛje] *vt* to bottle (up), jam, block; *vr* to get jammed.

embranchement [ɑ̃brɑ̃ʃmɑ̃] *nm* branching off, junction, branch-line.

embrancher [ɑ̃brɑ̃ʃe] *vt* to join up, together.

embrasement [ɑ̃brazmɑ̃] *nm* conflagration.

embraser [ɑ̃braze] *vt* to set fire to, fire; *vr* to catch fire.

embrassade [ɑ̃brasad] *nf* embrace, hug.

embrasser [ɑ̃brase] *vt* to embrace, hug, kiss, enfold, take up, include.

embrasure [ɑ̃brazyːr] *nf* recess, embrasure.

embrayage [ɑ̃brɛjaːʒ] *nm* connecting, coupling-gear, putting into gear.

embrayer [ɑ̃brɛje] *vt* to connect, couple, throw into gear; *vi* to let in the clutch.

embrocher [ɑ̃brɔʃe] *vt* to spit, put on the spit.

embrouillement [ɑ̃brujmɑ̃] *nm* entanglement, intricacy, muddle, confusion.

embrouiller [ɑ̃bruje] *vt* to tangle, muddle, embroil, complicate, confuse; *vr* to become entangled, complicated, confused.

embrun [ɑ̃brœ̃] *nm* spray, spindrift.

embryon [ɑ̃briɔ̃] *nm* embryo.

embûche [ãby(ː)ʃ] nf ambush; dresser une — à to waylay.

embuer [ãbɥe] vt to cloud, cover with vapor.

embuscade [ãbyskad] nf ambush, ambuscade.

embusqué [ãbyske] nm shirker, dodger, sharpshooter.

embusquer [ãbyske] vt to place in ambush, put under cover; vr to lie in ambush, take cover, shirk war service.

éméché [emeʃe] a slightly tipsy, rather merry.

émeraude [emroːd] nf emerald.

émerger [emɛrʒe] vi to emerge, come out.

émeri [ɛmri] nm emery.

émérite [emerit] a emeritus, retired, experienced.

émerveillement [emɛrvɛjmã] nm amazement.

émerveiller [emɛrvɛje] vt to amaze, astonish; vr to marvel, wonder.

émétique [emetik] nm emetic.

émetteur, -trice [emɛtœːr, tris] a issuing, transmitting, broadcasting; n issuer transmitter.

émettre [emɛtr] vt to emit, issue, utter, give out, express, transmit, broadcast.

émeute [emøːt] nf riot, disturbance.

émeutier [emøtje] nm rioter.

émietter [emjete] vtr to crumble.

émigrant [emigrã] a emigrating, migratory; n emigrant.

émigré [emigre] n political exile.

émigrer [emigre] vi to emigrate, migrate.

éminence [eminãːs] nf eminence, height, prominence.

éminent [eminã] a distinguished.

émissaire [emisɛːr] nm emissary; bouc — scapegoat.

émission [emisjɔ̃] nf issue, transmission, broadcast; poste d'— broadcasting station.

emmagasinage [ãmagazinaːʒ] nm storing, storage.

emmagasiner [ãmagazine] vt to store (up).

emmailloter [ãmajɔte] v. to swaddle, swathe.

emmancher [ãmãʃe] vt to put a handle on; joint; vr to fit (into dans), get going.

emmanchure [ãmãʃyːr] nf armhole.

emmêler [ãmɛle] vt to mix up, muddle, implicate.

emménager [ãmenaʒe] vt to move in, furnish; vi to move in.

emmener [ãmne] vt to lead, take away, take.

emmitoufler [ãmitufle] vt to muffle up.

émoi [emwa] nm emotion, excitement, stir, flutter; en — agog, astir, in a flutter.

émoluments [emolymã] nm pl emoluments, fees.

émonder [emɔ̃de] vt to prune, trim.

émotion [emosjɔ̃] nf emotion, feeling, excitement.

émotionnable [emosjɔnabl] a emotional, excitable.

émotionner [emosjɔne] vt to excite, stir, thrill; vr to get excited.

émoudre [emudr] vt to grind.

émoulu [emuly] a sharpened; frais — de just out of, fresh from.

émousser [emuse] vt to blunt, deaden; vr to become blunt, dulled.

émoustillant [emustijã] a piquant, exhilarating.

émoustiller [emustije] vt to stir (up), rouse, titillate, stimulate; vr to come to life, sparkle.

émouvant [emuvã] a moving, exciting, thrilling.

émouvoir [emuvwaːr] vt to move, stir up, excite; vr to be moved, get excited.

empailler [ãpaje] vt to pack, cover in straw, stuff.

empailleur, -euse [ãpajœːr, øːz] n taxidermist.

empaler [ãpale] vt to impale.

empaqueter [ãpakte] vt to pack up, parcel up, bundle.

s'emparer [sãpare] vr to seize, take possession (of de), secure.

empâté [ãpate] a coated, clogged, thick.

empâter [ãpate] vt to cover with paste, make sticky, fatten; vr to put on fat.

empêchement [ãpɛʃmã] nm impediment, obstacle, hindrance.

empêcher [ãpɛʃe] vt to prevent, impede, hamper; vr to refrain; je ne peux m'— de rire I cannot help laughing.

empeigne [ãpɛɲ] nf upper (of shoe).

empennage [ãpenaːʒ] nm feathers, feathering, fur, vanes.

empereur [ãprœːr] nm emperor.

empesé [ãpəze] a starched, stiff, starchy.

empeser [ãpəze] vt to starch, stiffen.

empester [ãpɛste] vt to infect, create a stink in.

empêtrer [ãpɛtre] vt to hobble, entangle, hamper; vr to get entangled, involved.

emphase [ãfaːz] nf grandiloquence, bombast.

emphatique [ãfatik] a bombastic, grandiloquent.

empierrer [ãpjɛre] vt to ballast, metal.

empiètement [ãpjɛtmã] nm encroachment, trespassing, infringement.

empiéter [ãpjete] vi to encroach, infringe.

empiffrer [ãpifre] vt to stuff; vr to stuff oneself, guzzle.

empiler [ãpile] vt to pile, stack.

empire [ãpiːr] nm empire, sway,

dominion; — **sur soi-même** self-control.

empirer [ăpire] *vt* to make worse, aggravate; *vr* to get worse.

empirique [ăpirik] *a* empirical.

emplacement [ăplasmă] *nm* site, location.

emplâtre [ăplɑːtr] *nm* plaster, poultice.

emplette [ăplɛt] *nf* purchase; **faire ses —s** to go shopping.

emplir [ăpliːr] *vt* to fill; *vr* to fill (up).

emploi [ăplwa] *nm* use, employment, job, post.

employé [ăplwaje] *n* employee, clerk, attendant.

employer [ăplwaje] *vt* to employ, use; *vr* to spend one's time, occupy oneself.

employeur, -euse [ăplwajœːr, øːz] *n* employer.

empocher [ăpɔʃe] *vt* to pocket.

empoignant [ăpwaɲă] *a* thrilling, gripping.

empoigner [ăpwaɲe] *vt* to grasp, grab, grip, hold.

empois [ăpwa] *nm* starch.

empoisonnant [ăpwazɔnă] *a* poisonous, rotten.

empoisonnement [ăpwazɔnmă] *nm* poisoning.

empoisonner [ăpwazɔne] *vt* to poison, infect, corrupt.

empoisonneur, -euse [ăpwazɔnœːr, øːz] *n* poisoner.

emporté [ăpɔrte] *a* hot-tempered, fiery, hasty.

emportement [ăpɔrtəmă] *nm* outburst, anger, rapture, passion.

emporte-pièce [ăpɔrtəpjɛs] *nm* punch; **réponse à l'—** caustic reply.

emporter [ăpɔrte] *vt* to carry away, off, sweep along, away, remove; *vr* to fly into a rage, bolt; **l'—** to carry the day, prevail, have the best of it; **— la balance** to turn the scale.

empoté [ăpɔte] *a* clumsy, unathletic; *n* bungler, duffer.

empoter [ăpɔte] *vt* to pot.

empourprer [ăpurpre] *vt* to tinge with crimson; *vr* to turn crimson, grow red.

empreindre [ăprɛ̃ːdr] *vt* to imprint, stamp.

empreinte [ăprɛ̃t] *nf* stamp, mark, imprint, print, impression, mold; **— digitale** fingerprint.

empressé [ăprɛse] *a* eager, solicitous, ardent, sedulous.

empressement [ăprɛsmă] *nm* eagerness, alacrity, haste, zeal.

s'empresser [săprɛse] *vr* to hurry, be eager, be attentive, dance attendance.

emprise [ăpriːz] *nf* expropriation, hold, power.

emprisonnement [ăprizɔnmă] *nm* imprisonment.

emprisonner [ăprizɔne] *vt* to imprison, put in prison, confine.

emprunt [ăprœ̃] *nm* borrowing, loan.

emprunté [ăprœ̃te] *a* borrowed, assumed, embarrassed, self-conscious.

emprunter [ăprœ̃te] *vt* to borrow, take, assume.

emprunteur, -euse [ăprœ̃tœːr, øːz] *n* borrower.

ému [emy] *a* moved, touched, excited, nervous.

émulation [emylasjɔ̃] *nf* emulation, rivalry.

émule [emyl] *n* rival.

en [ă] *prep* in, into, to, as, like, while; *pn* of it, of them, about it, about them, for that, because of that, some, any.

encadrement [ăkɑdrəmă] *nm* framing, framework, setting, commanding.

encadrer [ăkɑdre] *vt* to frame, set, surround, command.

encaisse [ăkɛs] *nf* cash in hand, cash-balance.

encaissé [ăkɛse] *a* boxed-in, sunken, steeply embanked, blind (corner).

encaissement [ăkɛsmă] *nm* encasing, packing in boxes, collection, embankment.

encaisser [ăkɛse] *vt* to pack in boxes, collect cash, embank, take (blow).

encaisseur [ăkɛsœːr] *nm* collector, cashier, payee.

encan [ăkă] *nm* **mettre à l'—** to put up for auction.

encanailler [ăkanaje] *vr* to keep bad company, go to the dogs.

encapuchonner [ăkapyʃɔne] *vt* to put a hood on, put the cover over.

encart [ăkaːr] *nm* inset.

en-cas [ăka] *nm* reserve, something to fall back on.

encastrer [ăkastre] *vt* to fit in, embed, dovetail.

encaustique [ăkostik] *nf* floor, furniture polish.

encaustiquer [ăkostike] *vt* to polish, beeswax.

enceindre [ăsɛ̃ːdr] *vt* to encircle, gird, surround.

enceinte [ăsɛ̃t] *a* pregnant; *nf* wall, fence, enclosure, circumference.

encens [ăsă] *nm* incense, flattery.

encenser [ăsăse] *vt* to cense, burn incense before, flatter.

encenseur [ăsăsœːr] *nm* censer-bearer, flatterer.

encensoir [ăsăswaːr] *nm* censer.

encercler [ăsɛrkle] *vt* to encircle, surround.

enchaînement [ăʃɛnmă] *nm* chaining, series, putting together.

enchaîner [ăʃɛne] *vt* to chain, link up, hold in check.

enchantement [ăʃătmă] *nm* magic, enchantment, charm, spell.

enchanter [ăʃăte] *vt* to enchant, delight, bewitch.

enchanteur, -eresse [ăʃătœːr, rɛːs]

a bewitching, entrancing; *n* enchanter, enchantress.
enchâsser [ăʃɑse] *vt* to enshrine, set, mount.
enchère [ăʃɛːr] *nf* bid(ding); **vente à l'—** auction sale.
enchérir [ăʃeriːr] *vt* to raise the price of; *vi* to go up in price, make a higher bid; **— sur qn** to outbid, outdo s.o.
enchérissement [ăʃerismă] *nm* rise, increase.
enchérisseur, -euse [ăʃerisœːr, øːz] *n* bidder.
enchevêtrement [ăʃvɛtrəmă] *nm* tangling up, confusion.
enchevêtrer [ăʃvɛtre] *vt* to halter, confuse, mix up; *vr* to get entangled, mixed up.
enclaver [ăklave] *vt* to enclose, dovetail.
enclencher [ăklăʃe] *vt* to put into gear, engage.
enclin [ăklɛ̃] *a* inclined, prone.
enclore [ăklɔːr] *vt* to enclose, fence in.
enclos [ăklo] *nm* enclosure, paddock.
enclume [ăklym] *nf* anvil.
encoche [ăkɔʃ] *nf* notch, last, slot; **avec —s** with thumb index.
encocher [ăkɔʃe] *vt* to notch, nick.
encoignure [ăkɔnyːr] *nf* corner, corner cupboard.
encoller [ăkɔle] *vt* to gum, glue, paste.
encolure [ăkɔlyːr] *nf* neck and shoulders, (*dress*) neck, (*collar*) size.
encombrant [ăkɔ̃bră] *a* clumsy, bulky, cumbersome.
encombre [ăkɔ̃ːbr] *nm* obstacle, hindrance, mishap.
encombrement [ăkɔ̃brəmă] *nm* obstruction, congestion, jam, litter, overcrowding, glut, bulkiness.
encombrer [ăkɔ̃bre] *vt* to encumber, burden, congest, crowd, glut, litter.
encontre [ăkɔ̃ːtr] *ad* **à l'—** to the contrary; *prep* **à l'— de** contrary to, unlike.
encore [ăkɔːr] *ad* still, yet, again, furthermore, even, even at that; **— que** although.
encouragement [ăkuraʒmă] *nm* encouragement, incentive, inducement.
encourager [ăkuraʒe] *vt* to encourage, hearten, foster, abet, egg on.
encourir [ăkuriːr] *vt* to incur, draw upon oneself.
encrasser [ăkrase] *vt* to dirty, clog, choke; *vr* to become dirty, clog.
encre [ăːkr] *nf* ink.
encrier [ăkrie] *nm* inkwell, inkstand.
encroûter [ăkrute] *vt* to encrust, cake; *vr* to become caked, stagnate.
encyclopédie [ăsiklɔpedi] *nf* encyclopedia.
endetter [ădɛte] *vt* to run into debt; *vr* to get into debt.
endiablé [ădjable] *a* reckless, wild, boisterous.

endiguer [ădige] *vt* to dam up, bank, dike.
s'endimancher [sădimăʃe] *vr* to dress in one's Sunday best.
endive [ădiːv] *nf* chicory.
endolori [ădɔlɔri] *a* painful, tender.
endommager [ădɔmaʒe] *vt* to damage, injure.
endormi [ădɔrmi] *a* asleep, sleeping, drowsy, sluggish, numb; *n* sleepyhead.
endormir [ădɔrmiːr] *vt* to put to sleep, make numb, give an anesthetic to; *vr* to fall asleep, drop off.
endosser [ădose] *vt* to put on, endorse.
endroit [ădrwa] *nm* place, spot, aspect, right side; **à l'— de** with regard to.
enduire [ădɥiːr] *vt* to coat, smear, daub.
enduit [ădɥi] *nm* coating, coat, plaster.
endurance [ădyrăːs] *nf* endurance, long-suffering.
endurant [ădyră] *a* patient, long-suffering.
endurcir [ădyrsiːr] *vt* to harden, inure; *vr* to harden, become hard, obdurate.
endurcissement [ădyrsismă] *nm* hardening, inuring, obduracy, callousness.
endurer [ădyre] *vt* to endure, put up with, bear.
énergie [enɛrʒi] *nf* energy, vigor, power, efficacy, drive.
énergique [enɛrʒik] *a* energetic, vigorous, drastic, strong-willed.
énergumène [enɛrgymɛn] *nm* madman.
énervant [enɛrvă] *a* enervating, annoying, nerve-racking.
énerver [enɛrve] *vt* to enervate, get on one's nerves; *vr* to grow soft, become irritable, get excited.
enfance [ăfăːs] *nf* childhood, boyhood, children.
enfant [ăfă] *n* child, little boy, girl; **— trouvé** foundling; *a* **bon —** easygoing.
enfantement [ăfătmă] *nm* childbirth, production.
enfanter [ăfăte] *vt* to bear, give birth to.
enfantillage [ăfătijaːʒ] *nm* childishness.
enfantin [ăfătɛ̃] *a* childish, childlike, children's.
enfer [ăfɛːr] *nm* hell.
enfermer [ăfɛrme] *vt* to shut in, lock up, enclose, sequester; *vr* to shut, lock oneself in.
enferrer [ăfɛre] *vt* to transfix, run s.o. through; *vr* to transfix oneself, swallow the hook, get caught out.
s'enfiévrer [săfjevre] *vr* to grow feverish, get excited.
enfilade [ăfilad] *nf* succession, string, raking fire.

enfiler [ãfile] *vt* to thread, string, pierce, go along, slip on.

enfin [ãfɛ̃] *ad* at last, finally, at length, in a word, after all.

enflammé [ãflɑme] *a* burning, fiery, blaze.

enflammer [ãflɑme] *vt* to inflame, set on fire, stir up; *vr* to catch fire, become inflamed.

enflé [ãfle] *a* swollen, inflated, grandiloquent.

enfler [ãfle] *vt* to swell, puff out, bloat; *vr* to swell.

enflure [ãfly:r] *nf* swelling, puffiness, grandiloquence.

enfoncement [ãfɔ̃smã] *nm* driving in, smashing in, depression, recess, bay.

enfoncer [ãfɔ̃se] *vt* to drive in, thrust, smash in; *vi* to sink, settle; *vr* to plunge, dive, sink.

enfouir [ãfwi:r] *vt* to bury, hide.

enfourcher [ãfurʃe] *vt* to stick a fork into, mount.

enfourchure [ãfurʃy:r] *nf* fork, bifurcation.

enfourner [ãfurne] *vt* to put in the oven, shovel in.

enfreindre [ãfrɛ̃:dr] *vt* to infringe, break, contravene.

s'enfuir [sãfɥi:r] *vr* to flee, escape, fly, run away, elope.

enfumé [ãfyme] *a* smoky, smoke-blackened.

enfumer [ãfyme] *vt* to fill (blacken) with smoke.

engagé [ãgaʒe] *a* pledged; *n* volunteer.

engageant [ãgaʒã] *a* winning, prepossessing, inviting, ingratiating.

engagement [ãgaʒmã] *nm* appointment, commitment, pawning, pledge, bond, engagement, enlistment.

engager [ãgaʒe] *vt* to engage, sign on, pawn, pledge, enter into, urge; *vr* to undertake, get involved, commit oneself, enlist, fit, jam, foul.

engainer [ãgɛne] *vt* to sheathe, envelop.

engeance [ãʒã:s] *nf* breed, race.

engelure [ãʒly:r] *nf* chilblain.

engendrer [ãʒãdre] *vt* to beget, engender, breed.

engin [ãʒɛ̃] *nm* engine, machine, device; *pl* tackle, appliances.

englober [ãglɔbe] *vt* to include, embrace, take in.

engloutir [ãgluti:r] *vt* to swallow up, gulp down, engulf; *vr* to be engulfed.

engoncé [ãgɔ̃se] *a* bunched-up, hunched-up.

engorgement [ãgɔrʒəmã] *nm* choking up, clogging, stoppage.

engorger [ãgɔrʒe] *vt* to choke up, clog, obstruct; *vr* to get choked up.

engouement [ãgumã] *nm* infatuation, craze.

engouer [ãgwe] *vt* to obstruct; *vr* to become infatuated, go crazy, mad

(about **de**), have a passion (for **de**).

engouffrer [ãgufre] *vt* to engulf, swallow up; *vr* to be engulfed, rush.

engourdi [ãgurdi] *a* numb, cramped, sluggish, lethargic; *n* dullard, sluggard.

engourdir [ãgurdi:r] *vt* to benumb, cramp, chill, dull; *vr* to grow numb, sluggish.

engourdissement [ãgurdismã] *nm* numbness, sluggishness.

engrais [ãgrɛ] *nm* fattening food, manure, fertilizer.

engraissement [ãgrɛsmã] *nm* fattening, growing fat, corpulence.

engraisser [ãgrɛse] *vt* to fatten, fertilize, manure; *vi* to grow fat, put on weight.

engranger [ãgrãʒe] *vt* (*corn*) to get in, to garner.

engrenage [ãgrəna:ʒ] *nm* gearing, gear, mesh; *pl* gear-wheels, works.

engrener [ãgrəne] *vt* to connect, engage; *vr* to interlock.

enhardir [ãardi:r] *vt* to make bolder, encourage; *vr* to venture, grow bolder.

enharnacher [ãarnaʃe] *vt* to put the harness on.

énigmatique [enigmatik] *a* enigmatic(al).

énigme [enigm] *nf* enigma, riddle, conundrum.

enivrement [ãnivrəmã] *nm* intoxication, rapture.

enivrer [ãnivre] *vt* to intoxicate, send into raptures; *vr* to get drunk, be carried away, be uplifted.

enjambée [ãʒãbe] *nf* stride.

enjambement [ãʒãbmã] *nm* enjambment.

enjamber [ãʒãbe] *vt* to step over, bestride; *vi* to stride along, encroach.

enjeu [ãʒø] *nm* (*betting*) stake.

enjoindre [ãʒwɛ̃:dr] *vt* to enjoin, exhort, call upon.

enjôler [ãʒole] *vt* to wheedle, cajole, coax.

enjoliver [ãʒɔlive] *vt* to embellish, embroider upon.

enjoué [ãʒwe] *a* playful, sportive, vivacious.

enjouement [ãʒumã] *nm* playfulness.

enlacement [ãlasmã] *nm* entwining, embrace.

enlacer [ãlase] *vt* to entwine, intertwine, clasp, embrace; *vr* to intertwine, twine, embrace each other.

enlaidir [ãlɛdi:r] *vt* to make ugly; *vi* to grow ugly.

enlèvement [ãlɛvmã] *nm* removal, carrying off, kidnapping, storming.

enlever [ãlve] *vt* to remove, carry off (away), storm, perform brilliantly, kidnap, abduct; *vr* to come off, boil over; **se laisser —** to elope.

enliser [ãlize] *vt* to draw in, engulf; *vr* to sink, get bogged.

enluminer [ãlymine] *vt* to illuminate, color.

enluminure [ãlyminy:r] *nf* illuminating, coloring, illumination.

ennemi [ɛnmi] *a* enemy, hostile; *n* enemy, foe.

ennoblir [ãnɔbli:r] *vt* to ennoble, exalt, elevate.

ennui [ãnɥi] boredom, tediousness, worry, trouble.

ennuyer [ãnɥije] *vt* to bore, bother, worry, annoy; *vr* to weary, be bored.

ennuyeux, -euse [ãnɥijø, ø:z] *a* tedious, irksome, tiresome, dull, drab, annoying.

énoncé [enɔ̃se] *nm* statement, wording, enunciation.

énoncer [enɔ̃se] *vt* to state, express, articulate.

énonciation [enɔ̃sjasjɔ̃] *nf* stating, articulation.

enorgueillir [ãnɔrgœji:r] *vt* to make proud; *vr* to become proud, pride oneself.

énorme [enɔrm] *a* huge, enormous, excessive, heinous.

énormément [enɔrmemã] *ad* enormously, awfully, a great many, a great deal.

énormité [enɔrmite] *nf* hugeness, enormity, incredible lie, excessiveness.

s'enquérir [sãkeri:r] *vr* to inquire, ask, make inquiries.

enquête [ãkɛt] *nf* inquiry, investigation, inquest.

enquêter [ãkɛte] *vi* to make investigations, hold an inquiry.

enraciner [ãrasine] *vt* to plant securely, establish; *vr* to take root, become ingrained.

enragé [ãraʒe] *a* mad, enthusiastic, rabid; *n* fan.

enrager [ãraʒe] *vt* to enrage, madden; *vi* to be mad, be in a rage.

enrayer [ãrɛje] *vt* to lock, check, stop, foul.

enregistrement [ãrəʒistrəmã] *nm* registration, recording; **bureau d'—** cloakroom; **bureau des bagages** checkroom.

enregistrer [ãrəʒistre] *vt* to register, record, enroll, enter.

enregistreur, -euse [ãrəʒistrœ:r, ø:z] *a* recording; *nm* registrar.

enrhumer [ãryme] *vt* to give s.o. a cold; *vr* to catch a cold.

enrichir [ãriʃi:r] *vt* to enrich, make wealthy, augment, increase; *vr* to grow wealthy, make money.

enrober [ãrɔbe] *vt* to cover, coat.

enrôler [ãrole] *vtr* to enroll, enlist.

enrouement [ãrumã] *nm* hoarseness, huskiness.

enroué [ãrwe] *a* hoarse, husky.

enrouer [ãrwe] *vt* to make hoarse; *vr* to become hoarse, husky.

enrouler [ãrule] *vt* to roll up, wind, wrap; *vr* to wind, coil.

enrubanner [ãrybane] *vt* to decorate with ribbon.

ensabler [ãsable] *vt* to sand, silt up.

ensanglanter [ãsãglãte] *vt* to stain, cover, with blood.

enseignant [ãsɛɲã] *a* teaching; **corps —** teaching profession.

enseigne [ãsɛɲ] *nf* mark, sign, token, shop-sign, ensign, (sub-) lieutenant; **logés à la même —** in the same boat.

enseignement [ãsɛɲmã] *nm* teaching, education, lesson.

enseigner [ãsɛɲe] *vt* to teach.

ensemble [ãsã:bl] *ad* together, at the same time; *nm* general effect, whole, set; **vue d'—** general view; **dans l'—** on the whole.

ensemencer [ãsmãse] *vt* to sow.

ensevelir [ãsəvli:r] *vt* to bury, entomb, cover.

ensevelissement [ãsəvlismã] *nm* burial, entombment.

ensoleillé [ãsɔlɛje] *a* sunny.

ensommeillé [ãsɔmɛje] *a* sleepy, drowsy.

ensorceler [ãsɔrsəle] *vt* to bewitch, cast a spell upon.

ensorcellement [ãsɔrsɛlmã] *nm* witchcraft, sorcery, spell.

ensuite [ãsɥit] *ad* then, afterward, next.

s'ensuivre [sãsɥi:vr] *vr* to follow, ensue.

entablement [ãtabləmã] *nm* coping, copestone.

entaille [ãtɑ:j] *nf* notch, nick, slot, dent, gash.

entailler [ãtɑje] *vt* to nick, notch, slot, gash.

entamer [ãtame] *vt* to cut, open, break, start.

entassement [ãtasmã] *nm* piling up, stacking.

entasser [ãtase] *vt* to heap (up), stack, accumulate, pack together; *vr* to accumulate, pile up, crowd together.

entendement [ãtãdmã] *nm* understanding, reason.

entendre [ãtã:dr] *vt* to hear, understand, mean, intend; *vr* to agree, know (about **en**), be good (at **à**); **—parler de** to hear of; **— dire que** to hear that; **laisser —** to imply.

entendu [ãtãdy] *a* capable, knowing, sensible, shrewd; *ad* **bien —** of course; **c'est —** all right, agreed.

entente [ãtã:t] *nf* agreement, understanding, knowledge.

entérite [ãterit] *nf* enteritis.

enterrement [ãtɛrmã] *nm* burial, funeral.

enterrer [ãtɛre] *vt* to bury, inter.

en-tête [ãtɛ:t] *nm* heading.

entêté [ãtɛte] *a* obstinate, stubborn.

entêtement [ãtɛtmã] *nm* obstinacy, doggedness.

s'entêter [sãtɛte] *vr* to be obstinate, persist.

enthousiasme [ãtuzjasm] *nm* enthusiasm.

enthousiasmer [ãtuzjasme] *vt* to fill with enthusiasm, send into raptures; *vr* to be, become, enthusiastic, rave (about **pour**).

enthousiaste [ãtuzjast] *a* enthusiastic; *n* enthusiast.

entiché [ãtiʃe] *a* infatuated, keen, mad; — **du théâtre** stage-struck.

entichement [ãtiʃmã] *nm* infatuation, craze.

s'enticher [sãtiʃe] *vr* to become infatuated (with **de**), take a fancy (to **de**).

entier, -ière [ãtje, jɛːr] *a* whole, entire, intact, downright, straightforward, possessive, whole-hearted.

entièrement [ãtjɛrmã] *ad* entirely, completely, quite.

entomologie [ãtɔmɔlɔʒi] *nf* entomology.

entonner [ãtɔne] *vt* to put into casks, strike up, intone; *vr* to rush, sweep.

entonnoir [ãtɔnwaːr] *nm* tunnel, crater, shell-hole.

entorse [ãtɔrs] *nf* sprain, twist, wrench.

entortiller [ãtɔrtije] *vt* to twine, twist, wind, coax, get around; *vr* to coil, wind.

entour [ãtuːr] *nm pl* neighborhood, surroundings; *ad* **à l'—** round about, around.

entourage [ãturaːʒ] *nm* circle of friends, following, environment.

entourer [ãture] *vt* to surround, encircle, encompass.

entournure [ãturnyːr] *nf* armhole.

entracte [ãtrakt] *nm* interval.

entra'de [ãtrɛ(ː)d] mutual aid.

s'entraider [sãtrɛde] *vr* to help one another.

entrai'les [ãtraːj] *nf pl* entrails, bowels, feeling.

entrain [ãtrɛ̃] *nm* spirit, dash, zest, whole-heartedness.

entraînant [ãtrɛnã] *a* stirring, rousing, catchy.

entraînement [ãtrɛnmã] *nm* dragging away, enticing away, enthusiasm, catchiness, training.

entraîner [ãtrɛne] *vt* to drag, carry away, entail, involve, lead astray, train, coach; *vr* to train, get into training.

entraîneur [ãtrɛnœːr] *nm* trainer, coach.

entrave [ãtraːv] *nf* fetter, shackle, obstacle, hobble.

entraver [ãtrave] *vt* to fetter, shackle, hobble, hamper, clog.

entre [ãːtr] *prep* between, among(st).

entrebâillement [ãtrəbajmã] *nm* chink, gap, slit, narrow opening.

entrebâiller [ãtrəbaje] *vt* to half-open, set ajar.

s'entrechoquer [sãtrəʃɔke] *vr* to clash, collide, clink.

entrecôte [ãtrəkɔt] *nf* (rib-)steak.

entrecouper [ãtrəkupe] *vt* to intersect, interrupt; *vr* to intersect, be interrupted.

entrecroiser [ãtrəkrwaze] *vt* to intersect, cross; *vr* to intersect.

entre-deux [ãtrədə] *nm* space between, partition, insertion.

entrée [ãtre] *nf* entry, entrance, way in, admission, inlet, import duty, entrée; — **interdite** no admittance.

entrefaite [ãtrəfɛt] *nf* **sur ces —s** meanwhile.

entrefilet [ãtrəfilɛ] *nm* paragraph.

entregent [ãrəʒã] *nm* tact, gumption.

entrelacement [ãtrəlasmã] *nm* interlacing, interweaving, intertwining.

entrelacer [ãtrəlase] *vtr* to interlace, intertwine.

entrelarder [ãtrəlarde] *vt* to lard, interlard.

entremêler [ãtrəmɛle] *vt* to intermingle, intervene.

entremets [ãtrəmɛ] *nm* side dish.

entremetteur -euse [ãtrəmɛtœːr, øːz] *n* intermediary, go-between, procurer.

s'entremettre [sãtrəmɛtr] *vr* to intervene, act as a go-between.

entremise [ãtrəmiːz] *nf* intervention, mediation, medium, agency.

entrepont [ãtrəpɔ̃] *nm* betweendecks.

entreposer [ãtrəpoze] *vt* to bond, warehouse, store.

entreposeur [ãtrəpozœːr] *nm* warehouseman.

entrepôt [ãtrəpo] *nm* bonded warehouse, mart, emporium.

entreprendre [ãtrəprãːdr] *vt* to undertake, contract for, take on.

entrepreneur, -euse [ãtrəprɑnœːr, øːz] *n* contractor; — **en bâtiments** builder, building contractor; — **de pompes funèbres** undertaker.

entreprise [ãtrəpriːz] *nf* enterprise, undertaking, concern.

entrer [ãtre] *vt* to bring in; *vi* to enter, come in, go in.

entresol [ãtrəsɔl] *nm* entresol, mezzanine.

entre-temps [ãtrətã] *nm* interval.

entretenir [ãtrətniːr] *vt* to maintain, keep (up), support, talk to, entertain; *vr* to keep oneself, converse; **s'— la main** to keep one's hand in.

entretien [ãtrətjɛ̃] *nm* maintenance, (up)keep, support, conversation, interview.

entrevoir [ãtrəvwaːr] *vt* to catch a glimpse of, glimpse, begin to see, foresee vaguely.

entrevue [ãtrəvy] *nf* interview, conference.

entr'ouvert [ãtruvɛr] *a* half-open, ajar. (*chasm*) gaping.

entr'ouvrir [ãtruviːr] *vt* to half-open; *vr* to gape.

énumération [enymɛrasjɔ̃] *nf*
enumeration, counting up.
énumérer [enymere] *vt* to enumerate, count up, detail.
envahir [ăvaːr] *vt* to invade, overrun, spread over.
envahisseur [ăvaisœːr] *nm* invader.
envaser [ăvaze] *vt* to silt up, choke up; *vr* to silt up, settle down in the mud.
enveloppe [ăvlɔp] *nf* envelope, cover, wrapping, sheath, outward appearance.
envelopper [ăvlɔpe] *vt* to envelop, wrap, cover, surround, shroud.
envenimer [ăvnime] *vt* to poison, inflame, embitter, aggravate; *vr* to fester, grow more bitter.
envergure [ăvɛrgyːr] *nf* breadth, span, scope; **de grande — far-reaching.
envers [ăvɛːr] *prep* toward; *nm* reverse, wrong side; **à l'— inside out, wrong way up.
envi [ăvi] *nm* **à l'— vying with one another.
enviable [ăvjabl] *a* enviable.
envie [ăvi] *nf* desire, longing, inclination, envy; **avoir — de** to want (to); **porter — à** to envy.
envier [ăvje] *vt* to envy, begrudge, long for, covet, be envious of.
envieux, -euse [ăvjø, øːz] *a* envious, jaundiced.
environ [ăvirɔ] *ad* about; *nm pl* neighborhood, outskirts, surroundings.
environner [ăvirɔne] *vt* to surround.
envisager [ăvisaʒe] *vt* to look at, face, view, foresee, anticipate.
envoi [ăvwa] *nm* sending, forwarding, consignment.
envol [ăvɔl] *nm* taking wing, taking off, take-off.
s'envoler [săvɔle] *vr* to fly away, off, take flight.
envoûtement [ăvutmă] *nm* (casting of a) spell, hoodoo, passion, craze.
envoûter [ăvute] *vt* to put a spell, a hoodoo on, hold enthralled.
envoyé [ăvwaje] *nm* envoy, representative.
envoyer [ăvwaje] *vt* to send, dispatch; **— chercher** to send for; **— dire** to send word; **— promener** to send about one's business.
épagneul [epaɲœl] *n* spaniel.
épais, -aisse [epɛ, ɛːs] *a* thick, dense.
épaisseur [epɛsœːr] *nf* thickness, density.
épaissir [epɛsiːr] *vt* to thicken, make dense; *vr* to thicken, grow dense, stout.
épanchement [epăʃmă] *nm* pouring out, effusion, outpouring.
épancher [epăʃe] *vt* to pour out, pour forth; *vr* to pour out one's heart, expand, unburden oneself.
épandre [epăːdr] *vt* to spread, shed; *vr* to spread.

épanoui [epanwi] *a* in full bloom, beaming, wreathed in smiles.
épanouir [epanwiːr] *vt* to make (*sth*) open, bring forth, — out; *vr* to open out, bloom, light up, beam.
épanouissement [epanwismă] *nm* opening up, blossoming.
épargne [eparɲ] *nf* economy, thrift, saving.
épargner [eparɲe] *vt* to save, economize, be sparing of, spare.
éparpiller [eparpije] *vtr* to scatter, disperse.
épars [epaːr] *a* scattered, stray, scant.
épatant [epată] *a* (*fam*) great, splendid, terrific.
épate [epat] *nf* **faire de l'— to show off.
épater [epate] *vt* astound, startle, stagger; to break the foot of.
épaule [epoːl] *nf* shoulder; **hausser les —s** to shrug one's shoulders.
épauler [epole] *vt* to shoulder; *vi* (*rifle*) to aim.
épaulette [epolɛt] *nf* shoulder-strap, epaulette.
épave [epaːv] *nf* wreck, waif, unclaimed object; *pl* flotsam, jetsam, wreckage.
épée [epe] *nf* sword.
épeler [eple] *vt* to spell.
éperdu [epɛrdy] *a* distracted, mad.
éperon [eprɔ̃] *nm* spur, buttress.
éperonner [eprɔne] *vt* to spur, urge on.
épervier [epɛrvje] *nm* sparrowhawk, fishing net.
éphémère [efemɛːr] *a* ephemeral, short-lived, fleeting; *nf* mayfly.
épi [epi] *nm* (*corn*) ear, cluster.
épice [epis] *nf* spice; **pain d'—** (type of) gingerbread.
épicé [epise] *a* spiced, seasoned, spicy.
épicer [epise] *vt* to spice, season.
épicerie [episri] *nf* spices, groceries, grocer's shop.
épicier, -ière [episje, jɛːr] *n* grocer.
épicurien, -ienne [epikyrjɛ̃, jɛn] *a* epicurean; *n* epicure, sybarite.
épicurisme [epikyrism] *nm* epicureanism.
épidémie [epidemi] *nf* epidemic.
épidémique [epidemik] *a* epidemic (al).
épiderme [epidɛrm] *nm* epiderm(is).
épier [epje] *vt* to spy upon, watch for, listen for.
épigramme [epigram] *nf* epigram.
épilepsie [epilɛpsi] *nf* epilepsy.
épiler [epile] *vt* to remove superfluous hair from, pluck.
épilogue [epilɔg] *nm* epilogue.
épiloguer [epilɔge] *vt* to criticize, find fault with; *vi* to carp.
épinard [epinaːr] *nm* spinach.
épine [epin] *nf* thorn-bush, thorn, prickle.
épinette [epinɛt] *nf* spruce, virginal, spinet.

épineux, -euse [epinø, øːz] *a* thorny, prickly, knotty, ticklish, tricky.

épingle [epɛ̃ːgl] *nf* pin; — **de nourrice** safety-pin; — **à linge** clothespin; **tiré à quatre** —**s** spruce, dapper.

épingler [epɛ̃gle] *vt* to pin, fasten with a pin.

épique [epik] *a* epic.

épiscopal [episkɔpal] *a* episcopal.

épiscopat [episkɔpa] *nm* episcopate.

épisode [epizɔd] *nm* episode.

épistolaire [epistɔlɛːr] *a* epistolary.

épitaphe [epitaf] *nf* epitaph.

épithète [epitɛt] *nf* epithet, adjective.

épître [epiːtr] *nf* epistle.

éploré [eplɔre] *a* tearful, in tears, weeping.

éplucher [eplyʃe] *vt* to clean, peel, sift, examine.

épluchures [eplyʃyːr] *nf pl* peelings, refuse.

épointer [epwɛ̃te] *vt* to blunt, break the point of.

éponge [epɔ̃ːʒ] *nf* sponge.

éponger [epɔ̃ʒe] *vt* to mop, sponge, dab, mop up.

épopée [epɔpe] *nf* epic.

époque [epɔk] *nf* epoch, era, age, period, time; **faire** — to mark an epoch, be a landmark.

s'époumoner [sepumɔne] *vr* to talk, shout, till one is out of breath.

épousailles [epuzaːj] *nf pl* wedding.

épouser [epuze] *vt* to marry, wed.

épousseter [epuste] *vt* to dust, beat.

époussette [epusɛt] *nf* feather-duster.

épouvantable [epuvɑ̃tabl] *a* dreadful, appalling.

épouvantail [epuvɑ̃taːj] *nm* scarecrow, bogy.

épouvante [epuvɑ̃ːt] *nf* terror, dread, fright.

épouvanter [epuvɑ̃te] *vt* to terrify; *vr* to be terror-stricken, take fright.

époux, -ouse [epu, uːz] *n* husband, wife.

s'éprendre [seprɑ̃ːdr] *vr* to fall in love (with de), take a fancy (to de).

épreuve [eprœːv] *nf* proof, test, trial, ordeal, print, impression, examination paper; **à l'**— **de** proof against; **à toute** — foolproof.

éprouvé [epruve] *a* well-tried, sorely tried, stricken.

éprouver [epruve] *vt* to test, try, feel, suffer.

éprouvette [epruvɛt] *nf* test-tube, gauge.

épuisement [epɥizmɑ̃] *nm* exhaustion, distress, depletion, using up, emptying.

épuiser [epɥize] *vt* to exhaust, use up, tire out.

épuisette [epɥizɛt] *nf* scoop, landing-net.

épuration [epyrasjɔ̃] *nf* purification, purging, expurgation, filtering.

épurer [epyre] *vt* to purify, filter.

équarrir [ekariːr] *vt* to square, broach, cut up.

équateur [ekwatœːr] *nm* equator.

équation [ekwasjɔ̃] *nf* equation.

équerre [ekɛːr] *nf* square, angle-iron, bevel.

équerrer [ekɛre] *vt* to square, bevel.

équestre [ekɛstr] *a* equestrian.

équilibre [ekilibr] *nm* equilibrium, balance, stability.

équilibrer [ekilibre] *vtr* to balance.

équilibriste [ekilibrist] *n* equilibrist, acrobat, tight-rope walker.

équinoxe [ekinɔks] *nm* equinox.

équipage [ekipaːʒ] *nm* crew, company, retinue, train, carriage and horses, apparel, rig-out, equipment; **maître d'**— master of the hounds, coxswain.

équipe [ekip] *nf* squad, gang, team, crew, shift, train (of barges); **chef d'**— foreman.

équipée [ekipe] *nf* escapade, frolic, lark.

équipement [ekipmɑ̃] *nm* equipment, accouterment, outfit, fitting out (up).

équiper [ekipe] *vt* to equip, appoint, fit out, man.

équipier [ekipje] *nm* one of a squad, member of a team.

équitable [ekitabl] *a* just, fair.

équitation [ekitasjɔ̃] *nf* horsemanship, riding.

équité [ekite] *nf* equity, fairness, justness.

équivalent [ekivalɑ̃] *a nm* equivalent.

équivaloir [ekivalwaːr] *vi* to be equal, be equivalent, be tantamount.

équivoque [ekivɔk] *a* ambiguous, equivocal, doubtful; *nf* ambiguity.

équivoquer [ekivɔke] *vi* to equivocate, quibble.

érable [erabl] *nm* maple.

érafler [erafle] *vt* to scratch, graze, score.

éraflure [eraflyːr] *nf* scratch, graze.

éraillement [erajmɑ̃] *nm* fraying, grazing, hoarseness.

érailler [eraje] *vt* to unravel, graze, roughen; *vr* to fray, become hoarse.

ère [ɛːr] *nf* era, period, epoch.

érection [ereksjɔ̃] *nf* putting up.

éreintant [erɛ̃tɑ̃] *a* back-breaking, killing.

éreinter [erɛ̃te] *vt* to break the back of, wear out, knock about, slate; *vr* to wear oneself out, slave.

ergot [ɛrgo] *nm* spur, dewclaw, ergot; **se dresser sur ses** —**s** to get on one's high horse.

ergotage [ɛrgotaːʒ] *nm* cavilling, quibbling.

ergoter [ɛrgote] *vi* to cavil, quibble, haggle.

ergoteur, -euse [ɛrgotœːr, øːz] *a* cavilling, quibbling; *n* quibbler.

ériger [eriʒe] *vt* to erect, put up, set up; *vr* to set oneself up (as en).
ermitage [ɛrmitaːʒ] *nm* hermitage.
ermite [ɛrmit] *nm* hermit.
éroder [erɔde] *vt* to erode, eat away.
erosion [erɔzjɔ̃] *nf* erosion.
érotique [erɔtik] *a* erotic.
érotisme [erɔtism] *nm* eroticism.
errements [ɛrmɑ̃] *nm pl* erring ways.
errer [ɛre] *vt* to wander, roam, ramble.
erreur [ɛrœːr] *nf* error, mistake, slip, fallacy.
erroné [ɛrɔne] *a* erroneous, false, mistaken.
éructer [erykte] *vi* to belch.
érudit [erydi] *a* learned, scholarly, erudite; *nm* scholar, scientist
érudition [erydisjɔ̃] *nf* learning, scholarship.
éruption [erypsjɔ̃] *nf* eruption.
ès [ɛs] = en + les; docteur — sciences, doctor of science.
escabeau [ɛskabo] *nm* stool, steps.
escadre [ɛskaːdr] *nf* (*naut*) squadron.
escadrille [ɛskadriːj] *nf* (*naut*) flotilla, (*av*) squadron.
escadron [ɛskadrɔ̃] *nm* (*cavalry*) squadron.
escalade [ɛskalad] *nf* climb(ing), scaling.
escalader [ɛskalade] *vt* to climb, scale.
escale [ɛskal] *nf* port of call, call; faire — à to put in at; sans — non-stop.
escalier [ɛskalje] *nm* staircase, stairs; — de service backstairs; — roulant escalator; il a l'esprit de l'— he has never a ready answer.
escalope [ɛskalɔp] *nf* cutlet.
escamotable [ɛskamotabl] *a* concealable, retractable.
escamotage [ɛskamɔtaːʒ] *nm* sleight of hand, conjuring, theft, pinching.
escamoter [ɛskamɔte] *vt* to conjure away, whisk away, hide, evade, pinch; (*av*) retract undercarriage.
escamoteur [ɛskamɔtœːr] *nm* conjurer.
escampette [ɛskɑ̃pɛt] *nf* prendre la poudre d'— to clear off, decamp.
escapade [ɛskapad] *nf* escapade, adventure, prank.
escarbille [ɛskarbiːj] *nf* cinder, clinker.
escarbot [ɛskarbo] *nm* cockchafer, blackbeetle.
escarboucle [ɛskarbukl] *nf* carbuncle.
escargot [ɛskargo] *nm* snail.
escarmouche [ɛskarmuʃ] *nf* skirmish.
escarpé [ɛskarpe] *a* steep, sheer, precipitous.
escarpement [ɛskarpəmɑ̃] *nm* escarpment.
escarpin [ɛskarpɛ̃] *nm* dancing-shoe, pump.
escarpolette [ɛskarpɔlɛt] *nf* swing.

escarre [ɛskaːr] *nf* bedsore, scab.
escient [ɛsjɑ̃] *nm* knowledge; à mon — to my knowledge; à son — wittingly.
s'esclaffer [sɛsklafe] *vr* to burst out laughing, guffaw.
esclandre [ɛsklɑ̃ːdr] *nm* scandal.
esclavage [ɛsklavaːʒ] *nm* slavery, bondage.
esclave [ɛsklaːv] *n* slave.
escompte [ɛskɔ̃ːt] *nm* discount, rebate.
escompter [ɛskɔ̃te] *vt* to discount, allow for, anticipate.
escorte [ɛskɔrt] *nf* escort, convoy.
escorter [ɛskɔrte] *vt* to escort.
escouade [ɛskwad] *nf* squad, section.
escrime [ɛskrim] *nf* fencing, swordsmanship, skirmishing.
escrimer [ɛskrime] *vi* to fence; *vr* to try hard, spar.
escrimeur [ɛskrimœːr] *nm* fencer, swordsman.
escroc [ɛskro] *nm* swindler, crook.
escroquer [ɛskrɔke] *vt* to rob, swindle, cheat.
escroquerie [ɛskrɔkri] *nf* swindling, swindle.
ésotérique [esɔterik] *a* esoteric.
espace [ɛspas] *nm* space, interval.
espacer [ɛspase] *vt* to space (out); *vr* to become more and more isolated, grow fewer and fewer.
espadrille [ɛspadriːj] *nf* rope-soled canvas shoe.
Espagne [ɛspaɲ] *nf* Spain.
espagnol [ɛspaɲɔl] *a* Spanish; *n* Spaniard.
espagnolette [ɛspaɲɔlɛt] *nf* window-catch.
espèce [ɛspɛs] *nf* kind, sort, species; *pl* cash.
espérance [ɛsperɑ̃ːs] *nf* hope, expectation.
espérer [ɛspere] *vt* to hope (for).
espiègle [ɛspjɛgl] *a* mischievous, arch, roguish.
espièglerie [ɛspjɛgləri] *nf* mischievousness, roguishness, trick, prank.
espion, -onne [ɛspjɔ̃, ɔn] *n* spy.
espionnage [ɛspjɔnaːʒ] *nm* espionage, spying.
espionner [ɛspjɔne] *vt* to spy (on).
esplanade [ɛsplanad] *nf* esplanade, parade.
espoir [ɛspwaːr] *nm* hope.
esprit [ɛspri] *nm* spirit, ghost, soul, mind, wit.
esquif [ɛskif] *nm* skiff.
esquimau, -aude [ɛskimo] *an* Eskimo.
esquinter [ɛskɛ̃te] *vt* to exhaust, run down, slate.
esquisse [ɛskis] *nf* sketch, draft, outline.
esquisser [ɛskise] *vt* to sketch, draft, outline.
esquiver [ɛskive] *vt* to evade, dodge, shirk; *vr* to slip away, dodge (off), abscond.

essai [ɛsɛ] nm trial, test, experiment, attempt, try, sample, essay; **à l'—** on trial, on approval; **coup d'—** first attempt, trial shot.

essaim [ɛsɛ̃] nm swarm, cluster, hive.

essaimer [eseme] vi to swarm.

essayage [esɛjɑːʒ] nm fitting.

essayer [esɛje] vt to test, try, try on, fit, attempt, assay; vr to try one's hand.

essence [ɛsɑ̃ːs] nf essence, extract, gasoline; **poste d'— filling-station.**

essentiel, -elle [ɛsɑ̃sjɛl] a essential, crucial, key; n the main thing, burden.

essieu [esjø] nm axle.

essor [ɛsɔːr] nm flight, rise, scope.

essoreuse [esɔrøːz] nf wringer, spin-drier.

essoufflé [esufle] a breathless, out of breath.

essoufflement [esufləmɑ̃] nm breathlessness.

essouffler [esufle] vt to wind, put out of breath; vr to get breathless, winded.

essuie-glace [esɥiglas] nm windshield wiper.

essuie-mains [esɥimɛ̃] nm towel.

essuie-pieds [esɥipje] nm doormat.

essuyer [esɥije] vt to wipe (up), clean, meet with.

est [ɛst] nm east.

estacade [ɛstakad] nf line of piles, pier, boom, stockade.

estafette [ɛstafɛt] nf courier, dispatch-rider.

estafilade [ɛstafilad] nf slash, gash, rent.

estaminet [ɛstaminɛ] nm café, bar, public-house.

estampe [ɛstɑ̃ːp] nf print, engraving.

estamper [ɛstɑ̃pe] vt to stamp, emboss, punch, sting.

estampille [ɛstɑ̃piːj] nf stamp, trade-mark, endorsement.

esthète [ɛstɛt] n aesthete.

esthétique [ɛstetik] a aesthetic.

estimateur, -trice [ɛstimatœːr, tris] n estimator.

estimation [ɛstimasjɔ̃] nf valuation, valuing, estimate.

estime [ɛstim] nf esteem, regard, estimation, reckoning.

estimer [ɛstime] vt to estimate, valuate, calculate, guess, consider, deem, value, esteem.

estival [ɛstival] a summer, estival.

estivant [ɛstivɑ̃] n summer visitor, holiday-maker.

estoc [ɛstɔk] nm stock, point of sword.

estocade [ɛstɔkad] nf thrust.

estomac [ɛstɔma] nm stomach.

estomaquer [ɛstɔmake] vt to take s.o.'s breath away, stagger.

estompé [ɛstɔ̃pe] a blurred, soft, hazy.

estomper [ɛstɔ̃pe] vt to stump, shade off, soften the outlines of.

estrade [ɛstrad] nf platform, stage, dais.

estropier [ɛstrɔpje] vt to maim, cripple, spoil, murder.

estuaire [ɛstɥɛːr] nm estuary, firth.

estudiantin [ɛstydjɑ̃tɛ̃] a student.

et [e] cj and; **et . . . et** both . . . and; **et vous?** what about you? do you? are you?; **— alors!** so what!

étable [etabl] nf cattle-shed, byre.

établi [etabli] nm (work-)bench.

établir [etabliːr] vt to establish, put up, set up, install, fix, draw up, lay down; vr to establish oneself, settle.

établissement [etablismɑ̃] nm establishment, setting up, installing, drawing up, laying down.

étage [etaːʒ] nm story, floor, tier, layer, rank.

étager [etaʒe] vt to arrange in tiers, terrace, stagger; vr to be tiered, terraced.

étagère [etaʒɛːr] nf rack, shelves.

étai [etɛ] nm stay, prop, strut, mainstay.

étain [etɛ̃] nm tin, pewter.

étal [etal] nm butcher's stall, shop.

étalage [etalaːʒ] nm show, display, window-dressing, show-window; **faire — de** to display, show off, flaunt.

étaler [etale] vt to display, spread out, lay out, exhibit, show off, air; vr to stretch (oneself out), sprawl, enlarge (upon), expatiate (on).

étalon [etalɔ̃] nm standard, stallion.

étalonner [etalɔne] vt to stamp, mark, standardize.

étamer [etame] vt to tinplate, silver, galvanize.

étameur [etamœːr] nm tinsmith.

étamine [etamin] nf coarse muslin, gauze, bunting, sieve, strainer, stamen.

étampe [etɑ̃ːp] nf stamp, die, punch·

étamper [etɑ̃pe] vt to stamp, mark, punch.

étanche [etɑ̃ːʃ] a impervious, tight, insulated; **— à l'air (à l'eau)** air-(water)tight.

étancher [etɑ̃ʃe] vt to stanch, stop (flow of), quench, make water(air) tight.

étançonner [etɑ̃sɔne] vt to prop up, shore up.

étang [etɑ̃] nm pond, pool.

étape [etap] nf stage, stopping-place, a day's march.

état [eta] nm state, condition, order, list, statement, profession; **mettre qn en — de** to enable s.o. to; **être dans tous ses —s** to be in a great state.

étatisme [etatism] nm state control.

état-major [etamaʒɔːr] nm general staff, headquarters.

étau [eto] nm (tec) vise.

étayer [etɛje] vt to prop up, shore up, support; vr to brace oneself.

été [ete] nm summer

éteignoir [etɛɲwaːr] *nm* damper, extinguisher.

éteindre [etɛ̃ːdr] *vt* to extinguish, put out, switch off, dim; *vr* to go out, die (out, away, down), fade (away).

éteint [etɛ̃] *a* extinguished, extinct, dim, faint, dull, dead.

étendard [etɑ̃daːr] *nm* standard, flag, colors.

étendre [etɑ̃ːdr] *vt* to stretch, spread, extend, enlarge; *vr* to stretch oneself out, lie down, extend, spread, dwell (upon), hold forth (on).

étendu [etɑ̃dy] *a* extensive, wide, far-reaching.

étendue [etɑ̃dy] *nf* extent, size, expanse, stretch.

éternel, -elle [etɛrnɛl] *a* eternal, everlasting, endless.

éterniser [etɛrnize] *vt* to perpetuate, drag (out, on); *vr* to drag on and on.

éternité [etɛrnite] *nf* eternity.

éternuement [etɛrnymɑ̃] *nm* sneeze, sneezing.

éternuer [etɛrnɥe] *vt* to sneeze.

éthéré [etere] *a* ethereal.

éthique [etik] *a* ethical; *nf* ethics.

ethnique [ɛtnik] *a* ethnical, ethnological.

étinceler [etɛ̃sle] *vi* to sparkle, glitter, flash.

étincelle [etɛ̃sɛl] *nf* spark, flash.

étincellement [etɛ̃sɛlmɑ̃] *nm* sparkling, glittering, twinkling

étioler [etjɔle] *vt* to blanch, make wilt, weaken; *vr* to blanch, wilt.

étique [etik] *a* emaciated, skinny, gaunt.

étiqueter [etikte] *vt* to label, ticket, docket.

étiquette [etikɛt] *nf* label, ticket, docket, etiquette, ceremonial; **— à œillets** tie-on label; **— gommée** stick-on label.

étoffe [etɔf] *nf* material, cloth, fabric, stuff, makings.

étoffé [etɔfe] *a* ample, rich, stuffed, stout, meaty.

étoile [etwal] *nf* star, asterisk; **dormir à la belle —** to sleep in the open.

étole [etɔl] *nf* stole.

étonnement [etɔnmɑ̃] *nm* surprise, astonishment.

étonner [etɔne] *vt* to surprise, astonish, amaze; *vr* to be surprised.

étouffant [etufɑ̃] *a* stifling, stuffy, sultry, airless.

étouffement [etufmɑ̃] *nm* choking, suffocation, attack of breathlessness.

étouffer [etufe] *vti* to suffocate, choke; *vi* damp, stifle, deaden, smother, hush up.

étoupe [etup] *nf* tow, oakum.

étourderie [eturdəri] *nf* thoughtlessness, giddiness.

étourdi [eturdi] *a* scatterbrained, hare-brained, dizzy, giddy; *n* scatterbrain.

étourdir [eturdiːr] *vt* to daze, bemuse, make one's head reel, deafen, astound.

étourdissement [eturdismɑ̃] *nm* giddiness, dizziness.

étourneau [eturno] *nm* starling, scatterbrain.

étrange [etrɑ̃ːʒ] *a* strange, queer, odd.

étranger, -ère [etrɑ̃ʒe, ɛːr] *a* foreign, alien, unfamiliar, irrelevant; *n* foreigner, alien, stranger; *nm* abroad.

étranglement [etrɑ̃gləmɑ̃] *nm* strangulation, constriction, narrows, narrowing, bottleneck.

étrangler [etrɑ̃gle] *vt* to throttle, strangle, choke, constrict; *vi* to choke; *vr* to narrow, gulp.

étrave [etraːv] *nf* (naut) bow, stem.

être [ɛːtr] *vi* to be, exist; *nm* being, existence, creature; **il est à écrire** he is busy writing; **où en êtes-vous?** how far have you got? **il n'en est rien** nothing of the kind; **le chapeau est à lui** the hat is his; **comme si de rien n'était** as if nothing had happened.

étreindre [etrɛ̃ːdr] *vt* to embrace, clasp, grasp, wring.

étreinte [etrɛ̃ːt] *nf* embrace, hug, clasp, grip, clutch.

étrenne [etrɛn] *nf* New Year's gift.

étrenner [etrɛne] *vt* to be the first to buy from, use for the first time, handsel.

étrier [etrie] *nm* stirrup; **coup de l'—** stirrup-cup.

étrille [etriːj] *nf* curry-comb.

étriller [etrije] *vt* to curry-comb, thrash, give a drubbing to.

étriper [etripe] *vt* to gut, clean, disembowel.

étriqué [etrike] *a* tight, skimped, cramped.

étroit [etrwa] *a* narrow, tight, close, hidebound.

étroitesse [etrwatɛs] *nf* narrowness, tightness, closeness.

étude [etyd] *nf* study, research, prep. (lessons), office, chambers; **à l'—** under consideration; **faire ses —s à** to be educated at.

étudiant [etydjɑ̃] *n* student, undergraduate.

étudié [etydje] *a* studied, affected, deliberate.

étudier [etydje] *vt* to study, read, investigate; *vr* to strive, make a point (of).

étui [etɥi] *nm* case, box.

étuve [etyːv] *nf* sweating-room, drying-room.

étuver [etyve] *vt* to dry, heat, stew, steam, jug.

étymologie [etimɔlɔʒi] *nf* etymology.

étymologique [etimɔlɔʒik] *a* etymological.

étymologiste [etimɔlɔʒist] *n* etymologist.

eucharistie [økaristi] *nf* Eucharist, Lord's Supper.

eunuque [ønyk] *nm* eunuch.

euphémisme [øfemism] *nm* euphemism.

euphonie [øfɔni] *nf* euphony.

Europe [ørɔp] *nf* Europe.

européen, -enne [ørɔpeɛ̃, ɛn] *an* European.

euthanasie [øtanazi] *nf* euthanasia.

évacuation [evakɥasjɔ̃] *nf* clearing, withdrawal, vacating.

évacué [evakɥe] *n* evacuee.

évacuer [evakɥe] *vt* to evacuate, empty, withdraw, vacate.

évadé [evade] *a* escaped; *n* escaped prisoner.

s'évader [sevade] *vr* to escape, run away, break out.

évaluation [evalɥasjɔ̃] *nf* valuation, assessment, estimate, appraisal.

évaluer [evalɥe] *vt* to evaluate, assess, appraise.

évangile [evɑ̃ʒil] *nm* gospel.

évanouir [evanwiːr] *vr* to vanish, disappear, faint.

évanouissement [evanwismɑ̃] *nm* disappearance, fading away, swoon.

évaporation [evapɔrasjɔ̃] *nf* evaporation, frivolousness.

évaporé [evapɔre] *a* giddy, light-headed.

évaporer [evapɔre] *vr* to evaporate, pass off, become silly and frivolous.

évasement [evɑzmɑ̃] *nm* widening out, flare, bell-mouth.

évaser [evɑze] *vtr* to open out, widen, flare.

évasif, -ive [evazif, iːv] *a* evasive.

évasion [evazjɔ̃] *nf* escape, evasion.

évêché [eveʃe] *nm* bishopric, bishop's palace.

éveil [eveːj] *nm* awakening, wide-awake state, alert, alarm.

éveillé [eveje] *a* awake, alert, bright, alive.

éveiller [eveje] *vt* to wake up, awake, arouse; *vr* to wake up, awaken.

événement [evenmɑ̃] *nm* event, incident, happening, occurrence; **dans l'**— as it transpired; **attendre l'**— to await the outcome.

éventail [evɑ̃taːj] *nm* fan.

éventaire [evɑ̃tɛːr] *nm* flat basket.

éventé [evɑ̃te] *a* flat, stale, musty.

éventer [evɑ̃te] *vt* to air, fan, catch the scent of, get wind of; *vr* to fan oneself, go flat, go stale.

éventrer [evɑ̃tre] *vt* to disembowel, gut, smash open.

éventualité [evɑ̃tɥalite] *nf* eventuality, contingency, possibility.

éventuel, -elle [evɑ̃tɥɛl] *ad* contingent, possible.

éventuellement [evɑ̃tɥɛlmɑ̃] *ad* possibly, should the occasion arise.

évêque [eveːk] *nm* bishop.

s'évertuer [severtɥe] *vr* to strive, make every effort.

éviction [eviksjɔ̃] *nf* eviction.

évidemment [evidamɑ̃] *ad* evidently, obviously.

évidence [evidɑ̃ːs] *nf* obviousness, conspicuousness; **se rendre à l'**— to accept the facts; **être en** — to be to the fore, in the limelight.

évident [evidɑ̃] *a* evident, obvious clear.

évider [evide] *vt* to hollow out groove, cut away.

évier [evje] *nm* sink.

évincer [evɛ̃se] to evict, turn out.

évitement [evitmɑ̃] *nm* avoiding, shunting, loop.

éviter [evite] *vt* to avoid, shun, evade, save (from).

évocateur, -trice [evɔkatœːr, tris] *a* evocative, picturesque.

évocation [evɔkasjɔ̃] *nf* evocation conjuring up, calling to mind.

évoluer [evɔlɥe] *vi* to maneuver, evolve, revolve.

évolution [evɔlysjɔ̃] *nf* evolution, maneuver.

évoquer [evɔke] *vt* to evoke, call forth, conjure up, call to mind.

exacerber [ɛgzasɛrbe] *vt* to exacerbate.

exact [ɛgzakt] *a* accurate, punctual, strict, express.

exactitude [ɛgzaktityd] *nf* exactness accuracy, punctuality.

exagération [ɛgzaʒerasjɔ̃] *nf* exaggeration, overstatement.

exagérer [ɛgzaʒere] *vt* to exaggerate, overrate, magnify, overdo, go too far.

exaltation [ɛgzaltasjɔ̃] *nf* exaltation, extolling, excitement.

exalté [ɛgzalte] *a* passionate, elated, impassioned, hot-headed, quixotic.

exalter [ɛgzalte] *vt* to exalt, extol, excite, uplift; *vr* to grow enthusiastic, excited.

examen [ɛgzamɛ̃] *nm* examination, inspection, scrutiny; **se présenter à un** — to take an examination.

examinateur, -trice [ɛgzaminatœːr, tris] *n* examiner.

examiner [ɛgzamine] *vt* to examine, inspect, scrutinize.

exaspération [ɛgzasperasjɔ̃] *nf* annoyance, aggravation.

exaspérer [ɛgzaspere] *vt* to exasperate, aggravate; *vr* to become exasperated.

exaucer [ɛgzose] *vt* to fulfill, grant.

excavation [ɛkskavasjɔ̃] *nf* excavation, digging out.

excédent [ɛksedɑ̃] *nm* surplus, excess.

excéder [ɛksede] *vt* to exceed, go beyond, overstrain, tire out, exasperate.

excellence [ɛkselɑ̃ːs] *nf* excellence.

excellent [ɛkselɑ̃] *a* excellent.

exceller [ɛksele] *vi* to excel.

excentricité [ɛksɑ̃trisite] *nf* eccentricity, oddity.

excentrique [ɛksãtrik] *a* eccentric, odd, outlying; *n* eccentric character.

excepté [eksɛpte] *prep* except, but, barring.

excepter [eksɛpte] *vt* to except, exclude.

exception [eksɛpsjɔ̃] *nf* exception; **sauf** — with certain exceptions.

exceptionnel, -elle [eksɛpsjɔnɛl] *a* exceptional.

excès [eksɛ] *nm* excess; **à l'** — to excess, to a fault, over-.

excessif, -ive [eksɛsif, iːv] *a* excessive, undue.

excessivement [eksɛsivmã] *a* exceedingly, over-.

excitabilité [eksitabilite] *nf* excitability.

excitant [eksitã] *a* stimulating, exciting, hectic; *nm* stimulant.

excitation [eksitasjɔ̃] *nf* excitation, stimulation, incitement.

exciter [eksite] *vt* to excite, stimulate, arouse, urge, incite, spur (on); *vr* to get worked up, roused.

exclamatif, -ive [ɛksklamatif, iːv] *a* exclamative, exclamatory.

exclamation [ɛksklamasjɔ̃] *nf* exclamation.

s'exclamer [sɛksklame] *vr* to exclaim.

exclure [ɛksklyːr] *vt* to exclude, leave out, debar.

exclusif, -ive [ɛksklyzif, iːv] *a* exclusive, sole.

exclusion [ɛksklyzjɔ̃] *nf* exclusion.

exclusivité [ɛksklyzivite] *nf* exclusiveness, sole rights.

excommunier [ɛkskɔmynje] *vt* to excommunicate.

excrément [ɛskremã] *nm* excrement, scum.

excursion [ɛkskyrsjɔ̃] *nf* excursion, trip, outing, raid.

excursionniste [ɛkskyrsjɔnist] *nm* excursionist, tourist.

excusable [ɛkskyzabl] *a* pardonable.

excuse [ɛkskyːz] *nf* excuse, apology.

excuser [ɛkskyze] *vt* to excuse, pardon, make excuses for; *vr* to apologize, excuse oneself; **se faire** — to withdraw, call off.

exécrable [egzɛkrabl] *a* execrable, abominable.

exécration [egzɛkrasjɔ̃] *nf* execration, loathing.

exécrer [egzekre] *vt* to execrate, loathe.

exécutable [egzekytabl] *a* feasible, practicable.

exécutant [egzekytã] *n* executant, performer.

exécuter [egzekyte] *vt* to execute, carry out, perform, enforce; *vr* to comply.

exécuteur, -trice [egzekytœːr, tris] *n* executor, -trix.

exécutif, -ive [egzekytif, iːv] *a* executive.

exécution [egzekysjɔ̃] *nf* execution, accomplishment, performance, en-

forcement; **mettre à** — to put into effect, carry out.

exemplaire [egzãplɛːr] *a* exemplary; *nm* specimen, copy.

exemple [egzãːpl] *nm* example, precedent, instance, lesson; **par** — for example, fancy that!

exempt [egzã] *a* exempt, free.

exempter [egzãte] *vt* to exempt excuse; *vr* to get out (o :.

exemption [egzãsjɔ̃] *nf* exemption, immunity.

exercé [egzɛrse] *a* trained, practiced

exercer [egzɛrse] *vt* to exercise, exert, carry on drill, train; *vr* to be exerted, practice.

exercice [egzɛrsis] *nm* drill, training, practice, exercise carrying out; financial year; **entrer en** — to take up one's duties; **en** — practicing, acting.

exhalaison [egzalɛzɔ̃] *nf* exhalation, odor.

exhalation [egzalasjɔ̃] *nf* exhalation exhaling.

exhaler [egzale] *v* to exhale, emit, vent, pour forth.

exhaustif [egzostif] *a* exhaustive.

exhiber [egzibe] *vt* to exhibit, show flaunt; *vr* to make an exhibition o oneself.

exhibition [egzibisjɔ̃] *nf* show showing.

exhorter [egzɔrte] *vt* to exhort, urge

exhumer [egzyme] *vt* to disinter unearth, exhume.

exigeant [egziʒã] *a* exacting, hard to please.

exigence [egziʒãːs] *nf* demand requirement.

exiger [egziʒe] *vt* to exact, demand require, call for.

exigu, -uë [egzigy] *a* tiny, slender scant, exiguous.

exiguïté [egziguite] *nf* smallness scantiness, exiguity.

exil [egzil] *nm* exile.

exilé [egzile] *n* exile.

exiler [egzile] *vt* to exile banish.

existence [egzistãːs] *nf* existence, life, subsistence; *pl* stock on hand.

exister [egziste] *vi* to exist, live, be extant.

exode [egzɔd] *nm* exodus.

exonérer [egzɔnere] *vt* to exonerate, exempt.

exorbitant [egzɔrbitã] *a* exorbitant, extortionate.

exorciser [egzɔrsize] *vt* to exorcize.

exotique [egzɔtik] *a* exotic.

expansif, -ive [ɛkspãsif] *a* expansive, effusive, forthcoming.

expansion [ɛkspãsjɔ̃] *nf* expansion, expansiveness.

expatriation [ɛkspatriasjɔ̃] *nf* expatriation.

expatrier [ɛkspatrie] *vt* to expatriate; *vr* to leave one's country.

expectative [ɛkspɛktatiːv] *nf* expectation, expectancy.

expectorer [ɛkspɛktɔre] *vi* to ex-
pectorate, spit.

expédient [ɛkspedjā] *a nm* expedient;
nm device, way.

expédier [ɛkspedje] *vt* to dispatch,
send off, expedite, hurry through,
get rid of.

expéditeur, -trice [ɛkspeditœːr, tris]
n sender, shipper, consigner.

expédition [ɛkspedisjɔ̃] *nf* dispatch,
shipping, consignment, expedition.

expéditionnaire [ɛkspedisjɔnɛːr] *a*
expeditionary; *nm* forwarding
agent.

expérience [ɛksperjāːs] *nf* experience, experiment, test.

expérimental [ɛksperimātal] *a* experimental, applied.

expérimentateur, -trice [ɛksperi-
mātatœːr, tris] *n* experimenter.

expérimentation [ɛksperimātasjɔ̃]
nf experimenting.

expérimenté [ɛksperimāte] *a* experienced, skilled.

expérimenter [ɛksperimāte] *vt* to
test, try; *vi* to experiment.

expert [ɛkspɛːr] *a* expert, skilled;
nm expert, valuator.

expert-comptable [ɛkspɛrkɔ̃tabl]
nm certified public accountant.

expertise [ɛkspɛrtiːz] *nf* survey,
valuation, assessment.

expertiser [ɛkspɛrtize] *vt* to value,
assess, survey.

expiation [ɛkspjasjɔ̃] *nf* expiation.

expier [ɛkspje] *vt* to expiate, atone
for.

expiration [ɛkspirasjɔ̃] *nf* breathing
out, expiration.

expirer [ɛkspire] *vi* to expire, to die.

explicatif, -ive [ɛksplikatif, iːv] *a*
explanatory.

explication [ɛksplikasjɔ̃] *nf* explanation.

explicite [ɛksplisit] *a* explicit, clear.

expliquer [ɛksplike] *vt* to explain,
expound, elucidate, account for;
vr to explain oneself, have it out
(with avec).

exploit [ɛksplwa] *nm* deed, feat, writ.

exploitation [ɛksplwatasjɔ̃] *nf* exploitation, cultivation, working,
trading upon; — des mines mining

exploiter [ɛksplwate] *vt* to exploit,
cultivate, work, take advantage of.

explorateur, -trice [ɛksplɔratœːr,
tris] *a* exploring; *n* explorer.

exploration [ɛksplɔrasjɔ̃] *nf* exploration.

explorer [ɛksplɔre] *vt* to explore.

exploser [ɛksploze] *vi* to explode,
blow up.

explosible [ɛksplozibl] *a* (high)
explosive.

explosif, -ive [ɛksplozif, iːv] *a nm*
explosive.

explosion [ɛksplozjɔ̃] *nf* explosion.

exportateur, -trice [ɛkspɔrtatœːr,
tris] *a* exporting; *n* exporter.

exportation [ɛkspɔrtasjɔ̃] *nf* exportation; *pl* exports, export trade.

exporter [ɛkspɔrte] *vt* to export.

exposant [ɛkspozā] *n* exhibitor,
petitioner.

exposé [ɛkspoze] *a* exposed, open;
nm account, statement.

exposer [ɛkspoze] *vt* to exhibit,
display, show, explain, expose,
expound, lay bare.

exposition [ɛkspozisjɔ̃] *nf* exhibition,
display, show, exposure, statement.

exprès, -esse [ɛksprɛ, ɛːs] *a* express,
clear, explicit; *ad* expressly, on
purpose.

expressément [ɛksprɛsemā] *ad* expressly.

express [ɛksprɛːs] *nm* express train,
repeating rifle.

expressif, -ive [ɛksprɛsif, iːv] *a*
expressive, emphatic.

expression [ɛksprɛsjɔ̃] *nf* expression,
squeezing, manifestation (of feeling),
(turn of) phrase.

exprimer [ɛksprime] *vt* to express,
voice, show, squeeze, press; *vr* to
express oneself.

expropriation [ɛksprɔpriasjɔ̃] *nf*
expropriation.

exproprier [ɛksprɔprie] *vt* to expropriate, dispossess.

expulser [ɛkspylse] *vt* to expel, drive
out, evict, eject.

expulsion [ɛkspylsjɔ̃] *nf* expulsion,
eviction, ejection.

expurger [ɛkspyrge] *vt* to expurgate,
bowdlerize.

exquis [ɛkski] *a* exquisite.

exsangue [ɛksāːg] *a* bloodless.

extase [ɛkstaːz] *nf* ecstasy, rapture,
trance.

s'extasier [sɛkstazje] *vr* to go into
raptures.

extatique [ɛkstatik] *a* ecstatic,
rapturous.

extensible [ɛkstāsibl] *a* extensible,
expanding.

extension [ɛkstāsjɔ̃] *nf* stretching,
spread, extent.

exténuation [ɛkstenɥasjɔ̃] *nf* extenuation, exhaustion.

exténuer [ɛkstenɥe] *vt* to extenuate,
exhaust, wear out; *vr* to wear
oneself out.

extérieur [ɛksterjœːr] *a* exterior,
outer, external; *nm* outside, exterior, outward appearance.

exterminer [ɛkstɛrmine] *vt* to exterminate, wipe out, annihilate; *vr*
to kill oneself.

externat [ɛkstɛrna] *nm* day-school,
out-patients' department.

externe [ɛkstɛrn] *a* external, outside,
outward; *n* day-pupil, non-resident
medical student.

extincteur, -trice [ɛkstɛ̃ktœːr, tris]
a extinguishing; *nm* fire-extinguisher.

extinction [ɛkstɛ̃ksjɔ̃] *nf* extinction,
putting out, suppression, quenching,
loss.

extirper [ɛkstirpe] *vt* to extirpate,

eradicate, root out, (corn) remove.

extorquer [ɛkstɔrke] vt to extort, squeeze (out of).

extorsion [ɛkstɔrsjɔ̃] nf extortion.

extra [ɛkstra] a nm extra.

extraction [ɛkstraksjɔ̃] nf extraction, getting (out), origin.

extradition [ɛkstradisjɔ̃] nf extradition.

extraire [ɛkstrɛːr] vt to extract, draw (out).

extrait [ɛkstrɛ] nm extract, abstract, excerpt, essence; — de mariage, de naissance marriage, birth, certificate.

extraordinaire [ɛkstr(a)ɔrdinɛːr] a extraordinary, unusual; par — for a wonder.

extra-sensoriel [ɛkstrasɑ̃sɔrjɛl] a extrasensory.

extravagance [ɛkstravagɑ̃ːs] nf folly, wild act or statement, fantasy.

extravagant [ɛkstravagɑ̃] a extravagant, foolish, immoderate, far-fetched, tall.

extrême [ɛkstrɛːm] a extreme, far, farthest, drastic, dire; nm extreme limit.

extrême-onction [ɛkstrɛmɔ̃ksjɔ̃] nf extreme unction.

extrémiste [ɛkstremist] n extremist.

extrémité [ɛkstremite] nf extremity, end, point, tip.

exubérance [ɛgzyberɑ̃ːs] nf exuberance, boisterousness, superabundance, ebullience.

exubérant [ɛgzyberɑ̃] a exuberant, high spirited, buoyant, ebullient, superabundant.

exultation [ɛgzyltasjɔ̃] nf exultation, elation.

exulter [ɛgzylte] vi to exult, rejoice, be elated.

F

fable [faːbl] nf fable, tale; la — de la ville laughing-stock.

fabricant [fabrikɑ̃] n manufacturer, maker.

fabricateur, -trice [fabrikatœːr, tris] n fabricator, forger.

fabrication [fabrikasjɔ̃] nf making, manufacture, forging, fabrication; — en série mass production.

fabrique [fabrik] nf factory, works; marque de — trade-mark; conseil de — church council.

fabriquer [fabrike] vt to manufacture, make, fabricate, invent; qu'est-ce qu'il fabrique là? what is he up to?

fabuleux, -euse [fabylø, øːz] a fabulous, prodigious.

façade [fasad] nf façade, front, face, figurehead; de — sham, superficial.

face [fas] nf face, aspect; faire — à to face up to, cope with; en — de opposite; — à facing.

face-à-main [fasamɛ̃] nm lorgnette.

facétie [fasesi] nf joke, jest.

facétieux, -euse [fasesjø, øːz] a facetious, jocular.

facette [fasɛt] nf facet, aspect.

fâché [faʃe] a angry, cross, annoyed, sorry.

fâcher [faʃe] vt to anger, make angry, grieve; vr to get angry.

fâcherie [faʃri] nf tiff, bickering.

fâcheux, -euse [faʃø, øːz] a annoying, tiresome, unfortunate, unwelcome.

facile [fasil] a easy, facile, ready, accommodating.

facilité [fasilite] nf easiness, ease, readiness, facility.

faciliter [fasilite] vt to facilitate, make easier.

façon [fasɔ̃] nf manner, fashion, way, making, workmanship; pl fuss, ado, ceremony; on travaille à — customer's own materials made up; à — bespoke, made to measure; de — à so as to; de — que so that.

faconde [fakɔ̃d] nf gift of the gab, glibness.

façonner [fasɔne] vt to shape, fashion, work, mold.

façonnier, -ière [fasɔnje, jɛːr] a ceremonious, fussy; nm jobbing tailor.

fac-similé [faksimile] nm facsimile.

factage [faktaːʒ] nm transport, carriage, delivery.

facteur, -trice [faktœːr, tris] n maker of musical instruments, carrier, postman; nm factor.

factice [faktis] a artificial, imitation, sham, dummy.

factieux, -euse [faksjø, øːz] a factious, seditious.

faction [faksjɔ̃] nf guard, sentry-duty, faction; faire — to be on guard.

factionnaire [faksjɔnɛːr] nm sentry, guard.

factorerie [faktɔrəri] nf trading station.

facture [faktyːr] nf bill, invoice, workmanship, treatment.

facturer [faktyre] vt to invoice.

facultatif, -ive [fakyltatif, iːv] a optional.

faculté [fakylte] nf option, power, property, ability, faculty, university.

fadaise [fadɛːz] nf silly remark; pl nonsense.

fade [fad] a insipid, tasteless, wishy-washy, tame.

fadeur [fadœːr] nf insipidity, colorlessness, lifelessness, tameness.

fagot [fago] nm faggot, bundle of firewood; sentir le — to smack of heresy.

fagoté [fagɔte] a mal — shabbily dressed, dowdy.

faiblard [fɛblaːr] a weakish.

faible [fɛbl] a feeble, weak, faint,

slender, scanty; *nm* weakness, liking.

faiblesse [fɛblɛs] *nf* feebleness, weakness, frailty, failing.

faiblir [fɛbliːr] *vi* to weaken, grow weak(er), fail, faulter.

faïence [fajãːs] *nf* crockery, delft, earthenware.

failli [faji] *nm* bankrupt.

faillibilité [fajibilite] *nf* fallibility.

faillible [fajibl] *a* fallible.

faillir [fajiːr] *vi* to fail; **il faillit tomber** he almost fell.

faillite [fajit] *nf* failure, bankruptcy; **faire —** to go bankrupt, fail.

faim [fɛ̃] *nf* hunger; **avoir —** to be hungry.

fainéant [fɛneɑ̃] *a* idle, lazy; *n* lazybones.

fainéanter [fɛneɑ̃te] *vi* to idle, laze about, loaf.

fainéantise [fɛneɑ̃tiːz] *nf* idleness, sloth.

faire [fɛːr] *vt* to make, do, get, be *etc*; **il n'y a rien à — there is** nothing can be done about it; **cela ne fait rien** it does not matter; **c'est bien fait** it serves you right; **c'en est fait de lui** he is done for; **il ne fait que de partir** he has just gone; **faites-le monter** show him up; **je lui ai fait écrire la lettre** I got him to write the letter; **cela fait très chic** that looks very smart; *vr* to become, to form, get accustomed, to mature; **il se fit un silence** silence fell, ensued; **comment se fait-il que vous ne l'ayez pas fait?** how does it come about that you did not do it?

faire-part [fɛrpaːr] *nm* card, letter.

faisable [fəzabl] *a* feasible.

faisan [fəzɑ̃] *nm* pheasant.

faisandé [fəzɑ̃de] *a* (*meat*) high.

faisceau [fɛso] *nm* bundle, pile, cluster, (*light*) beam.

faiseur, -euse [fəzœːr, øːz] *n* maker, doer, boaster.

fait [fɛ] *a* fully grown, developed; *nm* deed, act, fact, exploit; **—s et gestes** doings; **prendre sur le —** to catch in the act; **dire son — à qn** to give s.o. some home-truths; **arriver au —** to come to the point; **mettre qn au —** to give s.o. all the facts; **de —** actual(ly); **en —** as a matter of fact, actually; **en — de** as regards, in the way of.

fait-divers [fɛdivɛːr] *nm* news item.

faîte [fɛt] *nm* top, summit, ridge, cope.

falaise [falɛːz] *nf* cliff.

falbalas [falbala] *nm pl* furbelows, flounces.

fallacieux, -euse [falasjø, øːz] *a* fallacious, deceitful, deceptive.

falloir [falwaːr] *v imp* to be necessary, must, need, take, require; *vr* **s'en —** to be lacking, be far from; **il lui faut une voiture** he needs a

car; **il m'a fallu une heure pour le faire** it took me an hour to do it; **il nous faut le faire** we must do it; **tant s'en faut qu'il ait tort** he is far from being wrong.

falot [falo] *nm* lantern; *a* dull, tame.

falsificateur, -trice [falsifikatœːr, tris] *n* falsifier, forger.

falsification [falsifikasjɔ̃] *nf* forgery, forging, adulteration.

falsifier [falsifje] *vt* to falsify, adulterate, debase, doctor.

famé [fame] *a* **bien (mal) —** of good (evil) repute.

famélique [famelik] *a* starving; *n* starveling.

fameux, -euse [famø, øːz] *a* famous, first-rate, rare, tiptop.

familial [familjal] *a* family.

familiariser [familjarize] *vt* to familiarize, acquaint; *vr* to make oneself become familiar (with **avec**).

familiarité [familjarite] *nf* familiarity.

familier, -ière [familje] *a* familiar, well-known, conversant; *n* regular visitor.

famille [famiːj] *nf* family.

famine [famin] *nf* famine, starvation.

fanal [fanal] *nm* lantern, beacon.

fanatique [fanatik] *a* fanatical; *n* fanatic.

fanatisme [fanatism] *nm* fanaticism.

faner [fane] *vt* to wither, (*hay*) toss; *vr* to wither, wilt, fade.

faneur, -euse [fanœːr, øːz] *n* haymaker.

faneuse [fanøːz] *nf* tedder.

fanfare [fɑ̃faːr] *nf* flourish, brass band.

fanfaron, -onne [fɑ̃farɔ̃, ɔn] *a* boasting; *n* braggart.

fanfaronnade [fɑ̃farɔnad] *nf* brag, bluster.

fange [fɑ̃ːʒ] *nf* mud, mire, filth.

fangeux [fɑ̃ʒø] *a* filthy, abject.

fanion [fanjɔ̃] *nm* flag.

fanon [fanɔ̃] *nm* dewlap, wattle, fetlock.

fantaisie [fɑ̃tɛzi] *nf* imagination, fancy, whim, freak, fantasia; **de —** fanciful; **articles de —** fancy goods.

fantaisiste [fɑ̃tɛzist] *a* fanciful, whimsical.

fantasmagorique [fɑ̃tasmagɔrik] *a* weird, fantastic.

fantasque [fɑ̃task] *a* capricious, quaint, odd, temperamental.

fantassin [fɑ̃tasɛ̃] *nm* infantryman.

fantastique [fɑ̃tastik] *a* fanciful, fantastic, eerie.

fantoche [fɑ̃tɔʃ] *nm* puppet, marionette.

fantôme [fɑ̃toːm] *nm* ghost, phantom.

faon [fɑ̃] *nm* fawn.

faraud [faro] *a* dressed up, cocky.

farce [fars] *nf* farce, trick, joke, stuffing, forcemeat.

farceur, -euse [farsœːr, øːz] *n* wag, humorist, practical joker.

farcir [farsiːr] *vt* to stuff.

fard [faːr] *nm* rouge, make-up, paint, deceit, pretense.

fardeau [fardo] *nm* load, burden.

farder [farde] *vt* to rouge, make up, disguise; *vr* to make up.

farfouiller [farfuje] *vti* to rummage (in, about), fumble.

faribole [faribɔl] *nf* idle story, nonsense.

farine [farin] *nf* flour, meal; **fleur de — wheat flour; — de manioc** garri, cassava flour.

farineux, -euse [farinø, øːz] *a* floury, mealy.

farouche [faruʃ] *a* fierce, wild, grim, shy, unsociable.

fascicule [fasikyl] *nm* fascicle, installment, part, bunch.

fascinateur, -trice [fasinatœːr, tris] *a* fascinating, glamorous.

fascination [fasinasjɔ̃] *nf* charm.

fasciner [fasine] *vt* to fascinate, bewitch.

fascisme [fas(s)ism] *nm* fascism.

fasciste [fas(s)ist] *an* fascist.

faste [fast] *nm* pomp, show, ostentation.

fastidieux, -euse [fastidjø, øːz] *a* boring, tedious, dull.

fastueux, -euse [fastɥø, øːz] *a* showy, ostentatious.

fat [fat] *a* foppish; *nm* fop.

fatal [fatal] *a* fatal, fateful, inevitable; **femme —e** vamp.

fatalisme [fatalism] *nm* fatalism.

fatalité [fatalite] *nf* fatality, fate, calamity.

fatidique [fatidik] *a* fateful, prophetical.

fatigant [fatigɑ̃] *a* tiring, tiresome, irksome.

fatigue [fatig] *nf* fatigue, weariness, wear and tear.

fatiguer [fatige] *vt* to tire, fag, strain; *vr* to get tired, tire oneself; **— un poisson** to play a fish.

fatras [fatrɑ] *nm* jumble, rubbish.

fatuité [fatɥite] *nf* fatuity, self-conceit, foppishness.

faubourg [fobuːr] *nm* suburb, outskirts.

faubourien, -ienne [foburjɛ̃, jɛn] *a* suburban.

fauché [foʃe] *a* stony-broke.

faucher [foʃe] *vt* to mow, reap, cut.

faucheur, -euse [foʃœːr, øːz] *n* reaper, mower.

faucheuse [foʃøːz] *nf* reaper, mowing-machine.

faucille [fosiːj] *nf* sickle.

faucon [fokɔ̃] *nm* falcon, hawk.

fauconnerie [fokɔnri] *nf* falconry, hawking, hawk-house.

faufiler [fofile] *vt* to baste, tack (on), insert, slip in; *vr* to pick one's way, slip (in, out), sneak (in, out).

faune [toːn] *nm* faun; *nf* fauna.

faussaire [fosɛːr] *n* forger.

fausser [fose] *vt* to buckle, warp, falsify, pervert.

fausset [fosɛ] *nf* falsetto, spigot.

fausseté [foste] *nf* falsity, duplicity, falsehood.

faute [foːt] *nf* mistake, fault, offense, lack, want, foul; **— de** for want of. failing.

fauteuil [fotœːj] *nm* easy-chair, armchair.

fauteur, -trice [fotœːr, tris] *n* abettor, instigator.

fautif, -ive [fotif, iːv] *a* faulty, wrong, at fault.

fauve [foːv] *a* fawn-colored, tawny; *nm* fawn (color), deer, wild beast.

fauvette [fovɛt] *nf* warbler.

faux, fausse [fo, foːs] *a* false, wrong, inaccurate, insincere, treacherous, sham, bogus; *ad* false(ly); *nm* false, fake, forgery, fabrication; *nf* scythe.

faux-filet [fofilɛ] *nm* sirloin.

faux-fuyant [fofɥijɑ̃] *nm* subterfuge, dodge.

faux-monnayeur [fomɔnɛjœːr] *nm* coiner, forger.

faveur [favœːr] *nf* favor, boon, kindness, grace; **billet de —** complimentary ticket.

favorable [favɔrabl] *a* favorable, auspicious.

favori, -ite [favɔri, it] *a* favorite; *nm pl* whiskers.

favoriser [favɔrize] *vt* to favor, encourage, promote.

fébrile [febril] *a* febrile, feverish.

fécond [fekɔ̃] *a* fertile, fruitful, prolific, rich.

féconder [fekɔ̃de] *vt* to fecundate.

fécondité [fekɔ̃dite] *nf* fertility, fruitfulness.

fécule [fekyl] *nf* starch.

fédération [federasjɔ̃] *nf* federation.

fédérer [federe] *vtr* to federate.

fée [fe] *nf* fairy.

féerie [feri] *nf* fairyland, enchantment.

féerique [ferik] *a* fairylike.

feindre [fɛ̃ːdr] *vt* to pretend, simulate, sham, feign.

feinte [fɛ̃t] *nf* feint, pretense, sham.

fêlé [fele] *a* cracked, mad.

fêler [fele] *vtr* to crack.

félicitations [felisitasjɔ̃] *nf pl* congratulations.

félicité [felisite] *nf* bliss, happiness, felicity.

féliciter [felisite] *vt* to congratulate, compliment; *vr* to be pleased (about, with de).

félin [felɛ̃] *a* feline, catlike.

fêlure [felyːr] *nf* crack, split, rift, flaw.

femelle [fəmɛl] *a nf* female, she-, hen-, cow-.

féminin [feminɛ̃] *a* feminine, female; *nm* feminine gender.

femme [fam] *nf* woman, female, wife; **— de ménage** cleaning lady.

fémur [femyːr] *nm* femur.
fenaison [fənɛzɔ̃] *nf* haymaking.
fendre [fɑ̃ːdr] *vtr* to split, cleave, rend.
fenêtre [f(ə)nɛːtr] *nf* window.
fenouil [fənuːj] *nm* fennel.
fente [fɑ̃ːt] *nf* crack, split, cleft, chink, crevice, slot.
féodal [feɔdal] *a* feudal.
féodalité [feɔdalite] *nf* feudal system.
fer [tɛːr] *nm* iron, sword, shoe; *pl* chains, irons, fetters; (*fig*) de — hard, inflexible; — **rouge** brand; — à **repasser** flat-iron; — à **friser** curling tongs.
fer-blanc [fɛrblɑ̃] *nm* tin.
ferblanterie [fɛrblɑ̃tri] *nf* tinplate, tinsmith's shop.
ferblantier [fɛrblɑ̃tje] *nm* tinsmith.
férié [ferje] *a* **jour** — holiday.
férir [feriːr] *vt* to strike.
fermage [fɛrmaːʒ] *nm* rent.
ferme [fɛrm] *a* firm, solid, steady; *ad* firmly, hard; *nf* farm, lease.
fermé [fɛrme] *a* closed, exclusive, expressionless, hidebound, blind; **être** — à **qch** to have no appreciation of sth.
fermentation [fɛrmɑ̃tasjɔ̃] *nf* fermentation, unrest.
fermenter [fɛrmɑ̃te] *vi* to ferment, be in a ferment.
fermer [fɛrme] *vt* to close, shut, fasten, turn off, switch off; *vir* to shut, to close.
fermeté [fɛrməte] *nf* firmness, steadiness, resolution.
fermeture [fɛrmətyːr] *nf* shutting, close, closing(-down); — **éclair** zipper.
fermier, -ière [fɛrmje, jɛːr] *n* farmer, farmer's wife, tenant, lessee.
fermoir [fɛrmwaːr] *nm* clasp, fastener, hasp.
féroce [ferɔs] *a* wild, savage, fierce, ferocious.
férocité [ferɔsite] *nf* ferocity, fierceness, savagery.
ferraille [fɛraːj] *nf* scrap-iron.
ferrant [fɛrɑ̃] *a* **maréchal** — blacksmith.
ferré [fɛre] *a* iron-shod, hob-nailed, good (at **en**); **voie** —e railway line.
ferrer [fɛre] *vt* to bind with iron, shoe, (*fish*) strike.
ferronnerie [fɛrɔnri] *nf* iron-foundry, ironmongery.
ferronnier [fɛrɔnje] *nm* ironworker, ironmonger.
ferroviaire [fɛrɔvjɛːr] *a* railway; **réseau** — railway system.
ferrure [fɛryːr] *nf* piece of iron work, iron fitting, shoeing.
fertile [fɛrtil] *a* fruitful, rich.
fertiliser [fɛrtilize] *vt* to fertilize, make fruitful.
fertilité [fɛrtilite] *nf* fertility, fruitfulness.
féru [fery] *a* enamored, struck (with **de**).

férule [feryl] *nf* ferrule, rod.
fervent [fɛrvɑ̃] *a* fervent, ardent; *n* enthusiast, fan.
ferveur [fɛrvœːr] *nf* fervor, ardor, enthusiasm.
fesse [fɛs] *nf* buttock.
fessée [fɛse] *nf* spanking, flogging, thrashing, whipping.
fesser [fɛse] *vt* to spank, whip.
feston [fɛstɔ̃] *nm* festoon, scallop.
festonner [fɛstɔne] *vt* to festoon, scallop.
festoyer [fɛstwaje] *vti* to feast.
fêtard [fɛtaːr] *n* reveler.
fête [fɛːt] *nf* feast, festival, holiday, festivity, treat, entertainment; **faire la** — to celebrate, go on a spree.
Fête-Dieu [fɛtdjø] *nf* Corpus Christi.
fêter [fɛte] *vt* to observe as a holiday, celebrate, entertain.
fétiche [fetiʃ] *nm* fetish, mascot.
fétide [fetid] *a* fetid, stinking.
fétu [fety] *nm* straw, wisp, jot.
feu [fø] *nm* fire, heat, light, beacon, ardor, spirit; *a* late, deceased, dead; — **roulant** drum-fire; **donner du** — à **qn** to give a light to s.o.; **faire long** — to peter out; **n'y voir que du** — to be taken in; — **d'artifice** fireworks.
feuillage [fœjaːʒ] *nm* foliage.
feuille [fœːj] *nf* leaf, sheet; — **de présence** time-sheet.
feuillée [fœje] *nf* foliage.
feuillet [fœjɛ] *nm* (*book*) leaf, sheet, plate.
feuilleter [fœjte] *vt* to divide into sheets, turn over, thumb.
feuilleton [fœjtɔ̃] *nm* feuilleton, article, serial story.
feuillu [fœjy] *a* leafy.
feutre [føːtr] *nm* felt, felt hat, padding.
feutrer [føtre] *vt* to felt, cover with felt.
fève [fɛːv] *nf* bean, broad-bean.
février [fevrie] *nm* February.
fiacre [fjakr] *nm* cab, hackney-carriage.
fiançailles [fjɑ̃saːj] *nf pl* engagement, betrothal.
fiancé [fjɑ̃se] *n* fiancé(e), betrothed.
fiancer [fjɑ̃se] *vt* to betroth; *vr* to become engaged.
fiasco [fjasko] *nm* fiasco; **faire** — to fizzle out, flop.
fibre [fibr] *nf* fiber, grain.
fibreux, -euse [fibrø, øːz] *a* fibrous, stringy.
ficeler [fisle] *vt* to tie up.
ficelle [fisɛl] *nf* string.
fiche [fiʃ] *nf* pin, slip of paper, form, index-card, chit.
ficher [fiʃe] *vt* to fix, drive in, do, give; — **le camp** to clear out; *vr* **se** — **de qn** to pull s.o.'s leg; **je m'en fiche** I don't give a damn.
fichier [fiʃje] *nm* card-index, card-index cabinet.

fichu [fiʃy] *nm* neckerchief, shawl, fichu.

fictif, -ive [fiktif, iːv] *a* fictitious, imaginary.

fiction [fiksjɔ̃] *nf* fiction, invention.

fidèle [fidɛl] *a* faithful, true, loyal.

fidélité [fidelite] *nf* fidelity, loyalty, allegiance.

fiduciaire [fidysjɛːr] *a* fiduciary; *nm* trustee.

fieffé [fjɛfe] *a* given in fief, double-dyed, arrant, arch.

fiel [fjɛl] *nm* gall, malice.

fier, fière [fjɛːr] *a* proud, haughty, fine, arrant.

se fier [səfje] *vr* to trust, rely, confide in (à).

fierté [fjɛrte] *nf* pride, haughtiness.

fièvre [fjɛːvr] *nf* fever, heat; **avoir un peu de —** to have a slight temperature; **— paludéenne** ague, malaria.

fiévreux, -euse [fjevrø, øːz] *a* feverish, fevered, hectic.

fifre [fifr] *nm* fife.

figer [fiʒe] *vt* to congeal, coagulate, clot, fix; *vr* to curdle, congeal, set; **il resta figé** he stood rooted to the spot.

fignoler [fiɲɔle] *vt* to fiddle, dawdle over; *vi* to fiddle about.

figue [fig] *nf* fig.

figuier [figje] *nm* fig-tree.

figurant [figyrɑ̃] *n* walker-on, extra.

figuratif, -ive [figyratif, iːv] *a* figurative.

figure [figyːr] *nf* figure, shape, face; **faire —** to cut a figure, figure (as de).

figuré [figyre] *a* figured, figurative; **ad au —** figuratively.

figurer [figyre] *vt* to represent; *vi* to look, appear, put on a show; *vr* to fancy, imagine, picture.

fil [fil] *nm* thread, yarn, wire, grain, edge, current, clue; **— de la vierge** gossamer; **de — en aiguille** bit by bit, gradually; **au — de l'eau** with the stream.

filage [filaːʒ] *nm* spinning.

filament [filamɑ̃] *nm* filament, fiber.

filandreux, -euse [filɑ̃drø, øːz] *a* stringy, long-winded.

filant [filɑ̃] *a* gluey, ropy; **étoile —e** shooting-star.

filasse [filas] *nf* tow, oakum.

filateur [filatœːr] *nm* mill-owner, spinner, shadower.

filature [filatyːr] *nf* spinning-mill, spinning, shadowing.

file [fil] *nf* file, rank; **chef de —** leader; **à la —** in single file.

filer [file] *vt* to spin, prolong, pay out, shadow; *vi* to flow gently, fly, tear along, buzz off; **— à l'anglaise** to take French leave; **— vingt nœuds** to do twenty knots.

filet [filɛ] *nm* thread, fillet, net, thin stream, streak.

fileur, -euse [filœːr, øːz] *n* spinner.

filial [filjal] *a* filial.

filiale [filjal] *nf* branch, branch-store, -company.

filière [filjɛːr] *nf* draw-plate, die; **— à vis** screw-plate; **passer par la —** to work one's way up; **— administrative** official channels.

filigrane [filigran] *nm* filigree, water-mark.

fille [fiːj] *nf* daughter; **jeune —** girl; **petite —** little girl; **vieille —** spinster, old maid; **— d'honneur** bridesmaid; **— de salle** waitress; **— (publique)** prostitute.

fillette [fijɛt] *nf* little girl.

filleul [fijœl] *n* godchild.

film [film] *nm* film, picture; **tourner un —** to make a film; **— sonore** talkie.

filmer [filme] *vt* to film.

filon [filɔ̃] *nm* vein, seam.

filou [filu] *nm* pickpocket, thief, rogue.

filouterie [filutri] *nf* cheating, swindle.

fils [fis] *nm* son, boy.

filtration [filtrasjɔ̃] *nf* filtration, percolation.

filtre [filtr] *nm* filter, strainer.

filtrer [filtre] *vt* to strain, filter; *vi* to percolate, filter, seep; **— un poste** to skip a station.

fin [fɛ̃] *a* fine, delicate, keen, subtle, choice; *nf* end, conclusion, close, aim, purpose, object; **mener à bonne —** to bring to a successful conclusion; **en — de compte** finally.

final, -als [final] *a* final, last; *nm* finale.

finale [final] *nf* end syllable, final (round).

finalité [finalite] *nf* finality.

finance [finɑ̃ːs] *nf* finance; **ministre des —s** Secretary of the Treasury; **ministère des —s** Treasury Department.

financer [finɑ̃se] *vt* to finance.

financier, -ière [finɑ̃sje, jɛːr] *a* financial; *nm* financier.

finasser [finase] *vi* to dodge, fox, finesse.

finaud [fino] *a* wily, cunning, foxy; *n* wily bird.

finesse [finɛs] *nf* fineness, delicacy, astuteness, discrimination, artful dodge.

fini [fini] *a* finished, ended, over, accomplished, done for, gone, finite; *nm* finish, perfection.

finir [finiːr] *vt* to finish, conclude, end; **cela n'en finit pas** there is no end to it; **en — avec** to have done with.

finlandais [fɛ̃lɑ̃dɛ] *a* Finnish; *n* Finn.

Finlande [fɛ̃lɑ̃ːd] *nf* Finland.

fiole [fjɔl] *nf* phial, flask.

fioritures [fjɔrityːr] *nf pl* flourish(es), ornamentation.

firmament [firmamã] *nm* firmament, heavens.
firme [firm] *nf* firm.
fisc [fisk] *nm* treasury, exchequer, internal revenue.
fiscal [fiskal] *a* fiscal.
fission [fisjɔ̃] *nf* — **nucléaire** nuclear fission.
fissure [fis(s)y:r] *nf* fissure, cleft.
fissurer [fis(s)yre] *vtr* to crack, split.
fixage [fiksa:ʒ] *nm* fixing, fastening.
fixatif [fiksatif] *nm* fixative, hair cream.
fixe [fiks] *a* fixed, firm, steady, settled.
fixé [fikse] *a* fixed, stated, fast; **être — sur** to be clear about.
fixe-chaussettes [fiks(ə)ʃosɛt] *nm* garter.
fixement [fiksəmã] *ad* fixedly, steadily, hard.
fixer [fikse] *vt* to fix, fasten, hold, determine, gaze at, stare at; *vr* to settle down.
flacon [flakɔ̃] *nm* bottle, flask, flagon.
flageller [flaʒɛlle] *vt* to scourge, flog.
flageoler [flaʒɔle] *vi* to tremble, shake.
flageolet [flaʒɔlɛ] *nm* flageolet, kidney-bean.
flagorner [flagɔrne] *vt* to flatter, toady to.
flagorneur, -euse [flagɔrnœ:r, ø:z] *n* flatterer, toady.
flagrant [flagrã] *a* flagrant, glaring; **pris en — délit** caught redhanded.
flair [flɛ:r] *nm* scent, flair.
flairer [flɛre] *vt* to scent, smell (out), sniff.
flamant [flamã] *nm* flamingo.
flambant [flãbã] *a* blazing, roaring, flaming; **— neuf** brand new.
flambeau [flãbo] *nm* torch, candlestick.
flambée [flãbe] *nf* blazing fire, blaze.
flamber [flãbe] *vt* to singe; *vi* to blaze, flame, kindle.
flamboyant [flãbwajã] *a* flaming, blazing, flashing, brilliant.
flamboyer [flãbwaje] *vi* to blaze, flash, glow.
flamme [fla:m] *nf* flame, passion, fire, pennant.
flammèche [flamɛʃ] *nf* spark.
flan [flã] *nm* flan, custard, (*tec*) mold.
flanc [flã] *nm* flank, side; **tirer au —** to goof off, shirk, goldbrick.
flancher [flãʃe] *vi* to flinch, falter.
flanelle [flanɛl] *nf* flannel.
flâner [flane] *vi* to stroll, dawdle, lounge about, idle.
flânerie [flanri] *nf* stroll, idling, dawdling.
flâneur, -euse [flanœ:r, ø:z] *n* stroller, idler, dawdler.
flanquer [flãke] *vt* to flank, support, throw, chuck.

flaque [flak] *nf* puddle, pool.
flasque [flask] *a* flabby, backboneless, spineless, limp.
flatter [flate] *vt* to flatter, blandish, stroke, delight; *vr* to flatter oneself, pride oneself.
flatterie [flatri] *nf* flattery.
flatteur, -euse [flatœ:r, ø:z] *a* flattering, pleasing, fond; *n* flatterer.
flatueux, -euse [flatɥø, ø:z] *a* flatulent, windy.
flatulence [flatylã:s] *nf* flatulence.
fléau [fleo] *nm* flail, scourge, plague, beam.
flèche [flɛʃ] *nf* arrow, dart, spire, pole, indicator; **faire — de tout bois** to make use of every means.
fléchir [fleʃi:r] *vt* to bend, bow, move to pity; *vi* to give way, sag, falter.
flegmatique [flɛgmatik] *a* phlegmatic, stolid.
flegme [flɛgm] *nm* phlegm, stolidness.
flemmard [flɛma:r] *a* lazy; *n* slacker, loafer, sluggard.
flemme [flɛm] *nf* laziness.
flétrir [fletri:r] *vt* to fade, wither, brand, sully; *vr* to wither, fade.
flétrissure [fletrisy:r] *nf* fading, withering; stigma.
fleur [flœ:r] *nf* flower, bloom, blossom, heyday; **fine —** flower, pick; **à — de** on the surface of.
fleurer [flœre] *vi* to smell of, be redolent of.
fleuret [flœrɛ] *nm* foil.
fleuri [flœri] *a* in bloom, flower, flowery, florid.
fleurir [flœri:r] *vt* to adorn with flowers; *vi* to flower, bloom, flourish.
fleuriste [flœrist] *n* florist.
fleuve [flœ:v] *nm* river.
flexible [flɛksibl] *a* flexible, pliant, pliable; *nm* flex.
flexion [flɛksjɔ̃] *nf* bending, buckling.
flibustier [flibystje] *nm* buccaneer, pirate.
flic [flik] *nm* (*sl*) cop.
flirt [flœrt] *nm* flirtation, flirting, flirt, boy-, girlfriend.
flirter [flœrte] *vi* to flirt.
flocon [flɔkɔ̃] *nm* flake, tuft.
floconneux, -euse [flɔkɔnø, ø:z] *a* fleecy, fluffy.
floraison [flɔrɛzɔ̃] *nm* blossoming, flowering (time).
floral [flɔral] *a* floral.
flore [flɔ:r] *nf* flora.
florissant [flɔrisã] *a* flourishing, prosperous.
flot [flo] *nm* wave, billow, surge, flood; *pl* sea; **à — afloat; à —s in** streams, in torrents.
flottaison [flɔtɛzɔ̃] *nf* water-line.
flottant [flɔtã] *a* floating, full, wide, irresolute.
flotte [flɔt] *nf* fleet, float, (*fam*) water.
flottement [flɔtmã] *nm* floating, swaying, fluctuation, hesitation.

flotter [flɔte] *vi* to float, wave, waft, waver, fluctuate.
flotteur [flɔtœːr] *nm* raftsman, float.
flotille [flɔtiːj] *nf* flotilla.
flou [flu] *a* blurred, hazy, fluffy.
fluorescent [flyɔrɛs(s)ɑ̃] *a* fluorescent.
fluctuer [flyktɥe] *vi* to fluctuate.
fluet, -ette [flyɛ, ɛt] *a* slender, thin, delicate, spindly.
fluide [flɥid] *a nm* fluid, liquid.
fluidité [flɥidite] *nf* fluidity.
flûte [flyːt] *nf* flute, flutist, long loaf, tall champagne glass.
flûté [flyte] *a* flute-like, reed-like.
flûtiste [flytist] *nm* flautist.
flux [fly] *nm* flow, flood, rush.
fluxion [flyksjɔ̃] *nf* inflammation, swelling; **— de poitrine** pneumonia.
foc [fɔk] *nm* jib, stay-sail.
foi [fwa] *nf* faith, trust, belief, confidence, credit.
foie [fwa] *nm* liver; **crise de —** bilious attack.
foin [fwɛ̃] *nm* hay.
foire [fwaːr] *nf* fair, market.
foireux [fwarø] *a* cowardly.
fois [fwa] *nf* time, occasion; **à la —** at a time, at the same time, both.
foison [fwazɔ̃] *nf* plenty, abundance.
foisonner [fwazɔne] *vi* to abound, multiply.
folâtre [fɔlaːtr] *a* playful, frisky, sportive.
folâtrer [fɔlɑtrɛ] *vi* to romp, gambol, frisk.
folichon, -onne [fɔliʃɔ̃, ɔn] *a* playful, frisky.
folie [fɔli] *nf* folly, piece of folly, madness, craze.
follet, -ette [fɔlɛ, ɛt] *a* merry, gay; **feu —** will o' the wisp.
fomenter [fɔmɑ̃te] *vt* to foment, stir up.
foncé [fɔ̃se] *a* (color) dark, deep.
foncer [fɔ̃se] *vt* to sink (shaft), drive in, bottom, darken; *vi* to rush, charge.
foncier, -ière [fɔ̃sje, jɛːr] *a* land(ed), fundamental, ground.
fonction [fɔ̃ksjɔ̃] *nf* function, office; **faire — de** to act as.
fonctionnaire [fɔ̃ksjɔnɛːr] *nm* civil servant.
fonctionnement [fɔ̃ksjɔnmɑ̃] *nm* functioning, working, behavior.
fonctionner [fɔ̃ksjɔne] *vi* to function, work, act, run.
fond [fɔ̃] *nm* bottom, back, far end, depth, foundation, background, substance; **à —** thoroughly, up to the hilt; **au —** at heart, at bottom; **article de —** editorial; **course de —** long-distance race.
fondamental [fɔ̃damɑ̃tal] *a* basic, fundamental.
fondateur, -trice [fɔ̃datœːr, tris] *n* founder, promoter.
fondation [fɔ̃dasjɔ̃] *nf* foundation, founding.

fondement [fɔ̃dmɑ̃] *nm* foundation, base, grounds, reliance.
fondé [fɔ̃de] *a* founded, entitled, justified; *nm* **— de pouvoir** proxy, attorney.
fonder [fɔ̃de] *vt* to institute, found, lay the foundations of, base, set up; *vr* to place reliance (on **sur**), base one's reasons (on **sur**), be based.
fonderie [fɔ̃dri] *nf* foundry, smelting works, smelting.
fondeur [fɔ̃dœːr] *nm* smelter, founder.
fondre [fɔ̃ːdr] *vt* to smelt, cast, melt, fuse, dissolve; *vi* melt, dissolve, pounce, fall upon; *vr* to blend, melt.
fondrière [fɔ̃drjɛːr] *nf* bog, quagmire.
fonds [fɔ̃] *nm* land, stock, fund, means; **acheter un —** to buy a business; **— publics** government stocks; **— consolidés** consols; **rentrer dans ses —** to get one's money back.
fondu [fɔ̃dy] *nm* fading in and out (of film), melted (butter), molten (metal), cast (bronze), well-blended (colors); **-e** *nf* fondue.
fontaine [fɔ̃tɛn] *nf* fountain, spring.
fonte [fɔ̃ːt] *nf* smelting, casting, cast iron, melting; **— brute** pig-iron.
fonts [fɔ̃] *nm pl* font.
football [futbɔl] *nm* football.
footing [futiŋ] *nm* walking, hiking.
for [fɔːr] *nm* **dans son — intérieur** in his inmost heart.
forage [fɔraːʒ] *nm* sinking, boring, (min) drilling.
forain [fɔrɛ̃] *a* itinerant, traveling, *n* peddler, stall-keeper, traveling showman.
forçat [fɔrsa] *nm* convict.
force [fɔrs] *nf* power, might, strength, prime, compulsion; *pl* strength, spring, shears; *ad* many, a lot of; **à — de** by (means of); **— leur fut d'accepter** they could do nothing but agree.
forcé [fɔrse] *a* forced, strained; **travaux —s** penal servitude.
forcément [fɔrsemɑ̃] *ad* necessarily, perforce.
forcené [fɔrsəne] *a* frenzied, frantic, desperate.
forcer [fɔrse] *vt* to force, compel, break open, strain.
forcir [fɔrsiːr] *vi* to fill out.
forer [fɔre] *vt* to sink, bore, (min) drill.
forestier, -ière [fɔrɛstje, jɛːr] *a* forest, forestry; *n* forester, ranger.
foret [fɔrɛ] *nm* drill, broach, bracebit, gimlet.
forêt [fɔrɛ] *nf* forest.
foreuse [fɔrøːz] *nf* drill.
forfait [fɔrfɛ] *nm* serious crime; contract; forfeit; **déclarer —** to scratch, call off.
forfaiture [fɔrfɛtyːr] *nf* maladministration, breach.
forfanterie [fɔrfɑ̃tri] *nf* bragging, boasting.

forge [fɔrʒ] *nf* forge, smithy, iron-works.

forger [fɔrʒe] *vt* to forge, counterfeit, invent, coin.

forgeron [fɔrʒərɔ̃] *nm* blacksmith.

forgeur, -euse [fɔrʒœːr, øːz] *n* forger, inventor, fabricator (of news), coiner (of words).

formaliser [fɔrmalize] *vt* to give offense to; *vr* to take offense (at **de**).

formalisme [fɔrmalism] *nm* conventionality.

formaliste [fɔrmalist] *a* formal, stiff, ceremonious, conventional.

formalité [fɔrmalite] *nf* formality, (matter of) form, ceremony, ceremoniousness.

format [fɔrma] *nm* format, size.

formation [fɔrmasjɔ̃] *nf* formation, molding, forming, training.

forme [fɔrm] *nf* form, shape, figure, mold, last, shoetree; **pour la —** as a matter of form; **être en —** to be in form, be fit.

formel, -elle [fɔrmɛl, ɛl] *a* strict, formal, definite.

former [fɔrme] *vt* to shape, form, create, mold, train; *vr* to take shape, set; **le train se forme à Dijon** the train starts from Dijon.

formidable [fɔrmidabl] *a* fearsome, terrific, stupendous.

formule [fɔrmyl] *nf* formula, form.

formuler [fɔrmyle] *vt* to formulate, draft, put into words, state.

forniquer [fɔrnike] *vi* to fornicate.

fort [fɔːr] *a* strong, large, stout, solid, loud, violent; *ad* very, hard, loud, fast; *nm* strong part, strong man, fort; **c'est plus — que moi I can't help it; le plus — c'est que the** best (worst) of it is . . .; **se faire — de** to undertake to; **vous y allez un peu —** you are going a bit too far; **au — de l'hiver** in the dead of winter.

forteresse [fɔrtərɛs] *nf* fortress, stronghold.

fortifiant [fɔrtifjɑ̃] *a* fortifying, invigorating, bracing; *nm* tonic.

fortification [fɔrtifikasjɔ̃] *nf* fortification, fortifying.

fortifier [fɔrtifje] *vt* to fortify, strengthen, invigorate; *vr* to grow stronger.

fortuit [fɔrtɥi] *a* chance, fortuitous, casual, accidental.

fortuité [fɔrtɥite] *nf* fortuitousness, casual nature.

fortune [fɔrtyn] *nf* fortune, (piece of) luck; **de — makeshift; dîner à la — du pot** to take pot luck; **homme à bonnes —s** lady's man, ladykiller.

fortuné [fɔrtyne] *a* fortunate, well-off, wealthy.

fosse [foːs] *nf* hole, pit, grave; **— d'aisances** cesspool.

fossé [fose] *nm* ditch, drain, moat.

fossette [fosɛt, fɔsɛt] *nf* dimple.

fossile [fɔsil] *nm* fossil.

fossoyer [foswaje, fɔswaje] *vt* to trench, ditch.

fossoyeur [foswajœːr, fɔswajœːr] *nm* grave-digger.

fou, fol, folle [fu, fɔl, fɔl] *a* mad, insane, foolish, silly, frantic, frenzied; *n* lunatic, madman, mad-woman, fool, (chess) bishop; **être — de** to be beside oneself with; **succès — terrific success, hit; monde —** enormous crowd.

foudre [fudr] *nf* thunderbolt, lightning; **coup de — thunderbolt, bolt** from the blue, love at first sight.

foudroyant [fudrwajɑ̃] *a* crushing, overwhelming, smashing, lightning.

foudroyé [fudrwaje] *a* blasted, dumbfounded.

foudroyer [fudrwaje] *vt* to blast, strike down.

fouet [fwɛ] *nm* whip, lash, whisk; **coup de —** cut, fillip.

fouetter [fwɛte] *vt* to whip, flog, whisk, lash; *vi* to batter (against), flap.

fougère [fuʒɛːr] *nf* fern, bracken.

fougue [fug] *nf* dash, fire.

fougueux, -euse [fugø, øːz] *a* spirited, dashing, mettlesome, fiery.

fouille [fuːj] *nf* excavation, searching.

fouiller [fuje] *vt* to excavate, dig, search, ransack, rifle; *vi* to rummage.

fouillis [fuji] *nm* confusion, jumble, muddle.

fouine [fwin] *nf* stone-marten.

fouiner [fwine] *vi* to ferret, nose about, interfere.

fouir [fwiːr] *vt* to dig, burrow.

foulard [fulaːr] *nm* silk handkerchief, foulard, neckerchief, scarf.

foule [ful] *nf* crowd, throng, mob.

foulée [fule] *nf* tread, stride; *pl* spoor, track.

fouler [fule] *vt* to crush, tread on, (ankle) sprain.

foulure [fulyːr] *nf* sprain, wrench.

four [fuːr] *nm* oven, kiln; failure; **faire —** to be a flop.

fourbe [furb] *a* crafty; *n* rascal, knave, double-dealer.

fourberie [furbəri] *nf* double-dealing, deceit, cheating, treachery.

fourbir [furbir] *vt* to polish, rub up.

fourbu [furby] *a* foundered, dead-beat, done.

fourche [furʃ] *nf* fork, pitchfork; **faire —** (of roads) to fork.

fourcher [furʃe] *vt* to fork; *vi* to branch off, fork; **la langue lui a fourché** he made a slip of the tongue.

fourchette [furʃɛt] *nf* (table) fork, wishbone; **c'est une bonne —** he is fond of his food.

fourchu [furʃy] *a* forked, cloven.

fourgon [furgɔ̃] *nm* baggage car, truck, wagon, poker, rake.

fourgonner [furgɔne] *vti* to poke, rake.
fourmi [furmi] *nm* ant; **avoir des —s dans le bras** to have pins and needles in one's arm.
fourmilier [furmilje] *nm* anteater.
fourmilière [furmiljɛːr] *nf* anthill, ants' nest.
fourmillement [furmijmɑ̃] *nm* tingling, prickly feeling, swarming.
fourmiller [furmije] *vi* to swarm, teem, tingle.
fournaise [furnɛːz] *nf* furnace.
fourneau [furno] *nm* furnace, stove, (*pipe*) bowl; **haut —** blast furnace.
fournée [furne] *nf* batch (of loaves).
fourni [furni] *a* stocked, plentiful, thick.
fournil [furni] *nm* bakery.
fourniment [furnimɑ̃] *nm* equipment, accouterment.
fournir [furniːr] *vt* to supply, provide, furnish; *vr* to provide oneself (with **de**).
fournisseur, -euse [furnisœːr, øːz] *n* purveyor, supplier, caterer, tradesman.
fourniture [furnityːr] *nf* supplying, providing; *pl* supplies, requisites.
fourrage [furaːʒ] *nm* fodder, forage.
fourrager [furaʒe] *vt* to pillage; *vi* to forage, rummage.
fourragère [furaʒɛːr] *nf* lanyard; forage wagon.
fourré [fure] *a* fur-lined; *n* thicket.
fourreau [furo] *nm* scabbard, case, sheath, sleeve.
fourrer [fure] *vt* to line with fur, cram, stuff, poke, stick; *vr* to thrust oneself, butt (into **dans**).
fourre-tout [furtu] *nm* hold-all.
fourreur [furœːr] *nm* furrier.
fourrier [furje] *nm* quarter-master.
fourrure [furyːr] *nf* fur, lining.
fourvoyer [furvwaje] *vt* to mislead, lead astray; *vr* to lose one's way, go wrong.
foyer [fwaje] *nm* hearth, firebox, seat, home, center.
frac [frak] *nm* dress-coat.
fracas [fraka] *nm* din, uproar, crash, clash.
fracasser [frakase] *vtr* to shatter, smash.
fraction [fraksjɔ̃] *nf* fraction.
fracture [fraktyːr] *nf* fracture, break, breaking open.
fracturer [fraktyre] *vt* to fracture, force; *vr* to break, fracture.
fragile [fraʒil] *a* fragile, flimsy, frail, breakable, brittle.
fragilité [fraʒilite] *nf* fragility, frailty, weakness.
fragment [fragmɑ̃] *nm* fragment, chip, snatch.
fragmentaire [fragmɑ̃tɛːr] *a* fragmentary.
fragmenter [fragmɑ̃te] *vt* to divide into fragments.
frai [frɛ] *nm* spawn(ing).

fraîcheur [frɛʃœːr] *nf* cool(ness), chilliness, freshness.
fraîchir [frɛʃiːr] *vi* to grow cooler, freshen.
frais, fraîche [frɛ, frɛʃ] *a* cool, fresh, recent, new, new-laid; *nm* coolness, cool air; **prendre le —** to take the air.
frais [frɛ] *nm pl* expenses, charge, outlay, cost; **faux —** incidental expenses; **— divers** sundries.
fraise [frɛːz] *nf* strawberry; ruff; milling cutter.
fraiser [frɛze] *vt* to plait, frill, mill.
framboise [frɑ̃bwaːz] *nf* raspberry.
franc, franche [frɑ̃, frɑ̃ːʃ] *a* free, frank, downright, open, honest, candid, above-board; *ad* frankly, candidly; *nm* (*coin*) franc; **jouer — jeu** to play fair, play the game; **corps —** volunteer corps.
français [frɑ̃sɛ] *a* French; *n* Frenchman, Frenchwoman.
France [frɑ̃ːs] *nf* France.
franchement [frɑ̃ʃmɑ̃] *ad* frankly, candidly, really, downright.
franchir [frɑ̃ʃiːr] *vt* to jump (over), clear, cross.
franchise [frɑ̃ʃiːz] *nf* freedom, immunity, frankness, straightforwardness.
franciser [frɑ̃size] *vt* to Gallicize, Frenchify.
franc-maçon [frɑ̃masɔ̃] *nm* freemason.
franc-maçonnerie [frɑ̃masɔ̃nri] *nf* freemasonry.
franco [frɑ̃ko] *ad* free, carriage-free, duty paid.
franc-parler [frɑ̃parle] *nm* frankness, plain-speaking.
franc-tireur [frɑ̃tirœːr] *nm* sniper, sharpshooter, freelance (journalist).
frange [frɑ̃ːʒ] *nf* fringe.
franquette [frɑ̃kɛt] *nf* **à la bonne —** simply, without fuss.
frappant [frapɑ̃] *a* striking, impressive.
frappe [frap] *nf* minting, striking, impression.
frapper [frape] *vt* to strike, smite, knock, insist, stamp, mint; **— le champagne** to ice champagne.
frasque [frask] *nf* escapade, prank, trick.
fraternel, -elle [fratɛrnɛl, ɛl] *a* fraternal, brotherly.
fraterniser [fratɛrnize] *vi* to fraternize.
fraternité [fratɛrnite] *nf* fraternity, brotherhood.
fratricide [fratrisid] *a* fratricidal; *nm* fratricide.
fraude [froːd] *nf* fraud, fraudulence, deceit, deception; **passer en —** to smuggle in, out.
frauder [frode] *vt* to defraud, swindle; *vi* to cheat.
fraudeur, -euse [frodœːr, øːz] *n* smuggler, defrauder.

fraududeux, -euse [frodylø, ø:z] *a* fraudulent.
frayer [frɛje] *vt* open up, clear; *vi* to spawn, associate (with **avec**).
frayeur [frɛjœ:r] *nf* fear, fright, dread.
fredaine [frədɛn] *nf* escapade, prank.
fredonner [frədɔne] *vt* to hum.
frégate [frɛgat] *nf* frigate.
frein [frɛ̃] *nm* bit, brake, curb; **serrer (desserrer) le —** to put on (release) the brake; **ronger son —** to champ at the bit, fret; **sans —** unbridled.
ïreiner [frɛne] *vt* to brake, check; *vi* to brake.
frelater [frəlate] *vt* to adulterate, water down.
frêle [frɛ:l] *a* frail, delicate, weak, spare.
frelon [frəlɔ̃] *nm* hornet, drone.
frémir [fremi:r] *vi* to quiver, rustle, tremble, flutter.
frémissement [fremismã] *nm* quivering, rustling, shaking, quaking.
frêne [frɛ:n] *nm* ash-tree.
frénésie [frenezi] *nf* frenzy, madness.
frénétique [frenetik] *a* frantic, frenzied.
fréquence [frekã:s] *nf* frequency, prevalence, rate.
fréquent [frekã] *a* frequent, quick.
fréquentation [frekãtasjɔ̃] *nf* frequenting.
fréquenter [frekãte] *vt* to frequent, haunt, associate with; *vi* to visit, go to.
frère [frɛ:r] *nm* brother, friar.
fresque [frɛsk] *nf* fresco.
fret [frɛ] *nm* freight, chartering, load.
fréter [frete] *vt* to freight, charter.
frétillant [fretijã] *a* frisky, lively.
frétiller [fretije] *vi* to wag, wriggle, quiver.
fretin [frətɛ̃] *nm* (*of fish*) fry; **menu —** small fry.
frette [frɛt] *nf* hoop, band.
fretter [frɛte] *vt* to hoop.
friable [friabl] *a* crumbly, friable.
friand [friã] *a* fond of (good things); **morceau —** titbit.
friandise [friãdi:z] *nf* fondness for good food, titbit; *pl* sweets.
fricassée [frikase] *nf* fricassee, hash.
friche [friʃ] *nf* waste land, fallow land.
fricoter [frikɔte] *vti* to stew, cook.
friction [friksjɔ̃] *nf* friction, rubbing, massage, rub-down, dry shampoo.
frictionner [friksjɔne] *vt* to rub, massage, rub down, give a dry shampoo to.
frigide [friʒid] *a* frigid.
frigo [frigo] *nm* (*sl*) frozen meat.
frigorifier [frigɔrifje] *vt* to chill, refrigerate.
frigorifique [frigɔrifik] *a* chilling, refrigerating; *nm* deepfreeze, frozen meat, refrigerator.

frileux, -euse [frilø, ø:z] *a* sensitive to the cold, chilly.
frimas [frima] *nm* hoarfrost, rime.
frime [frim] *nf* pretense, sham, eyewash.
frimousse [frimus] *nf* face of child, girl, cat.
fringale [frɛ̃gal] *nf* **avoir la —** to be ravenous.
fringant [frɛ̃gã] *a* lively, frisky, spruce, smart.
friper [fripe] *vt* to crush, crumple; *vr* to get crushed.
fripier, -ière [fripje, jɛ:r] *n* old-clothes dealer.
fripon, -onne [fripɔ̃, ɔn] *a* roguish; *n* rogue, rascal, hussy.
friponnerie [fripɔnri] *nf* roguery.
fripouille [fripu:j] *nf* rotter, bad egg, cad.
frire [fri:r] *vti* to fry.
frise [fri:z] *nf* frieze.
frisé [frize] *a* curly, frizzy.
friser [frize] *vt* to curl, frizz, skim, graze, verge on; *vi* to curl, be curly.
frisoir [frizwa:r] *nm* curling-tongs, curler.
frisson [frisɔ̃] *nm* shudder, thrill, shiver, tremor.
frissonnement [frisɔnmã] *nm* shudder(ing), shiver(ing).
frissonner [frisɔne] *vt* to shudder, shiver, quiver.
frit [fri] *a* fried; (**pommes de terres**) **—es** chips, French fried (potatoes).
friture [frity:r] *nf* frying, fry; *pl* crackling noises, static.
frivole [frivɔl] *a* frivolous, empty, flimsy.
frivolité [frivɔlite] *nf* frivolity, emptiness, trifle.
froc [frɔk] *nm* monk's cowl, habit, gown.
froid [frwa] *a* cold, chilly, cool, frigid, unimpressed; *nm* cold, chill, coldness, coolness; **il fait —** it is cold; **il a —** he is cold; **— de loup** bitter cold; **prendre —** to catch cold; **battre — à** to cold-shoulder.
froideur [frwadœ:r] *nf* coldness, chilliness, frigidity.
froissement [frwasmã] *nm* crumpling, bruising, rustle, causing offense.
froisser [frwase] *vt* to bruise, crumple, jostle, offend, ruffle; *vr* to take offense, become crumpled.
frôler [frole] *vt* to graze, brush (against).
fromage [frɔma:ʒ] *nm* cheese; **— de tête** headcheese.
fromager [frɔmaʒe] *nm* silk cotton tree.
froment [frɔmã] *nm* wheat.
fronce [frɔ̃:s] *nf* gather, pucker.
froncement [frɔ̃smã] *nm* puckering, wrinkling.
froncer [frɔ̃se] *vt* to pucker, wrinkle, gather; **— les sourcils** to knit one's brows, frown, scowl.

frondaison [frɔ̃dɛzɔ̃] *nf* foliation, foliage.
fronde [frɔ̃:d] *nf* catapult, sling, Fronde.
fronder [frɔ̃de] *vt* to sling, criticize, jeer at.
frondeur, -euse [frɔ̃dœ:r, ø:z] *a* critical, always against authority; *n* slinger, critic, scoffer.
front [frɔ̃] *nm* brow, forehead, face, front, cheek, effrontery; **de —** abreast.
frontière [frɔ̃tjɛ:r] *nf* frontier, border, line, boundary.
frontispice [frɔ̃tispis] *nm* title page, frontispiece.
fronton [frɔ̃tɔ̃] *nm* pediment, fronton, ornamental front.
frottement [frɔtmɑ̃] *nm* rubbing, chafing, friction.
frotter [frɔte] *vt* to rub, polish, chafe, (*match*) strike; *vi* to rub; *vr* to rub, come up (against à), keep company (with à).
frottoir [frɔtwa:r] *nm* polisher, scrubbing brush.
frou-frou [frufru] *nm* rustle, swish.
frousse [frus] *nf* funk.
fructifier [fryktifje] *vi* to fructify, bear fruit.
fructueux, -euse [fryktɥø, ø:z] *a* fruitful, profitable.
frugal [frygal] *a* frugal, thrifty.
frugalité [frygalite] *nf* frugality.
fruit [frɥi] *nm* fruit; *pl* fruits, advantages, benefits; **— sec** (*person*) failure.
fruiterie [frɥitri] *nf* fruit trade, fruiterer's, greengrocer's shop.
fruitier, -ière [frɥitje, jɛ:r] *a* fruit; *n* fruiterer, greengrocer.
frusques [frysk] *nf pl* togs, clothes.
fruste [fryst] *a* worn, defaced, rough, coarse.
frustrer [frystre] *vt* to frustrate, deprive, do (out of **de**).
fugace [fygas] *a* fleeting, transient.
fugacité [fygasite] *nf* transience.
fugitif, -ive [fyʒitif, i:v] *a* fleeting, passing; *n* fugitive.
fugue [fyg] *nf* fugue, escapade, flying visit, jaunt.
fuir [fɥi:r] *vt* to run away from, shun, avoid; *vi* to flee, run away, recede, leak.
fuite [fɥit] *nf* flight, escape, leak(age).
fulgurant [fylgyrɑ̃] *a* flashing, striking.
fuligineux, -euse [fyliʒinø, ø:z] *a* soot-colored, sooty.
fulminer [fylmine] *vt* to fulminate; *vi* to inveigh.
fume-cigarette [fymsigarɛt] *nm* cigarette-holder.
fumée [fyme] *nf* smoke, steam; *pl* fumes.
fumer [fyme] *vt* to smoke, cure, manure; *vi* to smoke, fume, steam.
fumet [fymɛ] *nm* smell, bouquet, aroma, scent.

fumeur, -euse [fymœ:r, ø:z] *n* smoker, curer.
fumeux, -euse [fymø, ø:z] *a* smoky, smoking, heady, hazy.
fumier [fymje] *nm* dung, manure, dunghill, stable-litter.
fumigation [fymigasjɔ̃] *nf* fumigation.
fumiger [fymiʒe] *vt* to fumigate.
fumiste [fymist] *nm* stove-setter, practical joker, hoaxer, leg-puller.
fumisterie [fymistri] *nf* stove-setting, hoax, practical joke, leg-pulling.
fumoir [fymwa:r] *nm* smoking room.
funambule [fynɑ̃byl] *n* tight-rope walker.
funambulesque [fynɑ̃bylɛsk] *a* fantastic, queer.
funèbre [fynɛbr] *a* funeral, funereal, dismal.
funérailles [fyneraːj] *nf pl* funeral.
funéraire [fynerɛ:r] *a* funeral, funerary.
funeste [fynɛst] *a* fatal, deadly, disastrous, baleful.
funiculaire [fynikylɛ:r] *a* funicular; *nm* cable-railway.
fur [fy:r] *cj* **au — et à mesure que** (gradually) as, in proportion as; **ad au — et à mesure** gradually, as one goes along.
furet [fyrɛ] *nm* ferret, Nosy Parker.
fureter [fyrte] *vi* to ferret, pry, cast about.
fureur [fyrœ:r] *nf* fury, rage, madness, passion, craze; **faire —** to be all the rage.
furibond [fyribɔ̃] *a* furious.
furie [fyri] *nf* fury, rage, passion.
furieux, -euse [fyrjø, jø:z] *a* furious, wild, raging, in a rage.
furoncle [fyrɔ̃kl] *nm* boil.
furtif, -ive [fyrtif, i:v] *a* stealthy, covert, furtive, secret, sneaking.
fusain [fyzɛ̃] *nm* spindletree, charcoal sketch.
fuseau [fyzo] *nm* spindle, bobbin.
fusée [fyze] *nf* spindle, fuse, rocket; **— à pétard** firework; **— éclairante** flare; **— porte-amarre** rocket apparatus.
fuselage [fyzla:ʒ] *nm* fuselage.
fuseler [fyzle] *vt* to taper.
fuser [fyze] *vi* to fuse, melt, run, spread.
fusible [fyzibl] *a* fusible, easily melted.
fusil [fyzi] *nm* gun, rifle, steel; **coup de —** gunshot, report; **attraper un coup de —** to get stung, overcharged.
fusilier [fyzilje] *nm* fusilier; **— marin** marine.
fusillade [fyzijad] *nf* firing, volley.
fusiller [fyzije] *vt* to shoot, execute.
fusion [fyzjɔ̃] *nf* fusion, melting, smelting, union, amalgamation.
fusionner [fyzjɔne] *vti* to merge, unite, amalgamate.

fustiger [fystiʒe] *vt* to flog, thrash.
fût [fy] *nm* stock, shaft, handle, barrel, cask, bole.
futaie [fytɛ] *nf* wood, forest, very large tree.
futaille [fytɑ:j] *nf* cask, barrel, tun.
futé [fyte] *a* crafty, smart.
futile [fytil] *a* futile, frivolous, trivial.
futilité [fytilite] *nf* futility, triviality.
futur [fyty:r] *a* future, to come; *nm* future tense; *n* future husband, wife.
fuyant [fɥijɑ̃] *a* fleeing, fleeting, receding, elusive, shifty.
fuyard [fɥija:r] *n* fugitive, runaway.

G

gabardine [gabardin] *nf* raincoat, gabardine.
gabarit [gabari] *nm* gauge, templet, model, mold, stamp.
gabegie [gabʒi] *nf* dishonesty, underhand dealings, muddle, mismanagement.
gabier [gabje] *nm* topman, seaman.
gâche [gɑ:ʃ] *nf* staple, wall-hook.
gâcher [gɑʃe] *vt* to mix, waste, spoil, bungle, make a mess of.
gâchette [gɑʃɛt] *nf* trigger.
gâchis [gɑʃi] *nm* wet mortar, mud, slush, mess.
gaffe [gaf] *nf* boat-hook, gaff, blunder, boner.
gaffer [gafe] *vt* to hook, gaff; *vi* blunder.
gaga [gaga] *a* doddering; *nm* dodderer.
gage [ga:ʒ] *nm* pledge, pawn, security, token, forfeit; *pl* wages, pay.
gager [gaʒe] *vt* to wager, bet, pay, hire.
gageure [gaʒy:r] *nf* wager, bet.
gagnant [gɑɲɑ̃] *a* winning; *n* winner.
gagne-pain [gɑɲpɛ̃] *nm* livelihood, bread-winner.
gagner [gɑɲe] *vt* to earn, gain, win (over), get, reach, overtake, catch up (on); *vr* to be catching, be infectious.
gai [ge, gɛ] *a* gay, merry, blithe, cheerful, bright.
gaieté [gete, gɛte] *nf* gaiety, mirth, merriment, cheerfulness.
gaillard [gaja:r] *a* strong, stalwart, hearty, merry, spicy; *nm* fellow, fine, jolly fellow; **— d'avant** forecastle; **— d'arrière** quarter-deck; **—e** *nf* wench, strapping, bold young woman.
gaillardise [gajardi:z] *nf* jollity, gaiety; *pl* broad humor, suggestive stories.
gain [gɛ̃] *nm* gain, profit, earnings, winning(s); **— de cause** decision in one's favor.

gaine [gɛ:n] *nf* case, cover, sheath, corset.
gala [gala] *nm* gala, fête.
galamment [galamɑ̃] *ad* gallantly, courteously, bravely.
galant [galɑ̃] *a* attentive to women, gay, amatory; **intrigue —e** love-affair; **— homme** gentleman; *nm* lover, ladies' man.
galanterie [galɑ̃tri] *nf* attention to women, love affair, compliment, gift.
galbe [galb] *nm* contour, outline, figure.
gale [gal] *nf* itch, scabies, mange, scab.
galère [galɛ:r] *nf* galley.
galerie [galri] *nf* gallery, arcade, balcony, circle.
galet [galɛ] *nm* pebble, shingle, roller, pulley.
galette [galɛt] *nf* cake, ship's biscuit; (*fam*) money, dough.
galeux, -euse [galø, ø:z] *a* itchy, mangy, scabby; **brebis —se** black sheep.
galimatias [galimatjɑ] *nm* nonsense, gibberish.
Galles [gal] *nm* **pays de —** Wales.
gallois [galwa] *a nm* Welsh; *n* Welshman.
galon [galɔ̃] *nm* braid, stripe, band.
galonner [galɔne] *vt* to trim with braid, lace.
galop [galo] *nm* gallop.
galoper [galɔpe] *vti* to gallop.
galopin [galɔpɛ̃] *nm* urchin, young scamp.
galvaniser [galvanize] *vt* to galvanize.
galvauder [galvode] *vt* to botch, besmirch; *vr* to sully one's name.
gambade [gɑ̃bad] *nf* gambol, caper.
gambader [gɑ̃bade] *vi* to gambol, caper, romp.
gamelle [gamɛl] *nf* tin-can, mess-tin.
gamin [gamɛ̃] *nm* urchin, youngster; **—e** *nf* (pert) little girl.
gamme [gam] *nf* gamut, scale, range.
gammée [game] *a* **croix —** swastika.
ganache [ganaʃ] *nf* lower jaw; duffer, old fogey.
gangrène [gɑ̃grɛn] *nf* gangrene, canker.
gangrener [gɑ̃grəne] *vt* to gangrene, canker; *vr* to mortify, become cankered.
gangreneux, -euse [gɑ̃grənø, ø:z] *a* gangrenous, cankerous.
ganse [gɑ̃:s] *nf* braid, gimp, piping, loop.
gant [gɑ̃] *nm* glove, gauntlet.
gantelé [gɑ̃tle] *a* gauntleted, mailed.
ganter [gɑ̃te] *vt* to glove, *vr* to put on one's gloves.
ganterie [gɑ̃tri] *nf* glove-making, -factory, -shop.
gantier [gɑ̃tje] *nm* glover.

garage [gara:ʒ] *nm* garage, shed, depot, storage, parking, shunting; **voie de —** siding.

garagiste [garaʒist] *nm* garage owner, proprietor.

garant [garɑ̃] *nm* guarantor, surety, bail, authority, warrant, guarantee.

garantie [garɑ̃ti] *nf* guarantee, pledge, security, safeguard, underwriting.

garantir [garɑ̃ti:r] *vt* to guarantee, warrant, vouch for, underwrite, shield, insure.

garçon [garsɔ̃] *nm* boy, lad, son, young man, chap, fellow, bachelor, servant, assistant, waiter; **— d'honneur** usher, best man; **— manqué** tomboy.

garçonnet [garsɔnɛ] *nm* little boy.

garçonnière [garsɔnjɛ:r] *nf* bachelor's, single man's flat.

garde [gard] *nf* guardianship, care, guard, watch(ing), keeping, charge, flyleaf, the Guards; **prendre —** to take care, beware (**à of**), be careful (**à of**), to take good care (**à to**), be careful not (**de to**); **sans y prendre —** inadvertently; *nm* keeper, guard, watchman, guardsman.

garde-à-vous [gardavu] *nm* **au —** at attention.

garde-barrière [gardbarjɛ:r] *n* (grade crossing) gatekeeper.

garde-boue [gardəbu] *nm* mudguard, fender.

garde-champêtre [gardʃɑ̃pɛtr] *nm* village policeman.

garde-chasse [gardəʃas] *nm* gamekeeper.

garde-corps [gardəkɔr] *nm* parapet, balustrade, rail.

garde-feu [gardəfø] *nm* fireguard, fender.

garde-fou [gardəfu] *nm* parapet, rail(ing).

garde-malade [gardmalad] *n* nurse.

garde-manger [gardmɑ̃ʒe] *nm* larder, pantry.

garder [garde] *vt* to guard, protect, look after, preserve, keep, remain in, observe, respect; *vr* to protect oneself, beware (**de of**), take care not (**de to**), refrain (**de from**).

garde-robe [gardərɔb] *nf* wardrobe, clothes.

gardeur, -euse [gardœ:r, ø:z] *n* keeper, herdsman.

gardien, -ienne [gardjɛ̃, jɛn] *n* guardian, caretaker, warder, attendant, goalkeeper; **— de la paix** policeman.

gare [ga:r] *excl* look out! take care! mind!; *nf* station; **— maritime** harbor station.

garer [gare] *vt* to shunt, garage, park; *vr* to stand aside, take cover, pull to one side, shunt.

se gargariser [səgargarize] *vr* to gargle.

gargarisme [gargarism] *nm* gargle.

gargouille [gargu:j] *nf* gargoyle.

garnement [garnəmɑ̃] *nm* **mauvais —** scamp, rascal.

garni [garni] *a* well-filled, garnished, furnished; *nm* furnished room(s).

garnir [garni:r] *vt* to furnish, provide, fill, stock, fit out, trim, garnish, garrison.

garnison [garnizɔ̃] *nf* garrison.

garniture [garnity:r] *nf* fittings, furnishings, trimming(s), decoration, lining, lagging, packing.

garrotter [garɔte] *vt* to strangle, to bind tightly.

gars [gɑ] *nm* boy, lad, young fellow.

Gascogne [gaskɔɲ] *nf* Gascony.

gascon, -onne [gaskɔ̃, ɔn] *an* Gascon.

gaspiller [gaspije] *vt* to waste, squander, spoil.

gastrique [gastrik] *a* gastric.

gastronome [gastrɔnɔm] *nm* gastronome.

gastronomie [gastrɔnɔmi] *nf* gastronomy.

gastronomique [gastrɔnɔmik] *a* gastronomical.

gâteau [gɑto] *nm* cake, tart; **— de miel** honeycomb.

gâter [gɑte] *vt* to spoil, pamper, damage, taint, mar; *vr* to deteriorate; **enfant gâté** spoiled child.

gâterie [gɑtri] *nf* excessive indulgence, spoiling; *pl* treats, dainties, delicacies.

gâteux, -euse [gɑtø, ø:z] *a* senile, in one's dotage; *n* dotard.

gauche [go:ʃ] *a* left, warped, clumsy, awkward; *nf* left.

gaucher [goʃe] *a* left-handed; *n* left-hander.

gaucherie [goʃri] *nf* clumsiness, awkwardness.

gauchir [goʃi:r] *vti* to warp, buckle.

gaudriole [godrijɔl] *nf* broad joke.

gaufre [go:fr] *nf* waffle.

gaufrer [gofre] *vt* to crimp, emboss, crinkle.

gaufrette [gofrɛt] *nf* water biscuit.

gaule [go:l] *nf* pole, stick, fishing-rod.

gaulois [golwa] *a* Gallic; **esprit —** free, broad, Gallic wit; *n* Gaul.

gauloiserie [golwazri] *nf* broad, free joke.

se gausser [səgose] *vr* to poke fun (**de** at), taunt.

gaver [gave] *vt* to cram, stuff; *vr* to gorge.

gaz [gɑ:z] *nm* gas; *pl* flatulence, wind; **à pleins —** flat out.

gaze [gɑ:z] *nf* gauze.

gazelle [gazɛl] *nf* gazelle.

gazer [gaze] *vt* to cover with gauze, gloss over, tone down, veil, gas; *vi* to speed, go well.

gazeux, -euse [gazø, ø:z] *a* gaseous, aerated, gassy.

gazogène [gazɔʒɛn] *a* gas-producing; *nm* gazogene, gas-generator.

gazomètre [gazɔmɛtr] *nm* gaso-meter.
gazon [gazɔ̃] *nm* grass, turf, sod, lawn, green.
gazouillement [gazujmã] *nm* twit-tering, warbling, babbling, prattling.
gazouiller [gazuje] *vi* to twitter, warble, babble, prattle.
geai [ʒɛ] *nm* jay.
géant [ʒeã] *a* gigantic, giant; *n* giant, giantess.
geignard [ʒɛɲaːr] *a* whining, fretful; *nm* whiner, sniveler.
geindre [ʒɛ̃dr] *vi* to whine, whimper.
gélatine [ʒelatin] *nf* gelatin.
gelé [ʒ(ə)le] *a* frozen, frostbitten.
gelée [ʒ(ə)le] *nf* frost, jelly.
geler [ʒ(ə)le] *vti* to freeze; *vr* to freeze, solidify.
gelure [ʒəlyːr] *nf* frostbite.
gémir [ʒemiːr] *vi* to moan, groan, wail.
gémissement [ʒemismã] *nm* moan(ing), groan(ing), wail(ing).
gênant [ʒɛnã] *a* in the way, awk-ward, embarrassing.
gencive [ʒãsiːv] *nf* gum.
gendarme [ʒãdarm] *nm* gendarme, policeman.
gendre [ʒãːdr] *nm* son-in-law.
gêne [ʒɛn] *nf* embarrassment, dis-comfort, constraint, want, straitened circumstances; **sans —** free and easy.
gêné [ʒene] *a* embarrassed, ill at ease, awkward, hard up.
généalogie [ʒenealɔʒi] *nf* genealogy, pedigree.
généalogique [ʒenealɔʒik] *a* genea-logical, family.
gêner [ʒene] *vt* to cramp, constrain, pinch, hamper, inconvenience, em-barrass; *vr* to inconvenience oneself; **ne pas se —** not to put oneself out, to make oneself at home.
général [ʒeneral] *a* general, pre-vailing; *nm* general; **— de division** major-general; **— de brigade** brigadier-general.
généralement [ʒeneralmã] *ad* gener-ally.
généralisation [ʒeneralizasjɔ̃] *nf* generalization.
généraliser [ʒeneralize] *vt* to generalize; *vr* to become general, spread.
généralissime [ʒeneralisim] *nm* generalissimo, commander-in-chief.
généralité [ʒeneralite] *nf* generality.
générateur, -trice [ʒeneratœːr, tris] *a* generating, generative; *nm* generator.
génération [ʒenerasjɔ̃] *nf* generation.
généreux, -euse [ʒenerø, øːz] *a* generous.
générique [ʒenerik] *a* generic; *nm* (*film*) credits.
générosité [ʒenerɔzite] *nf* generosity.
genèse [ʒənɛːz] *nf* genesis.
genêt [ʒ(ə)nɛ] *nm* (*bot*) broom.
genévrier [ʒənevrie] *nm* juniper.

génial [ʒenjal] *a* inspired, bright, brilliant.
génie [ʒeni] *nm* genius, spirit, (army) engineers; **— civil** engineering.
genièvre [ʒənjɛːvr] *nm* juniper, gin.
génisse [ʒenis] *nf* heifer.
genou [ʒənu] *nm* knee.
genre [ʒãːr] *nm* kind, sort, type, genus, family, style.
gens [ʒã] *n pl* people, folk(s), men, servants.
gentiane [ʒãsjan] *nf* gentian.
gentil, -ille [ʒãti, iːj] *a* nice, pretty, kind, sweet, good.
gentilhomme [ʒãtijɔm] *nm* noble-man.
gentillesse [ʒãtijɛs] *nf* prettiness, graciousness, kindness; *pl* nice things.
gentiment [ʒãtimã] *ad* nicely, prettily, sweetly.
géographie [ʒeɔgrafi] *nf* geography.
géographique [ʒeɔgrafik] *a* geo-graphical.
geôle [ʒoːl] *nf* jail, prison.
geôlier [ʒolje] *nm* jailer, warder.
géologie [ʒeɔlɔʒi] *nf* geology.
géologue [ʒeɔlɔg] *nm* geologist.
géométrie [ʒeɔmetri] *nf* geometry.
géométrique [ʒeɔmetrik] *a* geo-metrical.
gérance [ʒerãːs] *nf* management, managership.
géranium [ʒeranjɔm] *nm* geranium.
gérant [ʒerã] *n* manager(ess), direc-tor, managing-.
gerbe [ʒɛrb] *nf* sheaf, spray, shower.
gerçure [ʒɛrsyːr] *nf* chap, crack, fissure.
gérer [ʒere] *vt* to manage.
germain [ʒɛrmɛ̃] *a* full, first.
germanique [ʒɛrmanik] *a* Germanic.
germe [ʒɛrm] *nm* germ, (*potato*) eye, seed.
germer [ʒɛrme] *vi* to germinate, sprout, shoot.
germination [ʒɛrminasjɔ̃] *nf* germ-ination.
gésier [ʒezje] *nm* gizzard.
gésir [ʒeziːr] *vi* to lie.
geste [ʒɛst] *nm* gesture, movement, motion, wave.
gesticuler [ʒɛstikyle] *vi* to gesticul-ate.
gestion [ʒɛstjɔ̃] *nf* management, administration, care.
gibecière [ʒipsjɛːr] *nf* game-bag, satchel.
giberne [ʒibɛrn] *nf* wallet, pouch, satchel.
gibier [ʒibje] *nm* game.
giboulée [ʒibule] *nf* (hail) shower.
giboyeux, -euse [ʒibwajø, øːz] *a* well stocked with game.
giclement [ʒikləmã] *nm* splashing, spurting.
gicler [ʒikle] *vi* to splash (up), squelch, spurt (out).
gicleur [ʒiklœːr] *nm* spray, jet.
gifle [ʒifl] *nf* slap, smack, cuff.

gifler [ʒifle] vt to slap, smack.
gigantesque [ʒigãtɛsk] a gigantic, huge.
gigot [ʒigo] nm leg of mutton.
gigue [ʒig] nf jig.
gilet [ʒilɛ] nm waistcoat, vest, jacket; — tricoté cardigan.
gingembre [ʒɛ̃ʒɑ̃:br] nm ginger.
girafe [ʒiraf] nf giraffe.
giratoire [ʒiratwa:r] a gyratory, roundabout.
girofle [ʒirɔfl] nm clove.
giroflée [ʒirɔfle] nf stock, wallflower.
giron [ʒirɔ̃] nm lap.
girouette [ʒirwɛt] nf weathercock, turncoat.
gisant [ʒizã] a lying, recumbent.
gisement [ʒizmã] nm layer, seam, stratum, bearing.
gîte [ʒit] nm resting-place, lair, home, shelter, bed, seam, leg of beef.
givre [ʒi:vr] nm hoarfrost.
glabre [glɑ:br] a smooth, hairless, clean-shaven.
glace [glas] nf ice, glass, mirror, window, icing, ice-cream.
glacé [glase] a frozen, icy, chilled, stony, iced, glossy.
glacer [glase] vt to freeze, chill, ice, glaze.
glacial [glasjal] a icy, frozen, frigid, stony.
glacier [glasje] nm glacier, ice-cream vendor, manufacturer of mirrors.
glacière [glasjɛ:r] nf ice-house, icebox, freezer.
glacis [glasi] nm slope, bank, glaze.
glaçon [glasɔ̃] nm block of ice, icefloe, icicle.
gladiateur [gladjatœ:r] nm gladiator.
glaïeul [glajœl] nm gladiolus.
glaise [glɛ:z] nf clay.
glaive [glɛv] nm sword, sword-fish.
gland [glã] nm acorn, tassel.
glande [glã:d] nf gland.
glaner [glane] vt to glean.
glaneur, -euse [glanœ:r, ø:z] n gleaner.
glapir [glapi:r] vi to yelp, yap, (fox) bark.
glas [glɑ] nm knell, death bell.
glauque [glo:k] a glaucous, sea-green.
glissade [glisad] nf slip, slide, sliding.
glissant [glisã] a slippery, sliding.
glissement [glismã] nm sliding, slip, gliding, glide.
glisser [glise] vi to slip, skid, slide, glide, pass over; vt to slip; vr to glide, creep, steal into (dans).
glisseur, -euse [glisœ:r, ø:z] n slider; nm speedboat, glider.
glissière [glisjɛ:r] nf groove, slide, shoot; à —s sliding.
global [glɔbal] a total, inclusive, lump.
globe [glɔb] nm globe, orb, ball.
globulaire [glɔbylɛ:r] a globular.

globule [glɔbyl] nm globule.
gloire [glwa:r] nf glory, fame, boast pride, halo.
glorieux, -euse [glɔrjø, ø:z] a glorious, proud, conceited, boastful; nm braggart.
glorifier [glɔrifje] vt to glorify, praise; vr to boast.
gloriole [glɔrjɔl] nf notoriety, vainglory, credit.
glose [glo:z] nf gloss, note, comment, criticism.
gloser [gloze] vt to gloss, criticize.
glossaire [glɔsɛ:r] nm glossary.
glouglou [gluglu] nm gurgle, gobblegobble.
glousser [gluse] vi to cluck, gobble, gurgle, chuckle.
glouton, -onne [glutɔ̃, ɔn] a greedy, gluttonous; n glutton.
gloutonnerie [glutɔnri] nf gluttony.
glu [gly] nf bird-lime.
gluant [glyã] a gluey, sticky.
glutineux [glytinø] a glutinous.
glycérine [gliserin] nf glycerine.
glycine [glisin] nf wisteria.
go [go] ad tout de — straight off.
gobelet [gɔblɛ] nm goblet, cup, tumbler.
gobe-mouches [gɔbmuʃ] nm flycatcher, ninny, wiseacre.
gober [gɔbe] vt to swallow, gulp down; vr to fancy oneself.
gobeur, -euse [gɔbœ:r, ø:z] n conceited person.
godasses [gɔdas] nf pl boots.
godet [gɔdɛ] nm mug, cup, flare, gore.
godille [gɔdi:j] nf scull.
godiller [gɔdije] vi to scull.
goéland [gɔelã] nm seagull.
goélette [gɔelɛt] nf schooner.
goémon [gɔemɔ̃] nm seaweed.
goguenard [gɔgna:r] a bantering, joking, jeering.
goinfre [gwɛ̃:fr] nm glutton.
goinfrerie [gwɛ̃frəri] nf gluttony, guzzling.
goitre [gwa:tr] nm goiter.
golf [gɔlf] nm golf, golf-course.
golfe [gɔlf] nm gulf, bay.
gombo [gɔ̃bo] nm okra.
gomme [gɔm] nf gum, (india)rubber, eraser.
gommeux, -euse [gɔmø, ø:z] a gummy, sticky; nm pretentious man, dude.
gond [gɔ̃] nm hinge.
gondolant [gɔ̃dɔlã] a funny, killing.
gondole [gɔ̃dɔl] nf gondola.
gondoler [gɔ̃dɔle] vi to warp, buckle, sag; vr to warp, buckle, shake with laughter.
gondolier [gɔ̃dɔlje] nm gondolier.
gonflage [gɔ̃fla:ʒ] nm inflation, tire pressure.
gonflement [gɔ̃fləmã] nm inflating, inflation, distension.
gonfler [gɔ̃fle] vt to swell, inflate, blow up; vir to swell, become distended.

gonfleur [gɔ̃flœːr] *nm* inflator, air-pump.

goret [gɔrɛ] *nm* piglet.

gorge [gɔrʒ] *nf* throat, gullet, breast, gorge, (*mountain*) pass; **rire à —** déployée to laugh heartily; **rendre —** to disgorge; **faire des —s chaudes de** to laugh heartily at the expense of.

gorgée [gɔrʒe] *nf* mouthful, gulp.

gorger [gɔrʒe] *vt* to stuff, gorge.

gorille [gɔriːj] *nm* gorilla.

gosier [gozje] *nm* throat, gullet.

gosse [gɔs] *n* youngster, child, kid.

gothique [gɔtik] *a* gothic.

goudron [gudrɔ̃] *nm* tar.

goudronner [gudrɔne] *vt* to tar, spray with tar.

gouffre [gufr] *nm* gulf, abyss, chasm.

goujat [guʒa] *nm* boor, cad, black-guard.

goujaterie [guʒatri] *nf* boorishness, churlish act.

goujon [guʒɔ̃] *nm* gudgeon, stud, pin.

goulet [gulɛ] *nm* gully, narrows, narrow channel.

goulot [gulo] *nm* (bottle)neck.

goulu [guly] *a* greedy, gluttonous.

goupille [gupiːj] *nf* (linch)pin.

goupillon [gupijɔ̃] *nm* holy-water sprinkler.

gourde [gurd] *nf* gourd, water-bottle, flask, fool.

gourdin [gurdɛ̃] *nm* cudgel.

gourmand [gurmɑ̃] *a* greedy, very fond (of); *n* gourmand, glutton.

gourmander [gurmɑ̃de] *vt* to guzzle; *vt* to scold.

gourmandise [gurmɑ̃diːz] *nf* greedi-ness, gluttony; *pl* sweet things.

gourme [gurm] *nf* impetigo, wild oats.

gourmet [gurmɛ] *nm* epicure.

gousse [gus] *nf* pod, shell; **— d'ail** clove of garlic.

gousset [gusɛ] *nm* waistcoat pocket, gusset.

goût [gu] *nm* taste, flavor, relish, liking, style, manner.

goûter [gute] *vt* to taste, enjoy, relish, take a snack between meals; *nm* (afternoon) snack, tea.

goutte [gut] *nf* drop, drip, dram, splash, spot, sip, gout.

goutteux, -euse [gutø, øːz] *a* gouty.

gouttière [gutjeːr] *nf* gutter, rain-pipe, spout.

gouvernail [guvɛrnaːj] *nm* rudder, helm.

gouvernante [guvɛrnɑ̃ːt] *nf* gover-ness, housekeeper.

gouverne [guvɛrn] *nf* guidance, direction, steering; *pl* controls.

gouvernement [guvɛrnəmɑ̃] *nm* government.

gouverner [guvɛrne] *vt* to govern, control, steer.

gouverneur [guvɛrnœːr] *nm* gover-nor.

goyavier [gwajavje] *nm* guava tree.

grabuge [grabyːʒ] *nm* quarrel, row.

grâce [grɑs] *nf* grace, gracefulness, favor, pardon, mercy; **de bonne —, de mauvaise —** willingly, un-willingly; **— à** thanks to.

gracier [grasje] *vt* to pardon, reprieve.

gracieux, -euse [grasjø, øːz] *a* graceful, gracious, free.

gracile [grasil] *a* slim, slender.

gradation [gradasjɔ̃] *nf* gradation.

grade [grad] *nm* grade, rank, degree.

gradé [grade] *nm* noncommissioned officer.

gradin [gradɛ̃] *nm* step, tier.

graduel, -elle [gradɥɛl] *a* gradual.

graduer [gradɥe] *vt* to graduate, grade.

grain [grɛ̃] *nm* grain, corn, berry, bean, particle, speck, squall; **— de beauté** beauty spot, mole; **— de plomb** pellet; **— de raisin** grape.

graine [grɛn] *nf* seed.

grainetier [grɛntje] *nm* seedsman, corn-chandler.

graissage [grɛsaːʒ] *nm* greasing, lubrication.

graisse [grɛːs] *nf* grease, fat; **— de rognon** suet; **— de rôti** drippings.

graisser [grɛse] *vt* to grease, lubricate.

graisseux, -euse [grɛsø, øːz] *a* greasy, oily, fatty.

grammaire [gramɛːr] *nf* grammar.

grammairien, -ienne [grammɛrjɛ̃, jɛn] *nm* grammarian.

grammatical [grammatikal] *a* gram-matical.

gramme [gram] *nm* gram.

gramophone [gramɔfɔn] *nm* gramo-phone, phonograph.

grand [grɑ̃] *a* tall, large, big, main, great, noble, high, grown up, grand; **en —** on a large scale, full size; *nm* grandee; *pl* grown-ups, great ones.

grand'chose [grɑ̃ʃoːz] *pr* much.

grandement [grɑ̃dmɑ̃] *ad* greatly, largely, grandly, ample, high.

grandeur [grɑ̃dœːr] *nf* size, height, magnitude, grandeur, Highness.

grandiloquence [grɑ̃dilɔkɑ̃ːs] *nf* grandiloquence.

grandiose [grɑ̃djoːz] *a* grandiose, imposing.

grandir [grɑ̃diːr] *vi* to grow (up, tall); *vt* to increase, make taller, magnify.

grand'mère [grɑ̃mɛːr] *nf* grand-mother.

grand'messe [grɑ̃mɛs] *nf* high mass.

grand'peine [grɑ̃pɛn] *ad* **à —** with great difficulty.

grand-père [grɑ̃pɛːr] *nm* grand-father.

grand'route [grɑ̃rut] *nf* highway, high road, main road.

grand'rue [grɑ̃ry] *nf* main street, high street.

grands-parents [grɑ̃parɑ̃] *nm* *pl* grandparents.

grange [grɑ̃ːʒ] *nf* barn.

granit [grani(t)] *nm* granite.
graphique [grafik] *a* graphic; *nm* diagram, graph.
graphite [grafit] *nm* graphite, plumbago.
grappe [grap] *nf* bunch, cluster.
grappin [grapɛ̃] *nm* grapnel, hook, grab; *pl* climbing-irons.
gras, -se [grɑ, grɑːs] *a* fat(ty), fatted, rich, oily, greasy, thick, ribald, heavy; **faire — to** eat meat; **jour —** meat day; *nm* fat.
grassement [grɑsmɑ̃] *ad* generously.
grasset, -ette [grɑsɛ, ɛt] *a* plump, fattish, chubby.
grasseyer [grɑsɛje] *vi* to burr, roll one's 'r's.
grassouillet, -ette [grɑsuje, ɛt] *a* plump, chubby.
gratification [gratifikasjɔ̃] *nf* bonus, gratuity.
gratifier [gratifje] *vt* to bestow, confer.
gratin [gratɛ̃] *nm* browned part, smart set; **au — with** bread-crumbs and grated cheese.
gratiné [gratine] *a* with breadcrumbs.
gratis [gratis] *ad* gratis, free (of charge).
gratitude [gratityd] *nf* gratitude, gratefulness.
gratte-ciel [gratsjɛl] *nm* skyscraper.
gratte-pieds [gratpje] *nm* scraper.
gratter [grate] *vt* to scratch, scrape (out).
gratuit [gratɥi] *a* gratuitous, free, uncalled for.
gratuité [gratɥite] *nf* gratuitousness.
grave [graːv] *a* grave, solemn, serious, low-pitched.
graveleux, -euse [gravlø, øːz] *a* gritty, ribald.
graver [grave] *vt* to engrave, cut, carve; **— à l'eau-forte** to etch.
graveur [gravœːr] *nm* engraver, carver.
gravier [gravje] *nm* gravel, grit.
gravir [graviːr] *vt* to climb .
gravitation [gravitasjɔ̃] *nf* gravitation.
gravité [gravite] *nf* gravity, severity, seriousness, weight, low pitch.
graviter [gravite] *vi* to gravitate, revolve.
gravure [gravyːr] *nf* engraving, print, illustration; **— à l'eau-forte** etching; **— sur bois** wood-cut.
gré [gre] *nm* liking, taste, will; **au — de** according to, at the mercy of; **bon —, mal — willy-nilly; de — à — by** mutual consent; **de — ou de force** by fair means or foul; **savoir — à** to be grateful to; **savoir mauvais — à** to be angry with.
grec, grecque [grɛk] *a nm* Greek; *n* Greek.
Grèce [grɛs] *nf* Greece.
gredin [grədɛ̃] *nm* rogue.
gréement [gremɑ̃] *nm* rigging, gear.

gréer [gree] *vt* to rig, sling.
greffe [grɛf] *nf* graft, grafting.
greffer [grɛfe] *vt* to graft.
greffier [grɛfje] *nm* clerk of court.
grêle [grɛːl] *a* small, slender, thin, high-pitched; *nf* hail, shower.
grêlé [grɛle] *a* pock-marked.
grêler [grɛle] *v imp* to hail.
grêlon [grɛlɔ̃] *nm* hailstone.
grelot [grəlo] *nm* bell.
grelotter [grəlɔte] *vi* to tremble, shake, shiver.
grenade [grənad] *nf* pomegranate, grenade; **— à main** hand-grenade; **— sous-marine** depth-charge.
grenadine [grənadin] *nf* grenadine.
grenier [grənje] *nm* granary, loft, attic, garret.
grenouille [grənuːj] *nf* frog, funds.
grès [grɛ] *nm* sandstone.
grésiller [grezije] *vi* to crackle, sputter, sizzle.
grève [grɛːv] *nf* beach, shore, strand, strike; **se mettre en — to** go on strike; **faire — to** be on strike; **— de solidarité** strike in sympathy; **— perlée** slowdown; **— sur le tas** sit-down strike; **— de zèle** work to rule.
grever [grəve] *vt* to burden, mortgage
gréviste [grevist] *n* striker.
gri(s)-gri(s) [grigri] *nm* amulet.
gribouillage [gribujaːʒ] *nm* scrawl, scribble.
gribouiller [gribuje] *vt* to scrawl, scribble.
grief [griɛf] *nm* grievance.
grièvement [grievmɑ̃] *ad* severely, seriously, deeply.
griffe [grif] *nf* claw, talon, clip, facsimile signature, writing; *pl* clutches.
griffer [grife] *vt* to scratch, claw, stamp.
griffonnage [grifɔnaːʒ] *nm* scrawl, scribble.
griffonner [grifɔne] *vt* to scrawl, scribble.
grignoter [griɲɔte] *vt* nibble, pick at.
grigou [grigu] *nm* skinflint, miser.
gril [gri] *nm* gridiron, grill.
grillade [grijad] *nf* grilled meat, grill.
grillage [grijaːʒ] *nm* grilling, toasting, roasting, grating, netting, lattice-work.
grille [griːj] *nf* grating, railings, iron-barred gate, entrance gate, grid.
griller [grije] *vt* to grill, toast, roast, scorch, rail in, grate.
grillon [grijɔ̃] *nm* (*insect*) cricket.
grimace [grimas] *nf* grimace, wry face.
grimacer [grimase] *vi* to grimace, make faces.
grimacier, -ière [grimasje, jɛːr] *a* grimacing, grinning, simpering.
se grimer [səgrime] *vr* to make up (one's face).

grimper [grɛ̃pe] *vti* to climb.
grimpeur, -euse [grɛ̃pœːr, øːz] *a* climbing; *n* climber.
grincer [grɛ̃se] *vi* to grate, grind, gnash, creak.
grincheux, -euse [grɛ̃ʃø, øːz] *a* grumpy, surly; *n* grumbler.
griot [grio] *nm* storyteller, praise singer.
grippe [grip] *nf* dislike, influenza.
grippé [gripe] *a* suffering from influenza.
grippe-sou [gripsu] *nm* skinflint, miser.
gris [gri] *a* gray, dull, cloudy, intoxicated.
grisâtre [grizɑːtr] *a* grayish.
griser [grize] *vt* to make tipsy, intoxicate; *vr* to become intoxicated, be carried away (with **de**).
griserie [grizri] *nf* tipsiness,intoxication, rapture.
grisonner [grizɔne] *vi* to turn gray.
grisou [grizu] *nm* firedamp.
grive [griːv] *nf* thrush.
grivois [grivwa] *a* broad, ribald, licentious.
grivoiserie [grivwazri] *nf* ribald, broad joke.
grog [grɔg] *nm* grog, toddy.
grognard [grɔɲaːr] *a* grumbling; *n* grumbler.
grognement [grɔɲəmɑ̃] *nm* grunt (ing), growl(ing), grumbling.
grogner [grɔɲe] *vi* to grunt, growl, snarl, grumble.
grognon [grɔɲɔ̃] *a* grumbling, querulous; *n* grumbler.
groin [grwɛ̃] *nm* snout.
grommeler [grɔmle] *vi* to grumble, mutter.
grondement [grɔ̃dmɑ̃] *nm* growl (ing), snarl(ing), rumble, roaring.
gronder [grɔ̃de] *vi* to growl, snarl, rumble, mutter, roar, grumble; *vt* to scold, rebuke.
gronderie [grɔ̃dri] *nf* scolding.
grondeur, -euse [grɔ̃dœːr, øːz] *a* grumbling, scolding; *n* grumbler, scold.
groom [grum] *nm* groom, page(boy).
gros, -se [gro, groːs] *a* big, large, heavy, stout, thick, coarse, plain, rough, loud, gruff, gross, pregnant; — **bonnets** bigwigs; — **mots** bad language; *nm* bulk, mass, chief part, hardest part; **en** — in bulk, wholesale.
groseille [grozɛːj] *nf* currant (red, white); — **à maquereau** gooseberry.
groseillier [grozɛje] *nm* currant-bush.
grossesse [grosɛs] *nf* pregnancy.
grosseur [grosœːr] *nf* size, bulk, thickness, swelling.
grossier, -ière [grosje, jɛːr] *a* coarse, rough, gross, vulgar, rude.
grossièreté [grosjerte] *nf* coarseness, roughness, rudeness, offensive remark.

grossir [grosiːr] *vt* to enlarge, magnify; *vi* to increase, swell, grow bigger.
grossissement [grosismɑ̃] *nm* increase, swelling, magnifying, enlargement.
grotesque [grɔtɛsk] *a* ludicrous.
grotte [grɔt] *nf* grotto.
grouiller [gruje] *vi* to swarm, be alive (with **de**); *vr* to get a move on, hurry up.
groupe [grup] *nm* group, clump, cluster, party.
groupement [grupmɑ̃] *nm* grouping, group.
grouper [grupe] *vt* to group, arrange; *vr* to form a group, gather.
gruau [gryo] *nm* wheat flour; — **d'avoine** oatmeal, gruel.
grue [gry] *nf* crane, prostitute.
gruger [gryʒe] *vt* to fleece, plunder, sponge on.
grumeau [grymo] *nm* clot, lump.
gué [ge] *nm* ford.
guenille [gəniːj] *nf* rag, tatter.
guenon [gənɔ̃] *nf* she-monkey, ugly woman.
guêpe [gɛːp] *nf* wasp; — **maçonne** mason wasp.
guêpier [gepje] *nm* wasps' nest, hornets' nest.
guère [gɛːr] *ad* hardly (any, ever), barely, not much, not many, but little, but few.
guéridon [geridɔ̃] *nm* pedestal table, occasional table.
guérilla [gerija, -illa] *nf* guerrilla.
guérir [geriːr] *vt* to cure, heal; *vi* to recover, heal.
guérison [gerizɔ̃] *nf* recovery, cure, healing.
guérissable [gerisabl] *a* curable.
guérite [gerit] *nf* sentry-box, signal-box.
guerre [gɛːr] *nf* war(fare), fighting, strife, quarrel, feud; — **d'usure** war of attrition; — **de mouvement** open warfare; — **de position** trench warfare; — **éclair** blitz war; **de bonne** — quite fair; **de** — **lasse** for the sake of peace.
guerrier, -ière [gɛrje, jɛːr] *a* warlike, war-; *nm* warrior.
guerroyer [gɛrwaje] *vi* to wage war.
guet [gɛ] *nm* watch, look-out.
guet-apens [gɛtapɑ̃] *nm* ambush, trap.
guêtre [gɛːtr] *nf* gaiter, spat.
guetter [gɛte] *vt* to lie in wait for, watch, be on the look-out for, listen for.
guetteur [gɛtœːr] *nm* lookout (man).
gueule [gœl] *nf* mouth, muzzle, face, mug; **ta** —! shut up! **casser la** — **à qn** to knock s.o.'s face in; **avoir la** — **de bois** to feel parched after excess of alcohol.
gueuler [gœle] *vti* to bawl, shout.
gueuleton [gœltɔ̃] *nm* blow-out, binge.

gueux, -euse [gø, ø:z] *a* poor, beggarly; *n* beggar.
gui [gi] *nm* mistletoe.
guichet [giʃɛ] *nm* wicket-gate, grating, turnstile, barrier, pay-desk, booking-office window.
guide [gid] *nm* guide, conductor, guidebook; *nf* rein.
guider [gide] *vt* to guide, conduct, drive, steer.
guidon [gidɔ̃] *nm* handlebar, marker flag, pennant, (*on gun*) bead.
guigne [giɲ] *nf* gean; bad luck.
guigner [giɲe] *vt* to peep at, cast an eye over, to leer, ogle.
guignol [giɲɔl] *nm* Punch and Judy show, Punch.
guillemets [gijmɛ] *nm pl* inverted commas, quotation marks.
guilleret, -ette [gijrɛ, ɛt] *a* lively, gay, perky, broad.
guillotine [gijɔtin] *nf* guillotine.
guillotiner [gijɔtine] *vt* to guillotine.
guimauve [gimo:v] *nf* marshmallow.
guimbarde [gɛ̃bard] *nf* jew's-harp, ramshackle vehicle.
guimpe [gɛ̃:p] *nf* wimple, blouse front.
guindé [gɛ̃de] *a* stiff, strained, starchy.
guingois [gɛ̃gwa] *nm* crookedness, skew, twistedness; **de — askew, awry.**
guinguette [gɛ̃gɛt] *nf* suburban tavern with music and dancing.
guipure [gipy:r] *nf* guipure, point-lace, pillow-lace.
guirlande [girlɑ̃:d] *nf* garland, festoon.
guirlander [girlɑ̃de] *vt* to garland, festoon.
guise [gi:z] *nf* way, manner; **à sa — as one pleases; en — de by way of.**
guitare [gita:r] *nf* guitar.
guttural [gytyral] *a* guttural.
gymnaste [ʒimnast] *nm* gymnast.
gymnastique [ʒimnastik] *a* gymnastic; **au pas — on the double; *nf* gymnastics.**
gynécologue [ʒinekɔlɔg] *n* gynecologist.
gypse [ʒips] *nm* gypsum, plaster of Paris.
gyroscope [ʒirɔskɔp] *nm* gyroscope.

H

The asterisk denotes that the initial h, which is never pronounced, is aspirate, i.e. there is no liaison or elision.

habile [abil] *a* clever, skillful, smart.
habileté [abilte] *nf* cleverness, skill, skillfulness, capability, smartness.
habillé [abije] *a* dressed (up), clad, smart, dressy.
habillement [abijmɑ̃] *nm* clothing, clothes, dress.
habiller [abije] *vt* to dress, clothe;

vr to dress, put one's clothes on.
habilleur, -euse [abijœːr, ø:z] *n* dresser (*theater*).
habit [abi] *nm* dress, coat, evening-dress; *pl* clothes.
habitable [abitabl] *a* (in)habitable.
habitant [abitɑ̃] *nm* inhabitant, dweller, resident, occupier; **loger chez l'— to billet privately.**
habitation [abitasjɔ̃] *nf* dwelling, residence, abode.
habiter [abite] *vt* to inhabit, live in, occupy; *vi* to live, reside, dwell.
habitude [abityd] *nf* habit, custom, use, practice, wont, knack; **d'— usually; comme d'— as usual.**
habitué [abitɥe] *nm* regular attendant, frequenter, regular customer.
habituel, -elle [abitɥel] *a* usual, habitual, customary.
habituer [abitɥe] *vt* to accustom, get into the habit; *vr* to get used, grow accustomed.
*****hâbleur** [ɑblœːr] *nm* braggart, boaster.
*****hache** [aʃ] *nf* ax, hatchet.
*****haché** [aʃe] *a* staccato, jerky, minced.
*****hacher** [aʃe] *vt* to chop (up), hash, hack, mince.
*****hachis** [aʃi] *nm* minced meat, mince, hash.
*****hachoir** [aʃwaːr] *nm* chopper, mincer, chopping-board.
*****hagard** [agaːr] *a* haggard, wild, drawn.
*****haie** [ɛ] *nf* hedge(row), hurdle, line.
*****haillon** [ajɔ̃] *nm* rag, tatter.
*****haine** [ɛn] *nf* hatred, aversion.
*****haineux, -euse** [ɛnø, ø:z] *a* full of hatred.
*****haïr** [aiːr] *vt* to hate, detest, loathe.
*****haïssable** [aisabl] *a* hateful, detestable.
*****halage** [ɑlaːʒ] *nm* towing.
*****hâle** [ɑːl] *nm* sunburn, tan.
*****hâlé** [ɑle] *a* sunburnt, tanned, weather-beaten.
haleine [alɛn] *nf* breath, wind; **travail de longue — work requiring a long effort; tenir en — to keep in suspense.**
haler [ɑle] *vt* to tow, pull, heave, haul up, in.
*****hâler** [ɑle] *vt* to sunburn, tan, brown.
*****haleter** [alte] *vi* to pant, gasp for breath.
*****hall** [al, ɔl] *nm* (entrance) hall, hotel lounge.
*****halle** [al] *nf* (covered) market.
*****hallebarde** [albard] *nf* halberd; **il pleut des —s it's raining cats and dogs.**
*****hallier** [alje] *nm* thicket.
hallucination [al(l)ysinasjɔ̃] *nf* hallucination.
*****halte** [alt] *nf* stop, halt.
haltère [altɛːr] *nm* dumb-bell.
*****hamac** [amak] *nm* hammock.

*hameau [amo] nm hamlet.
hameçon [amsɔ̃] nm hook, bait.
*hampe [ɑ̃:p] nf staff, pole, handle, shaft.
*hanche [ɑ̃:ʃ] nf hip, haunch.
*handicaper [ɑ̃dikape] vt to handicap.
*hangar [ɑ̃ga:r] nm shed, outhouse.
*hanneton [antɔ̃] nm cockchafer.
*hanter [ɑ̃te] vt to frequent, haunt.
*hantise [ɑ̃ti:z] nf obsession.
*happer [ape] vt to snap up, catch, seize.
*haranguer [arɑ̃ge] vt to harangue, lecture.
*haras [arɑ] nm stud farm, stud.
harasser [arase] vt to exhaust, wear out.
*harceler [arsəle] vt to harass, worry, harry, pester.
*hardes [ard] nf pl old clothes, get-up, gear.
*hardi [ardi] a bold, daring, fearless, rash, forward.
*hardiesse [ardjɛs] nf boldness, daring, fearlessness, forwardness, impudence.
*hareng [arɑ̃] nm herring; — salé et fumé kipper; — saur red herring.
*hargneux [arnjø] a snarling, ill-tempered, peevish, snappish.
*haricot [ariko] nm kidney bean, haricot bean; —s verts string beans.
harmonie [armɔni] nf harmony, accord, band; en — harmoniously, in keeping.
harmonieux, -euse [armɔnjø, ø:z] a harmonious, melodious.
harmonique [armɔnik] a nm harmonic.
harmoniser [armɔnize] vt to harmonize, attune; vr to be in keeping, tone in.
*harnachement [arnaʃmɑ̃] nm harnessing, trappings.
*harnais [arnɛ] nm harness, gear, tackle.
*harpe [arp] nf harp.
*harpie [arpi] nf harpy, shrew.
*harpiste [arpist] n harpist.
*harpon [arpɔ̃] nm harpoon.
*harponner [arpɔne] vt to harpoon.
*hasard [aza:r] nm chance, luck, accident, risk, hazard; au — at random; à tout — on the off chance.
*hasarder [azarde] vt to hazard, risk, venture; vr to take risks, venture.
*hasardeux, -euse [azardø, ø:z] a hazardous, risky, daring.
*hâte [ɑ:t] nf haste, hurry; avoir — de to be in a hurry to, be eager to; à la — hastily, hurriedly.
*hâter [ɑte] vt to hasten, hurry on, quicken; vr to hurry, make haste.
*hâtif, -ive [ɑtif, i:v] a hasty, hurried, early, premature.
*hausse [o:s] nf rise, rising, elevation, range, sight; jouer à la — to bull the market.

*haussement [osmɑ̃] nm raising, lifting, shrug(ging).
*hausser [ose] vt to raise, lift, shrug; vi to rise.
*haussier [osje] nm (Stock Exchange) bull.
*haut [o] a high, tall, lofty, raised, loud, upper, higher, important, remote; ad high, up, above, aloud, back; — les mains hands up; nm height, top, head; en — above, aloft, upstairs; de — en bas from top to bottom, downward, up and down; les —s et les bas ups and downs.
*hautain [otɛ̃] a haughty.
*hautbois [obwa] nm oboe.
*hauteur [otœ:r] nf height, elevation, altitude, eminence, hill(top), haughtiness, loftiness, pitch (of note); à la — de level with, equal to.
*haut-le-cœur [oləkœ:r] nm heave, retch.
*haut-le-corps [oləkɔ:r] nm start, jump.
*haut-parleur [oparlœ:r] nm loudspeaker.
*hauturier, -ière [otyrje, jɛ:r] a of the high seas; pilote — deep-sea pilot.
*hâve [ɑ:v] a hollow, gaunt.
*havre [ɑ:vr] nm haven, harbor.
*havresac [ɑvrəsak] nm knapsack.
*hé [e] excl hi! hullo! hey!
hebdomadaire [ɛbdɔmadɛ:r] a nm weekly.
héberger [ebɛrʒe] vt to harbor, lodge, put up, shelter.
hébéter [ebete] vt to daze, dull, stupefy, bewilder.
hébreu [ebrø] a nm Hebrew.
hécatombe [ekatɔ̃:b] nf hecatomb, slaughter.
hégémonie [eʒemɔni] nf hegemony.
*hein [ɛ̃] excl eh! what!
hélas [elɑ:s] excl alas!
*héler [ele] vt to hail, call.
hélice [elis] nf spiral, propeller, (of ship) screw.
hélicoptère [elikɔptɛ:r] nm helicopter.
héliotrope [eljɔtrɔp] a nm heliotrope, sunflower.
hellénique [elenik] a Hellenic.
helvétique [ɛlvetik] a Swiss.
hémicycle [emisikl] nm hemicycle.
hémisphère [emisfɛ:r] nm hemisphere.
hémorragie [emɔraʒi] nf hemorrhage, bleeding.
hémorroïdes [emɔrɔid] nf pl piles.
*hennir [ɛni:r] vi to neigh, whinny.
héraldique [eraldik] a heraldic; nf heraldry.
*héraut [ero] nm herald.
herbage [ɛrba:ʒ] nm grassland, pasture, greens.
herbe [ɛrb] nf herb, plant, weed, grass; en — budding, in embryo.
herbeux, -euse [ɛrbø, ø:z] a grassy.
herbivore [ɛrbivɔ:r] a herbivorous.

herboriser [ɛrbɔrize] *vi* to herborize, botanize.
herboriste [ɛrbɔrist] *n* herbalist.
herculéen, -enne [ɛrkyleɛ̃, ɛn] *a* herculean.
héréditaire [ereditɛːr] *a* hereditary.
hérédité [eredite] *nf* heredity, right of inheritance.
hérésie [erezi] *nf* heresy.
hérétique [eretik] *a* heretical; *n* heretic.
*****hérissé** [erise] *a* bristly, prickly, bristling.
*****hérisser** [erise] *vt* to bristle (up), ruffle; *vr* to bristle, stand on end.
*****hérisson** [erisɔ̃] *nm* hedgehog, (sea)urchin.
héritage [erita:ʒ] *nm* inheritance, heritage.
hériter [erite] *vti* to inherit.
héritier, -ière [eritje, jɛːr] *n* heir, heiress.
hermétique [ɛrmetik] *a* hermetically sealed, tight.
hermine [ɛrmin] *nf* stoat, ermine.
herniaire [ɛrnjɛːr] *a* hernial; **bandage** — truss.
*****hernie** [ɛrni] *nf* hernia, rupture.
héroïne [erɔin] *nf* heroine.
héroïque [erɔik] *a* heroic.
héroïsme [erɔism] *nm* heroism.
*****héron** [erɔ̃] *nm* heron.
*****héros** [ero] *nm* hero.
*****herse** [ɛrs] *nf* harrow, portcullis.
hésitation [ezitasjɔ̃] *nf* hesitation.
hésiter [ezite] *vi* to hesitate, falter.
hétéroclite [eterɔklit] *a* odd, queer.
hétérodoxe [eterɔdɔks] *a* heterodox.
hétérogène [eterɔʒɛn] *a* heterogeneous, mixed.
*****hêtre** [ɛːtr] *nm* beech.
heure [œːr] *nf* hour, time, o'clock; **la dernière** — stop-press news; **de bonne** — early, in good time; **sur l'**— at once; **tout à l'**— just now, a few minutes ago, presently; **à tout à l'**— see you later; **à la bonne** — that's right, well done!
heureusement [œrøzmɑ̃] *ad* happily, luckily.
heureux, -euse [œrø, øːz] *a* happy, pleased, lucky, successful, blessed.
*****heurt** [œːr] *nm* knock, shock, bump; **sans heurt** smoothly.
*****heurter** [œrte] *vt* to knock against, run against, shock; *vr* to run (into), knock up (against), collide.
*****heurtoir** [œrtwaːr] *nm* doorknocker, buffer.
hévéa [evea] *nm* rubber tree.
hexagone [ɛksagɔn] *a* hexagonal; *nm* hexagon.
*****hibou** [ibu] *nm* owl.
*****hideur** [idœːr] *nf* hideousness.
*****hideux, -euse** [idø, øːz] *a* hideous.
hier [iɛːr] *ad* yesterday.
*****hiérarchie** [jerarʃi] *nf* hierarchy.
*****hiérarchique** [jerarʃik] *a* hierarchical; **par voie** — through official channels.

hiéroglyphe [jerɔglif] *nm* hieroglyph.
hilarité [ilarite] *nf* hilarity, merriment.
hindou [ɛ̃du] *an* Hindu.
hippique [ippik] *a* horse, equine; **concours** — horse-show.
hippodrome [ip(p)ɔdrɔm] *nm* race-course.
hippopotame [ippɔpɔtam] *nm* hippopotamus.
hirondelle [irɔ̃dɛl] *nf* swallow.
hirsute [irsyt] *a* hairy, hirsute, shaggy.
*****hisser** [ise] *vt* to hoist (up), pull up, run up; *vr* to pull oneself up, raise oneself.
histoire [istwaːr] *nf* history, story, tale; **faire des** —s to make a fuss; — **de s'amuser** just for a lark.
historien, -ienne [istɔrjɛ̃, jɛn] *n* historian.
historique [istɔrik] *a* historic(al); *nm* statement, account.
hiver [ivɛːr] *nm* winter.
hivernant [ivɛrnɑ̃] *a* wintering; *nm* winter visitor.
hiverner [ivɛrne] *vi* to (lie up for) winter, hibernate.
*****hocher** [ɔʃe] *vt* to shake, nod.
hoirie [wari] *nf* succession, inheritance.
*****hollandais** [ɔlɑ̃dɛ] *a nm* Dutch; *n* Dutchman, Dutchwoman.
*****Hollande** [ɔlɑ̃:d] *nf* Holland.
holocauste [ɔlɔkɔst] *nm* holocaust, sacrifice.
*****homard** [ɔmaːr] *nm* lobster.
homicide [ɔmisid] *a* homicidal; *n* homicide; *nm* homicide (crime).
hommage [ɔmaːʒ] *nm* tribute, token of esteem; *pl* respects.
hommasse [ɔmas] *a* masculine, mannish.
homme [ɔm] *nm* man, mankind, husband
homogène [ɔmɔʒɛn] *a* homogeneous.
homologuer [ɔmɔlɔge] *vt* to confirm, endorse, ratify, prove, record.
homonyme [ɔmɔnim] *nm* homonym, namesake.
homosexuel [ɔmɔsɛksɥɛl] *a* homosexual.
*****Hongrie** [ʒgri] *nf* Hungary.
*****hongrois** [ʒgrwa] *a nm* Hungarian.
honnête [ɔnɛt] *a* honest upright, decent, well-bred, seemly, reasonable.
honnêteté [ɔnɛtte] *nf* honesty, uprightness, decency, courtesy.
honneur [ɔnœːr] *nm* honor, credit; **faire** — **à** to honor, meet.
honorable [ɔnɔrabl] *a* honorable, respectable.
honoraire [ɔnɔrɛːr] *a* honorary; *nm pl* fees, honorarium.
honorer [ɔnɔre] *vt* to honor, respect, favor, do credit to.
honorifique [ɔnɔrifik] *a* honorary, honorific.

*honte [ɔ̃:t] *nf* shame, disgrace, scandal; avoir — to be ashamed; faire — à to put to shame, disgrace.
*honteux, -euse [ɔ̃tø, øːz] *a* ashamed, shamefaced, bashful, disgraceful.
hôpital [ɔpital] *nm* hospital, infirmary.
*hoquet [ɔkɛ] *nm* hiccup, gasp.
horaire [ɔrɛːr] *nm* timetable.
*horde [ɔrd] *nf* horde.
horizon [ɔrizɔ̃] *nm* horizon.
horizontal [ɔrizɔ̃tal] *a* horizontal.
horloge [ɔrlɔ:ʒ] *nf* clock.
horloger [ɔrlɔʒe] *nm* clock and watchmaker.
horlogerie [ɔrlɔʒri] *nf* clock and watchmaking, clockwork.
*hormis [ɔrmi] *prep* except, but, save.
hormone [ɔrmɔn] *nf* hormone.
horreur [ɔrrœːr] *nf* horror, abhorrence; *pl* horrid things, atrocities.
horrible [ɔrribl] *a* horrid, frightful.
horrifier [ɔrrifje] *vt* to horrify.
horrifique [ɔrrifik] *a* horrific, hair-raising.
horripilant [ɔrripilɑ̃] *a* hair-raising.
horripiler [ɔrripile] *vt* to make someone's flesh creep, irritate.
*hors [ɔ:r] *prep* out of, outside, except, all but; — de out(side) of; — de combat out of action, disabled; être — de soi to be beside oneself.
*hors-bord [ɔrbɔːr] *nm* outboard motor boat.
*hors-d'œuvre [ɔrdøːvr] *nm* extraneous matter, hors-d'œuvre.
hortensia [ɔrtɑ̃sja] *nm* hydrangea.
horticole [ɔrtikɔl] *a* horticultural, flower-.
horticulteur [ɔrtikyltœːr] *nm* horticulturist.
horticulture [ɔrtikyltyːr] *nf* horticulture.
hospice [ɔspis] *nm* hospice, home, asylum, poorhouse.
hospitalier, -ière [ɔspitalje, jɛːr] *a* hospitable.
hospitaliser [ɔspitalize] *vt* to send, admit to a hospital, a poorhouse.
hospitalité [ɔspitalite] *nf* hospitality.
hostie [ɔsti] *nf* (Eucharistic) host.
hostile [ɔstil] *a* adverse, inimical, unfriendly.
hostilité [ɔstilite] *nf* hostility, enmity.
hôte, -esse [oːt, otɛs] *n* host, hostess, landlord, landlady, guest, visitor, inmate, dweller.
hôtel [otɛl] *nm* hotel, mansion, townhouse; — de ville town hall; — des postes general post office; — des ventes auction rooms; — meublé, garni lodging house, furnished apartments.
hôtel-Dieu [otɛldjø] *nm* hospital.
hôtelier, -ière [otəlje, jɛːr] *n* hotelkeeper, landlord.
hôtellerie [otɛlri] *nf* inn, restaurant, hotel trade.

*hotte [ɔt] *nf* basket (carried on back), hod.
*houblon [ublɔ̃] *nm* (bot) hop(s).
*houblonnière [ublɔnjɛːr] *nf* hopfield.
*houe [u] *nf* hoe.
*houille [uːj] *nf* coal; — blanche hydro-electric power.
*houiller, -ère [uje, jɛːr] *a* coal (bearing).
*houillère [ujɛːr] *nf* coalmine, pit, colliery.
*houle [ul] *nf* swell, surge, hearing.
*houlette [ulɛt] *nf* crook (shepherd's, of umbrella), crozier, trowel.
*houleux, -euse [ulø, øːz] *a* stormy, surging.
*houppe [up] *nf* tuft, bunch, crest, powder-puff.
*houppé [upe] *a* tufted, crested.
*houppette [upɛt] *nf* small tuft, powder-puff.
*houspiller [uspije] *vt* to hustle, jostle, maul, abuse.
*housse [us] *nf* cover(ing), dust-sheet, horse-cloth.
*houx [u] *nm* holly.
*hoyau [wajo] *nm* hoe.
*hublot [yblo] *nm* scuttle, porthole.
*huche [yʃ] *nf* trough, bin.
*hue [y] *excl* gee-up!
*huée [ye] *nf* boo(ing), hoot(ing), jeer(ing).
*huer [ye] *vi* to shout, whoop; *vt* to boo, hoot.
huile [ɥil] *nf* oil; — de copra coconut oil.
huiler [ɥile] *vt* to oil.
huileux, -euse [ɥilø, øːz] *a* oily, greasy.
huilier [ɥilje] *nm* oilcan, oil and vinegar cruet.
huis [ɥi] *nm* à — clos in camera, behind closed doors.
huissier [ɥisje] *nm* usher, bailiff, sheriff's officer.
*huit [ɥit] *a* eight; — jours week; d'aujourd'hui en — a week from today; donner ses — jours to give a week's notice; *nm* eight, eighth.
*huitaine [ɥitɛn] *nf* (about) eight, week.
*huitième [ɥitjɛm] *a nm* eighth.
huître [ɥiːtr] *nf* oyster.
humain [ymɛ̃] *a* human, humane.
humaniser [ymanize] *vt* to humanize; *vr* to become more humane.
humanitaire [ymanitɛːr] *a* humanitarian, humane.
humanité [ymanite] *nf* humanity.
humble [œ̃:bl] *a* humble, lowly.
humecter [ymɛkte] *vt* to moisten, damp, wet.
*humer [yme] *vt* to suck in, (up), breathe in, sniff.
humeur [ymœːr] *nf* humor, mood, temper, ill-humor.
humide [ymid] *a* damp, humid, moist, wet.
humidité [ymidite] *nf* damp(ness),

humidity, moisture, moistness; **craint l'**— to be kept dry.
humiliation [ymiljasjɔ̃] *nf* affront.
humilier [ymilje] *vt* to humiliate, humble.
humilité [ymilite] *nf* humility, humbleness.
humoriste [ymɔrist] *a* humorous; *nm* humorist.
humoristique [ymɔristik] *a* humorous.
humour [ymuːr] *nm* humor.
***hune** [yn] *nf* top; — **de vigie** crow's nest.
***hunier** [ynje] *nm* topsail.
***huppe** [yp] *nf* tuft, crest.
***huppé** [ype] *a* tufted, crested, (*fam*) well-dressed.
***hure** [yːr] *nf* head, brawn, headcheese.
***hurlement** [yrləmɑ̃] *nm* howl(ing), yell(ing).
***hurler** [yrle] *vi* to howl, yell, roar; *vt* to bawl out.
***hutte** [yt] *nf* hut, shed.
hybride [ibrid] *a nm* hybrid.
hydrate [idrat] *nm* hydrate.
hydraulique [idrɔlik] *a* hydraulic, water-; *nf* hydraulics.
hydravion [idravjɔ̃] *nm* sea-plane.
hydrogène [idrɔʒɛn] *nm* hydrogen; **bombe à** — hydrogen bomb.
hydroglisseur [idrɔglisœːr] *nm* speed-boat.
hydrophile [idrɔfil] *a* absorbent.
hydrophobie [idrɔfɔbi] *nf* hydrophobia, rabies.
hydropisie [idrɔpizi] *nf* dropsy.
hyène [jɛn] *nf* hyena.
hygiène [iʒjɛn] *nf* hygiene, health, sanitation.
hygiénique [iʒjenik] *a* hygienic, healthy, sanitary; **papier** — toilet paper.
hymne [im(n)] *nm* song, (national) anthem; *nf* hymn.
hyperbole [ipɛrbɔl] *nf* hyperbole, exaggeration.
hypnose [ipnoːz] *nf* hypnosis, trance.
hypnotiser [ipnɔtize] *vt* to hypnotize.
hypnotisme [ipnɔtism] *nm* hypnotism.
hypocondriaque [ipɔkɔ̃driak] *an* hypochondriac.
hypocrisie [ipɔkrizi] *nf* hypocrisy, cant.
hypocrite [ipɔkrit] *a* hypocritical; *n* hypocrite.
hypodermique [ipɔdɛrmik] *a* hypodermic.
hypothécaire [ipɔtekɛːr] *a* mortgage; *nm* mortgagee.
hypothèque [ipɔtɛk] *nf* mortgage.
hypothéquer [ipɔteke] *vt* to mortgage.
hypothèse [ipɔtɛːz] *nf* hypothesis, assumption.
hystérie [isteri] *nf* hysteria.
hystérique [isterik] *a* hysteric(al).

I

ici [isi] *ad* here, now; **par** — this way; **d'**— **huit jours** a week today; **d'**— **là** between now and then; **d'**— **peu** before long; **jusqu'**— hitherto, as far as this; — **bas** here below.
iconoclaste [ikɔnɔklast] *a* iconoclastic; *nm* iconoclast.
idéal [ideal] *a nm* ideal.
idéaliser [idealize] *vt* to idealize.
idéalisme [idealism] *nm* idealism.
idéaliste [idealist] *a* idealistic; *n* idealist.
idée [ide] *nf* idea, thought, notion, fancy, mind; **il lui est venu à l'**— **que** it occurred to him that; — **fixe** obsession.
identification [idɑ̃tifikasjɔ̃] *nf* identification.
identifier [idɑ̃tifje] *vt* to identify.
identique [idɑ̃tik] *a* identical.
identité [idɑ̃tite] *nf* identity.
idéologie [ideɔloʒi] *nf* ideology.
idéologue [ideɔlɔg] *a* ideological; *nm* ideologue.
idiomatique [idjɔmatik] *a* idiomatic.
idiome [idjɔm] *nm* language, idiom.
idiosyncrasie [idjɔsɛ̃krasi] *nf* idiosyncrasy.
idiot [idjo] *a* idiot(ic), senseless; *n* idiot, silly ass.
idiotie [idjɔsi] *nf* idiocy, imbecility, stupidity.
idiotisme [idjɔtism] *nm* idiom, idiomatic expression, idiocy.
idolâtre [idɔlaːtr] *a* idolatrous; *n* idolater, idolatress.
idolâtrer [idɔlatre] *vt* to idolize, worship.
idolâtrie [idɔlatri] *nf* idolatry.
idole [idɔl] *nf* idol, image, god.
idylle [idil] *nf* idyll.
idyllique [idilik] *a* idyllic.
if [if] *nm* yew(tree).
igname [iɲam] *nf* yam.
ignare [iɲaːr] *a* ignorant, uneducated; *n* ignoramus.
ignoble [iɲɔbl] *a* vile, base.
ignominie [iɲɔmini] *nf* ignominy, shame.
ignominieux, -euse [iɲɔminjø, øːz] *a* ignominious, disgraceful.
ignorance [iɲɔrɑ̃ːs] *nf* ignorance.
ignorant [iɲɔrɑ̃] *a* ignorant; *n* ignoramus.
ignorer [iɲɔre] *vt* to be ignorant of, not to know, to be unaware of.
il, ils [il] *pn* he, it, they, there.
île [il, iːl] *nf* island, isle.
illégal [illegal] *a* illegal.
illégalité [illegalite] *nf* illegality, unlawfulness.
illégitime [illeʒitim] *a* illegitimate, unlawful, unreasonable.
illégitimité [illeʒitimite] *nf* illegitimacy, unlawfulness.
illettré [illetre] *a* illiterate, uneducated.
illicite [illisit] *a* illicit, unlawful.

illimité [illimite] *a* unlimited, boundless.

illisibilité [illizibilite] *nf* illegibility.

illisible [illizibl] *a* illegible, unreadable.

illogique [illɔʒik] *a* illogical, inconsistent.

illogisme [illɔʒism] *nm* illogicality, inconsistency.

illumination [illyminasjɔ̃] *nf* illumination, lighting, understanding; *pl* lights, illuminations.

illuminer [illymine] *vt* to illuminate, enlighten, throw light on.

illusion [illyzjɔ̃] *nf* illusion, delusion.

illusionniste [illyzjɔnist] *n* illusionist, conjurer.

illusoire [illyzwaːr] *a* illusory.

illustration [illystrasjɔ̃] *nf* illustrating, illustration.

illustre [illystr] *a* illustrated, made famous, renowned.

illustré [illystre] *nm* picture-paper, illustrated newspaper.

illustrer [illystre] *vt* to make famous, illustrate; *vr* to win renown.

îlot [ilo] *nm* islet.

image [imaːʒ] *nf* image, picture, likeness, simile, metaphor, reflection; faire — to be vivid.

imagé [imaʒe] *a* full of imagery, picturesque.

imaginaire [imaʒinɛːr] *a* imaginary.

imagination [imaʒinasjɔ̃] *nf* imagination, fancy, invention.

imaginer [imaʒine] *vtr* to imagine, fancy, picture; *vt* invent, devise.

imbattable [ɛ̃batabl] *a* unbeatable, invincible.

imbécile [ɛ̃besil] *a* imbecile, halfwitted, silly; *n* fool, half-wit.

imbécilité [ɛ̃besilite] *nf* imbecility, silliness.

imberbe [ɛ̃bɛrb] *a* beardless.

imbiber [ɛ̃bibe] *vt* to imbibe, absorb, soak, impregnate, steep; *vr* to become absorbed, soak in, absorb.

imbrisable [ɛ̃brizabl] *a* unbreakable.

imbu [ɛ̃by] *a* soaked, steeped (de in).

imbuvable [ɛ̃byvabl] *a* undrinkable; (of person) unbearable.

imitateur, -trice [imitatœːr, tris] *a* imitative; *n* imitator.

imitation [imitasjɔ̃] *nf* copy, copying, mimicking, impersonation.

imiter [imite] *vt* to imitate, copy, mimic.

immaculé [imakyle] *a* immaculate, pure, spotless.

immangeable [imɑ̃ʒabl] *a* uneatable.

immanquablement [imɑ̃kabləmɑ̃] *ad* inevitably, without fail.

immatériel, -elle [immaterjɛl] *a* immaterial, incorporeal.

immatriculation [immatrikylasjɔ̃] *nf* matriculation, enrolling, registration; plaque d'— license plate.

immatriculer [immatrikyle] *vtr* to register, enroll, matriculate.

immaturité [immatyrite] *nf* immaturity.

immédiat [immedja] *a* immediate, direct, urgent.

immémorial [immemɔrjal] *a* immemorial.

immense [immɑ̃ːs] *a* immense, vast, huge.

immensité [immɑ̃site] *nf* vastness.

immerger [imɛrʒe] *vt* to immerse, plunge, dip.

immérité [immerite] *a* unmerited, undeserved.

immersion [immɛrsjɔ̃] *nf* immersion, dipping, submersion.

immeuble [immœbl] *a* real, fixed; *nm* real estate, house, tenement, premises.

immigrant [immigrɑ̃] *an* immigrant.

immigré [immigre] *n* immigrant, settler.

imminence [imminɑ̃ːs] *nf* imminence.

imminent [imminɑ̃] *a* imminent.

immiscer [immise] *vt* to mix up, involve; *vr* to get involved, interfere.

immixtion [immiksjɔ̃] *nf* interference.

immobile [immɔbil] *a* motionless, still, immovable.

immobilier, -ière [immɔbilje, jɛːr] *a* real (estate), building (society).

immobiliser [immɔbilize] *vt* to immobilize, tie up, convert into real estate.

immobilité [immɔbilite] *nf* immobility.

immodéré [immɔdere] *a* immoderate, excessive.

immodeste [immɔdɛst] *a* immodest, shameless.

immoler [immɔle] *vt* to sacrifice, immolate.

immonde [immɔ̃ːd] *a* filthy, foul.

immondices [immɔ̃dis] *nf pl* dirt, refuse, filth.

immoral [immɔral] *a* immoral.

immoralité [immɔralite] *nf* immorality, immoral act.

immortaliser [immɔrtalize] *vt* to immortalize.

immortalité [immɔrtalite] *nf* immortality.

immortel, -elle [immɔrtɛl] *a* immortal, undying.

immuable [immɥabl] *a* unalterable, unchanging.

immuniser [immynize] *vt* to immunise.

immunité [immynite] *nf* immunity.

immutabilité [immytabilite] *nf* immutability.

impact [ɛ̃pakt] *nm* impact.

impair [ɛ̃pɛːr] *a* odd, uneven; *nm* blunder, bloomer.

impalpable [ɛ̃palpabl] *a* intangible.

impardonnable [ɛ̃pardɔnabl] *a* unpardonable, unforgivable.

imparfait [ɛ̃parfɛ] *a* imperfect, defective, incomplete.

impartial [ɛ̃parsjal] *a* impartial, unprejudiced.
impassable [ɛ̃pasabl] *a* impassable, unfordable.
impasse [ɛ̃pɑːs] *nf* blind-alley, dilemma, fix, deadlock, (*cards*) finesse.
impassibilité [ɛ̃pasibilite] *nf* impassiveness.
impassible [ɛ̃pasibl] *a* impassive, unmoved, callous.
impatience [ɛ̃pasjɑ̃ːs] *nf* impatience, eagerness.
impatient [ɛ̃pasjɑ̃] *a* impatient, anxious, eager.
impatienter [ɛ̃pasjɑ̃te] *vt* to make impatient; *vr* to lose patience.
impayable [ɛ̃pɛjabl] *a* invaluable, priceless, terribly funny.
impeccable [ɛ̃pɛkabl] *a* faultless, flawless.
impécunieux [ɛ̃pekynjø] *a* impecunious.
impénétrable [ɛ̃penɛtrabl] *a* impenetrable, impervious, inscrutable.
impénitence [ɛ̃penitɑ̃ːs] *nf* impenitence, obduracy.
impénitent [ɛ̃penitɑ̃] *a* obdurate, unrepentant.
impératif, -ive [ɛ̃pɛratif, iːv] *a* imperative, imperious; *nm* imperative.
impératrice [ɛ̃pɛratris] *nf* empress.
imperceptible [ɛ̃pɛrsɛptibl] *a* imperceptible, inaudible.
imperfection [ɛ̃pɛrfɛksjɔ̃] *nf* imperfection, defectiveness, incompleteness, flaw.
impérial [ɛ̃perjal] *a* imperial.
impériale [ɛ̃perjal] *nf* top-deck, top, imperial, double-decker bus.
impérialisme [ɛ̃perjalism] *nm* imperialism.
impérieux [ɛ̃perjø, øːz] *a* imperious, peremptory, domineering, urgent.
impérissable [ɛ̃perisabl] *a* imperishable.
imperméabiliser [ɛ̃pɛrmeabilize] *vt* to proof, make waterproof.
imperméable [ɛ̃pɛrmeabl] *a* impervious; *nm* waterproof.
impersonnel, -elle [ɛ̃pɛrsɔnɛl] *a* impersonal.
impertinence [ɛ̃pɛrtinɑ̃ːs] *nf* impertinence.
impertinent [ɛ̃pɛrtinɑ̃] *a* impertinent, rude.
imperturbable [ɛ̃pɛrtyrbabl] *a* cool, calm and collected.
impétueux [ɛ̃petɥø, -øːz] *a* impetuous, impulsive.
impétuosité [ɛ̃petɥozite] *nf* impetuosity, impulsiveness.
impie [ɛ̃pi] *a* impious, blasphemous.
impiété [ɛ̃pjete] *nf* impiety, ungodliness, blasphemy.
impitoyable [ɛ̃pitwajabl] *a* pitiless, ruthless.
implacabilité [ɛ̃plakabilite] *nf* implacability, relentlessness.

implacable [ɛ̃plakabl] *a* implacable, relentless.
implanter [ɛ̃plɑ̃te] *vt* to plant, implant; *vr* to take root, take hold.
implicite [ɛ̃plisit] *a* implicit, absolute.
impliquer [ɛ̃plike] *vt* to implicate, involve.
implorer [ɛ̃plɔre] *vt* to implore, entreat, beseech.
impoli [ɛ̃pɔli] *a* impolite, unmannerly.
impolitesse [ɛ̃pɔlitɛs] *nf* unmannerliness, rude act, word.
impolitique [ɛ̃pɔlitik] *a* impolitic, illadvised.
impondérable [ɛ̃pɔ̃dɛrabl] *a* imponderable.
impopulaire [ɛ̃pɔpylɛːr] *a* unpopular.
impopularité [ɛ̃pɔpylarite] *nf* unpopularity.
importance [ɛ̃pɔrtɑ̃ːs] *nf* importance, moment, magnitude.
important [ɛ̃pɔrtɑ̃] *a* important, large, extensive, considerable, selfimportant; *nm* the main thing.
importateur, -trice [ɛ̃pɔrtatœːr, tris] *a* importing; *n* importer.
importation [ɛ̃pɔrtasjɔ̃] *nf* importing, import.
importer [ɛ̃pɔrte] *vt* to import; *vi* to be important, matter; **n'importe** never mind, it does not matter; **n'importe qui, quoi, comment, quand** anyone, anything, anyhow, anytime.
importun [ɛ̃pɔrtœ̃] *a* importunate, tiresome, unwelcome; *n* intruder, nuisance.
importuner [ɛ̃pɔrtyne] *vt* to importune, bother, trouble, dun.
importunité [ɛ̃pɔrtynite] *nf* importunity.
imposable [ɛ̃pozabl] *a* taxable, ratable, assessable.
imposant [ɛ̃pozɑ̃] *a* imposing, impressive.
imposé [ɛ̃poze] *n* ratepayer, taxpayer.
imposer [ɛ̃poze] *vt* to impose, set, prescribe, enforce, tax, rate; *vi* to command respect; *vr* to assert oneself, force oneself, itself (upon), be imperative; **en — à** to impose upon, take in, overawe.
imposition [ɛ̃pozisjɔ̃] *nf* imposition, imposing, setting, prescribing, taxation, rates.
impossibilité [ɛ̃pɔsibilite] *nf* impossibility.
impossible [ɛ̃pɔsibl] *a* impossible.
imposteur [ɛ̃pɔstœːr] *nm* impostor, hypocrite.
imposture [ɛ̃pɔstyːr] *nf* imposture, sham, swindle.
impôt [ɛ̃po] *nm* tax, duty; **frapper d'un — to** tax.
impotence [ɛ̃pɔtɑ̃ːs] *nf* helplessness, infirmity.

impotent [ɛ̃pɔtɑ̃] *a* infirm, helpless, crippled; *n* cripple, invalid.

impracticable [ɛ̃pratikabl] *a* impracticable, unfeasible, (*road*) impassable.

imprécation [ɛ̃prɛkasjɔ̃] *nf* imprecation, curse.

imprécis [ɛ̃presi] *a* vague, inaccurate.

imprécision [ɛ̃presizjɔ̃] *nf* vagueness, inaccuracy.

imprégner [ɛ̃preɲe] *vt* to impregnate, saturate; *vr* to become saturated, soak up.

imprenable [ɛ̃prənabl] *a* impregnable.

impression [ɛ̃presjɔ̃] *nf* impression, stamp(ing), print(ing).

impressionnable [ɛ̃presjɔnabl] *a* impressionable, nervous, sensitive.

impressionnant [ɛ̃presjɔnɑ̃] *a* impressive.

impressionner [ɛ̃presjɔne] *vt* to impress, make an impression on, move; *vr* to be moved, get nervous.

impressionisme [ɛ̃presjɔnism] *nm* impressionism.

imprévoyable [ɛ̃prevwajabl] *a* unforeseeable.

imprévoyance [ɛ̃prevwajɑ̃:s] *n* lack of foresight.

imprévoyant [ɛ̃prevwajɑ̃] *a* shortsighted, improvident.

imprévu [ɛ̃prevy] *a* unforeseen, unexpected; *nm* unexpected, emergency.

imprimé [ɛ̃prime] *nm* printed matter, paper, form, leaflet; **envoyer en — to send by book-post.**

imprimer [ɛ̃prime] *vt* to (im)print, impress, stamp.

imprimerie [ɛ̃primri] *nf* printing, printing house, press.

imprimeur [ɛ̃primœ:r] *nm* printer.

improbabilité [ɛ̃prɔbabilite] *nf* improbability, unlikelihood.

improbable [ɛ̃prɔbabl] *a* improbable, unlikely.

improbité [ɛ̃prɔbite] *nf* dishonesty.

improductif, -ive [ɛ̃prɔdyktif, i:v] *a* unproductive.

impromptu [ɛ̃prɔ̃(p)ty] *a* extempore; *ad* without preparation; *nm* impromptu.

impropriété [ɛ̃prɔpriete] *nf* impropriety, unsuitableness, incorrectness.

improvisation [ɛ̃prɔvizasjɔ̃] *nf* improvisation, extemporization.

improvisé [ɛ̃prɔvize] *a* improvised, extempore, makeshift.

improviser [ɛ̃prɔvize] *vt* to improvise, put together, make up; *vi* to speak extempore.

improviste (à l') [alɛ̃prɔvist] *ad* unexpected(ly).

imprudence [ɛ̃prydɑ̃:s] *nf* rashness, indiscretion.

impudence [ɛ̃pydɑ̃:s] *nf* insolence, (piece of) impudence.

impudent [ɛ̃pydɑ̃] *a* impudent, insolent, shameless.

impudicité [ɛ̃pydisite] *nf* lewdness, immodesty.

impudique [ɛ̃pydik] *a* lewd, immodest, unchaste.

impuissance [ɛ̃pɥisɑ̃:s] *nf* helplessness, powerlessness, impotence.

impuissant [ɛ̃pɥisɑ̃] *a* helpless, powerless, impotence, futile.

impulsif, -ive [ɛ̃pylsif, i:v] *a* impulsive.

impulsion [ɛ̃pylsjɔ̃] *nf* impulse, impetus.

impunément [ɛ̃pynemɑ̃] *ad* with impunity.

impunité [ɛ̃pynite] *nf* impunity.

impur [ɛ̃py:r] *a* impure, unchaste, unclean, foul.

impureté [ɛ̃pyrte] *nf* impurity, foulness.

imputable [ɛ̃pytabl] *a* imputable, attributable, chargeable.

imputation [ɛ̃pytasjɔ̃] *nf* imputation, charge, attribution.

imputer [ɛ̃pyte] *vt* to impute, ascribe, charge.

inabordable [inabɔrdabl] *a* inaccessible, prohibitive.

inacceptable [inaksɛptabl] *a* unacceptable.

inaccessible [inaksɛsibl] *a* inaccessible, unapproachable.

inaccoutumé [inakutyme] *a* unaccustomed, unusual, unwonted.

inachevé [inaʃve] *a* unfinished, incomplete.

inactif, -ive [inaktif, i:v] *a* inactive, inert.

inaction [inaksjɔ̃] *nf* inaction, inertia.

inactivité [inaktivite] *nf* inactivity, inertness.

inadmissible [inadmisibl] *a* inadmissible, who has failed in written examination.

inadvertance [inadvɛrtɑ̃:s] *nf* inadvertence, oversight, mistake.

inadvertant [inadvɛrtɑ̃] *a* careless.

inaliénable [inaljenabl] *a* inalienable, untransferable.

inaltérable [inaltɛrabl] *a* unalterable, unfailing.

inamovible [inamɔvibl] *a* irremovable, fixed, held for life.

inanimé [inanime] *a* lifeless, inanimate, unconscious.

inanité [inanite] *nf* inanity, inane remark.

inanition [inanisjɔ̃] *nf* starvation, inanition.

inaperçu [inapɛrsy] *a* unnoticed, unseen.

inapparent [inaparɑ̃] *a* unapparent.

inapplication [inaplikasjɔ̃] *nf* lack of diligence, of assiduity.

inappliqué [inaplike] *a* inattentive, careless, unapplied.

inappréciable [inapresjabl] *a* inappreciable, not perceptible, invaluable.

inapprivoisé [inaprivwaze] *a* untamed, wild.

inapte [inapt] *a* unfit, unsuited, inapt, unemployable

inaptitude [inaptityd] *nf* unfitness.

inarticulé [inartikyle] *a* inarticulate, not jointed.

inassouvi [inasuvi] *a* unappeased, unsatisfied.

inassouvissable [inasuvisabl] *a* insatiable.

inattaquable [inatakabl] *a* unassailable, unquestionable.

inattendu [inatɑ̃dy] *a* unexpected, unlooked for.

inattentif, -ive [inatɑ̃tif, iːv] *a* inattentive, careless, unobservant.

inattention [inatɑ̃sjɔ̃] *nf* inattention, carelessness.

inaugural [inogyral] *a* inaugural, opening.

inauguration [inogyrasjɔ̃] *nf* opening, unveiling.

inaugurer [inogyre] *vt* to inaugurate, open, unveil.

inavouable [inavwabl] *a* shameful, foul, low.

incalculable [ɛ̃kalkylabl] *a* incalculable, countless.

incandescence [ɛ̃kɑ̃dɛssɑ̃ːs] *nf* white heat.

incantation [ɛ̃kɑ̃tasjɔ̃] *nf* incantation.

incapable [ɛ̃kapabl] *a* inefficient, unfit, unable.

incapacité [ɛ̃kapasite] *nf* incapacity, inefficiency, inability, disablement.

incarcérer [ɛ̃karsere] *vt* to incarcerate, imprison.

incarnadin [ɛ̃karnadɛ̃] *a* incarnadine, rosy, pink.

incarnat [ɛ̃karna] *a* rosy, pink, flesh colored; *nm* rosiness, rosy hue.

incarnation [ɛ̃karnasjɔ̃] *nf* embodiment.

incarné [ɛ̃karne] *a* incarnate, ingrowing.

incarner [ɛ̃karne] *vt* to incarnate, embody, be the incarnation of.

incartade [ɛ̃kartad] *nf* outburst, tirade, prank.

incendiaire [ɛ̃sɑ̃djɛːr] *a* incendiary, inflammatory; *n* incendiary.

incendie [ɛ̃sɑ̃di] *nm* fire, conflagration, burning; **échelle à — fire-escape; pompe à — fire-engine; poste d'— fire-station.

incendier [ɛ̃sɑ̃dje] *vt* to set on fire, burn down.

incertain [ɛ̃sɛrtɛ̃] *a* uncertain, doubtful, unreliable.

incertitude [ɛ̃sɛrtityd] *nf* uncertainty, doubt.

incessamment [ɛ̃sɛsamɑ̃] *ad* immediately.

incessant [ɛ̃sɛsɑ̃] *a* unceasing, ceaseless.

inceste [ɛ̃sɛst] *nm* incest.

incestueux, -euse [ɛ̃sɛstɥø, øːz] *a* incestuous.

incidence [ɛ̃sidɑ̃ːs] *nf* incidence.

incident [ɛ̃sidɑ̃] *a* parenthetical, incidental; *nm* incident, occurrence.

incinérateur [ɛ̃sinɛratœːr] *nm* incinerator.

incinérer [ɛ̃sinere] *vt* to incinerate, cremate.

incisif [ɛ̃sisif] *a* incisive.

incision [ɛ̃sizjɔ̃] *nf* incision, cutting, lancing, tapping.

inciter [ɛ̃site] *vt* to incite, urge.

incivilisé [ɛ̃sivilize] *a* uncivilized.

incivilité [ɛ̃sivilite] *nf* incivility, (piece of) rudeness.

inclassable [ɛ̃klasabl] *a* unclassifiable, nondescript.

inclémence [ɛ̃klɛmɑ̃ːs] *nf* inclemency

inclinaison [ɛ̃klinɛzɔ̃] *nf* inclination, incline, gradient, tilt, slope.

inclination [ɛ̃klinasjɔ̃] *nf* inclination, bending, bow, nod, bent.

incliner [ɛ̃kline] *vt* to incline, slope, bow, tilt, dip, predispose; *vi* to be predisposed, inclined; *vr* to slope, slant, bow, give way.

inclure [ɛ̃klyːr] *vt* to enclose.

inclus [ɛ̃kly] *a* including.

inclusif, -ive [ɛ̃klyzif, iːv] *a* inclusive.

inclusion [ɛ̃klyzjɔ̃] *nf* inclusion, enclosing.

incohérence [ɛ̃kɔɛrɑ̃ːs] *nf* incoherence, disjointedness

incohérent [ɛ̃kɔɛrɑ̃] *a* incoherent, disjointed.

incolore [ɛ̃kɔlɔːr] *a* colorless.

incomber [ɛ̃kɔ̃be] *vi* to fall, devolve, be incumbent.

incombustible [ɛ̃kɔ̃bystibl] *a* incombustible, uninflammable.

incomestible [ɛ̃kɔmɛstibl] *a* inedible.

incommensurable [ɛ̃kɔm(m)ɑ̃syrabl] *a* incommensurable, incommensurate, immeasurable.

incommode [ɛ̃kɔmɔd] *a* inconvenient, uncomfortable, awkward, tiresome.

incommoder [ɛ̃kɔmɔde] *vt* to inconvenience, upset, disagree with.

incommodité [ɛ̃kɔmɔdite] *nf* inconvenience, discomfort.

incomparable [ɛ̃kɔ̃parabl] *a* incomparable, matchless.

incompatible [ɛ̃kɔ̃patibl] *a* incompatible.

incompétence [ɛ̃kɔ̃pɛtɑ̃ːs] *nf* incompetence, inefficiency.

incompétent [ɛ̃kɔ̃pɛtɑ̃] *a* incompetent, inefficient, unqualified.

incompréhensible [ɛ̃kɔ̃preɑ̃sibl] *a* incomprehensible.

incompréhension [ɛ̃kɔ̃preɑ̃sjɔ̃] *nf* obtuseness, want of understanding.

incompris [ɛ̃kɔ̃pri] *a* misunderstood, not appreciated.

inconcevable [ɛ̃kɔ̃s(ə)vabl] *a* inconceivable, unthinkable.

inconciliable [ɛ̃kɔ̃siljabl] *a* irreconcilable, incompatible.

inconduite [ɛ̃kɔ̃dɥit] *nf* bad living, misconduct.

incongru [ɛ̃kɔ̃gry] *a* incongruous, unseemly, stupid.

incongruité [ɛ̃kɔ̃gryite] *nf* incongruity, unseemliness, stupid remark.

inconnu [ɛ̃kɔny] *a* unknown; *n* stranger, unknown person; *nm* (the) unknown.

inconscience [ɛ̃kɔ̃sjɑ̃:s] *nf* unconsciousness, want of principle.

inconscient [ɛ̃kɔ̃sjɑ̃] *a* unconscious, unaware; *nm* subconscious mind.

inconséquent [ɛ̃kɔ̃sekɑ̃] *a* inconsistent, irresponsible, illogical.

inconsidéré [ɛ̃kɔ̃sideɾe] *a* inconsiderate, thoughtless, heedless.

inconsistant [ɛ̃kɔ̃sistɑ̃] *a* soft, flabby.

inconsolable [ɛ̃kɔ̃sɔlabl] *a* inconsolable.

inconstance [ɛ̃kɔ̃stɑ̃:s] *nf* inconstancy, fickleness, changeableness.

inconstant [ɛ̃kɔ̃stɑ̃] *a* inconstant, fickle, changeable.

incontestable [ɛ̃kɔ̃testabl] *a* indisputable, beyond question.

incontesté [ɛ̃kɔ̃teste] *a* undisputed.

incontinent [ɛ̃kɔ̃tinɑ̃] *a* incontinent; *ad* straightway, forthwith.

incontrôlable [ɛ̃kɔ̃trolabl] *a* not verifiable, unable to be checked.

inconvenance [ɛ̃kɔvnɑ̃:s] *nf* unsuitability, impropriety, unseemliness, improper act or word.

inconvenant [ɛ̃kɔ̃vnɑ̃] *a* improper, unseemly.

inconvénient [ɛ̃kɔvenjɑ̃] *nm* disadvantage, drawback, objection.

incorporer [ɛ̃kɔrpɔre] *vt* to incorporate, embody.

incorrect [ɛ̃kɔr(r)ɛkt] *a* wrong, illmannered.

incorrection [ɛ̃kɔr(r)ɛksjɔ̃] *nf* incorrectness, inaccuracy, ill-bred act.

incorrigible [ɛ̃kɔr(r)iʒibl] *a* incorrigible, hopeless.

incorruptible [ɛ̃kɔr(r)yptibl] *a* incorruptible.

incrédibilité [ɛ̃kredibilite] *nf* incredibility.

incrédule [ɛ̃kredyl] *a* incredulous; *n* unbeliever.

incrédulité [ɛ̃kredylite] *nf* incredulity.

incriminer [ɛ̃krimine] *vt* to incriminate, accuse.

incroyable [ɛ̃krwajabl] *a* incredible, unbelievable.

incroyant [ɛ̃krwajɑ̃] *a* unbelieving; *n* unbeliever.

incrustation [ɛ̃krystasjɔ̃] *nf* encrustation, inlaying, inlaid work, furring.

incruster [ɛ̃kryste] *vt* to encrust, fur, inlay; *vr* to become encrusted, furred up.

incubation [ɛ̃kybasjɔ̃] *nf* incubation, hatching.

inculpable [ɛ̃kylpabl] *a* chargeable, indictable.

inculpation [ɛ̃kylpasjɔ̃] *nf* charge, indictment.

inculpé [ɛ̃kylpe] *n* accused, defendant.

inculper [ɛ̃kylpe] *vt* to charge, indict.

inculquer [ɛ̃kylke] *vt* to inculcate, instill.

inculte [ɛ̃kylt] *a* uncultivated, wild, uncultured.

incurable [ɛ̃kyrabl] *a* incurable.

incurie [ɛ̃kyri] *nf* carelessness, negligence.

incuriosité [ɛ̃kyrjɔzite] *nf* want of curiosity.

incursion [ɛ̃kyrsjɔ̃] *nf* inroad, raid.

Inde [ɛ̃:d] *nf* India; *pl* Indies.

indébrouillable [ɛ̃debrujabl] *a* tangled, inextricable.

indécence [ɛ̃desɑ̃:s] *nf* immodesty, indecency.

indécent [ɛ̃desɑ̃] *a* immodest, indecent, improper.

indéchiffrable [ɛ̃deʃifrabl] *a* undecipherable, illegible, unintelligible.

indécis [ɛ̃desi] *a* undecided, irresolute, doubtful, open, vague.

indécision [ɛ̃desizjɔ̃] *nf* indecision, irresolution.

indéfendable [ɛ̃defɑ̃dabl] *a* indefensible.

indéfini [ɛ̃defini] *a* indefinite, undefined.

indéfinissable [ɛ̃definisabl] *a* indefinable.

indélébile [ɛ̃delebil] *a* indelible.

indélicat [ɛ̃delika] *a* indelicate, tactless.

indélicatesse [ɛ̃delikatɛs] *nf* indelicacy, tactlessness, coarse act or remark.

indémaillable [ɛ̃demajabl] *a* runproof.

indemne [ɛ̃demn] *a* undamaged, unhurt.

indemniser [ɛ̃dɛmnize] *vt* to compensate, indemnify.

indemnité [ɛ̃dɛmnite] *nf* indemnity, compensation, grant, allowance; — **de chômage** unemployment benefit.

indéniable [ɛ̃denjabl] *a* undeniable.

indépendance [ɛ̃depɑ̃dɑ̃:s] *nf* independence.

indépendant [ɛ̃depɑ̃dɑ̃] *a* independent, unattached, self-contained.

indescriptible [ɛ̃dɛskriptibl] *a* indescribable.

indésirable [ɛ̃dezirabl] *a* undesirable, objectionable.

indestructible [ɛ̃dɛstryktibl] *a* indestructible.

indéterminé [ɛ̃determine] *a* irresolute, indefinite, indeterminate.

index [ɛ̃dɛks] *nm* forefinger, index, indicator.

indicateur, -trice [ɛ̃dikatœːr, tris] *a* indicatory; *nm* time-table, gauge, indicator, detector, informer; **poteau** — signpost.

indicatif, -ive [ɛ̃dikatif, iːv] *a*

indicative; *nm* indicative (mood), signature tune.
indication [ɛ̃dikasjɔ̃] *nf* indication, information, sign, clue, pointing out; *pl* instructions, directions.
indice [ɛ̃dis] *nm* sign, mark, indication, clue.
indicible [ɛ̃disibl] *a* unspeakable, indescribable.
indien, -ienne [ɛ̃djɛ̃, jɛn] *an* Indian.
indienne [ɛ̃djɛn] *nf* chintz, print, overarm stroke.
indifférence [ɛ̃difɛrɑ̃:s] *nf* indifference, apathy.
indifférent [ɛ̃diferɑ̃] *a* apathetic, immaterial, all the same.
indigence [ɛ̃diʒɑ̃:s] *nf* want, poverty.
indigène [ɛ̃diʒɛn] *a* indigenous, native; *n* native.
indigent [ɛ̃diʒɑ̃] *a* indigent, needy.
indigeste [ɛ̃diʒɛst] *a* indigestible, heavy, undigested.
indigestion [ɛ̃diʒɛstjɔ̃] *nf* attack of indigestion.
indignation [ɛ̃diɲasjɔ̃] *nf* indignation.
indigne [ɛ̃diɲ] *a* unworthy, undeserving, vile.
indigné [ɛ̃diɲe] *a* indignant.
indigner [ɛ̃diɲe] *vt* to make indignant; *vr* to be, to become, indignant.
indignité [ɛ̃diɲite] *nf* indignity, unworthiness, infamy.
indiquer [ɛ̃dike] *vt* to indicate, point (to, out), show, appoint; c'était indiqué it was the obvious thing to do.
indirect [ɛ̃dirɛkt] *a* indirect, devious.
indiscipliné [ɛ̃disipline] *a* unruly, undisciplined.
indiscret, -ète [ɛ̃diskrɛ, ɛt] *a* indiscreet, unguarded, tactless, prying.
indiscrétion [ɛ̃diskresjɔ̃] *nf* indiscretion, tactless remark or action.
indiscutable [ɛ̃diskytabl] *a* unquestionable, indisputable.
indispensable [ɛ̃dispɑ̃sabl] *a* indispensable, necessary, essential, requisite.
indisponibilité [ɛ̃dispɔnibilite] *nf* unavailability.
indisposé [ɛ̃dispoze] *a* indisposed, unwell, ill-disposed.
indisposer [ɛ̃dispoze] *vt* to upset, disagree with, make unwell, antagonize.
indisposition [ɛ̃dispozisjɔ̃] *nf* indisposition.
indissoluble [ɛ̃dissɔlybl] *a* insoluble (*chem*), indissoluble.
indistinct [ɛ̃distɛ̃(:kt)] *a* indistinct, faint, blurred.
individu [ɛ̃dividy] *nm* individual, fellow, character.
individualiser [ɛ̃dividɥalize] *vt* to individualize, specify.
individuel, -elle [ɛ̃dividɥɛl] *a* individual, personal.
indivisible [ɛ̃divizibl] *a* indivisible.

Indochine [ɛ̃dɔʃin] *nf* Indochina.
indocile [ɛ̃dɔsil] *a* intractable, willful, disobedient.
indolence [ɛ̃dɔlɑ̃:s] *nf* apathy.
indolent [ɛ̃dɔlɑ̃] *a* indolent, slack, slothful.
indomptable [ɛ̃dɔ̃tabl] *a* untamable, ungovernable, unmanageable, invincible.
Indonésie [ɛ̃dɔnézi] *nf* Indonesia.
indu [ɛ̃dy] *a* not due, undue, unwarranted, unreasonable
indubitable [ɛ̃dybitabl] *a* unquestionable.
induire [ɛ̃dɥi:r] *vt* to induce, tempt.
indulgence [ɛ̃dylʒɑ̃:s] *nf* indulgence, forbearance, leniency.
indulgent [ɛ̃dylʒɑ̃] *a* forbearing, lenient.
indûment [ɛ̃dymɑ̃] *ad* unduly.
industrialiser [ɛ̃dystrialize] *vt* to industrialize.
industrialisme [ɛ̃dystrialism] *nm* industrialism.
industrie [ɛ̃dystri] *nf* industry, trade, activity, industriousness; vivre d'— to live by one's wits.
industriel, -ielle [ɛ̃dystriɛl] *a* industrial; *nm* industrialist, manufacturer.
industrieux, -euse [ɛ̃dystriø, ø:z] *a* industrious, active.
inébranlable [inebrɑ̃labl] *a* unshakable, steadfast, unswerving.
inédit [inedi] *a* unpublished, new.
ineffable [inefabl] *a* ineffable, unutterable.
ineffaçable [inefasabl] *a* indelible.
inefficace [inefikas] *a* ineffective, ineffectual.
inefficacité [inefikasite] *nf* inefficacy, ineffectiveness, ineffectualness.
inégal [inegal] *a* unequal, uneven, irregular, unsteady.
inégalité [inegalite] *nf* inequality, unevenness, roughness, unsteadiness.
inéligible [ineliʒibl] *a* ineligible.
inéluctable [inelyktabl] *a* inevitable.
inénarrable [inenarabl] *a* indescribable, beyond words.
inepte [inɛpt] *a* inept, foolish.
ineptie [inɛpsi] *nf* ineptitude, stupid remark.
inépuisable [inepɥizabl] *a* inexhaustible, abundant.
inéquitable [inekitabl] *a* unfair.
inerte [inɛrt] *a* inert, dull, sluggish, listless.
inespéré [inɛspere] *a* unexpected, unhoped-for.
inestimable [inɛstimabl] *a* priceless, invaluable.
inévitable [inevitabl] *a* inevitable.
inexact [inɛgzakt] *a* inexact, inaccurate, unpunctual.
inexactitude [inɛgzaktityd] *nf* inaccuracy, unpunctuality.
inexcusable [inɛkskyzabl] *a* unpardonable, unwarranted.

inexécutable [inɛgzekytabl] *a* impracticable.

inexercé [inɛgzɛrse] *a* unexercised, unpracticed.

inexistant [inɛgzistɑ̃] *a* non-existent.

inexorable [inɛgzɔrabl] *a* inexorable.

inexpérience [inɛksperjɑ̃:s] *nf* inexperience.

inexpérimenté [inɛksperimɑ̃te] *a* inexperienced, unpracticed, untried, raw.

inexplicable [inɛksplikabl] *a* inexplicable, unaccountable.

inexpliqué [inɛksplike] *a* unexplained, unaccounted for.

inexploité [inɛksplwate] *a* unworked, undeveloped.

inexpressif, -ive [inɛksprɛsif, i:v] *a* expressionless.

inexprimable [inɛksprimabl] *a* inexpressible, beyond words.

inextricable [inɛkstrikabl] *a* inextricable.

infaillibilité [ɛ̃fajibilite] *nf* infallibility.

infaillible [ɛ̃fajibl] *a* infallible, sure, unerring.

infâme [ɛ̃fɑ:m] *a* infamous, foul.

infamie [ɛ̃fami] *nf* infamy, foul deed or word.

infanterie [ɛ̃fɑ̃tri] *nf* infantry.

infatigable [ɛ̃fatigabl] *a* tireless, untiring, indefatigable.

infatuation [ɛ̃fatɥasjɔ̃] *nf* self-conceit, infatuation.

infécond [ɛ̃fekɔ̃] *a* barren, sterile, unfruitful.

infécondité [ɛ̃fekɔ̃dite] *nf* sterility, barrenness.

infect [ɛ̃fɛkt] *a* stinking, tainted, rotten, foul.

infecter [ɛ̃fɛkte] *vt* to infect, taint, stink of.

infectieux, -euse [ɛ̃fɛksjø, ø:z] *a* infectious.

infection [ɛ̃fɛksjɔ̃] *nf* infection, contamination, stink.

s'inféoder [sɛ̃feɔde] *vr* to give one's support, join.

inférer [ɛ̃fere] *vt* to infer.

inférieur [ɛ̃ferjœ:r] *a* inferior, lower; *n* inferior.

infériorité [ɛ̃ferjɔrite] *nf* inferiority.

infernal [ɛ̃fɛrnal] *a* infernal, devilish, diabolical.

infertile [ɛ̃fɛrtil] *a* barren, infertile, unfruitful.

infester [ɛ̃fɛste] *vt* to infest, overrun.

infidèle [ɛ̃fidɛl] *a* unfaithful, faithless, false; *n* infidel, unbeliever.

infidélité [ɛ̃fidelite] *nf* infidelity, unfaithfulness.

infiltration [ɛ̃filtrasjɔ̃] *nf* infiltration, percolation.

s'infiltrer [sɛ̃filtre] *vr* to infiltrate, seep, soak in.

infime [ɛ̃fim] *a* lowly, mean, tiny.

infini [ɛ̃fini] *a* infinite, endless, boundless, countless; *nm* infinite, infinity.

infiniment [ɛ̃finimɑ̃] *ad* infinitely.

infinité [ɛ̃finite] *nf* infinity, infinitude, countless number.

infirme [ɛ̃firm] *a* infirm, disabled, crippled, feeble; *n* cripple, invalid.

infirmer [ɛ̃firme] *vt* to weaken, invalidate, quash.

infirmerie [ɛ̃firmɔri] *nf* infirmary, sick-room.

infirmier, -ière [ɛ̃firmje, ɛ:r] *n* (male) nurse, hospital orderly.

infirmité [ɛ̃firmite] *nf* infirmity, weakness, disability.

inflammation [ɛ̃flamasjɔ̃] *nf* inflammation.

inflation [ɛ̃flasjɔ̃] *nf* inflation.

inflexible [ɛ̃flɛksibl] *a* inflexible, unbending, rigid.

inflexion [ɛ̃flɛksjɔ̃] *nf* inflection, modulation.

infliger [ɛ̃fliʒe] *vt* to inflict.

influence [ɛ̃flyɑ̃:s] *nf* influence, effect, sway.

influencer [ɛ̃flyɑ̃se] *vt* to influence, sway.

influent [ɛ̃flyɑ̃] *a* influential.

influer [ɛ̃flye] *vi* to have an influence, an effect.

informateur, -trice [ɛ̃fɔrmatœ:r, tris] *n* informant.

information [ɛ̃fɔrmasjɔ̃] *nf* inquiry, preliminary investigation; *pl* news bulletin.

informe [ɛ̃fɔrm] *a* shapeless, ill-formed, misshapen; (*jur*) irregular.

informer [ɛ̃fɔrme] *vt* to inform, apprise; *vi* to inform (against contre); *vr* to make inquiries.

infortune [ɛ̃fɔrtyn] *nf* misfortune.

infortuné [ɛ̃fɔrtyne] *a* unfortunate, unlucky.

infraction [ɛ̃fraksjɔ̃] *nf* infringement, breach.

infranchissable [ɛ̃frɑ̃ʃisabl] *a* impassable, insuperable.

infructueux, -euse [ɛ̃fryktɥø, ø:z] *a* unsuccessful, barren, fruitless.

infuser [ɛ̃fyse] *vt* to infuse, steep; *vr* to infuse, brew.

infusion [ɛ̃fyzjɔ̃] *nf* infusion.

ingambe [ɛ̃gɑ̃:b] *a* active.

s'ingénier [sɛ̃ʒenje] *vr* to contrive, use all one's wits.

ingénieur [ɛ̃ʒenjœ:r] *nm* engineer.

ingénieux, -euse [ɛ̃ʒenjø, ø:z] *a* ingenious, clever.

ingéniosité [ɛ̃ʒenjɔzite] *nf* ingenuity, ingeniousness.

ingénu [ɛ̃ʒeny] *a* ingenuous, simple, artless, unsophisticated.

ingénuité [ɛ̃ʒenɥite] *nf* ingenuousness, simplicity.

s'ingérer [sɛ̃ʒere] *vr* to interfere, meddle (with dans).

ingouvernable [ɛ̃guvɛrnabl] *a* unmanageable, uncontrollable.

ingrat [ɛ̃gra] *an* ungrateful, thankless, unprofitable, barren.

ingratitude [ɛ̃gratityd] *nf* ingratitude, thanklessness.

ingrédient [ɛ̃gredjɑ̃] *nm* ingredient.
inguérissable [ɛ̃gerisabl] *a* incurable.
ingurgiter [ɛ̃gyrʒite] *vt* to gulp down, swallow.
inhabile [inabil] *a* awkward, unskilled, clumsy.
inhabitable [inabitabl] *a* uninhabitable.
inhabité [inabite] *a* uninhabited, untenanted, vacant.
inhabituel(le) [inabitɥɛl] *a* unusual, unwonted.
inharmonieux, -euse [inarmɔnjø, øːz] *a* discordant, unmusical.
inhérent [inerɑ̃] *a* inherent.
inhibition [inibisjɔ̃] *nf* inhibition.
inhospitalier, -ière [inɔspitalje, jɛːr] *a* inhospitable.
inhumain [inymɛ̃] *a* inhuman, heartless.
inhumer [inyme] *vt* to bury, inter.
inimaginable [inimaʒinabl] *a* unimaginable, unthinkable.
inimitable [inimitabl] *a* inimitable, peerless.
inimitié [inimitje] *nf* enmity, ill-will, ill-feeling.
ininflammable [inɛ̃flamabl] *a* fireproof.
inintelligent [inɛ̃teliʒɑ̃] *a* unintelligent, obtuse.
inintelligible [inɛ̃teliʒibl] *a* unintelligible.
ininterrompu [inɛ̃terɔ̃py] *a* uninterrupted, unbroken.
iniquité [inikite] *nf* injustice, wickedness.
initial [inisjal] *a* initial, starting.
initiale [inisjal] *nf* initial (letter).
initiateur, -trice [inisjatœːr, tris] *n* initiator.
initiative [inisjatiːv] *nf* initiative, push; **syndicat d'—** information bureau.
initier [inisje] *vt* to initiate.
injecter [ɛ̃ʒɛkte] *vt* to inject; *vr* to become bloodshot.
injection [ɛ̃ʒɛksjɔ̃] *nf* injection.
injonction [ɛ̃ʒɔ̃ksjɔ̃] *nf* injunction, behest.
injudicieux, -euse [ɛ̃ʒydisjø, øːz] *a* injudicious.
injure [ɛ̃ʒyːr] *nf* insult, wrong.
injurier [ɛ̃ʒyrje] *vt* to insult, call names, abuse.
injurieux, -euse [ɛ̃ʒyrjø, øːz] *a* insulting, abusive.
injuste [ɛ̃ʒyst] *a* unfair, unjust.
injustice [ɛ̃ʒystis] *nf* injustice, unfairness, wrong.
injustifiable [ɛ̃ʒystifjabl] *a* unjustifiable.
inlassable [ɛ̃lɑsabl] *a* untiring, tireless.
innavigable [inavigabl] *a* unnavigable, unseaworthy.
inné [inne] *a* innate, inborn.
innocence [inɔsɑ̃ːs] *nf* innocence, harmlessness.
innocent [inɔsɑ̃] *a* innocent, simple,

guileless, harmless; *n* half-wit, idiot.
innocenter [inɔsɑ̃te] *vt* to clear, declare innocent.
innocuité [innɔkɥite] *nf* innocuousness, harmlessness.
innombrable [innɔ̃brabl] *a* countless, innumerable.
innover [innɔve] *vt* to innovate; *vi* to break new ground.
inobservation [inɔpsɛrvasjɔ̃] *nf* disregard, breach.
inobservé [inɔpsɛrve] *a* unnoticed, unobserved.
inoccupé [inɔkype] *a* unoccupied, idle, vacant.
inoculer [inɔkyle] *vt* to inoculate, inject.
inodore [inɔdor] *a* odorless, scentless.
inoffensif, -ive [inɔfɑ̃sif, iːv] *a* inoffensive, harmless.
inondation [inɔ̃dasjɔ̃] *nf* flood.
inonder [inɔ̃de] *vt* to flood, inundate; **être inondé de** to be flooded with, soaked in.
inopiné [inɔpine] *a* unexpected, unforeseen.
inopportun [inɔpɔrtœ̃] *a* inopportune, unseasonable, ill-timed.
inopportunité [inɔpɔrtynite] *nf* inopportuneness, unseasonableness.
inoubliable [inubliabl] *a* unforgettable.
inouï [inui, -w-] *a* unheard of, outrageous.
inoxydable [inɔksidabl] *a* rustproof, stainless; *nm* stainless steel.
inqualifiable [ɛ̃kalifjabl] *a* unspeakable.
inquiet, -ète [ɛ̃kjɛ, ɛt] *a* anxious, uneasy, concerned.
inquiéter [ɛ̃kjete] *vt* to make anxious, disturb, disquiet, alarm; *vr* to worry, grow anxious.
inquiétude [ɛ̃kjetyd] *nf* anxiety, misgivings.
insaisissable [ɛ̃sɛzisabl] *a* elusive, imperceptible.
insalissable [ɛ̃salisabl] *a* dirtproof.
insalubre [ɛ̃salybr] *a* unhealthy, insanitary.
insanité [ɛ̃sanite] *nf* insanity; *pl* (*fam*) nonsense.
insatiable [ɛ̃sasjabl] *a* insatiable, unquenchable.
inscription [ɛ̃skripsjɔ̃] *nf* inscription, writing down, enrollment; **droit d'—** entrance fee, registration fee.
inscrire [ɛ̃skriːr] *vt* to inscribe, write down, enroll, register; *vr* to enroll, put down one's name.
insecte [ɛ̃sɛkt] *nm* insect.
insécurité [ɛ̃sekyrite] *nf* insecurity.
insensé [ɛ̃sɑ̃se] *a* mad, senseless, wild, crazy.
insensibiliser [ɛ̃sɑ̃sibilize] *vt* to anesthetize.
insensibilité [ɛ̃sɑ̃sibilite] *nf* insensibility, callousness, lack of feeling.

insensible [ɛ̃sãsibl] *a* insensitive, callous, unfeeling, imperceptible.

inséparable [ɛ̃separabl] *a* inseparable.

insérer [ɛ̃sere] *vt* to insert.

insidieux, -euse [ɛ̃sidjø, øːz] *a* insidious.

insigne [ɛ̃siɲ] *a* distinguished, signal, notorious; *nm* badge, emblem; *pl* insignia.

insignifiance [ɛ̃siɲifjãːs] *nf* insignificance.

insignifiant [ɛ̃siɲifjã] *a* insignificant, trivial, meaningless.

insinuation [ɛ̃sinɥasjɔ̃] *nf* insinuation, innuendo, insertion.

insinuer [ɛ̃sinɥe] *vt* to insinuate, hint at, insert; *vr* to steal, slip, creep (into **dans**).

insipide [ɛ̃sipid] *a* insipid, tasteless, dull, flat.

insistance [ɛ̃sistãːs] *nf* insistence, persistence.

insister [ɛ̃siste] *vi* to insist, persist; **— sur** stress.

insociable [ɛ̃sɔsjabl] *a* unsociable.

insolation [ɛ̃sɔlasjɔ̃] *nf* insolation, sunstroke.

insolence [ɛ̃sɔlãːs] *nf* insolence, impertinence.

insolent [ɛ̃sɔlã] *an* insolent, impudent, impertinent.

insolite [ɛ̃sɔlit] *a* unusual, strange.

insoluble [ɛ̃sɔlybl] *a* insoluble, unsolvable.

insolvabilité [ɛ̃sɔlvabilite] *nf* insolvency.

insolvable [ɛ̃sɔlvabl] *a* insolvent.

insomnie [ɛ̃sɔmni] *nf* insomnia, sleeplessness.

insondable [ɛ̃sɔ̃dabl] *a* fathomless, bottomless, unfathomable.

insonore [ɛ̃sɔnɔːr] *a* soundproof.

insouciance [ɛ̃susjãːs] *nf* unconcern, casualness.

insouciant [ɛ̃susjã] *a* care-free, heedless.

insoucieux -euse [ɛ̃susjø. øːz] *a* heedless, regardless.

insoumis [ɛ̃sumi] *a* unsubdued, unruly, refractory.

insoumission [ɛ̃sumisjɔ̃] *nf* insubordination.

insoupçonnable [ɛ̃supsɔnabl] *a* beyond suspicion.

insoutenable [ɛ̃sutnabl] *a* untenable, indefensible.

inspecter [ɛ̃spɛkte] *vt* to inspect, examine.

inspecteur, -trice [ɛ̃spɛktœːr, tris] *n* inspector, inspectress, examiner, overseer.

inspection [ɛ̃spɛksjɔ̃] *nf* inspection, examination, survey.

inspiration [ɛ̃spirasjɔ̃] *nf* inspiration, breathing in.

inspirer [ɛ̃spire] *vt* to inspire, breathe in, prompt; *vr* to find inspiration (in **de**).

instabilité [ɛ̃stabilite] *nf* instability,

unsteadiness, uncertainty, fickleness.

instable [ɛ̃stabl] *a* unstable, unsteady, unreliable.

installation [ɛ̃stalasjɔ̃] *nf* setting up, fittings, plant.

installer [ɛ̃stale] *vt* to install, fit up, equip; *vr* to settle down, move in.

instamment [ɛ̃stamã] *ad* earnestly, urgently.

instance [ɛ̃stãːs] *nf* solicitation, lawsuit; *pl* entreaties, requests.

instant [ɛ̃stã] *a* urgent, pressing; *nm* instant, moment; **à l'—** at once, a moment ago; **par —s** off and on.

instantané [ɛ̃stãtane] *a* instantaneous; *nm* snapshot.

instar [ɛ̃staːr] *prep* **à l'— de** after the manner of, like.

instigateur, -trice [ɛ̃stigatœːr, tris] *n* instigator.

instigation [ɛ̃stigasjɔ̃] *nf* instigation, incitement.

instinct [ɛ̃stɛ̃] *nm* instinct.

instinctif, -ive [ɛ̃stɛ̃ktif, iːv] *a* instinctive.

instituer [ɛ̃stitɥe] *vt* to institute, set up, appoint.

institut [ɛ̃stity] *nm* institute, institution.

instituteur, -trice [ɛ̃stitytœːr, tris] *n* primary school-teacher, founder.

institution [ɛ̃stitysjɔ̃] *nf* setting up, institution, establishment.

instructeur [ɛ̃stryktœːr] *nm* instructor; **sergent —** drill sergeant.

instructif, -ive [ɛ̃stryktif, iːv] *a* instructive.

instruction [ɛ̃stryksjɔ̃] *nf* education, training, (*jur*) preliminary investigation; *pl* directions, orders.

instruire [ɛ̃strɥiːr] *vt* to instruct, train, (*jur*) investigate, inform.

instruit [ɛ̃strɥi] *a* educated, learned, trained.

instrument [ɛ̃strymã] *nm* instrument, tool.

instrumentation [ɛ̃strymãtasjɔ̃] *nf* instrumentation, orchestration.

instrumenter [ɛ̃strymãte] *vt* to score, orchestrate; *vi* to order proceedings to be taken.

insu [ɛ̃sy] *nm* **à l'— de** without the knowledge of; **à son —** without his knowing.

insubmersible [ɛ̃sybmɛrsibl] *a* unsinkable.

insubordination [ɛ̃sybɔrdinasjɔ̃] *nf* insubordination.

insuccès [ɛ̃syksɛ] *nm* failure.

insuffisance [ɛ̃syfizãːs] *nf* insufficiency, shortage, inadequacy, incompetence.

insuffisant [ɛ̃syfizã] *a* insufficient, inadequate, incompetent.

insulaire [ɛ̃sylɛːr] *a* insular; *n* islander.

insularité [ɛ̃sylarite] *nf* insularity.

insulte [ɛ̃sylt] *nf* insult.

insulter [ɛ̃sylte] *vt* to insult; *vi* to be an insult to.

insupportable [ɛ̃sypɔrtabl] *a* unbearable, insufferable, intolerable.
insurgé [ɛ̃syrʒe] *n* rebel, insurgent.
s'insurger [sɛ̃syrʒe] *vr* to revolt, rise in revolt.
insurmontable [ɛ̃syrmɔ̃tabl] *a* insuperable.
insurrection [ɛ̃syrrɛksjɔ̃] *nf* rebellion, insurrection.
intact [ɛ̃takt] *a* intact, whole, undamaged.
intangible [ɛ̃tãʒibl] *a* intangible, inviolable.
intarissable [ɛ̃tarisabl] *a* inexhaustible, endless.
intégral [ɛ̃tɛgral] *a* integral, full, complete.
intégrant [ɛ̃tɛgrã] *a* integral.
intègre [ɛ̃tɛgr] *a* upright, honest, just.
intégrer [ɛ̃tegre] *vt* integrate.
intégrité [ɛ̃tegrite] *nf* integrity, honesty, entirety.
intellectuel, -elle [ɛ̃tɛl(l)ɛktɥɛl] *a* intellectual, mental; *n* intellectual, highbrow.
intelligence [ɛ̃tɛl(l)iʒã:s] *nf* intelligence, intellect, understanding; **vivre en bonne — avec** to live on good terms with; **être d'— avec** to be in league with.
intelligent [ɛ̃tɛl(l)iʒã] *a* intelligent, clever.
intelligible [ɛ̃tɛl(l)iʒibl] *a* audible, understandable.
intempérance [ɛ̃tãpɛrã:s] *nf* intemperance, license.
intempérant [ɛ̃tãpɛrã] *a* intemperate.
intempérie [ɛ̃tãperi] *nf* inclemency (of weather).
intempestif, -ive [ɛ̃tãpɛstif, i:v] *a* unseasonable, inopportune.
intenable [ɛ̃tnabl] *a* untenable.
intendance [ɛ̃tãdã:s] *nf* stewardship, commissariat, Army Service Corps, supply depot, finance office.
intendant [ɛ̃tãdã] *nm* steward (of household); bursar; **— général** quartermaster general.
intense [ɛ̃tã:s] *a* intense, intensive, severe.
intensité [ɛ̃tãsite] *nf* intensity, strength.
intenter [ɛ̃tãte] *vt* **— un procès** to bring an action.
intention [ɛ̃tãsjɔ̃] *nf* intention, purpose; **à votre —** for you, meant for you.
intentionné [ɛ̃tãsjɔne] *a* intentioned, meaning, disposed.
intentionnel, -elle [ɛ̃tãsjɔnɛl] *a* intentional.
inter [ɛ̃tɛ:r] *nm (telephone)* trunks.
intercaler [ɛ̃tɛrkale] *vt* to insert, add.
intercéder [ɛ̃tɛrsede] *vi* to intercede.
intercepter [ɛ̃tɛrsɛpte] *vt* to intercept, cut off.
interception [ɛ̃tɛrsɛpsjɔ̃] *nf* interception, tackle.

intercession [ɛ̃tɛrsɛsjɔ̃] *nf* intercession.
interchangeable [ɛ̃tɛrʃãʒabl] *a* interchangeable.
interdiction [ɛ̃tɛrdiksjɔ̃] *nf* interdiction, prohibition.
interdire [ɛ̃tɛrdi:r] *vt* to prohibit, forbid, ban, suspend, nonplus, take aback.
interdit [ɛ̃tɛrdi] *a* suspended, forbidden, taken aback, nonplused; *nm* interdict; **sens —** no entry.
intéressant [ɛ̃tɛresã] *a* interesting.
intéressé [ɛ̃tɛrese] *a* interested, concerned, selfish.
intéresser [ɛ̃tɛrese] *vt* to interest, concern; *vr* to be interested, take an interest.
intérêt [ɛ̃tɛrɛ] *nm* interest, advantage, stake; **avoir — à le faire** to be to one's interest to do it; **porter — à** to take an interest in.
interférer [ɛ̃tɛrfere] *vt* to interfere.
intérieur [ɛ̃tɛrjœ:r] *a* interior, inward, home, domestic, inland; *nm* inside, interior, home, house, **à l'—** inside.
intérim [ɛ̃terim] *nm* interim.
interjection [ɛ̃tɛrʒɛksjɔ̃] *nf* interjection.
interligne [ɛ̃tɛrliɲ] *nm* space between two lines.
interlocuteur, -trice [ɛ̃tɛrlɔkytœ:r, tris] *n* interlocutor, speaker.
interloquer [ɛ̃tɛrlɔke] *vt* to disconcert, take aback; *vr* to become embarrassed.
intermède [ɛ̃tɛrmɛd] *nm* interlude.
intermédiaire [ɛ̃tɛrmedjɛ:r] *a* intermediate, intervening, middle; *nm* intermediary, agency, agent, gobetween, middleman.
interminable [ɛ̃tɛrminabl] *a* neverending, endless.
intermittent [ɛ̃tɛrmittã] *a* intermittent, irregular.
internat [ɛ̃tɛrna] *nm* boardingschool.
international, -e, -aux [ɛ̃tɛrnasjonal, o] *a* international; *nf* the International.
interne [ɛ̃tɛrn] *a* internal, interior, inner, inward; *n* boarder, resident doctor, intern.
interner [ɛ̃tɛrne] *vt* to intern, confine.
interpellation [ɛ̃tɛrpɛl(l)asjɔ̃] *nf* question, interruption, challenge.
interpeller [ɛ̃tɛrpɛl(l)e] *vt* to call upon s.o. for an explanation, challenge.
interplanétaire [ɛ̃tɛrplanete:r] *a* interplanetary.
interpoler [ɛ̃tɛrpɔle] *vt* to interpolate.
interposer [ɛ̃tɛrpoze] *vt* to interpose, place between; *vr* to intervene.
interprétation [ɛ̃tɛrpretasjɔ̃] *nf* interpretation, rendering.
interprète [ɛ̃tɛrprɛt] *n* interpreter, player, actor.

interpréter [ɛ̃tɛrprete] *vt* to interpret, expound, render.
interrogateur, -trice [ɛ̃tɛrɔgatœːr, tris] *a* inquiring, questioning; *n* interrogator, examiner.
interrogatif, -ive [ɛ̃tɛrɔgatif, iːv] *a* interrogative.
interrogation [ɛ̃tɛrɔgasjɔ̃] *nf* interrogation, question(ing), oral test; **point d'—** question mark.
interrogatoire [ɛ̃tɛrɔgatwaːr] *nm* interrogation, cross-examination.
interroger [ɛ̃tɛrɔʒe] *vt* to interrogate, question.
interrompre [ɛ̃tɛrɔ̃ːpr] *vt* to interrupt, break (off), stop.
interrupteur [ɛ̃tɛryptœːr] *nm* switch, cut-out.
interruption [ɛ̃tɛrypsjɔ̃] *nf* interruption, breaking off, switching off.
intersection [ɛ̃tɛrseksjɔ̃] *nf* intersection.
interstice [ɛ̃tɛrstis] *nm* chink.
interurbain [ɛ̃tɛryrbɛ̃] *a* interurban, trunk (call).
intervalle [ɛ̃tɛrval] *nm* interval, space, distance, period.
intervenir [ɛ̃tɛrvəniːr] *vi* to intervene, interfere.
intervention [ɛ̃tɛrvɑ̃sjɔ̃] *nf* intervention.
interversion [ɛ̃tɛrvɛrsjɔ̃] *nf* inversion.
intervertir [ɛ̃tɛrvɛrtiːr] *vt* to invert, reverse.
interviewer [ɛ̃tɛrvju(v)e] *vt* to interview.
intestin [ɛ̃tɛstɛ̃] *a* internal, civil; *nm* intestine.
intimation [ɛ̃timasjɔ̃] *nf* notification, notice.
intime [ɛ̃tim] *a* intimate, inner, inmost.
intimer [ɛ̃time] *vt* to notify.
intimider [ɛ̃timide] *vt* to intimidate, frighten.
intimité [ɛ̃timite] *nf* intimacy, privacy.
intituler [ɛ̃tityle] *vi* to entitle.
intolérable [ɛ̃tɔlerabl] *a* intolerable, unbearable.
intolérance [ɛ̃tɔlerɑ̃ːs] *nf* intolerance.
intolérant [ɛ̃tɔlerɑ̃] *a* intolerant.
intonation [ɛ̃tɔnasjɔ̃] *nf* intonation, pitch.
intoxication [ɛ̃tɔksikasjɔ̃] *nf* poisoning.
intoxiquer [ɛ̃tɔksike] *vt* to poison.
intraduisible [ɛ̃tradɥizibl] *a* untranslatable.
intraitable [ɛ̃trɛtabl] *a* unmanageable, uncompromising.
intransigeance [ɛ̃trɑ̃siʒɑ̃ːs] *nf* strictness, intolerance.
intransigeant [ɛ̃trɑ̃siʒɑ̃] *a* uncompromising, unbending, adamant.
intransportable [ɛ̃trɑ̃spɔrtabl] *a* not fit to travel.
intrépide [ɛ̃trepid] *a* intrepid, fearless, dauntless.

intrépidité [ɛ̃trepidite] *nf* fearlessness, dauntlessness.
intrigant [ɛ̃trigɑ̃] *a* intriguing, scheming; *n* intriguer, schemer.
intrigue [ɛ̃trig] *nf* intrigue, scheme, plot.
intriguer [ɛ̃trige] *vt* to intrigue, puzzle; *vi* to plot, scheme.
intrinsèque [ɛ̃trɛ̃sɛk] *a* intrinsic.
introduction [ɛ̃trɔdyksjɔ̃] *nf* introduction, bringing in, admission.
introduire [ɛ̃trɔdɥiːr] *vt* to introduce, put in, show in; *vr* to enter, get in.
introniser [ɛ̃trɔnize] *vt* to enthrone, establish.
introspection [ɛ̃trɔspɛksjɔ̃] *nf* introspection.
introuvable [ɛ̃truvabl] *a* not to be found, untraceable.
intrus [ɛ̃try] *a* intruding; *n* intruder.
intrusion [ɛ̃tryzjɔ̃] *nf* intrusion, trespass.
intuition [ɛ̃tɥisjɔ̃] *nf* intuition.
inusité [inyzite] *a* unusual.
inutile [inytil] *a* useless, vain, unavailing, needless.
inutilisable [inytilizabl] *a* useless, unserviceable.
inutilité [inytilite] *nf* uselessness.
invalide [ɛ̃valid] *a* infirm, disabled, invalid; *nm* disabled soldier.
invalider [ɛ̃valide] *vt* to invalidate, declare void, (*elected member*) unseat.
invalidité [ɛ̃validite] *nf* disablement, disability, invalidity.
invariable [ɛ̃varjabl] *a* invariable, unchanging.
invasion [ɛ̃vazjɔ̃] *nf* invasion.
invective [ɛ̃vɛktiːv] *nf* invective.
invectiver [ɛ̃vɛktive] *vt* to abuse, call s.o. names; *vi* to revile (**contre**).
invendable [ɛ̃vɑ̃dabl] *a* unsalable.
inventaire [ɛ̃vɑ̃tɛːr] *nm* inventory; **dresser l'—** to take stock.
inventer [ɛ̃vɑ̃te] *vt* to invent, devise, discover, make up.
inventeur [ɛ̃vɑ̃tœːr] *nm* inventor, discoverer.
invention [ɛ̃vɑ̃sjɔ̃] *nf* invention, inventiveness, device, made-up story.
inventorier [ɛ̃vɑ̃tɔrje] *vt* to make a list of, inventory.
inverse [ɛ̃vɛrs] *a* inverse, inverted, opposite; *nm* opposite, reverse.
inversion [ɛ̃vɛrsjɔ̃] *nf* inversion, reversal.
invertir [ɛ̃vɛrtiːr] *vt* to invert, reverse.
investigateur, -trice [ɛ̃vɛstigatœːr, tris] *a* investigating, searching; *n* investigator.
investir [ɛ̃vɛstiːr] *vt* to invest, entrust; beleaguer.
investiture [ɛ̃vɛstityːr] *nf* nomination, induction.
invétéré [ɛ̃vetere] *a* inveterate, deep-rooted, hardened, confirmed.
invincible [ɛ̃vɛ̃sibl] *a* invincible, insuperable.

inviolable [ɛ̃vjɔlabl] *a* inviolable, sacred.
invisibilité [ɛ̃vizibilite] *nf* invisibility.
invisible [ɛ̃vizibl] *a* invisible, never to be seen.
invitation [ɛ̃vitasjɔ̃] *nf* invitation.
invite [ɛ̃vit] *nf* invitation, inducement, (*cards*) lead.
invité [ɛ̃vite] *n* guest.
inviter [ɛ̃vite] *vt* to invite, ask, call for.
involontaire [ɛ̃vɔlɔ̃tɛːr] *a* involuntary, unintentional.
invoquer [ɛ̃vɔke] *vt* to invoke, call upon, bring forward.
invraisemblable [ɛ̃vrɛsɑ̃blabl] *a* unlikely, improbable, extraordinary.
invraisemblance [ɛ̃vrɛsɑ̃blɑ̃ːs] *nf* unlikelihood, improbability.
invulnérable [ɛ̃vylnɛrabl] *a* invulnerable.
iode [jɔd, iɔd] *nm* iodine.
irascible [irassibl] *a* crusty, quick-tempered.
iris [iris] *nm* iris.
irisé [irize] *a* iridescent, rainbow-colored.
irlandais [irlɑ̃dɛ] *an* Irish, Irishman, Irishwoman.
Irlande [irlɑ̃ːd] *nf* Ireland.
ironie [irɔni] *nf* irony.
ironique [irɔnik] *a* ironical.
irradier [irradje] *vi* to radiate, spread, irradiate.
irraisonnable [irrezɔnabl] *a* irrational.
irrecevable [irrəsəvabl] *a* inadmissible.
irréconciliable [irrekɔ̃siljabl] *a* irreconcilable.
irrécusable [irrekyzabl] *a* irrefutable, unimpeachable.
irréel, -elle [irreɛl] *a* unreal.
irréfléchi [irrefleʃi] *a* unconsidered, thoughtless.
irréflexion [irreflɛksjɔ̃] *nf* thoughtlessness.
irréfutable [irrefytabl] *a* irrefutable, indisputable.
irrégularité [irregylarite] *nf* irregularity, unsteadiness, unpunctuality.
irrégulier, -ière [irregylje, jɛːr] *a* irregular, loose (*life*).
irrémédiable [irremedjabl] *a* irremediable, irreparable.
irremplaçable [irrɑ̃plasabl] *a* irreplaceable.
irréparable [irreparabl] *a* irreparable, irretrievable.
irrépressible [irreprɛsibl] *a* irrepressible.
irréprochable [irreprɔʃabl] *a* irreproachable, faultless, impeccable.
irrésistible [irrezistibl] *a* irresistible.
irrésolu [irrezɔly] *a* irresolute, unsteady, unsolved.
irrésolution [irrezɔlysjɔ̃] *nf* hesitancy, uncertainty, wavering.

irrespectueux, -euse [irrɛspɛktɥø, øːz] *a* disrespectful.
irresponsable [irrɛspɔ̃sabl] *a* irresponsible.
irrévérencieux, -euse [irrevɛrɑ̃sjø, øːz] *a* irreverent, disrespectful.
irrévocable [irrevɔkabl] *a* irrevocable, binding.
irrigation [irrigasjɔ̃] *nf* irrigation.
irriguer [irrige] *vt* to irrigate.
irritable [irritabl] *a* irritable, short-tempered, sensitive, jumpy.
irritation [irritasjɔ̃] *nf* irritation.
irriter [irrite] *vt* to irritate, annoy, rouse, inflame; *vr* to become angry, inflamed.
irruption [irrypsjɔ̃] *nf* irruption, inrush, raid.
islandais [islɑ̃dɛ] *a* Icelandic; *n* Icelander.
Islande [islɑ̃ːd] *nf* Iceland.
isolateur, -trice [izɔlatœːr, tris] *a* insulating; *nm* insulator.
isolement [izɔlmɑ̃] *nm* isolation, loneliness, insulation.
isolé [izɔle] *a* isolated, lonely, insulated.
isoler [izɔle] *vt* to isolate, insulate.
Israël [israɛl] *nf* Israel.
israélien [israɛljɛ̃] *an* Israeli.
issu [isy] *a* sprung (from), descended (from).
issue [isy] *nf* issue, outlet, exit, end, conclusion.
isthme [ism] *nm* isthmus.
Italie [itali] *nf* Italy.
italien, -ienne [italjɛ̃, jɛn] *an* Italian.
italique [italik] *a* italic; *nm* italics.
item [itɛm] *ad* likewise.
itinéraire [itinerɛːr] *nm* itinerary, route.
itinérant [itinerɑ̃] *a* itinerant.
ivoire [ivwaːr] *nm* ivory.
ivraie [ivrɛ] *nf* tares, chaff.
ivre [iːvr] *a* drunk, tipsy, intoxicated, wild, mad.
ivresse [ivrɛs] *nf* intoxication, rapture.
ivrogne [ivrɔɲ] *a* drunken; *nm* drunkard, drunken man, sot.
ivrognerie [ivrɔɲri] *nf* drunkenness.

J

jabot [ʒabo] *nm* jabot, ruffle, frill.
jacasser [ʒakase] *vi* to chatter, jabber.
jachère [ʒaʃɛːr] *nf* untilled land, fallow.
jacinthe [ʒasɛ̃t] *nf* hyacinth.
Jacques [ʒaːk] James.
jacquet [ʒakɛ] *nm* backgammon.
jactance [ʒaktɑ̃ːs] *nf* boasting, brag, boastfulness.
jadis [ʒadis] *ad* once, formerly, in bygone days.
jaillir [ʒajiːr] *vi* to spout, gush (out), spurt, flash.

jaillissement [ʒajismã] *nm* spouting, gushing.

jais [ʒɛ] *nm* jet.

jalon [ʒalɔ̃] *nm* surveyor's staff, rod; landmark.

jalonner [ʒalɔne] *vt* to stake out, mark out, blaze.

jalouser [ʒaluze] *vt* to be jealous of, envy.

jalousie [ʒaluzi] *nf* jealousy, venetian blind, shutter.

jaloux, -ouse [ʒalu, uːz] *a* jealous, anxious.

jamais [ʒamɛ] *ad* ever, never; **ne . . . jamais** never.

jambage [ʒɑ̃baːʒ] *nm* jamb, leg, downstroke.

jambe [ʒɑ̃ːb] *nf* leg, strut; **prendre ses —s à son cou** to take to one's heels; **à toutes —s** as fast as one can.

jambière [ʒɑ̃bjɛːr] *nf* elastic stocking; *pl* leggings, shin-guards, waterproof overtrousers.

jambon [ʒɑ̃bɔ̃] *nm* ham.

jansénisme [ʒɑ̃senism] *nm* Jansenism.

jante [ʒɑ̃ːt] *nf* rim.

janvier [ʒɑ̃vje] *nm* January.

Japon [ʒapɔ̃] *nm* Japan.

japonais [ʒapɔnɛ] *an* Japanese.

jappement [ʒapmɑ̃] *nm* yelping, yapping.

japper [ʒape] *vi* to yelp, yap.

jaquette [ʒakɛt] *nf* (woman's) jacket, morning coat.

jardin [ʒardɛ̃] *nm* garden; **— public** public park; **— potager** kitchen garden; **— d'enfants** kindergarten.

jardinage [ʒardinaːʒ] *nm* gardening.

jardiner [ʒardine] *vi* to garden.

jardinière [ʒardinjɛːr] *nf* flowerstand, window box, market-gardener's cart, mixed vegetables.

jargon [ʒargɔ̃] *nm* jargon, gibberish.

jarre [ʒaːr] *nf* earthenware jar.

jarret [ʒarɛ] *nm* hough, ham, hock

jarretelle [ʒartɛl] *nf* suspender, garter; **porte-jarretelles** *nm* suspender belt, garter belt.

jars [ʒaːr] *nm* gander.

jaser [ʒaze] *vi* to chatter.

jaseur, -euse [ʒazœːr, øːz] *a* talkative; *n* chatterbox.

jasmin [ʒasmɛ̃] *nm* jasmine.

jaspe [ʒasp] *nm* jasper.

jasper [ʒaspe] *vt* to mottle, marble.

jatte [ʒat] *nf* bowl, basin, pan.

jauge [ʒoːʒ] *nf* gauge, tonnage, dipstick.

jauger [ʒoʒe] *vt* to gauge, measure, draw.

jaunâtre [ʒonɑːtr] *a* yellowish.

jaune [ʒoːn] *a nm* yellow; (slang) blackleg; **— d'œuf** yolk (of an egg); **rire —** to smile wryly.

jaunir [ʒoniːr] *vt* to make yellow; *vi* to turn yellow.

jaunisse [ʒonis] *nf* jaundice.

javel [ʒavɛl] *nm* eau de **—** (type of) bleach.

javelle [ʒavɛl] *nf* bundle, swath.

javelot [ʒavlo] *nm* javelin.

je [ʒə] *pn* I.

jésuite [ʒezɥit] *nm* Jesuit.

jet [ʒɛ] *nm* throw(ing), cast, jet, spurt, ray, shoot; **— d'eau** fountain; **d'un seul —** in one piece, at one attempt.

jetée [ʒəte] *nf* jetty, pier.

jeter [ʒəte] *vt* to throw (away), cast, fling, utter; *vr* to throw oneself, attack, fall (upon **sur**), flow (into **dans**).

jeton [ʒətɔ̃] *nm* counter, token.

jeu [ʒø] *nm* game, playing, acting, gambling, stake(s), child's play; **— de cartes** pack of cards; **— de mot** pun; **— de société** parlor game; **ce n'est pas de —** it is not fair (play); **prendre du —** to work loose; **hors —** offside.

jeudi [ʒødi] *nm* Thursday.

jeun [ʒœ̃] *ad* **à —** fasting, on an empty stomach.

jeune [ʒœn] *a* young, youthful, junior.

jeûne [ʒøːn] *nm* fast(ing).

jeûner [ʒøne] *vi* to fast.

jeunesse [ʒœnɛs] *nf* youth, boyhood, girlhood, youthfulness, young people.

joaillerie [ʒwajri] *nf* jeweler's trade, jewelry.

joaillier, -ière [ʒwaje, jɛːr] *n* jeweler.

jobard [ʒɔbaːr] *nm* simpleton, dupe, mug.

joie [ʒwa] *nf* joy, gladness, mirth, merriment; **à cœur —** to one's heart's content; **feu de —** bonfire.

joindre [ʒwɛ̃ːdr] *vtr* to join, unite, combine, add.

joint [ʒwɛ̃] *nm* joint, join.

jointoyer [ʒwɛ̃twaje] *vt* to point.

jointure [ʒwɛ̃tyːr] *nf* join, joint.

joli [ʒɔli] *a* pretty, fine, nice; **c'est du —!** what a mess!

joliment [ʒɔlimɑ̃] *ad* prettily, nicely, awfully.

jonc [ʒɔ̃] *nm* rush, reed, cane.

joncher [ʒɔ̃ʃe] *vt* to strew, litter.

jonction [ʒɔ̃ksjɔ̃] *nf* junction, joining.

jongler [ʒɔ̃gle] *vi* to juggle.

jonglerie [ʒɔ̃gləri] *nf* jugglery, juggling.

jongleur [ʒɔ̃glœːr] *nm* juggler, tumbler.

jonquille [ʒɔ̃kiːj] *nf* jonquil, daffodil.

joue [ʒu] *nf* cheek; **mettre en —** to aim (at).

jouer [ʒwe] *vt* to play, stake, back, act, feign, cheat; *vi* to play, gamble, work, be loose; *vr* to make fun (of **de**); **faire —** to work, set in motion.

jouet [ʒwɛ] *nm* toy, plaything.

joueur, -euse [ʒwœːr, øːz] *a* fond of play, fond of gambling; *n* player, performer, gambler; **être beau —** to be a (good) sport.

joufflu [ʒufly] *a* chubby.

joug [ʒug] *nm* yoke.
jouir [ʒwiːr] *vi* (de) to enjoy.
jouissance [ʒwisãːs] *nf* pleasure, enjoyment, possession.
jouisseur, -euse [ʒwisœːr, øːz] *n* pleasure-seeker, sensualist.
joujou [ʒuʒu] *nm* toy.
jour [ʒuːr] *nm* day, daylight, light, opening; **en plein — ** in broad daylight; **mettre au — ** to bring to light; **sous un autre — ** in another light; **de — en — ** from day to day.
journal [ʒurnal] *nm* newspaper, diary; **— de bord** logbook.
journalier, -ière [ʒurnalje, jeːr] *a* daily; *n* day-laborer.
journalisme [ʒurnalism] *nm* journalism.
journaliste [ʒurnalist] *n* journalist, reporter.
journée [ʒurne] *nf* day, day's work, day's pay.
journellement [ʒurnɛlmã] *ad* daily, every day.
joute [ʒut] *nf* joust, tilting.
jouter [ʒute] *vi* to tilt, joust, fight.
jovial [ʒɔvjal] *a* jovial, jolly.
jovialité [ʒɔvjalite] *nf* joviality, jollity.
joyau [ʒwajo] *nm* jewel.
joyeux, -euse [ʒwajø, øːz] *a* joyous, joyful, merry.
jubilation [ʒybilasjɔ̃] *nf* glee.
jubilé [ʒybile] *nm* jubilee.
jubiler [ʒybile] *vi* to be gleeful, to gloat.
jucher [ʒyʃe] *vti* to perch; *vr* to roost, perch.
juchoir [ʒyʃwaːr] *nm* perch, roosting-place.
judas [ʒyda] *nm* traitor, spy-hole.
judiciaire [ʒydisjeːr] *a* judicial, legal.
judicieux, -euse [ʒydisjø, øːz] *a* judicious, sensible.
juge [ʒyːʒ] *nm* judge, umpire; **— d'instruction** examining magistrate; **— de paix** magistrate.
jugé [ʒyʒe] *nm* **au — ** by guesswork.
jugement [ʒyʒmã] *nm* judgment, trial, sentence, opinion, discrimination.
jugeote [ʒyʒɔt] *nf* common sense, gumption.
juger [ʒyʒe] *vt* to judge, try, sentence, deem, imagine; *vi* to form an opinion of, imagine.
jugulaire [ʒygylɛːr] *a* jugular; *nf* jugular vein, chin-strap.
juif, -ive [ʒɥif, ʒɥiːv] *a* Jewish; *n* Jew, Jewess.
juillet [ʒɥije] *nm* July.
juin [ʒɥɛ̃] *nm* June.
juiverie [ʒɥivri] *nf* Jewry, ghetto.
jujube [ʒyʒyb] *nm* jujube.
jumeau, -elle [ʒymo, ɛl] *an* twin.
jumeler [ʒymle] *vt* to arrange in pairs.
jumelles [ʒymɛl] *nf pl* opera-glasses, field-glasses, binoculars.

jument [ʒymã] *nf* mare.
jungle [ʒɔ̃ːgl] *nf* jungle.
jupe [ʒyp] *nf* skirt.
jupe-culotte [ʒypkylɔt] *nf* divided skirt.
jupon [ʒypɔ̃] *nm* petticoat, underskirt.
juré [ʒyre] *a* sworn; *nm* juryman, juror; *pl* jury.
jurer [ʒyre] *vt* to vow, pledge, swear; *vi* to curse, swear, (*colors*) clash.
juridiction [ʒyridiksjɔ̃] *nf* jurisdiction.
juridique [ʒyridik] *a* juridical, legal, judicial.
juriste [ʒyrist] *nm* jurist.
juron [ʒyrɔ̃] *nm* oath, curse, swearword.
jury [ʒyri] *nm* jury, examining board, selection committee.
jus [ʒy] *nm* juice, gravy.
jusque [ʒysk(ə)] *prep* up to, as far as, until, even; **jusqu'ici** so far, until now; **—là** up to that point, until then; **jusqu'à ce que** until.
juste [ʒyst] *a* just, fair, right, righteous, accurate, tight, scanty; *ad* just. exactly, accurately, barely; **au — ** exactly; **comme de — ** as is only right.
justement [ʒystəmã] *ad* justly, precisely, just; as a matter of fact.
justesse [ʒystɛs] *nf* correctness, accuracy, exactness, soundness; **de — ** only just, just in time.
justice [ʒystis] *nf* justice, fairness, law; **se faire — ** to take the law into one's own hands, to kill oneself.
justicier [ʒystisje] *nm* justiciary.
justifiable [ʒystifjabl] *a* justifiable.
justification [ʒystifikasjɔ̃] *nf* justification, vindication.
justifier [ʒystifje] *vt* to justify, warrant, vindicate, clear; *vr* to justify, vindicate, clear oneself.
jute [ʒyt] *nm* jute.
juteux, -euse [ʒytø, øːz] *a* juicy.
juvénile [ʒyvenil] *a* juvenile, youthful.
juxtaposer [ʒykstapoze] *vt* to place side by side.

K

kangourou [kãguru] *nm* kangaroo.
kapokier [kapɔkje] *nm* silk cotton tree.
karité [karite] *nm* shea butter.
képi [kepi] *nm* peaked cap.
kermesse [kɛrmɛs] *nf* fair.
kif-kif [kifkif] *a inv* (*fam*) likewise.
kilogramme [kilɔgram] *nm* kilogram.
kilomètre [kilɔmɛtr] *nm* kilometer.
kilométrique [kilɔmetrik] *a* kilometric; **borne — ** milestone.
kiosque [kjɔsk] *nm* kiosk, stall, stand, conning-tower.
klaxon [klaksɔ̃] *nm* auto horn.

klaxonner [klaksɔne] *vi* to sound the horn.

kleptomane [klɛptɔman] *an* kleptomaniac.

kolatier [kɔlatje] *nm* kola nut tree.

krach [krak] *nm* (financial) crash, failure.

kyrielle [kirjɛl] *nf* rigmarole, string.

L

l' see **le**.

la [la] *def art pn f* see **le**.

la [la] *nm* musical note A.

là [la] *ad* there, then, that; *excl* there now! c'est — la question that is the question; **d'ici** — in the meantime; oh — —! oh, dear!

là-bas [labɑ] *ad* over there, yonder.

labeur [labœ:r] *nm* labor, hard work.

labial [labjal] *a* labial.

laboratoire [labɔratwa:r] *nm* laboratory.

laborieux, -euse [labɔrjø, ø:z] *a* laborious, hard-working, arduous, hard, slow.

labour [labu:r] *nm pl* plowed land.

labourable [laburabl] *a* arable.

labourage [labura:ʒ] *nm* plowing, tilling.

labourer [labure] *vt* to till, plow (up), furrow.

laboureur [laburœ:r] *nm* plowman.

labyrinthe [labirɛ̃:t] *nm* labyrinth, maze.

lac [lak] *nm* lake, (Scot) loch.

lacer [lase] *vt* to lace (up); *vr* to lace oneself up.

lacérer [lasere] *vt* to lacerate, slash, tear.

lacet [lasɛ] *nm* lace, noose, snare; **en** — winding.

lâchage [lɑʃa:ʒ] *nm* releasing, dropping.

lâche [lɑ:ʃ] *a* cowardly, loose, lax, slack; *n* coward.

lâchement [lɑʃmɑ̃] *ad* in a cowardly way.

lâcher [lɑʃe] *vt* to release, drop, let go, let fly, let loose, let out, set free, divulge, blab out; — **pied** to give ground, give way; — **prise** to let go (one's hold); *nm* release.

lâcheté [lɑʃte] *nf* cowardice, craven, cowardly action.

lacis [lasi] *nm* network.

laconique [lakɔnik] *a* laconic.

lacrymogène [lakrimɔʒɛn] *a* **gaz** — tear gas.

lacté [lakte] *a* milky, lacteal.

lacune [lakyn] *nf* lacuna, gap, break, blank.

là-dedans [ladədɑ̃] *ad* in there, within, in it, in them.

là-dehors [ladəɔ:r] *ad* outside, without.

là-dessous [latsu] *ad* under there,

under that, under it, under them, underneath.

là-dessus [latsy] *ad* on that, on it, on them, thereupon.

ladre [lɑ:dr] *a* mean, stingy; *nm* miser, skinflint.

ladrerie [lɑdrəri] *nf* meanness, niggardliness.

lagune [lagyn] *nf* lagoon.

là-haut [lao] *ad* up there.

laïciser [laisize] *vt* to secularize.

laid [lɛ] *a* ugly, despicable.

laideron, -onne [lɛdrɔ̃, ɔn] *n* plain person.

laideur [lɛdœ:r] *nf* ugliness, meanness.

lainage [lɛna:ʒ] *nm* woolen article, fleece; *pl* woolen goods.

laine [lɛn] *nf* wool; — **filée** yarn; — **peignée** worsted.

lainerie [lɛnri] *nf* woolen mill, -trade, wool-shop.

laineux, -euse [lɛnø, ø:z] *a* woolly, fleecy.

lainier, -ière [lenje, jɛ:r] *a* **industrie lainière** wool trade; *n* woolen-goods manufacturer.

laïque [laik] *a* lay, secular; *nm* layman.

laisse [lɛs] *nf* leash, lead.

laissé-pour-compte [lɛsepu:rkɔ̃:t] *nm* returned goods, rejects, unsold stock.

laisser [lɛse] *vt* to leave, let, allow; **se** — **faire** to submit; — **là quelque-chose** to give up doing something; **ne pas** — **de faire** not to fail to do, to do nevertheless.

laisser-aller [lɛseale] *nm* untidiness, carelessness, neglect.

laisser-faire [lɛsefɛ:r] *nm* non-interference, non-resistance.

laissez-passer [lɛsepase] *nm* pass, permit.

lait [lɛ] *nm* milk; **frère, sœur de** — foster-brother, sister.

laitage [lɛta:ʒ] *nm* dairy produce, milk foods.

laiterie [lɛtri] *nf* dairy.

laiteux, -euse [lɛtø, ø:z] *a* milky.

laitier, -ière [lɛtje, jɛ:r] *a* dairy-, milk-; *n* dairyman, milkman, milkmaid, dairymaid; *nm* slag, dross.

laiton [lɛtɔ̃] *nm* brass.

laitue [lɛty] *nf* lettuce.

laïus [lajy:s] *nm* (fam) speech.

lama [lama] *nm* (animal) llama; (priest) lama.

lambeau [lɑ̃bo] *nm* scrap, shred, rag, tatter.

lambin [lɑ̃bɛ̃] *a* (fam) slow, sluggish; *n* slow-coach.

lambris [lɑ̃bri] *nm* wainscoting, paneling, paneled ceiling.

lambrissage [lɑ̃brisa:ʒ] *nm* wainscoting, paneling.

lame [lam] *nf* blade, strip, slat, wave; — **de fond** groundswell.

lamé [lame] *a* spangled.

lamentable [lamɑ̃tabl] *a* pitiful,

woeful, lamentable, deplorable.
lamentation [lamɑ̃tasjɔ̃] *nf* lament (ation), wail(ing).
se lamenter [səlamɑ̃te] *vr* to lament, wail.
laminer [lamine] *vt* to laminate, roll, calender.
laminoir [laminwa:r] *nm* rolling-mill, roller, calender.
lampadaire [lɑ̃padɛ:r] *nm* standard lamp, candelabrum.
lampe [lɑ̃:p] *nf* lamp, light, torch, valve.
lamper [lɑ̃pe] *vt* to gulp, swig.
lampion [lɑ̃pjɔ̃] *nm* fairy light, Chinese lantern.
lampiste [lɑ̃pist] *n* lampman.
lampisterie [lɑ̃pistəri] *nf* lamproom, lamp works.
lance [lɑ̃:s] *nf* spear, lance, nozzle.
lancé [lɑ̃se] *a* under way, flying; **un homme — a** man who has made his name.
lance-bombes [lɑ̃sbɔ̃:b] *nm* trench mortar, bomb rack.
lance-flammes [lɑ̃sfla:m] *nm* flame-thrower.
lancement [lɑ̃smɑ̃] *nm* throwing, putting, launching, floating, promoting.
lance-pierres [lɑ̃spjɛ:r] *nm* catapult.
lancer [lɑ̃se] *vt* to throw, cast, drop (*bombs*), launch, float, start, set (on, going, on one's feet), put on the market; *vr* to rush, dash, launch (out), plunge.
lance-torpille [lɑ̃stɔrpi:j] *nm* torpedo-tube.
lancette [lɑ̃sɛt] *nf* lancet.
lancier [lɑ̃sje] *nm* lancer.
lancinant [lɑ̃sinɑ̃] *a* shooting, throbbing.
lande [lɑ̃:d] *nf* heath, moor.
langage [lɑ̃ga:ʒ] *nm* language, speech, talk.
lange [lɑ̃:ʒ] *nf* baby's diaper; *pl* swaddling-clothes.
langoureux, -euse [lɑ̃gurø, ø:z] *a* languorous, languid.
langouste [lɑ̃gust] *nf* (spiny) lobster.
langue [lɑ̃:g] *nf* tongue, language, speech; — **verte** slang; **mauvaise —** mischief-maker, slandermonger; **donner sa — aux chats** to give it up.
languette [lɑ̃gɛt] *nf* strip, tongue.
langueur [lɑ̃gœ:r] *nf* languor, list-lessness.
languir [lɑ̃gi:r] *vi* to languish, pine.
languissant [lɑ̃gisɑ̃] *a* listless, languid, dull.
lanière [lanjɛ:r] *nf* strip, strap, thong, lash.
lanterne [lɑ̃tɛrn] *nf* lantern, lamp, light.
lapalissade [lapalisad] *nf* truism, obvious remark.
laper [lape] *vt* to lap (up).
lapidaire [lapidɛ:r] *a* lapidary, concise; *nm* lapidary.

lapider [lapide] *vt* to throw stones at, vilify.
lapin [lapɛ̃] *nm* rabbit, coney; — **de garenne** wild rabbit; **poser un —** to fail to turn up.
laps [laps] *nm* lapse, space of time.
lapsus [lapsy:s] *nm* lapse, mistake, slip.
laquais [lakɛ] *nm* lackey, footman.
laque [lak] *nf* lake, hair-lacquer; — **en écailles** shellac; *nm* lacquer.
laquer [lake] *vt* to lacquer, japan, enamel.
laquelle *rel pn* see **lequel.**
larbin [larbɛ̃] *nm* flunky.
larcin [larsɛ̃] *nm* larceny, petty theft.
lard [la:r] *nm* fat, bacon.
larder [larde] *vt* to lard, inflict, shower, interlard.
large [larʒ] *a* broad, wide, ample, liberal, generous; *nm* space, open sea, breadth; **au — out** at sea; **prendre le — to** put to sea, make off; **au — de off.**
largesse [larʒɛs] *nf* liberality, generosity, largess(e).
largeur [larʒœ:r] *nf* breadth, broadness, width.
larguer [large] *vt* to loose, cast off, unfurl, release.
larme [larm] *nf* tear, drop.
larmoyant [larmwajɑ̃] *a* tearful, maudlin.
larmoyer [larmwaje] *vi* to snivel, shed tears, (*eyes*) water.
larron [larɔ̃] *nm* thief.
larve [larv] *nf* larva, grub.
laryngite [larɛ̃ʒit] *nf* laryngitis.
larynx [larɛ̃:ks] *nm* larynx.
las, lasse [la, la:s] *a* tired, weary.
lascif, -ive [lasif, i:v] *a* lewd.
lasser [lase] *vt* to tire, weary; *vr* to grow tired, weary.
lassitude [lasityd] *nf* weariness.
latent [latɑ̃] *a* latent.
latéral [lateral] *a* lateral, side-cross-.
latin [latɛ̃] *a nm* Latin; — **de cuisine** pig Latin.
latitude [latityd] *nf* latitude, scope.
latte [lat] *nf* lath, slat.
lattis [lati] *nm* lathing, lattice-work.
lauréat [lɔrea, -at] *nm* laureate, prize-winner.
laurier [lɔrje] *nm* laurel, bay.
laurier-rose [lɔrjero:z] *nm* oleander.
lavabo [lavabo] *nm* wash-hand basin, lavatory.
lavande [lavɑ̃:d] *nf* lavender.
lavandière [lavɑ̃djɛ:r] *nf* washer-woman.
lave [la:v] *nf* lava.
lavement [lavmɑ̃] *nm* rectal injection, enema.
laver [lave] *vt* to wash, bathe; *vr* to wash (oneself), have a wash; — **la tête à qn** to give s.o. a good dressing-down.
lavette [lavɛt] *nf* mop, dish-cloth.

laveur, -euse [lavœːr, øːz] n washer, washerwoman, washer-up.

lavis [lavi] nm washing, wash-tint, wash-drawing.

lavoir [lavwaːr] nm wash-house, washboard.

laxatif, -ive [laksatif, iːv] a nm laxative, aperient.

layette [lɛjɛt] nf layette, outfit of baby linen.

lazzi [lazi, ladzi] nm pl jeers.

le, la, l', les [lə, la, l, lɛ] def art the, a (often untranslated); pn him, her, it, them; neut pn so (often untranslated).

léché [leʃe] a finicking, over-polished.

lécher [leʃe] vt to lick.

lécheur, -euse [leʃœːr, øːz] n toady, parasite.

leçon [ləsɔ̃] nf lesson; — de choses object-lesson; **faire la — à qn** to lecture, drill s.o.

lecteur, -trice [lɛktœːr, tris] n reader, (foreign) assistant in French university.

lecture [lɛktyːr] nf reading, perusal; **salle de — reading room.**

ledit, ladite, lesdits, lesdites [lədi, ladit, ledi, ledit] a the aforesaid.

légal [legal] a legal, lawful.

légaliser [legalize] vt to attest, authenticate, legalize.

légalité [legalite] nf legality, lawfulness.

légataire [legateːr] nm legatee, heir.

légation [legasjɔ̃] nf legation.

légendaire [leʒɑ̃dɛːr] a legendary.

légende [leʒɑ̃d] nf legend, inscription, caption, key.

léger, -ère [leʒe, ɛːr] a light, agile, flighty, frivolous, slight, mild, weak; ad **à la légère** lightly, scantily, without due reflection.

légèreté [leʒɛrte] nf lightness, fickleness, levity, agility, mildness, weakness.

légion [leʒjɔ̃] nf legion.

législateur, -trice [leʒislatœːr, tris] a legislative; n legislator, lawgiver.

législatif, -ive [leʒislatif, iːv] a legislative.

législation [leʒislasjɔ̃] nf legislation, laws.

législature [leʒislatyːr] nf legislature, legislative body.

légitime [leʒitim] a legitimate, lawful, justifiable, sound.

légitimer [leʒitime] vt to legitimate, legitimatize, justify.

legs [lɛ] nm legacy, bequest.

léguer [lege] vt to bequeath, leave, will.

légume [legym] nm vegetable; **grosse — bigwig.**

lendemain [lɑ̃dmɛ̃] nm next day, day after, morrow; **sans — short-lived; du jour au — very quickly, from one day to the next.**

lénifiant [lenifjɑ̃] a soothing, relaxing.

lent [lɑ̃] a slow, lingering.

lenteur [lɑ̃tœːr] nf slowness, dilatoriness.

lentille [lɑ̃tiːj] nf lentil, lens.

léopard [leɔpaːr] nm leopard.

lèpre [lɛpr] nf leprosy.

lépreux, -euse [leprø, øːz] a leprous; n leper.

lequel, laquelle, lesquels, lesquelles [ləkɛl, lakɛl, lekɛl] rel pn who, whom, which; inter pn which (one).

léser [leze] vt to injure, wrong.

lésiner [lezine] vi to be mean, close-fisted, haggle (over).

lésion [lezjɔ̃] nf lesion, injury, wrong.

lessive [lɛsiːv] nf wash(ing).

lessiver [lɛsive] vt to wash, scrub.

lessiveuse [lɛsivøːz] nf clothes boiler, washing machine.

lest [lɛst] nm ballast.

leste [lɛst] a light, nimble, smart, flippant, free, spicy (humor).

léthargie [letarʒi] nf lethargy.

léthargique [letarʒik] a lethargic, dull.

lettre [lɛtr] nf letter, note; pl literature, letters; — de change bill of exchange; — de voiture consignment note; **au pied de la — literally; écrire quelque chose en toutes —s** to write something out in full.

lettré [lɛtre] a lettered, literate, well-read; nm scholar.

leu [lø] nm **à la queue — — in single file.**

leur [lœ(ː)r] pos a their; pos pn **le, la —, les —s** theirs; nm their own; pl their own people; pn dat (to) them.

leurre [lœːr] nm lure, decoy, bait, allurement, catch.

leurrer [lœre] vt to lure, decoy, allure, entice; vr to be taken in.

levain [ləvɛ̃] nm leaven, yeast.

levant [ləvɑ̃] a rising (sun); nm East, Orient.

levé [ləve] a raised, up, out of bed; **voter à main —e** vote by show of hands; nm survey.

levée [ləve] nf lifting, adjourning, collection, levy, embankment, (cards) trick.

lever [ləve] vt to raise, lift (up), collect, levy, remove, cut off, (camp) strike, adjourn, (anchor) weigh, (survey) effect; vi to shoot, rise; vr to stand up, get up, rise, (day) dawn; nm rising, levee, survey; — de rideau curtain-raiser; — du soleil sunrise.

levier [ləvje] nm lever, crowbar; — de commande control lever.

lèvre [lɛːvr] nf lip, rim; **du bout des —s** forced, disdainful.

lévrier [levrie] nm greyhound.

levure [ləvyːr] nf yeast.

lexicographe [lɛksikɔgraf] nm lexicographer.

lexique [lɛksik] nm lexicon, glossary.

lézard [lezaːr] nm lizard; **faire le —** to bask in the sun.
lézarde [lezard] nf crevice, crack, chink.
lézarder [lezarde] vt to crack, split; vir to lounge, sun oneself.
liaison [ljɛzɔ̃] nf joining, binding, connection, linking, liaison, slur, (mus) tie.
liant [ljɑ̃] a friendly, engaging, responsive, flexible, pliant; nm friendly disposition, flexibility.
liasse [ljas] nf bundle, wad.
libation [libasjɔ̃] nf libation, drinking.
libelle [libɛl] nm lampoon, libel.
libeller [libɛlle] vt to draw up.
libellule [libɛllyl] nf dragonfly.
libéral [liberal] an liberal, broad, generous.
libéralité [liberalite] nf liberality, generosity.
libérateur, -trice [liberatœːr, tris] a liberating; n liberator.
libération [liberasjɔ̃] nf liberation, release, discharge.
libérer [libere] vt to liberate, release, free, discharge.
liberté [libɛrte] nf liberty, freedom.
libertin [libɛrtɛ̃] a licentious, dis-solute, wayward; n libertine, rake, free-thinker.
libertinage [libɛrtinaːʒ] nm dissolute ways.
libraire [librɛːr] nm bookseller.
librairie [librɛri] nf book-trade, bookshop.
libre [libr] a free, clear, open, disengaged, unoccupied, vacant, for hire.
libre-échange [librefɑ̃ːʒ] nm free-trade.
libre-service [librəsɛrvis] nm self-service.
licence [lisɑ̃ːs] nf license, excessive liberty, permission, certificate, bachelor's degree.
licencié [lisɑ̃sje] nm licentiate, licensee, license-holder; **— ès lettres** (approx) B.A.; **— en droit** (approx) Ll.B.; **— ès sciences** (approx) B.Sc.
licencier [lisɑ̃sje] vt to disband, sack, dismiss.
licencieux, -euse [lisɑ̃sjø, øːz] a licentious.
licite [lisit] a licit, lawful.
licorne [likɔrn] nf unicorn.
licou [liku] nm halter.
lie [li] nf lees, dregs.
lié [lje] a bound, tied, friendly, intimate.
liebig [libig] nm beef extract.
liège [ljɛːʒ] nm cork.
lien [ljɛ̃] nm bond, tie.
lier [lje] vt to bind, tie (up), link, join, (sauce) thicken; **— amitié avec qn** to strike up an acquaintance with s.o.; vr to become friendly, intimate (with avec).
lierre [ljɛːr] nm ivy.

lieu [ljø] nm place, spot, scene; pl premises; **en premier, dernier —** firstly, lastly; **avoir — to take place, have every reason (to); donner — to give rise (to à); tenir — to take the place (of de); au — de instead of.
lieue [ljø] nf league.
lieuse [ljøːz] nf (mechanical) binder.
lieutenant [ljøtnɑ̃] nm lieutenant, mate; **— de vaisseau** lieutenant-commander.
lièvre [ljɛːvr] nm hare; **mémoire de — memory like a sieve.
liftier, -ière [liftje, jɛːr] n elevator man, boy, girl, operator.
ligaturer [ligatyre] vt to tie up, bind, ligature.
ligne [liɲ] nf line, cord, row; **hors — outstanding, out of the common; **à la — new paragraph.
lignée [liɲe] nf issue, stock, descendants.
lignite [liɲit] nf lignite.
ligoter [ligɔte] vt to bind, tie up.
ligue [lig] nf league.
liguer [lige] vt to league; vr to form a league.
lilas [lila] a nm lilac.
limace [limas] nf slug.
limaçon [limasɔ̃] nm snail; **en — spiral.
limande [limɑ̃ːd] nf dab.
lime [lim] nf file.
limer [lime] vt to file (up, off, down), (verses) polish.
limier [limje] nm bloodhound.
limitation [limitasjɔ̃] nf restriction.
limite [limit] nf limit, boundary; pl bounds; a maximum.
limiter [limite] vt to limit, mark the bounds of.
limitrophe [limitrɔf] a adjacent, bordering.
limoger [limɔʒe] vt to relegate.
limon [limɔ̃] nm mud, silt, lime.
limonade [limɔnad] nf lemonade.
limoneux, -euse [limɔnø, øːz] a muddy.
limpide [lɛ̃pid] a limpid.
limpidité [lɛ̃pidite] nm limpidity, clarity.
lin [lɛ̃] nm flax, linseed, linen.
linceul [lɛ̃sœl] nm shroud.
linéaire [lineɛːr] a linear.
linéal [lineal] a lineal.
linéament [lineamɑ̃] nm lineament, feature.
linge [lɛ̃ːʒ] nm linen.
lingère [lɛ̃ʒɛːr] nf seamstress.
lingerie [lɛ̃ʒri] nf underwear, linen-room.
linguiste [lɛ̃gɥist] n linguist.
linguistique [lɛ̃gɥistik] a linguistic; nf linguistics.
linoléum [linɔleɔm] nm linoleum.
linon [linɔ̃] nm lawn, buckram.
linotte [linɔt] nf linnet; **tête de — feather-brained person.
linteau [lɛ̃to] nm lintel.
lion. -onne [ljɔ̃, ɔn] n lion, lioness.

lionceau [ljɔ̃so] nm lion cub.
lippu [lipy] a thick-lipped.
liquéfier [likefje] vt to liquefy.
liqueur [likœːr] nm liquor, drink, liqueur, liquid.
liquidation [likidasjɔ̃] nf liquidation, settlement, clearing, selling off.
liquide [likid] a liquid, ready; nm liquid.
liquider [likide] vt to liquidate, settle, sell off, finish off.
liquoreux, -euse [likɔrø, øːz] a liqueur-like, sweet.
lire [liːr] vt to read.
lis [lis] nm lily.
liséré [lizere] nm border, edge, piping, binding.
lisérer [lizere] vt to border, edge, pipe.
liseron [lizrɔ̃] nm bindweed.
liseur, -euse [lizœːr, øːz] a reading; n reader.
liseuse [lizøːz] nf dust-jacket, bookmarker, bed-jacket.
lisibilité [lizibilite] nf legibility.
lisible [lizibl] a legible.
lisière [lizjɛːr] nf edge, border, selvage, list, leading-strings.
lisse [lis] a smooth, polished.
lisser [lise] vt to smooth, polish, preen.
liste [list] nf list, roster, register.
lit [li] nm bed, layer, bottom; — de sangle camp-bed; **enfant du second** — child of the second marriage.
litanie [litani] nf litany, rigmarole.
lit-armoire [liarmwaːr] nm boxbed.
literie [litri] nf bedding.
lithographie [litɔgrafi] nf lithograph(y).
litière [litjɛːr] nf litter.
litige [litiːʒ] nm litigation, lawsuit; en — under dispute.
litigieux, -euse [litiʒjø, øːz] a litigious.
litre [litr] nm liter.
littéraire [literɛːr] a literary.
littéral [literal] a literal, written.
littérateur [literatœːr] nm man of letters.
littérature [literatyːr] nf literature.
littoral [litɔral] a littoral, coastal; nm seaboard.
liturgie [lityrʒi] nf liturgy.
liturgique [lityrʒik] a liturgical.
livide [livid] a livid, ghastly.
livraison [livrɛzɔ̃] nf delivery, part, installment; à — on delivery.
livre [liːvr] nf pound; nm book; — de poche paperback.
livrée [livre] nf livery.
livrer [livre] vt to deliver, surrender, give up, hand over; — bataille to give, join battle; vr to give oneself up, confide (in à), indulge (in), take (to).
livresque [livrɛsk] a book, bookish.
livret [livrɛ] nm small book, booklet, handbook, libretto.

livreur, -euse [livrœːr, øːz] n delivery-man, -boy, -girl.
lobe [lɔb] nm lobe, flap.
local [lɔkal] a local; nm premises, building, quarters.
localiser [lɔkalize] vt to localize, locate.
localité [lɔkalite] nf locality, place, spot.
locataire [lɔkatɛːr] n tenant, lessee, lodger.
location [lɔkasjɔ̃] nf hiring, letting, renting, booking; en — on hire; **agent de** — renting agent.
locomotive [lɔkɔmɔtiv] nf locomotive, engine.
locomotion [lɔkɔmosjɔ̃] nf locomotion.
locution [lɔkysjɔ̃] nf expression, phrase.
lof [lɔf] nm (naut) windward side.
logarithme [lɔgaritm] nm logarithm.
loge [lɔːʒ] nf lodge, box, dressing-room.
logement [lɔʒmɑ̃] nm lodging(s), accommodation, billet(ing), housing.
loger [lɔʒe] vi to lodge, live, be billeted; vt to lodge, house, billet, stable, put, place; vr to lodge, find a home, a place.
logeur, -euse [lɔʒœːr, øz] n landlord -lady.
logique [lɔʒik] a logical, reasoned; nf logic.
logis [lɔʒi] nm dwelling, home, lodgings, accommodations.
loi [lwa] nf law, act, rule; **projet de** — bill.
loin [lwɛ̃] ad far, a long way off; au — in the distance, far and wide; de — from a distance; de — en — at long intervals, now and then.
lointain [lwɛ̃tɛ̃] a distant, far-off; nm distance.
loir [lwaːr] nm dormouse.
loisible [lwazibl] a permissible, convenient.
loisir [lwaziːr] nm leisure, spare time.
londonien, -enne [lɔ̃dɔnjɛ̃, jɛn] n Londoner.
Londres [lɔ̃ːdr] nm London.
long [lɔ̃] a long, lengthy, slow; nm length; à la longue in the long run; de — en large up and down, to and fro; le — de along(side); tout le — du jour the whole day long; en dire — to speak volumes; en savoir — to know a lot.
longe [lɔ̃ːʒ] nf halter.
longer [lɔ̃ʒe] vt to skirt, hug, run alongside.
longeron [lɔ̃ʒrɔ̃] nm girder, beam, tail-boom, spar.
longévité [lɔ̃ʒevite] nf longevity, expectation of life.
longitude [lɔ̃ʒityd] nf longitude.
longtemps [lɔ̃tɑ̃] ad long, a long time.
longuement [lɔ̃gmɑ̃] ad for a long time, at length.

longueur [lɔ̃gœːr] *nf* length; *pl* tedious passages; **tirer en — to** drag on, spin out.

longue-vue [lɔ̃gvy] *nf* telescope, field-glass.

looping [lupiŋ] *nm* **faire du —** to loop the loop.

lopin [lɔpɛ̃] *nm* plot, allotment.

loquace [lɔkwas] *a* loquacious, talkative.

loquacité [lɔkwasite] *nf* loquacity, talkativeness.

loque [lɔk] *nf* rag.

loquet [lɔkɛ] *nm* latch.

loqueteux, -euse [lɔktø, øːz] *a* tattered, ragged.

lorgnade [lɔrɲad] *nf* sidelong glance.

lorgner [lɔrɲe] *vt* to cast a (sidelong) glance at, have a covetous eye on, make eyes at, ogle.

lorgnette [lɔrɲɛt] *nf* opera-glasses.

lorgnon [lɔrɲɔ̃] *nm* eyeglasses, pince-nez.

loriot [lɔrjo] *nm* oriole.

lors [lɔːr] *ad* **depuis, dès —** from that time, ever since then; — **même que** even when; — **de** at the time of.

lorsque [lɔrsk(ə)] *cj* when.

losange [lɔzɑ̃ːʒ] *nm* lozenge; **en —** diamond-shaped.

lot [lo] *nm* share, portion, lot, prize; **gros —** first prize.

loterie [lɔtri] *nf* lottery, raffle, draw.

lotion [losjɔ̃] *nf* lotion.

lotir [lɔtiːr] *vt* to divide into lots, sort out, allot.

lotissement [lɔtismɑ̃] *nm* dividing into lots, selling in lots, building site, housing estate.

lotte [lɔt] *nf* burbot.

louable [lwabl, lu-] *a* praiseworthy, commendable.

louage [lwaːʒ, lu-] *nm* hire, hiring, letting out.

louange [lwɑ̃ːʒ] *nf* praise.

louche [luʃ] *a* ambiguous, suspicious, queer; *nf* ladle.

loucher [luʃe] *vi* to squint, (*fam*) to look enviously (at **sur**).

louer [lwe, lue] *vt* to hire (out), let (out), rent, reserve, praise, commend; *vr* to engage, hire oneself, be pleased, satisfied (with), congratulate oneself (upon **de**).

loueur, -euse [lwœːr, lu-, øːz] *n* hirer, renter.

loufoque [lufɔk] *a* cracked, crazy.

loulou [lulu] *nm* Pomeranian dog.

loup [lu] *nm* wolf, black velvet mask, flaw, error; **à pas de —** stealthily; **avoir une faim de —** to be ravenously hungry; **un froid de —** bitter cold; **quand on parle du —, on en voit la queue** talk of the devil and he's sure to appear; **— de mer** old salt, sea dog.

loup-cervier [lusɛrvje] *nm* lynx.

loupe [lup] *nf* lens, magnifying glass, wen.

louper [lupe] *vt* to bungle, make a mess of.

loup-garou [lugaru] *nm* werewolf.

lourd [luːr] *a* heavy, ponderous, ungainly, dull(witted), close, sultry.

lourdaud [lurdo] *a* loutish, clumsy, dullwitted; *n* lout, blockhead.

lourdeur [lurdœːr] *nf* heaviness, ponderousness, ungainliness, dullness, sultriness.

loustic [lustik] *nm* joker, wag.

loutre [lutr] *nf* otter.

louve [luːv] *nf* she-wolf.

louveteau [luvto] *nm* wolf-cub.

louvoyer [luvwaje] *vi* to tack, maneuver.

loyal [lwajal] *a* loyal, true, upright, fair.

loyauté [lwajote] *nf* loyalty, fidelity, uprightness, honesty, fairness.

loyer [lwaje] *nm* rent.

lubie [lybi] *nf* whim, fad.

lubricité [lybrisite] *nf* lewdness.

lubrifiant [lybrifjɑ̃] *a* lubricating; *nm* lubricant.

lubrique [lybrik] *a* lewd.

lucarne [lykarn] *nf* attic window, skylight.

lucide [lysid] *a* lucid, clear.

lucidité [lysidite] *nf* lucidity, clearness.

luciole [lysjɔl] *nf* fire-fly.

lucratif, -ive [lykratif, iːv] *a* lucrative, profitable.

luette [lɥɛt] *nf* uvula.

lueur [lɥœːr] *nf* gleam, glimmer, light.

luge [lyːʒ] *nf* toboggan.

lugubre [lygyːbr] *a* lugubrious, gloomy, dismal.

lui [lɥi] *pers pn dat* (to) him, her, it, from him, her, it; *disj pn* he, him; **—-même** himself.

luire [lɥiːr] *vi* to shine, gleam.

luisant [lɥizɑ̃] *a* shining, gleaming; *nm* gloss, sheen.

lumière [lymjɛːr] *nf* light; *pl* understanding, knowledge, enlightenment.

lumignon [lymiɲɔ̃] *nm* candle-end, dim light.

lumineux, -euse [lyminø, øːz] *a* luminous, bright.

luminosité [lyminozite] *nf* luminosity.

lunaire [lynɛːr] *a* lunar.

lunatique [lynatik] *a* whimsical, capricious, moody.

lundi [lœ̃di] *nm* Monday.

lune [lyn] *nf* moon; **clair de —** moonlight; **être dans la —** to be wool-gathering; **— de miel** honeymoon.

lunetier [lyntje] *nm* spectacle-maker, optician.

lunette [lynɛt] *nf* telescope, wishbone, (*toilet*) seat; *pl* spectacles, goggles; **— de soleil** sunglasses.

lupin [lypɛ̃] *nm* lupin.

lurette [lyrɛt] *nf* **il y a belle —** a long time ago.

luron,-onne [lyrɔ̃, ɔn] *n* strapping lad (lass), lively fellow, tomboy.
lustre [lystr] *nm* polish, gloss, chandelier, period of five years.
lustrer [lystre] *vt* to polish (up), gloss, glaze.
lustrine [lystrin] *nf* cotton luster.
luth [lyt] *nm* lute.
luthier [lytje] *nm* violin-maker.
lutin [lytɛ̃] *a* mischievous; *nm* sprite, imp.
lutiner [lytine] *vt* to tease, torment.
lutrin [lytrɛ̃] *nm* lectern.
lutte [lyt] *nf* struggle, contest, strife, wrestling; **de haute —** by force (of arms), hard-won.
lutter [lyte] *vi* to struggle, compete, fight, wrestle.
luxe [lyks] *nm* luxury, profusion, superfluity; **de —** first-class, luxury.
luxer [lykse] *vt* to dislocate, put out of joint.
luxueux, -euse [lyksɥø, ø:z] *a* luxurious, sumptuous.
luxure [lyksy:r] *nf* lewdness.
luxurieux, -euse [lyksyrjø, ø:z] *a* lewd, lustful.
luzerne [lyzɛrn] *nf* lucerne, alfalfa.
lycée [lise] *nm* secondary school.
lycéen, -enne [liseɛ̃, ɛn] *n* pupil, schoolboy, -girl.
lymphatique [lɛ̃fatik] *a* lymphatic.
lyncher [lɛ̃ʃe] *vt* to lynch.
lynx [lɛ̃ks] *nm* lynx.
lyre [li:r] *nf* lyre.
lyrique [lirik] *a* lyric(al); *nm* lyric poet.
lyrisme [lirism] *nm* lyricism, enthusiasm.
lys [lis] *nm* lily.

M

ma [ma] *af* see **mon.**
maboul [mabul] *a* crazy, cracked, mad.
macabre [maka:br] *a* grim, gruesome; **danse —** Dance of Death.
macadamiser [makadamize] *vt* to macadamize.
macaron [makarɔ̃] *nm* macaroon, rosette.
macaroni [makarɔni] *nm* macaroni.
macédoine [masedwan] *nf* salad, hodgepodge.
macérer [masere] *vt* to macerate, steep, mortify.
mâchefer [maʃfɛ:r] *nm* clinker, slag, dross.
mâché [maʃe] *a* chewed, worn, ragged, frayed.
mâcher [maʃe] *vt* to chew, munch, champ; **ne pas — ses mots** not to mince one's words.
machiavélique [makjavelik] *a* Machiavellian.
mâchicoulis [maʃikuli] *nm* machicolation.

machin [maʃɛ̃] *nm* thing, contraption, thingummy.
machinal [maʃinal] *a* mechanical.
machinateur, -trice [maʃinatœ:r, tris] *n* machinator, schemer, intriguer.
machination [maʃinasjɔ̃] *nf* machination, plot.
machine [maʃin] *nf* machine, engine, contraption; *pl* machinery; **— à écrire** typewriter; **fait à la —** machine made.
machine-outil [maʃinuti] *n* machine-tool.
machiner [maʃine] *vt* to plot, scheme.
machinerie [maʃinri] *nf* machine construction, machinery, plant, engine-room.
machinisme [maʃinism] *nm* mechanism, (use of) machinery.
machiniste [maʃinist] *nm* stagehand.
mâchoire [maʃwa:r] *nf* jaw, jawbone.
mâchonner [maʃɔne] *vt* to chew, munch, mumble.
maçon [masɔ̃] *nm* mason, bricklayer.
maçonner [masɔne] *vt* to build, face with stone, brick up.
maçonnerie [masɔnri] *nf* masonry, stonework.
maçonnique [masɔnik] *a* masonic.
macule [makyl] *nf* stain, blemish, spot.
maculer [makyle]*vti* to stain, spot, blur.
madame [madam] *nf* Mrs, madam.
madeleine [madlɛn] *nf* sponge-cake.
mademoiselle [madmwazɛl] *nf* Miss.
madone [madɔn] *nf* Madonna.
madré [madre] *a* wily, mottled; *n* wily bird.
madrier [madrie] *nm* beam, joist, thick plank.
madrigal [madrigal] *nm* madrigal.
madrilène [madrilɛn] *a* of Madrid.
magasin [magazɛ̃] *nm* shop, store, warehouse, (*mil*) magazine.
magasinage [magazina:ʒ] *nm* storing, warehouse dues.
magasinier [magazinje] *nm* warehouseman, storekeeper.
magazine [magazin] *nm* magazine.
mage [ma:ʒ] *nm* seer; *pl* wise men.
magicien, -ienne [maʒisjɛ̃, ɛn] *n* magician, wizard.
magie [maʒi] *nf* magic, wizardry.
magique [maʒik] *a* magic(al).
magistral [maʒistral] *a* magisterial, masterly.
magistrat [maʒistra] *nm* magistrate, judge.
magistrature [maʒistraty:r] *nf* magistracy.
magnanerie [maɲanri] *nf* rearing-house for silkworms, sericulture.
magnanime [maɲanim] *a* magnanimous, great-hearted.

magnanimité [maɲanimite] *nf* magnanimity.

magnésie [maɲezi] *nf* magnesia.

magnétique [maɲetik] *a* magnetic.

magnétiser [maɲetize] *vt* to magnetize, hypnotize, mesmerize.

magnétisme [maɲetism] *nm* magnetism, hypnotism, mesmerism.

magnéto [maɲeto] *nm* magneto.

magnétophone [maɲetɔfɔn] *nm* tape-recorder.

magnificence [maɲifisɑ̃:s] *nf* magnificence, splendor, liberality, munificence.

magnifier [maɲifje] *vt* to glorify, exalt.

magnifique [maɲifik] *a* magnificent, sumptuous, grand.

magot [mago] *nm* small ape, grotesque porcelain figure, ugly man, (*money*) hoard.

mahométan [maɔmetɑ̃] *a* Mohammedan, Moslem.

mai [mɛ] *nm* May.

maigre [mɛ:gr] *a* thin, lean, scanty, frugal, meager, poor; *nm* lean (*of meat*); **faire —** to fast; **jour —** fast-day; **repas —** meatless meal.

maigreur [mɛgrœ:r] *nf* leanness, thinness, scantiness.

maigrir [mɛgri:r] *vt* to make thin (ner), thin down; *vi* to grow thin, lose weight.

mail [ma:j] *nm* avenue, public walk, mall.

maille [mɑ:j] *nf* mesh, link, stitch, speckle; **cotte de —s** coat of mail.

maillet [majɛ] *nm* mallet.

maillon [majɔ̃] *nm* link, shackle; **— tournant** swivel.

maillot [majo] *nm* swaddling-clothes, jersey, singlet, tights; **— de bain** bathing suit.

main [mɛ̃] *nf* hand, handwriting, (*cards*) hand, quire; **— courante** handrail; **coup de —** surprise attack, helping hand; **sous la —** to, at hand; **à pleines —s** liberally, in handfuls; **fait à la —** handmade; **se faire la —** to get one's hand in; **avoir perdu la —** to be out of practice; **gagner haut la —** to win hands down; **ne pas y aller de — morte** to go at it; **avoir la — dure** to be a martinet; **en venir aux —s** to come to blows; **mettre la dernière — à** to put the finishing touch to.

main d'œuvre [mɛ̃dœ:vr] *nf* manpower, labor.

main-forte [mɛ̃fɔrt] *nf* help, assistance.

mainmise [mɛ̃mi:z] *nf* seizure.

mainmorte [mɛ̃mɔrt] *nf* mortmain.

maint [mɛ̃] *a* many a; **à —es reprises** many a time.

maintenant [mɛ̃tnɑ̃] *ad* now; **dès —** from now on, even now.

maintenir [mɛ̃tni:r] *vt* to support, hold up, maintain, uphold; *vr* to keep, continue, hold one's own.

maintien [mɛ̃tjɛ̃] *nm* maintenance, keeping, demeanor, bearing.

maire [mɛ:r] *nm* mayor.

mairie [mɛri] *nf* town hall, municipal buildings.

mais [mɛ] *but; excl* why! *adv* more; **je n'en peux —** I can't help it.

maïs [mais] *nm* maize, Indian corn.

maison [mɛzɔ̃] *nf* house, household, family, dynasty, firm; **— de santé** nursing-home; **— de fous** lunatic asylum; **— de correction** reformatory; **garder la —** to stay indoors, at home.

maisonnée [mɛzɔne] *nf* household, family.

maisonnette [mɛzɔnɛt] *nf* cottage, small house.

maître, -esse [mɛ:tr, mɛtrɛs] *a* principal, main, chief, out and out, utter; *n* master, mistress; **— de conférences** lecturer; **— d'équipage** boatswain; **premier —** chief petty officer; **— d'hôtel** butler, head-waiter, chief steward; **maîtresse femme** capable woman.

maître-autel [mɛtrotɛl] *nm* high altar.

maîtrise [mɛtri:z] *nf* command, mastery, control, self-control; choir-school.

maîtriser [mɛtrize] *vt* to master, curb, subdue; *vr* to keep control of oneself.

majesté [maʒɛste] *nf* majesty, grandeur.

majestueux, -euse [maʒɛstɥø, ø:z] *a* majestic, stately.

majeur [maʒœ:r] *a* major, greater, chief, important, of age; **force —e** absolute necessity, compulsion.

major [maʒɔ:r] *nm* regimental adjutant, medical officer.

majoration [maʒɔrasjɔ̃] *nf* overvaluation, increase, additional charge.

majordome [maʒɔrdɔm] *nm* majordomo, steward.

majorer [maʒɔre] *vt* to overvalue, raise, put up the price of, make an additional charge.

majorité [maʒɔrite] *nf* majority, coming of age.

majuscule [maʒyskyl] *a nf* capital (letter).

mal [mal] *nm* evil, wrong, harm, hurt, ache, malady, difficulty, trouble; *ad* badly, ill; **— lui en a pris** he had cause to rue it; **prendre en —** to take amiss; **avoir — au cœur** to feel sick; **avoir — à la tête** to have a headache; **se trouver —** to feel faint; **avoir le — du pays** to be homesick; **se donner du — pour** to take pains to; **tant bien que —** somehow or other; **pas — de** a good lot of, a good many; **elle n'est pas — ** she is not bad looking; **on est très — ici** we are very uncomfortable here.

malade [malad] *a* ill, sick, upset, sore, painful; *n* invalid, sick person, patient; **se faire porter —** to report sick.

maladie [maladi] *nf* illness, complaint, ailment, disease, disorder.

maladif, -ive [maladif, iːv] *a* sickly, unhealthy.

maladresse [maladrɛs] *nf* awkwardness, clumsiness, lack of skill, slip, blunder.

maladroit [maladrwa] *a* clumsy, unskillful; *n* blunderer.

malaise [malɛːz] *nm* discomfort, faintness, indisposition, uneasiness.

malappris [malapri] *a* uncouth; *n* ill-bred person.

malavisé [malavize] *a* indiscreet, unwise, rash.

malchance [malʃɑ̃ːs] *nf* (piece of) bad luck.

malchanceux, -euse [malʃɑ̃sø, øːz] *a* unlucky, unfortunate.

maldonne [maldɔn] *nf* misdeal.

mâle [mɑːl] *a* male, manly, he-, dog-, cock-, buck-; *nm* male.

malédiction [malediksjɔ̃] *nf* curse.

maléfice [malefis] *nm* evil spell.

maléfique [malefik] *a* evil, baleful, maleficent.

malencontreux, -euse [malɑ̃kɔ̃trø, øːz] *a* untoward, unlucky, tiresome.

malentendu [malɑ̃tɑ̃dy] *nm* misunderstanding.

malfaçon [malfasɔ̃] *nf* bad workmanship.

malfaisant [malfəzɑ̃] *a* evil, harmful.

malfaiteur, -trice [malfɛtœːr, tris] *n* malefactor, evil-doer.

malfamé [malfame] *a* of ill repute.

malgache [malgaʃ] *an* Madagascan.

malgré [malgre] *prep* in spite of, notwithstanding; *cj* **— que** in spite of, although.

malhabile [malabil] *a* awkward, clumsy.

malheur [malœːr] *nm* misfortune, ill luck; **jouer de —** to be out of luck.

malheureux, -euse [malœrø, øːz] *a* unhappy, wretched, unfortunate, unlucky.

malhonnête [malɔnɛt] *a* dishonest, rude, improper.

malhonnêteté [malɔnɛtte] *nf* dishonesty, dishonest action, rudeness, rude remark.

malice [malis] *nf* malice, spitefulness, mischievousness, roguishness, trick; **n'y pas entendre —** to mean no harm.

malicieux, -euse [malisjø, øːz] *a* mischievous, naughty.

malignité [maliɲite] *nf* spite, malignancy.

malin, -igne [malɛ̃, iɲ] *a* malicious, mischievous, sly, shrewd, malignant; **ce n'est pas —** that's easy enough.

malingre [malɛ̃ːgr] *a* sickly, weakly, puny.

malintentionné [malɛ̃tɑ̃sjɔne] *a* ill-disposed, evil-minded.

malle [mal] *nf* trunk, box; **faire sa —** to pack one's trunk.

malléable [maleabl] *a* malleable, pliable, soft.

malle-poste [malpɔst] *nf* mail car.

mallette [malɛt] *nf* small trunk.

malmener [malməne] *vt* to ill-treat, ill-use, treat roughly, put through it.

malodorant [malɔdɔrɑ̃] *a* evil-smelling.

malotru [malɔtry] *a* ill-bred, coarse; *nm* boor, lout.

malpeigné [malpɛɲe] *n* slut, slovenly person.

malpropre [malprɔpr] *a* dirty, untidy, indecent, dishonest.

malpropreté [malprɔprəte] *nf* dirtiness, untidiness, unsavoriness, dishonesty.

malsain [malsɛ̃] *a* unhealthy, unwholesome, corrupting.

malséant [malseɑ̃] *a* unseemly, unbecoming.

malt [malt] *nm* malt.

maltraiter [maltrɛte] *vt* to ill-treat.

malveillance [malvɛjɑ̃ːs] *nf* malevolence, spitefulness, foul play.

malveillant [malvɛjɑ̃] *a* malevolent, spiteful.

malvenu [malvəny] *a* ill-advised, unjustified.

malversation [malvɛrsasjɔ̃] *nf* embezzlement.

maman [mamɑ̃] *nf* mummy, mama.

mamelle [mamɛl] *nf* breast, udder.

mamelon [mamlɔ̃] *nf* nipple, teat, rounded hillock.

mammifère [mamifɛːr] *nm* mammal.

mamour [mamuːr] *nm* my love; *pl* **faire des —s à quelqu'un** to cuddle, coax someone.

manche [mɑ̃ːʃ] *nf* sleeve, hose-pipe, game, set, round, heat; **la Manche** the English Channel; *nm* handle, shaft, stock, joy-stick.

mancheron [mɑ̃ʃrɔ̃] *nm* handle (of plow), short sleeve.

manchette [mɑ̃ʃɛt] *nf* cuff, wristband, newspaper headline, marginal note; *pl* handcuffs.

manchon [mɑ̃ʃɔ̃] *nm* muff, socket, sleeve, casing, gas-mantle.

manchot [mɑ̃ʃo] *an* one-armed (person); penguin.

mandarine [mɑ̃darin] *nf* tangerine.

mandat [mɑ̃da] *nm* mandate, commission, money order, warrant; **— de comparution** summons.

mandataire [mɑ̃datɛːr] *n* mandatory, agent, proxy.

mandat-poste [mɑ̃dapɔst] *nm* postal money order.

mander [mɑ̃de] *vt* to send for, summon, send word to; *vi* to report.

mandibule [mɑ̃dibyl] *nf* mandible.

mandoline [mɑ̃dɔlin] *nf* mandolin.

mandragore [mãdragɔːr] *nf* mandragora, mandrake.

manège [manɛːʒ] *nm* training of horses, horsemanship, riding-school, trick, little game; — de chevaux de bois roundabout, merry-go-round.

manette [manɛt] *nf* hand lever, handle.

manganèse [mãganɛːz] *nm* manganese.

mangeable [mãʒabl] *a* eatable, edible.

mangeaille [mãzaːj] *nf* food, grub.

mangeoire [mãʒwaːr] *nf* manger, trough.

manger [mãʒe] *vt* to eat (up, away, into), squander; *nm* food; **donner à** — à to feed, give sth to eat to.

mange-tout [mãʒtu] *nm* spendthrift, string-bean.

mangouste [mãgust] *nf* mongoose.

mangue [mãːg] *nf* mango.

maniable [manjabl] *a* manageable, easily handled, handy.

maniaque [manjak] *a* raving mad, faddy; *n* maniac, crank.

manie [mani] *nf* mania, craze, fad.

maniement [manimã] *nm* handling; — d'armes rifle drill.

manier [manje] *vt* to handle, ply, wield, control, feel.

manière [manjɛːr] *nf* manner, way; *pl* manners, affected airs; à sa — in his own way; à la — de after, in the manner of; de cette — in this way; d'une — ou d'une autre somehow or other; en — de by way of; arranger qn de la belle — to give s.o. a thorough dressing-down.

maniéré [manjere] *a* affected, mincing.

maniérisme [manjerism] *nm* mannerism.

manifestant [manifɛstã] *n* demonstrator.

manifestation [manifɛstasjɔ̃] *nf* (public) demonstration, manifestation.

manifeste [manifɛst] *a* manifest, obvious, evident, patent; *nm* manifesto.

manifester [manifɛste] *vt* to manifest, display, reveal, show, express; *vi* to demonstrate; *vr* to show, reveal itself, appear, become apparent.

manigance [manigãːs] *nf* intrigue, scheme, game; *pl* underhand work, trickery.

manigancer [manigãse] *vt* to plot, scheme, arrange, be up to.

manille [maniːj] *nf* ankle-ring, shackle, manille.

manioc [manjɔk] *nm* cassava.

manipulateur, -trice [manipylatœːr, tris] *n* manipulator.

manipuler [manipyle] *vt* to manipulate, operate, handle, arrange.

manitou [manitu] *nm* **le grand** — the big boss.

manivelle [manivɛl] *nf* handle, crank, starting-handle.

manne [man] *nf* manna, basket, hamper.

mannequin [mankɛ̃] *nm* small hamper, manikin, dummy, mannequin.

manœuvrable [manœvrabl] *a* easily handled.

manœuvre [manœːvr] *nf* working, handling, maneuver, drill, shunting, scheme, move; *nm* laborer.

manœuvrer [manœvre] *vt* to work, operate, handle, maneuver, shunt; *vi* to maneuver, scheme.

manoir [manwaːr] *nm* manor, country house.

manomètre [manɔmɛtr] *nm* pressure-gauge.

manquant [mãkã] *a* missing, wanting, absent; *n* absentee.

manque [mãːk] *nm* lack, want, shortage, deficiency, breach; — de mémoire forgetfulness; à la — dud.

manqué [mãke] *a* unsuccessful, missed, wasted; **un garçon** — tomboy.

manquement [mãkmã] *nm* failure, omission, breach, oversight, lapse.

manquer [mãke] *vt* to miss, waste; *vi* to be short (of de), lack, run short, be missing, fail; **il manqua (de) tomber** he almost fell; — **à sa parole** to break one's word; **il leur manque** they miss him; **ne pas** — **de** to be sure to.

mansarde [mãsard] *nf* attic, garret.

mansardé [mãsarde] *a* with sloping ceiling, roof.

mansuétude [mãsɥetyd] *nf* gentleness.

mante [mãːt] *nf* mantis; — **religieuse** praying mantis.

manteau [mãto] *nm* coat, cloak, mantle; mantelpiece.

manucure [manykyːr] *n* manicurist.

manuel, -elle [manɥɛl] *a* manual; *nm* handbook.

manufacture [manyfaktyːr] *nf* factory, works.

manufacturer [manyfaktyre] *vt* to manufacture.

manufacturier, -ière [manyfaktyrje, jɛːr] *a* manufacturing; *n* manufacturer.

manuscrit [manyskri] *nm* manuscript.

manutention [manytãsjɔ̃] *nf* administration, handling, stores.

mappemonde [mapmɔ̃ːd] *nf* map of the world.

maquereau [makro] *nm* mackerel.

maquette [makɛt] *nf* clay model, model, dummy, mock-up.

maquignon, -onne [makiɲɔ̃, ɔn] *n* horse-dealer, shady dealer, jobber.

maquignonnage [makiɲɔnaːʒ] *nm* horse-dealing, faking, shady dealing.

maquignonner [makiɲɔne] *vt* to doctor, arrange, fix.

maquillage [makija:ʒ] *nm* make-up, making-up.
maquiller [makije] *vt* to make up, fake, doctor, cook up; *vr* to make up.
maquis [maki] *nm* bush, scrub; Resistance Movement.
maquisard [makiza:r] *n* member of the Resistance Movement.
maraîcher, -ère [marɛʃe, ɛːr] *a* market-gardening; *n* market gardener.
marais [marɛ] *nm* marsh, bog; floating vote; **— salant** salt-pan.
marasme [marasm] *nm* wasting, stagnation, depression.
marâtre [marɑːtr] *nf* stepmother, hard-hearted mother.
maraude [maroːd] *nf* marauding, looting, plundering; **être en —** to be on the prowl.
marbre [marbr] *nm* marble.
marbrer [marbre] *vt* to marble, vein, mottle, blotch.
marbrier [marbrie] *nm* marble cutter.
marbrure [marbryːr] *nf* marbling, veining, mottling, blotch.
marc [maːr] *nm* residue; **— de café** coffee grounds.
marcassin [markasɛ̃] *nm* young wild boar.
marchand [marʃɑ̃] *a* commercial, trading, merchant; *n* shopkeeper, tradesman, dealer; **valeur —e** market value; **— des quatre saisons** hawker, huckster.
marchander [marʃɑ̃de] *vt* to bargain, haggle over, be sparing of, grudge.
marchandise [marʃɑ̃diːz] *nf* merchandise, commodity, wares, goods.
marche [marʃ] *nf* walk(ing), gait, march(ing), working, running, progress, course, step, stair; **en —** moving, running, under way; **mettre en —** to get going, start up; **faire —** **arrière** to reverse, go astern.
marché [marʃe] *nm* market, bargain, deal(ing), contract; **(à) bon —** cheap(ly); **par-dessus le — into the bargain; faire bon —** **de** to attach little value to.
marchepied [marʃəpje] *nm* step, running-board.
marcher [marʃe] *vi* to walk, tread, go, run, work, get along; **il ne marche pas** he is not having any, he won't do as he is told; **faire —** **qn** to make s.o. do as he is told, pull s.o.'s leg.
marcheur, -euse [marʃœːr, øːz] *n* walker; **vieux —** old rake.
mardi [mardi] *nm* Tuesday; **— gras** Shrove Tuesday.
mare [maːr] *nf* pool, pond.
marécage [marɛkaːʒ] *nm* marsh (land), swamp.
marécageux, -euse [marɛkaʒø, øːz] *a* marshy, swampy, boggy.

maréchal [marɛʃal] *nm* marshal; **—** **ferrant** farrier, blacksmith; **— des** **logis** sergeant; **— de France** fieldmarshal.
marée [mare] *nf* tide, fresh fish; **—** **montante** flood tide; **— descendante** ebb tide; **arriver comme — en** **carême** to come at the right time.
marelle [marɛl] *nf* hopscotch.
mareyeur, -euse [marɛjœːr, øːz] *n* fish merchant, fish porter.
margarine [margarin] *nf* margarine.
marge [marʒ] *nf* margin, edge, border, fringe.
margelle [marʒɛl] *nf* edge.
marguerite [margərit] *nf* daisy, marguerite.
marguillier [margije] *nm* churchwarden.
mari [mari] *nm* husband.
mariage [marja:ʒ] *nm* marriage, matrimony.
Marie [mari] Mary.
marié [marje] *a* married; *n* bridegroom, bride.
marier [marje] *vt* to marry, give in marriage, unite, blend, cross; *vr* to get married, marry, harmonize.
marie-salope [marisalɔp] *nf* dredger, slut.
marigot [marigo] *nm* small stream.
marin [marɛ̃] *a* marine, sea-; *nm* sailor, seaman, seafaring man; **avoir le pied —** to be a good sailor; **se faire —** to go to sea; **— d'eau** **douce** landlubber.
marinade [marinad] *nf* pickle, brine.
marine [marin] *nf* navy, seamanship, seascape; **— marchande** merchant marine; **bleu —** navy blue.
mariner [marine] *vt* to pickle, souse, marinate; *vi* to be in a pickle.
marinier, -ière [marinje, jɛːr] *a* naval, marine; *nm* bargeman, boatman.
marionnette [marjɔnɛt] *nf* marionette, puppet.
maritime [maritim] *a* maritime, naval, seaside, sea(borne); **agent —** shipping agent; **courtier —** shipbroker.
marivaudage [marivoda:ʒ] *nm* affected, flippant conversation, mild flirtation.
marlou [marlu] *nm* pimp.
marmaille [marmaːj] *nf (fam)* brats, children.
marmelade [marməlad] *nf* compote, marmalade.
marmite [marmit] *nf* pot, pan, camp-kettle, heavy shell; **— de** **géants** pothole.
marmiter [marmite] *vt* to shell, bombard.
marmiton [marmitɔ̃] *nm* cook's boy, scullion.
marmonner [marmɔne] *vt* to mutter, mumble.
marmot [marmo] *nm* brat, child.

marmotte [marmɔt] *nf* marmot, kerchief.

marmotter [marmɔte] *vt* to mumble, mutter.

marne [marn] *nf* marl.

Maroc [marɔk] *nm* Morocco.

marocain [marɔkɛ̃] *an* Moroccan.

maroquinerie [marɔkinri] *nf* (morocco-) leather trade, goods, shop.

marotte [marɔt] *nf* cap and bells, bauble, hobby, fad.

marquant [markɑ̃] *a* outstanding, notable.

marque [mark] *nf* mark, stamp, make, token, proof, marker, tally, score, scoring; — **de fabrique** trademark; — **déposée** registered trademark; **vin de** — first class wine; **personnage de** — prominent person.

marqué [marke] *a* marked, pronounced, appointed.

marquer [marke] *vt* to mark, put a mark on, show, note down, record, score; *vi* to stand out, make one's mark; **elle marque bien** she is a good-looker; — **son âge** to look one's age; — **les points** to keep the score; — **le pas** to mark time.

marqueter [markəte] *vt* to speckle, spot, inlay.

marqueterie [markətri] *nf* marquetry, inlaid-work.

marqueur, -euse [markœːr, øːz] *n* marker, stamper, scorer.

marquis [marki] *nm* marquis, marquess.

marquise [markiːz] *nf* marchioness; awning, glass porch, marquee.

marraine [marɛn] *nf* godmother, sponsor.

marrant [marɑ̃] *a* terribly funny, killing.

marre [maːr] *nf* **j'en ai** — I'm fed up.

marrer [mare] *vr* to split one's sides laughing.

marron, -onne [marɔ̃, ɔn] *a* chestnut-colored; unlicensed, quack, sham; *nm* chestnut.

marronnier [marɔnje] *nm* chestnut-tree.

mars [mars] *nm* March, Mars; **champ de** — parade-ground.

marsouin [marswɛ̃] *nm* porpoise, colonial infantry soldier.

marteau [marto] *nm* hammer, door-knocker.

marteler [martəle] *vt* to hammer (out); *vi* to knock.

martial [marsjal] *a* martial, warlike, soldierlike.

martinet [martinɛ] *nm* strap, whip, swift.

martingale [martɛ̃gal] *nf* martingale, half-belt.

martin-pêcheur [martɛ̃pɛʃœːr] *nm* kingfisher.

martre [martr] *nm* marten, sable.

martyr [martiːr] *n* martyr.

martyre [martiːr] *nm* martyrdom.

martyriser [martirize] *vt* to martyr, torture.

marxisme [marksism] *nm* Marxism.

mascarade [maskarad] *nf* masquerade.

mascaret [maskarɛ] *nm* bore, tidal wave.

mascotte [maskɔt] *nf* mascot, charm.

masculin [maskylɛ̃] *a* masculine, male, mannish; *nm* masculine gender.

masque [mask] *nm* mask, features, expression, masque.

masquer [maske] *vt* to mask, hide, screen, disguise; **virage masqué** blind corner.

massacre [masakr] *nm* massacre, slaughter; **jeu de** — Aunt Sally (*game*).

massacrer [masakre] *vt* to massacre, slaughter, butcher, spoil; **être d'une humeur massacrante** to be in a vile temper.

massage [masaːʒ] *nm* massage, rubbing down.

masse [mas] *nf* mass, bulk, crowd, mace, sledge-hammer.

masser [mase] *vt* to mass, massage, rub down; *vr* to mass, throng together.

masseur, -euse [masœːr, øːz] *n* masseur, masseuse.

massif, -ive [masif, iːv] *a* solid, massive, bulky; *nm* clump, group, range.

massue [masy] *nf* club, bludgeon.

mastic [mastik] *nm* mastic, putty, cement.

mastication [mastikasjɔ̃] *nf* mastication, chewing.

mastiquer [mastike] *vt* to masticate, chew, putty, fill with cement.

m'as-tu-vu [matyvy] *nm* smart aleck, show-off.

masure [mazyːr] *nf* hovel, tumble-down house.

mat [mat] *a* dull, unpolished, mat, checkmated; *nm* checkmate.

mât [mɑ] *nm* mast, pole, strut; — **de cocagne** greasy pole.

match [matʃ] *nm* match; — **de sélection** trial match.

matelas [matlɑ] *nm* mattress.

matelasser [matlase] *vt* to pad, cushion; **porte matelassée** baize-covered door.

matelot [matlo] *nm* sailor, seaman; — **de première (deuxième) classe** leading (able) seaman.

mater [mate] *vt* to dull, mat, checkmate, humble.

matérialiser [materjalize] *vtr* to materialize.

matérialiste [materjalist] *a* materialistic; *n* materialist.

matériaux [materjo] *nm pl* material(s).

matériel, -elle [materjɛl] *a* material, sensual, physical; *nm* material, plant, implements, equipment; — **roulant** rolling stock.

maternel, -elle [matɛrnɛl] *a* maternal, mother(ly); **école** —**le** infant school.
maternité [matɛrnite] *nf* maternity, motherhood, maternity hospital.
mathématicien, -ienne [matematisjɛ̃, jɛn] *n* mathematician.
mathématique [matematik] *a* mathematical; *nf pl* mathematics.
matière [matjɛːr] *nf* matter, substance, material, subject.
matin [matɛ̃] *nm* morning; **de grand, de bon** — early in the morning.
mâtin [matɛ̃] *nm* mastiff.
matinal [matinal] *a* morning, early rising; **il est** — he is up early.
matinée [matine] *nf* morning, matinee; **faire la grasse** — to lie late in bed.
matines [matin] *nf pl* matins.
matineux, -euse [matinø, øːz] *a* early rising; **il est** — he gets up early.
matois [matwa] *a* sly, crafty, cunning; *n* cunning person; **fin** — sly, wily, bird.
matou [matu] *nm* tom-cat.
matraque [matrak] *nf* bludgeon.
matrice [matris] *nf* matrix, womb, mold, die.
matricide [matrisid] *a* matricidal; *n* matricide.
matricule [matrikyl] *nf* register, roll, registration (certificate); *nm* (registration) number; **plaque** — license plate.
matriculer [matrikyle] *vt* to enroll, enter in a register, stamp a number on.
matrimonial [matrimɔnjal] *a* matrimonial.
maturation [matyrasjɔ̃] *nf* maturation, ripening.
mâture [matyːr] *nf* masts; **dans la** — aloft.
maturément [matyremɑ̃] *ad* after due deliberation.
maturité [matyrite] *nf* maturity, ripeness, mellowness.
maudire [modiːr] *vt* to curse.
maudit [modi] *a* cursed, damned, damnable, confounded.
maugréer [mogree] *vi* to curse, (fret and) fume.
mausolée [mozɔle] *nm* mausoleum.
maussade [mosad] *a* glum, sullen, dismal, dull.
mauvais [movɛ] *a* bad, wrong, poor, nasty; *ad* **sentir** — to have a bad smell; **il fait** — the weather is bad.
mauve [moːv] *a nm* mauve.
mauviette [movjɛt] *nf* chit, softy.
maxime [maksim] *nf* maxim.
maximum [maksimɔm] *a nm* maximum.
mazout [mazu] *nm* fuel oil.
me [m(ə)] *pn* me, to me, myself, to myself.
méandre [meɑ̃ːdr] *nm* meander, bend, winding.

mécanicien, -ienne [mekanisjɛ̃, jɛn] *a* mechanical; *n* mechanic, machinist, engineer, engine-driver.
mécanique [mekanik] *a* mechanical, clockwork; *nf* mechanics, machinery, mechanism.
mécanisation [mekanizasjɔ̃] *nf* mechanization.
mécaniser [mekanize] *vt* to mechanize.
mécanisme [mekanism] *nm* mechanism, machinery, works, technique.
mécano [mekano] *nm* (*fam*) mechanic.
méchanceté [meʃɑ̃ste] *nf* wickedness, spitefulness, naughtiness, illnatured word or act.
méchant [meʃɑ̃] *a* wicked, bad, naughty, ill-natured, spiteful, vicious, wretched, sorry.
mèche [mɛʃ] *nf* wick, fuse, match, (*hair*) lock, wisp, gimlet, spindle, drill; **éventer la** — to give the game away; **être de** — **avec** to be in league with.
mécompte [mekɔ̃ːt] *nm* miscalculation, error, misjudgment, disappointment.
méconnaissable [mekɔnɛsabl] *a* unrecognizable.
méconnaissance [mekɔnɛsɑ̃ːs] *nf* refusal to recognize or appreciate, ignoring, disavowal.
méconnaître [mekɔnɛːtr] *vt* to fail (refuse) to recognize, not to appreciate, to ignore, misunderstand, disavow.
mécontent [mekɔ̃tɑ̃] *a* discontented, displeased, dissatisfied.
mécontentement [mekɔ̃tɑ̃tmɑ̃] *nm* discontent, dissatisfaction.
mécontenter [mekɔ̃tɑ̃te] *vt* to displease, dissatisfy, annoy.
mécréant [mekreɑ̃] *a* misbelieving, unbelieving; *n* infidel.
médaille [medaːj] *nf* medal, badge; **revers de la** — other side of the coin.
médaillon [medajɔ̃] *nm* medallion, locket, inset.
médecin [medsɛ̃] *nm* doctor, physician.
médecine [medsin] *nf* medicine.
médiateur, -trice [medjatœːr, tris] *a* mediatory, mediating; *n* mediator.
médiation [medjasjɔ̃] *nf* mediation.
médical [medikal] *a* medical.
médicament [medikamɑ̃] *nm* medicine, medicament.
médicinal [medisinal] *a* medicinal.
médiéval [medjeval] *a* medieval.
médiocre [medjɔkr] *a* mediocre, moderate, second-rate; *nm* mediocrity.
médiocrité [medjɔkrite] *nf* mediocrity, feebleness, nonentity.
médire [mediːr] *vi* to slander, speak ill of.
médisance [medizɑ̃ːs] *nf* calumny, scandal.

médisant [medizɑ̃] *a* slanderous, calumnious, backbiting; *n* slanderer.
méditatif, -ive [meditatif, iːv] *a* meditative.
méditation [meditasjɔ̃] *nf* meditation, contemplation.
méditer [medite] *vt* to contemplate, ponder; *vi* to meditate, muse.
Méditerranée [mediterane] *nf* Mediterranean.
méditerranéen, -enne [mediteranẽ, ɛn] *a* Mediterranean.
médium [medjɔm] *nm* medium.
médius [medjys] *nm* middle finger.
méduse [medyːz] *nf* jellyfish.
méduser [medyze] *vt* to petrify, paralyze.
méfait [mefɛ] *nm* misdeed; *pl* damage.
méfiance [mefjɑ̃ːs] *nf* distrust, mistrust, suspicion.
méfiant [mefjɑ̃] *a* distrustful, suspicious.
se méfier [səmefje] *vr* to distrust, mistrust, be watchful, be on one's guard.
mégalomanie [megalɔmani] *nf* megalomania.
mégaphone [megafɔn] *nm* megaphone.
mégarde [megard] *ad* **par —** inadvertently.
mégère [meʒɛːr] *nf* shrew.
mégot [mego] *nm* cigarette-end.
méhari [meari] *nm* racing camel.
meilleur [mɛjœːr] *a* better, best; *comp sup of* **bon**; *nm* best, best thing.
mélancolie [melɑ̃kɔli] *nf* melancholy, dejection, melancholia, sadness.
mélange [melɑ̃ːʒ] *nm* mixing, mingling, blending, mixture, blend, mélange.
mélanger [melɑ̃ʒe] *vtr* to mix, mingle, blend.
mélasse [melas] *nf* molasses, treacle.
mêlée [mele] *nf* conflict, fray, scuffle, scrimmage.
mêler [mele] *vt* to mix, mingle, blend, tangle, involve, implicate, shuffle; *vr* to mix, mingle, interfere, meddle.
mélèze [melɛːz] *nm* larch.
méli-mélo [melimelo] *nm* jumble.
mélodie [melɔdi] *nf* melody, tune, harmony, song.
mélodieux, -euse [melɔdjø, øːz] *a* melodious, tuneful, harmonious.
mélodique [melɔdik] *a* melodic.
mélodramatique [melɔdramatik] *a* melodramatic.
mélodrame [melɔdram] *nm* melodrama.
mélomane [melɔman] *a* music-loving; *n* music-lover.
melon [məlɔ̃] *nm* melon, bowler hat.
mélopée [melɔpe] *nf* art of recitative, chant, singsong.
membrane [mɑ̃bran] *nf* membrane, web.
membre [mɑ̃ːbr] *nm* member, limb.

membré [mɑ̃ːbre] *a* -limbed.
membrure [mɑ̃bryːr] *nf* limbs, framework.
même [mɛm] *a* same, very, -self; *ad* even; **de lui —** of his own accord; **de —** likewise; **il en est de — de lui** it is the same with him; **tout de —** all the same; **à — la bouteille** out of the bottle; **revenir au —** to come to the same thing; **à — de** in a position to.
mémento [memɛ̃to] *nm* memorandum, notebook, memento, synopsis.
mémoire [memwaːr] *nm* memoir, paper, memorial, bill, account; *nf* memory, recollection.
mémorable [memɔrabl] *a* memorable, eventful.
mémorandum [memɔrɑ̃dɔm] *nm* memorandum, notebook.
mémorial [memɔrjal] *nm* memorial, memoirs, daybook.
menaçant [mənasɑ̃] *a* threatening, menacing.
menace [mənas] *nf* threat, menace; *pl* intimidation.
menacer [mənase] *vt* to threaten, menace; **— ruine** to be falling to pieces; **— qn du poing** to shake one's fist at s.o.
ménage [menaːʒ] *nm* household, family, married couple, housekeeping, housework; **se mettre en —** to set up house; **faire bon — ensemble** to get on well together; **femme de —** housekeeper, cleaning woman.
ménagement [menaʒmɑ̃] *nm* consideration, caution, care.
ménager [menaʒe] *vt* to be sparing of, save, humor, spare, arrange, contrive; *vr* to take care of oneself; to spare oneself.
ménager, -ère [menaʒe, jɛːr] *a* domestic, house-, thrifty, careful, housewifely; *nf* housewife, housekeeper.
ménagerie [menaʒri] *nf* menagerie.
mendiant [mɑ̃djɑ̃] *a* begging, mendicant; *n* beggar.
mendicité [mɑ̃disite] *nf* begging, beggary.
mendier [mɑ̃dje] *vt* to beg (for); *vi* to beg.
menée [məne] *nf* track, intrigue; *pl* maneuvers.
mener [məne] *vt* to lead, take, drive, steer, manage, control; **— à bonne fin** to carry through; **n'en pas — large** to feel small.
ménétrier [menetrie] *nm* (strolling) fiddler.
meneur, -euse [mənœːr, øːz] *n* leader, agitator, ringleader.
méningite [menẽʒit] *nf* meningitis.
menotte [mənɔt] *nf* tiny hand; *pl* handcuffs, manacles.
menotter [mənɔte] *vt* to manacle, handcuff.
mensonge [mɑ̃sɔ̃ːʒ] *nm* lie, falsehood, illusion.

mensonger, -ère [mãsɔ̃ʒe, ɛːr] *a* lying, deceitful, illusory.
mensualité [mãsɥalite] *nf* monthly payment.
mensuel, -elle [mãsɥɛl] *a* monthly.
mensuration [mãsyrasjɔ̃] *nf* measurement, measuring, mensuration.
mental [mãtal] *a* mental.
mentalité [mãtalite] *nf* mentality.
menterie [mãtri] *nf* fib, tale, story.
menteur, -euse [mãtœːr, øːz] *a* lying, deceptive, false; *n* liar.
menthe [mãːt] *nf* mint, peppermint.
mention [mãsjɔ̃] *nf* endorsement; **reçu avec —** passed with distinction; **faire — de** to mention.
mentionner [mãsjɔne] *vt* to mention, speak of.
mentir [mãtiːr] *vi* to lie, tell lies.
menton [mãtɔ̃] *nm* chin.
mentonnière [mãtonjɛːr] *nf* chinstrap, chinpiece, chinrest.
mentor [mɛ̃tɔːr] *nm* mentor, tutor, guide.
menu [məny] *a* small, tiny, fine, minute, slight, trifling, petty; *ad* small, fine; *nm* menu, bill of fare; **par le — in** detail.
menuet [mənɥɛ] *nm* minuet.
menuiserie [mənɥizri] *nf* carpentry, woodwork.
menuisier [mənɥizje] *nm* joiner, carpenter.
méplat [mepla] *a* flat; *nm* flat part, plane.
se méprendre [səmeprãːdr] *vr* to be mistaken, make a mistake (about **sur**); **il n'y a pas à s'y —** there is no mistake about it.
mépris [mepri] *nm* scorn, contempt.
méprisable [meprizabl] *a* contemptible, despicable.
méprisant [meprizã] *a* contemptuous, scornful.
méprise [mepriːz] *nf* error, mistake, misapprehension.
mépriser [meprize] *vt* to despise, scorn.
mer [mɛːr] *nf* sea; **en pleine —** on the high seas; **prendre la —** to put out to sea; **mettre à la —** to lower (*a boat*).
mercantile [mɛrkãtil] *a* commercial, money-grabbing, mercenary.
mercantilisme [mɛrkãtilism] *nm* profiteering, commercialism.
mercenaire [mɛrsənɛːr] *an* mercenary.
mercerie [mɛrsəri] *nf* haberdashery.
merci [mɛrsi] *nf* mercy; *ad* thanks, thank you, no thanks, no thank you.
mercier, -ière [mɛrsje, jɛːr] *n* haberdasher.
mercredi [mɛrkrədi] *nm* Wednesday; **— des Cendres** Ash Wednesday.
mercure [mɛrkyːr] *nm* mercury, quicksilver.
mercuriale [mɛrkyrjal] *nf* market price-list, reprimand.

merde [mɛrd] *nf* shit, excrement.
mère [mɛːr] *nf* mother, source; *a* **main.**
méridien, -ienne [meridjɛ̃, jɛn] *a* meridian, meridional; *nm* meridian; *nf* meridian line.
méridional [meridjɔnal] *a* meridional, Southern; *n* Southerner.
meringue [mərɛ̃g] *nf* meringue.
mérinos [merinɔs] *nm* merino.
merisier [mərizje] *nm* wild cherry-tree.
méritant [meritã] *a* deserving, meritorious, worthy.
mérite [merit] *nm* merit, worth, credit, ability.
mériter [merite] *vt* to deserve, merit, earn.
méritoire [meritwaːr] *a* deserving, worthy, meritorious.
merlan [mɛrlã] *nm* whiting; (*fam*) barber.
merle [mɛrl] *nm* blackbird.
merluche [mɛrlyʃ] *nf* hake, dried cod.
merrain [mɛrɛ̃] *nm* caskwood.
merveille [mɛrvɛːj] *nf* marvel, wonder; **à — wonderfully** well, excellently.
merveilleux, -euse [mɛrvɛjø, øːz] *a* marvelous, wonderful; *nm* supernatural.
mes [me] *a pl* see **mon.**
mésalliance [mezaljãːs] *nf* misalliance, unsuitable marriage.
se mésallier [səmezalje] *vr* to marry beneath one.
mésange [mezãːʒ] *nf* tit; **— charbonnière** tomtit, great tit.
mésaventure [mezavãtyːr] *nf* misadventure, mishap.
mésentente [mezãtãt] *nf* misunderstanding, disagreement.
mésestime [mezɛstim] *nf* low esteem, poor opinion.
mésestimer [mezɛstime] *vt* to underestimate, have a poor opinion of.
mésintelligence [mezɛ̃teliʒãːs] *nf* misunderstanding, disagreement, discord.
mesquin [mɛskɛ̃] *a* mean, petty, shabby, paltry.
mesquinerie [mɛskinri] *nf* meanness, pettiness, shabbiness, paltriness, stinginess, mean action.
mess [mɛs] *nm* officers' mess.
message [mɛsaːʒ] *nm* message.
messager, -ère [mɛsaʒe, ɛr] *n* messenger, carrier.
messagerie [mɛsaʒri] *nf* freight trade; **les —s** central newsagency; **— maritime** shipping office.
messe [mɛs] *nf* mass; **— des morts** requiem mass.
messie [mɛsi] *nm* Messiah.
mesure [məzyːr] *nf* measure, standard (size), gauge, extent, bounds, moderation; *pl* measures, steps; **en — de** in a position to; **donner sa —** to show what one can

do; **dépasser la —** to overstep the mark; **fait sur —** made to measure; **à — que** as.

mesure-étalon [məzyretalɔ̃] *nf* standard measure.

mesuré [məzyre] *a* measured, moderate, restrained.

mesurer [məzyre] *vt* to measure (out, off), judge, calculate; *vr* to measure oneself (with), tackle; **— qn des yeux** to eye s.o. up and down.

métairie [metɛri] *nf* small farm.

métal [metal] *nm* metal.

métallique [metallik] *a* metallic; **toile —** wire gauze.

métalliser [metallize] *vt* to metalize, plate.

métallurgie [metallyrʒi] *nf* metallurgy.

métallurgiste [metallyrʒist] *nm* metallurgist, metal-worker.

métamorphose [metamɔrfoz] *nf* metamorphosis, transformation.

métaphore [metafɔːr] *nf* metaphor.

métaphorique [metafɔrik] *a* metaphorical.

métaphysicien, -ienne [metafizisjɛ̃, jɛn] *n* metaphysician.

métaphysique [metafizik] *a* metaphysical; *nf* metaphysics.

métayer, -ère [meteje, jɛːr] *n* farmer, share-cropper.

métempsychose [metɑ̃psikoːz] *nf* metempsychosis, transmigration of souls.

météore [meteɔːr] *nm* meteor.

météorologie [meteɔrɔlɔʒi] *nf* meteorology.

météorologique [meteɔrɔlɔʒik] *a* meteorological; **bulletin —** weather report.

métèque [metɛk] *nm* (*pej*) foreigner.

méthode [metɔd] *nf* method, system, orderliness, primer.

méthodique [metɔdik] *a* methodical.

méticuleux, -euse [metikylø, øːz] *a* meticulous, particular, punctilious.

métier [metje] *nm* trade, profession, craft(smanship), loom; **homme de — craftsman; — manuel** handicraft; **sur le —** on the stocks, in preparation.

métis, -isse [metis] *a* half-bred, cross-bred, mongrel; *n* half-cast, half-breed, mongrel.

métisser [metise] *vt* to cross(breed).

métrage [metraːʒ] *nm* measuring, metric area or volume, length; **(film à) court —** a short.

mètre [metr] *nm* meter, rule; **— à ruban** tape-measure.

métrique [metrik] *a* metric(al); *nf* metrics, prosody.

métro [metro] *nm* underground (railway), subway.

métropole [metrɔpɔl] *nf* metropolis, mother country.

métropolitain [metrɔpɔlitɛ̃] *a* metropolitan, home-; *nm* underground (railway), subway.

mets [mɛ] *nm* dish, food.

mettable [metabl] *a* wearable.

metteur, -euse [metœːr, øːz] *n* **— en scène** producer, director.

mettre [metr] *vt* to put (up, on), place, set (up), lay, wear; *vr* to go, stand, sit, put on; **se — à** to begin, set about; **mettons qu'il l'ait fait** suppose he did do it; **se — en colère** to get angry; **—en scène** to produce (*a play*).

meuble [mœbl] *a* movable; *nm* piece or suite of furniture; *pl* furniture.

meublé [mœble] *a* furnished, stocked; *nm* furnished room(s).

meubler [mœble] *vt* to furnish, stock; *vr* to furnish (one's house).

meugler [møgle] *vi* to low.

meule [møːl] *nf* millstone, stack, rick.

meuler [møle] *vt* to grind.

meulière [møljɛːr] *nf* millstone, -quarry.

meunerie [mønri] *nf* milling, milling-trade.

meunier, -ière [mønje, jɛːr] *n* miller.

meurtre [mœrtr] *nm* murder.

meurtrier, -ière [mœrtrie, iɛːr] *a* murderous, deadly; *n* murderer, murderess.

meurtrière [mœrtriɛːr] *nf* loophole.

meurtrir [mœrtriːr] *vt* to bruise, batter.

meurtrissure [mœrtrisyːr] *nf* bruise.

meute [møt] *nf* pack, mob, crowd.

mexicain [mɛksikɛ̃] *an* Mexican.

Mexique [mɛksik] *nm* Mexico.

mi [mi] *ad* half, semi, mid-; **à la — -septembre** in mid-September; **à — -chemin** half way; **à — -côte** half way up; **à — -corps** to the waist; *nm* note E.

miasme [mjasm] *nm* miasma.

miauler [mjole] *vi* to mew, caterwaul.

mi-carême [mikarɛm] *nm* Mid-Lent.

miche [miʃ] *nf* round loaf.

Michel [miʃɛl] Michael.

micmac [mikmak] *nm* trickery, scheming.

micocoulier [mikɔkulje] *nm* nettle-tree.

micro [mikro] *nm* mike, microphone.

microbe [mikrɔb] *nm* microbe, germ.

microbicide [mikrɔbisid] *a* germ-killing; *nm* germ-killer.

microcosme [mikrɔkɔsm] *nm* microcosm.

microscope [mikrɔskɔp] *nm* microscope.

microsillon [mikrɔsijɔ̃] *nm* long-playing record.

midi [midi] *nm* noon, midday, south; **chercher — à quatorze heures** to see difficulties when there are none.

midinette [midinɛt] *nf* workgirl, young dressmaker.

mie [mi] *nf* crumb, soft part of a loaf.

miel [mjɛl] *nm* honey.

mielleux, -euse [mjɛlø, øːz] *a* honeyed, sugary, bland.

mien, mienne [mjɛ̃, mjɛn] *pos pn* le(s) —(s), la mienne, les miennes mine; *nm* my own; *pl* my own people.

miette [mjɛt] *nf* crumb, morsel, tiny bit, atom.

mieux [mjø] *ad* better, (the) best, *comp sup of* bien; *nm* best thing, improvement; **de — en —** better and better; **à qui — —** one more than the other; **c'est on ne peut —** it could not be better; **faire de son —** to do one's best; **être au — avec** to be on the best terms with; **tant —!** all the better!

mièvre [mjɛːvr] *a* affected, pretty-pretty, delicate.

mièvrerie [mjɛvrəri] *nf* affectation, insipid prettiness.

mignard [miɲaːr] *a* affected, simpering, mincing, pretty-pretty.

mignardise [miɲardiːz] *nf* affectation, mincing manner, prettiness, garden pink.

mignon, -onne [miɲɔ̃, ɔn] *a* dainty, sweet, tiny; *n* darling, pet, favorite; **péché —** besetting sin.

mignonnette [miɲɔnɛt] *nf* mignonette lace, coarsely ground pepper, London pride.

migraine [migrɛn] *nf* migraine, sick headache.

migrateur, -trice [migratœːr, tris] *a* migratory, migrant.

migration [migrasjɔ̃] *nf* migration.

mijaurée [miʒɔre] *nf* affected woman.

mijoter [miʒɔte] *vt* to stew slowly, let simmer, plot; *vi* to stew, simmer; *vr* to simmer.

mil [mil] *a* thousand.

milan [milɑ̃] *nm* kite.

milice [milis] *nf* militia.

milieu [miljø] *nm* middle, midst, environment, circle, set, class, mean, middle course; **au beau — de** right in the middle of; **juste —** happy medium.

militaire [militɛːr] *a* military, soldierlike; *nm* soldier.

militant [militɑ̃] *an* militant (supporter).

militariser [militarize] *vt* to militarize.

militer [milite] *vi* to militate, tell.

mille [mil] *a* thousand; *nm* thousand; mile; **avoir des — et des cents** to have tons of money.

mille-feuille [milfœːj] *nf* flaky pastry, yarrow.

millénaire [millenɛːr] *a* millenial; *nm* thousand years.

millénium [millenjɔm] *nm* millenium.

mille-pattes [milpat] *nm* centipede.

millésime [mil(l)ezim] *nm* date (coin), year of manufacture, of vintage.

millet [mijɛ] *nm* millet.

milliardaire [miljardɛːr] *a nm* multimillionaire.

millier [milje] *nm* thousand.

milligramme [milligram] *nm* milligram.

millimètre [mil(l)imɛtr] *nm* millimeter.

million [miljɔ̃] *nm* million.

millionnaire [miljɔnɛːr] *an* millionaire(ss).

mime [mim] *nm* mimic, mime.

mimique [mimik] *a* mimic; *nf* mimicry.

mimosa [mimoza] *nm* mimosa.

minable [minabl] *a* shabby, seedy-looking, pitiable.

minaret [minarɛ] *nm* minaret.

minauder [minode] *vi* to smirk, simper, mince.

minaudier, -ière [minodje, jɛːr] *a* smirking, simpering, mincing, affected.

mince [mɛ̃ːs] *a* thin, slim, slight, scanty; *excl* **— alors!** hang it all, well I never!

minceur [mɛ̃sœːr] *nf* thinness, slimness.

mine [min] *nf* appearance, look, mine, lead; **— de plomb** graphite; **de bonne (mauvaise) —** prepossessing (evil-looking); **avoir bonne (mauvaise) —** to look well (ill); **faire — de** to make as if to; **faire bonne — à** to be pleasant to; **cela ne paie pas de —** it is not much to look at.

miner [mine] *vt* to (under)mine, sap.

minerai [minrɛ] *nm* ore.

minéral [mineral] *a nm* mineral.

minet, -ette [minɛ, ɛt] *n* pussy.

mineur, -eure [minœːr] *a* minor, underage, lesser; *n* minor; *nm* miner, sapper.

miniature [minjatyːr] *nf* miniature, small scale.

minier, -ière [minje, jɛːr] *a* mining.

minime [minim] *a* small, trifling, trivial.

minimum [minimɔm] *a nm* minimum.

ministère [ministɛːr] *nm* ministry, office, government; **— des Affaires Etrangères** State Department; **— de l'Intérieur** Interior Department **— de la Guerre** Defense Department.

ministériel, -elle [ministerjɛl] *a* ministerial, cabinet.

ministre [ministr] *nm* minister, clergyman; **premier —** Prime Minister; **— des Affaires Etrangères** Secretary of State; **— de l'Intérieur** Secretary of the Interior; **— des Finances** Secretary of The Treasury

minois [minwa] *nm* pretty face.

minorité [minɔrite] *nf* minority, infancy.
minoterie [minɔtri] *nf* flour-mill, -milling.
minotier [minɔtje] *nm* miller.
minuit [minɥi] *nm* midnight.
minuscule [minyskyl] *a* small, tiny, diminutive, minute.
minute [minyt] *nf* minute, record, draft; *excl* not so fast! hold on! **réparations à la —** repairs while you wait.
minuter [minyte] *vt* to minute, record, enter, draw up.
minuterie [minytri] *nf* time switch.
minutie [minysi] *nf* minute detail, trifle, fussiness over detail, thoroughness.
minutieux, -euse [minysjø, øːz] *a* minute, detailed, thorough, meticulous.
mioche [mjɔʃ] *n* (*fam*) small child, kid.
mi-parti [miparti] *a* half and half, parti-colored.
mirabelle [mirabɛl] *nf* mirabelle plum.
miracle [mirakl] *nm* miracle, wonder.
miraculeux, -euse [mirakylø, øːz] *a* miraculous, marvelous, wonderful.
mirage [miraːʒ] *nm* mirage.
mire [miːr] *nf* aiming, sight, surveyor's pole, (*TV*) test pattern; **point de —** cynosure.
mirer [mire] *vt* to sight, aim at, have one's eye on, examine; *vr* to look at oneself, admire oneself.
mirifique [mirifik] *a* amazing, wonderful.
mirobolant [mirɔbɔlɑ̃] *a* amazing, astounding.
miroir [mirwaːr] *nm* mirror, looking-glass, speculum; **œufs au —** eggs cooked in butter.
miroiter [mirwate] *vi* to gleam, sparkle, shimmer; **faire — qch** to dazzle, entice with sth.
misaine [mizɛn] *nf* foresail; **mât de — foremast.**
misanthrope [mizɑ̃trɔp] *a* misanthropic; *nm* misanthrope, misanthropist.
misanthropie [mizɑ̃trɔpi] *nf* misanthropy.
mise [miz] *nf* putting, setting, placing, stake, bid, dress; **— à l'eau** launching; **— en scène** setting, staging; **— en retraite** pensioning; **— en plis** setting (of hair); **— en marche** starting up; **cela n'est pas de —** that is not done, (worn, permissible).
miser [mize] *vt* to stake, gamble, lay, bid.
misérable [mizɛrabl] *a* wretched, miserable, despicable; *n* wretch, scoundrel.
misère [mizɛːr] *nf* misery, poverty,

want, distress, trouble, worry, wretchedness, shabbiness, trifle; **crier —** to plead poverty, be shabby; **faire des —** à to tease unmercifully.
miséreux, -euse [mizerø, øːz] *an* destitute, poverty-stricken (person).
miséricorde [mizerikɔrd] *nf* mercy; *excl* goodness gracious!
miséricordieux, -euse [mizerikɔrdjø, øːz] *a* merciful.
misogyne [mizɔʒin] *a* misogynous; *nm* misogynist, woman-hater.
misogynie [mizɔʒini] *nf* misogyny.
missel [misɛl] *nm* missal.
missile [misil] *nm* missile.
mission [misjɔ̃] *nf* mission; **en —** on a mission.
missionnaire [misjɔnɛːr] *nm* missionary.
missive [misiːv] *nf* missive.
mistral [mistral] *nm* mistral (wind).
mitaine [mitɛn] *nf* mitten.
mite [mit] *nf* moth, mite.
mité [mite] *a* moth-eaten.
mi-temps [mitɑ̃] *nf* half-time, interval, half.
miteux, -euse [mitø, øːz] *a* shabby, seedy-looking.
mitigation [mitigasjɔ̃] *nf* mitigation.
mitiger [mitiʒe] *vt* to mitigate.
mitonner [mitɔne] *vt* to let simmer, concoct; *vi* to simmer.
mitoyen, -enne [mitwajɛ̃, ɛn] *a* dividing, intermediate.
mitraille [mitraːj] *nf* grapeshot; (*fam*) change (*money*).
mitrailler [mitraje] *vt* to machine-gun, (*fam*) take shots of; **— de questions** to fire questions at.
mitraillette [mitrajɛt] *nf* tommy-gun.
mitrailleur [mitrajœːr] *nm* machine-gunner; **fusil —** automatic rifle, **bren-gun; fusilier —** bren-gunner.
mitrailleuse [mitrajøːz] *nf* machine-gun.
mitre [mitr] *nf* miter, chimney-pot, chimney-cowl.
mi-vitesse [mivitɛs] *ad* **à —** at half-speed.
mi-voix [mivwa] *ad* **à —** under one's breath, in an undertone.
mixte [mikst] *a* mixed, composite, joint.
mixture [mikstyːr] *nf* mixture.
mnémonique [mnemɔnik] *a* mnemonic; *nf* mnemonics.
mobile [mɔbil] *a* a mobile, moving, movable, detachable, changeable, unstable; *nm* moving body, motive, motive power.
mobilier, -ière [mɔbilje, jɛːr] *a* movable, personal; *nm* (suite of) furniture.
mobilisable [mɔbilizabl] *a* mobilizable, available.
mobilisation [mɔbilizasjɔ̃] *nf* mobilization, liquidation.
mobiliser [mɔbilize] *vt* to mobilize, call up, liquidate.

mobilité [mɔbilite] *nf* mobility, instability.
mocassin [mɔkasɛ̃] *nm* moccasin.
moche [mɔʃ] *a* (*fam*) ugly, lousy, rotten.
modalité [mɔdalite] *nf* modality; *pl* clauses, terms.
mode [mɔd] *nf* fashion, manner, vogue; *pl* millinery, fashions; *nm* mood, mode, method; **à la —** in fashion; **magasin de —s** milliner's shop; **— d'emploi** directions for use.
modèle [mɔdɛl] *a* model, exemplary; *nm* model, pattern; **prendre — sur** to model oneself on.
modelé [mɔdle] *nm* relief, modeling.
modeler [mɔdle] *vt* to model, fashion, shape, mold; *vr* to model oneself.
modérateur, -trice [mɔdɛratœːr, tris] *a* moderating, restraining; *n* moderator; *nm* regulator, governor, control.
modération [mɔdɛrasjɔ̃] *nf* moderation, temperance, restraint, mitigation, reduction.
modéré [mɔdere] *a* moderate, restrained temperate.
modérer [mɔdere] *vt* to moderate, restrain, temper, control, regulate, mitigate, reduce; *vr* to control oneself, calm down, abate.
moderne [mɔdɛrn] *a* modern.
moderniser [mɔdɛrnize] *vt* to modernize.
modeste [mɔdɛst] *a* modest, quiet, retiring, unpretentious.
modestie [mɔdɛsti] *nf* modesty, unpretentiousness.
modicité [mɔdisite] *nf* moderateness, reasonableness, slenderness (of means).
modificateur, -trice [mɔdifikatœːr, tris] *a* modifying; *n* modifier.
modificatif, -ive [mɔdifikatif, iːv] *a* modifying, modal.
modification [mɔdifikasjɔ̃] *nf* modification, change, alteration.
modifier [mɔdifje] *vt* to modify, change, alter.
modique [mɔdik] *a* moderate, slender, reasonable.
modiste [mɔdist] *n* milliner, modiste.
modulation [mɔdylasjɔ̃] *nf* modulation, inflexion.
module [mɔdyl] *nm* module, unit, modulus.
moduler [mɔdyle] *vti* to modulate.
moelle [mwal] *nf* marrow, substance, pith, medulla; **jusqu'à la —** to the backbone, to the core.
moelleux, -euse [mwalø, øːz] *a* mellow, velvety, soft; *nm* mellowness, velvetiness, softness.
moellon [mwalɔ̃] *nm* quarry stone.
mœurs [mœrs] *nf pl* customs, habits, manners, morals.
moi [mwa] *pn* I, me; *nm* self, ego; **moi-même** myself; **à moi!** help! **un ami à —** a friend of mine; **de vous à —** between you and me.

moignon [mwaɲɔ̃] *nm* stump.
moindre [mwɛːdr] *a* lesser, least, *comp sup* of **petit**.
moine [mwan] *nm* monk, friar.
moineau [mwano] *nm* sparrow.
moins [mwɛ̃] *ad* less, not so (much, many), (the) least, *comp sup* of **peu**; *prep* less, minus; **— de** less than; **au —** at least; **du —** at least, at any rate; **pas le — du monde** not in the least; **en — de rien** in no time, in a jiffy; **à — de** unless, barring; **à — que** unless; **rien — que** anything but, nothing less than.
moins-value [mwɛ̃valy] *nf* depreciation.
moire [mwaːr] *nf* watered silk.
moiré [mware] *a* moiré, watered.
mois [mwa] *nm* month.
moïse [mɔiːz] *nm* wicker cradle.
moisir [mwaziːr] *vt* to mildew, make moldy; *vi* to mildew, go moldy, vegetate.
moisi [mwazi] *a* mildewed, moldy, musty, fusty; *nm* mildew, mold; **sentir le —** to have a musty smell.
moisissure [mwazisyːr] *nf* mildew, moldiness, mustiness.
moisson [mwasɔ̃] *nf* harvest, harvest-time, crop.
moissonner [mwasɔne] *vt* to harvest, gather (in), reap.
moissonneur, -euse [mwasɔnœːr, øːz] *n* harvester, reaper.
moissonneuse [mwasɔnøːz] *nf* reaping-machine; **— -batteuse** combine-harvester.
moite [mwat] *a* moist, damp, clammy.
moiteur [mwatœːr] *nf* moistness, clamminess.
moitié [mwatje] *nf* half, (*fam*) better half; **plus grand de —** half as big again; **se mettre de — avec** to go halves with; **couper par —** to cut in halves; **— — fifty-fifty.**
molaire [mɔlɛːr] *a nf* molar.
môle [mol] *nm* mole, breakwater.
molécule [mɔlekyl] *nf* molecule.
moleskine [mɔlɛskin] *nf* imitation leather.
molester [mɔlɛste] *vt* to molest.
molette [mɔlɛt] *nf* small pestle, knob, (*of spur*) rowel, trimmer.
mollasse [mɔlas] *a* soft, flabby, spineless, apathetic.
mollesse [mɔlɛs] *nf* softness, flabbiness, indolence, apathy.
mollet, -ette [mɔlɛ, ɛt] *a* softish; *nm* (leg) calf; **œuf —** soft-boiled egg.
molletière [mɔltjɛːr] *nf* puttee.
molleton [mɔltɔ̃] *nm* flannel, swansdown.
mollir [mɔliːr] *vt* to ease, slacken; *vi* to become soft, abate, slacken, weaken.
mollusque [mɔlysk] *nm* mollusk, spineless person, vegetable.
môme [moːm] *n* (*fam*) kid.
moment [mɔmɑ̃] *nm* moment,

momentum; **en ce** — at the moment, just now; **sur le** — on the spur of the moment, for a moment; **d'un** — à l'autre any moment; **à tout** — constantly; **du** — **que** from the time when, seeing that.
momentané [mɔmɑ̃tane] *a* momentary.
momie [mɔmi] *nf* mummy.
mon, ma, mes [mɔ̃, ma, me] *a* my; **un de mes amis** a friend of mine.
monacal [mɔnakal] *a* monastic, monkish.
monarchie [mɔnarʃi] *nf* monarchy.
monarchiste [mɔnarʃist] *an* monarchist.
monarque [mɔnark] *nm* monarch.
monastère [mɔnastɛːr] *nm* monastery.
monastique [mɔnastik] *a* monastic.
monceau [mɔ̃so] *nm* heap, pile.
mondain [mɔ̃dɛ̃] *a* worldly, society, fashionable; *n* man about town, society woman.
mondanité [mɔ̃danite] *nf* worldliness, mundaneness; *pl* social events, society news.
monde [mɔ̃ːd] *nm* world, society, company, crowd, people; **tout le** — everybody; **homme du** — society man, socialite; **beau** — society; **aller dans le** — to move in society, go out; **avoir du** — to have company; **être le mieux du** — **avec** to be on the best of terms with; **savoir son** — to know how to behave in company.
mondial [mɔ̃djal] *a* world-, worldwide.
monégasque [mɔnegask] *an* of Monaco.
monétaire [mɔnetɛːr] *a* monetary, financial.
monétiser [mɔnetize] *vt* to mint.
moniteur, -trice [mɔnitœːr, tris] *n* monitor, instructor, supervisor, coach.
monnaie [mɔnɛ] *nf* money, currency, change; — **du pape** honesty *(flower)*; **rendre à qn la** — **de sa pièce** to pay s.o. back in his own coin.
monnayer [mɔnɛje] *vt* to coin, mint, exploit.
monnayeur [mɔnɛjœːr] *nm* minter; **faux** — counterfeiter, coiner.
monocle [mɔnɔkl] *nm* monocle.
monogame [mɔnɔgam] *a* monogamous.
monogramme [mɔnɔgram] *nm* monogram.
monographie [mɔnɔgrafi] *nm* monograph.
monolithe [mɔnɔlit] *a* monolithic; *nm* monolith.
monologue [mɔnɔlɔg] *nm* monologue, soliloquy.
monologuer [mɔnɔlɔge] *vi* to soliloquize.
monôme [mɔnoːm] *nm* monomial,

procession of students in single file.
monoplan [mɔnɔplɑ̃] *nm* monoplane.
monopole [mɔnɔpɔl] *nm* monopoly.
monopoliser [mɔnɔpɔlize] *vt* to monopolize.
monoprix [mɔnɔpri] *nm* a department store chain.
monorail [mɔnɔraːj] *a nm* monorail.
monosyllabe [mɔnɔsillab] *a* monosyllabic; *nm* monosyllable.
monosyllabique [mɔnɔsillabik] *a* monosyllabic.
monotone [mɔnɔtɔn] *a* monotonous, dreary, dull.
monotonie [mɔnɔtɔni] *nf* monotony, sameness, dullness.
monseigneur [mɔ̃sɛnjœːr] *nm* His (Your) Grace, His (Your) Lordship, His (Your) Royal Highness, my Lord; **pince** — *nf* jimmy, crowbar.
monsieur [m(ə)sjø] *nm* Mr, master, sir, gentleman.
monstre [mɔ̃ːstr] *a (fam)* huge, monstrous, colossal; *nm* monster, monstrosity.
monstrueux, -euse [mɔ̃stryø, øːz] *a* monstrous, colossal, gigantic, unnatural, scandalous.
mont [mɔ̃] *nm* mount mountain; **par** —**s et par vaux** up hill and down dale.
montage [mɔ̃taːʒ] *nm* carrying up, assembling, equipping, fitting up (on, out), setting, staging, producing, editing.
montagnard [mɔ̃taɲaːr] *a* highland, mountain; *n* highlander, mountaindweller.
montagne [mɔ̃taɲ] *nf* mountain(s); —**s russes** scenic railway.
montagneux, -euse [mɔ̃taɲø, øːz] *a* mountainous.
montant [mɔ̃tɑ̃] *a* rising, climbing, uphill, high-necked; *nm* post, upright, pole, amount, total, pungency.
mont-de-piété [mɔ̃dəpjete] *nm* pawnbroker's office, shop.
monte [mɔ̃ːt] *nf* mating (season), mount(ing), horsemanship.
monte-charge [mɔ̃tʃarʒ] *nm* hoist.
monte-plats [mɔ̃tpla] *nm* serviceelevator.
monté [mɔ̃te] *a* mounted, fitted, equipped, stocked; **coup** — put-up job, frame-up; **être** — **contre** have a grudge against.
montée [mɔ̃te] *nf* rise, gradient, slope, climb(ing).
monter [mɔ̃te] *vt* to climb, go up, mount, ride, bring up, carry up, take up, assemble, fit up (out, on), set (up), produce, stage; *vi* to climb, go (come) up, ascend, come (to), rise, get in; *vr* to amount; **se** — **la tête** to get excited; **je l'ai fait** — **à côté de moi** I gave him a lift.
monteur, -euse [mɔ̃tœːr, øːz] *n* mounter, setter, fitter, producer, editor.

monticule [mɔ̃tikyl] *nm* hillock, hummock.

montrable [mɔ̃trabl] *a* presentable, fit to be seen.

montre [mɔ̃ːtr] *nf* watch, display, show, show-case; — **-bracelet** wrist-watch; **faire — de** to display, show; **mettre qch en —** to display sth. in the window.

montrer [mɔ̃tre] *vt* to show (how to), display, point out, prove; *vr* to appear, prove, turn out (to be).

montreur, -euse [mɔ̃trœːr, øːz] *n* showman, -woman.

montueux, -euse [mɔ̃tɥø, øːz] *a* hilly.

monture [mɔ̃tyːr] *nf* mount, setting, frame, handle.

monument [mɔnymɑ̃] *nm* monument, memorial, historic building.

monumental [mɔnymɑ̃tal] *a* monumental, colossal.

se moquer [səmɔke] *vr* to make fun (of **de**), laugh at; **il s'en moque** he doesn't care.

moquerie [mɔkri] *nf* mockery, derision, scoffing.

moquette [mɔkɛt] *nf* moquette.

moqueur, -euse [mɔkœːr, øːz] *a* mocking, derisive, scoffing; *n* scoffer.

moral [mɔral] *a* ethical, moral, intellectual, mental; *nm* morale, mind; **remonter le — à qn** to raise s.o.'s spirits, buck s.o. up.

morale [mɔral] *nf* moral, morals, ethics, moral philosophy, preachifying; **faire la — à qn** to sermonize, lecture.

moralisateur, -trice [mɔralizatœːr, tris] *a* moralizing, edifying; *n* moralizer.

moraliser [mɔralize] *vt* to sermonize, raise the morals of, lecture; *vi* to moralize.

moraliste [mɔralist] *n* moralist.

moralité [mɔralite] *nf* morality, morals, moral (lesson).

moratoire [mɔratwaːr] *a* moratory.

morbide [mɔrbid] *a* morbid.

morbidité [mɔrbidite] *nf* morbidity, morbidness.

morceau [mɔrso] *nm* morsel, piece, bit, scrap.

morceler [mɔrsəle] *vt* to cut into small pieces, break up.

morcellement [mɔrsɛlmɑ̃] *nm* cutting up, breaking up, dismemberment.

mordant [mɔrdɑ̃] *a* caustic, biting, pungent, piercing, corrosive; *nm* mordancy, pungency.

mordicus [mɔrdikys] *ad* tenaciously, stoutly.

mordiller [mɔrdije] *vt* to nibble, snap playfully at.

mordoré [mɔrdɔre] *a* bronze; *nm* bronze color.

mordre [mɔrdr] *vt* to bite; *vi* to bite, catch, take (to à); **s'en — les doigts** to be sorry for it.

mordu [mɔrdy] *a* mad (about); *n* fan.

morfondre [mɔrfɔ̃ːdr] *vt* to chill to the bone; *vr* to freeze, be bored, wait impatiently.

morganatique [mɔrganatik] *a* morganatic.

morgue [mɔrg] *nf* pride, arrogance, mortuary.

moribond [mɔribɔ̃] *a* moribund, dying.

moricaud [mɔriko] *a* dark-skinned, swarthy; *n* blackamoor.

morigéner [mɔriʒene] *vt* to lecture, haul over the coals.

morne [mɔrn] *a* dismal, dreary, gloomy, dull.

morose [mɔroːz] *a* morose, surly, gloomy.

morosité [mɔrɔzite] *nf* surliness, gloominess.

morphine [mɔrfin] *nf* morphia, morphine.

morphinomane [mɔrfinɔman] *n* morphia addict, drug addict.

morphologie [mɔrfɔlɔʒi] *nf* morphology.

mors [mɔːr] *nm* bit, chap, joint.

morse [mɔrs] *nm* walrus, Morse code.

morsure [mɔrsyːr] *nf* bite.

mort [mɔːr] *a* dead, deceased, spent; *nf* death; *n* dead man, dead woman, dummy; **arrêt de —** death-sentence; **avoir la — dans l'âme** to be sick at heart; **se donner la —** to take one's life; **point —** neutral, deadlock; **nature —e** still life; **eau —e** stagnant water; **faire le —** to pretend to be dead, lie low, (*bridge*) be dummy.

mortadelle [mɔrtadɛl] *nf* bologna sausage.

mortaise [mɔrtɛːz] *nf* slot, mortise.

mortalité [mɔrtalite] *nf* mortality.

morte-eau [mɔrto] *nf* neap tide.

mortel, -elle [mɔrtɛl] *a* mortal, fatal, deadly, (*fam*) deadly dull.

morte-saison [mɔrtsɛzɔ̃] *nf* slack season, off season.

mortier [mɔrtje] *nm* mortar, mortar-board.

mortifier [mɔrtifje] *vt* to hang (*game*), mortify, hurt.

mort-né [mɔrne] *a* stillborn.

mortuaire [mɔrtɥeːr] *a* mortuary, burial, funeral; **drap —** pall.

morue [mɔry] *nf* cod.

morutier [mɔrytje] *nm* cod-fishing boat, cod-fisher.

morve [mɔrv] *nf* glanders, nasal mucus.

morveux, -euse [mɔrvø, øːz] *a* glandered, snotty; *n* (*fam*) brat.

mosaïque [mɔzaik] *a nf* mosaic.

mosquée [mɔske] *nf* mosque.

mot [mo] *nm* word, term, saying; **bon —** witticism; **— de passe (ralliement)** pass word, catchword; **— d'ordre** watchword, directive; **— pour —** word for word; **—s croisés** crossword puzzle; **comprendre à demi-—** to take the hint.

motard [mɔtaːr] *nm* motorcycle policeman.

motet [mɔtɛ] *nm* motet, anthem.

moteur, -trice [mɔtœːr, tris] *a* motive, driving; *nm* motor, engine.

motif, -ive [mɔtif, iːv] *a* motive; *nm* reason, motive, cause, grounds, theme, pattern, design.

motion [mɔsjɔ̃] *nf* motion, proposal.

motiver [mɔtive] *vt* to motivate, warrant, give cause for, give the reason for.

moto [mɔto] *nf* motorcycle, motor-bike.

motocycliste [mɔtɔsiklist] *nm* motor cyclist.

motorisé [mɔtɔrize] *a* fitted with a motor, motorized.

motte [mɔt] *nf* mound, lump, clod, pat; — de gazon turf.

motus [mɔtys] *excl* mum's the word!

mou, molle [mu, mɔl] *a* soft, flabby, feeble, limp, slack, close; *nm* slack (*of rope*), lights (*animal lungs*).

mouchard [muʃar] *nm* sneak, spy, informer, telltale.

moucharder [muʃarde] *vt* to spy on, inform against, squeal; *vi* to spy.

mouche [muʃ] *nf* fly, speck, spot, bull's eye, beauty-spot; — bleue blue-bottle; bateau — river steamer; faire — to hit the bull's-eye; prendre la — to get into a huff.

moucher [muʃe] *vt* to wipe (s.o.'s) nose, snuff, trim, (*fam*) tell off; *vr* to blow one's nose; il ne se mouche pas du pied he thinks a lot of himself.

moucheron [muʃrɔ̃] *nm* gnat, midge.

moucheté [muʃte] *a* speckled, flecked, brindle(d).

moucheture [muʃtyːr] *nf* speckle, spot, fleck.

mouchoir [muʃwaːr] *nm* handkerchief, kerchief.

moudre [mudr] *vt* to grind, mill.

moue [mu] *nf* pout; faire la — to pout.

mouette [mwɛt] *nf* seagull.

mouflard [muflaːr] *n* fat-faced, heavy-jowled person.

moufle [mufl] *nf* mitten, pulley-block, clamp, muffle-furnace.

mouflon [muflɔ̃] *nm* moufflon, wild sheep.

mouillage [mujaːʒ] *nm* wetting, damping, moistening, mooring, anchorage, watering-down.

mouiller [muje] *vt* to wet, damp, moisten, anchor, moor, lay (*mines*); *vr* to get wet, fill (*eyes*); poule mouillée cissy, milksop.

mouilleur [mujœːr] *nm* damper; — de mines minelayer.

moulage [mulaːʒ] *nm* milling, grinding, molding, casting.

moule [mul] *nm* mold, cast, matrix, shape, cake pan; *nf* mussel, blockhead.

moulé [mule] *a* molded, well-proportioned, copperplate; *nm* print.

mouler [mule] *vt* to mold, cast, fit closely.

mouleur [mulœːr] *nm* molder, caster.

moulin [mulɛ̃] *nm* mill; jeter son bonnet par-dessus les —s to throw propriety to the winds.

moulinet [mulinɛ] *nm* turnstile, current-meter, (fishing) reel; faire le — to twirl one's stick.

moulure [mulyːr] *nf* molding.

mourant [murɑ̃] *a* dying, feeble; *n* dying person.

mourir [muriːr] *vi* to die (away); *vr* to be dying, fade (away, out); c'était à — de rire it was killingly funny.

mouron [murɔ̃] *nm* chickweed; — rouge scarlet pimpernel.

mousquetaire [muskətɛːr] *nm* musketeer.

mousse [mus] *nm* ship's boy, cabin-boy; *nf* moss, froth, foam, cream, lather.

mousseline [muslin] *nf* muslin; — de soie chiffon; gâteau — sponge cake; pommes — mashed potatoes.

mousser [muse] *vi* to froth, foam, effervesce, lather.

mousseux, -euse [musø, øːz] *a* foaming, frothy, sparkling, fizzy.

mousson [musɔ̃] *nm* monsoon.

moussu [musy] *a* mossy, moss-grown.

moustache [mustaʃ] *nf* mustache; *pl* whiskers.

moustachu [mustaʃy] *a* having a mustache, whiskered.

moustiquaire [mustikɛːr] *nf* mosquito net.

moustique [mustik] *nm* mosquito, gnat.

moutard [mutaːr] *nm* small boy, youngster, kid.

moutarde [mutard] *nf* mustard.

moutardier [mutardje] *nm* mustard-pot, mustard-maker.

mouton [mutɔ̃] *nm* sheep, mutton, sheepskin, (*fam*) spy; *pl* white-caps (*waves*).

moutonnant [mutɔnɑ̃] *a* foam-flecked.

moutonner [mutɔne] *vi* foam, be covered with whitecaps.

moutonneux, -euse [mutɔnø, øːz] *a* foaming.

mouture [mutyːr] *nf* milling, grinding, milling dues, (*cereals, coffee*) ground mixture, rehash.

mouvant [muvɑ̃] *a* moving, unstable, changeable; sables —s quick-sands.

mouvement [muvmɑ̃] *nm* movement, motion, change, action, impulse, outburst, thrill, stir, traffic; de son propre — of one's own accord; être dans le — to be in the swim.

mouvementé [muvmɑ̃te] *a* lively,

exciting, thrilling, eventful, animated.

mouvoir [muvwaːr] *vt* to move, drive, propel, move to action, prompt; *vr* to move.

moyen, -enne [mwajɛ̃, jɛn] *a* medium, average, mean, middle; *nm* means, way, course; *pl* resources, ability; — âge Middle Ages; **il n'y a pas** — it can't be done; **au** — **de** by means of; **employer les grands** —**s** to take drastic measures.

moyennant [mwajɛnɑ̃] *prep* for, at (price); — **que** on condition that; — **argent** for a consideration.

moyenne [mwajɛn] *nf* average, mean, passing mark; **en** — on an average.

moyeu [mwajø] *nm* hub, nave, boss.

mû [my] *a* driven, propelled.

muable [mɥabl] *a* changeable, unstable.

mue [my] *nf* molting, slough(ing), casting of skin or coat, molting time, breaking of the voice, coop.

muer [mɥe] *vi* to molt, cast skin or coat, slough, break; *vr* **se** — **en** to change into.

muet, -ette [mɥɛ, ɛt] *a* mute, dumb, silent, unsounded; *n* mute, dumb person.

mufle [myfl] *nm* muzzle, snout, nose, mug, fathead, swine.

muflerie [myfləri] *nf* vulgar behavior, mean trick.

mugir [myʒiːr] *vi* to low, bellow, roar, moan, howl.

mugissement [myʒismɑ̃] *nm* lowing, bellowing, roaring, moaning.

muguet [mygɛ] *nm* lily of the valley.

muid [mɥi] *nm* hogshead.

mulâtre [mylɑːtr] *a* mulatto, halfcast; *n* (*f* **mulâtresse**) mulatto.

mule [myl] *nf* (she-)mule; bedroom slipper, mule.

mulet [mylɛ] *nm* (he-)mule; gray mullet.

muletier [myltje] *nm* muleteer, mule-driver.

mulot [mylo] *nm* field mouse.

multicolore [myltikɔlɔːr] *a* multicolored.

multiple [myltipl] *a* multiple, multifarious, manifold; *nm* multiple.

multiplicateur, -trice [myltiplikatœːr, tris] *a* multiplying; *nm* multiplier.

multiplication [myltiplikasjɔ̃] *nf* multiplication.

multiplicité [myltiplisite] *nf* multiplicity, multifariousness.

multiplier [myltiplie] *vti* to multiply; *vr* to be on the increase, be everywhere at once.

multitude [myltityd] *nf* multitude, crowd.

municipal [mynisipal] *a* municipal; **conseil** — town-council; **conseiller** — town-councilor; **loi** —**e** bylaw.

municipalité [mynisipalite] *nf* municipality, town-council.

munificence [mynifisɑ̃ːs] *nf* munificence, bounty.

munificent [mynifisɑ̃] *a* munificent, bountiful.

munir [myniːr] *vt* to provide, supply, furnish, fit.

munition [mynisjɔ̃] *nf* munitioning, provisioning, *pl* ammunition, munitions.

munitionner [mynisjɔne] *vt* to munition, supply.

muqueux, -euse [mykø, øːz] *a* mucous.

mur [myːr] *nm* wall; **mettre qn au pied du** — to corner s.o.

mûr [myːr] *a* ripe, mature, mellow.

mûraie [myrɛ] *nf* mulberry plantation.

muraille [myraːj] *nf* wall, rampart, barrier, (*of ship*) side.

mural [myral] *a* mural, wall-.

mûre [myːr] *nf* mulberry; — **sauvage** blackberry.

murer [myre] *vt* to wall in, brick up, block up.

mûrier [myrje] *nm* mulberry bush; — **sauvage** blackberry bush, bramble bush.

mûrir [myriːr] *vt* to ripen, mature, develop; *vi* to grow ripe, reach maturity.

murmure [myrmyːr] *nm* murmur (ing), whisper, babbling.

murmurer [myrmyre] *vti* to murmur, whisper.

musaraigne [myzarɛɲ] *nf* shrewmouse.

musarder [myzarde] *vi* to idle, moon about, dawdle.

musc [mysk] *nm* musk.

muscade [myskad] *nf* nutmeg.

muscat [myska] *nm* muscat grape, muscatel (wine).

muscle [myskl] *nm* muscle.

musclé [myskle] *a* muscular, brawny.

musculature [myskylatyːr] *nf* musculature.

muse [myːz] *nf* muse.

museau [myzo] *nm* muzzle, snout; (*fam*) mug.

musée [myze] *nm* museum; — **de peinture** picture-gallery.

museler [myzle] *vt* to muzzle.

muselière [myzəljɛːr] *nf* muzzle.

muser [myze] *vi* to idle, moon about, trifle.

muserolle [myzrɔl] *nf* noseband.

musette [myzɛt] *nf* bagpipe, nosebag, haversack, school-bag; **bal** — popular dance hall.

musical [myzikal] *a* musical.

musicien, -enne [myzisjɛ̃, jɛn] *a* musical; *n* musician, bandsman.

musicomane [myzikɔman] *n* music-lover.

musique [myzik] *nf* music, band.

musqué [myske] *a* musk-scented, affected.

musulman [myzylmɑ̃] *an* Moslem, Mohammedan.

mutabilité [mytabilite] *nf* mutability.

mutation [mytasjɔ̃] *nf* mutation, change, transfer.

mutilation [mytilasjɔ̃] *nf* mutilation, defacement.

mutilé [mytile] *a* mutilated, maimed; *nm* disabled soldier.

mutiler [mytile] *vt* to mutilate, maim, deface.

mutin [mytɛ̃] *a* unruly, roguish, arch, *nm* mutineer.

se mutiner [səmytine] *vr* to rebel, mutiny, refuse to obey.

mutinerie [mytinri] *nf* unruliness, mutiny.

mutisme [mytism] *nm* muteness, dumbness.

mutualité [mytɥalite] *nf* mutuality, (system of) friendly societies.

mutuel, -elle [mytɥel] *a* mutual; **société de secours —** friendly society.

myope [mjɔp] *a* short-sighted.

myopie [mjɔpi] *nf* short-sightedness.

myosotis [mjɔzɔtis] *nm* forget-me-not.

myriade [mirjad] *nf* myriad.

myrrhe [miːr] *nf* myrrh.

myrte [mirt] *nm* myrtle.

mystère [mistɛːr] *nm* mystery, mystery play; **il n'en fait pas —** he makes no bones about it, no secret of it.

mystérieux, -euse [misterjø, øːz] *a* mysterious, weird, eerie, uncanny.

mysticisme [mistisism] *nm* mysticism.

mystificateur, -trice [mistifikatœːr, tris] *a* mystifying; *n* hoaxer, leg-puller.

mystification [mistifikasjɔ̃] *nf* mystification, hoax, leg-pull.

mystifier [mistifje] *vt* to mystify, hoax, pull s.o.'s leg.

mystique [mistik] *a* mystical; *n* mystic.

mythe [mit] *nm* myth, legend.

mythique [mitik] *a* mythical, legendary.

mythologie [mitɔlɔʒi] *nf* mythology.

mythologique [mitɔlɔʒik] *a* mythological.

N

nabot [nabo] *n* midget, dwarf.

nacelle [nasɛl] *nf* skiff, gondola.

nacre [nakr] *nf* mother of pearl.

nacré [nakre] *a* pearly.

naevus [nevyːs] *nm* birthmark, mole.

nage [naːʒ] *nf* swimming, rowing, sculling, stroke; **en —** bathed in perspiration.

nageoire [naʒwaːr] *nf* fin, float.

nager [naʒe] *vi* to swim, float, row, scull.

nageur, -euse [naʒœːr, øːz] *n* swimmer, oarsman.

naguère [nagɛːr] *ad* not long since, a little while ago.

naif, -ive [naif, iːv] *a* artless, ingenuous, unaffected.

nain [nɛ̃] *an* dwarf.

naissance [nɛsɑ̃ːs] *nf* birth, descent, root, rise, dawn.

naissant [nɛsɑ̃] *a* newborn, dawning, budding, incipient, nascent.

naître [nɛːtr] *vi* to be born, spring up, grow, originate; **faire —** to give rise to, arouse; **à —** unborn.

naïveté [naivte] *nf* artlessness, ingenuousness.

nantir [nɑ̃tiːr] *vt* to give security to, provide.

naphtaline [naftalin] *nf* mothballs, naphthalene.

nappe [nap] *nf* tablecloth, cover, cloth, sheet (*of water*).

napperon [naprɔ̃] *nm* traycloth, napkin.

narcisse [narsis] *nm* narcissus.

narcotique [narkɔtik] *a nm* narcotic.

narguer [narge] *vt* to flout.

narine [narin] *nf* nostril.

narquois [narkwa] *a* quizzical, waggish.

narrateur, -trice [narratœːr, tris] *n* narrator, teller.

narratif, -ive [narratif, iːv] *a* narrative.

narration [narrasjɔ̃] *nf* narration, story, narrative.

nasal [nazal] *a* nasal.

naseau [nazo] *nm* nostril.

nasillard [nazijaːr] *a* nasal, through one's nose, with a nasal twang.

nasiller [nazije] *vi* to speak through one's nose.

nasse [nas] *nf* net, trap, eel-pot.

natal [natal] *a* native, natal, birth-.

natalité [natalite] *nf* birth-rate.

natation [natasjɔ̃] *nf* swimming.

natif, -ive [natif, iːv] *a* native, inborn.

nation [nasjɔ̃] *nf* nation.

national [nasjɔnal] *a nm* national; **route—e** main road.

nationaliser [nasjɔnalize] *vt* to nationalize.

nationalisme [nasjɔnalism] *nm* nationalism.

nationalité [nasjɔnalite] *nf* nationality.

nativité [nativite] *nf* nativity.

natte [nat] *nf* mat(ting), plait, braid.

naturalisation [natyralizasjɔ̃] *nf* naturalization.

naturaliser [natyralize] *vt* to naturalize.

naturaliste [natyralist] *a* naturalistic; *n* naturalist.

nature [natyːr] *nf* nature, kind, character, disposition; **— morte** still-life; **grandeur —** life-size; *a* plain, natural; **café —** black coffee.

naturel, -elle [natyrɛl] *a* natural, unaffected, illegitimate; *nm* disposition, naturalness, simplicity.

naufrage [nofra:ʒ] *nm* shipwreck; **faire** — to be shipwrecked.
naufragé [nofraʒe] *a* shipwrecked; *n* castaway.
nauséabond [nozeabɔ̃] *a* nauseous, foul.
nausée [noze] *nf* nausea, sickness, disgust.
nautique [notik] *a* nautical, aquatic.
naval [naval] *a* naval, sea-.
navet [navɛ] *nm* turnip; (*fam*) rubbish, daub.
navette [navɛt] *nf* shuttle, incense box; rape seed; **faire la** — go to and fro.
navigable [navigabl] *a* navigable, seaworthy.
navigateur [navigatœːr] *nm* navigator, seafarer; *a* seafaring.
navigation [navigasjɔ̃] *nf* navigation, sailing, shipping.
naviguer [navige] *vti* to navigate, sail.
navire [naviːr] *nm* ship, vessel, boat.
navrant [navrɑ̃] *a* heartbreaking, -rending.
navrer [navre] *vt* to break one's heart, grieve.
ne [n(ə)] *neg ad* used mostly with pas, point, *etc*, not.
néanmoins [neɑ̃mwɛ̃] *ad* nevertheless, notwithstanding, yet, still.
néant [neɑ̃] *nm* nothing(ness), worthlessness, naught.
nébuleux, -euse [nebylø, øːz] *a* nebulous, cloudy, hazy.
nécessaire [nesɛsɛːr] *a* necessary, needful, required, requisite; *nm* necessaries, what is necessary, bag, case, outfit.
nécessité [nesɛsite] *nf* necessity, straitened circumstances.
nécessiter [nesɛsite] *vt* to necessitate, entail.
nécessiteux, -euse [nesɛsitø, øːz] *a* necessitous, needy.
nécrologie [nekrɔlɔʒi] *nf* obituary notice.
nécromancien, -ienne [nekrɔmɑ̃sjɛ̃, jɛn] *n* necromancer.
nectarine [nɛktarin] *nf* nectarine peach.
nef [nɛf] *nf* nave.
néfaste [nefast] *a* luckless, baneful, ill-fated, evil.
nèfle [nɛfl] *nf* medlar.
négatif, -ive [negatif, iːv] *a nm* negative.
négligé [negliʒe] *a* neglected, careless, slovenly; *nm* undress, negligee, dishabille.
négligeable [negliʒabl] *a* negligible.
négligence [negliʒɑ̃ːs] *nf* negligence, neglect, carelessness.
négligent [negliʒɑ̃] *a* negligent, careless, neglectful, off-hand.
négliger [negliʒe] *vt* to neglect, be neglectful of, disregard, leave undone; *vr* to neglect oneself, be careless of one's appearance.

négoce [negɔs] *nm* trade, business.
négociable [negɔsjabl] *a* negotiable, transferable.
négociant [negɔsjɑ̃] *n* trader, merchant.
négociation [negɔsjasjɔ̃] *nf* negotiation, transaction, treaty, dealing.
négocier [negɔsje] *vt* to negotiate.
nègre [nɛːgr] *nm* Negro, black; hackwriter; *a* Negro; **parler petit** — to speak pidgin.
négresse [negrɛs] *nf* negress.
neige [nɛːʒ] *nf* snow; — **fondue** sleet, slush; **œufs à la** — floating islands; **tempête de** — snowstorm.
neiger [neʒe] *vi* to snow.
neigeux, -euse [neʒø, øːz] *a* snowy, snow-covered.
nénufar, nénuphar [nenyfaːr] *nm* water-lily.
néologisme [neɔlɔʒism] *nm* neologism.
néophyte [neɔfit] *nm* neophyte, beginner.
néo-zélandais [neozelɑ̃dɛ] *an* New Zealander, from New Zealand.
néphrite [nefrit] *nf* nephritis.
népotisme [nepɔtism] *nm* nepotism.
nerf [nɛːr] *nm* nerve, sinew, (fig) energy, stamina; *pl* hysterics; **porter sur les** — **à qn** to get on s.o.'s nerves.
nerveux, -euse [nɛrvø, øːz] *a* excitable, highly-strung, sinewy, nervous.
nervosité [nɛrvozite] *nf* irritability, nerves.
nervure [nɛrvyːr] *nf* rib, nervure, vein.
net, nette [nɛt] *a* clean, clear, distinct, plain, sharp, fair, (*of prices*) net; **mettre au** — to make a fair copy of; **faire place nette** to clear out; *ad* plainly, flatly, clearly, dead.
netteté [nɛt(ə)te] *nf* cleanness, cleanliness, distinctness, downrightness.
nettoyage [nɛtwajaːʒ] *nm* cleaning, cleansing.
nettoyer [nɛtwaje] *vt* to clean (out), clear, mop up.
nettoyeur, -euse [nɛtwajœːr, øːz] *n* cleaner.
neuf [nœf] *a nm* nine, ninth.
neuf, neuve [nœf, nœːv] *a* new; **à** — anew, like new; **quoi de** — what is the news? what's new?
neurasthénie [nørasteni] *nf* neurasthenia.
neutraliser [nøtralize] *vt* to neutralize, counteract.
neutralité [nøtralite] *nf* neutrality.
neutre [nøːtr] *a nm* neuter; *a* neutral; **zone** — no man's land.
neuvième [nœvjɛm] *a nm* ninth.
neveu [n(ə)vø] *nm* nephew.
névralgie [nevralʒi] *nf* neuralgia.
névrite [nevrit] *nf* neuritis.
névrose [nevroːz] *nf* neurosis.
névrosé [nevroze] *an* neurotic, neurasthenic.

nez [ne] *nm* nose, face, nose-piece, sense of smell.
ni [ni] *cj* nor, or, neither . . . nor.
niais [niɛ, njɛ] *a* simple, foolish, silly; *n* fool, simpleton.
niaiserie [niɛzri, njɛ-] *nf* silliness, foolishness; *pl* nonsense.
niche [niʃ] *nf* niche, recess, dog-kennel, trick, prank.
nichée [niʃe] *nf* nest(ful), brood.
nicher [niʃe] *vi* to nest; *vt* to put, lodge; *vr* to build a nest, lodge.
nid [ni] *nm* nest.
nièce [njɛs] *nf* niece.
nier [nie, nje] *vt* to deny, plead not guilty.
nigaud [nigo] *a* silly; *n* simpleton, booby, fool.
nimbe [nɛ̃:b] *nm* nimbus, halo.
se nipper [sənipe] *vr* to rig oneself out.
nippes [nip] *nf pl* (old) clothes, things.
nique [nik] *nf* **faire la — à** to pull a face at, turn up one's nose.
nitouche [nituʃ] *nf* **sainte —** little prude.
nitrate [nitrat] *nm* nitrate.
niveau [nivo] *nm* level, standard; **passage à —** grade crossing.
niveler [nivle] *vt* to level, even up, survey.
nobiliaire [nɔbiljɛ:r] *n* peerage (-book, -list).
noble [nɔbl] *a* noble, lofty, high-minded; *n* noble(man, woman).
noblesse [nɔblɛs] *nf* nobility, noble birth, nobleness.
noce [nɔs] *nf* wedding, wedding-party; **voyage de —s** honeymoon; **faire la —** to live it up.
noceur, -euse [nɔsœ:r, ø:z] *n* fast liver, dissolute man, rake.
nocif, -ive [nɔsif, i:v] *a* noxious, injurious.
noctambule [nɔktɑ̃byl] *nm* sleep-walker, night-prowler.
nocturne [nɔktyrn] *a* nocturnal, night-; *nm* nocturne.
Noël [nɔɛl] *nm* Christmas, Christmas carol.
nœud [nø] *nm* knot, bow, bond, crux.
noir [nwa:r] *a* black, swarthy, dark, gloomy, dirty, base, foul; *nm* black, black man, bull's eye; **broyer du —** to be in the dumps.
noire [nwa:r] *nf* quarter note, black-ball.
noirâtre [nwarɑ:tr] *a* blackish, darkish.
noirceur [nwarsœ:r] *nf* blackness, darkness, smut, base action.
noircir [nwarsi:r] *vi* to grow black; *vt* to blacken, darken, sully.
noisetier [nwaztje] *nm* hazel tree.
noisette [nwazɛt] *nf* hazel-nut; *a* hazel, nut-brown.
noix [nwa] *nf* walnut, nut.
nom [nɔ̃] *nm* name, noun; **— de famille** surname; **petit —** Christian

pet name; **— de guerre** assumed name; **qui n'a pas de —** beyond words, unspeakable.
nomade [nɔmad] *a* nomadic, wandering.
nombre [nɔ̃:br] *nm* number.
nombrer [nɔ̃bre] *vt* to count, number.
nombreux, -euse [nɔ̃brø, ø:z] *a* numerous, many.
nombril [nɔ̃bri] *nm* navel.
nominatif, -ive [nɔminatif, i:v] *a* nominal, registered; *nm* nominative.
nomination [nɔminasjɔ̃] *nf* appointment, nomination.
nommément [nɔmemɑ̃] *ad* namely, by name.
nommer [nɔme] *vt* to name, call, mention by name, appoint, nominate, elect; *vr* to be called, give one's name.
non [nɔ̃] *ad* no, not; non-, un-, in-; *nm* no; **faire signe que —** to shake one's head.
nonagénaire [nɔnaʒenɛ:r] *n* non-agenarian.
nonchalance [nɔ̃ʃalɑ̃:s] *nf* nonchalance, unconcern.
non-lieu [nɔ̃ljø] *nm* no case.
nonne [nɔn] *nf* nun.
nonobstant [nɔnɔbstɑ̃] *prep* notwithstanding; *ad* nevertheless.
nonpareil, -eille [nɔ̃parɛj] *a* matchless.
non-sens [nɔ̃sɑ̃:s] *nm* meaningless sentence, remark.
non-valeur [nɔ̃valœ:r] *nf* valueless object, bad debt, worthless security, unproductiveness, inefficient person, non-effective unit.
nord [nɔ:r] *nm* north; *a* north, northern; **perdre le —** be all at sea.
nord-est [nɔr(d)ɛst] *nm* north-east.
nordique [nɔrdik] *a* Nordic.
nord-ouest [nɔr(d)wɛst] *nm* north-west.
normal [nɔrmal] *a* normal, standard, average.
normalien, -ienne [nɔrmaljɛ̃, jɛn] *n* student at the *Ecole Normale Supérieure*.
normand [nɔrmɑ̃] *a* Norman, non-committal, shrewd; *n* Norman.
Normandie [nɔrmɑ̃di] *nf* Normandy.
norme [nɔrm] *nf* norm, standard.
Norvège [nɔrvɛ:ʒ] *nf* Norway.
norvégien, -ienne [nɔrveʒjɛ̃, jɛn] *an* Norwegian.
nostalgie [nɔstalʒi] *nf* nostalgia, home-sickness.
notable [nɔtabl] *a* notable, considerable, eminent.
notaire [nɔtɛ:r] *nm* notary, solicitor.
notamment [nɔtamɑ̃] *ad* notably, especially, among others.
note [nɔt] *nf* note, memorandum, mark, bill, account; **changer de —** to change one's tune; **forcer la —** to lay it on, overdo it.

noté [nɔte] *a* **bien, mal —** of good, bad, reputation.
noter [nɔte] *vt* to note, take a note of, write down.
notice [nɔtis] *nf* notice, account, review.
notification [nɔtifikasjɔ̃] *nf* notification, intimation.
notifier [nɔtifje] *vt* to notify, intimate.
notion [nɔsjɔ̃] *nf* notion, ídea.
notoire [nɔtwaːr] *a* well-known, notorious.
notoriété [nɔtɔrjete] *nf* notoriety, repute; **— publique** common knowledge.
notre, nos [nɔtr, no] *pos a* our.
nôtre [noːtr] *pos pn* **le, la —, les —s** ours; *nm* ours, our own; *pl* our own people *etc*.
nouer [nwe, nue] *vt* to tie (up), knot; *vr* to become knotted, become stiff; **— conversation avec** to enter into conversation with.
noueux, -euse [nuø, øːz] *a* knotty, gnarled, stiff.
nougat [nuga] *nm* nougat.
nouilles [nuːj] *nf pl* ribbon vermicelli, noodles.
nounou [nunu] *nf* nanny, children's nurse.
nourri [nuri] *a* fed, nourished, furnished, copious, full, sustained, prolonged.
nourrice [nuris] *nf* (wet) nurse; auxiliary tank, feed-pipe.
nourricier, -ière [nurisje, jɛːr] *a* nutritious, nutritive, foster-.
nourrir [nuriːr] *vt* to nourish, feed, suckle, nurse, rear, maintain, board, foster, cherish, fill out.
nourrissant [nurisɑ̃] *a* nourishing, nutritious.
nourrisson [nurisɔ̃] *nm* baby at the breast, infant, foster-child.
nourriture [nurityːr] *nf* food, board, feeding.
nous [nu] *pn* we, us, ourselves, each other; **à — ours.**
nouveau, -elle [nuvo, ɛl] *a* new, recent, fresh, another, further, second; **du —** something new; **de —** again; **à — afresh, anew.**
nouveau-né [nuvone] *an* new-born (child).
nouveauté [nuvote] *nf* novelty, change, innovation, new publication, play *etc*; *pl* new styles, latest fashions; **magasin de —s** drapery store.
nouvelle [nuvɛl] *nf* piece of news, short story.
nouvellement [nuvɛlmɑ̃] *ad* newly, lately.
Nouvelle-Zélande [nuvɛlzelɑ̃d] *nf* New Zealand.
nouvelliste [nuvɛlist] *nm* short-story writer.
novateur, -trice [nɔvatœːr, tris] *n* innovator.

novembre [nɔvɑ̃ːbr] *nm* November.
novice [nɔvis] *a* inexperienced, new, fresh, unpracticed; *n* novice, beginner, probationer, apprentice.
noviciat [nɔvisja] *nm* novitiate, probationary period, apprenticeship.
noyade [nwajad] *nf* drowning.
noyau [nwajo] *nm* stone, kernel, nucleus, cell, hub, core.
noyautage [nwajotaːʒ] *nm* (communist) infiltration.
noyé [nwaje] *a* drowned, flooded, sunken, choked, suffused; *n* drowned, drowning man, woman.
noyer [nwaje] *nm* walnut-tree.
noyer [nwaje] *vt* to drown, sink, flood, swamp, (*fish*) play; *vr* to drown, be drowned.
nu [ny] *a* naked, nude, bare, plain; *nm* nude; **à — uncovered, exposed,** bareback.
nuage [nɥaːʒ] *nm* cloud, haze, drop (of milk in tea).
nuageux, -euse [nɥaʒø, øːz] *a* cloudy, overcast, hazy.
nuance [nɥɑ̃ːs] *nf* shade, hue, tinge, slight suggestion.
nuancer [nɥɑ̃se] *vt* to blend, shade, vary.
nubile [nybil] *a* nubile; **âge — age of** consent.
nucléaire [nykleɛːr] *a* nuclear.
nudisme [nydism] *nm* nudism.
nudité [nydite] *nf* nudity, nakedness, bareness.
nue [ny] *nf* cloud.
nuée [nɥe] *nf* (large) cloud, swarm, host, shower.
nuire [nɥiːr] *vt* to harm, hurt, injure, prejudice.
nuisible [nɥizibl] *a* harmful, injurious.
nuit [nɥi] *nf* night, dark(ness); **cette — last night, tonight; à la — tombante** at nightfall.
nul, nulle [nyl] *a* no, not one, not any, worthless, of no account, null, invalid, non-existent; **course nulle** dead heat; **partie nulle** tie, tie game; **nulle part** nowhere; *pn* no one, none, nobody.
nullement [nylmɑ̃] *ad* not at all, by no means, in no way.
nullité [nyllite] *nf* nullity, invalidity, emptiness, incapacity, nonentity.
nûment [nymɑ̃] *ad* frankly; without embellishment.
numéral [nymeral] *a nm* numeral.
numérique [nymerik] *a* numerical.
numéro [nymero] *nm* number, item, turn; **c'est un — he is a character.**
nuptial, -ive [nypsjal] *a* nuptial, bridal, wedding-.
nuque [nyk] *nf* nape of the neck.
nutritif, -ive [nytritif, iːv] *a* nutritious, nourishing, food-.
nymphe [nɛ̃ːf] *nf* nymph.

O

obéir [ɔbeiːr] *vt* to obey, comply (with à).

obéissance [ɔbeisãːs] *nf* obedience, submission.

obéissant [ɔbeisã] *a* obedient, dutiful.

obélisque [ɔbelisk] *nm* obelisk.

obèse [ɔbɛːz] *a* fat, corpulent, stout.

obésité [ɔbezite] *nf* obesity, corpulence.

objecter [ɔbʒɛkte] *vt* to raise (as) an objection.

objecteur [ɔbʒɛktœːr] *nm* (conscientious) objector.

objectif, -ive [ɔbʒɛktif, iːv] *a* objective; *nm* objective, target, lens.

objection [ɔbʒɛksjɔ̃] *nf* objection.

objet [ɔbʒɛ] *nm* object, thing, aim, purpose, subject.

obligation [ɔbligasjɔ̃] *nf* obligation, duty, agreement, bond, debenture.

obligatoire [ɔbligatwaːr] *a* obligatory, compulsory, binding.

obligé [ɔbliʒe] *a* obliged, bound, indispensable, inevitable, grateful.

obligeance [ɔbliʒãːs] *nf* obligingness, kindness.

obliger [ɔbliʒe] *vt* to oblige, compel, do (s.o.) a favor.

oblique [ɔblik] *a* oblique, slanting, indirect, underhand.

obliquer [ɔblike] *vi* to edge, slant, turn off (*direction*).

oblitération [ɔblitɛrasjɔ̃] *nf* obliteration, canceling.

oblitérer [ɔblitere] *vt* to obliterate, cancel.

obole [ɔbɔl] *nf* mite.

obscène [ɔpsɛ(ː)n] *a* obscene.

obscénité [ɔpsenite] *nf* obscenity.

obscur [ɔpskyːr] *a* obscure, indistinct, unknown, dark.

obscurcir [ɔpskyrsiːr] *vt* to obscure, darken, dim, make unintelligible; *vr* to grow dark, become obscure, dim.

obscurcissement [ɔpskyrsismã] *nm* darkening, growing dim, blackout.

obscurité [ɔpskyrite] *nf* obscurity, darkness, dimness, unintelligibility.

obséder [ɔpsede] *vt* to obsess, haunt, worry.

obsèques [ɔpsɛk] *nf pl* obsequies, funeral.

obséquieux, -euse [ɔpsekjø, øːz] *a* obsequious.

observance [ɔpsɛrvãːs] *nf* observance.

observateur, -trice [ɔpsɛrvatœːr, tris] *a* observant, observing; *n* observer.

observation [ɔpsɛrvasjɔ̃] *nf* observation, remark, comment, reprimand, observance.

observatoire [ɔpsɛrvwatwaːr] *nm* observatory.

observer [ɔpsɛrve] *vt* to observe, keep (to), watch, note; **faire —** to

point out; *vr* to be careful, discreet.

obsession [ɔpsesjɔ̃] *nf* obsession.

obstacle [ɔpstakl] *nm* obstacle, impediment.

obstination [ɔpstinasjɔ̃] *nf* obstinacy.

obstiné [ɔpstine] *a* obstinate, stubborn.

obstruction [ɔpstryksjɔ̃] *nf* obstruction, blocking, choking.

obstruer [ɔpstrɥe] *vt* to obstruct, block, choke; *vr* to become blocked, choked.

obtempérer [ɔptãpere] *vt* to comply (with à).

obtenir [ɔptəniːr] *vt* to obtain, get, procure, achieve.

obtention [ɔptãsjɔ̃] *nf* obtaining.

obtus [ɔpty] *a* obtuse, dull, blunt.

obus [ɔby(ːs)] *nm* shell.

obusier [ɔbyzje] *nm* howitzer.

oc [ɔk] *ad* **langue d'—** dialect of South of France.

occasion [ɔkazjɔ̃, -kɑ-] *nf* occasion, opportunity, motive, bargain; **à l'—** when the opportunity occurs, in case of need, once in a while, on the occasion (of **de**), with regard (to **de**), **d'—** second-hand.

occasionner [ɔkazjɔne, -kɑ-] *vt* to occasion, give rise to.

occident [ɔksidã] *nm* West.

occidental [ɔksidãtal] *a* West(ern).

occlusion [ɔklyzjɔ̃] *nf* occlusion, closing, obstruction.

occulte [ɔkylt] *a* occult, hidden.

occupant [ɔkypã] *a* occupying; *n* occupying (power, army *etc*), occupier.

occupation [ɔkypasjɔ̃] *nf* occupation, occupancy, business, employment.

occupé [ɔkype] *a* occupied, busy, engaged.

occuper [ɔkype] *vt* to occupy, inhabit, fill, hold, employ; *vr* to keep oneself busy, go in (for **de**), turn one's attention (to **de**), attend (to **de**); **occupez-vous de ce qui vous regarde** mind your own business.

occurrence [ɔkyrãːs] *nf* occurrence, event; **en l'—** under the circumstances.

océan [ɔseã] *nm* ocean.

océanique [ɔseanik] *a* ocean(ic).

ocre [ɔkr] *nf* ochre.

octave [ɔktaɪv] *nf* octave.

octobre [ɔktɔbr] *nm* October.

octogénaire [ɔktɔʒenɛːr] *an* octogenarian.

octogone [ɔktɔgɔn] *a* octagonal; *nm* octagon.

octroi [ɔktrwa] *nm* concession, tollhouse.

octroyer [ɔktrwaje] *vt* to concede, grant, allow, bestow.

oculaire [ɔkylɛːr] *a* ocular, eye-; *nm* eyepiece.

oculiste [ɔkylist] *nm* oculist.

ode [ɔd] *nf* ode.

odeur [ɔdœːr] *nf* odor, smell, scent.

odieux, -euse [ɔdjø, øːz] *a* odious, hateful, heinous; *nm* odiousness, odium.

odorant [ɔdɔrɑ̃] *a* sweet-smelling.

odorat [ɔdɔra] *nm* sense of smell.

œil [œːj] *nm, pl* **yeux** [jø] eye, sight, look; **regarder dans le blanc des yeux** to look full in the face; **cela saute aux yeux** it is obvious; **coûter les yeux de la tête** to cost an outrageous price; **à l'—** on credit, free; **à vue d'—** visibly, at a glance; **coup d'—** view, glance; **faire de l'—à** to give the glad eye to, wink at.

œillade [œjad] *nf* glance; *pl* sheep's eyes.

œillère [œjɛːr] *nf* blinker, eyecup, eye-tooth.

œillet [œjɛ] *nm* eyelet, pink, carnation; **— de poète** sweet-william.

œsophage [ezɔfaːʒ] *nm* esophagus, gullet.

œuf [œf] *nm* egg; *pl* spawn, roe; **— dur** hard-boiled egg; **— sur le plat** egg fried in butter; **faire d'un — un bœuf** to make a mountain out of a molehill.

œuvre [œːvr] *nf* work; **— de bienfaisance** charitable society, charity; **mettre en —** to put in hand, bring into play; *nm* works.

offensant [ɔfɑ̃sɑ̃] *a* offensive, objectionable.

offense [ɔfɑ̃ːs] *nf* offense.

offenser [ɔfɑ̃se] *vt* to offend, injure, be offensive to; *vr* to take offense.

offensif, -ive [ɔfɑ̃sif, iːv] *a* offensive.

office [ɔfis] *nm* office, functions, service, worship, department; **faire — de** to act as; **d'—** officially, automatically; **— des morts** burialservice; *nf* pantry, servants' hall.

officiel, -elle [ɔfisjɛl] *a* official, formal.

officier [ɔfisje] *nm* officer; **— de l'état civil** registrar; *vi* to officiate.

officieux, -euse [ɔfisjø, øːz] *a* officious, semi-official; **à titre —** unofficially; *n* busybody.

officine [ɔfisin] *nf* drugstore, den, hotbed.

offrande [ɔfrɑ̃d] *nf* offering.

offrant [ɔfrɑ̃] *a nm* **le plus —** the highest bidder.

offre [ɔfr] *nf* offer, tender; **l'— et la demande** supply and demand.

offrir [ɔfriːr] *vt* to offer, proffer, stand, bid, afford, put up; *vr* to offer oneself, present itself.

offusquer [ɔfyske] *vt* to offend, shock; *vr* to take offense (at de).

ogival [ɔʒival] *a* pointed, ogival, gothic.

ogive [ɔʒiːv] *nf* ogive, pointed arch.

ogre, -esse [ɔgr, ɔgrɛs] *n* ogre, ogress.

oie [wa] *nf* goose.

oignon [ɔɲɔ̃] *nm* onion, bulb, bunion.

oindre [wɛ̃ːdr] *vt* to oil, anoint.

oiseau [wazo] *nm* bird, individual; **à vol d'—** as the crow flies.

oiseau-mouche [wazomuʃ] *nm* humming-bird.

oiselet [wazlɛ] *nm* small bird.

oiseleur [wazlœːr] *nm* bird-catcher.

oiseux, -euse [wazø, øːz] *a* idle, useless, trifling.

oisif, -ive [wazif, iːv] *a* idle; *n* idler.

oisillon [wazijɔ̃] *nm* fledgling.

oisiveté [wazivte] *nf* idleness.

oison [wazɔ̃] *nm* gosling, simpleton.

oléagineux, -euse [ɔleaʒinø, øːz] *a* oleaginous, oily, oil.

olfactif, -ive [ɔlfaktif, iːv] *a* olfactory.

oligarchie [ɔligarʃi] *nf* oligarchy.

olivâtre [ɔlivɑːtr] *a* olive-hued, sallow.

olive [ɔliːv] *a* olive-green, -shaped; *nf* olive.

olivier [ɔlivje] *nm* olive-tree, -wood.

Olympe [ɔlɛ̃ːp] *nm* Olympus.

olympique [ɔlɛ̃pik] *a* Olympic.

ombilical [ɔ̃bilikal] *a* umbilical, navel.

ombrage [ɔ̃braːʒ] *nm* shade, umbrage.

ombrager [ɔ̃braʒe] *vt* to shade, overshadow.

ombrageux, -euse [ɔ̃braʒø, øːz] *a* touchy, (*horse*) shy.

ombre [ɔ̃ːbr] *nf* shade, shadow, darkness, ghost.

ombrelle [ɔ̃brɛl] *nf* sunshade, parasol.

ombreux, -euse [ɔ̃brø, øːz] *a* shady.

omelette [ɔmlɛt] *nf* omelet; **— aux fines herbes** savory omelet.

omettre [ɔmɛtr] *vt* to omit.

omission [ɔmisjɔ̃] *nf* omission.

omnibus [ɔmnibyːs] *nm* (omni)bus; **train —** local, milk train.

omnipotence [ɔmnipɔtɑ̃ːs] *nf* omnipotence.

omnivore [ɔmnivɔːr] *a* omnivorous.

omoplate [ɔmoplat] *nf* shoulderblade.

on [ɔ̃] *pn* one, people, a man, we, you, they; **— demande** wanted; **— dit** it is said; **— ne passe pas** no thoroughfare.

oncle [ɔ̃ːkl] *nm* uncle.

onction [ɔ̃ksjɔ̃] *nf* oiling, anointing, unction, unctuousness.

onctueux, -euse [ɔ̃ktɥø, øːz] *a* unctuous, oily, greasy.

onde [ɔ̃ːd] *nf* wave, ocean, water.

ondé [ɔ̃de] *a* wavy, waved, watered.

ondée [ɔ̃de] *nf* heavy shower.

on-dit [ɔ̃di] *nm pl* hearsay, idle talk.

ondoyant [ɔ̃dwajɑ̃] *a* undulating, waving.

ondoyer [ɔ̃dwaje] *vi* to undulate, wave, sway.

ondulant [ɔ̃dylɑ̃] *a* undulating, waving, flowing.

ondulation [ɔ̃dylasjɔ̃] *nf* undulation, wave.

ondulé [ɔ̃dyle] *a* wavy, undulating, corrugated.

onduler [ɔ̃dyle] *vi* to undulate; *vt*

to corrugate, wave; **se faire** — to have one's hair waved.

onéreux, -euse [ɔnerø, øːz] *a* onerous, heavy.

ongle [ɔ̃ːgl] *nm* nail, claw, talon; **se faire les** —s to trim one's nails.

onglée [ɔ̃gle] *nf* numbness, tingling (of the fingers).

onglet [ɔ̃glɛ] *nm* guard, tab.

onguent [ɔ̃gɑ̃] *nm* ointment, salve.

onomatopée [ɔnɔmatɔpe] *nf* onomatopœia.

onyx [ɔniks] *nm* onyx.

onze [ɔ̃ːz] *a nm* eleven, eleventh.

onzième [ɔ̃zjɛm] *an* eleventh.

opacité [ɔpasite] *nf* opacity.

opale [ɔpal] *nf* opal.

opaque [ɔpak] *a* opaque.

opéra [ɔpɛra] *nm* opera, opera-house.

opérateur [ɔpɛratœːr] *nm* operator, cameraman.

opération [ɔpɛrasjɔ̃] *nf* operation, process, transaction; **salle d'**— operating room.

opératoire [ɔpɛratwaːr] *a* operative.

opéré [ɔpere] *n* person operated upon, surgical case.

opérer [ɔpere] *vt* to operate, perform an operation on, effect, work, carry out, make; **se faire** —to undergo an operation.

opérette [ɔpɛrɛt] *nf* operetta, light opera, musical comedy.

ophtalmique [ɔftalmik] *a* ophthalmic.

opiner [ɔpine] *vi* to express an opinion, vote; — **du bonnet** to nod approval.

opiniâtre [ɔpinjaːtr] *a* obstinate, opinionated, stubborn, dogged, persistent.

opiniâtrer [ɔpinjatre] *vr* to be obstinate, persist (in à).

opiniâtreté [ɔpinjatrəte] *nf* obstinacy.

opinion [ɔpiɲɔ̃] *nf* opinion, view.

opium [ɔpjɔm] *nm* opium.

opportun [ɔpɔrtœ̃] *a* opportune, timely, advisable.

opportunisme [ɔpɔrtynism] *nm* opportunism.

opportuniste [ɔpɔrtynist] *n* opportunist, time-server.

opportunité [ɔpɔrtynite] *nf* opportuneness, timeliness, advisability.

opposé [ɔpoze] *a* opposed, opposite, opposing; *nm* contrary, opposite, reverse; **à l'**— **de** contrary to.

opposition [ɔpozisjɔ̃] *nf* opposition, objection, injunction, contrast; **par** — **à** as opposed to, in contradiction to.

oppresser [ɔprɛse] *vt* to oppress.

oppresseur [ɔprɛsœːr] *a* oppressive, tyrannical; *nm* oppressor.

oppressif, -ive [ɔprɛsif, iv] *a* oppressive.

oppression [ɔprɛsjɔ̃] *nf* oppression.

opprimer [ɔprime] *vt* to oppress.

opprobre [ɔprɔbr] *nm* opprobrium' disgrace.

opter [ɔpte] *vt* to choose, decide (in favor of **pour**).

opticien [ɔptisjɛ̃] *nm* optician.

optimisme [ɔptimism] *nm* optimism.

optimiste [ɔptimist] *a* optimistic; *n* optimist.

option [ɔpsjɔ̃] *nf* choice, option

optique [ɔptik] *a* optic, visual, optical; *nf* optics.

opulence [ɔpylɑ̃ːs] *nf* opulence, affluence.

opulent [ɔpylɑ̃] *a* opulent, affluent, rich.

opuscule [ɔpyskyl] *nm* pamphlet.

or [ɔːr] *nm* gold; **à prix d'**— at an exorbitant price; **affaire d'**— good bargain, good thing; *cj* now.

oracle [ɔraːkl] *nm* oracle.

orage [ɔraːʒ] *nm* (thunder)storm.

orageux, -euse [ɔraʒø, øːz] *a* stormy, thundery.

oraison [ɔrɛzɔ̃] *nf* oration, prayer.

oral [ɔral] *a* oral, verbal; *nm* oral examination.

orange [ɔrɑ̃ːʒ] *nf* orange.

orangé [ɔrɑ̃ʒe] *a* orange(-colored).

orangeade [ɔrɑ̃ʒad] *nf* orangeade.

oranger [ɔrɑ̃ʒe] *nm* orange-tree; **fleur(s) d'**— orange-flower, -blossom.

orangerie [ɔrɑ̃ʒri] *nf* orange-grove, -greenhouse.

orang-outan(g) [ɔrɑ̃utɑ̃] *nm* orang-outang.

orateur [ɔratœːr] *nm* orator, speaker.

oratoire [ɔratwaːr] *a* oratorical; *nm* chapel, oratory.

orbe [ɔrb] *nm* orb, globe, heavenly body.

orbite [ɔrbit] *nf* orbit, socket.

orchestration [ɔrkɛstrasjɔ̃] *nf* orchestration.

orchestre [ɔrkɛstr] *nm* orchestra; **chef d'**— conductor.

orchestrer [ɔrkɛstre] *vt* to orchestrate, score.

orchidée [ɔrkide] *nf* orchid.

ordinaire [ɔrdinɛːr] *a* usual, common, ordinary, vulgar; **vin** — table wine; *nm* custom, wont, normal habit, daily fare; **d'**— as a rule; **comme d'**— as usual.

ordinal [ɔrdinal] *a* ordinal.

ordinateur [ɔrdinatœːr] *nm* computer.

ordonnance [ɔrdɔnɑ̃ːs] *nf* order, arrangement, ordinance, regulation, ruling, orderly, batman, medical prescription; **officier d'**— orderly officer, aide-de-camp.

ordonné [ɔrdɔne] *a* orderly, tidy, methodical.

ordonner [ɔrdɔne] *vt* to arrange, order, command, prescribe, ordain.

ordre [ɔrdr] *nm* order, method, discipline, class, character, command, warrant; **mettre en** — to put in order; **à l'**—! order! — **du jour**

order of the day, agenda; **cité à l'— du jour** mentioned in dispatches; **passer à l'— du jour** to proceed with the business; **jusqu'à nouvel — ** until further notice; **billet à — ** promissory note.

ordure [ɔrdyːr] *nf* dirt, filth(iness); *pl* rubbish, refuse; **boîte à —s** trash, garbage can.

ordurier, -ière [ɔrdyrje, jɛːr] *a* filthy, obscene.

oreille [ɔrɛːj] *nf* ear, lug; **avoir l'— dure** to be hard of hearing; **avoir de l'— ** to have a good ear; **dresser l'— ** to prick up one's ears; **se faire tirer l'— ** to have to be asked twice; **faire la sourde — ** to turn a deaf ear; **rebattre les —s à qn** to din in s.o.'s ears.

oreiller [ɔrɛje] *nm* pillow.

oreillon [ɔrɛjɔ̃] *nm* earflap; *pl* mumps.

ores [ɔːr] *ad* **d'— et déjà** here and now.

orfèvre [ɔrfɛːvr] *nm* goldsmith.

orfèvrerie [ɔrfɛvrəri] *nf* goldsmith's craft, shop, (gold, silver) plate.

orfraie [ɔrfrɛ] *nf* sea-hawk.

organdi [ɔrgɑ̃di] *nm* organdy.

organe [ɔrgan] *nm* organ, agency, mouthpiece.

organique [ɔrganik] *a* organic.

organisateur, -trice [ɔrganizatœːr, tris] *a* organizing; *n* organizer.

organisation [ɔrganizasjɔ̃] *nf* organization, organizing, constitution, body.

organiser [ɔrganize] *vt* to organize, arrange.

organisme [ɔrganism] *nm* organism, constitution, system.

organiste [ɔrganist] *nm* organist.

orge [ɔrʒ] *nf* barley.

orgelet [ɔrʒəlɛ] *nm* sty.

orgie [ɔrʒi] *nf* orgy, riot.

orgue [ɔrg] *nm* (*pl* is *f*) organ; **— de Barbarie** barrel-organ.

orgueil [ɔrgœːj] *nm* pride.

orgueilleux, -euse [ɔrgœjø, øːz] *a* proud.

orient [ɔrjɑ̃] *nm* Orient, East.

oriental [ɔrjɑ̃tal] *a* Eastern, East, Oriental; *n* Oriental.

orientation [ɔrjɑ̃tasjɔ̃] *nf* orientation, guidance, direction, trend.

orienter [ɔrjɑ̃te] *vt* to orient, guide, direct, point, take the bearings of; *vr* to find one's bearings, turn (to).

orifice [ɔrifis] *nm* opening, orifice.

originaire [ɔriʒinɛːr] *a* original, native, originating.

originairement [ɔriʒinɛrmɑ̃] *ad* originally.

original [ɔriʒinal] *a* original, first, novel, odd; *nm* original, top copy, eccentric.

originalement [ɔriʒinalmɑ̃] *ad* in an original manner, oddly.

originalité [ɔriʒinalite] *nf* originality, eccentricity.

origine [ɔriʒin] *nf* origin, beginning, extraction, source; **à l'— ** originally.

originel, -elle [ɔriʒinɛl] *a* original, primordial; **péché — ** original sin.

oripeau [ɔripo] *nm* tinsel; *pl* gaudy finery.

orme [ɔrm] *nm* elm-tree.

ornement [ɔrnəmɑ̃] *nm* ornament, adornment.

ornemental [ɔrnəmɑ̃tal] *a* ornamental, decorative.

ornementer [ɔrnəmɑ̃te] *vt* to ornament.

orner [ɔrne] *vt* to ornament, adorn.

ornière [ɔrnjɛːr] *nf* rut, groove.

ornithologie [ɔrnitɔlɔʒi] *nf* ornithology.

orphelin [ɔrfəlɛ̃] *a* orphan(ed); *n* orphan; **— de mère** motherless.

orphelinat [ɔrfəlina] *nm* orphanage.

orteil [ɔrtɛːj] *nm* toe.

orthodoxe [ɔrtɔdɔks] *a* orthodox, conventional.

orthodoxie [ɔrtɔdɔksi] *nf* orthodoxy.

orthographe [ɔrtɔgraf] *nf* spelling.

orthographier [ɔrtɔgrafje] *vt* to spell.

ortie [ɔrti] *nf* nettle.

os [ɔs; *pl* o] *nm* bone; **trempé jusqu'aux — ** soaked to the skin.

oscillateur [ɔsil(l)atœːr] *nm* oscillator.

oscillation [ɔsil(l)asjɔ̃] *nf* oscillation, fluctuation.

osciller [ɔsije, ɔsile] *vi* to oscillate, swing, flicker, fluctuate, waver.

osé [oze] *a* daring, bold.

oseille [ozɛːj, o-] *nf* sorrel.

oser [oze] *vt* to dare.

osier [ozje] *nm* osier; **panier d'— ** wicker-basket.

ossature [ɔsatyːr] *nf* frame(work), skeleton.

osselet [ɔslɛ] *nm* knuckle-bone.

ossements [ɔsmɑ̃, os-] *nm pl* bones.

osseux, -euse [ɔsø, øːz] *a* bony.

ossifier [ɔsifje] *vt* to ossify; *vr* to harden.

ossuaire [ɔsɥɛːr] *nm* charnel-house.

ostensible [ɔstɑ̃sibl] *a* ostensible.

ostensoir [ɔstɑ̃swaːr] *nm* monstrance.

ostentation [ɔstɑ̃tasjɔ̃] *nf* ostentation, show.

ostraciser [ɔstrasize] *vt* to ostracize.

ostréiculture [ɔstreikyltyːr] *nf* oyster-breeding.

otage [ɔtaːʒ] *nm* hostage.

ôter [ote] *vt* to remove, take away, take off; *vr* to remove oneself.

otite [ɔtit] *nf* otitis.

ottomane [ɔt(t)ɔman] *nf* divan, ottoman.

ou [u] *cj* or; **— ... — ** either ... or.

où [u] *ad inter* where?; *rel* where, in which, to which, when; **n'importe — ** anywhere; **d'— ? ** whence? where? where from? **d'— vient que ...?** how does it happen that ...? **jusqu'— ? ** how far? **partout — ** wherever.

ouailles [wɑːj] *nf pl* flock.
ouate [wat] *nf* wadding, cotton wool.
ouaté [wate] *a* padded, quilted, fleecy, soft.
ouater [wate] *vt* to pad, line with wadding, quilt.
oubli [ubli] *nm* forgetfulness, oblivion, omission, oversight; **par —** inadvertently.
oublie [ubli] *nf* cone, wafer.
oublier [ublie] *vt* to forget, neglect, overlook; *vr* to be unmindful of oneself, forget oneself.
oubliettes [ubliɛt] *nf pl* dungeon.
oublieux, -euse [ubliø, øːz] *a* forgetful, oblivious.
oued [wɛd] *nm* watercourse, wadi.
ouest [wɛst] *a* west(ern); *nm* west.
ouf [uf] *excl* ah! phew!
oui [wi] *ad* yes, ay(e); **je crois que —** I think so.
oui-dire [widiːr] *nm* hearsay.
ouïe [wi] *nf* (sense of) hearing; *pl* gills.
ouïr [wiːr, uiːr] *vt* to hear.
ouragan [uragɑ̃] *nm* hurricane.
ourdir [urdiːr] *vt* to warp, hatch, (*plot*) weave.
ourler [urle] *vt* to hem.
ourlet [urlɛ] *nm* hem, edge.
ours [urs] *nm* bear; **— blanc** polar bear; **— en peluche** teddy-bear; **— mal léché** unlicked cub, boorish fellow; **il ne faut pas vendre la peau de l'— avant de l'avoir tué** don't count your chickens before they are hatched.
oursin [ursɛ̃] *nm* sea-urchin.
ourson [ursɔ̃] *nm* bear's cub.
ouste [ust] *excl* **allez —!** off you go! clear out!
outil [uti] *nm* tool.
outillage [utijaːʒ] *nm* tools, gear, plant; **— national** national capital equipment.
outiller [utije] *vt* to equip, fit out; provide with tools, equip with plant.
outrage [utraːʒ] *nm* outrage, offense, contempt.
outrageant [utraʒɑ̃] *a* outrageous, insulting.
outrager [utraʒe] *vt* to outrage, insult, offend.
outrance [utrɑ̃ːs] *nf* excess; **à —** to the utmost, to the bitter end.
outre [uːtr] *prep* beyond, in addition to, ultra-; *ad* **passer — to** go on, take no notice (of), disregard; **en —** besides, over and above; **en — de** in addition to; **d'— en —** through and through; **— que** apart from the fact that.
outré [utre] *a* exaggerated, overdone.
outrecuidance [utrəkɥidɑ̃ːs] *nf* presumptuousness.
outre-Manche [utrəmɑ̃ːʃ] *ad* across the Channel.
outre-mer [utrəmɛːr] *ad* beyond the sea(s), oversea(s).

outrepasser [utrəpase] *vt* to exceed, go beyond.
outrer [utre] *vt* to exaggerate, overdo, carry to excess, revolt, provoke beyond measure.
ouvert [uvɛːr] *a* open, gaping, unfortified, frank; **grand —** wide open.
ouvertement [uvɛrtəmɑ̃] *ad* openly, frankly.
ouverture [uvɛrtyːr] *nf* opening, outbreak, overture, aperture, gap, width, span; **heures d'—** business hours, visiting hours.
ouvrable [uvrabl] *a* workable, working.
ouvrage [uvraːʒ] *nm* work, workmanship.
ouvragé [uvraʒe] *a* worked, wrought.
ouvrager [uvraʒe] *vt* to work, figure.
ouvrant [uvrɑ̃] *a* opening; *nm* leaf (of door).
ouvre-boîtes [uvrəbwat] *nm* can opener.
ouvre-bouteilles [uvrəbutɛːj] *nm* bottle-opener, can opener.
ouvrer [uvre] *vt* to work.
ouvreuse [uvrøːz] *nf* usher(ette).
ouvrier, -ière [uvrie, ɛːr] *a* working, labor; *n* worker, workman, operative, laborer, hand; *f* factory girl.
ouvrir [uvriːr] *vt* to open, turn (on), draw back, cut (through, open), lance, begin, start; *vi* to open (onto **sur**); *vr* to open, begin, open one's heart.
ovaire [ɔvɛːr] *nm* ovary.
ovale [ɔval] *a nm* oval.
ovation [ɔvasjɔ̃] *nf* ovation, acclamation.
oxydable [ɔksidabl] *a* oxidizable, liable to rust.
oxyde [ɔksid] *nm* oxide.
oxygène [ɔksiʒɛn] *nm* oxygen.
oxygéné [ɔksiʒene] *a* oxygenated; **eau —e** hydrogen peroxide; **cheveux —s** peroxided hair.
ozone [ɔzɔn, -oːn] *nm* ozone.

P

pacage [pakaːʒ] *nm* pasture, grazing.
pachyderme [paʃidɛrm, paki-] *a* thick-skinned; *nm* pachyderm.
pacificateur, -trice [pasifikatœːr, tris] *a* pacifying; *n* peace-maker.
pacification [pasifikasjɔ̃] *nf* pacification, peace-making.
pacifier [pasifje] *vt* to pacify, appease, quiet, calm down.
pacifique [pasifik] *a* pacific, peaceful.
pacifisme [pasifism] *nm* pacifism.
pacotille [pakɔtiːj] *nf* cheap goods; **de —** tawdry.
pacte [pakt] *nm* pact.
pactiser [paktize] *vi* to come to terms, treat.
pagaie [pagɛ] *nf* paddle.

pagaïe [pagaːj] *nf* rush, disorder, chaos.
paganisme [paganism] *nm* paganism.
pagayer [pagɛje] *vti* to paddle.
page [paːʒ] *nf* page; *nm* page(boy); **à la —** up to date.
pagination [paʒinasjɔ̃] *nf* paging, pagination.
pagne [paɲ] *nm* loincloth, (*Africa*) cloth (*toga*).
païen, -enne [pajɛ̃, jɛn] *a nf* pagan, heathen.
paillard [pajaːr] *a* lewd, ribald.
paillardise [pajardiːz] *nf* ribaldry, ribald joke.
paillasse [pajas] *nf* straw mattress, palliasse.
paillasson [pajasɔ̃] *nm* (door)mat, matting.
paille [paːj] *nf* straw, chaff, mote, flaw; **feu de —** flash in the pan; **homme de —** figurehead.
pailleter [pajte] *vt* to spangle.
paillette [pajɛt] *nf* spangle, flaw, flash, flake.
paillotte [pajɔt] *nf* straw, reed hut.
pain [pɛ̃] *nm* bread, loaf; **petit —** roll; **— de savon** cake of soap; **cela se vend comme du — frais** that sells like hot cakes; **pour une bouchée de —** for a mere song.
pair [pɛːr] *a* equal, even; *nm* equal, peer, par; **être au —** to have board and lodging but unpaid; **aller de — avec** to be in keeping with; **marcher de — avec** to keep abreast of; **traiter qn de — à égal** to treat someone as an equal.
paire [pɛːr] *nf* pair, brace.
pairie [pɛri] *nf* peerage.
paisible [pɛzibl] *a* peaceful, quiet.
paître [pɛːtr] *vt* to pasture, graze, crop; *vi* to browse, graze; **envoyer — qn** to send s.o. about his business.
paix [pɛ] *nf* peace(fulness), quiet (ness).
palabrer [palabre] *vi* to palaver.
palace [palas] *nm* magnificent hotel.
palais [palɛ] *nm* palace, palate; **P— de Justice** law-courts.
palan [palɑ̃] *nm* pulley-block, tackle.
palatal [palatal] *a* palatal.
pale [pal] *nf* blade, sluice.
pâle [pɑːl] *a* pale, pallid, wan.
palefrenier [palfrənje] *nm* groom, ostler.
palet [palɛ] *nm* quoit, puck.
paletot [palto] *nm* coat, overcoat.
palette [palɛt] *nf* palette, bat, blade; **roue à —s** paddle-wheel.
pâleur [pɑlœːr] *nf* pallor, paleness.
palier [palje] *nm* (*stair*) landing, stage, level stretch.
pâlir [pɑliːr] *vt* to make pale; *vi* to turn pale, grow dim.
palissade [palisad] *nf* palisade, fence, stockade.
palissandre [palisɑ̃ːdr] *nm* rosewood.

palliatif, -ive [palljatif, iːv] *a nm* palliative.
palmarès [palmarɛːs] *nm* prize list, honors list.
palme [palm] *nf* palm(-branch); **noix de —** palm nut.
palmier [palmje] *nm* palm-tree.
palonnier [palɔnje] *nm* swing-bar, rudder-bar.
pâlot, -otte [palo, ɔt] *a* palish, drawn.
palpable [palpabl] *a* palpable, obvious.
palpabilité [palpabilite] *nf* palpability, obviousness.
palper [palpe] *vt* to feel, finger.
palpitant [palpitɑ̃] *a* quivering, throbbing, fluttering, exciting.
palpiter [palpite] *vi* to palpitate, quiver, throb, flutter.
paludéen, -enne [palydeɛ̃, ɛn] *a* marsh.
paludisme [palydism] *nm* malaria.
pâmer [pame] *vir* to faint, swoon; **se — d'admiration devant** to go into raptures over.
pâmoison [pɑmwazɔ̃] *nf* swoon, faint.
pamphlet [pɑ̃flɛ] *nm* pamphlet, lampoon.
pamphlétaire [pɑ̃fletɛːr] *nm* pamphleteer.
pamplemousse [pɑ̃pləmus] *nf* grapefruit.
pampre [pɑ̃ːpr] *nm* vine-branch.
pan [pɑ̃] *nm* skirt, tail, flap, side, bit.
pan! [pɑ̃] *excl* bang!
panacée [panase] *nf* panacea.
panache [panaʃ] *nm* plume, tuft, trail, wreath, somersault; **avoir du —** to have style; **avoir son —** to be slightly intoxicated.
panaché [panaʃe] *a* plumed, mixed, motley; **bière —e** shandygaff.
panade [panad] *nf* **être dans la —** to be in a fix, to be in want.
panard [panaːr] *nm* (*fam*) foot.
panaris [panari] *nm* whitlow.
pancarte [pɑ̃kart] *nf* bill, placard.
panégyrique [paneʒirik] *a* eulogistic; *nm* panegyric.
paner [pane] *vt* to cover with breadcrumbs.
panier [panje] *nm* basket, hamper; **— à salade** salad shaker, black Maria; **— percé** spendthrift.
panique [panik] *a nf* panic.
panne [pan] *nf* plush, fat, breakdown; **en — hove** to, stranded, broken down; **rester en — d'essence** to run out of gas.
panneau [pano] *nm* panel, board, hoarding, trap.
panoplie [panɔpli] *nf* panoply, suit of armor.
panorama [panɔrama] *nm* panorama.
panoramique [panɔramik] *a* panoramic.
panse [pɑ̃ːs] *nf* paunch.

pansement [pãsmã] *nm* dressing.
panser [pãse] *vt* to dress, groom, rub down.
pansu [pãsy] *a* pot-bellied.
pantalon [pãtalɔ̃] *nm* trousers, knickers.
pantelant [pãtlã] *a* panting.
panthéisme [pãteism] *nm* pantheism.
panthère [pãtɛːr] *nf* panther.
pantin [pãtɛ̃] *nm* jumping-jack, puppet, nobody.
pantois [pãtwa] *a* flabbergasted, speechless.
pantomime [pãtɔmim] *nf* pantomime, dumb show.
pantoufle [pãtufl] *nf* slipper.
panure [panyːr] *nf* bread-crumbs.
paon, -onne [pã, pan] *n* peacock, -hen.
papa [papa] *nm* daddy, papa; à la — unhurriedly; **de** — old-fashioned.
papauté [papote] *nf* papacy.
papaye [papɛ] *nf* pawpaw.
pape [pap] *nm* Pope.
papelard [paplaːr] *a nmf* sanctimonious (person).
paperasse [papras] *nf* official paper, old paper, red tape.
paperassier, -ière [paprasje, jɛːr] *a* who likes to accumulate papers, bureaucratic.
papeterie [paptri] *nf* paper manufacture, trade, mill, stationer's shop.
papetier, -ière [paptje, jɛːr] *n* paper-manufacturer, stationer.
papier [papje] *nm* paper, document; — **à lettres** notepaper; — **de soie** tissue paper; — **peint** wallpaper; — **hygiénique** toilet paper.
papillon [papijɔ̃] *nm* butterfly, moth, leaflet, inset, ticket.
papillonner [papijɔne] *vi* to flit, flutter about.
papillote [papijɔt] *nf* curl paper, oiled paper for cooking.
papilloter [papijɔte] *vt* to put into curl papers; *vi* to flicker, blink.
papyrus [papiryːs] *nm* papyrus.
pâque [pɑːk] *nf* Passover.
paquebot [pakbo] *nm* steamer, liner, packet-boat.
pâquerette [pɑkrɛt] *nf* daisy.
Pâques [pɑːk] *nm* Easter; *nf pl* Easter sacrament; — **fleuries** Palm Sunday.
paquet [pakɛ] *nm* parcel, package, bundle; — **de mer** mass of sea water, heavy sea.
par [par] *prep* by, through, for, with, in, from, out, over, about, on, out of; — **où a-t-il passé?** which way did he go? — **ici (là)** this way (that way); — **trop difficile** far too difficult; —**ci**, —**là** here and there.
parabole [parabɔl] *nf* parable, parabola.
parabolique [parabɔlik] *a* parabolic.

parachever [paraʃve] *vt* to finish off, complete.
parachute [paraʃyt] *nm* parachute.
parachutiste [paraʃytist] *n* parachutist, paratrooper.
parade [parad] *nf* parade, show, display, parry.
paradis [paradi] *nm* paradise, heaven, gallery.
paradoxal [paradɔksal] *a* paradoxical.
paradoxe [paradɔks] *nm* paradox.
paraffine [parafin] *nf* (liquid) paraffin.
parage [paraːʒ] *nm* trimming, birth, lineage; *pl* regions, parts, latitudes.
paragraphe [paragraf] *nm* paragraph.
paraître [parɛːtr] *vi* to appear, seem, look, be published, show; il y **paraît** that is quite obvious; **à ce qu'il me paraît** as far as I can judge.
parallèle [parallɛl] *a nm* parallel, comparison.
parallélogramme [parallelɔgram] *nm* parallelogram.
paralyser [paralize] *vt* to paralyze, cripple.
paralysie [paralizi] *nf* paralysis.
paralytique [paralitik] *a nmf* paralytic.
parangon [parãgɔ̃] *nm* paragon, flawless gem.
parapet [parapɛ] *nm* parapet.
paraphe [paraf] *nm* flourish, initial.
parapher [parafe] *vt* to initial.
paraphrase [parafrɑːz] *nf* paraphrase.
paraphraser [parafraze] *vt* to paraphrase.
parapluie [paraplɥi] *nm* umbrella.
parasite [parazit] *a* parasitic; *nm* parasite; *pl* (*radio*) interference.
parasol [parasɔl] *nm* sunshade, parasol.
paratonnerre [paratɔnɛːr] *nm* lightning conductor.
paratyphoïde [paratifɔid] *a nf* paratyphoid.
paravent [paravã] *nm* folding-screen.
parbleu [parblø] *excl* I should think so! you bet!
parc [park] *nm* park, pen, paddock, parking lot; — **à huîtres** oyster bed.
parcage [parkaːʒ] *nm* penning, (*cars*) parking.
parcelle [parsɛl] *nf* particle, scrap, plot.
parce que [pars(ə)kə] *cj* because.
parchemin [parʃəmɛ̃] *nm* parchment, vellum.
parcimonie [parsimɔni] *nf* parsimony, meanness.
parcimonieux, -euse [parsimɔnjø, øːz] *a* parsimonious, niggardly.
parcourir [parkuriːr] *vt* to go through, travel over (through), read through, glance through, cover.

parcours [parku:r] *nm* distance, mileage, run, course.

par-dessous [pardəsu] *prep* under, beneath; *ad* underneath, under it, them.

par-dessus [pardəsy] *prep* over; *ad* over it, them, on top (of it, them); *nm* overcoat.

par-devant [pardəvã] *prep* before, in the presence of.

pardon [pardɔ̃] *nm* pardon, forgiveness, pilgrimage.

pardonner [pardɔne] *vt* to forgive, pardon, excuse.

pare-boue [parbu] *nm* fender.

pare-brise [parbri:z] *nm* windscreen, windshield.

pare-chocs [parʃɔk] *nm* bumper.

pareil, -eille [parɛ:j] *a* similar, like, same, equal, such; *nmf* peer, equal, match; **rendre la —le à qn** to get even with s.o.

pareillement [parɛjmã] *ad* likewise, also.

parement [parmã] *nm* cuff, altar cloth, facing, curbstone.

parent [parã] *nm* relative, kinsman; *pl* parents, relations.

parenté [parãte] *nf* relationship, kinship.

parenthèse [parãtɛ:z] *nf* parenthesis, digression, bracket; **entre —s** in parentheses, by the way.

parer [pare] *vt* to adorn, deck out, trim, pare, ward off; *vi* **— à qch** to guard against sth.

paresse [parɛs] *nf* laziness, sloth, sluggishness.

paresser [parɛse] *vi* to idle, laze.

paresseux, -euse [parɛsø, ø:z] *a* lazy, idle, sluggish; *n* lazybones.

parfaire [parfɛ:r] *vt* to finish off, complete.

parfait [parfɛ] *a* perfect, real; *nm* perfect tense.

parfaitement [parfɛtmã] *ad* perfectly, absolutely, exactly, quite so.

parfois [parfwa] *ad* sometimes, occasionally, at times.

parfum [parfœ̃] *nm* perfume, scent, flavor.

parfumé [parfyme] *a* perfumed, scented, fragrant, flavored.

parfumerie [parfymri] *nf* perfumery.

pari [pari] *nm* bet, wager; **— mutuel** totalizator.

paria [parja] *nm* outcast.

parier [parje] *vt* to bet, lay wager.

parieur, -euse [parjœ:r, ø:z] *n* backer, punter.

parisien, -ienne [parizjɛ̃, jɛn] *nmf* Parisian, from Paris.

paritaire [paritɛ:r] *a* **représentation — equal** representation.

parité [parite] *nf* parity, equality, evenness.

parjure [parʒy:r] *a* perjured; *n* perjurer; *nm* perjury.

parlant [parlã] *a* talking; **film — talkie.**

parlement [parləmã] *nm* parliament.

parlementaire [parləmãtɛ:r] *a* parliamentary; **drapeau — flag of truce.**

parlementer [parləmãte] *vi* to parley.

parler [parle] *vti* to speak, talk; *nm* speech, speaking; **façon de — manner of speaking.**

parleur, -euse [parlœ:r, ø:z] *n* speaker, talker.

parloir [parlwa:r] *nm* parlour.

parmi [parmi] *prep* among(st), amid(st).

Parnasse [parna:s] *nf* Parnassus.

parodie [parɔdi] *nf* parody, skit.

parodier [parɔdje] *vt* to parody, do a skit on.

paroi [parwa] *nf* partition, wall, lining.

paroisse [parwas] *nf* parish.

paroissial [parwasjal] *a* parochial.

paroissien, -enne [parwasjɛ̃, jɛn] *a* parochial; *n* parishioner; *nm* prayerbook.

parole [parɔl] *nf* word, remark, parole, promise, (power of) speech; **porter la —** to be the spokesman.

paroxysme [parɔksism] *nm* paroxysm, fit, outburst.

parquer [parke] *vt* to pen up, imprison, park.

parquet [parkɛ] *nm* floor(ing), public prosecutor's department.

parqueter [parkəte] *vt* to parquet, floor.

parqueterie [parkətri] *nf* laying of floors, parquetry.

parrain [parɛ̃] *nm* godfather, sponsor.

parricide [parisid] *a* parricidal; *nm* parricide.

parsemer [parsəme] *vt* to sprinkle, strew, dot.

part [pa:r] *nf* share, portion, part; **billet de faire—invitation, announcement** (*wedding, funeral*): **prendre— à** to take part in, join in; **faire — de qch à qn** to acquaint s.o. with sth; **de — en —** through and through; **de — et d'autre** on both sides; **d'une —, d'autre —** on the one hand, on the other hand; **à — aside,** except for.

partage [parta:ʒ] *nm* sharing, portion, allotment.

partager [partaʒe] *vt* to divide, share (out), apportion.

partance [partã:s] *nf* departure; **en — (outward) bound, outgoing.**

partant [partã] *a* departing; *nm* *pl* departing guests, starters; *ad* therefore.

partenaire [partənɛ:r] *nmf* partner.

parterre [partɛ:r] *nm* flower-bed, pit.

parti [parti] *nm* party, side, advantage, decision, course, match; **se ranger du — de** to side with; **en prendre son —** to make the best of it; **tirer — de** to take advantage of;

— pris prejudice; *a* gone, away tipsy.
partial [parsjal] *a* partial, prejudiced.
partialité [parsjalite] *nf* partiality, prejudice.
participation [partisipasjɔ̃] *nf* participation, share.
participe [partisip] *nm* participle.
participer [partisipe] *vi* to participate, share; — **de** to partake of, have something of.
particulariser [partikylarize] *vt* to particularize, specify; *vr* to be different from others.
particularité [partikylarite] *nf* particularity, peculiarity.
particule [partikyl] *nf* particle.
particulier, -ière [partikylje, jɛːr] *a* particular, peculiar, special, personal, private; *n* private individual.
partie [parti] *nf* part, party, game; **faire — de** to belong to, be part of; **se mettre de la —** to join in; **prendre à —** to call to account.
partiel [parsjɛl] *a* partial.
partir [partiːr] *vi* to depart, leave, set off, go away, start; — **(d'un éclat) de rire** to burst out laughing.
partisan [partizɑ̃] *nm* partisan, supporter, follower, guerrilla soldier.
partition [partisjɔ̃] *nf* partition, score.
partout [partu] *ad* everywhere; — **où** wherever.
parure [paryːr] *nf* adorning, ornament, dress, set of jewelry.
parution [parysjɔ̃] *nf* appearance, publication.
parvenir [parvəniːr] *vi* to arrive, reach, attain, manage, succeed.
parvenu [parvəny] *n* upstart.
parvis [parvi] *nm* parvis, square.
pas [pɑ] *ad* not; *nm* step, pace, tread, threshold, strait, pass; **mauvais —** awkward predicament; **à deux — d'ici** nearby, just round the corner; **au —** at walking pace, dead slow; **prendre le — sur** to take precedence over.
passable [pɑsabl] *a* passable, fair.
passage [pɑsaːʒ] *nm* passage, way through, passing, crossing, transition; **être de —** to be passing through; — **interdit** no thoroughfare.
passager, -ère [pɑsaʒe, ɛːr] *a* fleeting, short-lived; *n* passenger.
passant [pɑsɑ̃] *a* busy; *n* passer-by.
passe [pɑːs] *nf* pass(ing), channel, permit, thrust; **en — de** in a fair way to.
passementerie [pɑsmɑ̃tri] *nf* lace (trade), trimmings.
passe-montagne [pɑsmɔ̃taɲ] *nm* Balaclava (helmet).
passe-partout [pɑspartu] *nm* master-, (skeleton-)key.
passe-passe [pɑspɑs] *nm* sleight of hand.

passeport [pɑspɔːr] *nm* passport.
passé [pɑse] *a* past, over, faded; *nm* past.
passer [pɑse] *vt* to pass, hand, cross, ferry across, exceed, excuse, spend, strain, slip on; *vi* to pass (on, over, off, by, through), fade, call, to be shown, be promoted; *vr* to happen, take place, go off, be spent; — **un examen** to take an examination; **faire —** to hand around; **se faire — pour** to pose as; **se—de** to do without.
passereau [pɑsro] *nm* sparrow.
passerelle [pɑsrɛl] *nf* foot-bridge, (ship) bridge, gangway.
passe-temps [pɑstɑ̃] *nm* pastime.
passeur, -euse [pɑsœːr, øːz] *n* ferryman (woman).
passible [pɑsibl] *a* liable.
passif, -ive [pasif, iːv] *a* passive; *nm* debit, liabilities, passive voice.
passion [pɑsjɔ̃] *nf* passion.
passionnel, -elle [pɑsjɔnɛl] *a* concerning the passions, caused by jealousy.
passionné [pɑsjɔne] *a* passionate, enthusiastic; *nmf* enthusiast.
passionner [pɑsjɔne] *vt* to impassion, thrill, excite, fill with enthusiasm; *vr* to become passionately fond (of **pour**), be enthusiastic (over **pour**).
passivité [pasivite] *nf* passivity.
passoire [pɑswaːr] *nf* strainer.
pastel [pastɛl] *nm* crayon, pastel (drawing).
pastèque [pastɛk] *nf* water-melon.
pasteur [pastœːr] *nm* shepherd, pastor, minister.
pasteuriser [pastœrize] *vt* to pasteurize.
pastiche [pastiʃ] *nm* pastiche, parody.
pastille [pastiːj] *nf* lozenge, drop, (rubber) patch.
pastis [pastis] *nm* aniseed aperitif, a muddle.
pastoral [pastɔral] *a* pastoral.
pat [pat] *a* nm stalemate.
pataquès [patakɛːs] *nm* faulty liaison.
patate [patat] *nf* (sweet) potato, (*fam*) spud.
patati [patati] **et — et patata** and so on and so forth.
pataud [pato] *a* clumsy, boorish.
patauger [patoʒe] *vi* to splash, flounder, paddle.
pâte [pɑːt] *nf* paste, dough, fufu (*W. African*); *pl* noodles, spaghetti *etc*; **être de la — des héros** to be of the stuff that heroes are made of; **quelle bonne — d'homme** what a good guy.
pâté [pate] *nm* pie, blot, block.
patée [pate] *nf* mash, food.
patelin [patlɛ̃] *a* glib, wheedling; *nm* village.
patenôtre [patnoːtr] *nf* Lord's prayer.

patent [patɑ̃] *a* patent, obvious.
patente [patɑ̃:t] *nf* license.
patenter [patɑ̃te] *vt* to license; **faire** — to patent.
patère [patɛ:r] *nf* (hat-) coat-peg.
paterne [patɛrn] *a* patronizing.
paternel, -elle [patɛrnɛl] *a* paternal, fatherly.
paternité [patɛrnite] *nf* paternity, fatherhood.
pâteux, -euse [patø, ø:z] *a* doughy, thick, coated.
pathétique [patetik] *a* pathetic, touching; *nm* pathos.
pathologie [patɔlɔʒi] *nf* pathology.
pathos [patɔs] *nm* bathos.
patibulaire [patibylɛ:r] *a* of the gallows, hangdog.
patiemment [pasjamɑ̃] *ad* patiently.
patience [pasjɑ̃:s] *nf* patience.
patient [pasjɑ̃] *a* patient, long-suffering; *n* patient.
patienter [pasjɑ̃te] *vi* to have patience.
patin [patɛ̃] *nm* skate, runner, skid; **—s à roulettes** roller skates.
patine [patin] *nf* patina.
patiner [patine] *vi* to skate, slip.
patineur, -euse [patinœ:r, ø:z] *n* skater.
patinoire [patinwa:r] *nf* skating-rink.
pâtir [pati:r] *vi* to suffer.
pâtisserie [patisri] *nf* pastry (-making), pastry-shop, tea-room; *pl* cakes.
pâtissier, -ière [patisje, jɛ:r] *n* pastry-cook, tea-room proprietor.
patois [patwa] *nm* patois, dialect, lingo.
patraque [patrak] *a* out of sorts, seedy, rotten.
pâtre [pa:tr] *nm* herdsman, shepherd.
patriarche [patriarʃ] *nm* patriarch.
patrie [patri] *nf* native land, father-land.
patrimoine [patrimwan] *nm* patrimony, heritage.
patriote [patriɔt] *a* patriotic; *nmf* patriot.
patriotique [patriɔtik] *a* patriotic.
patriotisme [patriɔtism] *nm* patriotism.
patron, -onne [patrɔ̃, ɔn] *n* patron, patron saint, protector, head, boss, skipper; *nm* pattern, model.
patronal [patrɔnal] *a* of a patron saint, of employers.
patronat [patrɔna] *nm* (body of) employers.
patronner [patrɔne] *vt* to patronize, support.
patrouille [patru:j] *nf* patrol.
patrouiller [patruje] *vi* to patrol.
patte [pat] *nf* paw, foot, leg, tab, flap; **— de mouches** scrawl.
patte-d'oie [patdwa] *nf* crossroads; *pl* crow's feet, wrinkles.
pattemouille [patmu:j] *f* damp cloth (*for ironing*).

pâturage [patyra:ʒ] *nm* grazing, pasture.
pâture [paty:r] *nf* food, pasture.
paturon [patyrɔ̃] *nm* pastern.
paume [po:m] *nf* palm (of hand), tennis.
paupière [popjɛ:r] *nf* eyelid.
paupiette [popjet] *nf* (veal) bird.
pause [po:z] *nf* pause, interval, rest; **—café** coffee-break.
pauvre [po:vr] *a* poor, scanty, sorry, wretched, shabby; *n* poor man, woman.
pauvresse [povrɛs] *nf* poor woman.
pauvreté [povrəte] *nf* poverty, want.
se pavaner [səpavane] *vr* to strut (about).
pavé [pave] *nm* pavement, paved road, paving-stone, slab; **battre le** — to walk the streets; **prendre le haut du** — to assume lordly airs.
pavillon [pavijɔ̃] *nm* pavilion, lodge, flag, ear- (mouth)piece, bell (of brass instrument); **— de jardin** summer-house.
pavoiser [pavwaze] *vt* to deck with flags, bunting.
pavot [pavo] *nm* poppy.
payable [pɛjabl] *a* payable.
payant [pɛjɑ̃] *a* paying; *n* payer.
paye [pɛ:j] *nf* pay, wages.
payement [pɛjmɑ̃] *nm* payment.
payer [pɛje] *vt* to pay (for), stand, treat; *vi* to pay; **—d'audace** to brazen it out, put a bold face on it; **— de mots** to put off with fine talk; **se — la tête de qn** to get a rise out of s.o.; **il est payé pour le savoir** he knows it to his cost.
payeur, -euse [pɛjœ:r, ø:z] *n* payer, teller, paymaster.
pays [pe(j)i] *nm* country, land, district, locality; *n* (*f* payse) fellow-countryman, -woman.
paysage [peiza:ʒ] *nm* landscape, scenery.
paysagiste [peizaʒist] *nm* landscape painter.
paysan, -anne [peizɑ̃, an] *an* peasant; *n* countryman.
péage [pea:ʒ] *nm* toll.
peau [po] *nf* skin, hide, peel; **avoir qn dans la** — to be head over heels in love with s.o.; **faire — neuve** to cast its skin, turn over a new leaf.
peau-rouge [poru:ʒ] *nm* redskin, Red Indian.
peccadille [pɛkadi:j] *nf* peccadillo.
pêche [pɛʃ] *nf* fishing, fishery, catch, peach.
péché [peʃe] *nm* sin.
pécher [peʃe] *vi* to sin.
pêcher [peʃe] *vt* to fish for, fish up; *vi* to fish.
pêcherie [pɛʃri] *nf* fishery, fishing-ground.
pécheur, -eresse [peʃœ:r, peʃrɛs] *a* sinning; *n* sinner.
pêcheur, -euse [pɛʃœ:r, ø:z] *a* fishing; *n* fisher, fisherman, -woman; **— à la ligne** angler.

péculateur [pekylatœːr] *nm* peculator, embezzler.

pécule [pekyl] *nf* savings, nest-egg, gratuity.

pécuniaire [pekynjɛːr] *a* pecuniary.

pédagogie [pɛdagɔʒi] *nf* pedagogy.

pédagogique [pɛdagɔʒik] *a* pedagogic.

pédale [pɛdal] *nf* pedal, treadle.

pédaler [pɛdale] *vi* to pedal, cycle.

pédant [pɛdɑ̃] *a* pedantic; *n* pedant.

pédicure [pedikyːr] *n* chiropodist.

pègre [pɛːgr] *nf* underworld.

peigne [pɛɲ] *nm* comb, card.

peigné [pɛɲe] *a* combed; **bien —** well-groomed; **mal —** unkempt, tousled.

peignée [pɛɲe] *nf* drubbing.

peigner [pɛɲe] *vt* to comb (out), card, dress down.

peignoir [pɛɲwaːr] *nm* (woman's) dressing-gown, wrap.

peindre [pɛ̃ːdr] *vt* to paint, depict.

peine [pɛn] *nf* penalty, punishment, affliction, sorrow, trouble, difficulty; **homme de — laborer; en être pour sa —** to have one's trouble for nothing; **à —** hardly, scarcely.

peiner [pɛne] *vt* to vex, grieve, pain; *vi* toil, drudge.

peintre [pɛ̃ːtr] *nm* painter, artist.

peinture [pɛ̃tyːr] *nf* painting, picture, paint.

péjoratif, -ive [peʒɔratif, iːv] *a* pejorative.

pelage [pəlaːʒ] *nm* coat, fur, wool.

pêle-mêle [pɛlmɛl] *ad* pell-mell, helter-skelter; *nm* jumble.

peler [p(ə)le] *vt* to peel, skin; *vi* to peel off.

pèlerin [pɛlrɛ̃] *n* pilgrim.

pèlerine [pɛlrin] *nf* cape.

pèlerinage [pɛlrinaːʒ] *nm* pilgrimage.

pélican [pelikɑ̃] *nm* pelican.

pelisse [p(ə)lis] *nf* pelisse, fur-lined coat.

pelle [pɛl] *nf* shovel, scoop.

pelleter [pɛlte] *vt* to shovel.

pelleterie [pɛltri] *nf* fur-trade, furriery.

pelletier, -ière [pɛltje, jɛːr] *n* furrier.

pellicule [pɛlikyl] *nf* pellicle, skin, film; *pl* dandruff.

pelote [plɔt] *nf* ball, wad, pincushion, pelota.

peloton [plɔtɔ̃] *nm* ball, group, squad, platoon.

pelotonner [plɔtɔne] *vt* to wind into a ball; *vr* to curl up, huddle together.

pelouse [pluːz] *nf* lawn, green, public enclosure.

peluche [plyʃ] *nf* plush, shag.

pelure [plyːr] *nf* peel, skin, rind; **papier — onionskin paper.**

pénal [penal] *a* penal.

pénalité [penalite] *nf* penalty.

penaud [pəno] *a* crestfallen, sheepish, abashed.

penchant [pɑ̃ʃɑ̃] *nm* slope, tendency.

penché [pɑ̃ʃe] *a* leaning, stooping.

pencher [pɑ̃ʃe] *vt* to bend, tilt; *vi* to lean, incline; *vr* to stoop, bend, lean.

pendable [pɑ̃dabl] *a* hanging, abominable.

pendaison [pɑ̃dɛzɔ̃] *nf* hanging.

pendant [pɑ̃dɑ̃] *a* hanging, pending, baggy; *nm* pendant, counterpoint; *prep* during, for; *cj* **— que** while, whilst.

pendeloque [pɑ̃dlɔk] *nf* pendant, drop, shred.

penderie [pɑ̃dri] *nf* wardrobe.

pendre [pɑ̃ːdr] *vt* to hang, hang up; *vi* to hang (down).

pendu [pɑ̃dy] *a* hanged, hanging.

pendule [pɑ̃dyl] *nf* clock; *nm* pendulum, balancer.

pêne [pɛːn] *nm* bolt, latch.

pénétrable [penɛtrabl] *a* penetrable.

pénétrant [penɛtrɑ̃] *a* penetrating, piercing, keen.

pénétration [penɛtrasjɔ̃] *nf* penetration, shrewdness, insight, perspicacity.

pénétré [penetre] *a* penetrated, imbued, full, earnest.

pénétrer [penetre] *vt* to penetrate, pierce, imbue, see through; *vi* to penetrate, enter, break (into); *vr* to become imbued, impregnated.

pénible [penibl] *a* painful, distressing, hard.

péniche [peniʃ] *nf* barge, lighter.

péninsule [penɛ̃syl] *nf* peninsula.

pénitence [penitɑ̃ːs] *nf* penitence, repentance, penance, disgrace.

pénitencier [penitɑ̃sje] *nm* penitentiary.

pénitent [penitɑ̃] *an* penitent.

pénitentiaire [penitɑ̃sjɛːr] *a* penitentiary.

penne [pɛn] *nf* quill, feather.

pénombre [penɔ̃ːbr] *nf* half-light, semi-darkness.

pensant [pɑ̃sɑ̃] *a* thinking; **bien —** orthodox, right-thinking, moral; **mal —** unorthodox, evil-thinking.

pensée [pɑ̃se] *nf* thought, idea, pansy.

penser [pɑ̃se] *vti* to think; **— à faire qch** to remember to do sth; **— le voir** to expect to see him; **il pensa mourir** he almost died; **vous n'y pensez pas** you don't mean it.

penseur, -euse [pɑ̃sœːr, øːz] *n* thinker.

pensif, -ive [pɑ̃sif, iːv] *a* pensive, thoughtful.

pension [pɑ̃sjɔ̃] *nf* pension, allowance, board and lodging, boarding-house, **-school; prendre — chez** to board, lodge with; **— de famille** residential hotel.

pensionnaire [pɑ̃sjɔnɛːr] *n* pensioner, boarder, inmate.

pensionnat [pɑ̃sjɔna] *nm* boarding-school, hostel.

pensum [pɛ̃sɔm] *nm* imposition, unpleasant task.

pentagonal [pɛ̃tagɔnal] *a* pentagonal.
pentagone [pɛ̃tagɔn] *a* pentagonal; *nm* pentagon.
pente [pɑ̃ːt] *nf* slope, gradient, bent.
Pentecôte [pɑ̃tkoːt] *nf* Pentecost.
pénurie [penyri] *nf* scarcity, shortage, poverty.
pépère [pepɛːr] *a* first-class, easy; *nm* granddad, old chap.
pépier [pepje] *vi* to peep, chirp.
pépin [pepɛ̃] *nm* pip, stone, umbrella, (*fam*) hitch, trouble.
pépinière [pepinjɛːr] *nf* nursery.
pepiniériste [pepinjerist] *nm* nurseryman.
pépite [pepit] *nf* nugget.
percale [pɛrkal] *nf* percale, chintz.
perçant [pɛrsɑ̃] *a* piercing, keen, shrill.
perce-neige [pɛrsnɛːʒ] *nm or f inv* snowdrop.
perce-oreille [pɛrsɔrɛːj] *nm* earwig.
percepteur, -trice [pɛrsɛptœːr, tris] *n* tax-collector.
perceptible [pɛrsɛptibl] *a* perceptible, audible, collectible.
perceptif, -ive [pɛrsɛptif, iːv] *a* perceptive.
perception [pɛrsɛpsjɔ̃] *nf* perception, collection, tax-office.
percée [pɛrse] *nf* cutting, opening, vista, break(through).
percer [pɛrse] *vt* to pierce, hole, go through, break through, broach, bore; *vi* to come through, break through.
perceuse [pɛrsøːz] *nf* drill.
percevable [pɛrsəvabl] *a* perceivable, leviable.
percevoir [pɛrsəvwaːr] *vt* to perceive, discern, collect.
perche [pɛrʃ] *nf* pole, rod, perch, lanky person.
percher [pɛrʃe] *vi* to roost, perch; *vr* to perch, alight.
percheron [pɛrʃərɔ̃] *nm* Percheron, draft horse.
perchoir [pɛrʃwaːr] *nm* perch, roost.
perclus [pɛrkly] *a* stiff, crippled, paralyzed.
perçoir [pɛrswaːr] *nm* gimlet, awl, broach.
percolateur [pɛrkɔlatœːr] *nm* percolator.
percussion [pɛrkysjɔ̃] *nf* percussion.
percutant [pɛrkytɑ̃] *a* percussive, percussion.
percuter [pɛrkyte] *vt* to strike, tap.
perdant [pɛrdɑ̃] *a* losing; *n* loser.
perdition [pɛrdisjɔ̃] *nf* perdition; **en** — sinking, on the road to ruin.
perdre [pɛrdr] *vt* to lose, waste, ruin. *vi* to lose, deteriorate; *vr* to get lost, go to waste, disappear; **il s'y perd** he can't make anything of it.
perdu [pɛrdy] *a* lost, ruined, doomed, wasted, spare, distracted; **à corps** — recklessly.
perdreau [pɛrdro] *nm* young partridge.

perdrix [pɛrdri] *nf* partridge.
père [pɛr] *nm* father, senior.
péremptoire [perɑ̃ptwaːr] *a* peremptory, final.
pérennité [perɛnnite] *nf* perenniality.
perfectible [pɛrfɛktibl] *a* perfectible.
perfection [pɛrfɛksjɔ̃] *nf* perfection, faultlessness.
perfectionnement [pɛrfɛksjɔnmɑ̃] *nm* perfecting, improving.
perfectionner [pɛrfɛksjɔne] *vt* to perfect, improve.
perfide [pɛrfid] *a* perfidious, treacherous.
perfidie [pɛrfidi] *nf* (act of) perfidy, perfidiousness.
perforant [pɛrfɔrɑ̃] *a* perforating, armor-piercing.
perforateur, -trice [pɛrfɔratœːr, tris] *a* perforating.
perforatrice [pɛrfɔratris] *nf* drill.
perforation [pɛrfɔrasjɔ̃] *nf* perforation, drilling.
performance [pɛrfɔrmɑ̃ːs] *nf* performance.
péricliter [periklite] *vi* to be shaky, in jeopardy.
péril [peril] *nm* peril, risk, danger.
périlleux, -euse [perijø, øːz] *a* perilous, hazardous; **saut** — somersault.
périmé [perime] *a* out of date, not valid, expired.
périmètre [perimɛtr] *nm* perimeter.
période [perjɔd] *nf* period, era, spell.
périodique [perjɔdik] *a* periodical, recurring; *nm* periodical.
péripétie [peripesi] *nf* vicissitude, change.
périphérie [periferi] *nf* periphery, circumference.
périphrase [perifraːz] *nf* periphrasis.
périr [periːr] *vi* to perish, die, be lost.
périscope [periskɔp] *nm* periscope.
périssable [perisabl] *a* perishable, mortal.
périssoire [periswaːr] *nf* canoe, skiff.
péristyle [peristil] *nm* peristyle.
péritonite [peritɔnit] *nf* peritonitis.
perle [pɛrl] *nf* pearl, bead, drop.
perler [pɛrle] *vt* to pearl, husk; *vi* to form in beads.
permanence [pɛrmanɑ̃ːs] *nf* permanence; **en** — continuous, permanent(ly).
permanent [pɛrmanɑ̃] *a* continuous, standing.
permanente [pɛrmanɑ̃t] *nf* permanent wave.
perméable [pɛrmeabl] *a* permeable, pervious.
permettre [pɛrmɛtr] *vt* to permit, allow, enable; *vr* to take the liberty, indulge (in de).
permis [pɛrmi] *a* permitted, allowed, permissible; *nm* permit, license.
permission [pɛrmisjɔ̃] *nf* permission, leave, pass.

permissionnaire [pɛrmisjɔnɛːr] *nm* person, soldier on leave.
permutation [pɛrmytasjɔ̃] *nf* permutation, exchange.
permuter [pɛrmyte] *vt* to exchange, permute.
pernicieux, -euse [pɛrnisjø, øːz] *a* pernicious, hurtful.
pérorer [perɔre] *vi* to deliver a harangue, expatiate.
perpendiculaire [pɛrpɑ̃dikylɛːr] *a nf* perpendicular.
perpétrer [pɛrpetre] *vt* to perpetrate.
perpétuel, -elle [pɛrpetɥɛl] *a* perpetual, endless.
perpétuer [pɛrpetɥe] *vt* to perpetuate; *vr* to last.
perpétuité [pɛrpetɥite] *nf* perpetuity; à — in perpetuity, for life.
perplexe [pɛrplɛks] *a* perplexed, at a loss, perplexing.
perplexité [pɛrplɛksite] *nf* perplexity, confusion.
perquisition [pɛrkizisjɔ̃] *nf* search, inquiry.
perquisitionner [pɛrkizisjɔne] *vi* to search.
perron [pɛrɔ̃] *nm* (flight of) steps.
perroquet [pɛrɔkɛ] *nm* parrot.
perruche [pɛryʃ] *nf* hen-parrot, parakeet.
perruque [pɛryk] *nf* wig.
perruquier, -ière [pɛrykje, jɛːr] *n* wigmaker.
pers [pɛːr] *a* bluish-green.
persan [pɛrsɑ̃] *an* Persian.
Perse [pɛrs] *nf* Persia.
persécuter [pɛrsekyte] *vt* to persecute, plague, dun.
persécution [pɛrsekysjɔ̃] *nf* persecution, pestering.
persévérance [pɛrseverɑ̃ːs] *nf* perseverance, doggedness, steadfastness.
persévérant [pɛrseverɑ̃] *a* persevering, dogged.
persévérer [pɛrsevere] *vi* to persevere, persist.
persienne [pɛrsjɛn] *nf* venetian blind, shutter.
persiflage [pɛrsiflaːʒ] *nm* persiflage, banter, chaff.
persil [pɛrsi] *nm* parsley.
persillé [pɛrsije] *a* blue-molded, spotted with fat.
persistance [pɛrsistɑ̃ːs] *nf* persistence, continuance, doggedness.
persistant [pɛrsistɑ̃] *a* persistent, dogged, steady.
persister [pɛrsiste] *vi* to persist, continue.
personnage [pɛrsɔnaːʒ] *nm* personage, character, individual, notability.
personnalité [pɛrsɔnalite] *nf* personality, personal remark, person of note.
personne [pɛrsɔn] *nf* person, individual; *pn* anyone, anybody, no one, nobody.
personnel, -elle [pɛrsɔnɛl] *a* person-

al, not transferable; *nm* personnel, staff.
personnification [pɛrsɔnifikasjɔ̃] *nf* personification.
personnifier [pɛrsɔnifje] *vt* to personify.
perspective [pɛrspɛktiːv] *nf* perspective, prospect, outlook, vista.
perspicace [pɛrspikas] *a* perspicacious, astute.
perspicacité [pɛrspikasite] *nf* perspicacity, insight, astuteness.
persuader [pɛrsɥade] *vt* to persuade, convince, induce.
persuasif, -ive [pɛrsɥazif, iːv] *a* persuasive.
persuasion [pɛrsɥazjɔ̃] *nf* persuasion, conviction.
perte [pɛrt] *nf* loss, waste, ruin; à — de vue as far as the eye can see.
pertinence [pɛrtinɑ̃ːs] *nf* pertinence, pertinency, relevancy.
pertinent [pɛrtinɑ̃] *a* pertinent, relevant.
perturbation [pɛrtyrbasjɔ̃] *nf* perturbation, disturbance, trepidation.
pervenche [pɛrvɑ̃ːʃ] *nf* periwinkle.
pervers [pɛrvɛːr] *a* perverse, depraved.
perversion [pɛrvɛrsjɔ̃] *nf* perversion, corruption.
perversité [pɛrvɛrsite] *nf* perversity, depravity.
pervertir [pɛrvɛrtiːr] *vt* to pervert, corrupt; *vr* to become depraved, corrupted.
pesage [pəzaːʒ] *nm* weighing, paddock.
pesant [pəzɑ̃] *a* heavy, ponderous; *nm* weight.
pesanteur [pəzɑ̃tœːr] *nf* weight, heaviness.
pesée [pəze] *nf* weighing, leverage.
pèse-lettres [pɛzlɛtr] *nm* postage scale.
peser [pəze] *vt* to weigh, ponder; *vi* to weigh, hang heavy, be a burden (to **sur**), stress.
pessimisme [pesimism] *nm* pessimism, despondency.
pessimiste [pesimist] *a* pessimistic; *n* pessimist.
peste [pɛst] *nf* plague, pestilence, pest.
pester [pɛste] *vi* to curse, storm (at **contre**).
pestifère [pɛstifɛːr] *a* pestiferous, pestilential.
pet [pɛ] *nm* fart; — de nonne fritter.
pétale [petal] *nm* petal.
pétarade [petarad] *nf* crackling, backfire, succession of bangs.
pétarader [petarade] *vi* to make a succession of bangs, backfire.
pétard [petaːr] *nm* detonator, blast, firecracker, torpedo (*railroad*).
péter [pete] *vi* to fart, pop, bang, crackle.
pétiller [petije] *vi* to spark(le), fizz, bubble, crackle.

petit [pəti] *a* small, little, tiny, petty; *n* little boy, girl, pup, kitten, cub, whelp.
petit-beurre [pətibœːr] *nm* biscuit.
petite-fille [pətitfiːj] *nf* granddaughter.
petitement [pətitmɑ̃] *ad* in a limited way, pettily, half-heartedly.
petitesse [pətitɛs] *nf* smallness, tininess, pettiness, mean act, thing.
petit-fils [pətifis] *nm* grandson.
petit-gris [pətigri] *nm* squirrel (fur).
pétition [petisjɔ̃] *nf* petition.
pétitionner [petisjɔne] *vi* to make a petition.
petit-lait [pətilɛ] *nm* whey.
petit-maître [pətimɛtr] *nm* fop, dandy.
petits-enfants [pətizɑ̃fɑ̃] *nm pl* grandchildren.
pétrifier [petrifje] *vt* to petrify; *vr* to be petrified, turn into stone.
pétrin [petrɛ̃] *nm* kneading-trough; **dans le — ** in the soup, in a fix.
pétrir [petriːr] *vt* to knead, mold, shape; **pétri d'orgueil** bursting with pride.
pétrole [petrɔl] *nm* petroleum, kerosene.
pétrolier [petrɔlje] *a* oil; *nm* oil-tanker.
pétrolifère [petrɔlifɛːr] *a* oil(bearing).
pétulance [petylɑ̃ːs] *nf* liveliness, impulsiveness.
peu [pø] *ad* little, not much, few, not many, not very, dis-, un-, -less; **un —** a little, rather, just; **à —** little by little; **avant —, d'ici —** before long; **à — près** almost; **quelque —** not a little, somewhat; **pour — que** however little.
peuplade [pœplad] *nf* tribe.
peuple [pœpl] *nm* people, nation, masses; **petit —** lower classes.
peupler [pœple] *vt* to populate, stock, throng; *vr* to become populous, peopled.
peuplier [pøplie] *nm* poplar.
peur [pœːr] *nf* fear, fright; **avoir une — bleue** to be in a blue funk; **à faire —** frightfully; **faire — à** to frighten; **de — que** lest, for fear that.
peureux, -euse [pœrø, øːz] *a* timorous, timid.
peut-être [pøtɛːtr] *ad* perhaps, maybe.
phacochère [fakɔʃɛːr] *nm* warthog.
phalange [falɑ̃ːʒ] *nf* phalanx, finger, toe-joint; host.
phalène [falɛn] *nf* moth.
pharamineux, -euse [faraminø, øːz] *a* colossal, terrific.
phare [faːr] *nm* lighthouse, beacon, headlight.
pharmaceutique [farmasøtik] *a* pharmaceutic(al).
pharmacie [farmasi] *nf* pharmacy,

drugstore, dispensary; **armoire à —** medicine-chest.
pharmacien, -enne [farmasjɛ̃, jɛn] *n* chemist, druggist.
pharyngite [farɛ̃ʒit] *nf* pharyngitis.
phase [fɑːz] *nf* phase, stage, phasis.
phénique [fenik] *a* carbolic.
phénix [feniks] *nm* phœnix, paragon.
phénoménal [fenɔmenal] *a* phenomenal.
phénomène [fenɔmɛn] *nm* phenomenon, freak, marvel.
philanthrope [filɑ̃trɔp] *nm* philanthropist.
philanthropie [filɑ̃trɔpi] *nf* philanthropy.
philatéliste [filatelist] *n* philatelist, stamp-collector.
philistin [filistɛ̃] *an* Philistine.
philologie [filɔlɔʒi] *nf* philology.
philosophe [filɔzɔf] *a* philosophical; *n* philosopher.
philosophie [filɔzofi] *nf* philosophy.
philosophique [filɔzɔfik] *a* philosophical.
phobie [fɔbi] *nf* phobia.
phonétique [fɔnetik] *a* phonetic; *nf* phonetics.
phonologie [fɔnɔlɔʒi] *nf* phonology, phonemics.
phoque [fɔk] *nm* seal.
phosphate [fɔsfat] *nm* phosphate.
phosphore [fɔsfɔːr] *nm* phosphorus.
phosphorescence [fɔsfɔressɑ̃ːs] *nf* phosphorescence.
photo [fɔto] *nf* photo.
photogénique [fɔtɔʒenik] *a* photogenic.
photographe [fɔtɔgraf] *nm* photographer.
photographie [fɔtɔgrafi] *nf* photography, photograph.
photographier [fɔtɔgrafje] *vt* to photograph.
phrase [frɑːz] *nf* sentence, phrase; **faire des —s** to use flowery language.
phraseur, -euse [frazœːr, øːz] *n* wordy speaker, empty talker.
phtisie [ftizi] *nf* phthisis, consumption.
phtisique [ftizik] *an* consumptive.
physicien, -enne [fizisjɛ̃, jɛn] *n* physicist, natural philosopher.
physiologie [fizjɔlɔʒi] *nf* physiology
physiologique [fizjɔlɔʒik] *a* physiological.
physionomie [fizjɔnɔmi] *nf* physiognomy, countenance.
physique [fizik] *a* physical, bodily; *nm* physique; *nf* physics, natural philosophy.
piaffer [pjafe] *vi* to prance, paw the ground, swagger.
piailler [pjaje] *vi* to cheep, squeal, squall.
pianiste [pjanist] *n* pianist.
piano [pjano] *nm* piano; **— à queue** grand piano.
pianoter [pjanɔte] *vi* to strum, drum, tap.

piauler [pjole] *vi* to cheep, whimper.
piaule [pjol] *nf* lodgings, rooms.
pic [pik] *nm* pick(ax), peak, woodpecker; à — sheer, steep(ly), at the right moment.
pichenette [piʃnɛt] *nf* flick, fillip.
picorer [pikɔre] *vt* to steal, pilfer; *vi* to scratch about for food, pick.
picoter [pikɔte] *vt* to peck (at), prick, sting; *vi* prickle, smart, tingle.
pic-vert [pivɛːr] *nm* green woodpecker.
pie [pi] *a* piebald; *n* piebald horse; *nf* magpie.
pièce [pjɛs] *nf* piece, part, patch, room, coin, document, cask; — de théâtre play; — d'eau ornamental lake; de toutes —s completely, out of nothing; travailler à la — to do piece-work; trois francs la — three francs a piece.
pied [pje] *nm* foot(ing), base, leg (*chair*), stem, scale; — de laitue head of lettuce; au — levé offhand, at a moment's notice; sur — afoot, up; perdre — to lose one's footing, to get out of one's depth; lever le — to clear out, elope.
pied-à-terre [pjetatɛːr] *nm* occasional residence.
pied-d'alouette [pjedalwɛt] *nm* larkspur.
piédestal [pjedɛstal] *nm* pedestal.
piège [pjɛʒ] *nm* snare, trap; tendre un — to set a trap.
pierraille [pjɛraːj] *nf* rubble, gravel for road making.
pierre [pjɛːr] *nf* stone; c'est une — dans votre jardin it is a dig at you.
Pierre [pjɛːr] Peter.
pierreries [pjɛrəri] *nf pl* jewels, gems.
pierreux, -euse [pjɛrø, øːz] *a* stony, gritty.
piété [pjete] *nf* piety, godliness.
piétiner [pjetine] *vt* to trample (down), tread, stamp on; *vi* to stamp; — sur place to mark time.
piéton [pjetɔ̃] *nm* pedestrian.
piètre [pjɛtr] *a* poor, paltry, sorry.
pieu [pjø] *nm* post, stake, pile, (*fam*) bed.
pieuvre [pjœːvr] *nf* octopus.
pieux, -euse [pjø, øːz] *a* pious, religious, reverent.
pige [piːʒ] *nf* measuring rod.
pigeon, -onne [piʒɔ̃, ɔn] *n* pigeon, greenhorn.
pigeonnier [piʒɔnje] *nm* dovecote.
piger [piʒe] *vt* to look at, twig, understand, catch; *vi* to understand, get it.
pigment [pigmɑ̃] *nm* pigment.
pignon [piɲɔ̃] *nm* gable, pinion.
pignouf [piɲuf] *nm* lout, skinflint.
pile [pil] *nf* pile, heap, battery, pier, thrashing; — ou face heads or tails; s'arrêter — to stop dead.
piler [pile] *vt* to crush, pound.

pilier [pilje] *nm* pillar, column, shaft.
pillage [pijaːʒ] *nm* pillage, looting, ransacking.
piller [pije] *vt* to pillage, loot, plunder, ransack, rifle.
pilon [pilɔ̃] *nm* pestle, steamhammer, (*fam*) drumstick.
pilori [pilɔri] *nm* pillory.
pilot [pilo] *nm* pile.
pilotage [pilɔtaːʒ] *nm* pile-driving, piloting, driving.
pilote [pilɔt] *nm* pilot.
piloter [pilɔte] *vt* to pilot, fly, drive.
pilotis [pilɔti] *nm* pile (*foundation*).
pilule [pilyl] *nf* pill.
pimbêche [pɛ̃bɛʃ] *nf* unpleasant, supercilious woman, sour puss, catty woman.
piment [pimɑ̃] *nm* spice, red pepper.
pimenter [pimɑ̃te] *vt* to season, spice.
pimpant [pɛ̃pɑ̃] *a* spruce.
pin [pɛ̃] *nm* pine, fir-tree.
pinacle [pinakl] *nm* pinnacle.
pinard [pinaːr] *nm* wine.
pince [pɛ̃ːs] *nf* pincers, tongs, pliers, forceps, tweezers, clip, peg, claw, grip; — monseigneur jimmy.
pinceau [pɛ̃so] *nm* (paint)brush.
pincé [pɛ̃se] *a* supercilious, huffy, prim; *nm* pizzicato.
pincée [pɛ̃se] *nf* pinch.
pince-nez [pɛ̃sne] *nm* eye-glasses, pince-nez.
pincer [pɛ̃se] *vt* to pinch, nip (off), pluck, nab, grip; — les lèvres to purse one's mouth.
pince-sans-rire [pɛ̃sɑ̃riːr] *nm* person with a dry sense of humor.
pingouin [pɛ̃gwɛ̃] *nm* penguin, auk.
pingre [pɛ̃ːgr] *a* stingy, mean; *nm* skinflint, miser.
pinson [pɛ̃sɔ̃] *nm* finch, chaffinch.
pintade [pɛ̃tad] *nf* guinea-fowl.
pioche [pjɔʃ] *nf* pickaxe, mattock.
piocher [pjɔʃe] *vt* to dig (with a pick).
piocheur, -euse [pjɔʃœːr, øːz] *nm* pickman, digger.
piolet [pjɔlɛ] *nm* ice ax.
pion [pjɔ̃] *nm* pawn, (*checkers*) piece; monitor.
pioncer [pjɔ̃se] *vi* to sleep, snooze.
pionnier [pjɔnje] *nm* pioneer.
pipe [pip] *nf* pipe, tube.
pipeau [pipo] *nm* reed-pipe, bird-call.
piper [pipe] *vt* to lure, decoy.
pipi [pipi] *nm* faire — to piddle, pee.
piquant [pikɑ̃] *a* stinging, prickly, cutting, pungent, piquant, spicy, tart; *nm* prickle, quill, pungency, point.
pique [pik] *nm* spade(s) (*cards*); *n* pike, spite.
piqué [pike] *a* quilted, padded, (worm)eaten, spotted, dotty, staccato; *nm* pique, quilting, nose-dive; bombarder en — to dive-bomb; pas — des vers first rate.

pique-assiette [pikasjɛt] *nm* sponger, parasite.

pique-nique [piknik] *nm* picnic; **faire (un)** — to picnic

piquer [pike] *vt* to prick, bite, sting, make smart, excite, spur, stitch, nettle, dive, give an injection to; — **une tête** to take a header; *vr* to prick oneself, to get nettled, excited, become eaten up (with **de**), to pride oneself (on **de**).

piquet [pikɛ] *nm* stake, peg, picket, (*cards*) piquet.

piqueter [pikte] *vt* to stake (out), peg out, picket, spot, dot.

piquette [pikɛt] *nf* poor wine.

piqueur, -euse [pikœːr, øːz] *n* whipper-in, huntsman.

piqûre [pikyːr] *nf* sting, bite, prick, injection, stitching.

pirate [pirat] *nm* pirate.

pire [piːr] *a* worse, worst; *comp sup* of **mauvais**; *nm* worst, worst of it.

pirogue [pirɔg] *nf* canoe, surf boat.

pirouette [pirwɛt] *nf* pirouette, whirligig.

pirouetter [pirwɛte] *vi* to pirouette.

pis [pis] *nm* udder, dug, pap; *ad* worse, worst; *comp sup* of **mal**; **de mal en** — from bad to worse.

pis-aller [pizale] *nm* makeshift, last resource; **au** — at the worst.

piscine [pissin] *nf* swimming pool.

pisé [pize] *nm* puddled clay.

pissenlit [pisɑ̃li] dandelion.

pissotière [pisɔtjɛːr] *nf* public urinal.

pistache [pistaʃ] *nf* pistachio (nut).

piste [pist] *nf* track, trail, race-track, rink, floor; — **de décollage** runway; **route à double** — divided highway; — **sonore** sound track; **faire fausse** — to be on the wrong track.

pistolet [pistɔlɛ] *nm* pistol.

piston [pistɔ̃] *nm* piston, ram, valve, influence.

pistonner [pistɔne] *vt* to push (on), use one's influence for, help on.

pitance [pitɑ̃s] *nf* allowance, pittance.

piteux, -euse [pitø, øːz] *a* piteous, sorry; **faire piteuse mine** to look woe-begone.

pitié [pitje] *nf* pity, mercy, compassion; **avec** — compassionately; **elle lui fait** — he is sorry for her; **prendre qn en** — to take pity on s.o.

piton [pitɔ̃] *nm* eyebolt, peak.

pitoyable [pɪtwajabl] *a* pitiful, piteous, wretched.

pitre [piːtr] *nm* clown.

pittoresque [pittɔrɛsk] *a* picturesque, graphic; *nm* picturesqueness.

pivert [pivɛr] *nm* green woodpecker.

pivoine [pivwan] *nf* peony.

pivot [pivo] *nm* pivot, pin, swivel.

pivoter [pivɔte] *vi* to pivot, swivel, hinge, turn.

placage [plakaːʒ] *nm* plating, veneering.

placard [plakaːr] *nm* cupboard, bill, poster, panel.

placarder [plakarde] *vt* to post up, stick bills on.

place [plas] *nf* place, seat, post, job, room, square; **faire** — à to make room, way, for; — **forte** fortress.

placement [plasmɑ̃] *nm* investing, investment, placing, sale, employment.

placer [plase] *vt* to place, put, find a seat (a post) for, invest, sell; *vr* to take up one's position, take a seat, get a post.

placet [plasɛ] *nm* petition.

placidité [plasidite] *nf* placidity.

plafond [plafɔ̃] *nm* ceiling, maximum.

plafonnier [plafɔnje] *nm* ceiling light.

plage [plaːʒ] *nf* beach, shore, seaside resort.

plagiaire [plaʒjɛːr] *a nm* plagiarist.

plagiat [plaʒja] *nm* plagiarism.

plagier [plaʒje] *vt* to plagiarize.

plaid [plɛ] *nm* plaid, traveling-rug.

plaider [plede] *vti* to plead, argue.

plaideur, -euse [plɛdœr, øːz] *n* suitor, litigant.

plaidoirie [plɛdwari] *nf* pleading, speech.

plaidoyer [plɛdwaje] *nm* speech for the defense.

plaie [plɛ] *nf* wound, sore, evil.

plaignant [plɛɲɑ̃] *n* plaintiff, prosecutor.

plain-chant [plɛ̃ʃɑ̃] *nm* plainsong.

plaindre [plɛ̃ːdr] *vt* to pity, be sorry for; *vr* to complain.

plaine [plɛn] *nf* plain, flat country, open country.

plain-pied [plɛ̃pje] *ad* **de** — level, on one floor, smoothly, straight.

plainte [plɛ̃ːt] *nf* complaint, moan, lament; **porter** — **contre** to make a complaint against.

plaintif, -ive [plɛ̃tif, iːv] *a* plaintive, doleful, mournful.

plaire [plɛːr] *vt* to please, appeal to; *vr* to take pleasure, thrive, like it, be happy; **s'il vous plaît** please; **plaît-il?** I beg your pardon?

plaisance [plɛzɑ̃ːs] *nf* **maison de** — country seat; **bateau de** — pleasure boat.

plaisant [plɛzɑ̃] *a* funny, amusing; *nm* joker, wag; **mauvais** — practical joker.

plaisanter [plɛzɑ̃te] *vi* to joke, jest; *vt* to banter, chaff.

plaisanterie [plɛzɑ̃tri] *nf* joke, jest(ing); **entendre la** — to be able to take a joke.

plaisir [plɛziːr] *nm* pleasure, enjoyment, favor; **à** — without reason, freely; **au** — I hope we shall meet again; **par** — for the fun of the thing; **partie de** — pleasure-trip, -party, outing, picnic.

plan [plɑ̃] *a* even, flat, level; *nm* plane, plan, scheme, draft; **gros** —

close-up; **premier** — foreground; **en** — in the lurch.

planche [plɑ̃:ʃ] *nf* plank, board, shelf, plate, engraving; *pl* boards, stage; — **de bord** dashboard; — **de salut** sheet-anchor, last hope; **faire la** — to float on one's back.

planchéier [plɑ̃ʃeje] *vt* to floor, board (over).

plancher [plɑ̃ʃe] *nm* floor(ing), floor-board.

planer [plane] *vt* to plane, smooth; *vi* to hover, glide, soar.

planète [planɛt] *nf* planet.

planeur [planœ:r] *nm* glider.

planquer [plɑ̃ke] (*fam*) *vt* to hide; *vr* to take cover.

plant [plɑ̃] *nm* plantation, patch, sapling, seedling.

plantain [plɑ̃tɛ̃] *nm* plantain.

plantation [plɑ̃tasjɔ̃] *nf* planting, plantation.

plante [plɑ̃:t] *nf* plant, sole (of foot); **jardin des** —s botanical gardens.

planter [plɑ̃te] *vt* to plant, set, fix, stick; *vr* to station oneself, stand; — **là** to leave in the lurch.

planteur [plɑ̃tœ:r] *nm* planter, grower.

planton [plɑ̃tɔ̃] *nm* orderly.

plantureux, -euse [plɑ̃tyrø, ø:z] *a* abundant, copious, rich, lush.

plaquage [plaka:ʒ] *nm* throwing over, tackle.

plaque [plak] *nf* sheet, plate, slab, tablet, plaque, disk.

plaqué [plake] *a* plated, veneered; *nm* veneered wood, plated metal, electroplate.

plaquer [plake] *vt* to plate, veneer, plaster, throw over, drop, tackle, lay flat; *vr* to lie down flat, pancake.

plaquette [plakɛt] *nf* tablet, booklet.

plastique [plastik] *a* plastic; *nf* (art of) modeling, plastic art, plastic.

plastron [plastrɔ̃] *nm* breast-plate, shirt-front.

plastronner [plastrɔne] *vi* to swagger, strut, pose.

plat [pla] *a* flat, level, dull, tame; *nm* flat, dish, course, flat-racing; à — flat, run down, all in; **faire du** — à to toady to, fawn upon; à — ventre flat on the ground.

platane [platan] *nm* plane-tree.

plat-bord [plabɔ:r] *nm* gunwale.

plateau [plato] *nm* tray, plateau, platform, turntable.

plate-bande [platbɑ̃:d] *nf* flowerbed.

plate-forme [platfɔrm] *nf* platform, footplate.

platine [platin] *nm* platinum.

platiner [platine] *vt* to platinum-plate.

platitude [platityd] *nf* platitude, dullness.

plâtras [platrɑ] *nm* broken plaster, rubbish.

plâtre [pla:tr] *nm* plaster; *pl* plaster-work.

plâtrer [platre] *vt* to plaster (up).

plausible [plozibl] *a* plausible.

plébiscite [plebissit] *nm* plebiscite.

plein [plɛ̃] *a* full, big, solid; **en** — right in the middle (of), out and out; *nm* **avoir son** — to be fully loaded; **battre son** — to be in full swing; **faire le** — to fill up (with de).

plénière [plenjɛ:r] *a* plenary, full, complete.

plénipotentiaire [plenipɔtɑ̃sjɛ:r] *a nm* plenipotentiary.

plénitude [plenityd] *nf* plenitude, fullness.

pléonastique [pleɔnastik] *a* pleonastic.

pleurard [plœra:r] *a* tearful, sniveling; *n* sniveler.

pleurer [plœre] *vt* to weep for, mourn (for); *vi* weep, cry, drip.

pleurésie [plœrezi] *nf* pleurisy.

pleureur, -euse [plœrœ:r, ø:z] *a* tearful, whimpering; *n* whimperer, mourner.

pleurnicher [plœrniʃe] *vi* to whine, snivel.

pleutre [pløtr] *nm* coward.

pleuvoir [plœvwa:r] *vi* to rain; — à verse to pour.

pli [pli] *nm* fold, pleat, crease, pucker, envelope, cover, note, habit, trick.

pliant [pliɑ̃] *a* pliant, flexible, collapsible; *nm* camp-stool, folding chair.

plie [pli] *nf* plaice.

plier [plie] *vt* to fold (up), bend; *vi* to bend, give way; *vr* to submit, yield.

plinthe [plɛ̃:t] *nf* plinth, base-board.

plissé [plise] *a* pleated; *nm* pleats, pleating.

plissement [plismɑ̃] *nm* pleating, creasing, crumpling.

plisser [plise] *vt* to pleat, crumple, crease, corrugate.

plomb [plɔ̃] *nm* lead, shot, fuse; **de** — leaden; à — vertical(ly); **fil à** — plumbline; **faire sauter les** —**s** to blow the fuses.

plombage [plɔ̃ba:ʒ] *nm* leading, (*tooth*) filling.

plombagine [plɔ̃baʒin] *nf* blacklead, graphite.

plomber [plɔ̃be] *vt* to (cover with) lead, fill (*tooth*).

plomberie [plɔ̃bri] *nf* plumbing, plumber's shop, lead-works.

plombier [plɔ̃bje] *nm* plumber, lead-worker.

plongeoir [plɔ̃ʒwa:r] *nm* diving-board.

plongeon [plɔ̃ʒɔ̃] *nm* dive, plunge, diver.

plongée [plɔ̃ʒe] *nf* dive, plunge.

plonger [plɔ̃ʒe] *vt* to plunge, immerse, thrust; *vi* to dive, plunge, dip; *vr* to immerse oneself, devote oneself (to dans).

plongeur, -euse [plɔ̃ʒœːr, øːz] *a* diving; *n* diver, bottlewasher, dishwasher.

ploutocrate [plutɔkrat] *nm* plutocrat.

ployer [plwaje] *vt* to bend; *vi* to give way, bow.

pluie [plɥi] *nf* rain.

plumage [plymaːʒ] *nm* plumage, feathers.

plumard [plymaːr] *nm* (*fam*) bed.

plume [plym] *nf* feather, quill, pen, nib.

plumeau [plymo] *vt* feather duster.

plumer [plyme] *vt* to pluck, fleece.

plumet [plymɛ] *nm* plume, ostrich feather.

plumier [plymje] *nm* pencil-case.

plupart (la) [(la)plypaːr] *nf* (the) most, greatest or greater part, majority; **pour la —** mostly.

plural [plyral] *a* plural.

pluralité [plyralite] *nf* plurality, multiplicity.

pluriel, -elle [plyrjɛl] *a nm* plural.

plus [ply(s)] *ad* more, most, plus, in addition; *nm* more, most; **— (et) — the more . . . the more; tant et —** any amount; **— de** more, more than, no more; **ne . . . plus** no more, no longer, not now, not again; **de —** more, besides; **en —** extra, into the bargain; **en — de** over and above; **non —** either; **tout au —** at the very most.

plusieurs [plyzjœːr] *a pn* several.

plus-que-parfait [plyskəparfɛ] *nm* pluperfect.

plus-value [plyvaly] *nf* appreciation, increase (in value).

plutôt [plyto] *ad* rather, sooner, on the whole.

pluvier [plyvje] *nm* plover.

pluvieux, -euse [plyvjø, øːz] *a* rainy, wet.

pneu [pnø] *nm* tire.

pneumatique [pnømatik] *a* pneumatic, air-; *nm* tire, express letter.

pneumonie [pnømɔni] *nf* pneumonia.

pochard [pɔʃaːr] *n* boozer.

poche [pɔʃ] *nf* pocket, pouch, bag; **acheter chat en —** to buy a pig in a poke; **y être de sa —** to be out of pocket.

pocher [pɔʃe] *vt* to poach, dash off; *vi* to get baggy, to crease; **— l'œil à qn** to give s.o. a black eye.

pochette [pɔʃɛt] *nf* small pocket, handbag, fancy handkerchief, small fiddle.

pochoir [pɔʃwaːr] *nm* stencil.

poêle [pwaːl, pwal] *nm* stove, pall; *nf* frying pan.

poème [pɔɛm] *nm* poem.

poésie [pɔezi] *nf* poetry, poem.

poète [pɔɛt] *a* poetic; *nm* poet.

poétique [pɔetik] *a* poetic(al); *nf* poetics.

pognon [pɔɲɔ̃] *nm* money, dough.

poids [pwɑ] *nm* weight, burden, importance; **prendre du —** to put on weight.

poignant [pwaɲɑ̃] *a* poignant, soul-stirring.

poignard [pwaɲaːr] *nm* dagger.

poignarder [pwaɲarde] *vt* to stab.

poigne [pwaɲ] *nf* grip, energy, firmness, drive.

poignée [pwaɲe] *nf* handful, handle; **— de main** handshake.

poignet [pwaɲɛ] *nm* wrist, cuff, wrist-band.

poil [pwal] *nm* hair, fur, coat, bristle, nap; **à —** naked, hairy; **au —!** wonderful! **reprendre du — de la bête** to take a hair of the dog that bit you.

poilu [pwaly] *a* hairy, shaggy; *nm* soldier, tommy.

poinçon [pwɛ̃sɔ̃] *nm* awl, piercer, punch, stamp.

poinçonner [pwɛ̃sɔne] *vt* to pierce, punch, stamp.

poindre [pwɛ̃ːdr] *vi* to dawn, break, come up.

poing [pwɛ̃] *nm* fist, hand; **coup de —** punch; **dormir à —s fermés** to sleep like a log.

point [pwɛ̃] *ad* not, not at all; *nm* point, speck, dot, mark, stitch, full stop; **à — done to a turn; à — nommé** in the nick of time; **de tous —s** in all respects; **mettre au —** to focus, tune up, adjust, clarify, perfect; **mise au —** focusing, tuning up, clarification; **faire le —** to take one's bearings, take stock of one's position.

pointage [pwɛ̃taːʒ] *nm* checking, ticking off, sighting.

pointe [pwɛ̃ːt] *nf* point, tip, top, head, touch, tinge, twinge, quip; **— sèche** etching-needle, dry-point etching; **— du jour** daybreak; **heures de —** rush hours; **pousser une — jusqu'à** to push on to, take a walk over to; **en —** pointed.

pointer [pwɛ̃te] *vt* to prick, stab, sharpen, tick off, check, point, aim; *vi* to appear, soar, rise, sprout.

pointeur [pwɛ̃tœːr] *nm* checker, time-keeper, scorer.

pointillé [pwɛ̃tije] *a* dotted, stippled; *nm* dotted line, stippling.

pointiller [pwɛ̃tije] *vt* to dot, stipple, pester, annoy; *vi* to cavil, quibble.

pointilleux, -euse [pwɛ̃tijø, øːz] *a* captious, critical.

pointu [pwɛ̃ty] *a* pointed, sharp, angular.

pointure [pwɛ̃tyːr] *nf* size.

poire [pwaːr] *nf* pear, bulb; (*fam*) oaf; **garder une — pour la soif** to put something by for a rainy day.

poireau [pwaro] *nm* leek.

poireauter [pwarote] *vi* to hang about (waiting).

poirier [pwarje] *nm* pear-tree.

pois [pwa] *nm* pea, spot; **petits —
green peas; — de senteur** sweet
peas; **— chiches** chick peas.
poison [pwazɔ̃] *nm* poison.
poissard [pwasaːr] *a* vulgar, coarse.
poisse [pwas] *nf* bad luck.
poisser [pwase] *vt* to coat with
pitch, wax, make sticky.
poisson [pwasɔ̃] *nm* fish; **— rouge**
goldfish; **— d'avril** April fool.
poissonnerie [pwasɔnri] *nf* fish-
market, fish-shop.
poissonneux, -euse [pwasɔnø, øːz]
a full of fish, stocked with fish.
poissonnier, -ière [pwasɔnje, jɛːr]
n fishmonger, fishwife.
poissonnière [pwasɔnjɛːr] *nf* fish-
kettle.
poitevin, -e [pwatvɛ̃, in] *a* from
Poitou or Poitiers.
poitrail [pwatrɑːj] *nm* chest, breast
(strap).
poitrinaire [pwatrinɛːr] *an* con-
sumptive.
poitrine [pwatrin] *nf* chest, breast,
bosom, brisket.
poivre [pwaːvr] *nm* pepper, spiciness.
poivré [pwavre] *a* peppery, spicy.
poivrier [pwavrie] *nm* pepper-pot,
pepper-plant.
poivron [pwavrɔ̃] *nm* Jamaica
pepper, capsicum.
poivrot [pwavro] *nm* boozer, drunkard.
poix [pwa] *nf* pitch, wax.
polaire [pɔlɛːr] *a* polar.
polariser [pɔlarize] *vt* to polarize;
vr to have a one-track mind.
pôle [poːl] *nm* pole.
polémique [pɔlemik] *a* polemic(al);
nf controversy.
polémiste [pɔlemist] *nm* polemist.
poli [pɔli] *a* polished, glossy, polite;
nm polish, gloss.
policer [pɔlise] *vt* to organize,
establish order in.
police [pɔlis] *nf* police, policing,
policy; **salle de —** guard-room;
faire la — to keep order.
polichinelle [pɔliʃinɛl] *nf* punch,
turncoat, puppet, buffoon; **théâtre
de —** Punch and Judy show; **secret
de —** open secret.
policier, -ière [pɔlisje, jɛːr] *a* police;
nm detective; **roman —** detective
story.
polir [pɔliːr] *vt* to polish.
polisson, -onne [pɔlisɔ̃, ɔn] *a*
ribald, naughty; *n* scamp, rascal,
scapegrace.
polissonnerie [pɔlisɔnri] *nf* naughtiness, smutty remark.
politesse [pɔlites] *nf* politeness,
courtesy, manners.
politicien, -enne [pɔlitisjɛ̃, jɛn] *n*
politician.
politique [pɔlitik] *a* political, politic,
diplomatic; *nm* politician; *nf* politics,
policy,
pollen [pɔllɛn] *nm* pollen.

polluer [pɔllɥe] *vt* to pollute, defile.
pollution [pɔlysjɔ̃] *nf* pollution,
defilement.
Pologne [pɔlɔɲ] *nf* Poland.
polonais [pɔlɔnɛ] *a nm* Polish; *n*
Pole.
poltron, -onne [pɔltrɔ̃, ɔn] *a*
cowardly, timid; *n* coward.
polycopié [pɔlikɔpje] *nm* mimeo-
graphed lecture.
polycopier [pɔlikɔpje] *vt* to mimeograph, stencil.
polygame [pɔligam] *a* polygamous;
n polygamist.
polyglotte [pɔliglɔt] *an* polyglot.
polygone [pɔligɔn] *nm* polygon,
experimental range.
polype [pɔlip] *nm* polyp, polypus.
polytechnicien [pɔlitɛknisjɛ̃] *nm*
student of the *Ecole polytechnique.*
pombe [pɔ̃ːb] *nm* millet beer.
pommade [pɔmad] *nf* pomade, hair-
cream, ointment, lip-salve.
pomme [pɔm] *nf* apple, knob, head;
— de terre potato; **— d'arrosoir**
rose of a watering-can; **— de pin**
fir-cone; **tomber dans les —** to pass
out.
pommeau [pɔmo] *nm* pommel.
pommeler [pɔmle] *vr* to become
dappled, mottled.
pommette [pɔmɛt] *nf* knob, cheekbone.
pommier [pɔmje] *nm* apple-tree.
pompe [pɔ̃ːp] *nf* pump, pomp,
display; **— à incendie** fire-engine;
entrepreneur de —s funèbres undertaker.
pomper [pɔ̃pe] *vt* to pump, suck up.
pompette [pɔ̃pɛt] *a* slightly tipsy.
pompeux, -euse [pɔ̃pø, øːz] *a*
pompous, turgid.
pompier [pɔ̃pje] *nm* fireman, pump-
maker; *a* uninspired.
pomponner [pɔ̃pɔne] *vt* to adorn,
titivate; *vr* to deck oneself out,
titivate.
ponce [pɔ̃ːs] *nf* **pierre —** pumice-
stone.
poncer [pɔ̃se] *vt* to pumice, sandpaper, pounce.
poncif [pɔ̃sif] *nm* pounced drawing,
conventional work, commonplace
effect, image *etc.*
ponctionner [pɔ̃ksjɔne] *vt* to tap,
puncture.
ponctualité [pɔ̃ktɥalite] *nf* punctuality.
ponctuation [pɔ̃ktɥasjɔ̃] *nf* punctuation.
ponctuel, -elle [pɔ̃ktɥɛl] *a* punctual.
ponctuer [pɔ̃ktɥe] *vt* to punctuate,
emphasize, dot.
pondération [pɔ̃dɛrasjɔ̃] *nf* balance,
level-headedness.
pondéré [pɔ̃dere] *a* thoughtful, level-
headed.
pondre [pɔ̃ːdr] *vt* to lay, produce.
pont [pɔ̃] *nm* bridge, deck, axle; **—
levis** drawbridge; **— roulant** gantry;

faire le — to take the intervening day(s) off.
ponte [pɔ̃:t] *nf* laying, eggs laid.
pontife [pɔ̃tif] *nm* pontiff, pundit.
pontifier [pɔ̃tifje] *vi* to lay down the law, dogmatize.
ponton [pɔ̃tɔ̃] *nm* landing-stage, ramp.
popote [pɔpɔt] *nf* kitchen, restaurant, cooking, mess.
populace [pɔpylas] *nf* riff-raff, rabble, mob.
populacier, -ière [pɔpylasje, jɛːr] *a* vulgar, common.
populaire [pɔpylɛːr] *a* popular, vulgar; chanson — folksong, street song.
populariser [pɔpylarize] *vt* to popularize.
popularité [pɔpylarite] *nf* popularity.
population [pɔpylasjɔ̃] *nf* population.
populeux, -euse [pɔpylø, øːz] *a* populous.
porc [pɔːr] *nm* pig, swine, pork.
porcelaine [pɔrsəlɛn] *nf* porcelain, china.
porc-épic [pɔrkepik] *nm* porcupine.
porche [pɔrʃ] *nm* porch.
porcherie [pɔrʃəri] *nf* pigsty, piggery.
pore [pɔːr] *nm* pore.
poreux, -euse [pɔrø, øːz] *a* porous.
pornographie [pɔrnɔgrafi] *nf* pornography.
porphyre [pɔrfiːr] *nm* porphyry, slab.
port [pɔːr] *nm* port, harbor, haven, carriage, postage, carrying, bearing; se mettre au — d'armes to shoulder arms; — dû carriage forward.
portable [pɔrtabl] *a* portable, presentable, wearable.
portage [pɔrtaːʒ] *nm* porterage, carrying, transport, portage.
portail [pɔrtaːj] *nm* portal, door.
portant [pɔrtɑ̃] *a* carrying, bearing; être bien (mal) portant to be well (ill).
portatif, -ive [pɔrtatif, iːv] *a* portable.
porte [pɔrt] *nf* door, gate(way); — battante swing-door; — tambour revolving door; — cochère carriage entrance; mettre à la — to turn (put) s.o. out; écouter aux —s to eavesdrop.
porte-affiches [pɔrtafiʃ] *nm* bulletin board.
porte-amarre [pɔrtamaːr] *nm* line-rocket.
porte-avions [pɔrtavjɔ̃] *nm* aircraft carrier.
porte-bagages [pɔrtbagaːʒ] *nm* luggage-rack.
porte-bonheur [pɔrtbɔnœːr] *nm* charm, mascot.
porte-clefs [pɔrtkle] *nm* keyring.
porte-documents [pɔrtdɔkymɑ̃] *nm* attaché-case.

portée [pɔrte] *nf* litter, brood, range, reach, scope, span; à — de la voix within call; d'une grande — far-reaching.
portefaix [pɔrtəfɛ] *nm* porter.
porte-fenêtre [pɔrtfənɛːtr] *nf* french window.
portefeuille [pɔrtəfœːj] *nm* portfolio, pocket-book, wallet, letter-case.
porte-flambeau [pɔrtflɑ̃bo] *nm* torch-bearer.
portemanteau [pɔrtmɑ̃to] *nm* clothes tree.
porte-mine [pɔrtəmin] *nm* mechanical pencil.
porte-monnaie [pɔrtmɔnɛ] *nm* purse.
porte-parole [pɔrtparɔl] *nm* spokesman, mouthpiece
porte-plume [pɔrtəplym] *nm* pen (holder).
porter [pɔrte] *vt* to carry, bear, wear, take, inscribe, produce, bring (in), induce; *vi* bear, carry, hit (home), tell; *vr* to go, proceed, be; — un coup to deal, aim a blow; — manquant to post as missing; il me porte sur les nerfs he gets on my nerves; se — candidat to stand as candidate; se — bien to be well.
porte-serviettes [pɔrtsɛrvjɛt] *nm* towel rack.
porteur, -euse [pɔrtœːr, øːz] *n* porter, bearer, carrier.
porte-voix [pɔrtəvwa] *nm* megaphone.
portier, -ière [pɔrtje, jɛːr] *n* door keeper, gate-keeper.
portière [pɔrtjɛːr] *nf* door.
portillon [pɔrtijɔ̃] *nm* sidegate, wicket-gate.
portion [pɔrsjɔ̃] *nf* portion, helping, share.
portique [pɔrtik] *nm* porch, portico.
porto [pɔrto] *nm* port (wine).
portrait [pɔrtrɛ] *nm* portrait, likeness; — en pied full-length portrait.
portraitiste [pɔrtrɛtist] *nm* portrait-painter.
portugais [pɔrtygɛ] *an* Portuguese.
Portugal [pɔrtygal] *nm* Portugal.
pose [poːz] *nf* pose, attitude, posing, affectation, (time) exposure, laying, posing.
posé [poze] *a* sitting, sedate, staid, steady.
poser [poze] *vt* to put (down), place, lay (down), set, fix up, admit, suppose; *vi* to pose, sit, rest; *vr* to settle, alight, set oneself up (as en).
poseur, -euse [pozœːr, øːz] *n* poseur, snob, layer.
positif, -ive [pozitif, iːv] *a* positive, actual, matter-of-fact; *nm* positive.
position [pozisjɔ̃] *nf* position, situation, site, status, posture, post.
possédant [pɔsedɑ̃] *a* classes —es propertied classes.
possédé [pɔsede] *a* possessed; *n* person possessed, maniac.

posséder [pɔsede] vt to possess, own, know thoroughly; vr to contain oneself.
possesseur [pɔsesœːr] nm possessor, owner.
possessif, -ive [pɔsesif, iːv] a nm possessive.
possession [pɔsesjɔ̃] nf possession, ownership.
possibilité [pɔsibilite] nf possibility, feasibility.
possible [pɔsibl] a possible, feasible; nm possible, utmost; **pas —** not really! well I never!
postal [pɔstal] a postal.
poste [pɔst] nm post, job, appointment, station; **— de T.S.F.** radio set, -station; nf post, post office; **mettre une lettre à la —** to mail a letter.
poster [pɔste] vt to post, station; vr to take up a position.
postérieur [pɔsterjœːr] a posterior, subsequent, rear, back; nm posterior, bottom.
postérité [pɔsterite] nf posterity, issue.
posthume [pɔstym] a posthumous.
postiche [pɔstiʃ] a false, imitation, sham, dummy.
postillon [pɔstijɔ̃] nm postilion; **envoyer des —s** to splutter.
postscolaire [pɔstskɔlɛːr] a further (education), after-school.
postulant [pɔstylɑ̃] n applicant, candidate.
postuler [pɔstyle] vt to apply for, solicit.
posture [pɔstyːr] nf posture, position, attitude.
pot [po] nm pot, jar, jug, mug, tankard; **payer les —s cassés** to pay the damage.
potable [pɔtabl] a drinkable.
potache [pɔtaʃ] nm schoolboy, pupil.
potage [pɔtaːʒ] nm soup.
potager, -ère [pɔtaʒe, ɛːr] a for the pot; nm kitchen-garden.
potasse [pɔtas] nf potash.
potasser [pɔtase] vt to bone up on; vi to bone up.
pot-au-feu [pɔtofø] a homely, plain; nm stock-pot, soup with boiled beef.
pot-de-vin [pɔdvɛ̃] nm bribe.
poteau [pɔto] nm post, pole; **— d'arrivée** finish line; **— de départ** starting-post.
potelé [pɔtle] a chubby, plump.
potence [pɔtɑ̃s] nf gibbet, gallows, jib, derrick.
potentiel, -elle [pɔtɑ̃sjɛl] a potential; nm potentialities.
poterie [pɔtri] nf pottery.
poterne [pɔtɛrn] nf postern.
potiche [pɔtiʃ] nf (Chinese) porcelain vase.
potier, -ière [pɔtje, jɛːr] n potter.
potin [pɔtɛ̃] nm piece of gossip, (fam) noise; pl tittle-tattle.
potiron [pɔtirɔ̃] nm pumpkin.

pou [pu] nm louse.
poubelle [pubɛl] nf trash can.
pouce [pus] nm thumb, big toe, inch; **manger sur le —** to take a snack.
poucet [puse] nm **le petit —** Tom Thumb.
poucier [pusje] nm thumb-stall, -piece.
poudre [puːdr] nf powder, dust; **— aux yeux** bluff, eyewash.
poudrer [pudre] vt to powder, dust; vr to put on powder.
poudreux, -euse [pudrø, øːz] a dusty, powdery.
poudrier [pudrie] nm powder-box, compact.
poudrière [pudriɛːr] nf powder-horn, magazine.
poudroyer [pudrwaje] vt to cover with dust; vi to form clouds of dust.
pouf [puf] nm pouf, puff.
pouffer [pufe] vir (se) **— de rire** to roar with laughter.
pouilleux, -euse [pujø, øːz] a lousy, verminous.
poulailler [pulaje] nm hen-house, -roost, (theater fam) peanut gallery.
poulain [pulɛ̃] nm colt, foal, pony-skin, skid.
poularde [pulard] nf fowl.
poule [pul] nf hen, fowl, pool, sweepstake; tart; **— d'eau** moorhen; **— mouillée** coward, chicken.
poulet [pulɛ] nm chick(en), love-letter.
poulette [pulɛt] nf pullet.
pouliche [puliʃ] nf filly.
poulie [puli] nf pulley, block.
poulpe [pulp] nm octopus.
pouls [pu] nm pulse.
poumon [pumɔ̃] nm lung; **crier à pleins —s** to shout at the top of one's voice; **respirer à pleins —s** to take a deep breath.
poupe [pup] nf poop, stern.
poupée [pupe] nf doll, (tailor's) dummy, puppet.
poupon, -onne [pupɔ̃, ɔn] n baby, baby-faced boy, girl.
pouponnière [pupɔnjɛːr] nf day-nursery.
pour [puːr] prep for, on behalf of, in favor of, because of, for the sake of, instead of, as, to, by, in order to, with regard to, although; **— que** in order that, so that; **— dix francs (de)** ten francs worth (of); **je n'y suis — rien** I have nothing to do with it; **il en a — une heure** it will take him an hour; **— ce qui est de l'argent** as far as the money is concerned.
pourboire [purbwaːr] nm tip, gratuity.
pourceau [purso] nm hog, swine, pig.
pour-cent [pursɑ̃] nm (rate) per cent.
pourcentage [pursɑ̃taːʒ] nm percentage.

pourchasser [purʃase] vt to pursue.
pourlécher [purleʃe] vt to lick around; vr to run one's tongue over one's lips.
pourparler [purparle] nm parley, negotiation.
pourpoint [purpwɛ̃] nm doublet.
pourpre [purpr] a nm deep red, crimson; nf purple.
pourquoi [purkwa] cj adv why?
pourri [puri] a rotten, bad.
pourrir [puriːr] vt to rot; vir to decay, rot, go bad.
pourriture [purityːr] nf rotting, rot(tenness).
poursuite [pursɥit] nf pursuit, tracking (down); pl proceedings, prosecution, suing.
poursuivant [pursɥivɑ̃] n prosecutor, plaintiff.
poursuivre [pursɥiːvr] vt to pursue, chase, prosecute, carry on, continue, dog; vr to continue, go on.
pourtant [purtɑ̃] ad however, yet, still.
pourtour [purtuːr] nm circumference, periphery, precincts, area.
pourvoir [purvwaːr] vt to provide (for, with de,) make provision (for à), furnish, supply, equip.
pourvoyeur, -euse [purvwajœːr, øːz] n purveyor, caterer, provider.
pousse [pus] nf growth, shoot.
poussé [puse] a thorough, exhaustive, deep.
pousse-café [puskafe] nm liqueur (after coffee), chaser.
poussée [puse] nf push(ing), shove, thrust, pressure.
pousse-pousse [puspus] nm rickshaw, go-cart (of child).
pousser [puse] vt to push (on), thrust, shove, urge (on), drive, impel, prompt, utter; vi to grow, shoot, push (on, forward); vr to push oneself forward.
poussier [pusje] nm coal-dust.
poussière [pusjɛːr] nf dust.
poussiéreux, -euse [pusjerø, øːz] a dusty.
poussif, -ive [pusif, iːv] a broken-winded, wheezy.
poussin [pusɛ̃] nm chick.
poutre [putr] nf beam, joist, girder.
poutrelle [putrɛl] nf small beam, girder, spar.
pouvoir [puvwaːr] nm power, influence, authority, power of attorney; vt to be able, can, manage, to be allowed, may, might etc; vr ro be possible; **il n'en peut plus** he is worn out; **on n'y peut rien** it can't be helped, nothing can be done about it; **c'est on ne peut plus difficile** nothing could be more difficult.
prairie [prɛri] nf meadow, field, grassland.
praline [pralin] nf burnt almond.
praliner [praline] vt to bake in sugar, crust.

praticabilité [pratikabilite] nf practicability, feasibility.
praticable [pratikabl] a practicable, feasible, passable.
praticien, -enne [pratisjɛ̃, jɛn] n practitioner, expert; a practicing.
pratiquant [pratikɑ̃] a practicing.
pratique [pratik] a practical, useful; nf practice, practical knowledge, experience, association, custom; pl practices, dealings.
pratiquer [pratike] vti to practice; vt put into practice, employ, make, associate with.
pré [pre] nm meadow.
préalable [prealabl] a previous, preliminary; au — previously, to begin with.
préambule [preɑ̃byl] nm preamble (to de).
préau [preo] nm yard, covered playground.
préavis [preavi] nm (previous) notice, warning.
précaire [prekɛːr] a precarious, shaky.
précaution [prekosjɔ̃] nf (pre) caution, care, wariness.
précautionneux, -euse [prekosjɔnø, øːz] a cautious, wary, guarded.
précédent [presedɑ̃] a preceding, previous; nm precedent.
précéder [presede] vt to precede, take precedence over; vi to have precedence.
précepte [presɛpt] nm precept.
précepteur, -trice [presɛptœːr, tris] n tutor, governess.
prêche [prɛːʃ] nm sermon.
prêcher [preʃe] vt to preach (to), recommend; vi to preach; — **d'exemple** to practice what one preaches; — **pour son saint** to talk in one's own interests.
prêchi-prêcha [preʃipreʃa] nm going on and on, preachifying.
précieux, -euse [presjø, øːz] a precious, valuable, affected.
préciosité [presjosite] nf preciosity, affectation.
précipice [presipis] nm precipice.
précipitamment [presipitamɑ̃] ad precipitately, hurriedly, headlong.
précipitation [presipitasjɔ̃] nf precipitancy, overhastiness, precipitation.
précipité [presipite] a precipitate, rushed, hurried, headlong; nm precipitate.
précipiter [presipite] vt to precipitate, rush, hurry, hurl down, into; vr to rush, dash, bolt.
précis [presi] a precise, definite, accurate; nm précis, summary.
précisément [presizemɑ̃] ad precisely, just, exactly, as a matter of fact.
préciser [presize] vt to state exactly, specify; vi to be precise, more explicit.

précision [presizjɔ̃] *nf* precision, accuracy, preciseness; *pl* fuller particulars.

précoce [prekɔs] *a* precocious, early.

précocité [prekɔsite] *nf* precociousness, earliness.

préconçu [prekɔ̃sy] *a* preconceived.

préconiser [prekɔnize] *vt* to advocate.

précurseur [prekyrsœːr] *nm* forerunner, precursor.

prédécesseur [predesɛsœːr] *nm* predecessor.

prédestiner [predɛstine] *vt* to predestine, foredoom, fix beforehand.

prédicateur [predikatœːr] *nm* preacher.

prédiction [prediksjɔ̃] *nf* prediction, foretelling.

prédilection [predilɛksjɔ̃] *nf* liking, fondness.

prédire [prediːr] *vt* to predict, foretell, forecast.

prédisposer [predispoze] *vt* to predispose, prejudice.

prédisposition [predispozisjɔ̃] *nf* predisposition, prejudice, propensity.

prédominance [predɔminɑ̃ːs] *nf* predominance, prevalence, supremacy.

prédominer [predɔmine] *vi* to predominate, prevail.

prééminence [preeminɑ̃ːs] *nf* preeminence, superiority.

prééminent [preeminɑ̃] *a* pre-eminent, outstanding.

préface [prefas] *nf* preface.

préfacer [prefase] *vt* to write a preface for.

préfectoral [prefɛktɔral] *a* prefectoral, of a prefect.

préfecture [prefɛktyːr] *nf* prefecture, prefect's house or office; — de police Paris police headquarters.

préférable [preferabl] *a* preferable, better.

préférence [preferɑ̃ːs] *nf* preference, priority.

préférer [prefere] *vt* to prefer, like better.

préfet [prefɛ] *nm* prefect; — de police chief commissioner of the Paris police.

préfixe [prefiks] *nm* prefix.

préfixer [prefikse] *vt* to settle beforehand, prefix.

préhistorique [preistɔrik] *a* prehistoric.

préjudice [preʒydis] *nm* injury, detriment, prejudice; porter — à qn to harm, injure, hurt.

préjudiciable [preʒydisjabl] *a* prejudicial, injurious, detrimental.

préjugé [preʒyʒe] *nm* prejudice, preconceived idea.

préjuger [preʒyʒe] *vti* to judge beforehand.

se prélasser [səprelase] *vr* to lounge, loll, laze.

prélat [prela] *nm* prelate.

prélèvement [prelɛvmɑ̃] *nm* deduction, levy.

prélever [prelve] *vt* to deduct, levy.

préliminaire [preliminɛːr] *a nm* preliminary.

prélude [prelyd] *nm* prelude.

prématuré [prematyre] *a* premature, untimely.

préméditer [premedite] *vt* to premeditate.

prémices [premis] *nf pl* first fruits.

premier, -ière [prəmje, jɛːr] *a* first, foremost, early, original; — rôle leading part, lead; — venu first comer, anybody; du — coup first shot, at the first attempt; nm au — first floor; jeune — juvenile lead.

première [prəmjɛːr] *nf* first night, first performance, first class, sixth form.

prémisse [premis] *nf* premise, premiss.

prémonition [premɔnisjɔ̃] *nf* premonition.

prémunir [premyniːr] *vt* to (fore)warn; *vr* to provide.

prendre [prɑ̃ːdr] *vt* to take (up, on, in), pick up, grasp, catch, assume; *vi* to freeze, seize, congeal, set, catch on; *vr* to catch, get caught, begin, clutch, cling; à tout — on the whole; bien lui en a pris de partir it was a good thing for him that he left; s'en — à to attack, blame; se — d'amitié pour to take a liking to; cela ne prend pas that won't take a trick; s'y prendre to set about it.

prénom [prenɔ̃] *nm* first name, Christian name.

préoccupation [preɔkypasjɔ̃] *nf* preoccupation, anxiety, concern, care.

préoccuper [preɔkype] *vt* to preoccupy, worry, engross; *vr* to attend, see (to de).

préparatif [preparatif] *nm* preparation.

préparation [preparasjɔ̃] *nf* preparing, preparation.

préparatoire [preparatwaːr] *a* preparatory.

préparer [prepare] *vt* to prepare, get ready, read for; *vr* to get ready, prepare, brew.

prépondérance [prepɔ̃derɑ̃ːs] *nf* preponderance, prevalency.

prépondérant [prepɔ̃derɑ̃] *a* preponderant, predominant; voix — deciding vote.

préposé [prepoze] *n* person in charge.

préposer [prepoze] *vt* to appoint.

préposition [prepozisjɔ̃] *nf* preposition.

prérogative [prerɔgatiːv] *nf* prerogative, privilege.

près [prɛ] *ad* near, near-by, close by; *prep* — de near, close to, by, on, about; à beaucoup — by far; à peu — nearly, about; à cela — with that exception; de — closely, at a short distance; il n'est pas à cent francs — 100 francs more or less does not matter to him.

présage [preza:ʒ] *nm* presage, foreboding, omen.

présager [prɛzaʒe] *vt* to presage, predict, portend.

pré-salé [presale] *nm* mutton, sheep (fattened in fields near the sea).

presbyte [prɛzbit] *a* far-sighted.

presbytère [prɛzbitɛːr] *nm* presbytery, rectory, manse.

prescience [presjã:s] *nf* prescience, foreknowledge.

prescription [prɛskripsjɔ̃] *nf* prescription, regulation, direction.

prescrire [prɛskriːr] *vt* to prescribe, stipulate, ordain.

préséance [preseã:s] *nf* precedence, priority.

présence [prezã:s] *nf* presence, attendance; faire acte de — to put in an appearance.

présent [prezã] *a* present, ready; *nm* present (time or tense), gift.

présentable [prezãtabl] *a* presentable.

présentation [prezãtasjɔ̃] *nf* presentation, introduction, get-up.

présenter [prezãte] *vt* to present, introduce, show; *vr* to introduce oneself, appear, call, arise, occur; le livre présente bien the book is attractively got up; se bien — to look promising, well.

préservatif, -ive [preservatif, iːv] *a nm* preservative, preventive.

préservation [prezɛrvasjɔ̃] *nf* preservation, protection, saving.

préserver [prezɛrve] *vt* to preserve, protect, save.

présidence [prezidã:s] *nf* presidency, president's house, chairmanship.

président [prezidã] *n* president, chairman.

présidentiel, -elle [prezidãsjɛl] *a* presidential, of the president.

présider [prezide] *vt* to preside over; *vi* to preside, be in the chair.

présomptif, -ive [prezɔ̃ptif, iːv] *a* presumptive, apparent.

présomption [prezɔ̃psjɔ̃] *nf* presumption, presumptuousness.

présomptueux, -euse [presɔ̃ptɥø, øːz] *a* presumptuous, presuming, forward.

presque [prɛsk] *ad* nearly, almost, hardly.

presqu'île [prɛskil] *nf* peninsula.

pressant [presã] *a* pressing, urgent.

presse [prɛːs] *nf* crowd, throng, hurry, press(ing-machine), press, newspapers; sous — printing; heures de — rush hours.

pressé [prese] *a* pressed, squeezed, crowded, hurried, in a hurry, urgent.

pressentiment [presãtimã] *nm* presentiment, forewarning, feeling.

presser [prɛse] *vt* to press, squeeze hasten, hurry (on), quicken, beset; *vi* to be urgent, press; *vr* to hurry (up), crowd.

pression [presjɔ̃] *nf* pressure, tension; bière à la — draft beer; bouton — push button.

pressoir [preswaːr] *nm* wine-, ciderpress.

pressurer [presyre] *vt* to press (out), squeeze.

prestance [prestã:s] *nf* fine presence.

prestation [prestasjɔ̃] *nf* loan, lending, prestation; — de serment taking an oath.

preste [prɛst] *a* nimble, alert, quick.

prestidigitateur [prɛstidiʒitatœːr] *nm* conjuror.

prestidigitation [prɛstidiʒitasjɔ̃] *nf* conjuring, sleight of hand.

prestige [prɛstiːʒ] *nm* prestige, fascination.

prestigieux, -euse [prɛstiʒjø, øːz] *a* amazing, marvelous, spellbinding.

présumer [prezyme] *vt* to presume, assume; trop — de to overrate.

présupposer [presypoze] *vt* to presuppose, take for granted.

prêt [prɛ] *a* ready, prepared; *nm* loan, lending.

prêt-bail [prɛbaj] *nm* lend-lease.

prétendant [pretãdã] *n* candidate, applicant, claimant; *nm* suitor.

prétendre [pretã:dr] *vt* to claim, require, intend, state, maintain, aspire.

prétendu [pretãdy] *a* alleged, socalled, would-be; *n* intended.

prétentieux, -euse [pretãsjø, øːz] *a* pretentious, snobbish, conceited.

prétention [pretãsjɔ̃] *nf* pretension, claim, aspiration, self-conceit.

prêter [prete] *vt* to lend, ascribe, attribute; *vi* lend itself (to à), give scope (for à); *vr* to fall in (with à), be a party (to à), indulge (in à).

prêteur, -euse [pretœːr, øːz] *a* (given to) lending; *n* lender; — sur gages pawnbroker.

prétexte [pretɛkst] *nm* pretext, excuse; sous aucun — on no account.

prétexter [pretɛkste] *vt* to pretext, plead, make the excuse of.

prêtre [prɛːtr] *nm* priest.

prêtrise [pretriːz] *nf* priesthood.

preuve [prœːv] *nf* proof, token, evidence; faire — de to show, display; faire ses —s to survive the test, show what one can do.

prévaloir [prevalwaːr] *vi* to prevail; *vr* to avail oneself, take advantage (of de).

prévenance [prevnã:s] *nf* attention, kindness.

prévenant [prevnã] *a* attentive, considerate, prepossessing.

prévenir [prevniːr] *vt* to prevent, avert, anticipate, inform, warn, tell, prejudice.

prévenu [prevny] *a* prejudiced, biased; *n* accused.
préventif, -ive [prevătif, iːv] *a* preventive, deterrent.
prévention [prevãsjɔ̃] *nf* prejudice, detention.
prévision [previzjɔ̃] *nf* forecast(ing), expectation, anticipation, likelihood.
prévoir [prevwaːr] *vt* to foresee, forecast, provide for.
prévoyance [prevwajãːs] *nf* foresight, forethought.
prévoyant [prevwajã] *a* foreseeing, far-sighted.
prie-Dieu [pridjø] *nm* prayer-stool.
prier [prie] *vt* to pray, beg, request, ask, invite; **sans se faire** — without having to be coaxed, readily; **je vous en prie** please do, don't mention it.
prière [prieːr] *nf* prayer, entreaty, request; — **de ne pas fumer** please do not smoke.
prieur [prioeːr] *n* prior, prioress.
prieuré [prioere] *nm* priory.
primaire [primeːr] *a* primary.
primat [prima] *nm* primate.
primauté [primote] *nf* primacy, pre-eminence.
prime [prim] *a* first, earliest; *nf* premium, bonus, option, subsidy, reward, free gift; **de** — **saut** on the first impulse; **faire** — to be at a premium.
primer [prime] *vt* to surpass, outdo, award a prize, bonus to, to give a subsidy, bounty, to.
prime-sautier, -ière [primsotje, jeːr] *a* impulsive, spontaneous.
primeur [primoeːr] *nf* newness, freshness; *pl* early vegetables.
primevère [primveːr] *nf* primrose, primula.
primitif, -ive [primitif, iːv] *a* primitive, earliest, original; **les** — **s** the early masters.
primordial [primɔrdjal] *a* primordial, primeval, of prime importance.
prince [prɛ̃ːs] *nm* prince.
princesse [prɛ̃sɛs] *nf* princess; **aux frais de la** — at the expense of the state, free, gratis.
princier, -ière [prɛ̃sje, jeːr] *a* princely.
principal [prɛ̃sipal] *a* principal, chief; *nm* chief, head(master), main thing.
principauté [prɛ̃sipote] *nf* principality.
principe [prɛ̃sip] *nm* principle; **sans** — **s** unscrupulous; **dès le** — from the beginning.
printanier, -ière [prɛ̃tanje, jeːr] *a* spring(-like).
printemps [prɛ̃tã] *nm* spring(time).
priorité [priɔrite] *nf* priority.
prise [priːz] *nf* hold, grip, capture, taking, pinch, prize, setting; — **d'air** air-intake; — **d'eau** hydrant, cock; — **de courant** plug; — **de**

vues filming, shooting; **donner** — à to leave oneself open to; **en venir aux** — s to come to grips; **lâcher** — to let go.
priser [prize] *vt* to snuff (up), value, prize; *vi* to take snuff.
prisme [prism] *nm* prism.
prison [prizɔ̃] *nf* prison, jail, imprisonment.
prisonnier, -ière [prizɔnje, jeːr] *a* captive; *n* prisoner.
privation [privasjɔ̃] *nf* (de)privation, hardship.
privé [prive] *a* private, privy; *nm* private life.
priver [prive] *vt* to deprive; *vr* to deny oneself.
privilège [privileːʒ] *nm* privilege, prerogative, preference.
privilégié [privileʒje] *a* privileged licensed, preference.
prix [pri] *nm* price, prize, reward, value, cost; — **de revient** cost price; — **du trajet** fare; **au** — **de** at the price of, compared with; **de** — expensive; **attacher beaucoup de** — à to set a high value on.
probabilité [prɔbabilite] *nf* probability, likelihood.
probable [prɔbabl] *a* probable, likely.
probant [prɔbã] *a* conclusive, convincing.
probe [prɔb] *a* upright, honest.
probité [prɔbite] *nf* integrity, probity.
problématique [prɔblɛmatik] *a* problematical.
problème [prɔblɛm] *nm* problem.
procédé [prɔsede] *nm* process, method, proceeding, conduct, dealing, tip; **bons** — s civilities, fair dealings.
procéder [prɔsede] *vi* to proceed, originate (in **de**), take proceedings.
procédure [prɔsedyːr] *nf* procedure, proceedings.
procès [prɔsɛ] *nm* (legal) action, proceedings, case; **sans autre forme de** — without further ado, at once.
procession [prɔsesjɔ̃] *nf* procession.
processus [prɔsesyːs] *nm* process, method.
procès-verbal [prɔsevɛrbal] *nm* minutes, report, particulars; **dresser un** — **à qn** to take s.o.'s name and address.
prochain [prɔʃɛ̃] *a* next, nearest, neighboring, approaching; *n* neighbor.
prochainement [prɔʃɛnmã] *ad* shortly.
proche [prɔʃ] *a* near, at hand; *ad* near.
proclamation [prɔklamasjɔ̃] *nf* proclamation.
proclamer [prɔklame] *vt* to proclaim, declare.
procréer [prɔkree] *vt* to procreate, beget.

procurer [prɔkyre] *vtr* to procure, get, obtain.

procureur, -atrice [prɔkyrœːr, prɔkyratris] *n* procurator, proxy, agent; *nm* attorney.

prodigalité [prɔdigalite] *nf* prodigality, extravagance, lavishness.

prodige [prɔdiːʒ] *nm* prodigy, marvel.

prodigieux, -euse [prɔdiʒjø, øːz] *a* prodigious.

prodigue [prɔdig] *a* prodigal, lavish, profuse, thriftless; *n* waster, prodigal.

prodiguer [prɔdige] *vt* to be prodigal of, be lavish of, waste; *vr* to strive to please, make o.s. cheap.

producteur, -trice [prɔdyktœːr, tris] *a* productive; *n* producer.

productif, -ive [prɔdyktif, iːv] *a* productive.

production [prɔdyksjɔ̃] *nf* product (ion), generation, yield, output.

productivité [prɔdyktivite] *nf* productivity, productiveness.

produire [prɔdɥiːr] *vt* to produce, bear, yield, bring out, forward; *vr* to occur.

produit [prɔdɥi] *nm* product, produce, takings; — **secondaire** by-product.

proéminence [prɔeminãːs] *nf* prominence, protuberance.

profane [prɔfan] *a* profane, lay; *n* layman, outsider.

profaner [prɔfane] *vt* to desecrate, misuse.

proférer [prɔfere] *vt* to utter, speak.

professer [prɔfɛse] *vt* to profess, teach.

professeur [prɔfɛsœːr] *nm* professor, teacher.

profession [prɔfɛsjɔ̃] *nf* profession, occupation, trade.

professionnel, -elle [prɔfɛsjɔnɛl] *an* professional; *a* vocational; **enseignement** — vocational training.

professorat [prɔfɛsɔra] *nm* teaching profession, professorship, body of teachers.

profil [prɔfil] *nm* profile, section.

profiler [prɔfile] *vt* to draw in profile, in section, shape; *vr* to be outlined, stand out.

profit [prɔfi] *nm* profit, advantage, benefit.

profiter [prɔfite] *vi* to profit, be profitable, take advantage (of **de**).

profiteur [prɔfitœːr] *nm* profiteer.

profond [prɔfɔ̃] *a* deep, profound, deep-seated; *nm* depth.

profondeur [prɔfɔ̃dœːr] *nf* depth, profundity.

profusion [prɔfyzjɔ̃] *nf* profusion, abundance.

progéniture [prɔʒenityːr] *nf* progeny, offspring.

programme [prɔgram] *nm* program, syllabus, curriculum.

progrès [prɔgrɛ] *nm* progress, improvement, headway.

progresser [prɔgrɛse] *vi* to progress, make headway.

progressif, -ive [prɔgrɛsif, iːv] *a* progressive, gradual.

progression [prɔgrɛsjɔ̃] *nf* progress (ion).

prohiber [prɔibe] *vt* to prohibit, forbid.

prohibitif, -ive [prɔibitif, iːv] *a* prohibitive.

proie [prwa] *nf* prey, quarry; **en** — **à** a prey to.

projecteur [prɔʒɛktœːr] *nm* projector, searchlight, spotlight.

projectile [prɔʒɛktil] *nm* projectile, missile.

projection [prɔʒɛksjɔ̃] *nf* projection, throwing out, beam, lantern slide.

projet [prɔʒɛ] *nm* project, scheme, plan, draft; — **de loi** bill.

projeter [prɔʒəte] *vt* to project, throw, plan; *vr* to be thrown, stand out.

prolétaire [prɔleteːr] *an* proletarian.

prolifique [prɔlifik] *a* prolific.

prolixe [prɔliks] *a* prolix, verbose.

prolixité [prɔliksite] *nf* prolixity, wordiness.

prologue [prɔlɔg] *nm* prologue.

prolongation [prɔlɔ̃gasjɔ̃] *nf* prolongation, protraction, extension; *pl* extra time.

prolongement [prɔlɔ̃ʒmã] *nm* prolongation, lengthening, extension.

prolonger [prɔlɔ̃ʒe] *vt* to prolong, protract, extend; *vr* to be prolonged, continue.

promenade [prɔmnad] *nf* walk(ing), outing, ramble, public walk; — **en auto** car ride, drive; — **en bateau** sail; **emmener en** — to take for a walk.

promener [prɔmne] *vt* to take for a walk, a sail, a run, take about; *vr* to go for a walk *etc*; **envoyer** — **qn** to send s.o. about his business.

promeneur, -euse [prɔmnœːr, øːz] *nmf* walker, rambler.

promenoir [prɔm(ə)nwaːr] *nm* lounge, lobby, promenade.

promesse [prɔmɛs] *nf* promise.

prometteur, -euse [prɔmɛtœːr, øːz] *a* promising, full of promise(s).

promettre [prɔmɛtr] *vt* to promise, look promising.

promiscuité [prɔmiskɥite] *nf* promiscuity.

promontoire [prɔmɔ̃twaːr] *nm* promontory, headland.

promoteur, -trice [prɔmɔtœːr, tris] *a* promoting; *n* promoter.

promotion [prɔmɔsjɔ̃] *nf* promotion.

prompt [prɔ̃] *a* prompt, quick, hasty, ready.

promptitude [prɔ̃tityd] *nf* promptitude, readiness.

promulguer [prɔmylge] *vt* to promulgate, issue.

prôner [prone] *vt* to praise, extol.

pronom [prɔnɔ̃] *nm* pronoun.

prononcer [prɔnɔ̃se] *vt* to pronounce, say, mention, deliver; *vr* to declare one's opinion, decision, speak out.

prononciation [prɔnɔ̃sjasjɔ̃] *nf* pronunciation, utterance, delivery.

pronostic [prɔnɔstik] *nm* prognostic (ation), forecast.

pronostiquer [prɔnɔstike] *vt* to forecast.

propagande [prɔpagɑ̃:d] *nf* propaganda, publicity.

propagation [prɔpagasjɔ̃] *nf* propagation, spreading

propager [prɔpaʒe] *vtr* to propagate, spread.

propension [prɔpɑ̃sjɔ̃] *nf* propensity.

prophète, prophétesse [prɔfɛːt, prɔfetɛs] *n* prophet, prophetess.

prophétie [prɔfesi] *nf* prophecy, prophesying.

prophétiser [prɔfetize] *vt* to prophesy, foretell.

propice [prɔpis] *a* propitious, favorable.

proportion [prɔpɔrsjɔ̃] *nf* proportion, ratio; *pl* size; **toute — gardée** within limits.

proportionné [prɔpɔrsjɔne] *a* proportionate, proportioned.

proportionnel, -elle [prɔpɔrsjɔnɛl] *a* proportional.

proportionner [prɔpɔrsjɔne] *vt* to proportion, adapt.

propos [prɔpo] *nm* purpose, remark, matter, subject; *pl* talk; **à —** by the way, appropriate(ly), opportune(ly); **mal à —** untimely.

proposer [prɔpoze] *vt* to propose, suggest; *vr* to come forward, propose (to).

proposition [prɔpozisjɔ̃] *nf* proposition, proposal, motion, clause.

propre [prɔpr] *a* own, very; suitable (for **à**); peculiar (to **à**); proper; clean, neat; *nm* characteristic, peculiarity; **au —** in the literal sense.

proprement [prɔprəmɑ̃] *ad* properly, nicely, neatly, appropriately.

propreté [prɔprəte] *nf* clean(li)ness, tidiness.

propriétaire [prɔprietɛːr] *n* owner, proprietor, landlord, -lady.

propriété [prɔpriete] *nf* property, estate, ownership, propriety.

propulser [prɔpylse] *vt* to propel.

propulseur [prɔpylsœːr] *a* propelling; *nm* propeller.

propulsion [prɔpylsjɔ̃] *nf* propulsion, drive.

prorogation [prɔrɔgasjɔ̃] *nf* prorogation, delay, extension

proroger [prɔrɔʒe] *vt* to adjourn, extend, delay.

prosaïque [prɔzaik] *a* prosaic, pedestrian.

prosateur, -trice [prɔzatœːr, tris] *n* prose writer.

proscription [prɔskripsjɔ̃] *nf* proscription, outlawing, banishment.

proscrire [prɔskriːr] *vt* to proscribe, outlaw, banish.

proscrit [prɔskri] *a* outlawed; *n* outlaw.

prose [proːz] *nf* prose.

prospecter [prɔspɛkte] *vt* to prospect, circularize.

prospectus [prɔspɛktyːs] *nm* prospectus, handbill.

prospère [prɔspɛːr] *a* prosperous, flourishing, favorable.

prospérer [prɔspere] *vi* to prosper, thrive.

prospérité [prɔsperite] *nf* prosperity.

prosterné [prɔstɛrne] *a* prostrate, prone.

se prosterner [səprɔstɛrne] *vr* to prostrate oneself, grovel.

prostituée [prɔstitɥe] *nf* prostitute, whore.

prostré [prɔstre] *a* prostrate(d), exhausted.

protagoniste [prɔtagɔnist] *nm* protagonist.

protecteur, -trice [prɔtɛktœːr, tris] *a* protective, patronizing; *n* protector, protectress, patron(ess).

protection [prɔtɛksjɔ̃] *nf* protection, patronage.

protégé [prɔteʒe] *n* protégé(e), ward.

protéger [prɔteʒe] *vt* to protect, patronize, be a patron of.

protéine [prɔtein] *nf* protein.

protestant [prɔtɛstɑ̃] *n* Protestant.

protestation [prɔtɛstasjɔ̃] *nf* protestation, protest.

protester [prɔtɛste] *vti* to protest.

protêt [prɔtɛ] *nm* protest.

protocole [prɔtɔkɔl] *nm* protocol, correct procedure, etiquette.

protubérance [prɔtyberɑ̃:s] *nf* protuberance, projection, bump.

proue [pru] *nf* prow, bows.

prouesse [pruɛs] *nf* prowess, exploit.

prouver [pruve] *vt* to prove, give proof of.

provenance [prɔvnɑ̃:s] *nf* origin, produce; **en — de** coming from.

provençal [prɔvɑ̃sal] *an* Provençal.

Provence [prɔvɑ̃:s] *nf* Provence.

provende [prɔvɑ̃:d] *nf* provender, fodder, supplies.

provenir [prɔvniːr] *vi* to originate, come, arise.

proverbe [prɔvɛrb] *nm* proverb.

proverbial [prɔvɛrbjal] *a* proverbial.

providence [prɔvidɑ̃:s] *nf* providence.

providentiel, -elle [prɔvidɑ̃sjɛl] *a* providential.

province [prɔvɛ̃:s] *nf* province(s).

provincial [prɔvɛ̃sjal] *a* provincial.

proviseur [prɔvizœːr] *nm* headmaster (of lycée).

provision [prɔvizjɔ̃] *nf* provision, supply, reserve, stock.

provisoire [prɔvizwaːr] *a* temporary, provisional; **à titre —** provisionally, temporarily.

provocant [prɔvɔkɑ̃] *a* provocative.

provocateur, -trice [prɔvɔkatœːr, tris] *a* provocative; *n* instigator, inciter.
provocation [prɔvɔkasjɔ̃] *nf* provocation, instigation, inciting, challenge.
provoquer [prɔvɔke] *vt* to provoke, arouse, cause, incite, challenge.
proxénète [prɔksenɛt] *n* procurer, procuress.
proximité [prɔksimite] *nf* proximity, nearness.
prude [pryd] *a* prudish; *nf* prude.
prudence [prydɑːs] *nf* prudence, caution, carefulness.
prudent [prydɑ̃] *a* prudent, careful, cautious.
prune [pryn] *nf* plum; **jouer pour des —s** to play for the fun of the thing.
pruneau [pryno] *nm* prune.
prunelle [prynɛl] *nf* sloe, pupil, apple (of eye).
prunier [prynje] *nm* plum-tree.
Prusse [prys] *nf* Prussia.
prussien, -enne [prysjɛ̃, jɛn] *an* Prussian.
psalmodier [psalmɔdje] *vt* to intone, chant, drone; *vi* to chant.
psaume [psoːm] *nm* psalm.
psautier [psotje] *nm* psalter.
pseudonyme [psødɔnim] *a* pseudonymous; *nm* pseudonym, assumed name.
psychanalyse [psikanaliːz] *nf* psychoanalysis.
psyché [psiʃe] *nf* psyche, cheval glass.
psychiatrie [psikjatri] *nf* psychiatry.
psychique [psiʃik] *a* psychic.
psychologie [psikɔlɔʒi] *nf* psychology.
psychologique [psikɔlɔʒik] *a* psychological.
psychologue [psikɔlɔg] *nm* psychologist.
psychose [psikoːz] *nf* psychosis.
puanteur [pɥɑ̃tœːr] *nf* stink, stench.
puberté [pybɛrte] *nf* puberty.
public, -ique [pyblik] *a nm* public.
publication [pyblikasjɔ̃] *nf* publication, publishing.
publiciste [pyblisist] *nm* publicist.
publicité [pyblisite] *nf* publicity, advertising; **faire de la — to** advertise.
publier [pyblie] *vt* to publish, proclaim.
puce [pys] *nf* flea; **mettre la — à** l'oreille de qn to arouse s.o.'s suspicions, start s.o. thinking.
pucelle [pysɛl] *nf* virgin, maid(en).
pudeur [pydœːr] *nf* modesty, decorousness, decency.
pudibond [pydibɔ̃] *a* prudish, easily shocked.
pudibonderie [pydibɔ̃dri] *nf* prudishness.
pudique [pydik] *a* modest, chaste, virtuous.
puer [pɥe] *vi* to stink, smell.

puéril [pɥeril] *a* puerile, childish.
puérilité [pɥerilite] *nf* puerility, childishness, childish statement.
pugilat [pyʒila] *nm* boxing, fight.
pugiliste [pyʒilist] *nm* pugilist, boxer.
puîné [pɥine] *a* younger.
puis [pɥi] *ad* then, next, afterwards; **et — après** what about it, what next?
puisard [pɥizaːr] *nm* cesspool, sump.
puiser [pɥize] *vt* to draw, take.
puisette [pɥizɛt] *nf* scoop, ladle.
puisque [pɥisk(ə)] *cj* as, since.
puissance [pɥisɑ̃ːs] *nf* power, strength, force.
puissant [pɥisɑ̃] *a* powerful, strong, mighty, potent.
puits [pɥi] *nm* well, shaft, pit, fount.
pulluler [pyllyle] *vi* to multiply rapidly, teem, swarm.
pulmonaire [pylmɔnɛːr] *a* pulmonary.
pulpe [pylp] *nf* pulp.
pulper [pylpe] *vt* to pulp.
pulpeux, -euse [pylpø, øːz] *a* pulpy.
pulsation [pylsasjɔ̃] *nf* pulsation, throb(bing).
pulvérisateur [pylverizatœːr] *nm* pulverizer, atomizer.
pulvériser [pylverize] *vt* to pulverize, grind (down), spray, atomize.
punaise [pynɛːz] *nf* bug, thumbtack.
punir [pyniːr] *vt* to punish.
punition [pynisjɔ̃] *nf* punishment, punishing.
pupille [pypil] *n* ward; *nf* pupil (of eye).
pupitre [pypiːtr] *nm* desk, stand, rack.
pur [pyːr] *a* pure, clear, sheer, mere, genuine.
purée [pyre] *nf* purée, thick soup, mash; **— de pommes de terre** mashed potatoes; **être dans la —** to be hard-up.
pureté [pyrte] *nf* pureness, purity, clearness.
purgatif, -ive [pyrgatif, iːv] *a nm* purgative.
purgatoire [pyrgatwaːr] *nm* purgatory.
purge [pyrʒ] *nf* purge, purgative, draining, cleaning.
purger [pyrʒe] *vt* to purge, clean (out), cleanse, clear; *vr* to take medicine; **— sa peine** to serve one's sentence.
purificateur, -trice [pyrifikatœːr, tris] *a* purifying, cleansing; *n* purifier, cleanser.
purification [pyrifikasjɔ̃] *nf* purification.
purifier [pyrifje] *vt* to purify, cleanse, refine; *vr* to clear, become pure.
purin [pyrɛ̃] *nm* liquid manure.
puritanisme [pyritanism] *nm* puritanism.

pur-sang [pyrsɑ̃] nm thoroughbred.
pus [py] nm pus, matter.
pusillanime [pyzillanim] a pusillanimous, faint-hearted.
pustule [pystyl] nf pustule, pimple.
putain [pytɛ̃] nf whore.
putatif, -ive [pytatif, iːv] a putative, supposed.
putois [pytwa] nm pole-cat, skunk.
putréfaction [pytrɛfaksjɔ̃] nf putrefaction.
putréfier [pytrefye] vtr to putrefy, rot.
putride [pytrid] a putrid, tainted.
pygmée [pigme] n pygmy.
pyjama [piʒama] nm pajamas.
pylône [piloːn] nm pylon, mast, pole.
pyorrhée [pjɔre] nf pyorrhea.
pyramide [piramid] nf pyramid.
pyromane [pirɔman] n pyromaniac.
python [pitɔ̃] nm python.

Q

quadragénaire [kwadraʒenɛːr] an quadragenarian.
quadrangulaire [kwadrɑ̃gylɛːr] a quadrangular.
quadrilatéral [kwadrilatɛral] a quadrilateral.
quadriller [kadrije] vt to rule in squares, cross-rule.
quadrupède [kwadrypɛd] a four-footed; nm quadruped.
quadrupler [kwadryple] vt to quadruple.
quai [ke] nm quay, wharf, embankment, platform.
qualificatif, -ive [kalifikatif, iːv] a qualifying.
qualification [kalifikasjɔ̃] nf qualifying, title.
qualifier [kalifje] vt to qualify, call, describe.
qualité [kalite] nf quality, property, capacity, qualification, rank; en — de as, in the capacity of.
quand [kɑ̃] cj ad when; — même cj even if; ad all the same.
quant [kɑ̃t] ad — à as for, as to, as regards.
quantième [kɑ̃tjɛm] nm day of the month.
quantité [kɑ̃tite] nf quantity, amount, lot.
quarantaine [karɑ̃tɛn] nf (about) forty, quarantine.
quarante [karɑ̃ːt] anm forty.
quarantième [karɑ̃tjɛm] anm fortieth.
quart [kaːr] nm quarter, quarter of a liter, watch; être de —, to be on watch, on duty.
quarteron [kart(ə)rɔ̃] an quadroon.
quartier [kartje] nm quarter, part, portion, district, ward, quarters; — général headquarters.
quartier-maître [kartjemɛːtr] nm quartermaster, leading seaman.

quasi [kazi] ad quasi, almost, all but.
quasiment [kazimɑ̃] ad as it were.
quatorze [katɔrz] anm fourteen, fourteenth.
quatorzième [katɔrzjɛm] anm fourteenth.
quatrain [katrɛ̃] nm quatrain.
quatre [katr] anm four, fourth; se mettre en quatre, to do all one can.
quatre-vingt-dix [katrəvɛ̃dis] anm ninety.
quatre-vingts [katrəvɛ̃] anm eighty.
quatrième [katriɛm] fourth.
quatuor [kwatɥɔːr] nm (mus) quartet.
que [k(ə)] cj that, but; ad than, as, how, how many; ne . . . que, only; (soit) — . . . (soit) — . . ., whether . . . or; qu'il parle, let him speak; pr that, whom, which, what; qu'est-ce qui? qu'est-ce que? what?
Québec [kebɛk] nm Quebec.
quel, -le [kɛl] a what, which, who, what a; — que whoever, whatever.
quelconque [kɛlkɔ̃k] a any, some, whatever, commonplace, ordinary.
quelque [kɛlk(ə)] a some, any; pl some, a few; . . . qui, que whatever, whatsoever; ad some, about; — . . . que ad however
quelque chose [kɛlkəʃoːz] pn something, anything.
quelquefois [kɛlkəfwa] ad sometimes.
quelque part [kɛlkəpaːr] ad somewhere.
quelqu'un, quelqu'une [kɛlkœ̃, kɛlkyn] pn someone, anyone, one; pl some, a few.
quémander [kemɑ̃de] vi to beg; vt to solicit, beg for.
qu'en dira-t-on [kɑ̃diratɔ̃] nm what people will say, gossip.
quenelle [kənɛl] nf fish ball, forcemeat ball.
quenouille [kənuːj] nf distaff.
querelle [kərɛl] nf quarrel, row.
quereller [kərɛle] vt to quarrel with; vr to quarrel.
querelleur, -euse [kərɛlœːr, øːz] a quarrelsome; n quarreler, wrangler.
question [kɛstjɔ̃] nf question, query, matter, point.
questionnaire [kɛstjɔnɛːr] nm list of questions.
questionner [kɛstjɔne] vt to question.
quête [kɛːt] nf search, quest, collection.
quêter [kɛte] vt to search for, collect.
queue [kø] nf tail, end, train, stalk, stem, rear, queue, file, cue; finir en — de poisson to peter out; piano à — grand piano; en, à la — in the rear.
queue d'aronde [kødarɔ̃ːd] nf dovetail.
queue-de-pie [kødpi] nf tails, evening dress.
queue-de-rat [kødra] nf small taper.
qui [ki] pn who, whom, which, that;

— **que** who(so)ever, whom(so)ever;
— **que ce soit** anyone; — **est-ce
que? whom?**
quiconque [kikɔ̃:k] *pn* who(so)ever,
anyone who.
quiétude [kμietyd, kje] *nf* quietude.
quignon [kiɲɔ̃] *nm* hunk, chunk.
quille [ki:j] *nf* skittle, ninepin, keel.
quincaillerie [kɛ̃kɑjri] *nf* hardware store.
quincaillier [kɛ̃kɑje] *nm* hardware
dealer.
quinine [kinin] *nf* quinine.
quinquennal [kμɛ̃kμɛnnal] *a* quin-
quennial, five-year.
quintal [kɛ̃tal] *nm* 100 kilograms.
quinte [kɛ̃:t] *nf* (*mus*) fifth; fit of
bad temper; — **de toux** fit of
coughing.
quintessence [kɛ̃tɛssɑ̃:s] *nf* quintessence.
quintette [k(μ)ɛ̃tɛt] *nm* quintet.
quinteux, -euse [kɛ̃tø, ø:z] *a* fitful,
restive, fretful.
quintupler [k(μ)ɛ̃typle] *vti* to
increase fivefold.
quinzaine [kɛ̃zɛn] *nf* (about) fifteen,
fortnight, two weeks.
quinze [kɛ̃:z] *a nm* fifteen, fifteenth;
— **jours** fortnight, two weeks.
quinzième [kɛ̃zjɛm] *a nm* fifteenth.
quiproquo [kiprɔko] *nm* mistake,
misunderstanding.
quittance [kitɑ̃:s] *nf* receipt, discharge.
quitte [kit] *a* quit, rid, free (of); **en
être — pour la peur** to get off with
a fright; — **à** even though, at the
risk of.
quitter [kite] *vt* to quit, leave; **ne
quittez pas!** hold the line!
qui-vive [kivi:v] *nm* challenge; **sur
le —** on the alert.
quoi [kwa] *pn* what, which; **avoir
de — vivre** to have enough to live
on; **il n'y a pas de —** don't mention
it; **de — écrire** writing materials;
sans — otherwise; — qui, que
whatever; — **qu'il en soit** be that
as it may; — **que ce soit** anything
whatever; **à — bon?** what's the use?
quoique [kwak(ə)] *cj* (al)though.
quolibet [kɔlibɛ] *nm* gibe.
quotidien, -enne [kɔtidjɛ̃, jɛn] *a*
daily, everyday; *nm* daily paper.

R

rabâcher [rabɑʃe] *vti* to repeat over
and over again.
rabais [rabɛ] *nm* reduction, rebate,
allowance; **au —** at a reduced price.
rabaisser [rabɛse] *vt* to lower,
reduce, belittle, humble.
rabat-joie [rabaʒwa] *n* killjoy,
spoilsport.
rabatteur, -euse [rabatœ:r, ø:z] *n*
tout; *nm* beater (*hunting*).

rabattre [rabatr] *vt* to lower, bring
down, turn down, take down,
reduce, beat (up); *vi* to turn off;
**en — to climb down; *vr* to fold
(down), fall back.
rabbin [rabɛ̃] *nm* rabbi.
rabiot [rabjo] *nm* surplus, buckshee,
extra (work).
râble [rɑ:bl] *nm* back, saddle (of
hare).
râblé [rɑble] *a* broadbacked, strapping.
rabot [rabo] *nm* plane.
raboter [rabɔte] *vt* to plane, polish.
raboteux, -euse [rabɔtø, øz] *a*
rough, bumpy.
rabougrir [rabugri:r] *vt* to stunt;
vir to become stunted.
rabougrissement [rabugrismɑ̃] *nm*
stuntedness.
rabrouer [rabrue] *vt* to scold,
rebuke, rebuff, snub.
racaille [rakɑ:j] *nf* rabble, riff-raff,
trash.
raccommodage [rakɔmɔdaːʒ] *nm*
mend(ing), repair(ing), darn(ing).
raccommodement [rakɔmɔdmɑ̃] *nm*
reconciliation.
raccommoder [rakɔmɔde] *vt* to
mend, repair, darn, reconcile; *vr* to
make it up.
raccord [rakɔ:r] *nm* join, joint, link,
connection.
raccorder [rakɔrde] *vt* to join, link
up, connect, bring into line; *vr* to
fit together.
raccourci [rakursi] *a* short(ened),
abridged; **à bras —(s)** with might
and main, with a vengeance; *nm*
abridgement, foreshortening, short
cut; **en —** in miniature, in short.
raccourcir [rakursi:r] *vt* to shorten,
curtail, foreshorten; *vir* to grow
shorter, draw in.
raccroc [rakro] *nm* fluke.
raccrocher [rakrɔʃe] *vt* to hook up,
hang up, get hold of again; *vr* to
clutch, catch on, recover, cling.
race [ras] *nf* race, descent, strain,
stock, breed; **avoir de la — to be
pure-bred, pedigreed; **bon chien
chasse de — what's bred in the
bone comes out in the flesh.
racé [rase] *a* thoroughbred.
rachat [raʃa] *a* repurchase, redemption.
rachetable [raʃtabl] *a* redeemable.
racheter [raʃte] *vt* to repurchase, buy
back, redeem, ransom, retrieve,
atone for.
rachitique [raʃitik] *a* rachitic,
rickety.
racine [rasin] *nf* root.
racisme [rasism] *nm* color bar,
prejudice, race, racism.
raclée [rakle] *nf* thrashing.
racler [rakle] *vt* to scrape, rake,
rasp; **se — la gorge** to clear one's
throat.
racloir [raklwa:r] *nf* scraper.

racoler [rakɔle] *vt* to recruit, enlist, tout for.

racoleur [rakɔlœːr] *nm* recruiting-sergeant, tout.

racontars [rakɔ̃taːr] *nm pl* gossip, tittle-tattle.

raconter [rakɔ̃te] *vt* to relate, tell (about), recount; *vi* to tell a story; **en —** to exaggerate, spin a yarn.

raconteur, -euse [rakɔ̃tœːr, øːz] *n* (story-)teller, narrator.

racornir [rakɔrniːr] *vtr* to harden, toughen.

rade [rad] *nf* roadstead, roads.

radeau [rado] *nm* raft.

radiateur [radjatœːr] *a* radiating; *nm* radiator.

radiation [radjasjɔ̃] *nf* erasure, cancellation, striking off, radiation.

radical [radikal] *a nm* radical.

radier [radje] *vt* to erase, cancel, strike off, radiate.

radieux, -euse [radjø, øːz] *a* radiant, beaming.

radio [radjo] *nf* radio, X-rays; **par —** broadcast; *nm* radio message, radio operator.

radio-actif [radjoaktif, iːv] *a* radio-active.

radio-diffusion [radjɔdifyzjɔ̃] *nf* broadcast(ing).

radiogramme [radjɔgram] *nm* radiogram, X-ray photograph.

radiographie [radjɔgrafi] *nf* radiography.

radiologie [radjɔlɔʒi] *nf* radiology.

radio-reportage [radjɔrəpɔrtaːʒ] *nm* running commentary.

radiotélégraphie [radjɔtelegrafi] *nf* radiotelegraphy.

radiothérapie [radjɔtɛrapi] *nf* radiotherapy.

radis [radi] *nm* radish.

radium [radjɔm] *nm* radium.

radotage [radɔtaːʒ] *nm* drivel, twaddle.

radoter [radɔte] *vi* to drivel, talk nonsense.

radoteur, -euse [radɔtœːr, øːz] *n* dotard.

radoub [radu] *nm* repair, refitting; **en —** in dry dock.

radoucir [radusiːr] *vt* to calm, soften, mollify; *vr* to grow milder.

rafale [rafal] *nf* squall, gust, burst.

raffermir [rafɛrmiːr] *vt* to harden, strengthen, fortify; *vr* to harden, improve, be restored.

raffiné [rafine] *a* refined, subtle, fine, polished.

raffiner [rafine] *vt* to refine; *vi* to be too subtle; *vr* to become refined.

raffinerie [rafinri] *nf* refinery.

raffoler [rafɔle] *vi* to be very fond (of **de**), dote (upon **de**), be mad (about **de**).

rafistoler [rafistɔle] *vt* to patch up, do up.

rafle [rɑːfl] *nf* raid, clean sweep, round-up.

rafler [rɑfle] *vt* to make a clean sweep of, round up, comb out.

rafraîchir [rafrɛʃiːr] *vt* to refresh, cool, freshen up, touch up, trim, brush up; *vr* to turn cooler, have sth to drink, rest.

rafraîchissement [rafrɛʃismɑ̃] *nm* refreshing, cooling, freshening up, brushing up; *pl* refreshments.

ragaillardir [ragajardiːr] *vtr* to cheer up, revive.

rage [raːʒ] *nf* rage, madness, rabies, mania, passion; **— de dents** violent attack of toothache; **faire —** to rage.

rager [raʒe] *vi* to rage; **faire — qn** to make s.o. wild.

rageur, -euse [raʒœːr, øːz] *a* hot-tempered, passionate.

ragot [rago] *nm* gossip.

ragoût [ragu] *nm* stew.

rahat-loukoum [raatlukum] *nm* Turkish delight.

raid [rɛd] *nm* raid, long-distance flight, l.-d. run.

raide [rɛd] *a* stiff, taut, unbending, steep; **coup —** stinging blow; **c'est un peu —!** that's too much! **— mort** stone-dead.

raideur [rɛdœːr] *nf* stiffness, tightness, steepness; **avec —** stiffly, arrogantly.

raidir [rɛdiːr] *vt* to stiffen, tighten; *vr* to stiffen, brace oneself, steel oneself.

raie [rɛ] *nf* line, stroke, streak, stripe, parting, ridge, ray, (*fish*) skate.

railler [rɑje] *vt* to jeer at, laugh at; *vi* to joke; *vr* to make fun (of **de**), scoff (at **de**).

raillerie [rɑjri] *nf* raillery, banter, joke.

railleur, -euse [rɑjœːr, øːz] *a* bantering, mocking; *n* joker, scoffer.

rainure [rɛnyːr] *nf* groove, slot, channel.

rais [rɛ] *nm* spoke.

raisin [rɛzɛ̃] *nm* grape; **—s secs** raisins; **—s de Corinthe** currants.

raison [rɛzɔ̃] *nf* reason, motive, right mind, sense(s), satisfaction, ratio; **avoir —** to be right; **avoir — de qn, de qch** to get the better of s.o., sth; **se faire une —** to make the best of it; **à — de** at the rate of.

raisonnable [rɛzɔnabl] *a* reasonable, fair, adequate.

raisonnement [rɛzɔnmɑ̃] *nm* reasoning, argument.

raisonner [rɛzɔne] *vi* to reason, argue; *vt* to reason with, study.

raisonneur, -euse [rɛzɔnœːr, øːz] *a* reasoning, argumentative; *n* reasoner, arguer.

rajeunir [raʒøniːr] *vt* to rejuvenate, make (s.o. look) younger, renovate; *vi* to look younger.

rajuster [raʒyste] *vt* to readjust, put straight.

râle [rɑːl] nm rattle (in the throat).

ralenti [ralɑ̆ti] a slow(er); nm slow motion; au — dead slow; mettre au — to slow down, throttle down.

ralentir [ralɑ̆tiːr] vti to slacken, slow down.

râler [rɑle] vi to rattle, be at one's last gasp, be furious.

ralliement [ralimɑ̆] nm rally(ing); mot de — password.

rallier [ralje] vt to rally, rejoin, win over; vr to rally, join.

rallonge [ralɔ̃ːʒ] nf extension piece, extra leaf.

rallonger [ralɔ̃ʒe] vt to lengthen, let down.

rallye [rali] nm auto race, rally.

ramage [ramaːʒ] nm floral design, warbling, singing.

ramassé [ramɑse] a thickset, stocky, compact.

ramasser [ramɑse] vt to gather, collect, pick up; vr to gather, crouch.

rame [ram] nf oar, ream, string, train.

rameau [ramo] nm branch, bough; le dimanche des R—x Palm Sunday.

ramener [ramne] vt to bring back, bring around, reduce, pull down, restore.

ramer [rame] vi to row, pull.

rameur [ramœːr] n rower, oarsman.

ramier [ramje] nm wood pigeon.

ramification [ramifikasjɔ̃] nf ramification, branch(ing).

se ramifier [səramifje] vr to branch out.

ramollir [ramɔliːr] vt to soften, enervate; vr to soften, grow soft (-headed).

ramollissement [ramɔlismɑ̆] nm softening.

ramoner [ramɔne] vt to sweep, rake out.

ramoneur [ramɔnœːr] nm (chimney-) sweep.

rampe [rɑ̆ːp] nf slope, gradient, handrail, footlights, ramp.

ramper [rɑ̆pe] vi to creep, crawl, grovel, cringe.

rancart [rɑ̆kaːr] nm mettre au — to cast aside.

rance [rɑ̆ːs] a rancid.

rancir [rɑ̆siːr] vi to become rancid.

rancœur [rɑ̆kœːr] nf rancor, bitterness, resentment.

rançon [rɑ̆sɔ̃] nf ransom.

rancune [rɑ̆kyn] nf rancor, grudge, spite, ill-feeling.

rancunier, -ière [rɑ̆kynje, jɛːr] a vindictive, spiteful.

randonnée [rɑ̆dɔne] nf tour, run, excursion.

rang [rɑ̆] nm row, line, rank, status; rompre les —s to disperse, dismiss; de premier — first-class.

rangé [rɑ̆ʒe] a orderly, well-ordered, steady, staid; bataille —e pitched battle.

rangée [rɑ̆ʒe] nf row, line.

ranger [rɑ̆ʒe] vt to arrange, draw up, put away, tidy, keep back, rank, range; vr to draw up, settle down, fall in (with à); se — du côté de to side with; se — de côté to stand aside.

ranimer [ranime] vt to revive, rekindle, stir up; vr to come to life again.

rapace [rapas] a rapacious.

rapacité [rapasite] nf rapaciousness.

rapatrier [rapatrie] vt to repatriate.

râpe [rɑːp] nf rasp, file, grater.

râpé [rɑpe] a grated, shabby, threadbare.

râper [rɑpe] vt to rasp, grate, wear out.

rapetasser [raptase] vt to patch (up).

rapetisser [raptise] vt to shorten, make smaller; vir to shrink, shorten.

rapide [rapid] a rapid, quick, swift, steep; nm express train.

rapidité [rapidite] nf rapidity, swiftness, steepness.

rapiécer [rapjese] vt to patch.

rapin [rapɛ̃] nm (fam) art student.

rappareiller [raparɛje] vt to match.

rapparier [raparje] vt to match.

rappel [rapɛl] nm recall, call(ing), reminder, repeal.

rappeler [raple] vt to recall, call back, remind, repeal; vr to recall, remember; rappelez-moi à son bon souvenir remember me kindly to him.

rapport [rapɔːr] nm return, yield, profit, report, relation, connection, contact; pl relations, terms; en — avec in keeping with; par — à with regard to; sous ce — in this respect.

rapporter [rapɔrte] vt to bring back, bring in, yield, report, tell tales, revoke, refer; vr to agree, tally, fit together, refer, relate; s'en — à to rely on, to leave it to, go by.

rapporteur, -euse [rapɔrtœːr, øːz] n tale bearer; nm reporter, recorder, protractor.

rapproché [raprɔʃe] a near, close (-set), related.

rapprochement [raprɔʃmɑ̆] nm bringing together, reconciling, comparing, nearness, reconciliation.

rapprocher [raprɔʃe] vt to bring together, bring near(er), draw up, compare, reconcile; vr to draw near(er), become reconciled.

rapt [rapt] nm kidnapping, abduction.

raquette [rakɛt] nf racket, snowshoe, prickly pear.

rare [raːr] a rare, unusual, sparse.

rarement [rarmɑ̆] ad seldom, rarely.

rareté [rarte] nf rarity, scarcity, unusualness, rare happening, curiosity.

ras [ra] a close-cropped, close-shaven, bare; en —e campagne in the open country; faire table —e

de to make a clean sweep of; **à, au — de** level with, flush with, up to.
rasade [rɑzad] *nf* bumper.
rase-mottes [rɑzmɔt] *nm* **voler à —** to hedge-hop.
raser [rɑze] *vt* to shave, bore, raze to the ground, skim (over, along), hug; *vr* to shave, be bored; **se faire — to** have a shave.
rasoir [rɑzwaːr] *nm* razor; **qu'il est —! how** boring, tiresome he is!
rassasier [rasazje] *vt* to satisfy, satiate, surfeit; *vr* to eat one's fill.
rassemblement [rasɑ̃bləmɑ̃] *nm* assembling, gathering, fall-in, crowd.
rassembler [rasɑ̃ble] *vtr* to assemble, gather together, muster.
rasséréner [raserene] *vt* to clear (up); *vr* to clear up, brighten up.
rassis [rasi] *a* settled, staid, sane, stale.
rassurer [rasyre] *vt* to reassure, strengthen; *vr* to feel reassured, set one's mind at rest.
rat [ra] *nm* rat, miser; **— de bibliothèque** bookworm; **— de cave** exciseman, wax taper; **— d'église** excessively pious person; **— d'hôtel** hotel thief; **mort aux —s** rat-poison.
ratatiné [ratatine] *a* shriveled, wizened.
rate [rat] *nf* spleen; **ne pas se fouler la —** to take things easy.
raté [rate] *a* miscarried, bungled, muffed; *n* failure, misfire.
râteau [rɑto] *nm* rake, cue-rest.
râteler [rɑtle] *vt* to rake up.
râtelier [rɑtəlje] *nm* rack, denture.
rater [rate] *vi* to miscarry, misfire, fail; *vt* to miss, fail, bungle, muff.
ratière [ratjɛːr] *nf* rat-trap.
ratifier [ratifje] *vt* to ratify.
ration [rasjɔ̃] *nf* ration, allowance.
rationnel, -elle [rasjɔnɛl] *a* rational.
rationnement [rasjɔnmɑ̃] *nm* rationing.
rationner [rasjɔne] *vt* to ration (out).
ratisser [ratise] *vt* to rake.
ratissoire [ratiswaːr] *nf* rake, hoe, scraper.
rattacher [rataʃe] *vt* to (re)fasten, tie up, bind, connect; *vr* to be connected (with à), fastened (to à).
rattraper [ratrape] *vt* to recapture, catch (again, up), overtake, recover; *vr* to save oneself, recoup oneself, make it up.
rature [ratyːr] *nf* erasure.
raturer [ratyre] *vt* to erase, cross out.
rauque [roːk] *a* raucous, hoarse, harsh.
ravage [ravaːʒ] *nm* (*usu pl*) havoc.
ravager [ravaʒe] *vt* to devastate, lay waste.
ravaler [ravale] *vt* to swallow (again, down), disparage, roughcast; *vr* to lower oneself; **— ses paroles** to eat one's words.
ravauder [ravode] *vt* to mend, darn.

ravi [ravi] *a* delighted, overjoyed, enraptured.
ravigoter [ravigɔte] *vtr* to revive, buck up.
ravin [ravɛ̃] *nm* ravine.
raviner [ravine] *vt* to gully, cut up, rut.
ravir [raviːr] *vt* to ravish, carry off, enrapture, delight; **à — ravishingly,** delightfully.
se raviser [səravize] *vr* to change one's mind.
ravissant [ravisɑ̃] *a* lovely, delightful, bewitching, ravishing.
ravitaillement [ravitajmɑ̃] *nm* revictualing, supply(ing); **service du — Army** Service Corps.
ravitailler [ravitaje] *vtr* to revictual; *vt* to supply.
ravitailleur [ravitajœːr] *nm* carrier, supply-ship.
raviver [ravive] *vtr* to revive, brighten.
rayer [rɛje] *vt* to scratch, rule, stripe, delete, strike off.
rayon [rɛjɔ̃] *nm* ray, beam, radius, drill, row, shelf, counter, department; **— visuel** line of sight; **— de miel** honeycomb; **chef de — floor-**walker, buyer.
rayonne [rɛjɔn] *nf* rayon.
rayonnement [rɛjɔnmɑ̃] *nm* radiation, radiance.
rayonner [rɛjɔne] *vi* to radiate, beam, be radiant.
rayure [rɛjyːr] *nf* scratch, stripe, erasure, striking off.
raz [rɑ] *nm* strong current; **— de marée** tide-race, tidal wave.
ré [re] *nm* the note D, D string.
réactif, iv [reaktif, iːv] *a* **papier — litmus** paper.
réacteur [reaktœːr] *nm* reactor, (*aut*) choke.
réaction [reaksjɔ̃] *nf* reaction; **avion à — jet-plane.**
réactionnaire [reaksjɔnɛːr] *an* reactionary.
réagir [reaʒiːr] *vi* to react.
réalisation [realizasjɔ̃] *nf* realization, carrying into effect, selling out.
réaliser [realize] *vt* to realize, carry out, sell out; *vr* to materialize, be realized.
réalisme [realism] *nm* realism.
réaliste [realist] *a* realistic; *n* realist.
réalité [realite] *nf* reality.
réarmement [rearməmɑ̃] *nm* rearming, refitting.
réassurer [reasyre] *vt* to reassure, reinsure.
rébarbatif, -ive [rebarbatif, iːv] *a* forbidding, grim, crabbed, repulsive.
rebattre [rəbatr] *vt* to beat again, reshuffle; **— les oreilles à qn** to repeat the same thing over and over again to s.o.
rebattu [rəbaty] *a* hackneyed, trite.
rebelle [rəbɛl] *a* rebellious, obstinate; *n* rebel.

rébellion [rebɛljɔ̃] *nf* rebellion, rising.
reboiser [rəbwaze] *vt* to retimber, (re)afforest.
rebondi [rəbɔ̃di] *a* plump, chubby, rounded.
rebondir [rəbɔ̃diːr] *vi* to rebound, bounce, start up all over again.
rebord [rəbɔːr] *nm* edge, hem, border, rim, flange.
rebours [rəbuːr] *nm* wrong way, contrary; **à, au** — against the grain, backward, the wrong way.
rebouteur [rəbutœːr] *nm* bonesetter.
rebrousse-poil [rəbruspwal] *ad* à — the wrong way, against the nap or hair.
rebuffade [rəbyfad] *nf* rebuff.
rébus [rebyːs] *nm* puzzle, riddle.
rebut [rəby] *nm* scrap, waste, rubbish, scum; *pl* rejects; **bureau des** —s dead-letter office.
rebutant [rəbytɑ̃] *a* discouraging, irksome, repulsive, forbidding
rebuter [rəbyte] *vt* to rebuff, repulse, discourage; *vr* to become discouraged, jib.
récalcitrant [rekalsitrɑ̃] *a* recalcitrant, refractory.
recaler [rəkale] *vt* to fail.
récapituler [rekapityle] *vt* to recapitulate.
recéler [rəsele] *vt* to conceal, hide, receive (stolen goods).
receleur, -euse [rəslœːr, øːz] *n* receiver, fence.
récemment [resamɑ̃] *ad* recently, lately.
recensement [rəsɑ̃smɑ̃] *nm* census, counting.
recenser [rəsɑ̃se] *vt* to take the census of, count, check off.
récent [resɑ̃] *a* recent, fresh, late.
récépissé [resepise] *nm* receipt.
réceptacle [resɛptakl] *nm* receptacle.
récepteur, -trice [resɛptœːr, tris] *a* receiving; *nm* receiver.
réception [resɛpsjɔ̃] *nf* receipt, reception, admission, welcome, receiving desk; **accuser** — **de** to acknowledge receipt of; **avis, (accusé) de** — notice (acknowledgment) of delivery; **jour de** — athome day.
recette [rəsɛt] *nf* receipt(s), takings, gate-money, recipe.
receveur, -euse [rəsəvœːr, øːz] *n* receiver, addressee, tax-collector, conductor, -tress; — **des Postes** postmaster.
recevoir [rəsəvwaːr] *vt* to receive, get, entertain, welcome, take in (*boarders*), accept, admit; *vi* be at home.
rechange [rəʃɑ̃ːʒ] *nm* replacement, spare, change, refill; *a* **de** — spare.
réchapper [reʃape] *vi* to escape, recover.
recharger [rəʃarʒe] *vt* to recharge, reload.

réchaud [reʃo] *nm* portable stove, (gas-)ring, hot-plate.
réchauffé [reʃofe] *nm* warmed-up dish, rehash.
réchauffer [reʃofe] *vt* to reheat, warm up, stir up.
rêche [rɛʃ] *a* harsh, rough, crabbed, sour.
recherche [rəʃɛrʃ] *nf* search, pursuit, studied refinement; *pl* research.
recherché [rəʃɛrʃe] *a* in great demand, choice, mannered, affected.
rechercher [rəʃɛrʃe] *vt* to search (for, into), seek.
rechigner [rəʃiɲe] *vi* to look surly, jib (at **à, devant**).
rechute [rəʃyt] *nf* relapse.
récidiver [residive] *vi* to offend again, recur.
récidiviste [residivist] *n* old offender.
récif [resif] *nm* reef.
récipient [resipjɑ̃] *nm* receiver, container, vessel.
réciprocité [resiprɔsite] *nf* reciprocity.
réciproque [resiprɔk] *a* reciprocal, mutual; *nf* the like.
réciproquement [resiprɔkmɑ̃] *ad* reciprocally, vice-versa, mutually.
récit [resi] *nm* recital, account, story, narrative.
récitation [resitasjɔ̃] *nf* reciting, recitation.
réciter [resite] *vt* to recite, say.
réclamation [reklamasjɔ̃] *nf* complaint, claim.
réclame [reklɑːm] *nf* publicity, advertising, advertisement, sign.
réclamer [reklame] *vi* to complain, protest; *vt* to claim, demand back, beg for, call (out) for; *vr* — **de qn** to quote s.o. as one's authority, to use s.o.'s name.
reclus [rəkly] *n* recluse.
réclusion [reklyzjɔ̃] *nf* reclusion, seclusion.
recoin [rəkwɛ̃] *nm* nook, recess.
récolte [rekɔlt] *nf* harvest(ing), crop(s).
récolter [rekɔlte] *vt* to harvest, gather (in).
recommandation [rəkɔmɑ̃dasjɔ̃] *nf* recommendation, advice; **lettre de** — letter of introduction, testimonial.
recommander [rəkɔmɑ̃de] *vt* to (re)commend, advise, register.
recommencer [rəkɔmɑ̃se] *vti* to recommence, begin again.
récompense [rekɔ̃pɑ̃ːs] *nf* recompense, reward, prize.
récompenser [rekɔ̃pɑ̃se] *vt* to recompense, reward, requite.
réconciliation [rekɔ̃siljasjɔ̃] *nf* reconciliation.
réconcilier [rekɔ̃silje] *vt* to reconcile; *vr* to make it up, make one's peace, become friends again.
reconduire [rəkɔ̃dɥiːr] *vt* to accompany back, escort, see home, show out.

réconfort [rek5fɔːr] *nm* comfort, consolation.

réconforter [rek5fɔrte] *vt* to comfort, console, fortify, refresh; *vr* to cheer up.

reconnaissance [rəkɔnɛsãːs] *nf* recognition, acknowledgment, admission, reconnoitering, reconnaissance, gratitude, thankfulness.

reconnaissant [rəkɔnɛsã] *a* grateful, thankful.

reconnaître [rəkɔnɛːtr] *vt* to recognize, acknowledge, reconnoiter; *vr* to acknowledge, get one's bearings; **ne plus s'y — to be quite lost**, bewildered.

reconstituant [rək5stituã] *a nm* restorative.

record [rəkɔːr] *nm* record.

recourbé [rəkurbe] *a* bent (back, down, round), curved, crooked.

recourir [rəkuriːr] *vi* to run (again, back), have recourse (to à), appeal (to à).

recours [rəkuːr] *nm* recourse, resort, claim, appeal.

recouvrement [rəkuvrəmã] *nm* recovery, collection, recovering, cover (ing), overlapping.

recouvrer [rəkuvre] *vt* to recover, regain, collect.

recouvrir [rəkuvriːr] *vt* to recover, cover (over), overlap; *vr* to become overcast.

récréation [rekreasj5] *nf* recreation, amusement, relaxation, playtime; **cour de — playground; en — at play.**

récréer [rekree] *vt* to enliven, refresh, entertain, amuse; *vr* to take some recreation.

se récrier [sərekrie] *vr* to cry out, exclaim, protest.

récriminer [rekrimine] *vi* to recriminate.

se recroqueviller [sərəkrɔkvije] *vr* to curl (up, in), shrivel (up).

recru [rəkry] *a* — **de fatigue** worn out, dead tired.

recrudescence [rəkrydɛssãːs] *nf* recrudescence.

recrue [rəkry] *nf* recruit.

recruter [rəkryte] *vt* to recruit, enlist.

rectangle [rɛktãːgl] *a* right-angled; *nm* rectangle.

rectangulaire [rɛktãgylɛːr] *a* rectangular.

recteur [rɛktœːr] *nm* rector.

rectification [rɛktifikasj5] *nf* rectification, rectifying, straightening, (re)adjustment.

rectifier [rɛktifje] *vt* to rectify, straighten, adjust.

rectiligne [rɛktiliɲ] *a* rectilinear.

rectitude [rɛktityd] *nf* straightness, rectitude.

reçu [rəsy] *pp* of **recevoir;** *nm* receipt.

recueil [rəkœːj] *nm* collection.

recueillement [rəkœjmã] *nm* meditation, composure, concentration.

recueilli [rəkœji] *a* meditative, rapt, concentrated, still.

recueillir [rəkœjiːr] *vt* to gather, collect, take in; *vr* to collect one's thoughts, commune with oneself.

recul [rəkyl] *nm* recoil, backward movement, room to move back.

reculade [rəkylad] *nf* backward movement, withdrawal.

reculé [rəkyle] *a* remote.

reculer [rəkyle] *vi* to move back, draw back; *vt* to move back, postpone.

reculons [rəkyl5] *ad* à — backward.

récupérer [rekypere] *vt* to recover, recoup, salvage; *vr* to recuperate.

récurer [rekyre] *vt* to scour.

récuser [rekyze] *vt* to challenge, take exception to; *vr* to refuse to give an opinion, disclaim competence, decline.

rédacteur, -trice [redaktœːr, tris] *n* writer, editor.

rédaction [redaksj5] *nf* writing, editing, editorial staff, newspaper office, composition, wording.

reddition [reddisj5] *nf* surrender.

rédempteur, -trice [redãptœːr, tris] *a* redeeming; *n* redeemer.

rédemption [redãpsj5] *nf* redemption.

redevable [rədvabl] *a* indebted, obliged.

redevance [rədvãːs] *nf* rent, tax, due.

rédiger [rediʒe] *vt* to draft, write, edit.

redingote [rədɛ̃gɔt] *nf* frock-coat.

redire [rədiːr] *vt* to repeat; **trouver à — à** to find fault with.

redite [rədit] *nf* repetition.

redondance [rəd5dãːs] *nf* redundance.

redoubler [rəduble] *vt* to redouble, reline, repeat (*a class*); *vi* to redouble.

redoutable [rədutabl] *a* formidable.

redoute [rədut] *nf* redoubt.

redouter [rədute] *vt* to dread.

redressement [rədrɛsmã] *nm* setting up again, righting, rectifying, straightening, redress.

redresser [rədrɛse] *vt* to set upright again, right, rectify, straighten; *vr* to sit up again, draw oneself up, right oneself.

réductible [redyktibl] *a* reducible.

réduction [redyksj5] *nf* reduction, cut, conquest.

réduire [redɥiːr] *vt* to reduce; *vr* to be reduced, confine oneself to, boil down.

réduit [redɥi] *nm* retreat, hovel, redoubt.

rééducation [reedykasj5] *nf* **centre de —** reformatory.

réel, -elle [reɛl] *a* real, actual; *nm* reality.

réexpédier [reɛkspedje] *vt* to forward, retransmit.

réfaction [refaksjɔ̃] *nf* rebate, allowance.

refaire [rəfɛːr] *vt* to remake, do again, make again, repair, take in; *vr* to recuperate.

réfection [refɛksjɔ̃] *nf* remaking, repairing.

réfectoire [refɛktwaːr] *nm* dining-hall.

référence [referɑ̃ːs] *nf* reference.

référer [refere] *vt* to refer, ascribe; *vir* to refer (to à).

refiler [rəfile] *vt* to fob off, pass on.

réfléchi [refleʃi] *a* thoughtful, considered, reflexive.

réfléchir [refleʃiːr] *vt* to reflect, throw back; *vi* to reflect, consider; *vr* to be reflected.

reflet [rəflɛ] *nm* reflection, gleam.

refléter [rəflete] *vt* to reflect, throw back.

réflexe [reflɛks] *a nm* reflex.

réflexion [reflɛksjɔ̃] *nf* reflection, thought, remark.

refluer [rəflye] *vi* to ebb, surge back.

reflux [rəfly] *nm* ebb(-tide), surging back.

refondre [rəfɔ̃ːdr] *vt* to recast, reorganize.

refonte [rəfɔ̃ːt] *nf* recasting, reorganization.

réformateur, -trice [reformatœːr, tris] *a* reforming; *n* reformer.

réformation [reformasjɔ̃] *nf* reformation.

réforme [reform] *nf* reform, reformation, discharge.

réformé [reforme] *n* Protestant, disabled soldier.

réformer [reforme] *vt* to reform, discharge (as unfit).

refoulement [rəfulmɑ̃] *nm* forcing back, repression.

refouler [rəfule] *vt* to drive back, repress.

réfractaire [refraktɛːr] *an* refractory, insubordinate.

réfracter [refrakte] *vt* to refract; *vr* to be refracted.

refrain [rəfrɛ̃] *nm* refrain, theme, chorus.

refréner [rəfrene] *vt* to restrain, curb.

réfrigérant [refriʒerɑ̃] *nm* refrigerator, cooler.

réfrigérer [refriʒere] *vt* to refrigerate, cool, chill.

refroidir [rəfrwadiːr] *vt* to chill, cool, damp; *vir* to grow cold, cool down.

refroidissement [rəfrwadismɑ̃] *nm* cooling (down), chill.

refuge [rəfyːʒ] *nm* shelter, refuge, traffic island.

réfugié [refyʒje] *n* refugee.

se réfugier [sərefyʒje] *vr* to take refuge.

refus [rəfy] *nm* refusal; **ce n'est pas de —** it is not to be refused.

refuser [rəfyze] *vtr* to refuse; *vt* to reject, fail, turn away, grudge.

réfuter [refyte] *vt* to refute, disprove.

regagner [rəgaɲe] *vt* to regain, recover, get back to.

regain [rəgɛ̃] *nm* aftercrop, renewal, fresh lease.

régal [regal] *nm* feast, treat.

régaler [regale] *vt* to entertain, treat.

regard [rəgaːr] *nm* look, glance, gaze; **au — de** compared with; **en — de** opposite.

regardant [rəgardɑ̃] *a* particular, mean, stingy.

regarder [rəgarde] *vt* to look at, consider, concern, watch; *vi* to look (on to **sur**), be particular (about **à**).

régate [regat] *nf* regatta, boater.

régence [reʒɑ̃ːs] *nf* regency, fob chain, necktie.

régénérer [reʒenere] *vt* to regenerate.

régent [reʒɑ̃] *n* regent, governor.

régenter [reʒɑ̃te] *vt* to lord it over, domineer.

régie [reʒi] *nf* management, stewardship, excise.

regimber [rəʒɛ̃be] *vi* to kick, jib (at **contre**).

régime [reʒim] *nm* diet, government, administration, system, rules, flow, bunch, object.

régiment [reʒimɑ̃] *nm* regiment.

région [reʒjɔ̃] *nf* region, district.

régional [reʒjɔnal] *a* regional, local.

régir [reʒiːr] *vt* to govern, manage.

régisseur [reʒisœːr] *nm* agent, steward, stage-manager.

registre [rəʒistr] *nm* register, account-book.

réglage [regla:ʒ] *nm* ruling, adjusting, turning.

règle [rɛgl] *nf* rule, ruler; **en —** in order; *pl* menses, period.

réglé [regle] *a* ruled, regular, steady.

règlement [regləmɑ̃] *nm* regulation, settlement, rule.

réglementaire [regləmɑ̃tɛːr] *a* statutory, regulation.

réglementer [regləmɑ̃te] *vt* to make rules for, regulate.

régler [regle] *vt* to rule, order, adjust, settle; *vr* to model oneself (on **sur**).

réglisse [reglis] *nf* licorice.

règne [rɛɲ] *nm* reign, sway, kingdom.

régner [reɲe] *vi* to reign, prevail.

regorger [rəgɔrʒe] *vt* to disgorge; *vi* to overflow (with **de**), abound (in **de**).

régression [regresjɔ̃] *nf* regression, recession, drop.

regret [rəgrɛ] *nm* regret, sorrow; **à — regretfully**; **être au — (de)** to be sorry.

regretter [rəgrete] *vt* to regret, be sorry (for), miss.

régulariser [regylarize] *vt* to regularize, put in order.

régularité [regylarite] *nf* regularity, steadiness, punctuality.

régulateur, -trice [regylatœːr, tris] *a* regulating; *nm* regulator, governor, throttle.

régulier, -ière [regylje, ɛːr] *a* regular, steady, punctual.

réhabiliter [reabilite] *vt* to rehabilitate, discharge.

rehausser [raose] *vt* to raise, heighten, enhance, accentuate, bring out.

rein [rɛ̃] *nm* kidney; *pl* back.

reine [rɛn] *nf* queen.

reine-claude [rɛnkloːd] *nf* greengage.

réintégrer [reɛ̃tegre] *vt* to reinstate, take up again.

réitérer [reitere] *vt* to repeat, reiterate.

rejaillir [rəʒajiːr] *vi* to gush out, be reflected come back (upon **sur**).

rejet [rəʒɛ] *nm* rejection, throwing up (out).

rejeter [rəʒ(ə)te] *vt* to reject, throw (back, out); *vr* to fall back (on **sur**).

rejeton [rəʒtɔ̃] *nm* shoot, offspring.

rejoindre [reʒwɛ̃ːdr] *vt* to (re)join, overtake; *vr* to meet (again).

réjouir [reʒwiːr] *vt* to delight, hearten, amuse; *vr* to rejoice, be delighted.

réjouissance [reʒwisɑ̃ːs] *nf* rejoicing, merrymaking.

relâche [rəlɑːʃ] *nm* relaxation, respite, no performance; *nf* (port of) call.

relâchement [rəlɑʃmɑ̃] *nm* slackening, relaxing, relaxation, looseness.

relâcher [rəlɑʃe] *vt* to slacken, loosen, relax, release; *vr* to slacken, get loose, abate, grow lax, milder.

relais [rəlɛ] *nm* relay, stage, shift, posthouse.

relancer [rəlɑ̃se] *vt* to throw back; to go after (s.o.); to be at (s.o.); restart.

relater [rəlate] *vt* to relate, report.

relatif, -ive [rəlatif, iːv] *a* relative, relating (to **à**).

relation [rəlasjɔ̃] *nf* relation, contact, connection, account.

relaxer [rəlakse] *vt* to release; *vr* to relax.

relayer [rəlɛje] *vt* to relay, relieve; *vi* to change horses.

relent [rəlɑ̃] *nm* stale smell, mustiness.

relève [rəlɛːv] *nf* relief, changing (of guard).

relevé [rəlve] *a* lofty, spicy; *nm* statement, account.

relever [rəlve] *vt* to raise up (again), turn up, pick up, relieve, set off, point out; *vi* to be dependent (on **de**); *vr* to rise (again), recover.

relief [rəljɛf] *nm* relief, prominence.

relier [rəlje] *vt* to bind (again), join, connect.

relieur, -euse [rəljœːr, øːz] *n* bookbinder.

religieux, -euse [rəliʒjø, øːz] *a* religious; *n* monk, nun.

religion [rəliʒjɔ̃] *nf* religion.

reliquaire [rəlikɛːr] *nm* shrine.

reliquat [rəlika] *nm* remainder, after-effects.

relique [rəlik] *nf* relic.

reliure [rəljyːr] *nf* (book)binding.

reluire [rəlɥiːr] *vi* to shine, gleam.

reluquer [rəlyke] *vt* to eye.

remailler [rəmaje] *vt* to remesh, mend.

remanier [rəmanje] *vt* to rehandle, recast.

remarquable [rəmarkabl] *a* remarkable (for **par**).

remarque [rəmark] *nf* remark.

remarquer [rəmarke] *vt* to remark, notice.

rembarrer [rɑ̃bare] *vt* to tell off, snub.

remblai [rɑ̃blɛ] *nm* embankment.

rembourrer [rɑ̃bure] *vt* to stuff, pad.

rembourser [rɑ̃burse] *vt* to refund, repay.

rembrunir [rɑ̃bryniːr] *vtr* to darken, become sad; *vt* to sadden.

remède [rəmɛd] *nm* remedy, cure.

remédier [rəmedje] *vt* — **à** to remedy.

remembrement [rəmɑ̃brəmɑ̃] *nm* reallocation of land.

remémorer [rəmemɔre] *vt* to remind (of); *vr* to remember.

remerciement [rəmɛrsimɑ̃] *nm* thanks.

remercier [rəmɛrsje] *vt* to thank, dismiss, decline.

remettre [rəmɛtr] *vt* to put back (again), hand (over, in), remit, postpone; *vr* to recover, begin; **s'en** — **à qn** to rely on s.o., leave it to s.o.

remise [rəmiːz] *nf* putting back, off, remittance, delivery, rebate, shed.

rémission [remisjɔ̃] *nf* remission, pardon.

remonter [rəmɔ̃te] *vt* to go up (again), carry up, pull up, wind up, buck up; *vi* to go up again, remount, go back (to **à**); *vr* to cheer up, regain strength.

remonte-pente [rəmɔ̃tpɑ̃ːt] *nm* skilift.

remontoir [rəmɔ̃twaːr] *nm* winder, key.

remontrance [rəmɔ̃trɑ̃ːs] *nf* remonstrance.

remontrer [rəmɔ̃tre] *vt* to show again; **en** — **à** to remonstrate with, outdo.

remords [rəmɔːr] *nm* remorse.

remorque [rəmɔrk] *nf* tow(ing), tow-line, trailer.

remorqueur [rəmɔrke] *nm* tug (-boat).

rémouleur [remulœːr] *nm* knifegrinder.

remous [rəmu] *nm* eddy, backwash.

rempart [rɑ̃paːr] *nm* rampart.

remplaçant [rãplasã] *n* substitute.
remplacement [rãplasmã] *nm* replacing, substitution.
remplacer [rãplase] *vt* to replace, deputize for.
rempli [rãpli] *nm* tuck.
remplir [rãpli:r] *vtr* to fill (up, in); *vt* fulfill, occupy.
remporter [rãpɔrte] *vt* to carry away, gain, win.
remuant [rəmɥã] *a* stirring, restless.
remue-ménage [rəmymena:ʒ] *nm* bustle, stir.
remuer [rəmɥe] *vti* to move, stir.
rémunérateur, -trice [remynɛratœːr, tris] *a* remunerative, paying.
rémunération [remynɛrasjɔ̃] *nf* remuneration.
renâcler [rənakle] *vi* to snort, hang back.
renaissance [rənɛsãːs] *nf* rebirth, revival.
renaître [rənɛːtr] *vi* to be born again, revive, reappear.
renard [rəna:r] *n* fox, vixen.
renchérir [rãʃeri:r] *vt* to raise the price of; *vi* to rise in price, outbid, outdo.
rencontre [rãkɔ̃:tr] *nf* meeting, encounter, collision, occasion; **de —** chance.
rencontrer [rãkɔ̃tre] *vt* to meet (with), run across; *vr* to meet, collide, agree.
rendement [rãdmã] *nm* yield, output, profit, efficiency.
rendez-vous [rãdevu] *nm* appointment, meeting-place.
rendre [rãːdr] *vt* to give back (up, out), yield, deliver, surrender, make; *vr* to proceed, go, surrender, yield.
rêne [rɛn] *nf* rein.
renégat [rənɛga] *n* renegade.
renfermé [rãfɛrme] *a* uncommunicative, reticent; *nm* musty smell.
renfermer [rãfɛrme] *vt* to shut up (again), lock up, include, contain.
renfler [rãfle] *vti* to swell (out).
renflouer [rãflue] *vt* to refloat.
renfoncement [rãfɔ̃smã] *nm* cavity, recess, knocking in.
renfoncer [rãfɔ̃se] *vt* to drive in, pull down.
renforcer [rãfɔrse] *vt* to reinforce, strengthen; *vir* to become stronger.
renfort [rãfɔːr] *nm* reinforcement(s).
se renfrogner [sərãfrɔɲe] *vr* to frown, scowl.
rengaine [rãgɛn] *nf* old story, old refrain, catchword.
rengainer [rãgɛne] *vt* to sheathe.
se rengorger [sərãgɔrʒe] *vr* to puff oneself out, swagger.
renier [rənje] *vt* to disown, repudiate.
renifler [rənifle] *vti* to sniff.
renne [rɛn] *nm* reindeer.
renom [rənɔ̃] *nm* renown, fame, repute.
renommé [rənɔme] *a* celebrated, famous.

renommée [rənɔme] *nf* fame, good name.
renoncement [rənɔ̃smã] *nm* renouncing, self-denial.
renoncer [rənɔ̃se] *vt* to renounce.
renoncule [rənɔ̃kyl] *nf* buttercup.
renouer [rənwe] *vt* to join again; to resume, renew.
renouveau [rənuvo] *nm* springtime, renewal.
renouveler [r(ə)nuvle] *vt* to renew, renovate; *vr* to be renewed, recur.
rénovation [renɔvasjɔ̃] *nf* renovation, revival.
renseignement [rãsɛɲmã] *nm* (piece of) information.
renseigner [rãsɛɲe] *vt* to inform; *vr* to inquire (about **sur**), find out.
rente [rãːt] *nf* unearned income, pension.
rentier, -ière [rãtje, jɛːr] *n* person of private means, stock-holder.
rentrée [rãtre] *nf* return, reopening, gathering (in).
rentrer [rãtre] *vt* to bring (take, get, pull) in; *vi* to come (go) in (again), come (go) home, reopen.
renverse [rãvɛrs] *nf* change, turn; **à la —** backward.
renversement [rãvɛrsəmã] *nm* overturning, overthrow, reversal, inversion.
renverser [rãvɛrse] *vt* to knock over (down), overthrow, spill, reverse, invert, flabbergast; *vr* to overturn, recline.
renvoi [rãvwa] *nm* sending back, reflecting, dismissal, reference, putting off, belch.
renvoyer [rãvwaje] *vt* to send back, reflect, dismiss, refer, defer.
repaire [rəpɛːr] *nm* lair, den, haunt.
repaître [rəpɛːtr] *vtr* to feed.
répandre [repãːdr] *vt* to spread, pour out, shed, scatter; *vr* to (be) spread, spill.
répandu [repãdy] *a* widespread, well-known.
réparation [reparasjɔ̃] *nf* repair(ing), reparation, amends.
réparer [repare] *vt* to mend, repair, redress, restore.
repartie [rəparti] *nf* repartee, retort.
repartir [rəparti:r] *vi* to set out again, retort.
répartir [reparti:r] *vi* to distribute, divide, allot.
répartition [repartisjɔ̃] *nf* distribution, sharing out, allotment.
repas [rəpɑ] *nm* meal.
repasser [rəpɑse] *vt* to pass again, cross again, go over, iron, sharpen; *vi* to pass again, call back.
repêcher [rəpɛʃe] *vt* to fish out (again), pick up, rescue; *vr* to get another chance (examination).
repentir [rəpãti:r] *nm* repentance; *vr* to repent, rue.
répercussion [repɛrkysjɔ̃] *nf* repercussion.

répercuter [repεrkyte] *vtr* to reverberate, reflect.

repère [rəpεːr] *nm* **point de —** reference, guide, landmark.

repérer [rəpere] *vt* to locate, spot; *vr* to take one's bearings.

répertoire [repεrtwaːr] *nm* repertory, list, collection.

répéter [repete] *vt* to repeat, rehearse; *vr* to recur.

répétiteur, -trice [repetitœːr, tris] *n* assistant-teacher, private tutor, chorus master.

répétition [repetisjɔ̃] *nf* repetition, rehearsal, private lesson; **— générale** dress rehearsal.

répit [repi] *nm* respite.

repli [rəpli] *nm* fold, crease, bend, coil, withdrawal.

replier [rəplie] *vtr* to fold up, turn in (back), coil up; *vr* to wind, withdraw.

réplique [replik] *nf* ready answer, cue, replica.

répliquer [replike] *vi* to retort.

répondre [repɔ̃ːdr] *vt* to answer, reply, respond, comply; *vi* to answer, be answerable (for **de**), correspond (to **à**), come up (to **à**).

réponse [repɔ̃ːs] *nf* answer.

report [rəpɔːr] *nm* carrying-forward, amount brought forward.

reportage [rəpɔrtaːʒ] *nm* report(ing).

reporter [rəpɔrte] *vt* to carry (take) back, bring forward; *vr* to refer.

reporter [rəpɔrtœːr, tεːr] *nm* reporter.

repos [rəpo] *nm* rest, peace.

reposé [rəpoze] *a* refreshed, calm; **à tête —e** at leisure, quietly.

reposer [rəpoze] *vt* to replace, put back, rest; *vi* to rest, lie; *vr* to rest, alight again, rely (on **sur**).

reposoir [rəpozwaːr] *nm* resting-place, temporary altar.

repoussant [rəpusɑ̃] *a* repulsive.

repousser [rəpuse] *vt* to push away (back, off), reject, repel; *vi* to grow again, recoil.

repoussoir [rəpuswaːr] *nm* foil, punch.

répréhensible [repreɑ̃sibl] *a* reprehensible.

reprendre [rəprɑ̃ːdr] *vt* to recapture, take back, recover, resume, reprove, correct; *vi* to begin again, set (in) again; *vr* to correct oneself, pull oneself together.

représailles [rəprezaːj] *nf pl* reprisals.

représentant [rəprezɑ̃tɑ̃] *an* representative.

représentatif, -ive [rəprezɑ̃tatif, iːv] *a* representative.

représentation [rəprezɑ̃tasjɔ̃] *nf* representation, performance, agency, protest.

représenter [rəprezɑ̃te] *vt* to represent, portray, perform, act, reintroduce; *vi* to put up a show, have a

fine appearance; *vr* to present oneself again, recur, describe oneself (as **comme**).

répression [represjɔ̃] *nf* repression.

réprimande [reprimɑ̃ːd] *nf* reproof, reprimand.

réprimander [reprimɑ̃de] *vt* to reprove, reprimand.

réprimer [reprime] *vt* to repress, quell, curb.

repris [rəpri] *n* **— de justice** old offender.

reprise [rəpriːz] *nf* recapture, taking back, resumption, revival, acceleration, darn(ing), round; **à plusieurs —** several times.

repriser [rəprize] *vt* to darn, mend.

réprobateur, -trice [reprɔbatœːr, tris] *a* reproachful, reproving.

réprobation [reprɔbasjɔ̃] *nf* reprobation.

reproche [rəprɔʃ] *nm* reproach, blame.

reprocher [rəprɔʃe] *vt* to reproach (with), begrudge, cast up.

reproduction [rəprɔdyksjɔ̃] *nf* reproduction, copy.

reproduire [rəprɔdɥiːr] *vt* to reproduce; *vr* to breed, recur.

réprouver [repruve] *vt* to disapprove of, reprobate.

reptile [rεptil] *a nm* reptile.

repu [rəpy] *a* satiated.

républicain [repyblikε̃] *an* republican.

république [repyblik] *nf* republic.

répudier [repydje] *vt* to repudiate, renounce.

répugnance [repyɲɑ̃ːs] *nf* repugnance, loathing, reluctance.

répugnant [repyɲɑ̃] *a* repugnant, loathsome.

répugner [repyɲe] *vi* to be repugnant, loathe, be reluctant.

répulsion [repylsjɔ̃] *nf* repulsion.

réputation [repytasjɔ̃] *nf* reputation, repute, name.

réputé [repyte] *a* of repute, well-known.

requérir [rəkeriːr] *vt* to ask (for), demand, summon.

requête [rəkεːt] *nf* request, petition.

requin [rəkε̃] *nm* shark.

requinquer [rəkε̃ke] *vt* to smarten up, repair; *vr* to smarten oneself up, recover.

requis [rəki] *a* requisite, necessary.

réquisition [rekizisjɔ̃] *nf* requisition (ing).

réquisitionner [rekizisjɔne] *vt* to requisition.

réquisitoire [rekizitwaːr] *nm* indictment, charge.

rescapé [rεskape] *a* rescued; *n* survivor.

rescinder [rεssε̃de] *vt* to annul, rescind.

rescousse [rεskus] *nf* rescue.

réseau [rezo] *nm* net(work), system.

réséda [resεda] *nm* mignonette.

réservation [rezɛrvasjɔ̃] *nf* reservation.

réserve [rezɛrv] *nf* reserve, reservation, aloofness, caution; **de** — spare, reserve.

réservé [rezɛrve] *a* reserved, cautious, aloof, private.

réserver [rezɛrve] *vt* to reserve, save, set aside.

réserviste [rezɛrvist] *nm* reservist.

réservoir [rezɛrvwaːr] *nm* reservoir, tank.

résidence [rezidɑ̃ːs] *nf* residence, abode.

résider [rezide] *vi* to reside, live, lie.

résidu [rezidy] *nm* residue, balance.

résignation [reziɲasjɔ̃] *nf* resignation.

résigner [reziɲe] *vt* to resign, give up.

résilier [rezilje] *vt* to cancel, annul.

résille [reziːj] *nf* hair-net, snood.

résine [rezin] *nf* resin.

résistance [rezistɑ̃ːs] *nf* resistance, opposition, endurance, strength; **pièce de** — main dish, feature.

résistant [rezistɑ̃] *a* resistant, strong, fast.

résister [reziste] *vt* to resist, withstand; *vi* to be fast.

résolu [rezɔly] *a* resolute.

résolution [rezɔlysjɔ̃] *nf* resolve, determination, solution, canceling.

résonance [rezɔnɑ̃ːs] *nf* resonance.

résonner [rezɔne] *vi* to resound, clang, ring.

résoudre [rezuːdr] *vt* to resolve, decide, (dis)solve, settle; *vr* to decide, dissolve.

respect [rɛspɛ] *nm* respect.

respectable [rɛspɛktabl] *a* respectable.

respecter [rɛspɛkte] *vt* to respect, have regard for.

respectif, -ive [rɛspɛktif, iːv] *a* respective.

respectueux, -euse [rɛspɛktɥø, øːz] *a* respectful.

respiration [rɛspirasjɔ̃] *nf* breathing.

respirer [rɛspire] *vt* to breathe (in), inhale; *vi* to breathe.

resplendir [rɛsplɑ̃diːr] *vi* to shine, glow, be resplendent.

responsabilité [rɛspɔ̃sabilite] *nf* responsibility, liability.

responsable [rɛspɔ̃sabl] *a* responsible.

resquilleur, -euse [rɛskijœːr, øːz] *n* gatecrasher, wangler.

ressac [rəsak] *nm* undertow, surf.

ressaisir [rəsɛziːr] *vt* to seize again; *vr* to pull oneself together, recover one's self-control.

ressasser [rəsase] *vt* repeat, harp on, resift.

ressemblance [rəsɑ̃blɑ̃ːs] *nf* resemblance, likeness.

ressemblant [rəsɑ̃blɑ̃] *a* (a)like.

ressembler [rəsɑ̃ble] *vt* to resemble, be like.

ressentiment [rəsɑ̃timɑ̃] *nm* resentment.

ressentir [rəsɑ̃tiːr] *vt* to feel; *vr* to feel the effects (of **de**).

resserrement [rəsɛrmɑ̃] *nm* contraction, tightness; — **du cœur** pang.

resserrer [rəsɛre] *vt* to contract, tighten, draw tight; *vr* to contract, shrink, narrow, retrench.

ressort [rəsɔːr] *nm* spring, resilience, line, province, resort.

ressortir [rəsɔrtiːr] *vt* to bring out again; *vi* to come, (go) out again, stand out, follow (from **de**), belong (to **à**); **faire** — to bring out.

ressortissant [rəsɔrtisɑ̃] *nm* national.

ressource [rəsurs] *nf* resource(fulness), expedient; **en dernière** — in the last resort.

ressusciter [resysite] *vti* to resuscitate, revive.

restant [rɛstɑ̃] *a* remaining, left; *nm* rest, remainder.

restaurant [rɛstɔrɑ̃] *nm* restaurant.

restaurateur, -trice [rɛstɔratœːr, tris] *n* restorer; *nm* restaurant-keeper.

restauration [rɛstɔrasjɔ̃] *nf* restoring, restoration.

restaurer [rɛstɔre] *vt* to restore, refresh; *vr* to take refreshment, build oneself up.

reste [rɛst] *nm* remainder, rest; *pl* remains, traces, scraps; **au (du)** — moreover; **de** — left.

rester [rɛste] *vi* to remain, stay, keep, stand, be left.

restituer [rɛstitɥe] *vt* to restore, return.

restitution [rɛstitysjɔ̃] *nf* restitution, restoration, refunding.

restreindre [rɛstrɛ̃ːdr] *vt* to restrict, limit; *vr* to restrict oneself, retrench.

restriction [rɛstriksjɔ̃] *nf* restriction, limitation.

résultat [rezylta] *nm* result, outcome.

résulter [rezylte] *vi* to result, be the result (of **de**).

résumé [rezyme] *nm* summary; **en** — in brief.

résumer [rezyme] *vtr* to sum up.

résurrection [rezyrɛksjɔ̃] *nf* resurrection, revival.

rétablir [retabliːr] *vt* to re-establish, restore, reinstate; *vr* to recover, re-establish oneself.

rétablissement [retablismɑ̃] *nm* re-establishment, restoration, reinstatement, recovery.

retaper [rətape] *vt* to do up, mend; *vr* to recover.

retard [rətaːr] *nm* delay, lateness; **en** — late, in arrears.

retardataire [rətardatɛːr] *a* late, backward; *n* laggard, straggler.

retarder [rətarde] *vt* to delay, make late, put back; *vi* to be late, lag.

retenir [rətniːr] *vt* to hold (back), retain, detain, restrain, reserve; *vr*

to refrain (from **de**), restrain oneself.
retentir [rətăti:r] *vi* to echo, reverberate, resound.
retentissement [rətătismă] *nm* reverberation, repercussion.
retenue [rətny] *nf* withholding, deduction, restraint, detention, discretion.
réticence [retisă:s] *nf* reserve, reticence.
rétif, -ive [retif, i:v] *a* stubborn.
retiré [rətire] *a* retired, remote.
retirer [rətire] *vt* to withdraw, obtain, remove; *vr* to retire, recede.
retomber [rətɔ̃be] *vi* to fall back, droop, hang down.
rétorquer [retɔrke] *vt* to retort, cast back.
retors [rətɔ:r] *a* twisted, bent, crafty, sly.
retouche [rətuʃ] *nf* retouch(ing), small alteration.
retoucher [rətuʃe] *vt* to touch up.
retour [rətu:r] *nm* return, turn, recurrence, change.
retourner [rəturne] *vt* to turn (inside out), turn (back, down, over, round, up), return; *vi* to return, go back; *vr* to turn around, over.
retracer [rətrase] *vt* to retrace, recall.
rétracter [retrakte] *vtr* to retract, withdraw.
retrait [rətrɛ] *nm* withdrawal, shrinkage, recess.
retraite [rətrɛt] *nf* retreat, retirement, refuge, (*mil*) tattoo.
retraité, -e [rətrɛte] *nmf* pensioner.
retranchement [rətrăʃmă] *nm* cutting off (down, out), entrenchment.
retrancher [rətrăʃe] *vt* to cut off (out, down); *vr* to entrench oneself, cut down one's expenses.
rétrécissement [retresismă] *nm* narrowing, shrinking.
rétrécir [retresi:r] *vtir* to narrow, shrink, contract.
rétribuer [retribɥe] *vt* to remunerate, pay.
rétribution [retribysjɔ̃] *nf* remuneration, reward.
rétrograde [retrograd] *a* retrograde, backward.
rétrograder [retrograde] *vt* to reduce in rank; *vi* to go back, change down.
rétrospectif, -ive [retrɔspɛktif, i:v] *a* retrospective.
retrousser [rətruse] *vt* to turn up, roll up, tuck up; **nez retroussé** snub nose.
rétroviseur [retrɔvizœ:r] *nm* driving-mirror.
réunion [reynjɔ̃] *nf* reunion, meeting, joining.
réunir [reyni:r] *vt* to reunite, collect, gather; *vr* to unite, meet.
réussi [reysi] *a* successful.
réussir [reysi:r] *vt* to make a success of; *vi* to succeed, be successful.

réussite [reysit] *nf* success, outcome (*cards*) patience.
revaloir [rəvalwa:r] *vt* to pay back.
revanche [rəvă:ʃ] *nf* revenge, return game; **en** — in return, on the other hand.
rêvasser [rɛvase] *vi* to daydream.
rêve [rɛ:v] *nm* dream.
revêche [rəvɛʃ] *a* rough, difficult, cantankerous.
réveil [revɛ:j] *nm* awakening.
réveille-matin [revɛjmatɛ̃] *nm* alarm-clock.
réveiller [revɛje] *vtr* to wake (up), revive.
réveillon [revɛjɔ̃] *nm* midnight party (at Christmas, New Year).
révélateur, -trice [revɛlatœ:r, tris] *a* revealing, telltale.
révélation [revɛlasjɔ̃] *nf* revelation, disclosure.
révéler [revele] *vt* to reveal, disclose.
revenant [rəvnă] *nm* ghost.
revendeur, -euse [rəvădœ:r, ø:z] *n* retailer, second-hand dealer.
revendication [rəvădikasjɔ̃] *nf* claim(ing).
revendiquer [rəvădike] *vt* to claim.
revenir [rəvni:r] *vi* to come back, amount (to **à**), recover (from **de**), go back on; **en** — to get over it; **faire** — (*cooking*) to brown.
revenu [rəvny] *nm* income, revenue.
rêver [rɛve] *vt* to dream (of); *vi* to dream, ponder.
réverbère [revɛrbɛ:r] *nm* street-lamp, reflector.
réverbérer [revɛrbere] *vt* to reverberate, reflect; *vi* to be reverberated, reflected.
révérence [reveră:s] *nf* reverence, bow, curtsy.
révérencieux, -euse [reverăsjø, ø:z] *a* ceremonious, deferential.
révérer [revere] *vt* to revere.
rêverie [rɛvri] *nf* dreaming, musing.
revers [rəvɛ:r] *nm* reverse, back, lapel, turn-up; backhand.
revêtement [rəvɛtmă] *nm* coating, facing, casing, surface, revetment.
revêtir [rəvɛti:r] *vt* to (re)clothe, dress, invest, coat, face, put on.
rêveur, -euse [rɛvœ:r, ø:z] *a* dreaming, dreamy; *n* dreamer.
revient [rəvjɛ̃] *nm* **prix de** — cost price.
revirement [rəvirmă] *nm* veering, sudden change.
réviser [revize] *vt* to revise, examine, overhaul.
révision [revizjɔ̃] *nf* revision, inspection, overhaul(ing); **conseil de** — draft board.
revivre [rəvi:vr] *vt* to relive; *vi* to live again, revive.
révocation [revɔkasjɔ̃] *nf* revocation, repeal, dismissal.
revoir [rəvwa:r] *vt* to see again, revise; **au** — good-bye.

révolte [revɔlt] *nf* revolt.
révolté [revɔlte] *n* rebel.
révolter [revɔlte] *vt* to revolt, shock, disgust; *vr* to revolt, rebel.
révolu [revɔly] *a* completed, past, ended.
révolution [revɔlysjɔ̃] *nf* revolution, complete change.
révolutionnaire [revɔlysjɔnɛːr] *an* revolutionary.
révolutionner [revɔlysjɔne] *vt* to revolutionize.
revolver [revɔlvɛːr] *nm* revolver.
révoquer [revɔke] *vt* to revoke, repeal, dismiss.
revue [rəvy] *nf* revue, inspection.
rez-de-chaussée [redʃose] *nm* ground floor.
rhabiller [rabije] *vt* to reclothe, repair; *vr* to dress oneself again, buy new clothes.
rhénan [renɑ̃] *a* Rhenish, of the Rhine.
rhétorique [retɔrik] *nf* rhetoric.
rhinocéros [rinɔserɔs] *nm* rhinoceros, rhinoceros beetle.
rhubarbe [rybarb] *nf* rhubarb.
rhum [rɔm] *nm* rum.
rhumatisant [rymatizɑ̃] *an* rheumatic(ky) (person).
rhumatisme [rymatism] *nm* rheumatism.
rhume [rym] *nm* cold; **— de cerveau** cold in the head.
riant [rjɑ̃] *a* laughing, smiling, pleasant.
ribambelle [ribɑ̃bɛl] *nf* (*fam*) long string.
ricaner [rikane] *vi* to sneer, laugh derisively.
riche [riʃ] *a* rich, wealthy, valuable.
richesse [riʃɛs] *nf* richness, wealth, fertility.
ricin [risɛ̃] *nm* castor-oil plant; **huile de —** castor oil.
ricocher [rikɔʃe] *vi* to ricochet, glance off, rebound.
ricochet [rikɔʃɛ] *nm* rebound, ricochet.
rictus [riktyːs] *nm* grin.
ride [rid] *nf* wrinkle, ripple.
ridé [ride] *a* wrinkled, shriveled, corrugated.
rideau [rido] *nm* curtain, screen, veil.
ridelle [ridɛl] *nf* rail, rack.
rider [ride] *vtr* to wrinkle, pucker, shrivel, ripple.
ridicule [ridikyl] *a* ridiculous, ludicrous; *nm* ridiculousness, absurdity.
ridiculiser [ridikylize] *vt* to ridicule.
rien [rjɛ̃] *pn* nothing, not anything; *nm* trifle, just a little; **comme si de — n'était** as if nothing had happened; **il n'en fera —** he will do nothing of the kind; **il n'y est pour —** he has (had) nothing to do with it; **cela ne fait —** it does not matter.
rieur, -euse [rjœːr, øːz] *a* laughing, gay; *n* laughter.

riflard [riflaːr] *nm* paring chisel, file.
rigide [riʒid] *a* tense, rigid, stiff.
rigidité [riʒidite] *nf* tenseness, rigidity, stiffness.
rigolade [rigɔlad] *nf* fun, joke, lark.
rigole [rigɔl] *nf* gutter, drain, channel.
rigoler [rigɔle] *vi* to laugh, have some fun.
rigolo, -ote [rigɔlo, ɔt] *a* funny, comical, queer; *n* wag.
rigoureux, -euse [rigurø, øːz] *a* rigorous, harsh, severe, strict.
rigueur [rigœːr] *nf* rigor, severity, harshness, strictness; **à la —** if need be, at a pinch; **être de —** to be obligatory.
rillettes [rijɛt] *nf pl* potted minced pork.
rime [rim] *nf* rhyme.
rimer [rime] *vt* to put into rhyme; *vi* to rhyme, write verse; **cela ne rime à rien** there is no sense in it.
rinçage [rɛ̃saːʒ] *nm* rinse, rinsing.
rincée [rɛ̃se] *nf* drubbing.
rincer [rɛ̃se] *vt* to rinse (out); **se — la dalle** to wet one's whistle.
riquiqui [rikiki] *a* undersized (*pers* or *thing*), runt, shrimp.
ripaille [ripaːj] *nf* feasting, carousing.
riposte [ripɔst] *nf* retort, counter (stroke), riposte.
riposter [ripɔste] *vi* to retort, counter, riposte.
rire [riːr] *vi* to laugh, joke, smile; *vr* to laugh (at de); *nm* laughter, laugh(ing); **vous voulez —!** you are joking! **pour —** for fun, make-believe; **fou —** wild laugh.
ris [ri] *nm* laugh(ter), reef; **— de veau** sweetbread.
risée [rize] *nf* laughing-stock, jeer.
risible [rizibl] *a* laughable, comical, ludicrous.
risque [risk] *nm* risk; **à ses —s et périls** at one's own risk.
risquer [riske] *vt* to risk, venture; *vr* to take a risk, venture.
ristourner [risturne] *vt* to repay, return.
rite [rit] *nm* rite.
rituel, -elle [rityɛl] *a nm* ritual.
rivage [rivaːʒ] *nm* bank, shore, side.
rival [rival] *an* rival.
rivaliser [rivalize] *vi* to vie (with), emulate.
rivalité [rivalite] *nf* rivalry.
rive [riːv] *nf* shore, bank, side, edge.
river [rive] *vt* to rivet, clinch.
riverain [rivrɛ̃] *a* water-, river-, wayside; *n* riverside resident.
rivet [rivɛ] *nm* rivet.
rivière [rivjɛːr] *nf* river, stream.
rixe [riks] *nf* brawl, scuffle.
riz [ri] *nm* rice.
rizière [rizjɛːr] *nf* rice-field.
robe [rɔb] *nf* dress, frock, gown, coat, skin; **— de chambre** dressing-gown.

robinet [rɔbinɛ] *nm* tap, cock, faucet.
robot [rɔbo] *nm* robot; (*aviation*) pilotless plane.
robuste [rɔbyst] *a* robust, strong, hardy, sturdy.
roc [rɔk] *nm* rock.
rocaille [rɔkaːj] *nf* rock.
rocailleux, -euse [rɔkajø, øːz] *a* rocky, stony, rugged.
roche [rɔʃ] *nf* rock, boulder.
rocher [rɔʃe] *nm* rock, crag.
rochet [rɔʃɛ] *nm* ratchet.
rocheux, -euse [rɔʃø, øːz] *a* rocky, stony.
rococo [rɔkɔko] *a nm* rococo, baroque.
rodage [rɔdaːʒ] *nm* running in.
rôder [rode] *vi* to prowl, roam.
rôdeur, -euse [rodœːr, øːz] *a* prowling; *n* prowler, vagrant.
rogatons [rɔgatɔ̃] *nm pl* scraps.
rogner [rɔɲe] *vt* to clip, trim, pare.
rognon [rɔɲɔ̃] *nm* kidney.
rognures [rɔɲyːr] *nf pl* clippings, trimmings, parings.
rogomme [rɔgɔm] *nm* liquor; **voix de —** husky, throaty voice.
rogue [rɔg] *a* haughty, arrogant.
roi [rwa] *nm* king; **fêtes des —s** Twelfth Night; **tirer les —s** to celebrate Twelfth Night.
roide, roideur, roidir [rwad] *see* **raide, raideur, raidir.**
roitelet [rwatlɛ] *nm* wren.
rôle [roːl] *nm* rôle, part, register, roster; **à tour de —** in turn.
romain [rɔmɛ̃] *a* Roman.
romaine [rɔmɛn] *nf* romaine lettuce.
roman [rɔmɑ̃] *a* Romanic, Romanesque; *nm* novel, romance; — **feuilleton** serial story.
romance [rɔmɑ̃ːs] *nf* sentimental song, ballad.
romancier, -ière [rɔmɑ̃sje, jɛːr] *n* novelist.
romanesque [rɔmanɛsk] *a* romantic.
romanichel, -elle [rɔmaniʃɛl] *n* gipsy, vagrant.
romantique [rɔmɑ̃tik] *a* romantic; *n* romanticist.
romantisme [rɔmɑ̃tism] *nm* romanticism.
romarin [rɔmarɛ̃] *nm* rosemary.
rompre [rɔ̃ːpr] *vt* to break (off, up, in, into), snap, burst; *vi* to break (off, up); *vr* to break (off, up), break oneself (in, to **à**).
rompu [rɔ̃py] *a* broken (in), tired out.
ronce [rɔ̃ːs] *nf* bramble, blackberry bush; *pl* thorns.
ronchonner [rɔ̃ʃɔne] *vi* to grouse, grumble, growl.
rond [rɔ̃] *a* round(ed), plump; *nm* ring, circle, round, disc, bean.
rond-de-cuir [rɔ̃dkɥiːr] *nm* clerk, bureaucrat.
ronde [rɔ̃ːd] *nf* round, beat, whole note; **à la —** around.

rondeau [rɔ̃do] *nm* rondeau, rondo.
rondelet, -ette [rɔ̃dlɛ, ɛt] *a* plump, roundish, tidy.
rondelle [rɔ̃dɛl] *nf* slice, small round, ring, disc.
rondement [rɔ̃dmɑ̃] *ad* roundly, smartly, frankly.
rondeur [rɔ̃dœːr] *nf* roundness, plumpness, frankness.
rond-point [rɔ̃pwɛ̃] *nm* traffic circle, rotary.
ronflement [rɔ̃fləmɑ̃] *nm* snore, snoring, rumbling, throbbing, hum.
ronfler [rɔ̃fle] *vi* to snore, roar, throb, whir, hum.
ronger [rɔ̃ʒe] *vt* to gnaw, corrode, erode; **se — le cœur** to eat one's heart out.
rongeur, -euse [rɔ̃ʒœːr, øːz] *a* rodent, gnawing; *nm* rodent.
rônier [ronje] *nm* fan-palm.
ronronnement [rɔ̃rɔnmɑ̃] *nm* purr(ing), hum(ming).
ronronner [rɔ̃rɔne] *vi* to purr, hum.
roquet [rɔkɛ] *nm* pug-dog, cur.
rosace [rozas] *nf* rose-window.
rosaire [rozɛːr] *nm* rosary.
rosâtre [rozaːtr] *a* pinkish.
rosbif [rɔsbif] *nm* roast beef.
rose [roːz] *nf* rose; *a* pink, rosy; — **des vents** compass-card; **découvrir le pot aux —s** to discover the secret.
rosé [roze] *a* rosy, roseate, (*wine*) rosé.
roseau [rozo] *nm* reed.
rosée [roze] *nf* dew.
roseraie [rozrɛ] *nf* rose-garden.
rosette [rozɛt] *nf* rosette, bow.
rosier [rozje] *nm* rose-bush.
rosir [roziːr] *vi* to turn pink, rosy.
rosse [rɔs] *nf* nag, nasty person, beast; *a* nasty, spiteful.
rossée [rɔse] *nf* thrashing, drubbing, licking.
rosser [rɔse] *vt* to thrash, beat.
rosserie [rɔsri] *nf* nasty remark, dirty trick, nastiness.
rossignol [rɔsiɲɔl] *nm* nightingale, skeleton-key, bit of junk.
rot [ro] *nm* belch.
rotatif, -ive [rɔtatif, iːv] *a* rotary.
rotation [rɔtasjɔ̃] *nf* rotation.
rotatoire [rɔtatwaːr] *a* rotative, rotatory.
roter [rɔte] *vi* to belch.
rotin [rɔtɛ̃] *nm* rattan, cane.
rôti [roti] *nm* roast (meat).
rôtir [rotiːr] *vti* to roast, toast, scorch.
rôtisserie [rotisri] *nf* restaurant.
rotonde [rɔtɔ̃ːd] *nf* rotunda, circular hall.
rotondité [rɔtɔ̃dite] *nf* roundness, rotundity, stoutness.
rotule [rɔtyl] *nf* knee-cap, ball-and-socket joint.
roturier, -ière [rɔtyrje] *a* of the common people; *n* commoner.
rouage [rwaːʒ] *nm* wheel(s), works.
roublard [rublaːr] *a n* crafty, wily (person).

roublardise [rublardiːz] *nf* craftiness, wily trick.
roucouler [rukule] *vi* to coo.
roue [ru] *nf* wheel; **faire la — to** turn cartwheels, spread its tail, strut.
roué [rwe] *a* sly, wily; *nm* rake.
rouennerie [rwanri] *nf* printed cotton goods.
rouer [rwe] *vt* to break on the wheel; **— de coups** to beat unmercifully.
rouet [rwɛ] *nm* spinning-wheel, pulley-wheel.
rouf(le) [rufl] *nm* deck-house.
rouge [ruːʒ] *a* red; *nm* red, rouge; **bâton de —** lipstick.
rougeâtre [ruʒɑːtr] *a* reddish.
rouge-gorge [ruʒgɔrːʒ] *nm* robin.
rougeole [ruʒɔl] *nf* measles.
rougeoyer [ruʒwaje] *vi* to glow, turn red.
rouget [ruʒɛ] *nm* gurnard, red mullet.
rougeur [ruʒœːr] *nf* redness, flush, blush.
rougir [ruʒiːr] *vt* to redden; *vi* blush, flush, turn red.
rouille [ruːj] *nf* rust, blight, mildew.
rouillé [ruje] *a* rusted, rusty.
rouiller [ruje] *vt* to rust, blight, mildew; *vr* to rust, be blighted, mildewed.
rouillure [rujyːr] *nf* rustiness, blight.
roulage [rulaːʒ] *nm* rolling, haulage, cartage.
roulant [rulɑ̃] *a* rolling, moving, sliding, smooth, killingly funny.
rouleau [rulo] *nm* roller, roll, coil, spool; **— compresseur** steamroller.
roulement [rulmɑ̃] *nm* rolling, rumbling, running, rotation; **— à billes** ball-bearing.
rouler [rule] *vt* to roll (up), haul, trick, take in, turn over; *vi* to roll (along, down, over), roam, rumble, run, turn (upon **sur**); *vr* to roll.
roulette [rulɛt] *nf* roller, caster, roulette.
roulier [rulje] *nm* truck driver.
roulis [ruli] *nm* rolling, lurching.
roulotte [rulɔt] *nf* caravan.
roumain [rumɛ̃] *an* Rumanian.
Roumanie [rumani] *nf* Rumania.
roupie [rupi] *nf* drop, rupee.
roupiller [rupije] *vi* (*fam*) to sleep.
rouquin [rukɛ̃] *a* red-haired, carroty; *n* ginger-head, red-head.
rouspéter [ruspete] *vi* (*fam*) to protest, cut up rough, kick.
roussâtre [rusɑːtr] *a* reddish.
rousseur [rusœːr] *nf* redness; **tache de —** freckle.
roussir [rusiːr] *vti* to redden, turn brown, singe.
route [rut] *nf* road, track, course, route; **— nationale** main road; **se mettre en —** to set out.
routier, -ière [rutje, jeːr] *a* road-; **café —** roadside diner; *nm* long distance truck driver, road racer; **vieux —** old campaigner.

routine [rutin] *nf* routine.
routinier, -ière [rutinje, jeːr] *a* routine, unenterprising.
rouvrir [ruvriːr] *vti* to reopen.
roux, rousse [ru, rus] *a* reddish-brown, russet, red; *nm* reddish-brown, russet, (*sauce*) roux.
royal [rwajal] *a* royal, regal, crown.
royaliste [rwajalist] *an* royalist.
royaume [rwajoːm] *nm* kingdom, realm.
royauté [rwajote] *nf* royalty.
ruade [rɥad] *nf* kicking.
ruban [rybɑ̃] *nm* ribbon, band, tape.
rubis [rybi] *nm* ruby; **payer — sur l'ongle** to pay on the nail.
rubrique [rybrik] *nf* heading, rubric, column, imprint, red ocher.
ruche [ryʃ] *nf* hive, ruche.
rude [ryd] *a* coarse, rough, harsh, uncouth, gruff, hard.
rudesse [rydɛs] *nf* coarseness, roughness, harshness, uncouthness, gruffness.
rudiments [rydimɑ̃] *nm pl* rudiments, first principles.
rudoyer [rydwaje] *vt* to treat roughly, bully, browbeat.
rue [ry] *nf* street.
ruée [rɥe] *nf* (on)rush.
ruelle [rɥel] *nf* lane, alley, space between bed and wall.
ruer [rɥe] *vi* to kick, lash out; *vr* to hurl oneself (upon **sur**).
rugir [ryʒiːr] *vi* to roar, howl.
rugissement [ryʒismɑ̃] *nm* roar(ing), howling.
rugosité [rygɔzite] *nf* ruggedness, wrinkle.
rugueux, -euse [rygø, øːz] *a* rough, rugged, wrinkled.
ruine [rɥin] *nf* ruin(ation), downfall; **menacer —** to be falling to pieces.
ruiner [rɥine] *vt* to ruin, undo, destroy; *vr* to fall to ruin, ruin oneself.
ruisseau [rɥiso] *nm* stream, brook, gutter.
ruisseler [rɥisle] *vi* to stream, run, trickle.
rumeur [rymœːr] *nf* rumor, hum, confused murmur, din.
ruminant [ryminɑ̃] *a nm* ruminant.
ruminer [rymine] *vti* to chew the cud, ruminate, ponder.
rupture [ryptyːr] *nf* breaking (off, down), fracture, rupture.
rural [ryral] *a* rural, country.
ruse [ryːz] *nf* trick, dodge, ruse, stratagem.
rusé [ryze] *a* sly, crafty, artful.
russe [rys] *an* Russian.
Russie [rysi] *nf* Russia.
rustaud [rysto] *a* uncouth, boorish; *n* boor.
rustique [rystik] *a* rustic, robust.
rustre [rystr] *a* boorish, churlish; *nm* boor, bumpkin.
rut [ryt] *nm* rut(ting).
rutabaga [rytabaga] *nm* swede.

rutilant [rytilɑ̃] *a* gleaming, glowing red.
rythme [ritm] *nm* rhythm.
rythmé [ritme] *a* rhythmic(al).
rythmique [ritmik] *a* rhythmic(al).

S

sa [sa] *see* son.
sable [sɑːbl] *nm* sand, gravel; —s mouvants quicksands.
sablé [sable] *a* sanded, graveled; *nm* shortbread.
sabler [sable] *vt* to sand, cover with gravel, drink.
sableux, -euse [sablø, øːz] *a* sandy.
sablier [sablie] *nm* hour-glass, egg-timer, sand-dealer.
sablière [sabliɛːr] *nf* sand-, gravel-pit.
sablonneux, -euse [sablɔnø, øːz] *a* sandy, gritty.
sablonnière [sablɔnjɛːr] *nf* sandpit.
sabord [sabɔːr] *nm* porthole.
saborder [sabɔrde] *vt* to scuttle.
sabot [sabo] *nm* clog, hoof.
sabotage [sabotaːʒ] *nm* clog-making, sabotage.
saboter [sabɔte] *vt* to shoe, bungle, scamp, sabotage.
saboteur, -euse [sabɔtœːr, øːz] *n* saboteur, bungler.
sabotier [sabɔtje] *nm* clog-maker.
sabre [sɑːbr] *nm* saber, sword, swordfish.
sabrer [sabre] *vt* to saber, cut (down), scamp.
sac [sak] *nm* sack, bag, pouch, knapsack, sackcloth, sacking; — de couchage sleeping-bag; — à main handbag.
saccade [sakad] *nf* jerk, jolt; par —s by fits and starts.
saccadé [sakade] *a* jerky.
saccager [sakaʒe] *vt* to pillage, sack, ransack.
saccharine [sakarin] *nf* saccharin.
sacerdoce [sasɛrdɔs] *nm* priesthood, ministry.
sacerdotal [sasɛrdɔtal] *a* sacerdotal, priestly.
sachet [saʃɛ] *nm* small bag, sachet.
sacoche [sakɔʃ] *nf* satchel, wallet, tool-bag, saddle-bag.
sacre [sakr] *nm* coronation, consecration.
sacrement [sakrəmɑ̃] *nm* sacrament.
sacré [sakre] *a* sacred, holy, damned, confounded.
sacrer [sakre] *vt* to crown, consecrate, anoint; *vi* to swear.
sacrifice [sakrifis] *nm* sacrifice.
sacrifier [sakrifje] *vt* to sacrifice, give up.
sacrilège [sakrilɛːʒ] *a* sacrilegious; *nm* sacrilege.
sacristain [sakristɛ̃] *nm* sexton, sacristan.
sacristie [sakristi] *nf* vestry, sacristy.

sadique [sadik] *a* sadistic.
sadisme [sadism] *nm* sadism.
safran [safrɑ̃] *a* saffron-colored; *nm* crocus, saffron.
sagace [sagas] *a* sagacious, shrewd.
sagacité [sagasite] *nf* sagacity, shrewdness.
sagaie [sagɛ] *nf* assegai, spear.
sage [saːʒ] *a* wise, sensible, discreet, good, well-behaved.
sage-femme [saʒfam] *nf* midwife.
sagesse [saʒɛs] *nf* wisdom, discretion, good behavior.
sagou [sagu] *nm* sago.
saignant [sɛɲɑ̃] *a* bleeding, raw, red, underdone.
saignée [sɛɲe] *nf* bleeding, blood-letting, bend of the arm, irrigation ditch.
saigner [sɛɲe] *vt* to bleed, let blood from; *vi* to bleed.
saillant [sajɑ̃] *a* projecting, jutting out, prominent, salient; *nm* salient.
saillie [saji] *nf* projection, protrusion, ledge, spring, bound, flash of wit.
saillir [sajiːr] *vi* to jut out, project, spurt out, stand out.
sain [sɛ̃] *a* healthy, wholesome, sound.
saindoux [sɛ̃du] *nm* lard.
saint [sɛ̃] *a* holy, hallowed, godly, saintly, blessed; *n* saint; **il ne sait plus à quel — se vouer** he does not know where to turn.
Saint-Esprit [sɛ̃tɛspri] *nm* Holy Ghost.
sainteté [sɛ̃tǝte] *nf* holiness, sanctity.
Saint-Martin [sɛ̃martɛ̃] *nf* Martinmas.
Saint-Michel [sɛ̃miʃɛl] *nf* Michaelmas.
Saint-Siège [sɛ̃sjɛːʒ] *nm* Holy See.
Saint-Sylvestre [sɛ̃silvɛstr] *nf* New Year's Eve, (*Scot*) Hogmanay.
saisie [sɛzi] *nf* seizure, distraint, foreclosure.
saisir [sɛziːr] *vt* to seize, grasp, catch hold of, grip, understand, perceive; *vr* to seize, lay hands (on de).
saisissant [sɛzisɑ̃] *a* thrilling, striking, keen, biting, piercing.
saisissement [sɛzismɑ̃] *nm* seizure, shock, thrill, chill.
saison [sɛzɔ̃] *nf* season.
saisonnier, -ière [sɛzɔnje, jɛːr] *a* seasonal.
salacité [salasite] *nf* salaciousness.
salade [salad] *nf* salad, lettuce, hodgepodge, mess.
saladier [saladje] *nm* salad-bowl.
salaire [salɛːr] *nm* wage(s), pay, reward, retribution.
salaison [salɛzɔ̃] *nf* salting, curing.
salamandre [salamɑ̃ːdr] *nf* salamander, stove.
salant [salɑ̃] *a* marais — salt-pans, salt-marsh.
salarié [salarje] *a* paid, wage-earning; *n* wage-earner.

salaud [salo] *n* dirty dog, rotter, swine, slattern.
sale [sal] *a* dirty, soiled, filthy, foul; — type rotter.
salé [sale] *a* salt(y), salted, spicy, exorbitant, stiff; *nm* pickled pork.
saler [sale] *vt* to salt, pickle, overcharge, fleece, punish severely.
saleté [salte] *nf* dirt, trash, dirtiness, dirty trick (act, remark).
salière [saljɛːr] *nf* saltcellar, salt shaker.
saligaud [saligo] *n* rotter, skunk, dirty person.
salin [salɛ̃] *a* saline, salty, briny; *nm* salt-marsh.
saline [salin] *nf* salt-pan, rock-salt mine.
salir [saliːr] *vt* to dirty, soil, defile, tarnish; *vr* to get dirty, soil, besmirch one's reputation.
salive [saliːv] *nf* saliva, spittle.
salle [sal] *nf* room, hall, ward, house, audience; — à manger dining-room; — d'opérations operating theater; — d'attente waiting room.
salon [salɔ̃] *nm* drawing-room, saloon, cabin; — de l'automobile auto show; — de beauté beauty parlor; — de coiffure hairdressing-salon; — de thé tea-room.
saloperie [salɔpri] *nf* filth(iness), trash, dirty trick.
salopette [salɔpɛt] *nf* overalls, dungarees.
salpêtre [salpɛːtr] *nm* saltpeter, niter.
saltimbanque [saltɛ̃bɑ̃ːk] *nm* acrobat; (*fig*) mountebank, charlatan.
salubre [salyːbr] *a* salubrious, wholesome, healthy.
salubrité [salybrite] *nf* salubrity, wholesomeness, healthiness.
saluer [salɥe] *vt* to salute, bow to, greet, acclaim.
salure [salyːr] *nf* saltness, tang.
salut [saly] *nm* greeting, bow, salute, safety, salvation; — à tout le monde! hello, everybody!
salutaire [salytɛːr] *a* salutary, beneficial, wholesome.
salutation [salytasjɔ̃] *nf* salutation, bow, salute, greeting; *pl* kind regards.
salutiste [salytist] *n* member of the Salvation Army.
salve [salv] *nf* salvo, volley, round, salute.
samara [samara] *nm* sandal.
samedi [samdi] *nm* Saturday.
sanatorium [sanatɔrjɔm] *nm* sanatorium, convalescent home.
sanctification [sɑ̃ktifikasjɔ̃] *nf* sanctification.
sanctifier [sɑ̃ktifje] *vt* to sanctify, hallow.
sanction [sɑ̃ksjɔ̃] *nf* sanction, assent, penalty.
sanctionner [sɑ̃ksjɔne] *vt* to sanction, ratify, approve, penalize.

sanctuaire [sɑ̃ktɥɛːr] *nm* sanctuary, sanctum.
sandale [sɑ̃dal] *nf* sandal, gym-shoe.
sandwich [sɑ̃dwitʃ] *nm* sandwich.
sang [sɑ̃] *nm* blood, gore, kin(ship); race; effusion de — bloodshed; coup de — apoplectic fit, stroke; se faire du mauvais — to worry, fret; son — n'a fait qu'un tour it gave him an awful shock.
sang-froid [sɑ̃frwa] *nm* composure, coolness, self-possession; de — coolly.
sanglade [sɑ̃glad] *nf* lash, cut.
sanglant [sɑ̃glɑ̃] *a* bloody, gory, bloodstained, cutting, scathing.
sangle [sɑ̃ːgl] *nf* strap, band; lit de — camp bed.
sangler [sɑ̃gle] *vt* to girth, strap (up); *vr* to lace (button) oneself up tightly.
sanglier [sɑ̃glie] *nm* wild boar.
sanglot [sɑ̃glo] *nm* sob.
sangloter [sɑ̃glɔte] *vi* to sob.
sangsue [sɑ̃sy] *nf* leech, blood-sucker.
sanguin [sɑ̃gɛ̃] *a* blood, full-blooded.
sanguinaire [sɑ̃ginɛːr] *a* blood-thirsty, bloody.
sanguine [sɑ̃gin] *nf* red chalk, drawing in red chalk, bloodstone, blood orange.
sanguinolent [sɑ̃ginɔlɑ̃] *a* tinged with blood.
sanitaire [sanitɛːr] *a* sanitary, medical, ambulance-, hospital-.
sans [sɑ̃] *prep* without, but for, were it not for, had it not been for, un-, less, -lessly; — que *cj* without.
sans-culotte [sɑ̃kylɔt] *nm* sans-culotte, rabid republican.
sans-façon [sɑ̃fasɔ̃] *a* homely, downright, outspoken, unceremonious, over-familiar, free and easy; *nm* homeliness, outspokenness, over-familiarity.
sans-fil [sɑ̃fil] *nm* radio message, radiogram.
sans-filiste [sɑ̃filist] *n* radio fan, radio operator.
sans-gêne [sɑ̃ʒɛn] *a* offhanded, unceremonious; *nm* offhandedness, over-familiarity, cheek; *nm pl* il est — he is a cool customer.
sans-logis [sɑ̃lɔʒi] *nm pl* homeless.
sansonnet [sɑ̃sɔnɛ] *nm* starling.
sans-souci [sɑ̃susi] *a* carefree, unconcerned; *n* easy-going person; *nm* unconcern.
sans-travail [sɑ̃travaːj] *nm pl* unemployed, workless.
santal [sɑ̃tal] *nm* sandalwood.
santé [sɑ̃te] *nf* health; service de — medical service.
sape [sap] *nf* sap(ping), undermining.
saper [sape] *vt* to sap, undermine.
sapeur [sapœːr] *nm* sapper, pioneer.
sapeur-pompier [sapœrpɔ̃pje] *nm* fireman.
sapeur-télégraphiste [sapœrtele-

grafist] *nm* telegraph operator; *pl* signal corps, signals.
saphir [safiːr] *nm* sapphire.
sapin [sapɛ̃] *nm* fir (tree), coffin.
sapinière [sapinjɛːr] *nf* fir plantation.
sapristi [sapristi] *excl* good heavens!
sarbacane [sarbakan] *nf* blowpipe, pea-shooter.
sarcasme [sarkasm] *nm* (piece of) sarcasm, taunt.
sarcastique [sarkastik] *a* sarcastic.
sarcler [sarkle] *vt* to hoe, weed, clean.
sarcloir [sarklwaːr] *nm* hoe.
sarcophage [sarkɔfaːʒ] *nm* sarcophagus.
sardine [sardin] *nf* sardine.
sardonique [sardɔnik] *a* sardonic, sarcastic.
sarment [sarmɑ̃] *nm* vine-shoot, -branch, bine.
sarrasin [sarazɛ̃] *nm* buckwheat, Saracen.
sarrau [saro] *nm* overall, smock.
sasser [sɑse] *vt* to sieve, riddle, sift.
satané [satane] *a* confounded, abominable.
satanique [satanik] *a* satanic, diabolical, fiendish.
satellite [satɛllit] *nm* satellite, henchman, planet.
satiété [sasjete] *nf* satiety, surfeit, repletion.
satin [satɛ̃] *nm* satin.
satiner [satine] *vt* to satin, make glossy, glaze.
satinette [satinɛt] *nf* sateen.
satire [satiːr] *nf* satire, satirizing.
satirique [satirik] *a* satiric(al); *nm* satirist.
satiriser [satirize] *vt* to satirize.
satisfaction [satisfaksjɔ̃] *nf* satisfaction, gratification, atonement, amends.
satisfaire [satisfɛːr] *vt* to satisfy, gratify, fulfill, meet.
satisfait [satisfɛ] *a* satisfied, contented, pleased.
satisfaisant [satisfəzɑ̃] *a* satisfactory, satisfying.
saturation [satyrasjɔ̃] *nf* saturation.
saturer [satyre] *vt* to saturate; *vr* to become saturated.
satyre [satiːr] *nm* satyr.
sauce [sos] *nf* sauce, soft black crayon.
saucée [sose] *nf* (*fam*) drenching, soaking, telling-off.
saucer [sose] *vt* to dip into sauce, drench, souse, tell off; se faire — to get soaked, get a scolding.
saucière [sosjɛːr] *nf* sauce-boat.
saucisse [sosis] *nf* sausage, observation or barrage balloon.
saucisson [sosisɔ̃] *nm* large dry sausage.
sauf, sauve [sof, soːv] *a* safe, saved, unhurt; *prep* but, except, save, barring; — que except that.

sauf-conduit [sofkɔ̃dɥi] *nm* safe-conduct, pass.
sauge [soːʒ] *nf* sage.
saugrenu [sogrəny] *a* ridiculous, absurd.
saule [soːl] *nm* willow.
saumâtre [somaːtr] *a* briny, brackish, bitter.
saumon [somɔ̃] *a* salmon-pink; *nm* salmon.
saumure [somyːr] *nf* pickle, brine.
saupoudrer [sopudre] *vt* to sprinkle, dust, powder.
saupoudroir [sopudrwaːr] *nm* sugarsifter, castor.
saur [sɔːr] *a* hareng — red herring.
saut [so] *nm* leap, jump, bound, vault, falls, jerk; — périlleux somersault; — d'obstacles hurdling; —de-mouton overpass.
saute [soːt] *nf* sudden rise, jump, change.
saute-mouton [sotmutɔ̃] *nm* leapfrog.
sauter [sote] *vt* to jump (over), leap (over), leave out, miss, skip; *vi* jump, leap, blow up, explode, crash, come off, change, veer, blow out; faire — to explode, burst, blow up, blow out.
sauterelle [sotrɛl] *nf* grasshopper, locust.
sauterie [sotri] *nf* dance, hop.
saute-ruisseau [sotrɥiso] *nm* errandboy.
sauteur, -euse [sotœːr, øːz] *a* jumping; *n* jumper, turncoat, weathercock.
sautiller [sotije] *vi* to hop (about), skip, jump about.
sautoir [sotwaːr] *nm* St Andrew's cross, neck-chain, jumping lathe; en — crosswise, over one's shoulder.
sauvage [sovaːʒ] *a* wild, savage, barbarous, uncivilized, shy, unsociable; *n* savage, unsociable person.
sauvagerie [sovaʒri] *nf* savagery, barbarousness, unsociability.
sauvegarde [sovgard] *nf* safeguard, safe-keeping, safe-conduct.
sauvegarder [sovgarde] *vt* to safeguard, protect.
sauve-qui-peut [sovkipø] *nm* stampede, rout, everyone for himself.
sauver [sove] *vt* to save, rescue; *vr* to escape, run away, be off.
sauvetage [sovtaːʒ] *nm* rescue, salvage; canot de — lifeboat.
sauveteur [sovtœːr] *nm* rescuer, life-saver.
sauveur [sovœːr] *nm* deliverer, Savior, Redeemer.
savamment [savamɑ̃] *ad* learnedly, knowingly, expertly, ably, cleverly.
savane [savan] *nf* savanna.
savant [savɑ̃] *a* learned, scholarly, skillful; *n* scholar, scientist; chien— performing dog.
savate [savat] *nf* old shoe, French

boxing; **traîner la —** to be down at heel.
savetier [savtje] *nm* cobbler.
saveur [savœːr] *nf* savor, flavor, taste, raciness, zest.
savoir [savwaːr] *nm* knowledge, learning; *vt* to know (how, of), be able, contrive, manage; **faire — qch à qn** to let s.o. know about sth, inform s.o of sth; **à —** to wit, namely; **sachez que** I would have you know that; **sans le —** unconsciously, unwittingly; **(au)tant que je le sache** as far as I know, to the best of my knowledge; **pas que je sache** not that I am aware of; **je ne sache pas l'avoir dit** I am not aware of having said so; **il n'a rien voulu —** he would not hear of it; **je ne sais qui** someone or other.
savoir-faire [savwarfɛːr] *nm* tact, cleverness, ability.
savoir-vivre [savwarviːvr] *nm* good-breeding, (good) manners, art of living.
savon [savɔ̃] *nm* soap, dressing down; **pain de —** cake of soap.
savonner [savɔne] *vt* to soap, wash, dress down.
savonnerie [savɔnri] *nf* soap-factory, soap-trade.
savonnette [savɔnɛt] *nf* cake of toilet soap.
savonneux, -euse [savɔnø, øːz] *a* soapy.
savonnier, -ière [savɔnje, jɛːr] *a* soap-; *nm* soap-manufacturer.
savourer [savure] *vt* to relish, enjoy.
savoureux, -euse [savurø, øːz] *a* savory, tasty, racy.
saxophone [saksɔfɔn] *nm* saxophone.
saynète [sɛnɛt] *nf* sketch.
sbire [zbiːr] *nm* policeman, hired ruffian.
scabreux, -euse [skabrø, øːz] *a* scabrous, smutty, dangerous, difficult, rough.
scalper [skalpe] *vt* to scalp.
scandale [skãdal] *nm* scandal, disgrace.
scandaleux, -euse [skãdalø, øːz] *a* scandalous, disgraceful.
scandaliser [skãdalize] *vt* to scandalize, shock; *vr* to be shocked, scandalized.
scander [skãde] *vt* to scan, stress, mark.
scaphandrier [skafãdrie] *nm* diver.
scarabée [skarabe] *nm* beetle.
scarlatine [skarlatin] *nf* scarlet fever.
sceau [so] *nm* seal, stamp, mark.
scélérat [selera] *a* wicked, cunning, nefarious; *n* scoundrel, villain.
scélératesse [seleratɛs] *nf* wickedness, low cunning.
scellé [sɛle] *a* sealed, under seal; *nm* seal.
sceller [sɛle] *vt* to seal (up), fix, fasten, confirm.

scène [sɛn] *nf* stage, scene, row; **mettre en —** to produce.
scénique [senik] *a* scenic, stage.
scepticisme [sɛptisism] *nm* skepticism.
sceptique [sɛptik] *a* skeptical; *n* skeptic.
sceptre [sɛptr] *nm* scepter.
schéma [ʃema] *nm* diagram, outline.
schématique [ʃematik] *a* diagrammatic, schematic.
schisme [ʃism] *nm* schism.
sciatique [sjatik] *a* sciatic; *nm* sciatic nerve; *nf* sciatica.
scie [si] *nf* saw, catchword, bore.
science [sjãːs] *nf* knowledge, learning, science.
scientifique [sjãtifik] *a* scientific.
scier [sje] *vt* to saw (off).
scierie [siri] *nf* sawmill.
scinder [sɛ̃de] *vt* to split up.
scintillation [sɛ̃tijasjɔ̃, -tillɑ-] *nf* scintillation, twinkling, sparkling.
scintiller [sɛ̃tije, -tille] *vi* to scintillate, twinkle, sparkle.
scission [sissjɔ̃] *nf* scission, split, division, secession.
sciure [sjyːr] *nf* **— de bois** sawdust; **— de fer** iron filings.
sclérose [skleroːz] *nf* sclerosis.
sclérosé [skleroze] *a* hardened, (fig) in a rut.
scolaire [skɔlɛːr] *a* school.
scolastique [skɔlastik] *a* scholastic; *nf* scholasticism.
scolopendre [skɔlɔpãːdr] *nf* centipede.
scorbut [skɔrby] *nm* scurvy.
scorie [skɔri] *nf* slag, cinders, dross.
scoutisme [skutism] *nm* scouting, Boy Scout movement.
scrofule [skrɔfyl] *nf* scrofula.
scrupule [skrypyl] *nm* scruple; **se faire un — de** to have scruples about.
scrupuleux, -euse [skrypylø, øːz] *a* scrupulous.
scrutateur, -trice [skrytatœːr, tris] *a* searching, keen, scrutinizing; *n* scrutinizer, teller.
scruter [skryte] *vt* to scrutinize, scan.
scrutin [skrytɛ̃] *nm* poll, ballot, voting; **— de liste** multiple voting; **procéder au —** to take the vote; **voter au —** to ballot; **dépouiller le —** to count the votes.
sculpter [skylte] *vt* to carve, sculpture.
sculpteur [skyltœːr] *nm* sculptor, carver.
sculptural [skyltyral] *a* sculptural, statuesque.
sculpture [skyltyːr] *nf* sculpture, carving.
se [s(ə)] *pn* oneself, himself, herself, itself, themselves, each other, one another.
séance [seãːs] *nf* session, sitting,

meeting, performance, séance.
séant [seɑ̃] *a* becoming, seemly, proper, sitting; *nm* bottom, behind; **se dresser sur son —** to sit up.
seau [so] *nm* pail, bucket
sec, sèche [sɛk, sɛʃ] *a* dry, dried, harsh, unfeeling, gaunt, spare, curt, tart, sharp; **boire —** to drink liquor straight, drink heavily; **parler —** to clip one's words; **à pied —** dry-shod; **à —** dry, dried-up, aground, hard-up.
sécateur [sekatœːr] *nm* pruning shears.
sécession [sesɛsjɔ̃] *nf* secession.
sèche [sɛʃ] *nf* (*fam*) fag, (*cigarette*).
sèchement [sɛʃmɑ̃] *ad* dryly, boldly, curtly.
sécher [seʃe] *vt* to dry (up), fail, cut, skip; *vi* to become or run dry, dry up, be stumped, stick; *vr* to dry oneself, dry up, run dry; **faire — qn** to stump s.o.; **— sur pied** to pine for.
sécheresse [seʃrɛs] *nf* dryness, drought, harshness, unfeelingness, gauntness, barrenness, curtness.
séchoir [seʃwar] *nm* drying place, drier, airer.
second [səgɔ̃, zgɔ̃] *a* second; *nm* first mate, chief officer, second in command; second floor.
secondaire [səgɔ̃dɛːr, zgɔ̃-] *a* secondary, subordinate, minor.
seconde [səgɔ̃ːd, zgɔ̃ːd] *nf* second, second class, eleventh grade.
seconder [səgɔ̃de, zgɔ̃-] *vt* to second, support, assist, promote, further.
secouer [səkwe] *vt* to shake (up, down, off), rouse, stir; *vr* to shake oneself, bestir oneself.
secourable [səkurabl] *a* helpful, ready to help, helping.
secourir [səkuriːr] *vt* to help, aid, succor, relieve.
secours [s(ə)kuːr] *nm* help, aid, succor, relief, assistance; **porter — à** to lend assistance to; **apporter les premiers — à** to apply first-aid to; **poste de —** first-aid station; **de —** spare, emergency, relief; **au —!** help!
secousse [səkus] *nf* shake, shaking, shock, jolt.
secret [səkrɛ] *a* secret; *nm* secret, secrecy; **au —** in solitary confinement.
secrétaire [səkretɛːr] *n* secretary; *nm* writing-desk.
secrétariat [səkrɛtarja] *nm* secretaryship, secretariat.
sécréter [sekrete] *vt* to secrete.
sectaire [sɛktɛːr] *n* sectarian.
secte [sɛkt] *nf* sect.
secteur [sɛktœːr] *nm* sector, beat (of policeman).
section [sɛksjɔ̃] *nf* cutting, section, division, branch, stage, platoon.
sectionner [sɛksjone] *vt* to divide into sections, cut into pieces.

séculaire [sekylɛːr] *a* century-old, venerable, secular.
séculier, -ière [sekylje, jɛːr] *a* secular; *n* layman, -woman.
sécurité [sekyrite] *nf* security, safety, safeness.
sédatif, -ive [sedatif, iːv] *a nm* sedative.
sédentaire [sedɑ̃tɛːr] *a* sedentary, fixed.
sédiment [sedimɑ̃] *nm* sediment, deposit.
séditieux, -euse [sedisjø, øːz] *a* seditious; *nm* mutineer, rebel.
sédition [sedisjɔ̃] *nf* sedition, mutiny.
séducteur, -trice [sedyktœːr, tris] *a* seductive, tempting, alluring, enticing; *n* seducer, enticer, tempter.
séduction [sedyksjɔ̃] *nf* seduction, enticement, bribing, seductiveness, charm.
séduire [sedɥiːr] *vt* to seduce, (al)lure, captivate, charm, suborn, lead astray.
séduisant [sedɥizɑ̃] *a* tempting, captivating, attractive, fascinating, alluring.
ségrégation [segregasjɔ̃] *nf* segregation, separation.
seiche [sɛʃ] *nf* cuttle-fish.
seigle [sɛgl] *nm* rye.
seigneur [sɛɲœːr] *nm* lord, nobleman, God, the Lord.
seigneurie [sɛɲœri] *nf* lordship, manor.
sein [sɛ̃] *nm* bosom, breast.
séisme [seism] *nm* seism, earthquake.
seize [sɛːz] *a nm* sixteen, sixteenth.
seizième [sɛzjɛm] *a nm* sixteenth.
séjour [seʒuːr] *nm* sojourn, stay, residence, abode.
séjourner [seʒurne] *vi* to stay, sojourn, reside.
sel [sɛl] *nm* salt, spice, wit; *pl* smelling salts.
sélection [selɛksjɔ̃] *nf* selection.
selle [sɛl] *nf* saddle, stool, movement of bowels.
seller [sɛle] *vt* to saddle.
sellette [sɛlɛt] *nf* stool of repentance, small stool; **tenir qn sur la —** to have s.o. on the carpet.
sellier [sɛlje] *nm* saddler.
selon [s(ə)lɔ̃] *prep* according to, after; **c'est —** it depends.
Seltz [sɛls] *nm* eau de S— soda-water.
semailles [s(ə)maːj] *nf pl* sowing(s).
semaine [s(ə)mɛn] *nf* week, working-week, week's pay; **faire la — anglaise** to stop work on Saturdays at midday.
semblable [sɑ̃blabl] *a* similar, like, alike, such; *n* fellow-man, like.
semblant [sɑ̃blɑ̃] *nm* semblance, show, sham, appearance; **faire — de** to pretend.
sembler [sɑ̃ble] *vi* to seem, appear, look; **à ce qu'il me semble** as far as I can see, to my mind.

semelle [s(ə)mɛl] *nf* sole, foot, tread; **battre la —** to stamp one's feet (for warmth).

semence [s(ə)mã:s] *nf* seed, (tin) tacks.

semer [s(ə)me] *vt* to sow, scatter, spread, dot, outpace, shake off.

semestre [s(ə)mɛstr] *nm* term, half-year, semester.

semestriel, -elle [s(ə)mɛstriɛl] *a* half-yearly.

semeur, -euse [s(ə)mœːr, øːz] *n* sower, spreader.

sémillant [semijã] *a* sprightly, lively, brisk.

séminariste [seminarist] *nm* seminarist.

semis [səmi] *nm* sowing, seed-bed, seedling.

sémitique [semitik] *a* Semitic.

semonce [səmɔ̃:s] *nf* rebuke, scolding, dressing-down.

semoncer [səmɔ̃se] *vt* to scold, rebuke, lecture.

semoule [s(ə)mul] *nf* semolina.

sénat [sena] *nm* senate.

sénateur [senatœːr] *nm* senator.

sénile [senil] *a* senile.

sénilité [senilite] *nf* senility.

sens [sã:s] *nm* sense, intelligence, meaning, direction; **bon —** common sense; **rue à — unique** one-way street; **— interdit** no entry; **— dessus dessous** upside down.

sensation [sãsasjɔ̃] *nf* sensation, feeling, stir.

sensationnel, -elle [sãsasjɔnɛl] *a* sensational, super.

sensé [sãse] *a* sensible, judicious.

sensibilisateur, -trice [sãsibilizatœːr, tris] *a* sensitizing; *nm* sensitizer.

sensibilité [sãsibilite] *nf* sensibility, sensitiveness, feeling, tenderness.

sensible [sãsibl] *a* sensitive, susceptible, tender, sore, palpable, perceptible.

sensiblerie [sãsibləri] *nf* mawkish sentiment.

sensitif, -ive [sãsitif] *a* sensitive, sensory.

sensualisme [sãsɥalism] *nm* sensualism.

sensualité [sãsɥalite] *nf* sensuality.

sensuel, -elle [sãsɥɛl] *a* sensual, sensuous, voluptuous; *n* sensualist.

sentence [sãtã:s] *nf* maxim, sentence.

sentencieux, -euse [sãtãsjø, øːz] *a* sententious.

senteur [sãtœːr] *nf* perfume, scent.

senti [sãti] *a* heartfelt, genuine.

sentier [sãtje] *nm* path.

sentiment [sãtimã] *nm* feeling, sense, sensation, sentiment, opinion; **faire du —** to play on the emotions.

sentimental [sãtimãtal] *a* sentimental.

sentimentalité [sãtimãtalite] *nf* sentimentality.

sentine [sãtin] *nf* bilge.

sentinelle [sãtinɛl] *nf* sentry,

sentinel; **en — on** sentry duty.

sentir [sãti:r] *vt* to feel, smell, be aware (of); *vi* to smell (of). taste of, smack of; *vr* to feel; **je ne peux pas le —** I can't stand him; **ne pas se — de joie** to be beside oneself with joy, overjoyed.

seoir [swaːr] *vi* to become, suit.

séparable [separabl] *a* separable.

séparation [separasjɔ̃] *nf* separation, breaking up, parting.

séparatisme [separatism] *nm* separatism.

séparé [separe] *a* separate, apart, distinct.

séparément [separemã] *ad* separately, apart, singly.

séparer [separe] *vt* to separate, divide, part, be between; *vr* to part, separate, divide, break up.

sept [sɛ(t)] *a nm* seven, seventh.

septembre [sɛptã:br] *nm* September.

septentrional [sɛptãtriɔnal] *a* northern; *n* Northerner.

septième [sɛtjɛm] *a nm* seventh.

septique [sɛptik] *a* septic.

septuagénaire [sɛptɥaʒenɛːr] *an* septuagenarian.

septuor [sɛptɥɔːr] *nm* septet.

sépulcral [sepylkral] *a* sepulchral.

sépulcre [sepylkr] *nm* sepulcher, tomb.

sépulture [sepyltyːr] *nf* burial-place, tomb, interment.

séquelle [sekɛl] *nf* gang, string; *pl* after-effects.

séquence [sekã:s] *nf* sequence, run.

séquestration [sekɛstrasjɔ̃] *nf* sequestration, seclusion, isolation.

séquestre [sekɛstr] *nm* sequestrator, trustee, sequestration, embargo; **sous —** sequestered.

séquestrer [sekɛstre] *vt* to sequester, sequestrate, confine, isolate.

séraphin [serafɛ̃] *nm* seraph.

séraphique [serafik] *a* seraphic, angelic

serein [sərɛ̃] *a* serene, calm, quiet.

sérénade [serenad] *nf* serenade.

sérénité [serenite] *nf* serenity, calmness.

serf, serve [sɛrf, sɛrv] *a* in bondage; *n* serf.

serge [sɛrʒ] *nm* serge.

sergent [sɛrʒã] *nm* sergeant; **— major** quartermaster-sergeant; **— de ville** policeman.

série [seri] *nf* series, succession, line, set, run, break; **fin de —** remnant; **article hors —** specially made article, outsize; **voiture de —** car of standard model.

sérieux, -euse [serjø, øːz] *a* serious, grave, solemn, earnest, genuine; *nm* seriousness, gravity; **manque de — levity; prendre qch au —** to take sth seriously; **garder son —** to keep a straight face.

serin [s(ə)rɛ̃] *nm* canary, simpleton.

seringue [sərɛ̃:g] *nf* syringe.

serment [sɛrmɑ̃] nm oath; **prêter —** to take an oath, be sworn in; **sous —** on oath.

sermon [sɛrmɔ̃] nm sermon, talking-to.

sermonner [sɛrmɔne] vt to lecture; vi to preachify, lay down the law.

sermonneur, -euse [sɛrmɔnœːr, øːz] a sermonizing; n sermonizer.

serpe [sɛrp] nf bill-hook.

serpent [sɛrpɑ̃] nm snake, serpent; **— à sonnettes** rattlesnake.

serpenter [sɛrpɑ̃te] vi to wind, meander.

serpentin [sɛrpɑ̃tɛ̃] a serpentine; nm worm (of still), coil, streamer.

serpette [sɛrpɛt] nf bill-hook, pruning-knife.

serpillière [sɛrpijɛːr] nf sacking, apron.

serpolet [sɛrpɔlɛ] nm wild thyme.

serrage [sɛraːʒ] nm tightening, clamping, grip; **— des freins** braking.

serre [sɛːr] nf greenhouse, pressing, talon, claw, grip, clip; **— chaude** hothouse.

serré [sɛre] a tight, close, serried, packed, closely-woven, compact, close-fisted.

serrement [sɛrmɑ̃] nm squeezing, pressure; **— de cœur** pang; **— de main(s)** handshake.

serre-papiers [sɛrpapje] nm file, paper-clip, -weight.

serrer [sɛre] vt to press, squeeze, clasp, shake (hands), clench, close (up), tighten, condense, put away; vr to stand or sit closer, huddle together, crowd, tighten.

serre-tête [sɛrtɛːt] nm head-band, crash-helmet.

serrure [sɛryːr] nf lock; **trou de la — keyhole.**

serrurerie [sɛryr(ə)ri] nf lock, locksmith's (shop), locksmithing, metal work.

serrurier [sɛryrje] nm locksmith, ironsmith.

sertir [sɛrtiːr] vt to set.

servage [sɛrvaːʒ] nm bondage, serf-dom.

serval [sɛrval] nm bush-cat, serval.

servant [sɛrvɑ̃] a serving; nm server; pl gun crew.

servante [sɛrvɑ̃ːt] nf maid-servant, dumb-waiter, tea wagon.

serveur, -euse [sɛrvœːr, øːz] n carver, barman, barmaid, waitress, server; f coffee pot.

serviable [sɛrvjabl] a obliging, helpful.

service [sɛrvis] nm service, disposition, attendance, good turn, department, course, set; **escalier de —** backstairs; **porte de —** tradesmen's entrance; **entrer en —** to go into service; **entrer au —** to go into the army; **être de —** to be on duty; **assurer le — entre ... et ...** to run

between ... and ...; **bon pour le —** fit for service, serviceable; **libre —** self-service.

serviette [sɛrvjɛt] nf napkin, towel, brief-case.

servile [sɛrvil] a slavish, servile.

servilité [sɛrvilite] nf servility, slavishness.

servir [sɛrviːr] vt to serve (up, out), attend to, wait on, help, work, operate; vi to serve, be in use, be useful, be used; vr to help oneself, shop, deal, use; **— de** to be used as, serve as; **cela ne sert à rien** that is no use.

serviteur [sɛrvitœːr] nm servant.

servitude [sɛrvityd] nf servitude, slavery, bondage.

ses [se] see son.

session [sɛsjɔ̃] nf session, sitting.

séton [setɔ̃] nm **blessure en —** flesh wound.

seuil [sœːj] nm threshold, doorstep.

seul [sœl] a single, alone, sole, one, only, by oneself.

seulement [sœlmɑ̃] ad only, merely, solely, even.

sève [sɛːv] nf sap, pith, vigor.

sévère [sevɛːr] a severe, stern, harsh, strict.

sévérité [severite] nf severity, sternness, harshness, strictness.

sévices [sevis] nm pl brutality, maltreatment, cruelty.

sévir [seviːr] vi to be rife, severe, to rage, deal severely (with **contre**).

sevrer [sevre] vt to wean, deprive.

sexagénaire [sɛksaʒenɛːr] an sexagenarian.

sexe [sɛks] nm sex.

sextant [sɛkstɑ̃] nm sextant.

sexualité [sɛksyalite] nf sexuality.

sexuel, -elle [sɛksɥɛl] a sexual.

seyant [sɛjɑ̃] a becoming.

shampooing [ʃɑ̃pwɛ̃] nm shampoo.

si [si] ad so, as, such, yes; cj if, whether, how, what about; nm B (mus); **si ... que** however; **si ce n'était** were it not for.⟨

siamois [sjamwa] an Siamese.

sidéré [sidere] a struck dumb, dazed, dumbfounded.

sidérurgie [sideryrʒi] nf metallurgy, iron smelting.

siècle [sjɛkl] nm century, age, period.

siège [sjɛːʒ] nm seat, chair, bottom (of chair), center, siege; **déclarer l'état de —** to declare martial law.

siéger [sjeʒe] vi to sit, be seated, be centered.

sien, sienne [sjɛ̃, sjɛn] pos pn **le(s) —(s), la sienne, les siennes** his, hers, its, one's; nm his, her, its, one's own; pl one's own people; **y mettre du —** to do one's share; **faire des siennes** to be up to one's tricks.

sieste [sjɛst] nf siesta, nap.

sifflant [siflɑ̃] a whistling, hissing, sibilant.

siffler [sifle] *vt* to whistle (for, to, after), pipe, boo, hiss, swig; *vi* to whistle, hiss, sizzle, whiz, wheeze.

sifflet [siflɛ] *nm* whistle, pipe, hiss, catcall.

siffleur, -euse [sifloe:r, øːz] *a* whistling, hissing, wheezy; *n* whistler, booer.

siffloter [siflɔte] *vti* to whistle softly.

sigle [sigl] *nm* initials, trade-name, trade-mark.

signal [siɲal] *nm* signal.

signalement [siɲalmɑ̃] *nm* description, particulars.

signalé [siɲale] *a* signal, well-known, conspicuous.

signaler [siɲale] *vt* to signal, distinguish, point out, report, give a description of; *vr* to distinguish oneself.

signaleur [siɲaloe:r] *nm* signaler, signalman.

signalisateur [siɲalizatoe:r] *nm* signaling apparatus, traffic indicator.

signalisation [siɲalizasjɔ̃] *nf* signaling.

signataire [siɲatɛ:r] *n* signatory.

signature [siɲaty:r] *nf* signature, signing.

signe [siɲ] *nm* sign, mark, symptom, indication, gesture; — de tête nod; **faire — à qn** to beckon, motion to s.o.

signer [siɲe] *vt* to sign, stamp; *vr* to cross oneself.

signet [siɲɛ] *nm* bookmark(er).

significatif, -ive [siɲifikatif, iːv] *a* significant.

signification [siɲifikasjɔ̃] *nf* signification, significance, meaning, notification.

signifier [siɲifje] *vt* to signify, mean, notify.

silence [silɑ̃:s] *nm* silence, stillness, hush, rest; **passer sous** — to ignore.

silencieux, -euse [silɑ̃sjø, øːz] *a* silent, still, noiseless; *nm* silencer.

silex [silɛks] *nm* silex, flint.

silhouette [silwɛt] *nf* silhouette, outline, figure.

silhouetter [silwɛte] *vt* to silhouette, outline; *vr* to stand out, show up.

sillage [sijaːʒ] *nm* wake, wash, track.

sillon [sijɔ̃] *nm* furrow, track, trail, wrinkle, groove, streak.

sillonner [sijɔne] *vt* to furrow, plow, cleave, wrinkle.

simagrée [simagre] *nf* usu *pl* affectation, affected airs.

simiesque [simjɛsk] *a* ape-like, monkey-like.

similaire [similɛ:r] *a* similar, like.

similarité [similarite] *nf* similarity, likeness.

simili [simili] *nm* imitation.

similitude [similityd] *nf* similitude, similarity, likeness.

simple [sɛ̃:pl] *a* simple, easy, mere, ordinary, plain, homely, guileless, single; *nm* single (game); *pl* herbs; — **soldat** private (soldier).

simplicité [sɛ̃plisite] *nf* simplicity, plainness, naturalness, simple-mindedness.

simplificateur, -trice [sɛ̃plifikatoe:r, tris] *a* simplifying.

simplification [sɛ̃plifikasjɔ̃] *nf* simplification.

simplifier [sɛ̃plifje] *vt* to simplify.

simpliste [sɛ̃plist] *a* over-simple.

simulacre [simylakr] *nm* semblance, sham, show, image.

simulateur, -trice [simylatoe:r, tris] *n* simulator, shammer.

simulation [simylasjɔ̃] *nf* simulation, shamming.

simuler [simyle] *vt* to simulate, sham, feign.

simultané [simyltane] *a* simultaneous.

sinapisme [sinapism] *nm* mustard plaster.

sincère [sɛ̃sɛ:r] *a* sincere, genuine, frank, candid.

sincérité [sɛ̃serite] *nf* sincerity, genuineness, candor.

singe [sɛ̃:ʒ] *nm* monkey, ape, mimic, (*sl*) bully-beef.

singer [sɛ̃ʒe] *vt* to ape, mimic.

singerie [sɛ̃ʒri] *nf* grimace, antic, affected airs, monkey-house.

singulariser [sɛ̃gylarize] *vt* to make conspicuous.

singularité [sɛ̃gylarite] *nf* peculiarity, unusualness, oddness, eccentricity.

singulier, -ière [sɛ̃gylje, jɛ:r] *a* peculiar, singular, unusual, remarkable, queer, odd; *nm* singular; **combat** — single combat.

sinistre [sinistr] *a* sinister, ominous, fatal; *nm* catastrophe, disaster, calamity.

sinistré [sinistre] *a* damaged (by fire *etc*); *n* victim.

sinon [sinɔ̃] *cj* if not, otherwise, except.

sinueux, -euse [sinɥø, øːz] *a* sinuous, winding, meandering.

sinuosité [sinɥozite] *nf* winding, meander, bend.

sinusite [sinyzit] *nf* sinusitis.

siphon [sifɔ̃] *nm* siphon, trap.

sire [siːr] *nm* sire; **triste** — sorry fellow.

sirène [sirɛn] *nf* siren, vamp, buzzer, hooter, foghorn.

sirop [siro] *nm* syrup.

siroter [sirɔte] *vt* to sip; *vi* to tipple.

sis [si] *pp* situated.

sismique [sismik] *a* seismic.

site [sit] *nm* beauty spot, site.

sitôt [sito] *ad* — **dit,** — **fait** no sooner said than done; **nous ne le reverrons pas de** — we will not see him for some time to come.

siuation [sitɥasjɔ̃] *nf* situation, site, position, post, state.

situer [sitɥe] *vt* to situate, locate, place.

six [si(s)] *a nm* six, sixth.

sixième [sizjɛm] *an* sixth; *nm* sixth (part).

ski [ski] *nm* ski, skiing; — **nautique** water-skiing.

skieur, -euse [skiœːr, øːz] *n* skier.

slip [slip] *nm* slip, slipway, briefs, underpants.

smoking [smɔkiŋ] *nm* dinner jacket.

snob [snɔb] *nm* snob, slavish imitator of popular fashion or opinion; *a* smart, snobbish.

snobisme [snɔbism] *nm* snobbery, slavish imitation of popular fashion or opinion.

sobre [sɔbr] *a* temperate, moderate, sparing, quiet.

sobriété [sɔbriete] *nf* sobriety, temperateness, moderation.

sobriquet [sɔbrikɛ] *nm* nickname.

soc [sɔk] *nm* plowshare.

sociabilité [sɔsjabilite] *nf* sociability, sociableness.

sociable [sɔsjabl] *a* sociable.

social [sɔsjal] *a* social; **raison —e** name of a firm.

socialisme [sɔsjalism] *nm* socialism.

socialiste [sɔsjalist] *a* socialist(ic); *n* socialist.

sociétaire [sɔsjetɛːr] *n* member, shareholder.

société [sɔsjete] *nf* society, association, club, companionship, company, partnership; **S — des Nations** League of Nations.

sociologie [sɔsjɔlɔʒi] *nf* sociology.

socle [sɔkl] *nm* pedestal, plinth, base, stand.

socque [sɔk] *nm* clog, patten, sock.

socquette [sɔkɛt] *nf* ankle sock.

sodium [sɔdjom] *nm* sodium.

sœur [sœːr] *nf* sister, nun.

sofa [sɔfa] *nm* sofa, settee.

soi [swa] *pn* oneself, him-, her-, it-; **— -même** oneself.

soi-disant [swadizɑ̃] *a* would-be, so-called, self-styled; *ad* supposedly.

soie [swa] *nf* silk, bristle; **papier de —** tissue paper.

soierie [swari] *nf* silk-fabric, silks, silk-trade, -factory.

soif [swaf] *nf* thirst; **avoir —** to be thirsty, eager (for **de**).

soigné [swaɲe] *a* neat, careful, carefully done, well-groomed, trim.

soigner [swaɲe] *vt* to take care of, attend (to), look after, nurse, take pains with; *vr* to take care of o.s., look after o.s.

soigneux, -euse [swaɲø, øːz] *a* careful, tidy, neat.

soin [swɛ̃] *nm* care, trouble, attention, pains, task; *pl* solicitude, attention(s), aid, treatment; **avoir — to** take care; **être aux petits —s auprès de qn** to be most attentive to.

soir [swaːr] *nm* evening, night.

soirée [sware] *nf* evening, party, reception.

soit [swa] *excl* right! agreed! *cj* — **l'un — l'autre** either one or the other; — **aujourd'hui ou demain** either today or tomorrow; — **qu'il le fasse ou qu'il ne le fasse pas** whether he does it or not.

soixantaine [swasɑ̃tɛn] *nf* about sixty.

soixante [swasɑ̃ːt] *a nm* sixty.

soixantième [swasɑ̃tjɛm] *a nm* sixtieth.

sol [sɔl] *nm* ground, soil, earth, G (*mus*).

solaire [sɔlɛːr] *a* solar.

soldat [sɔlda] *nm* soldier; **simple —** private; — **de première classe** lance-corporal; — **de plomb** tin soldier.

solde [sɔld] *nm* balance, settlement, job lot, surplus stock, clearance sale; *nf* pay; **prix de —** bargain price; **être à la — de** to be in the pay of.

solder [sɔlde] *vt* to balance, settle, clear off, sell off.

sole [sɔl] *nf* sole.

solécisme [sɔlesism] *nm* solecism.

soleil [sɔlɛːj] *nm* sun, sunshine, sunflower, monstrance, Catherine wheel; **coup de —** sunburn, sunstroke, sunny interval; **il fait du —** it is sunny.

solennel, -elle [sɔlanɛl] *a* solemn, grave, official.

solenniser [sɔlanize] *vt* to solemnize, celebrate.

solennité [sɔlanite] *nf* solemnity, solemn ceremony.

solfège [sɔlfɛːʒ] *nm* sol-fa.

solidaire [sɔlidɛːr] *a* interdependent, jointly responsible, binding, bound up (with **de**).

solidariser [sɔlidarize] *vt* to make responsible.

solidarité [sɔlidarite] *nf* joint responsibility, interdependence, solidarity; **faire la grève de —** to strike in sympathy.

solide [sɔlid] *a* solid, secure, sound, strong, hefty, staunch; *nm* solid; **viser au —** to have an eye to the main chance.

solidifier [sɔlidifje] *vtr* to solidify.

solidité [sɔlidite] *nf* solidity, soundness, stability, strength, staunchness.

soliloque [sɔlilɔk] *nm* soliloquy.

soliste [sɔlist] *a* solo; *n* soloist.

solitaire [sɔlitɛːr] *a* solitary, lonely; *nm* hermit, recluse, solitaire.

solitude [sɔlityd] *nf* solitude, loneliness, wilderness.

solive [sɔliːv] *nf* beam, joist, rafter.

sollicitation [sɔllisitasjɔ̃] *nf* solicitation, entreaty, canvassing.

solliciter [sɔllisite] *vt* to solicit, beg for, canvass, apply for, attract.

solliciteur, -euse [sɔllisitœːr, øːz] *n*

petitioner, canvasser, applicant.
sollicitude [sɔllisityd] *nf* solicitude, concern, care, anxiety.
solo [sɔlo] *a nm* solo.
solstice [sɔlstis] *nm* solstice.
soluble [sɔlybl] *a* soluble, solvable.
solution [sɔlysjɔ̃] *nf* solution, answer, settlement.
solvabilité [sɔlvabilite] *nf* solvency.
solvable [sɔlvabl] *a* solvent.
sombre [sɔ̃:br] *a* somber, dark, dismal, gloomy, dull.
sombrer [sɔ̃bre] *vi* to sink, founder, go down.
sommaire [sɔmmɛːr] *a* summary, succinct, hasty, scant; *nm* summary, synopsis.
sommation [sɔmasjɔ̃] *nf* notice, summons.
somme [sɔm] *nf* sum, amount, pack-saddle; *nm* nap, snooze; **bête de —** beast of burden; **— toute, en —** on the whole, in short.
sommeil [sɔmɛːj] *nm* sleep, slumber, sleepiness; **avoir —** to be sleepy, drowsy; **avoir le — léger (profond)**, to be a light (heavy) sleeper.
sommeiller [sɔmɛje] *vi* to slumber, be asleep, nod.
sommelier [sɔmǝlje] *nm* wine-waiter.
sommer [sɔme] *vt* to summon, call upon.
sommet [sɔmɛ] *nm* summit, top, crown, crest, apex; **conférence au —** summit conference.
sommier [sɔmje] *nm* bed-springs, register.
sommité [sɔmmite] *nf* summit, top, leading figure.
somnambule [sɔmnɑ̃byl] *a* somnambulistic; *n* somnambulist, sleep-walker.
somnifère [sɔmnifɛːr] *a nm* sleeping-pill, soporific.
somnolence [sɔmnɔlɑ̃ːs] *nf* somnolence, drowsiness.
somnolent [sɔmnɔlɑ̃] *a* somnolent, drowsy, sleepy.
somnoler [sɔmnɔle] *vi* to doze, nod, drowse.
somptueux, -euse [sɔ̃ptɥø, øːz] *a* sumptuous.
son, sa, ses [sɔ̃, sa, se] *a* his, her, its, one's.
son [sɔ̃] *nm* sound, bran; **tache de —** freckle.
sonate [sɔnat] *nf* sonata.
sondage [sɔ̃daːʒ] *nm* sounding, boring, probing, bore-hole.
sonde [sɔ̃ːd] *nf* plummet, sounding-line, -rod, boring-machine, probe, taster.
sonder [sɔ̃de] *vt* to sound, bore, probe, investigate, fathom.
sondeuse [sɔ̃døːz] *nf* drilling-machine.
songe [sɔ̃ːʒ] *nm* dream.
songe-creux [sɔ̃ʒkrø] *nm* dreamer, visionary.

songer [sɔ̃ʒe] *vi* to dream, muse, imagine, remember, think.
songerie [sɔ̃ʒri] *nf* reverie, musing, daydream(ing), brown study.
songeur, -euse [sɔ̃ʒœːr, øːz] *a* dreamy, pensive; *n* dreamer.
sonnaille [sɔnaːj] *nf* cowbell.
sonnant [sɔnɑ̃] *a* ringing, striking; **à une heure —e** on the stroke of one; **espèces —es** hard cash.
sonner [sɔne] *vt* to ring (for), strike; *vi* to ring, sound, toll, strike.
sonnerie [sɔnri] *nf* ringing, chimes, bell, system of bells, bugle call; **— électrique** electric bell; **— aux morts** last post.
sonnet [sɔnɛ] *nm* sonnet.
sonnette [sɔnɛt] *nf* small bell, housebell, handbell; **coup de —** ring.
sonneur [sɔnœːr] *nm* bell-ringer.
sonore [sɔnɔːr] *a* sonorous, resounding, resonant, ringing, voiced, with good acoustics; **bande —** sound-track.
sonoriser [sɔnɔrize] *vt* to add the sound effects to (*a film*), to install amplifiers.
sonorité [sɔnɔrite] *nf* sonority, resonance.
sophisme [sɔfism] *nm* sophism, fallacy.
sophiste [sɔfist] *nm* sophist.
sophistiqué [sɔfistike] *a* sophisticated, adulterated.
soporifique [sɔpɔrifik] *a* soporific, tiresome.
sorbier [sɔrbje] *nm* service-tree, rowan-tree.
sorcellerie [sɔrsɛlri] *nf* witchcraft, sorcery.
sorcier, -ière [sɔrsje, jɛːr] *n* sorcerer, sorceress, wizard, witch, hag.
sordide [sɔrdid] *a* squalid, sordid, mean, dirty.
sornettes [sɔrnɛt] *nf pl* nonsense, trash.
sort [sɔːr] *nm* fate, chance, lot, spell; **tirer au —** to draw lots, ballot.
sortable [sɔrtabl] *a* suitable, eligible, presentable.
sortant [sɔrtɑ̃] *a* outgoing, retiring.
sorte [sɔrt] *nf* kind, sort, way, manner; **de la —** in that way; **de — que** so that; **en quelque —** in a way.
sortie [sɔrti] *nf* going out, coming out, exit, way out, leaving, sortie, trip, outburst; **— de secours** emergency exit; **jour de —** day out; **— de bain** bathing wrap.
sortilège [sɔrtilɛːʒ] *nm* charm, spell.
sortir [sɔrtiːr] *vt* to take (put, bring, pull) out; *vi* to go out (come, walk) out, protrude, stand out, spring, descend; *nm* coming out; **— de table** to rise from table; **faire —** to put out, take out; **il est sorti** he is out; **au — de l'école** on coming out of school, on leaving school.

sosie [sɔzi] *nm* double.

sot, sotte [so, sɔt] *a* stupid, foolish, silly; *n* fool, dolt.

sottise [sɔtiːz] *nf* stupidity, folly, silliness, foolish thing.

sou [su] *nm* sou; **cent —s** five francs; **il n'a pas le —** he is penniless; **il n'a pas pour deux —s de curiosité** he is not the least bit curious.

soubassement [subasmɑ̃] *nm* base, basement, substructure.

soubresaut [subrəso] *nm* leap, start, jump, jolt, gasp; *pl* spasmodic movements, convulsions.

soubrette [subrɛt] *nf* soubrette, lady's maid.

souche [suʃ] *nf* stump, log, dolt, counterfoil, origin; **faire — to found a family; de bonne —** of good stock, pedigree.

souci [susi] *nm* care, worry, anxiety, solicitude, marigold.

se soucier [səsusje] *vr* to concern o.s., worry, trouble, care, mind, bother.

soucieux, -euse [susjø, øːz] *a* anxious, mindful, worried.

soucoupe [sukup] *nf* saucer.

soudain [sudɛ̃] *a* sudden; *ad* suddenly.

soudaineté [sudɛnte] *nf* suddenness.

soudard [sudaːr] *nm* old soldier.

soude [sud] *nf* soda; **bicarbonate de — bicarbonate of soda, baking soda.

souder [sude] *vt* to solder, weld; *vr* to weld, knit; **lampe à —** blowtorch.

soudoyer [sudwaje] *vt* to hire, bribe.

soudure [sudyːr] *nf* soldering, welding, soldered joint, solder.

soufflage [suflaːʒ] *nm* blowing, blast.

souffle [sufl] *nm* breath, breathing, blast, puff, inspiration; **couper le — à qn** to take s.o.'s breath away; **à bout de —** out of breath.

soufflé [sufle] *a* unvoiced; *nm* soufflé.

souffler [sufle] *vt* to blow (out, off, up), breathe, utter, filch, pinch; *vi* to blow, pant, puff, recover one's breath; **— (son rôle à) qn** to prompt s.o.

soufflet [suflɛ] *nm* bellows, gore, insult, box on the ear, slap.

souffleter [suflɔte] *vt* to slap, box s.o.'s ears, insult.

souffleur, -euse [suflœːr, øːz] *n* prompter; *nm* blower.

souffrance [sufrɑ̃s] *nf* suffering, pain; **en — in suspense, awaiting delivery.

souffrant [sufrɑ̃] *a* suffering, unwell, ailing.

souffre-douleur [sufrədulœːr] *nm* butt, drudge.

souffreteux, -euse [sufrətø, øːz] *a* sickly, seedy, needy.

souffrir [sufriːr] *vt* to suffer, endure, bear, allow (of); *vi* to be in pain, suffer.

soufre [sufr] *nm* sulphur, brimstone.

soufrer [sufre] *vt* to sulphurate.

souhait [swɛ] *nm* wish, desire; **à — to one's liking.

souhaitable [swɛtabl] *a* desirable.

souhaiter [swɛte] *vt* to wish (for), desire.

souiller [suje] *vt* to soil, pollute, stain, sully.

souillon [sujɔ̃] *n* sloven, slut; *nf* scullery maid.

souillure [sujyːr] *nf* stain, spot, blemish, blot.

soûl [su] *a* drunk, surfeited; **tout son — one's fill.

soulagement [sulaʒmɑ̃] *nm* relief, comfort, alleviation.

soulager [sulaʒe] *vt* to relieve, alleviate, ease; *vr* to relieve one's feelings, relieve oneself.

soûlard [sulaːr] *nm* drunkard.

soûler [sule] *vt* to stuff with food, make drunk; *vr* to gorge, get drunk.

soûlerie [sulri] *nf* drinking bout, drunken orgy.

soulèvement [sulɛvmɑ̃] *nm* rising, upheaval, revolt, indignant outburst.

soulever [sulve] *vt* to raise, lift, rouse, stir up; *vr* to revolt, heave.

soulier [sulje] *nm* shoe.

souligner [suliɲe] *vt* to underline, stress, emphasize.

soumettre [sumɛtr] *vt* to subdue, subject, refer, lay, submit; *vr* to submit, comply, yield, defer.

soumis [sumi] *a* submissive, amenable, biddable, liable, subject.

soumission [sumisjɔ̃] *nf* submission, submissiveness, compliance, tender.

soupape [supap] *nf* valve.

soupçon [supsɔ̃] *nm* suspicion, touch, dash, flavor.

soupçonner [supsɔne] *vt* to suspect, guess, conjecture, surmise.

soupçonneux, -euse [supsɔnø, øːz] *a* suspicious, distrustful.

soupe [sup] *nf* soup.

soupente [supɑ̃t] *nf* garret, loft, recess, brace, strap.

souper [supe] *vi* to have supper; *nm* supper; **j'en ai soupé** I am fed up (with it).

soupeser [supəze] *vt* to weigh in the hand, feel the weight of.

soupière [supjɛːr] *nf* soup-tureen.

soupir [supiːr] *nm* sigh.

soupirail [supiraːj] *nm* ventilator, air-hole.

soupirant [supirɑ̃] *nm* suitor.

soupirer [supire] *vi* to sigh, gasp, long (for **après**).

souple [supl] *a* supple, flexible, adaptable, pliant.

souplesse [suplɛs] *nf* suppleness, pliability, flexibility, litheness; **— d'esprit** adaptability.

source [surs] *nf* source, spring, well, fount(ain), origin, root; **de bonne — on good authority.

sourcier, -ière [sursje, jɛːr] *n* water-diviner.

sourcil [sursi] *nm* eyebrow.
sourciller [sursije] *vi* to frown, flinch, wince.
sourcilleux, -euse [sursijø, øːz] *a* frowning, supercilious.
sourd [suːr] *a* deaf, muffled, dull, veiled, muted, sound-proof, unvoiced; **bruit** — thud; **lanterne** —e dark-lantern; — **comme un pot** as deaf as a door post.
sourdement [surdəmã] *ad* with a dull hollow sound, dully, secretly.
sourdine [surdin] *nf* mute, damper, dimmer; **en** — on the sly.
sourd-muet, sourde-muette [surmɥɛ, surdmɥɛt] *a* deaf-and-dumb; *n* deaf-mute.
sourdre [surdr] *vi* to well up, spring, arise.
souricière [surisjɛːr] *nf* mousetrap, trap.
sourire [suriːr] *vi* to smile, appeal; *nm* smile.
souris [suri] *nf* mouse; *nm* smile.
sournois [surnwa] *a* sly, crafty, artful, underhand; *n* sneak, shifty character, sly boots.
sournoiserie [surnwazri] *nf* craftiness, underhand piece of work.
sous [su] *prep* under(neath), below, beneath, within (time), sub-; — **la pluie** in the rain; — **peine de mort** on pain of death.
sous-alimentation [suzalimãtasjɔ̃] *nf* malnutrition.
sous-bois [subwa] *nm* underwood, undergrowth.
sous-chef [suʃɛf] *nm* deputy chief, assistant manager, chief assistant.
souscription [suskripsjɔ̃] *nf* subscription, contribution, signing, signature; **verser une** — to make a contribution.
souscrire [suskriːr] *vt* to subscribe (to), sign.
sous-développé [sudevlɔpe] *a* underdeveloped.
sous-directeur, -trice [sudirɛktœːr, tris] *n* assistant-manager(ess), vice-principal.
sous-entendre [suzãtãːdr] *vt* to imply, understand.
sous-entendu [suzãtãdy] *nm* implication; **parler par** —s to hint, insinuate.
sous-entente [suzãtãt] *nf* mental reservation.
sous-estimer [suzɛstime] *vt* to under-estimate.
sous-gouverneur [suguvɛrnœːr] *nm* deputy-, vice-governor.
sous-jacent [suʒasã] *a* subjacent, underlying.
sous-lieutenant [suljøtnã] *nm* second-, sub-lieutenant.
sous-location [sulɔkasjɔ̃] *nf* sublet (ting).
sous-louer [sulwe] *vt* to sub-let, sub-lease.
sous-main [sumɛ̃] *nm* writing-pad, blotting-pad; **en** — behind the scenes.
sous-marin [sumarɛ̃] *a* submarine, submerged; *nm* submarine.
sous-officier [suzɔfisje] *nm* non-commissioned officer, (*naut*) petty officer.
sous-pied [supje] *nm* under-strap.
sous-préfecture [suprefɛktyːr] *nf* sub-prefecture.
sous-produit [suprɔdɥi] *nm* by-product.
sous-secrétaire [susəkrɛtɛːr] *n* under-secretary.
sous-seing [susɛ̃] *nm* private contract, agreement.
soussigner [susiɲe] *vt* to sign, undersign.
sous-sol [susɔl] *nm* basement, subsoil.
sous-titre [sutiːtr] *nm* sub-title, caption.
soustraction [sustraksjɔ̃] *nf* subtraction, removal.
soustraire [sustrɛːr] *vt* to subtract, remove, take away, shield, screen; *vr* to elude, avoid, dodge, get out (of à); **se** — **à la justice** to abscond.
sous-ventrière [suvɑ̃trjɛːr] *nf* belly-band, saddle-girth.
sous-vêtement [suvɛtmã] *nm* undergarment.
soutache [sutaʃ] *nf* braid.
soutane [sutan] *nf* cassock.
soute [sut] *nf* store-room, coal-bunker; — **à eau** water-tank; — **à munitions** magazine.
soutenable [sutnabl] *a* bearable, tenable, arguable.
soutenance [sutnɑ̃ːs] *nf* maintaining (thesis).
souteneur [sutnœːr] *nm* upholder, pimp.
soutenir [sutniːr] *vt* to sustain, support, withstand, maintain, keep, back (up), assert; *vr* to support oneself, keep up, be maintained.
soutenu [sutny] *a* sustained, unflagging, constant, continued, steady, elevated.
souterrain [sutɛrɛ̃] *a* subterranean, underground; *nm* tunnel, underground passage.
soutien [sutjɛ̃] *nm* support, prop, supporter.
soutien-gorge [sutjɛ̃gɔrʒ] *nm* brassière.
soutier [sutje] *nm* trimmer.
soutirer [sutire] *vt* to rack, draw off, squeeze.
souvenance [suvnɑ̃ːs] *nf* recollection.
souvenir [suvniːr] *v imp* to come to mind; *vr* to remember, recall; *nm* memory, recollection, remembrance, memento, souvenir, memorial, keepsake.
souvent [suvã] *ad* often.
souverain [suvrɛ̃] *a* sovereign, supreme; *n* sovereign, ruler.
souveraineté [suvrɛnte] *nf* sovereignty.

soviétique [sɔvjetik] _a_ soviet; _n_ Soviet citizen.

soyeux, -euse [swajø, øːz] _a_ silky, silken.

spacieux, -euse [spasjø, øːz] _a_ spacious, roomy.

sparadrap [sparadra] _nm_ sticking-plaster.

sparte [spart] _nm_ esparto grass.

spartiate [sparsjat] _a_ spartan.

spasme [spasm] _nm_ spasm.

spasmodique [spasmɔdik] _a_ spasmodic.

spatule [spatyl] _nf_ spatula.

speaker, -ine [spikœːr, krin] _n_ (radio) announcer.

spécial [spesjal] _a_ special, particular.

se spécialiser [səspesjalize] _vr_ to specialize.

spécialiste [spesjalist] _n_ specialist, expert.

spécialité [spesjalitɛ] _nf_ specialty, special feature.

spécieux, -euse [spesjø, øːz] _a_ specious.

spécification [spesifikasjɔ̃] _nf_ specification.

spécifier [spesifje] _vt_ to specify, determine.

spécifique [spesifik] _a_ specific, precise.

spécimen [spesimɛn] _a nm_ specimen.

spéciosité [spesjɔzite] _nf_ speciousness.

spectacle [spɛktakl] _nm_ spectacle, scene, sight, display, theater, show; **salle de** — theater; **pièce à grand** — spectacular play; **se donner en** — to make an exhibition of o.s.

spectaculaire [spɛktakylɛːr] _a_ spectacular.

spectateur, -trice [spɛktatœːr, tris] _n_ spectator, onlooker, bystander.

spectral [spɛktral] _a_ spectral, ghostly, ghostlike, of the spectrum.

spectre [spɛktr] _nm_ ghost, specter, apparition, spectrum.

spéculaire [spekylɛːr] _a_ specular.

spéculateur, -trice [spekylatœːr, tris] _n_ speculator, theorizer.

spéculatif, -ive [spekylatif, iːv] _a_ speculative.

spéculation [spekylasjɔ̃] _nf_ speculation, theorizing, conjecture.

spéculer [spekyle] _vi_ to speculate, theorize, cogitate; — **à la baisse (hausse)** to speculate on a rise (fall).

spermatozoïde [spɛrmatɔzɔid] _nm_ spermatozoon.

sperme [spɛrm] _nm_ sperm.

sphère [sfɛr] _nf_ sphere, orb, globe.

sphérique [sferik] _a_ spherical.

sphéroïde [sferɔid] _nm_ spheroid.

sphinx [sfɛ̃ːks] _nm_ sphinx.

spider [spidɛːr] _nm_ trunk (of car), rumble seat.

spinal [spinal] _a_ spinal.

spiral [spiral] _a_ spiral.

spirale [spiral] _nf_ spiral; **escalier en** — winding staircase.

spirite [spirit] _a_ spiritualistic; _n_ spiritualist.

spiritisme [spiritism] _nm_ spiritualism.

spiritualiste [spirityalist] _a_ spiritualistic; _n_ spiritualist.

spirituel, -elle [spirityɛl] _a_ spiritual, sacred, witty.

spiritueux, -euse [spirityø, øːz] _a_ spirituous, alcoholic; _nm pl_ spirits.

spleen [splin] _nm_ spleen, depression; **avoir le** — to have the blues.

splendeur [splɑ̃dœːr] _nf_ splendor, grandeur, magnificence, brilliance, pomp.

splendide [splɑ̃did] _a_ splendid, magnificent, grand, gorgeous, glorious.

spoliateur, -trice [spɔljatœːr, tris] _a_ spoliatory, despoiling; _n_ despoiler, plunderer.

spoliation [spɔljasjɔ̃] _nf_ spoliation, despoiling, plundering.

spolier [spɔlje] _vt_ to despoil, rob, plunder.

spongieux, -euse [spɔ̃ʒjø, øːz] _a_ spongy.

spontané [spɔ̃tane] _a_ spontaneous, involuntary.

spontanéité [spɔ̃taneite] _nf_ spontaneity.

sporadique [spɔradik] _a_ sporadic.

spore [spɔːr] _nf_ spore.

sport [spɔːr] _nm_ sport(s), games; _a_ sporting, casual.

sportif, -ive [spɔrtif, iːv] _a_ sport (ing), athletic; _n_ sportsman, -woman, lover of games; **réunion sportive** sports, athletic meeting.

sportsman [spɔrt(s)man] _nm_ sportsman, race-goer.

spumeux, -euse [spymø, øːz] _a_ spumy, frothy, foamy.

square [skwɛːr, skwaːr] _nm_ small public garden.

squelette [skəlɛt] _nm_ skeleton, framework, outline.

squelettique [skəletik] _a_ skeleton-like.

stabilisateur, -trice [stabilizatœːr, tris] _a_ stabilizing, steadying; _nm_ stabilizer.

stabiliser [stabilize] _vt_ to stabilize, steady; _vr_ to become steady, stable.

stabilité [stabilite] _nf_ stability, steadiness, firmness, balance, durability.

stable [stabl] _a_ stable, steady, firm, durable.

stade [stad] _nm_ stadium, sports-ground, stage.

stage [staːʒ] _nm_ probationary period, course.

stagiaire [staʒɛːr] _a_ probationary; _n_ probationer.

stagnant [stagnɑ̃] _a_ stagnant, dull.

stagnation [stagnasjɔ̃] _nf_ stagnation, stagnancy, standstill.

stalactite [stalaktit] _nf_ stalactite.

stalagmite [stalagmit] _nf_ stalagmite.

stalle [stal] *nf* stall, box, seat, pew.
stance [stɑ̃ːs] *nf* stanza.
stand [stɑ̃ːd] *nm* stand, shooting-gallery.
standard [stãdaːr] *nm* switchboard, standard.
standardisation [stãdardizasjɔ̃] *nf* standardization.
standardiser [stãdardize] *vt* to standardize.
station [stasjɔ̃] *nf* stop, station, stage, taxi-stand, position, post, standing; — **centrale** power-house; — **balnéaire** seaside resort, spa; — **thermale** spa, watering place; — **d'hiver** winter resort; **faire une** — **à** to halt at.
stationnaire [stasjɔnɛːr] *a* stationary, fixed.
stationnement [stasjɔnmã] *nm* standing, stopping, stationing, taxi-stand; **parc de** — parking place; — **interdit** no parking.
stationner [stasjɔne] *vi* to stand, park, stop, be stationed.
statique [statik] *a* static.
statistique [statistik] *a* statistical; *nf* statistics.
statuaire [statɥɛːr] *a* statuary; *n* sculptor; *nf* statuary.
statue [staty] *nf* statue.
statuer [statɥe] *vt* to ordain, decree, enact; — **sur une affaire** to decide, give a decision on a matter.
stature [statyːr] *nf* stature, height.
statut [staty] *nm* statute, regulation, article, ordinance, bylaw.
statutaire [statytɛːr] *a* statutory.
sténodactylo(graphe) [stenɔdaktilɔ(graf)] *n* shorthand-typist.
sténodactylographie [stenɔdaktilɔgrafi] *nf* shorthand and typing.
sténographe [stenɔgraf] *n* stenographer, shorthand writer.
sténographie [stenɔgrafi] *nf* stenography, shorthand.
sténographier [stenɔgrafje] *vt* to take down in shorthand.
stentor [stãtɔːr] *nm* **voix de** — stentorian voice.
steppe [stɛp] *n* steppe.
stère [stɛːr] *nm* stere, cubic meter.
stéréophonie [stereɔfɔni] *nf* stereophony.
stéréotype [stereɔtip] *a* stereotype(d); *nm* stereotype plate.
stérile [steril] *a* sterile, barren, fruitless.
stérilisation [sterilizasjɔ̃] *nf* sterilization.
stériliser [sterilize] *vt* to sterilize.
stérilité [sterilite] *nf* sterility, barrenness, fruitlessness.
sternum [stɛrnɔm] *nm* sternum, breastbone.
stigmate [stigmat] *nm* stigma, scar, brand.
stigmatiser [stigmatize] *vt* to stigmatize, brand (with infamy), pock-mark.

stimulant [stimylã] *a* stimulating; *nm* stimulant, stimulus, incentive.
stimulation [stimylasjɔ̃] *nf* stimulation.
stimuler [stimyle] *vt* to stimulate, incite, rouse.
stipulation [stipylasjɔ̃] *nf* stipulation.
stipuler [stipyle] *vt* to stipulate, lay down.
stock [stɔk] *nm* stock; — **en magasin** stock in hand.
stockiste [stɔkist] *nm* stocker, wholesale warehouseman, agent; **agence** — service-station.
stoïcien, -enne [stɔisjɛ̃, jɛn] *a* stoic(al); *n* stoic.
stoïcisme [stɔisism] *nm* stoicism.
stoïque [stɔik] *a* stoic(al).
stomacal [stɔmakal] *a* gastric.
stomachique [stɔmaʃik] *a* stomach-, stomachic.
stoppage [stɔpaːʒ] *nm* stopping, stoppage, invisible mending.
stopper [stɔpe] *vt* to stop, fine-darn; *vi* to (come to a) stop.
store [stɔːr] *nm* blind, window shade.
strabisme [strabism] *nm* squinting.
strangulation [strãgylasjɔ̃] *nf* strangulation, throttling, constriction.
strapontin [strapɔ̃tɛ̃] *nm* folding-seat, jump seat.
strass [stras] *nm* strass, paste jewelry.
stratagème [strataʒɛm] *nm* stratagem.
stratégie [strateʒi] *nf* strategy, generalship, craft.
stratégique [strateʒik] *a* strategic (al).
stratosphère [stratɔsfɛːr] *nf* stratosphere.
strict [strikt] *a* strict, severe; **le** — **nécessaire** the bare necessities.
strident [stridã] *a* strident, harsh, grating.
strie [stri] *nf* score, streak.
strier [strie] *vt* to score, scratch, streak, groove.
striure [striyːr] *nf* score, scratch, streak, groove, striation.
strophe [strɔf] *nf* stanza, verse.
structure [stryktyːr] *nf* structure.
strychnine [striknin] *nf* strychnine.
stuc [styk] *nm* stucco.
studieux, -euse [stydjø, øːz] *a* studious.
studio [stydjo] *nm* (film) studio, artist's studio.
stupéfaction [stypefaksjɔ̃] *nf* stupefaction, amazement, bewilderment.
stupéfait [stypefɛ] *a* stupefied, amazed, astounded.
stupéfiant [stypefjã] *a* stupefying, astounding; *nm* narcotic, drug.
stupéfier [stypefje] *vt* to stupefy, bemuse, astound.
stupeur [stypœːr] *nf* stupor, astonishment, amazement.

stupide [stypid] *a* stupid, foolish, silly.
stupidité [stypidite] *nf* stupidity, foolishness, stupid thing.
stupre [stypr] *nm* debauchery.
style [stil] *nm* style, pin, etching-needle; **robe de** — period dress.
styler [stile] *vt* to train, school.
stylet [stilɛ] *nm* stiletto.
styliser [stilize] *vt* to stylize, conventionalize.
stylo(graphe) [stilɔ(graf)] *nm* fountain-pen, stylograph.
styptique [stiptik] *a nm* styptic, astringent.
su [sy] *nm* **au** — **de** to the knowledge of; **à mon vu et** — to my certain knowledge.
suaire [sɥɛːr] *nm* shroud, winding-sheet.
suave [sɥaːv] *a* bland, suave, sweet, mild, soft, mellow.
suavité [sɥavite] *nf* blandness, suavity, sweetness, mildness, mellowness.
subalterne [sybaltɛrn] *a* subordinate, junior; *nm* subaltern, underling.
subdiviser [sybdivize] *vtr* to subdivide.
subdivision [sybdivizjɔ̃] *nf* subdivision.
subir [sybiːr] *vt* to undergo, go through, sustain, suffer.
subit [sybi] *a* sudden, unexpected.
subjacent [sybʒasɑ̃] *a* subjacent, underlying.
subjectif, -ive [sybʒɛktif, iːv] *a* subjective.
subjonctif, -ive [sybʒɔ̃ktif, iːv] *a nm* subjunctive.
subjuguer [sybʒyge] *vt* to subjugate, subdue, overcome, captivate.
sublime [syblim] *a* sublime, exalted, lofty; *nm* sublime.
sublimer [syblime] *vt* to sublimate, purify.
submerger [sybmɛrʒe] *vt* to submerge, immerse.
submersible [sybmɛrsibl] *a* submersible, sinkable; *nm* submersible, submarine.
submersion [sybmɛrsjɔ̃] *nf* submersion, immersion.
subordination [sybɔrdinasjɔ̃] *nf* subordination.
subordonné [sybɔrdɔne] *a* subordinate, dependent; *n* subordinate, underling.
subordonner [sybɔrdɔne] *vt* to subordinate.
subornation [sybɔrnasjɔ̃] *nf* subornation, bribing.
suborner [sybɔrne] *vt* to suborn, bribe.
subreptice [sybrɛptis] *a* surreptitious, stealthy.
subrogation [sybrɔgasjɔ̃] *nf* subrogation, substitution, delegation.
subroger [sybrɔʒe] *vt* to subrogate, appoint as deputy.

subséquent [sypsekɑ̃] *a* subsequent ensuing.
subside [sypsid] *nm* subsidy.
subsidence [sypsidɑ̃ːs] *nf* subsidence.
subsidiaire [sypsidjɛːr] *a* subsidiary, accessory.
subsistance [sypsistɑ̃ːs] *nf* subsistence, keep, sustenance.
subsister [sypsiste] *vi* to subsist, exist, hold good.
substance [sypstɑ̃ːs] *nf* substance, matter, material.
substantiel, -elle [sypstɑ̃sjɛl] *a* substantial.
substantif, -ive [sypstɑ̃tif, iːv] *a* substantive; *nm* noun.
substituer [sypstitɥe] *vt* to substitute, entail; *vr* to take the place (of à).
substitut [sypstity] *nm* deputy, assistant, delegate.
substitution [sypstitysjɔ̃] *nf* substitution.
subterfuge [syptɛrfyːʒ] *nm* subterfuge, dodge.
subtil [syptil] *a* subtle, shrewd, discerning, fine, tenuous, thin.
subtiliser [syptilize] *vt* to subtilize, refine, make too subtle, pinch.
subtilité [syptilite] *nf* subtlety, rarity, shrewdness, acuteness.
subvenir [sybvəniːr] *vt* to provide for, supply; — **aux frais d'un voyage** to defray the expenses of a journey.
subvention [sybvɑ̃sjɔ̃] *nf* subsidy, grant.
subventionner [sybvɑ̃sjɔne] *vt* to subsidize; **théâtre subventionné par l'état** state-aided theater.
subversif, -ive [sybvɛrsif, iːv] *a* subversive.
subversion [sybvɛrsjɔ̃] *nf* subversion, overthrow.
suc [syk] *nm* juice, sap, pith, essence, substance.
succédané [syksedane] *nm* substitute.
succéder [syksede] *vt* to follow, succeed.
succès [syksɛ] *nm* success, (favorable) outcome, result; **remporter un** — **fou** to bring the house down.
successeur [syksesœːr] *nm* successor.
successif, -ive [syksesif, iːv] *a* successive.
succession [syksesjɔ̃] *nf* succession, sequence, estate, inheritance; **prendre la** — **de** to take over (from).
succinct [syksɛ̃] *a* succinct, concise, brief.
succion [syksjɔ̃] *nf* suction, sucking.
succomber [sykɔ̃be] *vi* to succumb, die, yield.
succulent [sykylɑ̃] *a* succulent, juicy, tasty.
succursale [sykyrsal] *nf* branch office.
sucer [syse] *vt* to suck.
sucette [sysɛt] *nf* pacifier, lollipop.
suçoir [syswaːr] *nm* sucker.

sucre [sykr] *nm* sugar; **— en pain** loaf sugar; **— en poudre** powdered sugar.
sucré [sykre] *a* sugared, sweet(ened), sugary.
sucrer [sykre] *vt* to sugar, sweeten.
sucrerie [sykrəri] *nf* sugar refinery; *pl* confectionery, sweets.
sucrier [sykrie] *nm* sugar bowl.
sud [syd] *a* south, southern, southerly; *nm* south.
sudation [sydasjɔ̃] *nf* sweating.
sud-est [sydɛst] *a* south-east(ern), south-easterly; *nm* south-east.
sud-ouest [sydwɛst] *a* south-west (ern), south-westerly; *nm* south-west.
Suède [sɥɛd] *nf* Sweden.
suédois [sɥedwa] *a* Swedish; *n* Swede.
suer [sɥe] *vi* to sweat, perspire, exude, toil.
sueur [sɥœːr] *nf* sweat, perspiration; **en — sweating.**
suffire [syfiːr] *vi* to suffice, be enough, be adequate, meet, cope (with à); *vr* to be self-sufficient.
suffisance [syfizɑ̃ːs] *nf* sufficiency, adequacy, (self-)conceit, priggishness.
suffisant [syfizɑ̃] *a* sufficient, enough, adequate, conceited, self-satisfied.
suffixe [syfiks] *nm* suffix.
suffocation [syfɔkasjɔ̃] *nf* choking, suffocation.
suffoquer [syfɔke] *vt* to suffocate, choke, stifle; *vi* to choke.
suffrage [syfraːʒ] *nm* suffrage, franchise, vote.
suffusion [syfyzjɔ̃] *nf* suffusion, blush.
suggérer [sygʒere] *vt* to suggest, hint (at).
suggestif, -ive [sygʒɛstif, iːv] *a* suggestive.
suggestion [sygʒɛstjɔ̃] *nf* suggestion, hint.
suicide [sɥisid] *a* suicidal; *nm* suicide.
suicidé [sɥiside] *n* suicide.
se suicider [səsɥiside] *vr* to commit suicide.
suie [sɥi] *nf* soot.
suif [sɥif] *nm* tallow, candle-grease.
suinter [sɥɛ̃te] *vi* to ooze, sweat, run, seep, leak.
Suisse [sɥis] *nf* Switzerland.
suisse [sɥis] *an* Swiss; *nm* church officer; **petit — cream cheese.**
suite [sɥit] *nf* continuation, succession, series, suite, retinue, train, sequel, result, consequence, coherence; **donner — à** to follow up, execute; **faire — à** to be a continuation of, a sequel to; **dans la —** subsequently; **par la — afterwards,** later on; **par — (de)** as a result (of); **tout de suite** immediately; **de — in** succession, one end; **sans — dis-** connected, incoherent.

suivant [sɥivɑ̃] *a* following, next; *nm* follower, attendant; *prep* according to, following; **— que** according as.
suivi [sɥivi] *a* coherent, steady, continuous, popular.
suivre [sɥiːvr] *vt* to follow (up), pursue, act upon, observe, escort; **— des cours** to attend lectures; **faire — to forward; à — to be** continued.
sujet, -ette [syʒɛ, ɛt] *a* subject, dependent, prone, liable, open; *n* subject; *nm* subject, topic, ground, theme, reason, fellow; **bon — steady** person; **mauvais — bad lot, worth-** less character; **au — de about, with** regard to.
sujétion [syʒɛsjɔ̃] *nf* subjection, servitude.
sulfate [sylfat] *nm* sulphate.
sulfater [sylfate] *vt* to sulphate, dress with copper sulphate.
sulfure [sylfyːr] *nm* sulphide.
sulfureux, -euse [sylfyrø, øːz] *a* sulphurous.
sulfurique [sylfyrik] *a* sulphuric.
sultan [syltɑ̃] *nm* sultan.
sultane [syltan] *nf* sultana.
superbe [sypɛrb] *a* superb, splendid, magnificent, stately, arrogant, haughty; *nf* arrogance, haughtiness.
super(carburant) [sypɛrkarbyrɑ̃] *nm* high-grade gasoline.
supercherie [sypɛrʃəri] *nf* fraud, hoax, deceit.
superficie [sypɛrfisi] *nf* area, surface.
superficiel, -elle [sypɛrfisjɛl] *a* superficial, shallow.
superflu [sypɛrfly] *a* superfluous, unnecessary; *nm* superfluity, over-abundance.
superfluité [sypɛrflyite] *nf* super-fluity.
supérieur [syperjœːr] *a* superior, upper, higher; *n* superior, head.
supériorité [syperjɔrite] *nf* superior-ity, supremacy, superiorship.
superlatif, -ive [sypɛrlatif, iːv] *a nm* superlative.
superposer [sypɛrpoze] *vt* to super-(im)pose.
superstitieux, -euse [sypɛrstisjø, øːz] *a* superstitious.
superstition [sypɛrstisjɔ̃] *nf* super-stition.
supplanter [syplɑ̃te] *vt* to supplant, supersede.
suppléance [sypleɑ̃ːs] *nf* deputyship, substitution.
suppléant [sypleɑ̃] *a* temporary, acting; *n* deputy, substitute.
suppléer [syplee] *vt* to deputize for, make up, make good; **— à to** compensate for.
supplément [syplemɑ̃] *nm* supple-ment, extra, addition, extra fare; **en — additional, extra.**
supplémentaire [syplemɑ̃tɛːr] *a* supplementary, extra, additional.

suppliant [sypliɑ̃] *a* suppliant, pleading, beseeching; *n* supplicant, suppliant.

supplication [syplikasjɔ̃] *nf* supplication.

supplice [syplis] *nm* torture, punishment, anguish, torment, agony.

supplier [syplie] *vt* to implore, beseech, beg.

support [sypɔːr] *nm* support, prop, stand, bracket, rest, holder.

supportable [sypɔrtabl] *a* bearable, tolerable.

supporter [sypɔrte] *vt* to hold up, support, prop, endure, suffer, put up with, tolerate.

supposé [sypoze] *a* supposed, alleged, fictitious, assumed, forged; — **que** supposing that.

supposer [sypoze] *vt* to suppose, assume, imply.

supposition [sypɔzisjɔ̃] *nf* supposition, assumption.

suppositoire [sypɔzitwaːr] *nm* suppository.

suppôt [sypo] *nm* tool.

suppression [sypresjɔ̃] *nf* suppression, canceling, discontinuance.

supprimer [syprime] *vt* to suppress, abolish, cancel, discontinue, omit.

suppurer [sypyre] *vi* to suppurate, run.

supputer [sypyte] *vt* to calculate, compute.

suprématie [sypremasi] *nf* supremacy.

suprême [sypreːm] *a* supreme, crowning, paramount, last.

sur [syːr] *prep* (up)on, over, above, about, towards, along, over-, super-; **un homme — dix** one man out of ten; **dix mètres — huit** ten yards by eight; — **ce (quoi)** whereupon.

sûr [syːr] *a* sure, certain, unerring, unfailing, safe, reliable, staunch; **à coup** — without fail, for certain.

surabondant [syrabɔ̃dɑ̃] *a* superabundant.

surabonder [syrabɔ̃de] *vi* to superabound, be surfeited (with **de**).

suraigu, -uë [syregy] *a* high-pitched, overshrill.

suralimenter [syralimɑ̃te] *vt* to feed up, overfeed.

suranné [syrane] *a* old-fashioned, out of date.

surcharge [syrʃarʒ] *nf* overload(ing), extra load, excess weight, surcharge, overtax.

surcharger [syrʃarʒe] *vt* to overload, overcharge, surcharge, overtax.

surchauffer [syrʃofe] *vt* to overheat, superheat.

surclasser [syrklase] *vt* to outclass.

surcomprimé [syrkɔ̃prime] *a* supercharged.

surcontrer [syrkɔ̃tre] *vt* to redouble.

surcroissance [syrkrwasɑ̃ːs] *nf* overgrowth.

surcroît [syrkrwa] *nm* increase, addition; **par** — in addition, into the bargain.

surdité [syrdite] *nf* deafness.

sureau [syro] *nm* elder (tree).

surélever [syrelve] *vt* to raise, heighten.

sûrement [syrmɑ̃] *ad* surely, certainly, safely, securely.

surenchère [syrɑ̃ʃɛːr] *nf* higher bid.

surenchérir [syrɑ̃ʃeriːr] *vi* to bid higher; *vt* — **sur** outbid.

surestimer [syrɛstime] *vt* to overestimate.

sûreté [syrte] *nf* sureness, soundness, safety, security, guarantee; **la Sûreté** the Criminal Investigation Department; **pour plus de** — to be on the safe side.

surexcitation [syrɛksitasjɔ̃] *nf* (over) excitement.

surexciter [syrɛksite] *vt* to excite, over-stimulate.

surexposer [syrɛkspoze] *vt* to overexpose.

surface [syrfas] *nf* surface, area.

surfaire [syrfɛːr] *vt* to overcharge, overrate; *vi* to overcharge.

surgir [syrʒiːr] *vi* to (a)rise, loom up, come into sight, crop up.

surhausser [syrose] *vt* to raise, heighten, increase.

surhumain [syrymɛ̃] *a* superhuman.

surimposer [syrɛ̃poze] *vt* to superimpose, increase the tax on.

suriner [syrine] *vt (fam)* to knife, do in.

surintendant [syrɛ̃tɑ̃dɑ̃] *nm* superintendent, steward.

surjet [syrʒe] *nm* overcasting, whipping (*of seams*).

sur-le-champ [syrləʃɑ̃] *ad* immediately.

surlendemain [syrlɑ̃dmɛ̃] *nm* next day but one, day after tomorrow; **le** — **de son départ** the second day after his departure.

surmenage [syrmənaːʒ] *nm* overworking, overdriving, strain.

surmené [syrməne] *a* overworked, jaded, fagged.

surmener [syrməne] *vt* to overwork, overexert; *vr* to overwork, overdo it.

surmontable [syrmɔ̃tabl] *a* surmountable.

surmonter [syrmɔ̃te] *vt* to surmount, top, overcome, get over; *vr* to master one's feelings.

surnaturel, -elle [syrnatyrɛl] *a* supernatural, uncanny; *nm* supernatural.

surnom [syrnɔ̃] *nm* nickname.

surnombre [syrnɔ̃ːbr] *nm* excessive number; **en** — supernumerary.

surnommer [syrnɔme] *vt* to nickname, call.

suroît [syrwa] *nm* sou'wester.

surpasser [syrpase] *vt* to surpass, outdo, outshine, exceed, excel, pass one's understanding.

surpayer [syrpɛje] *vt* to overpay, pay too much for.

surpeuplement [syrpœpləmã] *nm* overcrowding.

surplis [syrpli] *nm* surplice.

surplomb [syrplɔ̃] *nm* overhang; **en — overhanging.**

surplomber [syrplɔ̃be] *vti* to overhang.

surplus [syrply] *nm* surplus, excess; **au — besides.**

surpoids [syrpwɑ] *nm* overweight; **en — in excess.**

surprenant [syrprənã] *a* surprising, astonishing.

surprendre [syrprɑ̃:dr] *vt* to surprise, astonish, catch unawares, overtake, overhear, intercept, catch, detect.

surprise [syrpri:z] *nf* surprise, astonishment, grab bag.

surproduction [syrprɔdyksjɔ̃] *nf* overproduction.

sursaut [syrso] *nm* start, jump; **en — with a start.**

sursauter [syrsote] *vi* to start, jump.

surseoir [syrswa:r] *vt* to postpone, delay, suspend.

sursis [syrsi] *nm* postponement, reprieve, deferment.

surtaux [syrto] *nm* overassessment.

surtaxe [syrtaks] *nf* surtax, supertax, surcharge.

surtout [syrtu] *ad* above all, particularly, especially.

surveillance [syrvɛjɑ̃:s] *nf* supervision, vigilance, watching.

surveillant [syrvɛjã] *n* supervisor, overseer, watchman, usher, invigilator.

surveiller [syrvɛje] *vt* to supervise, superintend, invigilate, look after, watch; *vr* to watch one's step.

survenir [syrv(ə)ni:r] *vi* to happen, arise, crop up.

survêtement [syrvɛtmã] *nm* tracksuit.

survie [syrvi] *nf* survival, survivorship, after-life.

survivance [syrvivɑ̃:s] *nf* survival.

survivant [syrvivã] *a* surviving; *n* survivor.

survivre [syrvi:vr] *vi* to survive; *vt* — à to outlive.

survoler [syrvɔle] *vt* to fly over.

survolté [syrvɔlte] *a* worked up, het up.

sus [sys] *ad* against, upon; *excl* come on! **courir — à qn** to rush at s.o.; **en — in addition, besides.**

susceptibilité [sysɛptibilite] *nf* susceptibility, touchiness.

susceptible [sysɛptibl] *a* susceptible, touchy, likely, liable, apt.

susciter [syssite] *vt* to arouse, stir up, raise up, give rise to, bring on.

susdit [sydi] *a* aforesaid, abovementioned.

suspect [syspɛ(kt)] *a* suspect, suspicious, doubtful; *nm* suspect.

suspecter [syspɛkte] *vt* to suspect, doubt.

suspendre [syspɑ̃:dr] *vt* to suspend,

hang, stop, defer; *vr* to hang (on).

suspendu [syspɑ̃dy] *a* suspended, hanging, sprung; **pont — suspension bridge.**

suspens [syspɑ̃] *ad* **en — in suspense,** undecided, in abeyance.

suspension [syspɑ̃sjɔ̃] *nf* suspension, hanging, interruption, springing, hanging lamp.

suspicion [syspisjɔ̃] *nf* suspicion.

sustenter [systɑ̃te] *vt* to sustain, support.

susurrer [sysyre] *vi* to murmur, rustle, sough.

suture [syty:r] *nf* suture, join; **point de — stitch.**

suturer [sytyre] *vt* to stitch.

suzerain [syzrɛ̃] *a* paramount, sovereign; *n* suzerain.

suzeraineté [syzrɛnte] *nf* suzerainty.

svelte [svɛlt] *a* slim, slender, slight.

sveltesse [svɛltɛs] *nf* slimness, slenderness.

sycomore [sikɔmɔ:r] *nm* sycamore.

syllabe [sillab] *nf* syllable.

sylphe [silf] *nm* sylph.

sylphide [silfid] *nf* sylph.

sylvestre [silvɛstr] *a* woodland, sylvan.

sylviculture [silvikylty:r] *nf* forestry.

symbole [sɛ̃bɔl] *nm* symbol, sign.

symbolique [sɛ̃bɔlik] *a* symbolic(al).

symboliser [sɛ̃bɔlize] *vt* to symbolize.

symétrie [simetri] *nf* symmetry.

symétrique [simetrik] *a* symmetrical.

sympathie [sɛ̃pati] *nf* liking, sympathy; **avoir de la — pour qn** to like s.o.

sympathique [sɛ̃patik] *a* likable, congenial, sympathetic; **encre — invisible ink.**

sympathiser [sɛ̃patize] *vi* to sympathize, have a fellow feeling (for **avec**).

symphonie [sɛ̃fɔni] *nf* symphony, orchestra.

symphonique [sɛ̃fɔnik] *a* symphonic.

symptomatique [sɛ̃ptɔmatik] *a* symptomatic.

symptôme [sɛ̃pto:m] *nm* symptom, sign.

synagogue [sinagɔg] *nf* synagogue.

synchroniser [sɛ̃krɔnize] *vt* to synchronize.

synchronisme [sɛ̃krɔnism] *nm* synchronism.

syncope [sɛ̃kɔp] *nf* faint, syncope.

syncoper [sɛ̃kɔpe] *vt* to syncopate.

syndic [sɛ̃dik] *nm* syndic, assignee, trustee.

syndical [sɛ̃dikal] *a* syndical, trade union.

syndicalisme [sɛ̃dikalism] *nm* trade unionism.

syndicaliste [sɛ̃dikalist] *nm* trade unionist.

syndicat [sɛ̃dika] *nm* syndicate, trusteeship, trade union, federation.
syndiquer [sɛ̃dike] *vt* to syndicate, unite in a trade union; *vr* to form a trade union, combine.
synonyme [sinɔnim] *a* synonymous; *nm* synonym.
syntaxe [sɛ̃taks] *nf* syntax.
synthèse [sɛ̃tɛːz] *nf* synthesis.
synthétique [sɛ̃tetik] *a* synthetic.
synthétiser [sɛ̃tetize] *vt* to synthesize
Syrie [siri] *nf* Syria.
systématique [sistematik] *a* systematic, stereotyped, hidebound.
systématiser [sistematize] *vt* to systematize.
système [sistɛm] *nm* system, type; **esprit de** — hidebound mentality, unimaginativeness; **employer le** — **D** (*fam*) to wangle it.

T

ta [ta] *see* **ton**.
tabac [taba] *nm* tobacco; — **à priser** snuff.
tabagie [tabaʒi] *nf* place smelling (full) of tobacco-smoke, smoking room.
tabatière [tabatjɛːr] *nf* snuff-box.
tabernacle [tabɛrnakl] *nm* tabernacle.
table [tabl] *nf* table, board, slab; **mettre la** — to set the table.
tableau [tablo] *nm* board, picture, scene, panel, roster; — **de bord** dashboard.
tabler [table] *vi* to reckon, count (on **sur**).
tablette [tablɛt] *nf* tablet, cake, slab, shelf, notebook; **inscrire sur ses** —**s** to make a note of.
tabletterie [tablɛtri] *nf* fancy-goods (industry).
tablier [tablie] *nm* apron, pinafore, footplate, floor (of bridge), dashboard.
tabouret [taburɛ] *nm* stool.
tac au tac [takotak] *ad* tit for tat.
tache [taʃ] *nf* spot, stain, blot.
tâche [taːʃ] *nf* task, job; **travail à la** — piecework, jobbing; **prendre à** — **de** to make a point of.
tacher [taʃe] *vt* to stain, spot; *vr* to stain (one's clothes).
tâcher [taʃe] *vi* to try.
tâcheron [taʃrɔ̃] *nm* pieceworker, jobber.
tacheter [taʃte] *vt* to speckle, mottle, fleck.
tacite [tasit] *a* tacit, understood.
taciturne [tasityrn] *a* taciturn, silent.
taciturnité [tasityrnite] *nf* taciturnity.
tacot [tako] *nm* ramshackle automobile, jalopy.

tact [takt] *nm* touch, feel, tact.
tacticien [taktisjɛ̃] *nm* tactician.
tactile [taktil] *a* tactile.
tactique [taktik] *a* tactical; *nf* tactics.
taffetas [tafta] *nm* taffeta.
taie [tɛ] *nf* pillowcase.
taillade [tajad] *nf* slash, gash, cut.
taillant [tajɑ̃] *nm* (cutting) edge.
taille [taːj] *nf* cut(ting), hewing, clipping, figure, waist, height, tax; **être de** — **à** to be fit to.
tailler [taje] *vt* to cut (out), hew, clip, carve, sharpen.
tailleur, -euse [tajœːr, øːz] *n* cutter, hewer, tailor(ess); *nm* (woman's) costume, suit.
taillis [taji] *nm* copse, brushwood.
tain [tɛ̃] *nm* silvering, foil.
taire [tɛːr] *vt* to say nothing about, keep dark; *vr* to be silent, hold one's tongue.
talent [talɑ̃] *nm* talent, gift, ability.
taloche [talɔʃ] *nf* cuff, (builder's) mortar-board.
talon [talɔ̃] *nm* heel, counterfoil, beading, flange, butt; **marcher sur les** —**s de qn** to follow close on s.o.'s heels, close behind s.o.
talonner [talɔne] *vt* to follow, dog, spur on, dun, heel.
talus [taly] *nm* slope, bank, ramp.
tambour [tɑ̃buːr] *nm* drum, drummer, barrel, spool, revolving door; — **de ville** town crier.
tambourin [tɑ̃burɛ̃] *nm* tambourine, tabor.
tambouriner [tɑ̃burine] *vi* to drum, knock.
tambour-major [tɑ̃burmaʒɔːr] *nm* drum-major.
tamis [tami] *nm* sifter, sieve, riddle.
tamiser [tamize] *vt* to sift, strain, filter, screen; *vi* to filter through.
tampon [tɑ̃pɔ̃] *nm* stopper, bung, plug, buffer, pad, stamp.
tamponnement [tɑ̃pɔnmɑ̃] *nm* collision, plugging.
tamponner [tɑ̃pɔne] *vt* to plug, dab, pad, collide with.
tam-tam [tamtam] *nm* African drum, dance.
tancer [tɑ̃se] *vt* to scold, chide.
tandis que [tɑ̃di(s)kə] *cj* while, whereas.
tangage [tɑ̃gaʒ] *nm* pitching.
tangent [tɑ̃ʒɑ̃] *a* tangent.
tangible [tɑ̃ʒibl] *a* tangible.
tanguer [tɑ̃ge] *vi* to pitch.
tanière [tanjɛːr] *nf* lair, den, hole.
tanin [tanɛ̃] *nm* tannin.
tanner [tane] *vt* to tan.
tannerie [tanri] *nf* tannery.
tanneur [tanœːr] *nm* tanner.
tant [tɑ̃] *ad* so much, so many, as much, so; — **que** as much as, as long as; **si** — **est que** if it is true that, if it is the case that; — **soit peu** somewhat, ever so little; **en** — **que** in so far as, as; — **pis** so much

the worse, can't be helped, too bad.
tante [tãːt] *nf* aunt.
tantième [tãtjɛm] *nm* percentage, quota.
tantinet [tãtinɛ] *nm* tiny bit, spot.
tantôt [tãto] *ad* presently, soon, a little while ago; **tantôt ... tantôt ...** now ... now; **à —!** see you later!
taon [tã] *nm* horse-fly.
tapage [tapaːʒ] *nm* din, row.
tapageur, -euse [tapaʒœːr, øːz] *a* rowdy, noisy, showy, flashy.
tape [tap] *nf* stopper, tap, pat, slap.
tape-à-l'œil [tapalœːj] *nm* flashy article; *a* flashy.
tapecul [tapky] *nm* pillion-seat, jalopy.
taper [tape] *vt* to tap, pat, hit, touch, type; **— dans l'œil à qn** to catch, fill s.o.'s eye; **— sur qn** to slate s.o.; (*fam*) **ça tape** it's hot.
tapinois [tapinwa] *ad* **en —** on the sly, slyly.
se tapir [sətapiːr] *vr* to crouch, cower, squat, take cover.
tapis [tapi] *nm* carpet, cloth, cover; **mettre qch sur le —** to bring sth up for discussion; **— roulant** conveyer belt, moving sidewalk.
tapisser [tapise] *vt* to paper, line, cover.
tapisserie [tapisri] *nf* tapestry (making), wallpaper; **faire —** to be a wallflower.
tapissier, -ière [tapisje, jɛːr] *n* tapestry-worker, upholsterer.
tapoter [tapɔte] *vt* to tap, strum.
taquin [takɛ̃] *a* teasing; *n* tease.
taquiner [takine] *vt* to tease.
taquinerie [takinri] *nf* teasing.
tarabiscoté [tarabiskɔte] *a* ornate, grooved.
tard [taːr] *ad* late; **sur le —** late in the day, late in life; **tôt ou —** sooner or later.
tarder [tarde] *vi* to delay, loiter, be long (in **à**); **il leur tarde de vous revoir** they are longing to see you.
tardif, -ive [tardif, iːv] *a* late, backward, belated, tardy, slow.
tare [taːr] *nf* blemish, defect, depreciation, tare.
tarer [tare] *vt* to damage, blemish, spoil.
se targuer [sətarge] *vr* to pride oneself (on **de**).
tarière [tarjɛːr] *nf* auger, drill.
tarif [tarif] *nm* tariff, price list, fare.
tarifer [tarife] *vt* to price.
tarir [tariːr] *vti* to dry up.
tarte [tart] *nf* tart.
tartine [tartin] *nf* slice of bread and butter, long story, rigmarole.
tartre [tartr] *nm* tartar, fur, scale.
tartufe [tartyf] *nm* hypocrite, impostor.
tas [tɑ] *nm* heap, pile, pack, lot(s); **grève sur le —** sit-down strike.
tasse [tɑːs] *nf* cup.
tassé [tɑse] *a* full, heaped, squat.

tasser [tɑse] *vt* to squeeze, pack, cram; *vr* to crowd together, squeeze up, settle.
tâter [tate] *vt* to feel, taste, try; *vr* to hesitate.
tatillonner [tatijɔne] *vi* to interfere, meddle, fuss, be fussy.
tâtonner [tatɔne] *vi* to feel one's way, grope (about).
tâtons (à) [tatɔ̃] *ad* groping(ly), warily.
tatouer [tatwe] *vt* to tattoo.
taudis [todi] *nm* hovel; *pl* slums.
taupe [toːp] *nf* mole(skin).
taupinière [topinjɛːr] *nf* molehill.
taureau [tɔro] *nm* bull.
tautologie [tɔtɔlɔʒi] *nf* tautology.
taux [to] *nm* rate, scale.
taverne [tavɛrn] *nf* tavern, public house.
taxe [taks] *nf* tax, duty, rate, charge.
taxer [takse] *vt* to tax, charge, fix the price of, accuse.
taxi [taksi] *nm* taxi.
Tchécoslovaquie [tʃɛkɔslɔvaki] *nf* Czechoslovakia.
tchèque [tʃɛk] *an* Czech.
te [t(ə)] *pn* you, to you, yourself, thee, to thee, thyself.
technicien [tɛknisjɛ̃] *nm* technician.
technique [tɛknik] *a* technical; *nf* technique, technics, engineering.
technologie [tɛknɔlɔʒi] *nf* technology.
technologique [tɛknɔlɔʒik] *a* technological.
teigne [tɛɲ] *nf* moth, scurf, ringworm, vixen.
teigneux, -euse [tɛɲø, øːz] *a* scurfy.
teindre [tɛ̃ːdr] *vt* to dye, tinge, stain; *vr* to be tinged, dye one's hair.
teint [tɛ̃] *nm* dye, color, complexion.
teinte [tɛ̃ːt] *nf* shade, hue, tint, tinge, touch.
teinter [tɛ̃te] *vt* to tint, tinge.
teinture [tɛ̃tyːr] *nf* dye(ing), tinting, hue, tincture, smattering.
teinturier, -ière [tɛ̃tyrje, jɛːr] *n* dyer.
tek [tɛk] *nm* teak.
tel, telle [tɛl] *a* such, like; *pn* such a one; **— que** such as, like; **— quel** as it (she, he) is, ordinary; **monsieur un —** Mr So-and-so.
télécinéma [telesinema] *nm* televised movie.
télécommander [telekɔmɑ̃de] *vt* to operate by remote control.
télégramme [telegram] *nm* telegram.
télégraphe [telegraf] *nm* telegraph.
télégraphie [telegrafi] *nf* telegraphy; **— sans fil** radiotelegraphy.
télégraphier [telegrafje] *vti* to telegraph, cable, wire.
téléguider [telegide] *vt* to radiocontrol.
télépathie [telepati] *nf* telepathy.
téléphérique [teleferik] *a nm* cable railway.

téléphone [telefɔn] nm (tele)phone.
téléphoner [telefɔne] vti to (tele)
phone, ring up.
téléphonique [telefɔnik] a tele-
phonic; **cabine** — telephone booth.
téléphoniste[telefɔnist] n telephone
operator.
télescope [teleskɔp] nm telescope.
télescoper [teleskɔpe] vti to telescope, crumple up.
télésiège [telesjɛːʒ] nm chair-lift.
télévision [televizjɔ̃] nf television.
tellement [tɛlmɑ̃] ad so, in such a
way.
téméraire [temɛrɛːr] a rash, reckless,
bold.
témérité [temerite] nf rashness,
temerity, rash act.
témoignage [temwaɲaːʒ] nm
evidence, testimony, token, mark.
témoigner [temwaɲe] vt to show,
display, prove, testify to; vi to give
evidence.
témoin [temwɛ̃] nm witness, second,
baton.
tempe [tɑ̃ːp] nf temple.
tempérament [tɑ̃peramɑ̃] nm constitution, nature; **vente à** — hire-
purchase.
tempérance [tɑ̃perɑ̃ːs] nf moderation.
tempérant [tɑ̃perɑ̃] a temperate,
moderate.
température [tɑ̃peratyːr] nf temperature.
tempéré [tɑ̃pere] a moderate,
temperate.
tempérer [tɑ̃pere] vt to moderate,
temper; vr to moderate, abate.
tempête [tɑ̃pɛːt] nf storm.
tempêter [tɑ̃pɛte] vi to storm, rage.
tempétueux, -euse [tɑ̃petɥø, øːz] a
stormy.
temple [tɑ̃ːpl] nm temple, (Protestant) church.
temporaire [tɑ̃pɔrɛːr] a provisional,
temporary.
temporel, -elle [tɑ̃pɔrɛl] a temporal.
temporiser [tɑ̃pɔrize] vi to temporize, procrastinate.
temps [tɑ̃] nm time, period, age,
weather, tense; **à** — in time; **de
tout** — at all times; **quel** — **fait-il?**
what is the weather like?
tenable [tənabl] a tenable, bearable.
tenace [tənas] a tenacious, adhesive,
retentive, rooted.
ténacité [tenasite] nf tenacity, ad-
hesiveness, retentiveness.
tenaille [tənɑːj] nf tongs; pl pincers.
tenancier, -ière [tənɑ̃sje, jɛːr] n
keeper, lessee, tenant.
tenant [tənɑ̃] a **séance** —**e** forthwith;
—**s et aboutissants** adjoining
properties, ins and outs; **d'un seul**
— in one piece.
tendance [tɑ̃dɑ̃ːs] nf tendency,
trend.
tendancieux, -euse [tɑ̃dɑ̃sjø, øːz] a
tendentious.

tendre [tɑ̃ːdr] vt to stretch (out),
strain, hang, set, tighten, spread,
hold out; vi to lead, tend; vr to
become tight, strained, taut, tense.
tendre [tɑ̃ːdr] a tender, delicate,
loving.
tendresse [tɑ̃drɛs] nf tenderness,
love.
ténèbres [tenɛːbr] nf pl darkness.
ténébreux, -euse [tenebrø, øːz] a
dark, sinister.
teneur [tənœːr, øːz] n holder,
keeper, taker; nf tenor, purport,
content.
ténia [tenja] nm tapeworm.
tenir [təniːr] vt to hold, keep, run,
occupy, contain; vi to hold, stick,
stand, last; vr to stand, sit, remain,
stay, contain oneself, behave oneself; — **à** to be close to, be the
result of; **s'il ne tient qu'à cela** if
that is all; **qu'à cela ne tienne**
never mind that; **je n'y tiens plus**
I can't stand it any longer; — **de**
to have sth of, take after, get from;
— **pour** to consider as, be in favor
of; **tiens, tiens**, well, well! indeed!
tiens, tenez (look) here; **on tient
quatre dans cette voiture** this car
holds four; **se** — **à** to keep to, hold
on to; **s'en** — **à** to abide by, be
content with.
tennis [tɛnis] nm tennis (court).
ténor [tenɔːr] nm tenor.
tension [tɑ̃sjɔ̃] nf tension, pressure,
stretching.
tentacule [tɑ̃takyl] nm feeler,
tentacle.
tentateur, -trice [tɑ̃tatœːr, tris] a
tempting; n tempter, temptress.
tentation [tɑ̃tasjɔ̃] nf temptation.
tentative [tɑ̃tatiːv] nf attempt.
tente [tɑ̃ːt] nf tent, canvas, awning.
tenter [tɑ̃te] vt to tempt, try.
tenture [tɑ̃tyːr] nf tapestry, hang-
ings, wallpaper.
tenu [təny] a kept, bound.
ténu [teny] a fine, tenuous, slender,
subtle.
tenue [təny] nf holding, sitting,
upkeep, behavior, dress, seat;
avoir de la — to behave oneself;
en grande — in full dress.
ténuité [tenɥite] nf fineness, slenderness, tenuousness.
térébenthine [terebɑ̃tin] nf turpentine.
tergiverser [tɛrʒivɛrse] vi to beg the
question, hesitate.
terme [tɛrm] nm term, expression,
end, limit, quarter; **mener qch à
bon** — to carry sth through.
terminaison [tɛrminɛzɔ̃] nf termination, ending.
terminer [tɛrmine] vtr to terminate,
finish, end.
terminologie [tɛrminɔlɔʒi] nf term-
inology.
terminus [tɛrminyːs] nm terminus.
terne [tɛrn] a dull, lifeless, flat.

ternir [tɛrniːr] *vt* to tarnish, dim, dull; *vr* to become dim, dull.
terrain [tɛrɛ̃] *nm* land, (piece of) ground, course.
terrasse [tɛras] *nf* terrace, bank.
terrassement [tɛrasmɑ̃] *nm* digging, banking, earthwork.
terrasser [tɛrase] *vt* to bank up, lay low, fell.
terrassier [tɛrasje] *nm* digger.
terre [tɛːr] *nf* earth, world, land, soil, estate; **par — on the ground, on the floor; descendre à — to go ashore; — à — commonplace.
Terre-Neuve [tɛrnœːv] *nf* Newfoundland; *nm* -dog.
terre-neuvien, -enne [tɛrnœvjɛ̃, jɛn] *a* Newfoundland; *n* Newfoundlander; *nm* fisherman, boat that goes to fishing grounds off Newfoundland.
terrestre [tɛrɛstr] *a* terrestrial, earthly.
terreur [tɛrœːr] *nf* terror, dread.
terrible [tɛribl] *a* terrible, dreadful.
terrien, -enne [tɛrjɛ̃, jɛn] *a* landed; landowner, landsman.
terrier [tɛrje] *nm* hole, burrow, terrier.
terrifier [tɛr(r)ifje] *vt* to terrify.
terrine [tɛrin] *nf* earthenware pot, pan, potted meat.
territoire [tɛritwaːr] *nm* territory.
territorial [tɛritɔrjal] *a* territorial.
terroir [tɛrwaːr] *nm* soil.
terroriser [tɛr(r)ɔrize] *vt* to terrorize.
tertre [tɛrtr] *nm* mound, hillock.
tes [te] *see* **ton.**
tesson [tɛsɔ̃] *nm* fragment, broken end.
testament [tɛstamɑ̃] *nm* testament, will.
testateur, -trice [tɛstatœːr, tris] *n* testator, testatrix.
testicule [tɛstikyl] *nm* testicle.
tétanos [tetanɔs] *nm* lockjaw, tetanus.
têtard [tɛtaːr] *nm* tadpole.
tête [tɛːt] *nf* head, face, top, front; **calcul de — mental arithmetic; mauvaise — unruly person; femme de — capable woman; forte — self-willed person; faire une — to pull a long face; en faire à sa — to have one's own way; monter la — à qn to rouse s.o., work s.o. up.
tête-à-queue [tɛtakø] *nm* **faire — to swing right around.
tête-à-tête [tɛtatɛːt] *nm* private conversation, tête-à-tête..
tête-bêche [tɛtbɛʃ] *ad* head to foot, head to tail.
tétée [tete] *nf* suck.
téter [tete] *vt* to suck.
têtière [tɛtjɛːr] *nf* baby's cap, headstall (*of harness*).
tétin [tetɛ̃] *nm* nipple, dug.
tétine [tetin] *nf* udder, dug, (rubber) teat.
téton [tetɔ̃] *nm* breast.

têtu [tety] *a* obstinate, stubborn.
teuton, -onne [tøtɔ̃, ɔn] *a* Teuton(ic); *n* Teuton.
teutonique [tøtɔnik] *a* Teutonic.
texte [tɛkst] *nm* text.
textile [tɛkstil] *a nm* textile.
textuel, -elle [tɛkstɥɛl] *a* textual.
texture [tɛkstyːr] *nf* texture.
thé [te] *nm* tea, tea-party.
théâtral [teatral] *a* theatrical.
théâtre [teaːtr] *nm* theater, stage, drama, scene.
théière [tejɛːr] *nf* teapot.
thème [tɛm] *nm* theme, topic, prose composition.
théologie [teɔlɔʒi] *nf* theology, divinity.
théologique [teɔlɔʒik] *a* theological.
théorème [teɔrɛm] *nm* theorem.
théoricien, -enne [teɔrisjɛ̃, jɛn] *n* theorist.
théorie [teɔri] *nf* theory.
théorique [teɔrik] *a* theoretical.
théoriser [teɔrize] *vti* to theorize.
thermal [tɛrmal] *a* thermal; **station —e** spa; **eaux —es** hot springs.
thermomètre [tɛrmɔmɛtr] *nm* thermometer.
thésauriser [tezɔrize] *vt* to hoard.
thèse [tɛːz] *nf* thesis, argument.
Thierry [tjɛri] *n pr* Theodore.
thon [tɔ̃] *nm* tuna fish.
thorax [tɔraks] *nm* thorax, chest.
thuriféraire [tyrifeɛːr] *nm* incense-bearer, flatterer.
thym [tɛ̃] *nm* thyme.
tibia [tibja] *nm* shin-bone, tibia.
tic [tik] *nm* twitching, mannerism.
ticket [tikɛ] *nm* ticket, check, slip.
tic-tac [tiktak] *nm* tick-tock, ticking, pit-a-pat.
tiède [tjed] *a* lukewarm, tepid.
tiédeur [tjedœːr] *nf* lukewarmness, tepidity, half-heartedness, coolness.
tiédir [tjediːr] *vt* to make tepid, cool; *vi* to become tepid, cool down, off.
tien, tienne [tjɛ̃, tjɛn] *poss pn* le(s) —(s), la tienne, les tiennes yours, thine; *nm* your own; *pl* your own people.
tierce [tjɛrs] *nf* tierce, third.
tiercé [tjɛrse] *nm* betting (*on horses*).
tiers, tierce [tjɛːr, tjɛrs] *a* third; *nm* third (part), third person, -party.
tige [tiːʒ] *nf* stalk, stem, trunk, shank, shaft.
tignasse [tiɲas] *nf* mop, shock.
tigre, tigresse [tigr, tigrɛs] *n* tiger, tigress.
tilleul [tijœl] *nm* lime-tree, infusion of lime-flowers.
timbale [tɛ̃bal] *nf* kettledrum, metal drinking mug, raised piedish.
timbre [tɛ̃ːbr] *nm* stamp, stamp-duty, bell, timbre.
timbré [tɛ̃bre] *a* stamped, postmarked, sonorous, (*fam*) crazy, cracked.
timbre-poste [tɛ̃brəpɔst] *nm* postage-stamp.

timbre-quittance [tɛ̃brəkitɑ̃:s] *nm* receipt-stamp.
timbrer [tɛ̃bre] *vt* to stamp.
timide [timid] *a* timid, coy, shy, diffident.
timidité [timidite] *nf* timidity, shyness, diffidence.
timon [timɔ̃] *nm* shaft, pole, helm.
timonerie [timɔnri] *nf* steering (-gear), signaling.
timonier [timɔnje] *nm* helmsman, signalman.
timoré [timɔre] *a* timorous, fearful.
tintamarre [tɛ̃tama:r] *nm* noise, racket, din.
tinter [tɛ̃te] *vti* to toll, ring; *vi* to clink, jingle, tinkle, tingle.
tir [ti:r] *nm* shooting, gunnery, firing, rifle-range, shooting-gallery.
tirade [tirad] *nf* (long) speech, tirade.
tirage [tira:ʒ] *nm* pulling, hauling, draft, drawing, printing, circulation.
tiraillement [tirajmɑ̃] *nm* pulling, tugging, friction, pang, **twinge**.
tirailler [tiraje] *vt* to pull about, tug; *vi* to fire away.
tirailleur [tirajœ:r] *nm* sharpshooter, freelance.
tirant [tirɑ̃] *nm* purse-string, stay, ship's draft; — **d'air** headroom.
tire [ti:r] *nf* pull; **voleur à la —** pickpocket.
tiré [tire] *a* drawn, pinched.
tire-bouchon [tirbuʃɔ̃] *nm* corkscrew.
tire-bouchonner [tirbuʃɔne] *vi* to curl up, wrinkle; *vt* to screw up.
tire-bouton [tirbutɔ̃] *nm* buttonhook.
tire-d'aile [tirdɛl] *ad* **à —** swiftly.
tire-larigot [tirlarigo] *ad* **boire à —** to drink heavily.
tirelire [tirli:r] *nm* money-box.
tirer [tire] *vt* to haul, draw, tug, pull off, out, fire, shoot, let off, print; *vi* to tug, pull, incline, verge (on **sur**); *vr* to extricate o.s., get out; **se — d'affaire, s'en —** to get out of trouble, manage.
tiret [tirɛ] *nm* dash, hyphen.
tireur, -euse [tirœ:r, ø:z] *n* drawer, marksman, shot.
tiroir [tirwa:r] *nm* drawer, slide (-valve).
tisane [tizan] *nf* infusion.
tison [tizɔ̃] *nm* brand, half-burned log.
tisonner [tizɔne] *vt* to poke, stir, fan.
tisonnier [tizɔnje] *nm* poker.
tisser [tise] *vt* to weave.
tisserand [tisrɑ̃] *n* weaver.
tissu [tisy] *nm* cloth, fabric, tissue.
titre [ti:tr] *nm* title, heading, qualification, right, claim, title-deed, diploma, bond; *pl* securities; **en —** titular; **à — d'office** ex officio; **à quel —?** on what grounds? **à — gratuit** free of charge.

titré [titre] *a* titled, certificated.
titrer [titre] *vt* to give a title to.
tituber [titybe] *vi* to stagger, reel.
titulaire [titylɛ:r] *a* titular; *n* holder.
toaster [toste] *vt* to toast.
toc [tɔk] *nm* faked stuff, imitation, rap, knock.
tocsin [tɔksɛ̃] *nm* alarm-signal, tocsin.
tohu-bohu [tɔybɔy] *nm* hubbub, hurly-burly.
toi [twa] *pn* you, thou, thee.
toile [twal] *nf* linen, cloth, canvas, painting; — **cirée** oilcloth, oilskin; — **d'araignée** spider's web, cobweb; — **de fond** back-cloth, -drop.
toilette [twalɛt] *nf* toilet, dress(ing), dressing-table, wash-stand, lavatory.
toise [twa:z] *nf* fathom, measuring apparatus.
toiser [twaze] *vt* to measure, look (s.o.) up and down.
toison [twazɔ̃] *nf* fleece.
toit [twa] *nm* roof, home.
toiture [twaty:r] *nf* roof(ing).
tôle [to:l] *nf* sheet-iron.
tolérance [tɔlerɑ̃:s] *nf* tolerance, toleration, allowance.
tolérer [tɔlere] *vt* to tolerate, suffer.
tolet [tɔlɛ] *nm* oarlock.
tollé [tɔlle] *nm* outcry; **crier — contre** to raise a hue and cry after.
tomate [tɔmat] *nf* tomato.
tombe [tɔ̃:b] *nf* tomb, grave, tombstone.
tombeau [tɔ̃bo] *nm* tomb, tombstone.
tombée [tɔ̃be] *nf* fall.
tomber [tɔ̃be] *vi* to fall, drop, die down, hang; *vt* to throw, take off; — **sur** to come across, fall upon; — **juste** to arrive, (happen), at the right time, guess right; **laisser —** to drop.
tombereau [tɔ̃bro] *nm* dump cart, tumbrel.
tombola [tɔ̃bɔla] *nf* tombola.
tome [tɔ:m] *nm* volume, tome.
ton, ta, tes [tɔ̃, ta, te] *a* your, thy.
ton [tɔ̃] *nm* tone, color, key, pitch, fashion; **le bon —** good form.
tonalité [tɔnalite] *nf* tonality.
tondeuse [tɔ̃dø:z] *nf* shears, lawnmower.
tondre [tɔ̃:dr] *vt* to clip, shear, mow, fleece.
tonifier [tɔnifje] *vt* to tone up, brace.
tonique [tɔnik] *a nm* tonic; *a* bracing.
tonitruant [tɔnitryɑ̃] *a* thunderous, blustering.
tonne [tɔn] *nf* tun, cask, ton.
tonneau [tɔno] *nm* barrel, cask, ton.
tonnelier [tɔnəlje] *nm* cooper.
tonnelle [tɔnɛl] *nf* arbor, bower.
tonnellerie [tɔnɛlri] *nf* cooper's shop, cooperage.
tonner [tɔne] *vi* to thunder.

tonnerre [tɔnɛːr] *nm* thunder; **du —** marvelous, terrific.
tonsure [tɔ̃syːr] *nf* tonsure.
tonte [tɔ̃ːt] *nf* clipping, shearing.
topaze [tɔpɑːz] *nf* topaz.
toper [tɔpe] *vi* to agree, shake hands on it; **tope-là!** done!
topinambour [tɔpinăbuːr] *nm* Jerusalem artichoke.
topo [tɔpo] *nm* lecture, demonstration, plan.
topographie [tɔpɔgrafi] *nf* topography, surveying.
topographique [tɔpɔgrafik] *a* topographic(al), ordnance.
toquade [tɔkad] *nf* craze, fancy.
toque [tɔk] *nf* toque, cap.
toqué [tɔke] *a* cracked, crazy, infatuated.
toquer [tɔke] *vt* to infatuate; *vr* to become infatuated (with **de**).
torche [tɔrʃ] *nf* torch pad.
torchon [tɔrʃɔ̃] *nm* duster, dishcloth, floor-cloth.
tordant [tɔrdă] *a* screamingly funny.
tordre [tɔrdr] *vt* to twist, wring, distort; *vr* to twist, writhe; **se — de rire** to split one's sides with laughter.
tornade [tɔrnad] *nf* tornado.
torpédo [tɔrpedo] *nm* open touring-car.
torpeur [tɔrpœːr] *nf* torpor.
torpille [tɔrpiːj] *nf* torpedo.
torpiller [tɔrpije] *vt* to torpedo.
torréfier [tɔrrefje] *vt* to roast, scorch.
torrent [tɔr(r)ă] *nm* torrent, stream.
torrentiel, -elle [tor(r)ăsjɛl] *a* torrential.
torride [tɔrrid] *a* torrid, broiling.
tors [tɔːr] *a* twisted, crooked.
torse [tɔrs] *nm* torso.
torsion [tɔrsjɔ̃] *nf* twist(ing), torsion.
tort [tɔːr] *nm* wrong, fault, harm, injury, injustice; **avoir —** to be wrong; **donner — à** to decide against; **à — et à travers** at random.
torticolis [tɔrtikɔli] *nm* stiff neck.
tortillard [tɔrtijaːr] *nm* small locomotive, railway.
tortiller [tɔrtije] *vt* to twist, twirl; *vi* to wriggle, shilly-shally; *vr* to wriggle.
tortue [tɔrty] *nf* tortoise.
tortueux, -euse [tɔrtɥø, øːz] *a* tortuous, winding.
torture [tɔrtyːr] *nf* torture, torment.
torturer [tɔrtyre] *vt* to torture, rack, twist.
tôt [to] *ad* soon, early; **— ou tard** sooner or later.
total [tɔtal] *a nm* total, whole.
totalisateur, -trice [tɔtalizatœːr, tris] *a* adding; *nm* pari-mutuel.
totaliser [tɔtalize] *vt* to total up.
totalitaire [tɔtalitɛːr] *a* totalitarian.
totalité [tɔtalite] *nf* totality, whole.
touchant [tuʃ ̆ă] *a* touching, moving; *prep* with regard to, concerning.

touche [tuʃ] *nf* touch, manner, key, bite, hit, look.
touche-à-tout [tuʃatu] *n* meddler.
toucher [tuʃe] *vt* to touch (on), hit, draw, cash, move, concern; *vi* **— à** to be close to, be in contact with, affect, meddle; *vr* to adjoin; *nm* touch, feel.
touer [twe] *vt* to tow, warp.
touffe [tuf] *nf* tuft, cluster, clump.
touffu [tufy] *a* thick, bushy, involved, intricate.
toujours [tuʒuːr] *ad* always, ever, still, all the same.
toupet [tupɛ] *nm* forelock, tuft, cheek.
toupie [tupi] *nf* top.
tour [tuːr] *nf* tower; *nm* turn, course, shape, revolution, round, circuit, feat, trick, stroll; **— à —** in turn; **à — de bras** with all one's might; **mon sang n'a fait qu'un —** it gave me an awful shock.
tourangeau, -elle [turăʒo, ɛl] *an* (inhabitant) of Touraine.
tourbe [turb] *nf* peat, rabble.
tourbière [turbjɛːr] *nf* peat-bog.
tourbillon [turbijɔ̃] *nm* whirlwind, -pool, eddy, whirl, giddy round.
tourbillonner [turbijɔne] *vi* to whirl, swirl, eddy.
tourelle [turɛl] *nf* turret.
tourisme [turism] *nm* touring, travel.
touriste [turist] *n* tourist, traveler.
tourment [turmă] *nm* torment, anguish.
tourmente [turmăːt] *nf* gale, turmoil.
tourmenter [turmăte] *vt* to torment, torture, worry, pester, tease, fiddle with; *vr* to worry, fret.
tournant [turnă] *nm* bend, corner, turning-point.
tournebroche [turnəbrɔʃ] *nm* roasting spit, turnspit.
tournedos [turnədo] *nm* filet steak.
tourné [turne] *a* turned, sour; **bien —** shapely, neat.
tournée [turne] *nf* circuit, round, tour.
tourner [turne] *vt* to turn, wind, dodge, get round; *vi* to turn (out), revolve, result, curdle; *vr* to turn; **— un film** to make a film, act in a film; **— autour du pot** to beat about the bush.
tournesol [turnəsɔl] *nm* sunflower.
tournevis [turnəvis] *nm* screwdriver.
tourniquet [turnikɛ] *nm* turnstile, tourniquet.
tournoi [turnwa] *nm* tournament.
tournoyer [turnwaje] *vi* to whirl, wheel, swirl.
tournure [turnyːr] *nf* shape, figure, turn, course bustle.
tourte [turt] *nf* pie, tart.
tourterelle [turtərɛl] *nf* turtle dove.
Toussaint [tusɛ̃] *nf* **la —** All Saints' day.
tousser [tuse] *vi* to cough.

tout [tu] *a* all, whole, every, any; *pr* everything, all, anything; *nm* whole, all, main thing; *ad* very, completely, entirely, quite, right, however, while; **pas du** — not at all; — **à vous** yours truly; — **au plus** at the very most; — **à fait** quite, entirely; — **fait** ready made.

toutefois [tutfwa] *ad* yet, however, nevertheless.

toutou [tutu] *nm* doggie.

tout-puissant [tupɥisã] *a* omnipotent, all-powerful.

toux [tu] *nf* cough.

toxique [tɔksik] *a* toxic, poisonous.

trac [trak] *nm* funk, stage-fright.

tracas [trakɑ] *nm* worry, bother.

tracasser [trakase] *vtr* to bother, worry.

tracasserie [trakasri] *nf* worry, fuss.

tracassier, -ière [trakasje, jɛːr] *a* meddlesome, fussy.

trace [tras] *nf* trace, track, trail, mark.

tracé [trase] *nm* outline, graph, lay-out, tracing, marking out, plotting.

tracer [trase] *vt* to outline, draw, sketch, plot, lay-out, mark out.

tractation [traktasjɔ̃] *nf* underhand deal(ing).

tracteur [traktœːr] *nm* tractor.

traction [traksjɔ̃] *nf* traction, pulling; — **avant** front-wheel drive (*car*).

tradition [tradisjɔ̃] *nf* tradition.

traditionnel, -elle [tradisjɔnɛl] *a* traditional.

traducteur, -trice [tradyktœːr, tris] *n* translator.

traduction [tradyksjɔ̃] *nf* translation, translating.

traduire [tradɥiːr] *vt* to translate, express; — **en justice** to prosecute.

trafic [trafik] *nm* traffic, trade, trading.

trafiquant [trafikã] *nm* trafficker, black-marketeer.

trafiquer [trafike] *vi* to trade, deal, traffic.

tragédie [traʒedi] *nf* tragedy.

tragique [traʒik] *a* tragic; *nm* tragic element, poet.

trahir [traiːr] *vt* to betray, give away, reveal.

trahison [traizɔ̃] *nf* betrayal, treachery, treason.

train [trɛ̃] *nm* train, line, string, suite, mood, movement, pace; **à fond de** — at full speed; **être en** — **de** to be busy, engaged in; **être en** — to be in the mood, in good form; **mener grand** — to live in great style; **mettre en** — to set going.

traînant [trɛnã] *a* dragging, drawling, listless.

traînard [trɛnaːr] *nm* laggard, straggler.

traîne [trɛːn] *nf* drag-net, train (*dress*); **à la** — in tow, behind.

traîneau [trɛno] *nm* sleigh, sled.

traînée [trɛne] *nf* trail, train.

traîner [trɛne] *vt* to drag (out, on), trail, haul, drawl; *vi* to trail, straggle, lag (behind), lie about, drag (on); *vr* to crawl, shuffle along.

train-train [trɛ̃trɛ̃] *nm* routine; **aller son** — to jog along.

traire [trɛːr] *vt* to milk.

trait [trɛ] *nm* dart, shaft, gibe, feature, characteristic, stroke; — **d'union** hyphen; **d'un** — at one gulp, go; **avoir** — **à** to refer to; **cheval de** — draft horse.

traitable [trɛtabl] *a* tractable, docile.

traite [trɛt] *nf* trade, slave-trade, draft, stage, stretch, milking; **d'une** — at a stretch.

traité [trɛte] *nm* treaty, treatise.

traitement [trɛtmã] *nm* treatment, salary.

traiter [trɛte] *vt* to treat, entertain, discuss, call; *vti* to negotiate; — **de** to deal with, treat for, with.

traiteur [trɛtœːr] *nm* caterer, restaurateur.

traître, -tresse [trɛːtr, trɛtrɛs] *a* treacherous; *n* traitor, traitress.

traîtrise [trɛtriːz] *nf* treachery.

trajectoire [traʒɛktwaːr] *nf* trajectory.

trajet [traʒɛ] *nm* journey, way, passage, course.

trame [tram] *nf* woof, web, plot.

tramer [trame] *vt* to weave.

tramontane [tramɔ̃tan] *nf* north wind, North.

tranchant [trãʃã] *a* sharp, keen, peremptory, contrasting; *nm* edge.

tranche [trãːʃ] *nf* slice, round, slab, edge, series, chisel.

tranchée [trãʃe] *nf* trench.

trancher [trãʃe] *vt* to cut (off, short), slice, settle; *vi* to contrast (with); — **le mot** to speak bluntly.

tranquille [trãkil] *a* calm, quiet, easy; **laisser** — to leave alone.

tranquillisant [trãkilizã] *nm* tranquilizer.

tranquilliser [trãkilize] *vt* to soothe, set at rest; *vr* to set one's mind at rest.

tranquillité [trãkilite] *nf* peace, calm, quiet.

transaction [trãzaksjɔ̃] *nf* transaction, compromise.

transatlantique [trãzatlãtik] *a* transatlantic; *nm* liner, deck-chair.

transborder [trãsbɔrde] *vt* to transship.

transbordeur [trãsbɔrdœːr] *nm* (**pont**) — transporter-bridge.

transcription [trãskripsjɔ̃] *nf* transcription, copy.

transcrire [trãskriːr] *vt* to transcribe, write out.

transe [trãːs] *nf* trance; *pl* fear.

transférer [trãsfere] *vt* to transfer, remove.

transfert [trãsfɛːr] *nm* transfer(ence).

transformateur [trãsfɔrmatœːr, tris] nm transformer.

transformer [trãsfɔrme] vt to transform; vr to change, turn.

transfuge [trãsfyːʒ] nm deserter, turncoat.

transfuser [trãsfyze] vt to transfuse.

transgresser [trãsgrese] vt to transgress, break.

transi [trãsi] a frozen, paralyzed.

transiger [trãziʒe] vi to (come to a) compromise.

transir [trãsiːr] vt to benumb, chill.

transition [trãzisjɔ̃] nf transition.

transitoire [trãzitwaːr] a transitory, temporary.

transmettre [trãsmɛtr] vt to transmit, convey, hand down.

transmission [trãsmisjɔ̃] nf transfer, transmission, handing down; — **directe** live broadcast.

transparaître [trãsparɛːtr] vi to show through.

transparent [trãsparã] a transparent, clear.

transpercer [trãsperse] vt to pierce, transfix.

transpirer [trãspire] vi to perspire, transpire.

transplanter [trãsplãte] vt to transplant.

transport [trãspɔːr] nm transport, carriage, rapture.

transporter [trãspɔrte] vt to transport, convey, assign, enrapture.

transporteur [trãspɔrtœːr] nm carrier, conveyer.

transposer [trãspoze] vt to transpose.

transversal [trãsversal] a transversal, cross-, side-.

trapèze [trapɛːz] nm trapezium, trapeze.

trappe [trap] nf trap(door).

trapu [trapy] a squat, stocky, thickset.

traquenard [traknaːr] nm trap, pitfall.

traquer [trake] vt to track down, run to earth, hunt, beat.

travail [travaːj] nm (piece of) work, labor, craftsmanship; **travaux forcés** hard labor.

travaillé [travaje] a wrought, elaborate.

travailler [travaje] vt to work (at, upon), obsess, torment; vi to work, toil.

travailleur, -euse [travajœːr, øːz] a hard-working; n worker.

travailliste [travajist] a Labour (Party); nm member of the Labour Party.

travée [trave] nf girder, bay, span.

travers [travɛːr] nm breadth, fault, failing; **à** —, **au** — **de** across, through; **en** — across, crosswise; **par le** — amidships; **de** — awry, askance.

traverse [travers] nf cross-beam, -bar, rung, sleeper; **chemin de** — crossroad, side-road.

traversée [traverse] nf crossing.

traverser [traverse] vt to cross, go through, thwart.

traversin [traversɛ̃] nm crossbar, bolster.

travestir [travestiːr] vt to disguise, misrepresent; **bal travesti** fancy-dress ball.

travestissement [travestismã] nm disguise, disguising, travesty.

trébucher [trebyʃe] vi to stumble, trip.

trèfle [trɛfl] nm clover, trefoil, clubs.

treillage [trejaːʒ] nm trellis, lattice-work.

treille [trɛːj] nf climbing vine, vine-arbor.

treillis [treji] nm lattice, trellis, dungarees; — **métallique** wire-netting, -screening.

treize [trɛːz] a nm thirteen, thirteenth.

treizième [trɛzjɛm] an thirteenth.

tréma [trema] nm diaeresis.

tremble [trãːbl] nm aspen.

tremblement [trãbləmã] n trembling, tremor, quivering, quavering; — **de terre** earthquake.

trembler [trãble] vi to tremble, shake, quiver, quaver.

trembloter [trãblɔte] vi to quiver, quaver, flicker.

trémière [tremjɛːr] a **rose** — hollyhock.

trémousser [tremuse] vir to flutter; vr to fidget; go to a lot of trouble.

trempe [trãːp] nf steeping, temper (ing), stamp.

tremper [trãpe] vt to steep, soak, drench, temper; vi to steep, have a hand (in).

trempette [trãpɛt] nf bread etc, dipped in coffee etc; quick bath.

tremplin [trãplɛ̃] nm spring-, diving-board.

trentaine [trãtɛn] nf about thirty.

trente [trãːt] a nm thirty, thirtieth.

trente-six [trãtsi, -sis, -siz] a nm thirty-six; **ne pas y aller par** — **chemins** not to beat about the bush; **voir** — **chandelles** to see stars.

trentième [trãtjɛm] an thirtieth.

trépaner [trepane] vt to drill, bore, trepan.

trépas [trepɑ] nm death.

trépasser [trepase] vi to die, pass away.

trépidation [trepidasjɔ̃] nf shaking, vibration, trepidation.

trépied [trepje] nm tripod.

trépigner [trepiɲe] vi to stamp, dance.

très [trɛ] ad very, (very) much, most.

trésor [trezɔːr] nm treasure, riches, treasury.

trésorerie [trezɔrri] nf treasury, treasurer's office.

trésorier, -ière [trezɔrje, jɛːr] *n* treasurer, paymaster, -mistress.

tressaillement [trɛsajmɑ̃] *nm* start, thrill.

tressaillir [trɛsajiːr] *vi* to start, shudder, bound, thrill.

tressauter [trɛsote] *vi* to start, jump.

tresse [trɛs] *nf* plait, tress.

tresser [trɛse] *vt* to plait, braid, weave.

tréteau [treto] *nm* trestle, stand; *pl* boards, stage.

treuil [trœːj] *nm* windlass, winch.

trêve [trɛːv] *nf* truce, respite; — de no more of.

tri [tri] *nm* sorting.

triage [triaːʒ] *nm* sorting; **gare de —** marshaling yard.

triangle [triɑ̃ːgl] *nm* triangle, set-square.

tribord [tribɔːr] *nm* starboard.

tribu [triby] *nf* tribe.

tribulation [tribylasjɔ̃] *nf* tribulation, trouble.

tribunal [tribynal] *nm* tribunal, (law) court, bench.

tribune [tribyn] *nf* tribune, platform, grandstand.

tribut [triby] *nm* tribute.

tricher [triʃe] *vti* to cheat, trick.

tricherie [triʃri] *nf* cheating, trickery.

tricheur, -euse [triʃœːr, øːz] *n* cheat, trickster.

tricolore [trikɔlɔːr] *a* tricolored.

tricorne [trikɔrn] *a nm* three-cornered (hat).

tricot [triko] *nm* knitting, cardigan, jumper, jersey.

tricoter [trikɔte] *vt* to knit.

triennal [triɛnnal] *a* triennial.

trier [trie] *vt* to sort (out), pick out.

trigonométrie [trigɔnɔmetri] *nf* trigonometry.

trimbaler [trɛ̃bale] *vt* to lug, trail, drag about.

trimer [trime] *vi* to toil, drudge.

trimestre [trimɛstr] *nm* quarter, term.

trimestriel, -elle [trimɛstriɛl] *a* quarterly.

tringle [trɛ̃ːgl] *nf* (curtain-) rod, bar.

trinquer [trɛ̃ke] *vi* to clink glasses, toast.

triomphal [triɔ̃fal] *a* triumphal.

triomphe [triɔ̃ːf] *nm* triumph.

triompher [triɔ̃fe] *vi* to triumph (over de), surmount.

tripatouiller [tripatuje] *vt* to tinker, tamper with.

tripes [trip] *nf pl* tripe, intestines, guts.

triple [tripl] *a nm* treble, triple, threefold.

tripler [triple] *vt* to treble.

tripot [tripo] *nm* gambling house.

tripotage [tripɔtaːʒ] *nm* fiddling about, jobbery.

tripoter [tripɔte] *vt* to fiddle with, tamper with, finger, paw; *vi* to

potter, fiddle, mess about, dabble.

trique [trik] *nf* cudgel.

triste [trist] *a* sad, mournful, dismal, bleak, wretched.

tristesse [tristɛs] *nf* sadness, gloom, sorrow, mournfulness.

triturer [trityre] *vt* to grind.

trivial [trivjal] *a* vulgar, commonplace, trite.

trivialité [trivjalite] *nf* vulgarity, coarse word, triteness.

troc [trɔk] *nm* barter, exchange, swap(ping).

troène [trɔɛn] *nm* privet.

troglodyte [trɔglɔdit] *nm* cave-dweller.

trogne [trɔɲ] *nf* face, dial.

trognon [trɔɲɔ̃] *nm* core, stump.

trois [trwa] *a nm* three, third.

troisième [trwazjɛm] *an* third.

trombe [trɔ̃ːb] *nf* water-spout, cloudburst, whirlwind.

trombone [trɔ̃bɔn] *nm* trombone, paper-clip.

trompe [trɔ̃ːp] *nf* trumpet, horn, (*elephant*) trunk.

trompe-l'œil [trɔ̃plœːj] *nm* sham, eyewash, window-dressing (*fig*).

tromper [trɔ̃pe] *vt* to deceive, cheat, beguile; *vr* to be mistaken, be wrong.

tromperie [trɔ̃pri] *nf* (piece of) deceit, fraud.

trompette [trɔ̃pɛt] *nf* trumpet, trumpeter.

trompeur, -euse [trɔ̃pœːr, øːz] *a* deceitful, deceptive, misleading; *n* deceiver, cheat.

tronc [trɔ̃] *nm* trunk, bole, collection-box.

tronçon [trɔ̃sɔ̃] *nm* stump, fragment, section.

tronçonner [trɔ̃sɔne] *vt* to cut into pieces.

trône [troːn] *nm* throne.

trôner [trone] *vi* to sit enthroned, lord it, queen it.

tronquer [trɔ̃ke] *vt* to truncate, mutilate.

trop [tro] *ad* too, too much, over-; **de —** too much, too many, unwanted.

trophée [trɔfe] *nm* trophy.

tropical [trɔpikal] *a* tropical.

tropiques [trɔpik] *nm pl* tropics.

trop-plein [trɔplɛ̃] *nm* overflow, excess.

troquer [trɔke] *vt* to barter, exchange, swap.

trot [tro] *nm* trot.

trotte [trɔt] *nf* stretch, bit, distance, walk.

trotter [trɔte] *vi* to trot, scamper.

trotteuse [trɔtøːz] *nf* go-cart.

trottiner [trɔtine] *vi* to scamper, toddle, jog along.

trottinette [trɔtinɛt] *nf* scooter.

trottoir [trɔtwaːr] *nm* pavement, footpath, platform.

trou [tru] *nm* hole, gap, dead-and-alive place; — **d'air** air-pocket; — **du souffleur** prompter's box.

trouble [trubl] *a* muddy, dim, cloudy; *nm* confusion, uneasiness; *pl* disturbances.

trouble-fête [trubləfɛːt] *nm* spoil-sport, killjoy.

troubler [truble] *vt* to disturb, upset, excite, blur, make muddy; *vr* to get upset, become excited, muddy, dim.

trouée [true] *nf* gap.

trouer [true] *vt* to hole, make holes in.

troupe [trup] *nf* troop, gang, company, flock, herd, other ranks; *pl* troops.

troupeau [trupo] *nm* flock, herd, drove.

troupier [trupje] *nm* soldier, seasoned campaigner.

trousse [trus] *nf* outfit, kit, bundle, truss; **à mes —s** after me, at my heels.

trousseau [truso] *nm* bunch, outfit, trousseau.

trousser [truse] *vt* to turn up, tuck up, truss.

trouvaille [truvaːj] *nf* find, windfall, godsend.

trouver [truve] *vt* to find, hit upon, think; *vr* to be, be found, happen, feel.

truc [tryk] *nm* knack, dodge, gadget, thingummy.

truchement [tryʃmɑ̃] *nm* inter-mediary, interpreter.

truculence [trykylɑ̃ːs] *nf* truculence.

truelle [tryɛl] *nf* trowel, fish-slice.

truffe [tryf] *nf* truffle, dog's nose.

truie [trɥi] *nf* sow.

truite [trɥit] *nf* trout.

trumeau [trymo] *nm* (*archit*) pier; pier-glass; leg of beef.

truquer [tryke] *vt* to fake, cook, rig.

tsé-tsé [tsetse] *nf* tsetse fly.

T.S.F. *nf* radio.

tu [ty] *pn* you, thou.

tube [tyb] *nm* tube, pipe; (*song*) hit.

tuberculeux, -euse [tybɛrkylø, øːz] *a* tubercular, tuberculous, con-sumptive.

tuberculose [tybɛrkyloːz] *nf* tuber-culosis.

tuer [tɥe] *vt* to kill, slay.

tuerie [tyri] *nf* slaughter, carnage.

tue-tête [tytɛt] *ad* **à —** at the top of one's voice.

tueur [tɥœːr] *nm* killer, slaughter-man.

tuile [tɥil] *nf* tile, bit of bad luck.

tulipe [tylip] *nf* tulip.

tulle [tyl] *nm* tulle.

tuméfier [tymefje] *vt* to make swell.

tumulte [tymylt] *nm* tumult, up-roar.

tumultueux, -euse [tymyltɥø, øːz] *a* tumultuous, noisy.

tunique [tynik] *nf* tunic.

tunnel [tynɛl] *nm* tunnel.

turbine [tyrbin] *nf* turbine.

turbulence [tyrbylɑ̃ːs] *nf* turbulence, boisterousness.

turbulent [tyrbylɑ̃] *a* turbulent, unruly.

turc, turque [tyrk] *a* Turkish; *n* Turk.

turf [tyrf] *nm* racing, racetrack.

turfiste [tyrfist] *nm* racegoer.

turpitude [tyrpityd] *nf* turpitude, baseness, base act.

Turquie [tyrki] *nf* Turkey.

turquoise [tyrkwaːz] *a nm* turquoise (color); *nf* turquoise.

tutelle [tytɛl] *nf* guardianship, pro-tection.

tuteur, -trice [tytœːr, tris] *n* guardian; *nm* stake, trainer.

tutoyer [tytwaje] *vt* to address as 'tu', be familiar with.

tuyau [tɥijo] *nm* tube, (hose-) pipe, stem, goffer, tip, hint.

tuyauter [tɥjote, tɥijote] *vt* to goffer, frill, give a tip, hint to.

tympan [tɛ̃pɑ̃] *nm* eardrum, tym-panum.

type [tip] *nm* type, fellow.

typhoïde [tifɔid] *a* typhoid.

typique [tipik] *a* typical.

typo(graphe) [tipɔgraf] *nm* printer, typographer.

typographie [tipɔgrafi] *nf* printing.

tyran [tirɑ̃] *nm* tyrant.

tyrannie [tirani] *nf* tyranny.

tyrannique [tiranik] *a* tyrannical, tyrannous.

tyranniser [tiranize] *vt* to tyrannize, oppress.

tzigane [tsigan] *n* gipsy.

U

ubiquité [ybikɥite] *nf* ubiquity.

ulcère [ylsɛːr] *nm* ulcer, sore.

ulcérer [ylsere] *vt* to ulcerate, hurt, embitter; *vr* to fester, grow em-bittered.

ultérieur [ylterjœːr] *a* ulterior, subsequent, further.

ultimatum [yltimatɔm] *nm* ultimat-um.

ultime [yltim] *a* ultimate, last, final.

un, une [œ̃, yn] *indef art* a; *a pn* one; *nm* one; *nf* first page; **— à —** one by one; **en savoir plus d'une** to know a thing or two.

unanime [ynanim] *a* unanimous.

unanimité [ynanimite] *nf* unanim-ity; **à l'—** unanimously.

uni [yni] *a* united, smooth, self-colored, plain.

unième [ynjɛm] *a* (*in compound numbers only*) first.

unification [ynifikasjɔ̃] *nf* unifica-tion, amalgamation.

unifier [ynifje] *vt* to unify, amalgam-ate.

uniforme [ynifɔrm] *a nm* uniform.

uniformiser [yniformize] *vt* to make uniform, standardize.
uniformité [yniformite] *nf* uniformity.
unilatéral [ynilateral] *a* unilateral, one-sided.
union [ynjɔ̃] *nf* union, unity, association.
uniprix [ynipri] *a* **magasin —** dime store.
unique [ynik] *a* single, only, sole, one, unique; **rue à sens —** one-way street.
unir [ynːir] *vt* to unite, join, make, smooth; *vr* to unite, join, become smooth.
unisson [ynisɔ̃] *nm* unison.
unité [ynite] *nf* unity, consistency, unit.
univers [yniveːr] *nm* universe.
universalité [yniversalite] *nf* universality.
universel, -elle [yniversɛl] *a* universal, world-wide, versatile.
universitaire [yniversiteːr] *a* university; *n* university teacher.
université [yniversite] *nf* university.
uranium [yranjɔm] *nm* uranium.
urbain [yrbɛ̃] *a* urban, town; *n* city-dweller.
urbanisme [yrbanism] *nm* town-planning.
urbanité [yrbanite] *nf* urbanity.
urgence [yrʒɑ̃ːs] *nf* urgency, emergency; **d'—** urgently, emergency.
urgent [yrʒɑ̃] *a* urgent, pressing.
urine [yrin] *nf* urine.
uriner [yrine] *vi* to urinate, make water.
urinoir [yrinwaːr] *nm* urinal.
urne [yrn] *nf* urn.
URSS *nf* USSR.
urticaire [yrtikeːr] *nf* nettle-rash.
us [y] *nm pl* **les — et coutumes** ways and customs.
usage [yzaːʒ] *nm* use, using, service, wear, practice, custom, breeding; **d'—** usual, for everyday use.
usagé [yzaʒe] *a* used, worn.
usager, -ère [yzaʒe, ɛr] *a* for personal use, of everyday use; *n* user.
usé [yze] *a* worn (out, away), threadbare, shabby, stale.
user [yze] *vt* to wear out (away); **— de** to use; *vr* to wear (out, away, down); **en bien (mal) — avec qn** to treat s.o. well (badly).
usine [yzin] *nf* factory, mill, works.
usiner [yzine] *vt* to machine(-finish).
usité [yzite] *a* used, current.
ustensile [ystɑ̃sil] *nm* utensil, tool.
usuel, -elle [yzɥɛl] *a* usual, customary; *nm* reference book.
usufruit [yzyfrɥi] *nm* life interest, usufruct.
usure [yzyːr] *nf* wear (and tear), wearing away, attrition, usury, interest.
usurier, -ière [yzyrje, jɛːr] *a* usurious; *n* usurer.
usurpateur, -trice [yzyrpatœːr, tris] *a* usurping; *n* usurper.
usurper [yzyrpe] *vti* to usurp.
ut [yt] *nm* musical note C, do.
utile [ytil] *a* useful, handy, serviceable, effective, due.
utilisation [ytilizasjɔ̃] *nf* utilization, using.
utiliser [ytilize] *vt* to utilize, use.
utilitaire [ytiliteːr] *an* utilitarian.
utilité [ytilite] *nf* utility, use(fulness), service.
utopie [ytɔpi] *nf* utopia.
utopique [ytɔpik] *a* utopian.
utopiste [ytɔpist] *an* utopian.
uvule [yvyl] *nf* uvula.

V

vacance [vakɑ̃ːs] *nf* vacancy; *pl* holidays, vacation; **en —s** on vacation; **grandes —s** summer vacation.
vacant [vakɑ̃] *a* vacant.
vacarme [vakarm] *nm* din, uproar, hullabaloo.
vaccin [vaksɛ̃] *nm* vaccine, lymph.
vaccination [vaksinasjɔ̃] *nf* vaccination, inoculation.
vacciner [vaksine] *vt* to vaccinate, inoculate.
vache [vaʃ] *nf* cow, cowhide, nasty person, beast; **manger de la — enragée** to have a hard time of it; **parler français comme une — espagnole** to murder the French language.
vachement [vaʃmɑ̃] *ad* damn(ed), terribly.
vacher, -ère [vaʃe, ɛːr] *n* cowherd.
vacherie [vaʃri] *nf* cowshed, dirty trick.
vacillant [vasilɑ̃, -ijɑ̃] *a* wavering, flickering, unsteady, wobbling, uncertain.
vaciller [vasille, -ije] *vi* to waver, flicker, stagger, wobble.
va-comme-je-te-pousse [vakɔmʒətpus] *a* easy-going; *ad* any old way.
vacuité [vakɥite] *nf* emptiness.
vacuum [vakɥɔm] *nm* vacuum.
vadrouille [vadruːj] *nf* spree, swab, mop.
vadrouiller [vadruje] *vi* to rove, roam, gallivant.
vadrouilleur, -euse [vadrujœːr, øːz] *n* gadabout, rake.
va-et-vient [vaevjɛ̃] *nm* coming and going, movement to and fro.
vagabond [vagabɔ̃] *a* vagabond, roving, wandering; *n* vagrant, vagabond, tramp.
vagabondage [vagabɔ̃daːʒ] *nm* vagabondage, vagrancy.
vagabonder [vagabɔ̃de] *vi* to wander, roam, rove.

vagin [vaʒɛ̃] *nm* vagina.
vagir [vaʒiːr] *vi* to wail.
vague [vag] *a* vague, hazy, indefinite, empty; *nm* vagueness, space; *nf* wave; **terrains —s** vacant land.
vaguemestre [vagmɛstr] *nm* postman, mail clerk.
vaguer [vage] *vi* to roam, ramble, wander.
vaillance [vajɑ̃ːs] *nf* valor, bravery.
vaillant [vajɑ̃] *a* valiant, gallant, brave, stout; **n'avoir pas un sou —** not to have a cent.
vain [vɛ̃] *a* vain, useless, empty, futile.
vaincre [vɛ̃ːkr] *vt* to vanquish, defeat, conquer.
vainqueur [vɛ̃kœːr] *a inv* victorious, conquering; *nm* victor, conqueror, winner.
vairon [vɛrɔ̃] *nm* minnow.
vaisseau [vɛso] *nm* vessel, ship, receptacle.
vaisselier [vɛsəlje] *nm* dresser.
vaisselle [vɛsɛl] *nf* plates and dishes, table-service; **faire la —** to wash up.
val [val] *nm* valley, vale; **par monts et par vaux** up hill and down dale.
valable [valabl] *a* valid, available, good.
valet [valɛ] *nm* valet, footman, knave, jack, servant, farm-hand.
valeur [valœːr] *nf* value, worth, valor, merit, asset; *pl* securities, bills; **objets de —** valuables; **mettre en —** to bring out, emphasize, develop; **—s actives** assets; **—s passives** liabilities.
valeureux, -euse [valœrø, øːz] *a* valorous, gallant.
valide [valid] *a* valid, able-bodied, fit.
valider [valide] *vt* to ratify, validate.
validité [validite] *nf* validity.
valise [valiːz] *nf* suitcase, bag, valise.
vallée [vale] *nf* valley.
vallon [valɔ̃] *nm* (small) valley, vale, dale.
vallonné [valɔne] *a* undulating.
valoir [valwaːr] *vti* to be worth, be as good (bad) as, deserve, be equivalent to, win, bring (in); **faire —** to assert, make the most of, develop, show off; **se faire —** to show off, push o.s. forward; **cela vaut la peine d'être vu** it is worth seeing; **cela vaut le coup** it is worth while; **il vaut mieux le vendre** it is better to sell it; **ne pas — grand'chose** not to be up to much; **vaille que vaille** at all costs.
valorisation [valɔrizasjɔ̃] *nf* valorization, stabilization.
valoriser [valɔrize] *vt* to valorize, stabilize.
valse [vals] *nf* waltz.
valser [valse] *vi* to waltz.
valve [valv] *nf* valve.

vampire [vɑ̃piːr] *nm* vampire.
vandale [vɑ̃dal] *nm* vandal.
vandalisme [vɑ̃dalism] *nm* vandalism.
vanille [vaniːj] *nf* vanilla.
vanité [vanite] *nf* vanity, conceit, futility; **tirer — de** to take pride in.
vaniteux, -euse [vanitø, øːz] *a* vain, conceited.
vanne [van] *nf* sluice-gate, floodgate.
vanneau [vano] *nm* lapwing, plover, peewit.
vanner [vane] *vt* to winnow, sift, tire out.
vannerie [vanri] *nf* basket-making, basket-, wicker-work.
vanneuse [vanøːz] *nf* winnowing-machine.
vannier [vanje] *nm* basket-maker.
vantail [vɑ̃taːj] *nm* leaf (of door *etc*).
vantard [vɑ̃taːr] *a* boastful, bragging; *n* boaster, braggart.
vantardise [vɑ̃tardiːz] *nf* boast (fulness), bragging.
vanter [vɑ̃te] *vt* to praise, extol; *vr* to brag, boast, pride o.s.
vanterie [vɑ̃tri] *nf* boast(ing), brag (ging).
va-nu-pieds [vanypje] *n* barefoot beggar, ragamuffin.
vapeur [vapœːr] *nm* steamer, steamship; *nf* steam, vapor, haze, dizziness; **à toute —** full steam (ahead).
vaporeux, -euse [vapɔrø, øːz] *a* vaporous, steamy, hazy.
vaporisateur [vapɔrizatœːr] *nm* atomizer, (scent-)spray, evaporator.
vaporisation [vapɔrizasjɔ̃] *nf* evaporation, atomization, vaporization.
vaporiser [vapɔrize] *vt* to atomize, vaporize, volatilize, spray; *vr* to vaporize, spray oneself.
vaquer [vake] *vi* to be vacant, (*jur*) not to be sitting; **— à** to attend to, look after.
varech [varɛk] *nm* seaweed, wrack, kelp.
vareuse [varøːz] *nf* (sailor's) jersey, pea-jacket, short tunic.
variable [varjabl] *a* variable, changeable, unsettled.
variante [varjɑ̃ːt] *nf* variant.
variation [varjasjɔ̃] *nf* variation, change.
varice [varis] *nf* varicose vein.
varicelle [varisɛl] *nf* chicken-pox.
varié [varje] *a* varied, miscellaneous, variegated.
varier [varje] *vt* to vary, change; *vi* to vary, differ, fluctuate.
variété [varjete] *nf* variety, diversity.
variole [varjɔl] *nf* smallpox.
vase [vaːz] *nm* vase, receptacle; **— de nuit** chamber-pot; **en — clos** in isolation; *nf* mud, slime.
vaseline [vazlin] *nf* vaseline.
vaseux, -euse [vazø, øːz] *a* muddy, slimy, off-color, woolly,

vasistas [vazistɑːs] *nm* transom.
vassal [vasal] *an* vassal.
vaste [vast] *a* vast, wide, spacious.
vau [vo] *ad* à — **l'eau** downstream, to rack and ruin, to the dogs.
vaurien, -enne [vorjɛ̃, jɛn] *n* good-for-nothing, waster, blackguard, scamp.
vautour [votuːr] *nm* vulture.
vautrer [votre] *vr* to wallow, sprawl.
veau [vo] *nm* calf, veal, calf-skin.
vécu [veky] *a* true to life, realistic.
vedette [vədɛt] *nf* mounted sentry, motor launch, small steamer, scout, star; **être en** — to be in the limelight, in large type; **être mis en** — **sur l'affiche** to top the bill.
végétal [veʒetal] *a* vegetable, plant-; *nm* plant.
végétarien, -enne [veʒetarjɛ̃, jɛn] *an* vegetarian.
végétarisme [veʒetarism] *nm* vegetarianism.
végétation [veʒetasjɔ̃] *nf* vegetation; *pl* adenoids.
végéter [veʒete] *vi* to vegetate.
véhémence [veemɑ̃ːs] *nf* vehemence.
véhément [veemɑ̃] *a* vehement, violent.
véhicule [veikyl] *nm* vehicle.
veille [vɛːj] *nf* vigil, wakefulness, watch(ing), late night, sitting up, eve, day before; **à la** — **de** on the brink of.
veillée [vɛje] *nf* social evening, vigil, wake, night-nursing.
veiller [vɛje] *vt* to sit up with, look after; *vi* to watch, be on the lookout, keep awake, sit up; — **à** to see to, look after.
veilleur, -euse [vɛjœːr, øːz] *n* watcher, keeper of a vigil; — **de nuit** night-watchman.
veilleuse [vɛjøːz] *nf* night-light, pilot-light; **mettre en** — to dim, turn down.
veinard [venaːr] *an* lucky (fellow).
veine [vɛn] *nf* vein, mood, luck; **coup de** — stroke of luck, fluke.
veineux, -euse [venø, øːz] *a* venous, veined.
vêler [vele] *vi* to calve.
vélin [velɛ̃] *nm* vellum.
velléité [vɛlleite] *nf* inclination, slight desire.
vélo [velo] *nm* bike, cycle; **faire du** — to go in for cycling.
vélocité [velɔsite] *nf* velocity, speed.
vélodrome [velɔdroːm] *nm* cycle-racing track.
velours [vəluːr] *nm* velvet; — **de coton** velveteen.
velouté [v(ə)lute] *a* velvety, smooth, soft; *nm* velvetiness, bloom, softness.
velu [vəly] *a* hairy.
venaison [vənɛzɔ̃] *nf* venison, game.
vénal [venal] *a* venal, corrupt(ible).
vénalité [venalite] *nf* venality.
venant [vənɑ̃] *a* thriving; *nm* **à tout**

— to all comers, to anyone at all.
vendable [vɑ̃dabl] *a* salable, marketable.
vendange [vɑ̃dɑ̃ːʒ] *nf* grape-gathering, wine harvest, vintage.
vendanger [vɑ̃dɑ̃ʒe] *vti* to gather in the grapes.
vendangeur, -euse [vɑ̃dɑ̃ʒœːr, øːz] *n* vintager, grape-gatherer.
vendeur, -euse [vɑ̃dœːr, øːz] *n* seller, salesman, -woman, sales-clerk, vendor.
vendredi [vɑ̃drədi] *nm* Friday; **le** — **saint** Good Friday.
vendre [vɑ̃ːdr] *vt* to sell, betray.
vendu [vɑ̃dy] *nm* traitor.
vénéneux, -euse [venenø, øːz] *a* poisonous.
vénérable [venerabl] *a* venerable.
vénération [venerasjɔ̃] *nf* veneration, reverence.
vénérer [venere] *vt* to venerate, revere, worship.
vénérien, -ienne [venerjɛ̃, jɛn] *a* venereal.
vengeance [vɑ̃ʒɑ̃ːs] *nf* vengeance, revenge, retribution; **tirer** — **de** to be avenged on.
venger [vɑ̃ʒe] *vt* to avenge; *vr* to revenge oneself, take vengeance.
vengeur, -eresse [vɑ̃ʒœːr, ərɛs] *a* avenging; *n* avenger.
véniel, -elle [venjɛl] *a* venial.
venimeux, -euse [vənimø, øːz] *a* venomous, poisonous, spiteful.
venin [vənɛ̃] *nm* venom, poison, spite.
venir [v(ə)niːr] *vi* to come, reach, grow, be the result (of **de**); — **à apparaître** to happen, chance to appear; — **de sortir** to have just gone out; **faire** — send for; — **chercher** to come for; **en** — **à** to come to the point of, be reduced to; **l'idée me vient que** it occurs to me that.
vent [vɑ̃] *nm* wind, blast, flatulence, vent, scent; **coup de** — gust of wind; **il fait du** — it is windy; **avoir** — **de** to get wind of; **mettre au** — to hang out to air.
vente [vɑ̃t] *nf* sale, selling; **en** — on sale; — **de charité** charity bazaar.
venter [vɑ̃te] *vi* to be windy, blow.
venteux, -euse [vɑ̃tø, øːz] *a* windy, windswept.
ventilateur [vɑ̃tilatœːr] *nm* ventilator, fan.
ventiler [vɑ̃tile] *vt* to ventilate.
ventouse [vɑ̃tuːz] *nf* cupping-glass, sucker, vent-hole.
ventre [vɑ̃ːtr] *nm* abdomen, belly, stomach, paunch, bulge; **prendre du** — to grow stout; **n'avoir rien dans le** — to be starving, have no guts; **se mettre à plat** — to lie flat, grovel.
ventriloque [vɑ̃trilɔk] *a* ventriloquous; *nm* ventriloquist.
ventru [vɑ̃try] *a* stout, portly, pot-bellied.

venu [vəny] *n* comer.
venue [vəny] *nf* coming, arrival, advent, growth.
vêpres [vɛːpr] *nf pl* vespers, evensong.
ver [vɛːr] *nm* worm, maggot; — luisant glow-worm; — solitaire tapeworm; — à soie silkworm; tirer les —s du nez de qn to worm it out of s.o.
véracité [vɛrasite] *nf* veracity, truth (fulness).
véranda [vɛrɑ̃da] *nf* veranda.
verbal [vɛrbal] *a* verbal.
verbaliser [vɛrbalize] *vi* to make out an official report.
verbe [vɛrb] *nm* verb, word; avoir le — haut to be loud-mouthed.
verbeux, -euse [vɛrbø, øːz] *a* verbose, long-winded.
verbiage [vɛrbjaːʒ] *nm* verbiage.
verbosité [vɛrbozite] *nf* verbosity, long-windedness.
verdâtre [vɛrdɑːtr] *a* greenish.
verdeur [vɛrdœːr] *nf* greenness, tartness, vigor.
verdict [vɛrdikt] *nm* verdict, finding.
verdier [vɛrdje] *nm* greenfinch.
verdir [vɛrdiːr] *vt* to paint or make green; *vi* to turn green, become covered with verdigris.
verdoyant [vɛrdwayɑ̃] *a* green, verdant.
verdure [vɛrdyːr] *nf* verdure, greenery, greenness, greens.
véreux, -euse [verø, øːz] *a* wormeaten, maggoty, shady.
verge [vɛrʒ] *nf* rod, switch, wand.
verger [vɛrʒe] *nm* orchard.
verglas [vɛrglɑ] *nm* ice, black ice.
vergogne [vɛrgɔɲ] *nf* shame; sans — shameless.
vergue [vɛrg] *nf* yard.
véridicité [veridisite] *nf* truth(fulness).
véridique [veridik] *a* veracious, truthful.
vérificateur [verifikatœːr] *nm* inspector, examiner, gauge, auditor.
vérification [verifikasjɔ̃] *nf* inspection, verification, overhauling, checking, auditing.
vérifier [verifje] *vt* to inspect, verify, check, overhaul, audit.
véritable [veritabl] *a* real, true, genuine, downright.
vérité [verite] *nf* truth(fulness), sincerity, fact.
vermeil, -eille [vɛrmɛːj] *a* vermilion, bright red, ruby; *nm* silver-gilt.
vermicelle [vɛrmisɛl] *nm* vermicelli.
vermillon [vɛrmijɔ̃] *nm* vermilion, bright red.
vermine [vɛrmin] *nf* vermin.
vermoulu [vɛrmuly] *a* wormeaten, decrepit.
verni [vɛrni] *a* varnished, patent (*leather*), lucky.
vernir [vɛrniːr] *vt* to varnish, glaze, polish, japan.

vernis [vɛrni] *nm* varnish, glaze, polish, gloss.
vernissage [vɛrnisaːʒ] *nm* varnishing, glazing, polishing, preview.
vernisseur, -euse [vɛrnisœːr] *n* varnisher, glazer, japanner.
vérole [verɔl] *nf* pox; petite — smallpox.
verrat [vɛra] *nm* boar.
verre [vɛːr] *nm* glass; — de lunettes lens; papier de — sandpaper; tempête dans un — d'eau tempest in a teapot.
verrerie [vɛr(ə)ri] *nf* glassmaking, glassware, glass-factory.
verrier [vɛrje] *nm* glassmaker, -blower.
verrière [vɛrjɛːr] *nf* glass casing, stained glass window.
verroterie [vɛrɔtri] *nf* small glassware, beads.
verrou [vɛru] *nm* bolt, bar, breechbolt; pousser (tirer) le — to bolt (unbolt) the door; sous les —s under lock and key.
verrouiller [vɛruje] *vt* to bolt, lock up.
verrue [vɛry] *nf* wart.
vers [vɛːr] *nm* line; *pl* poetry, verse; *prep* toward, to, about.
versant [vɛrsɑ̃] *nm* slope, side.
versatile [vɛrsatil] *a* changeable, unstable, fickle.
versatilité [vɛrsatilite] *nf* instability, fickleness.
verse [vɛrs] *ad* à — in torrents.
versé [vɛrse] *a* versed, conversant, well up.
versement [vɛrs(ə)mɑ̃] *nm* pouring (out), payment, installment, deposit; bulletin de — deposit slip.
verser [vɛrse] *vt* to pour (out), shed, deposit, assign, lay, overturn; *vi* to be laid flat, overturn; — à boire to pour out a drink.
verset [vɛrse] *nm* verse.
versification [vɛrsifikasjɔ̃] *nf* versification.
versifier [vɛrsifje] *vt* to put into verse; *vi* to write poetry.
version [vɛrsjɔ̃] *nf* version, account, translation.
verso [vɛrso] *nm* back, verso; voir au — see overleaf.
vert [vɛːr] *a* green, unripe, spicy, sharp, vigorous, hale; *nm* green.
vert-de-gris [vɛrdəgri] *nm* verdigris.
vertébral [vɛrtebral] *a* vertebral; colonne —e spine.
vertèbre [vɛrtɛːbr] *nf* vertebra.
vertement [vɛrtəmɑ̃] *ad* sharply, severely.
vertical [vɛrtikal] *a* vertical, perpendicular, upright.
verticale [vɛrtikal] *nf* vertical.
vertige [vɛrtiːʒ] *nm* giddiness, dizziness, vertigo; avoir le — to be giddy.
vertigineux, -euse [vɛrtiʒinø, øːz] *a* giddy, dizzy.

vertu [vɛrty] nf virtue chastity, property, quality; **en — de** by virtue of.

vertueux, -euse [vɛrtɥø, øːz] a virtuous, chaste.

verve [vɛrv] nf verve, zest, go, vigor, high spirits; **être en —** to be in fine fettle.

verveine [vɛrvɛn] nf verbena, vervain.

vesce [vɛs] nf vetch, tare.

vésicatoire [vezikatwaːr] a nm vesicatory.

vésicule [vezikyl] nf vesicle, blister, air-cell; **— biliaire** gall-bladder.

vespasienne [vɛspazjɛn] nf street urinal.

vespéral [vɛspɛral] a evening.

vessie [vɛsi] nf bladder; **prendre des —s pour des lanternes** to think the moon is made of green cheese.

veste [vɛst] nf jacket.

vestiaire [vɛstjɛːr] nm cloakroom, changing-room, robing-room.

vestibule [vɛstibyl] nm (entrance-) hall, lobby, vestibule.

vestige [vɛstiːʒ] nm trace, mark, vestige.

vestimentaire [vɛstimɑ̃tɛːr] a vestimentary.

veston [vɛstɔ̃] nm jacket.

vêtement [vɛtmɑ̃] nm garment; pl clothing, clothes; **—s de dessous** underwear.

vétéran [vetɛrɑ̃] nm veteran.

vétérinaire [veterinɛːr] a veterinary; nm veterinarian.

vétille [vetiːj] nf trifle.

vétilleux, -euse [vetijø, øːz] a captious, finicky.

vêtir [vɛtiːr] vt to dress, clothe; vr to dress oneself.

veto [veto] nm veto; **mettre son — à** to veto.

vétusté [vetyste] nf decrepitude, old age.

veuf, veuve [vœf, vœːv] a widowed; n widower, widow.

veule [vœːl] a weak, soft, flabby, inert, drab.

veulerie [vœlri] nf weakness, flabbiness, drabness.

veuvage [vœvaːʒ] nm widow(er)hood.

vexation [vɛksasjɔ̃] nf vexation, annoying word or deed.

vexatoire [vɛksatwaːr] a vexatious.

vexer [vɛkse] vt to vex, annoy, pester, upset, irritate; vr to get annoyed.

viable [vjabl, vjabl] a strong enough to live, viable, fit for traffic.

viaduc [vjadyk] nm viaduct.

viager, -ère [vjaʒe, ɛːr] a for life; nm life interest; **rente viagère** life annuity.

viande [vjɑ̃ːd] nf meat, flesh.

viatique [vjatik] nm viaticum.

vibrant [vibrɑ̃] a vibrant, ringing, rousing, vibrating.

vibration [vibrasjɔ̃] nf vibration, resonance.

vibratoire [vibratwaːr] a vibratory, oscillatory.

vibrer [vibre] vi to vibrate, throb; **faire —** to thrill, rouse.

vicaire [vikɛːr] nm curate.

vice [vis] nm vice, flaw, defect.

vice-consul [viskɔ̃syl] nm viceconsul.

vice-roi [visrwa] nm viceroy.

vicier [visje] vt to vitiate, contaminate, corrupt, taint; vr to become corrupted, tainted, foul, spoiled.

vicieux, -euse [visjø, øːz] a vicious, depraved, bad-tempered, faulty.

vicinal [visinal] a **route —e** back road, by-road.

vicissitude [visissityd] nf vicissitude; pl ups and downs.

vicomte [vikɔ̃t] nm viscount.

vicomtesse [vikɔ̃tɛs] nf viscountess.

victime [viktim] nf victim, sacrifice.

victoire [viktwaːr] nf victory.

victorieux, -euse [viktɔrjø, øːz] v victorious.

victuailles [viktɥaːj] nf pl victuals, eatables.

vidange [vidɑ̃ːʒ] nf emptying, draining, clearing; nf pl night-soil.

vidanger [vidɑ̃ʒe] vt to empty, drain.

vidangeur [vidɑ̃ʒœːr] nm scavenger, cesspool clearer.

vide [vid] a empty, unoccupied, blank; nm empty space, emptiness, blank, gap, vacuum.

vider [vide] vt to empty, drain (off), blow, clean, gut, core, stone, bale, settle; vr to empty; **— une question** to settle a question; **— les arçons** to be unsaddled.

vie [vi] nf life, existence, lifetime (way of) living, livelihood, vitality; **à —** for life; **avoir la — dure** to die hard, be hard to kill.

vieillard [vjejaːr] nm old man.

vieilleries [vjejri] nf pl old things, dated ideas.

vieillesse [vjejɛs] nf (old) age, oldness.

vieillissement [vjejismɑ̃] nm aging, growing old.

vieillir [vjejiːr] vt to age, make look older; vi to age, grow old, become antiquated.

vieillot, -otte [vjejo, ɔt] a oldish, old-fashioned.

vierge [vjɛrʒ] a virgin(al), pure, blank; nf virgin, maiden.

vieux, vieil, vieille [vjø, vjɛ(ː)j] a old, ancient, stale; nm pl old people; **il est — jeu** he is old-fashioned, antiquated; **mon —** old man; **un — de la vieille** one of the old brigade, an old-timer.

vif, vive [vif, viːv] a lively, brisk, sharp, keen, quick, alive, high-spirited, vivid, bright; nm living

flesh, quick heart; **haie vive** quick-set hedge; **peindre sur le —** to paint from life.
vif-argent [vifarȝɑ̃] *nm* quicksilver, mercury.
vigie [viȝi] *nf* look-out (man), watch-tower.
vigilance [viȝilɑ̃:s] *nf* vigilance, care.
vigilant [viȝilɑ̃] *a* vigilant, watchful.
vigne [viɲ] *nf* vine, vineyard; — **vierge** Virginia creeper; **être dans les —s du Seigneur** to be in one's cups.
vigneron, -onne [viɲrɔ̃, ɔn] *n* vine-grower, vineyard worker.
vignette [viɲɛt] *nf* excise stamp, Internal Revenue stamp, vignette.
vignoble [viɲɔbl] *nm* vineyard.
vigoureux, -euse [viguro, ø:z] *a* vigorous, sturdy, strong, hardy.
vigueur [vigœ:r] *nf* vigor, sturdiness, strength, effect; **entrer en —** to come into effect, force; **mettre en —** to enforce.
vil [vil] *a* vile, base, low(ly), cheap.
vilain [vilɛ̃] *a* bad, naughty, nasty, dirty, mean, scurvy, ugly, wretched; *nm* rascal, villain.
vilebrequin [vilbrəkɛ̃] *nm* brace, drill; **arbre à —** crankshaft.
vilenie [viləni] *nf* nastiness, meanness, foul word, low action.
vilipender [vilipɑ̃de] *vt* to abuse, run down.
villa [vil(l)a] *nf* villa.
village [vila:ȝ] *nm* village.
villageois [vilaȝwa, wa:z] *a* country, boorish; *n* villager.
ville [vil] *nf* town, city; **— d'eau** spa.
villégiateur [vil(l)eȝjatœ:r] *nm* visitor, holiday-maker.
villégiature [vil(l)eȝjaty:r] *nf* holiday, stay in the country.
vin [vɛ̃] *nm* wine; **— de Bordeaux** claret; **— de Bourgogne** burgundy; **— de Xérès** sherry; **— en cercle** wine in the cask; **— millésimé** vintage wine; **avoir le — triste** to be maudlin in drink.
vinaigre [vinɛ:gr] *nm* vinegar.
vinaigrette [vinɛgrɛt] *nf* oil and vinegar dressing.
vinaigrier [vinɛgrie] *nm* vinegar-maker, vinegar-cruet.
vindicatif, -ive [vɛ̃dikatif, i:v] *a* vindictive, revengeful.
vineux, -euse [vino, ø:z] *a* wine-flavored, wine-stained, full-bodied, strong, rich in wine.
vingt [vɛ̃] *a nm* twenty, twentieth.
vingtaine [vɛ̃tɛn] *nf* about twenty, a score.
vingtième [vɛ̃tjɛm] *a nm* twentieth.
vinicole [vinikɔl] *a* wine-growing.
viol [vjɔl] *nm* rape.
violacé [vjɔlase] *a* purplish-blue.
violateur, -trice [vjɔlatœ:r, tris] *n* violator, transgressor.
violation [vjɔlasjɔ̃] *nf* violation, breach, breaking, infringement.

violence [vjɔlɑ̃:s] *nf* violence, force, vehemence.
violent [vjɔlɑ̃] *a* violent, fierce, strong, high.
violenter [vjɔlɑ̃te] *vt* to do violence to.
violer [vjɔle] *vt* to violate, break, transgress, rape.
violet, -ette [vjɔlɛ, ɛt] *a nm* purple, violet.
violette [vjɔlɛt] *nf* violet.
violon [vjɔlɔ̃] *nm* violin, fiddle, violinist, jail, clink.
violoncelle [vjɔlɔ̃sɛl] *nm* violoncello, cello (player).
violoniste [vjɔlɔnist] *n* violinist.
vipère [vipɛ:r] *nf* viper, adder.
virage [vira:ȝ] *nm* turn(ing), swinging round, tacking, cornering, bend.
virement [virmɑ̃] *nm* turn(ing), transfer; **banque de —** clearing-bank.
virer [vire] *vt* to turn over, clear, transfer; *vi* to turn, swing round, tack, veer, corner, bank, change color.
virevolte [virvɔlt] *nf* quick circling, sudden change.
virevolter [virvɔlte] *vi* to circle, spin round.
virginal [virȝinal] *a* virginal.
virginité [virȝinite] *nf* virginity, maidenhood.
virgule [virgyl] *nf* comma, decimal point; **point et —** semi-colon.
viril [viril] *a* virile, manly, male; **l'âge —** manhood.
virilité [virilite] *nf* virility, manliness.
virole [virɔl] *nf* ferrule, binding-ring.
virtuel, -elle [virtɥɛl] *a* virtual, potential.
virtuose [virtɥo:z] *n* virtuoso.
virtuosité [virtɥozite] *nf* virtuosity.
virulence [virylɑ̃:s] *nf* virulence.
vis [vis] *nf* screw, thread.
visa [viza] *nm* visa, initials.
visage [viza:ȝ] *nm* face, visage, countenance; **trouver — de bois** to find nobody at home, the door shut.
vis-à-vis [vizavi] *ad* opposite; *prep* **— de** opposite, facing, with regard to, towards; *nm* person opposite, partner.
viscère [vissɛ:r] *nm* viscus; *pl* viscera.
viscosité [viskozite] *nf* viscosity, stickiness.
visée [vize] *nf* aim(ing), sight(ing), design.
viser [vize] *vt* to aim at, sight, allude to, initial, countersign; *vi* to aim, aspire.
viseur, -euse [vizœ:r, ø:z] *n* aimer; *nm* view-finder, sights, sighting-tube.
visibilité [vizibilite] *nf* visibility.
visible [vizibl] *a* visible, obvious, perceptible, open; **il n'est pas —** he is not at home.

visière [vizjɛːr] *nf* visor, eye-shade, peak; **rompre en — avec** to quarrel openly with, attack openly.

vision [vizjɔ̃] *nf* vision, (eye)sight, fantasy.

visionnaire [vizjɔnɛːr] *a* visionary; *n* dreamer.

visite [vizit] *nf* visit, call, inspection, visitor, caller; **faire (rendre) — à** to visit, call on; **rendre à qn sa —** to return s.o.'s visit; **— des bagages** customs inspection.

visiter [vizite] *vt* to visit, attend, inspect, examine, go over, search; **faire — la maison à qn** to show s.o. over the house.

visiteur, -euse [vizitœːr, øːz] *n* visitor, caller, inspector.

vison [vizɔ̃] *nm* vison, mink.

visqueux, -euse [viskø, øːz] *a* viscous, sticky, gluey, thick.

visser [vise] *vt* to screw (down, in, on, up), put the screw on, keep down.

visuel, -elle [vizɥɛl] *a* visual; **champ —** field of vision.

vital [vital] *a* vital.

vitalité [vitalite] *nf* vitality.

vitamine [vitamin] *nf* vitamin.

vite [vit] *a* speedy, fast, fleet, swift; *ad* quickly, fast, soon; **avoir — fait de** to be quick about; **faites vite!** hurry up!

vitesse [vitɛs] *nf* speed, rapidity, rate; **à toute —** at full speed; **en petite —** by freight train; **gagner qn de —** to outstrip s.o., outrun, steal a march on s.o.; **prendre de la —** to gather speed.

viticole [vitikɔl] *a* wine.

viticulteur [vitikyltœːr] *nm* vine-grower.

viticulture [vitikyltyːr] *nf* wine-growing.

vitrage [vitraːʒ] *nm* glazing, windows.

vitrail [vitraːj] *nm* stained glass window.

vitre [vitr] *nf* (window) pane.

vitrer [vitre] *vt* to glaze.

vitreux, -euse [vitrø, øːz] *a* vitreous, glazed, glassy.

vitrier [vitrie] *nm* glazier.

vitrine [vitrin] *nf* shop-window, glass-case, showcase, cabinet.

vitriol [vitriɔl] *nm* vitriol.

vitupération [vityperasjɔ̃] *nf* vituperation.

vitupérer [vitypere] *vt* to blame.

vivace [vivas] *a* long-lived, undying, hardy, perennial.

vivacité [vivasite] *nf* vivacity, vivaciousness, vividness, intensity, hastiness, burst of temper.

vivant [vivɑ̃] *a* living, alive, lively, lifelike, vivid; **langues —es** modern languages; *nm* living person, lifetime; **bon —** person who enjoys life, boon companion; **de mon —** in my lifetime.

vivat [vivat] *nm* hurrah.

vive-eau [vivo] *nf* spring-tide.

vivement [vivmɑ̃] *ad* briskly, sharply, warmly.

viveur, -euse [vivœːr, øːz] *n* rake, fast liver.

vivier [vivje] *nm* fish-pond.

vivifiant [vivifjɑ̃] *a* vivifying, bracing, invigorating.

vivisection [vivisɛksjɔ̃] *nf* vivisection.

vivoter [vivɔte] *vi* to live from hand to mouth.

vivre [viːvr] *vi* to live; *nm* food, living; *pl* provisions, supplies; **avoir de quoi —** to have enough to live on; **apprendre à — à qn** to teach s.o. manners; **être commode à —** to be easy to get on with.

vlan [vlɑ̃] *excl* whack! bang!

vocable [vɔkabl] *nm* vocable, word.

vocabulaire [vɔkabylɛːr] *nm* vocabulary.

vocal [vɔkal] *a* vocal.

vocalise [vɔkaliːz] *nf* exercise in vocalization.

vocation [vɔkasjɔ̃] *nf* vocation, bent, call(ing).

vociférant [vɔsiferɑ̃] *a* vociferous.

vociférer [vɔsifere] *vi* to vociferate, yell, shout.

voeu [vø] *nm* vow, wish.

vogue [vɔg] *nf* vogue, fashion; **être en —** to be popular; **c'est la grande —** it's all the rage.

voguer [vɔge] *vi* to sail.

voici [vwasi] *prep* here is, here are, this is, these are; **me — here** I am; **le — qui arrive** here he comes.

voie [vwa] *nf* way, track(s), thoroughfare, passage; **— d'eau** leak; **— ferrée** railway line; **— de garage** siding; **être en — de** to be in a fair way to.

voilà [vwala] *prep* there is, there are, that is, those are; **le —** there he is; **— un an a year ago; en — une idée** what an idea! **ne —-t-il pas qu'il pleure** there now, if he isn't crying.

voile [vwal] *nm* veil, cloak; *nf* sail; **mettre à la —** to set sail.

voiler [vwale] *vt* to veil, muffle, cloud, shade, hide; *vr* to cloud over.

voilette [vwalɛt] *nf* (hat) veil, half-veil.

voilier [vwalje] *nm* sailing ship, sail-maker.

voilure [vwalyːr] *nf* sails.

voir [vwaːr] *vt* to see, notice, imagine, look into; *vr* to be seen, show, be obvious; **faire — to** show, reveal; **faites —** let's see it; **— sur** to look out on; **à ce que je vois** as far as I can see; **il ne peut pas me — he** can't stand the sight of me; **il n'y voit pas** he can't see; **se faire bien —** to get into s.o.'s good books; **vous n'avez rien à — là-dedans** it is none of your business; **cela n'a rien à — à l'affaire** that has nothing to do with it.

voire [vwaːr] *ad* nay, in truth; —
même and indeed.
voirie [vwari] *nf* roads, refuse
(-heap); **le service de** — Highways
Department.
voisin [vwazɛ̃] *a* neighboring, next,
adjoining, bordering; *n* neighbor.
voisinage [vwazinaːʒ] *nm* neighborhood, vicinity, nearness, proximity.
voisiner [vwazine] *vi* to adjoin, be
side by side, visit neighbors.
voiturage [vwatyraːʒ] *nm* carriage,
cartage.
voiture [vwatyːr] *nf* automobile,
vehicle, carriage, cart, van; — **à
bras** hand-cart, barrow; — **d'enfant**
perambulator, baby carriage; — **de
malade** wheelchair; — **de place** cab
taxi; **aller en** — to drive; **en** —!
all aboard!
voiturer [vwatyre] *vt* to transport,
convey.
voiturier, -ière [vwatyrje, jɛːr] *a*
carriage(able); *nm* carter, carrier.
voix [vwa] *nf* voice, vote; **à haute** —
aloud; **à mi-** — under one's breath;
avoir — **au chapitre** to have a say
in the matter; **de vive** — by word
of mouth, viva voce; **mettre aux** —
to put to the vote.
vol [vɔl] *nm* flight, flying, flock, theft,
robbery, stealing, stolen goods; **à** —
d'oiseau as the crow flies; — **à la
roulotte** theft from an automobile;
— **à l'étalage** shop-lifting; — **à la
lire** pocket-picking, bag-snatching;
— **à l'américaine** confidence trick.
volage [vɔlaːʒ] *a* fickle, flighty.
volaille [vɔlaːj] *nf* poultry, fowl.
volailler [vɔlaːje] *nm* poultry-yard,
poultry dealer.
volant [vɔlɑ̃] *a* flying, detachable,
loose, fluttering; *nm* shuttlecock,
flywheel, steering-wheel, flounce.
volatil [vɔlatil] *a* volatile.
volatile [vɔlatil] *nm* winged creature,
bird.
volatiliser [vɔlatilize] *vt* to volatilize;
vr to volatilize, vanish, disappear
into thin air.
vol-au-vent [vɔlovɑ̃] *nm* vol-au-
vent, puff pastry pie.
volcan [vɔlkɑ̃] *nm* volcano.
volcanique [vɔlkanik] *a* volcanic.
volée [vɔle] *nf* flight, flock, volley,
shower, thrashing; **à la** — in flight,
on the wing; **semer à la** — to
broadcast; **sonner à toute** — to ring
a full peal; **de la première** — of the
first rank, crack.
voler [vɔle] *vt* to steal, rob, swindle;
vi to fly, soar; **il ne l'a pas volé** he
deserved it.
volet [vɔlɛ] *nm* shutter, sorting-
board; **trié sur le** — select, hand-
picked.
voleter [vɔlte] *vi* to flutter, flit.
voleur, -euse [vɔlœːr, øːz] *a* flying,
thievish, thieving; *nm* thief, robber;
au —! stop thief!

volière [vɔljɛːr] *nf* aviary.
volontaire [vɔlɔ̃tɛːr] *a* voluntary,
willful, determined, self-willed; *nm*
volunteer.
volonté [vɔlɔ̃te] *nf* will; *pl* caprices,
whims; **dernières** —s **de** last will and
testament of; **de bonne** — with a
good grace, with a will; **à** — ad lib,
at will; **de sa propre** — of one's own
accord; **faire ses quatre** —s to do
as one pleases.
volontiers [vɔlɔ̃tje] *ad* willingly,
gladly, readily.
volt [vɔlt] *nm* volt.
voltage [vɔltaːʒ] *nm* voltage.
voltampère [vɔltɑ̃pɛːr] *nm* watt.
volte-face [vɔltfas] *nf* volte-face,
turning-around, about-face **faire**
— to face about, reverse one's
opinions.
voltige [vɔltiːʒ] *nf* slack-rope, flying
trapeze exercises, trick-riding,
vaulting.
voltiger [vɔltiʒe] *vi* to flutter, flit,
flap, perform on the flying trapeze
or on horseback.
voltigeur, -euse [vɔltiʒœːr, øːz] *n*
trapeze artist, trick-rider, equestrian
performer; *nm* light infantryman.
volubilité [vɔlybilite] *nf* volubility,
fluency.
volume [vɔlym] *nm* volume, bulk,
capacity, tome.
volumineux, -euse [vɔlyminø, øːz]
a voluminous, bulky.
volupté [vɔlypte] *nf* pleasure, delight,
sensuousness.
voluptueux, -euse [vɔlyptɥø, øːz] *a*
sensuous, voluptuous; *n* sensualist.
volute [vɔlyt] *nf* volute, scroll,
wreath.
vomir [vɔmiːr] *vti* to vomit; *vt*
bring up, belch forth.
vomissement [vɔmismɑ̃] *nm* vomit
(ing).
vomitif, -ive [vɔmitif, iːv] *a nm*
emetic.
vorace [vɔras] *a* voracious.
voracité [vɔrasite] *nf* voraciousness,
voracity.
votant [vɔtɑ̃] *a* voting, having a
vote; *n* voter.
vote [vɔt] *nm* vote, voting, poll,
passing; **bulletin de** — voting-
paper; **droit de** — franchise.
voter [vɔte] *vt* to vote, pass, carry;
vi to vote; — **à main levée** to vote
by show of hands.
votre, vos [vɔtr, vo] *pos a* your.
vôtre [voːtr] *pos pn* le, la —, les —s
yours; *nm* yours, your own; *pl* your
own people *etc*; **vous avez encore
fait des** —s you have been up to
your tricks again.
vouer [vwe] *vt* to vow, devote,
pledge, dedicate; **je ne sais à quel
saint me** — I don't know what to
do next.
vouloir [vulwaːr] *vt* to want, wish,
like, will, be willing, consent, be

determined, insist, intend, require, need, try; *vr* to try to be; *nm* will; **que voulez-vous?** what can you expect? what do you want? **il ne veut pas de nous** he won't have anything to do with us; **en — à** to bear (s.o.) a grudge, be angry with; **je veux bien** I don't mind; **sans le —** unintentionally.

voulu [vuly] *a* required, due, intentional, deliberate.

vous [vu] *pn* you, to you, (to) yourself, (to) each other, one another; **—-même(s)** yourself, yourselves.

voussoir [vuswaːr] *nm* arch-stone.

voussure [vusyːr] *nf* curve, arching.

voûte [vut] *nf* arch, vault, dome, canopy, roof.

voûter [vute] *vt* to arch, vault, bow; *vr* to become bent.

vouvoyer [vuvwaje] *vt* to address as 'vous'.

voyage [vwajaːʒ] *nm* journey, voyage, trip; *pl* travel; **compagnon de —** fellow-traveler, traveling companion; **— de noces** honeymoon.

voyager [vwajaʒe] *vi* to travel, journey, migrate.

voyageur, -euse [vwajaʒœːr, øːz] *a* traveling, migratory; *n* traveler, passenger, fare; **pigeon —** homing pigeon.

voyant [vwajɑ̃] *a* gaudy, conspicuous, loud, showy, clairvoyant; *n* seer, clairvoyant.

voyelle [vwajɛl] *nf* vowel.

voyer [vwaje] *nm* road surveyor.

voyou, -oute [vwaju, ut] *n* hooligan, guttersnipe.

vrac [vrak] *nm* **en —** in bulk, loose, wholesale, pell-mell.

vrai [vrɛ] *a* true, real, genuine, downright; *ad* really, truly; *nm* truth; **à — dire** as a matter of fact; **pour de —** in earnest; **il y a du —** there is something in it.

vraiment [vrɛmɑ̃] *ad* truly, really, indeed, is that so?

vraisemblable [vrɛsɑ̃blabl] *a* likely, probable; *nm* what is probable.

vraisemblance [vrɛsɑ̃blɑ̃ːs] *nf* likelihood, probability.

vrille [vriːj] *nf* tendril, gimlet, borer; **descente en —** spiral dive, spin.

vriller [vrije] *vt* to bore; *vi* to twist, corkscrew.

vrombir [vrɔ̃biːr] *vi* to throb, buzz, hum.

vrombissement [vrɔ̃bismɑ̃] *nm* throbbing, buzzing, drone, humming.

vu [vy] *a* seen; *prep* in view of, considering; *cj* **— que** seeing that, whereas; *nm* sight, presentation; **mal —** unpopular, disliked; **bien —** well thought of; **ni — ni connu** nobody is any the wiser for it; **au — de tous** openly; **au — et au su de tous** as everyone knows.

vue [vy] *nf* (eye)sight, view, prospect, purpose, intention, design, slide; **de — by** sight; **en — de** in sight of, with a view to; **perdre qn de — to** lose sight of s.o.

vulcaniser [vylkanize] *vt* to vulcanize.

vulcanite [vylkanit] *nf* ebonite, vulcanite.

vulgaire [vylgɛːr] *a* vulgar, common, coarse, low; *nm* common people, vulgarity.

vulgarisation [vylgarizasjɔ̃] *nf* popularization.

vulgariser [vylgarize] *vt* to popularize, vulgarize; *vr* to become popular, vulgar.

vulgarité [vylgarite] *nf* vulgarity.

vulnérabilité [vylnerabilite] *nf* vulnerability.

vulnérable [vylnerabl] *a* vulnerable.

W

wagon [vagɔ̃] *nm* carriage, coach, truck, wagon.

wagon-couloir [vagɔ̃kulwaːr] *nm* corridor-coach.

wagon-lit [vagɔ̃li] *nm* sleeping-car, sleeper.

wagon-poste [vagɔ̃pɔst] *nm* mail-car.

wagon-restaurant [vagɔ̃rɛstɔrɑ̃] *nm* dining-car.

watt [wat] *nm* watt.

wattman [watman] *nm* driver.

wolfram [vɔlfram] *nm* tungsten ore, wolfram.

X

xérès [keres, gzeres] *nm* sherry.

xylographe [ksilɔgraf] *nm* wood-engraver.

xylographie [ksilɔgrafi] *nf* wood-engraving, wood-cut.

xylophone [ksilɔfɔn] *nm* xylophone.

Y

y [i] *ad* here, there; *pn* at, to, on, in, by, of it or them; **j'y suis** I've got it, I understand; **ça y est** that's it, there you are, right!; **il y a** there is, there are; **il n'y est pour rien** he had nothing to do with it.

yacht [jak(t), jat, jɔt] *nm* yacht.

yaourt [jaurt] *nm* yoghourt.

yeuse [jøːz] *nf* holm-oak.

yole [jɔl] *nf* yawl, skiff.

yougoslave [jugɔslaːv] *an* Yugoslav.

Yougoslavie [jugɔslavi] *nf* Yugoslavia.

youyou [juju] *nm* dinghy.

ypérite [iperit] *nf* mustard-gas.

Z

zazou [zazu] *nm* weirdie, crank.
zèbre [zɛbr] *nm* zebra.
zébré [zebre] *a* striped.
zélateur, -trice [zɛlatœːr, tris] *a* zealous; *n* zealot, enthusiast.
zèle [zɛːl] *nm* zeal, enthusiasm; **faire du —** to be over-eager, bustle about.
zélé [zele] *a* zealous.
zénith [zenit] *nm* zenith, height.
zéphyr [zefiːr] *nm* zephyr, light breeze.
zéro [zero] *nm* zero, cipher, nought.
zest [zɛst] *nm* **être entre le zist et le —** to be betwixt and between, be so-so.
zeste [zɛst] *nm* peel.
zézayement [zezɛmɑ̃] *nm* lisp(ing).
zézayer [zezɛje] *vi* to lisp.

zibeline [ziblin] *nf* sable.
zigouiller [ziguje] *vt* to kill, knife.
zigzag [zigzag] *nm* zigzag; **faire des —s** to zigzag, stagger along; **éclair en —** forked lightning.
zigzaguer [zigzage] *vi* to zigzag.
zinc [zɛ̃ːg] *nm* zinc, bar, counter.
zinguer [zɛ̃ge] *vt* to (cover with) zinc, galvanize.
zodiaque [zɔdjak] *nm* zodiac.
zona [zɔna] *nm* (*med*) shingles.
zone [zoːn] *nf* zone, area, belt; **— neutre** no man's land.
zoologie [zɔɔlɔʒi] *nf* zoology.
zoologique [zɔɔlɔʒik] *a* zoological; **jardin —** zoological gardens, zoo
zoologiste [zɔɔlɔʒist] *nm* zoologist.
zut [zyt] *excl* darn it! hang it all!
zyeuter [zjøte] *vt* to take a squint at.

English — French

A

a [ei, ə] *indef art* un, une.

aback [ə'bæk] *ad* en arrière, par derrière (surprise), abasourdi, interdit.

abandon [ə'bændən] *vt* abandonner, délaisser.

abandoned [ə'bændənd] *a* dissolu, abandonné.

abandonment [ə'bændənmənt] *n* abandon *m*, dévergondage *m*.

abase [ə'beis] *vt* abaisser, humilier.

abasement [ə'beismənt] *n* abaissement *m*, dégradation *f*.

abash [ə'bæʃ] *vt* déconcerter.

abashment [ə'bæʃmənt] *n* ébahissement *m*, confusion *f*.

abate [ə'beit] *vt* diminuer, rabattre; *vi* se calmer.

abatement [ə'beitmənt] *n* apaisement *m*, diminution *f*, rabais *m*.

abbess ['æbis] *n* abbesse *f*.

abbey ['æbi] *n* abbaye *f*.

abbot ['æbət] *n* abbé *m*.

abbreviate [ə'briːvieit] *vt* abréger.

abbreviation [ə,briːvi'eiʃən] *n* abréviation *f*.

abdicate ['æbdikeit] *vti* abdiquer.

abdication [,æbdi'keiʃən] *n* abdication *f*.

abduct [æb'dʌkt] *vt* enlever.

abduction [æb'dʌkʃən] *n* enlèvement *m*, rapt *m*.

abed [ə'bed] *ad* au lit.

aberration [,æbə'reiʃən] *n* aberration *f*, égarement *m*.

abet [ə'bet] *vt* encourager, assister.

abetment [ə'betmənt] *n* instigation *f*.

abettor [ə'betə] *n* fauteur, -trice, complice *mf*.

abeyance [ə'beiəns] *n* suspens *m*, souffrance *f*, sommeil *m*, carence *f*, vacance *f*.

abhor [əb'hɔː] *vt* abhorrer.

abhorrence [əb'hɔrəns] *n* horreur *f*.

abhorrent [əb'hɔrənt] *a* odieux.

abide [ə'baid] *vt* attendre, souffrir; *vi* rester fidèle (à by), demeurer.

abiding [ə'baidiŋ] *a* permanent.

ability [ə'biliti] *n* capacité *f*, talent *m*, moyens *m pl*; **to the best of my** — de mon mieux.

abject ['æbdʒekt] *a* abject.

abjection [æb'dʒekʃən] *n* abjection *f*.

abjuration [,æbdʒuə'reiʃən] *n* abjuration *f*.

abjure ['əb'dʒuə] *vt* abjurer, renoncer à.

ablaze [ə'bleiz] *a ad* enflammé, en feu.

able ['eibl] *a* capable, en état (de to); —-bodied *a* valide.

ablution [ə'bluːʃən] *n* ablution *f*.

abnegation [,æbni'geiʃən] *n* abnégation *f*, renoncement *m*, répudiation *f*.

abnormal [æb'nɔːməl] *a* anormal.

aboard [ə'bɔːd] *ad* à bord; *prep* à bord de.

abode [ə'boud] *n* demeure *f*.

abolish [ə'bɔliʃ] *vt* abolir.

abolition [,æbə'liʃən] *n* abolition *f*.

abominable [ə'bɔminəbl] *a* abominable.

abominate [ə'bɔmineit] *vt* avoir en abomination.

abortion [ə'bɔːʃən] *n* avortement *m*, avorton *m*.

abound [ə'baund] *vi* abonder, foisonner.

about [ə'baut] *ad* à peu près, environ, çà et là; *prep* autour de, près de, sur le point de, au sujet de.

above [ə'bʌv] *prep* au dessus de, en amont de; *ad* plus que (de), ci-dessus, en amont, au-dessus.

above-board [ə'bʌv'bɔːd] *ad* net, loyal; *ad* loyalement.

above-named [ə'bʌv'neimd] *a* susnommé.

abrasion [ə'breiʒən] *n* écorchure *f*.

abreast [ə'brest] *ad* de front.

abridge [ə'bridʒ] *vt* abréger, restreindre.

abridgment [ə'bridʒmənt] *n* raccourcissement *m*, abrégé *m*.

abroad [ə'brɔːd] *ad* à l'étranger, au large, dehors.

abrogate ['æbrougeit] *vt* abroger.

abrogation [,æbrou'geiʃən] *n* abrogation *f*.

abrupt [ə'brʌpt] *a* brusque.

abruptness [ə'brʌptnis] *n* brusquerie *f*, escarpement *m*.

abscess ['æbsis] *n* abcès *m*.

abscond [əb'skɔnd] *vi* s'esquiver, décamper.

absence ['æbsəns] *n* absence *f*.

absent [æb'sent] *vi* to — oneself s'absenter.

absent ['æbsənt] *a* absent.

absently ['æbsəntli] *ad* d'un air absent, distraitement.

absolute ['æbsəlut] *an* absolu *m*.

absolutely ['æbsəluːtli] *ad* absolument.

absolution [,æbsə'luːʃən] *n* absolution *f*, acquittement *m*.

absolutism ['æbsəluːtizəm] *n* absolutisme *m*.
absolutist ['æbsəluːtist] *n* absolutiste *mf*.
absolve [əb'zɔlv] *vt* absoudre, dispenser.
absorb [əb'zɔːb] *vt* absorber.
absorption [əb'zɔːpʃən] *n* absorption *f*.
abstain [əb'stein] *vi* s'abstenir.
abstemious [æb'stiːmjəs] *a* sobre, abstinent.
abstention [æb'stenʃən] *n* abstention *f*.
abstinence ['æbstinəns] *n* abstinence *f*.
abstinent ['æbstinənt] *a* abstinent.
abstract ['æbstrækt] *n* précis *m*, extrait *m*; *a* abstrait.
abstract [æb'strækt] *vt* faire abstraction de, soustraire, distraire, résumer.
abstracted [æb'stræktid] *a* distrait.
abstraction [æb'strækʃən] *n* abstraction *f*.
absurd [əb'səːd] *a* absurde.
absurdity [əb'səːditi] *n* absurdité *f*.
abundance [ə'bʌndəns] *n* abondance *f*.
abundant [ə'bʌndənt] *a* abondant.
abundantly [ə'bʌndəntli] *ad* abondamment.
abuse [ə'bjuːs] *n* abus *m*, insulte *f*.
abuse [ə'bjuːz] *vt* abuser de, mésuser de, insulter, injurier.
abusive [ə'bjuːsiv] *a* abusif, outrageant, injurieux.
abut [ə'bʌt] *vi* se toucher.
abyss [ə'bis] *n* abîme *m*.
academy [ə'kædəmi] *n* académie *f*, institution *f*, école *f*.
accede [æk'siːd] *vi* arriver (à **to**), adhérer (à **to**).
accelerate [æk'seləreit] *vti* accélérer, activer.
acceleration [æk,selə'reiʃən] *n* accélération *f*.
accelerator [ək'seləreitə] *n* accélérateur *m*.
accent ['æksənt] *n* accent *m*.
accent [æk'sent] *vt* accentuer.
accentuate [æk'sentjueit] *vt* faire ressortir, souligner, accentuer.
accentuation [æk,sentju'eiʃən] *n* accentuation *f*.
accept [ək'sept] *vt* accepter, agréer, admettre.
acceptance [ək'septəns] *n* bienvenue *f* acceptation *f*.
access ['ækses] *n* accès *m*, abord *m*.
accessible [æk'sesəbl] *a* accessible.
accessory [æk'sesəri] *n* complice *mf*; *an* accessoire *m*.
accident ['æksidənt] *n* accident *m*, avarie *f*; **—prone** sujet aux accidents.
accidental [,æksi'dentl] *a* accidentel, fortuit.
accidentally [,æksi'dentəli] *ad* par accident.

acclaim [ə'kleim] *vt* acclamer.
acclamation [,æklə'meiʃən] *n* acclamation *f*.
acclimatization [ə'klaimətai'zeiʃən] *n* acclimatation *f*.
acclimatize [ə'klaimətaiz] *vt* acclimater.
acclivity [ə'kliviti] *n* montée *f*, rampe *f*.
accommodate [ə'kɔmədeit] *vt* adapter, arranger, fournir, obliger, loger.
accommodating [ə'kɔmədeitiŋ] *a* accommodant, serviable, complaisant.
accommodation [ə,kɔmə'deiʃən] *n* adaptation *f*, accommodement *m*, commodités *f pl*, logement *m*, prêt *m*.
accompaniment [ə'kʌmpənimənt] *n* accompagnement *m*.
accompanist [ə'kʌmpənist] *n* accompagnateur, -trice.
accompany [ə'kʌmpəni] *vt* accompagner.
accomplice [ə'kɔmplis] *n* complice *mf*.
accomplish [ə'kʌmpliʃ] *vt* accomplir, parachever, faire.
accomplishment [ə'kʌmpliʃmənt] *n* accomplissement *m*, exécution *f*; *pl* talents *m*, grâces *f pl*.
accord [ə'kɔːd] *n* accord *m*, assentiment *m*; **with one** — d'une seule voix; **of one's own** — de son propre mouvement; *vt* accorder; *vi* s'accorder.
accordance [ə'kɔːdəns] *n* conformité *f*, accord *m*.
according [ə'kɔːdiŋ] *ad* — **to** *prep* selon; — **as** *cj* selon que.
accordingly [ə'kɔːdiŋli] *ad* en conséquence.
accost [ə'kɔst] *vt* accoster, aborder.
account [ə'kaunt] *n* compte *m*, importance *f*, compte-rendu *m*; *vt* regarder (comme); **to** — **for** rendre compte de, répondre de, expliquer; **— rendered** rappel; **on one's own** — à ses risques et périls, de sa propre initiative; **on** — **of** en raison (vue) de; **on no** — à aucun prix.
accountable [ə'kauntəbl] *a* responsable, explicable.
accountancy [ə'kauntənsi] *n* tenue *f* des livres, comptabilité *f*.
accountant [ə'kauntənt] *n* comptable *m*.
accouterment [ə'kuːtrəmənt] *n* équipement *m*, fourniment *m*, caparaçon *m*.
accredit [ə'kredit] *vt* (ac)créditer.
accrue [ə'kruː] *vi* résulter, s'ajouter (à **to**), s'accumuler.
accumulate [ə'kjuːmjuleit] *vt* accumuler; *vi* s'accumuler.
accumulation [ə,kjuːmju'leiʃən] *n* accumulation *f*, amas *m*.
accumulative [ə'kjuːmjulətiv] *a* cumulatif.

accumulator [ə'kjuːmjuleitə] *n* (*motor etc*) accu(mulateur) *m*, accumulateur, -trice.

accuracy ['ækjurəsi] *n* exactitude *f*, précision *f*.

accurate ['ækjurit] *a* exact, correct, précis.

accursed [ə'kəːsid] *a* maudit.

accusation [ˌækju(ː)'zeiʃən] *n* accusation *f*.

accuse [ə'kjuːz] *vt* accuser.

accuser [ə'kjuːzə] *n* accusateur, -trice.

accustom [ə'kʌstəm] *vt* habituer; **to — oneself** se faire (à), s'habituer.

ace [eis] *n* un *m*, as *m*; **within an —** of à deux doigts de.

acerbity [ə'səːbiti] *n* acerbité *f*.

ache [eik] *n* mal *m*; *vi* avoir mal, souffrir, faire mal.

achieve [ə'tʃiːv] *vt* exécuter, acquérir, atteindre.

achievement [ə'tʃiːvmənt] *n* exécution *f*, succès *m*.

aching ['eikiŋ] *a* douloureux.

acid ['æsid] *an* acide *m*.

acidity [ə'siditi] *n* acidité *f*.

acidulous [ə'sidjuləs] *a* acidulé.

acknowledge [ək'nɔlidʒ] *vt* reconnaître, accuser réception de, répondre à.

acknowledgment [ək'nɔlədʒmənt] *n* reconnaissance *f*, accusé *m* de réception.

acme ['ækmi] *n* apogée *m*.

acne [ækni] *n* acné *m*.

acorn ['eikɔːn] *n* gland *m*.

acquaint [ə'kweint] *vt* informer; **to — oneself with** se familiariser avec, faire connaissance avec, prendre connaissance de.

acquainted [ə'kweintid] *a* en relation (avec), versé (dans).

acquaintance [ə'kweintəns] *n* connaissance *f*.

acquiesce [ˌækwi'es] *vi* acquiescer.

acquiescence [ˌækwi'esns] *n* assentiment *m*.

acquire [ə'kwaiə] *vt* acquérir, prendre.

acquirement [ə'kwaiəmənt] *n* acquisition *f*; *pl* talents *m pl*.

acquisition [ˌækwi'ziʃən] *n* acquisition *f*.

acquit [ə'kwit] *vti* acquitter, s'acquitter (de).

acquittal [ə'kwitl] *n* quittance *f*, acquittement *m*, accomplissement *m*.

acquittance [ə'kwitəns] *n* paiement *m*, décharge *f*, reçu *m*.

acre ['eikə] *n* acre *f*.

acrid ['ækrid] *a* âcre, acerbe.

acridity [æ'kriditi] *n* âcreté *f*.

acrimonious [ˌækri'mounjəs] *a* acrimonieux.

acrimony ['ækriməni] *n* acrimonie *f*.

acrobat ['ækrəbæt] *n* acrobate *mf*.

acrobatics [ˌækrə'bætiks] *n* acrobatie *f*.

across [ə'krɔs] *prep* à travers; *ad* en travers, en croix.

act [ækt] *n* acte *m*; *vti* jouer; *vt* représenter; *vi* agir, servir.

acting ['æktiŋ] *n* action *f*, représentation *f*, jeu *m*; *a* qui joue, qui fait semblant, en exercice, suppléant, par intérim.

action ['ækʃən] *n* action *f*.

actionable ['ækʃnəbl] *a* sujet à poursuites.

activate ['æktiveit] *vt* activer, organiser.

active ['æktiv] *a* actif, ingambe.

actively ['æktivli] *ad* **to be — involved in** prendre une part active à.

activity [æk'tiviti] *n* activité *f*, animation *f*.

actor ['æktə] *n* acteur *m*.

actress ['æktris] *n* actrice *f*.

actual ['æktjuəl] *a* réel, de fait, actual.

actuality [ˌæktju'æliti] *n* réalité *f*.

actually ['æktjuəli] *ad* en fait, présentement.

actuate ['æktjueit] *vt* actionner mettre en marche, motiver, pousser.

acumen ['ækjumen] *n* sagacité *f*, perspicacité *f*.

acute [ə'kjuːt] *a* aigu, -uë.

acuteness [ə'kjuːtnis] *n* acuité *f*, vivacité *f*.

adage ['ædidʒ] *n* adage *m*.

adamant ['ædəmənt] *a* inflexible, intransigeant.

adapt [ə'dæpt] *vt* adapter.

adaptability [əˌdæptə'biliti] *n* faculté *f* d'adaptation, souplesse *f*.

adaptable [ə'dæptəbl] *a* adaptable, souple.

adaptation [ˌædæp'teiʃən] *n* adaptation *f*.

A.D.C. ['ei'diː'siː] *n* aide de camp *m*.

add [æd] *vt* ajouter, additionner.

adder ['ædə] *n* vipère *f*.

addict ['ædikt] *n* personne adonnée à, -mane *mf*, morphinomane *mf etc*.

addicted [ə'diktid] *a* adonné (à to); **to be — to** s'adonner à.

addiction [ə'dikʃən] *n* besoin *m*, habitude *f*, goût *m*.

addition [ə'diʃən] *n* addition *f*; **in —** par surcroît.

additional [ə'diʃənl] *a* additionnel, supplémentaire.

addle ['ædl] *a* pourri, couvi; confus; *vt* brouiller, pourrir.

address [ə'dres] *n* adresse *f*, tenue *f*, allocution *f*; *pl* avances *f pl*, cour *f*; *vt* s'adresser à, adresser.

addressee [ˌædre'siː] *n* destinataire *mf*.

adduce [ə'djuːs] *vt* alléguer.

adept ['ædept] *a* expert (en **at**); *n* passé maître *m*.

adequate ['ædikwit] *a* adéquat, suffisant.

adhere [əd'hiə] *vi* adhérer, se coller, maintenir (**to** à).

adherence [əd'hiərəns] *n* adhérence *f*, adhésion *f*.
adherent [əd'hiərənt] *an* adhérent(e) *mf*.
adhesion [əd'hiːʒən] *n* adhésion *f*.
adhesive [əd'hiːsiv] *a* collant.
adjacent [ə'dʒeisənt] *a* adjacent, attenant.
adjective ['ædʒiktiv] *n* adjectif *m*.
adjoin [ə'dʒɔin] *vt* joindre, attenir à; *vi* se toucher.
adjoining [ə'dʒɔiniŋ] *a* contigu, -uë, attenant.
adjourn [ə'dʒəːn] *vt* ajourner, remettre.
adjournment [ə'dʒəːnmənt] *n* ajournement *m*.
adjudge [ə'dʒʌdʒ] *vt* décider, condamner, adjuger.
adjudicate [ə'dʒuːdikeit] *vti* juger.
adjudication [ə.dʒuːdi'keiʃən] *n* jugement *m*.
adjudicator [ə'dʒuːdikeitə] *n* juge *m*.
adjunct ['ædʒʌŋkt] *n* accessoire *m*, auxiliaire *mf*.
adjuration [.ædʒuə'reiʃən] *n* adjuration *f*.
adjure [ə'dʒuə] *vt* adjurer, conjurer.
adjust [ə'dʒʌst] *vt* ajuster, régler.
adjustment [ə'dʒʌstmənt] *n* ajustement *m*, réglage *m*.
ad-lib [æd'lib] *vi* improviser.
administer [əd'ministə] *vt* administrer, (*oath*) déférer, gérer.
administration [əd.minis'treiʃən] *n* administration *f*, gérance *f*.
administrative [əd'ministrətiv] *a* administratif.
administrator [əd'ministreitə] *n* administrateur *m*, gérant *m*.
admirable ['ædmərəbl] *a* admirable.
admiral ['ædmərəl] *n* amiral *m*; **rear—** contre-amiral *m*; **vice—** vice-amiral *m*.
admiralty ['ædmərəlti] *n* Amirauté *f*; **First Lord of the A—** Ministre de la Marine.
admiration [.ædmə'reiʃən] *n* admiration *f*.
admire [əd'maiə] *vt* admirer.
admirer [əd'maiərə] *n* admirateur, -trice.
admiring [əd'maiəriŋ] *a* admiratif.
admiringly [əd'maiəriŋli] *ad* avec admiration.
admissible [əd'misəbl] *a* admissible.
admission [əd'miʃən] *n* confession *f*, admission *f*, aveu *m*, entrée *f*.
admit [əd'mit] *vt* admettre, avouer, laisser entrer; **to — of** permettre, comporter.
admittance [əd'mitəns] *n* entrée *f*, accès *m*.
admittedly [əd'mitidli] *ad* sans conteste.
admonish [əd'mɔniʃ] *vt* admonester, avertir, exhorter.
admonishment [əd'mɔniʃmənt] *n* admonestation *f*, exhortation *f*, avertissement *m*.

ado [ə'duː] *n* affaire *f*, embarras *m*, bruit *m*.
adolescence [.ædə'lesns] *n* adolescence *f*.
adolescent [.ædə'lesnt] *a* adolescent.
adopt [ə'dɔpt] *vt* adopter, suivre, embrasser.
adoption [ə'dɔpʃən] *n* adoption *f*, choix *m*.
adoptive [ə'dɔptiv] *a* adoptif.
adorable [ə'dɔːrəbl] *a* adorable.
adoration [.ædɔː'reiʃən] *n* adoration *f*.
adore [ə'dɔː] *vt* adorer.
adorer [ə'dɔːrə] *n* adorateur, -trice.
adorn [ə'dɔːn] *vt* orner.
adornment [ə'dɔːnmənt] *n* ornement *m*, parure *f*.
adrift [ə'drift] *ad* à la dérive.
adroit [ə'drɔit] *a* adroit.
adroitness [ə'drɔitnis] *n* adresse *f*.
adulation [.ædju'leiʃən] *n* adulation *f*.
adult ['ædʌlt] *an* adulte *mf*.
adulterate [ə'dʌltəreit] *vt* frelater, falsifier.
adulteration [ə.dʌltə'reiʃən] *n* falsification *f*.
adulterer, -ess [ə'dʌltərə, is] *n* homme, femme adultère.
adulterine [ə'dʌltərain] *a* adultérin.
adultery [ə'dʌltəri] *n* adultère *m*.
adumbrate ['ædʌmbreit] *vt* esquisser, ébaucher.
advance [əd'vaːns] *n* avance *f*, hausse *f*, progrès *m*; *vti* avancer, pousser; *vi* faire des progrès, hausser.
advancement [əd'vaːnsmənt] *n* avancement *m*, progrès *m*.
advantage [əd'vaːntidʒ] *n* avantage *m*, dessus *m*; **to take — of** profiter de; *vt* avantager.
advantageous [.ædvən'teidʒəs] *a* avantageux.
advent ['ædvənt] *n* Avent *m*, arrivée *f*, venue *f*.
adventure [əd'ventʃə] *n* aventure *f*, hasard *m*; *vt* risquer; *vi* s'aventurer (à, dans **upon**).
adventurer, -ess [əd'ventʃərə, is] *a* aventurier, -ière, chevalier d'industrie *m*.
adventurous [əd'ventʃərəs] *a* aventureux.
adverb ['ædvəːb] *n* adverbe *m*.
adversary ['ædvəsəri] *n* adversaire *mf*.
adverse ['ædvəːs] *a* adverse, hostile, contraire.
adversity [əd'vəːsiti] *n* adversité *f*.
advert [æd'vəːt] *vi* faire allusion (à to).
advertise ['ædvətaiz] *vt* annoncer, faire valoir, faire de la réclame pour; *vi* faire de la publicité.
advertisement [əd'vəːtismənt] *n* publicité *f*, réclame *f*, affiche , annonce *f*.

advertising ['ædvətaiziŋ] n publicité f.
advice [əd'vais] n avis m, conseil(s) m (pl).
advisable [əd'vaizəbl] a recommendable, sage.
advisability [əd,vaizə'biliti] n convenance f, sagesse f.
advise [əd'vaiz] vt conseiller.
advised [əd'vaizd] a (bien, mal) avisé.
advisedly [əd'vaizidli] ad sagement, en connaissance de cause.
adviser [əd'vaizə] n conseiller, -ère.
advisory [əd'vaizəri] a consultatif.
advocacy ['ædvəkəsi] n plaidoyer (en faveur de) m.
advocate ['ædvəkit] n avocat m.
advocate ['ædvəkeit] vt defendre, préconiser.
aerate ['eiəreit] vt aérer.
aerated ['eiəreitid] a gazeux.
aeration [,eiə'reiʃen] n aération f.
aerial ['ɛəriəl] n antenne f; a aérien, de l'air.
aerobatics [,ɛərə'bætiks] n acrobatie aérienne f.
aerodrome ['ɛərədroum] n aérodrome m.
aeronaut ['ɛərənɔːt] n aéronaute m.
aeronautics [,ɛərə'nɔːtiks] n aéronautique f.
aeroplane ['ɛərəplein] n avion m.
æsthete ['iːsθiːt] n esthète mf.
æsthetics [iːs'θetiks] n esthétique f.
afar [ə'faː] ad de loin, au loin.
affability [,æfə'biliti] n affabilité f.
affable ['æfəbl] a affable.
affair [ə'fɛə] n affaire f.
affect [ə'fekt] vt affecter, poser à, attaquer, toucher.
affectation [,æfek'teiʃən] n affectation f, simagrées f pl.
affection [ə'fekʃən] n affection f, disposition f.
affectionate [ə'fekʃnit] a affectueux.
affianced [ə'faiənst] a fiancé.
affidavit [,æfi'deivit] n déclaration assermentée f.
affiliate [ə'filieit] vt (s')affilier.
affiliation [ə,fili'eiʃən] n attribution de paternité f, affiliation f.
affinity [ə'finiti] n affinité f.
affirm [ə'fəːm] vt affirmer.
affirmation [,æfə'meiʃən] n affirmation f.
affirmative [ə'fəːmətiv] n affirmative f; a affirmatif.
affix [ə'fiks] vt apposer.
afflict [ə'flikt] vt affliger.
affliction [ə'flikʃən] n affliction f.
afflictive [ə'fliktiv] a affligeant.
affluence ['æfluəns] n affluence f, richesse].
affluent 'jæfluənt] a riche.
afford [ə'fɔːd] vt s'offrir, se permettre, fournir.
affray [ə'frei] n bagarre f, rixe f.
affright [ə'frait] n effroi m; vt effrayer.

affront [ə'frʌnt] n affront m; vt offenser, faire honte à.
afloat [ə'flout] ad à flot; to get — lancer; to get — again renflouer.
afoot [ə'fut] ad à (sur) pied.
aforesaid [ə'fɔːsed] a susdit.
aforethought [ə'fɔːθɔːt] a with malice — avec préméditation.
afraid [ə'freid] a effrayé; to be — avoir peur.
Africa ['æfrikə] n Afrique f.
African ['æfrikən] a africain.
aft [aːft] ad à l'arrière.
after ['aːftə] prep (d')après, selon; ad ensuite; cj après que, quand.
aftermath ['aːftəmæθ] n regain m, suites f pl.
afternoon ['aːftə'nuːn] n après-midi m or f inv.
afterthought ['aːftəθɔːt] n réflexion f après coup, second mouvement m.
afterwards ['aːftəwədz] ad ensuite, plus tard.
again [ə'gen] ad encore, de plus, de nouveau; re-; — and — à maintes reprises; now and — de temps à autre; as much — as deux fois autant (plus, aussi).
against [ə'genst] prep contre, sur, à, en vue de.
agape [ə'geip] ad grand ouvert, bouche bée.
age [eidʒ] n âge m, génération f; of — majeur; under — mineur; pl siècles m pl; vti vieillir.
aged ['eidʒid] a âgé, vieux.
agency ['eidʒənsi] n opération f, entremise f, agence f, bureau m.
agenda [ə'dʒendə] n ordre m du jour, agenda m.
agent ['eidʒənt] n agent m, cause f, représentant m.
agglomerate [ə'gləməreit] n agglomérat m; vt agglomérer.
agglomeration [ə,gləmə'reiʃən] n agglomération f.
aggravate ['ægrəveit] vt aggraver, exaspérer.
aggravation [,ægrə'veiʃən] n aggravation f, exaspération f, envenimement m.
aggregate ['ægrigit] n agrégat m, ensemble m, total m.
aggregate ['ægrigeit] vt aggréger; vi se monter à.
aggression [ə'greʃən] n aggression f.
aggressive [ə'gresiv] a agressif.
aggressor [ə'gresə] n agresseur m.
aggrieved [ə'griːvd] a affligé, blessé.
aghast [ə'gaːst] a terrifié, stupéfait, interdit.
agile ['ædʒail] a agile.
agility [ə'dʒiliti] n agilité f.
agitate ['ædʒiteit] vt agiter, débattre; vi faire de l'agitation.
agitator ['ædʒiteitə] n agitateur m, meneur m.
aglow [ə'glou] a luisant, rayonnant, embrasé.
ago [ə'gou] ad il y a.

agog [ə'gɔg] *a* ardent, en émoi, impatient.

agonize ['ægənaiz] *vt* torturer.

agony ['ægəni] *n* agonie *f*, angoisse *f*, supplice *m*.

agree [ə'gri:] *vi* consentir (à to), être d'accord, convenir (de to), accepter.

agreeable [ə'griəbl] *a* agréable, disposé, qui consent, qui convient, d'accord.

agreed [ə'gri:d] *a* d'accord.

agreement [ə'gri:mənt] *n* accord *m*, convention *f*.

agricultural [.ægri'kʌltʃərəl] *a* agricole.

agriculture ['ægrikʌltʃə] *n* agriculture *f*.

aground [ə'graund] *ad* à la côte, échoué, par le fond.

ague ['eigju:] *n* fièvre paludéenne *f*.

ahead [ə'hed] *ad* en tête, ⎣ l'avant, de l'avant, en avant.

aid [eid] *n* aide *mf*, assistance *f*; *vt* aider, contribuer à.

ail [eil] *vt* tracasser; *vi* avoir mal, souffrir.

ailment ['eilmənt] *n* indisposition *f*.

aim [eim] *n* but *m*, visée *f*; *vt* viser, pointer; **to — at** viser.

aimless ['eimlis] *a* sans but.

aimlessly ['eimlisli] *ad* au hasard, sans but.

air [ɛə] *n* air *m*; *vt* aérer, sécher, étaler, mettre à l'évent; *vi* prendre l'air.

air- (cushion *etc*) gonflé d'air.

airborne ['ɛəbɔ:n] *a* aéroporté.

air-brake ['ɛəbreik] *n* frein *m* pneumatique.

aircraft ['ɛəkrɑ:ft] *n* avion; **— carrier** *n* porte-avions *m*; **—-man** *n* mécanicien *m*.

air-cushion ['ɛə.kuʃin] *m* coussin à air *m*.

Air Force ['ɛəfɔ:s] *m* Armée de l'Air *f*.

airhole ['ɛəhoul] *n* soupirail *m*.

air-hostess ['ɛə'houstis] *n* hôtesse de l'air.

airily ['ɛərili] *ad* d'un air dégagé.

airing ['ɛəriŋ] *n* aération *f*, éventage *m*, tour *m*.

airless ['ɛəlis] *a* sans air, renfermé, étouffant.

airliner ['ɛəlainə] *n* avion de ligne *m*.

airmail ['ɛəmeil] *n* courrier *m* aérien; **by —** par avion.

airman ['ɛəmən] *n* aviateur *m*.

airplane ['ɛə.plein] *n* avion *m*.

airport ['ɛə.pɔ:t] *n* aéroport *m*.

air-pump ['ɛə'pʌmp] *n* pompe *f*.

air-raid ['ɛəreid] *n* raid aérien *m*.

airship ['ɛəʃip] *n* aérostat *m*, (ballon) dirigeable *m*.

airtight ['ɛətait] *a* étanche, hermétique.

airworthy ['ɛə.wə:ði] *a* qui tient l'air, bon pour voler, navigable.

airy ['ɛəri] *a* aéré, aérien, gracieux, désinvolte.

aisle [ail] *n* bas-côté *m*.

ajar [ə'dʒɑ:] *ad* entr'ouvert.

akimbo [ə'kimbou] *ad* les poings sur les hanches.

akin [ə'kin] *a* parent (de to), analogue, qui tient (de to).

alacrity [ə'lækriti] *n* vivacité *f*, empressement *m*.

Alan ['ælən] Alain *m*.

alarm [ə'lɑ:m] *n* alarme *f*, alerte *f*; *vt* alarmer, alerter.

alarm-bell [ə'lɑ:mbel] *n* cloche, sonnette d'alarme *f*, tocsin *m*.

alarm-clock [ə'lɑ:mklɔk] *n* réveille-matin *m*.

alarmist [ə'lɑ:mist] *n* alarmiste *mf*.

alas [ə'læs] *excl* hélas!

albeit [ɔ:l'bi:it] *cj* bien que, quoique.

album ['ælbəm] *n* album *m*.

alchemy ['ælkimi] *n* alchimie *f*.

alcohol ['ælkəhɔl] *n* alcool *m*.

alcoholic [.ælkə'hɔlik] *an* alcoolique.

alcoholism ['ælkəhɔlizəm] *n* alcoolisme *m*.

alcove ['ælkouv] *n* niche *f*, retrait *m*, renfoncement *m*.

alder ['ɔ:ldə] *n* aune *m*.

alderman ['ɔ:ldəmən] *n* adjoint au maire *m*.

ale [eil] *n* bière *f*.

ale-house ['eilhaus] *n* brasserie *f*, cabaret *m*.

alert [ə'lə:t] *n* alerte *f*, qui-vive *m*; *a* vigilant, alerte, vif.

alertness [ə'lə:tnis] *n* vigilance *f*, promptitude *f*, vivacité *f*.

algebra ['æ ldʒibrə] *n* algèbre *f*.

alias ['eiljəs] *n* autre nom *m*, faux nom *m*; *ad* autrement dit, connu sous le nom de.

alibi ['ælibai] *n* alibi *m*.

alien ['eiljən] *n* étranger, -ère; *a* étranger, différent, répugnant (à to).

alienate ['eiljəneit] *vt* (s')aliéner, détourner.

alienation [.eiljə'neiʃən] *n* aliénation *f*.

alight [ə'lait] *a* allumé, éclairé, en feu; *vi* descendre, atterrir, se poser.

align [ə'lain] *vt* aligner.

alignment [ə'lainmənt] *n* alignement *m*.

alike [ə'laik] *a* pareil, ressemblant; *ad* de même, de la même manière.

alimony ['æliməni] *n* pension alimentaire *f*.

alive [ə'laiv] *a* en vie, vif, éveillé, grouillant; **to be — and kicking** être plein de vie; **to keep —** entretenir, soutenir.

all [ɔ:l] *n* tous *m pl*, tout *m*, tout le monde *m*; *a* tout, tous, toute(s); *ad* tout, entièrement; **— but** à peu près, autant dire; **I — but fell** j'ai failli tomber; **— clear** fin d'alerte *f*; **All Fools' Day** le premier avril; **All Hallows' Day** (le jour de) la Toussaint; **— in —** tout compris, à tout prendre; **— of you** vous tous; **— one** tout un; **— out** total, complètement, à plein rendement, à toute vitesse; — **powerful** tout-puissant; — **right** très bien, ça va bien, entendu, soit!; **All Saints' Day** (le jour de) la Toussaint; **All Souls' Day** le jour des Morts *m*; **at** — du tout; **one and** — tous sans exception; **to stake one's** — jouer son va-tout.

allay [ə'lei] *vt* soulager, apaiser.

allegation [,æle'geiʃən] *n* allégation *f*.

allege [ə'ledʒ] *vt* alléguer.

allegiance [ə'liːdʒəns] *n* hommage *m*, foi *f*, fidélité *f*.

allegory ['æligəri] *n* allégorie *f*.

alleviate [ə'liːvieit] *vt* alléger, adoucir.

alleviation [ə,liːvi'eiʃən] *n* soulagement *m*, allègement *m*.

alley ['æli] *n* allée *f*, ruelle *f*; **blind** — impasse *f*, cul de sac *m*.

alliance [ə'laiəns] *n* alliance *f*.

allied ['ælaid] *a* allié, connexe.

allocate ['æləkeit] *vt* allouer, assigner, distribuer.

allocation [,ælə'keiʃən] *n* allocation *f*, attribution *f*.

allot [ə'lɔt] *vt* lotir, assigner, répartir, destiner, attribuer.

allotment [ə'lɔtmənt] *n* attribution *f*, répartition *f*, lot *m*, lopin *m*, lotissement *m*.

allow [ə'lau] *vt* laisser, permettre, admettre, allouer; **to** — **for** tenir compte de, compter, faire la part de, prévoir.

allowance [ə'lauəns] *n* permission *f*, pension *f*, remise *f*, concession *f*, indemnité *f*, ration *f*; **to make** — **for** tenir compte de, faire la part de, se montrer indulgent pour.

alloy ['ælɔi] *n* titre *m*, aloi *m*, alliage *m*; *vt* allier, dévaloriser, modérer.

allude [ə'luːd] *vi* faire allusion (à **to**).

allure [ə'ljuə] *vt* tenter, attirer, aguicher, séduire.

allurement [ə'ljuəmənt] *n* attrait *m*, charme *m*.

alluring [ə'ljuəriŋ] *a* séduisant, attrayant.

allusion [ə'luːʒən] *n* allusion *f*.

ally ['ælai] *n* allié.

ally [ə'lai] *vt* allier, unir; *vi* s'allier.

almanac ['ɔːlmənæk] *n* almanach *m*, annuaire *m*.

almighty [ɔːl'maiti] *an* tout-puissant *m*; *a* (*fam*) formidable.

almond ['aːmənd] *n* amande *f*; **burnt** — praline *f*; **sugared** — dragée *f*; — **tree** *n* amandier *m*.

almoner ['aːmənə] *a* aumônier *m*.

almost ['ɔːlmoust] *ad* presque, à peu près; **he** — **fell** il faillit tomber.

alms [aːmz] *n* aumône *f*; —**house** *n* hospice *m*, asile *m*.

aloft [ə'lɔft] *ad* (en) haut, en l'air.

alone [ə'loun] *a* seul, tranquille; **to let, leave s.o., sth** — laisser tranquille, laisser en paix; **leave me** — laissez-moi, fichez-moi la paix; **let** — encore moins, loin de, sans compter, sans parler de.

along [ə'lɔŋ] *prep* le long de; *ad* tout au (du) long; **all** — tout le temps; **all** — **the line** sur toute la ligne.

alongside [ə'lɔŋ'said] *prep* le long de, au bord de, à côté de; *ad* côte à côte; **to come** — accoster, aborder.

aloof [ə'luːf] *a* distant; *ad* à l'écart.

aloofness [ə'luːfnis] *n* réserve *f*, quant à soi *m*.

aloud [ə'laud] *ad* à haute voix, tout haut.

alphabet ['ælfəbit] *n* alphabet *m*.

alphabetical [,ælfə'betikəl] *a* alphabétique.

already [ɔːl'redi] *ad* déjà.

also ['ɔːlsou] *ad* aussi, en outre.

altar ['ɔːltə] *n* autel *m*.

alter ['ɔːltə] *vt* altérer, changer (de), remanier, transformer, déplacer; **to** — **for the better** s'améliorer; **to** — **for the worse** s'altérer.

alteration [,ɔːltə'reiʃən] *n* retouche *f*, changement *m*, modification *f*.

altercation [,ɔːltə'keiʃən] *n* altercation *f*, dispute *f*.

alternate [ɔːl'təːnit] *a* alterne, alternatif; **on** — **days** tous les deux jours.

alternate ['ɔːltəːneit] *vt* faire alterner; *vi* alterner.

alternately [ɔːl'təːnitli] *ad* alternativement, tour à tour.

alternation [,ɔːltə'neiʃən] *n* alternance *f*, alternative *f*.

alternative [ɔːl'təːnətiv] *n* alternative *f*, choix *m*.

although [ɔːl'ðou] *cj* bien que, quoique.

altitude ['æltitjuːd] *n* altitude *f*, hauteur *f*, profondeur *f*.

altogether [,ɔːltə'geðə] *ad* tout compte fait, en tout, entièrement, absolument.

aluminum [,ælju'minjəm] *n* aluminium *m*.

alumnus [ə'lʌmnəs] *n* élève *mf*, pensionnaire *mf*.

always ['ɔːlweiz] *ad* toujours.

amalgam [ə'mælgəm] *n* amalgame *m*.

amalgamate [ə'mælgəmeit] *vt* amalgamer; *vi* s'amalgamer.

amass [ə'mæs] *vt* amasser.

amateur ['æmətə] *n* amateur *m*.

amaze [ə'meiz] *vt* stupéfier, confondre, renverser.

amazement [ə'meizmənt] *n* stupéfaction *f*, stupeur *f*.

amazing [ə'meiziŋ] *a* renversant.

ambassador [æm'bæsədə] *n* ambassadeur *m*.

ambassadress [æm'bæsədris] *n* ambassadrice *f*.

amber ['æmbə] *n* ambre *m*; *a* ambre; — **light** feu jaune *m*.

ambidextrous ['æmbi'dekstrəs] *a* ambidextre.

ambiguity [,æmbi'gjuiti] *n* ambiguïté *f*.

ambiguous [æm'bigjuəs] *a* ambigu, -uë, équivoque, obscur.

ambition [æm'biʃən] *n* ambition *f*.

ambitious [æm'biʃəs] *a* ambitieux.

amble ['æmbl] *vi* aller (à) l'amble; **to — along** marcher d'un pas tranquille, à la papa.

ambulance ['æmbjuləns] *n* ambulance *f*.

ambush ['æmbuʃ] *n* embuscade *f*; *vt* attirer dans un piège, dans un guet-apens; **to lie in —** *vi* s'embusquer.

ameliorate [ə'mi:ljəreit] *vt* améliorer; *vi* s'améliorer, s'amender.

amelioration [ə,mi:ljə'reiʃən] *n* amélioration *f*.

amen ['ɑː'men] *excl* amen, ainsi soit-il.

amenable [ə'mi:nəbl] *a* responsable, sensible (à **to**), soumis, maniable, passable, docile; **— to reason** raisonnable.

amend [ə'mend] *vt* amender, modifier, corriger; *vi* s'amender, se corriger.

amendment [ə'mendmənt] *n* modification *f*, rectification *f*, amendement *m*.

amends [ə'mendz] *n* dédommagement *m*, réparation *f*; **to make — for** dédommager, réparer

amenity [ə'mi:niti] *n* agrément *m*, aménité *f*; *pl* commodités *f pl*.

America [ə'merikə] *n* Amérique *f*; **North —**, **South —** l'Amérique du Nord, l'Amérique du Sud.

American [ə'merikən] *a* américain *n* Américain(e) *m(f)*.

amiability [,eimjə'biliti] *n* amabilité *f*, cordialité *f*, concorde *f*.

amiable ['eimjəbl] *a* aimable.

amicable ['æmikəbl] *a* amical, à l'amiable.

amid(st) [ə'mid(st)] *prep* au milieu de, parmi.

amidships [ə'midʃips] *ad* par le travers.

amiss [ə'mis] *a* insuffisant, fâcheux, qui cloche; *ad* (en) mal, de travers.

amity ['æmiti] *n* amitié *f*, bonne intelligence *f*.

ammonia [ə'mounjə] *n* ammoniaque *f*.

ammunition [,æmju'niʃən] *n* munitions *f pl*; *a* de munition, réglementaire.

amnesia [æm'ni:zjə] *n* amnésie *f*.

amnesty ['æmnəsti] *n* amnistie *f*; *vt* amnistier.

among(st) [ə'mʌŋ(st)] *prep* parmi, au milieu de, (d')entre.

amorous ['æmərəs] *a* porté à l'amour, amoureux.

amorousness ['æmərəsnis] *n* penchant à l'amour *m*.

amorphous [ə'mɔːfəs] *a* amorphe.

amount [ə'maunt] *n* montant *m*, compte *m*, somme *f*, quantité *f*; *vi* (se) monter (à **to**), s'élever (à **to**), revenir (à **to**).

amour [ə'muə] *n* liaison *f*, intrigue galante *f*.

ample ['æmpl] *a* ample, vaste, abondant.

ampleness ['æmplnis] *n* ampleur *f*, abondance *f*.

amplification [,æmplifi'keiʃən] *n* amplification *f*.

amplifier ['æmplifaiə] *n* amplificateur *m*.

amplify ['æmplifai] *vt* amplifier, développer.

amplitude ['æmplitju:d] *n* ampleur *f*, abondance *f*, dignité *f*.

amputate ['æmpjuteit] *vt* amputer.

amputation [,æmpju'teiʃən] *n* amputation *f*.

amuck [ə'mʌk] *ad* comme un fou, furieux.

amulet ['æmjulit] *n* amulette *f*, gri(s)-gri(s) *m*.

amuse [ə'mju:z] *vt* amuser, divertir.

amusement [ə'mju:zmənt] *n* amusement *m*, divertissement *m*, distraction *f*.

Amy ['eimi] Aimée *f*.

an [æn, ən, n] *art* un, une.

analogous [ə'næləgəs] *a* analogue.

analogy [ə'nælədʒi] *n* analogie *f*.

analysis [ə'næləsis] *n* analyse *f*.

analyst ['ænəlist] *n* analyste *m*.

analytic(al) [,ænə'litik(əl)] *a* analytique.

analyze ['ænəlaiz] *vt* analyser, faire l'analyse de.

anarchist ['ænəkist] *n* anarchiste *mf*.

anarchy ['ænəki] *n* anarchie *f*.

anathema [ə'næθəmə] *n* anathème *m*.

anathematize [ə'næθəmətaiz] *vt* jeter l'anathème sur.

anatomist [ə'nætəmist] *n* anatomiste *m*.

anatomize [ə'nætəmaiz] *vt* disséquer.

anatomy [ə'nætəmi] *n* anatomie *f*.

ancestor ['ænsistə] *n* ancêtre *m*, aïeul, -eux *m*.

ancestral [æn'sestrəl] *a* ancestral.

ancestry ['ænsistri] *n* race *f*, lignée *f*.

anchor ['æŋkə] *n* ancre *f*; *vt* ancrer, mettre au mouillage; *vi* jeter l'ancre, mouiller; **to cast —** jeter l'ancre; **to weigh —** lever l'ancre.

anchovy ['æntʃəvi] *n* anchois *m*.

ancient ['einʃənt] *a* ancien, antique.

ancientness ['einʃəntnis] *n* ancienneté *f*.

and [ænd, ənd, ən] *cj* et; **— so on** et ainsi de suite; **wait — see** attendez voir.

andiron ['ændaiən] *n* chenet *m*.

Andrew ['ændru:] André *m*.

anecdote ['ænikdout] *n* anecdote *f*.

anecdotic(al) [,ænek'dɔtik(əl)] *a* anecdotique.

anemia [ə'niːmjə] n anémie f.
anemic [ə'niːmik] a anémique.
anemone [ə'neməni] n anémone f.
anesthesia [.ænis'θiːzjə] n anesthésie f.
anesthetic [.ænis'θetik] n anesthétique m.
anesthetize [æ'niːsθətaiz] vt anesthésier, insensibiliser, endormir.
aneurysm ['ænjuərizəm] n anévrisme m.
anew [ə'njuː] ad de nouveau, autrement.
angel ['eindʒəl] n ange m.
Angela ['ændʒələ] Angèle f.
angelic [æn'dʒelik] a angélique, d'ange.
anger ['æŋgə] n colère f; vt mettre en colère, irriter.
angina [æn'dʒainə] n angine f; — **pectoris** angine de poitrine.
angle ['æŋgl] n angle m, coin m; vi pêcher à la ligne.
angler ['æŋglə] n pêcheur m à la ligne.
Anglicanism ['æŋglikənizəm] n anglicanisme m.
angling ['æŋgliŋ] n pêche f.
angry ['æŋgri] a en colère, fâché, enflammé, douloureux; **to get —** se mettre en colère, se fâcher, s'irriter; **to get — with s.o.** se fâcher contre qn; **I am — with myself for doing it** je m'en veux de l'avoir fait.
anguish ['æŋgwiʃ] n angoisse f, supplice m.
angular ['æŋgjulə] a angulaire, anguleux.
animal ['æniməl] an animal m.
animate ['ænimeit] vt animer, inspirer, inciter.
animated ['ænimeitid] a animé, vif.
animation [.æni'meiʃən] n animation f, entrain m, vivacité f, vie f, encouragement m.
animator ['ænimeitə] n animateur, -trice.
animosity [.æni'mɔsiti] n animosité f.
ankle ['æŋkl] n cheville f.
Ann [æn] Anne f.
annals ['ænls] n annales f pl.
anneal [ə'niːl] vt tremper, tempérer.
annex ['æneks] n annexe f; [ə'neks] vt annexer.
annexation [.ænek'seiʃən] n annexion f.
annihilate [ə'naiəleit] vt annihiler, anéantir.
annihilation [ə.naiə'leiʃən] n anéantissement m.
anniversary [.æni'vəːsəri] n anniversaire m.
annotate ['ænouteit] vt annoter, commenter.
annotation [.ænou'teiʃən] n annotation f, commentaire m.

annotator ['ænouteitə] n annotateur m, commentateur m.
announce [ə'nauns] vt annoncer, faire part de.
announcement [ə'naunsmənt] n annonce f, avis n, faire-part m.
announcer [ə'naunsə] n annonceur m, speaker m.
annoy [ə'nɔi] vt contrarier, ennuyer.
annoyance [ə'nɔiəns] n contrariété f, dégoût m, ennui m.
annoying [ə'nɔiiŋ] a contrariant, fâcheux, ennuyeux.
annual ['ænjuəl] n annuaire m, plante annuelle f; a annuel.
annuity [ə'nju(ː)iti] n annuité f, rente f; **life —** rente viagère f.
annul [ə'nʌl] vt annuler, abroger, résilier.
annulment [ə'nʌlmənt] n annulation f, abrogation f.
annunciate [ə'nʌnsieit] vt annoncer.
annunciation [ə.nʌnsi'eiʃən] n annonce f, annonciation f.
anoint [ə'nɔint] vt oindre.
anointing [ə'nɔintiŋ] n onction f, sacre m.
anomalous [ə'nɔmələs] a anormal, irrégulier.
anomaly [ə'nɔməli] n anomalie f.
anon [ə'nɔn] ad tantôt; **ever and —** de temps à autre.
anonymity [.ænə'nimiti] n anonymat m.
anonymous [ə'nɔniməs] a anonyme.
another [ə'nʌðə] a pron un (une) autre; encore (un, une); **one —** l'un l'autre, les unes les autres; **one way or —** d'une façon ou d'une autre; **that's — matter** c'est tout autre chose.
answer ['aːnsə] n réponse f; vti répondre; **to — for** répondre de (vouch), répondre pour (instead of).
answerable ['aːnsərəbl] a responsable.
answering ['aːnsəriŋ] a sympathique, qui répond à, qui correspond à.
ant [ænt] n fourmi f; **—eater** fourmilier m; **—-hill** n fourmilière f.
antagonism [ænt'ægənizəm] n antagonisme m.
antagonist [æn'tægənist] n adversaire m.
antagonize [æn'tægənaiz] vt contrecarrer, se faire un ennemi de.
antecedent [.ænti'siːdənt] n antécédent m; a antérieur.
antedate [.ænti'deit] vt antidater.
antenatal [.ænti'neitl] a prénatal.
antenna [æn'tenə] n antenne f.
anterior [æn'tiəriə] a antérieur.
anteriority [æntiəri'ɔriti] n antériorité f.
anthem ['ænθəm] n antienne f, hymne m.
Anthony ['æntəni] Antoine m.
anti-aircraft ['ænti'səkraːft] a contre-avions, anti-aérien.

antibiotic ['æntibai'ɔtik] *n* antibiotique *f.*
antibody ['ænti.bɔdi] *n* anticorps *m.*
Antichrist ['æntikraist] *n* Antéchrist *m.*
anticipate [æn'tisipeit] *vt* anticiper (sur), prévenir, devancer, s'attendre à.
anticipation [æn.tisi'peiʃən] *n* anticipation *f*, prévision *f*, attente *f*; **in** — d'avance, par avance.
antics ['æntiks] *n pl* pitreries *f pl*, singeries *f pl*, cabrioles *f pl.*
antidote ['æntidout] *n* antidote *m.*
anti-glare [.ænti'glɛə] *a* antiaveuglant; — **headlights** pharescode *m pl.*
antipathetic(al) [.æntipə'θetik(l)] *a* antipathique.
antipathy [æn'tipəθi] *n* antipathie *f.*
antipodes [æn'tipədiːz] *n* antipodes *m pl.*
antiquarian [.ænti'kwɛəriən] *n* antiquaire *m*; —'**s shop** magasin d'antiquités *m.*
antiquated ['æntikweitid] *a* suranné, vieilli, désuet.
antique [æn'tiːk] *a* antique, ancien; *n* antique *m*, objet antique *m*; — **dealer** antiquaire *m*; — **shop** magasin *m* d'antiquités.
antiquity [æn'tikwiti] *n* antiquité *f.*
antiseptic [.ænti'septik] *an* antiseptique *m.*
antitheft [ænti'θeft] *a* antivol.
antithesis [æn'tiθəsis] *n* antithèse *f*, contraire *m.*
antithetic(al) [.ænti'θetik(əi)] *a* antithétique.
antler ['æntlə] *n* andouiller *m*; *pl* bois *m pl.*
anvil ['ænvil] *n* enclume *f.*
anxiety [æŋ'zaiəti] *n* anxiété *f*, inquiétude *f*, désir *m.*
anxious ['æŋkʃəs] *a* anxieux, inquiet, soucieux, désireux, inquiétant.
any ['eni] *a* du, de la, des; quelque, tout, un, en; **not** — ne . . . aucun, nul; *pn* quiconque; *ad* en rien.
anybody, anyone ['enibɔdi, 'eniwʌn] *pn* quelqu'un, n'importe qui, tout le monde, quiconque; **not** — ne . . . personne.
anyhow ['enihau] *ad* n'importe comment, de toute façon, en tout cas; — **you can try** vous pouvez toujours essayer.
anyone *see* **anybody.**
anything ['eniθiŋ] *pn* quelque chose, n'importe quoi, tout; **not** — ne . . . rien; — **else, sir?** et avec cela, monsieur? — **you like** tout ce que vous voudrez; **I would give** — **to know** je donnerais gros pour savoir; **to run like** — courir à toutes jambes.
anyway ['eniwei] *ad* n'importe comment, de toute façon, en tout cas; en fait, en fin de compte.
anywhere ['eniwɛə] *ad* n'importe où,

dans quelque endroit que ce soit; **not** — ne . . . nulle part.
apace [ə'peis] *ad* vite, vivement, à grands pas.
apart [ə'paːt] *ad* à part, de côté, à l'écart, indépendamment (de **from**); **to come** — se détacher; *a* espace; **they are 10 miles** — ils sont à 10 milles l'un de l'autre.
apartment [ə'paːtmənt] *n* chambre *f*, pièce *f*, logement *m*, appartement *m.*
apathetic [.æpə'θetik] *a* apathique, indifférent.
apathy ['æpəθi] *n* apathie *f.*
ape [eip] *n* singe *m*; *vt* singer.
aperient [ə'piəriənt] *n* laxatif *m*, purge *f.*
aperture ['æpətjuə] *n* orifice *m*, ouverture *f.*
apex ['eipeks] *n* sommet *m.*
apiary ['eipjəri] *n* rucher *m.*
apiece [ə'piːs] *ad* (la) pièce, chaque, chacun, par tête.
apish ['eipiʃ] *a* simiesque, de singe, sot.
apogee ['æpoudʒiː] *n* apogée *m.*
apologetic(al) [ə.pɔlə'dʒetik(əl)] *a* apologétique, d'excuse.
apologetics [ə.pɔlə'dʒetiks] *n* apologétique *f.*
apologist [ə'pɔlədʒist] *n* apologiste *m.*
apologize [ə'pɔlədʒaiz] *vi* s'excuser, demander pardon.
apology [ə'pɔlədʒi] *n* excuses *f pl*, apologie *f.*
apoplectic [.æpə'plektik] *a* apoplectique; **an** — **fit, stroke** une attaque (d'apoplexie).
apoplexy ['æpəpleksi] *n* apoplexie *f*, congestion cérébrale *f.*
apostasy [ə'pɔstəsi] *n* apostasie *f.*
apostate [ə'pɔstit] *n* apostat *m.*
apostle [ə'pɔsl] *n* apôtre *m.*
apostleship [ə'pɔslʃip] *n* apostolat *m.*
apostolic [.æpəs'tɔlik] *a* apostolique.
apothecary [ə'pɔθikəri] *n* apothicaire *m*, pharmacien *m.*
appalling [ə'pɔːliŋ] *a* effroyable, épouvantable.
apparatus [.æpə'reitəs] *n* dispositif *m*, appareil *m*, attirail *m.*
apparel [ə'pærəl] *n* habit *m*, vêtement(s) *m(pl)*; *vt* habiller, vêtir.
apparent [ə'pærənt] *a* manifeste, évident; (*heir*) présomptif.
apparently [ə'pærəntli] *ad* apparemment.
apparition [.æpə'riʃən] *n* apparition *f*, fantôme *m.*
appeal [ə'piːl] *n* appel *m*; *vi* interjeter appel; **to** — **to** recourir à, en appeler à, faire appel à, plaire à, s'adresser à; **that doesn't** — **to me** cela ne me dit rien; **the idea** —**s to me** l'idée me sourit.
appear [ə'piə] *vi* apparaître, paraître, sembler, se présenter,

appearance [ə'piərəns] n apparition f, apparence f, mine f, tournure f; to put in an — faire acte de présence; for the sake of —(s) pour la forme; to, by all —(s) selon toute apparence.

appease [ə'piːz] vt apaiser, calmer.

appeasement [ə'piːzmənt] n apaisement m, conciliation f.

append [ə'pend] vt attacher, ajouter, apposer, joindre.

appendage [ə'pendidʒ] n addition f, apanage m.

appendicitis [ə,pendi'saitis] n appendicite f.

appendix [ə'pendiks] n appendice m, annexe f.

appertain [,æpə'tein] vi appartenir, se rapporter.

appertaining [,æpə'teiniŋ] a relatif, qui incombent.

appetite ['æpitait] n appétit m, soif f; to whet someone's — mettre qn en appétit.

appetizer ['æpitaizə] n apéritif m.

appetizing ['æpitaiziŋ] a appétissant.

applaud [ə'plɔːd] vti applaudir.

applause [ə'plɔːz] n applaudissements m pl.

apple ['æpl] n pomme f, (of the eye) pupille f, prunelle f.

apple-dumpling ['æpl'dʌmpliŋ] n chausson m.

apple-pie ['æpl'pai] n tourte aux pommes f; in — order en ordre parfait; — bed n lit en porte-feuille m.

apple tree ['æpltriː] n pommier m.

appliance [ə'plaiəns] n moyen m, dispositif m, machine f, appareil m.

applicable ['æplikəbl] a applicable, approprié.

applicant ['æplikənt] n postulant m, requérant m.

application [,æpli'keiʃən] n application f, demande f.

apply [ə'plai] vt appliquer; vi s'appliquer (à to), s'addresser (à to), se présenter; to — for demander, solliciter.

appoint [ə'pɔint] vt fixer, nommer, équiper, meubler.

appointment [ə'pɔintmənt] n rendez-vous m, nomination f, emploi m; pl équipement| m, installation f; to make an — with donner un rendez-vous à.

apportion [ə'pɔːʃən] vt répartir, assigner.

apportionment [ə'pɔːʃənmənt] n répartition f, distribution f, allocation f.

apposite ['æpəzit] a approprié, à propos.

appositeness ['æpəzitnis] n convenance f, justesse f.

apposition [,æpə'ziʃən] n apposition f.

appraisal [ə'preizəl] n évaluation f, mise à prix f.

appraise [ə'preiz] vt évaluer.

appraiser [ə'preizə] n commissaire-priseur m.

appreciate [ə'priːʃieit] vt évaluer, apprécier, faire cas de, se rendre compte de, goûter; vi prendre de la valeur, augmenter de valeur.

appreciation [ə,priːʃi'eiʃən] n évaluation f, hausse f, appréciation f, compte-rendu m, critique f.

apprehend [,æpri'hend] vt appréhender, comprendre.

apprehension [,æpri'henʃən] n compréhension f, appréhension f, crainte f, arrestation f.

apprehensive [,æpri'hensiv] a intelligent, inquiet, craintif.

apprentice [ə'prentis] n apprenti m; vt mettre en apprentissage.

apprenticeship [ə'prentiʃip] n apprentissage m.

apprise [ə'praiz] vt informer, apprendre, prévenir.

approach [ə'proutʃ] n approche f, approximation f, accès m; pl avances f pl; vt approcher de, aborder, faire des offres à; vi (s')approcher.

approachable [ə'proutʃəbl] a abordable.

approbation [,æprə'beiʃən] n approbation f; on — à condition, à l'essai.

appropriate [ə'proupriit] a propre (à to), approprié; [ə'prouprieit] vt s'approprier, destiner.

approval [ə'pruːvəl] n approbation f; on — à condition, à l'examen, à l'essai.

approve [ə'pruːv] vt approuver.

approver [ə'pruːvə] n approbateur, -trice.

approximate [ə'prɔksimit] a approximatif, proche.

approximation [ə,prɔksi'meiʃən] n approximation f.

appurtenance [ə'pəːtinəns] a appartenance f; pl dépendances f pl, accessoires m pl.

apricot ['eiprikɔt] n abricot m; — tree abricotier m.

April ['eiprəl] n avril m; to make an — fool of s.o. donner un poisson d'avril à qn.

apron ['eiprən] n tablier m; to be tied to one's mother's — strings être pendu aux jupes de sa mère.

apt [æpt] a approprié, juste, porté (à to), sujet (à to), prompt d'esprit, doué, habile.

aptitude ['æptitjuːd] n aptitude f, disposition f.

aptly ['æptli] ad (avec) à propos, habilement.

aptness ['æptnis] n justesse f, tendance f, propriété f.

aqualung ['ækwə'lʌŋ] n scaphandre m.

aqueduct ['ækwidʌkt] n aqueduc m.

aqueous ['eikwiəs] a aqueux.

aquiline ['ækwilain] *a* aquilin.
Arab ['ærəb] *an* arabe.
Arabic ['ærəbik] *a* arabique.
arable ['ærəbl] *a* arable.
arbitrage ['a:bitridʒ] *n* arbitrage m.
arbitrary ['a:bitrəri] *a* arbitraire.
arbitrate ['a:bitreit] *vti* arbitrer.
arbitration [,a:bi'treiʃən] *n* arbitrage m.
arbitrator ['a:bitreitə] *n* arbitre m.
arbor ['a:bə] *n* bosquet m, berceau m de verdure, tonnelle f.
arc [a:k] *n* arc m.
arcade [a:'keid] *n* arcade f.
arch [a:tʃ] *n* arche f, voûte f, cintre m; *vt* voûter, cintrer, arquer; *vi* former voûte; *a* espiègle, malicieux.
arch- ['a:tʃ] *a* maître, fieffé, archi-, consommé.
archaeologist [,a:ki'ɔlədʒist] *n* archéologue m.
archaeology [,a:ki'ɔlədʒi] *n* archéologie f.
archaic [a:'keiik] *a* archaïque.
archaism ['a:keiizəm] *n* archaïsme m.
archangel ['a:k,eindʒəl] *n* archange m.
archbishop ['a:tʃ'biʃəp] *n* archevêque m.
archbishopric [a:tʃ'biʃəprik] *n* archevêché m.
archdeacon ['a:tʃ'di:kən] *n* archidiacre m.
archdeaconship [a:tʃ'di:kənʃip] *n* archidiaconat m.
archduchess ['a:tʃ'dʌtʃis] *n* archiduchesse f.
archduke ['a:tʃ'dju:k] *n* archiduc m.
arched [a:tʃt] *ad* en arc, voûté, arqué, cintré, busqué, cambré.
archer ['a:tʃə] *n* archer m.
archery ['a:tʃəri] *n* tir à l'arc m.
archetype ['a:kitaip] *n* archétype m.
archipelago [,a:ki'peligou] *n* archipel m.
architect ['a:kitekt] *n* architecte m.
architecture ['a:kitektʃə] *n* architecture f.
archives ['a:kaivz] *n* archives f pl.
archivist ['a:kivist] *n* archiviste mf.
archness ['a:tʃnis] *m* malice f, espièglerie f.
archway ['a:tʃwei] *n* arcades f pl.
arctic ['a:ktik] *a* arctique.
ardent ['a:dənt] *a* ardent, fervent.
ardently ['a:dəntli] *ad* ardemment, avec ardeur.
ardor ['a:də] *a* ardeur f.
arduous ['a:djuəs] *a* ardu, pénible, escarpé, énergique.
area ['εəriə] *n* aire f, cour en sous-sol f, surface f, étendue f, zone f.
arena [ə'ri:nə] *n* arène f.
arguable ['a:gjuəbl] *a* soutenable, discutable.
argue [a:gju] *vt* prouver, soutenir; *vi* argumenter, discuter, raisonner, se disputer.
argument ['a:gjumənt] *n* argument m, débat m, discussion f, argumentation f.
arid ['ærid] *a* aride.
aridity [æ'riditi] *n* aridité f.
aright [ə'rait] *ad* à juste titre, à bon droit.
arise [ə'raiz] *vi* se lever, s'élever, survenir, surgir, se présenter.
arisen [ə'rizen] *pp* of arise.
aristocracy [,æris'tɔkrəsi] *n* aristocratie f.
aristocrat ['æristəkræt] *n* aristocrate mf.
aristocratic [,æristə'krætik] *a* aristocratique, aristocrate.
arithmetic [ə'riθmətik] *n* arithmétique f.
ark [a:k] *n* coffre m, arche f.
arm [a:m] *n* bras m; arme f; pl armoiries f pl; **fore—** avant-bras m; **— in —** bras dessus bras dessous; **with open —s** à bras ouverts; **at —'s length** à longueur de bras; **fire—** arme à feu f; **to lay down one's —s** mettre bas les armes; *vt* armer.
armament ['a:məmənt] *n* armement m, artillerie f.
armature ['a:mətjuə] *n* armature f.
armband ['a:m'bænd] *n* brassard m.
armchair ['a:m'tʃεə] *n* fauteuil m.
armful ['a:mful] *n* brassée f.
armhole ['a:mhoul] *n* emmanchure f.
armistice ['a:mistis] *n* armistice m.
armlet ['a:mlit] *n* brassard m, bracelet m.
armor ['a:mə] *n* armure f, blindage m, les blindés m pl; **—clad** *a* cuirassé, blindé; **— plates** n (plaques de) blindage f pl.
armorer ['a:mərə] *n* armurier m.
armory ['a:məri] *n* armurie f, arsenal m.
armpit ['a:mpit] *n* aisselle f.
army ['a:mi] *n* armée f.
aroma [ə'roumə] *n* arome m, bouquet m.
arose [ə'rouz] *pt* of arise.
around [ə'raund] *prep* autour de; *ad* à l'entour, à la ronde.
arouse [ə'rauz] *vt* soulever, exciter, éveiller.
arraign [ə'rein] *vt* mettre en accusation f, attaquer.
arraignment [ə'reinmənt] *n* mise en accusation f.
arrange [ə'reindʒ] *vt* ranger; *vi* (s')arranger (pour to).
arrangement [ə'reindʒmənt] *n* arrangement m, dispositions f pl.
arrant ['ærənt] *a* insigne, fieffé, pur.
array [ə'rei] *n* ordre m, cortège m, atours m pl; *vt* rassembler, disposer, parer.
arrear [ə'riə] *n* arrière m; pl arriéré m, arrérages m pl; **in —s** en retard, arriéré.
arrearage [ə'riəridʒ] *n* arrérages m pl.

arrest [ə'rest] n arrêt m, saisie f, arrestation f; vt arrêter, suspendre, captiver.
arrival [ə'raivəl] n arrivée f, arrivage m.
arrive [ə'raiv] vi arriver.
arrogance ['ærəgəns] n arrogance f.
arrogant ['ærəgənt] a arrogant, rogue.
arrogantly ['ærəgəntli] ad arrogamment.
arrogate ['ærəgeit] vt s'arroger, attribuer.
arrow ['ærou] n flèche f.
arson ['ɑːsn] n incendie volontaire m.
art [ɑːt] n art m, artifice m; black — magie noire f.
arterial [ɑː'tiəriəl] a artériel.
artery ['ɑːtəri] n artère f.
artful ['ɑːtful] a rusé, habile, malin.
artfulness ['ɑːtfulnis] n ingéniosité f, art(ifice) m.
artichoke ['ɑːtitʃouk] n (Jerusalem) topinambour m; (globe) artichaut m.
article ['ɑːtikl] n article m, objet m, pièce f; vt passer un contrat d'apprentissage à.
articulate [ɑː'tikjuleit] vti articuler.
articulation [ɑː,tikju'leiʃən] n articulation f.
artifice ['ɑːtifis] n artifice m, habileté f, ruse f.
artificial [,ɑːti'fiʃəl] a artificiel, simili-, faux, factice.
artillery [ɑː'tiləri] n artillerie f; —man artilleur m.
artisan [,ɑːti'zæn] n artisan m; ouvrier qualifié m.
artist ['ɑːtist] n artiste mf.
artistic [ɑː'tistik] a artistique, artiste.
artless ['ɑːtlis] a sans art, naturel, ingénu, innocent.
Aryan ['ɛəriən] an aryen.
as [æz, əz] ad aussi, si, comme, en (qualité de); cj que, comme, tout . . . que, si . . . que, pendant que, puisque; so good — to assez bon pour; — for, — to quant à; — from à dater de, provenant de; — though comme si; — it were pour ainsi dire; — yet jusqu'ici.
asbestos [æs'bestɔs] n asbeste m.
ascend [ə'send] vt gravir; vi s'élever; vti (re)monter.
ascendancy [ə'sendənsi] n ascendant m, suprématie f.
ascension [ə'senʃən] n ascension f.
ascent [ə'sent] n escalade f, montée f, ascension f.
ascertain [,æsə'tein] vt constater, s'assurer, savoir.
ascetic [ə'setik] an ascétique mf.
asceticism [ə'setisizəm] n ascétisme m.
ascribe [əs'kraib] vt attribuer, imputer.
asepsis [æ'sepsis] n asepsie f.
aseptic [æ'septik] a aseptique.

ash [æʃ] n frêne m; cendre f; —bin n boîte f à ordures; —tray n cendrier m.
ashamed [ə'ʃeimd] a honteux; to be — avoir honte.
ashen ['æʃn] a en bois de frêne, en cendres, cendré; —faced blême.
ashore [ə'ʃɔː] ad à terre, à la côte; to go — débarquer; to run — s'échouer.
aside [ə'said] n aparté m; ad de côté, à part, à l'écart.
ask [ɑːsk] vti demander; vt inviter, (question) poser; to — for chercher, demander; to — about se renseigner sur; to — after s'informer de; for the asking sur demande, pour rien.
askance [əs'kæns] ad de travers, avec méfiance.
askew [əs'kjuː] ad obliquement, de biais, de travers.
aslant [ə'slɑːnt] ad obliquement, de biais.
asleep [ə'sliːp] a endormi; to be — dormir.
asp [æsp] n tremble m, aspic m.
asparagus [əs'pærəgəs] n asperge f.
aspect ['æspekt] n aspect m, mine f, exposition f.
aspen ['æspən] n tremble m.
asperity [æs'periti] n rudesse f, aspérité f.
asperse [əs'pəːs] vt calomnier, éclabousser.
aspersion [əs'pəːʃən] n aspersion f, calomnie f.
asphalt ['æsfælt] n asphalte m.
asphyxia [æs'fiksiə] n asphyxie f.
asphyxiate [æs'fiksieit] vt asphyxier.
aspirate ['æspərit] vt aspirer.
aspiration [,æspə'reiʃən] n aspiration.
aspire [əs'paiə] vi aspirer.
aspirin ['æspərin] n aspirine f.
aspiring [əs'paiəriŋ] a ambitieux, qui aspire (à to).
ass [æs] n âne m; she — ânesse f; young — ânon m; to behave like an — faire l'âne, le sot, l'idiot.
assail [ə'seil] vt assaillir.
assailable [ə'seiləbl] a attaquable.
assailant [ə'seilənt] n assaillant m.
assassin [ə'sæsin] n assassin m.
assassinate [ə'sæsineit] vt assassiner.
assassination [ə,sæsi'neiʃən] n assassinat m.
assault [ə'sɔːlt] n assaut m, agression f, attentat m; by — d'assaut; vt attaquer, donner l'assaut à, attenter à l'assaut m.
assay [ə'sei] n essai m; vt essayer, titrer.
assegai ['æsigai] n sagaie f.
assemblage [ə'semblidʒ] n assemblage m, réunion f.
assemble [ə'sembl] vt assembler; vi s'assembler, se rassembler.
assembly [ə'sembli] n assemblée f, rassemblement m.
assent [ə'sent] n assentiment m,

consentement *m*; *vi* consentir, déférer (à to), convenir (de to).

assert [ə'səːt] *vt* revendiquer, affirmer, faire valoir.

assertion [ə'səːʃən] *n* revendication *f*, affirmation *f*.

assertive [ə'səːtiv] *a* péremptoire, autoritaire.

assertiveness [ə'səːtivnis] *n* ton péremptoire *m*.

assess [ə'ses] *vt* imposer, taxer, évaluer, estimer.

assessable [ə'sesəbl] *a* imposable, évaluable.

assessment[ə'sesmənt]*n*répartition*f*, évaluation *f*, taxation *f*, imposition *f*.

assessor [ə'sesə] *n* répartiteur *m*, assesseur *m*, contrôleur *m*.

assets ['æsets] *n* actif *m*, biens *m pl*.

asseverate [ə'sevəreit] *vt* attester, affirmer.

asseveration [ə,sevə'reiʃən] *n* attestation *f*.

assiduity [,æsi'dju(ː)iti] *n* assiduité *f*.

assiduous [ə'sidjuəs] *a* assidu.

assign [ə'sain] *vt* assigner, attribuer, fixer, transférer.

assignation [,æsig'neiʃən] *n* assignation *f*, transfert *m*, rendez-vous *m*, attribution *f*.

assignment [ə'sainmənt] *n* assignation *f*, attribution *f*, allocation *f*.

assimilable [ə'similəbl] *a* assimilable.

assimilate [ə'simileit] *vt* assimiler.

assimilation [ə,simi'leiʃən] *n* assimilation *f*.

assist [ə'sist] *vt* assister, aider; *vi* assister (à at).

assistance [ə'sistəns] *n* assistance *f*, aide *f*.

assistant [ə'sistənt] *a* adjoint, sous-; *n* aide *mf*, assistant(e) *mf*, adjoint(e) *mf*, employé(e) *mf*.

assize [ə'saiz] *n* assises *f pl*.

associate [ə'souʃiit] *an* associé *m*, camarade *mf*.

associate [ə'souʃieit] *vt* associer, mettre en contact; *vi* fréquenter, frayer (avec with) s'associer, s'allier (à with).

association [ə,sousi'eiʃən] *n* association *f*, fréquentation *f*, société *f*, amicale *f*.

assort [ə'sɔːt] *vt* classer, assortir; *vi* s'associer.

assortment [ə'sɔːtmənt] *n* assortiment *m*, classement *m*.

assuage [ə'sweidʒ] *vt* apaiser.

assuagement [ə'sweidʒmənt] *n* apaisement *m*.

assume [ə'sjuːm] *vt* prendre, assumer, affecter, présumer.

assuming [ə'sjuːmiŋ] *a* arrogant, prétentieux; *cj* en admettant que.

assumption [ə'sʌmpʃən] *n* hypothèse *f*, arrogance *f*, Assomption *f*; — **of office** entrée en fonctions *f*.

assurance [ə'ʃuərəns] *n* assurance *f*.

assure [ə'ʃuə] *vt* assurer.

assuredly [ə'ʃuəridli] *ad* assurément.

asterisk ['æstərisk] *n* astérisque *m*.

astern [əs'təːn] *ad* (*naut*) à l'arrière, derrière.

asthma ['æsmə] *n* asthme *m*.

astir [ə'stəː] *ad* en mouvement, en émoi, levé, debout.

astonish [əs'tɔniʃ] *vt* étonner.

astonishing [əs'tɔniʃiŋ] *a* étonnant.

astonishingly [əs'tɔniʃiŋli] *ad* étonnamment.

astonishment [əs'tɔniʃmənt] *n* étonnement *m*.

astound [əs'taund] *vt* stupéfier, abasourdir.

astraddle [ə'strædl] *ad* à califourchon, à cheval.

astray [əs'trei] *a* égaré; *ad* hors du droit chemin; **to go** — s'égarer, faire fausse route, se dévoyer; **to lead** — égarer, dévoyer.

astride [əs'traid] *ad* à califourchon, à cheval.

astrologer [əs'trɔledʒə] *n* astrologue *m*.

astrology [əs'trɔledʒi] *n* astrologie *f*.

astronaut ['æstrənɔːt] *n* astronaute *m*.

astronautics [,æstrə'nɔːtiks] *n* astronautique *f*.

astronomer [əs'trɔnəmə] *n* astronome *m*.

astronomy [əs'trɔnəmi] *n* astronomie *f*.

astute [əs'tjuːt] *a* sagace, astucieux, fin.

astuteness [əs'tjuːtnis] *n* finesse *f*, astuce *f*.

asunder [ə'sʌndə] *ad* à part, en pièces, en deux.

asylum [ə'sailəm] *n* asile *m*.

at [æt] *prep* à, chez *etc*; — **one** d'accord; — **that** et de plus, tel quel; — **hand** sous la main; — **all events** en tout cas; **to be** — s.o. s'en prendre à qn.

ate [et] *pt of* eat.

atheism ['eiθiizəm] *n* athéisme *m*.

atheist ['eiθiist] *n* athée *mf*.

athlete ['æθliːt] *n* athlète *m*.

athletic [æθ'letik] *a* athlétique, sportif, bien taillé.

athleticism [æθ'letisizəm] *n* athlétisme *m*.

athletics [æθ'letiks] *n pl* sports *m pl*, culture physique *f*.

at-home [ət'houm] *n* réception *f*, jour *m*.

athwart [ə'θwɔːt] *prep* en travers de; *ad* en travers, par le travers.

atmosphere ['ætməsfiə] *n* atmosphère *f*, ambiance *f*.

atmospheric [,ætməs'ferik] *a* atmosphérique; *n pl* parasites *m pl*, fritures *f pl*, perturbations *f pl*.

atom ['ætəm] *n* atome *m*.

atomic [ə'tɔmik] *a* atomique.

atomize ['ætəmaiz] *vt* vaporiser, pulvériser.

atone [ə'toun] *vti* expier.

atonement [ə'tounmənt] n expiation f, réparation f.
atrocious [ə'trouʃəs] a atroce, exécrable, affreux.
atrocity [ə'trɔsiti] **atrociousness** [ə'trouʃəsnis] n atrocité f.
attach [ə'tætʃ] vt attacher, fixer, lier, saisir.
attaché [ə'tæʃei] n attaché m; — **case** serviette f, mallette f, porte-documents m.
attachment [ə'tætʃmənt] n attachement m, attache f, saisie f.
attack [ə'tæk] n attaque f, assaut m, accès m, crise f; vt attaquer, s'attaquer à.
attain [ə'tein] vt atteindre.
attainable [ə'teinəbl] a accessible, à portée.
attainder [ə'teində] n mort civile f.
attainment [ə'teinmənt] n réalisation f, arrivée f; pl talents m pl, succès m pl, connaissances f pl.
attempt [ə'tempt] n tentative f, coup de main m, essai m, attentat m; vt tenter, essayer, attaquer.
attend [ə'tend] vt s'occuper de, soigner, assister à; vi faire attention; **to** — to se charger de, s'occuper de.
attendance [ə'tendəns] n présence f, service m, assistance f.
attendant [ə'tendənt] n employé(e) mf, appariteur m, gardien, -ienne, ouvreuse f; a présent, qui sui(ven)t.
attention [ə'tenʃən] n attention f, garde-à-vous m.
attentive [ə'tentiv] a attentif, plein d'attentions, prévenant, soucieux.
attenuate [ə'tenjueit] vt atténuer.
attenuation [ə.tenju'eiʃən] n atténuation f.
attest [ə'test] vt attester, déférer le serment à.
attestation [.ætes'teiʃən] n attestation f, déposition f.
attic ['ætik] n mansarde f, grenier m, combles m pl.
attire [ə'taiə] n habit m, atours m pl, costume m; vt habiller, parer.
attitude ['ætitjuːd] n attitude f, pose f.
attorney [ə'təːni] n fondé de pourvois m, procureur (général) m, avoué m; **power of** — procuration f.
attract [ə'trækt] vt attirer.
attraction [ə'trækʃən] n attraction f, séduction f.
attractive [ə'træktiv] a attrayant, séduisant.
attractiveness [ə'træktivnis] n attrait m, charme m.
attribute ['ætribjuːt] n attribut m, apanage m, qualité f.
attribute [ə'tribjuːt] vt attribuer, prêter.
attribution [.ætri'bjuːʃən] n attribution f.
attrition [ə'triʃən] n attrition f, usure f.
attune [ə'tjuːn] vt accorder.

auburn ['ɔːbən] a châtain, auburn (no f).
auction ['ɔːkʃən] n vente aux enchères f; vt mettre aux enchères.
auctioneer [.ɔːkʃə'niə] n commissaire-priseur m, crieur m.
audacious [ɔː'deiʃəs] a audacieux, hardi.
audacity [ɔː'dæsiti] n audace f.
audible ['ɔːdəbl] a qui s'entend, intelligible, perceptible.
audibly ['ɔːdəbli] ad distinctement.
audience ['ɔːdjəns] n audience f, auditoire m, assistance f.
audio-visual ['ɔːdiou'vizjuəl] a audio-visuel.
audit ['ɔːdit] n apurement de comptes m; vt apurer, vérifier.
audition [ɔː'diʃən] n ouïe f, audition f, séance f.
auditor ['ɔːditə] n expert-comptable m.
auger ['ɔːgə] n tarière f.
aught [ɔːt] n **for** — **I know** autant que je sache.
augment [ɔːg'ment] vti augmenter.
augmentation [.ɔːgmen'teiʃən] n augmentation f.
augur ['ɔːgə] n augure m; vti augurer.
augury ['ɔːgjuri] n augure m, présage m.
August ['ɔːgəst] n août m.
august [ɔː'gʌst] a auguste.
aunt [aːnt] n tante f.
aurora [ɔː'rɔːrə] n aurore f, aube f.
auspices ['ɔːspisiz] n pl auspices m pl.
auspicious [ɔːs'piʃəs] a favorable, propice.
austere [ɔs'tiə] a austere, âpre.
austerity [ɔs'teriti] n austérité f.
Australia [ɔs'treiljə] n Australie f.
Austria ['ɔstriə] n Autriche f.
Austrian ['ɔstriən] a autrichien.
authentic [ɔː'θentik] a authentique.
authenticate [ɔː'θentikeit] vt authentiquer, certifier, légaliser.
authenticity [.ɔːθen'tisiti] n authenticité f.
author ['ɔːθə] n auteur m.
authoritative [ɔː'θɔritətiv] a qui fait autorité, autorisé, péremptoire, autoritaire.
authority [ɔː'θɔriti] n autorité f, mandat m.
authorization [.ɔːθərai'zeiʃən] n autorisation f, mandat m.
authorize ['ɔːθəraiz] vt autoriser.
authorship ['ɔːθəʃip] n paternité f.
autocracy [ɔː'tɔkrəsi] n autocratie f.
autocrat ['ɔːtəkræt] n autocrate m.
autograph ['ɔːtəgraːf] n autographe m; vt signer, autographier.
automatic [.ɔːtə'mætik] a automatique, machinal.
automation [.ɔːtə'meiʃən] n automatisation f.
automaton [ɔː'tɔmətən] n automate m.

automobile [ɔːtəməbiːl] n auto-mobile *f*.
autonomous [ɔːˈtɔnəməs] a auto-nome.
autonomy [ɔː tɔnəmi] n autonomie *f*.
autumn [ˈɔːtəm] n automne *m*.
autumnal [ɔː tʌmnəl] a automnal, d automne.
auxiliary [ɔːgˈziljəri] an auxiliaire *mf*.
avail [ə veil] n utilité *f*; **without —** sans effet; *vi* servir à, être utile à; **to — oneself of** profiter de.
available [ə veiləbl] a utile, acces-sible, disponible, existant, valable.
avarice [ævəris] n cupidité *f*.
avaricious [ævə riʃəs] a cupide, avaricieux, avare.
avenge [ə vendʒ] vt venger.
avenger [ə vendʒə] n vengeur, -eresse.
avenue [ævinjuː] n avenue *f*.
aver [əˈvəː] vt affirmer.
average [ævəridʒ] n moyenne *f*, a moyen, courant; vt compter (faire) en moyenne, établir la moyenne de.
averse [ə vəːs] a opposé, hostile (à to).
aversion [ə vəːʃən] n aversion *f*; **pet —** bête *f* noire.
avert [ə vəːt] vt détourner, écarter, prévenir.
aviary [eivjəri] n volière *f*.
aviation [eivi eiʃən] n aviation *f*.
aviator [eivieitə] n aviateur, -trice.
avid [ævid] a avide.
avidity [əˈviditi] n avidité *f*.
avocation [ævou keiʃən] n vocation *f*, métier *m*.
avoid [ə vɔid] vt éviter.
avoidable [ə vɔidəbl] a évitable.
avoirdupois [ævədə pɔiz] n système *m* des poids et mesures.
avow [ə vau] vt avouer.
avowal [ə vauəl] n aveu *m*.
avowedly [ə vauidli] ad franchement.
await [əˈweit] vt attendre.
awake [əˈweik] vi s'éveiller, se réveiller; vt éveiller, réveiller; a éveillé, vigilant, averti, informé (de to).
awakening [əˈweikniŋ] n (r)éveil *m*.
award [əˈwɔːd] n jugement *m*, attribution *f*; vt adjuger, accorder, décerner.
aware [ə wɛə] a instruit (de of), informé (de of); **to be — of** savoir, avoir conscience de.
awash [əˈwɔʃ] a baigné, lavé, inondé, à fleur d eau.
away [ə wei] ad à distance, au loin; **go —!** sortez!; **out and —** de loin, sans arrêter; **to make — with** détruire, enlever; **far and — de** beaucoup; **right —** sur-le-champ, tout de suite.
awe [ɔː] n stupeur sacrée *f*, respect craintif *m*, effroi *m*, terreur *f*; **— stricken, —struck** frappé de ter-reur, intimidé.

awful [ˈɔːful] a terrible, affreux solennel.
awfully [ˈɔːfuli] ad terriblement, infiniment; **thanks —** merci mille fois.
awhile [əˈwail] ad un moment.
awkward [ˈɔːkwəd] a gauche, gêné, embarrassant, peu commode.
awkwardness [ˈɔːkwədnis] n gaucherie *f*, embarras *m*, incon-vénient *m*, gêne *f*.
awl [ɔːl] n alène *f*.
awn [ɔːn] n barbe *f*.
awning [ˈɔːniŋ] n marquise *f*, tente *f*, bâche *f*, abri *m*.
awoke [əˈwouk] pt of awake.
awry [əˈrai] a tortueux, pervers; ad de travers.
ax [æks] n hache *f*; vt porter la hache dans; **to have an — to grind** avoir un intérêt au jeu.
axiom [ˈæksiəm] n axiome *m*.
axis [ˈæksis] n axe *m*.
axle [ˈæksl] n essieu *m*.
ay(e) [ai] n oui; [ei] ad toujours.
azure [ˈeiʒə] n azur *m*; a d'azur, azure.

B

babble [ˈbæbl] n babil *m*; vi babiller.
baboon [bəˈbuːn] n babouin *m*, cynocéphale *m*.
baby [ˈbeibi] n bébé *m*; **— carriage** voiture *f* d'enfant.
babyhood [ˈbeibihud] n enfance *f*, bas âge *m*.
babyish [ˈbeibiiʃ] a enfantin, puéril.
bachelor [ˈbætʃələ] n célibataire *m*, garçon *m*, bachelier, -ière.
bachelorhood [ˈbætʃələhud] n céli-bat *m*.
back [bæk] n dos *m*, arrière *m*, dossier *m*, envers *m*, verso *m*, fond *m*; vt (faire) reculer, appuyer, parier pour, endosser; vi reculer, faire marche arrière; **to — down** de-scendre à reculons, en rabattre; **to — out** sortir à reculons, se dégon-fler, s'excuser; a arrière, de derrière; ad en arrière, à l'arrière, dans le sens contraire, de retour; **there and —** aller et retour.
backbite [ˈbækbait] vt médire de.
backbiter [ˈbæk,baitə] n mauvaise langue *f*.
backbiting [ˈbækbaitiŋ] n médisance *f*.
backbone [ˈbækboun] n épine dor-sale *f*; **to the —** jusqu'à la moelle des os.
backdate [ˈbæk deit] vt antidater.
backdoor [ˈbæk dɔː] n porte de service *f*, porte basse *f*; a souterrain.
backfiring [ˈbæk faiəriŋ] n retour de flamme *m*, (aut) pétarade *f*.
backgammon [bækˈgæmən] n tric-trac *m*.

background ['bækgraund] n arrière-plan m, fond m.
backing ['bækiŋ] n recul m, appui m, soutien m.
back-scratcher ['bæk'skrætʃə] n scratch m.
backsliding ['bæk'slaidiŋ] n rechute f.
backstairs ['bæk'stɛəz] n escalier de service m.
backward ['bækwəd] a rétrograde, arriéré, en retard, en arrière.
backwardness ['bækwədnis] n lenteur f, retard m, état m arriéré.
backwards ['bækwədz] ad à reculons, à la renverse, à rebours, en arrière.
bacon ['beikən] n lard m, bacon m.
bad [bæd] n mauvais m, ruine f; a mauvais, méchant, malade, fort, gros.
bade [beid] pt of **bid**.
badge [bædʒ] n (in)signe m.
badger ['bædʒə] n blaireau m.
badly ['bædli] ad mal, gravement; — off gêné.
badness ['bædnis] n méchanceté f, pauvreté f, maladie f.
baffle ['bæfl] vt déjouer, contre-carrer, défier.
bag [bæg] n sac m, gibecière f, tableau m, (cows) pis m, (eyes) poche f; pl pantalon m; vt mettre en sac, empocher, chiper, prendre; vi bouffer, s'enfler.
bagful ['bægful] n sac m, sachée f.
baggage ['bægidʒ] n bagage m; donzelle f.
baggy ['bægi] a bouffant.
bagpipe ['bægpaip] n cornemuse f, biniou m.
bail [beil] n caution f; batflanc m, anse f; vt se porter (donner) caution pour, vider, écoper.
bailiff ['beilif] n bailli m, huissier m, régisseur m.
bait [beit] n amorce f; vt amorcer, tourmenter.
baize [beiz] n serge f.
bake [beik] vt (faire) cuire au four, rissoler; vi cuire, se rôtir.
bakehouse ['beikhaus] n fournil m.
baker ['beikə] n boulanger, -ère.
baker's (shop) ['beikəz] n boulangerie f.
baking ['beikiŋ] n cuisson m; — powder levure f, poudre f à lever.
balance ['bæləns] n équilibre m, balance f, bilan m; — in hand avoir; — due manque; vt peser, équilibrer, balancer; vi osciller, s'équilibrer, se faire contre-poids.
balance-sheet ['bælənsʃi:t] n bilan m.
balance-wheel ['bælənswi:l] n balancier m.
balcony ['bælkəni] n balcon m.
bald [bɔ:ld] a chauve, pelé, dégarni.
balderdash ['bɔ:ldədæʃ] n balivernes f pl.
baldness ['bɔ:ldnis] n calvitie f.

bale [beil] n ballot m, paquet m, malheur m.
baleful ['beilful] a funeste.
balk [bɔ:k] n obstacle m, poutre f; vt contrecarrer, contrarier, esquiver; vi se dérober, reculer (devant at).
ball [bɔ:l] n bal m, boule f, bille f, ballon m, balle f, boulet m, peloton m.
ballad [bæ'la:d] n ballade f.
ballast ['bæləst] n lest m, ballast m; vt lester, empierrer.
ball-bearing ['bɔ:l'bɛəriŋ] n roulement à billes m.
balloon [bə'lu:n] n ballon m.
ballot ['bælət] n boule f, scrutin m, bulletin m; vote à main levée m; vt voter; vti tirer au sort.
ballot-box ['bælətbɔks] n urne f.
balm [ba:m] n baume m.
balmy ['ba:mi] a embaumé, toqué.
baluster ['bæləstə] n rampe f, balustre m.
balustrade [.bæləs'treid] n balustrade f.
bamboo [bæm'bu:] n bambou m.
bamboozle [bæm'bu:zl] vt mystifier, filouter.
bamboozlement [bæm'bu:zlmənt] n mystification f.
ban [bæn] n ban m, interdit m, mise hors la loi f, malédiction f; vt mettre au ban, interdire, mettre à l'index.
banana [bə'na:nə] n banane f.
band [bænd] n bande f, musique f, orchestre m; vt bander; vi to — together s'associer, se bander.
bandage ['bændidʒ] n bandage m, bandeau m.
bandbox ['bændbɔks] n carton à chapeaux m.
bandmaster ['bænd,ma:stə] n chef m de musique.
bandstand ['bændstænd] n kiosque m, estrade f.
bandy ['bændi] vt échanger; a bancal, arqué.
bane [bein] n poison m, ruine f.
baneful ['beinful] a empoisonné, ruineux, funeste.
bang [bæŋ] n coup sonore m, claquement m, détonation f; vti claquer, frapper; excl pan! v'lan!
bangle ['bæŋgl] n anneau m, bracelet m.
banish ['bæniʃ] vt bannir, proscrire, exiler.
banishment ['bæniʃmənt] n bannissement m, exil m.
banister ['bænistə] n rampe f.
bank [bæŋk] n rive f, berge f, bord m, banque f, talus m, banc m; vt endiguer, relever, mettre en banque; vi virer, miser (sur on).
banker ['bæŋkə] n banquier m.
banknote ['bæŋknout] n billet de banque m.
bankrupt ['bæŋkrəpt] n banque-

routier, -ière, failli(e) *m*; *vt* réduire à la faillite.
bankruptcy ['bæŋkrəptsi] *n* banque-route *f*, faillite *f*.
banner ['bænə] *n* bannière *f*, étandard *m*.
banns [bænz] *n* bans *m pl.*
banquet ['bæŋkwit] *n* banquet *m*; *vt* traiter; *vi* banqueter.
banter ['bæntə] *n* plaisanterie *f*; *vti* plaisanter.
baptism ['bæptizəm] *n* baptême *m*.
baptismal [bæp'tizməl] *a* baptismal, de baptême.
baptize [bæp'taiz] *vt* baptiser.
bar [baː] *n* barre *f*, bar *m*, comptoir *m*, barrière *f*, (*law*) barreau *m*; *vt* barrer. exclure; *prep* moins, sauf.
barb [baːb] *n* barbe *f*, pointe *f*.
barbarian [baː'beəriən] *an* barbare *mf*.
barbarism ['baːbərizəm] *n* barbarie *f*.
barbarous ['baːbərəs] *a* cruel, grossier.
barbed [baːbd] *a* barbelé, acéré.
barbed-wire ['baːbd'waiə] *n* fil de fer barbelé *m*.
barber ['baːbə] *n* barbier *m*, coiffeur *m*.
bard [baːd] *n* barde *f*.
bare [beə] *a* nu, vide, seul, simple; *vt* mettre à nu, dégainer, dépouiller.
bareback ['beəbæk] *ad* à cru.
barefaced ['beəfeist] *a* impudent, cynique, effronté.
barefooted ['beə'futid] *a* nu-pieds.
bareheaded ['beə'hedid] *a* nu-tête, découvert.
barely ['beəli] *ad* à peine, tout juste.
bareness ['beənis] *n* nudité *f*, dénuement *m*.
bargain ['baːgin] *n* marché *m*, occasion *f*; **into the** — par dessus le marché; *vi* traiter, négocier; **to** — **over, with** marchander.
barge [baːdʒ] *n* chaland *m*, barque *f*, péniche *f*.
bargee [baː'dʒiː] *n* batelier *m*.
baritone ['bæritoun] *n* (*mus*) baryton *m*.
bark [baːk] *n* écorce *f*, aboiement *m*, trois-mâts *m*; *vt* écorcer, écorcher; *vi* aboyer.
barley ['baːli] *n* orge *m*.
barm ['baːm] *n* levure *f*.
barmaid ['baːmeid] *n* serveuse *f*.
barman ['baːmən] *n* garçon *m* de comptoir, barman *m*.
barn [baːn] *n* grange *f*; écurie *f*, étable *f*, hangar *m*.
barometer [bə'rɔmitə] *n* baromètre *m*.
baron ['bærən] *n* baron *m*.
baroness ['bærənis] *n* baronne *f*.
baronet ['bærənit] *n* baronnet *m*.
baronetcy ['bærənitsi] *n* baronnie *f*.
barrack(s) ['bærəks] *n* caserne *f*, baraque *f*.
barrage ['bæruːʒ] *n* barrage *m*.

barrel ['bærəl] *n* baril *m*, barrique *f*, canon de fusil *m*, barillet *m*; **double-barreled** à deux coups.
barren ['bærən] *a* stérile, aride.
barrenness ['bærənnis] *n* stérilité *f*, aridité.
barricade [,bæri'keid] *n* barricade *f*; *vt* barricader.
barrier ['bæriə] *n* barrière *f*; **sound** — mur *m* du son.
barring ['baːriŋ] *prep* excepté.
barrister ['bæristə] *n* avocat *m*.
barrow ['bærou] *n* brouette *f*, charrette *f* à bras.
bartender ['baːtendə] *n* barman *m*.
barter ['baːtə] *n* troc *m*, échange *m*; *vt* troquer.
base [beis] *n* base *f*; *vt* baser, fonder; *a* bas, vil.
baseless ['beislis] *a* sans fondement, sans base.
basement ['beismənt] *n* soubassement *m*, sous-sol *m*.
baseness ['beisnis] *n* bassesse *f*.
bash [bæʃ] *vt* cogner; **to** — **in** enfoncer.
bashful ['bæʃful] *a* timide.
bashfulness ['bæʃfulnis] *n* timidité *f*, fausse honte *f*.
basic ['beisik] *a* fondamental, de base.
basin ['beisn] *n* cuvette *f*, bassine *f*, bassin *m*, jatte *f*.
basis ['beisis] *n see* **base**.
bask [baːsk] *vi* se chauffer.
basket ['baːskit] *n* panier *m*, corbeille *f*; éventaire *m*; *vt* mettre dans un (au) panier.
bass [beis] *n* basse *f*, bar *m*; *a* de basse, grave.
bastard ['bæstəd] *an* bâtard(e) *mf*.
bastardy ['bæstədi] *n* bâtardise *f*.
baste [beist] *vt* faufiler, bâtir, arroser, rosser.
bat [bæt] *n* chauve-souris *f*, crosse *f*.
batch [bætʃ] *n* fournée *f*; tas *m*.
bath [baːθ] *n* bain *m*, baignoire *f*.
bathe [beið] *vt* baigner; *vi* se baigner.
bather ['beiðə] *n* baigneur, -euse.
bathos ['beiθɔs] *n* chute *f*, dégringolade *f*.
bathroom ['baːθrum] *n* salle de bain *f*.
batman ['bætmən] *n* ordonnance *f*, brosseur *m*.
battalion [bə'tæljən] *n* bataillon *m*.
batten ['bætn] *vi* s'empiffrer, s'engraisser, se repaître.
batter ['bætə] *n* pâte *f*; *vt* battre, malmener, cabosser.
battering-ram ['bætəriŋræm] *n* bélier *m*.
battery ['bætəri] *n* batterie *f*, pile *f*, voies de fait *f pl.*
battle ['bætl] *n* bataille *f*; *vi* se battre, lutter.
battle-ax ['bætlæks] *n* hache *f* d'armes.
battledore ['bætldɔː] *n* raquette *f*.

battlement ['bætlmənt] *n* créneau *m*.
battleship ['bætlʃip] *n* cuirassé *m*.
bauble ['bɔːbl] *n* babiole *f*, (*fool's*) marotte *f*.
bawdiness ['bɔːdinis] *n* obscénité *f*.
bawdy ['bɔːdi] *a* obscène.
bawl [bɔːl] *vi* vociférer, gueuler, brailler; *vt* — **out** engueuler.
bay [bei] *n* laurier *m*, baie *f*; entredeux *m*; aboiement *m*, abois *m pl*; *vi* aboyer, hurler; *a* bai, en saillie.
bayonet ['beiənit] *n* baïonnette *f*; *vt* embrocher.
bazaar [bə'zɑː] *n* bazar *m*.
be [biː] *vi* être, exister, avoir, aller, faire (froid *etc*).
beach [biːtʃ] *n* plage *f*, grève *f*; *vt* atterrir, échouer.
beacon ['biːkən] *n* balise *f*, feu *m*, poteau *m*.
bead [biːd] *n* grain *m*, perle *f*, bulle *f*; *pl* chapelet *m*.
beadle ['biːdl] *n* bedeau *m*, appariteur *m*.
beak [biːk] *n* bec *m*, éperon *m*, magistrat *m*.
beaker ['biːkə] *n* coupe *f*.
beam [biːm] *n* poutre *f*, fléau *m*, rayon *m*; *vi* rayonner.
bean [biːn] *n* haricot *m*; **broad** — fève *f*; **French** — haricot vert *m*.
bear ['bɛə] *n* ours *m*; baissier *m*; *vi* jouer à la baisse; *vt* (em-, rem-, sup-, se con-)porter, souffrir, endurer, mettre au jour; **to** — **out** confirmer.
bearable ['bɛərəbl] *a* supportable.
beard [biəd] *n* barbe *f*; *vt* défier, narguer.
bearded ['biədid] *a* barbu.
beardless ['biədlis] *a* imberbe, sans barbe.
bearer ['bɛərə] *n* porteur, -euse.
bearing ['bɛəriŋ] *n* conduite *f*; rapport *m*, aspect *m*, maintien *m*, port *m*, position *f*.
beast [biːst] *n* bête *f*, bétail *m*, brute *f*, porc *m*.
beastliness ['biːstlinis] *n* gloutonnerie *f*, bestialité *f*.
beastly ['biːstli] *a* bestial, répugnant; *ad* terriblement.
beat [biːt] *n* coup de baguette *m*, cadence *f*; battement *m*, ronde *f*, tournée *f*; (*mus*) mesure *f*; *vti* battre; **to** — **about the bush** tourner autour du pot; **to** — **one's brains** se creuser la cervelle.
beaten ['biːtn] *a* (re)battu.
beater ['biːtə] *n* rabatteur *m*, battoir *m*, fléau *m*.
beatification [bi(ː).ætifi'keiʃən] *n* béatification *f*.
beatify [bi(ː)'ætifai] *vt* béatifier.
beatitude [bi(ː)'ætitjuːd] *n* béatitude *f*.
beau [bou] *n* dandy *m*.
beautiful ['bjuːtəful] *a* beau, (*before vowels*) bel, belle.

beauty ['bjuːti] *n* beauté *f*; — **spot** *n* mouche *f*, site *m*.
beaver ['biːvə] *n* castor *m*.
becalm [bi'kɑːm] *vt* déventer.
became [bi'keim] *pt of* **become**.
because [bi'kɔz] *cj* parce que; *prep* — **of** à cause de.
beck [bek] *n* signe *m*, ordre *m*.
beckon ['bekən] *vt* faire signe à, appeler; *vi* faire signe.
become [bi'kʌm] *vi* devenir; *vt* aller bien à.
becoming [bi'kʌmiŋ] *a* seyant, convenable.
becomingly [bi'kʌmiŋli] *ad* avec grâce, convenablement.
bed [bed] *n* lit *m*, plate-bande *f*, banc *m*, gisement *m*; *a* de lit; *vt* coucher, repiquer, dépoter, sceller.
bed-chamber ['bed.tʃeimbə] *n* chambre *f*.
bedclothes ['bedklouðz] *n pl* draps *m pl* de lit.
bedding ['bediŋ] *n* literie *f*.
bedizen [bi'daizn] *vt* pomponner, affubler.
bed-ridden ['bed.ridn] *a* alité.
bedroom ['bedrum] *n* chambre *f* à coucher.
bedside ['bedsaid] *n* chevet *m*.
bedsore ['bedsɔː] *n* escarre *f*.
bedspread ['bedspred] *n* couvre-lit *m*.
bedstead ['bedsted] *n* bois de lit *m*.
bedtime ['bedtaim] *n* heure *f* d'aller au lit.
bee [biː] *n* abeille *f*.
beech [biːtʃ] *n* hêtre *m*.
beef [biːf] *n* bœuf *m*, bifteck *m*.
beehive ['biːhaiv] *n* ruche *f*.
beekeeper ['biːkiːpə] *n* apiculteur *m*.
beeline ['biːlain] *n* ligne *f* droite.
been [biːn] *pp of* **be**.
beer [biə] *n* bière *f*; **millet** — pombe *m*.
beerhouse ['biəhaus] *n* brasserie *f*.
beet [biːt] *n* bette *f*.
beetle ['biːtl] *n* (*tool*) maillet *m*, masse *f*, demoiselle *f*, (*insect*) blatte *f*, scarabée *m*; *vi* surplomber.
beetling ['biːtliŋ] *a* saillant, menaçant, bombé, broussailleux, en surplomb.
beetroot ['biːtruːt] *n* betterave *f*.
befall [bi'fɔːl] *vti* arriver (à), advenir, survenir.
befit [bi'fit] *vt* aller à, convenir à.
befitting [bi'fitiŋ] *a* seyant, convenable.
before [bi'fɔː] *prep* avant, devant, par-devant; *ad* (aupar)avant, devant, en avant; *cj* avant que, plutôt que.
beforehand [bi'fɔːhænd] *ad* d'avance, au préalable, par avance, déjà.
befriend [bi'frend] *vt* traiter (*etc*) en ami, protéger, venir en aide à.
beg [beg] *vt* prier, supplier, demander, solliciter, mendier; *vi* faire le beau, mendier.
began [bi'gæn] *pt of* **begin**.

beget [bi'get] *vt* engendrer, procréer, enfanter.

begetter [bi'getə] *n* père *m*.

beggar ['begə] *n* mendiant(e) *mf*, gueux, -se, quémandeur, -euse; *vt* réduire à la misère, mettre sur la paille, défier.

beggarliness ['begəlinis] *n* misère *f*, mesquinerie *f*.

beggarly ['begəli] *a* miséreux, misérable, mesquin.

beggary ['begəri] *n* misère *f*, mendicité *f*.

begin [bi'gin] *vti* commencer; **to —** **with** pour commencer; *vt* amorcer, entamer, se mettre à.

beginner [bi'ginə] *n* débutant(e) *mf*, novice *mf*, auteur *m*.

beginning [bi'giniŋ] *n* commencement *m*, début *m*, origine *f*.

begone [bi'gɔn] *excl* sortez! allez-vous en!

begot(ten) [bi'gɔt(n)] *pt of* **beget**.

begrudge [bi'grʌdʒ] *vt* mesurer, envier, donner à contre-cœur.

beguile [bi'gail] *vt* tromper, charmer, distraire, séduire.

begun [bi'gʌn] *pp of* **begin**.

behalf [bi'hɑːf] *n* **in, on —** of au nom de, de la part de, au compte de.

behave [bi'heiv] *vi* se conduire, se comporter, fonctionner.

behaved [bi'heivd] *a* **well—**sage, bien élevé; **badly —** mal élevé.

behavior [bi'heivjə] *n* conduite *f*, maintien *m*, tenue *f*, manières *f pl*, fonctionnement *m*.

behead [bi'hed] *vt* décapiter.

beheading [bi'hediŋ] *n* décapitation *f*, décollation *f*.

beheld [bi'held] *pt of* **behold**.

behest [bi'hest] *n* commandement *m*, ordre *m*.

behind [bi'haind] *prep* derrière, en arrière de, en retard sur; *ad* (par) derrière, en arrière.

behold [bi'hould] *vt* apercevoir, voir, regarder.

beholden [bi'houldən] *a* obligé, redevable.

beholder [bi'houldə] *n* spectateur, -trice, témoin *m*.

behoof [bi'huːf] *n* bien *m*; **on s.o.'s —** à l'intention de, à l'avantage de.

behoove [bi'huːv] *vt* incomber à, seoir à, appartenir à.

being ['biːiŋ] *n* être *m*.

belabor [bi'leibə] *vt* rosser, rouer de coups.

belated [bi'leitid] *a* retardé, en retard, attardé, tardif.

belch [beltʃ] *n* rot *m*, renvoi *m*, grondement *m*, jet de flamme *m*; *vi* roter, éructer; *vt* vomir.

beleaguer [bi'liːgə] *vt* assiéger.

belfry ['belfri] *n* beffroi *m*.

Belgian ['beldʒən] *an* belge *mf*.

Belgium ['beldʒəm] *n* Belgique *f*.

belie [bi'lai] *vt* démentir, donner un démenti à.

belief [bi'liːf] *n* foi *f*, croyance *f*, conviction *f*.

believe [bi'liːv] *vti* croire; *vt* ajouter foi à; **to make —** faire semblant.

believer [bi'liːvə] *n* croyant(e) *mf*, partisan *m*.

belittle [bi'litl] *vt* diminuer, décrier, rabaisser.

bell [bel] *n* cloche *f*, sonnette *f*, sonnerie *f*, timbre *m*, grelot *m*, clochette *f*.

bellboy ['belbɔi], **bellhop** ['belhɔp] *n* groom *m*.

bellied ['belid] *a* ventru.

belligerency [bi'lidʒərənsi] *n* état de guerre *m*.

belligerent [bi'lidʒərənt] *an* belligérant(e) *mf*.

bellow ['belou] *n* mugissement *m*, beuglement *m*, grondement *m*; *vi* mugir, gronder; *vti* beugler, brailler.

bellows ['belouz] *n* soufflet *m*.

belly ['beli] *n* ventre *m*, panse *f*, bedaine *f*; *vt* gonfler; *vi* se gonfler, s'enfler.

bellyful ['beliful] *n* ventrée *f*; **to have had one's —** en avoir plein le dos.

belong [bi'lɔŋ] *vi* appartenir (à **to**), être (à **to**).

belongings [bi'lɔŋiŋz] *n* biens *m pl*, affaires *f pl*, effets *m pl*.

beloved [bi'lʌvd] *an* (bien-)aimé(e) *mf*, chéri(e) *mf*.

below [bi'lou] *prep* au dessous de, en aval de; *ad* (au, en, là-) dessous, ci-dessous, plus loin, en bas, en aval.

belt [belt] *n* ceinture *f*, ceinturon *m*, courroie *f*, bande *f*, zone *f*; *vt* ceindre, entourer.

bemoan [bi'moun] *vt* pleurer, se lamenter de.

bemuse [bi'mjuːz] *vt* étourdir, stupéfier.

bench [bentʃ] *n* banc *m*, banquette *f*, gradin *m*; établi *m*, tribunal *m*, magistrature *f*.

bend [bend] *n* nœud *m*, courbe *f*, virage *m*, tournant *m*, coude *m*; *pl* mal *m* des caissons; *vti* courber, ployer, plier, fléchir, pencher, arquer; *vi* se courber, s'incliner, tourner, faire un coude (*road etc*); **to — back** *vt* replier, recourber; *vi* se replier, se recourber; **to — down** *vi* se baisser, se courber.

beneath [bi'niːθ] *prep* au dessous de, sous; *ad* (au-)dessous, en bas.

Benedictine [ˌbeni'diktiːn] *an* bénédictin(e) *mf*; *n* (*liqueur*) bénédictine.

benediction [ˌbeni'dikʃən] *n* bénédiction *f*.

benefaction [ˌbeni'fækʃən] *n* bienfait *m*, don *m*.

benefactor, -tress ['benifæktə, tris] *n* bienfaiteur, -trice, donateur, -trice.

beneficence [bi'nefisəns] *n* bienfaisance *f*.

beneficent [bi'nefisənt] *a* bienfaisant, salutaire.

beneficently [bi'nefisəntli] *ad* généreusement, salutairement.

beneficial [‚beni'fiʃəl] *a* avantageux, salutaire.

beneficiary [‚beni'fiʃəri] *n* bénéficiaire *m*, bénéficier, -ière.

benefit ['benifit] *n* bénéfice *m*, bien *m*, gouverne *f*, secours (mutuels) *m pl*; *vt* profiter à; *vi* bénéficier, profiter (de **by**).

benevolence [bi'nevələns] *n* bienveillance *f*, bienfait *m*.

benevolent [bi'nevələnt] *a* bienveillant; — **society** société *f* de secours mutuels.

benighted [bi'naitid] *a* surpris par la nuit, aveuglé, plongé dans l'ignorance.

benign [bi'nain] *a* bénin, -igne, affable, heureux, doux.

benignity [bi'nigniti] *n* bénignité *f*; bienveillance *f*.

bent [bent] *pt of* **bend**; *n* pli *m*, tour *m*, penchant *m*, dispositions *f pl*; *a* courbé, plié, voûté, arqué, résolu.

benumb [bi'nʌm] *vt* engourdir, transir, frapper de stupeur.

benzine ['benziːn] *n* benzine *f*.

bequeath [bi'kwiːð] *vt* léguer.

bequest [bi'kwest] *n* legs *m*.

bereave [bi'riːv] *vt* enlever, ravir, priver.

bereaved [bi'riːvd] *pp a* affligé, en deuil.

bereavement [bi'riːvmənt] *n* perte *f*, deuil *m*.

bereft [bi'reft] *pp of* **bereave**.

berry ['beri] *n* baie *f*, grain *m*.

berth [bəːθ] *n* cabine *f*, couchette *f*; mouillage *m*, place *f*; *vi* mouiller; *vt* amarre r à quai.

beseech [bi'siːtʃ] *vt* supplier, implorer, conjurer.

beset [bi'set] *vt* cerner, entourer, assaillir, obséder.

besetting [bi'setiŋ] — **sin** *n* péché mignon *m*.

beside [bi'said] *prep* à côté de, près de; **to be** — o.s. être hors de soi.

besides [bi'saidz] *ad* d'ailleurs, en outre, en plus, du reste; *prep* en outre de, sans compter.

besiege [bi'siːdʒ] *vt* assiéger.

besieger [bi'siːdʒə] *n* assiégeant *m*.

besmear [bi'smiə] *vt* graisser, tacher, barbouiller.

besmirch [bi'sməːtʃ] *vt* salir, obscurcir, ternir, souiller.

besom ['biːzəm] *n* balai de bruyère *m*.

besot [bi'sɔt] *vt* abrutir.

besought [bi'sɔːt] *pt of* **beseech**.

bespatter [bi'spætə] *vt* éclabousser.

bespeak [bi'spiːk] *vt* commander, retenir, annoncer.

bespoke [bi'spouk] *a* sur mesure, à façon.

best [best] *a* le meilleur; *ad* le mieux; *n* le mieux *m*; **to do one's** — faire de son mieux; **to look one's** — être

à son avantage; **to the** — **of one's ability** de son mieux; **to get the** — **of it** avoir le dessus; **to make the** — **of it** en prendre son parti; **to the** — **of my knowledge** autant que je sache; **the** — **of it is that** . . . le plus beau de l'affaire, c'est que...; — **man** garçon d'honneur.

best-seller ['best'selə] *n* best-seller *m*, livre à succès *m*, grand favori *m*.

bestir [bi'stəː] *vi* **to** — o.s. se remuer.

bestow [bi'stou] *vt* conférer, octroyer.

bestowal [bi'stouəl] *n* octroi *m*, don *m*.

bestrew [bi'struː] *vt* joncher, parsemer.

bestride [bi'straid] *vt* enfourcher, enjamber, se mettre à califourchon sur.

bet [bet] *n* pari *m*; *vt* parier; *pt of* **bet**.

betake [bi'teik] *vt* **to** — o.s. se rendre.

betimes [bi'taimz] *ad* de bonne heure, à temps.

betoken [bi'toukən] *vt* indiquer, annoncer, révéler.

betray [bi'trei] *vt* livrer, vendre, trahir, montrer.

betrayal [bi'treiəl] *n* trahison *f*, révélation *f*.

betrayer [bi'treiə] *n* traître, -esse.

betrothal [bi'trouðəl] *n* fiançailles *f pl*.

betrothed [bi'trouðd] *an* fiancé(e) *mf*.

better ['betə] *n* parieur *m*; *a* meilleur; *ad* mieux; *vt* améliorer, surpasser; **to be** — aller mieux, valoir mieux; **to get** — s'améliorer, se rétablir, guérir; **to get the** — **of** l'emporter sur; **to think** — se raviser; — **and** — de mieux en mieux.

betterment ['betəmənt] *n* amélioration *f*.

between [bi'twiːn] *prep* entre; **far** — clairsemé, rare.

bevel ['bevəl] *n* équerre *f*, biais *m*, biseau *m*; *vt* biseauter, tailler en biais, chanfreiner.

beveled ['bevəld] *a* biseauté, de biais.

beverage ['bevəridʒ] *n* breuvage *m*, boisson *f*.

bevy ['bevi] *n* compagnie *f*, troupe *f*, bande *f*.

bewail [bi'weil] *vt* se lamenter sur, pleurer.

bewailing [bi'weiliŋ] *n* lamentation *f*.

beware [bi'wɛə] *vi* prendre garde; *vt* **to** — **of** prendre garde à (de), se garder de, se méfier de.

bewilder [bi'wildə] *vt* abasourdir, ahurir, dérouter, désorienter, confondre.

bewilderment [bi'wildəmənt] *n* ahurissement *m*, confusion *f*.

bewitch [bi'witʃ] *vt* ensorceler, charmer, enchanter.

bewitchment [bi'witʃmənt] n ensorcellement m.

beyond [bi'jɔnd] n l'au-delà m; prep au-delà de, après, par-delà, derrière, outre; ad au-delà, plus loin, par-delà.

bias ['baiəs] n biais m, penchant m, tendance f, prévention f, parti-pris m.

biased ['baiəst] a prévenu, tendancieux, partial.

bib [bib] n bavette f, bavoir m.

bibber ['bibə] n soiffard m, buveur m.

Bible ['baibl] n bible f.

biblical ['biblikəl] a biblique.

bibliographer [,bibli'ɔgrəfə]n bibliographe m.

bibliographical [,bibliə'græfikəl] a bibliographique.

bibliography [,bibli'ɔgrəfi] n bibliographie f.

bibliophile ['biblioufail] n bibliophile m.

bicker ['bikə] vi se quereller, se chamailler, murmurer, crépiter, briller.

bickering ['bikəriŋ] n prise de bec f, chamailleries f pl, bisbille f.

bicycle ['baisikl] n bicyclette f.

bid [bid] n offre f, enchère f, demande f; vti commander, dire, inviter, offrir, demander; **to — for** faire une offre pour; **to — s.o. good-day** donner le bonjour à qn.

bidden ['bidn] pp of **bid.**

bidder ['bidə] n enchérisseur m; **to the highest — au plus offrant.**

bide [baid] vti attendre.

biennial [bai'eniəl] a bisannuel, biennal.

bier [biə] n brancard m, civière f.

big [big] a gros(se), grand.

bigamist ['bigəmist] n bigame mf.

bigamous ['bigəməs] a bigame mf.

bigamy ['bigəmi] n bigamie f.

bight [bait] n baie f, anse f, crique f.

bigness ['bignis] n grosseur f, importance f, grandeur f.

bigot ['bigət] n bigot(e) mf, fanatique mf.

bigotry ['bigətri] n bigoterie f, fanatisme f.

bigwig ['bigwig] n gros bonnet m.

bike [baik] n bécane f, vélo m.

bile [bail] n bile f.

bilge [bildʒ] n sentine f, fond de cale m; vi faire eau; **to talk — dire des balivernes.**

bilious ['biljəs] a bilieux, cholérique; **— attack, crise f de foie.**

bilk [bilk] vt filouter, éluder, tromper.

bill [bil] n bec m, facture f, note f, traite f, effet m, addition f; **— of fare** carte f, affiche f; **hand—** prospectus m; vt annoncer, afficher, placarder; vi se becqueter; **to — and coo** faire les tourtereaux.

billet ['bilit] n bûche f, (billet m de) logement m, place f; vt loger, cantonner.

billiard-ball ['biljədbɔːl] n bille f.

billiard-cloth ['biljədklɔθ] n drap m.

billiard-cue ['biljədkjuː] n queue f.

billiard-room ['biljədrum] n salle de billard f.

billiards ['biljədz] n billard m.

billiard-table ['biljəd,teibl] n billard m.

billion ['biljən] n milliard m, billion m.

billow ['bilou] n grande vague f, houle f, lame f; vi se soulever, s'enfler.

billowy ['biloui] a houleux.

bill-sticker ['bil,poustə, ,stikə] n afficheur m.

bill-posting ['bil,poustiŋ] n affichage m.

billy-goat ['biligout] n bouc m.

bin [bin] n seau m, huche f, boîte à ordures f, panier m, coffre m.

bind [baind] vt lier, attacher, ligoter, bander, obliger, relier, engager.

binder ['baində] n (re)lieur, -euse, botteleur, -euse, bandage m, lieuse f, ceinture f.

binding ['baindiŋ] n reliure f, bordure f, bandage m, liséré m; a obligatoire.

binoculars [bi'nɔkjuləz] n pl jumelle(s) f pl.

biographer [bai'ɔgrəfə] n biographe m.

biographical [,baiou'græfikəl] a biographique.

biography [bai'ɔgrəfi] n biographie f.

biological [,baiə'lɔdʒikəl] a biologique.

biologist [bai'ɔlədʒist] n biologue m.

biology [bai'ɔlədʒi] n biologie f.

biped ['baiped] an bipède m.

biplane ['baiplein] n biplan m.

birch [bəːtʃ] n bouleau m, verges f pl; vt donner les verges à, flageoler.

bird [bəːd] n oiseau m, perdreau m, volaille f, type m; **a — in the hand is worth two in the bush un 'tiens' vaut mieux que deux 'tu l'auras';** **to give s.o. the — siffler qn, envoyer promener qn;** **bird's-eye view vue à vol d'oiseau.**

bird-call ['bəːdkɔːl] n appeau m.

bird-catcher ['bəːd,kætʃə] n oiseleur m.

bird-lime ['bəːdlaim] n glu f.

bird-seed ['bəːdsiːd] n mouron m.

birth [bəːθ] n naissance f, origine f, lignée f; **to give — to donner le jour à, enfanter, mettre bas; — certificate** acte m de naissance.

birthday ['bəːθdei] n anniversaire m, fête f.

birthplace ['bəːθpleis] n lieu natal m, lieu de naissance, berceau m.

birth-rate ['bəːθreit] n natalité f.

birthright ['bəːθrait] n droit m d'aînesse, de naissance.

biscuit ['biskit] n biscuit m, gateau sec m.

bishop ['biʃəp] *n* évêque *m*, (*chess*) fou *m*.
bishopric ['biʃəprik] *n* évêché *m*.
bison ['baisn] *n* bison *m*.
bissextile [bi'sekstail] *a* bissextile.
bit(ten) [bit, 'bitn] *pt* (*pp*) *of* **bite**.
bit [bit] *n* mors *m*, frein *m*; morceau *m*, brin *m*, miette *f*, bout *m*, **two — s** pièce *f* de ¼ dollar.
bitch [bitʃ] *n* chienne *f* etc, femelle *f*.
bite [bait] *n* morsure *f*, piqûre *f*, bouchée *f*, touche *f*, coup de dent *m*, mordant *m*; *vt* mordre, piquer, sucer, prendre, donner un coup de dent à, attraper; *vi* mordre.
biting ['baitiŋ] *a* mordant, piquant, cuisant, cinglant, âpre.
bitter ['bitə] *a* amer, aigre, âpre, rude, cruel, acharné; — **cold** *n* froid de loup *m*; **to the — end** jusqu'au bout.
bittern ['bitə(ː)n] *n* butor *m*.
bitterness ['bitənis] *n* amertume *f*, acrimonie *f*, aigreur *f*, âpreté *f*, rancune *f*.
bitumen ['bitjumin] *n* bitume *m*.
bituminous [bi'tjuːminəs] *a* bitumineux.
bivouac ['bivuæk] *n* bivouac *m*; *vi* bivouaquer.
blab [blæb] *vt* révéler; *vi* parler au bout vendre la mèche.
blabber ['blæbə] *n* bavard(e) *mf*, indiscret, -ète *mf*.
black [blæk] *a* noir, triste, sombre; **to be — and blue** être couvert de bleus; — **eye** œil poché *m*, œil au beurre noir *m*; — **Maria** panier *m* à salade; — **pudding** boudin *m*; — **sheep** brebis *f* galeuse; — noir(e) *mf*, nègre, négresse; *vt* noircir, cirer.
blackball ['blækbɔːl] *n* boule *f* noire; *vt* blackbouler.
blackbeetle ['blækbiːtl] *n* cafard *m*.
blackberry ['blækbəri] *n* mûre *f*; — **bush** ronce *f*, mûrier *m*.
blackbird ['blækbəːd] *n* merle *m*.
blackboard ['blækbɔːd] *n* tableau noir *m*.
blackcurrant(s) ['blæk'kʌrənt(s)] *n* cassis *m*.
blacken ['blækən] *vt* noircir, assombrir, obscurcir; *vi* (se) noircir, s'assombrir.
Blackfriar ['blæk'fraiə]ǁ*n* dominicain *m*.
blackguard ['blægɑːd] *n* canaille *f*, vaurien *m*.
blacking ['blækiŋ] *n* cirage noir *m*.
blackish ['blækiʃ] *a* noirâtre.
blacklead ['blæk'led] *n* mine *f* de plomb, plombagine *f*.
blackleg ['blækleg] *n* escroc *m*, renard *m*, jaune *m*.
blackmail ['blækmeil] *n* chantage *m*; *vt* faire chanter.
blackmailer ['blækmeilə] *n* maître chanteur *m*.
blackness ['blæknis] *n* noirceur *f*, obscurité *f*.

blackout ['blækaut] *n* couvre-feu *m*, obscurcissement *m*, black-out *m*; *vt* obscurcir.
blacksmith ['blæksmiθ] *n* forgeron *m*, maréchal ferrant *m*; — **'s forge** *f*.
blackthorn ['blækθɔːn] *n* prunellier *m*, épine noire *f*.
bladder ['blædə] *n* vessie *f*, outre *f* gonflée de vent, vésicule *f*.
blade [bleid] *n* feuille *f*, brin *m*, plat *m*, pale *f*, lame *f*; tranchant *m*, omoplate *f*, épaule *f*, boute-en-train *m*, luron *m*.
blame [bleim] *n* blâme *m*, faute *f*; *vt* blâmer, reprocher, attribuer.
blameless ['bleimlis] *a* irréprochable, innocent.
blameworthy ['bleim.wəːði] *a* blâmable, répréhensible.
blanch [blɑːntʃ] *vti* blanchir, pâlir; *vi* blêmir.
bland [blænd] *a* aimable, flatteur, doux, affable, doucereux, suave.
blandish ['blændiʃ] *vt* flatter, cajoler, amadouer.
blandishment ['blændiʃmənt] *n* flatterie *f*, cajolerie *f*.
blank [blæŋk] *n* blanc *m*, billet blanc *m*, vide *m*, trou *m*; *a* blanc, en (à) blanc, inexpressif, vide, confondu, net.
blanket ['blæŋkit] *n* couverture *f*; **to toss s.o. in a —** verner qn; **wet —** rabat-joie *m*.
blankly ['blæŋkli] *ad* vaguement, d'un air déconcerté.
blare [blɛə] *n* sonnerie *f*, accents cuivrés *m pl*; *vi* sonner, retentir; *vt* faire retentir, brailler.
blarney ['blɑːni] *n* eau *f* bénite de cour, boniments *m pl*, flagornerie *f*, pommade *f*.
blaspheme [blæs'fiːm] *vti* blasphémer.
blasphemer [blæs'fiːmə] *n* blasphémateur, -trice.
blasphemous ['blæsfiməs] *a* blasphématoire, blasphémateur, impie.
blasphemy ['blæsfimi] *n* blasphème *m*.
blast [blɑːst] *n* souffle *m*, coup de vent *m*, charge explosive *f*, rafale *f*, sonnerie *f*; *vt* faire sauter, foudroyer, flétrir, brûler, détruire, anéantir.
blast-furnace ['blɑːst.fəːnis] *n* haut-fourneau *m*.
blasting ['blɑːstiŋ] *n* sautage *m*, coups *m pl* de mine, foudroiement *m*, anéantissement *m*.
blast-off ['blɑːstɔːf] *n* mise *f* à feu.
blatant ['bleitənt] *a* bruyant, criard, criant.
blaze [bleiz] *n* flamme *f*, flambée *f*, éclat *m*, conflagration *f*; **go to —s!** allez au diable! *vt* trompeter; *vi* flamber, flamboyer, resplendir; **to — up** s'enflammer, s'emporter, se révolter.
blazon ['bleizn] *n* blason *m*, armoiries *f pl*; *vt* blasonner; **to — forth**

proclamer, publier, crier du haut des toits.

bleach [bli:tʃ] vti blanchir; vi décolorer; n décolorant m, agent de blanchiment m.

bleak [bli:k] n ablette f; a blême, battu des vents, désolé, glacial, désert.

bleary [bliəi] a confus, vague, chassieux; vt brouiller, estomper, rendre trouble.

bleat [bli:t] n bêlement m; vi bêler.

bleed [bli:d] vti saigner.

bleeding ['bli:diŋ] n saignement m, saignée f; a saignant, ensanglanté.

blemish ['blemiʃ] n tache f, défaut m, tare f; vt gâter, (en)tacher, souiller.

blench [blentʃ] vi broncher, pâlir, blêmir.

blend [blend] n mélange m, alliance f; vt mêler, mélanger, fondre, marier; vi se mêler, se mélanger, se marier, se confondre.

bless [bles] vt bénir, consacrer, accorder.

blessed ['blesid] a béni, comble, bienheureux, saint, fichu.

blessedness ['blesidnis] n félicité f.

blessing ['blesiŋ] n bénédiction f, bénédicité m.

blew [blu:] pt of **blow**.

blight [blait] n mildiou m, rouille f, nielle f, brouissure f, fléau m; vt frapper de mildiou, rouiller, nieller, brouir, moisir, flétrir.

blind [blaind] n store m, jalousie f, feinte f; a aveugle, invisible, masqué; vt aveugler, crever les yeux à, éblouir.

blindfold ['blaindfould] a ad les yeux bandés; vt bander les yeux à.

blindly ['blaindli] ad aveuglément, à l'aveugle(tte).

blindman's buff ['blaindmænz'bʌf] n colin-maillard m.

blindness ['blaindnis] n cécité f, aveuglement m.

blink [bliŋk] n lueur f, coup d'œil m, clignement d'yeux m, échappée f; vi ciller, cligner, clignoter, papilloter; to — at fermer les yeux sur.

blinkers ['bliŋkəz] n œillères f pl.

bliss [blis] n félicité f, béatitude f.

blister ['blistə] n ampoule f, cloque f, boursuflure f.

blithe [blaið] a joyeux.

blitz [blits] n guerre-éclair f; bombardement m.

blizzard ['blizəd] n tempête f, tourmente de neige f.

bloat [blout] vt saler et fumer, enfler, gonfler, bouffir.

bloated ['bloutid] a bouffi, gonflé, congestionné.

bloater ['bloutə] n hareng saur m.

blob [blɔb] n tache f, pâté d'encre m.

block [blɔk] n bûche f, souche f, billot m, bloc m, obstruction f, tronçon m; **traffic** — embouteillage

m; — **of houses** pâté de maisons m; — **of flats** immeuble m; vt bloquer, obstruer, boucher, encombrer, barrer.

blockade [blɔ'keid] n blocus m; to **run the** — braver le blocus; vt bloquer, obstruer, faire le blocus de.

blockhead ['blɔkhed] n tête f de bois, bûche f.

blockhouse ['blɔkhaus] n blokhaus m.

bloke [blouk] n (fam) type m, individu m, coco m.

blood [blʌd] n sang m; **in cold** — de sang-froid; **his** — **was up** il était monté.

blood-donor ['blʌd'dounə] n donneur de sang m.

bloodhound ['blʌdhaund] n limier m, détective m.

bloodless ['blʌdlis] a exsangue, anémié, sans effusion de sang.

bloodletting ['blʌd'letiŋ] n saignée f.

blood poisoning ['blʌd.pɔizniŋ] n empoisonnement m du sang, toxémie f.

bloodshed ['blʌdʃed] n massacre m, carnage m.

bloodshot ['blʌdʃɔt] a injecté de sang.

bloodsucker ['blʌd.sʌkə] n sangsue f.

bloodthirsty ['blʌd.θə:sti] a sanguinaire, assoiffé de sang.

bloodvessel ['blʌd.vesl] n vaisseau sanguin m.

bloody ['blʌdi] a sanglant, en (de, du) sang, ensangianté, sanguinaire; ad rudement, diablement.

bloom [blu:m] n fleur f, épanouissement m, duvet m, velouté m; vi fleurir, être dans sa, en, fleur.

bloomer ['blu:mə] n gaffe f, bévue f, bourde f.

blooming ['blu:miŋ] n fleuraison f; a en fleur, fleurissant, florissant, sacré.

blossom ['blɔsəm] n fleur f; vi fleurir; to — **out** s'épanouir.

blot [blɔt] n tache f, pâté m, défaut m; vt faire des taches sur, noircir (du papier), sécher, boire; to — **out** effacer, anéantir.

blotch [blɔtʃ] n pustule f, tache f; vt marbrer, couvrir de taches.

blotchy ['blɔtʃi] a marbré, couperosé.

blotting-paper ['blɔtiŋ.peipə] n buvard m.

blouse [blauz] n blouse f, chemisette f; camisole f, chemisier m.

blow [blou] n coup m, souffle m d'air, floraison f; vi souffler, venter, fleurir, fondre, sauter; vt souffler, essoufler, chasser, faire sauter; to — **a kiss** envoyer un baiser; to — **one's nose** se moucher; to — **away** emporter; to — **down** (r)abattre, renverser; to — **out** souffler, éteindre, enfler; vi s'éteindre; to — **up** vi sauter; vt faire sauter, gonfler.

blower ['bloua] n souffleur m, tablier de cheminée m.

blowfly ['blouflai] n mouche f à viande.

blown [bloun] pp of **blow**.

blowpipe ['bloupaip] n chalumeau m, canne f, sarbacane f.

blowy ['bloui] a venteux, balayé par le vent.

blubber ['blʌbə] n graisse f de baleine, vi pleurer bruyamment, pleurnicher, pleurer comme un veau.

blubberer ['blʌbərə] n pleurnicheur, -euse, pleurard(e) mf.

bludgeon ['blʌdʒən] n trique f, matraque f; vt assommer, asséner un coup de matraque à.

blue [bluː] a bleu; n bleu m, ciel m, la grande bleue f; **to have the —s** avoir le cafard, les papillons noirs; **light — bleu clair; dark — bleu** foncé; **navy — bleu marine; Prussian — bleu de Prusse; sky — bleu de** ciel; vt bleuir, passer au bleu, gaspiller.

bluebell ['bluːbel] n clochette f, campanule f.

bluebottle ['bluː botl] n bluet m, mouche bleue f.

bluejacket ['bluː dʒækit] n matelot m.

blue-stocking ['bluːstɔkiŋ] n bas-bleu m.

bluff [blʌf] n cap escarpé m, bluff m; vti bluffer; vi faire du bluff; a à pic, brusque, cordial.

bluffness ['blʌfnis] n brusquerie f cordiale, franc-parler m.

bluish ['bluːiʃ] a bleuâtre, bleuté.

blunder ['blʌndə] n bévue f, gaffe f; vi faire une gaffe, gaffer; **to — into** heurter; **to — along** marcher à l'aveuglette.

blunderbuss ['blʌndəbʌs] n tromblon m.

blundering ['blʌndəriŋ] a maladroit, brouillon.

blunt [blʌnt] a émoussé, brusque, franc; vt émousser.

bluntly ['blʌntli] ad rudement, carrément.

bluntness ['blʌntnis] n rudesse f, brusquerie f, état émoussé m.

blur [bləː] n tache f, macule f, buée f, effet confus m; vt tacher, obscurcir, troubler, brouiller, voiler, estomper.

blurb [bləːb] n annonce f, fadaises f pl.

blurt [bləːt] vt **to — out** lâcher, raconter de but en blanc.

blush [blʌʃ] n rougeur f; vi rougir.

blushingly ['blʌʃiŋli] ad en rougissant.

bluster ['blʌstə] n fracas m, rodomontades f pl, jactance f, menaces f pl; vi faire rage, s'emporter, le prendre de haut, fanfaronner, faire du fracas.

blusterer ['blʌstərə] n fanfaron m, rodmont m.

blustering ['blʌstəriŋ] a soufflant en rafales, bravache.

boa ['bouə] n boa m.

boar [bɔː] n verrat m, sanglier m.

board [bɔːd] n planche f, madrier m, tableau m, carton m, pension f, commission f, ministère m, conseil m, comité m; **above — franc, net; on — à bord (de); vi être en pension,** prendre pension; vt planchéier, prendre en pension, aborder, aller à bord de, s'embarquer sur; **to — out** mettre en pension; **to — up** condamner, boucher.

boarder ['bɔːdə] n pensionnaire mf.

boarding-house ['bɔːdiŋhaus] n pension f.

boarding-school ['bɔːdiŋskuːl] n pensionnat m, internat m.

boast [boust] n hâblerie f, vanterie f; vi se vanter, se faire gloire (de about).

boaster ['boustə] n vantard m, fanfaron m, hâbleur m.

boastful ['boustful] a vantard, glorieux.

boat [bout] n bateau m, barque f, canot m, embarcation f; **to be in the same — être logés à la même** enseigne; vi aller, se promener en bateau, faire du canotage.

boater ['boutə] n (hat) canotier m.

boat-hook ['bouthuk] n gaffe f.

boating ['boutiŋ] n canotage m, partie de canotage f.

boatman ['boutmən] n batelier m, loueur de canots m.

boat-race ['boutreis] n course de bateaux f, match d'aviron m, régate f.

boatswain ['bousn] n maître d'équipage m.

bob [bɔb] n bouche f, bonchon m, plomb m, coiffure f à la Ninon, courbette f, petit bond m; vt couper court, écourter; vi danser, s'agiter, faire la courbette.

bobbin ['bɔbin] n bobine f.

bobby ['bɔbi] n (fam) sergot m, flic m.

bode [boud] vt présager.

bodice ['bɔdis] n corsage m, cache-corset m.

bodily ['bɔdili] a corporel, physique; ad corporellement, en corps.

boding ['boudiŋ] n présage m, pressentiment m.

bodkin ['bɔdkin] n passelacet m, épingle f.

body ['bɔdi] n corps m, cadavre m, carrosserie f, fuselage m, substance f, consistance f.

bog [bɔg] n marais m, bourbier m, fondrière f, marécage m; vt enliser, embourber; **to get bogged** s'enliser.

bogey ['bougi] n épouvantail m, lutin m, croquemitaine m, le Père Fouettard m.

boggle ['bɔgl] vi **to — at, over** réchigner à, devant, reculer, hésiter devant.

boggy ['bɔgi] *a* marécageux, tourbeux.

bogle ['bougl] *n* fantôme *m*, épouvantail *m*.

bogus ['bougəs] *a* faux, véreux.

boil [bɔil] *n* furoncle *m*, clou *m*; *vi* bouillir, bouillonner; *vt* faire bouillir, faire cuire; **to — down** *vt* condenser, réduire; *vi* se réduire; **to — over** déborder.

boiler ['bɔilə] *n* chaudière *f*, bouilloire *f*, lessiveuse *f*.

boiler-maker ['bɔiləmeikə] *n* chaudronnier *m*.

boiling ['bɔiliŋ] *n* ébullition *f*, remous *m*, bouillonnement *m*.

boisterous ['bɔistərəs] *a* violent, exuberant, tapageur, bruyant, tempétueux.

boisterousness ['bɔistərəsnis] *n* violence *f*, exubérance *f*, turbulence *f*.

bold [bould] *a* hardi, téméraire, audacieux, effronté; **to make — to** se permettre de, oser.

boldness ['bouldnis] *n* hardiesse *f*, effronterie *f*, audace *f*.

bole [boul] *n* tronc *m*, fût *m*.

Bolshevism ['bɔlʃivizəm] *n* bolchevisme *m*.

Bolshevist ['bɔlʃivist] *n* bolcheviste *mf*.

bolster ['boulstə] *n* traversin *m*, coussinet *m*; *vt* soutenir, préserver, appuyer.

bolt [boult] *n* verrou *m*, pêne *m*, boulon *m*, coup de foudre *m*, culasse *f*; *vt* verrouiller, enfermer, boulonner, avaler tout rond, gober, bouffer; *vi* s'emballer, détaler, déguerpir, décamper, filer, lever le pied.

bolter ['boultə] *n* blutoir *m*; *vt* bluter.

bolting ['boultiŋ] *n* blutage *m*.

bomb [bɔm] *n* bombe *f*; **time —** bombe *f* à retardement; **—proof** à l'abri des bombes.

bombard [bɔm'baːd] *vt* bombarder, pilonner.

bombast ['bɔmbæst] *n* emphase *f*, grandiloquence *f*.

bombastic [bɔm'bæstik] *a* ampoulé, emphatique.

bomb-crater ['bɔmkreitə] *n* entonnoir *m*.

bomber ['bɔmə] *n* bombardier *m*.

bond [bɔnd] *n* attache *f*, lien *m*, engagement *m*, obligation *f*, depôt *m*, bon *m*, entrepôt *m*, douane *f*; *pl* fers *m pl*; *vt* assembler, entreposer, mettre en dépôt.

bondage ['bɔndidʒ] *n* servitude *f*, esclavage *m*, emprisonnement *m*.

bondholder ['bɔnd,houldə] *n* obligataire *m*, porteur *m* de bons.

bondsman ['bɔndzmən] *n* esclave *m*.

bone [boun] *n* os *m*, (*fish*) arêt̃ *f*; ossements *m pl*; *vt* désosser, escamoter.

boneless ['bounlis] *a* mou, désossé, sans arêtes.

bonfire ['bɔn,faiə] *n* feu *m* de joie.

bonnet ['bɔnit] *n* bonnet *m*, béguin *m*, capot *m*; **bee in the —** araignée dans le plafond.

bonny ['bɔni] *a* beau, joli.

bonus ['bounəs] *n* boni *m*, prime *f*, gratification *f*.

bony ['bouni] *a* osseux, décharné, anguleux, tout os, plein d'arêtes.

boo [buː] *n* huée; *vti* huer.

booby ['buːbi] *n* niais(e) *mf*, nigaud(e) *mf*.

booby-trap ['buːbitræp] *n* attrape-nigaud *m*.

book [buk] *n* livre *m*, bouquin *m*, livret *m*, cahier *m*, carnet *m*; *vt* entrer, inscrire, retenir, louer.

bookbinder ['buk,baində] *n* relieur *m*.

bookbinding ['buk,baindiŋ] *n* reliure *f*.

bookcase ['bukkeis] *n* bibliothèque *f*.

book-ends ['bukendz] *n pl* serre-livres *m inv*.

booking ['bukiŋ] *n* location *f*, inscription *f*, réservation *f*.

booking-office ['bukiŋ,ɔfis] *n* bureau *m* de location, guichet *m*.

bookish ['bukiʃ] *a* livresque.

book-keeper ['buk,kiːpə] *n* teneur *m* de livres, comptable *m*.

book-keeping ['buk,kiːpiŋ] *n* tenue *f* de livres, comptabilité *f*.

booklet ['buklit] *n* livret *m*, brochure *f*.

bookmaker ['buk,meikə] *n* bookmaker *m*.

bookmark ['bukmaːk] *n* signet *m*.

bookseller ['buk,selə] *n* libraire *m*.

book-sewer ['buk,souə] *n* brocheur *m*.

bookshop ['bukʃɔp] *n* librairie *f*.

bookstall ['bukstɔːl] *n* étalage *m* de livres, (*station*) bibliothèque *f*.

bookworm ['bukwəːm] *n* rat de bibliothèque *m*.

boom [buːm] *n* emballement *m*, vogue *f*, hausse rapide *f*, boom *m*, grondement *m*, ronflement *m*, barrage *m*; *vt* faire de la réclame pour, faire du tapage, du battage, autour de; *vi* entrer en hausse, s'emballer, trouver la grande vente, retentir, ronfler, tonner.

boon [buːn] *n* faveur *f*, don *m*, bénédiction *f*, avantage *m*; **— companion** bon vivant *m*, bon compagnon *m*.

boor [buə] *n* rustre *m*, goujat *m*, paysan *m*.

boorishness ['buəriʃnis] *n* rusticité *f*, grossièreté *f*.

boost [buːst] *vt* faire du tapage autour de, faire de la réclame pour, lancer, chauffer.

boot [buːt] *n* bottine *f*, botte *f*, brodequin *m*, coffre *m*.

bootblack ['buːtblæk] n cireur m.
booth [buːð] n tente f, baraque f, salle f de scrutin.
boot-jack ['buːtdʒæk] n tirebottes m.
bootleg ['buːt‚leg] vi faire la contrebande des boissons alcooliques.
bootmaker ['buːt‚meikə] n bottier m, cordonnier m.
boot polish ['buːt‚pɔliʃ] n cirage m, crème f à chaussures.
boots [buːts] n garçon m d'étage, cireur m de chaussures.
booty ['buːti] n butin m.
booze [buːz] n (fam) boisson f; vi chopiner, être en ribote.
bopeep [bou'piːp] n cache-cache m.
border ['bɔːdə] n bord m, bordure f, marge f, lisière f, frontière f; vt border; **to — upon** frôler, toucher à, tirer sur, friser, côtoyer.
borderer ['bɔːdərə] n frontalier, -ière.
borderline ['bɔːdəlain] n ligne de démarcation f; **— case** cas limite m.
bore [bɔː] pt of **bear**; n (gun) âme f, calibre m, trou m, mascaret m, raseur m, importun(e) mf, corvée f, scie f; vt forer, percer, assommer, ennuyer; vi (horse) encenser.
boredom ['bɔːdəm] n ennui m.
boring ['bɔːriŋ] a ennuyeux, assommant.
born [bɔːn] pp né; **to be —** naître; **he was —** il est né, il naquit; **to be — again** renaître.
borne [bɔːn] pp of **bear**.
borough ['bʌrə] n bourg m.
borrow ['bɔrou] vt emprunter.
borrower ['bɔrouə] n emprunteur, -euse.
borrowing ['bɔrouiŋ] n emprunt m.
bosh [bɔʃ] n blague f, fariboles f pl, chansons f pl.
bosom ['buzəm] n sein m, giron m, poitrine f, cœur m, surface f; a intime.
boss [bɔs] n bosse f, patron, -onne.
bossy ['bɔsi] a autoritaire.
botanist ['bɔtənist] n botaniste mf.
botany ['bɔtəni] n botanique f.
botch [bɔtʃ] n travail malfait m, ravaudage m; vt ravauder, saboter; **to — up** retaper, rafistoler.
both [bouθ] pn tous (les) deux, l'un et l'autre; a deux; ad à la fois, tant ... que ...
bother ['bɔðə] n ennui m, tracas m, embêtement m; vt ennuyer, tourmenter, tracasser, embêter; vi s'inquiéter, se faire de la bile; excl zut!
bottle ['bɔtl] n bouteille f, flacon m, bocal m, (hay) botte f, (baby's) biberon m; **hot-water —** bouillote f, moine m; vt mettre en bouteilles, botteler; **to — up** ravaler, refouler, étouffer, embouteiller.
bottleneck ['bɔtlnek] n étranglement m, goulot m, embouteillage m.

bottle-washer ['bɔtl‚wɔʃə] n plongeur m.
bottom ['bɔtəm] n fond m, derrière m, siège m, lit m, bas bout m, queue f, bas m, dessous m; vt mettre un fond, siège, à; vi toucher le fond; **to get to the — of** approfondir.
bottomless ['bɔtəmlis] a sans fond, insondable.
bough [bau] n rameau m, branche f.
boulder ['bouldə] n gros galet m, roche f, pierre f roulée.
bounce [bauns] n bond m, vantardise f, épate f; vt faire rebondir; vi (re)bondir, se vanter, faire de l'épate.
bouncer ['baunsə] n hâbleur m, épateur m, mensonge impudent m, expulseur m, videur m.
bound [baund] pt pp of **bind**; n limite f, bornes f pl, saut m, bond m; vt borner, limiter; vi (re)bondir, (sur)sauter; a à destination de, en route (pour), lié (à to), tenu (de to); **he is — to come** il ne peut pas manquer de venir.
boundary ['baundəri] n frontière f, limite f, bornes f pl.
bounden ['baundən] a sacré, impérieux.
boundless ['baundlis] a illimité, infini, sans bornes.
bounteous ['bauntiəs] a abondant, généreux.
bountiful ['bauntiful] a généreux, bienfaisant.
bounty ['baunti] n générosité f, munificence f, fondation f, prime f, subvention f.
bouquet [bu'kei] n bouquet m.
bout [baut] n tour m, orgie f, crise f, accès m, lutte f.
bow [bou] n courbe f, arc m, (coup d')archet m, nœud m; a arqué, cintré.
bow [bau] n révérence f, salut m, avant m, étrave f; vt courber, incliner, baisser, plier, voûter; vi s'incliner, faire une révérence.
bowels ['bauəlz] n boyaux m pl, entrailles f pl, intestins m pl.
bower ['bauə] n charmille f, tonnelle f.
bowl [boul] n bol m, jatte f, coupe f, (pipe) fourneau m, boule f; pl (jeu de) boules f pl; vt rouler, lancer; vi jouer aux boules; **to — over** renverser.
bowler ['boulə] n joueur m de boules, (hat) melon m.
bowling-green ['bouliŋgriːn] n boulingrin m, jeu m de boules.
bowman ['boumən] n archer m.
bowsprit ['bousprit] n beaupré m.
bow-window ['bou'windou] n fenêtre cintrée f, en saillie.
box [bɔks] n boîte f, caisse f, coffre m, carton m, tirelire f, tronc m, loge f, barre f, siège m du cocher, guérite f, pavillon m de chasse,

(*horse*) box *m*, stalle *f*; — **on the ear** gifle *f*, claque *f*; *vt* **to** — **s.o.'s ears** gifler qn, calotter; *vi* boxer, faire de la boxe.

boxer ['bɔksə] *n* boxeur *m*.

boxing ['bɔksiŋ] *n* boxe *f*.

box-office ['bɔks'ɔfis] *n* bureau *m* de location.

box-room ['bɔksrum] *n* (chambre *f* de) débarras *m*.

boxwood ['bɔkswud] *n* buis *m*.

boy [bɔi] *n* enfant *m*, garçon *m*, gars *m*, élève *m*, gamin *m*, boy *m*.

boycott ['bɔikət] *vt* boycotter.

boycotting ['bɔikətiŋ] *n* boycottage *m*.

boyhood ['bɔihud] *n* enfance *f*, adolescence *f*.

boyish ['bɔiiʃ] *a* garçonnier, puéril, enfantin, de garçon, d'enfant.

brace [breis] *n* attache *f*, croisillon *m*, acolade *f*, vilebrequin *m*, paire *f*, couple *f*; *pl* bretelles *f pl*; *vt* attacher, armer, ancrer, tendre, coupler, fortifier; **to** — **up** ravigoter, remonter, retremper; **to** — **o.s.** se raidir.

bracelet ['breislit] *n* bracelet *m*.

bracing ['breisiŋ] *a* fortifiant, tonique, tonifiant.

bracken ['brækən] *n* fougère *f*.

bracket ['brækit] *n* applique *f*, console *f*, tasseau *m*, (*gas*) bras *m*, parenthèse *f*, crochet *m*; *vt* mettre entre parenthèses, accoler.

bracket-seat ['brækit,siːt] *n* strapontin *m*.

brackish ['brækiʃ] *a* saumâtre.

brag [bræg] *n* vantardise *f*, fanfaronnade *f*; *vi* se vanter.

braggart ['brægət] *n* vantard *m*, fanfaron *m*.

braid [breid] *n* natte *f*, tresse *f*, galon *m*, lacet *m*, ganse *f*, soutache *f*; *vt* natter, border, soutacher, galonner, passementer.

brain [brein] *n* cerveau *m*, cervelle *f*; **to rack one's** —**s** se creuser la cervelle; *a* cérébral; *vt* assommer, casser la tête à.

brain-child ['breintʃaild] *n* conception personnelle *f*.

brain-drain ['breindrein] *n* brain-drain *m*.

brain-fever ['brein,fiːvə] *n* fièvre cérébrale *f*.

brainless ['breinlis] *a* idiot, stupide.

brainwave ['breinweiv] *n* idée géniale *f*, trouvaille *f*, inspiration *f*.

brainy ['breini] *a* (*fam*) intelligent; **to be** — avoir de la tête.

braise [breiz] *vt* braiser.

brake [breik] *n* fourré *m*, hallier *m*, frein *m*; *vti* freiner; *vi* serrer le frein.

brakeman ['breikmən] *n* serre-frein *m*.

bramble ['bræmbl] *n* ronce *f*, mûrier *m* des haies; — **berry** mûre sauvage *f*.

bran [bræn] *n* son *m*.

branch [braːntʃ] *n* branche *f*, rameau *m*, bras *m*, embranchement *m*, filiale *f*, succursale *f*; *vi* **to** — **out** se ramifier; **to** — **off** bifurquer.

branch-line, -road ['braːntʃlain, roud] *n* embranchement *m*, bifurcation *f*.

brand [brænd] *n* tison *m*, brandon *m*, marque *f*, fer rouge *m*; *vt* marquer au fer rouge, cautériser, stigmatiser, flétrir.

brandish ['brændiʃ] *vt* brandir.

brand-new ['brænd'njuː] *a* flambant neuf.

brandy ['brændi] *n* cognac *m*, eau *f* de vie; **liqueur** — **fine champagne** *f*.

brass [braːs] *n* cuivre jaune *m*, laiton *m*, les cuivres *m pl*, toupet *m*, (*sl*) galette *f*.

brass-band ['braːs'bænd] *n* fanfare *f*.

brass-hat ['braːs'hæt] *n* officier d'état-major *m*, galonnard *m*.

brassière ['bræsiə] *n* soutien-gorge *m*.

brass-plate ['braːs'pleit] *n* plaque *f*.

brassware ['braːsweə] *n* dinanderie *f*.

brat [bræt] *n* mioche *mf*, moutard *m*.

bravado [brə'vaːdou] *n* crânerie *f*, bravade *f*.

brave [breiv] *a* brave, courageux, beau, élégant; *vt* braver, affronter.

bravery ['breivəri] *n* bravoure *f*, courage *m*, élégance *f*, atours *m pl*.

brawl [brɔːl] *n* dispute *f*, rixe *f*, bagarre *f*, murmure *m*, bruissement *m*; *vi* se chamailler, se bagarrer, brailler, bruire, murmurer.

brawn [brɔːn] *n* muscle *m*, fromage *m* de tête.

brawny ['brɔːni] *a* musclé, costaud.

bray [brei] *n* braiment *m*; *vti* braire; *vt* broyer.

braze [breiz] *vt* souder, braser.

brazen ['breizn] *a* d'airain, effronté, cynique; **to** — **it out** payer d'audace.

brazier ['breizjə] *n* chaudronnier *m*, braséro *m*.

breach [briːtʃ] *n* brèche *f*, rupture *f*, contravention *f*, violation *f*, infraction *f*; *vt* faire (une) brèche dans, percer.

bread [bred] *n* pain *m*; **fresh** — pain frais; **stale** — pain rassis; **brown** — pain bis; **whole-wheat** — pain complet; — **bin** huche *f* au pain, maie *f*.

bread-crumbs ['bredkrʌmz] *n pl* chapelure *f*, gratin *m*.

breadth [bredθ] *n* largeur *f*, ampleur *f*.

break [breik] *n* fracture *f*, cassure *f*, rupture *f*, alinéa *m*, percée *f*, trouée *f*, lacune *f*, trou *m*, arrêt *m*, répit *m*; — **of day** point du jour *m*; *vt* (inter)rompre, casser, briser, entamer, violer, manquer à, amortir, résilier; *vi* (se) briser, (se) rompre, (se) casser, poindre, muer, s'altérer, déferler; **to — down** vt démolir, supprimer, venir à bout de; vi s'effrondrer, échouer, demeurer court, fondre en larmes, rester en panne; **to — in** vt défoncer, enfoncer, dresser; vi intervenir, entrer par effraction, faire irruption; **to — off** vt détacher, casser, (inter)rompre; vi se détacher, s'(inter)rompre; **to — out** s'évader, se déclarer, éclater; **to — through** vt enfoncer, percer, trouer; vi faire une percée, se frayer un passage; **to — up** vt démolir, séparer, désarmer, démembrer, morceler, disperser, rompre; vi se désagréger, se séparer, se disperser, se démembrer, entrer en vacances.

breakable ['breikəbl] a fragile.

breakage ['breikidʒ] n casse f, fracture f.

breakdown ['breikdaun] n panne f, effondrement nerveux m, rupture f, insuccès m, interruption f.

breaker ['breikə] n dresseur, -euse, dompteur, -euse, brisant m, violateur, -trice.

breakfast ['brekfəst] n petit déjeuner m; vi déjeuner.

breakneck ['breiknek] a à se rompre le cou.

break-through ['breik'θruː] n percée f, trouée f.

break-up ['breik'ʌp] n dissolution f, dispersion f, affaissement m, entrée f en vacances.

breakwater ['breik,wɔːtə] n brise-lames m, môle m.

bream [briːm] n brème f.

breast [brest] n poitrine f, sein m, poitrail m, blanc m, devant m.

breastbone ['brestboun] n sternum m.

breasted ['brestid] a single-— droit; double-— croisé.

breastplate ['brestpleit] n cuirasse f, plastron m.

breast-stroke ['breststrouk] n brasse f (sur le ventre).

breath [breθ] n souffle m, haleine f, bouffée f; last — dernier soupir m, âme f; under one's — à mi-voix, en sourdine.

breathe [briːð] vti souffler, respirer; vt exhaler, murmurer; **to — in** aspirer; **to — out** exhaler.

breather ['briːðə] n moment de répit m; **to give a — to** s.o. laisser souffler qn; **to go for a —** aller prendre l'air.

breathing ['briːðiŋ] n respiration f.

breathless ['breθlis] a essoufflé.

breathlessness ['breθlisnis] n essouflement m.

bred [bred] pp pt of **breed**.

breech [briːtʃ] n culasse f, derrière m; pl culotte f.

breed [briːd] n race f, lignée f, couvée f, espèce f; vt porter, élever,

produire, engendrer, procréer; vi multiplier, se reproduire, faire de l'élevage.

breeder ['briːdə] n éleveur m, réproducteur, -trice.

breeding ['briːdiŋ] n élevage m, reproduction f, éducation f, savoir vivre m.

breeze [briːz] n brise f, grabuge m.

breezy ['briːzi] a venteux, désinvolte, bruyant.

brethren ['breðrin] n pl frères m pl.

Breton ['bretən] an Breton, -onne.

breviary ['briːvjəri] n bréviaire m.

brevity ['breviti] n brièveté f.

brew [bruː] vt brasser, faire infuser, fomenter; vi fermenter, s'infuser, se préparer, se mijoter, se tramer.

brewer ['bruːə] n brasseur m.

brewery ['bruəri] n brasserie f.

brewing ['bruːiŋ] n brassage m.

briar ['braiə] n ronce f, bruyère f, églantier m; — **rose** églantine f.

bribe [braib] n pot-de-vin m; vt acheter, soudoyer, graisser la patte à.

bribery ['braibəri] n corruption f.

bribing ['braibiŋ] n corruption f, subornation f.

brick [brik] n brique f; **to drop a —** faire une gaffe.

brick-kiln ['brikkiln] n four m à briques.

bricklayer ['brikleiə] n maçon m.

brickwork ['brikwəːk] n maçonnerie f.

bridal ['braidl] a de noce, de mariée, nuptial, de mariage.

bride [braid] n mariée f, jeune mariée f.

bridegroom ['braidgrum] n marié m.

bridesmaid ['braidzmeid] n demoiselle d'honneur f.

bridge [bridʒ] n pont m, passerelle f, (nose) dos m, (violin) chevalet m, (cards) bridge m; vt jeter un pont sur, relier, combler.

bridgehead ['bridʒhed] n tête de pont f, point d'appui m.

Bridget ['bridʒit] Brigitte f.

bridge-train ['bridʒtrein] n les pontonniers m pl, train de pontons m.

bridle ['braidl] n bridon m, bride f, frein m; vt brider, refréner; vi se rebiffer, se redresser, regimber.

brief [briːf] n bref m, dossier m, exposé m, cause f; vt engager, constituer, rédiger; a bref, court; **in —** bref, en résumé.

briefless ['briːflis] a sans cause.

briefly ['briːfli] ad brièvement.

brig [brig] n brick m.

brigade [bri'geid] n brigade f.

brigadier [brigə'diə] n général m de brigade.

brigand ['brigənd] n bandit m, brigand m.

bright [brait] a clair, vif, éclatant, lumineux, brillant, éveillé.

brighten ['braitn] *vt* animer, éclairer, égayer, dérider, fourbir; *vi* s'animer, s'éclairer, se dérider, s'épanouir, s'éclaircir.
brightness ['braitnis] *n* éclat *m*, splendeur *f*, vivacité *f*.
brilliant ['briljənt] *a* brillant.
brilliantly ['briljəntli] *ad* brillamment, avec brio.
brim [brim] *n* bord *m*, *vt* remplir jusqu'au bord; **to — over** déborder.
brimstone ['brimstən] *n* soufre *m*.
brine [brain] *n* saumure *f*; *vt* saler.
bring [briŋ] *vt* apporter, amener, faire venir; **to — about** causer, amener, produire, effectuer, opérer, entraîner, occasionner; **to — down** abattre, (r)abaisser, terrasser, faire crouler, descendre; **to — forth** produire, mettre au monde, mettre bas, provoquer; **to — forward** avancer, reporter; **to — in** introduire, faire entrer, rapporter, faire intervenir; **to — off** mener à bien, réussir, sauver, renflouer; **to — out** faire (res)sortir, faire valoir, mettre en relief, lancer; **to — round** ranimer, (r)amener; **to — together** réunir, réconcilier; **to — up** élever, (faire) monter, avancer, mettre sur le tapis, rendre.
brink [briŋk] *n* bord *m*; **on the — of** près de, à la veille de.
briny ['braini] *a* salé, saumâtre; *n* (*fam*) mer *f*.
brisk [brisk] *a* vif, actif, fringant, animé, gazeux, vivifiant, frais.
brisket ['briskit] *n* poitrine *f* (de bœuf).
briskness ['brisknis] *n* vivacité *f*, activité *f*.
bristle ['brisl] *n* soie *f*, crin *m*, poil *m*; *vt* faire dresser, hérisser; *vi* se hérisser, se rebiffer, regimber.
bristling ['brisliŋ] *a* hérissé.
Britain ['britn] *n* Angleterre *f*; **Great —** Grande Bretagne *f*.
British ['britiʃ] *a* anglais, britannique.
Briton ['britn] *n* Anglais(e) *mf*.
Brittany ['britəni] *n* Bretagne *f*.
brittle ['britl] *a* fragile, cassant.
brittleness ['britlnis] *n* fragilité *f*.
broach [broutʃ] *n* broche *f*, flèche *f*, perçoir *m*, foret *m*; *vt* percer, mettre en perce, entamer, embrocher.
broad [brɔːd] *a* large, plein, grivois, hardi, libre, marqué; *n* (*sl*) poupée *f*.
broadcast ['brɔːdkaːst] *vt* radiodiffuser, répandre, disséminer; *n* émission *f*, radio-reportage *m*, audition *f*.
broadcaster ['brɔːdkaːstə] *n* microphoniste *mf*, artiste *mf* de la radio.
broadcasting ['brɔːdkaːstiŋ] *n* radiodiffusion *f*; **— station** poste émetteur *m*.
broaden ['brɔːdn] *vt* élargir; *vi* s'élargir, s'évaser.

broadening ['brɔːdniŋ] *n* élargissement *m*.
broad-minded ['brɔːdmaindid] *a* tolérant, aux idées larges.
broadness ['brɔːdnis] *n* largeur *f*, grossièrté *f*.
broadside ['brɔːdsaid] *n* bordée *f*, flanc *m*, travers *m*.
brocade [brə'keid] *n* brocart *m*.
broil [brɔil] *n* dispute *f*, rixe *f*; *vti* (faire) griller.
broiling ['brɔiliŋ] *a* ardent, torride.
broke [brouk] *pt of* **break**; *a* sans le sou, dans la dèche.
broken ['broukən] *pp of* **break**; *a* brisé, détraqué, raboteux, incertain, en pièces, (entre)coupé, agité, décousu.
brokenly ['broukənli] *ad* sans suite, par à-coups.
broken-winded ['broukən'windid] *a* poussif.
broker ['broukə] *n* revendeur, -euse, courtier *m*, agent *m* de change, brocanteur *m*.
brokerage ['broukəridʒ] *n* courtage *m*.
bronchitis [brɔŋ'kaitis] *n* bronchite *f*.
bronze [brɔnz] *n* bronze *m*; *vt* bronzer; *vi* se bronzer.
brooch [broutʃ] *n* broche *f*.
brood ['bruːd] *n* couvée *f*, nichée *f*, volée *f*; *vi* couver, méditer, rêver; **to — over** remâcher, couver.
brook [bruk] *n* ruisseau *m*; *vt* souffrir.
brooklet ['bruklit] *n* ruisselet *m*.
broom [bruːm] *n* genêt *m*; balai *m*; **—stick** manche *m* à balai.
broth [brɔθ] *n* bouillon *m*, potage *m*.
brother ['brʌðə] *n* frère *m*, confrère *m*.
brotherhood ['brʌðəhud] *n* confrérie *f*, société *f*, fraternité *f*.
brother-in-law ['brʌðərinlɔː] *n* beau-frère *m*.
brotherly ['brʌðəli] *a* fraternel.
brought [brɔːt] *pt of* **bring**.
brow [brau] *n* sourcil *m*, front *m*, surplomb *m*, crête *f*.
browbeat ['braubiːt] *vt* malmener, intimider, rabrouer.
brown [braun] *an* brun *m*, marron *m*; *a* châtain, fauve; *vt* brunir, faire dorer, rissoler.
brownish ['brauniʃ] *a* brunâtre.
browse [brauz] *vti* brouter, bouquiner.
bruise [bruːz] *n* meurtrissure *f*, contusion *f*, bleu *m*, noir *m*; *vt* meurtrir, contusionner.
brunette [bruː'net] *an* brune *f*.
brunt [brʌnt] *n* choc *m*, poids *m*, fort *m*.
brush [brʌʃ] *n* brosse *f*, balai *m*, pinceau *m*, coup *m* de brosse, (*fox*) queue *f*; échauffourée *f*; *vt* brosser, balayer; **to — aside** écarter; **to — out** balayer; **to — up, down** donner un coup de brosse à;

to — up repolir, rafraîchir, dérouiller; to — against frôler, effleurer.

brushwood ['brʌʃwud] n broussailles f pl, fourré m, brindilles f pl.

brusque [brusk] a brusque, bourru, rude.

Brussels ['brʌslz] n Bruxelles; — sprouts choux m pl de Bruxelles.

brutal ['bruːtl] a brutal, de brute, sensuel.

brutality [bruːˈtæliti] n brutalité f.

brutalize ['bruːtəlaiz] vt abrutir.

brute [bruːt] n bête f, brute f; a brut, stupide.

brutish ['bruːtiʃ] a bestial, de brute, abruti.

bubble ['bʌbl] n bulle f, bouillon m, chimère f; vi bouillonner, pétiller, glouglouter; to — over déborder.

buccaneer [ˌbʌkəˈniə] n flibustier m, pirate m.

buck [bʌk] n daim m, chevreuil m, mâle m, dandy m; to — off désarçonner; vt to — up remonter le courage à, ravigoter; vi reprendre courage, se remuer.

bucket ['bʌkit] n seau m, baquet m.

buckle ['bʌkl] n boucle f, agrafe f, voile m, benne f; vt boucler, agrafer, serrer, voiler; vi se mettre (à to), s'appliquer (à to); to — up se voiler, se gondoler.

buckler ['bʌklə] n bouclier m.

buckram ['bʌkrəm] n bougran m.

buckshee ['bʌkˈʃiː] ad à l'œil, gratis.

buckskin ['bʌkskin] n peau f de daim.

buckwheat ['bʌkwiːt] n sarrasin m.

bud [bʌd] n bourgeon m, bouton m; vi bourgeonner, boutonner.

budding ['bʌdiŋ] a qui bourgeonne, qui boutonne, en herbe.

budge [bʌdʒ] vi bouger, remuer, reculer.

budget ['bʌdʒit] n sac m, budget m; to — for sth porter qch au budget.

buff [bʌf] n buffle m; a couleur buffle; vt polir; to strip to the — se mettre à poil.

buffalo ['bʌfəlou] n buffle m.

buffer ['bʌfə] n tampon m, amortisseur m; —-state état-tampon m.

buffer-stop ['bʌfəstɔp] n butoir m.

buffet ['bʌfit] n soufflet m; vt souffleter, ballotter, secouer; vi lutter.

buffet ['bufei] n buffet m.

buffoon [bʌˈfuːn] n bouffon m.

buffoonery [bʌˈfuːnəri] n bouffonnerie f.

bug [bʌg] n punaise f, insecte m; big — grosse légume.

bugbear ['bʌgbɛə] n épouvantail m, cauchemar m, bête noire f, loup-garou m.

bugle ['bjuːgl] n clairon m; vi sonner du clairon.

bugler ['bjuːglə] n clairon m.

build [bild] vt construire, bâtir, fonder; to — up échafauder,

affermir, créer; n construction f, charpente f.

builder ['bildə] n entrepreneur m, constructeur m, fondateur, -trice.

building ['bildiŋ] n bâtiment m, édifice m. construction f.

built [bilt] pp pt of build; —-up area agglomération urbaine f.

bulb [bʌlb] n bulbe m, ampoule f, poire f, oignon m.

Bulgaria [bʌlˈgɛəriə] n Bulgarie f.

Bulgarian [bʌlˈgɛəriən] a bulgare; n Bulgare mf.

bulge [bʌldʒ] n gonflement m, renflement m, bombement m; vti bomber, ballonner; vi faire saillie.

bulk [bʌlk] n chargement m, grande carcasse f, masse f, gros m, volume m, grandeur f; in — en vrac, en gros; vt empiler, grouper; to — large occuper une place importante.

bulkhead ['bʌlkhed] n cloison f étanche.

bulky ['bʌlki] a volumineux, encombrant.

bull [bul] n taureau m, mâle m, haussier m, bulle f, bourde f, mouche f.

bulldog ['buldɔg] n bouledogue m.

bulldozer ['bulˌdouzə] n niveleuse f, bulldozer m.

bullet ['bulit] n balle f.

bulletin ['bulitin] n bulletin m, communiqué m; news — informations f pl, journal parlé m.

bullfight ['bulfait] n course f de taureaux.

bullfinch ['bulfintʃ] n bouvreuil m.

bullheaded ['bulˈhedid] a têtu, gaffeur, impétueux.

bullion ['buljən] n lingot m.

bullock ['bulək] n bœuf m.

bull's eye ['bulzai] n noir m, mouche f, hublot m, œil de bœuf m, lanterne sourde f, lentille f.

bully ['buli] n brute f, brimeur m, souteneur m; vt rudoyer, brutaliser, malmener.

bully-beef ['buliˈbiːf] n (fam) singe m.

bulwark ['bulwək] n rempart m, bastingage m.

bumble-bee ['bʌmblbiː] n bourdon m.

bump [bʌmp] n heurt m, secousse f, cahot m, bosse f; vt heurter, cogner, secouer; vi (se) heurter, (se) cogner, buter; to — along cahoter; to — into tamponner, buter contre; excl pan!

bumper ['bʌmpə] n (aut) pare-chocs m; rasade f; a monstre, comble etc.

bumpkin ['bʌmpkin] n rustre m.

bumptious ['bʌmpʃəs] a arrogant, présomptueux.

bumptiousness ['bʌmpʃəsnis] n arrogance f, suffisance f, outrecuidance f.

bumpy ['bʌmpi] a en creux et en bosses, cahoteux, inégal.

bunch [bʌntʃ] n bouquet m, (grapes)

grappe *f*, (*radishes*) botte *f*, (*bananas*) régime *m*, (*keys*) trousseau *m*, (*people*) bande *f*, groupe *m*, peloton *m*; *vt* lier, attacher, botteler, réunir, grouper; *vi* se pelotonner, se serrer.

bundle ['bʌndl] *n* paquet *m*, fagot *m*, liasse *f*, ballot *m*, faisceau *m*; *vt* mettre en paquet, empaqueter, fourrer; **to — off** envoyer paître; **to — out** flanquer à la porte.

bungle ['bʌngl] *n* gâchis *m*; *vt* gâcher, bousiller, rater, massacrer.

bungler ['bʌnglə] *n* maladroit(e) *mf*, bousilleur *m*.

bunion ['bʌnjən] *n* oignon *m*.

bunk [bʌnk] *n* couchette *f*; *vi* décamper, filer.

bunker ['bʌnkə] *n* soute *f*, banquette *f*, (*golf*) bunker *m*.

bunkum ['bʌnkəm] *n* blague *f*, balivernes *f pl*.

bunting ['bʌntiŋ] *n* étamine *f*, drapeaux *m pl*.

buoy [bɔi] *n* bouée *f*.

buoyancy ['bɔiənsi] *n* insubmersibilité *f*, élasticité *f*, entrain *m*, ressort *m*.

buoyant ['bɔiənt] *a* élastique, exubérant, flottable, insubmersible, qui a du ressort.

burble ['bə:bl] *n* murmure *m*, gloussement *m*; *vi* murmurer, glousser.

burden ['bə:dn] *n* charge *f*, fardeau *m*, tonnage *m*, poids *m*, refrain *m*, essentiel *m*, fond *m*; *vt* charger, encombrer.

burdensome ['bə:dnsəm] *a* pesant, encombrant, fâcheux, onéreux.

bureau ['bjuərou] *n* bureau *m*, secrétaire *m*.

bureaucracy [bjuə'rɔkrəsi] *n* bureaucratie *f*.

bureaucrat ['bjuəroukræt] *n* bureaucrate *m*, rond-de-cuir *m*.

burgess ['bə:dʒis] *n* bourgeois *m*, citoyen *m*.

burgh ['bʌrə] *n* (*Scot*) bourg *m*.

burglar ['bə:glə] *n* cambrioleur *m*.

burglary ['bə:gləri] *n* cambriolage *m*.

burgle ['bə:gl] *vt* cambrioler.

burgomaster ['bə:gə,ma:stə] *n* bourgmestre *m*.

Burgundian [bə:'gʌndjən] *a* bourguignon; *n* Bourguignon, -onne.

Burgundy ['bə:gəndi] *n* Bourgogne *f*, (*wine*) bourgogne *m*.

burial ['beriəl] *n* enterrement *m*.

burlesque [bə:'lesk] *an* burlesque *m*; *n* parodie *f*; *vt* parodier.

burly ['bə:li] *a* massif, solide, costaud.

Burma ['bə:mə] *n* Birmanie *f*.

Burmese [bə:'mi:z] *an* birman.

burn [bə:n] *n* brûlure *f*; *vti* brûler.

burner ['bə:nə] *n* brûleur, -euse, bec *m*, brûleur *m*.

burnish ['bə:niʃ] *vt* polir.

burnt [bə:nt] *pp of* **burn**; **— offering** holocauste *m*.

burrow ['bʌrou] *n* terrier *m*; *vt* creuser; *vi* se terrer, fouiller.

bursar ['bə:sə] *n* économe *mf*, boursier, -ière.

burst [bə:st] *n* éclatement *m*, explosion *f*, salve *f*, éclat *m*; *vti* éclater, crever; *vt* faire éclater, faire sauter, percer, rompre; *vi* faire explosion, exploser, sauter, se rompre, éclore, regorger; **to — in** *vt* enfoncer; *vi* faire irruption; **to — out** jaillir, éclater, s'exclamer, sortir en coup de vent.

bury ['beri] *vt* enterrer, enfouir, ensevelir, enfoncer, plonger.

bus [bʌs] *n* autobus *m*, (auto)car *m*; **to miss the —** manquer l'autobus, manquer le coche.

bush [buʃ] *n* arbuste *m*, arbrisseau *m*, buisson *m*, brousse *f*, coussinet *m*, bague *f*; **—cat** serval *m*.

bushel ['buʃl] *n* boisseau *m*.

bushy ['buʃi] *a* touffu, broussailleux, épais.

busily ['bizili] *ad* activement, avec affairement.

business ['biznis] *n* affaire(s) *f pl*, occupation *f*, établissement *m*; **it is none of your —** cela ne vous regarde pas; **to make it one's —** to se faire un devoir de; **to send s.o. about his —** envoyer promener qn; **big —man** brasseur d'affaires; **—man** homme d'affaires.

businesslike ['biznislaik] *a* actif, pratique, sérieux.

buskin ['bʌskin] *n* cothurne *m*.

bust [bʌst] *n* buste *m*, gorge *f*.

bustle ['bʌsl] *n* agitation *f*, remue-ménage *m*; *vi* s'agiter, s'affairer, faire l'empressé; *vt* bousculer.

busy ['bizi] *a* occupé, actif, affairé; *vt* occuper.

busybody ['bizibɔdi] *n* mouche *f* du coche, officieux, -euse *mf*.

but [bʌt] *cj* mais, sans (que), que . . . ne (*after a negative*); *ad* seulement, ne . . . que, excepté, autre que, sinon, si ce n'est; **— for** sans, à part; **all —** presque, autant dire; **anything —** riens moins que.

butcher ['butʃə] *n* boucher *m*; *vt* massacrer, égorger; **—'s** boucherie *f*.

butchery ['butʃəri] *n* boucherie *f*, massacre *m*, tuerie *f*.

butler ['bʌtlə] *n* sommelier *m*, dépensier *m*, maître d'hôtel *m*.

butt [bʌt] *n* crosse *f*, gros bout *m*, mégot *m*, butte *f*, coup *m* de tête, tête *f* de turc, souffre-douleur *m*, cible *f*; *pl* champ *m* de tir; *vt* donner un coup de tête à; *vi* fourrer le nez (dans **into**), foncer (dans **into**), donner de la tête (contre **against**).

butter ['bʌtə] *n* beurre *m*; **shea —** karité *f*; *vt* beurrer; **— would not melt in his mouth** c'est une sainte nitouche.

butter-bean ['bʌtəbi:n] *n* haricot beurre *m*.

buttercup ['bʌtəkʌp] *n* bouton *m* d'or.
butter-dish ['bʌtədiʃ] *n* beurrier *m*.
butter-fingers ['bʌtə,fiŋgəz] *n* empoté(e) *mf*, maladroit(e) *mf*.
butterfly ['bʌtəflai] *n* papillon *m*.
buttermilk ['bʌtəmilk] *n* petit-lait *m*, babeurre *m*.
buttock ['bʌtək] *n* fesse *f*.
button ['bʌtn] *n* bouton *m*; *vt* boutonner; — -**hook** tire-bouton *m*.
buttonhole ['bʌtnhoul] *n* boutonnière *f*; *vt* accrocher, cueillir.
buttress ['bʌtris] *n* contrefort *m*, arc-boutant *m*; *vt* soutenir, renforcer, étayer.
buxom ['bʌksəm] *a* rebondi, avenant
buy [bai] *vt* acheter; **to — back** racheter; **to — off** acheter; **to — out** désintéresser; **to — up** accaparer.
buyer ['baiə] *n* acheteur, -euse, chef *m* de rayon.
buzz [bʌz] *n* bourdonnement *m*, brouhaha *m*, fritures *f pl*; *vi* bourdonner, tinter; **to — off** déguerpir, filer.
buzzard ['bʌzəd] *n* buse *f*.
by [bai] *prep* par, près de, à côté de, à, en, pour, avec, de, sur, envers; *ad* près, à (de) côté; — **and** — avant peu, tout à l'heure.
bygone ['baigɔn] *an* passé *m*.
bylaw ['bailɔː] *n* arrêté municipal *m*.
by-name ['baineim] *n* sobriquet *m*.
by-pass ['baipɑːs] *n* route *f* d'évitement *m*; *vt* éviter, contourner, filtrer.
by-product ['bai,prɔdəkt] *n* sous-produit *m*.
by-road ['bairoud] *n* rue écartée *f*.
bystander ['bai,stændə] *n* spectateur, -trice, curieux -euse.
byway ['baiwei] *n* chemin détourné *m*, raccourci *m*; *pl* à-côtés *m pl*.
byword ['baiwəːd] *n* proverbe *m*, risée *f*, fable *f*.

C

cab [kæb] *n* fiacre *m*, voiture de place *f*, cabine *f*.
cabbage ['kæbidʒ] *n* chou *m*.
cabbage-patch ['kæbidʒpætʃ] *n* plant *m*, carré de choux *m*.
cabin ['kæbin] *n* cabane *f*, cabine *f*, case *f*, poste *m* de conduite.
cabinet ['kæbinit] *n* vitrine *f*, bonheur du jour *m*, coffret *m*, ministère *m*; *a* ministériel, d'état.
cabinet-maker ['kæbinit,meikə] *n* ébéniste *m*.
cabinet-work ['kæbinit,wəːk] *n* ébénisterie *f*.
cabin-trunk ['kæbin,trʌŋk] *n* malle *f* (de) paquebot.
cable ['keibl] *n* câble *m*, chaîne *f*, câblogramme *m*; *vt* câbler, aviser par câble.

cable-railway ['keibl'reilwei] *n* funiculaire *m*.
cabman ['kæbmən] *n* cocher *m*, chauffeur *m*.
caboodle [kə'buːdl] *n* **the whole —** tout le bazar, tout le fourbi.
caboose [kə'buːs] *n* wagon *m* de queue.
cabstand ['kæbstænd] *n* station *f* de voitures.
ca' canny [kɔ'kæni] *a* tout doux, hésitant; *vi* faire la grève perlée.
cackle ['kækl] *n* caquet *m*; *vi* caqueter.
cacophony [kæ'kɔfəni] *n* cacophonie *f*.
cad [kæd] *n* goujat *m*, mufle *m*, canaille *f*.
caddie ['kædi] *n* cadet *m*, caddie *m*.
caddishness ['kædiʃnis] *n* goujaterie *f*, muflerie *f*.
caddy ['kædi] *n* boîte *f* à thé.
cadence ['keidəns] *n* cadence *f*, rythme *m*.
cadet [kə'det] *n* cadet *m*, élève officier, *m* membre *m* d'un bataillon scolaire.
cadge [kædʒ] *vti* colporter, mendier, écornifler.
cadger ['kædʒə] *n* colporteur *m*, camelot *m*, mendiant(e) *mf*, écornifleur *m*.
cage [keidʒ] *n* cage *f*.
cahoot [kə'huːt] *n* **to be in —s with** (*sl*) être de mèche avec.
cajole [kə'dʒoul] *vt* cajoler, enjôler.
cajolery [kə'dʒouləri] *n* cajolerie *f*, enjôlement *m*.
cajoling [kə'dʒouliŋ] *a* enjôleur.
cake [keik] *n* gâteau *m*, tablette *f*, morceau *m*, pain *m*; **to sell like hot —s** se vendre comme du pain frais.
cake-shop ['keikʃɔp] *n* pâtisserie *f*.
calabash ['kæləbæʃ] *n* calebasse *f*, gourde *f*.
calamitous [kə'læmitəs] *a* désastreux.
calamity [kə'læmiti] *n* calamité *f*, désastre *m*, malheur *m*.
calculate ['kælkjuleit] *vti* calculer, estimer, évaluer; *vi* faire un (des) calcul(s).
calculated ['kælkjuleitid] *a* délibéré, calculé, propre (à to).
calculating ['kælkjuleitiŋ] *a* calculateur, avisé, réfléchi.
calculation [,kælkju'leiʃən] *n* calcul *m*.
calendar ['kælində] *n* calendrier *m*, répertoire *m*.
calf [kɑːf] *n* veau *m*, mollet *m*.
calibrate ['kælibreit] *vt* calibrer, étalonner, graduer.
caliber ['kælibə] *n* calibre *m*, alésage *m*.
call [kɔːl] *n* appel *m*, cri *m*, rappel *m*, visite *f*, invitation *f*, demande *f*, invite *f*, communication *f*, coup de téléphone *m*; **on —** sur demande; **within —** à portée de la voix; *vti*

crier, appeler; *vt* héler, convoquer, ordonner, déclarer; *vi* faire escale, toucher (à at); to — **aside** prendre à part; to — **back** *vt* rappeler; *vi* repasser; to — **for** demander, venir chercher; to — **forth** évoquer, provoquer, faire appel à; to — **off** *vt* décommander, rompre, rappeler; *vi* s'excuser, se retirer; to — **on** faire une visite à, passer chez, se présenter chez; to — out *vti* appeler; *vt* provoquer, réquisitionner; to — **together** réunir, convoquer; to — up évoquer, appeler au téléphone, mobiliser; to — upon sommer.

callbox ['kɔːlbɔks] *n* cabine téléphonique *f*.

caller ['kɔːlə] *n* visiteur, -euse, visite *f*.

calling ['kɔːliŋ] *n* appel *m*, vocation *f*, profession *f*, état *m*.

callosity [kæ'lɔsiti] *n* callosité *f*, durillon *m*.

call-up ['kɔːlʌp] *n* mobilisation *f*.

callous ['kæləs] *a* calleux, brutal, dur, endurci.

callousness ['kæləsnis] *n* dureté *f*, manque *m* de cœur.

callow ['kælou] *a* sans plumes, novice, inexpérimenté; a — youth un blancbec.

calm [kɑːm] *a* calme, tranquille; *n* calme *m*, tranquillité *f*; *vt* calmer, tranquilliser, apaiser; to — down s'apaiser, se calmer.

calumniate [kə'lʌmnieit] *vt* calomnier.

calumniator [kə'lʌmnieitə] *n* calomniateur, -trice.

calumny ['kæləmni] *n* calomnie *f*.

calvary ['kælvəri] *n* calvaire *m*.

calve [kɑːv] *vi* vêler.

cam [kæm] *n* came *f*.

camber ['kæmbə] *n* cambrure *f*, bombement *m*.

Cambodia [kæm'boudjə] *n* Cambodge *m*.

cambric ['keimbrik] *n* batiste *f*.

came [keim] *pt of* **come**.

camel ['kæməl] *n* chameau *m*.

cameo ['kæmiou] *n* camée *m*.

camera ['kæmərə] *n* appareil *m* photographique; in — à huis clos; **movie** — caméra *f*.

cameraman ['kæmərəmæn] *n* photographe *m*, opérateur *m*.

cami-knickers ['kæminikəz] *n* chemise-culotte *f*.

camouflage ['kæməflɑːʒ] *n* camouflage *m*; *vt* camoufler.

camp [kæmp] *n* camp *m*, campement *m*; *vti* camper; to go —ing faire du camping.

campaign [kæm'pein] *n* campagne *f*; *vi* faire campagne.

camper ['kæmpə] *n* amateur (-trice) de camping, campeur *m*.

camphor ['kæmfə] *n* camphre *m*.

can [kæn] *n* broc *m*, pot *m*, bidon *m*, boîte *f*, (oil) burette *f*, (beer) canette *f*; *vt* mettre, conserver, en boîte.

can [kæn] *vi* pouvoir, savoir; **all one** — de son mieux; **he cannot but do it** il ne peut pas ne pas le faire.

Canada ['kænədə] *n* Canada *m*.

Canadian [kə'neidjən] *a* canadien; *n* Canadien, -ienne.

canal [kə'næl] *n* canal *m*.

canalization [ˌkænəlai'zeiʃən] *n* canalisation *f*.

canalize ['kænəlaiz] *vt* canaliser.

canary [kə'nɛəri] *n* canari *m*, serin *m*.

cancel ['kænsəl] *vt* annuler, biffer, révoquer, résilier, supprimer, décommander, contremander; to — out s'éliminer.

cancellation [ˌkænse'leiʃən] *n* annulation *f*, résiliation *f*, révocation *f*, contre-ordre *m*.

cancer ['kænsə] *n* cancer *m*.

cancerous ['kænsərəs] *a* cancéreux.

candid ['kændid] *a* franc, sincère, impartial, sans malice.

candidate ['kændidit] *n* candidat(e) *mf*, aspirant *m*, pretendant(e) *mf*.

candidature ['kændiditʃə] *n* candidature *f*.

candle ['kændl] *n* bougie *f*, chandelle *f*, cierge *f*.

candlestick ['kændlstik] *n* chandelier *m*, bougeoir *m*.

candor ['kændə] *n* franchise *f*, impartialité *f*, bonne foi *f*.

candy ['kændi] *n* sucre candi *m*; *vt* glacer, faire candir, confire.

cane [kein] *n* tige *f*, canne *f*, badine *f*, rotin *m*; — **chair** chaise cannée *f*; *vt* bâtonner, fouetter.

canine ['keinain] *n* canine *f*; *a* canin.

caning ['keiniŋ] *n* bastonnade *f*, correction *f*.

canister ['kænistə] *n* boîte *f*.

canker ['kæŋkə] *n* chancre *m*, fléau *m*, plaie *f*; *vt* ronger, corrompre.

canned [kænd] *a* en boîte; en conserve.

cannibal ['kænibəl] *an* cannibale *mf*.

cannibalism ['kænibəlizəm] *n* cannibalisme *m*.

cannon ['kænən] *n* canon *m*, pièce *f*, carambolage *m*; *vi* caramboler, se heurter.

cannonade [ˌkænə'neid] *n* cannonade *f*; *vt* canonner.

cannon-ball ['kænənbɔːl] *n* boulet *m*.

cannon-fodder ['kænənfɔdə] *n* chair à canon *f*.

canny ['kæni] *a* avisé, sûr, rusé, finaud, économe.

canoe [kə'nuː] *n* canoë *m*, pirogue *f*, périssoire *f*.

canon ['kænən] *n* canon *m*, chanoine *m*, règle *f*.

canoness ['kænənis] *n* chanoinesse *f*.

canonize ['kænənaiz] *vt* canoniser.

canonry ['kænənri] *n* canonicat *m*.

can-opener ['kænoupnə] n ouvre-boîte m.

canopy ['kænəpi] n dais m, baldaquin m, ciel m, marquise f.

cant [kænt] n argot m, pharisaïsme m, tartuferie f, plan incliné m; vt incliner.

cantankerous [kən'tæŋkərəs] a revêche, batailleur, acariâtre.

canteen [kæn'ti:n] n cantine f, gamelle f, bidon m, caisse f; — of cutlery service m de table en coffre.

canter ['kæntə] n petit galop m; vi aller au petit galop.

canticle ['kæntikl] n cantique m.

cantilever ['kæntili:və] n encorbellement m, cantilever m.

canto ['kæntou] n chant m.

canvas ['kænvəs] n toile f, tente f, voile f; **under** — sous voile, sous la tente.

canvass ['kænvəs] vt discuter, solliciter, briguer; vi (com) faire la place, faire une tournée électorale.

canvasser ['kænvəsə] n agent électoral m, solliciteur, -euse, placier m.

cap [kæp] n bonnet m, casquette f, toque f, calotte f; vt coiffer, couronner, surpasser, saluer; **to** — **it** pour comble; **if the** — **fits, wear it** qui se sent morveux, se mouche.

capability [.keipə'biliti] n pouvoir m, moyens m pl, capacité f, faculté f.

capable ['keipəbl] a capable,: compétent, susceptible (de).

capacious [kə'peiʃəs] a spacieux, ample, grand.

capacity [kə'pæsiti] n capacité f, contenance f, débit m, rendement m, aptitude f, qualité f, mesure f; **to** — à plein, comble.

cape [keip] n cap m, collet m, pèlerine f, cape f.

caper ['keipə] n câpre f, cabriole f; vi cabrioler, gambader.

capital ['kæpitl] n capitale f, majuscule f, capital m, chapiteau m; a capital, fameux.

capitalism ['kæpitəlizəm] n capitalisme m.

capitalist ['kæpitəlist] n capitaliste mf.

capitalize ['kæpitəlaiz] vt capitaliser.

capitulate [kə'pitjuleit] vi capituler.

capitulation [kə.pitju'leiʃən] n capitulation f.

capon ['keipən] n chapon m.

caprice [kə'pri:s] b caprice m.

capricious [kə'priʃəs] a capricieux.

capriciousness [kə'priʃəsnis] n humeur capricieuse f, inconstance f.

capsize [kæp'saiz] vi chavirer, capoter; vt faire chavirer.

capstan ['kæpstən] n cabestan m.

capsule ['kæpsju:l] n capsule f, (of spaceship) cabine f.

captain ['kæptin] n capitaine m, chef m (d'équipe); vt commander, diriger.

caption ['kæpʃən] n arrestation f, légende f, soustitre m, rubrique f, manchette f.

captious [kæpʃəs] a captieux, chicaneur, pointilleux.

captivate ['kæptiveit] vt séduire, captiver, charmer.

captive ['kæptiv] an prisonnier, -ière, captif, -ive.

captivity [kæp'tiviti] n captivité f.

capture ['kæptʃə] n capture f, prise f; vt prendre, capturer, capter.

car [ka:] n char m, wagon m, voiture f, auto f; **dining** — wagon-restaurant m; **sleeping** — wagon-lit m.

carafe [kə'ra:f] n carafe f.

caramel ['kærəmel] n caramel m, bonbon m au caramel.

caravan ['kærəvæn] n caravane f, roulotte f.

carbide ['ka:baid] n carbure m.

carbine ['ka:bain] n carabine f.

carbon ['ka:bən] n (papier) carbone m.

carbonize ['ka:bənaiz] vt carboniser, carburer.

carboy ['ka:bɔi] n bonbonne f.

carbuncle ['ka:bʌnkl] n anthrax m, escarboucle f.

carburetor ['ka:bjuretə] n carburateur m.

carcass ['ka:kəs] n corps m, cadavre m, carcasse f.

card [ka:d] n carte f; **visiting** — carte f de visite; **he is a** — c'est un numéro; **a queer** — un drôle de type.

cardboard ['ka:dbɔ:d] n carton m.

card-case ['ka:dkeis] n porte-cartes m.

cardigan ['ka:digən] n tricot m, cardigan m.

cardinal ['ka:dinl] an cardinal m.

card-index ['ka:d'indeks] n classeur m, fichier m.

card-sharper ['ka:d.ʃa:pə] n bonneteur m, tricheur, -euse, escroc m.

care [kɛə] n soin m, souci m, attention f, peine f, solicitude f, préoccupation f, entretien m; vi s'inquiéter, se soucier; c/o (care of) aux bons soins de; **with** — fragile; **to take** — prendre garde; **to take** — **not to** se garder de, prendre garde de; **to take** — **of** prendre soin de, se charger de; **to** — **for** vt aimer, soigner; **I don't** — **a rap** je m'en fiche, je m'en moque pas mal; **I don't** — **for this tobacco** ce tabac ne me dit rien.

career [kə'riə] n course f, cours m, carrière f; vi marcher (courir) comme un fou.

careerist [kə'riərist] n arriviste mf.

careful ['kɛəful] a soigneux, prudent, attentif.

carefulness ['kɛəfulnis] n soin m, attention f, prudence f, circonspection f.

careless ['kɛəlis] a sans soin, négligent, insouciant.

carelessness ['kεəlisnis] n négligence f, insouciance f.

caress [kə'res] n caresse f; vt caresser.

caretaker ['kεə,teikə] n concierge mf, gardien, -ienne.

cargo ['ka:gou] n cargaison f.

cargo-boat ['ka:goubout] n cargo m.

caricature [,kærikə'tjuə] n caricature f, charge f; vt caricaturer, charger.

carmine ['ka:main] an carmin m; a carminé.

carnage ['ka:nidʒ] n carnage m, tuerie f.

carnal ['ka:nl] a charnel, sensuel, de la chair.

carnation [ka:'neiʃən] n œillet m; an incarnat m.

carnival ['ka:nivəl] n carnaval m.

carnivore ['ka:nivɔ:] n carnassier m.

carnivorous [ka:'nivərəs] a carnassier, carnivore.

carol ['kærəl] n chant m; **Christmas** — (chant de) Noël m; vti chanter, tirelirer.

carousal [kə'rauzəl] n buverie f, orgie f, bombe f.

carouse [kə'rauz] vi faire la noce, faire la bombe.

carp [ka:p] n carpe f; vi mordre sur tout; **to** — **at** crier après, gloser sur, chicaner.

carpenter ['ka:pintə] n charpentier m.

carpet ['ka:pit] n tapis m; **to be on the** — être sur la sellette; vt poser un (des) tapis sur, recouvrir d'un tapis.

carping ['ka:piŋ] a mordant, chicanier, malveillant, pointilleux.

carport ['ka:pɔ:t] n abri m.

carriage ['kæridʒ] n (trans)port m, voiture f, wagon m, affût m, allure f, maintien m; — **free** franco; — **forward** en port dû; — **paid** franco de port.

carriageway ['kæridzwei] n dual — route jumelée f.

carrier ['kæriə] n camionneur m, roulier m, porteur, -euse, porte-avions m, porte-bagages m.

carrion ['kæriən] n charogne f.

carrot ['kærət] n carotte f.

carroty ['kærəti] a rouquin, roux, rouge de carotte.

carry ['kæri] n trajet m, trajectoire f, portée f; vti porter; vt transporter, rouler, amener, conduire, emporter, enlever, supporter, voter, adopter; **to** — **away** emporter, enlever, entrainer; **to** — **back** rapporter, ramener, reporter; **to** — **down** descendre; **to** — **forward**· avancer, reporter; **to** — **off** enlever, (r)emporter; **to** — **on** vt soutenir, entretenir, poursuivre; vi continuer, persister, se conduire; **to** — **out** exécuter, mettre à exécution, appliquer, réussir, exercer, porter dehors; **to** — **through** mener à bonne fin;

to — **weight** peser, avoir de l'influence, avoir du poids, être handicapé.

cart [ka:t] n charrette f, tombereau m, camion m; vt transporter, charroyer, charrier; **to** — **about** trimbaler.

cartage ['ka:tidʒ] n charroi m, charriage m, transport m.

carter ['ka:tə] n charretier m, roulier m, camionneur m.

cart-horse ['ka:thɔ:s] n cheval m de trait.

cart-load ['ka:tloud] n charretée f, tombereau m.

cart-shed ['ka:tʃed] n remise f, hangar m.

Carthusian [ka:'θju:zjən] an chartreux m.

cartilage ['ka:tilidʒ] n cartilage m.

cartoon [ka:'tu:n] n carton m, dessin m (satirique, humoristique, animé), portrait caricaturé m.

cartridge ['ka:tridʒ] n cartouche f.

cartwright ['ka:trait] n charron m.

carve [ka:v] vt tailler, sculpter (sur bois), ciseler, découper.

carver ['ka:və] n ciseleur m, serveur m, découpeur m, couteau m à découper.

carving ['ka:viŋ] n sculpture f, découpage m.

cascade [kæs'keid] n cascade f, chute f d'eau; vi tomber en cascade.

case [keis] n cas m, affaire f, cause f, boîte f, caisse f, trousse f, fourreau m, étui m, écrin m, vitrine f, boîtier m; **in** — au cas où; **in any (no)** — en tout (aucun) cas; vt emballer, encaisser, envelopper.

casement ['keismənt] n battant m, croisée f.

cash [kæʃ] n monnaie f, argent comptant m, espèces f pl; vt encaisser, toucher; — **account** compte m en banque; **petty** — argent m de poche, petite caisse f; — **down** comptant; — **on delivery** paiement m à la livraison; — **book** livre m de caisse; — **box** n caisse f.

cashier [kæ'ʃiə] n caissier, -ière; vt casser.

cashmere ['kæʃmiə] n cachemire m.

casino [kə'si:nou] n casino m.

cask [ka:sk] n tonneau m, fût m.

casket ['ka:skit] n écrin m, boîte f, coffret m, cassette f.

cassava [kə'sa:və] n manioc m.

cassock ['kæsək] n soutane f.

cast [ka:st] n lancement m, jet m, calcul m, moule m, moulage m, modèle m, coulée f, bas de ligne m, (dice) coup m, (eye) faux-trait m, (mind) type m, trempe f, qualité f, (theatre) troupe f, distribution f des rôles; vt lancer, (pro)jeter, ôter, couler, mouler, fondre, assigner un rôle à; **to** — **about** fureter; **to** — **aside** rejeter, se débarrasser de, mettre de côté; **to** — **away** jeter (au loin); **to — back** renvoyer, reporter; **to — down** déprimer, abattre, jeter bas; **to — off** rejeter, larguer, renier; **to — up** rejeter, reprocher.

castaway ['kɑːstəwei] *n* naufragé(e) *mf*, réprouvé(e) *mf*, proscrit(e) *mf*.

caste [kɑːst] *n* caste *f*; **half-— an,** metis, -isse.

castigate ['kæstigeit] *vt* corriger, châtier.

castigation [ˌkæsti'geiʃən] *n* correction *f*, châtiment *m*.

casting ['kɑːstiŋ] *n* jet *m*, fronte *f*, moulage *m*, modelage *m*, distribution des rôles; *f a* (*vote*) qui départage.

cast-iron ['kɑːst'aiən] *n* fonte *f*; *a* de fer, de fonte.

castle ['kɑːsl] *n* château *m*; **—s in the air** des châteaux en Espagne; *vi* (*chess*) roquer.

castor ['kɑːstə] *n* saupoudroir *m*, poivrière *f*, roulette *f*.

castor-oil ['kɑːstər'ɔil] *n* huile *f* de ricin.

castrate [kæs'treit] *vt* châtrer, émasculer.

casual ['kæʒjuəl] *a* fortuit, accidentel, banal, désinvolte, insouciant.

casually ['kæʒjuəli] *ad* en passant, avec désinvolture.

casualty ['kæʒjuəlti] *n* accident *m*, blessé(e) *mf*, mort(e) *mf*, malheur *m*; *pl* pertes *f pl.*

cat [kæt] *n* chat, -tte; **tom**—matou *m*.

cataclysm ['kætəklizəm] *n* cataclysme *m*.

catacombs ['kætəkoumz] *n* catacombes *f pl.*

catalepsy ['kætəlepsi] *n* catalepsie *f*.

catalogue ['kætələg] *n* catalogue *m*, liste *f*, prix-courant *m*; *vt* cataloguer.

catapult ['kætəpʌlt] *n* lance-pierres *m inv*, fronde *f*, catapulte *f*; *vt* lancer.

cataract ['kætərækt] *n* cataracte *f*.

catarrh [kə'tɑː] *n* catarrhe *m*.

catastrophe [kə'tæstrəfi] *n* catastrophe *f*, désastre *m*, dénouement *m*.

catcalls ['kætkɔːlz] *n pl* miaulements *m pl*, sifflets *m pl*, huées *f pl.*

catch [kætʃ] *n* prise *f*, capture *f*, pêche *f*, attrape *f*, piège *m*, agrafe *f*, loquet *m*, déclic *m*, cran d'arrêt *m*; *vti* prendre; *vt* attraper, saisir, accrocher, surprendre; *vi* se prendre, s'engager, mordre; **to — on** prendre, réussir; **to — up** saisir, rattraper, rejoindre.

catching ['kætʃiŋ] *a* séduisant, contagieux, communicatif.

catchword ['kætʃwəːd] *n* mot *m* d'ordre, mot *m* de ralliement, slogan *m* scie *f*.

catchy ['kætʃi] *a* entraînant, insidieux.

catechism ['kætikizəm] *n* catéchisme *m*.

categorical [ˌkæti'gɔrikəl] *a* catégorique.

category ['kætigəri] *n* catégorie *f*.

cater ['keitə] *vi* pourvoir; **to — for** pourvoir à, approvisionner.

caterer ['keitərə] *n* fournisseur, -euse, pourvoyeur, -euse, traiteur *m*.

catering ['keitəriŋ] *n* approvisionnement *m*; **to do the —** fournir le buffet.

caterpillar ['kætəpilə] *n* chenille *f*.

caterwaul ['kætəwɔːl] *vi* miauler, faire du tapage.

caterwauling ['kætəwɔːliŋ] *n* miaulements *m pl*, tapage *m*, sabbat *m* de chats.

catgut ['kætgʌt] *n* catgut *m*.

cathedral [kə'θiːdrəl] *n* cathédrale *f*.

catholic ['kæθəlik] *an* catholique *mf*; *a* universel, tolérant.

Catholicism [kə'θɔlisizəm] *n* catholicisme *m*.

catholicity [ˌkæθə'lisiti] *n* catholicité *f*, orthodoxie *f*, universalité *f*, tolérance *f*.

cat-o'-nine-tails ['kætə'nainteilz] *n* garcette *f*.

cat's-paw ['kætspɔː] *n* instrument *m*, dupe *f*.

cattish ['kætiʃ] *a* méchant, rosse.

cattle ['kætl] *n* bétail *m*, bestiaux *m pl*; **— show** comice agricole *m*.

cattle-drover ['kætldrouvə] *n* bouvier *m*.

cattle-shed ['kætlʃed] *n* étable *f*.

caucus ['kɔːkəs] *n* comité *m*, clique politique *f*.

caught [kɔːt] *pt pp of* catch.

cauldron ['kɔːldrən] *n* chaudron *m*, chaudière *f*.

cauliflower ['kɔliflauə] *n* chou-fleur *m*.

caulk [kɔːk] *vt* calfater, calfeutrer, mater.

cause [kɔːz] *n* cause *f*, motif *m*, occasion *f*, raison *f*, sujet *m*; *vt* causer, occasionner, provoquer.

causeway ['kɔːzwei] *n* chaussée *f*, digue *f*.

caustic ['kɔːstik] *a* caustique, mordant.

cauterize ['kɔːtəraiz] *vt* cautériser.

caution ['kɔːʃən] *n* prudence *f*, précaution *f*, circonspection *f*, réprimande *f*, avertissement *m*; *vt* avertir, mettre sur ses gardes.

cautious ['kɔːʃəs] *a* prudent, circonspect.

cautiousness ['kɔːʃəsnis] *n* prudence *f*, circonspection *f*.

cavalier [ˌkævə'liə] *n* cavalier *m*, gentilhomme *m*, cavalier servant *m*, galant *m*; *a* cavalier, désinvolte.

cavalry ['kævəlri] *n* cavalerie *f*.

cavalryman ['kævəlrimən] *n* cavalier *m*, soldat *m* de cavalerie.

cave [keiv] *n* caverne *f*, grotte *f*; **to — in** s'affaisser, s'effondrer, s'enfoncer, céder.

cavern ['kævən] *n* souterrain *m*, caverne *f*.
cavil ['kævil] *vi* ergoter, chicaner.
caviling ['kæviliŋ] *n* argutie *f*, ergotage *m*, chicanerie *f*; *a* ergoteur.
cavity ['kæviti] *n* cavité *f*, creux *m*, trou *m*, fosse *f*.
caw [kɔ:] *vi* croasser.
cease [si:s] *n* cesse *f*; *vti* cesser.
cease-fire [si:s'faiə] *n* cessez-le-feu *m*.
ceaseless ['si:slis] *a* incessant.
ceaselessly ['si:slisli] *ad* incessament, sans cesse.
Cecilia [ɔɪ'siljə] Cécile *f*.
cedar ['si:də] *n* cèdre *m*.
ceiling ['si:liŋ] *n* plafond *m*.
celebrate ['selibreit] *vt* célébrer, fêter, commémorer; *vi* faire la fête.
celebration [.seli'breiʃən] *n* fête *f*, commémoration *f*.
celebrity [si'lebriti] *n* célébrité *f*, renommée *f*, sommité *f*.
celeriac [sə'leriæk] *n* céleri-rave *m*.
celery ['seləri] *n* céleri *m*.
celestial [si'lestjəl] *a* céleste.
celibacy ['selibəsi] *n* célibat *m*.
celibate ['selibit] *n* célibataire *mf*.
cell [sel] *n* cellule *f*, cachot *m*.
cellar ['selə] *n* cave *f*, caveau *m*.
cellophane ['seləfein] *n* cellophane *f*.
celluloid ['seljulɔid] *n* celluloïde *m*.
cellulose ['seljulous] *n* cellulose *f*.
Celtic ['keltik] *a* celtique, celte.
cement [si'ment] *n* ciment *m*; *vt* cimenter.
cemetery ['semitri] *n* cimetière *m*.
cense [sens] *vt* encenser.
censer ['sensə] *n* encensoir *m*.
censor ['sensə] *n* censeur *m*, *vt* interdire, supprimer, contrôler; **to be —ed** passer par la censure.
censoring ['sensəriŋ] *n* censure *f*.
censorious [sen'sɔ:riəs] *a* réprobateur, dénigrant, sévère.
censorship ['sensəʃip] *n* censure *f*, contrôle *m*.
censurable ['senʃərəbl] *a* répréhensible, censurable.
censure ['senʃə] *n* censure *f*, blâme *m*; *vt* censurer, condamner, critiquer
census ['sensəs] *n* recensement *m*.
cent [sent] *n* cent *m*; **he hasn't a —** il n'a pas le sou.
centenarian [.senti'nɛəriən] *an* centenaire *mf*.
centenary [sen'ti:nəri] *an* centenaire *m*.
center ['sentə] *n* centre *m*, milieu *m*, foyer *m*; *vt* centrer, concentrer; *vi* se centrer, se concentrer.
center-forward [.sentə'fɔ:wəd] *n* avant-centre *m*.
center-half [.sentə'hɑ:f] *n* demi-centre *m*.
centigram ['sentigræm] *n* centigramme *m*.
centimeter ['senti.mitə] *n* centimètre *m*.
centipede ['sentipi:d] *n* mille-pattes *m inv*.

central ['sentrəl] *a* central.
centralize ['sentrəlaiz] *vt* centraliser.
centrifugal [sen'trifjugəl] *a* centrifuge.
centripetal [sen'tripətl] *a* centripète.
centuple ['sentjupl] *an* centuple *m*; *vt* centupler.
century ['sentʃuri] *n* siècle *m*.
cereal ['siəriəl] *an* céréale *f*.
cerebral ['seribrəl] *a* cérébral.
ceremonial [.seri'mounjəl] *n* cérémonial *m*, étiquette *f*; *a* de cérémonie.
ceremonious [.seri'mounjəs] *a* cérémonieux.
ceremony ['seriməni] *n* cérémonie *f*, façon(s) *f pl*.
certain ['sə:tn] *a* certain, sûr; **to make —** s'assurer.
certainly ['sə:tnli] *ad* certainement, certes, assurément, à coup sûr; — **not!** non, par example.
certainty ['sə:tnti] *n* certitude *f*.
certificate [sə'tifikit] *n* certificat *m*, attestation *f*, titre *m*, diplôme *m*; diplômer.
certify ['sə:tifai] *vt* certifier, déclarer, attester.
certifying ['sə:tifaiiŋ] *n* attestation *f*, homologation *f*, approbation *f*.
certitude ['sə:titju:d] *n* certitude *f*.
cessation [se'seiʃən] *n* cessation *f*, arrêt *m*.
cession ['seʃən] *n* cession *f*, abandon *m*.
cesspool ['sespu:l] *n* fosse *f*, puisard *m*.
chafe [tʃeif] *vt* frotter, irriter, écorcher, frictionner, érailler; *vi* se frotter, s'irriter, s'énerver, s'agiter.
chaff [tʃɑ:f] *n* balle *f*, paille *f*, blague *f*, persiflage *m*; *vt* blaguer, railler.
chaffinch ['tʃæfintʃ] *n* pinson *m*.
chafing ['tʃeifiŋ] *n* irritation *f*, frottement *m*, friction *f*, écorchement *m*.
chagrin ['ʃægrin] *n* chagrin *m*, dépit *m*; *vt* chagriner, mortifier.
chain [tʃein] *n* chaîne *f*, enchaînement *m*, série *f*, suite *f*; *vt* enchaîner, attacher; **—gang** chaîne de galériens.
chair [tʃɛə] *n* chaise *f*, siège *m*, fauteuil *m*, chaire *f*; **to be in the —** présider.
chairman ['tʃɛəmən] *n* président *m*.
chalice ['tʃælis] *n* calice *m*.
chalk [tʃɔ:k] *n* craie *f*, pastel *m*, blanc *m*; *vt* marquer, tracer *etc* à la craie.
chalky ['tʃɔ:ki] *a* crayeux.
challenge ['tʃælindʒ] *n* défi *m*, provocation *f*, qui vive *m*, interpellation *f*, récusation *f*; *vt* défier, crier qui vive à, porter un défi à, provoquer (en duel), mettre en question, récuser.
chamber ['tʃeimbə] *n* chambre *f*, cabinet *m*, salle *f*, étude *f*.

chamberlain ['tʃeimbəlin] n chambellan m.

chambermaid ['tʃeimbəmeid] n femme f de chambre.

chamber-pot ['tʃeimbəpɔt]‿n pot m de chambre.

champ [tʃæmp] vt mâcher, ronger.

Champagne [ʃæm'pein] n Champagne f; (wine) champagne m.

champion ['tʃæmpjən] n champion, -onne; vt soutenir.

championship ['tʃæmpjənʃip] n championnat m.

chance [tʃɑ:ns] n chance f, sort m, occasion f, hasard m; a fortuit, de rencontre; vt risquer; vi venir (à to); to — upon rencontrer (par hasard), tomber sur.

chancel ['tʃɑ:nsəl] n chœur m.

chancellor ['tʃɑ:nsələ] n chancelier m.

chancellory ['tʃɑ:nsələri] n chancellerie f.

chancy ['tʃɑ:nsi] a chanceux, incertain, risqué.

chandelier [‚ʃændi'liə] n lustre m, candélabre m.

change [tʃeindʒ] n changement m, change f, revirement m, monnaie f; vt changer, transformer, modifier; vi (se) changer, se modifier, se transformer.

changeable ['tʃeindʒəbl] a changeant, variable.

changeableness ['tʃeindʒəblnis] n mobilité f, inconstance f, variabilité f.

channel ['tʃænl] n lit m, canal m, rainure f, voie f; the Channel la Manche; Irish Channel mer d'Irlande f.

chant [tʃɑ:nt] n (plain-)chant m, psalmodie f; vt chanter, psalmodier.

chanty ['tʃɑ:nti] n chanson de bord f.

chaos ['keiɔs] n chaos m.

chaotic [kei'ɔtik] a chaotique, sans ordre, désorganisé.

chap [tʃæp] n gerçure f, crevasse f, bajoue f, type m; vt gercer, crevasser.

chapel ['tʃæpl] n chapelle f, oratoire m.

chaperon ['ʃæpəroun] n chaperon m; vt chaperonner.

chaplain ['tʃæplin] n aumônier m; army chaplain, aumônier (mil).

chaplet ['tʃæplit] n guirlande f, chapelet m.

chapter ['tʃæptə] n chapitre m, suite f; branche d'une société f.

char [tʃɑ:] vt carboniser.

character ['kæriktə] n caractère m, moralité f, certificat m (de moralité), réputation f, numéro m, original(e) mf, personnage m, individu m; a bad — un mauvais sujet.

characteristic [‚kæriktə'ristik] n trait m (de caractère), particularité f; a caractéristique.

characterize ['kæriktəraiz] vt caractériser, être caractéristique de.

charcoal ['tʃɑ:koul] n charbon m de bois, fusain m.

charcoal-burner ['tʃɑ:koul‚bə:nə] n charbonnier m.

charge [tʃɑ:dʒ] vti charger; vt accuser, demander; n charge f, prix m, frais m pl, fonction f, emploi m, soin m, garde f, accusation f; to — s.o. with sth accuser qn de qch, reprocher qch à qn; to — sth to s.o. mettre qch au compte de qn; on a — of sous l'inculpation de; free of — franco, gratuitement, gratis.

chargeable ['tʃɑ:dʒəbl] a imputable, inculpable.

charger ['tʃɑ:dʒə] n chargeur m, plateau m, cheval m de bataille.

charily ['tʃɛərili] ad prudemment, chichement.

chariness ['tʃɛərinis] n prudence f, parcimonie f.

chariot ['tʃæriət] n char m.

charitable ['tʃæritəbl] a charitable, de bienfaisance.

charity ['tʃæriti] n charité f, bienfaisance f, aumônes f pl.

charm [tʃɑ:m] n charme m, agrément m, sort m, sortilège m, portebonheur m, fétiche m; vt charmer, enchanter, jeter un sort sur.

charnel-house ['tʃɑ:nlhaus] n charnier m.

chart [tʃɑ:t] n carte f, diagramme m; vt relever la carte de, porter sur une carte, établir le graphique de, l'hydrographie de, explorer.

charter ['tʃɑ:tə] n charte f; vt accorder une charte à, affréter, louer.

chartering ['tʃɑ:təriŋ] n nolisement m, affrètement m.

charwoman ['tʃɑ:wumən] n femme de ménage f.

chary ['tʃɛəri] a prudent, chiche, avare.

chase [tʃeis] n chasse f, poursuite f; vt poursuivre, (pour)chasser, ciseler, repousser.

chaser ['tʃeisə] n chasseur m, pousse-café m.

chasing ['tʃeisiŋ] n ciselure f, repoussage m.

chasm ['kæzəm] n crevasse f, abîme m, gouffre m, vide m.

chassis ['ʃæsi] n chassis m.

chaste [tʃeist] a chaste, pudique, pur.

chasten ['tʃeisn] vt châtier, assagir, dégonfler.

chastise [tʃæs'taiz] vt châtier, corriger.

chastisement ['tʃæstizmənt] n châtiment m.

chastity ['tʃæstiti] n chasteté f, pureté f, sobriété f.

chat [tʃæt] n (brin de) causerie f, causette f; vi bavarder, causer.

chattel ['tʃætl] n propriété f, bien

m, mobilier m; **goods and —s** biens et effets m pl.

chatter ['tʃætə] n babil m, caquetage m, bavardage m, claquement m; vi bavarder, jaser, caqueter, claquer.

chatterbox ['tʃætəbɔks] n moulin m à paroles, bavard m.

chatty ['tʃæti] a bavard, causant, causeur.

chauffeur ['ʃoufə] n chauffeur m.

cheap [tʃiːp] a bon marché, (à prix) réduit, trivial, facile; **it's dirt —** c'est donné.

cheapen ['tʃiːpən] vt déprécier, baisser le prix de.

cheaply ['tʃiːpli] ad (à) bon marché, à peu de frais, à bon compte.

cheat [tʃiːt] n tricheur, -euse, escroc m, filou m; vti tricher; vt tromper, voler.

cheating ['tʃiːtiŋ] n tricherie f, tromperie f, fourberie f.

check [tʃek] n échec m, arrêt (brusque) m, contrôle m, contremarque f, rebuffade f, bulletin m, ticket m, étoffe à carreaux f; vt tenir en échec, arrêter, retenir, contenir, freiner, réprimer, réprimander, contrôler, vérifier, réviser, compulser; n (bank) chèque m; **blank —** chèque en blanc; **traveler's —** chèque de voyage; **to cross a —** barrer un chèque.

checkbook ['tʃekbuk] n carnet m de chèques, chéquier m.

checker ['tʃekə] n contrôleur m, pointeur m, damier m; pl carreaux m pl, quadrillage m; vt disposer en damier, quadriller, diaprer, varier.

checker-board ['tʃekəbɔːd] n damier m.

checkered ['tʃekəd] a varié, diapré, inégal, quadrillé, en damier, à carreaux, accidenté.

checkmate ['tʃek'meit] vt faire échec et mat à, déjouer, contrecarrer.

cheek [tʃiːk] n joue f, toupet m, effronterie f.

cheekbone ['tʃiːkboun] n pommette f.

cheekiness ['tʃiːkinis] n effronterie f.

cheeky ['tʃiːki] a effronté.

cheep [tʃiːp] vi piauler, pépier.

cheer [tʃiə] n belle humeur f, bonne chère f, acclamations f pl, applaudissements m pl, vivats m pl; vt réconforter, égayer, acclamer; **to give three —s for** accorder un ban à; vti applaudir; **to — up** vi reprendre courage, se regaillardir; vt réconforter, remonter le moral à; **— up!** courage!

cheerful ['tʃiəful] a joyeux, gai, réconfortant, égayant.

cheerfully ['tʃiəfuli] ad gaîment, de bon cœur.

cheerfulness ['tʃiəfulnis] n gaieté f, belle humeur f, entrain m.

cheering ['tʃiəriŋ] n applaudissements m pl, acclamation f; a réjouissant, encourageant, réconfortant.

cheerio ['tʃiəri'ou] excl à bientôt! à tantôt! à la vôtre!

cheerless ['tʃiəlis] a sombre, morne, triste.

cheery ['tʃiəri] a gai, joyeux.

cheese [tʃiːz] n fromage m.

chef [ʃef] n chef m (de cuisine).

chemical ['kemikəl] a chimique; n pl produits chimiques m pl.

chemist ['kemist] n chimiste m, pharmacien m; **—'s shop** pharmacie f.

chemistry ['kemistri] n chimie f.

cherish ['tʃeriʃ] vt chérir, soigner, caresser.

cherry ['tʃeri] n cerise f.

cherry tree ['tʃeritri] n cerisier m.

cherub ['tʃerəb] n chérubin m.

chervil ['tʃəːvil] n cerfeuil m.

chess [tʃes] n échecs m pl.

chessboard ['tʃesbɔːd] n échiquier m.

chest [tʃest] n poitrine f, poitrail m, coffre m, caisse f; **— of drawers** commode f.

chestnut ['tʃesnʌt] n châtaigne f, marron m; a châtain, marron, alezan.

chestnut tree ['tʃesnʌttri] n châtaignier m, marronnier m.

chew [tʃuː] vt (re)mâcher, mastiquer, chiquer, ruminer.

chicanery [ʃi'keinəri] n chicanerie f, arguties f pl.

chick [tʃik] n poussin m.

chicken ['tʃikin] n poulet m.

chicken-pox ['tʃikinpɔks] n varicelle f.

chickweed ['tʃikwiːd] n mouron m des oiseaux.

chicory ['tʃikəri] n endive f.

chidden ['tʃidn] pp of **chide**.

chide [tʃaid] vti gronder.

chief [tʃiːf] n chef m, patron m; a en chef, principal.

chiefly ['tʃiːfli] ad notamment.

chilblain ['tʃilblein] n engelure f.

child [tʃaild] n enfant mf.

childbed ['tʃaildbed] n couches f pl.

childbirth ['tʃaildbəːθ] n accouchement m.

childhood ['tʃaildhud] n enfance f.

childish ['tʃaildiʃ] a enfantin, d'enfant, puéril.

childishness ['tʃaildiʃnis] n puérilité f, enfantillage m.

childless ['tʃaildlis] a sans enfant, stérile.

childlike ['tʃaildlaik] a enfantin, d'enfant.

children ['tʃildrən] pl of **child**.

chill [tʃil] n froid m, refroidissement m, chaud et froid m, frisson m; a glacial, froid; vt glacer, refroidir; vt se glacer, se refroidir.

chilled [tʃild] a transi de froid, glacé, frigorifié.

chilly ['tʃili] *a* froid, frileux, glacial, frisquet.

chime [tʃaim] *n* carillon *m*; *vti* sonner, carillonner; *vi* s'harmoniser (avec **with**); **to — in** placer son mot, intervenir.

chimera [kai'miərə] *n* chimère *f*.

chimney ['tʃimni] *n* cheminée *f*.

chimney-pot ['tʃimnipɔt] *n* cheminée *f*.

chimney-sweep ['tʃimniswiːp] *n* ramoneur *m*.

chin [tʃin] *n* menton *m*.

chinstrap ['tʃinstræp] *n* jugulaire *f*.

china ['tʃainə] *n* porcelaine *f*.

China ['tʃainə] *n* Chine *f*.

Chinese ['tʃai'niːz] *an* chinois *m*; *n* Chinois(e) *mf*.

chink [tʃiŋk] *n* fente *f*, crevasse *f*, lézarde *f*, entrebâillement *m*, tintement *m*; *vi* sonner, tinter; *vt* faire sonner, faire tinter.

chintz [tʃints] *n* perse *f*.

chip [tʃip] *n* copeau *m*, éclat *m*, tranche *f*, écornure *f*, écaille *f*, jeton *m*; *vt* couper, ébrécher, écorner; *vi* s'ébrécher, s'écorner; **to — in** intervenir, placer son mot.

chips [tʃips] *n pl* (pommes *f pl* de terre) frites *f pl*.

chiropodist [ki'rɔpədist] *n* pédicure *m*.

chirp [tʃəːp] **chirrup** ['tʃirəp] *n* pépiement *m*, gazouillement *m*; *vi* pépier, gazouiller, grésiller; **—ing** pépiement.

chisel ['tʃizl] *n* ciseau *m*, burin *m*; *vt* ciseler, sculpter.

chit [tʃit] *n* marmot *m*, mioche *mf*, brin *m*.

chit-chat ['tʃittʃæt] *n* commérages *m pl*.

chivalrous ['ʃivəlrəs] *a* chevaleresque.

chivalry ['ʃivəlri] *n* chevalerie *f*, courtoisie *f*.

chive [tʃaiv] *n* ciboulette *f*.

chlorine ['klɔːriːn] *n* chlore *m*.

chloroform ['klɔrəfɔːm] *n* chloroforme *m*.

chock [tʃɔk] *n* cale *f*; *vt* caler, mettre sur cale, bourrer.

chock-full ['tʃɔkful] *a* bourré, bondé.

chocolate ['tʃɔkəlit] *n* chocolat *m*; **— button, candy** crotte de chocolat *f*.

choice [tʃɔis] *n* choix *m*, préférence *f*, élection *f*; *a* de choix, choisi.

choir ['kwaiə] *n* chœur *m*, maîtrise *f*.

choke [tʃouk] *n* étranglement *m*, étrangleur *m*, (aut) starter *m*; *vti* étrangler, suffoquer, étouffer; *vt* boucher, obstruer; *vi* se boucher, obstruer; *vi* se boucher, s'obstruer; **to — back** refouler; **to — down** avaler.

choking ['tʃoukiŋ] *n* suffocation *f*, étranglement *m*, étouffement *m*, obstruction *f*.

cholera ['kɔlərə] *n* choléra *m*.

choleric ['kɔlərik] *a* cholérique, irascible.

choose [tʃuːz] *vt* choisir, opter, élire, adopter.

choosy ['tʃuːzi] *a* difficile, chipoteur.

chop [tʃɔp] *n* coup *m* (de hache), côtelette *f*, clapotis *m*; *vt* hacher, tailler, couper, fendre; *vi* clapoter; **to — down** abattre; **to — off** couper, trancher.

chopper ['tʃɔpə] *n* hachoir *m*, couperet *m*; hélicoptère *m*.

choppy ['tʃɔpi] *a* agité, haché.

chopstick ['tʃɔpstik] *n* baguette *f*.

chord [kɔːd] *n* corde *f*, accord *m*.

chorister ['kɔristə] *n* choriste *m*, chantre *m*, enfant de chœur *m*.

chorus ['kɔːrəs] *n* chœur *m*, refrain *m*; **—girl** girl *f*.

chose [tʃouz] *pt of* **choose**.

Christ [kraist] *n* le Christ.

christen ['krisn] *vt* baptiser.

Christendom ['krisndəm] *n* chrétienté *f*.

christening ['krisniŋ] *n* baptême *m*.

Christian ['kristjən] *an* chrétien, -ienne.

Christianity [ˌkristi'æniti] *n* christianisme *m*.

Christmas ['krisməs] *n* Noël *m*; **Father —** le Père Noël.

Christmas-box ['krisməsbɔks] *n* étrennes *f pl*.

Christmas-carol ['krisməs'kærəl] *n* noël *m*.

Christopher ['kristəfə] Christophe *m*.

chromium ['kroumjəm] *n* chrome *m*.

chromium-plated ['kroumjəm.pleitid] *a* chromé.

chronic ['krɔnik] *a* chronique, constant.

chronicle ['krɔnikl] *n* chronique *f*; *vt* relater, faire la chronique de.

chronicler ['krɔniklə] *n* chroniqueur *m*.

chronological [ˌkrɔnə'lɔdʒikl] *a* chronologique.

chronology [krə'nɔlədʒi] *n* chronologie *f*.

chronometer [krə'nɔmitə] *n* chronomètre *m*.

chrysalis ['krisəlis] *n* chrysalide *f*.

chrysanthemum [kri'sænθəməm] *n* chrysanthème *m*.

chubby ['tʃʌbi] *a* joufflu, potelé.

chuck [tʃʌk] *n* tape *f*; *vt* jeter, plaquer; **to — out** flanquer à la porte; **to — up** abandonner, balancer.

chuckle ['tʃʌkl] *n* rire étouffé *m*, gloussement *m*; *vi* rire sous cape, glousser.

chum [tʃʌm] *n* copain *m*, copine *f*, camarade *mf*.

chunk [tʃʌŋk] *n* gros morceau *m*, (bread) quignon *m*.

church [tʃəːtʃ] *n* église *f*, temple *m*.

churchwarden ['tʃəːtʃ'wɔːdn] n marguillier m.
churchyard ['tʃəːtʃ'jɑːd] n cimetière
m.
churl [tʃəːl] n rustre m, ladre m.
churlish ['tʃəːliʃ] a grossier, mal
élevé, grincheux, hargneux, bourru.
churlishness ['tʃəːliʃnis] n rusticité
f, grossièreté f.
churn [tʃəːn] n baratte f; vt battre;
vi (sea) bouillir, bouillonner.
cicada [si'kɑːdə] n cigale f.
cider ['saidə] n cidre m.
cigar [si'gɑː] n cigare m.
cigarette [ˌsigə'ret] n cigarette f.
cigarette-case [ˌsigəˈretkeis] n étui
m à cigarettes.
cigarette-holder [ˌsigə'retˌhouldə] n
fume-cigarette m.
cinder ['sində] n cendre f; pl cendres
f pl, escarbilles f pl.
Cinderella [ˌsindəˈrelə] n Cendrillon.
cine-camera ['siniˈkæmərə] n
caméra f.
cinema ['sinimə] n cinéma m.
cine-projector ['siniprəˌdʒektə] n
ciné-projecteur m.
cinnamon ['sinəmən] n canelle f.
cipher ['saifə] n zéro m, chiffre m,
clé f; vt chiffrer.
circle ['səːkl] n cercle m, milieu m;
vicious — cercle vicieux; vt encercler,
entourer, faire le tour de; vi tourner
en rond, tournoyer.
circuit ['səːkit] n circuit m, ressort
m, tournée f, tour m, enceinte f,
parcours m, pourtour m, détour m.
circuitous [səˈkjuitəs] a tournant,
détourné.
circular ['səːkjulə] an circulaire f.
circularize ['səːkjuləraiz] vt envoyer des circulaires à.
circulate ['səːkjuleit] vi circuler; vt
faire circuler.
circulation [ˌsəːkjuˈleiʃən] n circulation f, (of newspaper) tirage m.
circumcise ['səːkəmsaiz] vt circoncire.
circumcision [ˌsəːkəmˈsiʒən] n cir-
concision f.
circumference [səˈkʌmfərəns] n circonférence f.
circumflex ['səːkəmfleks] an circonflexe m.
circumlocution [ˌsəːkəmləˈkjuːʃən]
n circonlocution f, ambages f pl.
circumscribe ['səːkəmskraib] vt circonscrire.
circumspect ['səːkəmspekt] a circonspect.
circumspection [ˌsəːkəmˈspekʃən] n
circonspection f.
circumstance ['səːkəmstəns] n circonstance f, situation f, cérémonie
f.
circumstantial [ˌsəːkəmˈstænʃəl] a
indirect, circonstancié, circonstan-
ciel.
circumvent [ˌsəːkəmˈvent] vt circonvenir.

circus ['səːkəs] n cirque m, rond-
point m.
cistern ['sistən] n réservoir m,
citerne f.
citadel ['sitədl] n citadelle f.
citation [saiˈteiʃən] n citation f.
cite [sait] vt citer, assigner.
citizen ['sitizn] n citoyen, citadin(e)
mf bourgeois(e) mf.
citizenship ['sitiznʃip] n civisme m.
citron ['sitrən] n cédrat m.
city ['siti] n (grande)ville f, cité f;
garden — cité jardin f.
civic ['sivik] a civique, municipal.
civics ['siviks] n instruction civique
f.
civil ['sivil] a civil, poli, honnête;
C— Service n administration f;
— servant n fonctionnaire m; in —
life dans le civil; C— War Guerre
f de sécession.
civilian [siˈviljən] n civil m, pékin m.
civility [siˈviliti] n politesse f,
civilité f.
civilization [ˌsivilaiˈzeiʃən] n civilisation f.
civilize ['sivilaiz] vt civiliser.
clack [klæk] n claquement m; vi
claquer, caqueter.
clad [klæd] pt pp of **clothe.**
claim [kleim] n revendication f,
réclamation f, titre m, droit m,
demande f, prétention f; vt réclamer, revendiquer, prétendre (à),
demander.
claimant ['kleimənt] n demandeur,
-eresse, réclamant(e) mf, prétendant
(e) mf, revendicateur m.
clairvoyant [kleəˈvɔiənt] a clairvoyant, doué de seconde vue; n
voyant(e) mf.
clam [klæm] n palourde f.
clamant ['kleimənt] a bruyant,
criant, urgent.
clamber ['klæmbə] vi grimper; n
escalade f.
clammy ['klæmi] a moite, humide,
gluant.
clamor ['klæmə] n clameur f; vi
pousser des cris, vociférer; to — for
demander, réclamer, à grand cris.
clamorous ['klæmərəs] a bruyant,
braillard.
clamp [klæmp] n crampon m,
mordache f, patte f d'attache,
(potato) silo m; vt consolider, brider,
agrafer.
clan [klæn] n clan m.
clandestine [klænˈdestin] a clandestin.
clang [klæŋ] n bruit m retentissant,
son m métallique; vt résonner,
retentir; vt faire résonner.
clank [klæŋk] n cliquetis m; vi
sonner; vt faire sonner.
clap [klæp] n éclat m, battement m,
applaudissements m pl, tape f; vi
battre (des mains); vti applaudir;
vt camper, fourrer.
clapper ['klæpə] n battant m,

crécelle *f*, claquet *m*, claqueur *m*.
claptrap ['klæptræp] *n* tape-à-l'œil *m*, boniment *m*.
claret ['klærət] *n* bordeaux *m* rouge.
clarify ['klærifai] *vt* clarifier, éclaircir; *vi* se clarifier, s'éclaircir.
clarinet [ˌklæri'net] *n* clarinette *f*.
clarion ['klæriən] *n* clairon *m*; *a* claironnant.
clarity ['klæriti] *n* clarté *f*, lucidité *f*.
clash [klæʃ] *n* choc *m*, heurt *m*, fracas *m*, cliquetis *m*, confit *m*; *vi* faire du fracas, se heurter, s'entrechoquer, jurer; *vt* faire résonner.
clasp [klɑːsp] *n* agrafe *f*, fermoir *m*, fermeture *f*, étreinte *f*; *vt* agrafer, serrer, étreindre.
clasp-knife ['klɑːspnaif] *n* couteau fermant, pliant *m*.
class [klɑːs] *n* classe *f*, catégorie *f*, type *m*, sorte *f*; *vt* classer.
classic ['klæsik] *an* classique *m*.
classicism ['klæsisizəm] *n* classicisme *m*.
classification [ˌklæsifi'keiʃən] *n* classement *m*.
classify ['klæsifai] *vt* classer.
clatter ['klætə] *n* bruit *m*, fracas *m*, brouhaha *m*, ferraillement *m*.
clause [klɔːz] *n* clause *f*, article *m*, proposition *f*.
clavicle ['klævikl] *n* clavicule *f*.
claw [klɔː] *n* serre *f*, pince *f*, griffe *f*; *vt* gratter, griffer, déchirer, égratigner.
clay [klei] *n* argile *f*, glaise *f*, pisé *m*.
clean [kliːn] *a* propre, net, bien fait, complet; *vt* nettoyer, vider, mettre en ordre, balayer, (re)curer, décrotter, décrasser.
cleaner ['kliːnə] *n* teinturier *m*, nettoyeur, -euse, décrotteur *m*, balayeur, -euse.
cleaning ['kliːniŋ] *n* nettoyage *m*, dégraissage *m*.
clean(li)ness ['klenlinis] *n* propreté *f*, netteté *f*.
cleanse [klenz] *vt* purifier, laver, curer, assainir.
clear [kliə] *a* clair, net, évident, libre, dégagé, sûr; **all — fin** d'alerte *f*; *vt* éclaircir, disculper, déblayer, dégager, franchir, solder, acquitter, gagner net, desservir, (*forest, bush*) débrousser; *vi* s'éclaircir, se dégager, se dissiper; **to — away** *vt* écarter, enlever; *vi* se dissiper; **to — off** enlever, solder; **to — out** *vt* nettoyer, balayer, vider; *vi* filer, ficher le camp, se sauver; **to — up** *vt* tirer au clair, éclaircir; *vi* s'éclaircir.
clearance ['kliərəns] *n* déblayage *m*, liquidation *f*, congé *m*, jeu *m*.
clear-cut ['kliə'kʌt] *a* distinct, net ciselé.
clear-headed ['kliə'hedid] *a* lucide, perspicace.
clearing ['kliəriŋ] *n* clairière *f*, levée *f*, dégagement *m*, déblaiement *m*, évacuation *f*, défrichement *m*.

clearness ['kliənis] *n* clarté *f*, netteté *f*.
clear-sighted ['kliə'saitid] *a* clairvoyant.
cleavage ['kliːvidʒ] *n* division *f*, scission *f*, (*fam*) décolleté *m*.
cleave [kliːv] *vt* fendre; *vi* se fendre, s'attacher.
cleaver ['kliːvə] *n* couperet *m*, fendoir *m*.
cleft [kleft] *pt pp of* **cleave**; *n* fente *f*, crevasse *f*, fissure *f*; *a* fourchu, (*palate*) fendu; **in a — stick** dans une impasse, mal pris.
clemency ['klemənsi] *n* clémence *f*, douceur *f*, indulgence *f*.
clement ['klemənt] *a* clément, indulgent, doux.
clench [klentʃ] *see* **clinch**; *vt* serrer; *vi* se serrer.
clergy ['kləːdʒi] *n* clergé *m*.
clergyman ['kləːdʒimən] *n* ecclésiastique *m*, pasteur *m*.
clerical ['klerikəl] *a* de clerc, d'écriture, de copiste.
clerk [klɑːk] *n* clerc *m*, commis *m*, employé(e) de bureau *mf*.
clever ['klevə] *a* habile, adroit, intelligent, ingénieux.
cleverness ['klevənis] *n* habileté *f*, adresse *f*, intelligence *f*, ingéniosité *f*.
click [klik] *n* (dé)clic *m*, cliquetis *m*; *vti* cliqueter, claquer; *vi* avoir de la veine, avoir des touches, cadrer.
client ['klaiənt] *n* client(e) *mf*.
clientele [ˌkliːãːn'tel] *n* clientèle *f*.
cliff [klif] *n* falaise *f*, paroi *f* rocheuse, rochers *m pl*.
climate ['klaimit] *n* climat *m*.
climatic [klai'mætik] *a* climat(ér)que.
climax ['klaimæks] *n* gradation *f*, comble *m*, apogée *f*.
climb [klaim] *n* escalade *f*, montée *f*, ascension *f*, côte *f*; *vti* monter, grimper; *vt* escalader, gravir, monter à, sur, grimper à, sur, faire l'ascension de; *vi* prendre de l'altitude; **to — down** *vti* descendre; *vi* baisser pavillon, en rabattre, se dégonfler; **to — over** escalader, franchir.
climber ['klaimə] *n* grimpeur *m*, alpiniste, plante grimpante *f*, arriviste *mf*.
clinch [klintʃ] *n* crampon *m*, corps à corps *m*; *vt* river, serrer, conclure.
clincher ['klintʃə] *n* argument décisif *m*.
cling [kliŋ] *vi* se cramponner, s'accrocher, se prendre, coller.
clinging ['kliŋiŋ] *a* étroit, collant.
clinic ['klinik] *n* clinique *f*.
clink [kliŋk] *n* tintement *m*, cliquetis *m*; prison *f*; *vi* tinter, s'entrechoquer; *vt* faire tinter, choquer; **to — glasses** trinquer.
clip [klip] *n* agrafe *f*, pince *f*, attache *f*; *vt* agrafer, pincer, tondre, rogner, tailler.

clippers ['klipəz] n tondeuse f.
clipping ['klipiŋ] n tonte f, tondage m, taille f, coupure f; pl rognures f pl.
cloak [klouk] n manteau m, masque m; vt couvrir, masquer.
cloakroom ['kloukrum] n consigne f, vestiaire m.
clock [klɔk] n pendule f, horloge f, baguette f; vt chronométrer.
clock-maker ['klɔk'meikə] n horloger m.
clock-making ['klɔk'meikiŋ] n horlogerie f.
clockwise ['klɔkwaiz] a dans le sens des aiguilles d'une montre, à droite.
clockwork ['klɔkwəːk] n mouvement d'horlogerie m, rouage m d'horloge; **to go like** — marcher comme sur des roulettes.
clod [klɔd] n motte f de terre, rustre m.
clog [klɔg] n entrave f, galoche f, sabot m; vt entraver, obstruer, arrêter, boucher; vi s'obstruer, se boucher.
cloister ['klɔistə] n cloître m; pl ambulatoire m.
close [klous] n (en)clos m, clôture f, enceinte f; a fermé, clos, confiné, lourd, compact, serré, secret, proche, étroit, exact, intime, avare; ad de près, étroitement; — **by** tout près; — **to** prep tout près de.
close [klouz] n clôture f, fermeture f, conclusion f, fin f; **to draw to a** — tirer à sa fin; vt fermer, clore, conclure, terminer, (res)serrer; vi (se) fermer, se terminer, faire relâche, en venir aux prises; **to** — **down** vti fermer; **to** — **up** vt boucher, barrer, obturer; vi s'obturer, se serrer.
closely ['klousli] ad de près.
closeness ['klousnis] n proximité f, rapprochement m, étroitesse f, intimité f, lourdeur f, avarice f, exactitude f, réserve f.
closet ['klɔzit] n cabinet m, armoire f; vt enfermer.
close-up ['klousʌp] n gros, premier plan m.
closing ['klouziŋ] n fermeture f, clôture f.
closure ['klouʒə] n clôture f.
clot [klɔt] n caillot m, grumeau m; vi se prendre, se coaguler, se figer, se cailler.
cloth [klɔθ] n toile f, étoffe f, nappe f, napperon m, linge m, torchon m, drap m, tapis m, habit ecclésiastique m; **to lay the** — mettre la nappe, le couvert.
clothe [klouð] vt (re)vêtir, habiller, couvrir.
clothes [klouðz] n pl habits m pl, vêtements m pl, effets m pl.
clothes-horse ['klouðzhɔːs] n séchoir m.
clothes-peg ['klouðzpeg] n patère f.
clothier ['klouðiə] n drapier m.

clothing ['klouðiŋ] n habillement m, vêtements m pl.
cloud [klaud] n nuage m, nue f, nuée f, buée f; vt assombrir, couvrir, obscurcir, voiler, ternir, embuer, troubler; vi s'assombrir, se couvrir, s'obscurcir, se voiler, se troubler, se ternir.
cloudy ['klaudi] a nuageux. couvert, trouble.
clout [klaut] n torchon m, linge m, chiffon m, taloche f.
clove [klouv] pt of **cleave**; n clou m de girofle; — **of garlic** gousse f d'ail.
cloven ['klouvn] pp of **cleave**; a fendu, fourchu.
clover ['klouvə] n trèfle m; **to be in** — être comme un coq en pâte.
clown [klaun] n clown m, bouffon m, pitre m; vi faire le clown.
cloy [klɔi] vt ressasier, affadir.
club [klʌb] n massue f, crosse f, gourdin m, club m, cercle m, (cards) trèfle m; vt frapper avec un gourdin, assommer; vi s'associer; **to** — **together** se cotiser.
club-foot ['klʌb'fut] n pied-bot m.
cluck [klʌk] n gloussement m; vi glousser.
clue [kluː] n indice m, indication f.
clump [klʌmp] n massif m, bouquet m, masse f; vi sonner, marcher lourdement.
clumsiness ['klʌmzinis] n gaucherie f, balourdise f, maladresse f.
clumsy ['klʌmzi] a gauche, maladroit.
clung [klʌŋ] pt pp of **cling**.
cluster ['klʌstə] n groupe m, grappe f, essaim m, bouquet m; vt grouper; vi se grouper.
clutch [klʌtʃ] n prise f, étreinte f, poigne f, griffes f pl, couvée f, (cheville d')embrayage f; **to let in (out) the** — embrayer, (débrayer); vt empoigner, étreindre, saisir; **to** — **at** s'agripper à, se raccrocher à.
clutter ['klʌtə] n encombrement m, pagaïe f; **to** — **up** encombrer.
coach [koutʃ] n coche m, carrosse m, voiture f, autocar m, répétiteur m, entraîneur m; vt donner des leçons à, entraîner.
coach-builder ['koutʃ'bildə] n carrossier m.
coach-building ['koutʃ'bildiŋ] n carrosserie f.
coach-house ['koutʃhaus] n remise f.
coaching ['koutʃiŋ] n leçons f pl, répétitions f pl, dressage m, entraînement m.
coachman ['koutʃmən] n cocher m.
coachwork ['koutʃwəːk] n carrosserie f.
coagulate [kou'ægjuleit] vt (faire) coaguler, figer; vi se coaguler, se figer.
coal [koul] n charbon m, houille f; **to haul s.o. over the** —s laver la tête à qn; vi faire le charbon.

coal-bed ['koul'bed] *n* banc *m*, couche *f* de houille.

coalesce [,kouə'les] *vi* s'unir, fusionner.

coalfield ['koulfiːld] *n* bassin houiller *m*.

coalition [,koulə'liʃən] *n* coalition *f*.

coalmine ['koulmain] *n* mine *f* de houille, houillère *f*.

coalminer ['koulmainə] *n* mineur *m*, houilleur *m*.

coal-tar ['koul'taː] *n* goudron *m*.

coarse [kɔːs] *a* gros(sier), rude, rêche.

coarseness ['kɔːsnis] *n* grossièreté *f*, rudesse *f*, grosseur *f*, brutalité *f*.

coast [koust] *n* côte *f*, rivage *m*, littoral *m*; *vi* côtoyer le rivage, faire le cabotage; **to — down a hill** descendre une côte en roue libre, le moteur débrayé.

coastal ['koustəl] *a* côtier.

coaster ['koustə] *n* caboteur *m*.

coasting ['koustiŋ] *n* cabotage *m*, navigation côtière.

coat [kout] *n* pardessus *m*, manteau *m*, habit *m*, robe *f*, poil *m*, couche *f*, revêtement *m*; *vt* couvrir, enduire, revêtir.

coat-hanger ['kout,hæŋə] *n* portevêtements *m*.

coat-peg ['koutpeg] *n* patère *f*.

coax [kouks] *vt* amadouer, câliner, cajoler, amener (à **to**).

coaxing ['kouksiŋ] *n* cajoleries *f pl*, enjôlement *m*; *a* cajoleur, câlin.

cob [kɔb] *n* cygne *m*, bidet *m*, torchis *m*, (*bread*) miche *f*, (*nut*) aveline *f*.

cobble ['kɔbl] *n* galet *m*, caillou *m*; *vt* paver, rapiécer.

cobbler ['kɔblə] *n* savetier *m*, cordonnier *m*.

cobra ['koubrə] *n* cobra *m*, serpent à lunettes *m*.

cobweb ['kɔbweb] *n* toile d'araignée *f*.

cock [kɔk] *n* coq *m*, mâle *m*, robinet *m*, (*gun*) chien *m*, (*hay*) meule *f*, (*scales*) aiguille *f*, retroussis *m*; *vt* dresser, retrousser, mettre de travers, armer.

cockade [kɔ'keid] *n* cocarde *f*.

cock-a-doodle-doo ['kɔkəduːdl'duː] *excl* cocorico!

cock-and-bull story ['kɔkən'bul-'stɔːri] *n* coq à l'âne *m*.

cockatoo [,kɔkə'tuː] *n* cacatoès *m*.

cockchafer ['kɔk,tʃeifə] *n* hanneton *m*.

cockle ['kɔkl] *n* coque *f*, bucarde *f*.

cockney ['kɔkni] *an* londonien, -ienne.

cockpit ['kɔkpit] *n* arène *f*, carlingue *f*.

cockroach ['kɔkroutʃ] *n* cafard *m*, blatte *f*, cancrelet *m*.

cockscomb ['kɔkskoum] *n* crête *f* de coq.

cocksure ['kɔk'ʃuə] *a* qui ne doute de rien, outrecuidant, très assuré.

cocky ['kɔki] *a* faraud, outrecuidant.

cocoa ['koukou] *n* cacao *m*; **— tree** cacaoyer *m*; **— plantation** cacaotière *f*.

coconut ['koukənʌt] *n* noix de coco *f*; **— palm** cocotier *m*; **— plantation** cocoteraie *f*; **— oil** huile *f* de copra.

cocoon [kə'kuːn] *n* cocon *m*.

cod [kɔd] *n* morue *f*, cabillaud *m*.

coddle ['kɔdl] *vt* dorloter, choyer.

code [koud] *n* code *m*, chiffre *m*; *vt* codifier, chiffrer.

codicil ['kɔdisil] *n* codicille *m*.

codliver-oil ['kɔdlivər'ɔil] *n* huile *f* de foie de morue.

coerce [kou'əːs] *vt* forcer, contraindre.

coercion [kou'əːʃən] *n* coercition *f*, contrainte *f*.

coercive [kou'əːsiv] *a* coercitif.

coffee ['kɔfi] *n* café *m*; **— bean** grain *m* de café; **— grounds** marc *m* de café **black —** café noir; **light —** café au lait, café crème.

coffee-mill ['kɔfimil] *n* moulin à café *m*.

coffee plant ['kɔfiplɑːnt] *n* caféier *m*.

coffee plantation ['kɔfiplæn,teiʃən] *n* caféière *f*.

coffeepot ['kɔfipɔt] *n* cafetière *f*.

coffer ['kɔfə] *n* coffre *m*.

coffin ['kɔfin] *n* cercueil *m*, bière *f*.

cog [kɔg] *n* dent *f*; **he's only a — in the wheel** il n'est qu'un rouage de la machine.

cogency ['koudʒənsi] *n* force *f*, puissance *f*, urgence *f*.

cogent ['koudʒənt] *a* décisif, valable, urgent.

cogitate ['kɔdʒiteit] *vi* réfléchir; *vti* méditer.

cogitation [,kɔdʒi'teiʃən] *n* réflexion *f*, délibération.

cognate ['kɔgneit] *a* parent, connexe, analogue, qui a du rapport, de même origine.

cognizance ['kɔgnizəns] *n* connaissance *f*, compétence *f*, ressort *m*.

cogwheel ['kɔgwiːl] *n* roue dentée *f*.

cohabit [kou'hæbit] *vi* cohabiter.

cohabitation [,kouhæbi'teiʃən] *n* cohabitation *f*.

coheir ['kou'ɛə] *n* cohéritier, -ière.

cohere [kou'hiə] *vi* se tenir ensemble, adhérer, s'agglomérer, être conséquent, se tenir.

coherence [kou'hiərəns] *n* cohésion *f*, cohérence *f*, suite *f*.

coherent [kou'hiərənt] *a* cohérent, qui a de la suite, conséquent.

cohesion [kou'hiːʒən] *n* cohésion *f*.

cohesive [kou'hiːsiv] *a* adhérent, cohésif.

coil [kɔil] *n* rouleau *m*, bobine *f*, anneau *m*, repli *m*; *vt* embobiner, (en)rouler; **to — up** *vi* s'enrouler, se lover, se mettre en rond, serpenter; *vti* enrouler.

coin [kɔin] *n* pièce *f*, monnaie *f*; *vt* frapper, forger, inventer.

coinage ['kɔinidʒ] *n* frappe *f*, monnaie *f*.

coincide [ˌkouin'said] *vi* coincider, s'accorder.

coincidence [kou'insidəns] *n* coïncidence *f*, concours *m*.

coiner ['kɔinə] *n* faux-monnayeur *m*, forgeur *m*, inventeur *m*.

coke [kouk] *n* coke *m*.

colander ['kɔləndə] *n* passoire *f*.

cold [kould] *a* froid, insensible; *n* froid *m*, rhume *m*; — **in the head** rhume de cerveau *m*; **it is** — il fait froid; **he is** — il a froid; **to catch** — prendre froid, s'enrhumer, attraper un rhume; **to grow** — se refroidir.

coldness ['kouldnis] *n* froideur *f*, froid *m*, froidure *f*.

cold-shoulder ['kould'ʃouldə] *vt* battre froid à.

colic ['kɔlik] *n* colique *f*.

collaborate [kə'læbəreit] *vi* collaborer.

collaboration [kə,læbə'reiʃən] *n* collaboration *f*.

collaborator [kə'læbəreitə] *n* collaborateur, -trice.

collapse [kə'læps] *n* effondrement *m*, écroulement *m*, dégringolade *f*, débâcle *f*; *vi* s'effondrer, s'écrouler, s'affaiser, se rabattre.

collapsible [kə'læpsəbl] *a* pliant, démontable, rabattable.

collar ['kɔlə] *n* (faux-)col *m*, collier *m*, collerette *f*, collet *m*; *vt* prendre au collet, saisir.

collarbone ['kɔləboun] *n* clavicule *f*.

colleague ['kɔliːg] *n* collègue *mf*.

collect [kə'lekt] *vr* rassembler, réunir, percevoir, ramasser; *vi* se rassembler, s'amasser, faire la quête.

collected [kə'lektid] *a* froid, posé, recueilli, de sang-froid.

collection [kə'lekʃən] *n* collecte *f*, quête *f*, levée *f*, collection *f*, rassemblement *m*, collectionnement *m*, recueil *m*, perception *f*.

collective [kə'lektiv] *a* collectif.

collector [kə'lektə] *n* collecteur, -trice, collectionneur, -euse, quêteur, -euse, percepteur, -trice, receveur, -euse, encaisseur *m*; **ticket** — contrôleur *m*.

college ['kɔlidʒ] *n* collège *m*, école *f*.

collide [kə'laid] *vi* se heurter.

collier ['kɔliə] *n* mineur *m* (de charbon), (navire) charbonnier *m*.

colliery ['kɔljəri] *n* mine *f* de houille.

collision [kə'liʒən] *n* collision *f*, tamponnement *m*.

colloquial [kə'loukwiəl] *a* familier, parlé.

colloquy ['kɔləkwi] *n* colloque *m*.

collusion [kə'luːʒən] *n* collusion *f*, connivence *f*.

colon ['koulən] *n* deux-points *m*.

colonel ['kəːnl] *n* colonel *m*.

colonial [kə'lounjəl] *a* colonial.

colonist ['kɔlənist] *n* colon *m*.

colonization [ˌkɔlənai'zeiʃən] *n* colonisation *f*.

colonize ['kɔlənaiz] *vt* coloniser.

colony ['kɔləni] *n* colonie *f*.

colossal [kə'lɔsl] *a* colossal.

colossus [kə'lɔsəs] *n* colosse *m*.

color ['kʌlə] *n* couleur *f*, coloris *m*, teint *m*; *pl* drapeau *m*, cocarde *f*, livrée *f*; *vt* colorer, colorier, présenter sous un faux jour; *vi* rougir, se colorer; **in its true** —**s** sous son vrai jour; **to be off** — n'être pas dans son assiette; **with flying** —**s** haut la main.

color-bar ['kʌləbɑː] *n* racisme *m*.

color-blind ['kʌləblaind] *a* daltonien.

color-blindness ['kʌləblaindnis] *n* daltonisme *m*.

colored ['kʌləd] *a* coloré, de couleur.

colorful ['kʌləful] *a* pittoresque, coloré.

coloring ['kʌləriŋ] *n* coloris *m*, coloration *f*, teint *m*.

colorless ['kʌləlis] *a* incolore, terne, pâle.

colt [koult] *n* poulain *m*, pouliche *f*.

column ['kɔləm] *n* colonne *f*.

comb [koum] *n* peigne *m*, étrille *f*, carde *f*, crête *f*; *vt* peigner, étriller, carder, fouiller; *vi* déferler; **to** — **out** démêler, faire une rafle dans.

combat ['kɔmbæt] *n* combat *m*; *vt* combattre, lutter contre, s'opposer à.

combatant ['kɔmbətənt] *n* combattant *m*.

combative ['kɔmbətiv] *a* combatif, batailleur.

combination [ˌkɔmbi'neiʃən] *n* combinaison *f*, mélange *m*, combiné *m*.

combine ['kɔmbain] *n* combinaison *f*, cartel *m*; [kəm'bain] *vt* combiner, unir, joindre, allier; *vi* se combiner, s'unir, fusionner, se syndiquer.

combined [kəm'baind] *a* combiné, joint (à **with**).

combustible [kəm'bʌstibl] *a* inflammable; *an* combustible *m*.

combustion [kəm'bʌstʃən] *n* combustion *f*.

come [kʌm] *vi* venir, arriver, en venir (à), en arriver (à); **to** — **about** arriver, se passer, se faire; **to** — **across** tomber sur, rencontrer, trouver; **to** — **along** s'en venir, s'amener, se dépêcher; **to** — **away** partir, se détacher; **to** — **back** revenir, en revenir (à); **to** — **by** *vi* passer par; *vt* obtenir; **to** — **down** *vti* descendre; *vi* baisser, s'abaisser, s'écrouler; **to** — **forward** (s')avancer; **to** — **in** entrer; **to** — **off** descendre, se détacher, s'effacer, avoir lieu, réussir, aboutir; **to** — **out** sortir, débuter, paraître, se montrer, s'effacer, se mettre en grève; **to** — **to** revenir à soi, reprendre connaissance; **to** — **up to** s'approcher de, venir à, répondre à, s'élever à; **to** — **up against** entrer en conflit avec, se heurter avec; **to — upon** tomber sur, surprendre.

come-back ['kʌmbæk] *n* retour *m* (à la charge), réplique *f*, réapparition *f*.

comedian [kə'miːdjən] *n* auteur *m*, (acteur) comique, comédien, -ienne.

comedy ['kɔmidi] *n* comédie *f*.

comeliness ['kʌmlinis] *n* grâce *f*.

comely ['kʌmli] *a* gracieux, avenant.

comer ['kʌmə] *n* (premier, -ière, nouveau, -elle) venu(e) *mf* arrivant(e) *mf*, venant(e) *mf*.

comet ['kɔmit] *n* comète *f*.

comfit ['kʌmfit] *n* dragée *f*, bonbon *m*.

comfort ['kʌmfət] *n* (ré)confort *m*, aisance *f*, bienêtre *m*, confortable *m*, consolation *f*, soulagement *m*; *pl* douceurs *f pl*, gâteries *f pl*; *vt* réconforter, consoler, soulager, mettre à l'aise.

comfortable ['kʌmfətəbl] *a* à l'aise, bien, confortable, aisé, commode.

comforter ['kʌmfətə] *n* consolateur, -trice, cache-nez *m*, écharpe *f*, tétine *f*, sucette *f*.

comic ['kɔmik] *an* comique *m*.

comical ['kɔmikəl] *a* comique, drôle.

coming ['kʌmiŋ] *a* prochain, à venir, futur, d'avenir; *n* venue *f*, arrivée *f*, approche *f*, avènement *m*; **— of age** majorité *f*.

comity ['kɔmiti] *n* affabilité *f*.

comma ['kɔmə] *n* virgule *f*; **inverted —s** guillemets *m pl*.

command [kə'mɑːnd] *n* ordre *m*, commandement *m*, maîtrise *f*; *vt* ordonner, commander (à), dominer.

commandeer [ˌkɔmən'diə] *vt* réquisitionner.

commander [kə'mɑːndə] *n* commandeur *m*, commandant *m* (en chef), capitaine de frégate *m*.

commanding [kə'mɑːndiŋ] *a* imposant, dominateur, dominant.

commandment [kə'mɑːndmənt] *n* commandement *m*.

commemorate [kə'meməreit] *vt* commémorer.

commemoration [kəˌmemə'reiʃən] *n* commémoration *f*.

commemorative [kə'memərətiv] *a* commémoratif.

commence [kə'mens] *vti* commencer.

commencement [kə'mensmənt] *n* commencement *m*.

commend [kə'mend] *vt* confier, recommander, louer.

commendable [kə'mendəbl] *a* recommandable, louable.

commendation [ˌkɔmen'deiʃən] *n* recommandation *f*, éloge *m*, louange *f*.

commensurate [kə'menʃərit] *a* proportionné, commensurable.

comment ['kɔment] *vi* commenter, faire des observations; *n* commentaire *m*, observation *f*.

commentary ['kɔmentəri] *n* com-

mentaire *m*, glose *f*; **running —** radio-reportage *m*.

commentator ['kɔmenteitə] *n* commentateur, -trice, radio-reporter *m*.

commerce ['kɔməːs] *n* commerce *m*, les affaires *f pl*.

commercial [kə'məːʃəl] *a* commercial, mercantile; *n* annonce publicitaire *f*; **— traveler** *n* commis-voyageur *m*.

commiserate [kə'mizəreit] *vi* compatir (à **with**), s'apitoyer (sur **with**).

commiseration [kəˌmizə'reiʃən] *n* commisération *f*.

commissary ['kɔmisəri] *n* délégué *m*, intendant *m*.

commission [kə'miʃən] *n* commission *f*, courtage *m*, guelte *f*, délégation *f*, mandat *m*, brevet *m*, nomination *f*, perpétration *f*; *vt* mandater, nommer, charger (de), commissionner, déléguer, (**ship**) armer.

commissionaire [kəˌmiʃə'nɛə] *n* commissionnaire *m*, chasseur *m*.

commissioned [kə'miʃənd] *a* commissionné; **non— officer** sous-officier *m*.

commissioner [kə'miʃənə] *n* commissaire *m*, délégué *m*.

commit [kə'mit] *vt* confier, remettre, commettre, compromettre, renvoyer, engager; **— to memory** apprendre par cœur; **— suicide** se suicider.

commitment [kə'mitmənt] *n* engagement *m*.

committal [kə'mitl] *n* engagement *m*, perpétration *f*.

committee [kə'miti] *n* comité *m*, commission *f*, conseil *m*.

commode [kə'moud] *n* commode *f*, chaise percée *f*.

commodious [kə'moudjəs] *a* spacieux, ample.

commodiousness [kə'moudjəsnis] *n* grandeur *f*.

commodity [kə'mɔditi] *n* denrée *f*, marchandise *f*, article *m*.

common ['kɔmən] *a* commun, public, vulgaire, ordinaire, courant, coutumier, (*mil*) simple, communal.

commonalty ['kɔmənəlti] *n* commun *m* des hommes, les roturiers *m pl*.

commoner ['kɔmənə] *n* bourgeois(e) *mf*, homme du peuple, roturier, -ière.

commonly ['kɔmənli] *ad* communément, vulgairement.

commonness ['kɔmənnis] *n* vulgarité *f*, trivialité *f*, fréquence *f*.

commonplace ['kɔmənpleis] *n* lieu commun *m*; *a* banal, terre à terre.

commons ['kɔmənz] *n* peuple *m*; **the House of Commons** = la Chambre des Députés.

commonsense ['kɔmənˌsens] *n* bon sens *m*, sens commun *m*.

commonweal ['kɔmənwiːl] *n* bien public *m*, chose publique *f*.

commonwealth ['kɔmənwelθ] *n* république *f*, commonwealth *m*.
commotion [kə'mouʃən] *n* commotion *f*, émoi *m*, agitation *f*, ébranlement *m*, brouhaha *m*, troubles *m pl*.
communal ['kɔmjuːnl] *a* communal, public, (*life*) collectif.
commune [kə'mjuːn] *vi* communier s'entretenir; **to — with oneself** se recueillir, vivre en soi.
communicable [kə'mjuːnikəbl] *a* communicable, contagieux.
communicant [kə'mjuːnikənt] *n* communiant(e) *mf*, informateur, -trice.
communicate [kə'mjuːnikeit] *vti* communiquer; *vi* communier, faire part de.
communication [kə.mjuːni'keiʃən] *n* communication *f*, rapports *m pl*.
communicative [kə'mjuːnikətiv] *a* communicatif, expansif.
communion [kə'mjuːnjən] *n* communion *f*, relations *f pl*.
communism ['kɔmjunizəm] *n* communisme *m*.
communist ['kɔmjunist] *an* communiste *mf*.
community [kə'mjuːniti] *n* communauté *f*, solidarité *f*, société *f*.
communize ['kɔmjunaiz] *vt* socialiser, communiser.
commutable [kə'mjuːtəbl] *a* échangeable, permutable, commuable.
commutation [.kɔmjuː'teiʃən] *n* commutation *f*.
commute [kə'mjuːt] *vt* (é)changer, commuer.
compact ['kɔmpækt] *n* contrat *m*, accord *m*, pacte *m*, poudrier *m*; [kəm'pækt] *a* compact, tassé, serré, concis.
compactness [kəm'pæktnis] *n* compacité *f*, concision *f*.
companion [kəm'pænjən] *n* compagnon *m*, compagne *f*, demoiselle (dame) de compagnie *f*.
companionable [kəm'pænjənəbl] *a* sociable.
companionship [kəm'pænjənʃip] *n* camaraderie *f*.
company ['kʌmpəni] *n* compagnie *f*, (*ship*) équipage *m*, société *f*, corporation *f*, bande *f*, troupe *f*; **to have — for dinner** avoir du monde à dîner.
comparable ['kɔmpərəbl] *a* comparable.
comparative [kəm'pærətiv] *a* comparatif, relatif.
comparatively [kəm'pærətivli] *ad* par comparaison, relativement.
compare [kəm'pɛə] *vt* comparer, confronter, collationner, expliquer.
compared [kəm'pɛəd] *pt pp of* **compare; — with** *prep* à côte de, par rapport à, au prix de, par comparaison à.
comparison [kəm'pærisn] *n* comparaison *f*.

compartment [kəm'pɑːtmənt] *n* compartiment *m*, case *f*.
compass ['kʌmpəs] *n* compas *m*, boussole *f*, portée *f*, limites *f pl*, détour *m*; *vt* faire le tour de, entourer, saisir, tramer, exécuter.
compassion [kəm'pæʃən] *n* compassion *f*, pitié *f*.
compassionate [kəm'pæʃənit] *a* compatissant.
compatibility [kəm.pæti'biliti] *n* compatibilité *f*.
compatible [kəm'pætibl] *a* compatible.
compatriot [kəm'pætriət] *n* compatriote *mf*.
compel [kəm'pel] *vt* contraindre, forcer, obliger, imposer.
compendious [kəm'pendiəs] *a* succinct.
compendium [kəm'pendiəm] *n* abrégé *m*.
compensate ['kɔmpenseit] *vt* (ré)compenser, rémunérer, dédommager; **to — for** racheter, compenser.
compensation [.kɔmpen'seiʃən] *n* dédommamgeent *m*, indemnité *f*.
compete [kəm'piːt] *vi* rivaliser, concourir, faire concurrence, disputer.
competence ['kɔmpitəns] *n* compétence *f*, aisance *f*.
competent ['kɔmpitənt] *a* compétent, capable.
competition [.kɔmpi'tiʃən] *n* concurrence *f*, concours *m*.
competitive [kəm'petitiv] *a* de concours, de concurrence.
competitor [kəm'petitə] *n* compétiteur, -trice, concurrent(e) *mf*, émule *mf*.
compilation [.kɔmpi'leiʃən] *n* compilation *f*.
compile [kəm'pail] *vt* compiler, dresser.
compiler [kəm'pailə] *n* compilateur, -trice.
complacency [kəm'pleisnsi] *n* contentement *m* (de soi), suffisance *f*.
complacent [kəm'pleisnt] *a* suffisant, content de soi-même.
complain [kəm'plein] *vi* se plaindre, porter plainte.
complainer [kəm'pleinə] *n* réclamant(e) *mf*, mécontent(e) *mf*.
complaint [kəm'pleint] *n* plainte *f*, grief *m*, maladie *f*.
complaisance [kəm'pleizəns] *n* complaisance *f*.
complaisant [kəm'pleizənt] *a* complaisant, obligeant.
complement ['kɔmplimənt] *n* complément *m*; [.kɔmpli'ment] *vt* compléter.
complete [kəm'pliːt] *a* complet, entier, total, absolu, accompli, achevé, au complet; *vt* compléter, accomplir, achever, mettre le comble à.

completion [kəm'pli:ʃən] *n* achèvement *m*, accomplissement *m*, satisfaction *f*.

complex ['kɔmpleks] *an* complexe *m*.

complexion [kəm'plekʃən] *n* teint *m*, jour *m*, couleur *f*, caractère *m*.

complexity [kəm'pleksiti] *n* complexité *f*.

compliance [kəm'plaiəns] *n* déférence *f*, acquiescement *m*; **in —** **with** conformément à.

compliant [kəm'plaiənt] *a* obligeant, docile.

complicate ['kɔmplikeit] *vt* compliquer.

complication [.kɔmpli'keiʃən] *n* complication *f*.

complicity [kəm'plisiti] *n* complicité *f*.

compliment ['kɔmplimənt] *n* compliment *m*; [.kɔmpli'ment] *vt* féliciter, complimenter.

complimentary [.kɔmpli'mentəri] *a* flatteur, (*ticket*) de faveur, (*book*) en hommage.

comply [kəm'plai] *vi* se conformer (à **with**), accéder (à **with**), obéir (à **with**). observer, se soumettre (à **with**), s'exécuter.

component [kəm'pounənt] *n* élément *m*, composant *m*; *a* constitutif, constituant.

compose [kəm'pouz] *vt* composer, arranger; **to — oneself** se calmer, se remettre.

composed [kəm'pouzd] *a* calme, posé, composé.

composer [kəm'pouzə] *n* compositeur, -trice.

composite ['kɔmpəzit] *a* composite, composé.

composition [.kɔmpə'ziʃən] *n* composition *f*, constitution *f*, arrangement *m*, composé *m*, mélange *m*, rédaction *f*, dissertation *f*.

compositor [kəm'pozitə] *n* typographe *m*, compositeur *m*.

composure [kəm'pouʒə] *n* calme *m*, maîtrise de soi *f*, sang-froid *m*.

compound ['kɔmpaund] *an* composé *m*, concession *f*; **— interest** intérêts composés; *a* complexe; *n* mastic *m*.

compound [kəm'paund] *vt* mélanger, combiner, arranger, composer; *vi* s'arranger, transiger.

comprehend [.kɔmpri'hend] *vt* comprendre.

comprehensible [.kɔmpri'hensəbl] *a* compréhensible.

comprehension [.kɔmpri'henʃən] *n* compréhension *f*.

comprehensive [.kɔmpri'hensiv] *a* compréhensif; **— school** collège pilote (mixte) *f*.

comprehensiveness [.kɔmpri'hensivnis] *n* étendue *f*, portée *f*.

compress ['kɔmpres] *n* compresse *f*.

compress [kəm'pres] *vt* comprimer, bander, condenser, concentrer.

comprise [kəm'praiz] *vt* comprendre, comporter, renfermer.

compromise ['kɔmprəmaiz] *n* compromis *m*; *vi* transiger; *vti* compromettre; **to — oneself** se compromettre.

compulsion [kəm'pʌlʃən] *n* force *f*, contrainte *f*.

compulsory [kəm'pʌlsəri] *a* obligatoire, coercitif.

compunction [kəm'pʌŋkʃən] *n* remords *m*, regret *m*, componction *f*.

computation [.kɔmpju'teiʃən] *n* calcul *m*, estimation *f*.

compute [kəm'pju:t] *vt* calculer, estimer.

computer [kəm'pju:tə] *n* ordinateur *m*, calculateur *m*.

comrade ['kɔmrid] *n* camarade *m*, compagnon *m*.

comradeship ['kɔmridʃip] *n* camaraderie *f*.

con [kɔn] *vt* étudier, diriger, escroquer.

concave ['kɔn'keiv] *a* concave, incurvé.

conceal [kən'si:l] *vt* cacher, dissimuler, céler, voiler, dérober, masquer.

concealment [kən'si:lmənt] *n* dissimulation *f*, réticence *f*.

concede [kən'si:d] *vt* accorder, concéder, admettre.

conceit [kən'si:t] *n* vanité *f*, suffisance *f*, pointe *f*, jugement *m*.

conceited [kən'si:tid] *a* vaniteux, suffisant, glorieux.

conceivable [kən'si:vəbl] *a* concevable.

conceive [kən'si:v] *vt* concevoir; *vi* s'imaginer.

concentrate ['kɔnsəntreit] *vt* concentrer; *vi* se concentrer.

concentration [.kɔnsən'treiʃən] *n* concentration *f*, application *f*, rassemblement *m*.

conception [kən'sepʃən] *n* conception *f*, idée *f*.

concern [kən'sə:n] *n* intérêt *m*, sympathie *f*, affaire *f*, souci *m*, sollicitude *f*, maison *f* de commerce, entreprise *f*; **the whole —** toute la boutique; *vt* regarder, concerner intéresser, importer; **to — oneself** **with** s'occuper de, s'intéresser à.

concerned [kən'sə:nd] *a* préoccupé (de **with**), intéressé, (à **with**), inquiet, soucieux.

concerning [kən'sə:niŋ] *prep* quant à, au sujet de, en ce qui concerne, pour ce qui est de.

concert ['kɔnsət] *n* concert *m*, accord *m*, unisson *m*; **— hall** salle *f* de concert; **in — with** de concert avec.

concert [kən'sə:t] *vt* concerter; *vi* se concerter.

concession [kən'seʃən] *n* concession *f*.

conciliate [kən'silieit] *v t* (ré)concilier

conciliation [kən͵sili'eiʃən] *n* conciliation *f*.
conciliatory [kən'siliətəri] *a* conciliant, conciliatoire.
concise [kən'sais] *a* concis.
concision [kən'siʒən] *n* concision *f*.
conclude [kən'kluːd] *vti* conclure; *vi* se terminer; *vt* terminer, achever, régler.
conclusion [kən'kluːʒən] *n* conclusion *f*, fin *f*.
conclusive [kən'kluːsiv] *a* concluant, décisif.
conclusiveness [kən'kluːsivnis] *n* force décisive *f*.
concoct [kən'kɔkt] *vt* confectionner, composer, combiner, imaginer, concevoir.
concoction [kən'kɔkʃən] *n* pot-pourri *m*, boisson *f*, confectionnement *m*, conception *f*, tissu *m*.
concord ['kɔŋkɔːd] *n* harmonie *f*, accord *m*.
concordance [kən'kɔːdəns] *n* concordance *f*, harmonie *f*, accord *m*.
concordant [kən'kɔːdənt] *a* concordant.
concourse ['kɔŋkɔːs] *n* concourse *m*, affluence *f*, foule *f*.
concrete ['kɔnkriːt] *n* ciment *m*, béton *m*; **reinforced —** béton armé; *a* concret *m*.
concrete [kən'kriːt] *vt* solidifier, cimenter, bétonner; *vi* se solidifier.
concur [kən'kəː] *vi* s'accorder, contribuer, concourir, être d'accord.
concurrence [kən'kʌrəns] *n* concours *m*, approbation *f*, assentiment *m*.
concurrent [kən'kʌrənt] *a* concurrent, simultané.
concurrently [kən'kʌrəntli] *ad* concurremment.
concussion [kən'kʌʃən] *n* commotion *f*, secousse *f*, ébranlement *m*, choc *m*.
condemn [kən'dem] *vt* condamner, censurer.
condemnation [͵kɔndem'neiʃən] *n* condamnation *f*, censure *f*.
condensation [͵kɔnden'seiʃən] *n* condensation *f*.
condense [kən'dens] *vt* condenser, concentrer, serrer; *vi* se condenser.
condenser [kən'densə] *n* condenseur *m*, distillateur *m*.
condescend [͵kɔndi'send] *vi* condescendre, s'abaisser.
condescending [͵kɔndi'sendiŋ] *a* condescendant.
condescension [͵kɔndi'senʃən] *n* condescendance *f*, déférence *f*.
condign [kən'dain] *a* juste, merité, exemplaire.
condiment ['kɔndimənt] *n* assaisonnement *m*, condiment *m*.
condition [kən'diʃən] *n* condition *f*, situation *f*, état *m*; *vt* conditionner.
conditional [kən'diʃənl] *a* conditionnel, dépendant.

condolatory [kən'doulətəri] *a* de condoléance.
condole [kən'doul] *vi* sympathiser (avec **with**), exprimer ses condoléances (à **with**).
condolence [kən'douləns] *n* condoléances *f pl*.
condone [kən'doun] *vt* pardonner.
conduce [kən'djuːs] *vi* aboutir, contribuer.
conducive [kən'djuːsiv] *a* qui conduit (à **to**), qui contribue (à **to**), favorable (à **to**).
conduct ['kɔndəkt] *n* conduite *f*, gestion *f*.
conduct [kən'dʌkt] *vt* conduire, mener, diriger, gérer; **to — oneself** se conduire, se comporter.
conduction [kən'dʌkʃən] *n* conduction *f*, transmission *f*.
conductor [kən'dʌktə] *n* guide *m*, conducteur *m*, chef *m* d'orchestre, (*bus*) receveur *m*.
conductress [kən'dʌktris] *n* conductrice *f*, receveuse *f*.
conduit ['kɔndit] *n* conduit *m*.
cone [koun] *n* cône *m*, pomme de pin *f*.
confection [kən'fekʃən] *n* confection *f*; bonbons *m pl*, confits *m pl*.
confectioner [kən'fekʃənə] *n* confiseur *m*.
confectioner's [kən'fekʃənəz] *n* confiserie *f*.
confectionery [kən'fekʃnəri] *n* confiserie *f*.
confederacy [kən'fedərəsi] *n* confédération *f*, conspiration *f*.
confederate [kən'fedərit] *an* confédéré *m*; *n* complice *m*, comparse *m*.
confer [kən'fəː] *vti* conférer; *vt* accorder, octroyer.
conference ['kɔnfərəns] *n* conférence *f*, congrès *m*, consultation *f*.
conferment [kən'fəːmənt] *n* octroi *m*, attribution *f*.
confess [kən'fes] *vt* confesser, avouer; *vi* se confesser, faire des aveux.
confession [kən'feʃən] *n* confession *f*, aveu *m*; **to go to —** aller à confesse.
confessional [kən'feʃənl] *n* confessional *m*; *a* confessionel.
confessor [kən'fesə] *n* confesseur *m*.
confide [kən'faid] *vt* confier, avouer en confidence; *vi* se fier (à **in**).
confidence ['kɔnfidəns] *n* confidence *f*, confiance *f* (en soi), assurance *f*; **— game** fraude *f*.
confident ['kɔnfidənt] *a* confiant, assuré, sûr.
confidential [͵kɔnfi'denʃəl] *a* confidential, de confiance.
confidentially [͵kɔnfi'denʃəli] *ad* en confidence, à titre confidentiel.
confidently ['kɔnfidəntli] *ad* avec confiance.
confine [kən'fain] *vt* limiter, confiner, borner, emprisonner, renfermer.

confined [kən'faind] *a* (*space*) resserré; — **to bed** alité, (*woman*) en couches.

confinement [kən'fainmənt] *n* réclusion *f*, emprisonnement *m*, restriction *f*, accouchement *m*, couches *f pl.*

confines ['kɔnfainz] *n pl* confins *m pl.*

confirm [kən'fəːm] *vt* confirmer, fortifier, raffermir.

confirmation [,kɔnfə'meiʃən] *n* confirmation *f*, raffermissement *m*.

confirmed [kən'fəːmd] *a* invétéré, endurci, incorrigible.

confiscate ['kɔnfiskeit] *vt* confisquer.

confiscation [,kɔnfis'keiʃən] *n* confiscation *f*.

conflagration [,kɔnflə'greiʃən] *n* conflagration *f*, incendie *m*, embrasement *m*.

conflict ['kɔnflikt] *n* conflit *m*, lutte *f*.

conflict [kən'flikt] *vi* être en conflit, jurer, se heurter.

confluent ['kɔnfluənt] *n* confluent *m*, affluent *m*.

conform [kən'fɔːm] *vt* conformer; *vi* se conformer, obéir, s'adapter.

conformation [,kɔnfɔː'meiʃən] *n* conformation *f*, structure *f*.

conformity [kən'fɔːmiti] *n* conformité *f*; **in — with** conformément à.

confound [kən'faund] *vt* confondre, embarrasser, déconcerter.

confounded [kən'faundid] *a* maudit, sacré.

confraternity [,kɔnfrə'təːniti] *n* confrérie *f*, bande *f*.

confront [kən'frʌnt] *vt* affronter, confronter, faire face à, se trouver en présence de.

confuse [kən'fjuːz] *vt* mettre en désordre, confondre, embrouiller, (em)mêler.

confused [kən'fjuːzd] *a* confus, interdit, ahuri, bouleversé, trouble.

confusedly [kən'fjuːzidli] *ad* confusément.

confusion [kən'fjuːʒən] *n* confusion *f*, désordre *m*, désarroi *m*, remue-ménage *m*.

confutation [,kɔnfjuː'teiʃən] *n* réfutation.

confute [kən'fjuːt] *vt* réfuter, démolir les arguments de.

congeal [kən'dʒiːl] *vt* (con)geler, coaguler, figer; *vi* se congeler, se coaguler, se figer, se prendre.

congenial [kən'dʒiːnjəl] *a* du même caractère que, au goût de, sympathique, agréable, convenable.

congeniality [kən,dʒiːniː'æliti] *n* sympathie *f*, caractère agréable *m*, accord *m* de sentiments.

congest [kən'dʒest] *vt* congestionner, encombrer, embouteiller.

congestion [kən'dʒestʃən] *n* congestion *f*, encombrement *m*, embouteillage *m*, surpeuplement *m*.

conglomerate [kən'glɔməreit] *vt* conglomérer; *vi* se conglomérer, s'agglomérer.

congratulate [kən'grætjuleit] *vt* féliciter.

congratulation [kən,grætju'leiʃən] *n* félicitation *f*.

congregate ['kɔngrigeit] *vt* rassembler, réunir; *vi* se réunir, se rassembler.

congregation [,kɔngri'geiʃən] *n* congrégation *f*, assemblée *f*, amas *m*, rassemblement *m*.

congress ['kɔngres] *n* congrès *m*, réunion *f*.

congruency ['kɔngruənsi] *n* accord *m*, conformité *f*.

congruous ['kɔngruəs] *a* approprié, conforme.

conifer ['kɔnifə] *n* conifère *m*.

conjecture [kən'dʒektʃə] *n* conjecture *f*; *vt* conjecturer.

conjugal ['kɔndʒugəl] *a* conjugal.

conjugate ['kɔndʒugeit] *vt* conjuguer.

conjugation [,kɔndʒu'geiʃən] *n* conjugaison *f*.

conjunction [kən'dʒʌŋkʃən] *n* connexion *f*, jonction *f*, coïncidence *f*; **in — with** conjointement avec.

conjuncture [kən'dʒʌŋktʃə] *n* conjoncture *f*, circonstance *f*.

conjuration [,kɔndʒuə'reiʃən] *n* conjuration *f*, évocation *f*.

conjure [kən'dʒuə] *vt* conjurer, évoquer.

conjure ['kʌndʒə] *vi* faire des tours de prestidigitation; **to — away** escamoter.

conjurer ['kʌndʒərə] *n* prestidigitateur *m*.

connect [kə'nekt] *vt* (re)lier, rattacher, réunir, associer; *vi* se (re)lier, se réunir, faire correspondance.

connection [kə'nekʃən] *n* lien *m*, rapport *m*, sens *m*, égard *m*, parenté *f*, clientèle *f*, correspondance *f*, prise *f* de courant.

conning-tower ['kɔniŋ,tauə] *n* (sous-marin **submarine**) capot *m*.

connivance [kə'naivəns] *n* connivence *f*, complicité *f*.

connive [kə'naiv] *vi* être de connivence (avec **with**), fermer les yeux (sur **at**).

connubial [kə'njuːbjəl] *a* conjugal.

conquer ['kɔŋkə] *vt* conquérir, vaincre.

conqueror ['kɔŋkərə] *n* conquérant *m*, vainqueur *m*.

conquest ['kɔŋkwest] *n* conquête *f*.

conscience ['kɔnʃəns] *n* conscience *f*.

conscientious [,kɔnʃi'enʃəs] *a* consciencieux, scrupuleux.

conscientiousness [,kɔnʃi'enʃəsnis] *n* conscience *f*.

conscious ['kɔnʃəs] *a* conscient; **to be — of** sentir, avoir conscience de, s'apercevoir de; **to become —** reprendre connaissance.

consciously ['kɔnʃəsli] *ad* consciemment.

consciousness ['kɔnʃəsnis] *n* conscience *f*, connaissance *f*, sens *m*.

conscript ['kɔnskript] *an* conscrit *m*.

conscript [kən'skript] *vt* engager, enrôler.

conscription [kən'skripʃən] *n* conscription *f*.

consecrate ['kɔnsikreit] *vt* consacrer, bénir.

consecration [.kɔnsi'kreiʃən] *n* consécration *f*.

consecutive [kən'sekjutiv] *a* consécutif, de suite.

consensus [kən'sensəs] *n* accord *m*, unanimité *f*, consensus *m*.

consent [kən'sent] *n* consentement *m*, assentiment *m*, agrément *m*; *vi* consentir.

consequence ['kɔnsikwəns] *n* conséquence *f*, importance *f*.

consequent ['kɔnsikwənt] *a* résultant.

consequential [.kɔnsi'kwenʃəl] *a* conséquent, consécutif, important, plein de soi.

consequently ['kɔnsikwəntli] *ad* conséquemment, en conséquence.

conservation [.kɔnsə'veiʃən] *n* conservation *f*.

conservative [kən'səːvətiv] *an* conservateur, -trice.

conservatory [kən'səːvətri] *n* serre *f*, jardin *m* d'hiver.

conserve [kən'səːv] *vt* conserver, préserver.

conserves [kən'səːvz] *n pl* confitures *f pl*, conserves *f pl*.

consider [kən'sidə] *vt* considérer, réfléchir à, regarder, estimer, examiner, envisager, avoir égard à.

considerable [kən'sidərəbl] *a* considérable.

considerate [kən'sidərit] *a* attentif, prévenant.

considerately [kən'sidəritli] *ad* avec égards, avec prévenance.

consideration [kən.sidə'reiʃən] *n* considération *f*, réflexion *f*, récompense *f*, importance *f*; **in — of** eu égard à; **under — à** l'étude, en délibération; **after due —** tout bien considéré, après mûre réflection; **for a —** moyennant finance; **on no — pour** rien au monde, à aucun prix.

considering [kən'sidəriŋ] *ad* somme toute; *prep* étant donné, vu, eu égard à; *cj* vu que, attendu que.

consign [kən'sain] *vt* livrer, expédier, déposer, consigner.

consignment [kən'sainmənt] *n* expédition *f*, envoi *m*, dépôt *m*; — **note** récépissé *m*, lettre de voiture *f*.

consist [kən'sist] *vi* consister (en, à **of**), se composer (de **of**).

consistence [kən'sistəns] *n* consistance *f*.

consistency [kən'sistənsi] *n* suite *f*,

logique *f*, uniformité *f*, régularité *f*.

consistent [kən'sistənt] *a* compatible, fidèle (à **with**), conséquent, logique, régulier.

consolation [.kɔnsə'leiʃən] *n* consolation *f*.

console [kən'soul] *vt* consoler.

console ['kɔnsoul] *n* console *f*.

consolidate [kən'sɔlideit] *vt* consolider, raffermir, unifier.

consolidation [kən.sɔli'deiʃən] *n* consolidation *f*, raffermissement *m*.

consols [kən'sɔlz] *n pl* fonds consolidés *m pl*.

consonance ['kɔnsənəns] *n* consonance *f*, accord *m*.

consonant ['kɔnsənənt] *n* consonne *f*; *a* compatible, harmonieux, qui s'accorde.

consort ['kɔnsɔːt] *n* consort(e) *mf*, époux, -se *mf*.

consort [kən'sɔːt] *vi* **to — with** fréquenter, frayer avec.

conspicuous [kən'spikjuəs] *a* marquant, insigne, remarquable, en vue, en évidence; **to make oneself — se** faire remarquer, se signaler.

conspiracy [kən'spirəsi] *n* conspiration *f*, conjuration *f*.

conspirator [kən'spirətə] *n* conspirateur, -trice, conjuré *m*.

conspire [kən'spaiə] *vi* conspirer, comploter, agir de concert, concourir.

constable ['kʌnstəbl] *n* agent *m* de police, gendarme *m*; **chief —** commissaire *m* de police.

constabulary [kən'stæbjuləri] *n* police *f*, gendarmerie *f*.

constancy ['kɔnstənsi] *n* constance *f*, régularité *f*, fidelité *f*, fermeté *f*.

constant ['kɔnstənt] *a* constant, continuel, fidèle, invariable.

constantly ['kɔnstəntli] *ad* constamment, toujours.

constellation [.kɔnstə'leiʃən] *n* constellation *f*.

consternation [.kɔnstə'neiʃən] *n* consternation *f*.

constipate ['kɔnstipeit] *vt* constiper.

constipation [.kɔnsti'peiʃən] *n* constipation *f*.

constituency [kən'stitjuənsi] *n* circonscription *f*, collège électoral *m*.

constituent [kən'stitjuənt] *n* électeur, -trice, élément *m*; *a* constituant, constitutif.

constitute ['kɔnstitjuːt] *vt* constituer.

constitution [.kɔnsti'tjuːʃən] *n* constitution *f*, composition *f*, santé *f*.

constitutional [.kɔnsti'tjuːʃənl] *a* constitutionnel.

constrain [kən'strein] *vt* contraindre, forcer.

constraint [kən'streint] *n* contrainte *f*, retenue *f*.

constrict [kən'strikt] *vt* rétrécir, (res)serrer, étrangler.

constriction [kən'strikʃən] *n* étranglement *m*, resserrement *m*.

construct [kən'strʌkt] vt construire, établir, charpenter.

construction [kən'strʌkʃən] n construction f, établissement m, édifice m, interprétation f.

construe [kən'struː] vt traduire, interpréter, expliquer, analyser.

consul ['kɔnsəl] n consul m.

consular ['kɔnsjulə] a consulaire.

consulate ['kɔnsjulit] n consulat m.

consult [kən'sʌlt] vti consulter.

consultation [.kɔnsəl'teiʃən] n consultation f, délibération f.

consume [kən'sjum] vt consumer, consommer, épuiser, perdre.

consumer [kən'sjumə] n consommateur, -trice.

consummate [kən'sʌmit] a consommé, achevé.

consummate ['kɔnsʌmeit] vt consommer.

consummation [.kɔnsʌ'meiʃən] n consommation f, comble m.

consumption [kən'sʌmpʃən] n consomption f, phtisie f, consommation f.

consumptive [kən'sʌmptiv] a phtisique, tuberculeux.

contact ['kɔntækt] n contact m, rapport m; vt se mettre en rapport avec, contacter.

contagion [kən'teidʒən] n contagion f.

contagious [kən'teidʒəs] a contagieux, communicatif.

contain [kən'tein] vt contenir, comporter, renfermer, retenir.

container [kən'teinə] n récipient m.

contaminate [kən'tæmineit] vt contaminer, vicier, corrompre.

contamination [kən.tæmi'neiʃən] n contamination f.

contemplate ['kɔntempleit] vt contempler, considérer, envisager; vi méditer, se recueillir.

contemplation [.kɔntem'pleiʃən] n contemplation f, recueillement m.

contemplative ['kɔntempleitiv] a contemplatif, recueilli.

contemporary [kən'tempərəri] an contemporain(e) mf.

contempt [kən'tempt] n mépris m.

contemptible [kən'temptəbl] a méprisable.

contemptuous [kən'temptjuəs] a méprisant, de mépris.

contend [kən'tend] vi lutter, disputer, rivaliser; vt soutenir, prétendre.

content [kən'tent] n contentement m, contenance f; a content; vt contenter.

contentedly [kən'tentidli] ad avec plaisir.

contention [kən'tenʃən] n discussion f, rivalité f, idée f, prétention f.

contentious [kən'tenʃəs] a disputeur, chicanier, discutable.

contentment [kən'tentmənt] n contentement m.

contents ['kɔntents] n pl contenu m, table des matières f.

contest ['kɔntest] n lutte f, concours m.

contest [kən'test] vt contester, disputer, débattre.

contestation [.kɔntes'teiʃən] n contestation f.

context ['kɔntekst] n contexte m.

contiguous [kən'tigjuəs] a contigu, -uë.

continence ['kɔntinəns] n continence f.

continent ['kɔntinənt] an continent m.

continental [.kɔnti'nentl] a continental.

contingent [kən'tindʒənt] n contingent m; a éventuel, subordonné.

continual [kən'tinjuəl] a continuel, sans cesse.

continuation [kən.tinju'eiʃən] n continuation f, durée f, suite f.

continue [kən'tinju] vti continuer; vt maintenir, poursuivre, prolonger; vi se prolonger.

continuity [.kɔnti'njuiti] n continuité f.

continuous [kən'tinjuəs] a continu, permanent.

continuously [kən'tinjuəsli] ad continûment, sans arrêt, sans désemparer.

contort [kən'tɔːt] vt tordre, crisper.

contortion [kən'tɔːʃən] n contorsion f, crispation f.

contour ['kɔntuə] n contour m, profil m, tracé m.

contraband ['kɔntrəbænd] n contrebande f.

contraceptive [.kɔntrə'septiv] n préservatif m; a anticonceptionnel.

contract ['kɔntrækt] n contrat m, entreprise f.

contract [kən'trækt] vt contracter, resserrer, crisper; vi s'engager, se rétrécir, se crisper, se contracter.

contraction [kən'trækʃən] n contraction f, rétrécissement m, crispement m.

contractor [kən'træktə] n entrepreneur m, (mil) fournisseur m.

contradict [.kɔntrə'dikt] vt démentir, contredire.

contradiction [.kɔntrə'dikʃən] n contradiction f, démenti m.

contradictory [.kɔntrə'diktəri] a contradictoire.

contraption [kən'træpʃən] n machin m, truc m, dispositif m.

contrary ['kɔntrəri] a contraire, opposé; on the — au contraire.

contrast ['kɔntrɑːst] n contraste m.

contrast [kən'trɑːst] vi contraster; vt mettre en contraste, opposer.

contravene [.kɔntrə'viːn] vt enfreindre, contrevenir à, s'opposer à.

contravention [.kɔntrə'venʃən] n violation f, contravention f.

contribute [kən'tribjut] vti con-

tribuer (à **to**), souscrire; **to — to a newspaper** collaborer à un journal.
contribution [ˌkɔntri'bju:ʃən] n contribution f.
contrite ['kɔntrait] a contrit.
contrivance [kən'traivəns] n invention f, manigance f, ingéniosité f, dispositif m.
contrive [kən'traiv] vt inventer, combiner; vi s'arranger (pour **to**), trouver moyen (de **to**).
control [kən'troul] n contrôle m, maîtrise f, autorité f; vt contrôler, maîtriser, diriger.
controller [kən'troulə] n contrôleur, -euse, commande f.
controversial [ˌkɔntrə'və:ʃəl] a controversable, (person) disputeur.
controversy ['kɔntrəvə:si] n controverse f.
contumacious [ˌkɔntju'meiʃəs] a rebelle, contumace.
contuse [kən'tju:z] vt contusionner.
contusion [kən'tju:ʒən] n contusion f.
conundrum [kə'nʌndrəm] n énigme f, problème m, devinette f.
convalesce [ˌkɔnvə'les] vi être en convalescence, relever de maladie.
convalescence [ˌkɔnvə'lesns] n convalescence f.
convalescent [ˌkɔnvə'lesnt] a convalescent.
convector [kən'vektə] n appareil m de chauffage par convection.
convene [kən'vi:n] vt convoquer; vi se réunir.
convenience [kən'vi:njəns] n convenance f, commodité f, avantage m; pl commodités f pl, agréments m pl.
convenient [kən'vi:njənt] a commode.
conveniently [kən'vi:njəntli] ad commodément, sans inconvénient.
convent ['kɔnvənt] n couvent m.
convention [kən'vənʃən] n convention f, convocation f, usage m; pl bienséances f pl.
conventional [kən'venʃənl] a conventionnel, normal, ordinaire, classique, stylisé.
conventionality [kən,venʃə'næliti] n formalisme m, bienséances f pl.
converge [kən'və:dʒ] vi converger.
convergence [kən'və:dʒəns] n convergence f.
conversant [kən'və:sənt] a familiar, versé, au courant (de **with**).
conversation [ˌkɔnvə'seiʃən] n conversation f, entretien m.
converse ['kɔnvə:s] an réciproque f, converse f.
converse [kən'və:s] vi causer, s'entretenir.
conversely ['kɔnvə:sli] ad réciproquement.
conversion [kən'və:ʃən] n conversion f.
convert ['kɔnvə:t] n converti(e) mf.

convert [kən'və:t] vt convertir, transformer.
convex ['kɔn'veks] a convexe, bombé.
convey [kən'vei] vt (trans)porter, transmettre, communiquer.
conveyance [kən'veiəns] n transport m, voiture f, transmission f.
convict ['kɔnvikt] n forçat m.
convict [kən'vikt] vt convaincre, condamner.
conviction [kən'vikʃən] n conviction f, condamnation f.
convince [kən'vins] vt convaincre, persuader.
convivial [kən'viviəl] a plein d'entrain, jovial, de fête.
convocation [ˌkɔnvə'keiʃən] n convocation f, assemblée f.
convoke [kən'vouk] vt convoquer.
convoy ['kɔnvɔi] n convoi m, escorte f.
convoy ['kɔnvɔi] vt convoyer, escorter.
convulse [kən'vʌls] vt bouleverser, décomposer, tordre, convulser.
convulsion [kən'vʌlʃən] n convulsion f, bouleversement m.
convulsive [kən'vʌlsiv] a convulsif.
coo [ku:] vi roucouler.
cook [kuk] n cuisinier, -ière; vti cuire, cuisiner; vt faire cuire; maquiller, truquer.
cooker ['kukə] n réchaud m, cuisinière f.
cookery ['kukəri] n cuisine f.
cool [ku:l] n frais m, fraîcheur f; a frais, rafraîchissant, impudent, imperturbable; vt rafraîchir, refroidir; vi se rafraîchir, se refroidir.
cooler ['ku:lə] n seau m à glace, refroidisseur m, taule f.
coolly ['ku:li] ad froidement, avec sang-froid.
coolness ['ku:lnis] n fraîcheur f, sang-froid m.
coop [ku:p] n mue f; vt enfermer, claustrer.
co-operate [kou'ɔpəreit] vi coopérer, collaborer.
co-operation [kou,ɔpə'reiʃən] n collaboration f, coopération f, concours m.
co-operative stores [kou'ɔpərətiv ˌstɔːz] n coopérative f.
co-opt [kou'ɔpt] vt coopter.
co-ordinate [kou'ɔ:dineit] vt co-ordonner.
co-ordination [kou,ɔ:di'neiʃən] n coordination f.
cop [kɔp] n fuseau m, flic m; vt pincer, attraper, écoper.
cope [koup] **to — with** faire face à, tenir tête à, venir à bout de.
copious ['koupjəs] a copieux, abondant.
copiousness ['koupjəsnis] n abondance f.
copper ['kɔpə] n cuivre m, billon m, sou m, lessiveuse f, sergot m.
copse [kɔps] n taillis m.

copy ['kɔpi] *n* copie *f*, exemplaire *m*, numéro *m*; *vt* copier, imiter, se modeler sur.

copyist ['kɔpiist] *n* copiste *mf*.

copyright ['kɔpirait] *n* proprieté littéraire *f*, droit d'auteur *m*.

coral ['kɔrəl] *n* corail *m*.

cord [kɔːd] *n* cordelette *f*, cordon *m*, (*vocal*) cordes *f pl*, étoffe *f* à côtes, ganse *f*; *vt* corder.

corded ['kɔːdid] *a* côtelé, à côtes.

cordial ['kɔːdjəl] *an* cordial *m*; *a* chaleureux.

cordiality [.kɔːdi'æliti] *n* cordialité *f*.

cordon ['kɔːdn] *n* cordon *m*; **to —off** *vt* isoler, entourer d'un cordon.

corduroy ['kɔːdərɔi] *n* velours côtelé *m*.

core [kɔː] *n* cœur *m*, trognon *m*.

co-respondent ['kouris.pɔndənt] *n* complice *mf* (d'adultère).

cork [kɔːk] *n* liège *m*, bouchon *m*; *vt* boucher.

corked [kɔːkt] *a* qui sent le bouchon.

corkscrew ['kɔːkskruː] *n* tire-bouchon *m*.

corn [kɔːn] *n* grain *m*, blé *m*, maïs *m*; (*foot*) cor *m*.

cornea ['kɔːniə] *n* cornée *f*.

corned [kɔːnd] *a* salé, de conserve.

corner ['kɔːnə] *n* coin *m*, angle *m*, tournant *m*, virage *m*, accaparement *m*; *vt* acculer, mettre au pied du mur, accaparer; *vi* virer.

corner-stone ['kɔːnəstoun] *n* pierre angulaire *f*.

cornet ['kɔːnit] *n* cornet *m* (à piston).

corn exchange ['kɔːniks'tʃeindʒ] *n* halle *f* aux blés.

cornflower ['kɔːnflauə] *n* bluet *m*.

cornice ['kɔːnis] *n* corniche *f*.

cornstarch ['kɔːnstɑːtʃ] *n* farine *f* de maïz.

coronation [.kɔrə'neiʃən] *n* couronnement *m*, sacre *m*.

corporal ['kɔːpərəl] *n* caporal *m*, brigadier *m*; *a* corporel.

corporate ['kɔːpərit] *a* constitué; **— spirit** esprit de corps *m*, solidarité.

corporation [.kɔːpə'reiʃən] *n* corporation *f*, conseil municipal *m*, bedaine *f*.

corpse [kɔːps] *n* cadavre *m*.

corpuscle ['kɔːpʌsl] *n* corpuscle *m*.

Corpus Christi ['kɔːpəs'kristi] *n* Fête-Dieu *f*.

correct [kə'rekt] *a* correct, juste, exact; *vt* corriger, reprendre, rectifier.

correction [kə'rekʃən] *n* correction *f*, redressement *m*.

corrector [kə'rektə] *n* correcteur, -trice.

correspond [.kɔris'pɔnd] *vi* correspondre (à **with, to**).

correspondence [.kɔris'pɔndəns] *n* correspondance *f*.

correspondent [.kɔris'pɔndənt] *n* correspondant(e) *mf*, envoyé *m*.

corridor ['kɔridɔː] *n* couloir *m*, corridor *m*.

corroborate [kə'rɔbəreit] *vt* corroborer, confirmer.

corroboration [kə.rɔbə'reiʃən] *n* corroboration *f*.

corrode [kə'roud] *vt* corroder, ronger; *vi* se corroder.

corrosion [kə'rouʒən] *n* corrosion *f*.

corrosive [kə'rousiv] *an* corrosif *m*.

corrugated ['kɔrugeitid] *a* ondulé, cannelé, gaufré.

corrupt [kə'rʌpt] *vt* corrompre, altérer; *a* corrompu.

corruption [kə'rʌpʃən] *n* corruption *f*, subornation *f*.

corsair ['kɔːsɛə] *n* corsaire *m*.

corset ['kɔːsit] *n* corset *m*.

Corsica ['kɔːsikə] *n* la Corse *f*.

Corsican ['kɔːsikən] *a nm* corse; *n* Corse *mf*.

cosmic ['kɔzmik] *a* cosmique.

cosmonaut ['kɔzmənɔːt] *n* cosmonaute *mf*.

cosmopolitan [.kɔsmə'pɔlitən] *an* cosmopolite *mf*.

cosmopolitanism [.kɔzmə'pɔlitənizəm] *n* cosmopolitisme *m*.

cost [kɔst] *n* prix *m*, coût *m*, dépens *m pl*, frais *m pl*; *vi* coûter; *vt* établir le prix de.

costermonger ['kɔstə.mʌngə] *n* marchand *m* des quatre saisons.

costly ['kɔstli] *a* coûteux, dispendieux, précieux, somptueux.

cot [kɔt] *n* abri *m*, berceau *m*, couchette *f*, hutte *f*.

cottage ['kɔtidʒ] *n* chaumière *f*.

cotton ['kɔtn] *n* coton *m*, fil *m*; **— plant** cotonnier *m*; **— plantation** cotonneraie *f*.

cotton-wool ['kɔtn'wul] *n* ouate *f*, coton hydrophile *m*.

couch [kautʃ] *n* lit *m*, divan *m*; *vt* coucher; *vi* se tapir, s'embusquer.

cough [kɔf] *n* toux *f*; *vi* tousser.

could [kud] *pt of* **can**.

council ['kaunsl] *n* concile *m*, conseil *m*.

councilor ['kaunsilə] *n* conseiller *m* (municipal).

counsel ['kaunsəl] *n* conseil *m*, délibération *f*, avocat *m*; *vt* conseiller, recommander.

counselor ['kaunsələ] *n* conseiller *m*.

count [kaunt] *n* compte *m*, calcul *m*, comte *m*; *vti* compter.

countdown ['kauntdaun] *n* compte à rebours *m*.

countenance ['kauntinəns] *n* expression *f*, visage *m*, sérieux *m*, contenance *f*, appui *m*; *vt* sanctionner, appuyer, approuver.

counter ['kauntə] *n* comptoir *m*, jeton *m*, contre *m*; *a* opposé; *vt* contrarier, contredire, aller à l'encontre de; *vi* riposter; *ad* en sens contraire.

counteract [.kauntə'rækt] *vt* neutraliser.

counterbalance [ˌkauntəˈbæləns] n contre-poids m; vt contrebalancer, faire contrepoids à, compenser.

countercharge [ˈkauntətʃɑːdʒ] n contre-accusation f.

counterfeit [ˈkauntəfit] n contre-façon f; — **coin** pièce fausse f; vt feindre, contrefaire, forger.

counterfoil [ˈkauntəfɔil] n talon m, souche f.

countermand [ˌkauntəˈmɑːnd] vt contremander, rappeler, décommander.

counterpane [ˈkauntəpein] n couvre-pied m, courtepointe f.

counterpart [ˈkauntəpɑːt] n contre-partie f, pendant m.

countersign [ˈkauntəsain] n mot m de passe, mot m d'ordre; vt viser, contresigner.

countess [ˈkauntis] n comtesse f.

countless [ˈkauntlis] a innombrable.

country [ˈkʌntri] n contrée f, pays m, campagne f, province f, patrie f.

country-house [ˈkʌntriˈhaus] n maison de campagne f.

countryman [ˈkʌntrimən] n campagnard m, compatriote m.

countryside [ˈkʌntrisaid] n campagne f, pays m.

county [ˈkaunti] n comté m.

couple [ˈkʌpl] n couple mf, laisse f; vt (ac)coupler, unir, associer.

coupon [ˈkuːpɔn] n coupon m, ticket m, estampille officielle f, bon(-prime) m.

courage [ˈkʌridʒ] n courage m.

courageous [kəˈreidʒəs] a courageux.

courier [ˈkuriə] n courrier m.

course [kɔːs] n course f, cours m, champ de courses m, carrière f, série f, marche f, direction f, route f, plat m, service m; **of** — naturellement; **matter of** — chose qui va de soi, positif, prosaïque.

court [kɔːt] n cour f, terrain de jeux m, court m (tennis); vt courtiser, inviter, chercher, solliciter, aller au-devant de.

courteous [ˈkəːtiəs] a courtois.

courtesy [ˈkəːtisi] n courtoisie f, politesses f pl.

courtesan [ˌkəːtiˈzæn] n courtisane f.

courtier [ˈkɔːtjə] n courtisan m.

courtliness [ˈkɔːtlinis] n élégance f, raffinement m.

courtly [ˈkɔːtli] a élégant, courtois.

courtship [ˈkɔːtʃip] n cour f.

courtyard [ˈkɔːtjɑːd] n cour f.

cousin [ˈkʌzn] n cousin(e) mf; **first** — cousin germain; **second** — issu de germain; **third** — au 3ᵉ degré etc.

cove [kouv] n (sea) anse f, crique f, type m.

covenant [ˈkʌvinənt] n pacte m, alliance f, contrat m.

cover [ˈkʌvə] n couverture f, housse f, bâche f, dessus m, couvercle m, abri m; couvert m, voile m, masque m; compte-rendu m; vt (re)couvrir, revêtir, embrasser; faire un compte-rendu.

covering [ˈkʌvəriŋ] a de couverture, confirmatif.

coverlet [ˈkʌvəlit] n couvre-pied m, dessus m de lit, couvre-lit m.

covert [ˈkʌvət] a couvert, furtif, voile, indirect.

covet [ˈkʌvit] vt convoiter.

covetous [ˈkʌvitəs] a convoiteux, avide.

covetousness [ˈkʌvitəsnis] n convoitise f, cupidité f.

covey [ˈkʌvi] n couvée f, compagnie f, vol m, troupe f.

cow [kau] n vache f, femelle f; vt intimider.

coward [ˈkauəd] an lâche mf.

cowardice [ˈkauədis] n lâcheté f.

cowardly [ˈkauədli] a lâche, poltron; ad lâchement.

cower [ˈkauə] vi s'accroupir, se blottir, se faire petit.

cowl [kaul] n capuchon m, capot m, mitre f, champignon m.

cowrie-shell [ˈkauriʃel] n cauri m.

coxcomb [ˈkɔkskoum] n poseur m, fat m, petit-maître m.

coxswain [ˈkɔksn] n homme de barre m, maître m d'équipage.

coy [kɔi] a timide, réservé, écarté.

coyness [ˈkɔinis] n timidité f, réserve f.

cozy [ˈkouzi] n couvre-théière m; a tiède, douillet, bon.

crab [kræb] n crabe m, (apple) pomme sauvage f, (tool) chèvre f.

crabbed [ˈkræbd] a revêche, raboteux, grincheux, aigre.

crack [kræk] n craquement m, coup sec m, fêlure f, lézarde f, fente f; a (fam) d'élite; —**brained** félé, timbré, toqué; vi craquer, claquer, se casser, se gercer, se fêler, muer; vt faire craquer (claquer), casser, fêler, (joke) faire.

cracker [ˈkrækə] n pétard m, casse-noix m, diablotin m.

crackle [ˈkrækl] n craquement m, crépitement m, friture f, craquelure f; vi crépiter, craqueter, grésiller, pétiller.

cracksman [ˈkræksmən] n (sl) cambrioleur m.

cradle [ˈkreidl] n berceau m; —**song** berceuse f; vt coucher, bercer.

craft [krɑːft] n habileté f, ruse f, art m, métier m, vaisseau m, avion m.

craftsman [ˈkrɑːftsmən] n ouvrier qualifié m, artisan m.

crafty [ˈkrɑːfti] a rusé, cauteleux, fin.

crag [kræg] n rocher m.

craggy [ˈkrægi] a rocheux, rocailleux.

cram [kræm] vt remplir, gaver, fourrer, enfoncer, bourrer, chauffer; vi se gaver, s'empiffrer, s'entasser.

cramming [ˈkræmiŋ] n gavage m, bourrage m, chauffage m.

cramp [kræmp] *n* crampe *f*, crampon *m*; *vt* donner des crampes à, engourdir.

cramped [kræmpt] *a* crispé, gêné, à l'étroit.

crane [krein] *n* grue *f*; *vt* tendre, soulever.

crank [krænk] *n* manivelle *f*, coude *m*, meule *f*, original(e) *mf*, toque(e) *mf*.

crape [kreip] *n* crêpe *m*.

crash [kræʃ] *n* fracas *m*, crac *m*, krach *m*, accident *m*; *vt* briser, fracasser, écraser; *vi* dégringoler, s'abattre, s'écraser, casser du bois; **to — into** heurter, tamponner, accrocher.

crass [kræs] *a* grossier, crasse.

crate [kreit] *n* manne *f*, cageot *m*.

crater ['kreitə] *n* cratère *m*, entonnoir *m*.

crave [kreiv] *vt* solliciter; **to — for** désirer violemment, avoir soif de.

craven ['kreivən] *an* lâche *mf*.

craving ['kreiviŋ] *n* besoin *m*, faim *f*, soif *f*.

crawl [krɔːl] *vi* se traîner, ramper, grouiller; *n* rampement *m*, (*swimming*) crawl *m*.

crawler ['krɔːlə] *n* (*cab*) maraudeur *m*, reptile *m*.

crayfish ['kreifiʃ] *n* langouste *f*, écrevisse *f*.

crayon ['kreiən] *n* fusain *m*, pastel *m*.

craze [kreiz] *n* folie *f*, manie *f*, toquade *f*.

crazy ['kreizi] *a* branlant, toqué, affolé, insensé, fou.

creak [kriːk] *n* grincement *m*; *vi* grincer, craquer, crier.

cream [kriːm] *n* crème *f*; *vi* crêmer, mousser; *vt* écrémer.

creamery ['kriːməri] *n* crémerie *f*.

creamy ['kriːmi] *a* crêmeux.

crease [kriːs] *n* pli *m*; *vt* plisser, froisser; *vi* se plisser, prendre un faux pli, se froisser.

create [kriː'eit] *vt* créer.

creation [kriː'eiʃən] *n* création *f*.

creator [kriː'eitə] *n* créateur, -trice.

creature ['kriːtʃə] *n* créature *f*, être *m*, homme *m*.

credentials [kri'denʃəlz] *n* lettres de créance *f*, certificat *m*.

credibility [,kredi'biliti] *n* crédibilité *f*.

credible ['kredibl] *a* croyable, digne de foi.

credibly ['kredibli] *ad* vraisemblablement.

credit ['kredit] *n* foi *f*, mérite *m*, honneur *m*, crédit *m*; **tax —s** déductions fiscales; *vt* croire, ajouter foi à, créditer, accorder, reconnaître.

creditable ['kreditəbl] *a* honorable, qui fait honneur (à **to**).

creditor ['kreditə] *n* créancier, -ière.

credulity [kri'djuːliti] *n* crédulité *f*.

credulous ['kredjuləs] *a* crédule.

creed [kriːd] *n* crédo *m*, foi *f*.

creek [kriːk] *n* crique *f*, anse *f*.

creep [kriːp] *vi* ramper, se glisser, grimper.

creeper ['kriːpə] *n* plante rampante *f*, grimpante.

creeps [kriːps] *n* chair *f* de poule.

cremate [kri'meit] *vt* brûler, incinérer.

cremation [kri'meiʃən] *n* incinération *f*.

crematorium [,kremə'tɔːriəm] *n* four crématoire *m*.

crept [krept] *pt pp of* **creep.**

crescent ['kresnt] *n* croissant *m*.

cress [kres] *n* cresson *m*.

crest [krest] *n* crête *f*, huppe *f*, plumet *m*, cimier *m*, armoiries *f pl*.

crestfallen ['krest,fɔːlən] *a* penaud, découragé.

crevice ['krevis] *n* crevasse *f*, fente *f*, fissure *f*.

crew [kruː] *n* équipage *m*, équipe *f*, bande *f*.

crib [krib] *n* mangeoire *f*, crèche *f*, lit d'enfant *m*, poste *m*; **to — from** plagier, copier sur.

crick [krik] *n* torticolis *m*.

cricket ['krikit] *n* cricket *m*, grillon *m*.

crier ['kraiə] *n* crieur *m*.

crime [kraim] *n* crime *m*, délit *m*.

criminal ['kriminl] *an* criminel, -elle.

criminality [,krimi'næliti] *n* criminalité *f*.

crimp [krimp] *vt* plisser, onduler, friser, racoler.

crimson ['krimzn] *an* cramoisi *m*, pourpre *m*.

cringe [krindʒ] *n* courbette obséquieuse *f*; *vi* s'aplatir, se tapir, faire le chien couchant.

crinkle ['kriŋkl] *n* pli *m*, ride *f*; *vt* chiffonner, froisser; *vi* se froisser.

cripple ['kripl] *n* estropié(e) *mf*, infirme *mf*; *vt* estropier, paralyser.

crisis ['kraisis] *n* crise *f*.

crisp [krisp] *a* cassant, croquant, vif, brusque, bouclé; *vti* boucler; *vt* crêper.

criss-cross ['kriskrɔs] *n* entrecroisement *m*; *a* entrecroisé, revêche; *vt* entrecroiser; *vi* s'entrecroiser.

criterion [krai'tiəriən] *n* critérium *m*, critère *m*.

critic ['kritik] *n* critique *m*.

critical ['kritikəl] *a* critique.

criticism ['kritisizəm] *n* critique *f*.

criticize ['kritisaiz] *vt* critiquer, censurer.

croak [krouk] *n* c(r)oassement *m*; *vi* c(r)oasser.

crochet ['krouʃei] *n* crochet *m*.

crockery ['krɔkəri] *n* faïence *f*, vaisselle *f*.

crocodile ['krɔkədail] *n* crocodile *m*, caïman *m*.

crocus ['kroukəs] *n* crocus *m*, safran *m*.

croft [krɔft] *n* clos *m*.

crook [kruk] *n* houlette *f*, crosse *f*.

croc *m*, crochet *m*, courbe *f*, escroc *m*; *vt* (re)courber.
crooked ['krukid] *a* courbé, tordu, tortueux, malhonnête.
croon [kru:n] *n* bourdonnement *m*, fredonnement *m*, plainte *f*; *vti* bourdonner, fredonner.
crop [krɔp] *n* récolte *f*, jabot *m*, manche *f* de fouet, cravache *f*, coupe *f* de cheveux (à ras); *vt* récolter, brouter, écourter, tondre, couper ras, planter; **to — up** *vi* affleurer, surgir, se présenter.
cross [krɔs] *n* croix *f*, barre *f*, croisement *m*; *a* croisé, fâché; *vt* croiser, traverser, barrer; *vi* se croiser; **to — out** *vt* biffer; **to — oneself** se signer.
crossbar ['krɔsbɑ:] *n* traverse *f*.
cross-belt ['krɔsbelt] *n* cartouchière *f*, bandoulière *f*.
crossbreed ['krɔsbri:d] *n* hybride *m*, métis, -isse.
cross-examination ['krɔsig,zæmi'-neiʃən] *n* contre-interrogatoire *m*.
cross-eyed ['krɔsaid] *a* louche.
cross-grained ['krɔsgreind] *a* à contre-fil, revêche, grincheux.
crossing ['krɔsiŋ] *n* croisement *m*, traversée *f*.
cross-legged ['krɔs'legd] *a* les jambes croisées.
crossroads ['krɔsroudz] *n* carrefour *m*.
cross-section ['krɔs'sekʃən] *n* coupe *f*, tranche *f*, catégorie *f*.
crossword ['krɔswə:d] *n* mots croisés *m pl.*
crotchet ['krɔtʃit] *n* noire *f*, caprice *m*.
crotchety ['krɔtʃiti] *a* fantasque, difficile.
crouch [krautʃ] *vi* s'accroupir, se blottir, se ramasser.
croup [kru:p] *n* croupe *f*, croup *m*.
crow [krou] *n* corneille *f*, corbeau *m*, cri du coq *m*; **as the — flies** à vol d'oiseau; *vi* chanter, crier de joie, chanter victoire, crâner.
crowbar ['kroubɑ:] *n* levier *m*, pince *f*.
crowd [kraud] *n* foule *f*, affluence *f*, bande *f*, monde *m*; *vt* remplir, tasser, serrer; *vi* se presser, s'entasser, s'empiler, affluer, s'attrouper.
crowded ['kraudid] *a* comble, bondé, encombré.
crown [kraun] *n* couronne *f*; *vt* couronner.
crucial ['kru:ʃəl] *a* essentiel, décisif, critique.
crucible ['kru:sibl] *n* creuset *m*.
crucifix ['kru:sifiks] *n* crucifix *m*.
crucifixion [,kru:si'fikʃən] *n* crucifiement *m*.
crucify ['kru:sifai] *vt* crucifier.
crude [kru:d] *a* cru, mal digéré, vert, rude, sommaire, brutal, frustre.
crudely ['kru:dli] *ad* crûment, rudement, grossièrement.

crudity ['kru:diti] *n* crudité *f*, grossièreté *f*.
cruel ['kruəl] *a* cruel.
cruelty ['kruəlti] *n* cruauté *f*.
cruet ['kru:it] *n* burette *f*.
cruet-stand ['kru:itstænd] *n* huilier *m*.
cruise [kru:z] *n* croisière *f*; *vi* croiser, marauder.
cruiser ['kru:zə] *n* croiseur *m*.
crumb [krʌm] *n* mie *f*, miette *f*.
crumble ['krʌmbl] *vt* briser en morceaux, émietter, effriter; *vi* s'écrouler, s'émietter, s'effriter.
crumple ['krʌmpl] *vt* froisser, chiffonner; *vi* se froisser, se friper, se télescoper.
crunch [krʌntʃ] *vt* croquer, écraser; *vi* craquer, grincer, crier.
crusade [kru:'seid] *n* croisade *f*, campagne *f*.
crush [krʌʃ] *n* écrasement *m*, cohue *f*, béguin *m*; *vt* écraser, froisser, terrasser, broyer.
crust [krʌst] *n* croûte *f*, croûton *m*, depôt *m*.
crutch [krʌtʃ] *n* béquille *f*.
crux [krʌks] *n* nœud *m*.
cry [krai] *n* cri *m*, crise *f* de larmes; *vi* crier, pleurer; **to — down** décrier; **to — off** renoncer, se faire excuser; **to — out** s'écrier; **to — up** louer.
crypt [kript] *n* crypte *f*.
crystal ['kristl] *n* cristal *m*, boule de cristal *f*; *a* cristallin, limpide.
cub [kʌb] *n* petit *m*, ourson *m*, ours mal léché, louveteau *m*.
Cuba ['kju:bə] *n* Cuba *m*.
Cuban ['kju:bən] *an* cubain.
cube [kju:b] *n* cube *m*.
cubic ['kju:bik] *a* cubique.
cuckoo ['kuku] *n* coucou *m*.
cucumber ['kju:kʌmbə] *n* concombre *m*.
cud [kʌd] **to chew the —** ruminer.
cuddle ['kʌdl] *vt* mignoter, peloter; **to — into** se pelotonner contre.
cudgel ['kʌdʒəl] *n* gourdin *m*; *vt* rosser.
cue [kju:] *n* queue *f*, invite *f*, indication *f*, mot *m*.
cuff [kʌf] *n* taloche *f*, claque *f*, manchette *f*; *vt* gifler, calotter.
cull [kʌl] *vt* (re)cueillir.
culling ['kʌliŋ] *n* cueillette *f*; *pl* glanures *f pl.*
culminant ['kʌlminənt] *a* culminant.
culminate ['kʌlmineit] *vi* s'achever (en in), se couronner (par in).
culmination [,kʌlmi'neiʃən] *n* point culminant *m*.
culpability [,kʌlpə'biliti] *n* culpabilité *f*.
cult [kʌlt] *n* culte *m*.
cultivate ['kʌltiveit] *vt* cultiver.
cultivation [,kʌlti'veiʃən] *n* cultivation *f*.
cultivator ['kʌltiveitə] *n* cultivateur, motoculteur *m*.
culture ['kʌltʃə] *n* culture *f*.

culvert ['kʌlvət] n canal m, canalisation f, tranchée f, cassis m.
cumbersome ['kʌmbəsəm] a encombrant, gênant.
cumbrous ['kʌmbrəs] a encombrant, gênant.
cumulate ['kju:mjuleit] vt (ac)cumuler.
cumulation [‚kju:mju'leiʃən] n accumulation f, cumul m.
cumulative ['kju:mjulətiv] a cumulatif.
cunning ['kʌniŋ] n finesse f, ruse f, habileté f, rouerie f; a entendu, retors, rusé, cauteleux.
cup [kʌp] n tasse f, coupe f, calice m.
cupboard ['kʌbəd] n buffet m, armoire f, placard m.
cupidity [kju:'piditi] n cupidité f.
cur [kə:] n roquet m, cuistre m.
curable ['kjuərəbl] a guérissable.
curate ['kjuərit] n vicaire m, abbé m.
curator [kjuə'reitə] n curateur m, conservateur m.
curb [kə:b] n gourmette f, margelle f, bordure f, frein m; vt refréner, brider.
curd [kə:d] n lait caillé m.
curdle ['kə:dl] vi se cailler, se figer, tourner.
cure [kjuə] n guérison f, remède m, cure f, soin m; vt guérir, saler, fumer, mariner.
curfew ['kə:fju:] n couvre-feu m.
curio ['kjuəriou] n pièce rare f, bibelot m, curiosité f.
curiosity [‚kjuəri'ɔsiti] n curiosité f.
curious ['kjuəriəs] a curieux, singulier, indiscret.
curl [kə:l] n boucle f, (lips) ourlet m; vt (en)rouler, friser; vi déferler, monter en spirale, friser.
curlew ['kə:lu:] n courlis m.
curling-tongs ['kə:liŋtɔŋz] n fer m à friser.
curl-paper ['kə:lpeipə] n papillotte f.
curly ['kə:li] a bouclé, frisé.
currant ['kʌrənt] n groseille f, raisin de Corinthe m.
currency ['kʌrənsi] n cours m, circulation monétaire f, monnaie (courante) f.
current ['kʌrənt] n courant m, cours m, tendance f; a courant, en cours.
currently ['kʌrəntli] ad couramment.
curry ['kʌri] n cari m; to — favor with amadouer, se mettre bien avec.
curse [kə:s] n malédiction f, fléau m, juron m; vt maudire; vi sacrer, blasphémer, jurer, pester.
cursory ['kə:səri] a superficiel, rapide.
curt [kə:t] a bref, sec.
curtail [kə:'teil] vt écourter, restreindre, réduire.
curtailment [kə:'teilmənt] n retranchement m, restriction f, réduction f.

curtain [kə:tn] n rideau m; excl tableau! **fireproof** — rideau de fer m; —**raiser** lever de rideau m.
curtly ['kə:tli] ad brièvement, sèchement.
curtness ['kə:tnis] n sécheresse f, brièveté f, rudesse f.
curtsy ['kə:tsi] n révérence f; vi faire une révérence.
curve [kə:v] n courbe f; vt (re)courber; vi se courber.
cushion ['kuʃən] n coussin m, (billiards) bande f.
cushy ['kuʃi] a (fam) moelleux, pépère, de tout repos.
custard ['kʌstəd] n flan de lait m, crème cuite f.
custody ['kʌstədi] n garde f, prison f.
custom ['kʌstəm] n usage m, coutume f, clientèle f; pl (droits m de) douane f.
customary ['kʌstəməri] a d'usage, habituel.
customarily ['kʌstəmərili] ad d'habitude.
customer ['kʌstəmə] n client(e) mf, chaland(‚) mf, type m, coco m.
custom-house ['kʌstəmhaus] n bureau m de la douane.
customs-officer ['kʌstəmz'ɔfisə] n douanier m.
cut [kʌt] n coupure f, coupe f, tranche f, incision f, coup m; vti couper; vt blesser, (teeth) faire, percer, (lecture) sécher, couper (au) court; **to — down** réduire; **to — off** amputer, trancher; **to — up** tailler en pièces.
cute [kju:t] a rusé, malin, coquet, mignon.
cutlass ['kʌtləs] n coutelas m, coupe-coupe m.
cutler ['kʌtlə] n coutelier m.
cutlery ['kʌtləri] n coutellerie f.
cutlet ['kʌtlit] n côtelette f.
cut-throat ['kʌtθrout] n coupe-jarret m.
cutting ['kʌtiŋ] n taille f, (dé)coupage m, incision f, coupure f, bouture f; a tranchant, mordant.
cycle ['saikl] n cycle m, bicyclette f; **motor —** motocyclette f; vi faire de la (aller à) bicyclette.
cycling ['saikliŋ] n cyclisme m.
cyclist ['saiklist] n cycliste mf.
cyclone ['saikloun] n cyclone m.
cygnet ['signit] n jeune cygne m.
cylinder ['silində] n cylindre m.
cylindrical [si'lindrikəl] a cylindrique.
cynic ['sinik] n cynique m, sceptique m.
cynical ['sinikəl] a cynique, sceptique.
cynicism ['sinisizəm] n cynisme m, scepticisme m.
cynosure ['sinəzjuə] n point de mir m.
cypress ['saipris] n cyprès m.
Cyprus ['saiprəs] n Chypre f.

cyst [sist] n kyste m.
czar [zɑː] n czar m, tsar m.
czarina [zɑː'riːnə] n tsarine f.

D

D-Day ['diːdei] n Jour J. m.
dab [dæb] n limande f, tape f, coup d'éponge m; vt tamponner, éponger, tapoter.
dabble ['dæbl] vt mouiller; vi patauger, jouer (à **in**), faire, s'occuper (de **in**).
dabbler ['dæblə] n amateur, -trice.
dad(dy) ['dædi] n papa m.
daddy-long-legs ['dædi'lɔŋlegz] n faucheux m.
daffodil ['dæfədil] n narcisse des bois m, jonquille f.
daft [dɑːft] a toqué, entiché.
dagger ['dægə] n poignard m; at —s drawn à couteaux tirés; **to look** —s at s.o. foudroyer qn du regard.
daily ['deili] an quotidien m; a journalier; ad tous les jours.
daintiness ['deintinis] n délicatesse f, beauté fine f.
dainty ['deinti] n morceau m de choix, friandise f; a délicat, mignon, exquis.
dairy ['dɛəri] n laiterie f.
dairymaid ['dɛərimeid] n laitière f.
dairyman ['dɛərimən] n laitier m.
dais ['deiis] n estrade f, dais m.
daisy ['deizi] n marguerite f, pâquerette f.
dale [deil] n vallée f, combe f.
dalliance ['dæliəns] n coquetteries f pl, flânerie f, badinage m, délai m.
dally ['dæli] vi jouer, coqueter, badiner, tarder.
dam [dæm] n barrage m, digue f; vt barrer, endiguer.
damage ['dæmidʒ] n dégats m pl, dommages m pl, pl dommages-intérêts m pl; vt endommager, nuire à, abîmer, faire tort à.
damaging ['dæmidʒiŋ] a dévastateur, nuisible.
dame [deim] n dame f.
damn [dæm] vt (con)damner, perdre, maudire, envoyer au diable; excl zut!; **I don't give a** — je m'en fiche.
damnable ['dæmnəbl] a damnable, maudit.
damnation [dæm'neiʃən] n damnation f.
damned [dæmd] a damné, perdu, sacré; ad vachement.
damp [dæmp] n humidité f; a humide, moite; vt mouiller, étouffer, décourager, refroidir.
damper ['dæmpə] n éteignoir m, sourdine f, rabat-joie m.
damson ['dæmzən] n prune f de Damas.
dance [dɑːns] n danse f, bal m, (African) tam-tam; vti danser; vi sauter, trépigner; vt faire danser.

dance-hall ['dɑːnshɔːl] n dancing m, salle f de danse.
dancer ['dɑːnsə] n danseur, -euse.
dandelion ['dændilaiən] n pissenlit m.
dandle ['dændl] vt dodeliner, dorloter.
dandruff ['dændrəf] n pellicules f pl.
dandy ['dændi] n dandy m.
Dane [dein] n Danois(e) mf.
danger ['deindʒə] n danger m, péril m, risque m.
dangerous ['deindʒrəs] a dangereux, périlleux.
dangle ['dæŋgl] vi pendre, se balancer, agiter, pendiller; vt faire balancer.
Danish ['deiniʃ] an danois m.
dapper ['dæpə] a net, soigné, tiré à quatre épingles.
dappled ['dæpld] a pommelé, tacheté.
dare [dɛə] vt oser, risquer, défier, braver.
dare-devil ['dɛə,devl] n casse-cou m.
daring ['dɛəriŋ] n audace f; a hardi, audacieux.
dark [dɑːk] n noir m, nuit f, obscurité f; a sombre, noir, foncé.
darken ['dɑːkən] vt assombrir, obscurcir, attrister; vi s'assombrir, s'obscurcir.
darkness ['dɑːknis] n obscurité f, ténèbres f pl.
darling ['dɑːliŋ] n chéri(e) mf, amour m.
darn [dɑːn] n reprise f; vt repriser, ravauder.
dart [dɑːt] n flèche f, dard m, fléchette f, lancement m; vt lancer, darder; vi s'élancer, foncer.
dash [dæʃ] n fougue f, allant m, brio m, trait m, tiret m, pointe f, (fig) goutte f, filet m; vt lancer, éclabousser, diluer, étendre, décevoir; vi se précipiter, s'élancer; **to** — **off** vt bâcler; vi filer en vitesse, se sauver.
dashboard ['dæʃbɔːd] n tablier m.
dashing ['dæʃiŋ] a fougueux, impétueux, tapageur, plein d'entrain, galant.
dastardly ['dæstədli] a infâme, lâche.
date [deit] n date f, rendezvous m, datte f; vti dater; **out of** — démodé, périmé; **up to** — au courant, à la page.
dating ['deitiŋ] **dating from** à dater de.
daub [dɔːb] n barbouillage m, croûte f, navet m; vt enduire, barbouiller.
daughter ['dɔːtə] n fille f.
daughter-in-law ['dɔːtərinlɔː] n belle-fille f.
daunt [dɔːnt] vt effrayer, intimider, décourager.
dauntless ['dɔːntlis] a intrépide, courageux.
dawdle ['dɔːdl] vi traîner, flâner; **to** — **away** gaspiller

dawdler ['dɔːdlə] *n* lambin(e) *mf*, flâneur, -euse.

dawn [dɔːn] *n* aube *f*, aurore *f*; *vi* poindre, naître, se faire jour.

day [dei] *n* jour *m*, journée *f*; — **before** veille *f*; — **after** lendemain *m*; **a week today** d'aujourd'hui en huit.

day-boarder ['dei,bɔːdə] *n* demi-pensionnaire *mf*.

day-boy ['deibɔi] *n* externe *m*.

daybreak ['deibreik] *n* point du jour *m*.

daydream ['deidriːm] *n* rêve (éveillé) *m*, rêverie *f*; *n* rêver, rêvasser.

day-laborer ['dei'leibərə] *n* ouvrier *m* à la journée.

daylight ['deilait] *n* (lumière *f* du) jour *m*, publicité *f*, notoriété *f*.

day-nursery ['dei,nəːsri] *n* crèche *f*, garderie *f*.

daze [deiz] *vt* ébahir, ahurir, étourdir, hébéter.

dazzle ['dæzl] *vt* éblouir, aveugler.

dazzling ['dæzliŋ] *n* éblouissement *m*; *a* éblouissant.

deacon ['diːkən] *n* diacre *m*.

deaconess ['diːkənis] *n* diaconesse *f*.

dead [ded] *n* morts *m pl*; *a* mort, défunt, feu, funèbre, éteint, amorti, (*loss*) net, sec, plat; *ad* droit, en plein, à fond; **in the** — **of** au cœur de, au plus fort de, au milieu de.

deaden ['dedn] *vt* étouffer, amortir, émousser, feutrer.

dead-end ['ded'end] *n* cul de sac *m*, impasse *f*.

dead-letter ['ded'letə] *n* lettre morte *f*, mise au rebut *f*.

deadline ['dedlain] *n* dernière limite *f*, date limite *f*.

deadlock ['dedlɔk] *n* point mort *m*, impasse *f*.

deadly ['dedli] *a* mortel.

deaf [def] *a* sourd.

deafen ['defn] *vt* rendre sourd, assourdir.

deafness ['defnis] *n* surdité *f*.

deal [diːl] *n* planche *f*, bois blanc *m*, sapin *m*, quantité *f*, nombre *m*, affaire *f*, (*cards*) donne *f*; *vt* donner, distribuer, asséner; *vi* avoir affaire (à, avec **with**), s'occuper (de **with**), traiter (de **with**), faire le commerce (de **in**), se conduire.

dealer ['diːlə] *n* marchand(e) *mf*, fournisseur *m*, donneur *m*.

dealing(s) ['diːliŋz] *n* relations *f pl*, affaire *f*, agissements *m pl*, menées *f pl*.

dean [diːn] *n* doyen *m*.

deanery ['diːnəri] *n* doyenne *m*.

dear ['diə] *a* cher, coûteux.

dearly ['diəli] *ad* cher, chèrement.

dearness ['diənis] *n* cherté *f*.

dearth [dəːθ] *n* disette *f*, pénurie *f*.

death [deθ] *n* mort *f*, décès *m*; — **certificate** acte *m* de déces.

deathbed ['deθbed] *n* lit *m* de mort.

death-bell ['deθbel] *n* glas *m*.

death-rate ['deθreit] *n* taux de mortalité *m*.

death-trap ['deθtræp] *n* souricière *f*, casse-cou *m*.

death-warrant ['deθwɔrənt] *n* ordre *m* d'exécution, arrêt *m* de mort.

debar [di'baː] *vt* exclure.

debase [di'beis] *vt* avilir, altérer.

debatable [di'beitəbl] *a* discutable.

debate [di'beit] *n* débat *m*, discussion *f*; *vt* débattre; *vti* discuter.

debauch [di'bɔːtʃ] *n* débauche *f*; *vt* débaucher, corrompre.

debauchee [,debɔːˈtʃiː] *n* débauché(e) *mf*.

debilitate [di'biliteit] *vt* débiliter.

debility [di'biliti] *n* débilité *f*.

debit ['debit] *n* débit *m*, doit *m*; *vt* porter au débit (de **with**), débiter.

debouch [di'bautʃ] *vi* déboucher.

debt [det] *n* dette *f*, passif *m*.

debt-collector ['detkəlektə] *n* huissier *m*.

debtor ['detə] *n* débiteur, -trice.

debunk [di'bʌŋk] *vt* dégonfler.

debut ['deibuː] *n* début *m*.

decade ['dekeid] *n* décade *f*.

decadence ['dekədəns] *n* décadence *f*.

decadent ['dekədənt] *a* décadent.

decamp [di'kæmp] *vi* décamper, filer.

decant [di'kænt] *vt* décanter.

decanter [di'kæntə] *n* carafe *f*.

decapitate [di'kæpiteit] *vt* décapiter.

decapitation [di,kæpi'teiʃən] *n* décapitation *f*.

decay [di'kei] *n* déclin *m*, décadence *f*, décomposition *f*; *vi* tomber en décadence, décliner, pourrir.

decease [di'siːs] *n* décès *m*; *vi* décéder.

deceased [di'siːst] *an* défunt(e) *mf*.

deceit [di'siːt] *n* fourberie *f*, apparence trompeuse *f*.

deceitful [di'siːtful] *a* trompeur, faux, perfide.

deceitfulness [di'siːtfulnis] *n* fausseté *f*, perfidie *f*.

deceive [di'siːv] *vt* tromper, décevoir.

December [di'sembə] *n* décembre *m*.

decency ['diːsnsi] *n* bienséance *f*, décence *f*.

decent ['diːsnt] *a* décent, passable, honnête.

decently ['diːsntli] *ad* décemment.

decentralization [diː,sentrəlai'zeiʃn] *n* décentralisation *f*.

decentralize [diː'sentrəlaiz] *vt* décentraliser.

deception [di'sepʃən] *n* tromperie *f*, déception *f*, fraude *f*.

deceptive [di'septiv] *a* trompeur.

decide [di'said] *vti* décider; *vt* régler, trancher; *vi* se décider.

decided [di'saidid] *a* décidé, net, arrêté.

decidedly [di'saididli] *ad* catégoriquement, incontestablement.

decimal ['desiməl] *n* décimale *f*; *a* décimal.

decimate ['desimeit] *vt* décimer.
decipher [di'saifə] *vt* déchiffrer.
deciphering [di'saifəriŋ] *n* déchiffrement *m*.
decision [di'siʒən] *n* décision *f*, arrêt *m*.
decisive [di'saisiv] *a* décisif, net, tranchant.
deck [dek] *n* pont *m*; *vt* orner, couvrir, pavoiser.
deck-chair ['dek'tʃɛə] *n* transatlantique *m*.
deck-house ['dekhaus] *n* (*naut*) rouf *m*.
declaim [di'kleim] *vti* déclamer.
declamation [,deklə'meiʃən] *n* déclamation *f*.
declamatory [di'klæmətəri] *a* déclamatoire.
declaration [,deklə'reiʃən] *n* déclaration *f*, (*pol*) proclamation *f*, annonce *f*.
declare [di'klɛə] *vt* déclarer, annoncer.
decline [di'klain] *n* déclin *m*, baisse *f*, phtisie *f*; *vti* décliner; *vt* refuser, repousser; *vi* baisser, s'incliner, descendre.
declivity [di'kliviti] *n* pente *f*.
decode ['di:'koud] *vt* déchiffrer.
decompose [,di:kəm'pouz] *vt* décomposer; *vi* se décomposer, pourrir.
decomposition [,di:kɔmpə'ziʃən] *n* décomposition *f*, putréfaction *f*.
decontrol ['di:kən'troul] *vt* décontrôler.
decorate ['dekəreit] *vt* décorer, pavoiser.
decoration [,dekə'reiʃən] *n* décoration *f*, décor *m*.
decorator ['dekəreitə] *n* décorateur *m*.
decorative ['dekərətiv] *a* décoratif.
decorous ['dekərəs] *a* séant.
decorum [di'kɔːrəm] *n* décorum *m*, bienséance *f*.
decoy [di'kɔi] *n* piège *m*, amorce *f*, appeau *m*, appât *m*, agent provocateur *m*; *vt* attraper, induire (à **into**), leurrer, attirer.
decrease ['di:kri:s] *n* diminution *f*, décroissance *f*.
decrease [di:'kri:s] *vti* diminuer; *vi* décroître.
decree [di'kri:] *n* décret *m*, arrêt *m*, édit *m*; *vt* décréter; — **nisi** divorce *m* sous conditions.
decrepit [di'krepit] *a* décrépit, caduc, délabré.
decrepitude [di'krepitjuːd] *n* décrépitude *f*, caducité *f*.
decry [di'krai] *vt* décrier, dénigrer, huer.
dedication [,dedi'keiʃən] *n* consécration *f*, dédicace *f*.
dedicate ['dedikeit] *vt* consacrer, dédier.
deduce [di'djuːs] *vt* déduire, conclure.
deduct [di'dʌkt] *vt* retrancher, rabattre.

deduction [di'dʌkʃən] *n* déduction *f*, rabais *m*, conclusion *f*.
deed [diːd] *n* acte *m*, (haut) fait *m*, exploit *m*.
deem [diːm] *vt* estimer, juger.
deep [diːp] *n* fond *m*, profondeur *f*, mer *f*, abîme *m*, gouffre *m*; *a* profond, (*mourning*) grand, (*colour*) chaud, foncé, (*sound*) riche, bas.
deepen ['diːpən] *vt* approfondir, creuser, augmenter; *vi* devenir plus profond *etc*.
deepening ['diːpniŋ] *n* approfondissement *m*.
deeply ['diːpli] *ad* profondément.
deer [diə] *n* daim *m*, cerf *m*.
deerskin ['diəskin] *n* peau *f* de daim.
deface [di'feis] *vt* défigurer, discréditer, mutiler, oblitérer.
defalcation [,diːfæl'keiʃən] *n* défalcation *f*, détournement *m*.
defalcate ['diːfælkeit] *vi* défalquer, détourner des fonds.
defamation [,defə'meiʃən] *n* diffamation *f*.
defamatory [di'fæmətəri] *a* diffamatoire.
defame [di'feim] *vt* diffamer.
default [di'fɔːlt] *n* défaut *m*, forfait *m*; *vi* faire défaut.
defaulter [di'fɔːltə] *n* défaillant *m*, contumace *mf*.
defeat [di'fiːt] *n* défaite *f*, annulation *f*; *vt* déjouer, battre, vaincre, contrarier.
defeatism [di'fiːtizəm] *n* défaitisme *m*.
defeatist [di'fiːtist] *n* défaitiste *mf*.
defect [di'fekt] *n* défaut *m*, manque *m*.
defection [di'fekʃən] *n* défection *f*.
defective [di'fektiv] *a* défectueux, anormal.
defend [di'fend] *vt* défendre, protéger.
defendant [di'fendənt] *n* défendeur, -eresse.
defender [di'fendə] *n* défenseur *m*.
defense [di'fens] *n* défense *f*.
defensible [di'fensəbl] *a* défendable.
defensive [di'fensiv] *n* défensive *f*; *a* défensif.
defer [di'fəː] *vt* différer, ajourner; *vi* déférer (à **to**).
deference ['defərəns] *n* déférence *f*.
deferment [di'fəːmənt] *n* ajournement *m*, remise *f*.
defiance [di'faiəns] *n* défi *m*, révolte *f*.
defiant [di'faiənt] *a* rebelle, défiant, provocant.
deficiency [di'fiʃənsi] *n* insuffisance *f*, manque *m*, défaut *m*, manquant *m*.
deficient [di'fiʃənt] *a* qui manque de, déficitaire, défectueux.
deficit ['defisit] *n* déficit *m*.
defile ['diːfail] *n* défilé *m*; [di'fail] *vi* marcher par files, défiler; *vt* souiller, profaner.

defilement [di'failmənt] n souillure f, profanation f.
definable [di'fainəbl] a définissable.
define [di'fain] vt définir, (dé)limiter.
definite ['definit] a défini, net, précis, définitif.
definiteness ['definitnis] n netteté f, précision f.
definition [.defi'niʃən] n définition f.
definitive [di'finitiv] a définitif.
deflate [di'fleit] vt dégonfler; vi pratiquer la déflation.
deflect [di'flekt] vt (faire) dévier, détourner.
deflection [di'flekʃən] n déviation f, déjettement m.
deform [di'fɔːm] vt déformer, défigurer.
deformed [di'fɔːmd] a difforme.
deformity [di'fɔːmiti] n difformité f.
deformation [.diːfɔː'meiʃən] n déformation f.
defraud [di'frɔːd] vt voler, frauder, frustrer.
defray [di'frei] vt défrayer, couvrir.
deft [deft] a adroit.
deftness ['deftnis] n adresse f.
defunct [di'fʌŋkt] a défunt.
defy [di'fai] vt défier.
degenerate [di'dʒenəreit] an dégénéré(e) mf; vi dégénérer.
degeneration [di.dʒenə'reiʃən] n dégénérescence f.
degradation [.degrə'deiʃən] n dégradation f, abrutissement m.
degrade [di'greid] vt avilir, dégrader, casser.
degree [di'griː] n degré m, grade m, titre m, échelon m, condition f; **to a** — au dernier point.
dehydrate [diː'haidreit] vt déshydrater.
deign [dein] vi daigner.
deity ['diːiti] n divinité f.
dejected [di'dʒektid] a déprimé, abattu.
dejection [di'dʒekʃən] n abattement m.
delay [di'lei] n délai m, retard m; vt remettre, retarder, différer.
delegate ['deligit] n délégué(e) mf.
delegate ['deligeit] vt déléguer.
delegation [.deli'geiʃən] n délégation f.
delete [di'liːt] vt effacer, rayer.
deleterious [.deli'tiəriəs] a délétère, nuisible.
deletion [di'liːʃən] n radiation f, rature f, suppression f.
deliberate [di'libərit] a délibéré, voulu, réfléchi.
deliberate [di'libəreit] vti délibérer.
deliberately [di'libəritli] ad délibérément, exprès.
deliberation [di.libə'reiʃən] n délibération f.
delicacy ['delikəsi] n délicatesse f, finesse f, friandise f.
delicate ['delikit] a délicat, fin, raffiné, épineux.

delicious [di'liʃəs] a délicieux, exquis.
delight [di'lait] n délices f, pl joie f; vt enchanter, ravir.
delightful [di'laitful] a délicieux, ravissant.
delineate [di'linieit] vt tracer, esquisser.
delineation [di.lini'eiʃən] n délinéation f, description f, tracé m.
delinquency [di'liŋkwənsi] n délit m, faute f, négligence f.
delinquent [di'liŋkwənt] an délinquant(e) mf, coupable mf.
delirious [di'liriəs] a délirant, en délire.
delirium [di'liriəm] n délire m.
deliver [di'livə] vt (dé)livrer, remettre, (letters) distribuer, (blow) asséner, (ball) lancer, (lectures) faire.
deliverance [di'livərəns] n délivrance f, libération f.
deliverer [di'livərə] n libérateur, -trice, livreur, -euse.
delivery [di'livəri] n livraison f, distribution f, remise f, débit m.
dell [del] n vallon m, combe f.
delude [di'luːd] vt tromper, duper.
deluge ['deljuːdʒ] n déluge m; vt inonder.
delusion [di'luːʒən] n leurre m, illusion f, hallucination f.
demand [di'mɑːnd] n requête f, (com) demande f, revendication f; vt requérir, exiger, réclamer.
demarcation [diːmɑː'keiʃən] n démarcation f.
demarcate ['diːmɑːkeit] vt délimiter.
demean [di'miːn] vi to — oneself s'abaisser.
demeanor [di'miːnə] n conduite f, tenue f.
demented [di'mentid] a (tombé) en démence, fou.
demise [di'maiz] n transfert m, carence f, mort f; vt transférer, céder.
demobilization ['diː.moubilai'zeiʃən] n démobilisation f.
demobilize [diː'moubilaiz] vt démobiliser.
democracy [di'mɔkrəsi] n démocratie f.
democrat ['deməkræt] n démocrate mf; membre mf du parti démocrate.
democratic [.demə'krætik] a démocratique, démocrate.
demolish [di'mɔliʃ] vt démolir.
demolition [.demə'liʃən] n démolition f.
demon ['diːmən] n démon m.
demonetize [diː'mʌnitaiz] vt démonétiser.
demonstrate ['demənstreit] vt démontrer; vi manifester.
demonstration [.demɔns'treiʃən] n démonstration f, manifestation f.
demonstrative [di'mɔnstrətiv] a démonstratif, expansif.
demonstrator ['demənstreitə] n dé-

monstrateur *m*, préparateur *m*, manifestant *m*.

demoralization [di͵mɔrəlaiˈzeiʃən] *n* démoralisation *f*.

demoralize [diˈmɔrəlaiz] *vt* démoraliser.

demur [diˈməː] *n* objection *f*; *vi* objecter, hésiter.

demure [diˈmjuə] *a* réservé, composé, faussement modeste, prude.

demureness [diˈmjuənis] *n* ingénuité feinte *f*, air prude *m*.

den [den] *n* tanière *f*, antre *m*, retraite *f*, turne *f*, cagibi *m*; (*fam*) cabinet *m* de travail.

denial [diˈnaiəl] *n* refus *m*, démenti *m*, désaveu *m*, reniement *m*.

denizen [ˈdenizn] *n* habitant(e) *mf*, hôte *m*.

Denmark [ˈdenmɑːk] *n* Danemark *m*.

denominate [diˈnɔmineit] *vt* dénommer.

denote [diˈnout] *vt* dénoter, accuser, respirer.

denounce [diˈnauns] *vt* dénoncer, déblatérer contre.

dense [dens] *a* dense, épais, lourd, bouché.

density [ˈdensiti] *n* densité *f*, lourdeur *f*.

dent [dent] *n* entaille *f*, bosselure *f*; *vt* entailler, bosseler.

dental [ˈdentl] *n* dentale *f*; *a* dentaire.

dentifrice [ˈdentifris] *n* dentifrice *m*.

dentist [ˈdentist] *n* dentiste *m*.

dentition [denˈtiʃən] *n* dentition *f*.

denture [ˈdentʃə] *n* dentier *m*, denture *f*.

denude [diˈnjuːd] *vt* dénuder, dépouiller.

denunciation [di͵nʌnsiˈeiʃən] *n* dénonciation *f*.

deny [diˈnai] *vt* (re)nier, refuser, démentir, désavouer.

depart [diˈpɑːt] *vi* partir, trépasser, se départir (de **from**).

department [diˈpɑːtmənt] *n* département *m*, rayon *m*, service *m*, bureau *m*; — **store** bazar *m*, grand magasin *m*.

departmental [͵diːpɑːtˈmentl] *a* départemental, de service.

departure [diˈpɑːtʃə] *n* départ *m*, déviation *f*.

depend [diˈpend] *vi* dépendre (de **on**), compter (sur **on**), tenir (à **on**).

dependable [diˈpendəbl] *a* sûr, (digne) de confiance.

dependence [diˈpendəns] *n* dépendance *f*, confiance *f*.

dependency [diˈpendənsi] *n* dépendance *f*.

dependent [diˈpendənt] *a* dépendant, subordonné.

depict [diˈpikt] *vt* (dé)peindre.

deplenish [diˈpleniʃ] *vt* vider, dégarnir.

deplete [diˈpliːt] *vt* vider, épuiser.

depletion [diˈpliːʃən] *n* épuisement *m*.

deplorable [diˈplɔːrəbl] *a* déplorable, lamentable.

deplore [diˈplɔː] *vt* déplorer.

deploy [diˈplɔi] *vt* déployer.

deployment [diˈplɔimənt] *n* déploiement *m*.

depopulate [diːˈpɔpjuleit] *vt* dépeupler.

depopulation [diː͵pɔpjuˈleiʃən] *n* dépopulation *f*.

deport [diˈpɔːt] *vt* déporter, expulser (*aliens*); **to — oneself** se comporter.

deportation [͵diːpɔːˈteiʃən] *n* déportation *f*, expulsion *f*.

deportment [diˈpɔːtmənt] *n* comportement *m*, tenue *f*.

depose [diˈpouz] *vt* déposer.

deposit [diˈpɔzit] *n* dépôt *m*, sédiment *m*, gisement *m*, gage *m*; *vt* déposer, verser en gage.

depositary [diˈpɔzitəri] *n* dépositaire *m*.

deposition [͵diːpəˈziʃən] *n* déposition *f*.

depository [diˈpɔzitəri] *n* garde-meubles *m*, entrepôt *m*.

depot [ˈdepou] *n* dépôt *m*, entrepôt *m*, garage *m*; gare *f*.

depravation [͵deprəˈveiʃən] *n* dépravation *f*.

deprave [diˈpreiv] *vt* dépraver.

deprecate [ˈdeprikeit] *vt* déconseiller (fortement), désapprouver.

depreciate [diˈpriːʃieit] *vt* déprécier; *vi* se déprécier.

depreciation [di͵priːʃiˈeiʃən] *n* dépréciation *f*, amortissement *m*.

depredation [͵depriˈdeiʃən] *n* déprédation *f*.

depress [diˈpres] *vt* (a)baisser, appuyer, déprimer, attrister.

depression [diˈpreʃən] *n* dépression *f*, abattement *m*.

deprival [diˈpraivəl] *n* privation *f*.

deprive [diˈpraiv] *vt* priver.

depth [depθ] *n* profondeur *f*, fond *m*, fort *m*, cœur *m*; **to get out of one's —** perdre pied.

deputation [͵depjuˈteiʃən] *n* délégation *f*.

depute [diˈpjuːt] *vt* déléguer.

deputize [ˈdepjutaiz] **to — for** *vt* représenter, remplacer.

deputy [ˈdepjuti] *n* délégué *m*, suppléant *m*, sous-.

derail [diˈreil] *vt* (faire) dérailler.

derailment [diˈreilmənt] *n* déraillement *m*.

derange [diˈreindʒ] *vt* déranger.

derangement [diˈreindʒmənt] *n* dérangement *m*.

derelict [ˈderilikt] *n* épave *f*; *a* abandonné.

dereliction [͵deriˈlikʃən] *n* abandon *m*, négligence *f*.

deride [diˈraid] *vt* tourner en dérision, bafouer, se gausser de.

derision [di'riʒən] *n* dérision *f*, objet *m* de dérision.

derisive [di'raisiv] *a* ironique, dérisoire, railleur.

derivation [,deri'veiʃən] *n* dérivation *f*.

derivative [di'rivətiv] *an* dérivatif *m*.

derive [di'raiv] *vti* tirer; *vi* dériver, provenir.

derogate ['derəgeit] *vi* déroger (à **from**), diminuer.

derogation [,derə'geiʃən] *n* dérogation *f*, abaissement *m*.

derogatory [di'rɔgətəri] *a* dérogatoire.

descend [di'send] *vti* descendre, dévaler; *vi* s'abaisser.

descent [di'sent] *n* descente *f*, lignage *m*, parage *m*, transmission *f*.

describe [dis'kraib] *vt* dépeindre, décrire, donner pour, qualifier, signaler.

description [dis'kripʃən] *n* description *f*, signalement *m*, espèce *f*.

descriptive [dis'kriptiv] *a* descriptif, de description.

descry [dis'krai] *vt* apercevoir, aviser.

desecrate ['desikreit] *vt* profaner.

desert [di'zə:t] *n* mérite *m*, dû *m*; *vt* abandonner; *vti* déserter.

desert ['dezət] *an* désert *m*.

deserter [di'zə:tə] *n* déserteur *m*.

desertion [di'zə:ʃən] *n* désertion *f*, abandon *m*.

deserve [di'zə:v] *vt* mériter.

deservedly [di'zə:vidli] *ad* à juste titre.

deserving [di'zə:viŋ] *a* méritant, méritoire.

de siccate ['desikeit] *vt* dessécher.

desiccation [,desi'keiʃən] *n* desiccation *f*.

design [di'zain] *n* dess(e)in *m*, esquisse *f*, modèle *m*, projet *m*; *vt* désigner, esquisser, projeter, créer, former, destiner.

designate ['dezigneit] *vt* désigner, nommer.

designation [,dezig'neiʃən] *n* désignation *f*, nom *m*.

designedly [di'zainidli] *ad* à dessein.

designer [di'zainə] *n* dessinateur, -trice, créateur, -trice, décorateur *m*.

designing [di'zainiŋ] *a* intrigant.

desirable [di'zaiərəbl] *a* désirable, souhaitable.

desire [di'zaiə] *n* désir *m*, souhait *m*; *vt* désirer, avoir envie de.

desirous [di'zaiərəs] *a* désireux.

desist [di'zist] *vi* renoncer (à **from**), cesser (de **from**).

desk [desk] *n* pupitre *m*, bureau *m*.

desolate ['desəlit] *a* solitaire, abandonné, désert, désolé.

desolate [,'desəleit] *vt* dépeupler, dévaster, désoler.

desolation [,desə'leiʃən] *n* désolation *f*, solitude *f*.

despair [dis'pɛə] *n* désespoir *m*; *vi* désespérer.

despairingly [dis pɛəriŋli] *ad* désespérément.

desperate ['despərit] *a* désespéré, forcené, acharné, affreux.

desperation [,despə'reiʃən] *n* désespoir *m*.

despicable [dis'pikəbl] *a* méprisable.

despise [dis'paiz] *vt* mépriser.

despite [dis'pait] *ad* malgré.

despoil [dis'pɔil] *vt* dépouiller, spolier.

despoiler [dis'pɔilə] *n* spoliateur, -trice.

despoliation [,dispɔli'eiʃən] *n* spoliation *f*.

despond [dis'pɔnd] *vi* se décourager.

despondency [dis'pɔndensi] *n* découragement *m*, abattement *m*.

despondent [dis'pɔndənt] *a* découragé, abattu.

despot ['despɔt] *n* despote *m*.

despotic [des'pɔtik] *a* despotique, arbitraire.

despotism ['despətizəm] *n* despotisme *m*.

dessert [di'zə:t] *n* dessert *m*, entremets *m*.

dessert-spoon [di'zə:tspu:n] *n* cuiller *f* à entremets.

destination [,desti'neiʃən] *n* destination *f*.

destine ['destin] *vt* destiner.

destiny ['destini] *n* destinée *f*, destin *m*, sort *m*.

destitute ['destitju:t] *a* sans ressources, dénué, indigent.

destitution [,desti'tju:ʃən] *n* dénuement *m*, misère *f*, indigence *f*.

destroy [dis'trɔi] *vt* détruire.

destroyer [dis'trɔiə] *n* destructeur, -trice, (*naut*) contre-torpilleur *m*.

destruction [dis'trʌkʃən] *n* destruction *f*.

destructive [dis'trʌktiv] *a* destructeur, destructif.

desultorily ['desəltərili] *ad* sans suite, à bâtons rompus.

desultoriness ['desəltərinis] *n* incohérence *f*, décousu *m*, manque de suite *m*.

desultory ['desəltəri] *a* décousu, sans suite.

detach [di'tætʃ] *vt* détacher, dételer.

detachedly [di'tætʃədli] *ad* d'un ton (air) détaché, avec désinvolture.

detachment [di'tætʃmənt] *n* détachement *m*, indifférence.

detail [di'teil] *n* détail *m*, détachement *m*; *vt* détailler, affecter (à **for**).

detailed ['di:teild] *a* détaillé, circonstancié; — **work** travail très fouillé.

detain [di'tein] *vt* retenir, empêcher, détenir.

detect [di'tekt] *vt* découvrir, apercevoir, repérer, détecter.

detection [di'tekʃən] *n* découverte *f*, détection *f*, repérage *m*.

detective [di'tektiv] *n* détective *m*; — **novel** roman policier *m*.

detention [di'tenʃən] *n* détention *f*,

arrestation *f*, arrêts *m pl*, retard *m*, retenue *f*.
deter [di'tə:] *vt* détourner, décourager, retenir.
deteriorate [di'tiəriəreit] *vt* détériorer; *vi* se détériorer, dégénérer, se gâter.
deterioration [di,tiəriə'reiʃən] *n* détérioration *f*, dégénération *f*.
determination [di,tə:mi'neiʃən] *n* détermination *f*, résolution *f*.
determine [di'tə:min] *vti* déterminer, décider; *vt* constater.
determined [di'tə:mind] *a* résolu.
deterrent [di'terənt] *n* mesure préventive *f*, arme *f* de dissuasion.
detest [di'test] *vt* détester.
detestation [,di:tes'teiʃən] *n* horreur *f*, haîne *f*.
detonate ['detəneit] *vi* détoner; *vt* faire détoner.
detonation [,detə'neiʃən] *n* détonation *f*.
detract [di'trækt] **to — from** retrancher, déprécier, diminuer.
detraction [di'trækʃən] *n* dénigrement *m*, détraction *f*.
detractor [di'træktə] *n* détracteur, -trice.
detriment ['detrimənt] *n* détriment *m*, préjudice *m*.
detrimental [,detri'məntl] *a* préjudiciable, nuisible.
deuce [dju:s] *n* deux *m*, diable *m*, diantre *m*.
deuced [dju:st] *a* sacré, satané.
devastate ['devəsteit] *vt* ravager, dévaster.
devastation [,devəs'teiʃən] *n* dévastation *f*.
devastating ['devəsteitiŋ] *a* dévastateur.
develop [di'veləp] *vt* exploiter, développer; *vi* se développer, se produire.
development [di'veləpmənt] *n* développement *m*.
deviate ['di:vieit] *vi* dévier, s'écarter.
deviation [,di:vi'eiʃən] *n* déviation *f*, écart *m*.
device [di'vais] *n* plan *m*, ruse *f*, moyen *m*, invention *f*, dispositif *m*, devise *f*.
devil ['devl] *n* diable *m*.
devilish ['devliʃ] *a* diabolique.
devilry ['devlri] *n* diablerie *f*, méchanceté *f*.
devious ['di:vjəs] *a* détourné, tortueux.
devise [di'vaiz] *vt* imaginer, combiner, tramer.
deviser [di'vaizə] *n* inventeur, -trice.
devoid [di'vɔid] *a* dénué, dépourvu.
devolve [di'vɔlv] *vt* passer (à **upon**), rejeter (sur **upon**), transmettre; *vi* échoir, incomber.
devote [di'vout] *vt* vouer, dévouer, consacrer.
devotee [,devou'ti:] *n* fanatique *mf*, fervent(e) *mf*.

devotion [di'vouʃən] *n* dévotion *f*, dévouement *m*, consécration *f*.
devour [di'vauə] *vt* dévorer.
devout [di'vaut] *an* dévôt, fervent, zélé.
dew [dju:] *n* rosée *f*.
dewy ['dju:i] *a* couvert de rosée.
dexterity [deks'teriti] *n* dextérité *f*.
dexterous ['dekstrəs] *a* adroit.
diabetes [,daiə'bi:ti:z] *n* diabète *m*.
diabetic [,daiə'betik] *an* diabétique *mf*.
diabolic(al) [,daiə'bɔlik(əl)] *a* diabolique, infernal.
diadem ['daiədem] *n* diadème *m*.
diagnose ['daiəgnouz] *vt* diagnostiquer.
diagnosis [,daiəg'nousis] *n* diagnostic *m*.
diagonal [dai'ægənl] *n* diagonale *f*; *a* diagonal.
diagram ['daiəgræm] *n* diagramme *m*, tracé *m*, schéma *m*.
dial ['daiəl] *n* cadran *m*.
dialogue ['daiəlɔg] *n* dialogue *m*.
diameter [dai'æmitə] *n* diamètre *m*.
diametrical [,daiə'metrikəl] *a* diamétral.
diamond ['daiəmənd] *n* diamant *m*, losange *m*, (*cards*) carreau *m*.
diaper ['daiəpə] *n* linge damassé *m*; couches *fpl*; *vt* damasser.
diaphragm ['daiəfræm] *n* diaphragme *m*, membrane *m*.
diary ['daiəri] *n* journal *m*, agenda *m*.
dibble ['dibl] *n* plantoir *m*.
dice [dais] *n* dés *m pl*; — **box** cornet *m*.
dicky ['diki] *n* faux-plastron *m*, tablier *m*, (*aut*) spider *m*; *a* flanchard.
dictate ['dikteit] *n* dictat *m*, ordre *m*, voix *f*; [dik'teit] *vt* dicter, ordonner; *vi* faire la loi.
dictation [dik'teiʃən] *n* dictée *f*.
dictator [dik'teitə] *n* dictateur *m*.
dictatorial [,diktə'tɔ:riəl] *a* dictatorial.
dictatorship [dik'teitəʃip] *n* dictature *f*.
diction ['dikʃən] *n* diction *f*, style *m*.
dictionary ['dikʃənri] *n* dictionnaire *m*.
did [did] *pt of* do.
die [dai] *n* (*pl* dice) dé *m*, (*pl* dies) coin *m*, matrice *f*; *vi* mourir, crever; **to — away, out** s'éteindre, tomber.
diehard ['daihɑ:d] *n* jusqu'au boutiste *m*; the **—s** le dernier carré *m*, les irréductibles *m pl*; *a* — **conservative** conservateur intransigeant.
diet ['daiət] *n* régime *m*, diète *f*; *vt* mettre au régime; *vi* suivre un régime.
differ ['difə] *vi* différer.
difference ['difrəns] *n* différence *f*, écart *m*, différend *m*.
different ['difrənt] *a* différent, divers.
differentiate [,difə'renʃieit] *vt* différencier; *vi* faire la différence.

differently ['difrəntli] *ad* différemment.

difficult ['difikəlt] *a* difficile.

difficulty ['difikəlti] *n* difficulté *f*, ennui *m*, peine *f*, gêne *f*.

diffidence ['difidəns] *n* défiance de soi *f*, timidité *f*.

diffident ['difidənt] *a* modeste, timide, qui manque d'assurance.

diffuse [di'fju:z] *vt* diffuser, répandre.

diffuse [di'fju:s] *a* diffus.

diffusion [di'fju:ʒən] *n* diffusion *f*.

dig [dig] *vt* creuser, bêcher, piocher, piquer; **to — up** déterrer, déraciner.

digest [dai'dʒest] *vt* digérer, assimiler; *vi* se digérer, s'assimiler.

digestible [di'dʒestəbl] *a* digestible.

digestion [di'dʒestʃən] *n* digestion *f*.

digestive [di'dʒestiv] *a* digestif.

dignified ['dignifaid] *a* digne, majestueux.

dignify ['dignifai] *vt* honorer, donner un air de majesté à.

dignity ['digniti] *n* dignité *f*.

digress [dai'gres] *vi* s'écarter (de **from**), faire une digression.

digression [dai'greʃən] *n* digression *f*.

digs [digz] *n pl* garni *m*, logement *m*, piaule *f*.

dike [daik] *n* levée *f*, digue *f*, remblai *m*; *vt* endiguer, remblayer.

dilapidated [di'læpideitid] *a* délabré, décrépit.

dilapidation [di,læpi'deiʃən] *n* délabrement *m*, dégradation *f*.

dilatation [,dailei'teiʃən] *n* dilatation *f*.

dilate [dai'leit] *vt* dilater; *vi* se dilater, s'étendre (sur **upon**).

dilatoriness ['dilətərinis] *n* temporisation *f*, tergiversation *f*, lenteur *f*.

dilatory ['dilətəri] *a* lent, tardif.

dilemma [dai'lemə] *n* dilemme *m*.

diligence ['dilidʒəns] *n* diligence *f*, application *f*.

diligent ['dilidʒənt] *a* diligent, appliqué.

diligently ['dilidʒəntli] *ad* diligemment.

dilute [dai'lju:t] *a* dilué, atténué; *vt* diluer, arroser, atténuer.

dim [dim] *a* indistinct, voilé, faible, sourd; *vt* assombrir, éclipser, ternir, mettre en veilleuse; *vi* s'affaiblir, baisser.

dime [daim] *n* pièce de dix cents; **— store** prix unique *m*.

dimension [di'menʃən] *n* dimension *f*.

diminish [di'miniʃ] *vti* diminuer.

diminution [,dimi'nju:ʃən] *n* diminution *f*.

diminutive [di'minjutiv] *an* diminutif *m*.

dimmer ['dimə] *n* phare code *m*.

dimness ['dimnis] *n* pénombre *f*, faiblesse *f*, imprécision *f*.

dim-out ['dimaut] *n* obscurcissement *m*.

dimple ['dimpl] *n* fossette *f*, ride *f*, creux *m*.

din [din] *n* tintamarre *m*, vacarme *m*; *vt* corner, rabattre.

dine [dain] *vi* dîner; **to — out** dîner en ville.

dinghy ['diŋgi] *n* canot *m*.

dingy ['dindʒi] *a* sale, crasseux, terne, sombre.

dining-room ['daininrum] *n* salle *f* à manger.

dinner ['dinə] *n* dîner *m*.

dinner-jacket ['dinə,dʒækit] *n* smoking *m*.

dint [dint] **by — of** à force de.

diocese ['daiəsis] *n* diocèse *m*.

dip [dip] *n* plongeon *m*, pent : *f*. immersion *f*, bain *m*; *vti* plonger, baisser, (*headlights*) basculer; *vt* puiser, tremper, baigner; *vi* pencher.

diphtheria [dip'θiəriə] *n* diphtérie *f*.

diphthong ['dipθɔŋ] *n* diphtongue *f*.

diploma [di'ploumə] *n* diplôme *m*.

diplomacy [di'ploum128si] *n* diplomatie *f*.

diplomat ['dipləmæt] *n* diplomate *m*.

diplomatic [,diplə'mætik] *a* diplomatique, prudent.

dire ['daiə] *a* affreux, cruel, dernier, extrême.

direct [dai'rekt] *a* direct, droit, catégorique, formel, franc; *vt* adresser, diriger, attirer, ordonner, indiquer.

direction [di'rekʃən] *n* direction *f*, sens *m*, adresse *f*; *pl* instructions *f pl*.

directly [di'rektli] *ad* tout de suite, (tout) droit, directement, tout à l'heure, bientôt, personnellement.

director [di'rektə] *n* directeur *m*, gérant *m*, administrateur *m*.

directorship [di'rektəʃip] *n* directorat *m*.

directory [di'rektəri] *n* indicateur *m*, annuaire *m*, bottin *m*, directoire *m*.

dirge [də:dʒ] *n* misérère *m*, chant funèbre *m*.

dirk [də:k] *n* poignard *m*.

dirt [də:t] *n* boue *f*, saleté *f*, ordure *f*, crasse *f*.

dirtiness ['də:tinis] *n* crasse *f*, saleté *f*.

dirty ['də:ti] *vt* salir; *vi* se salir; *a* sale, malpropre, crasseux, vilain, polisson.

disability [,disə'biliti] *n* incapacité *f* (de travail), infirmité *f*.

disable [dis'eibl] *vt* rendre impropre au travail, mettre hors de combat, désemparer.

disabled [dis'eibld] *a* invalide, estropié, désemparé.

disabuse [,disə'bju:z] *vt* désabuser.

disaffected [,disə'fektid] *a* détaché, refroidi.

disaffection [ˌdisə'fekʃən] n désaffection f.

disagree [ˌdisə'griː] vi n'être pas d'accord, ne pas convenir.

disagreeable [ˌdisə'griːəbl] a désagréable, fâcheux.

disagreement [ˌdisə'griːmənt] n disconvenance f, désaccord m, mésentente f.

disallow ['disə'lau] vt désavouer, interdire, ne pas admettre, rejeter.

disappear [ˌdisə'piə] vi disparaître.

disappearance [ˌdisə'piərəns] n disparition f.

disappoint [ˌdisə'pɔint] vt désappointer, décevoir.

disappointed [ˌdisə'pɔintəd] a déçu; manqué.

disappointment [ˌdisə'pɔintmənt] n déception f, désappointement m, déboire m.

disapproval [ˌdisə'pruːvəl] n désapprobation f.

disapprove [ˌdisə'pruːv] vti désapprouver.

disapproving [ˌdisə'pruːviŋ] a désapprobateur.

disarm [dis'ɑːm] vti désarmer.

disarmament [dis'ɑːməmənt] n désarmement m.

disarrange ['disə'reindʒ] vt déranger.

disarrangement [ˌdisə'reindʒmənt] n désorganisation f, désordre m, dérangement m.

disarray ['disə'rei] n désarroi m, désordre m, déroute f.

disaster [di'zɑːstə] n désastre m, sinistre m, catastrophe f.

disastrous [di'zɑːstrəs] a désastreux, funeste.

disavow [ˌdisə'vau] vt désavouer, renier.

disavowal [ˌdisə'vauəl] n désaveu m, reniement m.

disband [dis'bænd] vt licencier; vi se débander.

disbanding [dis'bændiŋ] n licenciement m.

disbelief ['disbi'liːf] n incrédulité f.

disc [disk] n disque m, plaque f; **slipped — hernie** discale f.

discard [dis'kɑːd] n écart m, défausse f; vt se défausser de, écarter, mettre au rancart, laisser de côté.

discern [di'səːn] vt distinguer, discerner.

discernible [di'səːnəbl] a discernable, perceptible.

discerning [di'səːniŋ] a perspicace, judicieux.

discernment [di'səːnmənt] n discernement m.

discharge [dis'tʃɑːdʒ] n déchargement m, décharge f, acquittement m, élargissement m, renvoi m, exécution f, paiement m; vt décharger, élargir, renvoyer, (s')acquitter (de), lancer; vi se jeter, se dégorger.

disciple [di'saipl] n disciple m.

disciplinary ['disiplinəri] a disciplinaire.

discipline ['disiplin] n discipline f; vt discipliner, mater, former.

disclaim [dis'kleim] vt répudier, désavouer, rénoncer à, dénier.

disclaimer [dis'kleimə] n répudiation f, désaveu m, déni m.

disclose [dis'klouz] vt découvrir, divulguer, révéler.

disclosure [dis'klouʒə] n révélation f, divulgation f.

discolor [dis'kʌlə] vt décolorer, ternir, délaver; vi se décolorer, se ternir.

discoloration [dis.kʌlə'reiʃən] n décoloration f.

discomfit [dis'kʌmfit] vt déconcerter, déconfire.

discomfiture [dis'kʌmfitʃə] n déconfiture f, déconvenue f.

discomfort [dis'kʌmfət] n malaise m, gêne f.

discomposure [ˌdiskəm'pouʒə] n confusion f, trouble m.

disconcert [ˌdiskən'səːt] vt déranger, déconcerter, interloquer.

disconnect ['diskə'nekt] vt couper, décrocher, disjoindre, débrayer.

disconnected ['diskə'nektid] a décousu, sans suite.

disconnection [ˌdiskə'nekʃən] n disjonction f, débrayage m.

disconsolate [dis'kɔnsəlit] a inconsolable, désolé.

discontent ['diskən'tent] n mécontentement m.

discontented ['diskən'tentid] a mécontent, insatisfait (de with).

discontinuance [ˌdiskən'tinjuəns] n discontinuation f, fin f.

discontinue ['disken'tinju] vt discontinuer; vti cesser.

discontinuity ['dis.kɔnti'njuiti] n discontinuité f.

discontinuous ['diskən'tinjuəs] a discontinu.

discord ['diskɔːd] n discorde f, discordance f, dissonance f.

discount ['diskaunt] n rabais m, escompte m; [dis'kaunt] vt escompter, laisser hors de compte.

discountenance [dis'kauntinəns] vt désapprouver, décontenancer.

discourage [dis'kʌridʒ] vt décourager, déconseiller.

discouragement [dis'kʌridʒmənt] n découragement m.

discourse ['diskɔːs] n traité m, sermon m, essai m, dissertation f.

discourse [dis'kɔːs] vi causer, discourir.

discourteous [dis'kəːtjəs] a discourtois, impoli.

discourtesy [dis'kəːtisi] n discourtoisie f, impolitesse f.

discover [dis'kʌvə] vt découvrir, révéler, s'apercevoir (de), constater.

discovery [dis'kʌvəri] n révélation f, découverte f, trouvaille f.

discredit [dis'kredit] n déconsidération f, discrédit m, doute m; vt discréditer, déconsidérer, mettre en doute.

discreditable [dis'kreditəbl] a indigne, déshonorant.

discreet [dis'kriːt] a discret, prudent.

discrepancy [dis'krepənsi] n désaccord m, inconsistance f, écart m.

discretion [dis'kreʃən] n prudence f, discrétion f, choix m.

discriminate [dis'krimineit] vt distinguer.

discriminating [dis'krimineitiŋ] a sagace, avisé, fin.

discrimination [dis,krimi'neiʃən] n finesse f, goût m, discernement m.

discuss [dis'kʌs] vt discuter, délibérer, débattre.

discussion [dis'kʌʃən] n discussion f.

disdain [dis'dein] n dédain m; vt dédaigner.

disdainful [dis'deinful] a dédaigneux.

disease [di'ziːz] n maladie f, affection f.

diseased [di'ziːzd] a malade; — **mind** esprit morbide m.

disembark ['disim'baːk] vti débarquer.

disembarkation [,disembaː'keiʃən] n débarquement m.

disembody ['disim'bɔdi] vt désincarner, désincorporer, licencier.

disembowel [,disim'bauəl] vt éventrer.

disengage ['disin'geidʒ] vt dégager, rompre, débrayer, déclencher; vi se dégager, rompre.

disengaged ['disin'geidʒd] a libre, visible.

disengagement ['disin'geidʒmənt] n dégagement m, rupture f.

disentangle ['disin'tæŋgl] vt débrouiller, démêler, dépêtrer.

disentanglement ['disin'tæŋglmənt] n débrouillement m, démêlage m.

disfavor [dis'feivə] n défaveur f, disgrâce f.

disfigure [dis'figə] vt défigurer, gâter.

disfranchise ['dis'fræntʃaiz] vt priver de droits politiques, de représentation parlementaire.

disgorge [dis'gɔːdʒ] vt rendre, dégorger; vi se jeter.

disgrace [dis'greis] n disgrâce f, honte f; vt disgrâcier, déshonorer.

disgraceful [dis'greisful] a honteux, scandaleux.

disgruntled [dis'grʌntld] a mécontent, bougon.

disguise [dis'gaiz] n déguisement m, feinte f; in — déguisé; vt déguiser, travestir.

disgust [dis'gʌst] n dégoût m; vt dégoûter, écœurer.

disgusting [dis'gʌstiŋ] a dégoûtant, dégueulasse.

dish [diʃ] n plat m, mets m, récipient m, bol m; vt servir, supplanter, rouler, déjouer.

dish-cloth ['diʃklɔθ] n lavette f, torchon m.

dish-cover ['diʃ kʌvə] n couvre-plat m.

dishearten [dis'haːtn] vt décourager, démoraliser.

disheveled [di'ʃevəld] a débraillé, dépeigné.

dishonest [dis'ɔnist] a malhonnête, déloyal.

dishonesty [dis'ɔnisti] n malhonnêteté f, improbité f.

dishonor |[dis'ɔnə] n déshonneur m; vt déshonorer.

dishonorable [dis'ɔnərəbl] a déshonorant, sans honneur.

dishwasher ['diʃ,wɔʃə] n plongeur m.

dishwater ['diʃ,wɔːtə] n eau de vaisselle f.

disillusion [,disi'luːʒən] vt désillusionner, désabuser.

disillusionment [,disi'luːʒənmənt] n désenchantement m, désillusionnement m.

disinclination [,disinkli'neiʃən] n aversion f, répugnance f.

disinfect [,disin'fekt] vt désinfecter.

disinfectant [,disin'fektənt] an désinfectant m.

disinfection [,disin'fekʃən] n désinfection f.

disingenuous [,disin'dʒenjuəs] a faux.

disingenuousness [,disin'dʒenjuəsnis] n fausseté f.

disinherit ['disin'herit] vt déshériter.

disintegrate [dis'intigreit] vt désintégrer, désagréger; vi se désintégrer, se désagréger.

disintegration [dis,inti'greiʃən] n désintégration f, désagrégation f.

disinterested [dis'intristid] a désintéressé.

disinterestedness [dis'intristidnis] n désintéressement m.

disjoin [dis'dʒɔin] vt disjoindre, désunir.

disjoint [dis'dʒɔint] vt disjoindre, disloquer, démettre, désarticuler.

disjointed [dis'dʒɔintid] a disloqué, décousu, incohérent.

dislike [dis'laik] n antipathie f; vt ne pas aimer, trouver antipathique, détester.

dislodge [dis'lɔdʒ] vt déloger, détacher, dénicher.

disloyal ['dis'lɔiəl] a déloyal, infidèle.

disloyalty ['dis'lɔiəlti] n déloyauté f, infidélité f.

dismal ['dizmal] a morne, lugubre.

dismantle [dis'mæntl] vt démanteler, démonter.

dismantling [dis'mæntliŋ] n démantèlement m, démontage m.

dismay [dis'mei] n consternation f, épouvante f, gêne f; vt effrayer, consterner, affoler.

dismember [dis'membə] *vt* démembrer.

dismiss [dis'mis] *vt* renvoyer, congédier, révoquer, rejeter, écarter, acquitter.

dismissal [dis'misəl] *n* renvoi *m*, révocation *f*, acquittement *m*.

disobedience [,disə'bi:djəns] *n* désobéissance *f*.

disobedient [,disə'bi:djənt] *a* désobéissant.

disobey [,disə'bei] *vt* désobéir à; *vi* désobéir.

disoblige ['disə'blaidʒ] *vt* désobliger.

disobliging ['disə'blaidʒiŋ] *a* désobligeant.

disorder [dis'ɔ:də] *n* désordre *m*, confusion *f*.

disorderly [dis'ɔ:dəli] *a* désordonné, turbulent, déréglé, en désordre.

disorganization [dis,ɔ:gənai'zeiʃən] *n* désorganisation *f*.

disorganize [dis'ɔ:gənaiz] *vt* désorganiser.

disown [dis'oun] *vt* désavouer, renier.

disparage [dis'pæridʒ] *vt* dénigrer déprécier.

disparagement [dis'pæridʒmənt] *n* dénigrement *m*, dépréciation *f*.

disparity [dis'pæriti] *n* inégalité *f*, différence *f*.

dispassionate [dis'pæʃnit] *a* calme, impartial, désintéressé.

dispatch [dis'pætʃ] *n* envoi *m*, rapidité *f*, dépêche *f*, expédition *f*, promptitude *f*; *vt* expédier, envoyer, dépêcher.

dispatch-rider [dis'pætʃ,raidə] *n* estafette *f*.

dispel [dis'pel] *vt* dissiper, chasser.

dispensary [dis'pensəri] *n* dispensaire *m*, pharmacie *f*.

dispensation [,dispen'seiʃən] *n* distribution *f*, dispensation *f*, dispense *f*.

dispense [dis'pens] *vt* distribuer, administrer; *vi* se dispenser (de with), se passer (de with).

disperse [dis'pə:s] *vt* disperser, dissiper; *vi* se disperser.

dispersion [dis'pə:ʃən] *n* dispersion *f*.

dispirit [dis'pirit] *vt* décourager.

displace [dis'pleis] *vt* déplacer, remplacer.

displacement [dis'pleismənt] *n* déplacement *m*.

display [dis'plei] *n* déploiement *m*, étalage *m*, parade *f*, manifestation *f*, montre *f*; *vt* déployer, faire parade, (montre, preuve) de, manifester, afficher.

displease [dis'pli:z] *vt* déplaire à, mécontenter.

displeasure [dis'pleʒə] *n* déplaisir *m*, mécontentement *m*.

disport [dis'pɔ:t] *vr* se divertir.

disposal [dis'pouzəl] *n* disposition *f*, vente *f*, cession *f*.

dispose [dis'pouz] *vt* disposer,

arranger, expédier; *vi* se disposer (de of), se débarrasser (de of).

dispossess [,dispə'zes] *vt* déposséder.

dispossession [,dispə'zeʃən] *n* dépossession *f*.

disproof [dis'pru:f] *n* réfutation *f*.

disproportion [,disprə'pɔ:ʃən] *n* disproportion *f*.

disproportionate [,disprə'pɔ:ʃnit] *a* disproportionné.

disprove [dis'pru:v] *vt* réfuter.

disputable [dis'pju:təbl] *a* discutable, contestable.

dispute [dis'pju:t] *n* dispute *f*, discussion *f*; *vt* discuter, débattre, contester; *vi* se disputer.

disqualification [dis,kwɔlifi'keiʃən] *n* disqualification *f*, inhabilité *f*.

disqualify [dis'kwɔlifai] *vt* disqualifier.

disquiet [dis'kwaiət] *n* inquiétude *f*; *vt* inquiéter.

disregard [,disri'gɑ:d] *n* indifférence *f*, mépris *m*; *vt* laisser de côté, ne tenir aucun compte de, mépriser.

disregarding [,disri'gɑ:diŋ] *prep* sans égard à (pour).

disrepair [,disri'pɛə] *n* délabrement *m*.

disreputable [dis'repjutəbl] *a* déconsidéré, de mauvaise réputation, minable.

disrepute ['disri'pju:t] *n* mauvaise réputation *f*, discrédit *m*.

disrespect ['disris'pekt] *n* manque de respect *m*.

disrespectful [,disris'pektful] *a* irrespectueux, irrévérencieux.

disruption [dis'rʌpʃən] *n* dislocation *f*, scission *f*, démembrement *m*.

dissatisfaction ['dis,sætis'fækʃən] *n* mécontentement *m*.

dissatisfy [dis'sætisfai] *vt* mécontenter.

dissect [di'sekt] *vt* disséquer.

dissection [di'sekʃən] *n* dissection *f*.

dissemble [di'sembl] *vt* dissimuler.

dissembler [di'semblə] *n* hypocrite *mf*.

disseminate [di'semineit] *vt* disséminer.

dissemination [di,semi'neiʃən] *n* dissémination *f*.

dissension [di'senʃən] *n* dissension *f*.

dissent [di'sent] *n* dissentiment *m*, dissidence *f*; *vi* différer.

dissenter [di'sentə] *n* dissident *m*.

dissipate ['disipeit] *vt* dissiper; *vi* se dissiper.

dissipation [,disi'peiʃən] *n* dissipation *f*, dispersion *f*, gaspillage *m*, dérèglement *m*.

dissolute ['disəlu:t] *a* dissolu, débauché.

dissoluteness ['disəlu:tnis] *n* dérèglement *m*, débauche *f*.

dissolution [,disə'lu:ʃən] *n* dissolution *f*, dissipation *f*.

dissolve [di'zɔlv] *vt* dissoudre; *vi* se dissoudre.

dissolvent [di'zɔlvənt] *an* dissolvant *m.*

distaff ['distɑːf] *n* quenouille *f.*

distance ['distəns] *n* distance *f*, lointain *m*, intervalle *m*, éloignement *m.*

distant ['distənt] *a* éloigné, lointain, distant, réservé.

distaste ['dis'teist] *n* répugnance *f*, aversion *f.*

distasteful [dis'teistful] *a* répugnant, antipathique.

distemper [dis'tempə] *n* maladie *f* (des chiens), badigeon *m*, détrempe *f*; *vt* badigeonner.

distend [dis'tend] *vt* gonfler, dilater; *vi* enfler, se dilater.

distill [dis'til] *vti* distiller; *vi* s'égoutter, se distiller.

distillation [‚disti'leiʃən] *n* distillation *f.*

distiller [dis'tilə] *n* distillateur *m.*

distillery [dis'tiləri] *n* distillerie *f.*

distinct [dis'tiŋkt] *a* distinct, net, clair.

distinction [dis'tiŋkʃən] *n* distinction *f.*

distinctive [dis'tiŋktiv] *a* distinctif.

distinctness [dis'tiŋktnis] *n* netteté *f.*

distinguish [dis'tiŋgwiʃ] *vt* distinguer; *vi* faire la distinction.

distinguishable [dis'tiŋgwiʃəbl] *a* perceptible, sensible.

distort [dis'tɔːt] *vt* déformer, travestir, tordre, convulser, fausser.

distract [dis'trækt] *vt* distraire, détourner, diviser, déranger.

distracted [dis'træktid] *a* fou, furieux, affolé.

distraction [dis'trækʃən] *n* distraction *f*, dérangement *m*, folie *f*, affolement *m.*

distress [dis'tres] *n* détresse *f*, dénuement *m*, misère *f*, angoisse *f*; *vt* tourmenter, affliger, épuiser.

distribute [dis'tribjuːt] *vt* distribuer, répartir.

distribution [‚distri'bjuːʃən] *n* distribution *f*, répartition *f.*

district ['distrikt] *n* district *m*, région *f.*

distrust [dis'trʌst] *n* méfiance *f*; *vt* se méfier de.

distrustful [dis'trʌstful] *a* méfiant, soupçonneux.

disturb [dis'təːb] *vt* troubler, agiter, déranger.

disturbance [dis'təːbəns] *n* trouble *m*, bagarre *f*, émeute *f*, tapage *m.*

disunion [dis'juːnjən] *n* désunion *f.*

disuse ['dis'juːs] *n* désuétude *f.*

disused [dis'juːzd] *a* hors de service, hors d'usage.

ditch [ditʃ] *n* tranchée *f*, fossé *m*; *vt* creuser, draîner; faire dérailler (train); **to be —ed** échouer, être dans le pétrin.

ditcher ['ditʃə] *n* fossoyeur *m.*

ditto ['ditou] *an* idem, amen.

ditty ['diti] *n* chanson (nette) *f.*

divagate ['daivəgeit] *vi* divaguer.

divagation [‚daivə'geiʃən] *n* divagation *f.*

divan [di'væn] *n* divan *m*; **—bed** divan-lit *m.*

dive [daiv] *n* plongeon *m*, plongée *f*, pique *m*; *vi* se plonger, piquer (une tête, du nez).

diver ['daivə] *n* plongeur *m*, scaphandrier *m.*

diverge [dai'vəːdʒ] *vi* diverger, s'écarter.

divergence [dai'vəːdʒəns] *n* divergence *f.*

diverse [dai'vəːs] *a* divers, différent.

diversify [dai'vəːsifai] *vt* diversifier.

diversion [dai'vəːʃən] *n* diversion *f*, divertissement *m*, détournement *m.*

divert [dai'vəːt] *vt* détourner, divertir, écarter, distraire.

divest [dai'vest] *vt* dévêtir, dépouiller, priver.

divide [di'vaid] *vt* partager, diviser; *vi* aller aux voix, se diviser, se partager, fourcher.

dividend ['dividend] *n* dividende *m.*

dividers [di'vaidəz] *n* compas *m.*

divine [di'vain] *n* théologien *m*, prêtre *m*; *a* divin; *vt* deviner, prédire.

diviner [di'vainə] *n* devin *m*, sourcier *m.*

diving ['daiviŋ] *n* (*sport*) plongeon *m*, (*av*) piqué *m*; **— board** plongeoire *m.*

divinity [di'viniti] *n* divinité *f*, théologie *f.*

division [di'viʒən] *n* division *f*, partage *m*, répartition *f*, frontière *f*, vote *m.*

divorce [di'vɔːs] *n* divorce *m*; *vt* divorcer.

divulge [dai'vʌldʒ] *vt* divulguer.

divulgement [dai'vʌldʒmənt] *n* divulgation *f.*

dizziness ['dizinis] *n* vertige *m*, étourdissement *m.*

dizzy ['dizi] *a* étourdi, vertigineux.

do [duː] *vt* faire, finir, cuire à point, rouler, refaire; *vi* se porter, aller, s'acquitter; **to — away with** supprimer, abolir, tuer; **to — up** remettre à neuf, retaper.

docile ['dousail] *a* docile.

docility [dou'siliti] *n* docilité *f.*

dock [dɔk] *n* bassin *m*, dock *m*, cale *f*, banc *m* des accusés, box *m*; *vt* mettre en bassin; *vi* entrer au bassin.

docker ['dɔkə] *n* débardeur *m.*

docket ['dɔkit] *n* bordereau *m*, fiche *f*, étiquette *f*; *vt* classer, étiqueter.

dockyard ['dɔkjɑːd] *n* chantier maritime *m.*

doctor ['dɔktə] *n* docteur *m*, médecin *m*; *vt* soigner, falsifier, cuisiner, doper, truquer, maquiller.

document ['dɔkjumənt] *n* document *m*; **—case** porte-documents *m.*

documentary [ˌdɔkju'mentəri] *a* documentaire

documentation [ˌdɔkjumen'teiʃən] *n* documentation *f*.

dodge [dɔdʒ] *n* tour *m*, faux-fuyant *m*, truc *m*, esquive *f*; *vi* se jeter de côté, s'esquiver, finasser; *vt* esquiver, éviter, tourner, éluder.

dodger ['dɔdʒə] *n* finaud *m*, tire-au-flanc *m*.

doe [dou] *n* daine *f*, lapine *f*.

doff [dɔf] *vt* ôter.

dog [dɔg] *n* chien *m*, chenet *m*, gaillard *m*; **dirty——** salaud *m*; **——tired** (*fam*) claqué.

dog-days ['dɔgdeiz] *n* canicule *f*.

dogged ['dɔgid] *a* tenace.

doggedness ['dɔgidnis] *n* ténacité *f*, persévérance *f*.

doggerel ['dɔgərəl] *n* poésie burlesque *f*; *a* trivial, boîteux, de mirliton.

dogma ['dɔgmə] *n* dogme *m*.

dogmatic [dɔg'mætik] *a* dogmatique, tranchant.

dog's ear ['dɔgz'iə] *n* corne *f*; *vt* faire une corne à, corner.

doily ['dɔili] *n* napperon *m*.

doings ['duːiŋz] *n pl* faits et gestes *m pl*, agissements *m pl*, exploits *m pl*.

doldrums ['dɔldrəmz] *n pl* **to be in the —** avoir le cafard, être dans le marasme.

dole [doul] *n* don *m*, aumône *f*, allocation de chômage *f*; **to — out** *vt* donner au compte-goutte.

doleful ['doulful] *a* triste, sombre, dolent, lugubre.

doll [dɔl] *n* poupée *f*.

dolphin ['dɔlfin] *n* dauphin *m*.

dolt [doult] *n* niais *m*, sot *m*.

domain [də'mein] *n* domaine *m*, propriété *f*.

dome [doum] *n* dôme *m*, coupole *f*.

domestic [də'mestik] *an* domestique *mf*; *a* d'intérieur, national, de ménage.

domesticate [də'mestikeit] *vi* domestiquer, apprivoiser.

domesticated [də'mestikeitid] *a* soumis, d'intérieur.

domesticity [ˌdɔmes'tisiti] *n* amour *m* du foyer, vie privée *f*, soumission *f*.

domicile ['dɔmisail] *n* domicile *m*.

dominate ['dɔmineit] *vti* dominer; *vt* commander.

domination [ˌdɔmi'neiʃən] *n* domination *f*.

domineer [ˌdɔmi'niə] *vt* tyranniser.

domineering [ˌdɔmi'niəriŋ] *a* dominateur, autoritaire.

Dominican [də'minikən] *an* dominicain(e) *mf*.

dominion [də'minjən] *n* domination *f*, empire *m*; *pl* dominions *m pl*, colonies *f pl*.

don [dɔn] *vt* enfiler, endosser, revêtir; *n* professeur *m*.

donation [dou'neiʃən] *n* donation *f*, don *m*.

done [dʌn] *pp of* do; *a* fourbu, fini, conclu! tope là, cuit à point; **over—** trop cuit; **under—** saignant; **well —**! bravo! bien cuit.

donkey ['dɔŋki] *n* âne *m*, baudet *m*.

donor ['dounə] *n* donateur, -trice.

doom [duːm] *n* jugement *m* (dernier), ruine *f*, malheur *m*, sort *m*; *vt* condamner, vouer, perdre.

door [dɔː] *n* porte *f*, portière *f*.

doorkeeper ['dɔːˌkiːpə] *n* concierge *mf*, portier *m*.

doormat ['dɔːmæt] *n* paillasson.

doorstep ['dɔːstep] *n* pas *m*, seuil *m*.

dope [doup] *n* narcotique *m*, stupéfiant *m*, tuyau *m*, bourrage de crâne *m*; *vt* droguer, doper, endormir.

dormer ['dɔːmə] *n* lucarne *f*.

dormitory ['dɔːmitri] *n* dortoir *m*.

dormouse ['dɔːmaus] *n* loir *m*.

Dorothy ['dɔrəθi] Dorothée *f*.

dose [dous] *n* dose *f*; *vt* doser, droguer.

dot [dɔt] *n* point *m*; *vt* mettre les points sur, semer, pointiller, piquer.

dotage ['doutidʒ] *n* radotage *m*, seconde enfance *f*.

dotard ['doutəd] *n* gaga *m*, gâteux *m*.

dote [dout] *vt* radoter, raffoler (de on).

double ['dʌbl] *n* double *m*, crochet *m*, sosie *m*; *a* double; *ad* double (ment), deux fois, à double sens, en partie double; *vt* doubler, plier en deux; *vi* (se) doubler, prendre le pas de gymnastique.

double-clutch [ˌdʌbl'klʌtʃ] *vi* (*aut*) faire un double débrayage.

double-dealer ['dʌbl'diːlə] *n* fourbe *m*.

double-dealing ['dʌbl'diːliŋ] *m* duplicité *f*.

double-dyed ['dʌbl'daid] *a* fieffé, achevé.

double-edged ['dʌbl'edʒd] *a* à deux tranchants.

double-lock ['dʌbl'lɔk] *vt* fermer à double tour.

double-quick ['dʌbl'kwik] *ad* au pas de course.

doubt [daut] *n* doute *m*; *vt* douter.

doubtful ['dautful] *a* douteux, incertain.

doubtless ['dautlis] *ad* sans doute.

dough [dou] *n* pâte *f*; (*sl*) fric *m*.

doughnut ['dounʌt] *n* beignet soufflé *m*, pet de nonne *m*.

doughy ['doui] *a* pâteux.

dour [duə] *a* sévère, obstiné, buté.

dove [dʌv] *n* colombe *f*.

dovecot(e) ['dʌvkɔt] *n* colombier *m*.

dovetail ['dʌvteil] *n* queue d'aronde *f*; *vi* s'encastrer; *vt* encastrer, assembler à queue d'aronde.

dowager ['dauədʒə] *n* douairière *f*.

dowdy ['daudi] *a* mal fagoté.

down [daun] *n* dune *f*; duvet *m*; bas *m*; *a* en bas, en pente, descendant; *prep* au (en) bas de; *ad* en bas, en aval, à bas! comptant, par écrit, en baisse; *vt* abattre, terrasser, descendre.

down-and-outer ['daunən'autə] *n* pouilleux *m*, miséreux.

downcast ['daunkɑːst] *a* abattu, déprimé.

downfall ['daunfɔːl] *n* chute *f*, ruine *f*.

downhearted ['daun'hɑːtid] *a* découragé, abattu.

downpour ['daunpɔː] *n* déluge *m*, forte pluie *f*.

downright ['daunrait] *a* franc, droit, net; *ad* carrément, catégoriquement; tout à fait.

downstairs ['daun'stɛəz] *ad* en bas.

downtrodden ['daun,trɔdn] *a* opprimé, foulé aux pieds.

downward ['daunwəd] *ad* en aval, en descendant.

downy ['dauni] *a* duveté.

dowry ['dauri] *n* dot *f*, douaire *m*.

doze [douz] *n* somme *m*; *vi* sommeiller, s'assoupir.

dozen ['dʌzn] *n* douzaine *f*.

drab [dræb] *a* brunâtre, terne, ennuyeux, prosaïque.

draft [drɑːft] *n* détachement *m*, traite *f*, effet *m*, tracé *m*, brouillon *m*, projet *m*; conscription *f*, *n* traction *f*, courant d'air *m*, tirant d'eau *m*, coup *m* (de vin *etc*), esquisse *f*, traite *f*; *pl* jeu de dames *m*; **on** — à la pression; *vt* détacher, désigner, esquisser, rédiger.

draft horse ['drɑːfthɔːs] *n* cheval *m* de trait.

draftsman ['drɑːftsmən] *n* dessinateur *m*, rédacteur *m*.

drag [dræg] *n* drague *f*, herse *f*, traîneau *m*, obstacle *m*, grappin *m*, sabot *m*, résistance *f*; *vt* draguer, (en)traîner; *vi* tirer, traîner.

dragon ['drægən] *n* dragon *m*.

dragonfly ['drægənflai] *n* libellule *f*.

dragoon [drə'guːn] *n* dragon *m*; *vt* persécuter, contraindre.

drain [drein] *n* fossé *m*, caniveau *m*, égout *m*, perte *f*, (*fig*) saignée *f*; *vt* drainer, assécher, assainir; *vi* s'écouler, s'égoutter.

drake [dreik] *n* canard *m*.

drama ['drɑːmə] *n* drame *m*, le théâtre *m*.

dramatic [drə'mætik] *a* dramatique.

dramatist ['dræmətist] *n* dramaturge *m*.

dramatize ['dræmətaiz] *vt* mettre au théâtre, adapter à la scène, dramatiser.

drank ['dræŋk] *pt of* **drink.**

drape [dreip] *vt* draper.

draper ['dreipə] *n* drapier *m*, marchand *m* de nouveautés.

drapery ['dreipəri] *n* draperie *f*.

drastic ['dræstik] *a* radical, énergique.

draw [drɔː] *n* tirage *m*, partie nulle *f*, question insidieuse *f*, loterie *f*, clou *m*, attraction *f*; *vt* (at-, re)tirer, traîner, tendre, aspirer, (*tooth*) extraire, (*salary*) toucher, faire parler, dessiner, rédiger; **to** — **aside** *vt* écarter, tirer; *vi* s'écarter; **to** — **back** *vt* retirer; *vi* reculer; **to** — **up** *vt* (re)lever, approcher; *vi* s'arrêter.

drawback ['drɔːbæk] *n* remise *f*, mécompte *m*, échec *m*, inconvénient *m*.

drawbridge ['drɔːbridʒ] *n* pont-levis *m*.

drawer ['drɔːə] *n* tiroir *m*; *pl* caleçon *m*, pantalon *m* de femme.

drawing ['drɔːiŋ] *n* dessin *m*.

drawing-board ['drɔːiŋbɔːd] *n* planche *f*.

drawing-pin ['drɔːiŋpin] *n* punaise *f*.

drawing-room ['drɔːiŋrum] *n* salon *m*.

drawl [drɔːl] *n* voix traînante *f*; *vt* traîner; *vi* parler d'une voix traînante

drawn [drɔːn] *pp of* **draw**; *a* tiré, nul.

dray [drei] *n* camion *m*, haquet *m*.

dread [dred] *n* effroi *m*; *vt* redouter.

dreadful ['dredful] *a* terrible, horrible

dreadnought ['drednɔːt] *n* cuirassé *m*.

dream [driːm] *n* rêve *m*, songe *m*; *vt* rêver.

dreamer ['driːmə] *n* rêveur, -euse, songe-creux *m*.

dreamy ['driːmi] *a* rêveur, songeur, vague.

dreary ['driəri] *a* lugubre, morne, ennuyeux, terne.

dredge [dredʒ] *n* drague *f*; *vt* draguer, curer, saupoudrer.

dredger ['dredʒə] *n* curemôle *m*, drague *f*.

dregs [dregz] *n* lie *f*.

drench [drentʃ] *vt* tremper, mouiller.

dress [dres] *n* vêtement *m*, tenue *f*, costume *m*, robe *f*, toilette *f*; **full** — grande tenue; **badly** —**ed** mal mis *m*, mal mise *f*; **well** —**ed** bien mis *m*, bien mise *f*; *vt* habiller, vêtir, coiffer, pavoiser, aligner, parer, panser, tailler; *vi* s'habiller, faire sa toilette, se mettre (en habit), s'aligner; **to get** —**ed** s'habiller.

dress-circle ['dres'səːkl] *n* fauteuils *m pl* de balcon.

dresser ['dresə] *n* dressoir *m*, habilleuse *f*, apprêteur, -euse; commode-toilette *f*.

dressing ['dresiŋ] *n* habillage *m*, toilette *f*, pansement *m*, assaisonnement *m*, apprêt *m*, alignement *m*; (*naut*) pavoisement *m*.

dressing-case ['dresiŋkeis] *n* nécessaire *m* de toilette.

dressing-down ['dresiŋ'daun] *n* semonce *f*, savonnage *m*.

dressing-gown ['dresiŋgaun] *n* robe *f* de chambre, peignoir *m*.

dressing-room ['dresiŋrum] *n* cabinet *m* de toilette.

dressing-table ['dresiŋ.teibl] *n* coiffeuse *f*.

dressmaker ['dres.meikə] *n* couturier, -ière.

dressy ['dresi] *a* élégant, chic, qui aime la toilette.

drew [dru:] *pt of* **draw**.

dribble ['dribl] *n* goutte *f*, dégouttement *m*, dribble *m*; *vi* dégoutter, baver, dribbler.

drift [drift] *n* débâcle *f*, dérive *f*, laisser-aller *m*, direction *f*, portée *f*, amas *m*; *vi* être emporté, dériver, s'amasser, se laisser aller; *vt* flotter, charrier.

drifter ['driftə] *n* chalutier *m*.

drill [dril] *n* foret *m*, mèche *f*, perforateur *m*, perceuse *f*, sillon *m*, semoir *m*, exercice *m*, manœuvre *f*; — **sergeant** sergent instructeur *m*; *vt* forer, semer, instruire, faire faire l'exercice à; *vi* faire l'exercice, manœuvrer.

drink [driŋk] *n* boisson *f*, alcool *m*, un verre *m*, ivrognerie *f*, boire *m*; *vt* boire.

drinkable ['driŋkəbl] *a* buvable, potable.

drinker ['driŋkə] *n* buveur, -euse, alcoolique *mf*.

drinking ['driŋkiŋ] *n* boire *m*, boisson *f*; —**water** eau potable *f*.

drip [drip] *vt* verser goutte à goutte; *vi* s'égoutter, dégoutter, dégouliner, suinter; *n* (d)égouttement *m*, dégoulinement *m*.

dripping ['dripiŋ] *n* graisse (à frire) *f*, (d)égouttement *m*; — **pan** lèchefrite *f*.

drive [draiv] *n* avance *f*, poussée *f*, randonnée *f*, promenade *f*, avenue *f*, tendance *f*, mouvement *m*, énergie *f*; *vt* pousser, entraîner, conduire, chasser, forcer, surmener, actionner; *vi* se promener, chasser, conduire; **driving school** auto-école *f*.

drivel ['drivl] *n* bave *f*, roupie *f*, radotage *n*; *vi* radoter, baver.

driver ['draivə] *n* mécanicien *m*, conducteur *m*, chauffeur, -euse.

drizzle ['drizl] *n* bruine *f*; *vi* bruiner.

droll [droul] *a* drôle.

drollery ['drouləri] *n* drôlerie *f*, bouffonnerie *f*.

dromedary ['drɔmədəri] *n* dromadaire *m*.

drone [droun] *n* bourdon *m*, bourdonnement *m*, ronronnement *m*, fainéant *m*; *vi* bourdonner, ronronner.

droop [dru:p] *n* attitude penchée *f*, découragement *m*; *vt* laisser tomber, pendre, (a)baisser, pencher; *vi* languir, se pencher, retomber, s'affaisser.

drop [drɔp] *n* goutte *f*, pastille *f*, chute *f*, baisse *f*, rideau *m*, pendant *m*; *vi* s'égoutter, se laisser tomber, tomber, plonger, baisser; *vt* laisser tomber, baisser, lâcher, abandonner, laisser, verser goutte à goutte; **to — in** entrer en passant; **to — off** partir, s'endormir.

dropsy ['drɔpsi] *n* hydropisie *f*.

drought [draut] *n* sécheresse *f*.

drove [drouv] *n* troupeau *m*, foule *f*.

drover ['drouvə] *n* toucheur de bœufs *m*.

drown [draun] *vt* noyer, tremper, inonder, couvrir; *vi* se noyer.

drowsiness ['drauzinis] *n* somnolence *f*.

drowsy ['drauzi] *a* assoupi, endormi, soporifique.

drubbing ['drʌbiŋ] *n* (*fam*) raclée *f*, tripotée *f*.

drudge [drʌdʒ] *n* tâcheron *m*, femme de peine *f*, souffre-douleur *mf*; *vi* trimer.

drudgery ['drʌdʒəri] *n* corvée *f*, travail ingrat *m*.

drug [drʌg] *n* drogue *f*, stupéfiant *m*, (*fig*) rossignol *m*; *vt* droguer, endormir.

druggist ['drʌgist] *n* droguiste *m*, pharmacien *m*.

drum [drʌm] *n* tympan *m*; bonbonne *f*, tambour *m*; **big —** grosse caisse; **African —** tam-tam *m*.

drummer ['drʌmə] *n* tambour *m*.

drum-fire ['drʌm'faiə] *m* feu roulant *m*.

drumming ['drʌmiŋ] *n* bourdonnement *m*, battement *m*, tambourinage *m*.

drunk [drʌŋk] *pp of* **drink**; *a* ivre, saoûl.

drunkard ['drʌŋkəd] *n* ivrogne, ivrognesse.

drunkenness ['drʌŋkənnis] *n* ivresse *f*, ivrognerie *f*.

dry [drai] *a* sec, à sec, tari, caustique; *n* prohibitionniste *m*; *vt* (faire) sécher, essuyer; *vi* sécher, se dessécher, tarir.

dryness ['drainis] *n* sécheresse *f*.

dub [dʌb] *vt* armer, traiter (de), doubler.

dubious ['dju:bjəs] *a* douteux, louche, incertain.

duchess ['dʌtʃis] *n* duchesse *f*.

duchy ['dʌtʃi] *n* duché *m*.

duck [dʌk] *n* canard *m*, cane *f*, plongeon *m*, courbette *f*, esquive *f*, coutil *m*; *vti* plonger; *vi* se baisser, esquiver de la tête.

duckling ['dʌkliŋ] *n* caneton *m*.

duct [dʌkt] *n* conduit *m*, conduite *f*.

dud [dʌd] *n* raté *m*; *pl* nippes *f pl*; *a* moche, faux.

dudgeon ['dʌdʒən] *n* colère *f*.

due [dju:] *n* dû *m*, dettes *f pl*, droits *m pl*; *a* dû, attendu.

duel ['djuəl] n duel m; vi se battre en duel.
duelist ['djuəlist] n duelliste m, bretteur m.
duet [dju'et] n duo m.
duffer ['dʌfə] n cancre m, empoté(e) mf, maladroit(e) mf.
dug [dʌg] pt pp of **dig**; n pis m, téton m.
dug-out ['dʌgaut] n trou m, abri m, cagna m.
duke [djuːk] n duc m.
dull [dʌl] a ennuyeux, stupide, insensible, émoussé, terne, sourd, mat, sombre; vt amortir, émousser, ternir, hébéter.
dullard ['dʌləd] n balourd(e) mf, cancre m.
dullness ['dʌlnis] n hébétude f, lourdeur f, monotonie f, marasme m.
duly ['djuːli] ad dûment, à point.
dumb [dʌm] a muet, sot; —**bell** haltère f; — **show** pantomime f.
dumbfounded [dʌm'faundid] a éberlué, interdit.
dumbness ['dʌmnis] n mutisme m.
dummy ['dʌmi] n homme de paille m, mannequin m, silhouette f, mort m, (of baby) sucette f, maquette f; a faux, postiche.
dump [dʌmp] n dépôt m (de munitions), (fam) trou m; vt décharger, déposer (avec un bruit sourd); vi faire du dumping.
dumpling ['dʌmpliŋ] n chausson m.
dumps [dʌmps] n pl cafard m; **to be in the —s** avoir le cafard, broyer du noir.
dumpy ['dʌmpi] a trapu, replet, boulot.
dun [dʌn] a gris-brun; vt relancer, importuner.
dunce [dʌns] n endormi(e) mf, cancre m, crétin m; —**'s cap** bonnet m d'âne.
dung [dʌŋ] n bouse f, fiente f, crottin m.
dungeon ['dʌndʒən] n cul-de-basse-fosse m, cachot m.
dunghill ['dʌŋhil] n fumier m.
dunk ['dʌŋk] vt tremper; vi faire trempette.
dupe [djuːp] n dupe f; vt duper.
duplex ['djuːpleks] a double.
duplicate ['djuːplikit] n double m; a double de rechange.
duplicate ['djuːplikeit] vt établir en double.
duplicity [djuː'plisiti] n duplicité f.
durable ['djuərəbl] a durable, résistant.
duration [djuə'reifən] n durée f.
duress [djuə'res] n contrainte f, emprisonnement m.
during ['djuəriŋ] prep pendant, au cours de.
durst [dəːst] pt (old) of **dare**.
dusk [dʌsk] n crépuscule m.
dusky ['dʌski] a sombre, brun, foncé, noiraud.

dust [dʌst] n poussière f; vt saupoudrer, couvrir de poussière, épousseter; — **coat** cache-poussière m; — **jacket** protège-livre m.
dustbin ['dʌstbin] n boîte à ordures f, poubelle f.
duster ['dʌstə] n torchon m, chiffon à épousseter m.
dusty ['dʌsti] a poussiéreux, poudreux.
Dutch [dʌtf] a Hollandais; n Hollandais (language).
dutiable ['djuːtjəbl] a imposable, taxable.
dutiful ['djuːtiful] a respectueux, soumis.
duty ['djuːti] n devoir m, taxe f, droits m pl; **on** — de service; — **paid** franco, franc de douane.
dwarf [dwɔːf] n nain m.
dwell [dwel] vi demeurer, s'étendre (sur on).
dwelling ['dweliŋ] n maison f, demeure f.
dwelt [dwelt] pt of **dwell**.
dwindle ['dwindl] vi fondre, dépérir,
dye [dai] n teinte f, teinture f, teint m; — **works** teinturerie f; vt teindre, teinter; vi se teindre.
dyer ['daiə] n teinturier m.
dying ['daiiŋ] a mourant, de mort.
dynamite ['dainəmait] n dynamite f; vt faire sauter à la dynamite.
dynasty ['dinəsti] n dynastie f.
dysentery ['disntri] n dysenterie f.
dyspepsia [dis'pepsiə] n dyspepsie f.
dyspeptic [dis'peptik] a dyspeptique.

E

each [iːtf] a chaque; pn chacun(e); **two francs** — deux francs la pièce; — **other** l'un l'autre, entre eux.
eager ['iːgə] a empressé, ardent, avide, impatient.
eagerly ['iːgəli] ad ardemment, avec empressement.
eagerness ['iːgənis] n ardeur f, empressement m.
eagle ['iːgl] n aigle m.
eaglet ['iːglit] n aiglon m.
ear [iə] n oreille f, (corn) épi m, (tec) anse f.
ear-drop ['iədrɔp] n pendant d'oreille m.
ear-drum ['iədrʌm] n tympan m.
early ['əːli] a matinal, précoce, prochain, premier; **in** — **summer** au début de l'été; ad de bonne heure, tôt.
ear-mark ['iəmaːk] vt réserver, assigner.
earn [əːn] vt gagner.
earnest ['əːnist] n présage m, (com) arrhes f pl, avant-goût m; a sérieux, sincère, consciencieux; **in** — pour de bon.
earnestly ['əːnistli] ad sérieusement, instamment.

earnestness ['əːnistnis] n sérieux m, sincérité f, ardeur f, ferveur f.
earnings ['əːniŋz] n gain(s) m, gages m pl.
earring ['iəriŋ] n boucle f d'oreille.
earshot ['iəʃɔt] n portée f de la voix.
earth [əːθ] n terre f, terrier m; vt relier au sol.
earthen ['əːθən] a de (en) terre.
earthenware ['əːθənwɛə] n faïence f, poterie f; — **pot** canari m.
earthliness ['əːθlinis] n mondanité f.
earthly ['əːθli] a terrestre.
earthquake ['əːθkweik] n tremblement m de terre.
earthworks ['əːθwəːks] n terrassements m pl.
earthworm ['əːθwəːm] n ver m de terre.
earthy ['əːθi] a terreux.
ear-trumpet ['iə,trʌmpit] n cornet acoustique m.
earwig ['iəwig] n perce-oreille(s) m.
ease [iːz] n facilité f, tranquillité f, aise f, soulagement m; (mil) repos m; vt soulager, calmer, détendre; **to — up** ralentir, freiner, se relâcher.
easel ['iːzl] n chevalet m.
easily ['iːzili] ad facilement, aisément, tranquillement.
east [iːst] n est m, levant m, orient m; **Near E—** proche Orient; **Middle E—** moyen Orient; **Far E—** extrême Orient.
Easter ['iːstə] n Pâques f pl.
easterly ['iːstəli] a oriental, d'est; ad vers l'est.
eastern ['iːstən] a oriental, de l'est.
eastward ['iːstwəd] ad vers l'est; a à l'est.
easy ['iːzi] a facile, aisé, à l'aise, tranquille, accommodant, dégagé.
easy-chair ['iːzi'tʃɛə] n fauteuil m.
easy-going ['iːzi,gouiŋ] a débonnaire, qui ne s'en fait pas, accommodant.
eat [iːt] vt manger.
eatable ['iːtəbl] a mangeable.
eatables ['iːtəblz] n pl comestibles m pl, provisions f pl.
eaten ['iːtn] pp of **eat**; — **up with** dévoré de, consumé par, pétri de.
eating ['iːtiŋ] n manger m; a à croquer, de dessert.
eaves [iːvz] n avance f de toit.
eavesdrop ['iːvzdrɔp] vi écouter aux portes.
ebb [eb] n reflux m, déclin m; vi refluer, décliner.
E-boat ['iːbout] n vedette lance-torpilles f.
ebony ['ebəni] n ébène f.
ebullience [i'bʌljəns] n exubérance f, effervescence f.
ebullient [i'bʌljənt] a exubérant, bouillant.
ebullition [,ebə'liʃən] n ébullition f, effervescence f.
eccentric [ik'sentrik] a excentrique, original.

eccentricity [,eksen'trisiti] n excentricité f.
echo ['ekou] n écho m; vt faire écho à, se faire l'écho de, répéter; vi faire écho, retentir.
eclipse [i'klips] n éclipse f; vt éclipser.
economic [,iːkə'nɔmik] a économique.
economical [,iːkə'nɔmikəl] a économe, économique.
economics [,iːkə'nɔmiks] n économie politique f, régime économique m.
economist [iː'kɔnəmist] n économiste m.
economize [iː'kɔnəmaiz] vt économiser; vi faire des économies.
economy [iː'kɔnəmi] n économie f.
ecstasy ['ekstəsi] n extase f, transe f, ravissement m.
ecstatic [eks'tætik] a extatique, en extase.
eddy ['edi] n remous m, volute f, tourbillon m.
edge [edʒ] n bord m, bordure f, fil m, tranchant m; **on —** agacé, énervé; vt border, aiguiser; **to — (in)**, **to — one's way (in)** se faufiler (dans); **to — away** s'écarter tout doucement.
edgeless ['edʒlis] a émoussé.
edgeways ['edʒweiz] ad de côté, de champ; **to get a word in —** glisser un mot dans la conversation.
edible ['edibl] a mangeable, comestible, bon à manger.
edict ['iːdikt] n édit m.
edify ['edifai] vt édifier.
edit ['edit] vt éditer, rédiger.
edition [i'diʃən] n édition f.
editor ['editə] n éditeur m, rédacteur en chef m, directeur m.
editorial [,edi'tɔːriəl] an éditorial m; n article de fond m.
educate ['edjukeit] vt instruire, élever, former; **he was educated in Paris** il a fait ses études à Paris.
education [,edju'keiʃən] n éducation f, instruction f, enseignement m.
educational [,edju'keiʃənl] a d'enseignement, éducateur.
educative ['edjukətiv] a éducatif.
educator ['edjukeitə] n éducateur, -trice.
Edward ['edwəd] Edouard m.
eel [iːl] n anguille f.
eerie ['iəri] a étrange, fantastique, surnaturel.
efface [i'feis] vt effacer, oblitérer.
effect [i'fekt] n effet m, influence f, conséquence f; **of no —** inutile, inefficace; **to no —** en vain; **for —** à effet; **to the same —** dans le même sens; **in —** en fait, en réalité; vt exécuter, accomplir.
effective [i'fektiv] n effectif m; a effectif, efficace, valide.
effectively [i'fektivli] ad en réalité, efficacement.
effectiveness [i'fektivnis] n efficacité f.

effeminate [i'feminit] *a* efféminé.
effervesce [,efə'ves] *vi* bouillonner, mousser.
effervescence [,efə'vesns] *n* effervescence *f*.
effete [e'fiːt] *a* épuisé, caduc.
efficacious [,efi'keiʃəs] *a* efficace.
efficaciousness [,efi'keiʃəsnis] *n* efficacité *f*.
efficacy ['efikəsi] *n* efficacité *f*, rapidité *f*.
efficiency [i'fiʃənsi] *n* efficience *f*, efficacité *f*, rendement *m*, capacité *f*, valeur *f*.
efficient [i'fiʃənt] *a* efficace, compétent, effectif, capable
efficiently [i'fiʃəntli] *ad* efficacement.
effigy ['efidʒi] *n* effigie *f*.
effort ['efət] *n* effort *m*.
effortless ['efətlis] *a* sans effort, passif, facile.
effrontery [e'frʌntəri] *n* effronterie *f*.
effulgence [e'fʌldʒəns] *n* éclat *m*, splendeur *f*.
effulgent [e'fʌldʒənt] *a* resplendissant, éclatant.
effusion [i'fjuːʒən] *n* effusion *f*, épanchement *m*.
effusive [i'fjuːsiv] *a* expansif, démonstratif.
effusiveness [i'fjuːsivnis] *n* exubérance *f*, effusion *f*.
egg [eg] *n* œuf *m*; **new-laid** — œuf frais; **boiled** — œuf à la coque; **hard-boiled** — œuf dur; **soft-boiled** — œuf mollet; **fried** — œuf sur le plat; **poached** — œuf poché; **scrambled** —s œufs brouillés; *vt* **to** — **on** encourager.
egg-cup ['egkʌp] *n* coquetier *m*.
egg-spoon ['egspuːn] *n* petite cuiller *f*.
egg-whisk ['egwisk] *n* fouet *m*.
eglantine ['egləntain] *n* églantine *f*, églantier *m*.
ego ['egou] *n* le moi.
egoist ['egouist] *an* égoïste *mf*.
egregious [i'griːdʒəs] *a* énorme, insigne.
egret ['iːgret] *n* aigrette *f*.
Egyptian [i'dʒipʃən] *an* égyptien.
eiderdown ['aidədaun] *n* édredon *m*.
eight [eit] *an* huit *m*.
eighteen ['ei'tiːn] *an* dixhuit *m*.
eighteenth ['ei'tiːnθ] *an* dixhuit *m*, dix-huitième *mf*.
eighth [eitθ] *an* huit *m*, huitième *mf*.
eightieth ['eitiiθ] *an* quatre-vingts *m*, quatre-vingtième *mf*.
eighty ['eiti] *an* quatre-vingts *m*.
either ['aiðə] *pn* l'un et (ou) l'autre; *a* chaque; **on** — **side** de chaque côté; *cj* ou, soit, non plus; — ... **or** ou ... ou, soit ... soit; **not** ... — ne ... non plus.
eject [iː'dʒekt] *vt* jeter (dehors), expulser, émettre.
eke out ['iːk 'aut] *vt* ajouter à, compléter, faire durer.
elaborate [i'læbəreit] *vt* élaborer.

elaborate [i'læbərit] *a* compliqué, soigné, tiré, recherché.
elaboration [i,læbə'reiʃən] *n* élaboration *f*.
elapse [i'læps] *vi* s'écouler.
elastic [i'læstik] *an* élastique *m*.
elasticity [,elæs'tisiti] *n* élasticité *f*.
elated [i'leitid] *a* gonflé, transporté, exultant, enivré.
elation [i'leiʃən] *n* orgueil *m*, ivresse *f*, exaltation *f*.
elbow ['elbou] *n* coude *m*; *vt* coudoyer, pousser des coudes; *vi* jouer des coudes; **to have** — **room** avoir ses coudées franches.
elder ['eldə] *n* (*bot*) sureau *m*; aîné(e) *mf*, Ancien *m*; *a* plus âgé, aîné.
elderly ['eldəli] *a* d'un certain âge.
eldest ['eldist] *a* aîné.
elect [i'lekt] *vt* choisir, élire; *a* désigné, élu.
election [i'lekʃən] *n* élection *f*.
electioneer [i,lekʃə'niə] *vi* mener une campagne électorale.
electioneering [i,lekʃə'niəriŋ] *n* campagne *f* (propagande *f*) électorale.
elector [i'lektə] *n* électeur *m*, votant *m*.
electorate [i'lektərit] *n* corps électoral *m*.
electric [i'lektrik] *a* électrique.
electrical [i'lektrikəl] *a* électrique.
electrician [ilek'triʃən] *n* électricien *m*.
electricity [ilek'trisiti] *n* électricité *f*.
electrification [i,lektrifi'keiʃən] *n* électrification *f*.
electrify [i'lektrifai] *vt* électrifier, électriser.
electrocute [i'lektrəkjuːt] *vt* électrocuter.
electrocution [i,lektrə'kjuːʃən] *n* électrocution *f*.
electrolier [i,lektrou'liə] *n* luster électrique *m*.
electron [i'lektrɔn] *n* électron *m*.
electroplate [i'lektroupleit] *n* ruolz *m*, articles *m pl* argentés; *vt* plaquer.
electrotyping [i'lektrou'taipiŋ] *n* galvanoplastie *f*.
elegance ['eligəns] *n* élégance *f*.
elegant ['eligənt] *a* élégant.
elegantly ['eligəntli] *ad* élégamment.
elegy ['elidʒi] *n* élégie *f*.
element ['elimənt] *n* élément *m*, facteur *m*; *pl* rudiments *m pl*.
elementary [,eli'mentəri] *a* élémentaire, primaire.
elephant ['elifənt] *n* éléphant *m*.
elevate ['eliveit] *n* élever.
elevation [,eli'veiʃən] *n* élévation *f*, altitude *f*.
elevator ['eliveitə] *n* élévateur *m*, ascenseur *m*.
eleven [i'levn] *an* onze *m*.
eleventh [i'levnθ] *n* onze; *an* onzième *mf*.
elf [elf] *n* elfe *m*, lutin *m*.
elicit [i'lisit] *vt* extraire, tirer.
elide [i'laid] *vt* élider.

eligible ['elidʒəbl] *a* éligible, admissible, désirable.
eliminate [i'limineit] *vt* éliminer.
elimination [i.limi'neiʃən] *n* élimination *f*.
elision [i'liʒən] *n* élision *f*.
elixir [i'liksə] *n* élixir *m*.
elk [elk] *n* élan *m*.
ell [el] *n* aûne *f*.
elm [elm] *n* orme *m*.
elongate ['iːlɔŋgeit] *vt* allonger; *vi* s'allonger.
elope [i'loup] *vi* se laisser (se faire) enlever, prendre la fuite.
elopement [i'loupmənt] *n* enlèvement *m*, fuite *f*.
eloquence ['eləkwəns] *n* éloquence *f*.
eloquent ['eləkwənt] *a* éloquent.
eloquently ['eləkwəntli] *ad* éloquemment.
else [els] *a* (d')autre de plus; *ad* autrement, ou bien; **something —** autre chose *m*; **everywhere —** partout ailleurs; **anybody —** quelqu'un d'autre.
elsewhere ['els'wɛə] *ad* ailleurs, autre part.
elucidate [i'luːsideit] *vt* élucider, éclaircir.
elucidation [i.luːsi'deiʃən] *n* élucidation *f*.
elude [i'luːd] *vt* éluder, échapper à, esquiver.
elusive [i'luːsiv] *a* fuyant, insaisissable, évasif, souple.
elusiveness [i'luːsivnis] *n* souplesse fuyante *f*, intangibilité *f*.
emaciated [i'meiʃieitid] *a* émacié, décharné.
emaciation [i.meisi'eiʃən] *n* maigreur extrême *f*.
emanate ['eməneit] *vi* émaner.
emanation [.emə'neiʃən] *n* émanation *f*.
emancipate [i'mænsipeit] *vt* émanciper.
emancipator [i'mænsipeitə] *n* émancipateur, -trice.
emasculate [i'mæskjuleit] *vt* châtrer, expurger.
embalm [im'baːm] *vt* embaumer.
embalming [im'baːmiŋ] *n* embaumement *m*.
embank [im'bæŋk] *vt* endiguer, remblayer.
embankment [im'bæŋkmənt] *n* quai *m*, remblai *m*, levée *f*.
embargo [em'baːgou] *n* embargo *m*, séquestre *m*; **to put an — on** mettre l'embargo sur, interdire.
embark [im'baːk] *vt* embarquer; *vi* s'embarquer.
embarkation [.embaː'keiʃən] *n* embarquement *m*.
embarrass [im'bærəs] *vt* gêner, embarrasser.
embarrassment [im'bærəsmənt] *n* embarrass *m*, gêne *f*.
embassy ['embəsi] *n* ambassade *f*.
embedded [im'bedid] *a* pris, enfoncé.

embellish [im'beliʃ] *vt* embellir, enjoliver.
embellishment [im'beliʃmənt] *n* embellissement *m*.
ember ['embə] *n* braise *f*; **— days** Quatre-Temps *m pl*.
embezzle [im'bezl] *vt* détourner.
embezzlement [im'bezlmənt] *n* détournement *m*.
embitter [im'bitə] *vt* envenimer, aigrir, aggraver.
embitterment [im'bitəmənt] *n* aigreur *f*, aggravation *f*, envenimement *m*.
emblem ['embləm] *n* emblème *m*, symbole *m*.
emblematic [.embli'mætik] *a* emblématique, figuratif.
embodiment [im'bɔdimənt] *n* incarnation *f*.
embody [im'bɔdi] *vt* incarner, donner corps à, exprimer, incorporer.
embolden [im'bouldən] *vt* enhardir.
embolism ['embəlizəm] *n* embolie *f*.
emboss [im'bɔs] *vt* estamper, repousser.
embossing [im'bɔsiŋ] *n* relief *m*, brochage *m* (d'étoffes), repoussage *m*.
embrace [im'breis] *n* embrassement *m*, étreinte *f*; *vt* embrasser, étreindre, saisir, adopter, comporter.
embrasure [im'breizə] *n* embrasure *f*.
embroider [im'brɔidə] *vt* broder.
embroidery [im'brɔidəri] *n* broderie *f*.
embroil [im'brɔil] *vt* (em)brouiller, envelopper, entraîner.
embroilment [im'brɔilmənt] *n* imbroglio *m*.
embryo ['embriou] *n* embryon *m*.
embryonic [.embri'ɔnik] *a* embryonnaire, en herbe.
emend [iː'mend] *vt* corriger.
emendation [.iːmen'deiʃən] *n* correction *f*, émendation *f*.
emerald ['emərəld] *n* émeraude *f*.
emerge [i'məːdʒ] *vi* émerger, sortir.
emergency [i'məːdʒənsi] *n* crise *f*, éventualité *f*; **— brake, — exit** frein *m*, sortie *f* de secours.
emery ['eməri] *n* émeri *m*; **— cloth** toile *f* d'émeri.
emetic [i'metik] *n* vomitif *m*.
emigrant ['emigrənt] *n* émigrant(e) *mf*, émigré *m*.
emigrate ['emigreit] *vi* émigrer.
emigration [.emi'greiʃən] *n* émigration *f*.
eminence ['eminəns] *n* éminence *f*, distinction *f*.
eminent ['eminənt] *a* éminent.
eminently ['eminəntli] *ad* éminemment, par excellence.
emissary ['emisəri] *n* émissaire *m*.
emission [i'miʃən] *n* émission *f*.
emit [i'mit] *vt* émettre.
emoluments [i'mɔljumənts] *n pl* émoluments *m pl*, traitement *m*, appointements *m pl*.

emotion [i'mouʃən] *n* émotion *f*, trouble *m*.

emotive [i'moutiv] *a* émotif.

emperor ['empərə] *n* empereur *m*.

emphasis ['emfəsis] *n* accent *m*, intensité *f*, insistance *f*, force *f*.

emphasize ['emfəsaiz] *vt* mettre en relief, souligner.

emphatic [im'fætik] *a* expressif, accentué, significatif, énergique, positif, net.

empire ['empaiə] *n* empire *m*.

employ [im'plɔi] *n* service *m*; *vt* employer.

employee [,emplɔi'iː] *n* employé(e) *mf*.

employer [im'plɔiə] *n* patron, -onne, employeur *m*, maître, -tresse.

employment [im'plɔimənt] *n* situation *f*, travail *m*, emploi *m*.

empower [im'pauə] *vt* autoriser, donner pouvoir à.

empress ['empris] *n* impératrice *f*.

emptiness ['emptinis] *n* vide *m*, néant *m*.

empty ['empti] *a* vide, vain, inoccupé; **to come back ——-handed** revenir bredouille; *vt* vider; *vi* se décharger, se vider.

emulate ['emjuleit] *vt* rivaliser avec, imiter.

emulation [,emju'leiʃən] *n* émulation *f*.

enable [i'neibl] *vt* mettre à même (de **to**), permettre (à), autoriser.

enact [i'nækt] *vt* ordonner, décréter, jouer.

enactment [i'næktmənt] *n* décret *m*, promulgation *f*.

enamel [i'næməl] *n* émail *m*, vernis *m*; *vt* émailler, vernir.

enameler [i'næmələ] *n* émailleur *m*.

encamp [in'kæmp] *vt* (faire) camper; *vi* camper.

encampment [in'kæmpmənt] *n* campement *m*, camp *m*.

encase [in'keis] *vt* enfermer, encaisser, revêtir.

enchant [in'tʃɑːnt] *vt* enchanter, ensorceler.

enchanting [in'tʃɑːntiŋ] *a* enchanteur, ravissant.

enchantment [in'tʃɑːntmənt] *n* enchantement *m*, ravissement *m*.

encircle [in'səːkl] *vt* encercler, entourer, cerner.

enclave ['enkleiv] *n* enclave *f*.

enclose [in'klouz] *vt* enclore, entourer, (r)enfermer, insérer.

enclosed [in'klouzd] *a* ci-inclus, ci-joint.

enclosure [in'klouʒə] *n* clôture *f*, enceinte *f*, (en)clos *m*, pièce incluse *f*.

encompass [in'kʌmpəs] *vt* entourer, contenir, renfermer.

encore [ɔŋ'kɔː] *excl* bis *m*; *vt* bisser.

encounter [in'kauntə] *n* rencontre *f*, combat *n*, assaut *m*; *vt* rencontrer, affronter, essuyer.

encourage [in'kʌridʒ] *vt* encourager, favoriser.

encouragement [in'kʌridʒmənt] *n* encouragement *m*.

encroach [in'kroutʃ] *vi* empiéter (sur **upon**).

encroachment [in'kroutʃmənt] *n* empiètement *m*, usurpation *f*.

encrust [in'krʌst] *vt* incruster, encroûter.

encumber [in'kʌmbə] *vt* gêner, embarrasser, encombrer, grever.

encumbrance [in'kʌmbrəns] *n* charge *f*, encombrement *m*, embarras *m*.

encyclic [en'siklik] *an* encyclique *f*.

encyclopedia [en'saiklou'piːdjə] *n* encyclopédie *f*.

encyclopedic [en,saiklou'piːdik] *a* encyclopédique.

end [end] *n* fin *f*, bout *m*, extrémité *f*; *vti* finir; *vt* terminer, achever; *vi* se terminer; **on** — debout, de suite; **in the** — au bout du compte, à la fin; **to the bitter** — jusqu'au bout.

endanger [in'deindʒə] *vt* mettre en danger, exposer.

endear [in'diə] *vt* rendre cher, faire aimer.

endeavor [in'devə] *n* effort *m*, tentative *f*; *vi* s'efforcer, tenter.

ending ['endiŋ] *n* fin *f*, conclusion *f*, dénouement *m*, terminaison *f*; *a* final, dernier.

endive ['endiv] *n* chicorée *f*.

endless ['endlis] *a* sans fin, interminable.

endorse [in'dɔːs] *vt* appuyer, endosser, estampiller.

endorsement [in'dɔːsment] *n* (fin) endossement *m*, (passport) mention *f*, approbation *f*.

endow [in'dau] *vt* doter, investir.

endowed [in'daud] *a* doué, muni.

endowment [in'daumənt] *n* dotation *f*, fondation *f*.

endurable [in'djuərəbl] *a* supportable.

endurance [in'djuərəns] *n* résistance *f*, endurance *f*.

endure [in'djuə] *vt* supporter, endurer.

enduring [in'duəriŋ] *a* durable, qui persiste.

enemy ['enimi] *an* ennemi(e) *mf*.

energetic [,enə'dʒetik] *a* énergique.

energy ['enədʒi] *n* énergie *f*, vigueur *f*, nerf *m*.

enervate ['enəːveit] *vt* énerver, amollir.

enervation [,enəː'veiʃən] *n* énervement *m*, mollesse *f*.

enfeeble [in'fiːbl] *vt* affaiblir.

enfeeblement [in'fiːblment] *n* affaiblissement *m*.

enfilade [,enfi'leid] *n* enfilade *f*; *vt* prendre d'enfilade.

enforce [in'fɔːs] *vt* imposer, faire respecter, mettre en vigueur, appliquer.

enforcement [in'fɔːsmənt] n application f, mise f en vigueur.

enfranchise [in'fræntʃaiz] vt donner le droit de vote à, ériger en circonscription.

engage [in'geidʒ] vt occuper, engager, retenir, embaucher, attirer.

engaged [in'geidʒd] a occupé, retenu, fiancé.

engagement [in'geidʒmənt] n engagement m, fiançailles f pl, combat m.

engender [in'dʒendə] vt engendrer, faire naître.

engine ['endʒin] n engin m, machine f, locomotive f, moteur m.

engine-driver ['endʒin,draivə] n mécanicien m.

engineer [,endʒi'niə] n ingénieur m, mécanicien m; pl (mil) le génie m; vt construire, machiner, combiner.

engineering [,endʒi'niəriŋ] n génie m, construction f, mécanique f.

England ['iŋglənd] n Angleterre f.

English ['iŋgliʃ] n Anglais(e) mf; an anglais m.

Englishman ['iŋgliʃmən] n Anglais m.

engrave [in'greiv] vt graver.

engraver [in'greivə] n graveur m.

engraving [in'greiviŋ] n gravure f.

engross [in'grous] vt accaparer, absorber.

engulf [in'gʌlf] vt engloutir.

enhance [in'hɑːns] vt (re)hausser, relever, mettre en valeur, accroître.

enhancement [in'hɑːnsmənt] n mise f en valeur.

enigma [i'nigmə] n énigme f.

enigmatic [,enig'mætik] a énigmatique.

enjoin [in'dʒɔin] vt enjoindre, recommander.

enjoy [in'dʒɔi] vt aimer, goûter, jouir de, prendre plaisir à; to — oneself s'amuser.

enjoyable [in'dʒɔiəbl] a agréable.

enjoyment [in'dʒɔimənt] n plaisir m, jouissance f.

enlarge [in'lɑːdʒ] vt accroître, agrandir, élargir, développer; vi s'élargir, s'agrandir; to — upon s'étendre sur.

enlargement [in'lɑːdʒmənt] n agrandissement m, accroissement m.

enlighten [in'laitn] vt éclairer.

enlightenment [in'laitnmənt] n lumières f pl.

enlist [in'list] vt enrôler; vi s'engager.

enlistment [in'listmənt] n enrôlement m.

enliven [in'laivn] vt animer, inspirer, égayer.

enmity ['enmiti] n hostilité f, inimitié f.

ennoble [i'noubl] vt anoblir, ennoblir.

enormity [i'nɔːmiti] n énormité f.

enormous [i'nɔːməs] a énorme, gigantesque.

enormously [i'nɔːməsli] ad énormément.

enough [i'nʌf] a n ad assez (de), suffisamment.

enquire [in'kwaiə] vi se renseigner (sur about), s'informer (de about).

enrage [in'reidʒ] vt exaspérer, faire enrager.

enrapture [in'ræptʃə] vt ravir, transporter.

enrich [in'ritʃ] vt enrichir.

enroll [in'roul] vt enrôler, immatriculer, enregistrer.

enrollment [in'roulmənt] n enrôlement m, enregistrement m, embauche f.

ensconce [in'skɔns] to — oneself se nicher, s'installer, se carrer.

enshrine [in'ʃrain] vt enchâsser.

enshroud [in'ʃraud] vt cacher, voiler, envelopper.

ensign ['ensain] n insigne m, pavillon m, porte-drapeau m.

enslave [in'sleiv] vt asservir.

enslavement [in'sleivmənt] n asservissement m.

ensnare [in'snɛə] vt prendre au piège, dans ses filets.

ensue [in'sjuː] vi s'ensuivre.

ensure [in'ʃuə] vt mettre en sûreté, (s')assurer.

entail [in'teil] vt impliquer, entraîner, occasionner.

entangle [in'tæŋgl] vt embrouiller, emmêler, empêtrer.

entanglement [in'tæŋglmənt] n enchevêtrement m; pl complications f pl.

enter ['entə] vt entrer dans; vi entrer, se faire inscrire; vt enregistrer, inscrire.

enterprise ['entəpraiz] n entreprise f, initiative f.

enterprising ['entəpraiziŋ] a entreprenant.

entertain [,entə'tein] vt recevoir, entretenir, caresser, amuser, régaler.

entertaining [,entə'teiniŋ] a amusant, divertissant.

entertainment [,entə'teinmənt] n amusement m, fête f, divertissement m.

enthrall [in'θrɔːl] vt ensorceler, charmer, envoûter.

enthrone [in'θroun] vt mettre sur le trône, introniser.

enthronement [in'θrounmənt] n couronnement m, intronisation f.

enthusiasm [in'θjuːziæzəm] n enthousiasme m.

enthusiast [in'θjuːziæst] n enthousiaste mf, fervent(e) mf.

enthusiastic [in,θjuːzi'æstik] a enthousiaste, passionné.

entice [in'tais] vt attirer, séduire; **enticing** séduisant.

enticement [in'taismənt] n attrait m, séduction f.

entire [in'taiə] a entier, complet, tout, pur.

entirely [in'taiəli] ad entièrement, tout à fait.

entirety [in'taiəti] *n* totalité *f*, intégralité *f*.
entitle [in'taitl] *vt* intituler, donner le titre, le droit, à, autoriser.
entomb [in'tu:m] *vt* enterrer.
entrails ['entreilz] *n* entrailles *f pl*.
entrain [en'trein] *vt* embarquer (dans le train).
entrance ['entrəns] *n* entrée *f*, accès *m*, admission *f*; — **examination** examen *m* d'entrée.
entrance [in'trɑ:ns] *vt* ravir, transporter.
entreat [in'tri:t] *vt* supplier.
entreaty [in'tri:ti] *n* supplication *f*; *pl* instances *f pl*.
entrench [in'trentʃ] *vt* retrancher.
entrust [in'trʌst] *vt* charger (de with), confier (à).
entry ['entri] *n* entrée *f*, inscription *f*; **by double** (**single**) — en partie double (simple).
entwine [in'twain] *vt* entrelacer, enlacer; *vi* s'entrelacer.
enumerate [i'nju:məreit] *vt* énumérer, dénombrer.
enumeration [i,nju:mə'reiʃən] *n* énumération *f*.
enunciate [i'nʌnsieit] *vt* articuler, énoncer.
enunciation [i,nʌnsi'eiʃən] *n* énonciation *f*.
envelop [in'veləp] *vt* envelopper.
envelope ['envəloup] *n* enveloppe *f*.
enviable ['enviəbl] *a* enviable, digne d'envie.
envious ['enviəs] *a* envieux, d'envie; **to be** — **of** porter envie à.
environment [in'vaiərənmənt] *n* milieu *m*, entourage *m*, ambiance *f*, atmosphère *f*.
environs [en'vaiərənz] *n pl* environs *m pl*.
envisage [in'vizidʒ] *vt* regarder en face, envisager.
envoy ['envɔi] *n* envoyé *m*.
envy ['envi] *n* envie *f*; *vt* envier, porter envie à.
epic ['epic] *n* épopée *f*; *a* épique.
epicure ['epikjuə] *n* gourmet *m*.
epidemic [,epi'demik] *n* épidémie *f*; *a* épidémique.
epidermis [,epi'də:mis] *n* épiderme *m*.
epigram ['epigræm] *n* épigramme *f*.
epigraph ['epigrɑ:f] *n* épigraphe *f*.
epilepsy ['epilepsi] *n* épilepsie *f*.
epileptic [,epi'leptik] *a* épileptique.
episcopacy [i'piskəpəsi] *n* épiscopat *m*.
episcopal [i'piskəpəl] *a* épiscopal.
episode ['episoud] *n* épisode *m*.
episodic [,epi'sɔdik] *a* épisodique.
epistle [i'pisl] *n* épître *f*.
epistolary [i'pistələri] *a* épistolaire.
epitaph ['epitɑ:f] *n* épitaphe *f*.
epithet ['epiθet] *n* épithète *f*.
epitome [i'pitəmi] *n* abrégé *m*, résumé *m*.
epoch ['i:pɔk] *n* époque *f*.

equable ['ekwəbl] *a* égal, uni(forme), régulier.
equal ['i:kwəl] *n* égal(e) *mf*, pareil(le) *mf*; *a* égal, de taille (à **to**); *vt* égaler.
equality [i:'kwɔliti] *n* égalité *f*.
equalization [,i:kwəlai'zeiʃən] *n* égalisation *f*.
equalize ['i:kwəlaiz] *vt* égaliser.
equally ['i:kwəli] *ad* également, pareillement.
equator [i'kweitə] *n* équateur *m*.
equatorial [,ekwə'tɔ:riəl] *a* équatorial.
equerry ['ekwəri] *n* écuyer *m*.
equestrian [i'kwestriən] *a* équestre.
equilibrate [,i:kwi'laibreit] *vt* équilibrer.
equilibrium [,i:kwi'libriəm] *n* équilibre *m*.
equinox ['i:kwinɔks] *n* équinoxe *m*.
equip [i'kwip] *vt* munir, équiper, monter.
equipage ['ekwipidʒ] *n* équipage *m*.
equipment [i'kwipmənt] *n* équipement *m*, outillage *m*, installation *f*, matériel *m*.
equipoise ['ekwipɔiz] *n* équilibre *m*, contre-poids *m*.
equitable ['ekwitəbl] *a* équitable.
equity ['ekwiti] *n* équité *f*.
equivalence [i'kwivələns] *n* équivalence *f*.
equivalent [i'kwivələnt] *an* équivalent *m*.
equivocal [i'kwivəkəl] *a* équivoque, ambigu -uë, douteux.
equivocate [i'kwivəkeit] *vi* jouer sur les mots, tergiverser.
era ['iərə] *n* ère *f*.
eradicate [i'rædikeit] *vt* extirper, déraciner.
eradication [i,rædi'keiʃən] *n* déracinement *m*.
erase [i'reiz] *vt* effacer, raturer.
eraser [i'reizə] *n* gomme *f*.
erasure [i'reiʒə] *n* rature *f*.
ere [ɛə] *prep* avant; *cj* avant que.
erect [i'rekt] *a* droit; *vt* dresser, bâtir, ériger.
erection [i'rekʃən] *n* érection *f*, construction *f*, montage *m*, édifice *m*.
ermine ['ə:min] *n* hermine *f*.
erode [i'roud] *vt* ronger, éroder, corroder.
erosion [i'rouʒən] *n* érosion *f*, usure *f*.
err [ə:] *vi* se tromper, faire erreur, être erroné, pécher.
errand ['erənd] *n* course *f*, commission *f*.
errand-boy ['erəndbɔi] *n* commissionnaire *m*, chasseur *m*.
erroneous [i'rouniəs] *a* erroné, faux.
error ['erə] *n* erreur *f*, faute *f*, méprise *f*.
erupt [i'rʌpt] *vi* faire éruption.
eruption [i'rʌpʃən] *n* éruption *f*.
escalator ['eskəleitə] *n* escalier mouvant *m*.

escapade [.eskə'peid] *n* escapade *f*, frasque *f*.

escape [is'keip] *n* évasion *f*, fuite *f*; *vi* s'évader, s'esquiver, (s')échapper; *vt* échapper à.

eschew [is'tʃuː] *vt* éviter, s'abstenir de, renoncer à.

escort ['eskɔːt] *n* escorte *f*, cavalier *m*.

escort [is'kɔːt] *vt* escorter, accompagner, reconduire.

escutcheon [is'kʌtʃən] *n* écu(sson) *m*, blason *m*.

Eskimo ['eskimou] *an* Esquimau *m*; — **woman** femme esquimau.

especial [is'peʃəl] *a* (tout) particulier, propre.

espouse [is'pauz] *vt* se marier avec, épouser.

espy [is'pai] *vt* apercevoir, aviser.

essay ['esei] *n* tentative *f*, essai *m*, dissertation *f*.

essay [e'sei] *vt* essayer, éprouver.

essence ['esns] *n* essence *f*, extrait *m*, fond *m*, suc *m*.

essential [i'senʃəl] *an* essentiel *m*, indispensable *m*.

establish [is'tæbliʃ] *vt* fonder, créer, établir.

establishment [is'tæbliʃmənt] *n* établissement *m*, fondation *f*, pied *m* (de guerre), train *m* de maison.

estate [is'teit] *n* condition *f*, rang *m*, succession *f*, domaine *m*, immeuble *m*.

esteem [is'tiːm] *n* estime *f*; *vt* estimer, tenir (pour).

estimate ['estimit] *n* estimation *f*, devis *m*, appréciation *f*; ['estimeit] *vt* évaluer, apprécier.

estimation [.esti'meiʃən] *n* estime *f*, jugement *m*.

estrange [is'treindʒ] *vt* (s')aliéner, indisposer.

estrangement [is'treindʒmənt] *n* désaffection *f*, refroidissement *m*, aliénation *f*.

estuary ['estjuəri] *n* estuaire *m*.

etch [etʃ] *vt* graver à l'eau forte.

etching ['etʃiŋ] *n* eau-forte *f*.

eternal [i'təːnl] *a* éternel.

eternity [i'təːniti] *n* éternité *f*.

ether ['iːθə] *n* éther *m*.

ethereal [i'θiəriəl] *a* éthéré.

ethical ['eθikəl] *a* moral.

ethics ['eθiks] *n* morale *f*.

etiquette ['etiket] *n* étiquette *f*, convenances *f pl*, cérémonial *m*, protocole *m*.

etymology [.ety'mɔlədʒi] *n* étymologie *f*.

eucharist ['juːkərist] *n* eucharistie *f*.

eulogize ['juːlədʒaiz] *vt* faire l'éloge de.

eulogy ['juːlədʒi] *n* éloge *m*, panégyrique *m*.

eunuch ['juːnək] *n* eunuque *m*.

Europe ['juərəp] *n* l'Europe *f*.

European [.juərə'piːən] *n* Européen, -enne *mf*; *a* européen.

evacuate [i'vækjueit] *vt* évacuer, expulser.

evacuation [i.vækju'eiʃən] *n* évacuation *f*.

evade [i'veid] *vt* esquiver, déjouer, éviter, tourner.

evaluate [i'væljueit] *vt* évaluer, estimer.

evangelic [.iːvæn'dʒelik] *a* évangélique.

evangelist [i'vændʒəlist] *n* évangéliste *mf*.

evaporate [i'væpəreit] *vt* faire évaporer; *vi* s'évaporer, se vaporiser.

vaporation [i.væpə'reiʃən] *n* évaporation *f*.

evasion [i'veiʒən] *n* subterfuge *m*, faux-fuyant *m*, échappatoire *f*.

evasive [i'veiziv] *a* évasif.

eve [iːv] *n* veille *f*.

even ['iːvən] *a* égal, uni, plat, pair; *ad* même, seulement, encore; *vt* égaliser, aplanir.

evening ['iːvniŋ] *n* soir *m*, soirée *f*.

evening-dress ['iːvniŋdres] *n* habit *m*, robe *f* de soirée, tenue *f* de soirée.

evenly ['iːvənli] *ad* également, régulièrement.

evensong ['iːvənsɔŋ] *n* office du soir *m*, vêpres *f pl*.

event [i'vent] *n* événement *m*, cas *m*, chance *f*, résultat *m*, épreuve *f*; **in the** — **of** au cas où; **at all** —**s** à tout hasard.

eventful [i'ventful] *a* mouvementé, mémorable, tourmenté.

ever ['evə] *ad* toujours, jamais.

everlasting [.evə'laːstiŋ] *a* éternel.

evermore ['evə'mɔː] *ad* pour toujours, à jamais.

every ['evri] *a* chaque, tout; — **other day** tous les deux jours.

everybody ['evribɔdi] *pn* tout le monde, tous, chacun.

everyday ['evridei] *a* quotidien, journalier, banal.

everyone ['evriwʌn] *pn* tout le monde, chacun, tous.

everything ['evriθiŋ] *pn* tout.

everywhere ['evriweə] *ad* partout.

evict [i'vikt] *vt* expulser.

eviction [i'vikʃən] *n* expulsion *f*, éviction *f*.

evidence ['evidəns] *n* évidence *f*, signe *m*, preuve *f*, témoignage *m*; *vt* indiquer, attester, manifester.

evident ['evidənt] *a* évident.

evil ['iːvl] *n* mal *m*, péché *m*; *a* mauvais, méchant, malin.

evilly ['iːvili] *ad* mal.

evince [i'vins] *vt* montrer.

evocation [.evou'keiʃən] *n* évocation *f*.

evoke [i'vouk] *vt* évoquer.

evolution [.iːvə'luːʃən] *n* évolution *f*, développement *m*.

evolve [i'vɔlv] *vt* dérouler, développer, élaborer; *vi* évoluer, se dérouler, se développer.

ewe [juː] *n* brebis *f*.

ewer ['juːə] n aiguière f, pot m à eau, broc m.

exact [ig'zækt] a juste, exact, précis; vt exiger, extorquer.

exacting [ig'zæktiŋ] a exigeant, fatigant.

exaction [ig'zækʃən] n exigence f, exaction f.

exactitude [ig'zæktitjuːd] n exactitude f, précision f.

exactly [ig'zæktli] ad précisément, justement, tout juste, juste.

exaggerate [ig'zædʒəreit] vti exagérer.

exaggeration [ig,zædʒə'reiʃən] n exagération f.

exalt [ig'zɔːlt] vt exalter, porter aux nues, élever.

exaltation [,egzɔːl'teiʃən] n exaltation f, élévation f.

examination [ig,zæmi'neiʃən] n examen m, inspection f, visite f, interrogatoire m, (term) composition f.

examine [ig'zæmin] vt examiner, visiter, vérifier.

examiner [ig'zæminə] n examinateur, -trice, inspecteur, -trice.

example [ig'zɑːmpl] n exemple m, précédent m.

exasperate [ig'zæspəreit] vt exaspérer, aggraver.

exasperation [ig,zæspə'reiʃən] n exaspération f.

excavate ['ekskəveit] vt fouiller, creuser, déterrer.

excavation [,ekskə'veiʃən] n excavation f, fouille f.

exceed [ik'siːd] vt dépasser, excéder, aller au-delà de.

exceedingly [ik'siːdiŋli] ad excessivement, extrêmement.

excel [ik'sel] vt surpasser, dépasser; vi exceller.

excellence ['eksələns] n excellence f, mérite m.

excellent ['eksələnt] a excellent, parfait.

except [ik'sept] vt excepter, exclure; prep excepté; cj sauf que.

exception [ik'sepʃən] n exception f, objection f.

exceptionable [ik'sepʃnəbl] a répréhensible.

exceptional [ik'sepʃənl] a exceptionnel.

excerpt ['eksəːpt] n extrait m.

excess [ik'ses] n excès m, surplus m, excédent m, supplément m.

excessive [ik'sesiv] a excessif, immodéré.

excessively [ik'sesivli] ad excessivement, démesurément, à l'excès.

exchange [iks'tʃeindʒ] n échange m, Bourse f, change m; vt (é)changer; vi permuter.

exchangeable [iks'tʃeindʒəbl] a échangeable.

exchequer [iks'tʃekə] n Echiquier m, ministère des finances m, Trésor m, fisc m.

excise ['eksaiz] n contributions indirectes f pl; excise f; vt couper, retrancher.

excision [ek'siʒən] n excision f, coupure f.

excitable [ik'saitəbl] a (sur)excitable, émotionnable.

excitation [,eksi'teiʃən] n excitation f.

excite [ik'sait] vt exciter, susciter, émouvoir, agiter.

excitement [ik'saitmənt] n agitation f, émotion f, surexcitation f, sensation(s) f pl.

exciting [ik'saitiŋ] a passionant, palpitant, mouvementé.

exclaim [iks'kleim] vi (s'é)crier, se récrier.

exclamation [,eksklə'meiʃən] n exclamation f.

exclude [iks'kluːd] vt exclure.

excluding [iks'kluːdiŋ] a sans compter.

exclusion [iks'kluːʒən] n exclusion f.

exclusive [iks'kluːsiv] a non compris, à l'exclusion (de of), exclusif, unique.

exclusively [iks'kluːsivli] ad exclusivement.

excommunicate [,ekskə'mjuːnikeit] vt excommunier.

excommunication ['ekskə,mjuːni'keiʃən] n excommunication f.

excoriate [eks'kɔːrieit] vt écorcher.

excrescence [iks'kresns] n excroissance f.

excruciating [iks'kruːʃieitiŋ] a atroce, déchirant.

excursion [iks'kəːʃən] n sortie f, excursion f.

excusable [iks'kjuːzəbl] a excusable, pardonnable.

excuse [iks'kjuːs] n excuse f, prétexte m.

excuse [iks'kjuːz] vt excuser, dispenser (de from).

executant [ig'zekjutənt] n exécutant(e) mf.

execute ['eksikjuːt] vt exécuter, valider, s'acquitter de.

execution [,eksi'kjuːʃən] n exécution f, validation f, saisie f.

executioner [,eksi'kjuːʃnə] n bourreau m.

executive [ig'zekjutiv] an exécutif m.

executor [ig'zekjutə] n exécuteur, -trice.

exemplar [ig'zemplə] n modèle m, exemplaire m.

exemplary [ig'zempləri] a exemplaire, caractérisque.

exemplify [ig'zemplifai] vt illustrer d'exemples, être l'exemple de.

exempt [ig'zempt] a exempt; vt dispenser.

exemption [ig'zempʃən] n exemption f, dispense f.

exercise ['eksəsaiz] n exercice m, devoir m; vt exercer, pratiquer, éprouver; vi s'entraîner.

exert [ig'zə:t] *vt* déployer, faire sentir, employer, exercer.

exertion [ig'zə:ʃən] *n* effort *m*, efforts *m pl*, fatigues *f pl*, emploi *m*.

exhalation [,ekshə'leiʃən] *n* exhalaison *f*, bouffée *f*, effluve *m*.

exhale [eks'heil] *vt* exhaler; *vi* se dilater, s'exhaler.

exhaust [ig'zɔ:st] *n* échappement *m*; *vt* épuiser, exténuer.

exhaustion [ig'zɔ:stʃən] *n* épuisement *m*.

exhaustive [ig'zɔ:stiv] *a* qui épuise, complet, minutieux.

exhibit [ig'zibit] *n* pièce à conviction *f*, objet exposé *m*; *vt* montrer, étaler, exhiber.

exhibition [,eksi'biʃən] *n* exposition *f*, exhibition *f*, spectacle *m*, étalage *m*.

exhort [ig'zɔ:t] *vt* exhorter.

exhortation [,egzɔ:'teiʃən] *n* exhortation *f*.

exhumation [,ekshju:'meiʃən] *n* exhumation *f*.

exhume [eks'hju:m] *vt* exhumer.

exigence ['eksidʒəns] *n* exigence *f*, nécessité *f*.

exigent ['eksidʒənt] *a* urgent, exigeant.

exiguity [,eksi'gju(:)iti] *n* exiguïté *f*.

exiguous [eg'zigjuəs] *a* exigu, -uë.

exile ['eksail] *n* exil *m*, exilé(e) *mf*; *vt* exiler, bannir.

exist [ig'zist] *vi* exister.

existence [ig'zistəns] *n* existence *f*, vie *f*.

existing [ig'zistiŋ] *a* existant, actuel.

exit ['eksit] *n* sortie *f*.

exodus ['eksədəs] *n* exode *m*, sortie *f*.

exonerate [ig'zɔnəreit] *vt* exonérer, décharger.

exoneration [ig,zɔnə'reiʃən] *n* exonération *f*.

exorbitance [ig'zɔ:bitəns] *n* énormité *f*, exorbitance *f*.

exorbitant [ig'zɔ:bitənt] *a* exorbitant, extravagant.

exorcise ['eksɔ:saiz] *vt* exorciser.

exorcising ['eksɔ:saiziŋ] *n* exorcisme *m*.

exotic [ig'zɔtik] *a* exotique.

expand [iks'pænd] *vt* étendre, dilater, épancher; *vi* se dilater, se développer.

expanse [iks'pæns] *n* étendue *f*.

expansion [iks'pænʃən] *n* expansion *f*, développement *m*.

expansive [iks'pænsiv] *a* expansif, étendu.

expatiate [eks'peiʃieit] *vi* s'étendre (sur **on**), pérorer.

expatriate [eks'pætrieit] *vt* expatrier.

expect [iks'pekt] *vt* (s')attendre (à), compter sur.

expectancy [iks'pektənsi] *n* attente *f*, expectative *f*.

expectation [,ekspek'teiʃən] *n* attente *f*, espérances *f pl*, prévision *f*.

expediency [iks'pi:djənsi] *n* convenance *f*, opportunité *f*.

expedient [iks'pi:djənt] *an* expédient *m*.

expedite ['ekspidait] *vt* hâter, expédier.

expedition [,ekspi'diʃən] *n* expédition *f*, rapidité *f*.

expeditious [,ekspi'diʃəs] *a* expéditif, prompt.

expel [iks'pel] *vt* chasser, expulser.

expend [iks'pend] *vt* dépenser, consommer, épuiser.

expenditure [iks'penditʃə] *n* dépense(s) *f pl*.

expense [iks'pens] *n* débours *m pl*, dépens *m pl*, frais *m pl*.

expensive [iks'pensiv] *a* cher, coûteux, dispendieux.

experience [iks'piəriəns] *n* expérience *f*, épreuve *f*.

experienced [iks'piəriənst] *a* expérimenté, exercé.

experiment [iks'perimənt] *n* essai *m*, expérience *f*; *vi* expérimenter, faire une expérience.

experimental [eks,peri'mentl] *a* expérimental.

experimentally [eks,peri'mentəli] *ad* expérimentalement, à titre d'essai.

expert ['ekspə:t] *an* expert *m*; *a* habile.

expiate ['ekspieit] *vt* expier.

expiation [,ekspi'eiʃən] *n* expiation *f*.

expiration [,ekspaiə'reiʃən] *n* expiration *f*, (d)échéance *f*.

expire [iks'paiə] *vti* exhaler, expirer; *vi* s'éteindre.

expiry [iks'paiəri] *n* fin *f*, terminaison *f*.

explain [iks'plein] *vt* expliquer, éclaircir.

explanation [,eksplə'neiʃən] *n* explication *f*.

explanatory [iks'plænətəri] *a* explicatif; explicateur, -trice.

explicable [eks'plikəbl] *a* explicable.

explicit [iks'plisit] *a* formel, clair.

explode [iks'ploud] *vt* faire sauter, dégonfler; *vi* sauter, faire explosion, éclater.

exploit ['eksplɔit] *n* exploit *m*; *vt* exploiter.

exploitation [,eksplɔi'teiʃən] *n* exploitation *f*.

exploration [,eksplɔ:'reiʃən] *n* exploration *f*.

explore [iks'plɔ:] *vt* explorer.

explorer [iks'plɔ:rə] *n* explorateur, -trice.

explosion [iks'plouʒən] *n* explosion *f*, détonation *f*.

explosive [iks'plouziv] *a* explosible, explosif, détonnant.

export [eks'pɔ:t] *vt* exporter.

export ['ekspɔ:t] *n* exportation *f*; *pl* exportations *f pl*.

exportation [,ekspɔ:'teiʃən] *n* exportation *f*.

exporter [eks'pɔːtə] n exportateur, -trice.

expose [iks'pouz] vt exposer, mettre à nu, démasquer.

expostulate [iks'pɔstjuleit] vi en remontrer (à **with**), faire des remontrances (à **with**).

expostulation [iks,pɔstju'leiʃən] n rémontrance f.

expound [iks'paund] vt exposer, expliquer.

express [iks'pres] n exprès m, rapide m, express m; compagnie f de messageries; a exact, exprès; vt exprimer.

expression [iks'preʃən] n expression f.

expressive [iks'presiv] a expressif.

expressly [iks'presli] ad expressément, formellement.

expropriate [eks'prouprieit] vt exproprier.

expropriation [eks,proupri'eiʃən] n expropriation f.

expulsion [iks'pʌlʃən] n expulsion f.

expunge [iks'pʌndʒ] vt biffer, rayer.

expurgate ['ekspəːgeit] vt expurger, épurer.

exquisite [eks'kwizit] n élégant m; a exquis, raffiné.

exquisiteness [eks'kwizitnis] n finesse exquise f, raffinement m.

extant [eks'tænt] a subsistant.

extempore [eks'tempəri] a improvisé; ad d'abondance.

extemporization [eks,tempərai'zeiʃən] n improvisation f.

extemporize [iks'tempəraiz] vti improviser.

extend [iks'tend] vt étendre, prolonger, accorder; vi se déployer, s'étendre.

extensible [iks'tensibl] a extensible.

extension [iks'tenʃən] n extension f, prolongement m, prolongation f, agrandissement m.

extensive [iks'tensiv] a extensif, étendu, ample.

extensively [iks'tensivli] ad **to use —** se servir largement, beaucoup.

extent [iks'tent] n étendue f, mesure f, point m.

extenuate [eks'tenjueit] vt atténuer, excuser.

extenuation [eks,tenju'eiʃən] n atténuation f, affaiblissement m, exténuation f.

exterior [eks'tiəriə] an extérieur m; n dehors m.

exterminate [eks'təːmineit] vt exterminer, extirper.

extermination [eks,təːmi'neiʃən] n extermination f, extirpation f.

external [eks'təːnl] a externe, extérieur.

extinct [iks'tiŋkt] a éteint.

extinction [iks'tiŋkʃən] n extinction f.

extinguish [iks'tiŋgwiʃ] vt éteindre, éclipser, anéantir.

extinguisher [iks'tiŋgwiʃə] n éteignoir m, extincteur m.

extirpate ['ekstəːpeit] vt extirper.

extol [iks'tɔl] vt porter aux nues, exalter.

extort [iks'tɔːt] vt extorquer, arracher.

extortion [iks'tɔːʃən] n extorsion f, arrachement m.

extortionate [iks'tɔːʃnit] a exorbitant, de pirate.

extra ['ekstrə] a supplémentaire, d'extra, de plus; ad extra, super, ultra, en plus; n supplément m; pl à-côtés m pl.

extract ['ekstrækt] n extrait m.

extract [iks'trækt] vt extraire, (sou) tirer.

extraction [iks'trækʃən] n extraction f, origine f.

extradite ['ekstrədait] vt extrader.

extradition [,ekstrə'diʃən] n extradition f.

extraneous [eks'treinjəs] a étranger, en dehors de.

extraordinary [iks'trɔːdnri] a extraordinaire.

extravagance [iks'trævəgəns] n extravagance f, folle dépense f, gaspillage m.

extravagant [iks'trævəgənt] a extravagant, dépensier.

extreme [iks'triːm] an extrême m.

extremely [iks'triːmli] ad extrêmement, au dernier point.

extremist [iks'triːmist] n extrémiste mf.

extremity [iks'tremiti] n extrémité f, bout m.

extricate ['ekstrikeit] vt tirer, sortir, dégager.

exuberance [ig'zuːbərəns] n exubérance f, luxuriance f.

exuberant [ig'zuːbərənt] a exubérant.

exult [ig'zʌlt] vi exulter.

exultation [,egzʌl'teiʃən] n jubilation f, exultation f.

eye [ai] n œil m, pl yeux m pl, (needle) chas m; vt regarder, lorgner.

eyeball ['aibɔːl] n pupille f, prunelle f.

eyebrow ['aibrau] n sourcil m.

eyeglass ['aiglaːs] n monocle m; pl lorgnon m.

eyelash ['ailæʃ] n cil m.

eyelet ['ailit] n œillet m.

eyelid ['ailid] n paupière f.

eyeshot ['aiʃɔt] n portée f de vue.

eyesight ['aisait] n vue f.

eyesore ['aisɔːr] n mal m d'yeux, tache f, hideur f.

eyetooth ['aituːθ] n canine f.

eyewash ['aiwɔʃ] n poudre aux yeux f.

eyewitness ['ai,witnis] n témoin oculaire m.

F

fable ['feibl] n fable f, conte m.
fabric ['fæbrik] n construction f, édifice m, tissu m.
fabricate ['fæbrikeit] vt fabriquer, inventer.
fabrication [.fæbri'keiʃən] n faux m, fabrication f.
fabulist ['fæbjulist] n fabuliste m.
fabulous ['fæbjuləs] a fabuleux, légendaire, prodigieux.
face [feis] n visage m, figure f, face f, air m, mine f, grimace f, toupet m, façade f, cadran m; — **cream** crème f de beauté; —**pack** masque m anti-ride; — **value** valeur f nominale; vt regarder en face, faire face à, confronter garnir, couvrir, donner sur; — **up to** affronter.
facet ['fæsit] n facette f.
facetious [fə'si:ʃəs] a facétieux, bouffon.
facial ['feiʃəl] a facial.
facile ['fæsail] a facile.
facility [fə'siliti] n facilité f.
facing ['feisiŋ] n parement m, revers m, revêt m.
fact [fækt] n fait m; **matter-of-—** (of person) pratique; **as a matter of —** en effet, en réalité.
faction ['fækʃən] n faction f, cabale f.
factious ['fækʃəs] a factieux.
factitious [fæk'tiʃəs] a factice, artificiel.
factor ['fæktə] n facteur m, agent m, régisseur m.
factory ['fæktəri] n usine f, manufacture f, fabrique f, factorerie f.
factotum [fæk'toutəm] n factotum m.
facultative ['fækəltətiv] a facultatif.
faculty ['fækəlti] n faculté f, pouvoir m, liberté f.
fad [fæd] n lubie f, manie f, marotte f.
faddist ['fædist] n maniaque mf.
fade [feid] vi se faner, se déteindre, s'éteindre; vt faner, décolorer.
faded ['feidid] a fané, décoloré, défraîchi.
fade-out ['feidaut] n fondu m.
fading ['feidiŋ] a pâlissant, estompé; n flétrissure f, décoloration f, (of sound) chute f d'intensité.
fag [fæg] n corvée f, (sl) sèche f; vi turbiner, trimer; vt fatiguer, éreinter.
fag-end ['fægend] n mégot m.
faggot ['fægət] n fagot m.
fail [feil] vi manquer, échouer, faire faillite, baisser; vt refuser, coller, manquer à; ad **without —** sans faute.
failing ['feiliŋ] prep faute de; n défaut m, défaillance f.
failure ['feiljə] n échec m, manque (ment) m, faillite f, raté(e) mf, four m, panne f.
fain [fein] a heureux; ad volontiers.
faint [feint] n défaillance f, syncope

f; vi s'évanouir; a faible, pâle, vague, léger.
fair [fɛə] a beau, blond, clair, loyal, juste, passable, moyen; n foire f.
fair-copy ['fɛə'kɔpi] n mise au net f, copie au net f.
fairly ['fɛəli] ad absolument, assez, loyalement.
fairness ['fɛənis] n justice f, loyauté f, impartialité f; in blancheur f, fraîcheur f; **in all —** en bonne conscience.
fair-play ['fɛə'plei] n franc jeu m.
fairy ['fɛəri] n fée f.
fairyland ['fɛərilænd] n féerie f.
fairy-like ['fɛərilaik] a féerique.
faith [feiθ] n foi f, parole f.
faithful ['feiθful] a fidèle.
faithfully ['feiθfuli] adv fidèlement; **yours —** agréez l'expression de nos sentiments distingués.
faithless ['feiθlis] a sans foi.
fake [feik] n truquage m, faux m; vt truquer, maquiller.
falcon ['fɔ:lkən] n faucon m.
fall [fɔ:l] n chute f, tombée f; automne m; vi tomber, baisser, échoir.
fallacy ['fæləsi] n illusion f, fausseté f, erreur f.
fallacious [fə'leiʃəs] a fallacieux, trompeur.
fallen ['fɔ:lən] pp of **fall.**
fallibility [.fæli'biliti] n faillibilité f.
fallible ['fæləbl] a faillible.
fall-out ['fɔ:laut] n retombée f.
fallow ['fælou] n friche f, jachère f.
false [fɔls] a faux, trompeur, perfide.
falsehood ['fɔlshud] n fausseté f, mensonge m.
falseness ['fɔlsnis] n duplicité f, mauvaise foi f.
falsification [.fɔlsifi'keiʃən] n falsification f.
falsify ['fɔlsifai] vt falsifier, tromper, rendre faux.
falter ['fɔltə] vi trébucher, balbutier, hésiter, flancher.
fame [feim] n réputation f, renom m, renommée f.
famed [feimd] a célèbre, famé.
familiar [fə'miljə] a familier, intime.
familiarity [fə.mili'æriti] n familiarité f, connaissance f.
familiarize [fə'miljəraiz] vt familiariser, habituer.
family ['fæmili] n famille f.
famine ['fæmin] n famine f.
famish ['fæmiʃ] vi être affamé.
famous ['feiməs] a célèbre, fameux.
fan [fæn] n éventail m, ventilateur m, aérateur m, fan m, fervent(e) mf, enragé(e) mf; — **palm** rômer m; vt éventer, souffler (sur), attiser, vanner.
fanatic [fə'nætik] n fanatique mf, enragé(e) mf.
fanatical [fə'nætikəl] a fanatique.
fanaticism [fə'nætisizəm] n fanatisme m.

fanciful ['fænsiful] *a* capricieux, fantaisiste, chimérique.

fancy ['fænsi] *n* imagination *f*, fantaisie *f*, chimère *f*, caprice *m*; *vt* (s')imaginer, se toquer de; **to —** **oneself** se gober.

fang [fæŋ] *n* croc *m*, crochet *m*, défense *f*, racine *f*.

fanner ['fænə] *n* vanneur, -euse.

fantastic [fæn'tæstik] *a* fantastique, fantasque.

fantasy ['fæntəzi] *n* imagination *f*, extravagance *f*.

far [fɑː] *a* éloigné, lointain; *ad* loin, au loin, avant, (de) beaucoup; **so —** jusqu'ici; **in so —** **as** dans la mesure où; **— afield** très loin.

faraway ['fɑːrəwei] *a* éloigné, lointain.

far-between ['fɑːbi'twiːn] *a* espacé.

far-fetched ['fɑː'fetʃt] *a* outré, tiré par les cheveux, extravagant.

far-off ['fɑːr'ɔf] *a* éloigné.

far-reaching ['fɑː'riːtʃiŋ] *a* de longue portée, de grande envergure.

far-sighted ['fɑː'saitid] *a* presbyte, à longue vue, prévoyant.

farce [fɑːs] *n* farce *f*.

farcical ['fɑːsikəl] *a* grotesque.

fare [fɛə] *n* prix *m* (du voyage), places *f pl*, voyageur, -euse, client(e) *mf*; **good —** bonne chère *f*; *vi* se faire, se porter, se trouver; **single —** aller *m*; **return —** aller et retour *m*.

farewell ['fɛə'wel] *n* adieu *m*.

farm [fɑːm] *n* ferme *f*; *vt* affermer, cultiver, exploiter; *vi* être cultivateur.

farmer ['fɑːmə] *n* fermier *m*, cultivateur *m*.

farming ['fɑːmiŋ] *n* culture *f*, affermage *m*, exploitation *f*.

farrier ['færiə] *n* maréchal ferrant *m*, vétérinaire *m*.

farther ['fɑːðə] *see* **further**.

farthing ['fɑːðiŋ] *n* liard *m*, sou *m*.

fascinate ['fæsineit] *vt* séduire, fasciner.

fascination [,fæsi'neiʃən] *n* fascination *f*, charme *m*.

fascism ['fæʃizəm] *n* fascisme *m*.

fascist ['fæʃist] *an* fasciste *mf*.

fashion ['fæʃən] *n* mode *f*, façon *f*, coutume *f*; *vt* façonner, former.

fashionable ['fæʃnəbl] *a* à la mode, élégant.

fast [fɑːst] *n* jeûne *m*; *vi* jeûner; *a* fixé, confiné, sûr, solide, bon teint, rapide, qui va fort, qui avance; *ad* solidement, rapidement, fort, vite.

fasten ['fɑːsn] *vt* attacher, ficeler, fermer, fixer, saisir; *vi* se cramponner, se fixer.

fastener ['fɑːsnə] *n* attache *f*, agrafe *f*, fermeture *f*.

fastidious [fæs'tidjəs] *a* difficile, délicat.

fastidiousness [fæs'tidjəsnis] *n* goût difficile *m*.

fastness ['fɑːstnis] *n* rapidité *f*

vitesse *f*, fermeté *f*, solidité *f*, forteresse *f*.

fat [fæt] *n* gros *m*, graisse *f*; *a* gras, gros.

fatal ['feitl] *a* fatal, mortel, funeste.

fatalism ['feitəlizəm] *n* fatalisme *m*.

fatalist ['feitəlist] *n* fataliste *mf*.

fatality [fə'tæliti] *n* fatalité *f*, sinistre *m*, accident mortel *m*.

fate [feit] *n* destin *m*, sort *m*, destinée *f*.

fateful ['feitful] *a* décisif, gros d'avenir, fatidique, fatal.

father ['fɑːðə] *n* père *m*; **—-in-law** beau-père *m*; *vt* reconnaître, avouer, imputer, patronner, engendrer.

fatherhood ['fɑːðəhud] *n* paternité *f*.

fatherland ['fɑːðəlænd] *n* patrie *f*.

fatherless ['fɑːðəlis] *a* sans père.

fatherly ['fɑːðəli] *a* paternel.

fathom ['fæðəm] *n* toise *f*, brasse *f*; *vt* sonder, approfondir.

fathomless ['fæðəmlis] *a* insondable, sans fond.

fatigue [fə'tiːg] *n* fatigue *f*, corvée *f*; *vt* fatiguer.

fatten ['fætn] *vtn* engraisser.

fatty ['fæti] *a* graisseux, onctueux, gras, gros.

fatuous ['fætjuəs] *a* sot, idiot.

fatuousness ['fætjuəsnis] *n* stupidité *f*.

faucet ['fɔːsit] *n* robinet *m*.

fault [fɔlt] *n* défaut *m*, faute *f*, faille *f*; **to a —** jusqu'à l'excès.

faultless ['fɔltlis] *a* impeccable, sans faute.

faulty ['fɔlti] *a* fautif, défectueux, inexact.

favor ['feivə] *n* faveur *f*; *vt* favoriser, approuver, appuyer.

favorable ['feivərəbl] *a* favorable, propice, avantageux.

favorite ['feivərit] *an* favori, -ite; *a* préféré.

favoritism ['feivəritizəm] *n* favoritisme *m*.

fawn [fɔːn] *n* faon *m*; *a* fauve; *vt* **to — upon** caresser, flagorner, faire le chien couchant devant.

fear [fiə] *n* peur *f*, crainte *f*; *vt* craindre, avoir peur de.

fearful ['fiəful] *a* terrible, affreux, craintif, peureux.

fearless ['fiəlis] *a* sans peur, intrépide.

fearsome ['fiəsəm] *a* hideux, redoutable.

feasible ['fiːzəbl] *a* faisable, praticable, probable.

feasibility [,fiːzə'biliti] *n* possibilité *f*, praticabilité *f*.

feast [fiːst] *n* fête *f*, régal *m*, festin *m*; *vt* fêter, régaler; *vi* se régaler, faire festin.

feat [fiːt] *n* exploit *m*, prouesse *f*, haut fait *m*, tour de force *m*.

feather ['feðə] *n* plume *f*, penne *f*, plumage *m*; *vt* garnir de plumes, empenner.

feathery ['feðəri] *a* léger comme une plume, plumeux.

feather-weight ['feðəweit] *n* poids plume *m*.

feature ['fi:tʃə] *n* trait *m* (saillant), caractéristique *f*, spécialité *f*; grand film *m*, long-métrage *m*; *vt* caractériser, esquisser, mettre en manchette, mettre en vedette.

featureless ['fi:tʃəlis] *a* terne.

February ['februəri] *n* février *m*.

fecund ['fi:kənd] *a* fécond.

fecundate ['fi:kəndeit] *vt* féconder.

fecundation [,fi:kən'deiʃən] *n* fécondation *f*.

fecundity [fi'kʌnditi] *n* fécondité *f*.

fed [fed] *pt pp of* **feed**; **to be — up** en avoir assez, marre.

federal ['fedərəl] *a* fédéral.

federalism [,fedərəlizəm] *n* fédéralisme *m*.

federate ['fedəreit] *vt* fédérer; *vi* se fédérer; *a* fédéré.

federation [,fede'reiʃən] *n* fédération *f*.

fee [fi:] *n* fief *m*, frais *m pl*, cachet *m*, honoraires *m pl*.

feeble ['fi:bl] *a* faible, infirme, chétif.

feebleness ['fi:blnis] *n* faiblesse *f*.

feeblish ['fi:bliʃ] *a* faiblard.

feed [fi:d] *n* repas *m*, tétée *f*, pâture *f*, picotin *m*, alimentation *f*, fourrage *m*; *vt* nourrir, alimenter, donner à manger à, ravitailler; *vi* manger, se nourrir, s'alimenter, brouter.

feeder ['fi:də] *n* mangeur, -euse, biberon *m*, tétine *f*, bavette *f*.

feed-back ['fi:dbæk] *n* rétroaction *f*, réaction *f*.

feel [fi:l] *n* toucher *m*, sensation *f*; *vt* toucher, tâter, palper, sentir; *vi* se sentir, tâtonner, fouiller.

feeler ['fi:lə] *n* antenne *f*, éclaireur *m*, sondage *m*.

feeling ['fi:liŋ] *n* toucher *m*, maniement *m*, sensation *f*, sentiment *m*, sensibilité *f*; *a* sensible.

feelingly ['fi:liŋli] *ad* avec émotion.

feign [fein] *vt* feindre, simuler.

feint [feint] *n* feinte *f*; *vi* faire une fausse attaque, feinter.

felicitous [fi'lisitəs] *a* heureux, bien trouvé.

felicity [fi'lisiti] *n* félicité *f*.

fell [fel] *n* peau *f*, toison *f*; *vt* abattre; *a* sinistre, cruel.

fellow ['felou] *n* type *m*, gars *m*, individu *m*, membre *m*, confrère *m*, pareil *m*.

fellowship ['felouʃip] *n* société *f*, amitié *f*, association *f*, camaraderie *f*.

felon ['felən] *n* auteur d'un crime *m*, criminel, -elle.

felonious [fi'lounjəs] *a* criminel.

felt [felt] *pp pt of* **feel**; *n* feutre *m*, *vt* feutrer, couvrir de carton goudronné.

female ['fi:meil] *n* femelle *f*, femme *f*; *a* féminin.

feminine ['feminin] *a* féminin, femelle.

fen [fen] *n* marais *m*.

fence [fens] *n* barrière *f*, clôture *f*, receleur, -euse; *vi* faire de l'escrime, s'escrimer; *vt* enclore, clôturer.

fencing ['fensiŋ] *n* escrime *f*, clôture *f*.

fend [fend] *vt* **to — for oneself** se débrouiller; *vt* **to — off** parer, écarter.

fender [['fendə] *n* garde-bove *m*; *n* garde-feu *m*.

ferment ['fə:ment] *n* ferment *m*.

ferment [fə:'ment] *vt* faire fermenter, fomenter; *vi* fermenter, travailler.

fermentation [,fə:men'teiʃən] *n* fermentation *f*, travail *m*, effervescence *f*.

fern [fə:n] *n* fougère *f*.

ferocious [fə'rouʃəs] *a* féroce.

ferocity [fə'rositi] *n* férocité *f*.

ferret ['ferit] *n* furet *m*; *vi* fureter; *vt* **to — out** débusquer, dénicher.

ferro-concrete ['ferou'kɔŋkri:t] *n* ciment armé *m*.

ferrule ['feru:l] *n* virole *f*, embout *m*.

ferry ['feri] *n* bac *m*; *vt* passer.

ferryman ['ferimən] *n* passeur *m*.

fertile ['fə:tail] *a* fertile.

fertility [fə:'tiliti] *n* fertilité *f*, fécondité *f*.

fertilize ['fə:tilaiz] *vt* fertiliser, féconder.

fertilizer ['fə:tilaizə] *n* engrais *m*.

fervent ['fə:vənt] *a* brûlant, fervent, ardent.

fervor ['fə:və] *n* chaleur *f*, ferveur *f*, zèle *m*

fester ['festə] *n* abcès *m*; *vi* suppurer; *vt* empoisonner, ulcérer.

festival ['festəvəl] *n* festival *m*, fête *f*.

festive ['festiv] *a* joyeux, de fête.

festivity [fes'tiviti] *n* festivité *f*, fête *f*.

festoon [fes'tu:n] *n* feston *m*; *vt* festonner.

fetch [fetʃ] *vt* aller chercher, apporter, atteindre, (*blow*) envoyer, (*sigh*) pousser, (*breath*) reprendre.

fetching ['fetʃiŋ] *a* intéressant.

fetid ['fetid] *a* fétide.

fetidness ['fetidnis] *n* fétidité *f*, puanteur *f*.

fetter ['fetə] *n* lien *m*; *pl* fers *m pl*, entraves *f pl*; *vt* enchaîner, entraver.

fettle ['fetl] *n* état *m*; **in good —** en train, en forme.

feud [fju:d] *n* vendetta *f*.

feudal ['fju:dl] *a* féodal.

feudalism ['fju:dəlizəm] *n* féodalité *f*.

fever ['fi:və] *n* fièvre *f*.

feverish ['fi:vəriʃ] *a* fiévreux, fébrile.

few [fju:] *a* peu de, un (le) petit nombre; **a — quelques.**

fewer ['fju:ə] *a* moins de, moins nombreux.

fewest ['fju:ist] *a* le moins de, le moins nombreux.

fez [fez] n chéchia m.
fiasco [fi'æskou] n fiasco m, four m.
fib [fib] n petit mensonge m, craque f, colle f; vi enconter (à **to**).
fiber ['faibə] n fibre f; **staple** — fibrane f.
fibrous ['faibrəs] a fibreux.
fickle ['fikl] a volage, changeant, inconstant.
fickleness ['fiklnis] n inconstance f.
fiction ['fikʃən] n fiction f, romans m pl.
fictitious [fik'tiʃəs] a fictif, imaginaire.
fiddle ['fidl] n violon m, crin-crin m; vi jouer du violon, râcler du violon; **to** — **with** tripoter, tourmenter.
fiddler ['fidlə] n ménétrier m, violoneux m; violiniste.
fiddlestick ['fidlstik] n archet m; pl sottises f pl.
fidelity [fi'deliti] n fidélité f, loyauté f, exactitude f.
fidget ['fidʒit] n **to have the** —s avoir la bougeotte; vi s'agiter, se trémousser.
fie [fai] excl fi!
field [fi:ld] n champ m, (mil) campagne f, terrain de jeux m, domaine m, candidatures f pl; a de campagne.
field glasses ['fi:ldglɑːsiz] n jumelles f pl.
field-marshal ['fi:ld'mɑːʃəl] n maréchal m.
field-mouse ['fi:ldmaus] n mulot m.
fiend [fi:nd] n démon m.
fiendish ['fi:ndiʃ] a diabolique, infernal.
fierce [fiəs] a féroce, violent.
fiercely ['fiəsli] ad violemment, âprement.
fierceness ['fiəsnis] n férocité f, sauvagerie f, violence f.
fiery ['faiəri] a de feu, ardent, emporté, fougueux.
fife [faif] n fifre m.
fifteen ['fif'ti:n] an quinze m.
fifteenth ['fif'ti:nθ] an quinzième mf, quinze m.
fifth [fifθ] an cinquième mf, cinq m.
fiftieth ['fiftiəθ] an cinquantième mf.
fifty ['fifti] an cinquante m.
fig [fig] n figue f, tenue f, forme f.
fight [fait] n lutte f, combat m, combat(t)ivité f; vi se battre, lutter, combattre; vt combattre, se battre avec.
fighter ['faitə] n combattant m, militant m, avion de combat m.
figment ['figmənt] n invention f, rêve m.
fig-tree ['figtri:] n figuier m.
figure ['figə] n forme f, corps m, taille f, personne f, ligne f, galbe m, chiffre m, emblème m, figure f; vt (se) figurer, estimer; vi calculer, faire figure, se chiffrer, figurer.
figurehead ['figəhed] n façade f, prête-nom m, figure de proue f.

filbert ['filbə(ː)t] n noisette f.
filch [filtʃ] vt voler, escamoter.
file [fail] n lime f, piquenotes m, classeur m, dossier m, liasse f, file f; vt limer, enfiler, classer, soumettre; vi défiler.
filial ['filjəl] a filial.
filiation [fili'eiʃən] n filiation f.
filibuster ['filibʌstə] n flibustier m; vi flibuster.
filigree ['filigriː] n filigrane m.
filing ['failiŋ] n limaille f, limage m; classement m.
fill [fil] n plein m, soûl m, pipée f; vt remplir, plomber, compléter, combler; vi se remplir, se garnir; **to** — **up** vi faire le plein.
filling ['filiŋ] n plombage m, chargement m, remplissage m.
filling-station ['filiŋˌsteiʃən] n poste d'essence m.
fillet ['filit] n bandeau m, filet m.
fillip ['filip] n chiquenaude f, stimulant m, coup de fouet m.
filly ['fili] n pouliche f.
film [film] n pellicule f, film m, voile m, (eye) taie f; vt filmer, tourner.
film-star ['filmstɑː] n vedette du cinéma f.
filter ['filtə] n filtre m; vti filtrer; vt tamiser.
filth [filθ] n saleté f, ordure f.
filthy ['filθi] a sale, crasseux, immonde.
fin [fin] n nageoire f, aileron m.
final ['fainl] a final, dernier, définitif, décisif.
finally ['fainəli] ad enfin, finalement.
finance [fai'næns] n finance f; vt financer.
financial [fai'nænʃəl] a financier.
financier [fai'nænsiə] n financier m.
finch [fintʃ] n pinson m.
find [faind] n trouvaille f, découverte f; vt trouver, constater, pourvoir, fournir; **all found** tout compris.
fine [fain] n amende f; vt mettre à l'amende; a beau, bon, fin, délié, élégant.
finely ['fainli] ad habilement, subtilement, magnifiquement, fin.
fineness ['fainnis] n beauté f, élégance f, finesse f, excellence f.
finery ['fainəri] n atours m pl, parure f.
finesse [fi'nes] n finesse f; vi user de finesse, faire une impasse.
finger ['fiŋgə] n doigt m; **fore**—index m; **middle** — médius m; **ring**— annulaire m; **little** — petit doigt m, auriculaire m; vt toucher, manier, jouer, tripoter.
finger-bowl ['fiŋgəboul] n rince-doigts m.
fingering ['fiŋgəriŋ] n maniement m, touche f, doigté m.
fingernail ['fiŋgəneil] n ongle de la main m.
fingerprint ['fiŋgəprint] n empreinte digitale f.

finish ['finiʃ] n fini m, dernière touche f; **to a** — à mort; vti finir, terminer; vt achever; vi prendre fin, se terminer.

finished ['finiʃt] a accompli.

Finland ['finlənd] n Finlande f.

Finn [fin] n Finlandais(e) mf.

Finnish ['finiʃ] an finlandais m.

fir [fəː] n sapin m.

fire ['faiə] n feu m, incendie m, tir m, ardeur f; vt allumer, incendier, mettre le feu à, enflammer; vi faire feu; — **away** allez!

fire-alarm ['faiərə.laːm] n avertisseur d'incendie m.

firearm ['faiəraːm] n arme à feu f.

firebrand ['faiəbrænd] n incendiaire m, boutefeu m, brandon m.

fire-brigade ['faiəbri.geid] n compagnie de sapeurs-pompiers f.

firedamp ['faiədæmp] n grisou m.

firedog ['faiədɔg] n chenet m.

fire-engine ['faiər.endʒin] n pompe à incendie f.

fire-escape ['faiəris.keip] n échelle de sauvetage f.

fireguard ['faiəgaːd] n garde-feu m.

fireman ['faiəmən] n pompier m, chauffeur m.

fireplace ['faiəpleis] n cheminée f.

fireproof ['faiəpruːf] a ignifuge.

fireside ['faiəsaid] n coin du feu m.

firework ['faiəwəːk] n feu d'artifice m.

firing-squad ['faiəriŋ.skwɔd] n peloton d'exécution m.

firm [fəːm] n firme f, maison de commerce f; a ferme, solide, résolu.

firmly ['fəːmli] ad fermement.

firmness ['fəːmnis] n fermeté f, solidité f.

first [fəːst] a premier; ad premièrement, primo.

first-aid ['fəːst'eid] n premiers secours m pl.

first-class ['fəːstklaːs] a de première classe, qualité.

first-rate ['fəːst'reit] a de premier ordre.

firth [fəːθ] n estuaire m.

fish [fiʃ] n poisson m; vti pêcher.

fishbone ['fiʃboun] n arête f.

fisherman ['fiʃəmən] n pêcheur m.

fishery ['fiʃəri] n pêcherie f.

fishing ['fiʃiŋ] n pêche f.

fishing-ground ['fiʃiŋgraund] n pêcherie f.

fishing-net n ['fiʃiŋnet] n épervier.

fishing-rod ['fiʃiŋrɔd] n canne à pêche f.

fish-kettle ['fiʃ'ketl] n poissonnière f.

fishmonger ['fiʃ.mʌŋgə] n marchand de poisson m.

fishmonger's ['fiʃ.mʌŋgəz] n poissonnerie f.

fish-pond ['fiʃpɔnd] n vivier m.

fishy ['fiʃi] a poissoneux, louche.

fissionable ['fiʃənəbl] a fissile.

fissure ['fiʃə] n fissure f.

fist [fist] n poing m.

fit [fit] n attaque f, accès m, ajustement m, coupe f; a apte, bon, convenable, en forme; vt aller à, ajuster, garnir, munir, préparer, équiper; vi s'adapter, s'ajuster; **to** — **on** monter, essayer; **to** — **out** garnir, équiper; **to** — **up** monter.

fitful ['fitful] a capricieux.

fitfully ['fitfuli] ad par accès, par à-coups.

fitly ['fitli] ad à propos, à point.

fitness ['fitnis] n parfait état m convenance f, aptitude f.

fitter ['fitə] n ajusteur m, essayeur m.

fitting ['fitiŋ] n ajustage m, essayage m; pl garnitures f pl; a bon, juste, approprié.

five [faiv] an cinq m.

fivefold ['faivfould] a quintuple.

fix [fiks] n embarras m, situation fâcheuse f; vt fixer, établir, arrêter, assujettir.

fixed [fikst] a fixe, arrêté.

fixedly ['fiksidli] ad fixement.

fixity ['fiksiti] n fixité f.

fixture(s) ['fikstʃə(s)] n garniture(s) fixe(s) f (pl), (fig) meuble m, match m.

fizz [fiz] n bruit de fusée m, pétillement m, (fam) champagne m; vi pétiller, siffler.

fizzle ['fizl] n pétillement m, grésillement m; vi fuser, grésiller; **to** — **out** faire long feu, faire four.

flabbergast ['flæbəgaːst] vt renverser, stupéfier.

flabby ['flæbi] a flasque, pendant.

flag [flæg] n drapeau m, pavillon m, dalle f, glaïeul m; vi pendre, languir, fléchir, se relâcher; vt jalonner, signaler, pavoiser.

flagbearer ['flæg'beərə] n porte-drapeau m.

flagging ['flægiŋ] n dallage m, ralentissement m.

flagon ['flægən] n flacon m, burette f.

flagrancy ['fleigrənsi] n éclat m, énormité f.

flagrant ['fleigrənt] a flagrant, énorme, scandaleux.

flagship ['flægʃip] n vaisseau-amiral m.

flagstaff ['flægstaːf] n mât m.

flail [fleil] n fléau m.

flair [fleə] n flair m.

flak [flæk] n tir m contre avion, la DCA.

flake [fleik] n flocon m, flammèche f, lamelle f, pelure f, écaille f; vi tomber à flocons, (s')écailler.

flaky ['fleiki] a floconneux, écailleux, feuilleté.

flame [fleim] n flamme f; vi flamber, s'enflammer.

flame-thrower ['fleim.θrouə] n lance-flammes m.

flaming ['fleimiŋ] a flambant.

Flanders ['flaːndəz] n Flandre f.

flank [flæŋk] n flanc m; vt flanquer, prendre de flanc.

flannel ['flænl] n flanelle f.

flap [flæp] n tape f, battement d'ailes m, patte f, claquement m, pan m, bord m; vti battre; vi s'agiter, claquer.

flare [flɛə] n flambée f, fusée éclairante f, flamme f, feu d'atterrissage m; vi flamber, s'évaser; vt évaser; **to — up** s'emporter, s'enflammer.

flash [flæʃ] n éclair m, lueur f; **in a —** en un clin d'œil; vi flamboyer, jeter des éclairs; vt faire étinceler, télégraphier.

flashing ['flæʃiŋ] n éclat m, clignotement m, projection f.

flashy ['flæʃi] a voyant, tapageur.

flask [flɑːsk] n gourde f, fiole f.

flat [flæt] n appartement m; plat m, plaine f, (mus) bémol m; a plat, tout sec, pur, éventé, catégorique, insipide.

flat-iron ['flæt,aiən] n fer à repasser m.

flatness ['flætnis] n platitude f, monotonie f, égalité f.

flatten ['flætn] vt aplatir, aplanir, niveler, laminer; vi s'aplatir, s'aplanir.

flatter ['flætə] vt flatter.

flatterer ['flætərə] n flatteur m.

flattery ['flætəri] n flatterie f.

flaunt [flɔːnt] vi s'exhiber, se pavaner; vt afficher, faire étalage de, étaler.

flautist ['flɔːtist] n flûtiste mf.

flavor ['fleivə] n saveur f, bouquet m, fumet m, goût m; vt assaisonner, relever, aromatiser.

flavoring ['fleivəriŋ] n assaisonnement m.

flaw [flɔː] n fêlure f, défaut m, paille f, tache f.

flawless ['flɔːlis] a impeccable, sans défaut.

flax [flæks] n lin m.

flaxen ['flæksən] a en (de) lin, blond, filasse.

flay [flei] vt étriller, écorcher, massacrer, rosser.

flea [fliː] n puce f, vétille f.

fleabite ['fliːbait] n morsure de puce f, rien m.

fleck [flek] n tache de son f, grain m, moucheture f; vt tacheter, moucheter.

fled [fled] pt pp of **flee**.

fledged [fledʒd] a couvert de plumes; **fully—** a dru, émancipé.

flee [fliː] vi fuir, se sauver.

fleece [fliːs] n toison f; vt tondre, estamper.

fleecy ['fliːsi] a laineux, cotonneux, moutonné.

fleet [fliːt] n flotte f; train m; vi passer, s'enfuir.

fleeting ['fliːtiŋ] a fugitif, éphémère.

flesh [fleʃ] n chair f.

fleshy ['fleʃi] a charnu, pulpeux.

flew [fluː] pt of **fly**.

flex [fleks] n flexible m; vti fléchir.

flexibility [,fleksi'biliti] n flexibilité f, souplesse f.

flexible ['fleksəbl] a flexible, souple.

flexion ['flekʃən] n flexion f, courbe f.

flick [flik] n chiquenaude f, pichenette f, petit coup m.

flicker ['flikə] n frémissement m, éclair m, clignement m; vi frémir, vaciller, flotter.

flight [flait] n fuite f, vol m, ligne f, essor m, saillie f, volée f, raid m; **— deck** pont m d'envol.

flighty ['flaiti] a volage, écervelé, frivole, pauvre.

flimsy ['flimzi] a fragile, trivial, frivole.

flinch [flintʃ] vi broncher, reculer, fléchir.

fling [fliŋ] n jet m, impulsion f; vt (re)jeter, lancer, émettre; vi se jeter, se précipiter.

flint ['flint] n silex m, pierre à briquet f.

flinty ['flinti] a dur comme pierre, caillouteux.

flip [flip] n chiquenaude f, tape f, petit tour de vol m; vt lancer, tapoter, (ear) pincer.

flippancy ['flipənsi] n désinvolture f, irrévérence f.

flippant ['flipənt] a impertinent, désinvolte.

flirt [fləːt] n coquette f, flirt m; vi flirter, conter fleurette (à **with**).

flit [flit] vi voltiger, passer, déménager; n déménagement m.

float [flout] n radeau m, bouchon m, flotteur m, rampe f; vt lancer, émettre, porter, mettre à flot, flotter; vi flotter, nager, faire la planche.

floatation [flou'teiʃən] n lancement m, émission f.

flock [flɔk] n troupeau m, troupe f, bourre m, flocon m; vi s'assembler, s'attrouper.

floe [flou] n banquise f.

flog [flɔg] vt fouetter, fouailler, bazarder.

flogging ['flɔgiŋ] n fessée f, flagellation f.

flood [flʌd] n inondation f, crue f, déluge m, flux m, marée f; vt inonder, irriguer, grossir; vi déborder, se noyer, être en crue.

floodgate ['flʌdgeit] n vanne f.

floodlight ['flʌdlait] vt illuminer par projecteurs.

floor [flɔː] n plancher m, parquet m, étage m; vt planchéier, terrasser, renverser.

floorcloth ['flɔːklɔθ] n torchon m.

flop [flɔp] n plouf!, bruit m sourd, four m; vi s'affaler, faire four.

florid ['flɔrid] a rubicond, fleuri, flamboyant.

florist ['flɔrist] n fleuriste mf.

floss [flɔs] n bourre f.

flotilla [flə'tilə] n flottille f.

flotsam ['flɔtsəm] n épave f flottante.

flounce [flauns] n sursaut m, volant m; to — out sortir en colère.

flounder ['flaundə] n carrelet m; vi patauger.

flour ['flauə] n farine f; **cassava** —, **garri** farine f de manioc.

flourish ['flʌriʃ] n fioritures f pl, parafe m, grand geste m, fanfare f; vi prospérer, embellir; vt brandir.

flourishing ['flʌriʃiŋ] a florissant, prospère.

flout [flaut] vt narguer, se moquer de.

flow [flou] n écoulement m, arrivée f, courant m, flux m, flot m; vi couler, affluer, flotter, résulter, se jeter.

flower ['flauə] n fleur f; vi fleurir; — **garden** jardin m d'agrément; — **shop** boutique f de fleuriste.

flowery ['flauəri] a fleuri.

flowing ['flouiŋ] a coulant, flottant, aisé.

flown [floun] pp of **fly**; a high — ampoulé.

flu [fluː] n see **influenza**.

fluctuate ['flʌktjueit] vi fluctuer, vaciller, flotter.

fluctuation [‚flʌktju'eiʃən] n fluctuation f, variations f pl.

flue [fluː] n tuyau m (de cheminée).

fluency ['fluːənsi] n aisance f, facilité f.

fluent ['fluːənt] a coulant, facile.

fluently ['fluːəntli] ad avec facilité, couramment.

fluff [flʌf] n duvet m.

fluffy ['flʌfi] a duveté, pelucheux.

fluid ['fluːid] an fluide m.

fluidity [fluːʼiditi] n fluidité f, inconstance f.

fluke [fluːk] n fer m, pointe f, (coup m de) raccroc m.

flung [flʌŋ] pt pp of **fling**.

flurry ['flʌri] n coup de vent m, excitation f, émoi m, rafale f, vt agiter, étourdir.

flush [flʌʃ] n rougeur f, accès m, transport m, flot m, jet m, vol m d'oiseau, chasse f (d'eau); a débordant, regorgeant, abondant, de niveau; vi jaillir, rougir; vt enivrer, inonder, laver à grande eau.

fluster ['flʌstə] n agitation f; vt énerver, agiter, faire perdre la tête à.

flute [fluːt] n flûte f, cannelure f; vi jouer de la flûte, parler d'une voix flûtée; vt canneler, rainurer.

flutist ['fluːtist] n flûtiste mf.

flutter ['flʌtə] n battement m (d'ailes), émoi m, sensation f, palpitation f, voltigement m; vti battre faiblement; vi palpiter, s'agiter, frémir, trémousser; vt agiter, secouer.

flux [flʌks] n flux m.

fly [flai] n mouche f, fiacre m, braguette f; a malin; vi voler,

courir, se sauver; vti fuir; vt faire voler, piloter; to — away s'envoler.

flyer, flier ['flaiə] n aviateur, -trice.

flying ['flaiiŋ] n vol m, aviation f; a flottant, au vent, volant — **visit** visite-éclair f.

flying-boat ['flaiiŋbout] n hydravion m.

flying-bomb ['flaiiŋ'bɔm] n bombe volante f.

flying-club ['flaiiŋ‚klʌb] n aéro-club m.

flying-squad ['flaiiŋ'skwɔd] n brigade volante f.

flysheet ['flaiʃiːt] n circulaire m, papillon m.

flywheel ['flaiwiːl] n volant m (de commande).

foal [foul] n poulain m.

foam [foum] n écume f; vi écumer, bouillonner, baver.

fob [fɔb] n gousset m, régence f; to — **off** vt refiler.

focus ['foukəs] n foyer m; vt mettre au point, concentrer; vi converger; out of — brouillé.

fodder ['fɔdə] n fourrage m.

foe [fou] n ennemi m.

fog [fɔg] n brouillard m, voile m; vt embruner, voiler.

foggy ['fɔgi] a épais, brumeux, brouillé.

foghorn ['fɔghɔːn] n sirène f.

fog-signal ['fɔg‚signl] n pétard m.

foil [fɔil] n feuille f, tain m, repoussoir m, fleuret m, piste f; vt donner le change à, tromper, déjouer, faire échouer.

foist [fɔist] vt repasser, refiler.

fold [fould] n parc à bestiaux m, bercail m, troupeau m, (re)pli m, creux m, battant m; vt parquer, plier, envelopper, serrer, croiser; vi se (re)plier.

folding ['fouldiŋ] n (re)pliage m; a pliant, rabattable.

foliage ['fouliidʒ] n feuillage n, feuillée f.

folk(s) [fouk(s)] n gens mf pl.

folksong ['fouksɔŋ] n chanson f populaire.

follow ['fɔlou] vti suivre; vt succéder à; vi s'ensuivre.

follower ['fɔlouə] n partisan m, serviteur m.

following ['fɔlouiŋ] n suite f; a suivant.

folly ['fɔli] n folie f.

foment [fou'ment] vt fomenter.

fond [fɔnd] a tendre, affectueux, indulgent, friand, amateur; to be — of aimer.

fondle ['fɔndl] vt câliner.

font [fɔnt] n fonts baptismaux m pl.

food [fuːd] n nourriture f, alimentation f, vivres m pl, pâture f, pâtée f; a alimentaire, nutritif.

fool [fuːl] n sot, sotte, fou, folle, imbécile mf, idiot(e) mf, bouffon m; vt rouler, duper; vi faire la bête.

foolhardiness ['fuːl,haːdinis] n témérité f.
foolhardy ['fuːl,haːdi] a téméraire, casse-cou.
foolish ['fuːliʃ] a stupide, fou, absurde, insensé.
foolishness ['fuːliʃnis] n folie f, bêtise f.
foolproof ['fuːlpruːf] a de sureté, à toute épreuve.
foot [fut] n pied m, patte f, base f, fond m, bas m, bas-bout m; vt danser, payer.
foot-and-mouth disease ['futən'mauθdi'ziːz] n fièvre aphteuse f.
football ['futbɔːl] n ballon m, football m.
footboard ['futbɔːd] n marchepied m.
footbridge ['futbridʒ] n passerelle f.
foothold ['futhould] n prise f, pied m.
footing ['futiŋ] n pied m, prise f.
footlights ['futlaits] n rampe f.
footman ['futmən] n valet de pied m, laquais m.
footmuff ['futmʌf] n chancelière f.
footnote ['futnout] n note f.
footpath ['futpaːθ] n sentier m, trottoir m.
footplate ['futpleit] n plateforme f.
footprint ['futprint] n empreinte f.
footslogger ['futslɔgə] n piéton m, fantassin m, biffin m.
footstep ['futstep] n pas m; pl traces f pl, brisées f pl.
footstool ['futstuːl] n tabouret m.
foot-warmer ['fut,wɔːmə] n bouillotte f, chaufferette f.
footwear ['futwɛə] n chaussures f pl.
foozle ['fuːzl] vt rater.
fop [fɔp] n gandin m, fat m.
for [fɔː] prep pour, à, quant à, comme, pendant, malgré; cj car.
forage ['fɔridʒ] n fourrage m; vt fourrager, marauder; vi aller au fourrage.
forage-cap ['fɔridʒ,kæp] n calot m.
forasmuch [fərəz'mʌtʃ] cj vu que, d'autant que.
foray ['fɔrei] n raid m, incursion f.
forbear [fɔː'bɛə] vt tolérer, s'abstenir de; vi patienter.
forbearance [fɔː'bɛərəns] n indulgence f, patience f.
forbid [fə'bid] vt défendre.
forbidden [fə'bidn] a interdit, défendu, prohibé; **smoking** — défense de fumer.
forbidding [fə'bidiŋ] a sévère, rébarbatif, sinistre.
force [fɔːs] n force f, contrainte f, violence f, puissance f, vigueur f; **task** — corps m expéditionnaire; vt forcer.
forced [fɔːst] a forcé, inévitable, faux.
forceful ['fɔːsful] a énergique, puissant.
force-land ['fɔːslænd] vi faire un atterrissage forcé.

forcible ['fɔːsəbl] a puissant, vigoureux.
ford [fɔːd] n gué m; vt passer à gué.
fordable ['fɔːdəbl] a guéable.
fore [fɔː] n avant m, premier plan m; **to the** — en vue.
forearm ['fɔːraːm] n avant-bras m.
forebear ['fɔːbɛə] n ancêtre m.
forebode [fɔː'boud] vt pressentir, augurer.
foreboding [fɔː'boudiŋ] n pressentiment m, mauvais augure m.
forecast ['fɔːkaːst] n prévision f, pronostic m; vt prévoir.
forecastle ['fouksl] n gaillard d'avant m.
foreclose [fɔː'klouz] vt défendre; (law) forclore, saisir.
forefather ['fɔː,faːðə] n ancêtre m, aïeul m.
forefinger ['fɔː,fiŋgə] n index m.
forefront ['fɔːfrʌnt] n premier rang m, premier plan m.
foregone ['fɔːgɔn] a acquis (couru) d'avance, prévu.
foreground ['fɔːgraund] n premier plan m.
forehead ['fɔrid] n front m.
foreign ['fɔrin] a étranger.
foreigner ['fɔrinə] n étranger, -ère.
foreland ['fɔːlənd] n promontoire m, cap m, pointe f.
forelock ['fɔːlɔk] n mèche f.
foreman ['fɔːmən] n contremaître n, chef d'équipe m, président du jury m.
foremost ['fɔːmoust] a premier, en tête.
forenoon ['fɔːnuːn] n matinée f.
forerunner ['fɔː,rʌnə] n précurseur m, avant-coureur m, avant-courrier, -ière.
foresee [fɔː'siː] vt prévoir.
foreshadow [fɔː'ʃædou] vt laisser prévoir, présager.
foresight ['fɔːsait] n prevoyance f, prévision f, (gun) bouton m de mire.
forest ['fɔrist] n forêt f.
forestall [fɔː'stɔːl] vt anticiper, devancer, prévenir.
forester ['fɔristə] n garde-forestier n.
foretaste ['fɔːteist] n avant-goût m.
foretell [fɔː'tel] vt prédire, présager.
forethought ['fɔːθɔːt] n prévoyance f, préméditation f.
forever [fə'revə] ad pour toujours, à jamais.
forewarn [fɔː'wɔːn] vt prévenir, avertir.
foreword ['fɔːwəːd] n avant-propos m, préface f.
forfeit ['fɔːfit] n prix m, rançon f, amende f, confiscation f, forfait m; vt perdre, avoir à payer, forfaire à.
forgave [fə'geiv] pt of **forgive**.
forge [fɔːdʒ] n forge f; vt forger, contrefaire, fabriquer; **to** — **ahead** prendre de l'avance, pousser de l'avant.

forger ['fɔːdʒə] n faussaire mf, forgeron m.
forgery ['fɔːdʒəri] n faux m, contrefaçon f.
forget [fə'get] vt oublier, négliger.
forgetful [fə'getful] a oublieux, négligent.
forgetfulness [fə'getfulnis] n oubli m.
forget-me-not [fə'getminɔt] n myosotis m.
forgivable [fə'givabl] a pardonnable.
forgive [fə'giv] vt pardonner.
forgiveness [fə'givnis] n pardon m.
forgiving [fə'giviŋ] a indulgent.
forgo [fɔː'gou] vt renoncer à.
forgot, -ten [fə'gɔt, -n] pt pp of **forget**.
fork [fɔːk] n fourche f, fourchette f, branche f, (em)branchement m; vi fourcher, bifurquer.
forked [fɔːkt] a fourchu.
forlorn [fə'lɔːn] a abandonné, désespéré, désolé.
form [fɔːm] n forme f, formule f, formulaire m, formalité f, manières f pl, classe f, banc m, gite f; vt former, façonner, contracter; vi prendre forme, se former, se faire.
formal ['fɔːmel] a formel, formaliste, gourmé, de cérémonie, protocolaire.
formality [fɔː'mæliti] n formalité f, cérémonie f.
formally ['fɔːməli] ad formellement.
formation [fɔː'meiʃən] n formation f, disposition f.
former ['fɔːmə] a antérieur, ancien, premier, précédent, celui-là, ceux-là, celle(s)-là.
formerly ['fɔːməli] ad antérieurement, autrefois.
formidable ['fɔːmidəbl] a formidable, redoutable.
formless ['fɔːmlis] a informe.
formula ['fɔːmjulə] n formule f.
formulate ['fɔːmjuleit] vt formuler.
forsake [fə'seik] vt renoncer à, retirer, abandonner.
forsaken [fə'seikən] pp of **forsake**.
forsook [fə'suk] pt of **forsake**.
forswear [fɔː'swɛə] vt renoncer sous serment à, renier.
fort [fɔːt] n fort m; **small** — fortin m.
forth [fɔːθ] ad en avant, en route; **and so** — et ainsi de suite, et caetera.
forthcoming [fɔːθ'kʌmiŋ] a proche, prochain, tout prêt, à venir.
forthright ['fɔːθrait] a droit, franc; ad tout droit.
forthwith ['fɔːθwið] ad sur-le-champ.
fortieth ['fɔːtiiθ] an quarantième mf.
fortification [ˌfɔːtifi'keiʃən] n fortification f.
fortify ['fɔːtifai] vt fortifier, affermir, armer.
fortitude ['fɔːtitjuːd] n force d'âme f, courage m.

fortnight ['fɔːtnait] n quinzaine f; **today** — d'aujourd'hui en quinze.
fortnightly ['fɔːtnaitli] ad tous les quinze jours; a bimensuel.
fortress ['fɔːtris] n forteresse f.
fortuitous [fɔː'tjuːitəs] a fortuit, imprévu.
fortunate ['fɔːtʃənit] a heureux, qui a de la chance.
fortunately ['fɔːtʃənitli] ad heureusement.
fortune ['fɔːtʃən] n fortune f, chance f, hasard m.
fortune-teller ['fɔːtʃən,telə] n diseuse de bonne aventure f.
forty ['fɔːti] an quarante m.
forward ['fɔːwəd] n avant m; a qui va de l'avant, précoce, avancé, effronté, présomptueux; ad en avant; vt promouvoir, hâter, faire suivre, expédier.
forwardness ['fɔːwədnis] n audace f, présomption f.
fossil ['fɔsil] an fossile m.
foster ['fɔstə] vt nourrir, élever, encourager.
foster-brother ['fɔstə,brʌðə] n frère de lait m.
foster-child ['fɔstətʃaild] n nourrisson, -onne.
foster-father ['fɔstə,faːðə] n père nourricier m.
foster-mother ['fɔstə,mʌðə] n nourrice f.
foster-sister ['fɔstə,sistə] n sœur de lait f.
fought [fɔːt] pt pp of **fight**.
foul [faul] n coup bas m, faute f; a sale, nauséabond, vicié, obscène, traître, ordurier, déloyal, emmêlé, enrayé; vt salir, enrayer, emmêler, obstruer; vi se rencontrer s'enrayer, s'encrasser.
found [faund] pp pt of **find**; vt fonder, établir.
foundation [faun'deiʃən] n fondation f, fondement m, établissement m, assise f.
founder ['faundə] n fondateur m, fondeur m; vi s'effondrer, sombrer, couler.
foundling ['faundliŋ] n enfant trouvé(e) mf.
foundry ['faundri] n fonderie f.
fountain ['fauntin] n fontaine f, source f, jet d'eau m, réservoir m.
fountain-pen ['fauntinpen] n stylo m.
four [fɔː] an quatre m; **—engined** quadriréacteur.
fourfold ['fɔːfould] a quadruple.
fourteen [fɔː'tiːn] an quatorze m.
fourteenth [fɔː'tiːnθ] an quatorzième mf, quatorze m.
fourth [fɔːθ] an quatrième mf, quatre m.
fowl [faul] n volaille f, oiseau m.
fox [fɔks] n renard m, rusé m, roublard m.
foxy ['fɔksi] a roublard, rusé.

fraction ['frækʃən] *n* fraction *f*, fragment *m*.
fractious ['frækʃəs] *a* hargneux, rétif.
fracture ['fræktʃə] *n* fracture *f*; *vt* fracturer, casser; *vi* se casser, se fracturer.
fragile ['frædʒail] *a* fragile.
fragility [frə'dʒiliti] *n* fragilité *f*.
fragment ['frægmənt] *n* fragment *m*.
fragrance ['freigrəns] *n* parfum *m*.
fragrant ['freigrənt] *a* embaumé, odorant, parfumé.
frail [freil] *n* bannette *f*; *a* frêle, éphémère.
frailty ['freilti] *n* fragilité *f*.
frame [freim] *n* cadre *m*, fuselage *m*, châssis *m*, charpente *f*, corps *m*, carcasse *f*; — **house** maison *f* démontable (en bois); *vt* encadrer, façonner, ajuster, construire, concevoir, monter un coup contre.
frame-up ['freimʌp] *n* coup monté *m*.
framework ['freimwə:k] *n* cadre *m*, charpente *f*.
France [frɑːns] *n* France *f*.
franchise ['fræntʃaiz] *n* droit de vote *m*, franchise *f*.
Frances ['frɑːnsis] Françoise *f*, Francine *f*.
Francis ['frɑːnsis] Francis *m*, François *m*.
frank [fræŋk] *a* franc.
frankincense ['fræŋkinsens] *n* encens *m*.
frantic ['fræntik] *a* frénétique, effréné.
fraternal [frə'tə:nl] *a* fraternel.
fraternity [frə'tə:niti] *n* amour fraternel *m*, confrérie *f*, compagnie *f*.
fraternize ['frætənaiz] *vi* fraterniser.
fraternizing ['frætə'naiziŋ] *n* fraternisation *f*.
fratricide ['frætrisaid] *n* fratricide *mf*.
fraud [frɔːd] *n* fraude *f*, supercherie *f*, imposteur *m*.
fraudulent ['frɔːdjulənt] *a* frauduleux.
fraught [frɔːt] *a* gros (de with).
fray [frei] *n* bagarre *f*; *vt* effilocher, effiler; *vi* s'effilocher, s'effiler.
frayed [freid] *a* frangeux.
freak [friːk] *n* caprice *m*, phénomène *m*, monstre *m*.
freakish ['friːkiʃ] *a* capricieux, fantasque.
freckle ['frekl] *n* tache de rousseur *f*.
freckled ['frekld] *a* couvert de taches de rousseur.
free [friː] *a* libre, exempt, gratuit, franco; *vt* affranchir, libérer, élargir.
freedom ['friːdəm] *n* liberté *f*.
freehold ['friːhould] *n* propriété libre *f*.
freelance ['friːlɑːns] *n* franc-tireur *m*, indépendant(e) *mf*.
freely ['friːli] *ad* librement, largement, franchement.

freemason ['friːˌmeisn] *n* franc-maçon *m*.
freemasonry ['friː'meisnri] *n* franc-maçonnerie *f*.
free-trade ['friː'treid] *n* libre échange *m*.
free-will ['friː'wil] *n* libre arbitre *m*; **of one's own** — de son propre gré.
freeze [friːz] *vti* geler; *vi* se figer, se congeler; *vt* glacer, congeler; *n* austerité *f*, blocage *m* des prix.
freezing ['friːziŋ] *a* de congélation, glacial; *n* gel *m*, réfrigération *f*.
freight [freit] *n* fret *m*, cargaison *f*, marchandises *f* *pl*; *vt* (af)fréter, charger, noliser.
French [frentʃ] *an* français *m*.
Frenchman ['frentʃmən] *n* Français *m*.
French-speaking ['frentʃ'spiːkiŋ] *a* francophone.
Frenchwoman ['frentʃˌwumən] *n* Française *f*.
frenzied ['frenzid] *a* fou, affolé, délirant, frénétique.
frenzy ['frenzi] *n* frénésie *f*, transport *m*.
frequency ['friːkwənsi] *n* fréquence *f*.
frequent ['friːkwənt] *a* fréquent, répandu.
frequent [friː'kwent] *vt* fréquenter, courir, hanter.
frequentation ['friːkwen'teiʃən] *n* fréquentation *f*.
frequently ['friːkwəntli] *ad* fréquamment, souvent.
fresco ['freskou] *n* fresque *f*.
fresh [freʃ] *a* frais, nouveau, novice, récent, (water) doux, (wind) vif, alerte, effronté.
freshen ['freʃn] *vi* rafraîchir, raviver.
freshness ['freʃnis] *n* fraîcheur *f*, vigueur *f*.
fret [fret] *n* grecque *f*, irritation *f*; *vt* ronger, irriter; *vi* s'agiter, se faire du mauvais sang.
fretful ['fretful] *a* irritable, agité.
fretfulness ['fretfulnis] *n* irritabilité *f*.
fretsaw ['fretsɔː] *n* scie à découper *f*.
fretwork ['fretwə:k] *n* découpage *m*, bois découpé *m*.
friable ['fraiəbl] *a* friable.
friar ['fraiə] *n* moine *m*, frère *m*.
friction ['frikʃən] *n* friction *f*, frottement *m*, tirage *m*.
Friday ['fraidi] *n* vendredi *m*; **Good** — vendredi saint.
friend [frend] *n* ami(e) *mf*.
friendly ['frendli] *a* amical.
friendship ['frendʃip] *n* amitié *f*.
frieze [friːz] *n* frise *f*.
frigate ['frigit] *n* frégate *f*.
fright [frait] *n* frayeur *f*, épouvante *f*, peur *f*.
frighten ['fraitn] *vt* terrifier, faire peur à.
frightful ['fraitful] *a* effrayant, affreux.

frightfulness ['fraitfulnis] n terreur f, horreur f.

frigid ['fridʒid] a glacial, froid, réfrigérant.

frill [fril] n ruche f, jabot m, volant m; vt plisser, tuyauter.

fringe [frindʒ] n frange f, bord m, zone f limitrophe.

frippery ['fripəri] n tralala m, fioritures f pl, babioles f pl.

frisk [frisk] vi gambader.

frisky ['friski] a fringant, frétillant, folâtre.

fritter ['fritə] n beignet m; **to —away** gaspiller.

frivolous ['frivələs] a frivole, futile.

frizz [friz] n frisette f, vti friser.

frizzle ['frizl] vi crépiter, grésiller; vt faire frire.

frock [frɔk] n blouse f, robe f.

frockcoat ['frɔk'kout] n redingote f.

frog [frɔg] n grenouille f.

frolic ['frɔlik] n cabriole f; pl gambades f pl; vi batifoler, s'ébattre.

frolicsome ['frɔliksəm] a espiègle, folâtre.

from [frɔm] prep de, avec, d'après, de chez, à, contre.

front [frʌnt] n front m, façade f, devant m, plastron m, devanture f; **in — of** devant, en avant de; vt affronter, donner sur.

frontage ['frʌntidʒ] n exposition f, vue f, façade f, devanture f.

frontier ['frʌntjə] n frontière f.

frontispiece ['frʌntispiːs] n frontispice m.

frost [frɔst] n gelée f, gel m, givre m, verglas m; vt geler, glacer, givrer, ferrer à glace.

frostbite ['frɔstbait] n gelure f, congélation f.

frostbitten ['frɔst,bitn] a gelé, brûlé par le froid.

frosty ['frɔsti] a gelé, givré, poudré, glacial.

froth [frɔθ] n écume f, mousse f.

frothy ['frɔθi] a écumeux, mousseux.

frown [fraun] n froncement de sourcils m, vi froncer les sourcils, se renfrogner; **to — upon** désapprouver.

frowzy ['frauzi] a moisi, renfermé, négligé.

froze, -zen [frouz, -n] pp pt of **freeze.**

fructify ['frʌktifai] vi porter fruit, fructifier; vt faire fructifier.

frugal ['fruːgəl] a frugal, économe, simple.

frugality [fruː'gæliti] n frugalité f, économie f.

fruit [fruːt] n fruit m.

fruiterer ['fruːtərə] n frutier, -ière.

fruiterer's ['fruːtərəz] n fruiterie f.

fruitful ['fruːtful] a fécond, fructueux, fertile.

fruitfulness ['fruːtfulnis] n fécondité f, productivité f.

fruition [fruː'iʃən] n jouissance f, maturation f.

fruitless ['fruːtlis] a stérile.

fruitlessness ['fruːtlisnis] n stérilité f.

fruit-tree ['fruːttriː] n arbre fruitier m.

frustrate [frʌs'treit] vt frustrer, déjouer, faire échouer.

frustration [frʌs'treiʃən] n frustration f, anéantissement m.

fry [frai] n fretin m, frai m; vt faire frire; vi frire.

frying-pan ['fraiiŋ,pæn] n poêle f.

fuddle ['fʌdl] n cuite f; vt griser, brouiller, enfumer.

fuel ['fjuəl] n combustible m, carburant m, essence f; **— pump** pompe à essence.

fugacious [fjuː'geiʃəs] a fugace.

fugitive ['fjuːdʒitiv] an fugitif, -ive mf; a éphémère.

fulcrum ['fʌlkrəm] m point m d'appui.

fulfill [ful'fil] vt remplir, accomplir, exaucer, exécuter.

fulfillment [ful'filmənt] n accomplissement m, exécution f, réalisation f.

full [ful] a plein, rempli, complet, riche, vigoureux, rond, ample, bouffant.

full-blown ['ful'bloun] a épanoui.

full-dress ['ful'dres] n grande tenue f; **— rehearsal** répétition générale f.

full-debate ['fuldiː'beit] n débat en règle m.

full-length ['ful'leŋθ] a en pied.

full-speed ['ful'spiːd] ad à toute vitesse, à fond de train.

full-stop ['ful'stɔp] n point m.

fullness ['fulnis] n plénitude f, ampleur f, rondeur f.

fully ['fuli] ad pleinement, en plein.

fulminate ['fulmineit] vi fulminer.

fulsome ['fulsəm] a écœurant, excessif.

fumble ['fʌmbl] vi tâtonner, fouiller; **to — with** tripoter.

fume [fjuːm] n fumée f, vapeur f; vi fumer (de rage), rager.

fun [fʌn] n plaisanterie f, amusement m; **for —** pour rire, histoire de rire.

function ['fʌŋkʃən] n fonction f, cérémonie f; vi fonctionner, marcher.

functionary ['fʌŋkʃənəri] n fonctionnaire m.

fund [fʌnd] n fonds m, caisse f, rente f; vt convertir, consolider.

fundamental [,fʌndə'mentl] a fondamental, essentiel, foncier; n pl essentiel m, principe m.

funeral ['fjuːnərəl] n enterrement m, funérailles f pl.

funereal [fjuː'niəriəl] a funéraire, funèbre, sépulcral.

funicular [fjuː'nikjuːlə] n funiculaire m.

funk [fʌnk] n frousse f, trouille f, trac m, froussard(e) mf; vt esquiver; vi avoir la frousse, se dégonfler.

funnel ['fʌnl] n entonnoir m, cheminée f.

funny ['fʌni] *a* drôle, marrant, comique.
fur [fəː] *n* fourrure *f*.
furbish ['fəːbiʃ] *vt* fourbir, astiquer.
furious ['fjuəriəs] *a* furieux, furibond, acharné.
furl [fəːl] *vt* rouler, serrer, plier, ferler.
furlough ['fəːlou] *n* permission *f*.
furnace ['fəːnis] *n* fourneau *m*, fournaise *f*, calorifère *m*, brasier *m*.
furnish ['fəːniʃ] *vt* fournir, garnir, meubler.
furniture ['fəːnitʃə] *n* mobilier *m*, meubles *m pl*; **piece of** — meuble *m*; — **polish** encaustique *f*.
furrier ['fʌriə] *n* fourreur *m*, pelletier, -ière.
furrow ['fʌrou] *n* sillon *m*, rainure *f*; *vt* labourer, sillonner.
furry ['fəːri] *a* fourré, garni de fourrure, sale, chargé, encrassé.
further ['fəːðə] *a* nouveau, supplémentaire, plus ample, plus éloigné; *ad* plus loin, d'ailleurs, davantage; *vt* appuyer, favoriser, avancer.
furtherance ['fəːðərəns] *n* avancement *m*.
furthermore ['fəːðə'mɔː] *ad* en outre, de plus.
furtive ['fəːtiv] *a* furtif.
fury ['fjuəri] *n* fureur *f*, rage *f*, furie *f*.
furze [fəːz] *n* genêt *m*, ajonc *m*.
fuse [fjuːz] *n* plomb *m*, amorce *f*, fusée *f*; *vti* fondre, fusionner; **the lights fused** les plombs ont sauté.
fuselage ['fjuːzəlɑːʒ] *n* fuselage *m*.
fusion ['fjuːʒən] *n* fusion *f*.
fuss [fʌs] *n* bruit *m*, agitation *f*, embarras *m pl*; *vt* tracasser; *vi* faire des embarras, faire des histoires.
fussy ['fʌsi] *a* agité, tracassier, méticuleux, tatillon.
fusty ['fʌsti] *a* moisi, ranci, renfermé, démodé.
futile ['fjuːtail] *a* futile, vain.
futility [fjuːˈtiliti] *n* futilité *f*, inutilité *f*.
future ['fjuːtʃə] *n* avenir *m*, futur *m*; *a* futur.
fuzzy ['fʌzi] *a* crépu, duveté, frisé, brouillé.

G

gab [gæb] *n* parole *f*; **gift of the** — bagout *m*, faconde *f*.
gabble ['gæbl] *n* bafouillage *m*; *vi* bredouiller, jacasser.
gable ['geibl] *n* pignon *m*.
gad [gæd] *vi* **to** — **about** courir (la prétentaine), papillonner.
gadfly ['gædflai] *n* taon *m*.
gadget ['gædʒit] *n* truc *m*, dispositif *m*.
gaff [gæf] *n* gaffe *f*.
gag [gæg] *n* bâillon *m*, gag *m*; *vt* bâillonner.

gage [geidʒ] *n* gage *m*, garantie *f*, défi *m*; *vt* gager, offrir en gage.
gaiety ['geiəti] *n* gaieté *f*, allégresse *f*.
gain [gein] *n* gain *m*, bénéfice *m*, avantage *m*; *vt* gagner.
gainer ['geinə] *n* gagnant(e) *mf*.
gainsay ['gein'sei] *vt* nier, démentir, contredire.
gait [geit] *n* port *m*, allure *f*, démarche *f*.
gaiter ['geitə] *n* guêtre *f*.
galaxy ['gæləksi] *n* voie *f* lactée, constellation *f*.
gale [geil] *n* rafale *f*, tempête *f*.
gall [gɔːl] *n* fiel *m*, rancœur *f*, amertume *f*, écorchure *f*; effronterie *f*, aplomb *m*; *vt* écorcher, blesser, irriter.
gallant ['gælənt] *n* élégant *m*, galant *m*; *a* vaillant, galant, brave, noble.
gallantly ['gæləntli] *ad* vaillamment, galamment.
gallantry ['gæləntri] *n* vaillance *f*, galanterie *f*.
gall-bladder ['gɔːl,blædə] *n* vésicule biliaire *f*.
gallery ['gæləri] *n* galerie *f*, tribune *f*, musée *m*.
galley ['gæli] *n* galère *f*, cambuse *f*, placard *m*.
galley-slave ['gælisleiv] *n* galérien *m*.
gallop ['gæləp] *n* galop *m*; *vi* galoper; *vt* faire galoper.
gallows ['gælouz] *n* potence *f*.
gallstone ['gɔːlstoun] *n* calcul biliaire *m*.
galore [gəˈlɔː] *n* abondance *f*, *ad* en abondance, à profusion, à gogo.
galosh [gəˈlɔʃ] *n* caoutchouc *m*.
galvanize ['gælvənaiz] *vt* galvaniser.
gamble ['gæmbl] *n* jeu *m*, spéculation *f*; *vti* jouer; *vt* risquer.
gambler ['gæmblə] *n* joueur, -euse.
gambol ['gæmbəl] *n* gambade *f*; *vi* gambader, s'ébattre.
game [geim] *n* jeu *m*, partie *f*, tour *m*, manche *f*, gibier *m*.
game-bag ['geimbæg] *n* gibecière *f*.
gamekeeper ['geim'kiːpə] *n* garde-chasse *m*.
game-licence ['geim'laisəns] *n* permis de chasse *m*.
gammon ['gæmən] *n* jambon *m*, blague *f*, attrape *f*; *vt* saler, fumer, mystifier.
gamp [gæmp] *n* pépin *m*, riflard *m*.
gamut ['gæmət] *n* gamme *f*.
gander ['gændə] *n* jars *m*.
gang [gæŋ] *n* équipe *f*, bande *f*.
gang-foreman ['gæŋ'fɔːmən] *n* brigadier *m*, chef d'équipe *m*.
gangrene ['gæŋgriːn] *n* gangrène *f*; *vt* gangrener; *vi* se gangrener.
gangrenous ['gæŋgrənəs] *a* gangreneux.
gangster ['gæŋstə] *n* bandit *m*, gangster *m*.
gangway ['gæŋwei] *n* passage *m*, passerelle *f*.

gap [gæp] n trou m, trouée f, brèche f, lacune f, différence f, écart m, intervalle f.

gape [geip] vi bâiller, rester bouche bée, être béant, s'ouvrir.

gaping ['geipiŋ] a béant, bouche bée.

garage ['gærɑːʒ] n garage m; vt remiser, garer.

garb [gɑːb] n costume m, tenue f; vt habiller, vêtir.

garbage ['gɑːbidʒ] n ordures f pl, détritus m pl, tripaille f.

garble ['gɑːbl] vt dénaturer, tronquer, mutiler.

garden ['gɑːdn] n jardin m; vi jardiner; — party réception en plein air, f.

gardener ['gɑːdnə] n jardinier m.

gargle ['gɑːgl] n gargarisme m; vi se gargariser.

gargoyle ['gɑːgɔil] n gargouille f.

garish ['gɛəriʃ] a criard, voyant.

garland ['gɑːlənd] n guirlande f, couronne f.

garlic ['gɑːlik] n ail m.

garment ['gɑːmənt] n vêtement m.

garner ['gɑːnə] n grenier m; vt accumuler, rentrer, engranger.

garnet ['gɑːnit] n grenat m.

garnish ['gɑːniʃ] n garniture f, vt parer, garnir; (jur) appeler en justice.

garotte [gə'rɔt] tourniquet m, garotte f; vt étrangler, garrotter.

garret ['gærit] n mansarde f.

garrison ['gærisən] n garnison f; vt tenir garnison à, garnir de troupes.

garrulity [gə'ruːliti] n loquacité f.

garrulous ['gæruləs] a bavard, loquace.

garter ['gɑːtə] n jarretière f.

gas [gæs] n gaz m, (poison-gas) les gaz m pl, essence f; vt gazer, asphyxier.

gas-burner ['gæs,bəːnə] n bec de gaz m.

gaseous ['geisiəs] a gazeux.

gas-fitter ['gæs,fitə] n gazier m.

gash [gæʃ] n balafre f, taillade f, entaille f; vt balafrer, entailler.

gas-holder ['gæshouldə] n gazomètre m.

gasket ['gæskit] n joint m.

gas-lamp ['gæs'læmp] n réverbère m.

gasman ['gæsmæn] n employé du gaz m.

gas-mantle ['gæs,mæntl] n manchon à gaz m.

gas-mask ['gæsmɑːsk] n masque à gaz m.

gas-meter ['gæs,miːtə] n compteur à gaz m, gazomètre m.

gasoline ['gæsəliːn] n essence f.

gasp [gɑːsp] n aspiration f convulsive, dernier soupir m; vi panteler, en rester bouche bée, avoir un hoquet, respirer avec peine.

gassy ['gæsi] a gazeux, mousseux.

gastronomy [gæs'trɔnəmi] n gastronomie f.

gasworks ['gæswəːks] n usine à gaz f.

gate [geit] n porte f, grille f, barrière f, vanne f; — keeper portier, -ière; — money recette f.

gatecrasher ['geitkræʃə] n resquilleur m.

gateway ['geitwei] n portail m, porte f.

gather ['gæðə] vt réunir, rassembler, cueillir, moissonner, amasser, gagner, froncer, imaginer; vi grossir, se réunir, s'accumuler, s'amonceler.

gathering ['gæðəriŋ] n assemblée f, réunion f, amoncellement m, moisson f, cueillette f, quête f, abcès m, fronçure f.

gathers ['gæðəz] n pl fronces f pl.

gaudy ['gɔːdi] a criard, voyant, éclatant.

gauge [geidʒ] n jauge f, mesure f, calibre m, indicateur m, (rails) écartement m; vt jauger, mesurer, estimer; narrow — voie étroite; standard — écartement normal.

gaunt [gɔːnt] a hâve, hagard, décharné.

gauntlet ['gɔːntlit] n gantelet m, gant m (à manchette).

gauze [gɔːz] n gaze f.

gave [geiv] pt of **give**.

gawky ['gɔːki] a dégingandé.

gay [gei] a gai, resplendissant.

gaze [geiz] n regard fixe m; vti regarder fixement; to — at fixer, contempler.

gazette [gə'zet] n gazette f, journal officiel m; vt publier à l'Officiel.

gazetteer [,gæzə'tiə] n gazetier m, dictionnaire m de géographie.

gear [giə] n harnais m, attirail m, ustensiles m pl, engrenage m, marche f, vitesse f; to throw into— embrayer; to put out of — débrayer.

gearbox ['giəbɔks] n boîte de vitesses f, carter m.

gearing ['giəriŋ] n engrenage m, embrayage m.

gearless ['giələs] a sans engrenage.

gear-lever ['giəliːvə] n levier m de vitesse.

gear-shift ['giəʃift] n levier m de vitesse.

gearwheel ['giəwiːl] n roue dentée f, rouage m.

gecko ['gekou] n margouillat m.

gel [dʒel] n gèle m; vi coaguler.

gelatine [,dʒelə'tiːn] n gélatine f; explosive — plastic m.

geld [geld] vt châtrer.

gelding ['geldiŋ] n hougre m, eunuque m.

gem [dʒem] n gemme f, perle f, joyau m.

gender ['dʒendə] n genre m

general ['dʒenərəl] an général m.

generalissimo [,dʒenəri'lisimou] n généralissime m.

generality [,dʒenə'ræliti] n généralité f, portée générale f.

generalization [,dʒenərəlai'zeiʃən] *n* généralisation *f*.

generalize ['dʒenərəlaiz] *vt* généraliser.

generalship ['dʒenərəlʃip] *n* stratégie *f*.

generate ['dʒenəreit] *vt* produire, générer.

generation [,dʒenə'reiʃən] *n* génération *f*, production *f*.

generosity [,dʒenə'rɔsiti] *n* générosité *f*.

generous ['dʒenərəs] *a* généreux, copieux.

genesis ['dʒenisis] *n* genèse *f*.

genial ['dʒiːnjəl] *a* jovial, cordial, doux, chaud.

geniality [,dʒiːni'æliti] *n* belle humeur *f*, cordialité *f*.

genius ['dʒiːnjəs] *n* génie *m*, aptitude *f*.

genteel [dʒen'tiːl] *a* distingué, élégant, qui affecte de la distinction.

Gentile ['dʒentail] *n* Gentil(e) *mf*.

gentility [dʒen'tiliti] *n* bonne société *f*.

gentle ['dʒentl] *a* bien né, doux, aimable.

gently ['dzentli] *ad* doucement.

gentlefolk ['dʒentlfouk] *n* personnes de distinction *f pl*.

gentleman ['dʒentlmən] *n* monsieur *m*, homme comme il faut *m*, gentleman *m*.

gentlemanly ['dʒentlmənli] *a* comme il faut, distingué, convenable.

gentleness ['dʒentlnis] *n* gentillesse *f*, douceur *f*.

gentry ['dʒentri] *n* haute bourgeoisie *f*, petite noblesse *f*.

genuine ['dʒenjuin] *a* authentique, naturel, sincère, franc, véritable.

geographer [dʒi'ɔgrəfə] *n* géographe *m*.

geographical [dʒiə'græfikəl] *a* géographique.

geography [dʒi'ɔgrəfi] *n* géographie *f*.

geologist [dʒi'ɔlədʒist] *n* géologue *m*.

geology [dʒi'ɔlədʒi] *n* géologie *f*.

geometric [dʒiə'metrik] *a* géométrique; — **drawing** dessin *m* géométrique, linéaire.

geometrician [,dʒioume'triʃən] *n* géometre *m*.

geometry [dʒi'ɔmitri] *n* géométrie *f*.

geomorphic [dʒiou'mɔːfik] *a* semblable à la terre.

geophysics ['dʒiou'fiziks] *n pl* géophysique, physique *f* du globe.

George [dʒɔːdʒ] Georges *m*.

germ [dʒəːm] *n* germe *m*, bacille *m*, microbe *m*.

German [dʒəːmən] *n* Allemand(e) *mf*; *an* allemand *m*.

Germany ['dʒəːməni] *n* Allemagne *f*.

germinate ['dʒəːmineit] *vi* germer.

germination [,dʒəːmi'neiʃən] *n* germination *f*.

gerrymander ['dʒerimændə] *vt* manipuler, truquer.

gesticulate [dʒes'tikjuleit] *vi* gesticuler.

gesticulation [dʒes,tikju'leiʃən] *n* gesticulation *f*.

gesture ['dʒestʃə] *n* geste *m*; *vi* faire des gestes.

get [get] *vt* se procurer, obtenir, acquérir, chercher, comprendre, piger, tenir, attraper, avoir, faire; *vi* devenir, arriver, aboutir; *(fam)* **get!** fiche le camp!; **to — across** *vt* traverser, franchir; *vi* passer la rampe; **to — away** partir, s'échapper; **to — back** revenir, reculer; **to — in** (r)entrer (dans), monter; **to — on** monter (sur); **to — up** se lever, monter.

ghastly ['gɑːstli] *a* livide, horrible.

gherkin ['gəːkin] *n* cornichon *m*.

ghost [goust] *n* fantôme *m*, revenant *m*, ombre *f*, esprit *m*.

ghostly ['goustli] *a* spectral, fantomatique, spirituel.

ghoul [guːl] *n* vampire *m*, strige *f*.

giant ['dʒaiənt] *n* géant *m*.

gibber ['dʒibə] *vi* baragouiner.

gibberish ['gibəriʃ] *n* baragouin *m*, charabia *m*.

gibbet ['dʒibit] *n* gibet *m*, potence *f*.

gibe [dʒaib] *n* sarcasme *m*, quolibet *m*; *vt* railler.

giblets ['dʒiblits] *n pl* abat(t)is *m pl*.

giddiness ['gidinis] *n* vertige *m*.

giddy ['gidi] *a* étourdi, vertigineux, volage.

gift [gift] *n* don *m*, cadeau *m*, prime *f*.

gifted ['giftid] *a* (bien) doué.

gig [gig] *n* cabriolet *m*, canot *m*.

gigantic [dʒai'gæntik] *a* gigantesque, colossal.

giggle ['gigl] *n* gloussement *m*, petit rire *m*; *vi* glousser, pousser des petits rires.

gild [gild] *vt* dorer.

gilder ['gildə] *n* doreur *m*.

gilding ['gildiŋ] *n* dorure *f*.

gill [gil] *n* ouïe(s) *f pl*, branchie(s) *f pl*, bajoues *f pl*.

gilt [gilt] *n* dorure *f*; *a* doré.

gimlet ['gimlit] *n* vrille *f*.

gimmick ['gimik] *n* machin, truc.

gin [dʒin] *n* trappe *f*, genièvre *m*, gin *m*, piège *m*.

ginger ['dʒindʒə] *n* gingembre *m*, énergie *f*; *a* roux.

gingerbread ['dʒindʒəbred] *n* (espèce de) pain d'épice *m*.

gingerly ['dʒindʒəli] *ad* avec précaution.

gingham ['giŋəm] *n* ginnham *m*.

gipsy ['dʒipsi] *n* bohémien, -ienne, romanichel, -elle.

giraffe [dʒi'rɑːf] *n* girafe *f*.

gird [gəːd] *vt* ceindre, entourer; **to — at** railler.

girder ['gəːdə] *n* poutre *f*, poutrelle *f*.

girdle ['gəːdl] *n* gaine *f*, ceinture *f*, cordelière *f*.

girl [gəːl] n (jeune) fille f, amie f.
girlish ['gəːliʃ] a de jeune fille, efféminé.
girth [gəːθ] n sangle f, tour m.
gist [dʒist] n fin mot m, fond m, essentiel m.
give [giv] vti donner; **to — away** trahir, conduire à l'autel; **— in** céder, se laisser faire; **— out** annoncer, distribuer; **— over** cesser, abandonner; **to — up** renoncer à, livrer.
given ['givn] pp of **give**; cj étant donné que.
giver ['givə] n donneur, -euse, donateur, -trice.
gizzard ['gizəd] n gésier m.
glacial ['gleisjəl] a glacial.
glacier ['glæsjə] n glacier m.
glad [glæd] a content, heureux, joyeux.
gladden ['glædn] vt réjouir.
glade [gleid] n clairière f.
gladly ['glædli] ad volontiers.
gladness ['glædnis] n plaisir m, joie f.
glamorous ['glæmərəs] a fascinant, charmeur, enchanteur.
glamour ['glæmə] n éclat m, charme m, fascination f.
glance [glɑːns] n coup d'œil m, regard m; vi jeter un coup d'œil (sur **at**); **to — through** parcourir; **to — off** glisser, ricocher, dévier.
gland [glænd] n glande f.
glare [glɛə] n lumière aveuglante f, éclat m, regard de défi m; vi flamboyer; **to — at** vt regarder d'un œil furibond.
glaring ['glɛəriŋ] a aveuglant, flagrant, éclatant, cru.
glass [glɑːs] n verre m, (beer) bock m, vitre f, baromètre m; pl lunettes f pl.
glassblower ['glɑːs,blouə] n verrier m.
glasscase ['glɑːs'keis] n vitrine f.
glasscutter ['glɑːs,kʌtə] n diamant m, tournette f.
glass-paper ['glɑːs,peipə] n papier de verre m.
glassware ['glɑːswɛə] n verrerie f.
glassy ['glɑːsi] a vitreux, transparent.
glaze [gleiz] n glacis m, lustre m; vt vitrer, glacer, lustrer, devenir vitreux.
glazier ['gleizjə] n vitrier m.
gleam [gliːm] n rayon m, lueur f, reflet m; vi luire, miroiter.
glean [gliːn] vt glaner.
gleaner ['gliːnə] n glaneur, -euse.
gleaning ['gliːniŋ] n glanage m; pl glanures f pl.
glee [gliː] n joie f, gaîté f.
glen [glen] n vallon m.
glib [glib] a spécieux, qui a de la faconde.
glibness ['glibnis] n faconde f, spéciosité f.
glide [glaid] n glissement m, glissade f, vol plané m; vi glisser, planer.

glider ['glaidə] n avion en remorque m, planeur m.
glimmer ['glimə] n lueur f; vi luire.
glimpse [glimps] n lueur passagère f, coup d'œil m, échappée f, aperçu m; vt entrevoir.
glint [glint] vi entreluire, étinceler; n trait m, meur f.
glisten ['glisn] vi étinceler, scintiller, luire.
glitter ['glitə] n scintillement m; vi scintiller, étinceler.
gloat [glout] **to — over** manger (couvrer) des yeux, se réjouir de.
globe [gloub] n globe m sphère f.
gloom [gluːm] n obscurité f, dépression f.
gloomy ['gluːmi] a obscur, sombre, lugubre.
glorification [,glɔːrifi'keiʃən] n glorification f.
glorify ['glɔːrifai] vt glorifier.
glorious ['glɔːriəs] a glorieux.
glory ['glɔːri] n gloire f; **to — in** se faire gloire de.
gloss [glɔs] n lustre m, vernis m; vt lustrer, glacer; **to — over** glisser sur.
glossary ['glɔsəri] n glossaire m, lexique m.
glossy ['glɔsi] a lustré, brillant, glacé.
glove [glʌv] n gant m; vt ganter.
glow [glou] n rougeur (diffuse) f, ardeur f, éclat m, rougeoiement m; vi briller, luire, rougeoyer, s'embraser, brûler.
glow-worm ['glouwəːm] n luciole f, ver luisant m.
glue [gluː] n colle forte f; vt coller.
glum [glʌm] a renfrogné, maussade.
glut [glʌt] n surabondance f, encombrement m; vt gorger, gaver, encombrer.
glutton ['glʌtn] n goinfre m, gourmand(e) mf.
gluttonous ['glʌtənəs] a vorace, goulu.
gnarled [nɑːld] a noueux, tordu.
gnash [næʃ] vt **to — one's teeth** grincer des dents.
gnashing ['næʃiŋ] n grincement m.
gnat [næt] n cousin m, moustique m.
gnaw [nɔː] vti grignoter, ronger.
go [gou] n aller m, allant m, affaire f; vi (s'en) aller, marcher, partir, tendre à, passer, faire loi, disparaître, devenir; **to — away** partir; **to — back** revenir, retourner, reculer; **to — down** descendre, se coucher, sombrer; **to — for** aller chercher; **to — in(to)** entrer (dans); **to — off** partir; **to — on** avancer, continuer; **to — out** sortir; **to — through** traverser, parcourir.
goad [goud] n aiguillon m; vt piquer, exciter.
goal [goul] n but m.
goalkeeper ['goul,kiːpə] n goal m, gardien de but m.
goat [gout] n chèvre f; **he——** bouc m·

go-between ['goubi'twi:n] *n* entremetteur *m*, truchement *m*.
gobble ['gɔbl] *vt* bâfrer, bouffer; *vi* glouglouter, glousser.
goblet ['gɔblit]*n* gobelet *m*, coupe *f*.
goblin ['gɔblin] *n* lutin *m*.
God [gɔd] *n* Dieu *m*.
godchild ['gɔdtʃaild] *n* filleul(e) *mf*.
goddess ['gɔːdis] *n* déesse *f*.
godfather ['gɔd,faːðə] *n* parrain *m*.
godmother ['gɔd,mʌðə] *n* marraine *f*.
godless ['gɔdlis] *a* athée, impie.
godliness ['gɔdlinis] *n* piété *f*.
godly ['gɔdli] *a* pieux, saint.
godsend ['gɔdsend] *n* aubaine *f*.
godspeed ['gɔd'spiːd] *excl* bonne chance! bon voyage!
goggle ['gɔgl] *vi* rouler les yeux; *n pl* lunettes d'automobile *f pl*; (*fam*) —**box** télé(vision) *f*.
goggle-eyed ['gɔglaid] *a* aux yeux saillants, de homard.
going ['gouiŋ] *n* terrain *m*, circonstances *m pl*.
gold [gould] *n* or *m*; — **dust** poudre *f* d'or.
gold-digger ['gould,digə] *n* chercheur d'or *m*.
golden ['gouldən] *a* d'or, doré.
goldfinch ['gouldfintʃ] *n* chardonneret *m*.
goldfish ['gouldfiʃ] *n* dorade *f*, poisson rouge *m*.
goldsmith ['gouldsmiθ] *n* orfèvre *m*.
gold-standard ['gould,stændəd] *n* étalon-or *m*.
golf [gɔlf] *n* golf *m*; —**course** (terrain *m* de) golf *m*.
gondola ['gɔndələ] *n* gondole *f*, nacelle *f*.
gone [gɔn] *pp of* go; *a* parti, fini, disparu, épris (de on).
good [gud] *n* bien *m*, bon *m*, profit *m*; *pl* marchandises *f pl*, effets *m pl*; *a* bon, sage; — **for nothing** propre à rien; **for** — pour de bon; — **Heavens**! Ciel! — **gracious**! bonté divine!
good-bye ['gud'bai] *excl n* au revoir *m*, adieu *m*.
good-looking ['gud'lukiŋ] *a* de bonne mine, bien, beau.
goodly ['gudli] *a* large, ample.
goodness ['gudnis] *n* bonté *f*, vertu *f*.
goodwill [gud'wil] *n* bon vouloir *m*, clientèle *f*.
goody ['gudi] *n* commère *f*; *a* édifiant; **to be a** — la faire à la vertu.
goose [guːs] *n* oie *f*.
gooseberry ['guzbəri] *n* groseille à maquereau *f*.
gooseflesh ['guːsfleʃ] *n* chair de poule *f*.
goose-step ['guːsstep] *n* pas de l'oie *m*.
gore [gɔː] *n* sang *m* (caillé), pointe *f*, pièce *f*, soufflet *m*, godet *m*; *vt* encorner, blesser d'un coup de cornes.

gorge [gɔːdʒ] *n* gorge *f*, défilé *m*, cœur *m*; *vt* rassasier, gorger; *vi* s'empiffrer, se gorger.
gorgeous ['gɔːdʒəs] *a* splendide, superbe.
gorgeousness ['gɔːdʒəsnis] *n* splendeur *f*.
gorilla [gə'rilə] *n* gorille *m*.
gormandize ['gɔːməndaiz] *vi* bâfrer.
gormandizer ['gɔːməndaizə] *n* gourmand(e) *mf*, goinfre *m*.
gorse [gɔːs] *n* ajonc *m*, genêt *m*.
gory ['gɔːri] *a* ensanglanté.
gosling ['gɔzliŋ] *n* oison *m*.
gospel ['gɔspəl] *n* évangile *m*.
gossamer ['gɔsəmə] *n* fils de la Vierge *m pl*, gaze *f*; *a* léger, ténu.
gossip ['gɔsip] *n* commérage *m*, mauvaise langue *f*, bavette *f*; *vi* cancaner, bavarder.
gouge [gaudʒ] *n* gouge *f*; *vt* arracher.
gourd [guəd] *n* potiron *m*, gourde *f*, calebasse *f*.
gourmet ['guəmei] *n* gourmet *m*, fine fourchette *f*.
gout [gaut] *n* goutte *f*.
gouty ['gauti] *a* goutteux.
govern ['gʌvən] *vt* gouverner, administrer.
governess ['gʌvənis] *n* gouvernante *f*.
governing ['gʌvəniŋ] *a* gouvernant, au pouvoir.
government ['gʌvnmənt] *n* gouvernement *m*, régime *m*, ministère *m*.
governor ['gʌvənə] *n* gouverneur *m*, gouvernant *m*, patron *m*.
gown [gaun] *n* robe *f*.
grab [græb] *n* rapacité *f*; *vt* saisir, happer, arracher.
grace [greis] *n* grâce *f*, bénédicité *m*; *pl* grâces *f pl*; *vt* orner, honorer.
graceful ['greisful] *a* gracieux.
graceless ['greislis] *a* sans grâce.
gracious ['greiʃəs] *a* gracieux, accueillant, bow; **good** —! bonté divine! mon Dieu!
gradation [grə'deiʃən] *n* gradation *f*.
grade [greid] *n* degré *m*, rang *m*, qualité *f*, pente *f*, rampe *f*; *vt* graduer, fondre, classer.
grade crossing ['greid'krɔsiŋ] *n* passage *m* à niveau.
gradient ['greidjənt] *n* pente *f*, rampe *f*, variation *f*.
gradual ['grædjuəl] *a* graduel.
gradually ['grædjuəli] *ad* doucement, peu à peu.
graduate ['grædjueit] *n* licencié(e) *mf*; *vt* passer sa licence, recevoir ses diplômes, conférer (un diplôme).
graft [graːft] *n* greffe *f*, tripotage *m*, gratte *f*, corruption *f*; *vt* greffer; *vi* tripoter, rabioter.
grain [grein] *n* grain *m*; **against the** — à contre-fil, à contre-cœur; **with a** — **of salt** avec réserve.
grammar ['græmə] *n* grammaire *f*; — **school** lycée.

gramophone ['græməfoun] n phonographe m.

granary ['grænəri] n grenier m.

grand [grænd] a grand(iose).

grandchildren ['græn͵tʃildrən] n pl petits-enfants m pl.

grand-daughter ['græn͵dɔːtə] n petite-fille f.

grandee [͵græn'diː] n Grand m.

grandeur ['grændjə] n grandeur f, splendeur f.

grandfather ['grænd͵faːðə] n grandpère m.

grandiloquence [græn'diləkwəns] n emphase f.

grandiose ['grændiouz] a grandiose, magnifique, pompeux.

grandmother ['græn͵mʌðə] n grand'mère f.

grandson ['grænsʌn] n petit-fils m.

grandstand ['grændstænd] n tribune f.

grange [greindʒ] n maison avec ferme f.

granite ['grænit] n granit m; a granitique.

granny ['græni] n bonne-maman f.

grant [graːnt] n subvention f, allocation f; vt accorder, admettre, octroyer.

grape [greip] n raisin m.

grapefruit ['greipfruːt] n pamplemousse f.

grape-harvest ['greip͵haːvist] n vendange f.

grapeshot ['greipʃɔt] n mitraille f.

graphic ['græfik] a graphique, vivant.

grapnel ['græpnəl] n grappin m, ancre f.

grapple ['græpl] n grappin m, prise f, étreinte f; to — with empoigner, colleter, en venir aux prises avec.

grasp [graːsp] n prise f, étreinte f, serre f, portée de la main f, compréhension f; vt saisir, serrer, empoigner.

grasping ['graːspiŋ] a rapace, cupide.

grass [graːs] n herbe f.

grasshopper ['graːs͵hɔpə] n sauterelle f.

grassy ['graːsi] a herbu, herbeux, verdoyant.

grate [greit] vt râper, racler; vi grincer, crier, crisser; to — on choquer, agacer.

grater ['greitə] n râpe f.

grateful ['greitful] n reconnaissant.

gratefully ['greitfuli] ad avec reconnaissance.

gratefulness ['greitfulnis] n reconnaissance f.

grating ['greitiŋ] a grinçant; n grille f, grillage m, râpage m, grincement m.

gratification [͵grætifi'keiʃən] n plaisir m, satisfaction f.

gratify ['grætifai] vt contenter, rémunérer, satisfaire.

gratis ['graːtis] ad gratis; a gratuit.

gratitude ['grætitjuːd] n gratitude f, reconnaissance f.

gratuitous [grə'tjuːitəs] a gratuit.

gratuity [grə'tjuːiti] n gratification f, pourboire m, pot de vin m.

gravamen [grə'veimen] n poids m, fond m.

grave [greiv] n fosse f, tombe f, tombeau m; a sérieux, grave; vt graver, radouber.

grave-digger ['greiv͵digə] n fossoyeur m.

gravel ['grævəl] n gravier m.

gravestone ['greivstoun] n pierre tombale f.

graveyard ['greivjaːd] n cimetière m.

graving-dock ['greiviŋdɔk] n bassin de radoub m.

graving-tool ['greiviŋtuːl] n burin m.

gravitate ['græviteit] vi graviter.

gravity ['græviti] n gravité f, sérieux m.

gravitation [͵grævi'teiʃən] n gravitation f, pesanteur f.

gravy ['greivi] n sauce f, jus m.

gray [grei] an gris m; to grow — grisonner.

grayish ['greiiʃ] a grisâtre.

graze [greiz] n égratignure f; vt égratigner, effleurer; vti brouter, paître.

grease [griːs] n graisse f; vt graisser.

greasy ['griːsi] a graisseux, gras.

great [greit] a grand, gros, fort.

greatcoat ['greitkout] n par-dessus m, capote f.

greatly ['greitli] ad énormément, puissamment, beaucoup.

greatness ['greitnis] n grandeur f, noblesse f.

Greece [griːs] n Grèce f.

greed [griːd] n convoitise f, cupidité f.

greediness ['griːdinis] n cupidité f, gloutonnerie f.

greedy ['griːdi] a gourmand, glouton, cupide, avide.

Greek [griːk] n Grec, Grecque; an grec m.

green [griːn] an vert m; a naïf, sot, inexpérimenté.

greengage ['griːngeidʒ] n reineclaude f.

greengrocer ['griːn͵grousə] n fruitier, -ière.

greenhorn ['griːnhɔːn] n blanc-bec m, bleu m.

greenhouse ['griːnhaus] n serre f.

greenish ['griːniʃ] a verdâtre.

Greenland ['griːnlənd] n Groenland m.

greet [griːt] vt saluer, accueillir.

greeting ['griːtiŋ] n salut m, salutation f.

gregarious [gri'gɛəriəs] a grégaire, de troupeau.

grenade [gri'neid] n grenade f.

grenadier [͵grenə'diə] n grenadier m.

grew [gruː] pt of grow.

greyhound ['greihaund] n lévrier m, levrette f.

grid [grid] n grille f.

gridiron ['grid‚aiən] n gril m, terrain m de football.

grief [gri:f] n chagrin m, mal m, peine f.

grievance ['gri:vəns] n grief m, tort m.

grieve [gri:v] vt affliger, faire de la peine à; vi se désoler, s'affliger.

grievous ['gri:vəs] a affligeant, douloureux.

grill [gril] n gril m, grillade f, grille f, grillage m; vt griller, cuisiner.

grim [grim] a sévère, farouche, sardonique, sinistre.

grimace [gri'meis] n grimace f; vi grimacer, faire la grimace.

grime [graim] n crasse f; vt salir.

grimy ['graimi] a crasseux, encrassé, noir.

grin [grin] n rictus m, sourire épanoui m; vi découvrir ses dents, sourire à belles dents.

grind [graind] vt moudre, broyer, écraser, affiler; vi grincer, (fig) piocher; n grincement m, turbin m.

grinder ['graində] n rémouleur m, broyeur m.

grinding ['graindiŋ] n broyage m, mouture f, grincement m.

grindstone ['graindstoun] n meule f.

grip [grip] n prise f, étreinte f, serre f; pl prises f pl, mains f pl; vt agripper, empoigner, saisir, serrer.

gripe [graip] vt donner la colique à.

grisly ['grizli] a terrifiant, macabre.

grist [grist] n blé m; **to bring — to the mill** faire venir l'eau au moulin.

gristle ['grisl] n cartilage m, croquant m.

grit [grit] n gravier m, sable m, grès m, cran m; vi grincer; vt sabler.

gritty ['griti] a graveleux, sablonneux.

grizzled ['grizld] a gris, grisonnant.

groan [groun] n gémissement m, grognement m; vi gémir, grogner.

grocer ['grousə] n épicier, -ière.

grocery ['grousəri] n épicerie f.

groggy ['grɔgi] a ivre, étourdi, titubant.

groin [grɔin] n aine f.

groom [gru:m] n palefrenier m, valet d'écurie m; vt panser.

groomed [gru:md] a **well——** (bien) soigné, tiré à quatre épingles.

grooming ['gru:miŋ] n pansage m.

groomsman ['gru:mzmən] n garçon d'honneur m.

groove [gru:v] n sillon m, rainure f, glissière f; vt rayer, sillonner; **micro——** microsillon m.

grope [group] vi tâtonner; **to — for** chercher à tâtons.

gross [grous] n grosse f; a dru, obèse, grossier, brut, gros.

ground [graund] pp of **grind**; a moulu, broyé; n sol m, terrain m,

fond m, fondement m raison f; vt fonder, appuyer, instruire, (arms) reposer, maintenir au sol; vi s'échouer.

ground floor ['graundflɔ:] n rez-de-chaussée m.

groundless ['graundlis] a sans fondement, immotivé.

groundnut ['graundnʌt] n arachide f.

grounds [graundz] n pl lie f, marc m.

groundsheet ['graundʃi:t] n bâche f de campement.

groundswell ['graundswel] n lame f de fond.

groundwork ['graundwə:k] n fond m, base f, assise f, plan m.

group [gru:p] n groupe m; vt grouper; vi se grouper.

grouse [graus] n coq m de bruyère; vi grogner, ronchonner, rouspéter.

grove [grouv] n bosquet m.

grovel ['grɔvl] vi s'aplatir, ramper.

groveler ['grɔvlə] n flagorneur m, sycophante m, piedplat m.

grow [grou] vt cultiver; vi pousser, grandir, croître, devenir.

growl [graul] n grondement m; vi gronder, grommeler, grogner.

grown [groun] pp of **grow**.

grown-up ['groun'ʌp] n adulte mf, grande personne f.

growth [grouθ] n croissance f, accroissement m, tumeur f.

grub [grʌb] n larve f, (sl) boustifaille f; vt bêcher, nettoyer; vi fouiller.

grudge [grʌdʒ] n dent f, rancune f; vt donner à contre-cœur, mesurer.

grudgingly ['grʌdʒiŋli] ad à contre-cœur.

gruel ['gruəl] n gruau m, brouet m.

grueling ['gruəliŋ] a éreintant, épuisant.

gruesome ['gru:səm] a macabre, répugnant.

gruff [grʌf] a bourru, revêche, rude, gros.

gruffly ['grʌfli] ad rudement.

gruffness ['grʌfnis] n rudesse f, ton bourru m.

grumble ['grʌmbl] n grognement m; vti grommeler, bougonner.

grumbler ['grʌmblə] n ronchonneur, -euse, grognard(e) mf, rouspéteur, -euse.

grumpy ['grʌmpi] a maussade, grincheux.

grunt [grʌnt] n grognement m; vi grogner.

guarantee [‚gærən'ti:] n garant(e) mf, garantie f, caution f; vt garantir, se porter garant pour.

guard [ga:d] n garde mf, chef de train m, geôlier m; vt garder, protéger; vi mettre (se tenir) en garde.

guarded ['ga:did] a circonspect.

guardedly ['ga:didli] ad prudemment, avec réserve.

guardian ['ga:djən] n gardien, -ienne, tuteur, -trice.

guardianship ['gɑːdjənʃip] *n* garde *f*, tutelle *f*.
guava ['gwɑːvə] *n* goyave *f*; — **tree** goyavier *m*.
gudgeon ['gʌdʒən] *n* goujon *m*.
guess [ges] *n* conjecture *f*; *vti* deviner; *vt* estimer; **at a** — au jugé.
guesswork ['geswəːk] *n* hypothèse *f*, conjecture *f*.
guest [gest] *n* invité(e) *mf*; **paying—** pensionnaire *mf*; — **house** pension *f*.
guffaw [gʌ'fɔː] *n* gros rire *m*; *vi* s'esclaffer.
guidance ['gaidəns] *n* conduite *f*, direction *f*, gouverne *f*, orientation *f*.
guide [gaid] *n* guide *m*; *vt* guider, conduire, diriger.
guidebook ['gaidbuk] *n* guide *m*.
guided ['gaidid] *a* (*of rockets*) téléguidé.
guidepost ['gaidpoust] *n* poteau indicateur *m*.
guild [gild] *n* corporation *f*, confrérie *f*.
guildhall ['gildhɔːl] *n* hôtel de ville *m*.
guile [gail] *n* astuce *f*.
guileful ['gailful] *a* retors.
guileless ['gaillis] *a* sans malice, naïf.
guilt [gilt] *n* culpabilité *f*.
guiltless ['giltlis] *a* innocent.
guilty ['gilti] *a* coupable.
guinea-fowl ['ginifaul] *n* pintade *f*.
guinea-pig ['ginipig] *n* cobaye *m*, cochon d'Inde *m*.
guise [gaiz] *n* forme *f*, apparence *f*, costume *m*.
guitar [gi'tɑː] *n* guitare *f*.
gulf [gʌlf] *n* golfe *m*, gouffre *m*, abîme *m*.
gull [gʌl] *n* mouette *f*, jobard *m*, gogo *m*; *vt* rouler.
gullet ['gʌlit] *n* œsophage *m*, gosier *m*.
gullibility [,gʌli'biliti] *n* crédulité *f*, jobardise *f*.
gullible ['gʌlibl] *a* crédule, jobard.
gully ['gʌli] *n* ravin *m*.
gulp [gʌlp] *n* lampée *f*, trait *m*; *vti* boire, avaler d'un trait; *vi* s'étrangler.
gum [gʌm] *n* gencive *f*, gomme *f*; *vt* gommer, coller.
gumboil ['gʌmbɔil] *n* abcès à la gencive *m*.
gumption ['gʌmpʃən] *n* jugeotte *f*, gingin *m*.
gun [gʌn] *n* fusil *m*, canon *m*, pièce *f*.
gunboat ['gʌnbout] *n* canonnière *f*.
gun-carriage ['gʌn,kæridʒ] *n* affût de canon *m*.
gunner ['gʌnə] *n* canonnier *m*, artilleur *m*.
gunnery ['gʌnəri] *n* tir au canon *m*.
gunpowder ['gʌn,paudə] *n* poudre *f*.
gunshot ['gʌnʃɔt] *n* portée de fusil *f* (canon), coup de feu *m*.
gunsmith ['gʌnsmiθ] *n* armurier *m*.
gurgle ['gəːgl] *n* glouglou *m*, gar-

gouillement *m*; *vi* glouglouter, gargouiller; *vti* glousser.
gush [gʌʃ] *n* jaillissement *m*, jet *m*, projection *f*, effusion *f*; *vi* jaillir, saillir, se répandre, la faire au sentiment.
gust [gʌst] *n* rafale *f*, ondée *f*, accès *m*.
gusto ['gʌstou] *n* brio *m*, entrain *m*.
gut [gʌt] *n* boyau *m*; *pl* entrailles *f pl*, cran *m*; *vt* vider, dévaster.
gutter ['gʌtə] *n* gouttière *f*, ruisseau *m*, rigole *f*.
guy [gai] *n* corde *f*, hauban *m*, type *m*, épouvantail *m*; *vt* railler, travestir.
guzzle ['gʌzl] *vt* boire à tire-larigot, bouffer; *vi* s'empiffrer, se gaver.
gymnasium [dʒim'neizjəm] *n* gymnase *m*.
gymnast ['dʒimnæst] *n* gymnaste *mf*.
gymnastics [dʒim'næstiks] *n pl* gymnastique *f*.

H

haberdasher ['hæbədæʃə] *n* mercier *m*.
haberdasher's ['hæbədæʃəz] *n* mercerie *f*.
habit ['hæbit] *n* habitude *f*, état *m*, constitution *f*.
habitable ['hæbitəbl] *a* habitable.
habitation [,hæbi'teiʃən] *n* habitation *f*, demeure *f*.
habitual [hə'bitjuəl] *a* habituel, invétéré.
hack [hæk] *n* pioche *f*, pic *m*, blessure *f*, cheval *m* (de louage), rosse *f*, corvée *f*, écrivassier *m*; *vt* couper, frapper, hacher, taillader; *vi* tousser sèchement.
hackneyed ['hæknid] *a* usé, rebattu, banal.
had [hæd] *pp pt of* **have.**
haddock ['hædək] *n* aiglefin *m*, aigrefin *m*.
haft [hɑːft] *n* manche *m*, poignée *f*.
hag [hæg] *n* sorcière *f*, chipie *f*.
haggard ['hægəd] *a* hagard, hâve, décharné, égaré.
haggle ['hægl] *vi* ergoter, chicaner.
hail [heil] *n* grêle *f*, salut *m*; *vi* grêler; *vt* saluer, héler, venir (de **from**), descendre (de **from**).
hailstone ['heilstoun] *n* grêlon *m*.
hair [hɛə] *n* cheveu *m*, chevelure *f*, poil *m*, crin *m*; **to comb one's —** se peigner.
haircut ['hɛə,kʌt] *n* coupe de cheveux *f*.
hairdresser ['hɛə,dresə] *n* coiffeur, -euse.
hairless ['hɛəlis] *a* chauve, sans poils, glabre.
hairline ['hɛəlain] *n* — **crack** gerçure *f*; (*fig*) distinction *f* subtile.

hairpin ['hɛəpin] *n* épingle à cheveux *f*.

hair-raising ['hɛə,reiziŋ] *a* horrifique, horripilant.

hair's breadth ['hɛəz'bredθ] *ad* à un cheveu (près).

hair-splitting ['hɛə,splitiŋ] *n* chinoiserie *f*, ergotage *m*.

hairy ['hɛəri] *a* chevelu, poilu, velu.

hake [heik] *n* merluche *f*, colin *m*.

hale [heil] *a* robuste; — **and hearty** frais et dispos.

half [haːf] *n* moitié *f*; *a* demi, mi-; *ad* à moitié, demi, en deux; — **as much again** une fois et demie autant, la moitié en plus; — **hearted** *a* tiède; **at—tide** à mi-marée.

half-back ['haːfbæk] *n* demi(-arrière) *m*.

half-bred ['haːfbred] *a* métis, demi-sang.

half-brother ['haːf,brʌðə] *n* demi-frère *m*.

half-caste ['haːfkaːst] *a* demi-sang; *an* métis, -isse, hybride *m*.

half-dozen ['haːf'dʌzn] *n* demi-douzaine *f*.

half-hour ['haːf'auə] *n* demi-heure *f*.

half-mast ['haːf'maːst] *ad* en berne, à mi-mât.

half-measure ['haːf'meʒə] *n* demi-mesure *f*.

half-pay ['haːf'pei] *n* demi-solde *f*.

halfway ['haːf'wei] *ad* à mi-chemin.

halibut ['hælibət] *n* flétan *m*.

hall [hɔːl] *n* salle *f*, vestibule *m*, hall *m*.

hallmark ['hɔːlmaːk] *n* contrôle *m*, poinçon *m*, empreinte *f*.

hallow ['hælou] *vt* sanctifier, bénir.

hallucinate [hə'luːsineit] *vt* halluciner.

hallucination [hə,luːsi'neiʃən] *n* hallucination *f*.

halo ['heilou] *n* halo *m*, nimbe *m*, auréole *f*.

halt [hɔlt] *n* halte *f*; *vi* s'arrêter, hésiter, boiter; *a* boiteux.

halter ['hɔltə] *n* licou *m*, corde *f*.

halve [haːv] *vt* couper en deux, partager.

ham [hæm] *n* jambon *m*, jarret *m*.

hamlet ['hæmlit] *n* hameau *m*.

hammer ['hæmə] *n* marteau *m*; *vt* marteler, battre.

hammock ['hæmək] *n* hamac *m*.

hamper ['hæmpə] *n* corbeille *f*, manne *f*, banne *f*; *vt* gêner, empêcher.

hand [hænd] *n* main *f*, (*watch*) aiguille *f*, jeu *m*, ouvrier, -ière; — **to** — corps à corps; **out of** — hors de contrôle; **on the one** — d'une part; **old** — vieux routier *m*; *vt* tendre, passer, remettre.

handbag ['hændbæg] *n* sac à main *m*, pochette *f*.

handbook ['hændbuk] *n* manuel *m*, guide *m*.

handcuff ['hændkʌf] *vt* passer les menottes à.

handcuffs ['hændkʌfs] *n pl* menottes *f pl*.

handful ['hændful] *n* poignée *f*.

handicap ['hændikæp] *n* handicap *m*, désavantage *m*; *vt* handicaper, désavantager.

handicraft ['hændikraːft] *n* habileté manuelle *f*, métier manuel *m*, travail manuel *m*.

handiwork ['hændiwəːk] *n* travail manuel *m*, ouvrage *m*.

handkerchief ['hæŋkətʃif] *n* mouchoir *m*, pochette *f*.

handle ['hændl] *n* poignée *f*, manche *m*, anse *f*, bouton *m*, bras *m*; *vt* manier, traiter, prendre en main.

handlebar ['hændlbaː] *n* guidon *m*.

handling ['hændliŋ] *n* maniement *m*, manœuvre *f*.

handrail ['hændreil] *n* rampe *f*, main courante *f*.

handshake ['hændʃeik] *n* poignée de main *f*.

handsome ['hænsəm] *a* beau, élégant, généreux.

handsomely ['hænsəmli] *ad* élégamment, libéralement.

handwriting ['hænd,raitiŋ] *n* écriture *f*, main *f*.

handy ['hændi] *a* sous la main, commode, adroit, maniable.

hang [hæŋ] *vt* pendre, accrocher, tapisser, poser; *vi* pendre, planer, peser, tomber; **to** — **about** rôder, flâner; **to** — **back** hésiter, rester en arrière.

hangar ['hæŋə] *n* hangar *m*.

hanger ['hæŋə] *n* portemanteau *m*, cintre *m*, crochet *m*.

hanging ['hæŋiŋ] *n* pose *f*, tenture *f*, suspension *f*, montage *m*, pendaison *f*.

hangman ['hæŋmən] *n* bourreau *m*.

hanker ['hæŋkə] *vi* aspirer (à **after**).

hankering ['hæŋkəriŋ] *n* aspiration *f*, forte envie *f*.

hanky-panky ['hæŋki'pæŋki] *n* boniment *m*, tour de passe-passe *m*.

hansom ['hænsəm] *n* cabriolet *m*.

haphazard ['hæp'hæzəd] *a* fortuit; *ad* au petit bonheur, à l'aveuglette.

hapless ['hæplis] *a* malchanceux, infortuné.

happen ['hæpən] *vi* arriver, se passer, se produire.

happening ['hæpniŋ] *n* événement *m*.

happily ['hæpili] *ad* heureusement, par bonheur.

happiness ['hæpinis] *n* bonheur *m*.

happy ['hæpi] *a* heureux.

harangue [hə'ræŋ] *n* harangue *f*, *vt* haranguer.

harass ['hærəs] *vt* harceler, tracasser, tourmenter.

harbinger ['haːbindʒə] *n* précurseur *m*, avant-coureur *m*, messager, -ère.

harbor ['hɑːbə] n port m, asile m; vt recéler, nourrir, abriter.

hard [hɑːd] a dur, difficile, sévère; — by tout près; — up à sec; — upon de près, sur les talons; ad dur, fort, durement.

harden ['hɑːdn] vt (en)durcir, tremper; vi durcir, s'endurcir, devenir dur.

hardfisted ['hɑːd'fistid] a pingre, radin.

hardhearted ['hɑːd'hɑːtid] a dur, inflexible.

hardihood ['hɑːdihud] n audace f.

hard labor ['hɑːd'leibə] n travaux forcés m pl.

hardly ['hɑːdli] ad à (avec) peine, ne . . . guère, sévèrement.

hardness ['hɑːdnis] n dureté f, difficulté f.

hardship ['hɑːdʃip] n privation f, épreuve f.

hardware ['hɑːdwɛə] n quincaillerie f.

hardwareman ['hɑːdwɛəmən] n quincailler m.

hardy ['hɑːdi] a résistant, robuste, vigoureux.

hare [hɛə] n lièvre m.

hare-brained ['hɛəbreind] a écervelé, insensé.

harelip ['hɛəʾlip] n bec-de-lièvre m.

haricot ['hærikou] n — bean haricot m vert etc; (stew) haricot de mouton m.

hark [hɑːk] vti écouter; to — back to revenir à.

harm [hɑːm] n mal m, tort m; vt faire tort à, faire (du) mal à, porter préjudice à.

harmful ['hɑːmful] a nuisible, pénible, nocif.

harmless ['hɑːmlis] a inoffensif.

harmlessly ['hɑːmlisli] ad innocemment.

harmonious [hɑːˈmounjəs] a harmonieux.

harmonize ['hɑːmənaiz] vt harmoniser, concilier; vi s'harmoniser, s'accorder.

harmony ['hɑːməni] n harmonie f, accord m.

harness ['hɑːnis] n harnais m; vt harnacher, capter, aménager.

harness-maker ['hɑːnis.meikə] n bourrelier m.

Harold ('hærəld] Henri m.

harp [hɑːp] n harpe f; vi jouer de la harpe; to — on ressasser, rabâcher.

harpoon [hɑːˈpuːn] n harpon m; vt harponner.

harpsichord ['hɑːpsikɔːd] n clavecin m.

harrow ['hærou] n herse f; vt herser, blesser, déchirer.

harrowing ['hærouiŋ] a déchirant, navrant.

harry ['hæri] vt ravaget, tracasser, harceler.

harsh [hɑːʃ] a rèche, âpre, cruel.

harshness ['hɑːʃnis] n rudesse f, âpreté f, rigueur f.

hart [hɑːt] n cerf m.

harum-scarum ['hɛərəmˈskɛərəm] an hurluberlu(e) mf, écervelé(e) mf.

harvest ['hɑːvist] n moisson f, récolte f, vendange f, fenaison f; vt moissonner, récolter; vi faire la moisson.

harvester ['hɑːvistə] n moissonneur, -euse, (machine) moissonneuse f.

hash [hæʃ] n hachis m, gâchis m, compte m; vt hacher, gâcher.

hassock ['hæsək] n coussin m.

haste [heist] n hâte f.

hasten ['heisn] vt presser, hâter, avancer; vi se presser, se dépêcher se hâter.

hastily ['heistili] ad à la hâte.

hasty ['heisti] a hâtif, vif, emporté.

hat [hæt] n chapeau m.

hat-box ['hætbɔks] n carton à chapeau m.

hatch [hætʃ] n écoutille f, couvaison f, couvée f, éclosion f; vt couver, tramer; vi éclore, se tramer.

hatchet ['hætʃit] n hachette f, cognée f.

hatching ['hætʃiŋ] n éclosion f, machination f.

hate [heit] n haine f, aversion f; vt haïr, détester.

hateful ['heitful] a haïssable, odieux.

hat-peg ['hætpeg] n patère f.

hatred ['heitrid] n haine f.

hatter ['hætə] n chapelier m.

hatter's ['hætəz] n chapellerie f.

haughtiness ['hɔːtinis] n hauteur f, morgue f.

haughty ['hɔːti] a hautain.

haul [hɔːl] n traction f, coup de filet m, butin m; vt haler, tirer, traîner.

haulage ['hɔːlidʒ] n halage m, roulage m, charriage m.

haunch [hɔːntʃ] n hanche f, cuissot m, quartier m.

haunt [hɔːnt] n rendez-vous m, repaire m; vt fréquenter, hanter, obséder.

have [hæv] vt avoir, permettre, savoir, soutenir, admettre, prendre, faire, tenir; I had better, rather je ferais (aimerais) mieux; to — it out with s'expliquer avec.

haven ['heivn] n port m.

haversack ['hævəsæk] n musette f, havresac m.

haves [hævz] n pl les possédants m pl.

havoc ['hævək] n ravage m, dégâts m pl.

hawk [hɔːk] n faucon m; vt colporter; vi chasser au faucon.

hawker ['hɔːkə] n camelot m, colporteur m, (fruit) marchand des quatre saisons m.

hawser ['hɔːzə] n haussière f, amarre f.

hawthorn ['hɔːθɔːn] n aubépine f.

hay [hei] n foin m.

hayloft ['heilɔft] n fenil m.
haymaker ['heimeikə] n faneur, -euse.
haymaking ['heimeikiŋ] n fenaison f.
haystack ['heistæk] n meule de foin f.
hazard ['hæzəd] n hasard m; vt hasarder, risquer.
haze [heiz] n brume f (de chaleur), harassement m, brimade f; vt brimer, bizuter.
hazel ['heizl] n noisetier m.
hazel-nut ['heizlnʌt] n noisette f.
hazy ['heizi] a brumeux, vague, estompé.
he [hi:] pr il, lui, celui; an mâle m.
head [hed] n tête f, face f, sommet m, source f, haut bout m, chef m, crise f; a premier, principal, (en) chef; vt conduire, intituler, venir en tête de; **to — for** se diriger vers, mettre le cap sur.
headache ['hedeik] n mal de tête m.
headdress ['heddres] n coiffure f.
heading ['hediŋ] n titre m, en-tête m, rubrique f.
headland ['hedlənd] n cap m, promontoire m.
headlight ['hedlait] n phare m.
headline ['hedlain] n titre m, manchette f.
headlong ['hedlɔŋ] a impétueux; ad la tête la première, tête baissée.
headman ['hedmən] n chef m.
headmaster ['hed'mɑːstə] n proviseur m, directeur m.
headmistress ['hed'mistris] n directrice f.
headphone ['hedfoun] n récepteur m, écouteur m.
headquarters ['hed'kwɔːtəz] n quartier général m, état major m.
headstone ['hedstoun] n pierre angulaire f, pierre tombale f.
headstrong ['hedstrɔŋ] a têtu, volontaire.
headway ['hedwei] n progrès m (pl), erre f.
heady ['hedi] a violent, capiteux.
heal [hi:l] vti guérir; vi se cicatriser.
healing ['hi:liŋ] n guérison f.
health [helθ] n santé f.
healthy ['helθi] a sain, bien portant, salubre.
heap [hi:p] n tas m, monceau m; vt entasser, amonceler, combler.
heaped [hi:pd] a entassé, amoncelé, comble.
hear [hiə] vt entendre, entendre dire, apprendre, faire répéter; **to — from** recevoir des nouvelles de.
heard [hə:d] pp pt of **hear**.
hearer ['hiərə] n auditeur, -trice.
hearing ['hiəriŋ] n ouïe f, oreille f, audition f, audience f.
hearken ['hɑːkən] vi écouter, prêter l'oreille (à **to**).
hearsay ['hiəsei] n ouï-dire m.
hearse [hə:s] n corbillard m.
heart [hɑːt] n cœur m, courage m.

heartbeat ['hɑːtbiːt] n battement de cœur m.
heartbreaking ['hɑːtbreikiŋ] a navrant, accablant, déchirant.
heartbroken ['hɑːt,broukən] a navré, accablé.
heartburn ['hɑːtbəːn] n aigreurs f pl.
hearten ['hɑːtn] vt réconforter, remonter le moral à.
heartfelt ['hɑːtfelt] a sincère, senti.
heartily ['hɑːtili] ad de bon cœur, avec appétit
heartiness ['hɑːtinis] n cordialité f, vigueur f.
heartless ['hɑːtlis] a sans cœur, cruel.
heartlessness ['hɑːtlisnis] n dureté f, manque de cœur m.
hearth [hɑːθ] n foyer m.
hearty ['hɑːti] a cordial, copieux, solide.
heat [hi:t] n chaleur f, colère f, épreuve f, manche f; vti chauffer; vt (r)échauffer, enflammer; vi s'échauffer.
heated ['hi:tid] a chaud, chauffé, animé.
heater ['hi:tə] n radiateur m.
heath [hi:θ] n lande f, bruyère f.
heathen ['hi:ðən] an paien, -ienne.
heather ['heðə] n bruyère f.
heating ['hi:tiŋ] n chauffage m, chauffe f.
heave [hi:v] n soulèvement m, effort m; vt soulever, pousser; vi palpiter, avoir des haut-le-cœur, se soulever, battre du flanc; **to — to** mettre en panne.
heaven ['hevn] n ciel m.
heavenly ['hevnli] a céleste, divin.
heavily ['hevili] ad pesamment, lourdement.
heaviness ['hevinis] n lourdeur f, poids m, lassitude f.
heavy ['hevi] a lourd, (sea) dur, violent, gros, triste.
Hebrew ['hi:bru:] an hébreu.
heckle ['hekl] vt harceler.
hectic ['hektik] a fiévreux, excitant.
hector ['hektə] vt rudoyer.
hedge [hedʒ] n haie f, (fig) mur m; vt enclore; vi se couvrir, esquiver la question.
hedgehog ['hedʒhɔg] n hérisson m.
heed [hi:d] n attention f; vt faire attention à.
heedful ['hi:dful] a attentif.
heedless ['hi:dlis] a inattentif, léger, insouciant.
heedlessly ['hi:dlisli] ad étourdiment.
heel [hi:l] n talon m; vt réparer le talon de; vti talonner; **to bring to —** mettre au pas; **to —! ici! down at —** éculé.
hefty ['hefti] a solide, costaud.
heifer ['hefə] n génisse f.
height [hait] n hauteur f, comble m.
heighten ['haitn] vt rehausser, faire ressortir.
heinous ['heinəs] a atroce, odieux.

heinousness ['heinəsnis] n atrocité f, énormité f.
heir [εə] n héritier m.
heiress ['εəris] n héritière f.
heirloom ['εəluːm] n bien inaliénable m, meuble m de famille.
held [held] pt pp of **hold.**
Helen ['helin] Hélène f.
hell [hel] n enfer m, diable m.
hellish ['heliʃ] a infernal.
helm [helm] n barre f, gouvernail m.
helmet ['helmit] n casque m.
helmsman ['helmzmən] n timonier m, homme de barre m.
help [help] n aide f, secours m, domestique mf, auxiliaire mf, collaborateur, -trice; vt aider, secourir, servir; **I can't — laughing** je ne peux m'empêcher de rire; **I can't — it** je n'y peux rien.
helpful ['helpful] a secourable, serviable, utile.
helpfulness ['helpfulnis] n serviabilité f.
helping ['helpiŋ] n portion f, morceau m.
helpless ['helplis] a sans défense désemparé, sans ressource.
helplessness ['helplisnis] n impuis sance f, faiblesse f.
helter-skelter ['heltə'skeltə] ad pêle mêle, à la débandade.
hem [hem] n ourlet m; vt ourler; **to — in** cerner.
hemlock ['hemlɔk] n ciguë f.
hemp [hemp] n chanvre m.
hen [hen] n poule f, femelle f.
hence [hens] ad d'ici.
henceforth ['hens'fɔːθ] ad à l'avenir dorénavant.
henchman ['hentʃmən] n partisan m, bras droit m.
henhouse ['hen'haus] n poulailler m.
henpecked ['henpekt] a dominé par sa femme.
henroost ['henrust] n perchoir m.
Henry ['henri] Henri m.
her [həː] a son, sa, ses; pn la, lui, à elle; **—self** elle-même; **—s** pn le sien, la sienne, les siens, les siennes.
herald ['herəld] n héraut m, messager, -ère, avant-coureur m, avant-courrier, -ière.
heraldry ['herəldri] n blason m, art héraldique m.
herb [həːb] n herbe f; pl simples m pl.
herbaceous [həː'beiʃəs] a herbacé.
herbalist ['həːbəlist] n herboriste mf.
herd [həːd] n troupeau m; vi vivre en troupe.
herdsman ['həːdzmən] n pâtre m, bouvier m.
here [hiə] ad ici.
hereafter [hiər'aːftə] n vie future f, au-delà m; ad à l'avenir, désormais, ci-dessous.
hereditary [hi'reditəri] a héréditaire.
heredity [hi'rediti] n hérédité f.

herein ['hiərin] ad ici, ci-dedans, ci-inclus.
heresy ['herəsi] n hérésie f.
heretic ['herətik] n hérétique mf.
heritage ['heritidʒ] n héritage m.
hermit ['həːmit] n ermite m.
hernia ['həːnjə] n hernie f.
hero ['hiərou] n héros m.
heroic [hi'rouik] a héroïque.
heroine ['herouin] n héroïne f.
heron ['herən] n héron m.
herring ['heriŋ] n hareng m; **red —** (fig) diversion.
hesitate ['heziteit] vi hésiter.
hesitation [ˌhezi'teiʃən] n hésitation f.
hew [hjuː] vt couper, ouvrir, tailler.
hewer ['hjuːə] n bûcheron m, tailleur m.
heyday ['heidei] n fleur f, apogée m, beaux jours m pl.
hiccup ['hikʌp] n hoquet m; vi avoir le hoquet.
hid, hidden [hid, 'hidn] pt pp of **hide.**
hide [haid] n peau f, cuir m; vt cacher; vi se cacher.
hide-and-seek ['haidan'siːk] n cache-cache m.
hidebound ['haidbaund] a étroit, fermé, systématique.
hideous ['hidjəs] a hideux, horrible, affreux, odieux.
hiding ['haidiŋ] n râclée f, dissimulation f.
hiding-place ['haidiŋpleis] n cachette f.
higgledy-piggledy ['higldi'pigldi] ad en confusion, pêle-mêle.
high [hai] a haut (placé), élevé, grand, gros, avancé, faisandé, (of drug addict) parti, en voyage; **— altar** maître-autel m; **— school** lycée m, collège m.
highborn ['haibɔːn] a de haute naissance.
highbrow ['haibrau] n intellectuel, -elle, pontife m, snob m.
highflown ['haifloun] a ampoulé, extravagant.
high-handed ['hai'hændid] a impérieux, arbitraire.
highly ['haili] ad fortement, hautement, fort, très; **—-strung** exalté, nerveux.
highness ['hainis] n Altesse f. hauteur f.
high-pitched ['hai'pitʃt] a aigu, -uë.
high-spirited ['hai'spiritid] a exubérant, courageux, enthousiaste.
highway ['haiwei] n route f nationale, principale, grande route f, grand chemin m, voie f; a routier; **divided —** route jumelée.
highwayman ['haiweimən] n voleur de grand chemin m.
hike [haik] n excursion f à pied; vi faire du footing, trimarder.
hilarious [hi'lεəriəs] a hilare.
hilarity [hi'læriti] n hilarité f.
hill [hil] n colline f, côte f, coteau m, montée f.

hillock ['hilək] n tertre m, butte f.
hilltop ['hiltɔp] n sommet m.
hilly ['hili] a accidenté, montueux.
hilt [hilt] n poignée f, garde f, crosse f.
him [him] pn le, lui; **—self** lui-même.
hind [haind] n biche f; a de derrière.
hinder ['hində] vt gêner, empêcher, entraver.
hindmost ['haindmoust] a dernier.
hindquarters ['haind'kwɔːtəz] n arrière train m.
hindrance ['hindrəns] n entrave f, obstacle m, empêchement m.
hinge [hindʒ] n gond m, pivot m, charnière f; vi tourner, dépendre.
hint [hint] n allusion f, insinuation f, mot m; vt insinuer, faire entendre; vi faire allusion (à at).
hip [hip] n hanche f.
hire ['haiə] n louage m, location f; **on, for — à** louer; vt louer, embaucher.
hireling ['haiəliŋ] n mercenaire m.
hire-purchase ['haiə'pəːtʃis] n paiements échelonnés m pl, vente à tempérament f.
hirsute ['həːsjuːt] a hirsute, velu.
his [hiz] a son, sa, ses; pn le sien, la sienne, les siens, les siennes, à lui.
hiss [his] n sifflement m, sifflets m pl; vti siffler.
historian [his'tɔːriən] n historien m.
historic [his'tɔrik] a historique.
history ['histəri] n histoire f.
hit [hit] n coup m (au but), succès m; vt frapper, atteindre, mettre le doigt sur; vi se cogner, donner.
hitch [hitʃ] n secousse f, accroc m, nœud m; vt pousser (tirer) brusquement, attacher, accrocher.
hitchhike ['hitʃhaik] vi faire de l'autostop.
hither ['hiðə] ad ici, y, çà.
hitherto ['hiðə'tuː] ad jusqu'ici.
hive [haiv] n ruche f, essaim m.
hoard [hɔːd] n stock m, magot m; vt amasser, thésauriser.
hoarding ['hɔːdiŋ] n palissade f, panneau-réclame m, thésaurisation f, amassage m.
hoarfrost ['hɔː'frɔst] n gelée blanche f, givre m.
hoarse [hɔːs] a rauque, enroué.
hoarseness ['hɔːsnis] n enrouement m.
hoary ['hɔːri] a chenu, vénérable, blanchâtre.
hoax [houks] n mystification f, vt mystifier.
hobble ['hɔbl] n boiterie f, entrave f, embarras m; vt entraver; vi aller clopin-clopant.
hobby ['hɔbi] n marotte f, dada m.
hobnail ['hɔbneil] n clou à ferrer m.
hock [hɔk] n jarret m, vin du Rhin m.
hod [hɔd] n hotte f, auge f.
hoe [hou] n houe f, sarcloir m, hoyeau m, daba m; vt biner, sarcler.

hog [hɔg] n porc m, pourceau m, cochon m.
hogshead ['hɔgzhed] n barrique f.
hoist [hɔist] n poulie f, treuil m, monte-charge m; vt hisser.
hold [hould] n prise f, mainmise f, influence f, empire m, cale f; vt (con-, dé-, main-, re-, sou-, tenir, porter; vi tenir (bon), se maintenir, persister, subsister; **to — back** vt retenir; vi hésiter, rester en arrière; **to — on** tenir bon, s'accrocher.
holdall ['houldɔːl] n valise f, fourre-tout m.
holder ['houldə] n manche m, poignée f, récipient m, porteur, -euse, détenteur, -trice, titulaire mf.
holdfast ['houldfɑːst] n crampon m.
holding ['houldiŋ] n propriété f, tenue f, conservation f, tenure f.
hold-up ['houldʌp] n embouteillage m, panne f, attaque f, coup à main armée m.
hole [houl] n trou m; vt trouer, percer.
holiday ['hɔlədi] n jour férié m, congé m, vacances f pl.
holiness ['houlinis] n sainteté f.
Holland ['hɔlənd] n la Hollande f.
hollow ['hɔlou] n creux m, cavité f, cuvette f; a creux, faux, sourd; vt creuser.
holly ['hɔli] n houx m.
hollyhock ['hɔlihɔk] n rose trémière f.
holm [houm] n îlot m, berge f; **—oak** chêne vert m.
holster ['houlstə] n fontes f pl, étui m.
holy ['houli] a saint, bénit, sacré; **the H— Ghost** le Saint-Esprit.
home [houm] n chez-soi m, maison f, foyer m, pays m, asile m, clinique f; a domestique, de famille, indigène, métropolitain, national, (coup) direct, bien appliqué; ad chez soi, de retour; **not at —** sorti; **to drive —** pousser à fond; **to strike —** frapper juste.
homecoming ['houm,kʌmiŋ] n retour m, rentrée f.
homeless ['houmlis] a sans logis.
homely ['houmli] a simple, commun.
home-made ['houm'meid] a fait chez soi, bricolé.
Home Office ['houm,ɔfis] n (UK) ministère de l'Intérieur m.
home rule ['houm'ruːl] n autonomie f.
Home Secretary ['houm'sekrətri] n (UK) ministre de l'Intérieur m.
homesickness ['houmsiknis] n mal du pays m.
homespun ['houmspʌn] a filé à la maison.
homeward ['houmwəd] ad vers la maison, vers le pays.
homily ['hɔmili] n homélie f.
homogeneity [,hɔmoudʒə'niːiti] n homogénéité f.
homogeneous [,hɔmə'dʒiːnjəs] a homogène.

hone [houn] *n* pierre *f* à aiguiser, (*razors*) cuir *m.*
honest ['ɔnist] *a* honnête, probe, loyal.
honestly ['ɔnistli] *ad* sincèrement, de bonne foi, honnêtement.
honesty ['ɔnisti] *n* honnêteté *f,* sincérité *f.*
honey ['hʌni] *n* miel *m.*
honeycomb ['hʌnikoum] *n* rayon de miel *m; vt* cribler.
honeydew ['hʌnidju:] *n* miellée *f.*
honeymoon ['hʌnimu:n] *n* lune de miel *f,* voyage de noces *m.*
honeysuckle ['hʌni.sʌkl] *n* chèvrefeuille *m.*
honor ['ɔnə] *n* honneur *m,* ¡distinction *f; vt* honorer.
honorable ['ɔnərəbl] *a* honorable, honnête.
honorary ['ɔnərəri] *a* honoraire, honorifique.
hood [hud] *n* capuchon *m,* cape (line) *f,* capote *f,* capot *m* (*de moteur*).
hooded ['hudid] *a* encapuchonné, mantelé.
hoodwink ['hudwiŋk] *vt* égarer, donner le change à.
hoof [hu:f] *n* sabot *m.*
hook [huk] *n* croc *m,* crochet *m,* hameçon *m,* faucille *f;* —**up** (*radio*) combinaison *f* d'intérêts, conjugaison *f* de postes; *vt* (ac)crocher, agrafer, (*fish*) ferrer.
hookah ['hukə] *n* narghileh *m.*
hooked [hukt] *a* crochu, busqué.
hooligan ['hu:ligən] *n* voyou *m.*
hoop [hu:p] *n* cercle *m,* cerceau *m,* arceau *m.*
hoot [hu:t] *n* hululement *m,* huée *f,* coup de klaxon *m; vi* hululer, corner, klaxonner; *vti* huer; *vt* siffler.
hooter ['hu:tə] *n* sirène *f,* corne *f.*
hop [hɔp] *n* houblon *m,* petit saut *m,* sauterie *f; vi* saut(ill)er; **to** — **it** ficher le camp.
hope [houp] *n* espoir *m,* espérance *f,* attente *f; vt* espérer; **to** — **for** espérer.
hopeful ['houpful] *a* qui a bon espoir, qui donne espoir.
hopefully ['houpfuli] *ad* avec confiance.
hopeless ['houplis] *a* désespéré, incurable.
hop-garden ['hɔp'ga:dn] *n* houblonnière *f.*
hopping ['hɔpiŋ] *n* sautillement *m,* cueillette du houblon *f.*
horde [hɔ:d] *n* horde *f.*
horizon [hə'raizn] *n* horizon *m.*
horizontal [.hɔri'zɔntl] *a* horizontal.
horn [hɔ:n] *n* cor *m,* corne *f.*
hornbill ['hɔ:nbil] *n* calao *m.*
hornet ['hɔ:nit] *n* frelon *m.*
horrible ['hɔribl] *a* horrible, affreux.
horrid ['hɔrid] *a* affreux.
horrify ['hɔrifai] *vt* horrifier.
horror ['hɔrə] *n* horreur *f.*

horror-struck ['hɔrəstrʌk] *a* saisi, glacé.
horse [hɔ:s] *n* cheval *m,* cavalerie *f,* chevalet *m.*
horseback ['hɔ:sbæk] *ad* **on** — à cheval.
horse-dealer ['hɔ:s.di:lə] *n* maquignon *m.*
horsefly ['hɔ:sflai] *n* taon *m.*
horseman ['hɔ:smən] *n* écuyer *m,* cavalier *m.*
horsemanship ['hɔ:smənʃip] *n* équitation *f.*
horseplay ['hɔ:splei] *n* jeu de vilain *m,* jeu brutal *m.*
horsepower ['hɔ:s.pauə] *n* chevalvapeur *m.*
horse-radish ['hɔ:s.rædiʃ] *n* raifort *m.*
horseshoe ['hɔ:sʃu:] *n* fer à cheval *m.*
horsewoman ['hɔ:s.wumən] *n* cavalière *f,* écuyère *f,* amazone *f.*
hose [houz] *n* tuyau *m,* bas *m pl.*
hosier's ['houʒəz] *n* bonneterie *f.*
hospitable [hɔs'pitəbl] *a* hospitalier.
hospitably [hɔs'pitəbli] *ad* à bras ouverts.
hospital ['hɔspitl] *n* hôpital *m.*
hospitality [.hɔspi'tæliti] *n* hospitalité *f.*
host ['houst] *n* hôte *m,* hostie *f,* armée *f.*
hostage ['hɔstidʒ] *n* ôtage *m.*
hostel ['hɔstəl] *n* foyer *m,* pension *f;* **youth** — auberge de la jeunesse *f.*
hostess ['houstes] *n* hôtesse *f,* maîtresse *f* de maison.
hostile ['hɔstail] *a* hostile, ennemi.
hostility [hɔs'tiliti] *n* hostilité *f.*
hot [hɔt] *a* très chaud, brûlant, qui emporte la bouche.
hotch-potch ['hɔtʃpɔtʃ] *n* salmigondis *m,* macédoine *f.*
hotel [hou'tel] *n* hôtel *m.*
hot-headed ['hɔt'hedid] *a* exalté, impétueux, emporté.
hothouse ['hɔthaus] *n* serre chaude *f.*
hot-line ['hɔtlain] *n* téléphone rouge *m.*
hotpot ['hɔtpɔt] *n* ragoût *m.*
hot-water bottle [hɔt'wɔ:tə.bɔtl] *n* bouillotte *f,* moine *m.*
hough [hɔk] *n* jarret *m.*
hound [haund] *n* chien courant *m; pl* meute *f; vt* chasser.
hour ['auə] *n* heure *f;* — **hand** petite aiguille *f.*
hourly ['auəli] *ad* à toute heure, à l'heure.
house [haus] *n* maison *f,* Chambre *f;* [hauz] *vt* loger, abriter, garer; **town** — hôtel *m* particulier.
house-agent ['haus.eidʒənt] *n* agent de location *m.*
housebreaking ['haus.breikiŋ] *n* vol *m* avec effraction, cambriolage *m.*
household ['haushould] *n* maisonnée *f,* ménage *m,* maison *f.*
householder ['haus.houldə] *n* occupant(e) *mf.*

housekeeper ['haus,ki:pə] n femme de charge f, ménagère f.

housekeeping ['haus,ki:piŋ] n ménage m.

housemaid ['hausmeid] n femme de chambre f, bonne f.

housetop ['haustɔp] n toit m; **to shout from the —s** crier qch sur les toits.

housewarming ['haus,wɔ:miŋ] n **to hold a —** pendre la crémaillère.

housewife ['hauswaif] n ménagère f.

housework ['hauswə:k] n ménage m.

housing ['hauziŋ] n logement m, rentrée f; **— problem** crise de logement f.

hovel ['hɔvəl] n masure f, taudis m.

hover ['hɔvə] vi planer, flâner, hésiter; **—craft** n aéroglisseur m.

how [hau] ad comment, comme, combien.

however [hau'evə] ad cependant; cj quelque (si) . . . que, de quelque manière que.

howitzer ['hauitsə] n obusier m.

howl [haul] n hurlement m; vi hurler, rugir, mugir.

hub [hʌb] n moyeu m, centre m.

huddle ['hʌdl] n tas m, fouillis m; vt entasser, serrer; vi se blottir, s'entasser, se serrer.

hue [hju:] n teinte f, nuance f; **to raise a — and cry against** crier tollé contre.

huff [hʌf] vt offusquer, froisser, souffler; **to take a —** prendre la mouche, s'offusquer; **to be |in a —** être offusqué.

hug [hʌg] n étreinte f; vt étreindre, presser, embrasser, serrer, longer, s'accrocher à.

huge [hju:dʒ] a immense, énorme.

hugeness ['hju:dʒnis] n énormité f, immensité f.

hulk [hʌlk] n carcasse f; pl pontons m pl.

hull [hʌl] n cosse f, coque f.

hullabaloo [,hʌləbə:'lu:] n vacarme m, charivari m.

hum [hʌm] n bourdonnement m, fredonnement m, ronron(nement) m; vi bourdonner, fredonner, ronronner.

human ['hju:mən] a humain.

humane [hju:'mein] a humain, humanitaire.

humanist ['hju:mənist] n humaniste m.

humanity [hju:'mæniti] n humanité f, genre humain m.

humanize ['hju:mənaiz] vt humaniser.

humble ['hʌmbl] a humble; vt humilier, rabattre.

humbug ['hʌmbʌg] n blagueur m, fumiste m, blague f, fumisterie f.

humdrum ['hʌmdrum] a plat, assommant, monotone, quotidien.

humid ['hju:mid] a humide.

humidity [hju:'miditi] n humidité f.

humiliate [hju:'milieit] vt humilier.

humiliation [hju:,mili'eiʃən] n humiliation f.

humility [hju:'militi] n humilité f.

hummock ['hʌmək] n mamelon m, monticule m.

humor ['hju:mə] n humeur f, humour m; vt flatter, se prêter à.

humorist ['hju:mərist] n plaisant m, humoriste m, comique m.

humorous ['hju:mərəs] a humoristique, comique, plaisant, drôle.

hump [hʌmp] n bosse f, cafard m.

humpback(ed) ['hʌmpbæk(t)] an bossu(e) mf.

hunch [hʌntʃ] n bosse f, pressentiment m; vt incurver, voûter.

hundred ['hʌndrid] an cent m.

hundredth ['hʌndridθ] a centième.

hung [hʌŋ] pp pt of **hang**.

Hungarian [hʌŋ'gɛəriən] a hongrois.

Hungary ['hʌŋgəri] n Hongrie f.

hunger ['hʌŋgə] n faim f; vi avoir faim, être affamé.

hunger-strike ['hʌŋgəstraik] n grève f de la faim.

hungry ['hʌŋgri] a qui a (donne) faim, affamé.

hunt [hʌnt] n chasse f; vti chasser; vi chasser à courre.

hunter ['hʌntə] n chasseur m, monture f.

hunting-box ['hʌntiŋbɔks] n pavillon de chasse m.

hunting-ground ['hʌntiŋgraund] n terrain de chasse m.

hunting-horn ['hʌntiŋhɔ:n] n cor de chasse m.

huntsman ['hʌntsmən] n piqueur m, veneur m, chasseur m.

hurdle ['hə:dl] n claie f, haie f, obstacle m; **— race** course de haies f, steeple-chase m.

hurl [hə:l] vt lancer, précipiter.

hurrah [hu'rɑ:] int n hourra m.

hurricane ['hʌrikən] n ouragan m; **—lamp** lampe-tempête f.

hurried ['hʌrid] a pressé, hâtif.

hurriedly ['hʌridli] ad précipitamment, à la hâte.

hurry ['hʌri] n hâte f, urgence f; vt hâter, presser; vi (se) presser, se dépêcher; **in a —** pressé, en toute hâte, de si tôt; **there is no —** rien ne presse.

hurt [hə:t] n mal m, blessure f, tort m, préjudice m; vt faire (du) mal à, blesser, faire tort à; vi faire mal.

hurtful ['hə:tful] a préjudiciable, nocif, nuisible.

husband ['hʌzbənd] n mari m; vt ménager, gérer sagement.

husbandman ['hʌzbəndmən] n fermier m, laboureur m.

husbandry ['hʌzbəndri] n culture f, gestion habile f.

hush [hʌʃ] n silence m, accalmie f; vt faire taire, étouffer; vi se taire; excl chut!

husk [hʌsk] n cosse f, gousse f, balle

f, peau f; vt écosser, décortiquer, éplucher.
husky ['hʌski] a enroué, altéré, fort, costaud; n chien esquimau m.
hussar [hu'zɑː] n hussard m.
hussy ['hʌsi] n effrontée f, luronne f.
hustle ['hʌsl] n bousculade f, activité f, vt bousculer, presser; vi jouer des coudes, se hâter.
hut [hʌt] n cabane f, baraque f; (mil) baraquement m; **straw —** paillotte.
hutch [hʌtʃ] n clapier m.
hyacinth ['haiəsinθ] n jacinthe f, hyacinthe f.
hybrid ['haibrid] an hybride m.
hydrangea [hai'dreindʒə] n hortensia m.
hydrant ['haidrənt] n prise d'eau f.
hydro-electric [‚haidroui'lektrik] a hydraulique; **—-power** houille f blanche.
hydrogen ['haidrədʒən] n hydrogène m.
hydrophobia [‚haidrə'foubjə] n hydrophobie f, rage f.
hyena [hai'iːnə] n hyène f.
hygiene ['haidʒiːn] n hygiène f.
hygienic [hai'dʒiːnik] a hygiénique.
hymn [him] n hymne m.
hyphen ['haifən] n trait d'union m.
hypnosis [hip'nousis] n hypnose f.
hypnotic [hip'nɔtik] a hypnotique.
hypnotism ['hipnətizəm] n hypnotisme m.
hypnotize ['hipnətaiz] vt hypnotiser.
hypocrisy [hi'pɔkrisi] n hypocrisie f.
hypocrite ['hipəkrit] n hypocrite mf.
hypocritical [‚hipə'kritikəl] a hypocrite.
hypothesis [hai'pɔθisis] n hypothèse f.
hypothetical [‚haipou'θetikəl] a hypothétique.
hysteria [his'tiəriə] n hystérie f.
hysterical [his'terikəl] a hystérique, sujet à des crises de nerfs.
hysterics [his'teriks] n crise de nerfs f.

I

I [ai] pn je, moi.
Iain ['iən] (Scot) Jean m.
Iberia [ai'biəriə] n Ibérie f.
Iberian [ai'biəriən] a ibérique; an ibérien, -ienne.
ibex ['aibeks] n chamois m.
ice [ais] n glace f; vt (con)geler, glacer, (wine) frapper.
iceberg ['aisbəːg] n iceberg m, glaçon m.
icebound ['aisbaund] a pris par les glaces.
icecream ['ais'kriːm] n glace f.
ice-floe ['aisflou] n banquise f.
ice-house ['aishaus] n glacière f.
icicle ['aisikl] n glaçon m.

icy ['aisi] a glacial, couvert de glace.
idea [ai'diə] n idée f, notion f.
ideal [ai'diəl] an idéal m.
idealize [ai'diəlaiz] vt idéaliser.
identical [ai'dentikəl] a identique, conforme.
identify [ai'dentifai] vt identifier, établir l'identité de.
identity [ai'dentiti] n identité f.
idiocy ['idiəsi] n idiotie f.
idiom ['idiəm] n dialecte m, locution f, idiome m, idiotisme m; **—atically** ad d'une manière idiomatique.
idiot ['idiət] n idiot(e) mf.
idiotic [‚idi'ɔtik] a idiot, bête.
idle ['aidl] a paresseux, désœuvré, perdu, vain; vi paresser, muser, marcher au ralenti.
idleness ['aidlnis] n paresse f, oisiveté f, chômage m, futilité f.
idler ['aidlə] n fainéant(e) mf, flâneur, -euse, désœuvré(e) mf.
idly ['aidli] ad paresseusement, vainement.
idol ['aidl] n idole f.
idolatrous [ai'dɔlətrəs] a idolâtre.
idolatry [ai'dɔlətri] n idolâtrie f.
idolize ['aidəlaiz] vt idolâtrer, adorer.
if [if] cj si.
igloo ['igluː] n igloo m.
ignite [ig'nait] vt allumer, mettre le feu à; vi prendre feu.
ignition [ig'niʃən] n allumage m, ignition f.
ignoble [ig'noubl] a né bas, ignoble, infâme.
ignominious [‚ignə'miniəs] a ignominieux.
ignominy ['ignəmini] n ignominie f.
ignorance ['ignərəns] n ignorance f.
ignorant ['ignərənt] a ignorant.
ignore [ig'nɔː] vt passer sous silence, méconnaître, ne pas tenir compte de.
ill [il] n mal m, tort m; a malade, mauvais; ad mal.
ill-bred ['il'bred] a mal élevé.
ill-considered ['ilkən'sidəd] a peu réfléchi, hâtif, -ive.
ill-disposed ['ildis'pouzd] a malveillant.
illegal [i'liːgəl] a illégal.
illegality [‚ili:'gæliti] n illégalité f.
illegible [i'ledʒəbl] a illisible.
illegitimacy [‚ili'dʒitiməsi] n illégitimité f.
illegitimate [‚ili'dʒitimit] a illégitime.
ill-fated ['il'feitid] a malchanceux, néfaste.
ill-feeling ['il'fiːliŋ] m rancune f, ressentiment m.
ill-gotten ['il'gɔtn] a mal acquis.
illiberal [i'libərəl] a borne, grossier, mesquin.
illicit [i'lisit] a illicite.
ill-informed ['ilin'fɔːmd] a mal renseigné.
illiterate [i'litərit] an illettré(e) mf.
illness ['ilnis] n maladie f.

ill-starred ['il'stɑːd] *a* né sous une mauvaise étoile, néfaste.

ill-timed ['il'taimd] *a* inopportun, malencontreux.

illuminate [i'luːmineit] *vt* illuminer, éclairer, enluminer.

illumination [i,luːmi'neiʃən] *n* illumination *f*, enluminure *f*.

ill-used ['il'juːzd] *a* malmené, maltraité.

illusion [i'luːʒən] *n* illusion *f*.

illusionist [i'luːʒənist] *n* prestidigitateur *m*.

illusive [i'luːsiv] *a* trompeur, mensonger.

illustrate ['iləstreit] *vt* éclairer, illustrer.

illustration [,iləs'treiʃən] *n* illustration *f*, explication *f*, exemple *m*.

illustrator ['iləstreitə] *n* illustrateur *m*.

illustrious [i'lʌstriəs] *a* illustre, célèbre.

image ['imidʒ] *n* image *f*, statuette *f*.

imagery ['imədʒəri] *n* images *fpl*.

imaginable [i'mædʒinəbl] *a* imaginable.

imaginary [i'mædʒinəri] *a* imaginaire.

imagination [i,mædʒi'neiʃən] *n* imagination *f*.

imaginative [i'mædʒinətiv] *a* imaginatif.

imagine [i'mædʒin] *vt* s'imaginer, se figurer, concevoir, croire, imaginer.

imbecile ['imbəsiːl] *an* imbécile *mf*; *a* faible.

imbecility [,imbi'siliti] *n* imbécillité *f*.

imbibe [im'baib] *vt* boire, absorber, imbiber, adopter.

imbue [im'bjuː] *vt* imprégner, inspirer.

imitate ['imiteit] *vt* imiter.

imitation [,imi'teiʃən] *n* imitation *f*.

imitative ['imitətiv] *a* imitatif, imitateur.

imitator ['imitəitə] *n* imitateur, -trice.

immaculate [i'mækjulit] *a* immaculé, irréprochable.

immaterial [,imə'tiəriəl] *a* immatériel, sans importance.

immature [,imə'tjuə] *a* pas mûr.

immeasurable [i'meʒərəbl] *a* incommensurable, infini.

immediate [i'miːdjət] *a* immédiat, direct, premier.

immediately [i'miːdjətli] *ad* aussitôt, tout de suite.

immemorial [,imi'mɔːriəl] *a* immémorial.

immense [i'mens] *a* immense, vaste.

immensely [i'mensli] *ad* énormément, immensément

immensity [i'mensiti] *n* immensité *f*.

immerse [i'məːs] *vt* immerger, plonger.

immigrant ['imigrənt] *an* immigrant(e) *mf*, immigré(e) *mf*.

immigrate ['imigreit] *vi* immigrer.

immigration [,imi'greiʃən] *n* immigration *f*.

imminence ['iminəns] *n* imminence *f*.

imminent ['iminənt] *a* imminent.

immobility [,imou'biliti] *n* immobilité *f*, fixité *f*.

immoderate [i'mɔdərit] *a* immodéré, démesuré.

immoderately [i'mɔdəritli] *ad* démesurément, immodérément.

immoderation ['i,mɔdər'eiʃən] *n* manque de mesure *m*.

immoral [i'mɔrəl] *a* immoral.

immorality [,imə'ræliti] *n* immoralité *f*.

immortal [i'mɔːtl] *a* immortel.

immortality [,imɔː'tæliti] *n* immortalité *f*.

immortalize [i'mɔːtəlaiz] *vt* immortaliser.

immovable [i'muːvəbl] *a* immuable, inébranlable, insensible.

immune [i'mjuːn] *a* à l'abri (de **to**), réfractaire (à **to**).

immunity [i'mjuːniti] *n* immunité *f*, exemption *f*.

immunize ['imjunaiz] *vt* immuniser.

immutability [i,mjuːtə'biliti] *n* immutabilité *f*.

immutable [i'mjuːtəbl] *a* immuable.

imp [imp] *n* diablotin *m*.

impact ['impækt] *n* choc *m*, collision *f*, impression *f*.

impair [im'pɛə] *vt* affaiblir, altérer.

impairment [im'pɛəmənt] *n* affaiblissement *m*, altération *f*.

impale [im'peil] *vt* empaler.

impart [im'pɑːt] *vt* faire part de, communiquer.

impartial [im'pɑːʃəl] *a* impartial, équitable.

impassable [im'pɑːsəbl] *a* infranchissable, impraticable.

impassibility [,impɑːsə'biliti] *n* impassibilité *f*.

impassioned [im'pæʃnd] *a* passionné.

impassive [im'pæsiv] *a* impassible.

impatience [im'peiʃəns] *n* impatience *f*.

impatient [im'peiʃənt] *a* impatient.

impeach [im'piːtʃ] *vt* mettre en accusation, mettre en cause, attaquer, blâmer.

impeccable [im'pekəbl] *a* impeccable.

impecuniosity [,impikjuːnj'ɔsiti] *n* dénuement *m*.

impecunious [,impi'kjuːnjəs] *a* sans le sou, besogneux.

impede [im'piːd] *vt* entraver, retarder.

impediment [im'pedimənt] *n* empêchement *m*, entrave *f*, obstacle *m*, embarras *m*.

impedimenta [im,pedi'mentə] *n pl* bagages *m pl*.

impel [im'pel] *vt* pousser.

impend [im'pend] *vt* menacer, être imminent.

impenetrable [im'penitrəbl] a impénétrable.

impenitence [im'penitəns] n impénitence f.

impenitent [im'penitənt] a impénitent.

imperative [im'perətiv] an impératif m; a péremptoire, impérieux.

imperceptible [impə'septəbl] a imperceptible, insensible, insaisissable.

imperfect [im'pə:fikt] a imparfait, défectueux.

imperfection [impə'fekʃən] n imperfection f, défectuosité f.

imperial [im'piəriəl] a impérial, majestueux.

imperialism [im'piəriəlizəm] n impérialisme m.

imperialist [im'piəriəlist] an impérialiste mf.

imperil [im'peril] vt mettre en danger.

imperious [im'piəriəs] a impérieux.

imperishable [im'periʃəbl] a impérissable.

impermeable [im'pə:mjəbl] a imperméable.

impersonal [im'pə:snl] a impersonnel.

impersonate [im'pə:səneit] vt se faire passer pour, représenter.

impersonation [im pə:sə'neiʃən] n personnification f, incarnation f, imitation f.

impertinence [im'pə:tinəns] n insolence f, impertinence f.

impertinent [im'pə:tinənt] a impertinent, insolent.

imperturbability [impətə:bə'biliti] n flegme m, imperturbabilité f, sang-froid m.

imperturbable [impə'tə:bəbl] a imperturbable, inaltérable, serein.

impervious [im'pə:vjəs] a impénétrable, imperméable.

impetuosity [im petju'ɔsiti] n impétuosité f.

impetuous [im'petjuəs] a impétueux.

impetus ['impitəs] n impulsion f, élan m.

impiety [im'paiəti] n impiété f.

impinge [im'pindʒ] vi to — upon frapper, se heurter à.

mpious ['impiəs] a impie.

implant [im'pla:nt] vt implanter, inspirer, inculquer.

implement ['implimənt] n instrument m, article m, outil m; pl attirail m, matériel m.

implement ['impliment] vt remplir, exécuter.

implicate ['implikeit] vt mettre en cause, emmêler, impliquer.

implication [impli'keiʃən] n implication f, insinuation f, portée f.

implicit [im'plisit] a implicite, tacite, absolu.

implore [im'plɔ:] vt implorer, supplier.

imploring [im'plɔ:riŋ] a suppliant.

imply [im'plai] vt impliquer, (faire) supposer.

impolite [impə'lait] a impoli.

impolitely [impə'laitli] ad impoliment.

impoliteness [impə'laitnis] n impolitesse.

import ['impɔ:t] n portée f, signification f; pl importations f pl.

import [im'pɔ:t] vt importer, introduire, signifier, dénoter.

importance- [im'pɔ:təns] n importance f, onséquence f.

important [im'pɔ:tənt] a important.

importing [im'pɔ:tiŋ] n importation f.

importunate [im'pɔ:tjunit] a importun, ennuyeux.

importune [impɔ:'tju:n] vt importuner, solliciter.

impose [im'pouz] vt imposer, infliger; to — upon abuser de, en imposer à.

imposition [impə'ziʃən] n imposition f, impôt m, imposture f, supercherie, pensum m.

impossibility [im pɔsə'biliti] n impossibilité f.

impossible [im'pɔsəbl] a impossible.

impostor [im'pɔstə] n imposteur m.

imposture [im'pɔstʃə] n imposture f.

impotence ['impətəns] n impuissance f.

impotent ['impətənt] a impuissant, impotent.

impound [im'paund] vt mettre à la fourrière, saisir, confisquer, enfermer.

impoverish [im'pɔvəriʃ] vt appauvrir.

impoverishment [im'pɔvəriʃmənt] n appauvrissement m.

impracticability [im præktikə'biliti] n impossibilité f.

impracticable [im'præktikəbl] a impraticable, intraitable, infaisable.

impregnable [im'pregnəbl] a imprenable, inexpugnable.

impregnate ['impregneit] vt saturer, imprégner.

impress ['impres] n empreinte f.

impress [im'pres] vt empreindre, timbrer, imprimer, impressionner, enrôler de force.

impression [im'preʃən] n impression f, tirage m.

impressionable [im'preʃnəbl] a impressionnable, susceptible.

impressionism [im'preʃənizəm] n impressionnisme m.

impressive [im'presiv] a frappant, impressionnant.

imprint ['imprint] n empreinte f, griffe f.

imprint [im'print] vt imprimer.

imprison [im'prizn] vt emprisonner.

imprisonment [im'priznmənt] n emprisonnement m, prison f.

improbability [im prɔbə'biliti] n invraisemblance f, improbabilité f.

improbable [im'prɔbəbl] *a* improbable, invraisemblable.

improper [im'prɔpə] *a* impropre, indécent.

impropriety [,imprə'praiəti] *n* impropriété *f*, inconvenance *f*.

improve [im'pru:v] *vt* améliorer, profiter de; *vi* s'améliorer, faire des progrès.

improved [im'pru:vd] *a* amélioré, perfectionné.

improvement [im'pru:vmənt] *n* amélioration *f*, progrès *m* pl, mieux *m*.

improvidence [im'prɔvidəns] *n* imprévoyance *f*.

improvident [im'prɔvidənt] *a* imprévoyant.

improvisation [,imprəvai'zeiʃən] *n* improvisation *f*.

improvise ['imprəvaiz] *vti* improviser.

imprudence [im'pru:dəns] *n* imprudence *f*.

imprudent [im'pru:dənt] *a* imprudent.

impudent ['impjudənt] *a* impudent.

impudently ['impjudəntli] *ad* impudemment.

impugn [im'pju:n] *vt* critiquer, contester.

impulse ['impʌls] *n* impulsion *f*, mouvement *m*, poussée *f*.

impulsive [im'pʌlsiv] *a* impulsif, prime-sautier.

impulsiveness [im'pʌlsivnis] *n* impulsivité *f*.

impunity [im'pjuniti] *n* impunité *f*; **with — impunément.**

impure [im'pjuə] *a* impur, rouillé.

impurity [im'pjuəriti] *n* impureté *f*.

imputable [im'pju:təbl] *a* imputable.

imputation [,impju'teiʃən] *n* imputation *f*, attribution *f*.

impute [im'pju:t] *vt* imputer, attribuer.

in [in] *prep* en, dans, pendant; à, de, sur, par; *ad* y, là, rentré, de retour, à la maison.

inability [,inə'biliti] *n* incapacité *f*, impuissance *f*.

inaccessibility ['inæk,sesə'biliti] *n* inaccessibilité *f*.

inaccessible [,inæk'sesəbil] *a* inaccessible, inabordable.

inaccuracy [in'ækjurəsi] *n* inexactitude *f*.

inaccurate [in'ækjurit] *a* inexact.

inaction [in'ækʃən] *n* inaction *f*, inertie *f*.

inactive [in'æktiv] *a* inactif, inerte.

inactivity [,inæk'tiviti] *n* inactivité *f*.

inadequacy [in'ædikwəsi] *n* insuffisance *f*.

inadequate [in'ædikwit] *a* inadéquat, insuffisant.

inadvertency [,inəd'və:tənsi] *n* inadvertance *f*.

inadvertent [,inəd'və:tənt] *a* inattentif, involontaire.

inadvertently [,inəd'və:təntli] *ad* par mégarde.

inane [i'nein] *a* vide, stupide, inepte.

inanimate ['inænimit] *a* inanimé.

inanity [in'æniti] *n* inanité *f*, niaiserie *f*.

inapposite [in'æpəzit] *a* déplacé.

inappropriate [,inə'proupriit] *a* déplacé, impropre.

inapt [in'æpt] *a* impropre, inapte, inexpert.

inarticulate [,inɑ:'tikjulit] *a* inarticulé, muet.

inasmuch as [inəz'mʌtʃ,æz] *cj* en tant que, vu que.

inattention [,inə'tenʃən] *n* inattention *f*.

inaudible [in'ɔ:dəbl] *a* insaisissable, imperceptible, faible.

inaugural [i'nɔ:gjurəl] *a* inaugural.

inaugurate [i'nɔ:gjureit] *vt* inaugurer, introniser.

inauguration [i,nɔ:gju'reiʃən] *n* inauguration *f*.

inauspicious [,inɔ:s'piʃəs] *a* de mauvais augure, malencontreux.

inborn ['in'bɔ:n] *a* inné, infus.

incandescent [,inkæn'desənt] *a* incandescent.

incapable [in'keipəbl] *a* incapable, incompétent, inaccessible.

incarcerate [in'kɑ:səreit] *vt* incarcérer, emprisonner.

incarceration [in,kɑ:sə'reiʃən] *n* incarcération *f*.

incarnate [in'kɑ:nit] *vt* incarner; *a* incarné.

incarnation [,inkɑ:'neiʃən] *n* incarnation *f*.

incendiary [in'sendjəri] *an* incendiaire *m*.

incense ['insens] *n* encens *m*.

incense [in'sens] *vt* offenser, exaspérer.

incentive [in'sentiv] *n* encouragement *m*, stimulant *m*; *a* stimulant.

inception [in'sepʃən] *n* commencement *m*, début *m*.

incessant [in'sesnt] *a* incessant, continuel.

incessantly [in'sesntli] *ad* incessamment, sans cesse.

incest ['insest] *n* inceste *m*.

incestuous [in'sestjuəs] *a* incestueux.

inch [intʃ] *n* pouce *m*; *vi* avancer, reculer, peu à peu.

incidence ['insidəns] *n* incidence *f*.

incident ['insidənt] *n* incident *m*.

incidental [,insi'dentl] *a* accessoire, fortuit, commun (à **to**); **— expenses** faux frais.

incidentally [,insi'dentəli] *ad* incidemment, en passant.

incinerator [in'sinəreitə] *n* incinérateur *m*.

incise [in'saiz] *vt* inciser.

incision [in'siʒən] *n* incision *f*, entaille *f*.

incisive [in'saisiv] *a* incisif, mordant, pénétrant.

incite [in'sait] *vt* inciter, pousser, exciter.
incitement [in'saitmənt] *n* incitation *f*, instigation *f*.
incivility [,insi'viliti] *n* impolitesse *f*.
inclemency [in'klemənsi] *n* inclémence *f*, rigueur *f*.
inclination [,inkli'neiʃən] *n* inclinaison *f*, pente *f*, inclination *f*.
incline ['inklain] *n* pente *f*, rampe *f*.
incline [in'klain] *vti* incliner, pencher.
include [in'kluːd] *vt* comprendre, englober.
inclusive [in'kluːsiv] *a* inclus, tout compris; — **sum** somme globale.
inclusively [in'kluːsivli] *ad* inclusivement.
incoherence [,inkou'hiərəns] *n* incohérence *f*.
incoherent [,inkou'hiərənt] *a* décousu, incohérent.
income ['inkʌm] *n* revenu *m*; — **tax** impôt *m* sur le revenu.
incomparable [in'kɔmpərəbl] *a* incomparable, hors ligne.
incompatible [,inkəm'pætibl] *a* incompatible, inconciliable.
incompetence [in'kɔmpitəns] *n* incapacité *f*, incompétence *f*.
incomplete [,inkəm'pliːt] *a* incomplet, inachevé.
incomprehensible [,inkɔmpri'hensibl] *a* incompréhensible.
incomprehension[,inkɔmpri'henʃən] *n* inintelligence *f*, incompréhension *f*.
inconceivable [,inkən'siːvəbl] *a* inconcevable.
inconclusive [,inkən'kluːsiv] *a* pas (non) concluant.
incongruity [,inkɔn'gruːiti] *n* incongruité *f*.
incongruous [in'kɔngruəs] *a* incongru, déplacé.
incongruously [in'kɔngruəsli] *ad* incongrûment.
inconsiderable [,inkən'sidərəbl] *a* négligeable, insignifiant.
inconsiderate [,inkən'sidərit] *a* irréflechi, étourdi, sans égard.
inconsistency [,inkən'sistənsi] *n* inconséquence, inconsistance.
inconsistent [,inkən'sistənt] *a* décousu, inconsistant, inconséquent, contradictoire.
inconsolable [,inkən'souləbl] *a* inconsolable.
inconspicuous [,inkən'spikjuəs] *a* effacé, discret.
inconstancy [in'kɔnstənsi] *n* inconstance *f*, instabilité *f*.
inconstant [in'kɔnstənt] *a* inconstant, volage.
incontinently [in'kɔntinəntli] *ad* incontinent, sur-le-champ.
inconvenience [,inkən'viːnjəns] *n* inconvénient *m*, incommodité *f*.
inconvenient [,inkən'viːnjənt] *a* incommode, inopportun.
incorporate [in'kɔːpəreit] *vt* in-

corporer; *vi* se former en société.
incorrect [,inkə'rekt] *a* inexact, incorrect.
incorrigible [in'kɔridʒəbl] *a* incorrigible.
increase ['inkriːs] *n* augmentation *f*,
increase [in'kriːs] *vt* accroître; *vti* augmenter; *vi* s'accroître, s'agrandir.
increasingly [in'kriːsiŋli] *ad* de plus en plus.
incredible [in'kredəbl] *a* incroyable.
incredulous [in'kredjuləs] *a* incrédule, sceptique.
increment ['inkrimənt] *n* accroissement *m*, plus-value *f*.
incriminate [in'krimineit] *vt* inculper, incriminer.
incriminating [in'krimineitiŋ] *a* accusateur, à conviction.
incubate ['inkjubeit] *vti* couver.
incubation [,inkju'beiʃən] *n* couvaison *f*, incubation *f*.
incubator ['inkju,beitə] *n* couveuse artificielle *f*.
inculcate ['inkʌlkeit] *vt* inculquer.
inculpate ['inkʌlpeit] *vt* inculper.
inculpation [,inkʌl'peiʃən] *n* inculpation *f*.
incumbent [in'kʌmbənt] *a* qui incombe (à **upon**).
incur [in'kəː] *vt* encourir, s'attirer, contracter.
incurable [in'kjuərəbl] *a* incurable.
incursion [in'kəːʃən] *n* incursion *f*.
indebted [in'detid] *a* endetté, redevable, obligé.
indebtedness [in'detidnis] *n* dette *f*, obligation *f*.
indecent [in'diːsnt] *a* indécent, inconvenant.
indecision [,indi'siʒən] *n* indécision *f*, irrésolution *f*.
indecisive [,indi'saisiv] *a* indécis(if), peu concluant.
indecorous [in'dekərəs] *a* inconvenant, malséant.
indecorousness [in'dekərəsnis] *n* inconvenance *f*.
indeed [in'diːd] *ad* vraiment, en vérité, en effet, de fait.
indefatigable [,indi'fætigəbl] *a* infatigable.
indefensible [,indi'fensibl] *a* insoutenable, indéfendable.
indefinable [,indi'fainəbl] *a* indéfinissable.
indefinite [in'definit] *a* indéfini, vague, indéterminé.
indelible [in'delibl] *a* indélébile, ineffaçable.
indelicate [in'delikit] *a* indélicat, inconvenant.
indemnify [in'demnifai] *vt* indemniser, dédommager.
indemnity [in'demniti] *n* indemnité *f*, sécurités *f pl*.
indent ['indent] *n* commande *f*, ordre de requisition *m*; [in'dent] *vt* entailler, échancrer; **to — for** commander, réquisitionner.

indentation [ˌinden'teiʃən] *n* échancrure *f*, entaille *f*.

indenture [in'dentʃə] *n* contrat *m*; *vt* lier par contrat.

independence [indi'pendəns] *n* indépendance *f*.

independent [ˌindi'pendənt] *a* indépendant.

independently [ˌindi'pendəntli] *ad* indépendamment, séparément.

indescribable [ˌindis'kraibəbl] *a* indescriptible, indicible.

indestructible [ˌindis'trʌktəbl] *a* indestructible.

index ['indeks] *n* table *f* alphabétique, indice *m*; classeur *m*; *vt* classer, repertorier.

index-card ['indeks,kɑːd] *n* fiche *f*.

India ['indjə] *n* l'Inde *f*.

Indian ['indjən] *an* Indien, -ienne.

india-rubber ['indjə'rʌbə] *n* caoutchouc *m*, gomme *f* (à effacer).

indicate ['indikeit] *vt* indiquer, désigner, dénoter.

indication [ˌindi'keiʃən] *n* indication *f*, signe *m*, indice *m*.

indicative [in'dikətiv] *an* indicatif *m*; *a* suggestif.

indicator ['indikeitə] *n* indicateur *m*, aiguille *f*.

indict [in'dait] *vt* accuser, traduire en justice.

indictment [in'daitmənt] *n* accusation *f*, inculpation *f*.

Indies ['indiz] *n pl* Indes *f pl*; **East** — les Grandes Indes *f*; **West** — les Antilles.

indifference [in'difrəns] *n* indifférence *f*, médiocrité *f*, impartialité.

indifferent [in'difrənt] *a* indifférent, égal, médiocre, impartial.

indigence ['indidʒəns] *n* indigence *f*, misère *f*.

indigenous [in'didʒinəs] *a* indigène, du pays, autochtone.

indigent ['indidʒənt] *a* indigène, nécessiteux.

indigestible [ˌindi'dʒestəbl] *a* indigeste.

indigestion [ˌindi'dʒestʃən] *n* indigestion *f*, mauvaise digestion *f*.

indignant [in'dignənt] *a* indigné.

indignation [ˌindig'neiʃən] *n* indignation *f*.

indignity [in'digniti] *n* indignité *f*, affront *m*.

indigo ['indigou] *n* indigo *m*.

indirect [ˌindi'rekt] *a* indirect, détourné.

indiscernible [ˌindi'səːnəbl] *a* imperceptible.

indiscreet [ˌindis'kriːt] *a* indiscret, imprudent.

indiscretion [ˌindis'kreʃən] *n* indiscrétion *f*, imprudence *f*, sottise *f*.

indiscriminate [ˌindis'kriminit] *a* fait au hasard.

indiscriminately [ˌindis'kriminitli] *ad* au petit bonheur, au hasard.

indispensable [ˌindis'pensəbl] *a* indispensable, de première nécessité.

indispose [ˌindis'pouz] *vt* indisposer (contre), incommoder; **to be** —d être indisposé, souffrant.

indisposition [ˌindispə'ziʃən] *n* indisposition *f*, aversion *f*, malaise *m*.

indisputable [ˌindis'pjuːtəbl] *a* indiscutable, incontestable.

indissoluble [ˌindi'sɔljubl] *a* indissoluble.

indistinct [ˌindis'tiŋkt] *a* confus, vague, indistinct.

indistinctness [ˌindis'tiŋktnis] *n* confusion *f*.

indistinguishable [ˌindis'tiŋgwiʃəbl] *a* impossible à distinguer, imperceptible, insaisissable.

individual [ˌindi'vidjuəl] *n* individu *m*; *a* individuel, particulier.

individuality [ˌindi,vidju'æliti] *n* individualité *f*.

indivisible [ˌindi'vizəbl] *a* indivisible.

Indochina ['indo'tʃainə] *n* Indochine *f*.

indoctrinate [in'dɔktrineit] *vi* endoctriner, instruire.

indolence ['indələns] *n* indolence *f*.

indolent ['indələnt] *a* indolent, paresseux.

indomitable [in'dɔmitəbl] *a* indomptable.

indoor ['indɔː] *a* de salon, de société, d'intérieur; *ad* —s à l'intérieur, à la maison.

induce [in'djuːs] *vt* induire, amener, provoquer, décider.

inducement [in'djuːsmənt] *n* invite *f*, encouragement *m*.

induct [in'dʌkt] *vt* installer, initier.

induction [in'dʌkʃən] *n* installation *f*, induction *f*.

indulge [in'dʌldʒ] *vt* satisfaire, nourrir, gâter; **to** — **in** s'abandonner à, se livrer à.

indulgence [in'dʌldʒəns] *n* goût excessif *m*, indulgence *f*.

indulgent [in'dʌldʒənt] *a* faible, indulgent.

industrial [in'dʌstriəl] *a* industriel.

industrialism [in'dʌstriəlizəm] *n* industrialisme *m*.

industrialist [in'dʌstriəlist] *n* industriel *m*.

industrialize [in'dʌstriəlaiz] *vt* industrialiser.

industrious [in'dʌstriəs] *a* actif, industrieux, laborieux.

industry ['indəstri] *n* industrie *f*, activité *f*, application *f*.

inebriate [i'niːbrieit] *vt* griser, enivrer; *n* ivrogne *m*.

inebriated [i'niːbrieitid] *a* ivre, enivré, grisé.

inebriety [ˌini'braiəti] *n* ébriété *f*, ivresse *f*.

ineffable [ˌin'efəbl] *a* ineffable, indicible.

ineffective [ˌini'fektiv] *a* inefficace, impuissant.

ineffectual [,ini'fektjuəl] *a* vain, stérile, inefficace.

inefficacious [,inefi'keiʃəs] *a* inefficace.

inefficiency [,ini'fiʃənsi] *n* inefficacité *f*, incapacité *f*.

inefficient [,ini'fiʃənt] *a* inefficace, incompétent.

inelastic [,ini'læstik] *a* raide, inélastique, fixe.

inept [i'nept] *a* déplacé, inepte.

ineptitude [i'neptitju:d] *n* ineptie *f*.

inequality [,ini'kwɔliti] *n* inégalité *f*, irrégularité *f*.

ineradicable [,ini'rædikəbl] *a* indéracinable, inextirpable.

inert [i'nə:t] *a* inerte.

inertia [i'nə:ʃə] *n* inertie *f*, paresse *f*.

inestimable [in'estiməbl] *a* inestimable, incalculable.

inevitable [in'evitəbl] *a* inévitable, fatal.

inexact [,inig'zækt] *a* inexact.

inexcusable [,iniks'kju:zəbl] *a* impardonnable, inexcusable.

inexhaustible [,inig'zɔ:stəbl] *a* inépuisable, intarissable.

inexorable [in'eksərəbl] *a* inexorable.

inexpedience [,iniks'pi:djəns] *n* inopportunité *f*.

inexpedient [,iniks'pi:djənt] *a* inopportun, malavisé.

inexpensive [,iniks'pensiv] *a* bon marché, pas cher.

inexperienced [,iniks'piəriənst] *a* inexpérimenté, inexercé.

inexpert [in'ekspə:t] *a* inexpert, maladroit.

inexpiable [in'ekspiəbl] *a* inexpiable.

inexplicable [,iniks'plikəbl] *a* inexplicable.

inexpressible [,iniks'presəbl] *a* inexprimable.

inextinguishable [,iniks'tingwiʃəbl] *a* inextinguible, inassouvissable.

inextricable [in'ekstrikəbl] *a* inextricable.

infallible [in'fæləbl] *a* infaillible.

infallibility [in,fæli'biliti] *n* infaillibilité *f*.

infamous ['infəməs] *a* infâme, abominable.

infamy ['infəmi] *n* infamie *f*.

infancy ['infənsi] *n* première enfance *f*, minorité *f*.

nfant ['infənt] *n* (petit) enfant *mf*, mineur(e) *mf*.

infantile ['infəntail] *a* infantile, enfantin, d'enfant.

infantry ['infəntri] *n* infanterie *f*.

infantryman ['infəntrimən] *n* fantassin *m*.

infatuate [in'fætjueit] *vt* engouer, affoler.

infatuation [in,fætju'eiʃən] *n* folie *f*, engouement *m*.

infect [in'fekt] *vt* infecter, vicier, contagionner.

infection [in'fekʃən] *n* infection *f*, contagion *f*.

infectious [in'fekʃəs] *a* contagieux, infectieux.

infer [in'fə:] *vi* inférer.

inference ['infərəns] *n* inférence *f*, conclusion *f*.

inferior [in'fiəriə] *an* inférieur(e) *mf*; *n* subalterne *m*, subordonné(e) *mf*.

inferiority [in,fiəri'ɔriti] *n* infériorité *f*.

infernal [in'fə:nl] *a* infernal.

infest [in'fest] *vt* infester.

infidel ['infidəl] *an* infidèle *mf*.

infidelity [,infi'deliti] *n* infidélité *f*.

infinite ['infinit] *an* infini *m*.

infinity [in'finiti] *n* infinité *f*.

infirm [in'fə:m] *a* faible, infirme.

infirmary [in'fə:məri] *n* infirmerie *f*, hôpital *m*.

infirmity [in'fə:miti] *n* faiblesse *f*, infirmité *f*.

inflame [in'fleim] *vt* enflammer, mettre le feu à; *vi* s'enflammer.

inflammable [in'flæməbl] *a* inflammable.

inflammation [,inflə'meiʃən] *n* inflammation *f*.

inflammatory [in'flæmətəri] *a* inflammatoire, incendiaire.

inflate [in'fleit] *vt* gonfler, grossir, hausser; *vi* faire de l'inflation.

inflated [in'fleitid] *a* enflé, gonflé, bouffi.

inflation [in'fleiʃən] *n* gonflement *m*, inflation *f*, hausse *f*, enflure *f*.

inflect [in'flekt] *vt* courber, fléchir, moduler.

inflexible [in'fleksəbl] *a* inflexible, inébranlable.

inflict [in'flikt] *vt* infliger, imposer.

influence ['influəns] *n* influence *f*; *vt* influencer.

influential [,influ'enʃəl] *a* influent.

influenza [,influ'enzə] *n* grippe *f*, influenza *f*.

influx ['inflʌks] *n* afflux *m*, affluence *f*.

inform [in'fɔ:m] *vt* informer, avertir, faire savoir à.

informal [in'fɔ:məl] *a* irrégulier, sans cérémonie.

informant [in'fɔ:mənt] *n* informateur, -trice.

information [,infə'meiʃən] *n* informations *f pl*, renseignements *m pl*; **a piece of** — un renseignement.

informative [in'fɔ:mətiv] *a* instructif.

informer [in'fɔ:mə] *n* dénonciateur, -trice, délateur *m*, mouchard *m*.

infraction [in'frækʃən] *n* infraction *f*, violation *f*.

infringe [in'frindʒ] *vt* violer, enfreindre, empiéter sur.

infringement [in'frindʒmənt] *n* infraction *f*, atteinte *f*, violation *f*.

infuriate [in'fjuərieit] *vt* mettre en fureur.

infuriated [in'fjuərieitid] *a* furieux, en fureur.

infuse [in'fju:z] *vti* infuser.

infusion [in'fju:ʒən] *n* infusion *f*, tisane *f*.
ingenious [in'dʒi:njəs] *a* ingénieux.
ingeniousness [in'dʒi:njəsnis] *n* ingéniosité *f*.
ingenuity[ˌindʒə'nju:iti]*n* ingéniosité *f*.
ingenuous [in'dʒenjuəs] *a* franc, ingénu, candide.
ingenuousness [in'dʒenjuəsnis] *n* franchise *f*, naïveté *f*.
inglorious [in'glɔ:riəs] *a* ignominieux.
ingot ['ingət] *n* lingot *m*.
ingrained [in'greind] *a* enraciné, encrassé.
ingratiate [in'greiʃieit] *vt* **to — oneself with** se pousser dans les bonnes grâces de.
ingratiating [in'greiʃieitiŋ] *a* insinuant, doucereux.
ingratitude [in'grætitju:d] *n* ingratitude *f*.
ingredient [in'gri:dʒənt] *n* ingrédient *m*, élément *m*.
ingress ['ingres] *n* entrée *f*.
ingrowing ['inˌgrouiŋ] *a* incarné.
ingrown ['ingroun] *a* incarné, invétéré.
inhabit [in'hæbit] *vt* habiter.
inhabitable [in'hæbitəbl] *a* habitable.
inhabitant [in'hæbitənt] *n* habitant (e) *mf*.
inhalation [ˌinhə'leiʃən] *n* inhalation *f*, aspiration *f*.
inhale [in'heil] *vt* inhaler, aspirer, avaler.
inherent [in'hiərənt] *a* inhérent, propre.
inherit [in'herit] *vt* hériter (de), succéder à.
inheritance [in'heritəns] *n* héritage *m*.
inhibit [in'hibit] *vt* reprimer, inhiber, défendre à.
inhibition [ˌinhi'biʃən] *n* inhibition *f*, défense *f*.
inhospitable [ˌinhɔs'pitəbl] *a* inhospitalier.
inhuman [in'hju:mən] *a* inhumain.
inhumanity [ˌinhju:'mæniti] *n* inhumanité *f*, cruauté *f*.
inhume [in'hju:m] *vt* inhumer, enterrer.
inimical [i'nimikəl] *a* hostile, ennemi.
inimitable [i'nimitəbl] *a* inimitable.
iniquitous [i'nikwitəs] *a* inique.
iniquity [i'nikwiti] *n* iniquité *f*.
initial [i'niʃəl] *n* initiale *f*; *pl* parafe *m*; *a* initial.
initiate [i'niʃieit] *vt* initier.
initiation [iˌniʃi'eiʃən] *n* initiation *f*.
initiative [i'niʃətiv] *n* initiative *f*.
initiator [i'niʃieitə] *n* initiateur, -trice.
inject [in'dʒekt] *vt* injecter, faire une piqûre à, piquer.
injection [in'dʒekʃən] *n* injection *f*, piqûre *f*.

injudicious [ˌindʒu:'diʃəs] *a* malavisé, peu judicieux.
injunction [in'dʒʌŋkʃən] *n* injonction *f*.
injure ['indʒə] *vt* blesser, faire tort à, léser, offenser.
injurious [in'dʒuəriəs] *a* préjudiciable, nocif, injurieux.
injury ['indʒəri] *n* préjudice *m*, blessure *f*, mal *m*, tort *m*.
injustice [in'dʒʌstis] *n* injustice *f*.
ink [iŋk] *n* encre *f*.
inkling ['iŋkliŋ] *n* vague idée *f*, soupçon *m*.
inkwell ['iŋkwel] *n* encrier.
inky ['iŋki] *a* taché d'encre, noir.
inlaid ['in'leid] *a* incrusté.
inland ['inlənd] *an* intérieur *m*; *ad* à (de) l'intérieur.
inlay ['in'lei] *vt* incruster, marqueter, encastrer.
inlaying ['in'leiiŋ] *n* marqueterie *f*, incrustation *f*.
inlet ['inlət] *n* crique *f*, arrivée *f*.
inmate ['inmeit] *n* habitant(e) *mf*, pensionnaire *mf*.
inmost ['inmoust] *a* le plus profond, intime.
inn [in] *n* auberge *f*.
innate [i'neit] *a* inné.
inner ['inə] *a* intérieur, intime.
innings ['iniŋz] *n* manche *f*.
innkeeper ['inki:pə] *n* aubergiste *mf*.
innocence ['inəsns] *n* innocence *f*, candeur *f*.
innocent ['inəsnt] *a* innocent, pur, vierge.
innocuous [i'nɔkjuəs] *a* inoffensif.
innovate ['inouveit] *vi* innover.
innovation [ˌinou'veiʃən] *n* innovation *f*, changement *m*.
innovator ['inouveitə] *n* (in)novateur -trice.
innuendo [ˌinju:'endou] *n* insinuation *f*, sous-entendu *m*.
innumerable [i'nju:mərəbl] *a* innombrable.
inoculate [i'nɔkjuleit] *vt* inoculer, vacciner.
inoculation [iˌnɔkju'leiʃən] *n* inoculation *f*.
inodorous [in'oudərəs] *a* inodore.
inoffensive [ˌinə'fensiv] *a* inoffensif.
inoperative [in'ɔpərətiv] *a* sans action (effet).
inopportune [in'ɔpətju:n] *a* intempestif, inopportun.
inopportunely [in'ɔpətju:nli] *ad* hors de propos.
inordinate [i'nɔːdinit] *a* démesuré, déréglé.
inquest ['inkwest] *n* enquête *f*.
inquire [in'kwaiə] *vti* s'informer (de **about**), demander, se renseigner (sur **about**).
inquiry [in'kwaiəri] *n* question *f*, enquête *f*.
inquisition [ˌinkwi'ziʃən] *n* investigation *f*, inquisition *f*.
inquisitive [in'kwizitiv] *a* curieux.

inquisitiveness [in'kwizitivnis] *n* curiosité aiguë *f*.
inroad ['inroud] *n* incursion *f*; **to make —s upon** entamer.
inrush ['inrʌʃ] *n* irruption *f*.
insane [in'sein] *a* fou, aliéné.
insanity [in'sæniti] *n* insanité *f*, démence *f*, folie *f*.
insatiable [in'seiʃəbl] *a* insatiable, inassouvissable.
inscribe [in'skraib] *vt* inscrire, graver.
inscription [in'skripʃən] *n* inscription *f*.
inscrutable [in'skruːtəbl] *a* impénétrable, fermé.
insect ['insekt] *n* insecte *m*.
insecticide [in'sektisaid] *n* insecticide *m*.
insecure [,insi'kjuə] *a* peu sûr, mal affermi, incertain.
insensible [in'sensəbl] *a* insensible, sans connaissance.
insensibility [in,sensə'biliti] *n* défaillance *f*, insensibilité *f*.
insert [in'səːt] *vt* insérer, introduire.
insertion [in'səːʃən] *n* insertion *f*.
inset ['inset] *n* médaillon *m*, horstexte *m*.
inside [in'said] *an* intérieur *m*; *n* dedans *m*; *ad* à l'intérieur, au dedans; *prep* à l'intérieur de, au dedans de, dans.
insidious [in'sidiəs] *a* insidieux, captieux.
insight ['insait] *n* intuition *f*, perspicacité *f*, aperçu *m*.
insignificance [,insig'nifikəns] *n* insignifiance *f*.
insignificant [,insig'nifikənt] *a* insignifiant.
insincere [,insin'siə] *a* faux, de mauvaise foi.
insincerity [,insin'seriti] *n* insincérité *f*.
insinuate [in'sinjueit] *vt* insinuer.
insinuation [in,sinju'eiʃən] *n* insinuation *f*.
insipid [in'sipid] *a* insipide, fade.
insipidity [,insi'piditi] *n* fadeur *f*, insipidité *f*.
insist [in'sist] *vi* insister, appuyer, soutenir, vouloir.
insistence [in'sistəns] *n* insistance *f*.
insistent [in'sistənt] *a* pressant, importun.
insolence ['insələns] *n* insolence *f*.
insolent ['insələnt] *a* insolent.
insolently ['insələntli] *ad* insolemment.
insoluble [in'sɔljubl] *a* insoluble.
insolvent [in'sɔlvənt] *a* insolvable.
insomnia [in'sɔmniə] *n* insomnie *f*.
inspect [in'spekt] *vt* inspecter, examiner, vérifier, visiter.
inspection [in'spekʃən] *n* inspection *f*, contrôle *m*, revue *f*, visite *f*.
inspector [in'spektə] *n* inspecteur *m*.
inspiration [,inspə'reiʃən] *n* inspiration *f*.
inspire [in'spaiə] *vt* inspirer, aspirer.

inspirit [in'spirit] *vt* animer, enflammer.
instability [,instə'biliti] *n* instabilité *f*.
install [in'stɔːl] *vt* installer, monter.
installation [,instə'leiʃən] *n* installation *f*, montage *m*.
installment [in'stɔːlmənt] *n* acompte *m*, tranche *f*; **on the — system** à tempérament.
instance ['instəns] *n* exemple *m*, cas *m*, instance(s) *f* *pl*; *vt* citer en exemple.
instancy ['instənsi] *n* urgence *f*, imminence *f*.
instant ['instənt] *n* instant *m*; *a* pressant, urgent, du courant.
instantaneous [,instən'teinjəs] *a* instantané.
instantly ['instəntli] *ad* à l'instant, sur-le-champ.
instead [in'sted] *ad* au lieu de cela; *prep* au lieu de (of).
instep ['instep] *n* cou de pied *m*, cambrure *f*.
instigate ['instigeit] *vt* inciter, provoquer.
instigation [,insti'geiʃən] *n* instigation *f*.
instigator ['instigeitə] *n* instigateur, -trice, fauteur *m*.
instill [in'stil] *vt* verser goutte à goutte, infiltrer, inculquer.
instinct ['instiŋkt] *n* instinct *m*; *a* plein.
instinctive [in'stiŋktiv] *a* instinctif.
institute ['institjuːt] *n* institut *m*; *vt* fonder, ouvrir.
institution [,insti'tjuːʃən] *n* institution *f*, établissement *m*.
instruct [in'strʌkt] *vt* former, instruire, ordonner.
instruction [in'strʌkʃən] *n* instruction(s) *f* *pl*; *pl* indications *f* *pl*, ordres *m* *pl*.
instructive [in'strʌktiv] *a* instructif.
instructor [in'strʌktə] *n* instructeur *m*, précepteur *m*.
instrument ['instrumənt] *n* instrument *m*, mécanisme *m*, appareil *m*; **— panel** tableau de bord *m*.
instrumental [,instrə'mentl] *a* qui trouve le moyen de, instrumental, contributif.
insubordinate [,insə'bɔːdinit] *a* insubordonné, mutin.
insubordination ['insə,bɔːdi'neiʃən] *n* insubordination *f*, insoumission *f*.
insufferable [in'sʌfərəbl] *a* intolérable, insupportable.
insufficiency [,insə'fiʃənsi] *n* insuffisance *f*.
insufficient [,insə'fiʃənt] *a* insuffisant.
insular ['insjələ] *a* insulaire.
insularity [,insju'læriti] *n* insularité *f*.
insulate ['insjuleit] *vt* isoler.
insult ['insʌlt] *n* insulte *f*, affront *m*; [in'sʌlt] *vt* insulter, injurier.

insuperable [in'sjuːpərəbl] a insurmontable.

insurance [in'ʃɔːrəns] n assurance f; **life** — assurance sur la vie f; — **company** compagnie f d'assurance(s).

insure [in'ʃɔː] vt assurer, garantir.

insurer [in'ʃɔːrə] n assureur m.

insurgent [in'səːdʒənt] n insurgé(e) mf.

insurrection [ˌinsə'rekʃən] n soulèvement m, émeute f.

intact [in'tækt] a intact, indemne.

intangibility [in.tændʒi'biliti] n intangibilité f.

intangible [in'tændʒəbl] a intangible, impalpable.

integral ['intigrəl] a intégral, intégrant.

integrate ['intigreit] vt compléter, intégrer.

integrity [in'tegriti] n intégrité f, probité f.

intellect ['intilekt] n intellect m, intelligence f.

intellectual [ˌinti'lektjuəl] a intellectuel.

intelligence [in'telidʒəns] n intelligence f, esprit m, sagacité f.

intelligent [in'telidʒənt] a intelligent

intelligible [in'telidʒəbl] a intelligible, compréhensible.

intemperance [in'tempərəns] n intempérance f, alcoolisme m.

intemperate [in'tempərit] a immodéré, intempérant.

intend [in'tend] vt avoir l'intention (de **to**), entendre, projeter (de **to**), vouloir (dire), destiner (à **to**).

intended [in'tendid] n futur(e) mf, prétendu(e) mf; a voulu, projeté.

intense [in'tens] a intense, vif, profond.

intensity [in'tensiti] n intensité f, violence f.

intent [in'tent] n intention f; a appliqué, absorbé, profond.

intention [in'tenʃən] n intention f, dessein m, but m.

intentional [in'tenʃənl] a intentionnel, voulu, fait exprès.

inter [in'təː] vt enterrer.

interaction [ˌintər'ækʃən] n interaction f.

intercede [ˌintəː'siːd] vi intercéder.

intercept [ˌintəː'sept] vt intercepter, arrêter, couper, capter.

interception [ˌintə'sepʃən] n interception f.

intercession [ˌintə'seʃən] n intercession f.

interchange [ˌintə'tʃeindʒ] n échange m, communication f, vt échanger.

intercourse ['intəkɔːs] n commerce m, relations f pl.

interdict ['intədikt] n interdit m, interdiction f; vt interdire (à).

interdiction [ˌintə'dikʃən] n interdiction f.

interest ['intrist] n intérêt m; participation f, crédit m; vt intéres-

ser; **to be** —**ed in** s'intéresser à, s'occuper de.

interesting ['intristiŋ] a intéressant.

interfere [ˌintə'fiə] vi se mêler (de **in**, **with**), s'immiscer (dans **in**), toucher (à **with**), intervenir; **don't** — mêlez-vous de vos affaires.

interference [ˌintə'fiərəns] n ingérence f, intervention f, brouillage m.

interfering [ˌintə'fiəriŋ] a indiscret, fouinard, importun.

interim ['intərim] n intérim m; a intérimaire; ad en attendant.

interior [in'tiəriə] an intérieur m; a interne.

interject [ˌintə'dʒekt] vt interjeter; vi s'écrier.

interjection [ˌintə'dʒekʃən] n interjection f.

interlace [ˌintə'leis] vt entrelacer, entrecroiser.

interlard [ˌintə'lɑːd] vt bigarrer, entremêler.

interlinear [ˌintə'liniə] a interlinéaire.

interlock [ˌintə'lɔk] vt emboîter, enclencher; vi s'emboîter, s'enclencher, s'engrener.

interlocutor [ˌintə'lɔkjutə] n interlocuteur m.

interloper ['intəloupə] n intrus(e) mf, courtier marron m, resquilleur, -euse.

interlude ['intəluːd] n intermède m.

intermediary [ˌintə'miːdjəri] an intermédiaire m.

intermediate [ˌintə'miːdjət] a intermédiaire, intermédiat.

interment [in'təːmənt] n enterrement m.

intermission [ˌintə'miʃən] n interruption f, relache f, pause f, entr'acte m, (school) récréation f.

intermit [ˌintə'mit] vt arrêter, suspendre.

intermittence [ˌintə'mitəns] n intermittence f.

intermittent [ˌintə'mitənt] a intermittent.

intern [in'təːn] vt interner; ['intəːn] n interne.

internal [in'təːnl] a interne, intérieur, intime; — **revenue** n fisc m.

international [ˌintə'næʃnəl] a international; n match international m.

internecine [ˌintə'niːsain] a — **war** guerre f d'extermination réciproque.

internee [ˌintə'niː] n interné(e) mf.

interplay ['intəplei] n jeu croisé m, effet m réciproque (combiné).

interpolate [in'təːpəleit] vt intercaler, interpoler.

interpose [ˌintə'pouz] vt interposer; vi s'interposer.

interpret [in'təːprit] vt interpréter; vi faire l'interprète.

interpretation [in.təːpri'teiʃən] n interprétation f.

interpreter [in'təːpritə] n interprète mf.

interrogate [in'terəgeit] *vt* interroger, questionner.

interrogation [in,terə'geiʃən] *n* interrogation *f*; — **mark** point d'interrogation *m*.

interrogative [,intə'rɔgətiv] *a* interrogateur.

interrupt [,intə'rʌpt] *vti* interrompre.

interrupter [,intə'rʌptə] *n* interrupteur, -trice, coupe-circuit *m*.

interruption [,intə'rʌpʃən] *n* interruption *f*.

intersect [,intə'sekt] *vt* entrecouper, entrecroiser.

intersection [,intə'sekʃən] *n* intersection *f*, croisement *m*.

interstice [in'tə:stis] *n* interstice *m*, alvéole *m*.

interval ['intəvəl] *n* intervalle *m*, entr'acte *m*, mi-temps *f*, récréation *f*.

intervene [,intə'vi:n] *vi* intervenir, séparer, s'interposer.

intervening [,intə'vi:niŋ] *a* qui sépare, qui intervient.

intervention [,intə'venʃən] *n* intervention *f*.

interview ['intəvju:] *n* interview *f*, entrevue *f*; *vt* interviewer, avoir une entrevue avec.

intestinal [in'testinl] *a* intestinal.

intestine [in'testin] *an* intestin *m*.

intimacy ['intiməsi] *n* intimité *f*.

intimate ['intimit] *an* intime *mf*; ['intimeit] *vt* intimer, indiquer, notifier.

intimation [,inti'meiʃən] *n* intimation *f*, avis *m*.

intimidate [in'timideit] *vt* intimider.

intimidation [in,timi'deiʃən] *n* intimidation *f*.

into ['intu] *prep* dans, en, entre.

intolerable [in'tɔlərəbl] *a* insupportable, intolérable.

intolerance [in'tɔlərəns] *n* intolérance *f*.

intolerant [in'tɔlərənt] *a* intolérant.

intonation [,intou'neiʃən] *n* intonation *f*.

intone [in'toun] *vt* psalmodier, entonner.

intoxicate [in'tɔksikeit] *vt* enivrer, tourner la tête à.

intoxication [in,tɔksi'keiʃən] *n* ivresse *f*, intoxication *f*, enivrement *m*.

intractable [in'træktəbl] *a* intraitable, opiniâtre.

intrepid [in'trepid] *a* intrépide.

intrepidity [,intri'piditi] *n* intrépidité *f*.

intricacy ['intrikəsi] *n* complication *f*, complexité *f*.

intricate ['intrikit] *a* compliqué, embrouillé.

intrigue [in'tri:g] *n* intrigue *f*, cabale *f*; *vti* intriguer.

intrinsic [in'trinsik] *a* intrinsèque.

introduce [,intrə'dju:s] *vt* introduire, présenter, initier.

introduction [,intrə'dʌkʃən] *n* introduction *f*, présentation *f*, avant-propos *m*.

introspection [,introu'spekʃən] *n* introspection *f*.

introverted [,introu'və:tid] *a* recueilli, introverti.

intrude [in'tru:d] *vi* faire intrusion, être importun, empiéter (sur **upon**).

intruder [in'tru:də] *n* intrus(e) *mf*, resquilleur, -euse.

intrusion [in'tru:ʒən] *n* intrusion *f*.

intuition [,intju:'iʃən] *n* intuition *f*.

inundate ['inʌndeit] *vt* inonder, déborder.

inundation [,inʌn'deiʃən] *n* inondation *f*.

inure [in'juə] *vt* habituer, endurcir.

invade [in'veid] *vt* envahir, violer.

invader [in'veidə] *n* envahisseur *m*.

invalid [in'vælid] *a* invalide.

invalid ['invəlid] *an* malade *mf*, infirme *mf*; *vt* réformer.

invalidate [in'vælideit] *vt* invalider, casser.

invalidation [in,væli'deiʃən] *n* invalidation *f*.

invalidity [,invə'liditi] *n* invalidité *f*.

invaluable [in'væljuəbl] *a* inestimable.

invariable [in'vɛəriəbl] *a* invariable.

invasion [in'veiʒən] *n* invasion *f*, envahissement *m*.

invective [in'vektiv] *n* invective *f*.

inveigh [in'vei] *vi* se déchaîner, invectiver.

inveigle [in'vi:gl] *vt* séduire, attirer, entraîner.

inveiglement [in'vi:glmənt] *n* séduction *f*, leurre *m*.

invent [in'vent] *vt* inventer.

invention [in'venʃən] *n* invention *f*.

inventiveness [in'ventivnis] *n* imagination *f*.

inventor [in'ventə] *n* inventeur *m*.

inverse [in'və:s] *an* inverse *m*; contraire *m*.

inversion [in'və:ʃən] *n* renversement *m*, inversion *f*.

invert [in'və:t] *vt* retourner, renverser.

invest [in'vest] *vt* (re)vêtir, investir, placer.

investigate [in'vestigeit] *vt* examiner, faire une enquête sur, informer sur.

investigation [in,vesti'geiʃən] *n* investigation *f*, enquête *f*.

investment [in'vestmənt] *n* placement *m*, investissement *m*.

investor [in'vestə] *n* actionnaire *m*, capitaliste *m*.

inveterate [in'vetərit] *a* invétéré, acharné.

invidious [in'vidiəs] *a* odieux, qui fait envie.

invigilate [in'vidʒileit] *vt* surveiller.

invigilation [in,vidʒi'leiʃən] *n* surveillance *f*.

invigilator [in'vidʒileitə] *n* surveillant(e) *mf*.

invigorating [in'vigəreitiŋ] *a* forti-fiant, tonifiant.
invincibility [in.vinsi'biliti] *n* in-vincibilité *f*.
invincible [in'vinsəbl] *a* invincible.
inviolability [in.vaiələ'biliti] *n* in-violabilité *f*.
inviolable [in'vaiələbl] *a* inviolable.
invisibility [in.vizə'biliti] *n* in-visibilité *f*.
invisible [in'vizəbl] *a* invisible, (*ink*) sympathique.
invitation [.invi'teiʃən] *n* invitation *f*.
invite [in'vait] *vt* inviter, demander.
invitingly [in'vaitiŋli] *ad* de manière engageante, tentante.
invocation [.invou'keiʃən] *n* in-vocation *f*.
invoice ['invɔis] *n* facture *f*.
invoke [in'vouk] *vt* invoquer, évo-quer.
involuntary [in'vɔləntəri] *a* in-volontaire.
involve [in'vɔlv] *vt* envelopper, im-pliquer, engager, entraîner, néces-siter.
inward ['inwəd] *a* intérieur, interne.
iodine ['aiədiːn] *n* (teinture *f* d')iode *m*.
irascibility [i.ræsi'biliti] *n* irasci-bilité *m*.
irascible [i'ræsibl] *a* irascible, colé-rique.
irate [ai'reit] *a* en colère, courroucé.
Ireland ['aiələnd] *n* Irlande *f*.
iris ['aiəris] *n* iris *m*.
Irish ['aiəriʃ] *an* irlandais *m*.
Irishman ['aiəriʃmən] *n* Irlandais *m*.
irksome ['əːksəm] *a* ennuyeux, fatigant, ingrat.
iron ['aiən] *n* fer *m*; *a* de fer; *vt* repasser; **to — out** aplatir, effacer au fer chaud.
iron age ['aiəneidʒ] *n* âge *m* de fer.
ironclad ['aiənklæd] *an* cuirassé *m*.
iron-foundry ['aiən.faundri] *n* fon-derie *f*.
iron-gray ['aiəngrei] *a* gris-fer.
ironical [ai'rɔnikəl] *a* ironique.
ironing ['aiəniŋ] *n* repassage *m*.
ironmonger ['aiən.mʌŋgə] *n* quin-cailler *m*.
ironmonger's ['aiən.mʌŋgəz] *n* quin-caillerie *f*.
iron-ore ['aiən'ɔː] *n* minéral *m* de fer.
iron rations ['aiən'ræʃənz] *n* *pl* vivres de réserve *m* *pl*.
ironwork ['aiənwəːk] *n* serrurerie *f*, charpenterie *f* en fer.
irony ['aiərəni] *n* ironie *f*.
irradiate [i'reidieit] *vi* rayonner, iradier.
irradiation [i.reidi'eiʃən] *n* irradia-tion *f*, rayonnement *m*.
irrational [i'ræʃənl] *a* absurde, déraisonnable, irrationnel.
irrecognizable [i'rekəgnaizəbl] *a* méconnaissable.
irreconcilable [i.rekən'sailəbl] *a*

irréconciliable, inconciliable, im-placable.
irrecoverable [.iri'kʌvərəbl] *a* irré-couvrable.
irredeemable [.iri'diːməbl] *a* non remboursable, irréparable, incor-rigible.
irreducible [.iri'djuːsəbl] *a* irré-ductible.
irrefutable [.iri'fjuːtəbl] *a* irréfu-table, irrécusable.
irregular [i'regjulə] *a* irrégulier, inégal.
irrelevant [i'reləvənt] *a* à côté de la question, hors de propos.
irreligious [.iri'lidʒəs] *a* irréligieux.
irremediable [.iri'miːdiəbl] *a* irré-médiable, sans remède.
irremovable [.iri'muːvəbl] *a* inamo-vible.
irreparable [i'repərəbl] *a* irrépa-rable.
irreplaceable [.iri'pleisəbl] *a* irrem-plaçable.
irreproachable [.iri'proutʃəbl] *a* irréprochable.
irresistible [.iri'zistəbl] *a* irrésistible.
irresolute [i'rezəluːt] *a* irrésolu, hésitant, indécis.
irresoluteness [i'rezəluːtnis] *n* irré-solution *f*, indécision *f*.
irrespective [.iri'spektiv] *a* sans égard (à **of**), indépendamment (de **of**), indépendant.
irresponsible [.iris'pɔnsəbl] *a* ir-réfléchi, étourdi.
irresponsive [.iris'pɔnsiv] *a* figé, froid.
irretentive [.iri'tentiv] *a* peu fidèle, peu sûr.
irretrievable [.iri'triːvəbl] *a* irrépa-rable.
irreverence [i'revərəns] *n* irrévé-rence *f*.
irreverent [i'revərənt] *a* irrévéren-cieux, irrévérent.
irrevocable [i'revəkəbl] *a* irrévo-cable.
irrigate ['irigeit] *vt* irriguer, arroser.
irrigation [.iri'geiʃən] *n* irrigation *f*.
irritability [.iritə'biliti] *n* irritabilité *f*.
irritable ['iritəbl] *a* irritable.
irritate ['iriteit] *vt* irriter.
irritating ['iriteitiŋ] *a* irritant, agaçant.
irritation [.iri'teiʃən] *n* irritation *f*.
irruption [i'rʌpʃən] *n* irruption *f*.
Isabel ['izəbel] Isabelle *f*.
island ['ailənd] *n* île *f*, (*street*) refuge *m*.
islander ['ailəndə] *n* insulaire *mf*.
isle [ail] *n* îlot *m*.
islet ['ailit] *n* îlot *m*.
isolate ['aisouleit] *vt* isoler.
isolation [.aisə'leiʃən] *n* isolement *m*, solitude *f*.
issue ['isjuː] *n* issue *f*, progéniture *f*, question *f*, émission *f*, discussion *f*, débouché *m*, terme *m*, tirage *m*,

numéro *m*; *vti* sortir, résulter; *vt*
émettre, publier, lancer.
isthmus ['isθməs] *n* isthme *m*.
Italian [i'tæliən] *n* Italien, -ienne;
an italien *m*.
italics [i'tæliks] *n* italiques *f pl*.
it [it] *pn* il, le; ce, c', cela, ça.
Italy ['itəli] *n* Italie *f*.
itch [itʃ] *n* démangeaison *f*, prurit *m*,
gale *f*; *vi* démanger.
itchy ['itʃi] *a* galeux, qui démange.
item ['aitəm] *n* item *m* de plus,
article *m*, détail *m*, rubrique *f*.
itinerant [i'tinərənt] *a* ambulant,
forain.
itinerary [ai'tinərəri] *n* itinéraire *m*.
its [its] *a* son, sa, ses.
itself [it'self] *pn* soi, lui-, elle-même,
se.
ivory ['aivəri] *n* ivoire *m*.
ivy ['aivi] *n* lierre *m*.

jabber ['dʒæbə] *n* bafouillage *m*; *vi*
bredouiller, baragouiner.
jack [dʒæk] *n* valet *m*, cric *m*,
tourne-broche *m*, cochonnet *m*,
pavillon *m*, brochet *m*; **to — up**
hisser, soulever avec un cric; **— of
all trades** *n* bricoleur *m*; **— o'
lantern** *n* feu follet *m*.
jackal ['dʒækɔːl] *n* chacal *m*.
jackdaw ['dʒækdɔː] *n* choucas *m*.
jacket ['dʒækit] *n* veston *m*, veste *f*,
(*women*) jaquette *f*, (*books*) chemise *f*.
jade [dʒeid] *n* jade *m*, rosse *f*,
effrontée *f*.
jaded ['dʒeïdid] *a* éreinté, fourbu,
excédé.
jaguar ['dʒægjuə] *n* jaguar *m*.
jail [dʒeil] *n* prison *f*, geôle *f*; *vt*
écrouer.
jailbird ['dʒeil.bəːd] *n* gibier de
potence *m*.
jailer ['dʒeilə] *n* gardien de prison
m, geôlier *m*.
jam [dʒæm] *n* confiture *f*, embarras
m, embouteillage *m*, encombrement
m; *vt* presser, bloquer, coincer,
caler, enfoncer, fourrer, brouiller; *vi*
se bloquer, se coincer, se caler.
Jane [dʒein] Jeanne *f*.
jangle ['dʒæŋgl] *vi* crier, grincer,
cliqueter, s'entrechoquer.
January ['dʒænjuəri] *n* janvier *m*.
Japan [dʒə'pæn] *n* Japon *m*.
japan [dʒə'pæn] *n* laque *m*; *vt*
laquer.
Japanese [.dʒæpə'niːz] *n* Japonais(e)
mf; *an* japonais *m*.
jar [dʒɑː] *n* jarre *f*, cruche *f*, bocal *m*,
pot *m*, choc *m*, secousse *f*, grincement *m*; *vt* secouer, ébranler,
agacer; *vi* jurer, détonner.
jargon ['dʒɑːgən] *n* jargon *m*,
baragouin *m*.
jasmine ['dʒæzmin] *n* jasmin *m*.
jasper ['dʒæspə] *n* jaspe *m*.

jaundice ['dʒɔːndis] *n* jaunisse *f*.
jaundiced ['dʒɔːndist] *a* envieux,
bilieux.
jaunt [dʒɔːnt] *n* excursion *f*, sortie *f*,
balade *f*.
jaunty ['dʒɔːnti] *a* enjoué, désinvolte,
vaniteux.
jaw [dʒɔː] *n* mâchoire *f*, mords *m*,
bec *m*, bouche *f*; *vi* bavarder, jaser;
vt semoncer.
jay [dʒei] *n* geai *m*.
jazz [dʒæz] *n* jazz *m*; **— band** jazz
m; *vi* danser le jazz.
jealous ['dʒeləs] *a* jaloux.
jealousy ['dʒeləsi] *n* jalousie *f*.
jeep [dʒiːp] *n* jeep *f*.
jeer [dʒiə] *n* sarcasme *m*, huée *f*; *vi*
ricaner; **to — at** se moquer de, huer.
jelly ['dʒeli] *n* gelée *f*.
jellyfish ['dʒelifiʃ] *n* méduse *f*.
jemmy ['dʒemi] *n* pince-monsei-
gneur *f*.
jeopardize ['dʒepədaiz] *vt* mettre en
danger.
jeopardy ['dʒepədi] *n* danger *m*.
jerk [dʒəːk] *n* saccade *f*, à-coup *m*,
secousse *f*, contraction *f*, convulsion
f; *vt* secouer, tirer d'un coup sec,
tirer par saccades.
jerkily ['dʒəːkili] *ad* par saccades.
jerky ['dʒəːki] *a* saccadé.
jersey ['dʒəːzi] *n* jersey *m*, tricot *m*,
maillot *m*, vareuse *f*.
jest [dʒest] *n* plaisanterie *f*; *vi*
plaisanter.
jester ['dʒestə] *n* bouffon *m*, fou *m*.
jet [dʒet] *n* jais *m*, jet *m*, gicleur *m*,
bec *m*; **— propulsion** autopropul-
sion *f*; **—propelled plane** avion à
réaction *m*.
jetsam ['dʒetsəm] *n* choses *fpl* jetées
par-dessus bord, épaves *f pl*.
jettison ['dʒetizn] *vt* jeter par-dessus
bord, se délester de.
jetty ['dʒeti] *n* jetée *f*, digue *f*.
Jew [dʒuː] *n* Juif *m*.
jewel ['dʒuːəl] *n* bijou *m*, joyau *m*.
jeweler ['dʒuːələ] *n* bijoutier *m*,
joaillier *m*.
jewelry ['dʒuːəlri] *n* bijouterie *f*,
joaillerie *f*.
Jew ['dʒuː] *n* Juif *m*, Juive *f*.
Jewish ['dʒuːiʃ] *a* juif.
Jewry ['dʒuəri] *n* monde juif *m*,
juiverie *f*.
jib [dʒib] *n* foc *m*; *vi* se refuser,
renâcler, regimber.
jiffy ['dʒifi] *n* clin d'œil *m*; **in a —**
en un clin d'œil.
jig [dʒig] *n* gigue *f*, calibre *m*; *vi*
danser la gigue, gigoter.
jigsaw puzzle ['dʒigsɔː'pʌzl] *n* puzzle
m, jeu m de patience.
jilt [dʒilt] *n* coquette *f*; *vt* planter là,
plaquer.
jingle ['dʒiŋgl] *n* tintement *m*,
cliquetis *m*; *vi* cliqueter, tinter; *vt*
faire sonner.
jingoism ['dʒiŋgouizəm] *n* chauvi-
nisme *m*.

jitters ['dʒitəz] n frousse f, trouille f.
Joan [dʒoun] Jeanne f.
job [dʒɔb] n besogne f, affaire f, travail m, place f; vi bricoler.
jobber ['dʒɔbə] n tâcheron m, bricoleur m, tripoteur m.
jobbery ['dʒɔbəri] n tripotage m.
jockey ['dʒɔki] n jockey m; vt duper; vi manœuvrer.
jocose [dʒə'kous] a goguenard, facétieux.
jocular ['dʒɔkjulə] a rieur, badin.
jocund ['dʒɔkʌnd] a enjoué, jovial.
jog [dʒɔg] n cahot m, coup de coude m, petit trot m; vt secouer; vi to — along aller son (petit) train.
John [dʒɔn] Jean m.
join [dʒɔin] n point m, (ligne f de) jonction f, jointure f; vt se joindre à, (re)joindre, (ré)unir, s'inscrire à, relier; vi se (re)joindre; to — up s'engager.
joiner ['dʒɔinə] n menuisier m.
joint [dʒɔint] n joint m, jointure f, articulation f, gond m, pièce f (de viande), rôti m; boîte f (malfamée); **gambling** — tripot m; **juice** — cabaret m borgne; a (con)joint, (ré)uni, en commun; out of — déboîté, démis, déréglé.
jointed ['dʒɔintid] a articulé.
joint-heir ['dʒɔintɛə] n cohéritier m.
jointly ['dʒɔintli] ad conjointement.
joint-stock company ['dʒɔintstɔk'kʌmpæni] n société anonyme f.
joist [dʒɔist] n solive f, poutre f.
joke [dʒouk] n farce f, bon mot m, plaisanterie f, blague f; vi plaisanter; **practical** — farce f.
joker ['dʒoukə] n plaisant m, farceur, -euse; **practical** — mauvais plaisant m.
jollity ['dʒɔliti] n fête f, réjouissance f.
jolly ['dʒɔli] a gai, joyeux, éméché; ad (fam) drôlement, rudement.
jolt [dʒoult] n cahot m, secousse f; vt secouer; vti cahoter.
jonquil ['dʒɔŋkwil] n jonquille f.
Jordan ['dʒɔːdn] n Jordanie f.
jostle ['dʒɔsl] vt pousser, bousculer; vi jouer des coudes.
jot [dʒɔt] n fétu m, brin m; vt to — down noter, griffonner.
journal ['dʒəːnl] n journal m.
journalism ['dʒəːnəlizəm] n journalisme m.
journalist ['dʒəːnəlist] n journaliste mf.
journey ['dʒəːni] n voyage m, trajet m; vi voyager.
journeyman ['dʒəːnimən] n journalier m, compagnon m.
jovial ['dʒouviəl] a jovial.
joviality [,dʒouvi'æliti] n jovialité f.
jowl [dʒaul] n mâchoire f, (ba)joue f.
joy [dʒɔi] n joie f.
joyful ['dʒɔiful] a joyeux.
jubilant ['dʒuːbilənt] a joyeux, réjoui; **to be** — jubiler, exulter.

jubilation [,dʒuːbi'leiʃən] n jubilation f.
jubilee ['dʒuːbiliː] n jubilé m.
Judas ['dʒuːdəs] n judas m.
judge [dʒʌdʒ] n juge m, arbitre m, connaisseur, -euse; vt juger, estimer.
judgment ['dʒʌdʒmənt] n jugement m, avis m, arrêt m, discernement m.
judicature ['dʒuːdikətʃə] n Justice f, Cour f.
judicial [dʒuː'diʃəl] a juridique, judiciaire, légal, impartial.
judicious [dʒuː'diʃəs] a judicieux.
jug [dʒʌg] n broc m, cruche f, (fam) violon m.
jugged [dʒʌgd] a cuit à l'étuvée, en civet; emprisonné, coffré.
juggle ['dʒʌgl] vi jongler, faire des tours de passe-passe; to — away escamoter.
juggler ['dʒʌglə] n jongleur m, bateleur m.
juggling ['dʒʌgliŋ] n jonglerie f, tours de passe-passe m pl.
juice [dʒuːs] n jus m.
juicy ['dʒuːsi] a juteux.
Julian ['dʒuːliən] n Julien m.
July [dʒuː'lai] n juillet m.
jumble ['dʒʌmbl] n fouillis m; vt mêler, brouiller.
jump [dʒʌmp] n saut m, bond m, haut-le-corps m; vi sauter, bondir, tressaillir; vt sauter, franchir.
jumper ['dʒʌmpə] n sauteur, -euse, tricot m, vareuse f.
jumpiness ['dʒʌmpinis] n nervosité f.
jump rope ['dʒʌmproup] n corde f à sauter.
junction ['dʒʌŋkʃən] n jonction f, bifurcation f, gare d'embranchement f.
juncture ['dʒʌŋktʃə] n jointure f, conjoncture f.
June [dʒuːn] n juin m.
jungle ['dʒʌŋgl] n jungle f.
junior ['dʒuːniə] an cadet, -ette; a jeune; n subalterne m.
juniper ['dʒuːnipə] n genièvre m.
junk [dʒʌŋk] n vieilleries f pl, jonque f; **piece of** — rossignol m; drogue f.
junket ['dʒʌŋkit] n lait caillé m, bombance f.
jurisdiction [,dʒuəris'dikʃən] n juridiction f, ressort m.
jurist ['dʒuərist] n juriste m.
jury ['dʒuəri] n jury m.
just [dʒʌst] a juste, équitable; ad (tout) juste, au juste, justement, précisément, seulement, simplement, à l'instant, rien que; **I have** — **seen him** je viens de le voir; **he** — **laughed** il ne fit que rire; — **as** tout comme.
justice [dʒʌstis] n justice f, juge m.
justifiable [,dʒʌsti'faiəbl] a justifiable, légitime.
justification [,dʒʌstifi'keiʃən] n justification f.

justify ['dʒʌstifai] vt justifier.
justness ['dʒʌstnis] n justice f,
justesse f.
jut [dʒʌt] vi — **out** faire saillie,
avancer.
jute [dʒuːt] n jute m
juvenile ['dʒuːvənail] a juvenile,
jeune.
juxtapose ['dʒʌkstəpouz] vt juxtaposer.

K

kangaroo [ˌkæŋgə'ruː] n kangourou
m.
keel [kiːl] n quille f.
keen [kiːn] a (objet) aiguisé, affilé;
vif, acerbe; fin, perçant; (pers) zélé,
passionné (de on), enragé (de); **I am
not — on it** je n'y tiens pas.
keenness ['kiːnnis] n (obj) acuité f;
(pers) empressement m, ardeur f,
enthousiasme m.
keep [kiːp] n donjon m, subsistance
f; vt garder, tenir, observer, célébrer;
— s.o. waiting faire attendre qn;
vi se tenir rester, se conserver,
continuer (de); **— from** s'empêcher de; **— in** entretenir; **kept in**
en retenue; **— on** continuer de, à;
— to tenir, garder.
keeper ['kiːpə] n gardien, -ienne,
conservateur m, garde mf.
keeping ['kiːpiŋ] n garde f, harmonie
f, observation f, célébration f.
keg [keg] n barillet m, caque f.
ken [ken] n portée f, connaissances
f pl.
kennel ['kenl] n chenil m, niche f.
kept [kept] pp pt of **keep**.
kerchief ['kəːtʃif] n fichu m, mouchoir de tête m.
kernel ['kəːnl] n amande f, chair f,
grain m, noyau m, essentiel m.
kettle ['ketl] n bouilloire f.
kettledrum ['ketldrʌm] n timbale f.
key [kiː] n clé f, clef f, touche f, mot
m, corrigé m; a essentiel, clé; vt
accorder; **to — up** stimuler.
keyboard ['kiːbɔːd] n clavier m.
keyhole ['kiːhoul] n trou de la
serrure m.
keynote ['kiːnout] n clé f, tonique f,
note dominante f.
key-ring ['kiːriŋ] n porte-clefs m inv.
keystone ['kiːstoun] n clé de voûte f.
kick [kik] n coup de pied m, ruade
f, recul m, ressort m; plaintes
f pl, critiques f pl; vi donner un coup
de pied, ruer, reculer; vt pousser du
pied, donner un coup de pied à,
botter.
kick-off ['kikɔf] n coup d'envoi m.
kid [kid] n chevreau m, (fam) gosse
mf.
kidnap ['kidnæp] vt enlever.
kidnapper ['kidnæpə] n ravisseur,
-euse.

kidney ['kidni] n rein m, rognon m,
acabit m, trempe f.
kill [kil] n mise à mort f; vt tuer,
abattre.
killing ['kiliŋ] n tuerie f, massacre m;
a meurtrier, tuant, mortel, tordant.
killjoy ['kildʒɔi] n rabat-joie m.
kiln [kiln] n four m.
kin [kin] n race f, souche f, parenté f,
parents m pl; a allié, apparenté;
next of — le plus proche parent,
famille f.
kind [kaind] n espèce f, sorte f,
genre m; **in —** en nature; a bon,
aimable.
kindergarten ['kindəˌgaːtn] n école
f maternelle, jardin m d'enfants.
kindle [kindl] vt allumer, enflammer;
vi s'allumer, prendre feu, flamber.
kindly ['kaindli] ad avec bonté, ayez
l'obligeance de; a bon, bienveillant.
kindness ['kaindnis] n bonté f,
amabilité f.
kindred ['kindrid] n parenté f; a
analogue.
king [kiŋ] n roi m, (draughts) dame f.
kingdom ['kiŋdəm] n royaume m,
règne m.
kingfisher ['kiŋfiʃə] n martin-
pêcheur m.
kingly ['kiŋli] a royal.
kingship ['kiŋʃip] n art de régner m,
royauté f.
kink [kiŋk] n nœud m, lubie f.
kinsfolk ['kinzfouk] n parenté f,
famille f.
kipper ['kipə] n hareng fumé m; vt
saler, fumer.
kirk [kəːk] n (Scot) église f.
kiss [kis] n baiser m; vt embrasser,
baiser.
kissing ['kisiŋ] n embrassade f.
kit [kit] n fourniment m, effets m pl,
fourbi m, baluchon m, trousse f.
kit-bag ['kitbæg] n sac m.
kitchen ['kitʃin] n cuisine f.
kitchen-garden ['kitʃin'gaːdn] n
jardin potager m.
kitchen-maid ['kitʃinmeid] n fille de
cuisine f.
kitchen-range ['kitʃin'reindʒ] n fourneau m, cuisinière f.
kite [kait] n milan m, ballon d'essai
m, cerf-volant m.
kitten ['kitn] n chaton m.
knack [næk] n tour m de main,
adresse f, coup m, truc m.
knacker ['nækə] n équarisseur m.
knapsack ['næpsæk] n sac m, havresac m.
knave [neiv] n gredin m, (cards) valet
m.
knead [niːd] vt pétrir, masser.
kneading-trough ['niːdiŋˌtrɔf] n pétrin m.
knee [niː] n genou m.
knee-breeches ['niːˌbriːtʃiz] n culotte f.
knee-cap ['niːkæp] n rotule f;
genouillère f.

kneel [niːl] *vi* s'agenouiller.
knell [nel] *n* glas *m*.
knew [njuː] *pt of* **know**.
knickerbockers ['nikəbɔkəz] *n* culotte *f*.
knickers ['nikəz] *n* pantalon *m* (de femme), culotte *f*.
knife [naif] *n* couteau *m*; *vt* donner un coup de couteau à, suriner.
knife-board ['naifbɔːd] *n* planche à couteaux *f*.
knife-grinder ['naif.graində] *n* rémouleur *m*.
knight [nait] *n* chevalier *m*; *vt* créer (armer) chevalier.
knighthood ['naithud] *n* rang de chevalier *m*
knit [nit] *vt* tricoter; **to — one's brows** froncer les sourcils; **well—** serré.
knitting ['nitiŋ] *n* tricotage *m*, tricot *m*; **— needle** aiguille à tricoter *f*.
knob [nɔb] *n* bosse *f*, bouton *m*, morceau *m*, pomme *f*.
knock [nɔk] *n* coup *m*; *vti* frapper, cogner; **to — about** *vt* bousculer, malmener; *vi* rouler sa bosse; **to — down** renverser, abattre, adjuger; **to — off** quitter le travail; **to — out** mettre hors de combat, mettre knock-out.
knocker ['nɔkə] *n* marteau *m*.
knock-kneed ['nɔk'niːd] *a* cagneux.
knoll [noul] *n* monticule *m*, tertre *m*.
knot [nɔt] *n* nœud *m*, groupe *m*; *vt* nouer, embrouiller.
knotty ['nɔti] *a* noueux, compliqué.
know [nou] *vt* connaître, reconnaître, savoir; **to be in the —** être dans le secret.
knowing ['nouiŋ] *a* averti, éveillé, fin, rusé, entendu.
knowingly ['nouiŋli] *ad* sciemment, finement, à bon escient.
knowledge ['nɔlidʒ] *n* connaissance *f*, savoir *m*, science *f*; **not to my —** pas que je sache; **without my —** à mon insu; **to have a thorough — of** connaître à fond.
knuckle ['nʌkl] *n* phalange *f*, articulation *f*, jointure *f*; **— of veal** jarret de veau *m*.
knuckle-bone ['nʌkl'boun] *n* osselet *m*.
knuckleduster ['nʌkl.dʌstə] *n* coup-de-poing américain *m*.
kola ['koulə] *n* **— nut** noix *f* de kola; **— tree** kolatier *m*.
Koran [kɔːˈræn] *n* Coran *m*.

L

label ['leibl] *n* étiquette *f*; *vt* étiqueter, classer.
labor ['leibə] *n* travail *m*, classe ouvrière *f*, main-d'œuvre *f*; **— exchange** bureau de placement *m*, bourse du Travail *f*; **— party** parti travailliste *m*; *vt* élaborer, travailler; *vi* travailler, peiner.
laboratory [ləˈbɔrətəri] *n* laboratoire *m*.
labored ['leibəd] *a* cherché, travaillé, pénible.
laborer ['leibərə] *n* manœuvre *m*.
laborious [ləˈbɔːriəs] *a* laborieux, ardu, pénible.
laboriousness [ləˈbɔːriəsnis] *n* application *f*.
laburnum [ləˈbəːnəm] *n* cytise *m*.
labyrinth ['læbərinθ] *n* labyrinthe *m*, dédale *m*.
lace [leis] *n* lacet *m*, galon *m*, dentelle *f*, point *m*; *vt* lacer, galonner, garnir de dentelle, nuancer, corser.
lace-maker ['leis'meikə] *n* fabricant de dentelles *m*, dentellière *f*.
lacerate ['læsəreit] *vt* lacérer.
lachrymal ['lækriməl] *a* lacrymal.
lachrymatory ['lækrimətəri] *a* lacrymogène.
lachrymose ['lækrimous] *a* larmoyant.
lack [læk] *n* manque *m*, défaut *m*, besoin *m*; **for — of** faute de; *vt* manquer de.
lackadaisical [.lækə'deizikəl] *a* maniéré, affecté, langoureux.
lackey ['læki] *n* laquais *m*.
lacking ['lækiŋ] *a* qui manque, en défaut; *prep* à défaut de, faute de.
lacquer ['lækə] *n* laque *m*, vernis-laque *m*; *vt* laquer.
lad [læd] *n* (jeune) garçon *m*, gars *m*, gaillard *m*.
ladder ['lædə] *n* échelle *f*, maille *f* filée.
lade [leid] *vt* charger; *n* bief *m*.
lading ['leidiŋ] *n* chargement *m*.
ladle ['leidl] *n* louche *f*.
lady ['leidi] *n* dame *f*, Lady; *pl* mesdames, mesdemoiselles; **—in-waiting** dame d'honneur *f*; **L— Day** Annonciation *f*.
ladybird ['leidibəːd] *n* bête à bon Dieu *f*, coccinelle *f*.
ladylike ['leidilaik] *a* de dame, comme il faut.
lag [læg] *n* retard *m*, décalage *m*, cheval de retour *m*, repris de justice *m*; *vi* traîner, rester en arrière.
laggard ['lægəd] *n* traînard *m*, lambin(e) *mf*; *a* lent.
lagging ['lægiŋ] *n* revêtement calorifuge *m*.
lagoon [ləˈguːn] *n* lagune *f*.
laic ['leiik] *n* laïque.
laicize ['leiisaiz] *vt* laïciser.
laid [leid] *pt pp of* **lay**; **— up** mis en réserve, remisé, alité.
lain [lein] *pp of* **lie** (être couché).
lair [lɛə] *n* tanière *f*, repaire *m*.
laity ['leiiti] *n* laïques *m pl*, amateurs *m pl*.
lake [leik] *n* lac *m*; *a* lacustre.
lamb [læm] *n* agneau *m*.
lambkin ['læmkin] *n* agnelet *m*.

lame [leim] *a* boiteux, faible; *vt* rendre boiteux, estropier.

lameness ['leimnis] *n* boiterie *f*, claudication *f*, faiblesse *f*.

lament [lə'ment] *n* lamentation *f*; *vt* déplorer, pleurer; *vi* se lamenter.

lamentable ['læməntəbl] *a* lamentable, déplorable.

lamented [lə'mentid] *a* regretté.

lamp [læmp] *n* lampe *f*, lanterne *f*; **standard —** lampadaire *m*, lampe *f* de parquet.

lamplighter ['læmp'laitə] *n* allumeur de réverbères *m*.

lampoon [læm'puːn] *n* libelle *m*; *vt* déchirer, chansonner.

lampoonist [læm'puːnist] *n* libelliste *m*.

lamp-post ['læmppoust] *n* réverbère *m*.

lampshade ['læmpʃeid] *n* abat-jour *m*.

lance [lɑːns] *n* lance *f*.

lancer ['lɑːnsə] *n* lancier *m*.

lancet ['lɑːnsit] *n* lancette *f*.

land [lænd] *n* terre *f*, sol *m*, pays *m*; *vti* débarquer; *vi* atterrir, descendre; *vt* asséner.

landed ['lændid] *a* foncier.

land-holder ['lænd,houldə] *n* propriétaire *mf*, foncier, -ière.

landing ['lændiŋ] *n* débarquement *m*, atterrissage *m*, palier *m*; **forced —** atterrissage forcé *m*.

landing-place ['lændiŋpleis] *n* débarcadère *m*, terrain d'atterrissage *m*.

landing-net ['lændiŋnet] *n* épuisette *f*.

landlady ['læn,leidi] *n* propriétaire *f*.

landlord ['lænlɔːd] *n* propriétaire *m*, patron *m*.

landowner ['lænd,ounə] *n* propriétaire *mf*, foncier, -ière.

landscape ['lænskeip] *n* paysage *m*.

landslide ['lændslaid] *n* éboulement *m*.

land-tax ['lændtæks] *n* impôt foncier *m*.

lane [lein] *n* sentier *m*, ruelle *f*.

language ['læŋgwidʒ] *n* langage *m*, langue *f*.

languid ['læŋgwid] *a* languissant, mou.

languidly ['læŋgwidli] *ad* languissamment, mollement.

languish ['læŋgwiʃ] *vi* languir.

languishing ['læŋgwiʃiŋ] *a* langoureux.

languor ['læŋgə] *n* langueur *f*.

languorous ['læŋgərəs] *a* langoureux.

lank [læŋk] *a* efflanqué, plat.

lantern ['læntən] *n* lanterne *f*, fanal *m*, falot *m*.

lap [læp] *n* giron *m*, sein *m*, pan *m*, lobe *m*, creux *m*, tour *m* (de piste), lapement *m*, lampée *f*, clapotis *m*; *vt* laper, lamper, (sea) lécher, faire le tour de; *vi* clapoter.

lapdog ['læpdɔg] *n* bichon *m*.

lapel [lə'pel] *n* revers *m*.

lapidary ['læpidəri] *n* lapidaire *m*.

Lapland ['læplænd] *n* Laponie *f*.

lapse [læps] *n* faux-pas *m*, lapsus *m*, laps de temps *m*, déchéance *f*; *vi* s'écouler, déchoir, manquer (à **from**).

lapsed [læpst] *a* déchu, périmé, caduc.

larboard ['lɑːbəd] *n* bâbord *m*.

larceny ['lɑːsni] *n* larcin *m*.

larch [lɑːtʃ] *n* mélèze *m*.

lard [lɑːd] *n* saindoux *m*.

larder ['lɑːdə] *n* garde-manger *m*.

large [lɑːdʒ] *a* large, gros, grand, vaste; **at —** au large, en liberté.

largeness ['lɑːdʒnis] *n* (width) largeur *f*, grandeur *f*, grosseur *f*.

lark [lɑːk] *n* alouette *f*, farce *f*.

larkspur ['lɑːkspə] *n* pied-d'alouette *m*.

laser ['leizə] *n* laser *m*.

lash [læʃ] *n* coup de fouet *m*, lanière *f*; *vti* fouailler, cingler; *vt* attacher, amarrer; **to — out** éclater, se ruer.

lass [læs] *n* fille *f*, bonne amie *f*.

lassitude ['læsitjuːd] *n* lassitude *f*.

last [lɑːst] *n* forme *f*, fin *f*; *a* dernier; **— but one** avant-dernier; **— night** cette nuit, la nuit dernière, hier soir; *vi* durer, tenir, faire.

lastly ['lɑːstli] *ad* enfin.

latch [lætʃ] *n* loquet *m*; **— key** passe-partout *m*; *vt* fermer au loquet.

late [leit] *a* tard, tardif, en retard, dernier, feu; **—comer** retardataire; **to be — for** être en retard pour; **the train is —** le train a du retard; **it is getting —** il se fait tard.

lately ['leitli] *ad* récemment.

lateness ['leitnis] *n* heure tardive *f*, retard *m*.

latent ['leitənt] *a* latent.

lateral ['lætərəl] *a* latéral, transversal.

laterite ['lætərait] *n* terre de barre *f*, latérite *f*.

lath [lɑːθ] *n* latte *f*.

lathe [leið] *n* tour *m*.

lather ['lɑːðə] *n* mousse *f*, écume *f*; *vt* savonner, rosser; *vi* mousser, écumer.

latitude ['lætitjuːd] *n* largeur *f*, latitude *f*, liberté *f*.

latter ['lætə] *a* dernier, second, celui-ci, celle-ci, ceux-ci, celles-ci.

lattice ['lætis] *n* treillis *m*, treillage *m*.

laudable ['lɔːdəbl] *a* louable.

laudatory ['lɔːdətəri] *a* élogieux.

laugh [lɑːf] *n* rire *m*; *vi* rire.

laughable ['lɑːfəbl] *a* risible, ridicule.

laughing ['lɑːfiŋ] *n* rire *m*; *a* à rire; **— gas** gaz hilarant *m*; **— stock** risée *f*.

laughter ['lɑːftə] *n* rire *m*; **to roar with —** rire aux éclats, rire à gorge déployée.

launch [lɔːntʃ] *n* lancement *m*, chaloupe *f*; *vt* lancer, déclencher; *vi* se lancer.

launderette [lɔːndə'ret] *n* laverie *f*, blanchisserie *f* automatique.
laundress ['lɔːndris] *n* blanchisseuse *f*.
laundry ['lɔːndri] *n* blanchissage *m*, blanchisserie *f*, linge *n*.
laureate ['lɔːriit] *n* lauréat *m*.
laurel ['lɔrəl] *n* laurier *m*.
lava ['lɑːvə] *n* lave *f*.
lavatory ['lævətəri] *n* lavabo *m*, cabinets *m pl*, toilette *f*.
lavender ['lævində] *n* lavande *f*.
lavish ['læviʃ] *a* prodigue, somptueux; *vt* prodiguer, gaspiller.
lavishness ['læviʃnis] *n* prodigalité *f*.
law [lɔː] *n* loi *f*, droit *m*; —**abiding** *a* respectueux de la loi; **L— Courts** Palais de Justice *m*.
lawful ['lɔːful] *a* légal, légitime.
lawfulness ['lɔːfulnis] *n* respect de la loi *m*, légalité *f*.
lawless ['lɔːlis] *a* sans foi ni loi, effréné, déréglé, anarchique.
lawlessness ['lɔːlisnis] *n* mépris de la loi *m*, anarchie *f*.
lawn [lɔːn] *n* pelouse *f*, gazon *m*.
lawn-mower ['lɔːn,mouə] *n* tondeuse *f*.
lawsuit ['lɔːsjuːt] *n* procès *m*.
lawyer ['lɔːjə] *n* homme de loi *m*, jurisconsulte *m*.
lax [læks] *a* lâche, relâché, vague, mou, inexact.
laxity ['læksiti] *n* laxité *f*, relâchement *m*, mollesse *f*.
lay [lei] *pt of* **lie** (être couché); *n* lai *m*, spécialité *m*; *a* lai, laïque, profane, amateur; *vt* coucher, étendre, abattre, placer, mettre, déposer, parier, pondre; **to — the table** mettre le couvert; **to — aside** se défaire de, mettre de côté; **to — down** déposer, quitter; **to — off** congédier; **to — out** étaler, aménager, assomer, tracer.
layer ['leiə] *n* couche *f*, marcotte *f*, banc *m*, pondeuse *f*.
lay-figure ['lei'figə] *n* mannequin *m*.
laying ['leiiŋ] *n* pose *f*, ponte *f*.
lay-off ['leiɔf] *n* (*workers*) mortesaison *f*.
layout ['leiaut] *n* tracé *m*, dessin *m*, disposition *f* typographique.
lazily ['leizili] *ad* nonchalamment, paresseusement.
laziness ['leizinis] *n* paresse *f*.
lazy ['leizi] *a* paresseux.
lead [liːd] *n* exemple *m*, tête *f*, (*dogs*) laisse *f*, (*cards*) main *f*, câble *m*, premier rôle *m*; *vti* mener, conduire; *vt* diriger, porter; *vi* (*cards*) avoir la main.
lead [led] *n* plomb *m*.
leaden ['ledn] *a* de plomb, plombé, lourd.
leader ['liːdə] *n* chef *m*, directeur *m*, meneur *m*, guide *m*, éditorial *m*.
leadership ['liːdəʃip] *n* direction *f*, commandement *m*.
leading ['liːdiŋ] *a* principal, de tête;

— case précédent *n*; **— question** question qui postule la réponse; **— strings** lisières *f pl*.
leaf, *pl* **leaves** [liːf, liːvz] *n* feuille *f*, rallonge *f*.
leafless ['liːflis] *a* sans feuilles, effeuillé, dépouillé.
leaflet ['liːflit] *n* feuillet *m*, prospectus *m*, papillon *m*.
leafy ['liːfi] *a* feuillu, touffu.
league [liːg] *n* lieue *f*, ligne *f*; **L— of Nations** Société des Nations *f*; *vi* se liguer.
leak [liːk] *n* fuite *f*, voie d'eau *f*; *vi* fuir, avoir une fuite, faire eau; **to — out** transpirer.
leakage ['liːkidʒ] *n* fuite *f*.
lean [liːn] *a* maigre; *n* inclinaison *f*; *vt* pencher, appuyer; *vi* s'appuyer, se pencher, incliner.
leaned [liːnd] *pt pp of* **lean**.
leaning ['liːniŋ] *n* penchant *m*, penchement *m*, tendance *f*.
leanness ['liːnnis] *n* maigreur *f*.
leap [liːp] *n* saut *m*; —**frog** sautemouton *m*; **— year** année bissextile *f*; *vti* sauter.
leapt [lept] *pt pp of* **leap**.
learn [ləːn] *vt* apprendre.
learned ['ləːnid] *a* savant.
learning ['ləːniŋ] *n* savoir *m*, érudition *f*.
lease [liːs] *n* bail *m*; **on —** à bail; *vt* louer, affermer.
leaseholder ['liːshouldə] *n* locataire *mf*.
leash [liːʃ] *n* laisse *f*; *vt* tenir en laisse.
least [liːst] *n* le moins; *a* le, la moindre; **at —** au (du) moins; **not in the —** pas le moins du monde; *ad* (le) moins.
leather ['leðə] *n* cuir *m*; **patent —** cuir verni *m*.
leave [liːv] *n* permission *f*, congé *m*; **on —** en permission, en congé; —**taking** départ *m*, adieu *m*; *vt* laisser, quitter; *vi* partir.
leaven ['levn] *n* levain *m*; *vt* faire lever, tempérer.
Lebanon ['lebənən] *n* Liban *m*.
lecherous ['letʃərəs] *a* lascif, lubrique.
lechery ['letʃəri] *n* lasciveté *f*, luxure *f*.
lectern ['lektə(ː)n] *n* lutrin *m*.
lecture ['lektʃə] *n* conférence *f*, semonce *f*; *vi* faire des conférences; *vt* faire la leçon à; **to — on** faire un cours de.
lecturer ['lektʃərə] *n* conférencier *m*, maître de conférences *m*, chargé de cours *m*.
lectureship ['lektʃəʃip] *n* maîtrise de conférences *f*.
led [led] *pt pp of* **lead**.
ledge [ledʒ] *n* rebord *m*, corniche *f*, banc de rochers *m*.
ledger ['ledʒə] *n* grand-livre *m*.
lee [liː] *n* abri *m*; *a* abrité.
leech [liːtʃ] *n* sangsue *f*.

leek [li:k] *n* poireau *m.*
leer [liə] *n* regard de côté *m,* œillade *f;* *vi* regarder de côté, faire de l'œil (à at).
lees [li:z] *n* lie *f.*
leeward ['li:wəd] *a ad* sous le vent.
leeway ['li:wei] *n* dérive *f,* retard *m.*
left [left] *pt pp of* **leave**; *n* gauche *f;* *a* gauche; **on the** — à gauche; —**handed** gaucher, morganatique, de la main gauche; —**wing** de gauche; — **over** laissé de côté; —**overs** restes *m pl.*
leg [leg] *n* jambe *f,* cuisse *f,* gigot *m,* pied *m.*
legacy ['legəsi] *n* legs *m.*
legal ['li:gəl] *a* légal, judiciaire, licite.
legality [li(:)'gæliti] *n* légalité *f.*
legalize ['li:gəlaiz] *vt* légaliser, autoriser.
legate ['legit] *n* légat *m.*
legatee [,legə'ti:] *n* légataire *mf.*
legation [li'geiʃən] *n* légation *f.*
legator ['legitə] *n* testateur *m.*
legend ['ledʒənd] *n* légende *f.*
leggings ['legiŋz] *n* jambières *f pl,* guêtres *f pl.*
leggy ['legi] *a* haut sur pattes, dégingandé.
legibility [,ledʒi'biliti] *n* lisibilité *f.*
legible ['ledʒəbl] *a* lisible.
legion ['li:dʒən] *n* légion *f.*
legionary ['li:dʒənəri] *n* légionnaire *m.*
legislate ['ledʒisleit] *vi* légiférer.
legislation [,ledʒis'leiʃən] *n* législation *f.*
legislative ['ledʒislətiv] *a* législatif.
legislator ['ledʒisleitə] *n* législateur *m.*
legislature ['ledʒisleitʃə] *n* législature *f.*
legitimacy [li'dʒitiməsi] *n* légitimité *f.*
legitimate [li'dʒitimit] *a* légitime.
legitimation [li.dʒiti'meiʃən] *n* légitimation *f.*
legitimize [li'dʒitimaiz] *vt* légitimer, reconnaître.
leisure ['leʒə] *n* loisir *m.*
leisurely ['leʒəli] *a* qui n'est jamais pressé, tranquille; *ad* à loisir, à tête reposée.
lemon ['lemən] *n* citron *m.*
lemonade [,lemə'neid] *n* limonade *f.*
lend [lend] *vt* prêter; — **lease** prêt-bail *m.*
lender ['lendə] *n* prêteur, -euse.
length [leŋθ] *n* longueur *f;* **full** — en pied; **at** — longuement, enfin.
lengthwise ['leŋθwaiz] *a ad* dans le sens de la longueur.
lengthy ['leŋθi] *a* long.
leniency ['li:niənsi] *n* douceur *f,* indulgence *f.*
lenient ['li:niənt] *a* indulgent, doux.
leniently ['li:niəntli] *ad* avec douceur (indulgence).
lenity ['leniti] *n* clémence *f.*
lens [lenz] *n* lentille *f,* loupe *f.*

lent [lent] *pt pp of* **lend.**
Lent [lent] *n* carême *m.*
lentil ['lentil] *n* lentille *f.*
leopard ['lepəd] *n* léopard *m.*
leper ['lepə] *n* lépreux, -euse.
leprosy ['leprəsi] *n* lèpre *f.*
lesbian ['lezbiən] *an* lesbien, -enne, saphiste.
lesion ['li:ʒən] *n* lésion *f.*
less [les] *n* (le) moins; *a* moindre, moins de; *prep ad* moins, (*in many compounds*) sans.
lessee [le'si:] *n* locataire *mf,* tenancier, -ière, preneur *m.*
lessen ['lesn] *vti* diminuer; *vi* décroître.
lesser ['lesə] *a* moindre.
lesson ['lesn] *n* leçon *f.*
lessor [le'sɔ:] *n* bailleur, -eresse.
lest [lest] *cj* de peur que.
let [let] *vt* laisser, louer; — **us go** partons; — **him do it** qu'il le fasse; — **alone** sans parler de; **to** — **alone** laisser tranquille; **to** — **down** baisser, descendre, laisser tomber; **to** — **in** faire, laisser entrer; **to** — **on** cafarder; **to** — **off** décharger; **to** — **out** laisser échapper, (re)lâcher; **to** — **through** laisser passer; **to** — **up** (*rain*) diminuer; se relâcher.
lethal ['li:θəl] *a* mortel, meurtrier.
lethargic [le'θa:dʒik] *a* léthargique.
lethargy ['leθədʒi] *n* léthargie *f.*
letter ['letə] *n* lettre *f;* — **bound** *a* esclave de la lettre; —**box** boîte aux lettres *f;* —**card** carte-lettre *f;* — **pad** bloc-notes *m.*
lettuce ['letis] *n* laitue *f.*
leukemia [lju'ki:miə] *n* leucémie *f.*
levee ['levi] *n* lever *m.*
level [levl] *n* niveau *m;* *a* uni, régulier, en palier; — **with** au même niveau que, au ras de; —**crossing** passage *m* à niveau; —**headed** pondéré; *vt* niveler, viser.
leveler ['levələ] *n* niveleur *m.*
leveling ['levliŋ] *n* nivellement *m.*
lever ['li:və] *n* levier *m,* manette *f.*
leveret ['levərit] *n* levraut *m.*
levity ['leviti] *n* légèreté *f.*
levy ['levi] *n* levée *f;* *vt* lever, imposer, percevoir.
lewd [lju:d] *a* luxurieux.
lewdness ['lju:dnis] *n* luxure *f,* lasciveté *f.*
Lewis ['lu(:)is] Louis *m.*
lexicon ['leksikən] *n* lexique *m.*
liability [,laiə'biliti] *n* responsabilité *f;* *pl* engagements *m pl,* passif *m.*
liable ['laiəbl] *a* passible (de for), responsable, sujet (à to).
liar ['laiə] *n* menteur, -euse.
libel ['laibəl] *n* diffamation *f,* libelle *m;* *vt* diffamer.
libeler ['laibələ] *n* diffamateur, -trice.
libelous ['laibələs] *a* diffamatoire, calomnieux.
liberal ['libərəl] *n* libéral *m;* *a* large, libéral, prodigue.

liberalism ['libərəlizəm] n libéralisme m.
liberality [.libə'ræliti] n libéralité f, générosité f.
liberate ['libəreit] vt libérer.
liberation [.libə'reiʃən] n libération f.
liberator ['libəreitə] n libérateur, -trice.
libertine ['libə(:)tiːn] an libertin m; n débauché m.
liberty ['libəti] n liberté f.
librarian [lai'brɛəriən] n bibliothécaire m.
library ['laibrəri] n bibliothèque f; lending — b. de prêt; free — b. publique; circulating — b. circulante.
lice [lais] n pl poux m pl.
license ['laisəns] n permission f, autorisation f, permis m, licence f, patente f.
license ['laisəns] vt autoriser, patenter, accorder un permis à.
licentious [lai'senʃəs] a libre, licencieux.
licentiousness [lai'senʃəsnis] n licence f.
lichen ['laikən] n lichen m.
licit ['lisit] a licite.
lick [lik] n coup m de langue; vt lécher, rosser, battre à plate couture, (sur)passer; to — up laper; to — into shape dégrossir.
licking ['likiŋ] n râclée f.
lid [lid] n couvercle m.
lie [lai] n mensonge m, démenti m; disposition f, tracé m, gîte m; vi mentir, être couché, étendu, être resté, se trouver, (bank) déposer; it lies with cela dépend de; to — down se coucher, filer doux; to — up garder la chambre, désarmer; — in n (fam) grasse matinée f.
lieutenant [lef'tenənt] n lieutenant m; second— sous-lieutenant m.
life [laif] n vie f; —boat canot m de sauvetage; —buoy bouée m de sauvetage; — estate propriété f en viager; — saving sauvetage m; — savings économies f pl.
lifeless ['laiflis] a inanimé.
lifelike ['laiflaik] a d'après nature, vivant.
life-size ['laif'saiz] a en pied.
lifetime ['laiftaim] n vie f, vivant m.
lift [lift] n ascenseur m, montecharge m, montée f, (in a car) place f, coup d'épaule m; vt lever, soulever, pendre, voler; vi s'élever, se dissiper.
light [lait] n lumière f, clarté f, jour m, phare m, feu m; vt allumer, éclairer; vi s'allumer, s'éclairer, s'abattre, tomber; a léger, clair; —handedness légèreté de main f; —headed étourdi; —hearted gai, allègre; — minded frivole.
lighten ['laitn] vt alléger, soulager, éclairer, éclaircir; vi s'éclairer, faire des éclairs.

lighter ['laitə n briquet m, chaland m.
lighthouse ['laithaus] n phare m.
lighting ['laitiŋ] n allumage m, éclairage m.
lightness ['laitnis] n légèreté f.
lightning ['laitniŋ] n éclair m, foudre f; a prompt comme l'éclair, foudroyant; — conductor paratonerre m.
light-ship ['laitʃip] n bateau-feu m, bouée lumineuse f.
lightweight ['laitweit] a léger, poids léger.
likable ['laikəbl] a sympathique.
like [laik] an semblable mf, pareil, -eille mf; a ressemblant; prep comme; vt aimer, vouloir, désirer.
likelihood ['laiklihud] n vraisemblance f, probabilité f.
likely ['laikli] a probable, propre, susceptible, plein de promesse; ad probablement.
liken ['laikən] vt comparer.
likeness ['laiknis] n ressemblance f, portrait m.
likewise ['laikwaiz] ad de même, aussi.
liking ['laikiŋ] n goût m, penchant m, sympathie f, gré m.
lilac ['lailək] n lilas m.
lily ['lili] n lis m; a de lis; — of the valley muguet m.
limb [lim] n membre m, bras m, branche maîtresse f.
limber ['limbə] n avant-train m; vt atteler; a souple.
limbo ['limbou] n limbes m pl.
lime [laim] n glu f, chaux f, tilleul m, limon m.
lime-juice ['laimdʒuːs] n limonade f, jus de limon m.
lime-kiln ['laimkiln] n four à chaux m.
limelight ['laimlait] n rampe f, feu de la publicité m, vedette f.
limestone ['laimstoun] n pierre à chaux f.
limit ['limit] n limite f, borne f; comble m; vt limiter, borner, restreindre.
limitation [.limi'teiʃən] n limitation f.
limited ['limitid] a à responsabilité limitée, restreint.
limp [limp] n claudication f; vi boiter; a souple, mou.
limpid ['limpid] a limpide.
limpidity [lim'piditi] n limpidité f.
limy ['laimi] a gluant, calcaire.
linden ['lindən] n tilleul m.
line [lain] n ligne f, file f, voie f, trait m, corde f, câble m, fil m, vers m; vt tracer, régler, sillonner, rider, aligner, border, doubler, remplir, garnir; vi s'aligner; to become lined se rider.
lineage ['liniidʒ] n lignage m, lignée f.
lineament ['liniəmənt] n linéament m.

linear ['liniə] *a* linéaire.
linen ['linin] *n* toile *f* (de lin), linge *m*.
liner ['lainə] *n* paquebot *m*.
linger ['liŋgə] *vi* tarder, trainer, subsister, s'attarder.
lingerer ['liŋgərə] *n* lambin(e) *mf*, retardataire *mf*.
lining ['lainiŋ] *n* doublure *f*, coiffe *f*, garniture *f*.
link [liŋk] *n* chaînon *m*, anneau *m*, lien *m*, maille *f*; *vt* (re)lier, enchaîner, unir, serrer; *vi* s'attacher (à **to**); **to** — **arms** se donner le bras.
links [liŋks] *n* (terrain *m* de) golf.
linnet ['linit] *n* linotte *f*.
linseed ['linsi:d] *n* graîne de lin *f*.
lint [lint] *n* charpie *f*.
lintel ['lintl] *n* linteau *m*.
lion ['laiən] *n* lion *m*; — **cub** lionceau *m*.
lioness ['laiənis] *n* lionne *f*.
lip [lip] *n* lèvre *f*, babine *f*, bord *m*; *vt* toucher des lèvres.
lipstick ['lipstik] *n* rouge à lèvres *m*, bâton de rouge *m*
liquefaction [,likwi'fækʃən] *n* liquéfaction *f*.
liquefy ['likwifai] *vt* liquéfier.
liqueur [li'kjuə] *n* liqueur *f*; — **stand** cabaret *m*, cave à liqueurs *f*.
liquid ['likwid] *an* liquide *m*.
liquidate ['likwideit] *vt* liquider.
liquidation [,likwi'deiʃən] *n* liquidation *f*.
liquidator ['likwideitə] *n* liquidateur *m*.
liquidizer ['likwidaizə] *m*, mixe(u)r *m*.
liquor ['likə] *n* boisson alcoolique *f*.
liquorice ['likəris] *n* réglisse *f*.
lisp [lisp] *n* zézaiement *m*, bruissement *m*; *vti* zézayer.
lissom ['lisəm] *a* souple.
list [list] *n* liste *f*, tableau *m*, lisière *f*, bourrelet *m*, gîte *f*, (*pl*) lice *f*; **wine** — **carte** *f* des vins; **honors** — palmarès *m*; *vt* cataloguer; *vi* donner de la bande.
listen ['lisn] *vti* écouter.
listener ['lisnə] *n* écouteur, -euse, auditeur, -trice.
listless ['listlis] *a* apathique.
listlessness ['listlisnis] *n* apathie *f*.
lit [lit] *pt pp of* **light**.
litany ['litəni] *n* litanie *f*.
literal ['litərəl] *a* littéral.
literary ['litərəri] *a* littéraire; — **man** littérateur *m*, homme de lettres *m*.
literature ['litəritʃə] *n* littérature *f*.
lithe [laið] *a* souple.
litheness ['laiðnis] *n* souplesse *f*.
litigant ['litigənt] *n* plaideur, -euse, partie *f*.
litigate ['litigeit] *vi* plaider, être en procès.
litigation [,liti'geiʃən] *n* litige *m*.
litigious [li'tidʒəs] *a* litigieux, processif.
litter ['litə] *n* litière *f*, détritus *m*,

fouillis *m*, portée *f*; — **bin** poubelle *f*; *vt* encombrer.
little ['litl] *n* peu *m* (de chose); *ad* peu; *a* petit; **a** — un peu.
live [laiv] *a* vivant, vrai, vital, ardent, chargé.
live [liv] *vi* vivre, demeurer, habiter, durer; **to** — **down** user, faire oublier; **to** — **up to** se hausser à, faire honneur à; **long** —! vive!
livelihood ['laivlihud] *n* gagne-pain *m*, vie *f*.
liveliness ['laivlinis] *n* vivacité *f*, entrain *m*.
lively ['laivli] *a* vivant, vif, animé, plein de vie.
liven ['laivn] *vt* animer; **to** — **up** *vi* s'animer.
liver ['livə] *n* foie *m*.
liverish ['livəriʃ] *a* bilieux, amer.
livery ['livəri] *n* livrée *f*, compagnie *f*.
livestock ['laivstɔk] *n* bétail *m*, bestiaux *m pl*.
livid ['livid] *a* livide.
living ['liviŋ] *n* vie *f*, gagne-pain *m*, poste *m*, cure *f*; — **room** salle *f* de séjour, living-room *m*.
lizard ['lizəd] *n* lézard *m*.
load [loud] *n* charge *f*, chargement *m*, poids *m*, tas *m*; *vt* charger, accabler, combler; *vi* prendre charge.
loaded ['loudid] *a* chargé; — **cane** canne plombée *f*; — **dice** dés pipés *m pl*.
loadstone ['loudstoun] *n* aimant *m*.
loaf [louf] *n* pain *m*; *vi* fainéanter.
loafer ['loufə] *n* fainéant *m*, voyou *m*.
loam [loum] *n* glaise *f*, torchis *m*.
loan [loun] *n* prêt *m*, emprunt *m*.
loath [louθ] *a* qui répugne à.
loathe [louð] *vt* détester, abhorrer.
loathsome ['louðsəm] *a* répugnant, écœurant.
lobby ['lɔbi] *n* salle *f*, vestibule *m*, couloirs *m pl*; *vi* intriguer.
lobster ['lɔbstə] *n* homard *m*; — **pot** casier à homard *m*, langouste *f*.
local ['loukəl] *a* local, du lieu, du pays, en ville; — **road** route vicinale *f*; *n pl* examens locaux *m pl*.
locality [lou'kæliti] *n* localité *f*, emplacement *m*, parages *m pl*, région *f*, endroit *m*.
localize ['loukəlaiz] *vt* localiser.
locate [lou'keit] *vt* situer, repérer; *vi* s'établir, trouver.
location [lou'keiʃən] *n* position *f*, repérage *m*.
loch [lɔx] *n* (*Scot*) lac *m*, bras de mer *m*.
lock [lɔk] *n* flocon *m*, mèche *f*, serrure *f*, écluse *f*, embouteillage *m*, enrayure *f*; *vt* fermer à clef, mettre sous clef, caler, serrer, écluser; *vi* se bloquer, s'empoigner.
locker ['lɔkə] *n* casier *m*, caisson *m*, armoire *f*.
locket ['lɔkit] *n* médaillon *m*.
lockjaw ['lɔkdʒɔ:] *n* tétanos *m*.

lock-out ['lɔkaut] *n* lockout *m*.
locksmith ['lɔksmiθ] *n* serrurier *m*.
lock-up ['lɔkʌp] *n* fermeture *f*, (*jail*) violon *m*, garage *m*, box *m*.
locomotive ['loukə,moutiv] *n* locomotive *f*.
locum ['loukəm] *n* remplaçant(e) *mf*.
locust ['loukəst] *n* sauterelle *f*, locuste *f*.
lode [loud] *n* filon *m*; —**stone** aimant *m*.
lodge [lɔdʒ] *n* loge *f*, atelier *m*, pavillon *m*; *vt* loger, (con)tenir, déposer; **to** — **a complaint** porter plainte; *vi* (se) loger.
lodger ['lɔdʒə] *n* locataire *mf*, pensionnaire *mf*.
lodging ['lɔdʒiŋ] *n* logement *m*, chambres *f pl* meublées, garni *m*; — **house** hôtel meublé *m*, hôtel à la nuit *m*.
loft [lɔft] *n* grenier *m*, soupente *f*, galerie *f*, pigeonnier *m*.
loftiness ['lɔftinis] *n* hauteur *f*, sublimité *f*, élévation *f*.
lofty ['lɔfti] *a* haut, hautain, élevé, sublime.
log [lɔg] *n* bûche *f*; *vt* débiter en bûches, enregistrer; — **book** livre de bord *m*, carnet de route *m*.
loggerhead ['lɔgəhed] *n* bûche *f*; **at —s** à couteaux tirés.
logic ['lɔdʒik] *n* logique *f*.
logical ['lɔdʒikəl] *a* logique.
loin [lɔin] *n* rein *m*, (*meat*) longe *f*; —**chop** côtelette de filet *f*; —**cloth** pagne *m*.
loiter ['lɔitə] *vi* traîner (en route), s'attarder.
loiterer ['lɔitərə] *n* flâneur, -euse, rôdeur *m*.
loll [lɔl] *vi* pendre, se prélasser; **to —back** se renverser, s'appuyer; **to — about** flâner, fainéanter; **to — out** its tongue tirer la langue.
lollipop ['lɔlipɔp] *n* sucette *f*, sucre d'orge *m*.
London ['lʌndən] *n* Londres *m*.
lone [loun] *a* solitaire.
loneliness ['lounlinis] *n* solitude *f*, isolement *m*.
lonely ['lounli] *ad* esseulé, seul, solitaire.
loner ['lounə] *n* solitaire *m*.
long [lɔŋ] *a* long; *ad* (depuis, pendant, pour) longtemps; *vi* aspirer (à to, for), avoir bien envie (de to, for), attendre avec impatience; —**sightedness** presbytie *f*, prévoyance *f*; —**suffering** *a* patient.
longevity [lɔn'dʒeviti] *n* longévité *f*.
longhand ['lɔŋhænd] *n* écriture *f* ordinaire, courante.
longing ['lɔŋiŋ] *n* aspiration *f*, nostalgie *f*, grande envie *f*.
longitude ['lɔŋgitjuːd] *n* longitude *f*.
long-standing [lɔŋ'stændiŋ] *a* de longue terme, durée, connaissance, date *f*.

longways ['lɔŋweiz] *ad* dans le sens de la longueur.
look [luk] *n* regard *m*, air *m*, mine *f*; *vi* regarder, avoir l'air (de); **to — after** prendre soin de; **to — at** regarder; **to — for** attendre, chercher, guetter; **to — in** regarder dans, entrer en passant; **to — out** regarder au dehors, prendre garde; **to — out on** donner sur; **to — through** parcourir, repasser.
looker-on ['lukər'ɔn] *n* spectateur, -trice, badaud(e) *mf*.
look-out ['luk'aut] *n* qui-vive *m*, guet *m*, poste d'observation *m*, vigie *f*, guetteur *m*, perspective *f*.
looking-glass ['lukiŋglɑːs] *n* miroir *m*, glace *f*.
loom [luːm] *n* métier *m*; *vi* se montrer à l'horizon, surgir; **to — ahead, large** paraître imminent, menacer.
loony ['luːni] *a* (*fam*) cinglé.
loop [luːp] *n* boucle *f*, anse *f*, huit *m*; *vt* boucler.
loophole ['luːphoul] *n* meurtrière *f*, trou *m*, échappatoire *f*.
loose [luːs] *a* libre, lâche, décousu, dissolu, desserré, détaché; *vt* délier, dénouer, défaire, détacher.
loosen ['luːsn] *vt* relâcher, desserrer, dénouer; *vi* se défaire, se relâcher, se desserrer.
loot [luːt] *n* butin *m*; *vt* piller, saccager.
lop [lɔp] *n* branchette *f*; *vt* élaguer, couper; *vi* pendre.
lopsided ['lɔp'saidid] *a* bancal, déjeté, de guingois.
lord [lɔːd] *n* Seigneur *m*, Lord *m*, maître *m*; *vi* **to — it** faire son grand seigneur.
lordly ['lɔːdli] *a* seigneurial, hautain.
lore [lɔː] *n* savoir *m*, science *f*.
lorry ['lɔri] *n* camion *m*.
lose [luːz] *vt* perdre.
loser ['luːzə] *n* perdant(e) *mf*.
loss [lɔs] *n* perte *f*; **at a —** à perte, désorienté; **at a — to** en peine de.
lost [lɔst] *pt pp of* **lose**; — **and found** bureau des objets trouvés *m*.
lot [lɔt] *n* (tirage *m* au) sort *m*, partage *m*, lot *m*, tas *m*; *ad* beaucoup de, nombre de, quantité de.
lotion ['louʃən] *n* lotion *f*.
lottery ['lɔtəri] *n* loterie *f*.
loud [laud] *a* haut, fort, bruyant, criard, tapageur.
loudly ['laudli] *ad* à voix haute, bruyamment.
loudness ['laudnis] *n* hauteur *f*, force *f*, fracas *m*.
loudspeaker ['laud'spiːkə] *n* haut-parleur *m*.
lounge [laundʒ] *n* flânerie *f*, divan *m*, hall *m*, salon *m* (d'attente); *vi* flâner, tuer le temps, se prélasser.
lounger ['laundʒə] *n* flâneur, -euse.
lour ['lauə] *vi* se renfrogner, se couvrir, menacer.

louse [laus] n pou m; pl poux m pl.
lousy ['lauzi] a pouilleux; — **trick** sale coup m, cochonnerie f.
lout [laut] n butor m, rustre m, lourdaud m.
love [lʌv] n amour m, amitiés f pl; vt aimer; —-**letter** billet-doux m, lettre d'amour f; —-**making** cour f; —-**match** mariage d'amour m.
loveliness ['lʌvlinis] n charme m, beauté f, fraîcheur f.
lovely ['lʌvli] a ravissant, charmant, adorable.
lover ['lʌvə] n amant m, amoureux m, fiancé m.
loving ['lʌviŋ] a affectueux, tendre.
lovingly ['lʌviŋli] ad tendrement, affectueusement.
low [lou] n beuglement m; vi beugler, meugler, mugir; a bas, décolleté, commun; —**down** n to give s.o. the —**down** renseigner qn; —-**grade** de qualité inférieure; ad bas; at — **level** à rase-mottes, bas, en contre-bas.
lower ['louə] a (plus) bas; vt baisser, abaisser, affaiblir.
lowliness ['loulinis] n humilité f.
lowly ['louli] a humble.
loyal ['bɔiəl] a loyal, fidèle.
loyalty ['bɔiəlti] n loyauté f, fidélité f.
lozenge ['bɔzindʒ] n losange m, tablette f.
lubber ['lʌbə] n pataud m, empoté m; **land**— terrien m, marin d'eau douce m.
lubricate ['lu:brikeit] vt lubrifier, graisser.
lucerne [lu:'sə:n] n luzerne f.
lucid ['lu:sid] a lucide.
lucidity [lu:'siditi] n lucidité f, transparence f.
luck [lʌk] n chance f, veine f; **bad** — malchance f, déveine f, guignon m.
luckily ['lʌkili] ad heureusement, par bonheur.
lucky ['lʌki] a heureux; — **dog** veinard(e) mf; — **penny** porte-bonheur m.
lucrative ['lu:krətiv] a lucratif.
lucre ['lu:kə] n lucre m.
Lucy ['lu:si] Lucie f, Luce f.
ludicrous ['lu:dikrəs] a absurde, grotesque.
lug [lʌg] vt traîner, trimbaler.
luggage ['lʌgidʒ] n bagages m pl; — **rack** filet m; — **room** salle des bagages f; — **ticket** bulletin m; — **van** fourgon m.
lugubrious [lu:'gu:briəs] a lugubre.
lukewarm ['lu:kwɔ:m] a tiède.
lull [lʌl] n accalmie f, trêve f; vt bercer, endormir; vi se calmer, s'apaiser.
lullaby ['lʌləbai] n berceuse f.
lumbago [lʌm'beigou] n lumbago m.
lumber ['lʌmbə] n vieilleries f pl, fatras m, gros bois m; vt encombrer, entasser, embarrasser; vi marcher gauchement; — **mill** scierie f;

—-**room** chambre de débarras f, capharnaüm m.
lumberjack ['lʌmbədʒæk] n bûcheron m.
luminosity [,lu:mi'nɔsiti] n luminosité f.
luminous ['lu:minəs] a lumineux.
lump [lʌmp] n morceau m, bosse f, (in the throat) boule f, tas m, enflure f, contusion f; **in the** — en bloc; — **sum** somme globale f; vt mettre dans le même sac, en tas.
lunacy ['lu:nəsi] n folie f.
lunar ['lu:nə] a lunaire.
lunatic ['lu:nətik] n fou, folle, aliéné(e) mf; a lunatique.
lunch [lʌntʃ] n déjeuner m, petit repas m.
lung [lʌŋ] n poumon m.
lunge [lʌndʒ] n longe f, (fencing) botte f, ruée f; vi se fendre, se ruer, lancer un coup (à at).
lurch [lə:tʃ] n embardée f, embarras m; **in the** — en plan; vi embarder, tituber.
lure [ljuə] n leurre m, appât m, fascination f; vt entraîner, leurrer, séduire.
lurid ['ljuərid] a sinistre.
lurk [lə:k] vi se tapir.
lurking ['lə:kiŋ] a furtif, vague; —-**place** cachette f.
luscious ['lʌʃəs] a doux, savoureux, écœurant, fleuri.
lush [lʌʃ] a succulent.
lust [lʌst] n concupiscence f, désir m, soif f; vt to — for désirer violemment, avoir soif de, convoiter.
luster ['lʌstə] n lustre m, lustrine f, éclat m.
lustily ['lʌstili] ad de toutes ses forces, à pleins poumons.
lustrous ['lʌstrəs] a lustré, glacé, éclatant.
lusty ['lʌsti] a robuste.
lute [lu:t] n luth m.
luxuriance [lʌg'zjuəriəns] n luxriance f.
luxuriant [lʌg'zjuəriənt] a luxuriant, abondant.
luxurious [lʌg'zjuəriəs] a somptueux, luxueux.
luxury ['lʌkʃəri] n luxe m, amour du luxe m, objet de luxe m.
lying ['laiiŋ] a menteur, étendu, couché; — **in** en couches.
lymph [limf] n lymphe f.
lymphatic [lim'fætik] a lymphatique.
lynch [lintʃ] vt lyncher.
lynx [liŋks] n lynx m.
lyre ['laiə] n lyre f.
lyrical ['lirikəl] a lyrique.
lyricism ['lirisizəm] n lyrisme m.

M

macaroni [,mækə'rouni] n macaroni m.

macaroon [ˌmækə'ruːn] *n* macaron *m*.

mace [meis] *n* masse *f*, (*spice*) macis *m*.

macebearer ['meisbɛərə] *n* massier *m*.

macerate ['mæsəreit] *vt* macérer.

maceration [ˌmæsə'reiʃən] *n* macération *f*.

machine [mə'ʃiːn] *n* machine *f*, automate *m*, appareil *m*; *vt* usiner, façonner.

machine-gun [mə'ʃiːngʌn] *n* mitrailleuse *f*.

machinery [mə'ʃiːnəri] *n* machinerie *f*, machines *f pl*, mécanisme *m*, rouages *m pl*.

machinist [mə'ʃiːnist] *n* mécanicien *m*, machiniste *m*.

mackerel ['mækrəl] *n* maquereau *m*.

mac(kintosh) ['mæk(intɔʃ)] *n* imper (méable) *m*.

mad [mæd] *a* fou, fol, insensé, enragé, effrené.

madam ['mædəm] *n* Madame *f*.

madcap ['mædkæp] *an* étourdi(e) *mf*, écervelé(e) *mf*.

madden ['mædn] *vt* rendre fou, exaspérer.

maddeningly ['mædniŋli] *ad* à en devenir fou.

made [meid] *pt pp of* **make**.

madhouse ['mædhaus] *n* asile d'aliénés *m*.

madman ['mædmən] *n* fou *m*, aliéné *m*, forcéné.

madness ['mædnis] *n* folie *f*.

madonna [mə'dɔnə] *n* madone *f*.

magazine [mægə'ziːn] *n* magasin *m*, dépôt *m*, magazine *m*, revue *f*; — **gun** fusil *m* à répétition.

Magdelene ['mægdəlin] Madeleine *f*.

maggot ['mægət] *n* larve *f*, ver *m*, asticot *m*.

magic ['mædʒik] *n* magie *f*; *a* magique, enchanté.

magician [mə'dʒiʃən] *n* magicien, -ienne.

magisterial [ˌmædʒis'tiəriəl] *a* magistral, de magistrat.

magistracy ['mædʒistrəsi] *n* magistrature *f*.

magistrate ['mædʒistreit] *n* magistrat *m*, juge *m*.

magnanimity [ˌmægnə'nimiti] *n* magnanimité *f*.

magnanimous [ˌmæg'næniməs] *a* magnanime.

magnate ['mægneit] *n* magnat *m*, gros bonnet *m*.

magnesia [mæg'niːʃə] *n* magnésie *f*.

magnet ['mægnit] *n* aimant *m*.

magnetic [mæg'netik] *a* magnétique, hypnotique.

magnetism ['mægnitizəm] *n* magnétisme *m*.

magnetize ['mægnitaiz] *vt* magnétiser, aimanter.

magneto [mæg'niːtou] *n* magnéto *f*.

magnificence [mæg'nifisns] *n* magnificence *f*.

magnificent [mæg'nifisnt] *a* magnifique, somptueux.

magnify ['mægnifai] *vt* (a)grandir, grossir, exalter.

magnifying glass ['mægnifaiŋˌglɑːs] *n* loupe *f*.

magniloquent [mæg'niləkwənt] *a* grandiloquent.

magnitude ['mægnitjuːd] *n* grandeur *f*, ampleur *f*.

magpie ['mægpai] *n* pie *f*.

mahogany [mə'hɔgəni] *n* acajou *m*.

maid [meid] *n* fille *f*, pucelle *f*, bonne *f*; — **of all work** bonne à tout faire *f*; — **of honor** demoiselle d'honneur *f*.

maiden ['meidn] *n* jeune fille *f*, vierge *f*; *a* de jeune fille, non mariée; — **voyage** voyage de baptème *m*; — **speech** début à la tribune *m*.

maidenhood ['meidnhud] *n* célibat *m*.

maidenly ['meidnli] *a* chaste, modeste.

mail [meil] *n* (cotte de) mailles *f pl*, courrier *m*, poste *f*; *vt* expédier; — **coach** wagon postal *m*; — **train** train poste *m*.

maim [meim] *vt* mutiler.

main [mein] *n* force *f*, conduite principale *f*, océan *m*; **in the** — en gros; *a* principal, premier, essentiel.

mainland ['meinlənd] *n* continent *m*, terre ferme *f*.

mainly ['meinli] *ad* surtout, en grande partie, pour la plupart.

mainstay ['meinstei] *n* armature *f*, soutien *m*.

maintain [men'tein] *vt* soutenir, maintenir, entretenir, garder, conserver.

maintenance ['meintinəns] *n* moyens d'existence *m pl*, soutien *m*, maintien *m*, entretien *m*, pension *f*.

maize [meiz] *n* maïs *m*.

majestic [mə'dʒestik] *a* majestueux, auguste.

majesty ['mædʒisti] *n* majesté *f*.

major ['meidʒə] *n* commandant *m*, chef d'escadron *m*, majeure *f*; *school*) sujet *m* special; *a* majeur, principal, plus grand, aîné; *vti* passer les examens universitaires.

major-general ['meidʒə'dʒenərəl] *n* général de brigade *m*.

majority [mə'dʒɔriti] *n* majorité *f*, la plus grande partie.

make [meik] *n* fabrication *f*, marque *f*, taille *f*, façon *f*; *vt* faire, façonner, fabriquer, confectionner, rendre, gagner, arriver à; **to** — **away with** se débarrasser de; **to** — **off** décamper, se sauver; **to** — **out** comprendre, distinguer, dresser, établir; **to** — **over** transférer, céder; **to** — **up** compléter, compenser, combler, rattraper, arranger, préparer, dresser,

inventer; **to — up to** faire des avances à.
make-believe['meikbi.li:v] *n* tromper l'œil *m*, feinte *f*.
maker ['meikə] *n* faiseur, -euse, fabricant *m*, Créateur *m*.
makeshift ['meikʃift] *n* pis-aller *m*, expédient *m*; *a* de fortune.
make-up ['meikʌp] *n* maquillage *m*; composition *f*; *vi* se maquiller, se grimer.
making ['meikiŋ] *n* fabrication *f*, façon *f*, construction *f*, création *f*, main d'œuvre *f*; *pl* étoffe *f*, gains *m pl*.
maladjusted ['mælə'dʒʌstid] *a* inadapté.
malaria [mə'lɛəriə] *n* malaria *f*, paludisme *m*.
male [meil] *an* mâle *m*.
malefactor ['mælifæktə] *n* malfaiteur, -trice.
maleficent [mə'lefisnt] *a* malfaisant, criminel.
malevolence [mə'levələns] *n* malveillance *f*.
malevolent [mə'levələnt] *a* malveillant.
malice ['mælis] *n* méchanceté *f*, malice *f*.
malicious [mə'liʃəs] *a* méchant, malveillant.
malign [mə'lain] *vt* calomnier, diffamer.
malignancy [mə'lignənsi] *n* méchanceté *f*, malignité *f*.
malignant[mə'lignənt]*a* malin, -gne, méchant.
malinger [mə'liŋgə] *vi* tirer au flanc.
malingerer [mə'liŋgərə] *n* tireur au flanc *m*.
mall [mɔ:l] *n* mail *m*.
mallard ['mæləd] *n* canard sauvage *m*.
mallet ['mælit] *n* maillet *m*.
mallow ['mælou] *n* mauve *f*.
malnutrition ['mælnju'triʃən] *n* sous-alimentation *f*, malnutrition *f*.
malodorous [mæ'loudərəs] *a* malodorant.
malpractice ['mæl'præktis] *n* négligence *f*, incurie *f*, malversation *f*.
malt [mɔ:lt] *n* malt m.
maltreat [mæl'tri:t] *vt* maltraiter.
maltreatment [mæl'tri:tmənt] *n* mauvais traitement *m*.
man [mæn] *n* homme *m*, domestique *m*, pion *m*, pièce *f*; — **in the street** homme moyen; — **of war** vaisseau *m* de guerre; *vt* servir, occuper, garnir (d'hommes), armer, équiper.
manacle(s)['mænəkl(z)]*n* menotte(s) *f pl*; *vt* passer les menottes à.
manage ['mænidʒ] *vt* manier, diriger, mener arranger, manœuvrer, maîtriser, réussir à, venir à bout de; *vi* s'arranger, en venir à bout, se débrouiller.
managed ['mænidʒd] *pp of* **manage** réussi, gouverné.

management ['mænidʒmənt] *n* direction *f*, conduite *f*, gestion *f*.
manager ['mænidʒə] *n* directeur *m*, régisseur *m*, gérant *m*, imprésario *m*.
manageress ['mænidʒəres] *n* directrice *f*, gérante *f*.
mandate ['mændeit] *n* mandat *m*.
mandate ['mændeit] *vt* mandater.
mandatory ['mændətəri] *an* mandataire *mf*, obligatoire.
mandible ['mændibl] *n* mandibule *f*.
mandrake ['mændreik] *n* mandragore *f*.
mane [mein] *n* crinière *f*.
man-eater ['mæn.i:tə] *n* cannibale *m*, mangeur d'hommes *m*.
maneuver [mə'nu:və] *vti* manœuvrer.
manful ['mænful] *a* viril, courageux.
mange [meindʒ] *n* gale *f*.
manger ['meindʒə] *n* mangeoire *f*, crèche *f*.
mangle ['mæŋgl] *n* calandreuse *f*; *vt* déchiqueter, estropier, défigurer, calandrer.
mango ['mæŋgou] *n* mangue *f*.
mangy ['meindʒi] *a* galeux.
manhandle ['mænhændl] *vt* faire à bras d'hommes, manutentionner, malmener.
manhood ['mænhud] *n* âge viril *m*, virilité *f*, humanité.
mania ['meiniə] *n* manie *f*.
maniac ['meiniæk] *n* fou furieux, maniaque *mf*, enragé(e) *mf*.
maniacal [mə'naiəkəl] *a* maniaque, de fou.
manicure ['mænikjuə] *vt* se faire faire les mains; *n* manucure *f*.
manicurist ['mænikjuərist] *n* manucure *mf*.
manifest ['mænifest] *a* manifeste; *vti* (se) manifester.
manifestation [.mænifes'teiʃən] *n* manifestation *f*.
manifesto [.mæni'festou] *n* manifeste *m*.
manifold ['mænifould] *a* divers, multiple; *vt* polycopier.
manikin ['mænikin] *n* mannequin *m*, gringalet *m*.
manipulate [mə'nipjuleit] *vt* manipuler, actionner, manœuvrer.
mankind [mæn'kaind] *n* humanité *f*, genre humain *m*.
manliness ['mænlinis] *n* virilité *f*.
manly ['mænli] *a* viril, mâle, d'homme.
manner ['mænə] *n* manière *f*, sorte *f*; *pl* manières *f pl*, mœurs *f pl*, savoir-vivre *m*.
mannered ['mænəd] *a* élevé, maniéré.
mannerism ['mænərizəm] *n* maniérisme *m*, particularité *f*, tic *m*.
mannerly ['mænəli] *a* poli, bien, courtois.
mannish ['mæniʃ] *a* masculin, hommassé, d'homme.

manor-house ['mænəhaus] n manoir m.

manpower ['mæn'pauə] n main d'œuvre f.

manse [mæns] n cure f, presbytère m.

mansion ['mænʃən] n résidence f, château m; hôtel m.

manslaughter ['mæn,slɔːtə] n homicide involontaire m.

mantelpiece ['mæntlpiːs] n manteau de cheminée m.

mantis ['mæntis] n mante f; **praying** — mante religieuse.

mantle ['mæntl] n mante f, manteau m, (gas) manchon m; vt couvrir, dissimuler.

manual ['mænjuəl] an manuel m; n clavier m.

manufacture [,mænju'fæktʃə] n fabrication f; vt fabriquer, confectionner.

manufacturer [,mænju'fæktʃərə] n manufacturier m, fabricant m, industriel m.

manure [mə'njuə] n fumier m, engrais m; vt fumer, engraisser.

manuscript ['mænjuskript] an manuscrit m.

many ['meni] n foule f, masse f; a beaucoup de, bien des, nombre de, nombreux; **as** — autant de, que; **how** —? combien?; **too** — trop (de), de trop.

many-sided ['meni'saidid] a complexe, multilatère.

many-sidedness ['meni'saididnis] n complexité f.

map [mæp] n carte f, (world) mappemonde f, plan m.

maple ['meipl] n érable m; — **sugar** sucre d'érable m.

mar [maː] vt ruiner, troubler, gâter.

maraud [mə'rɔːd] vti marauder.

marauder [mə'rɔːdə] n maraudeur m.

marble ['maːbl] n marbre m, bille f; — **quarry** carrière de marbre f.

March [maːtʃ] n mars m.

march [maːtʃ] vi marcher, défiler; vt faire marcher; n marche f, pas m, frontière f; **forced** — marche forcée f; **quick** — pas accéléré m; — **past** défilé m.

marchioness ['maːʃənis] n marquise f.

mare [mɛə] n jument f.

Margaret ['maːgərit] Marguerite f.

margarine [,maːdʒə'riːn] n margarine f.

margin ['maːdʒin] n bordure f, lisière f, Marge f.

marginal ['maːdʒinl] a marginal.

marigold ['mærigould] n souci m.

marine [mə'riːn] n marine f, fusilier marin m; a marin, maritime.

mariner ['mærinə] n marin m.

mark [maːk] n but m, point m, note f, marque f, empreinte f, signe m, repère m; **up to the** — à la hauteur; **of** — d'importance; vt marquer, repérer, montrer; — **you** remarquez bien.

markedly ['maːkidli] ad nettement.

marker ['maːkə] n marqueur m, signet m, jeton m, carnet-bloc m.

market ['maːkit] n marché m, débouché m; vt trouver un débouché pour; vi faire son marché.

marketable ['maːkitəbl] a qui a un marché, d'un débit facile.

market-gardener ['maːkit'gaːdnə] n maraîcher, -ère.

market research ['maːkitri'səːtʃ] n étude f des marchés

marksman ['maːksmən] n bon tireur m.

marl [maːl] n marne f.

marmalade ['maːməleid] n marmelade f.

marmoset ['maːməzet] n ouistiti m.

marmot ['maːmət] n marmotte f.

maroon [mə'ruːn] an marron pourpré m; n pétard m, nègre marron m; **to be** —**ed** être coupé, isolé.

marquee [maː'kiː] n (tente-)marquise f.

marquess, marquis ['maːkwis] n marquis m.

marriage ['mæridʒ] n mariage m; — **lines** extrait de mariage m.

marriageable ['mæridʒəbl] a nubile, mariable, à marier.

married ['mærid] a en ménage.

marrow ['mærou] n moelle f, courge f.

marry ['mæri] vt épouser, (of parent, priest) marier; vi se marier.

marsh [maːʃ] n marais m.

marshal ['maːʃəl] n maréchal m, maître des cérémonies m; vt ranger, rassembler, introduire, trier.

marshmallow [maːʃ'mælou] n guimauve f.

marshy ['maːʃi] a marécageux.

marten ['maːtin] n martre f: **stone-** — fouine f; **pine** — martre m des pins.

martial ['maːʃəl] a martial, guerrier.

martin ['maːtin] n martinet m

martinet [,maːti'net] n **to be a** — être à cheval sur la discipline.

martyr ['maːtə] n martyr(e) mf.

martyrdom ['maːtədəm] n martyre m.

marvel ['maːvəl] n merveille f, prodige m; vi s'étonner, s'émerveiller (de at).

marvelous ['maːviləs] a merveilleux, prodigieux.

Mary ['mɛəri] Marie f.

masculine ['mæskjulin] an masculin m.

mash [mæʃ] n moût m, mixture f, pâtée f; vt brasser, écraser, mettre en purée, broyer.

mask [maːsk] n masque m; vt masquer, déguiser, voiler.

mason ['meisn] n maçon m.

masquerade [,mæskə'reid] n bal

masqué m, déguisement m, mascarade f; vi se déguiser, poser (pour as).
mass [mæs] n messe f; **high** —
grand'messe; **low** — messe basse;
foule f, masse f; — **meeting** meeting
m; vt masser; vi se masser, s'amonceler.
massacre ['mæsəkə] n massacre m;
vt massacrer.
massage ['mæsɑːʒ] n massage m; vt
masser, malaxer.
massive ['mæsiv] a massif.
mass-production [ˌmæsprə'dʌkʃən]
m fabrication f en série.
mast [mɑːst] n mât m, faîne f.
master ['mɑːstə] n maître m; vt
maîtriser, surmonter, dompter, posséder à fond
masterful ['mɑːstəful] a impérieux,
autoritaire.
master-key ['mɑːstəkiː] n passe-
partout m.
masterly ['mɑːstəli] ad de maître.
masterpiece ['mɑːstəpiːs] n chef
d'œuvre m.
masterstroke ['mɑːstəstrouk] n
coup de maître m.
mastery ['mɑːsteri] n maîtrise f,
connaissance parfaite f.
mastic ['mæstik] n mastic m.
masticate ['mæstikeit] vt mâcher.
mastication [ˌmæsti'keiʃən] n mastication f.
mastiff ['mæstif] n mâtin m, dogue
m.
mat [mæt] n natte f, paillasson m,
dessous de plat m; vt emmêler,
tresser; vi s'emmêler.
match [mætʃ] n allumette f, match
m, partie f; assortiment m, parti m,
égal(e) mf, pareil, -eille; vt unir (à
with), opposer (à), assortir, apparier,
rivaliser avec, égaler; vi s'assortir;
well—cd bien assorti.
matchet ['mætʃet] n coupe-coupe.
matchless ['mætʃlis] a sans égal,
incomparable.
match-maker ['mætʃˌmeikə] n ma-
rieuse f.
mate [meit] n camarade mf, copain
m, compagnon m, compagne f,
second m, aide m, époux m, épouse
f; vi se marier, s'accoupler; vt
accoupler.
material [mə'tiəriəl] n matériaux
m pl, matière(s) f pl, matériel m,
fournitures f pl; **raw** — matières
premières f pl; a matériel, important,
sensible.
materialism [mə'tiəriəlizəm] n
matérialisme m.
materialist [mə'tiəriəlist] n matérialiste mf.
materialize [mə'tiəriəlaiz] vi se
matérialiser, prendre corps, se
réaliser.
maternal [mə'təːnl] a maternel.
maternity [mə'təːniti] n maternité f.
mathematician [ˌmæθimə'tiʃən] n
mathématicien, -ienne.

mathematics [ˌmæθi'mætiks] n ma-
thématiques f pl.
matriculate [mə'trikjuleit] vt immatriculer; vi s'inscrire (à l'université).
matriculation [məˌtrikju'leiʃən] n
(university) inscription f.
matrimonial [ˌmætri'mouniəl] a
matrimonial, conjugal.
matrimony ['mætriməni] n mariage
m.
matron ['meitrən] n mère f, matrone
f, infirmière en chef f.
matter ['mætə] n matière f, pus m,
affaire f, question f; vi importer,
suppurer; — **of course** a tout
naturel, positif, prosaïque; **no** —
n'importe; **what is the** — qu'est ce
qu'il y a; **for that** — quant à cela;
—of-fact pratique.
Matthew ['mæθjuː] Mathieu m.
mattock ['mætək] n hoyau m.
mattress ['mætris] n matelas m;
spring — sommier m.
mature [mə'tjuə] a mûr; vti mûrir;
vi échoir.
maturity [mə'tjuəriti] n maturité f,
échéance f.
Maud [mɔːd] Mathilde f.
maudlin ['mɔːdlin] a larmoyant,
pompette.
maul [mɔːl] n maillet m; vt battre,
abîmer, malmener.
mausoleum [ˌmɔːsə'liəm] n mausolée
m.
maw [mɔː] n panse f, gueule f.
mawkish ['mɔːkiʃ] a fade.
mawkishness ['mɔːkiʃnis] n fadeur
f, sensiblerie f.
maxim ['mæksim] n maxime f.
maximum ['mæksiməm] n maximum m.
May [mei] n mai m.
may [mei] n aubépine f; v aux
pouvoir; **maybe** peut-être.
mayor [mɛə] n maire m.
mayoress ['mɛəris] n mairesse f.
maze [meiz] n labyrinthe m, dédale
m.
me [miː] pn me, moi.
meadow ['medou] n pré m, prairie f.
meager ['miːgə] a maigre, rare,
chiche.
meagerness ['miːgənis] n maigreur
f, rareté f.
meal [miːl] n repas m, farine f.
mealy ['miːli] a farineux, en bouillie,
doucereux.
mean [miːn] n milieu m, moyen-
terme m, moyenne f; pl moyens
m pl, ressources f pl; a moyen,
intermédiaire, minable, médiocre;
— **job** besogne ennuyeuse; **to feel** —
se sentir mal en train, mesquin,
vilain, ladre; vt signifier, vouloir
dire, avoir l'intention (de **to**),
destiner, adresser.
meander [mi'ændə] n méandre m;
vi serpenter.
meaning ['miːniŋ] n sens f.
meanness ['miːnnis] n mesquinerie f,

ladrerie *f*, médiocrité *f*, bassesse *f*.
means [miːnz] *n* moyens *m pl*.
means-test ['miːnztest] *n* relevé *m* des revenus.
meantime, -while ['miːntaim, -wail] *ad* en attendant, cependant.
measles ['miːzlz] *n* rougeole *f*.
measure ['meʒə] *n* mesure *f*, démarche *f*; *vt* mesurer; *vi* — **up** égaler qn, être l'égal de.
measurement ['meʒəmənt] *n* mesurage *m*, dimension *f*, tour *m*, mesure *f*.
meat [miːt] *n* viande *f*.
Mecca ['mekə] *n* La Mecque.
mechanic [mi'kænik] *n* méchanicien *m*; *pl* mécanique *f*.
mechanical [mi'kænikəl] *a* mécanique, machinal, automatique.
mechanism ['mekənizəm] *n* mécanisme *m*, appareil *m*.
medal ['medl] *n* médaille *f*.
medallion [mi'dæljən] *n* médaillon *m*.
meddle ['medl] *vi* se mêler (de **with**), s'immiscer (dans **in**), toucher (à **with**).
meddlesome ['medlsəm] *a* indiscret, fouinard, officieux.
mediate ['miːdieit] *vi* s'entremettre, s'interposer.
mediator ['miːdieitə] *n* médiateur, -trice.
medical ['medikəl] *a* médical, de (en) médecine.
medicine ['medsin] *n* médecine *f*, médicament *m*, purgatif *m*, sorcellerie *f*.
medicinal [me'disnl] *a* médicinal.
medieval [ˌmedi'iːvəl] *a* médiéval, moyenâgeux.
mediocre [ˌmiːdi'oukə] *a* médiocre, quelconque.
meditate ['mediteit] *vti* méditer; *vi* se recueillir.
meditation [ˌmedi'teiʃən] *n* méditation *f*, recueillement *m*.
meditative ['meditətiv] *a* méditatif, pensif, recueilli.
Mediterranean [ˌmeditə'reiniən] *a* méditerranéen; — **Sea** *n* Méditerranée *f*.
medium ['miːdjəm] *n* milieu *m*, moyen *m*, médium *m*, intermédiaire *m*; *a* moyen.
medlar ['medlə] *n* nèfle *f*.
medley ['medli] *n* mélange *m*, bigarrure *f*, pot pourri *m*.
meek [miːk] *a* doux, résigné.
meekness ['miːknis] *n* douceur *f*, humilité.
meet [miːt] *n* rendez-vous *m* de chasse; *vt* faire la connaissance de, se retrouver, aller à la rencontre, joindre, se croiser, payer; **to — with** trouver, subir; *vi* se recontrer, se retrouver, se rejoindre.
meeting ['miːtiŋ] *n* rencontre *f*, réunion *f*, meeting *m*; *a* convenable, séant.

megalomania ['megəlou'meiniə] *n* mégalomanie *m*.
megaton ['megətʌn] *n* mégatonne *f*.
melancholy ['melənkəli] *n* mélancolie *f*; *a* mélancolique, triste.
mellow ['melou] *a* succulent, moëlleux, adouci, mûr, cordial; *vti* mûrir; *vt* adoucir; *vi* s'adoucir.
melodious [mi'loudiəs] *a* mélodieux, harmonieux.
melodrama ['melə.drɑːmə] *n* mélodrame *m*.
melodramatic [ˌmeloudrə'mætik] *a* mélodramatique.
melody ['melədi] *n* mélodie *f*, air *m*.
melon ['melən] *n* melon *m*.
melt [melt] *vti* fondre; *vt* attendrir; *vi* se fondre, s'attendrir.
melting ['meltiŋ] *n* fonte *f*.
melting-pot ['meltiŋpɔt] *n* creuset *m*.
member ['membə] *n* membre *m*.
membership ['membəʃip] *n* nombre des membres *m*, qualité de membre *f*.
memento [mi'mentou] *n* mémento *m*, souvenir *m*.
memoir ['memwɑː] *n* mémoire *m*.
memorable ['memərəbl] *a* mémorable.
memorandum [ˌmemə'rændəm] *n* mémorandum *m*.
memorial [mi'mɔːriəl] *n* monument *m*, pétition *f*; *a* commémoratif.
memorize ['meməraiz] *vt* apprendre par cœur.
memory ['meməri] *n* mémoire *f*.
menace ['menəs] *n* menace *f*; *vt* menacer.
mend [mend] *n* réparation *f*; *vt* raccommoder, réparer, (*fig*) améliorer, arranger; *vi* se rétablir, se corriger.
mendacious [men'deiʃəs] *a* menteur, mensonger.
mendacity [men'dæsiti] *n* penchant au mensonge *m*, fausseté *f*.
mendicant ['mendikənt] *an* mendiant(e) *mf*.
mendicity [men'disiti] *n* mendicité *f*.
menial ['miːniəl] *n* domestique *mf*; *a* servile.
meningitis [ˌmenin'dʒaitis] *n* méningite *f*.
menses ['mensiːz] *n pl* menstrues *f*, règles *f*.
mental ['mentl] *a* mental, de tête.
mentality [men'tæliti] *n* mentalité *f*.
mention ['menʃən] *n* mention *f*; *vt* mentionner, citer, prononcer, faire mention de.
mercantile ['məːkəntail] *a* marchand, mercantile, commerçant.
mercenary ['məːsinəri] *an* mercenaire *m*.
mercer ['məːsə] *n* mercier, -ière.
merchandise ['məːtʃəndaiz] *n* marchandise *f*.
merchant ['məːtʃənt] *n* négociant(e), commerçant(e); *a* marchand.

merciful ['məːsiful] *a* clément.
mercifulness ['məːsifulnis] *n* clémence *f*.
merciless ['məːsilis] *a* inexorable, impitoyable.
mercilessness ['məːsilisnis] *n* implacabilité *f*.
mercurial [məː'kjuəriəl] *a* vif, inconstant, (*med*) mercuriel.
mercury ['məːkjuri] *n* mercure *m*, vif-argent *m*.
mercy ['məːsi] *n* pitié *f*, merci *f*, grâce *f*.
mere ['miə] *a* pur, simple, seul; *n* lac *m*.
merely ['miəli] *ad* tout simplement.
merge [məːdʒ] *vt* fondre, fusionner, amalgamer; *vi* se (con)fondre, s'amalgamer.
merger ['məːdʒə] *n* fusion *f*, combine *f*.
meridian [mə'ridiən] *n* méridian *m*.
merino [mə'riːnou] *n* mérinos *m*.
merit ['merit] *n* mérite *m*, valeur *f*; *vt* mériter.
meritorious [ˌmeri'tɔːriəs] *a* méritoire, méritant.
mermaid ['məːmeid] *n* sirène *f*.
merriment ['merimənt] *n* gaieté *f*, réjouissance *f*.
merry ['meri] *a* joyeux, gai.
merry-go-round ['merigouˌraund] *n* chevaux de bois *m pl*, carrousel *m*.
mesh [meʃ] *n* maille *f*, filets *m pl*; *vt* prendre, engrener; *vi* s'engrener.
mesmerize ['mezməraiz] *vt* hypnotiser.
mess [mes] *n* (*food*) plat *m*, pâtée *f*; saleté *f*, désordre *m*, pétrin *m*; (*army*) mess *m*; *vt* salir, gâcher; *vi* manger au mess, faire table.
message ['mesidʒ] *n* message *m*, course *f*, commission *f*.
messenger ['mesindʒə] *n* messager, -ère, chasseur *m*.
Messiah [mi'saiə] *n* Messie *m*.
metal ['metl] *n* métal *m*; — **fatigue** fatigue *f* des métaux.
metallic [mi'tælik] *a* métallique.
metallurgy [me'tælədʒi] *n* métallurgie *f*.
metamorphosis [ˌmetə'mɔːfəsis] *n* métamorphose *f*.
metaphor ['metəfə] *n* métaphore *f*, image *f*.
meteor ['miːtiə] *n* météore *m*.
meteorology [ˌmiːtjə'rɔlədʒi] *n* météorologie *f*.
meter ['miːtə] *n* compteur *m*, mètre *m*, mesure *f*.
method ['meθəd] *n* méthode *f*, ordre *m*, façon *f*, procédé *m*, manière *f*.
methodical [mi'θɔdikəl] *a* méthodique, réglé, qui a de l'ordre.
methylated spirits ['meθileitid 'spirits] *n* alcool à brûler *m*.
meticulous [mi'tikjuləs] *a* méticuleux, exact.
metric ['metrik] *a* métrique.

metropolis [mi'trɔpəlis] *n* métropole *f*.
metropolitan [ˌmetrə'pɔlitən] *an* métropolitain *m*.
mettle ['metl] *n* fougue *f*, ardeur *f*, courage *m*.
mettlesome ['metlsəm] *a* fougueux, ardent.
mew [mjuː] *n* mue *f*, mouette *f*, miaulement *m*, piaillement *m*; *vt* enfermer; *vi* miauler, piailler.
mew *see* **miaow**.
Mexican ['meksikən] *a* mexicain.
miaow [mi'au] *vi* miauler, piailler; *n* miaulement, piaillement.
miasma [mi'æzmə] *n* miasme *m*.
mice [mais] *n pl* souris *f pl*.
Michael ['maikl] Michel *m*.
microbe ['maikroub] *n* microbe *m*.
microphone ['maikrəfoun] *n* micro *m*.
microscope ['maikrəskoup] *n* microscope *m*.
microscopic [ˌmaikrəs'kɔpik] *a* microscopique.
midday ['middei] *n* midi *m*.
middle ['midl] *n* milieu; *a* du milieu, moyen.
middle-aged ['midl'eidʒd] *a* d'âge mûr.
middle class ['midl'klɑːs] *n* (haute) bourgeoisie *f*.
middleman ['midlmæn] *n* intermédiaire *mf*.
middling ['midliŋ] *a* passable.
midge [midʒ] *n* moucheron *m*, cousin *m*.
midget ['midʒit] *n* nain(e) *mf*, nabot(e) *mf*.
midlands ['midləndz] *n* comtés *m pl* du centre (de l'Angleterre).
midnight ['midnait] *n* minuit *m*.
midshipman ['midʃipmən] *n* aspirant *m*, midship *m*.
midsummer ['midˌsʌmə] *n* mi-été *f*, la Saint-Jean.
midwife ['midwaif] *n* sage-femme *f*.
mien [miːn] *n* mine *f*, air *m*.
might [mait] *pt of* **may**; *n* puissance *f*, force *f*.
mighty ['maiti] *a* puissant; *ad* très.
migrate [mai'greit] *vi* émigrer.
migratory ['maigrətəri] *a* — **bird(s)**, oiseau(x) migrateur(s).
milch-cow ['miltʃkau] *n* vache à lait *f*.
mild [maild] *a* doux, faible, mou.
mildness ['maildnis] *n* douceur *f*, clémence *f*.
mile [mail] *n* mille *m*.
mileage ['mailidʒ] *n* indemnité *f* de déplacement; carnets de billets de chemin de fer.
milestone ['mailstoun] *n* borne milliaire *f*, étape *f*, événement *m*.
militant ['militənt] *a* militant, activiste.
militarist ['militərist] *n* militariste *m*.

military ['militəri] *a* militaire; *n* armée *f.*
militate ['militeit] *vi* militer.
militia [mi'liʃə] *n* milice *f.*
milk [milk] *n* lait *m*; *vt* traire; *a* de lait, lacté.
milkman, -maid ['milkmən, -meid] *n* laitier, -ière.
milksop ['milksɔp] *n* poule mouillée *f.*
milky ['milki] *a* laiteux, lacté; the M— Way la Voie Lactée.
mill [mil] *n* moulin *m*, usine *f*; moteur *m* d'avion; *vti* moudre; *vt* fouler, fraiser, battre; *vi* tourner en rond.
millennial [mi'leniəl] *an* millénaire *m.*
miller ['milə] *n* meunier *m*, minotier *m.*
millet ['milit] *n* mil *m*, millet *m.*
milliard ['miljaːd] *n* milliard *m.*
milliner ['milinə] *n* modiste *f.*
millinery ['milinəri] *n* modes *f pl.*
million ['miljən] *n* million *m.*
millionaire [,miljə'nɛə] *n* millionnaire *mf*, milliardaire *mf.*
millstone ['milstoun] *n* meule *f*; (*fig*) boulet *m.*
mimeograph ['mimiəgraːf] *n* autocopiste *m* (au stencil).
mimic ['mimik] *n* imitateur -trice, mime *m*; *vt* contrefaire, singer, imiter.
mimicry ['mimikri] *n* mimique *f*, imitation *f.*
mince [mins] *n* hachis *m*; *vt* hacher; not to — one's words ne pas mâcher ses mots.
mincing ['minsiŋ] *a* affecté, minaudier.
mind [maind] *n* pensée *f*, esprit *m*, avis *m*, décision *f*, attention *f*, souvenir *m*, parti *m*; *vt* s'occuper de, garder, avoir soin de, faire attention à, regarder à, soigner, s'inquiéter de; I don't — cela m'est égal, je veux bien, ça ne me fait rien.
minded ['maindid] *a* disposé.
mindful ['maindful] *a* réfléchi, attentif, soucieux.
mine [main] *n* mine *f*; *vt* miner, creuser, mouiller des mines dans; *pn* le(s) mien(s), la mienne, les miennes, à moi.
minefield ['mainfiːld] *n* région *f* minière, champ *m* de mines.
minelayer ['main,leiə] *n* mouilleur *m* de mines.
miner ['mainə] *n* mineur *m.*
mineralogy [,minə'rælədʒi] *n* minéralogie *f.*
minesweeper ['main,swiːpə] *n* dragueur *m* de mines.
mingle ['miŋgl] *vt* mêler, mélanger; *vi* se mêler, se mélanger.
miniature ['minətʃə] *n* miniature *f*; *a* en miniature, en petit.
miniaturist ['minətjuərist] *n* miniaturiste *mf.*

minimize ['minimaiz] *vt* diminuer, minimiser.
minimum ['miniməm] *n* minimum *m.*
mining ['mainiŋ] *a* minier; *n* industrie *f* minière.
minion ['minjən] *n* favori, -ite.
minister ['ministə] *n* ministre *m*, pasteur *m*; to — to soigner, veiller, subvenir à.
ministerial [,minis'tiəriəl] *a* ministériel, exécutif.
ministration [,minis'treiʃən] *n* bons soins *m pl*, bons offices *m pl.*
ministry ['ministri] *n* ministère *m.*
mink [miŋk] *n* vision *m.*
minor ['mainə] *an* mineur(e) *mf*; *a* moindre, jeune.
minority [mai'nɔriti] *n* minorité *f.*
minster ['minstə] *n* cathédrale *f.*
minstrel ['minstrəl] *n* ménestrel *m*, chanteur *m.*
mint [mint] *n* Monnaie *f*, trésor *m*, menthe *f*; *vt* frapper, forger.
minuet [,minju'et] *n* menuet *m.*
minus ['mainəs] *prep* moins, en moins; *a* négatif.
minute ['minit] *n* minute *f*; *pl* procès-verbal *m.*
minute [mai'njuːt] *a* menu, tout petit, minutieux.
minuteness [mai'njuːtnis] *n* minutie *f*, petitesse *f.*
minx [miŋks] *n* luronne *f*, friponne *f.*
miracle ['mirəkl] *n* miracle *m*, prodige *m.*
miraculous [mi'rækjuləs] *n* miraculeux, extraordinaire.
mirage ['miraːʒ] *n* mirage *m.*
mire ['maiə] *n* bourbier *m*, fange *f*, bourbe *f*, boue *f.*
mirror ['mirə] *n* miroir *m*, glace *f*; *vt* refléter.
mirth [məːθ] *n* gaieté *f.*
misadventure ['misəd'ventʃə] *n* mésaventure *f.*
misalliance ['misə'laiəns] *n* mésalliance *f.*
misanthrope ['mizənθroup] *n* misanthrope *m.*
misapprehend ['mis,æpri'hend] *vt* comprendre de travers, se méprendre sur.
misapprehension ['mis,æpri'henʃən] *n* malentendu *m*, méprise *f.*
misappropriate ['misə'prouprieit] *vt* détourner.
misbegotten ['misbi'gɔtn] *a* illégitime.
misbehave ['misbi'heiv] *vi* se conduire mal.
miscalculate ['mis'kælkjuleit] *vt* mal calculer; *vi* se tromper.
miscarriage [mis'kæridʒ] *n* fausse couche *f*, égarement *m*, déni de justice *m.*
miscarry [mis'kæri] *vi* échouer, faire une fausse couche.
miscellaneous [,misi'leinəis] *a* varié, divers.

miscellany [mi'seləni] *n* mélange *m*, recueil *m*.

mischance [mis'tʃɑːns] *n* malchance *f*, malheur *m*.

mischief ['mistʃif] *n* malice *f*, méchant tour *m*, tort *m*, mal *m*.

mischievous ['mistʃivəs] *a* malicieux, malfaisant, méchant.

misconduct [mis'kɔndəkt] *n* inconduite *f*, mauvaise gestion *f*.

misconduct ['miskən'dʌkt] *vt* mal gérer.

misconstrue ['miskən'struː] *vt* interpréter de travers.

miscount ['mis'kaunt] *n* malcompte *m*, erreur d'addition *f*; *vi* mal compter.

miscreant ['miskriənt] *n* mécréant *m*, gredin *m*.

misdeal ['mis'diːl] *n* mal donne *f*; *vt* mal donner.

misdeed ['mis'diːd] *n* méfait *m*, crime *m*.

misdemeanor [ˌmisdi'miːnə]ˑ *n* délit *m*, méfait *m*.

misdirect ['misdi'rekt] *vt* mal diriger, mal adresser.

miser ['maizə] *n* avare *mf*.

miserable ['mizərəbl] *a* malheureux, misérable.

miserliness ['maizəlinis] *n* avarice *f*.

miserly ['maizəli] *a* avare, sordide.

misery ['mizəri] *n* misère *f*.

misfire ['mis'faiə] *vi* rater, faire long feu, manquer son effet.

misfit ['misfit] *n* malfaçon *f*, laissé-pour-compte *m*, misfit *m*.

misfortune [mis'fɔːtʃən] *n* malchance *f*, malheur *m*.

misgiving [mis'giviŋ] *n* défiance *f*, soupçon *m*, inquiétude *f*.

misguided ['mis'gaidid] *a* mal dirigé.

mishap ['mishæp] *n* accident *m*, mésaventure *f*.

misinformed ['misin'fɔːmd] *a* mal informé.

misjudge ['mis'dʒʌdʒ] *v t* maljuger.

mislay, -lead [mis'lei, -'liːd] *vt* égarer.

mismanage ['mis'mænidʒ] *vt* mal diriger, gâcher.

mismanagement ['mis'mænidʒmənt] *n* gestion inhabile *f*.

misplace ['mis'pleis] *vt* mal placer, déplacer, égarer.

misprint ['misprint] *n* coquille *f*, faute d'impression *f*.

misrepresent ['misˌrepri'zent] *vt* fausser, dénaturer, travestir.

miss [mis] *n* Mademoiselle *f*; ratage *m*, raté *m*, coup manqué *m*; *vt* manquer, rater.

missal ['misəl] *n* missel *m*.

missile ['misail] *n* projectile *m*, missile *m*.

missing ['misiŋ] *a* manquant, qui manque.

mission ['miʃən] *n* mission *f*.

missionary ['miʃnəri] *m* missionnaire *mf*.

miss out [mis'aut] *vt* oublier, omettre; *n* omission *f*.

misspell ['mis'spel] *vt* mal orthographier.

misspent ['mis'spent] *a* dissipé, dépensé à tort et à travers, mal employé.

mist [mist] *n* brume *f*, brouillard *m*.

mistake [mis'teik] *n* erreur *f*, méprise *f*, faute *f*; *vt* mal comprendre, se méprendre sur, se tromper de, confondre.

mistaken [mis'teikn] *a* dans l'erreur, faux, erroné.

mistakenly [mis'teiknli] *ad* par erreur.

mister ['mistə] *n* Monsieur *m*.

mistletoe ['misltou] *n* gui *m*.

mistress ['mistris] *n* maîtresse *f*.

mistrust ['mistrʌst] *n* méfiance *f*; *vt* se méfier de.

misty ['misti] *a* brumeux, confus, vague, estompé.

misunderstand ['misʌndə'stænd] *vt* mal comprendre, se méprendre sur.

misunderstanding ['misʌndə'stændiŋ] *n* malentendu *m*, mésintelligence *f*.

misuse ['mis'juːs] *n* mauvais usage *m*, abus *m*.

misuse ['mis'juːz] *vt* mésuser de, maltraiter.

mite [mait] *n* obole *f*, brin *m*, un rien *m*, (*fam*) môme *mf*.

miter ['maitə] *n* mitre *f*.

mitigate ['mitigeit] *vt* apaiser, soulager, mitiger, atténuer.

mitigation [ˌmiti'geiʃən] *n* adoucissement *m*, atténuation *f*.

mitten ['mitn] *n* mitaine *f*.

mix [miks] *vt* mêler, mélanger, brasser, confondre; *vi* se mêler, se mélanger, frayer.

mixture ['mikstʃə] *n* mélange *m*, mixture *f*, panaché *m*.

mix-up ['miks'ʌp] *n* mélange *f*; *vi* confondre.

moan [moun] *n* gémissement *m*, plainte *f*; *vt* gémir.

moat [mout] *n* fossé *m*, douves *f pl*.

mob [mɔb] *n* foule *f*, racaille *f*, ramassis *m*; *vt* faire foule autour de, malmener.

mobile ['moubail] *a* mobile.

mobilization [ˌmoubilai'zeiʃən] *n* mobilisation *f*.

mock [mɔk] *a* d'imitation, simili, faux; *vt* se moquer de, narguer, en imposer à, contrefaire.

mockery ['mɔkəri] *n* raillerie *f*, parodie *f*, farce *f*.

mode [moud] *n* (*fashion*) mode *f*, mode *m*, manière *f*.

model ['mɔdl] *n* modèle *m*, (*fashion*) mannequin; *vt* modeler, copier.

modeling ['mɔdliŋ] *n* modelage *m*.

moderate ['mɔdərit] *a* modéré, médiocre, moyen, sobre.

moderate ['mɔdəreit] *vt* modérer, tempèrer; *vi* se modérer.

moderation [ˌmɔdəˈreiʃən] n modération f, sobriété f, mesure f.
modern [ˈmɔdən] a moderne.
modernize [ˈmɔdənaiz] vt moderniser, renover.
modest [ˈmɔdist] a modeste, chaste, modéré.
modesty [ˈmɔdisti] n modestie f, modération f.
modification [ˌmɔdifiˈkeiʃən] n modification f.
modify [ˈmɔdifai] vt modifier, atténuer.
modish [ˈmoudiʃ] a à la mode, faraud.
modulate [ˈmɔdjuleit] vt moduler, ajuster.
modulation [ˌmɔdjuˈleiʃən] n modulation f.
mohair [ˈmouhɛə] n mohair m.
moist [mɔist] a humide, moite, mouillé.
moisten [ˈmɔisn] vt humecter, mouiller.
moisture [ˈmɔistʃə] n humidité f, buée f, moiteur f.
molar [ˈmoulə] an molaire f.
molasses [məˈlæsiz] n pl mélasse f.
mold [mould] n terreau m, moule m, moisissure f; vt mouler, façonner, pétrir, former.
molder [ˈmouldə] vi tomber en poussière, pourrir; n mouleur m.
molding [ˈmouldiŋ] n moulage m, moulure f, formation f.
moldy [ˈmouldi] a moisi.
mole [moul] n jetée f, môle m, taupe f, grain de beauté m.
molecular [mouˈlekjulə] a moléculaire.
molecule [ˈmɔlikjuːl] n molécule m.
molehill [ˈmoulhil] n taupinière f.
molest [mouˈlest] vt molester.
mollify [ˈmɔlifai] vt apaiser, adoucir.
mollusk [ˈmɔləsk] n mollusque m.
molt [moult] n mue f; vi muer.
molten [ˈmoultən] a fondu.
moment [ˈmoumənt] n moment m, instant m, importance f; **of —** d'importance.
momentarily [ˈmouməntərili] ad momentanément, pour l'instant.
momentary [ˈmouməntəri] a momentané, passager.
momentous [mouˈmentəs] a important, de conséquence.
monarch [ˈmɔnək] n monarque m.
monarchy [ˈmɔnəki] n monarchie f.
monastery [ˈmɔnəstəri] n monastère m.
monastic [məˈnæstik] a monastique, monacal.
Monday [ˈmʌndi] n lundi m.
money [ˈmʌni] n argent m; monnaie f; **—-box** n tire-lire f, caisse f; **—-changer** n changeur m; **—-grubber** n grippe-sous m; **—-lender** n usurier m, bailleur de fonds m; **—-market** n marché financier m; **—-order** n mandat m; **ready —**

argent comptant; **public —** trésor m public.
moneyed [ˈmʌnid] a riche.
monger [ˈmʌŋgə] n marchand (de . . .).
mongrel [ˈmʌŋgrəl] n métis, -isse, bâtard(e) mf.
monk [mʌŋk] n moine m.
monkey [ˈmʌŋki] n singe m (f guenon); vti singer; vi jouer des tours; **— business** filouterie f; **— wrench** clé anglaise f.
monkish [ˈmʌŋkiʃ] a monastique, monacal.
monogamy [mɔˈnɔgəmi] n monogamie f.
monogram [ˈmɔnəgræm] n monogramme m.
monologue [ˈmɔnəlɔg] n monologue m.
monomania [ˌmɔnouˈmeiniə] n monomanie f.
monopolist [məˈnɔpəlist] n accapareur, -euse.
monopoly [məˈnɔpəli] n monopole m.
monosyllabic [ˌmɔnəsiˈlæbik] a monosyllabique.
monosyllable [ˈmɔnəˌsiləbl] n monosyllabe m.
monotonous [məˈnɔtənəs] a monotone.
monotony [məˈnɔtəni] n monotonie f.
monsoon [mɔnˈsuːn] n mousson f.
monster [ˈmɔnstə] n monstre m.
monstrance [ˈmɔnstrəns] n ostensoir m.
monstrosity [mɔnsˈtrɔsiti] n monstruosité f, énormité f.
monstrous [ˈmɔnstrəs] a monstrueux, énorme.
month [mʌnθ] n mois m.
monthly [ˈmʌnθli] a mensuel; ad mensuellement.
monument [ˈmɔnjumənt] n monument m.
monumental [ˌmɔnjuˈmentl] a monumental.
mood [muːd] n humeur f, mode m, disposition f.
moody [ˈmuːdi] a morose, qui a des lubies, mal luné.
moon [muːn] n lune f; vi rêvasser; **to — about** musarder.
moonlight [ˈmuːnlait] n clair de lune m.
moonshine [ˈmuːnʃain] n clair de lune m, blague f.
moonstruck [ˈmuːnstrʌk] a lunatique, toqué.
moor [muə] n lande f, bruyère f; vt amarrer; vi s'amarrer.
Moor [muə] n Maure m, Mauresque f.
moorhen [ˈmuəhen] n poule f d'eau.
mooring [ˈmuəriŋ] n amarrage m, mouillage m; pl amarres f pl.
mooring rope [ˈmuəriŋroup] n amarre f.
Moorish [ˈmuəriʃ] a maure, mauresque.

moot [muːt] *a* discutable.
mop [mɔp] *n* balai *m* à laver, lavette *f*, (*hair*) tignasse, (*naut*) faubert; *vt* éponger, s'essuyer, fauberder.
mope [moup] *n* ennuyé(e) *mf*, *pl* le cafard; *vi* s'ennuyer, avoir le spleen.
moral ['mɔrəl] *a* moral; *n* moralité *f*; *pl* mœurs *f pl*.
morale [mɔ'rɑːl] *n* moral *m*.
moralist ['mɔrəlist] *n* moraliste *mf*.
moralize ['mɔrəlaiz] *vi* moraliser.
morass [mə'ræs] *n* marais *m*, fondrière *f*.
morbid ['mɔːbid] *a* morbide, maladif.
more [mɔː] *a ad* plus (de); *prep* davantage; — **and** — de plus en plus; **the** — ... **the** — ... plus ... plus ...
moreover [mɔː'rouvə] *ad* en outre, d'ailleurs.
morning ['mɔːniŋ] *n* matin *m*, matinée *f*; *a* du matin, matinal.
Moroccan [mə'rɔkən] *an* marocain *m*; *n* Marocain(e) *mf*.
Morocco [mə'rɔkou] *n* Maroc *m*, (*leather*) maroquin *m*.
morose [mə'rous] *a* morose.
moroseness [mə'rousnis] *n* maussaderie *f*, morosité *f*.
morphia ['mɔːfiə] *n* morphine *f*.
morrow ['mɔrou] *n* lendemain *m*.
morsel ['mɔːsəl] *n* morceau *m*, bouchée *f*.
mortal ['mɔːtl] *a* mortel, funeste; — **fear** peur jaune *f*.
mortality [mɔː'tæliti] *n* mortalité *f*.
mortar ['mɔːtə] *n* mortier *m*; *vt* cimenter.
mortgage ['mɔːgidʒ] *n* hypothèque *f*; *vt* hypothéquer.
mortification [ˌmɔːtifi'keiʃən] *n* mortification *f*, (*med*) gangrène *f*.
mortify ['mɔːtifai] *vti* mortifier, (*med*) se gangrener.
mortise ['mɔːtis] *n* mortaise *f*.
mortuary ['mɔːtjuəri] *n* morgue *f*; *a* mortuaire.
mosaic [mə'zeiik] *a n* mosaïque *f*.
Moscow ['mɔskou] *n* Moscou *m*.
Moslem ['mɔzlem] *an* musulman(ne).
mosque [mɔsk] *n* mosquée *f*.
mosquito [məs'kiːtou] *n* moustique *m*; — **net** moustiquaire *f*.
moss [mɔs] *n* mousse *f*.
mossy ['mɔsi] *a* moussu.
most [moust] *a* le plus, la plupart de; *ad* le (au) plus, très; presque.
mostly ['moustli] *ad* surtout, pour la plupart.
motel [mou'tel] *n* motel *m*.
moth [mɔθ] *n* phalène *f*, mite *f*.
moth-ball ['mɔθbɔːl] *n* boule de naphtaline *f*.
moth-eaten ['mɔθˌiːtn] *a* mangé aux mites, des vers.
mother ['mʌðə] *n* mère *f*; *vt* choyer, servir de mère à; — **country** mère-patrie *f*; —**in-law** belle-mère *f*; —**of-pearl** nacre *f*; — **tongue**

langue maternelle *f*.
motherhood ['mʌðəhud] *n* maternité *f*.
motion ['mouʃən] *n* mouvement *m*, geste *m*, signe *m*; motion *f*, proposition *f*; — **picture** cinéma *m*; *vt* diriger d'un geste, faire signe à.
motionless ['mouʃənlis] *a* immobile.
motivate ['moutiveit] *vt* motiver.
motivating ['moutiveitiŋ] *a* moteur.
motive ['moutiv] *n* motif *m*, mobile *m*.
motley ['mɔtli] *n* bariolage *m*; *a* bariolé, mêlé.
motor ['moutə] *a* moteur, automobile; *n* moteur *m*, automobile *f*; *vt* conduire en automobile; *vi* voyager, aller, en automobile; — **car** *n* auto(mobile) *f*; —**-cycle** *n* motocyclette *f*.
motoring ['moutriŋ] *n* automobilisme *m*.
motorist ['moutərist] *n* automobiliste *mf*.
motorway ['moutəwei] *n* autoroute *f*.
mottle ['mɔtl] *n* marbrure *f*, veine *f*; *vt* marbrer, veiner.
motto ['mɔtou] *n* devise *f*.
mound [maund] *n* tertre *m*.
mount [maunt] *n* mont *m*, monture *f*, cadre *m*; *vti* monter; *vt* monter sur.
mountain ['mauntin] *n* montagne *f*.
mountaineer [ˌmaunti'niə] *n* alpiniste *mf*, montagnard(e) *m(f)*.
mountaineering [ˌmaunti'niəriŋ] *n* alpinisme *m*.
mountainous ['mauntinəs] *a* de montagne, montagneux.
mountebank ['mauntibæŋk] *n* saltimbanque *m*, charlatan *m*.
mourn [mɔːn] *vti* pleurer; *vi* se lamenter, être en deuil.
mourners ['mɔːnəz] *n pl* le cortège *m* funèbre.
mournful ['mɔːnful] *a* triste, lugubre, endeuillé.
mournfulness ['mɔːnfulnis] *n* tristesse *f*.
mourning ['mɔːniŋ] *n* deuil *m*.
mouse [maus] *n* souris *f*; *vi* chasser les souris, fureter.
mousetrap ['maustræp] *n* souricière *f*.
mouth [mauθ] *n* bouche *f*, embouchure *f*, orifice *m*, grimace *f*, gueule *f*; *vti* déclamer; *vi* grimacer, discourir.
mouthful ['mauθful] *n* bouchée *f*.
mouthpiece ['mauθpiːs] *n* embouchure *f*, porte-parole *m*.
movable ['muːvəbl] *a* mobile, mobilier; *n pl* biens meubles *m pl*, effets mobiliers *m pl*.
move [muːv] *n* mouvement *m*, coup *m*, démarche *f*; *vt* (é)mouvoir, exciter, pousser, proposer, déplacer; *vi* bouger, déménager; *vi* — **on** (faire) circuler; **to** — **back** *vt* faire reculer; *vi* (se) reculer; **to** — **forward** *vti* avancer; **to** — **in**

emménager; **to — on** s'avancer,
circuler; **to — out** déménager.
movement ['muːvmənt] *n* mouvement *m*, déplacement *m*.
movies ['muːviz] *n* ciné(ma) *m*.
moving ['muːviŋ] *a* émouvant,
mobile, en marche.
mow [mou] *vt* faucher.
mower ['mouə] *n* faucheur, -euse,
(*machine*) tondeuse *f*.
mown [moun] *pp of* **mow**.
Mr ['mistə] Monsieur *m*.
Mrs ['misiz] *n* Madame *f*.
much [mʌtʃ] *a* beaucoup de; *pn*
beaucoup; *ad* de beaucoup, très;
too — *pn* trop; *a* trop de.
mucilage ['mjuːsilidʒ] *n* colle *f* (de
bureau).
muck [mʌk] *n* fumier *m*, ordure *f*;
vt salir, gâcher.
mud [mʌd] *n* boue *f*, banco *m*;
mud walls murs en banco.
muddle ['mʌdl] *n* confusion *f*,
désordre *m*, pagaille *f*, gâchis *m*;
vt (em)brouiller, emmêler; **to —
through** se débrouiller, finir par s'en
tirer.
muddleheaded ['mʌdl‚hedid] *a*
brouillon.
muddy ['mʌdi] *a* boueux, terne,
épais, trouble, limoneux.
mudguard ['mʌdgɑːd] *n* pareboue *m*.
muff [mʌf] *n* manchon *m*, pataud(e)
mf, empoté(e) *mf*; *vt* rater.
muffle ['mʌfl] *n* mufle *m*, moufle *m*;
vt emmitoufler, assourdir, étouffer.
muffled ['mʌfld] *a* étouffé, feutré,
voilé.
muffler ['mʌflə] *n* cache-nez *m inv*.
mug [mʌg] *n* gobelet *m*, chope *f*,
poire *f*, nigaud(e) *mf*.
muggy ['mʌgi] *a* étouffant, lourd et
humide.
mulatto [mjuˈlætou] *n* mulâtre, -esse.
mulberry ['mʌlbəri] *n* mûre *f*.
mulberry-tree ['mʌlbəritriː] *n* mûrier *m*.
mulct [mʌlkt] *n* amende *f*; *vt*
mettre à l'amende.
mule [mjuːl] *n* mule *f*, mulet *m*.
multifarious [‚mʌltiˈfɛəriəs] *a* multiple, divers, varié.
multiple ['mʌltipl] *an* multiple *m*.
multiplication [‚mʌltipliˈkeiʃən] *n*
multiplication *f*.
multiplicity [‚mʌltiˈplisiti] *n* multiplicité *f*.
multiply ['mʌltiplai] *vt* multiplier;
vi se multiplier.
multitude ['mʌltitjuːd] *n* multitude
f, foule *f*.
mum [mʌm] *a* silencieux; *n* maman
f; *excl* silence! motus!
mumble ['mʌmbl] *n* marmottage *m*;
vti marmonner, marmotter.
mummify ['mʌmifai] *vt* momifier.
mummy ['mʌmi] *n* maman *f*,
momie *f*.
mumps [mʌmps] *n* *pl* oreillons
m pl.

munch [mʌnʃ] *vti* mastiquer; *vt*
mâcher.
mundane ['mʌndein] *a* mondain,
terrestre.
municipal [mjuˈnisipəl] *a* municipal.
municipality [mju‚nisiˈpæliti] *n* municipalité *f*.
munificent [mjuˈnifisnt] *a* généreux,
munificent.
munitions [mjuˈniʃəns] *n* *pl* munitions *f pl*.
mural ['mjuərəl] *a* mural.
murder ['məːdə] *n* meurtre *m*,
assassinat *m*; *vt* assassiner, (fig)
massacrer.
murderer ['məːdərə] *n* meurtrier
m, assassin *m*.
murderous ['məːdərəs] *a* meurtrier,
homicide.
murky ['məːki] *a* sombre, épais,
ténébreux.
murmur ['məːmə] *n* murmure *m*;
vti murmurer.
muscle ['mʌsl] *n* muscle *m*; *vi*
s'immiscer (dans in), usurper.
muscular ['mʌskjulə] *a* musclé,
musculaire.
muse [mjuːz] *n* muse *f*; *vi* méditer,
rêver.
museum [mjuˈziəm] *n* musée *m*.
mushroom ['mʌʃrum] *n* champignon
m; *vi* champignonner.
music ['mjuːzik] *n* musique *f*; **—
stand** pupitre *m*; **— stool** tabouret
m.
musical ['mjuːzikəl] *a* musical,
mélodieux, musicien; *n* opérette *f*.
musician [mjuˈziʃən] *n* musicien,
-ienne.
musing ['mjuːziŋ] *n* rêverie *f*,
méditation *f*.
musk [mʌsk] *n* musc *m*.
musket ['mʌskit] *n* mousquet *m*.
musketeer [‚mʌskiˈtiə] *n* mousquetaire *m*.
muslin ['mʌzlin] *n* mousseline *f*.
musquash ['mʌskwɔʃ] *n* rat musqué
m, castor *m*.
mussel ['mʌsl] *n* moule *f*.
mussy ['mʌsi] *a* dérangé, sale.
must [mʌst] *n* moût *m*, moisissure
f; *v aux* devoir, falloir; **they — go**
il leur faut partir, ils doivent
partir.
mustard ['mʌstəd] *n* moutarde *f*; **—
plaster** sinapisme *m*.
muster ['mʌstə] *n* appel *m*, rassemblement *m*; *vt* rassembler, faire
l'appel de, compter; *vi* se rassembler.
musty ['mʌsti] *a* moisi, désuet.
mutable ['mjuːtəbl] *a* sujet à déplacement, changeant.
mutation [mjuˈteiʃən] *n* mutation *f*.
mute [mjuːt] *a* muet, sourd; *vt*
assourdir, mettre la sourdine à.
mutilate ['mjuːtileit] *vt* mutiler.
mutilation [‚mjuːtiˈleiʃən] *n* mutilation *f*.
mutineer [‚mjuːtiˈniə] *n* révolté *m*,
mutiné *m*.

mutinous ['mju:tinəs] *a* mutin, rebelle.
mutiny ['mju:tini] *n* mutinerie *f*, révolte *f*.
mutter ['mʌtə] *n* murmure *m*; *vti* murmurer, marmotter.
mutton ['mʌtn] *n* mouton *m*; — chop côtelette *f*.
mutual ['mju:tjuəl] *a* mutuel, réciproque, respectif, commun.
mutuality [.mju:tju'æliti] *n* mutualité *f*.
muzzle ['mʌzl] *n* museau *m*, (gun) gueule *f*, muselière *f*; *vt* museler, bâillonner.
my [mai] *a* mon, ma, mes.
myrtle ['mə:tl] *n* myrte *m*.
myself [mai'self] *pn* moi-même.
mysterious [mis'tiəriəs] *a* mystérieux.
mystery ['mistəri] *n* mystère *m*.
mystic ['mistik] *an* mystique *mf*.
mysticism ['mistisizəm] *n* mysticisme *m*.
mystification [.mistifi'keiʃən] *n* mystification *f*, fumisterie *f*.
myth [miθ] *n* mythe *m*.
mythical ['miθikəl] *a* mythique.
mythology [.mi'θɔlədʒi] *n* mythologie *f*.
myxomatosis [.miksəmə'tousis] *n* myxomatose *f*.

N

nab [næb] *vt* pincer.
nabob ['neibɔb] *n* nabab *m*.
nag [næg] *n* bidet *m*; *vt* chamailler; *vi* grogner sur tout.
nagging ['nægiŋ] *a* hargneux; — woman chipie *f*.
nail [neil] *n* clou *m*, ongle *m*; *vt* clouer, fixer, empoigner.
naïve [naː'iːv] *a* naïf, ingénu.
naked ['neikid] *a* nu, à poil.
nakedness ['neikidnis] *n* nudité *f*.
name [neim] *n* nom *m*, renom *m*, mot *m*; *vt* nommer, dire, fixer; **Christian** — prénom *m*; assumed — nom d'emprunt, pseudonyme *m*.
nameless ['neimlis] *a* sans nom, innommable, anonyme.
namely ['neimli] *ad* à savoir.
namesake ['neimseik] *n* homonyme *m*.
nap [næp] *n* somme *m*, poil *m*; *vi* sommeiller.
napalm ['neipaːm] *n* napalm *m*.
nape [neip] *n* nuque *f*.
napkin ['næpkin] *n* serviette *f*.
napping ['næpiŋ] *a* endormi, hors de garde, au dépourvu.
narcissus [naː'sisəs] *n* narcisse *m*.
narcotic [naː'kɔtik] *n* narcotique *m*; *an* stupéfiant *m*.

narrate [næ'reit] *vt* conter.
narration [næ:'reiʃən] *n* narration *f*, récit *m*.
narrative ['nærətiv] *n* récit *m*, narration *f*.
narrator [næ'reitə] *n* narrateur, -trice.
narrow ['nærou] *a* étroit, étranglé; *vt* rétrécir, resserrer, restreindre; *vi* se resserrer, se rétrécir, s'étrangler.
narrowness ['nærounis] *n* étroitesse *f*, exiguïté *f*.
narrows ['nærouz] *n* détroit *m*, défilé *m*, étranglement *m*.
nasal ['neizəl] *n* nasale *f*; *a* nasal, de nez.
nastily ['naːstili] *ad* méchamment.
nastiness ['naːstinis] *n* méchanceté *f*, saleté *f*.
nasty ['naːsti] *a* méchant, vilain, sale.
natal ['neitl] *a* natal.
nation ['neiʃən] *n* nation *f*.
national ['næʃənl] *a* national.
nationalism ['næʃnəlizəm] *n* nationalisme *m*.
nationality [.næʃə'næliti] *n* nationalité *f*.
nationalize ['næʃnəlaiz] *vt* nationaliser.
native ['neitiv] *n* originaire *mf*, indigène *mf*; *a* naturel, de naissance, natif du pays.
nativity [nə'tiviti] *n* nativité *f*.
natty ['næti] *a* soigné, adroit.
natural ['nætʃrəl] *a* naturel, inné, foncier.
naturalism ['nætʃrəlizəm] *n* naturalisme *m*.
naturalist ['nætʃrəlist] *n* naturaliste *m*.
naturalization [.nætʃrəlai'zeiʃən] *n* naturalisation *f*.
naturalize ['nætʃrəlaiz] *vt* naturaliser.
naturally ['nætʃrəli] *ad* naturellement, bien sûr.
naturalness ['nætʃrəlnis] *n* naturel *m*, simplicité *f*.
nature ['neitʃə] *n* nature *f*, sorte *f*, tempérament *m*.
naught [nɔːt] *n* rien *m*, zéro *m*; **to come to** — échouer.
naughtiness ['nɔːtinis] *n* méchanceté *f*.
naughty ['nɔːti] *a* vilain, méchant, polisson.
nausea ['nɔːsiə] *n* nausée *f*.
nauseating ['nɔːsieitiŋ] *a* écœurant, nauséabond.
nauseous ['nɔːsiəs] *a* nauséabond, dégoûtant.
naval ['neivəl] *a* naval, maritime, de marine; — **base** port de guerre *m*.
nave [neiv] *n* nef *f*, moyeu *m*.
navel ['neivəl] *n* nombril *m*.
navigate ['nævigeit] *vi* naviguer; *vt* diriger, gouverner, piloter.
navigation [.nævi'geiʃən] *n* navigation *f*, manœuvre *f*, conduite *f*.

navigator ['nævigeitə] *n* navigateur *m*, pilote *m*.
navvy ['nævi] *n* terrassier *m*.
navy ['neivi] *n* marine *f*.
nay [nei] *ad* non, ou plutôt, voire.
near [niə] *a* proche, prochain, (r)approché; *prep* près de; *ad* (de) près, à peu de chose près.
nearly ['niəli] *ad* de près, presque.
nearness ['niənis] *n* proximité *f*, ladrerie *f*, fidélité *f*.
neat [niːt] *a* net, élégant, bien tenu, en ordre, adroit, nature, (*drink*) pur.
neatness ['niːtnis] *n* netteté *f*, (bon) ordre *m*, finesse *f*.
nebulous ['nebjuləs] *n* nébuleux.
necessary ['nesisəri] *n* nécessaire, indispensable.
necessitate [ni'sesiteit] *vt* nécessiter.
necessitous [ni'sesitəs] *a* nécessiteux, besogneux.
necessity [ni'sesiti] *n* nécessité *f*, besoin *m*, contrainte *f*.
neck [nek] *n* cou *m*, col *m*, collet *m*, encolure *f*, goulot *m*.
neckerchief ['nekətʃif] *n* fichu *m*, foulard *m*.
necklace ['neklis] *n* collier *m*.
necktie ['nektai] *n* cravate *f*.
need [niːd] *n* besoin *m*, nécessité *f*; *vt* avoir besoin de, exiger, réclamer, falloir; **he needs money** il lui faut une livre.
needful ['niːdful] *an* nécessaire *m*.
needle ['niːdl] *n* aiguille *f*; **—woman** *n* lingère *f*, couturière *f*.
needless ['niːdlis] *a* inutile.
needs [niːdz] *ad* nécessairement; **he must — refuse** force lui est de refuser.
needy ['niːdi] *a* nécessiteux, besogneux.
nefarious [ni'fɛəriəs] *a* inique, abominable.
negative ['negətiv] *a* négatif; *n* négative *f*, négatif *m*, cliché *m*; *vt* rejeter, nier, neutraliser.
neglect [ni'glekt] *n* négligence *f*, incurie *f*; *vt* négliger.
neglectful [ni'glektful] *a* négligent, insoucieux.
negligently ['neglidʒəntli] *ad* négligemment.
negligible ['neglidʒəbl] *a* négligeable.
negotiable [ni'gouʃjəbl] *a* négociable.
negotiate [ni'gouʃieit] *vti* négocier; *vt* conclure, surmonter, franchir.
negotiation [ni,gouʃi'eiʃən] *n* négociation *f*.
negotiator [ni'gouʃieitə] *n* négociateur, -trice.
Negress ['niːgris] *n* négresse *f*.
Negro ['niːgrou] *n* nègre *m*.
neigh [nei] *n* hennissement; *vi* hennir.
neighbor ['neibə] *n* voisin(e) *mf*.
neighborhood ['neibəhud] *n* voisinage *m*, région *f*.
neighboring ['neibəriŋ] *a* voisin, avoisinant.

neither ['naiðə] *pn* ni l'un ni l'autre; *ad* ni, non plus.
neo-colonialism [,nioukə'louniəlizm] *n* néo-colonialisme *m*.
nephew ['nevju] *n* neveu *m*.
nephritis [ne'fraitis] *n* néphrite *f*.
nepotism ['nepətizəm] *n* népotisme *m*.
nerve ['nəːv] *n* nerf *m*, sang-froid *m*, toupet *m*; *vt* fortifier; **to — oneself** se raidir, s'armer de courage.
nerveless ['nəːvlis] *a* mou, inerte.
nervous ['nəːvəs] *a* nerveux, excitable.
nervousness ['nəːvəsnis] *n* timidité *f*, nervosité *f*, peur *f*.
nest [nest] *n* nid *m*, nichée *f*; *vi* faire son nid, (se) nicher.
nestle ['nesl] *vi* se blottir, se nicher.
nestling ['nesliŋ] *n* oisillon *m*.
net [net] *n* filet *m*, réseau *n*, résille *f*, tulle *m*; *vt* rapporter net, prendre au filet, tendre des filets sur, dans; *vi* faire du filet; *vt* prendre au filet, couvrir de filets, tendre des filets dans; *a* net.
nether ['neðə] *a* inférieur, infernal.
Netherlands ['neðələndz] *n* Pays-Bas *m pl*.
netting ['netiŋ] *n* filet *m*, treillis *m*, pose de filets *f*.
nettle ['netl] *n* ortie *f*; *vt* piquer, irriter; **—rash** *n* urticaire *f*.
network ['netwəːk] *n* réseau *m*, ligne *f*.
neuralgia [njuə'rældʒə] *n* neuralgie *f*.
neurasthenia [,njuərəs'θiːniə] *n* neurasthénie *f*.
neurasthenic ['njuərəs'θenik] *a* neurasthénique.
neuritis [njuə'raitis] *n* névrite *f*.
neurology [njuə'rɔlədʒi] *n* neurologie *f*.
neuropath [njuərə'pɑːθ] *n* névropathe *m*.
neurosis [njuə'rousis] *n* névrose *f*.
neurotic [njuə'rɔtik] *a* névrosé.
neuter ['njuːtə] *an* neutre *m*.
neutral ['njuːtrəl] *a* neutre.
neutrality [nju'træliti] *n* neutralité *f*.
neutralize ['njuːtrəlaiz] *vt* neutraliser.
neutron ['njuːtrɔn] *n* neutron *m*.
never ['nevə] *ad* jamais, ne . . . jamais.
nevertheless [,nevəðə'les] *ad* cependant, néanmoins.
new [njuː] *a* neuf, nouveau, jeune, frais; **—born** nouveau-né; **New Year** Le Nouvel An; **New Year's Day** le jour de l'an.
newly ['njuːli] *ad* nouvellement, fraîchement.
newness ['njuːnis] *n* nouveauté *f*, fraîcheur *f*.
news [njuːz] *n* nouvelle(s) *f pl*, (*radio*) informations *f pl*; **a piece of** — une nouvelle; **—agent**, **—dealer** — marchand *m* de journeaux; **—boy** *n* vendeur de journaux *m*.

newspaper ['njuːsˌpeipə] *n* journal *m*.

news-reel ['njuːzriːl] *n* informations *f pl*, actualités *f pl*.

news-stand ['njuːzstænd] *n* kiosque à journaux *m*.

newt [njuːt] *n* salamandre *f*.

next [nekst] *a* le plus proche, prochain, suivant; *prep* près de, sur, à même; *ad* ensuite, après, près.

nib [nib] *n* bec *m*, pointe *f*.

nibble ['nibl] *vt* grignoter, mordiller, égratigner.

nice [nais] *a* délicat, gentil, joli, doux, fin, subtil.

nicely ['naisli] *ad* gentiment, précisément, bien.

nicety ['naisiti] *n* subtilité *f*; **to a —** exactement, à point.

niche [nitʃ] *n* niche *f*.

nick [nik] *n* entaille *f*, encoche *f*; *vt* entailler, deviner, attraper, pincer, couper au court; **in the — of time** juste à temps.

nickname ['nikneim] *n* surnom *m*, sobriquet *m*; *vt* baptiser, surnommer.

niece [niːs] *n* nièce *f*.

niggard ['nigəd] *n* ladre *m*, pingre *m*.

niggardliness ['nigədlinis] *n* ladrerie *f*, pingrerie *f*.

niggardly ['nigədli] *a* ladre, pingre, mesquin.

nigh [nai] *a* proche; *ad* presque.

night [nait] *n* nuit *f*, soir *m*; *a* du soir, nocturne; **last night** hier soir; **tonight** ce soir.

night-club ['naitklʌb] *n* boîte de nuit *f*.

nightdress ['naitdres] *n* chemise de nuit *f*.

nightfall ['naitfɔːl] *n* tombée de la nuit *f*.

nightingale ['naitiŋgeil] *n* rossignol *m*.

nightlight ['naitlait] *n* veilleuse *f*.

nightly ['naitli] *a* nocturne, de nuit.

nightmare ['naitmɛə] *n* cauchemar *m*.

night-watchman ['nait'wɔtʃmən] *n* veilleur de nuit *m*.

nil [nil] *n* rien *m*, zéro *m*; *a* nul.

nimble ['nimbl] *a* agile, délié, ingambe.

nincompoop ['ninkəmpuːp] *n* gros bêta *m*, nigaud *m*.

nine [nain] *an* neuf *m*, équipe *f* de baseball.

ninepins ['nain'pinz] *n* quilles *f pl*.

nineteen ['nain'tiːn] *an* dix-neuf *m*.

nineteenth ['nain'tiːnθ] *an* dix-neuvième *mf*.

ninetieth ['naintiiθ] *an* quatre-vingt-dixième *mf*.

ninety ['nainti] *an* quatre-vingt-dix *m*.

ninny ['nini] *n* benêt *m*, niais(e) *mf*.

ninth [nainθ] *a* neuvième.

nip [nip] *n* pincement *m*, pinçon *m*, morsure *f*, sarcasme *m*, goutte *f*;

vt pincer, mordre, piquer, flétrir.

nipper ['nipə] *n* gosse *m*; *pl* pince *f*, tenailles *f pl*.

nipple ['nipl] *n* tétin *m*, mamelon *m*.

no [nou] *nm ad* non; *a* aucun, nul; **— longer** ne . . . plus.

nobility [nou'biliti] *n* noblesse *f*.

noble ['noubl] *an* noble *mf*; *a* grandiose, majestueux.

nobody ['noubədi] *pn* personne; *n* nullité *m*, pauvre type *m*.

nocturnal [nɔk'təːnl] *a* nocturne.

nod [nɔd] *n* signe de tête *m*; *vi* faire un signe de tête, dodeliner, somnoler.

nodding ['nɔdiŋ] *a* à la tête dodelinante.

node [noud] *n* nœud *m*.

noise [nɔiz] *n* bruit *m*, vacarme *m*; *vt* répandre, ébruiter.

noiseless ['nɔizlis] *a* sans bruit, silencieux.

noisily ['nɔizili] *ad* bruyamment.

noisome ['nɔisəm] *a* nuisible, offensant, malodorant, désagréable.

noisy ['nɔizi] *a* bruyant.

no-man's-land ['noumænzlænd] *n* zone neutre *m*, terrains *mpl* vagues, zone *m*.

nominal ['nɔminl] *a* nominal.

nominally ['nɔminəli] *ad* de nom, soi-disant.

nominate ['nɔmineit] *vt* proposer, désigner, nommer.

nomination [ˌnɔmi'neiʃən] *n* nomination *f*.

non-aligned countries *npl* le tiers monde *m*.

non-alignement ['nɔnə'lainmənt] *n* neutralisme *m*.

non-appearance ['nɔnə'piərəns] *n* absence *f*; (*law*) défaut *m*.

non-committal ['nɔnkə'mitl] *a* évasif, (de) normand.

nondescript ['nɔndiskript] *a* vague, hétéroclite.

none [nʌn] *a pn* aucun, nul; *pn* pas une personne; *ad* en rien, pas.

nonentity [nɔ'nentiti] *n* nullité *f*, zéro *m*.

non-intervention ['nɔnˌintə'venʃən] *n* non-intervention *f*.

non-payment ['nɔn'peimənt] *n* défaut de payement *m*.

nonplus ['nɔn'plʌs] *vt* interloquer, interdire.

nonsense ['nɔnsəns] *n* nonsens *m*, galimatias *m*, absurdité *f*, bêtise *f*.

nonsensical [nɔn'sensikəl] *a* absurde.

non-stop ['nɔn'stɔp] *a* sans arrêt, direct

noodle ['nuːdl] *n* nigaud(e) *mf*, benêt *m*; *pl* nouilles *f pl*.

nook [nuk] *n* (re)coin *m*.

noon [nuːn] *n* midi *m*.

noose [nuːs] *n* nœud coulant *m*.

nor [nɔː] *ad* ni, et ne pas.

normal ['nɔːməl] *a* normal, moyen, ordinaire.

Norman ['nɔːmən] *n* Normand(e) *mf*; *a* normand.

Normandy ['nɔːməndi] *n* Normandie *f*.

north [nɔːθ] *an* nord *m*; *a* du nord, septentrional.

northward ['nɔːθwəd] *a* vers le nord, au nord.

Norway ['nɔːwei] *n* Norvège *f*.

nose [nouz] *n* nez *m*, flair *m*; *vt* sentir, flairer; **to — about** fureter; **to — out** éventer, flairer; **—bag** musette *f*; **—dive** descente en piqué *f*; *vi* piquer du nez.

nosegay ['nouzgei] *n* bouquet *m*.

nostril ['nɔstril] *n* narine *f*, naseau *m*.

nostrum ['nɔstrəm] *n* orviétan *m*, panacée *f*.

not [nɔt] *ad* ne . . . pas, pas, non.

notable ['noutəbl] *a* notable, éminent, insigne.

notch [nɔtʃ] *n* (en)coche *f*, défilé *m*, gorge *f*; *vt* encocher, faire une coche à.

note [nout] *n* note *f*, ton *m*, signe *m*, mot *m*, marque *f*, réputation *f*; *vt* noter.

notebook ['noutbuk] *n* carnet *m*, bloc-notes *m*.

noted ['noutid] *a* connu, remarquable, célèbre (par **for**).

notepaper ['nout.peipə] *n* papier à lettres *m*.

noteworthy ['nout.wəːði] *a* remarquable.

nothing ['nʌθiŋ] *n* *pn* rien *m*; *n* zéro *m*, néant *m*; *ad* en rien, nullement.

no:hingness ['nʌθiŋnis] *n* néant *m*.

notice ['noutis] *n* avis *m*, informé *m*, avertissement *m*, affiche *f*, annonce *f*, compte *m*, connaissance *f*, congé *m*, notice *f*; *vt* remarquer, prendre garde à, s'apercevoir de, apercevoir.

noticeable ['noutisəbl] *a* sensible, perceptible, digne de remarque.

noticeboard ['noutisbɔːd] *n* panneau *m*, écriteau *m*.

notifiable ['noutifaiəbl] *a* à déclarer.

notification [,noutifi'keiʃən] *n* avis *m*, déclaration *f*, notification *f*.

notify ['noutifai] *vt* avertir, notifier, déclarer.

notion ['nouʃən] *n* notion *f*, idée *f*.

notoriety [,noutə'raiəti] *n* notoriété *f*.

notorious [nou'tɔːriəs] *a* notoire, malfamé.

notwithstanding [,nɔtwiθ'stændiŋ] *prep* malgré; *ad* néanmoins; *cj* bien que.

nought [nɔːt] *n* rien *m*, zéro *m*.

noun [naun] *n* nom *m*.

nourish ['nʌriʃ] *vt* nourrir, sustenter, alimenter.

nourishment ['nʌriʃmənt] *n* nourriture *f*.

Nova Scotia ['nouvə'skouʃə] la Nouvelle-Écosse.

novel ['nɔvəl] *a* original, étrange, nouveau; *n* roman *m*.

novelist ['nɔvəlist] *n* romancier *m*.

novelty ['nɔvəlti] *n* nouveauté *f*, innovation *f*.

November [nou'vembə] *n* novembre *m*.

novice ['nɔvis] *a* apprenti(e) *mf*, débutant(e) *mf*, novice *mf*.

now [nau] *ad* à présent, maintenant, tout de suite, dès lors, alors, tantôt, or; *cj* maintenant que.

nowadays ['nauədeiz] *ad* de nos jours, aujourd'hui.

nowhere ['nouwɛə] *ad* nulle part.

noxious ['nɔkʃəs] *a* nuisible, nocif.

nozzle ['nɔzl] *n* bec *m*, lance *f*, tuyau *m*, buse *f*.

nuclear ['njuːkliə] *a* nucléaire, atomique.

nucleus ['njuːkliəs] *n* noyau *m*.

nude [njuːd] *an* nu *m*.

nudge [nʌdʒ] *n* coup de coude *m*; *vt* pousser du coude.

nudity ['njuːditi] *n* nudité *f*.

nugget ['nʌgit] *n* pépite *f*.

nuisance ['njuːsns] *n* délit *m*, ennui *m*; **to be a —** être gênant, assommant.

null [nʌl] *a* nul, nulle.

nullify ['nʌlifai] *vt* annuler, infirmer.

numb [nʌm] *a* engourdi; *vt* engourdir.

number ['nʌmbə] *n* nombre *m*, numéro *m*, chiffre *m*; *vt* compter, numéroter.

numberless ['nʌmbəlis] *a* innombrable.

numbness ['nʌmnis] *n* engourdissement *m*.

numerator ['njuːməreitə] *n* numérateur *m*.

numerical [nju(ː)'merikəl] *a* numérique.

numerous ['njuːmərəs] *a* nombreux.

nun [nʌn] *n* nonne *f*, religieuse *f*.

nunnery ['nʌnəri] *n* couvent *m*.

nuptial ['nʌpʃəl] *a* nuptial; *pl* noces *f pl*.

nurse [nəːs] *n* infirmière *f*, nurse *f*, nourrice *f*, bonne *f*; *vt* nourrir, élever, soigner, bercer, ménager, entretenir.

nursery ['nəːsri] *n* (*plants*) pépinière *f*, garderie *f*, nursery *f*.

nurseryman ['nəːsrimən] *n* pépiniériste *m*.

nursing-home ['nəːsiŋhoum] *n* clinique *f*, maison *f* de santé.

nursling ['nəːsliŋ] *n* nourrisson *m*, poupon, -onne.

nurture ['nəːtʃə] *n* éducation *f*, soin *m*, nourriture *f*, soin *m*, nourriture *f*; *vt* nourrir, élever, soigner.

nut [nʌt] *n* noix *f*, écrou *m*, (*fam*) tête *f*, caboche *f*; cinglé *m*; **—crackers** *n* casse-noix *m*.

nutmeg ['nʌtmeg] *n* muscade *f*.

nutrition [nju(ː)'triʃən] *n* nutrition *f*.

nutritious [nju(ː)'triʃəs] *a* nourrissant.

nutritive ['njuːtritiv] *a* nutritif.

nutshell ['nʌtʃel] *n* coquille de noix *f*; **in a —** en deux mots.

nut-tree ['nʌttriː] *n* noyer *m*.

nutty ['nʌti] *a* à goût de noisette, toqué.
nuzzle ['nʌzl] *vt* flairer, fouiller, fourrer son nez dans, (contre); *vi* se blottir.
nymph [nimf] *n* nymphe *f*.

O

oak [ouk] *n* chêne *m*.
oakum ['oukəm] *n* étoupe *f*.
oar [ɔː] *n* rame *f*, aviron *m*; *vi* ramer.
oarsman ['ɔːzmən] *n* rameur *m*, nageur *m*.
oasis [ou'eisis] *n* oasis *f*.
oat(s) [outs] *n* avoine *f*; **to sow one's wild —** jeter sa gourme.
oath [ouθ] *n* serment *m*, juron *m*.
oatmeal ['outmiːl] *n* gruau *m*.
obduracy ['ɔbdjurəsi] *n* endurcissement *m*, obstination *f*.
obdurate ['ɔbdjurit] *a* endurci, obstiné.
obedience [ə'biːdjəns] *n* obéissance *f*, obédience *f*.
obedient [ə'biːdjənt] *a* obéissant, docile.
obeisance [ou'beisəns] *n* révérence *f*, hommage *m*.
obelisk ['ɔbilisk] *n* obélisque *m*.
obese [ou'biːs] *a* obèse.
obesity [ou'biːsiti] *n* obésité *f*.
obey [ə'bei] *vi* obéir; *vt* obéir à.
obituary [ə'bitjuəri] *n* notice nécrologique *f*.
object ['ɔbdʒikt] *n* objet *m*, but *m*, complément *m*.
object [əb'dʒekt] *vt* objecter; *vi* to — to trouver à redire à, s'opposer à, désapprouver.
objection [əb'dʒekʃən] *n* objection *f*, inconvénient *m*.
objectionable [əb'dʒekʃnəbl] *a* choquant, répugnant, désagréable.
objective [ɔb'dʒektiv] *an* objectif *m*; *n* but *m*.
objectivity [,ɔbdʒek'tiviti] *n* objectivité *f*.
obligation [,ɔbli'geiʃən] *n* obligation *f*, engagement *m*.
obligatory [ɔ'bligətəri] *a* obligatoire, de rigueur.
oblige [ə'blaidʒ] *vt* obliger, rendre service à.
obliging [ə'blaidʒiŋ] *a* obligeant, serviable.
oblique [ə'bliːk] *a* oblique.
obliterate [ə'blitəreit] *vt* effacer, oblitérer.
oblivion [ə'bliviən] *n* oubli *m*.
oblivious [ə'bliviəs] *a* oublieux.
oblong ['ɔblɔŋ] *a* oblong.
obloquy ['ɔbləkwi] *n* blâme *m*, opprobre *m*.
obnoxious [əb'nɔkʃəs] *a* offensa t déplaisant, odieux.
oboe ['oubou] *n* hautbois *m*.
obscene [ɔb'siːn] *a* impur, immonde, obscène.

obscenity [ɔb'seniti] *n* obscénité *f*, impieté *f*.
obscure [əb'skjuə] *a* obscur; *vt* obscurcir, éclipser, cacher.
obscurity [əb'skjuəriti] *n* obscurité *f*.
obsequies ['ɔbsikwiz] *n* obsèques *f pl*.
obsequious [əb'siːkwiəs] *a* obséquieux.
obsequiousness [əb'siːkwiəsnis] *n* obséquiosité *f*.
observable [əb'zəːvəbl] *a* observable.
observance [əb'zəːvəns] *n* observation *f*, observance *f*.
observant [əb'zəːvənt] *a* observateur.
observation [,ɔbzəː'veiʃən] *n* observation *f*.
observatory [əb'zəːvətri] *n* observatoire *m*.
observe [əb'zəːv] *vt* observer, faire remarquer.
obsess [əb'ses] *vt* obséder.
obsession [əb'seʃən] *n* obsession *f*, hantise *f*.
obsolete ['ɔbsəliːt] *a* désuet, hors d'usage.
obstacle ['ɔbstəkl] *n* obstacle *m*.
obstinacy ['ɔbstənəsi] *n* obstination *f*.
obstinate ['ɔbstinit] *a* obstiné, têtu, acharné.
obstinately ['ɔbstinitli] *ad* obstinément.
obstreperous [əb'strepərəs] *a* bruyant, turbulent.
obstreperousness [əb'strepərisnis] *n* rouspétance *f*.
obstruct [əb'strʌkt] *vt* obstruer, boucher, entraver, encombrer.
obstruction [əb'strʌkʃən] *a* obstruction *f*, encombrement *m*, obstacle *m*.
obtain [əb'tein] *vt* se procurer, obtenir; *vi* prévaloir, régner.
obtainable [əb'teinəbl] *a* qui peut s'obtenir, procurable.
obtrude [əb'truːd] *vti* (s')imposer, (se) mettre en avant.
obtrusion [əb'truːʒən] *n* ingérence *f*, intrusion *f*.
obtrusive [əb'truːsiv] *a* importun, indiscret.
obtuse [əb'tjuːs] *a* émoussé, obtus.
obtuseness [əb'tjuːsnis] *n* stupidité *f*.
obviate ['ɔbvieit] *vt* parer à, prévenir.
obvious ['ɔbviəs] *a* évident, manifeste, indiqué.
occasion [ə'keiʒən] *n* cause *f*, occasion *f*, sujet *m*, affaires *f pl*; *vt* occasionner.
occasional [ə'keiʒənl] *a* de circonstance, occasionnel; **— hand** extra *m*; épars.
occasionally [ə'keiʒənəli] *ad* à l'occasion, de temps en temps.
occident ['ɔksidənt] *n* occident *m*.
occult [ɔ'kʌlt] *a* occulte.
occultism ['ɔkəltizəm] *n* occultisme *m*.

occupant ['ɔkjupənt] *n* occupant(e) *mf*, habitant(e) *mf*, locataire *mf*.

occupation [ˌɔkju'peiʃən] *n* métier *m*, occupation *f*.

occupy ['ɔkjupai] *vt* occuper, habiter, tenir.

occur [ə'kəː] *vi* arriver, se produire, venir à l'esprit.

occurrence [ə'kʌrəns] *n* occurrence *f*, événement *m*.

ocean ['ouʃən] *n* océan *m*.

October [ɔk'toubə] *n* octobre *m*.

octopus ['ɔktəpəs] *n* pieuvre *f*.

ocular ['ɔkjulə] *a* oculaire.

oculist ['ɔkjulist] *n* oculiste *mf*.

odd [ɔd] *a* impair, de plus, de reste, dépareillé, curieux, bizarre.

oddity ['ɔditi] *n* bizarrerie *f*, curiosité *f*, excentricité *f*.

oddments ['ɔdmənts] *n pl* fins de série *f pl*, articles soldés *m pl*, fonds de boutique *m pl*.

odds [ɔdz] *n* inégalité *f*, avantage *m*, chances *f pl*; — **and ends** pièces et morceaux.

odious ['oudiəs] *a* odieux.

odor ['oudə] *n* odeur *f*.

odorless ['oudəlis] *a* inodore, sans odeur.

odorous ['oudərəs] *a* odorant.

of [ɔv] *prep* de, d'entre, depuis, par, à, en.

off [ɔf] *prep* de, sur, sans, de dessus, au large de, à la hauteur de; *a* éloigné, extérieur, de liberté; *ad* coupé, fermé, libre, parti, éloigné; **I'm —** je m'en vais; **day —** jour de congé.

offal ['ɔfəl] *n* abats *m pl*, rebut *m*.

offend [ə'fend] *vt* offenser, enfreindre, blesser.

offender [ə'fendə] *n* délinquant(e) *mf*, coupable *mf*.

offense ['əfens] *n* contravention *f*, délit *m*, offense *f*.

offensive [ə'fensiv] *n* offensive *f*; *a* offensant, répugnant, offensif.

offer ['ɔfə] *n* offre *f*; *vt* offrir; *vi* s'offrir, se présenter.

offering ['ɔfəriŋ] *n* offrande *f*.

offertory ['ɔfətəri] *n* quête *f*.

offhand ['ɔf'hænd] *a* improvisé, désinvolte.

offhandedly ['ɔf'hændidli] *ad* de haut, avec désinvolture.

office ['ɔfis] *n* poste *m*, bureau *m*, office *m*; **good —s** bons offices *m pl*.

officer ['ɔfisə] *n* officier *m*.

official [ə'fiʃəl] *a* officiel, réglementaire; *n* employé *m*, fonctionnaire *m*.

officialdom [ə'fiʃəldəm] *n* monde officiel *m*, bureaucratie *f*.

officiate [ə'fiʃieit] *vi* officier, remplir les fonctions (de **as**).

officious [ə'fiʃəs] *a* trop zélé, officieux.

officiousness [ə'fiʃəsnis] *n* excès de zèle *m*.

offing ['ɔfiŋ] *n* (*sea*) large *m*, perspective *f*.

off-peak ['ɔfpiːk] *a* — **hours** heures creuses *f pl*; — **tariff** tarif de nuit *m*.

off-season ['ɔf'siːzn] *n* morte saison *f*.

offset ['ɔfset] *n* œilleton *m*, rejeton *m*, éperon *m*, compensation *f*, repoussoir *m*.

offshoot ['ɔfʃuːt] *n* rejeton *m*.

offshore ['ɔfʃɔː] *ad a* de terre, éloigné de la côte.

offside ['ɔf'said] *a* hors jeu.

offspring ['ɔfspriŋ] *n* rejeton *m*, résultat *m*.

often ['ɔfn] *ad* souvent; — **and —** à mainte reprise.

ogle ['ougl] *n* œillade *f*; *vt* lorgner, faire de l'œil à.

oil [ɔil] *n* huile *f*, pétrole *m*; **crude —** mazout *m*; *vt* huiler, graisser; *vi* faire son plein de mazout; **—can** *n* burette *f*; **—painting** *n* peinture à l'huile; **coconut —** huile *f* de copra.

oilcake ['ɔilkeik] *n* tourteau *m*.

oilcloth ['ɔilklɔθ] *n* toile cirée *f*.

oiliness ['ɔilinis] *n* onctuosité *f*, état graisseux *m*.

oilskin ['ɔilskin] *n* ciré *m*.

oil-tanker ['ɔiltæŋkə] *n* pétrolier *m*.

oil-well ['ɔilwel] *n* puits pétrolifère *m*.

oily ['ɔili] *a* huileux, onctueux.

ointment ['ɔintmənt] *n* onguent *m*, pommade *f*.

old [ould] *a* vieux, vieil, vieille, ancien, âgé; **to grow —** vieillir; — **age** vieillesse *f*; **—timer** *n* vieillard *m*.

old-fashioned ['ould'fæʃənd] *a* démodé, suranné.

oldish ['ouldiʃ] *a* vieillot.

olive ['ɔliv] *n* olive *f*; *a* d'olive; — **tree** olivier *m*.

omen ['oumen] *n* présage *m*, augure *m*.

ominous ['ɔminəs] *a* menaçant, de mauvais augure.

omission [ou'miʃən] *n* omission *f*, oubli *m*.

omit [ou'mit] *vt* omettre, oublier.

omnifarious [ˌɔmni'fɛəriəs] *a* de toute espèce.

omnipotence [ɔm'nipətəns] *n* toute-puissance *f*.

omnivorous [ɔm'nivərəs] *a* omnivore.

on [ɔn] *prep* sur, à, lors de, en, sous, par, contre; *ad* en cours, en avant! mis, passé, allumé, ouvert.

once [wʌns] *ad* une fois; **at —** immédiatement, à la fois; **—over** *n* un coup d'œil scrutateur.

one [wʌn] *a* un, un seul; *pn* on.

one-eyed ['wʌn'aid] *a* borgne.

one's [wʌnz] *a* son, sa, ses.

oneself [wʌn'self] *pn* soi-même.

one-sided ['wʌn'saidid] *a* unilatéral, borné.

one-way ['wʌn'wei] *n* sens unique *m*; *a* à sens unique.

onerous ['ounərəs] *a* onéreux.

onion ['ʌnjən] *n* oignon *m.*
only ['ounli] *a* unique, seul; *ad* seulement; *cj* sauf que, mais.
onset ['ɔnset] *n* attaque *f*, assaut *m*, départ *m*, début *m.*
onslaught ['ɔnslɔːt] *see* **onset.**
onus ['ounəs] *n* poids *m*, charge *f*, responsabilité *f.*
onward ['ɔnwəd] *a* progressif, avancé, avançant; *ad* en avant, dorénavant.
ooze [uːz] *n* boue *f*, limon *m*, suintement *m*; *vi* suinter, dégoutter.
opal ['oupəl] *n* opale *f*; *a* opalin.
opaque [ou'peik] *a* opaque.
opaqueness [ou'peiknis] *n* opacité *f.*
open ['oupən] *a* ouvert, public, exposé, franc, débouché, libre; **in the — (air)** en plein air, au grand air; *vt* ouvrir, entamer, déboucher, percer, engager; *vi* s'ouvrir, débuter, commencer, s'épanouir.
opening ['oupəniŋ] *n* ouverture *f*, début *m*, débouché *m*, inauguration *f.*
opera ['ɔpərə] *n* opéra *m.*
operate ['ɔpəreit] *vti* opérer; *vt* accomplir, actionner, faire marcher; *vi* fonctionner, agir; gérer, exploiter.
operation [,ɔpə'reiʃən] *n* opération *f*, action *f*, fonctionnement *m.*
operative ['ɔpərətiv] *n* ouvrier, -ière; *a* efficace, actif, opératif, en vigueur.
opinion [ə'pinjən] *n* opinion *f*, avis *m.*
opinionated [ə'pinjəneitəd] *a* obstiné, entier.
opium ['oupjəm] *n* opium *m.*
opponent [ə'pounənt] *n* adversaire *m*, antagoniste *mf.*
opportune ['ɔpətjuːn] *a* opportun.
opportunely ['ɔpətjuːnli] *ad* à propos, en temps opportun.
opportunism ['ɔpətjuːnizəm] *n* opportunisme *m.*
opportunity [,ɔpə'tjuːniti] *n* occasion *f*, chance *f.*
oppose [ə'pouz] *vt* s'opposer à, opposer.
opposite ['ɔpəzit] *a* opposé, correspondant; *prep* face à, en face de; *ad* en face, en regard; *n* contraire *m*, contre-pied *m.*
opposition [,ɔpə'ziʃən] *n* opposition *f*, concurrence *f.*
oppress [ə'pres] *vt* opprimer.
oppression [ə'preʃən] *a* oppression *f.*
oppressive [ə'presiv] *a* oppressif, lourd.
oppressor [ə'presə] *n* oppresseur *m.*
opprobrious [ə'proubriəs] *a* déshonorant, injurieux.
opprobrium [ə'proubriəm] *n* opprobre *m.*
opt [ɔpt] *vi* opter; **— out** s'esquiver.
optic ['ɔptik] *a* optique.
optician [ɔp'tiʃən] *n* opticien *m*
optics ['ɔptiks] *n* optique *f.*
optimism ['ɔptimizəm] *n* optimisme *m.*

optimistic [,ɔpti'mistik] *a* optimiste.
option ['ɔpʃən] *n* option *f*, choix *m.*
optional ['ɔpʃənl] *a* facultatif.
opulence ['ɔpjuləns] *n* opulence *f.*
opulent ['ɔpjulənt] *a* opulent.
or [ɔː] *cj* ou, sinon.
oracle ['ɔrəkl] *n* oracle *m.*
oracular [ə'rækjulə] *a* oraculaire, obscur.
oral ['ɔːrəl] *a* oral.
orange ['ɔrindʒ] *n* orange *f.*
oration [ɔː'reiʃən] *n* discours *m*, harangue *f.*
orator ['ɔrətə] *n* orateur *m.*
oratorical [,ɔrə'tɔrikəl] *a* oratoire, ampoulé, disert.
orb [ɔːb] *n* orbe *m*, globe *m*, sphère *f.*
orbit ['ɔːbit] *n* orbite *f.*
orchard ['ɔːtʃəd] *n* verger *m.*
orchestra ['ɔːkistrə] *n* orchestre *m.*
orchestrate ['ɔːkistreit] *vt* orchestrer.
orchid ['ɔːkid] *n* orchidée *f.*
ordain [ɔː'dein] *vt* ordonner, conférer les ordres à.
ordeal [ɔː'diːl] *n* épreuve *f.*
order ['ɔːdə] *n* ordre *m*; **to —** sur commande; **out of —** détraqué, déplacé, irrégulier; **in — to** afin de; *vt* commander, ordonner.
orderliness ['ɔːdəlinis] *n* (esprit *m* d') ordre *m.*
orderly ['ɔːdəli] *n* infirmier militaire *m*, planton *m*; *a* en ordre, rangé, discipliné.
ordinary ['ɔːdnri] *a* ordinaire, typique, normal.
ordnance ['ɔːdnəns] *n* artillerie *f*, intendance *f.*
ore [ɔː] *n* minéral *m.*
organ ['ɔːgən] *n* organe *m*, orgue *m.*
organic [ɔː'gænik] *a* organique.
organism ['ɔːgənizəm] *n* organisme *m.*
organist ['ɔːgənist] *n* organiste *mf.*
organization [,ɔːgənai'zeiʃən] *n* organisation *f*, organisme *m.*
organize ['ɔːgənaiz] *vt* organiser, arranger.
organizer ['ɔːgənaizə] *n* organisateur, -trice.
orient ['ɔːriənt] *n* orient *m.*
oriental [,ɔːri'entl] *a* oriental, d'orient.
orientation [,ɔːrien'teiʃən] *n* orientation *f.*
orifice ['ɔrifis] *n* orifice *m*, ouverture *f.*
origin ['ɔridʒin] *n* origine *f.*
original [ə'ridʒənl] *an* original *m*; *a* originel.
originality [ə,ridʒi'næliti] *n* originalité *f.*
originate [ə'ridʒineit] *vt* donner naissance à; *vt* descendre, provenir, naître.
originator [ə'ridʒineitə] *n* auteur *m*, source *f.*
ornament ['ɔːnəmənt] *n* ornement *m.*
ornament [ɔːnə'ment] *vt* orner, agrémenter.

ornamental [ˌɔːnəˈmentl] *a* ornemental, décoratif.
ornamentation [ˌɔːnəmenˈteiʃən] *n*
ornementation *f*, décoration *f*.
orphan [ˈɔːfən] *n* orphelin(e) *mf*.
orphanage [ˈɔːfənidʒ] *n* orphelinat
m.
orthodox [ˈɔːθədɔks] *a* orthodoxe.
orthodoxy [ˈɔːθədɔksi] *n* orthodoxie
f.
orthography [ɔːˈθɔgrəfi] *n* orthographe *f*.
oscillate [ˈɔsileit] *vi* osciller.
osier [ˈouʒə] *n* osier *m*.
ostensible [ɔsˈtensəbl] *a* soi-disant,
prétendu.
ostentation [ˌɔstenˈteiʃən] *n* ostentation *f*, faste *m*.
ostentatious [ˌɔstenˈteiʃəs] *a*
fastueux.
ostler [ˈɔslə] *n* garçon d'écurie *m*.
ostracize [ˈɔstrəsaiz] *vt* ostraciser,
mettre au ban.
ostrich [ˈɔstritʃ] *n* autruche *f*.
other [ˈʌðə] *an pn* autre; *pl* d'autres,
les autres.
otherwise [ˈʌðəwaiz] *ad* autrement,
sans quoi.
otter [ˈɔtə] *n* loutre *f*.
ought [ɔːt] *v aux* devoir.
ounce [auns] *n* once *f*.
our [ˈauə] *a* notre, nos; **—self,
(selves)** *pn* nous-même(s), nous.
ours [ˈauəz] *pn* le, la, les nôtre(s),
à nous, nôtre.
oust [aust] *vt* jeter dehors, évincer,
supplanter.
out [aut] *ad* dehors, au dehors, au
large, sur pied, en grève; *a* épuisé,
à bout, sorti, éteint, éclos; **— of**
prep hors de, à l'abri de, dans, à,
par, d'entre, parmi.
outbid [autˈbid] *vt* (r)enchérir sur.
outboard [ˈautbɔːd] *an* hors bord *m*.
outbreak [ˈautbreik] *n* explosion *f*,
éruption *f*, émeute *f*, accès *m*.
outbuilding [ˈautbildiŋ] *n* dépendance *f*, annexe *f*.
outburst [ˈautbəːst] *n* explosion *f*,
éclat *m*, élan *m*.
outcast [ˈautkɑːst] *n* paria *m*,
proscrit(e) *mf*, exilé(e) *mf*.
outclass [autˈklɑːs] *vt* surclasser,
surpasser.
outcome [ˈautkʌm] *n* résultat *m*,
issue *f*.
outcrop [ˈautkrɔp] *n* affleurement *m*.
outcry [ˈautkrai] *n* clameur *f*, tollé
m.
outdo [autˈduː] *vt* surpasser.
outer [ˈautə] *a* plus éloigné, extérieur,
externe.
outfall [ˈautfɔːl] *n* embouchure *f*.
outfit [ˈautfit] *n* équipement *m*,
trousseau *m*, trousse *f*, attirail *m*,
équipe *f* d'ouvriers.
outflank [ˈautˈflæŋk] *vt* déborder,
circonvenir.
outflow [ˈautflou] *n* écoulement *m*,
décharge *f*; *vi* provenir.

outgrow [autˈgrou] *vt* dépasser,
devenir trop grand pour, faire
craquer.
outhouse [ˈauthaus] *n* dépendance *f*.
outing [ˈautiŋ] *n* sortie *f*, excursion *f*.
outlandish [autˈlændiʃ] *a* étranger,
étrange, barbare, écarté, reculé.
outlaw [ˈautlɔː] *n* hors-la-loi *m*,
proscrit(e) *mf*; *vt* proscrire.
outlay [ˈautlei] *n* dépenses *f pl*, frais
m pl.
outlet [ˈautlet] *n* issue *f*, débouché *m*,
départ *m*.
outline [ˈautlain] *n* contour *m*,
esquisse *f*, silhouette *f*; *vt* esquisser,
silhouetter.
outlive [autˈliv] *vt* survivre à.
outlook [ˈautluk] *n* (point *m* de) vue
f, perspective *f*, philosophie *f*,
aguets *m pl*.
outlying [ˈautˌlaiiŋ] *a* éloigné, excentrique.
outmatch [ˈautmætʃ] *vt* surpasser
en finesse.
outpost [ˈautpoust] *n* avant poste *m*.
outpouring [ˈautˌpɔːriŋ] effusion *f*,
débordement *m*.
output [ˈautput] *n* production *f*,
rendement *m*.
outrage [ˈautreidʒ] *n* outrage *m*; *vt*
outrager, violenter.
outrageous [autˈreidʒəs] *a* outra-
geux, outrageant, excessif, indigne.
outrageously [autˈreidʒəsli] *ad* outre
mesure, immodérément.
outright [ˈautrait] *a* net, direct; *ad*
du (sur le) coup, complètement; *a*
franc.
outset [ˈautset] *n* début *m*.
outshine [autˈʃain] *vt* éclipser, dépasser.
outside [ˈautˈsaid] *n* dehors *m*,
impériale *f*, extérieur *m*, maximum
m; *a* extérieur, du dehors; *ad* (en)
dehors, à l'extérieur; *prep* hors de,
en (au) dehors de.
outsider [ˈautˈsaidə] *n* étranger, -ère,
intrus(e) *mf*, outsider *m*.
outskirts [ˈautskəːts] *n* lisière *f*,
banlieue *f*, faubourgs *m pl*.
outspoken [autˈspoukən] *a* franc,
brutal, rond, entier.
outstanding [autˈstændiŋ] *a* éminent, marquant, en suspens, à
recouvrer.
outstretch [autˈstretʃ] *vt* (é)tendre,
déployer.
outstrip [autˈstrip] *vt* dé-,sur-
passer, distancer.
outward [ˈautwəd] *a* extérieur, de
dehors, externe; *ad* pour l'étranger,
vers le dehors.
outwards [ˈautwədz] *ad see* **outward**.
outwit [autˈwit] *vt* déjouer, rouler,
dépister.
outworn [autˈwɔːn] *a* usé jusqu'à la
corde, désuet.
oval [ˈouvəl] *an* ovale *m*.
ovary [ˈouvəri] *n* ovaire *m*.
ovation [ouˈveiʃən] *n* ovation *f*.

oven ['ʌvn] n four m.
over ['ouvə] prep sur, contre, par
dessus, au dessus de, plus de; ad
au dessus, et plus, au delà, de trop,
à l'excès.
overall ['ouvərɔ:l] n salopette f,
combinaison f, bleu m de travail,
blouse f; a général.
overawe [ˌouvər'ɔ:] vt en imposer à,
intimider.
overbalance [ˌouvə'bæləns] vi perdre
l'équilibre; vt renverser.
overbearing [ˌouvə'bɛəriŋ] a arrogant, autoritaire.
overboard ['ouvəbɔ:d] ad par dessus
bord, à la mer.
overcast ['ouvəka:st] a couvert,
assombri.
overcharge ['ouvə'tʃa:dʒ] n majoration f, prix excessif m, surcharge f;
vt surfaire, faire payer trop cher à,
surcharger.
overcoat ['ouvəkout] n pardessus m.
overcome [ˌouvə'kʌm] vt surmonter,
dominer, venir à bout de, triompher
de, vaincre, accabler.
overdo [ˌouvə'du:] vt exagérer,
outrer, trop cuire.
overdose ['ouvədous] n dose excessive f.
overdraft ['ouvədra:ft] n dépasse-
ment de crédit m, découvert m.
overdraw ['ouvə'drɔ:] vt tirer à
découvert, charger.
overdrive ['ouvə'draiv] n vitesse
surmultipliée f.
overdue ['ouvə'dju:] a en retard,
périmé, échu.
overestimate ['ouvər'estimeit] vt surestimer.
overflow ['ouvəflou] n trop plein m,
déversoir m; [ouvə'flou] vi déborder;
vt inonder.
overflowing [ˌouvə'flouiŋ] n débordement m, inondation f; a
débordant.
overgrow ['ouvə'grou] vt envahir; vi
trop grandir.
overhang ['ouvə'hæŋ] vt surplomber.
overhaul ['ouvəhɔ:l] vt réviser,
remettre en état, rattraper; n
remise en état f, révision f, examen
détaillé m.
overhead ['ouvəhed] a ad aérien;
n pl frais généraux m pl.
overhear [ˌouvə'hiə] vt surprendre.
overheat ['ouvə'hi:t] vt surchauffer.
overjoyed [ˌouvə'dʒɔid] a transporté de joie, enchanté.
overland ['ouvəlænd] a ad par voie
de terre.
overlap ['ouvəlæp] vt chevaucher; vi
se chevaucher.
overleaf ['ouvə'li:f] ad au revers, au
verso.
overlook [ˌouvə'luk] vt avoir vue sur,
dominer, oublier, laisser passer,
négliger, surveiller.
overmuch ['ouvə'mʌtʃ] ad par trop,
excessif.

overpass ['ouvəpa:s] n enjambement m.
overpopulated ['ouvə'pɔpjuleitid] a
surpeuplé.
overpower [ˌouvə'pauə] vt terrasser,
subjuger, maîtriser, accabler.
overpowering [ˌouvə'pauəriŋ] a irrésistible, accablant.
overproduction ['ouvəprə'dʌkʃən] n
surproduction f.
overrate ['ouvə'reit] vt surfaire,
surtaxer, présumer de.
overreach [ˌouvə'ri:tʃ] vt duper, dépasser; to — oneself se surmener,
se donner un effort.
overripe ['ouvə'raip] a trop mûr,
trop fait, blet.
overrule [ˌouvə'ru:l] vt annuler par
autorité supérieure, casser, passer
outre à.
overrun [ˌouvə'rʌn] vt envahir,
infester, excéder, dépasser, surmener.
oversea(s) ['ouvə'si:(z)] a d'outre-
mer; ad outre-mer.
oversee ['ouvə'si:] vt surveiller.
overseer ['ouvəsiə] n surveillant(e)
mf, contremaître, -tresse.
overshadow [ˌouvə'ʃædou] vt ombrager, éclipser.
overshoes ['ouvəʃu:z] n pl caout-
choucs m pl.
overshoot [ˌouvə'ʃu:t] vi tirer trop
loin; vt dépasser.
oversight ['ouvəsait] n inadvertance
f, oubli m.
overspill ['ouvəspil] n déversement
m de population.
overstate ['ouvə'steit] vt exagérer.
overstatement ['ouvə'steitmənt] n
exagération f.
overstep ['ouvə'step] vt outrepasser,
dépasser.
overstrain ['ouvəstrein] vt tendre à
l'excès, surmener.
overstrung ['ouvə'strʌŋ] a hyper-
tendu.
overt ['ouvə:t] a public, évident.
overtake [ˌouvə'teik] vt dépasser,
doubler, rattraper, surprendre.
overthrow [ˌouvə'θrou] vt renverser,
mettre à bas.
overtime ['ouvətaim] n heures
supplémentaires f pl; ad au delà du
temps normal.
overtly ['ouvə:tli] ad au grand jour.
overture ['ouvətjuə] n ouverture f.
overturn ['ouvətə:n] vt tourner sens
dessus dessous, renverser; vi verser,
chavirer, se renverser, capoter.
overvaluation ['ouvəˌvælju'eiʃən] n
surestimation f.
overvalue ['ouvə'vælju:] vt surestimer.
overweening [ˌouvə'wi:niŋ] a présomptueux.
overweight ['ouvə'weit] n excédent
m, prépondérance f.
overwhelm [ˌouvə'welm] vt accabler,
écraser, combler.

overwork ['ouvə'wəːk] n surmenage m.

overwork ['ouvə'wəːk] vt surmener; vi se surmener.

overwrought ['ouvə'rɔːt] a surmené, surexcité.

owe [ou] vt devoir.

owing ['ouiŋ] a dû; — **to** grâce à.

owl [aul] n hibou m, chouette f.

owlish ['auliʃ] a solennel, prétentieux, de hibou.

own [oun] a propre, à moi etc; vt posséder, admettre, reconnaître, avouer.

ownership ['ounəʃip] n propriété f, possession f.

ox [ɔks] (pl **oxen**) n bœuf m.

oxide ['ɔksaid] n oxyde m.

oxidize ['ɔksidaiz] vt oxyder; vi s'oxyder.

oxygen ['ɔksidʒən] n oxygène m.

oxygenate [ɔk'sidʒineit] vt oxygéner.

oyster ['ɔistə] n huître f; — **bed** banc d'huîtres m.

P

pace [peis] n pas m, allure f, vitesse f; vt arpenter, mesurer au pas, entraîner; vi marcher (à pas mesurés).

pacific [pə'sifik] a pacifique, paisible; n Pacifique m.

pacification [ˌpæsifi'keiʃən] n pacification f.

pacifier ['pæsifaiə] n pacificateur, -trice.

pacifism ['pæsifizəm] n pacifisme m.

pacifist ['pæsifist] n pacifiste mf.

pacify ['pæsifai] vt pacifier, apaiser.

pack [pæk] n paquet m, ballot m, jeu m (de cartes), bande f, meute f; —**ice** banquise f; vt empaqueter, emballer, envelopper, entasser, bourrer; vi se presser, s'attrouper, se tasser, faire ses malles.

package ['pækidʒ] n empaquetage m, paquet m; — **tour** voyage organisé m.

packer ['pækə] n emballeur m.

packet ['pækit] n paquet m, colis m, paquebot m.

packing ['pækiŋ] n emballage m, tassement m.

pact [pækt] n pacte m.

pad [pæd] n bourrelet m, tampon m, coussin m, sous-main m, (paper) bloc m, (fam) pieu m; vt rembourrer, capitonner, garnir.

padding ['pædiŋ] n rembourrage m, capitonnage m, remplissage m.

paddle ['pædl] n pagaie f, palette f, aube f; vti pagayer; vi patauger, barboter, faire trempette.

paddock ['pædək] n pré m, paddock m, pesage m.

padlock ['pædlɔk] n cadenas m; vt cadenasser.

pagan ['peigən] an païen, -ïenne.

paganism ['peigənizəm] n paganisme m.

page [peidʒ] n page f, (boy) page m, chasseur m, groom m; vt paginer.

pageant ['pædʒənt] n cortège m, cavalcade f, fête f, spectacle m.

pail(ful) ['peil(ful)] n seau m.

pain [pein] n peine f, douleur f; vt faire mal à, faire de la peine à.

painful ['peinful] a douloureux, pénible.

pain-killer ['peinkilə] n calmant m, anodin m.

painless ['peinlis] a indolore, sans douleur.

painstaking ['peinzˌteikiŋ] a laborieux, assidu, soigné.

paint [peint] n peinture f; vti peindre; vi faire de la peinture.

painter ['peintə] n peintre m, peintre décorateur m.

pair [pɛə] n paire f, couple mf; vt accoupler, apparier, assortir.

pajamas [pə'dʒɑːməz] n pyjama(s) m (pl).

pal [pæl] n copain m, copine f.

palace ['pælis] n palais m.

palatable ['pælətəbl] a délectable, agréable.

palate ['pælit] n palais m.

palaver [pə'lɑːvə] n palabre f; vi palabrer.

pale [peil] n pieu m, pal m; a pâle; vi pâlir.

palette ['pælit] n palette f.

paling ['peiliŋ] n palissade f, clôture f.

palish ['peiliʃ] a pâlot.

pall [pɔːl] n drap mortuaire m, voile m; vi s'affadir, se blaser.

pallbearer ['pɔːlˌbɛərə] n qui tient un cordon du poêle.

pallet ['pælit] n paillasse f.

palliate ['pælieit] vt pallier, atténuer.

palliative ['pæliətiv] an palliatif m.

pallid ['pælid] a blême, pâle.

palm [pɑːm] n paume f, palmier m, palme f, rameau m; **P— Sunday** dimanche des Rameaux; —**nut** noix f de palme; — **wine** vin n de palme; vt escamoter; **to** — **off** repasser, refiler.

palmist ['pɑːmist] n chiromancien, -ienne.

palmistry ['pɑːmistri] n chiromancie f.

palmy ['pɑːmi] a triomphant, beau, heureux.

palpable ['pælpəbl] a palpable, évident.

palpitate ['pælpiteit] vi palpiter.

palsy ['pɔːlzi] n paralysie f.

paltry ['pɔːltri] a mesquin, pauvre, malheureux.

pamper ['pæmpə] vt dorloter, gâter.

pamphlet ['pæmflit] n brochure f, opuscule m.

pamphleteer [ˌpæmfli'tiə] n publiciste m, auteur m de brochures.

pan [pæn] n casserole f, sauteuse f,

poêle *f*, bac *m*; **to — out** se passer, s'arranger.
panacea [,pænə'siə] *n* panacée *f*.
pancake ['pænkeik] *n* crêpe *f*.
pandemonium [,pændi'mouniəm] *n* charivari *m*, tapage infernal *m*.
pander ['pændə] **to — to** se prêter à, encourager.
pane [pein] *n* carreau *m*, vitre *f*.
panel ['pænl] *n* tableau *m*, panneau *m*, lambris *m*, jury *m*; *vt* lambrisser, plaquer.
paneling ['pænliŋ] *n* lambrissage *m*.
pang [pæŋ] *n* serrement de cœur *m*, douleur *f*; **—s of death** affres de la mort *f pl*.
panic ['pænik] *an* panique *f*; *vi* s'affoler; **—-monger** *n* fauteur *m* de panique, paniquard *m*.
panicky ['pæniki] *a* alarmiste, qui s'affole pour rien.
panoply ['pænəpli] *n* panoplie *f*.
pansy ['pænzi] *n* pensée *f*.
pant [pænt] *vi* haleter, panteler, aspirer (à **after**).
panties ['pæntiz] *n pl* slip *m*, culotte *f*.
pantheism ['pænθiizəm] *n* panthéisme *m*.
panther ['pænθə] *n* panthère *f*.
pantry ['pæntri] *n* office *m*, garde-manger *m*.
pants [pænts] *n* caleçon *m*, pantalon *m*.
pap [pæp] *n* tétin *m*, mamelon *m*, bouillie *f*.
papacy ['peipəsi] *n* papauté *f*.
paper ['peipə] *n* papier *m*, journal *m*, article *m*, essai *m*, épreuve *f*, copie *f*; *vt* tapisser; **—hanger** *n* colleur de papier *m*; **—knife** *n* coupe-papier *m*; **—weight** *n* presse-papier *m*; **—clip** *n* trombone *m*; pince *f*.
papermill ['peipəmil] *n* papeterie *f*.
papist ['peipist] *n* papiste *mf*.
par [pɑː] *n* égalité *f*, pair *m*, moyenne *f*.
parable ['pærəbl] *n* parabole *f*.
parachute ['pærəʃuːt] *n* parachute *m*.
parachutist ['pærəʃuːtist] *n* parachutiste *mf*.
parade [pə'reid] *n* parade *f*, revue *f*, défilé *m*; *vt* faire étalage de, faire défiler, passer en revue; *vi* défiler, parader.
paradise ['pærədais] *n* paradis *m*.
paradox ['pærədɔks] *n* paradoxe *m*.
paradoxical [,pærə'dɔksikəl] *a* paradoxal.
paraffin ['pærəfin] *n* paraffine *f*, pétrole *m*.
paragon ['pærəgən] *n* parangon *m*.
paragraph ['pærəgrɑːf] *n* paragraphe *m*, alinéa *m*, entrefilet *m*.
parakeet ['pærəkiːt] *n* perruche *f*.
parallel ['pærəlel] *a* parallèle, pareil; *n* parallèle *mf*; *vt* mettre en parallèle, comparer.

paralysis [pə'rælisis] *n* paralysie *f*.
paralyze ['pærəlaiz] *vt* paralyser.
paramount ['pærəmaunt] *a* suprême.
parapet ['pærəpit] *n* parapet *m*, garde-fou *m*.
paraphernalia [,pærəfə'neiljə] *n* attirail *m*, boutique *f*, bataclan *m*, affaires *f pl*.
paraphrase ['pærəfreiz] *n* paraphrase *f*; *vt* paraphraser.
parasite ['pærəsait] *n* parasite *m*, pique-assiette *m*.
paratrooper ['pærətruːpə] *n* parachutiste *m*.
parasol ['pærəsɔl] *n* parasol *m*, ombrelle *f*.
parcel ['pɑːsl] *n* paquet *m*, colis *m*, parcelle *f*, bande *f*; *vt* morceler, emballer.
parch [pɑːtʃ] *vt* rôtir, (des)sécher, griller.
parchment ['pɑːtʃmənt] *n* parchemin *m*.
pardon ['pɑːdn] *n* pardon *m*; *vt* pardonner.
pardonable ['pɑːdnəbl] *a* pardonnable, excusable.
pare [pɛə] *vt* peler, rogner, tailler.
parent ['pɛərənt] *n* père *m*, mère *f*; *pl* parents *m pl*.
parentage ['pɛərəntidʒ] *n* extraction *f*, naissance *f*.
parenthesis [pə'renθisis] *n* parenthèse *f*.
pariah ['pæriə] *n* paria *m*.
parish ['pæriʃ] *n* paroisse *f*.
parishioner [pə'riʃənə] *n* paroissien, -ienne.
Parisian [pə'riziən] *an* parisien.
park [pɑːk] *n* parc *m*, jardin public *m*; *vt* parquer; *vi* stationner.
parking ['pɑːkiŋ] *n* stationnement *m*, parcage *m*; **— meter** *n* parcomètre *m*, compteur *m*.
parley ['pɑːli] *n* pourparlers *m pl*; *vi* parlementer, entrer en pourparlers.
parliament ['pɑːləmənt] *n* parlement *m*.
parliamentary [,pɑːlə'mentəri] *a* parlementaire.
parlor ['pɑːlə] *n* salle *f*, petit salon *m*, parloir *m*; **beauty —** salon de coiffure *m*.
parochial [pə'roukiəl] *a* paroissial, étroit.
parochialism [pə'roukiəlizem] *n* esprit de clocher *m*.
parody ['pærədi] *n* parodie *f*, pastiche *m*; *vt* parodier, pasticher.
parole [pə'roul] *n* parole *f*.
paroxysm ['pærəksizəm] *n* paroxysme *m*, crise *f*.
parricide ['pærisaid] *n* parricide (*crime*) *m*, (*person*) *mf*.
parrot ['pærət] *n* perroquet *m*.
parry ['pæri] *n* parade *f*; *vt* parer, détourner.
parse [pɑːz] *vt* analyser.

parsimonious [ˌpɑːsiˈmouniəs] *a* parcimonieux, ladre.

parsimony [ˈpɑːsiməni] *n* parcimonie *f*, ladrerie *f*.

parsley [ˈpɑːsli] *n* persil *m*.

parsnip [ˈpɑːsnip] *n* panais *m*.

parson [ˈpɑːsn] *n* prêtre *m*, pasteur *m*.

parsonage [ˈpɑːsnidʒ] *n* cure *f*, presbytère *m*.

part [pɑːt] *n* partie *f*, parti *m*, région *f*, (*theatre*) rôle *m*, côté *m*; *vt* diviser, séparer; *vi* se séparer, se rompre; **to — with** céder, se séparer de.

partake [pɑːˈteik] **to — of** participer à, prendre part à, partager, tenir de, sentir.

partial [ˈpɑːʃəl] *a* partial, qui a un faible (pour **to**).

partiality [ˌpɑːʃiˈæliti] *n* partialité *f*, penchant *m*.

participate [pɑːˈtisipeit] *vi* participer (à, de **in**).

participation [pɑːˌtisiˈpeiʃən] *n* participation *f*.

participle [ˈpɑːtsipl] *n* participe *m*.

particle [ˈpɑːtikl] *n* particule *f*, parcelle *f*, brin *m*, semblant *m*.

particular [pəˈtikjulə] *a* spécial, minutieux, difficile; *n* *pl* détails *m pl*, renseignements *m pl*.

particularity [pəˌtikjuˈlæriti] *n* particularité *f*, minutie *f*.

particularize [pəˈtikjuləraiz] *vt* spécifier; *vi* préciser.

parting [ˈpɑːtiŋ] *n* séparation *f*, rupture *f*, (*hair*) raie *f*, (*ways*) croisée *f*; *a* de départ, d'adieu.

partisan [ˌpɑːtiˈzæn] *n* partisan *m*.

partition [pɑːˈtiʃən] *n* partage *m* démembrement *m*, morcellement *m*, cloison *f*; *vt* démembrer, morceler, partager, cloisonner.

partner [ˈpɑːtnə] *n* partenaire *mf*, associé(e) *mf*, cavalier *m*, danseuse *f*; *vt* associer, être associé à, mener, être le partenaire de.

partnership [ˈpɑːtnəʃip] *n* association *f*, société *f*.

partridge [ˈpɑːtridʒ] *n* perdrix *f*.

part-time [ˈpɑːtˈtaim] *a* à mi-temps.

party [ˈpɑːti] *n* parti *m*, réception *f*, partie *f*, bande *f*, détachement *m*.

pass [pɑːs] *n* défilé *m*, col *m*, permission *f*, passe *f*, (*school*) moyenne *f*; *vt* (faire) passer, passer près de, disparaître, dépasser, franchir, doubler, voter, approuver, réussir à (un examen), recevoir; *vi* passer, s'écouler, se passer, être reçu.

passable [ˈpɑːsəbl] *a* passable, praticable, traversable.

passage [ˈpæsidʒ] *n* passage *m*, corridor *m*, échange *m*, passe d'armes *f*, traversée *f*.

pass-book [ˈpɑːsbuk] *n* carnet de comptes *m*.

passenger [ˈpæsindʒə] *n* passager, -ère, voyageur, -euse.

passer-by [ˈpɑːsəˈbai] *n* passant(e) *mf*.

passing [ˈpɑːsiŋ] *n* passage *m*, mort *f*, écoulement *m*; *a* passager, fugitif.

passion [ˈpæʃən] *n* passion *f*, colère *f*.

passionate [ˈpæʃənit] *a* ardent, passionné, irascible.

passionately [ˈpæʃənitli] *ad* passionnément.

passive [ˈpæsiv] *a* passif.

passiveness [ˈpæsivnis] *n* passivité *f*, inertie *f*.

pass-key [ˈpɑːskiː] *n* passe-partout *m*.

passport [ˈpɑːspɔːt] *n* passeport *m*.

password [ˈpɑːswəːd] *n* mot de passe *m*.

past [pɑːst] *an* passé *m*; *a* ancien, ex—; *prep* après, au delà de, plus loin que.

paste [peist] *n* pâte *f*, colle *f*; *vt* coller, (*fam*) rosser.

pasteboard [ˈpeistbɔːd] *n* carton *m*.

pastel [ˈpæstəl] *n* pastel *m*.

pasteurize [ˈpæstəraiz] *vt* pasteuriser.

pastime [ˈpɑːstaim] *n* passetemps *m*, distraction *f*.

pastor [ˈpɑːstə] *n* pasteur *m*.

pastoral [ˈpɑːstərəl] *a* pastoral.

pastry [ˈpeistri] *n* pâtisserie *f*, pâte *f*; **—cook** *n* pâtissier, -ière; **—shop** *n* pâtisserie *f*.

pasture [ˈpɑːstʃə] *n* pâture *f*, pâturage *m*, pacage *m*; *vt* faire paître.

pasty [ˈpeisti] *n* pâté *m*; *a* pâteux, terreux.

pat [pæt] *n* tape *f*, coquille *f*, motte *f*, rondelle *f*; *vt* tapoter, caresser; *ad* à point, du tac au tac, tout prêt.

patch [pætʃ] *n* pièce *f*, emplâtre *m*, mouche *f*, tache *f*, (*peas*) planche *f*, carré *m*; *vt* rapiécer; **to — up** replâtrer, rafistoler.

patchwork [ˈpætʃwəːk] *n* rapiéçage *m*, mosaïque *f*.

patchy [ˈpætʃi] *a* fait de pièces et de morceaux, inégal, irrégulier.

paten [ˈpætən] *n* patène *f*.

patent [ˈpeitənt] *n* brevet *m*, lettres patentes *f pl*; *a* breveté, patenté, manifeste; *vt* faire breveter.

paternal [pəˈtəːnl] *a* paternel.

paternity [pəˈtəːniti] *n* paternité *f*.

path [pɑːθ] *n* sentier *m*, course *f*, chemin *m*.

pathetic [pəˈθetik] *a* pathétique, triste, attendrissant.

pathfinder [ˈpɑːθˌfaində] *n* éclaireur *m*, pionnier *m*.

patience [ˈpeiʃəns] *n* patience *f*, (*cards*) réussite *f*.

patient [ˈpeiʃənt] *n* malade *mf*, patient(e) *mf*; *a* patient.

patiently [ˈpeiʃəntli] *ad* patiemment, avec patience.

patriarch [ˈpeitriɑːk] *n* patriarche *m*.

patriarchal [ˌpeitri'ɑːkəl] a patriarcal.

Patrick ['pætrik] Patrice m.

patrimony ['pætriməni] n patrimoine m.

patriot ['peitriət] n patriote mf.

patriotic [ˌpætri'ɔtik] a patriotique, (person) patriote.

patriotism ['pætriətizəm] n patriotisme m.

patrol [pə'troul] n patrouille f, ronde f; vti patrouiller.

patron, -ess ['peitrən, is] n patron, -onne, protecteur, -trice, client(e) mf, habitué(e) mf.

patronage ['pætrənidʒ] n patronage m, protection f, clientèle f, airs protecteurs m pl.

patronize ['pætrənaiz] vt patronner, protéger, traiter de haut, accorder sa clientèle à, se fournir chez.

patter ['pætə] n crépitement m, trottinement m, piétinement m, fouettement m, bagout m, boniment m; vi crépiter, trottiner, jaser.

pattern ['pætən] n modèle m, échantillon m, dessin m.

patty ['pæti] n petit pâté m.

paucity ['pɔːsiti] n rareté f, disette f, manque m.

Paul [pɔːl] Paul m.

paunch ['pɔːntʃ] n panse f, bedaine f.

pauper ['pɔːpə] n indigent(e) mf, mendiant(e) mf.

pause [pɔːz] n pause f, arrêt m, silence m, point d'orgue m; vi s'arrêter, faire la pause, hésiter.

pave [peiv] vt paver, carreler, frayer (la voie).

pavement ['peivmənt] n pavé m, pavage m, trottoir m; chaussée f.

pavilion [pə'viljən] n tente f, pavillon m.

paw [pɔː] n patte f; vt frapper du pied, tripoter; vi piaffer.

pawn [pɔːn] n pion m, gage m; vt mettre en gage.

pawnbroker ['pɔːnˌbroukə] n prêteur m sur gages.

pawnshop ['pɔːnʃɔp] n mont-de-piété m; (fam) tante f.

pawpaw ['pɔːpɔː] n papaye f.

pay [pei] n paie f, gages m pl, salaire m, solde f; vt payer, rétribuer, acquitter, faire; — in verser, encaisser; — a visit rendre visite (à to).

payer ['peiə] n payeur, -euse, payant(e) mf.

paying-guest ['peiiŋˌgest] n hôte payant m.

paymaster ['peiˌmɑːstə] n trésorier m, payeur m.

payment ['peimənt] n paiement m, rémunération f, règlement m, versement m.

pea [piː] n pois m; green —s petits pois; sweet — pois de senteur.

peace [piːs] n paix f; justice of the

— juge de paix m; vi to hold one's — se taire.

peaceful ['piːsful] a paisible, pacifique.

peacefulness ['piːsfulnis] n paix f, humeur paisible f.

peacemaker ['piːsˌmeikə] n pacificateur, -trice.

peach [piːtʃ] n pêche f.

peach-tree ['piːtʃtriː] n pêcher m.

peacock ['piːkɔk] n paon m.

peahen ['piːhen] n paonne f.

peak [piːk] n pic m, cime f, pointe f, visière f, apogée f, plus fort m; a maximum, de pointe.

peaked [piːkt] a à (en) pointe, pointu, hâve.

peal [piːl] n carillon m, volée de cloches f, coup m, grondement m; vti sonner; vi carillonner, gronder, retentir.

peanut ['piːnʌt] n cacahuète f.

pear [peə] n poire f.

pearl [pəːl] n perle f.

pearly ['pəːli] a nacré, perlé.

pear-tree ['peətriː] n poirier m.

peasant ['pezənt] n paysan, -anne.

peasantry ['pezəntri] n paysans m pl.

peat [piːt] n tourbe f; — bog tourbière.

pebble ['pebl] n galet m, caillou m.

peck [pek] n coup de bec m, bécot m; vt picoter, donner un coup de bec à, bécoter; vti manger du bout des lèvres; vi picorer.

peculiar [pi'kjuːliə] a particulier, excentrique, singulier.

peculiarity [piˌkjuːli'æriti] n singularité f, particularité f.

pecuniary [pi'kjuːniəri] a pécuniaire, d'argent.

pedal ['pedl] n pédale f; vi pédaler.

pedant ['pedənt] n pédant(e) mf.

pedantic [pi'dæntik] a pédantesque, pédant.

pedantry ['pedəntri] n pédantisme m.

peddle ['pedl] vt colporter; vi faire le colportage.

peddler ['pedlə] n colporteur m, porteballe m; itinerant — dioula m.

pedestrian [pi'destriən] n piéton m; a à pied, terre à terre, banal; — crossing passage clouté m.

pedigree ['pedigriː] n généalogie f, pedigree m.

pediment ['pedimənt] n fronton m.

peel [piːl] n peau f, écorce f, pelure f; vti peler; vt éplucher; vi s'écailler.

peep [piːp] n coup d'œil m, point du jour m, pépiement m, piaulement m; vi pépier, risquer un coup d'œil, se montrer; —hole n judas m.

peer [piə] n pair m, pareil, -eille, égal(e) mf; vi risquer un coup d'œil; to — at scruter.

peerage ['piəridʒ] n pairie f.

peerless ['piəlis] a incomparable, sans pareil.

peevish ['piːviʃ] *a* bougon, revêche, irritable, maussade.

peevishness ['piːviʃnis] *n* humeur bourrue *f*.

peg [peg] *n* cheville *f*, patère *f*, piquet *m*; **to come down a** — en rabattre; *vt* cheviller, marquer, accrocher; — **away** bûcher.

pellet ['pelit] *n* boulette *f*, pilule *f*, grain de plomb *m*.

pelt [pelt] *n* peau *f*; **at full** — à toutes jambes; *vt* bombarder; *vi* (*rain*) tomber à verse.

pen [pen] *n* parc *m*, plume *f*, stylo *m*; *vt* enfermer, parquer, écrire.

penal ['piːnl] *a* pénal, punissable; — **servitude** *n* travaux forcés *m pl*.

penalty ['penlti] *n* amende *f*, peine *f*, sanction *f*, pénalité *f*; (*football*) penalty *m*; inconvénient *m*, rançon *f*.

penance ['penəns] *n* pénitence *f*.

pencil ['pensl] *n* crayon *m*, faisceau *m*; *vt* crayonner, marquer au crayon.

pendant ['pendənt] *n* pendant(if) *m*, pendeloque *f*, (*flag*) flamme *f*.

pending ['pendiŋ] *prep* pendant, en attendant.

pendulum ['pendjuləm] *n* pendule *m*, balancier *m*.

penetrate ['penitreit] *vti* pénétrer.

penetrating ['penitreitiŋ] *a* pénétrant, perçant.

penguin ['peŋgwin] *n* pingouin *m*.

penholder ['pen,houldə] *n* porte-plume *m*.

penicillin [,peni'silin] *n* pénicilline *f*.

peninsula [pi'ninsjulə] *n* péninsule *f*.

penitence ['penitəns] *n* pénitence *f*.

penitent ['penitənt] *an* pénitent(e) *mf*; *a* contrit.

penitentiary [,peni'tenʃəri] *n* pénitencier *m*, prison *f*.

penknife ['pennaif] *n* canif *m*.

pen-name ['penneim] *n* pseudonyme *m*.

pennant ['penənt] *n* flamme *f*, banderole *f*.

penniless ['penilis] *a* sans le sou.

penny ['peni] *n* sou *m*, deux sous *m pl*; —**worth** pour deux sous; —**wise** *a* lésineur.

pension ['penʃən] *n* pension *f*, retraite *f*; *vt* pensionner; **to** — **off** mettre à la retraite.

pensive ['pensiv] *a* pensif.

pensiveness ['pensivnis] *n* rêverie *f*, air rêveur *m*.

pent [pent] *a* — **in** renfermé, confiné; — **up** contenu, refoulé.

Pentecost ['pentikɔst] *n* Pentecôte *f*.

penthouse ['penthaus] *n* appentis *m*, auvent *m*.

penurious [pi'njuəriəs] *a* pauvre, avare.

penury ['penjuri] *n* pénurie *f*, misère *f*.

peony ['piəni] *n* pivoine *f*.

people ['piːpl] *n* peuple *m*, habitants

m pl, gens *m pl*, personnes *f pl*, monde *m*, famille *f*, on, vous; *vt* peupler.

pep [pep] *n* vigueur *f*, allant *m*; **to** — **up** remonter.

pepper ['pepə] *n* poivre *m*; *vt* poivrer, cribler.

pepper-box, -pot ['pepəbɔks, -pɔt] *n* poivrière *f*.

peppermint ['pepəmint] *n* menthe poivrée *f*.

peppery ['pepəri] *a* poivré, emporté, colérique.

pep-pill ['pep'pil] *n* remontant *m*.

per [pəː] *prep* par, pour, à, par l'entremise de.

peradventure [pərəd'ventʃə] *ad* d'aventure, par hasard.

perambulate [pə'ræmbjuleit] *vi* déambuler, se promener.

perambulator ['præmbjuleitə] *n* voiture d'enfant *f*.

perceive [pə'siːv] *vt* percevoir, comprendre, s'apercevoir (de).

percentage [pə'sentidʒ] *n* pourcentage *m*, proportion *f*.

perceptible [pə'septəbl] *a* perceptible, sensible.

perception [pə'sepʃən] *n* perception *f*.

perch [pəːtʃ] *n* perche *f*, perchoir *m*; *vi* se percher, se jucher.

perchance [pə'tʃɑːns] *ad* par hasard.

percolate ['pəːkəleit] *vt* filtrer.

percolator ['pəːkəleitə] *n* percolateur *m*, filtre *m*.

percussion [pəː'kʌʃən] *n* percussion *f*, choc *m*.

perdition [pəː'diʃən] *n* ruine *f*, perte *f*.

peremptory [pə'remptəri] *a* péremptoire, catégorique, absolu.

perennial [pə'reniəl] *a* perpétuel, vivace.

perfect ['pəːfikt] *a* parfait.

perfect [pə'fekt] *vt* perfectionner, parfaire, achever.

perfection [pə'fekʃən] *n* perfection *f*.

perfidious [pəː'fidiəs] *a* perfide, traître.

perfidy ['pəːfidi] *n* perfidie *f*.

perforate ['pəːfəreit] *vt* perforer, percer.

perforation [,pəːfə'reiʃən] *n* perforation *f*, percement *m*.

perforce [pə'fɔːs] *ad* de (par) force.

perform [pə'fɔːm] *vt* remplir, exécuter; *vti* jouer.

performance [pə'fɔːməns] *n* exécution *f*, (*theatre*) représentation *f*, (*cine*) séance *f*, exploit *m*, fonctionnement *m*, performance *f*.

performer [pə'fɔːmə] *n* exécutant(e) *mf*, artiste *mf*.

perfume ['pəːfjuːm] *n* parfum *m*.

perfume [pə'fjuːm] *vt* parfumer.

perfumery [pə'fjuːməri] *n* parfumerie *f*.

perfunctory [pə'fʌŋktəri] *a* de pure forme, superficiel, négligent.

perhaps [pə'hæps] *ad* peut-être.
peril ['peril] *n* péril *m*, danger *m*; **at your —** à vos risques et périls.
perilous ['periləs] *a* périlleux, dangereux.
period ['piəriəd] *n* période *f*, délai *m*, époque *f*, point *m*, phase *f*, style *m*; *pl (med)* règles *f pl*.
perish ['periʃ] *vi* périr, mourir, se détériorer.
perishable ['periʃəbl] *a* périssable, éphémère.
perished ['periʃt] *a* mort, détérioré.
peritonitis [,peritə'naitis] *n* péritonite *f*.
periwinkle ['peri,wiŋkl] *n* pervenche *f*, bigorneau *m*.
perjure ['pə:dʒə] *vt* **to — oneself** se parjurer.
perjurer ['pə:dʒərə] *n* parjure *mf*.
perjury ['pə:dʒəri] *n* parjure *m*, faux témoignage *m*.
perk [pə:k] *vt* **to — up** ravigoter, remettre le moral à; *vi* se ranimer, se retaper.
perky ['pə:ki] *a* impertinent, coquet, dégagé, guilleret.
permanent ['pə:mənənt] *a* permanent, fixe.
permanent wave ['pə:mənənt'weiv] *n* ondulation *f* permanente.
permanently ['pə:mənəntli] *ad* de façon permanente, à titre définitif.
permeable ['pə:miəbl] *a* perméable.
permeate ['pə:mieit] *vt* pénétrer; *vi* s'insinuer, filtrer.
permission [pə'miʃən] *n* permission *f*, autorisation *f*.
permit ['pə:mit] *n* permis *m*, autorisation *f*.
permit [pə'mit] *vt* permettre (à), autoriser.
pernicious [pə:'niʃəs] *a* pernicieux, fatal.
perpendicular [,pə:pən'dikjulə] *an* perpendiculaire *f*.
perpetrate ['pə:pitreit] *vt* commettre, perpétrer.
perpetration [,pə:pi'treiʃən] *n* perpétration *f*.
perpetrator ['pə:pitreitə] *n* auteur *m*.
perpetual [pə'petjuəl] *a* éternel, perpétuel.
perpetuate [pə'petjueit] *vt* perpétuer.
perpetuity [,pə:pi'tju(:)iti] *n* perpétuité *f*.
perplex [pə'pleks] *vt* embarrasser.
perplexed [pə'plekst] *a* perplexe, embarrassé.
perplexity [pə'pleksiti] *n* perplexité *f*.
perquisite ['pe:kwizit] *n* profit *m*, pourboire *m*, casuel *m*, gratte *f*.
persecute ['pə:sikju:t] *vt* persécuter.
persecution [,pə:si'kju:ʃən] *n* persécution *f*.
perseverance [,pə:si'viərəns] *n* persévérance *f*.

persevere [,pə:si'viə] *vi* persévérer, s'obstiner.
persevering [,pə:si'viəriŋ] *a* persévérant, assidu.
Persia ['pə:ʃə] *n* Perse *f*.
Persian ['pə:ʃən] *n* Persan(e) *mf*; *an* persan *m*.
persist [pə'sist] *vi* persister, s'obstiner, s'entêter.
persistency [pə'sistənsi] *n* persistance *f*, obstination *f*.
person ['pə:sn] *n* personne *f*.
personage ['pə:snidʒ] *n* personnage *m*.
personal ['pə:snl] *a* personnel, individuel.
personality [,pə:sə'næliti] *n* personnalité *f*, personnage *m*.
personification [pə:,sɔnifi'keiʃən] *n* personnification *f*.
personify [pə:'sɔnifai] *vt* personnifier.
personnel [,pə:sə'nel] *n* personnel *m*.
perspective [pə'spektiv] *n* perspective *f*.
perspicacious [,pə:spi'keiʃəs] *a* perspicace.
perspicacity [,pə:spi'kæsiti] *n* perspicacité *f*.
perspicuity [,pə:spi'kju(:)iti] *n* clarté *f*, netteté *f*.
perspicuous [pə'spikjuəs] *a* clair, évident.
perspiration [,pə:spə'reiʃən] *n* transpiration *f*.
perspire [pəs'paiə] *vi* transpirer.
persuade [pə'sweid] *vt* persuader, décider.
persuasion [pə'sweiʒən] *n* persuasion *f*, conviction *f*, confession *f*.
persuasive [pə'sweisiv] *a* persuasif.
pert [pə:t] *a* effronté, impertinent.
pertinacious [,pə:ti'neiʃəs] *a* opiniâtre, entêté, obstiné.
pertinacity [,pə:ti'næsiti] *n* opiniâtreté *f*.
pertinence ['pə:tinəns] *n* pertinence *f*, à-propos *m*.
pertinent ['pə:tinənt] *a* pertinent, juste.
pertinently ['pə:tinəntli] *ad* pertinemment, à-propos.
perturb [pə'tə:b] *vt* bouleverser, troubler, inquiéter.
perturbation [,pə:tə:'beiʃən] *n* bouleversement *m*, inquiétude *f*, trouble *m*.
perusal [pə'ru:zəl] *n* examen *m*, lecture *f*.
peruse [pə'ru:z] *vt* étudier, prendre connaissance de.
pervade [pə:'veid] *vt* pénétrer, animer, régner dans.
perverse [pə'və:s] *a* pervers, contrariant.
perversion [pə'və:ʃən] *n* perversion *f*, travestissement *m*.
perversity [pə'və:siti] *n* perversité *f*, esprit de contradiction *m*.
pervert ['pə:və:t] *n* perverti(e) *mf*, apostat *m*.

pervert [pə'vəːt] *vt* pervertir, fausser.
pervious ['pəːviəs] *a* perméable, accessible.
pessimism ['pesimizəm] *n* pessimisme *m*.
pessimistic [.pesi'mistik] *a* pessimiste.
pest [pest] *n* peste *f*, fléau *m*.
pester ['pestə] *vt* tracasser, importuner, infester.
pestilence ['pestiləns] *n* pestilence *f*.
pestilential [.pesti'lenʃəl] *a* pestilentiel, pernicieux.
pestle ['pesl] *n* pilon *m*; *vt* piler, broyer.
pet [pet] *a* animal *m* familier, favori *m*, chouchou *m*; **to take the —** prendre la mouche; *vt* caresser, choyer.
petal ['petl] *n* pétale *m*.
Peter ['piːtə] Pierre *m*.
peter out ['piːtə'aut] *vi* faire long feu, s'épuiser, s'arrêter.
petition [pə'tiʃən] *n* pétition *f*, prière *f*, demande *f*; *vt* adresser une pétition à.
petitioner [pə'tiʃənə] *n* pétitionaire *mf*, requérant(e) *mf*.
petrel ['petrəl] *n* pétrel *m*.
petrify ['petrifai] *vt* pétrifier.
petrol ['petrəl] *n* essence *f*.
petroleum [pi'trouliəm] *n* pétrole *m*.
petticoat ['petikout] *n* jupon *m*, jupe *f*.
pettifoggery ['petifɔgəri] *n* chicane *f*.
pettiness ['petinis] *n* mesquinerie *f*.
pettish ['petiʃ] *a* grincheux.
petty ['peti] *a* petit, mesquin; **— cash** menue monnaie *f*.
petty-officer ['peti'ɔfisə] *n* contremaître *m*; *pl* maistrance *f*.
petulance ['petjuləns] *n* pétulance *f*, vivacité *f*.
petulant ['petjulənt] *a* pétulant, vif.
pew [pjuː] *n* banc *m*.
pewit ['piːwit] *n* vanneau *m*.
pewter ['pjuːtə] *n* étain *m*.
phantom ['fæntəm] *n* fantôme *m*; *a* illusoire.
Pharisee ['færisiː] *n* pharisien *m*.
pharyngitis [.færin'dʒaitis] *n* pharingite *f*.
pharynx ['færiŋks] *n* pharynx *m*.
phase [feiz] *n* phase *f*.
pheasant ['feznt] *n* faisan *m*, faisane *f*.
phenomenal [fi'nɔminl] *a* phénoménal.
phenomenon [fi'nɔminən] *n* phénomène *m*.
phial [faiəl] *n* fiole *f*.
philander [fi'lændə] *vi* papillonner, conter fleurette (à).
philanderer [fi'lændərə] *n* flirteur *m*.
philologist [fi'blədʒist] *n* philologue *m*.
philology [fi'blədʒi] *n* philologie *f*.
philosopher [fi'bsəfə] *n* philosophe *m*.
philosophy [fi'bsəfi] *n* philosophie

f; **moral —** morale *f*; **natural —** physique *f*.
philter ['filtə] *n* philtre *m*.
phlebitis [fli'baitis] *n* phlébite *f*.
phlegm [flem] *n* flegme *m*.
phlegmatic [fleg'mætik] *a* flegmatique.
phonetician [.fɔni'tiʃən] *n* phonéticien *m*.
phonetics [fə'netiks] *n* phonétique *f*.
phony ['founi] *a* drôle, faux.
phosphate ['fɔsfeit] *n* phosphate *m*.
phosphorous ['fɔsfərəs] *a* phosphoreux.
phosphorus ['fɔsfərəs] *n* phosphore *m*.
photograph ['foutəgrɑːf] *n* photographie *f*; *vt* photographier.
photographer [fə'tɔgrəfə] *n* photographe *m*.
photographic [.foutə'græfik] *a* photographique.
phrase [freiz] *n* phrase *f*, locution *f*, expression *f*; *vt* exprimer, rédiger.
phraseology [.freizi'ɔlədʒi] *n* phraséologie *f*.
phthisis ['θaisis] *n* phtisie *f*.
physic ['fizik] *n* (*fam*) médecine *f*, médicaments *m pl*.
physical ['fizikəl] *a* physique.
physician [fi'ziʃən] *n* médecin *m*.
physicist ['fizisist] *n* physicien, -ienne.
physics ['fiziks] *n* physique *f*.
physiognomy [.fizi'ɔnəmi] *n* physionomie *f*.
pianist ['piənist] *n* pianiste *mf*.
piano ['piænou] *n* piano *m*; *ad* piano; **grand —** piano à queue; **upright —** piano droit.
pick [pik] *n* pic *m*, pioche *f*, élite *f*, dessus du panier *m*; *vt* piocher, picorer, cueillir, choisir, trier, (*lock*) crocheter; **to — out** repérer, choisir, faire le tri de; **to — up** *vt* ramasser, prendre, relever, racoler, draguer; *vi* reprendre des forces.
pickaback ['pikəbæk] *ad* sur le dos.
pickax ['pikæks] *n* pioche *f*.
picket ['pikit] *n* piquet *m*, pieu *m*.
picking ['pikiŋ] *n* cueillette *f*, épluchage *m*, crochetage *m*; *pl* bribes *f pl*, glanures *f pl*, gratte *f*.
pickle ['pikl] *n* saumure *f*, marinade *f*; *pl* condiments *m pl*, conserves au vinaigre *f pl*; *vt* conserver, mariner.
pickpocket ['pik.pɔkit] *n* pickpocket *m*, voleur à la tire *m*.
picnic ['piknik] *n* piquenique *m*; *vi* faire un piquenique.
pictorial [pik'tɔːriəl] *a* illustré, pittoresque.
picture ['piktʃə] *n* tableau *m*, image *f*; *pl* cinéma *m*; *vt* représenter, se figurer.
picturesque [.piktʃə'resk] *a* pittoresque.
picturesqueness [.piktʃə'resknis] *n* pittoresque *m*.

pie [pai] *n* pâté *m*, tourte *f*, tarte *f*.

piece [piːs] *n* morceau *m*, pièce *f*; *vt* assembler, rapiécer.

piecemeal ['piːsmiːl] *ad* pièce à pièce, un à un.

piecework ['piːswəːk] *n* travail à la pièce *m*.

pier [piə] *n* jetée *f*, pile *f*, pilier *m*.

pierce [piəs] *vt* percer, pénétrer.

piety ['paiəti] *n* piété *f*.

pig [pig] *n* porc *m*, pourceau *m*, cochon *m*.

pigeon ['pidʒin] *n* pigeon *m*; —**hole** *n* casier *m*; **to** —**hole** *vt* classer.

pigheaded ['pig'hedid] *a* buté, têtu.

pigsty ['pigstai] *n* porcherie *f*, étable *f*, bauge *f*.

pigtail ['pigteil] *n* natte *f*.

pike [paik] *n* pique *f*, brochet *m*, tourniquet *m*.

pikestaff ['paikstaːf] *n* hampe *f*.

pile [pail] *n* pieu *m*, pilotis *m*, pile *f*, (*fam*) fortune *f*, poil *m*; *pl* hémorroïdes *f pl*; *vt* empiler, entasser, (*fam*) charrier.

pilfer ['pilfə] *vt* chaparder.

pilferer ['pilfərə] *n* chapardeur, -euse.

pilfering ['pilfəriŋ] *n* chapardage *m*.

pilgrim ['pilgrim] *n* pèlerin(e) *mf*.

pilgrimage ['pilgrimidʒ] *n* pèlerinage *m*.

pill [pil] *n* pilule *f*.

pillage ['pilidʒ] *n* pillage *m*; *vt* piller, saccager.

pillar ['pilə] *n* pilier *m*, colonne *f*.

pillar-box ['piləbɔks] *n* boîte aux lettres *f*.

pill-box ['pilbɔks] *n* blockhaus *m*, boîte *f* à pilules.

pillow ['pilou] *n* oreiller *m*.

pillow-case ['piloukeis] *n* taie *f*.

pilot ['pailət] *n* pilote *m*; *vt* piloter.

pimple ['pimpl] *n* bouton *m*, pustule *f*.

pimply ['pimpli] *a* boutonneux.

pin [pin] *n* épingle *f*, cheville *f*, (*fam*) quille *f*; *vt* épingler, clouer, lier, accrocher, goupiller; —**s and needles** fourmis *f pl*.

pinafore ['pinəfɔː] *n* tablier *m*.

pincers ['pinsəz] *n* pince *f*, tenailles *f pl*.

pinch [pintʃ] *n* pincée *f*, prise *f*, pincement *m*; *vt* pincer, blesser, gêner, chiper.

pincushion ['pin,kuʃin] *n* pelote à épingles *f*.

pine [pain] *n* pin *m*; *vi* languir, dépérir; **to** — **for** soupirer après, aspirer à.

pineapple ['pain,æpl] *n* ananas *m*.

pinion ['pinjən] *n* aileron *m*, aile *f*, (*tec*) pignon *m*; *vt* couper les ailes à, lier.

pink [pink] *n* œillet *m*; *an* rose *m*; *vt* percer; *vi* (*motor*) cliqueter.

pin-money ['pin,mʌni] *n* argent de poche *m*.

pinnacle ['pinəkl] *n* clocheton *m*, cime *f*, apogée *f*.

pinprick ['pinprik] *n* piqûre d'épingle *f*.

pint [paint] *n* pinte *f*.

pioneer [,paiə'niə] *n* pionnier *m*.

pious ['paiəs] *a* pieux.

pip [pip] *n* pépie *f*, pépin *m*, point *m*, cafard *m*.

pipe [paip] *n* tuyau *m*, pipe *f*, pipée *f*, sifflet *m*, chalumeau *m*; *pl* cornemuse *f*; *vi* jouer de la cornemuse, siffler, crier; *vt* jouer sur la cornemuse.

piper ['paipə] *n* joueur de cornemuse *m*.

pippin ['pipin] *n* reinette *f*.

piquancy ['piːkənsi] *n* piquant *m*, sel *m*.

pique [piːk] *n* pique *f*, dépit *m*; *vt* piquer, dépiter.

pirate ['paiərit] *n* pirate *m*.

pistol ['pistl] *n* pistolet *m*.

piston ['pistən] *n* piston *m*.

pit [pit] *n* trou *m*, puits *m*, fosse *f*, creux *m*, marque *f*, arène *f*, aisselle *f*; *vt* enfouir, mettre face à face, marquer, opposer.

pitch [pitʃ] *n* poix *m*, degré *m*, hauteur *f*, diapason *m*, comble *m*, terrain *m*, tangage *m*; *a* noir; *vt* dresser, poisser, régler le ton de, lancer, jeter; *vi* tanguer, tomber.

pitched [pitʃt] *a* rangé, en règle.

pitcher ['pitʃə] *n* cruche *f*, broc *m*.

pitchfork ['pitʃfɔːk] *n* fourche *f*.

piteous ['pitiəs] *a* lamentable, piteux.

pitfall ['pitfɔːl] *n* trappe *f*, traquenard *m*, piège *m*.

pith [piθ] *n* moelle *f*, essence *f*, vigueur *f*, sève *f*.

pitiable ['pitiəbl] *a* pitoyable.

pitiful ['pitiful] *a* compatissant, lamentable, qui fait pitié.

pitiless ['pitilis] *a* impitoyable, cruel.

pittance ['pitəns] *n* pitance *f*.

pitted ['pitid] *a* troué, marqué.

pity ['piti] *n* pitié *f*; **it is a** — c'est dommage; *vt* plaindre.

pivot ['pivət] *n* pivot *m*; *vt* monter sur pivot, faire pivoter; *vi* pivoter.

placard ['plækaːd] *n* affiche *f*; *vt* placarder, afficher, couvrir d'affiches.

placate [plə'keit] *vt* calmer, apaiser.

place [pleis] *n* place *f*, endroit *m*, lieu *m*, résidence *f*; *vt* placer, mettre, situer, poser, classer.

placebo [plə'siːbou] *n* remède factice *m*.

plagiarism ['pleidʒjərizəm] *n* plagiat *m*.

plagiarist ['pleidʒjərist] *n* plagiaire *m*.

plagiarize ['pleidʒjəraiz] *vt* plagier, contrefaire.

plague [pleig] *n* peste *f*, fléau *m*; *vt* tracasser.

plaice [pleis] *n* plie *f*, carrelet *m*.

plain [plein] *n* plaine *f*; *a* plan, plat,

clair, uni, franc, simple, commun, ordinaire; **in — clothes** en civil; **she is —** elle n'est pas belle; **—-dealing** *n* loyauté *f*; **—-spoken** *a* franc, rond, carré.

plainly ['pleinli] *ad* clairement, simplement, sans détours.

plainness ['pleinnis] *n* air *m*, commun, clarté *f*, netteté *f*, franchise *f*, simplicité *f*.

plaint [pleint] *n* plainte *f*.

plaintiff ['pleintif] *n* plaignant(e) *mf*, demandeur, -eresse.

plaintive ['pleintiv] *a* plaintif.

plait [plæt] *n* pli *m*, tresse *f*, natte *f*; *vt* plisser, natter.

plan [plæn] *n* plan *m*, projet *m*; *vt* relever, projeter, arrêter le plan de, combiner.

plane [plein] *n* platane *m*, rabot *m*, plan *m*, niveau *m*, avion *m*; *a* plan, uni; *vt* raboter, aplanir; *vi* voler, planer.

planet ['plænit] *n* planète *f*.

plank [plæŋk] *n* planche *f*, programme *m*.

plant [plɑ:nt] *n* plante *f*, outillage *m*, machinerie *f*; *vt* planter (là), établir, fonder; **to — out** dépoter, déplanter.

plantation [plæn'teiʃən] *n* plantation *f*, bosquet *m*.

planter ['plɑ:ntə] *n* planteur *m*.

plash [plæʃ] *n* flac *m*, clapotis *m*, éclaboussure *f*; *vi* faire flac, clapoter, éclabousser.

plaster ['plɑ:stə] *n* (em)plâtre *m*; *vt* plâtrer, enduire, couvrir.

plasterer ['plɑ:stərə] *n* plâtrier *m*.

plastic ['plæstik] *an* plastique *m*.

plate [pleit] *n* plaque *f*, planche *f*, assiette *f*, vaisselle *f*, dentier *m*; *vt* plaquer; **—-ful** *n* assiettée *f*; **—-rack** *n* égouttoir *m*.

platform ['plætfɔ:m] *n* plate-forme *f*, estrade *f*, quai *m*, trottoir *m*.

platinum ['plætinəm] *n* platine *m*.

platitude ['plætitju:d] *n* platitude *f*, lieu commun *m*.

platoon [plə'tu:n] *n* peloton *m*, section *f*.

plausible ['plɔ:zəbl] *a* plausible, vraisemblable.

plausibility [,plɔ:zə'biliti] *n* plausibilité *f*.

play [plei] *n* jeu *m*, pièce *f* (de théâtre), carrière *f*; **fair —** franc jeu *m*; *vti* jouer; *vi* folâtrer, gambader.

player ['pleiə] *n* joueur *m*, -euse, acteur, -trice, exécutant(e) *mf*.

playful ['pleiful] *a* enjoué.

playground ['pleigraund] *n* terrain de jeu *m*, cour *f*.

playmate ['pleimeit] *n* camarade *mf* de jeu, ami(e) d'enfance.

playpen ['pleipen] *n* parc *m* (d'enfant).

playtime ['pleitaim] *n* récréation *f*.

plaything ['pleiθiŋ] *n* jouet *m*.

playwright ['pleirait] *n* auteur dramatique *m*.

plea [pli:] *n* argument *m*, plaidoyer *m*. excuse *f*.

plead [pli:d] *vti* plaider; *vt* prétexter, invoquer; *vi* s'avouer.

pleader ['pli:də] *n* défenseur *m*, plaideur *m*.

pleasant ['pleznt] *a* agréable, aimable.

pleasantly ['plezntli] *ad* agréablement.

pleasantness ['plezntnis] *n* agrément *m*, affabilité *m*, charme *m*.

please [pli:z] *vt* plaire à; *vi* plaire; s'il vous plaît.

pleased [pli:zd] *a* très heureux, content.

pleasure ['pleʒə] *n* plaisir *m*, gré *m*, plaisance *f*.

pleat [pli:t] *n* pli *m*: *vt* plisser.

plebiscite ['plebisit] *n* plébiscite *m*.

pledge [pledʒ] *n* gage *m*, promesse *f*, toast *m*; *vt* mettre en gage, engager, porter un toast à.

plenipotentiary [,plenipə'tenʃəri] *an* plénipotentiaire *m*.

plentiful ['plentiful] *a* abondant, copieux.

plenty ['plenti] *n* abondance *f*.

pleurisy ['pluərisi] *n* pleurésie *f*.

pliability [,plaiə'biliti] *n* souplesse *f*, flexibilité *f*.

pliant ['plaiənt] *a* souple, flexible, complaisant.

pliers ['plaiəz] *n* pince *f*.

plight [plait] *n* (triste) état *m*; *vt* engager.

plighted ['plaitid] *a* engagé, lié.

plod [plɔd] *n* lourde tâche *f*; *vi* avancer (cheminer) péniblement, travailler laborieusement, bûcher.

plot [plɔt] *n* lopin *m*, complot *m*, intrigue *f*; *vt* tracer, relever; *vti* comploter; *vi* conspirer.

plotter ['plɔtə] *n* intrigant(e) *mf*, conspirateur, -trice.

plover ['plʌvə] *n* pluvier *m*.

plow [plau] *n* charrue *f*; *vt* labourer, rider, sillonner, (*exam*) refuser, recaler.

plowman ['plaumən] *n* laboureur *m*.

plowshare ['plauʃeə] *n* soc *m*.

pluck [plʌk] *n* courage *m* cran *m*; *vt* cueillir, arracher, plumer, tirer; **to — up courage** prendre courage.

plug [plʌg] *n* cheville *f*, bouchon *m*, tampon *m*, prise de courant *f*; *vt* boucher, tamponner.

plum [plʌm] *n* prune *f*, meilleur morceau *m*, poste *etc*.

plumage ['plu:midʒ] *n* plumage *m*.

plumb [plʌm] *n* plomb *m*; *a* d'aplomb, vertical, tout pur; *vt* sonder; *ad* d'aplomb, juste, en plein.

plumber ['plʌmə] *n* plombier *m*.

plumb-line ['plʌmlain] *n* fil à plomb *m*.

plume [plu:m] *n* plume *f*, plumet *m*, panache *m*; **to — oneself on** se piquer de, se flatter de.

plummet ['plʌmit] *n* plomb *m*, sonde *f*.

plump [plʌmp] *a* rondelet, dodu, bien en chair; *n* chute *f*, bruit sourd *m*, plouf *m*; *ad* tout net; *vt* laisser tomber, flanquer; *vi* tomber, se laisser tomber lourdement.

plum-tree ['plʌmtriː] *n* prunier *m*.

plunder ['plʌndə] *n* pillage *m*, butin *m*; *vt* piller.

plunderer ['plʌndərə] *n* pillard *m*.

plunge [plʌndʒ] *n* plongeon *m*; *vti* plonger; *vi* se jeter, s'enfoncer, piquer du nez, tanguer.

plural ['pluərəl] *an* pluriel *m*; *a* plural.

plus [plʌs] *n* *prep* plus; *a* positif, actif.

plush [plʌʃ] *n* peluche *f*.

plutocracy [pluːˈtɔkrəsi] *n* ploutocratie *f*.

ply [plai] *n* pli *m*, épaisseur *f*; *vt* manier, exercer, travailler, gorger, assaillir; *vi* faire la navette, faire le service.

plywood ['plaiwud] *n* contre-plaqué *m*.

pneumatic [nju(ː)ˈmætik] *an* pneumatique *m*.

pneumonia [nju(ː)ˈmouniə] *n* pneumonie *f*.

poach [poutʃ] *vt* pocher; *vi* braconner; *vt* braconner (dans); *vi* to — upon empiéter sur.

poacher ['poutʃə] *n* braconnier *m*.

poaching ['poutʃiŋ] *n* braconnage *m*.

pocket ['pɔkit] *n* poche *f*, sac *m*; —-book calepin *m*, portefeuille *m*; *vt* empocher, mettre dans sa poche.

pock-marked ['pɔk,maːkt] *a* grêlé.

pod [pɔd] *n* cosse *f*, (coco) cabosse *f*; *vt* écosser, écaler.

poem ['pouim] *n* poème *m*.

poet ['pouit] *n* poète *m*.

poetry ['pouətri] *n* poésie *f*.

poignant ['pɔinənt] *a* âpre, piquant, poignant.

point [pɔint] *n* point *m*, pointe *f*, extrémité *f*, sujet *m*; (rl) aiguille *f*; —-blank à bout portant; **on — duty** de faction; *vt* tailler, aiguiser, pointer, diriger, braquer; **to — out** indiquer, représenter, montrer du doigt, faire observer; **to — at** montrer du doigt; **to — to** annoncer, laisser supposer.

pointed ['pɔintid] *a* pointu, aigu, en pointe, mordant, direct.

pointer ['pɔintə] *n* aiguille *f*, baguette *f*, chien d'arrêt *m*, tuyau *m*, indication *f*.

pointless ['pɔintlis] *a* émoussé, qui manque d'à-propos, fade.

pointsman ['pɔintsmən] *n* aiguilleur *m*.

poise [pɔiz] *n* équilibre *m*, port *m*, dignité *f*, attente *f*; *vt* équilibrer, soupeser, balancer.

poison ['pɔizn] *n* poison *m*; *vt* empoisonner, intoxiquer.

poisoning ['pɔizniŋ] *n* empoisonnement *m*, intoxication *f*.

poisonous ['pɔiznəs] *a* empoisonné, toxique, (plant) vénéneux, (animal) venimeux.

poke [pouk] *n* coup *m* (de coude etc), poussée *f*; *vt* piquer, pousser du coude, tisonner, fourrer, passer; **to — about** fureter, fouiller; **to — fun at** se moquer de.

poker ['poukə] *n* tisonnier *m*, (game) poker *m*.

Poland ['poulənd] *n* Pologne *f*.

polar ['poulə] *a* polaire; **— bear** ours *m* blanc.

pole [poul] *n* perche *f*, échalas *m*, mât *m*, poteau *m*, montant *m*, timon *m*, pôle *m*; —-jump saut *m* à la perche.

Pole [poul] *n* Polonais(e) *mf*.

police [pəˈliːs] *n* police *f*; *vt* maintenir l'ordre dans, policer.

policeman [pəˈliːsmən] *n* agent *m*.

police station [pəˈliːsˈsteiʃən] *n* commissariat *m* de police, poste *m*.

policy ['pɔlisi] *n* politique *f*, police d'assurance *f*.

polish ['pɔliʃ] *n* poli *m*, éclat *m*, cirage *m*, encaustique *f*, vernis *m*, blanc d'Espagne *m*, raffinement *m*; *vt* cirer, astiquer, fourbir, polir; **to — off** finir, régler son compte à, expédier.

Polish ['pouliʃ] *an* polonais *m*.

polite [pəˈlait] *a* poli, cultivé, élégant.

politely [pəˈlaitli] *ad* poliment.

politeness [pəˈlaitnis] *n* politesse *f*, courtoisie *f*.

political [pəˈlitikəl] *a* politique.

politician [,pɔliˈtiʃən] *n* homme politique *m*, politicien *m*.

politics ['pɔlitiks] *n* politique *f*.

poll [poul] *n* scrutin *m*, vote *m*; *vt* obtenir les voix, étêter, écorner; *vi* voter.

pollute [pəˈluːt] *vt* polluer, profaner.

poltroon [pɔlˈtruːn] *n* poltron *m*.

polygamist [pɔˈligəmist] *n* polygame *m*.

polygamy [pɔˈligəmi] *n* polygamie *f*.

polyglot ['pɔliglɔt] *an* polyglotte *mf*.

polygon ['pɔligən] *n* polygone *m*.

pomegranate ['pɔmi,grænit] *n* grenade *f*.

pomp [pɔmp] *n* pompe *f*, faste *m*, apparat *m*.

pomposity [pɔmˈpɔsiti] *n* solennité *f*, pompe *f*, suffisance *f*, emphase *f*.

pompous ['pɔmpəs] *a* pompeux, suffisant, ampoulé.

pond [pɔnd] *n* bassin *m*, étang *m*, vivier *m*.

ponder ['pɔndə] *vt* peser, réfléchir sur, considérer; *vi* ruminer, réfléchir.

ponderous ['pɔndərəs] *a* pesant, lourd.

pontiff ['pɔntif] *n* pontife *m*, prélat *m*.

pontificate [pɔn'tifikeit] n pontificat m; vi pontifier.
pontoon [pɔn'tuːn] n ponton m.
pontoon bridge [pɔn'tuːnbridʒ] n pont de bateaux m.
pony ['pouni] n poney m.
poodle ['puːdl] n caniche mf.
pooh-pooh [puːˈpu] vt tourner en dérision; excl bah!
pool [puːl] n mare f, flaque f, (swimming-) piscine f, (games) poule f, fonds commun m, cartel m; vt mettre en commun, répartir.
poop [puːp] n poupe f, dunette f.
poor [puə] a pauvre, malheureux, médiocre, maigre, piètre, faible; the — les pauvres.
poorly ['puəli] ad tout doucement, pas fort, médiocrement; a souffrant.
poorness ['puənis] n pauvreté f, manque m, infériorité f.
pop [pɔp] n bruit sec m; excl pan! vi sauter, péter, éclater; vt faire sauter, fourrer, mettre au clou.
pope [poup] n pape m, pope m.
popery ['poupəri] n papisme m.
poplar ['pɔplə] n peuplier m.
poplin ['pɔplin] n popeline f.
poppy ['pɔpi] n coquelicot m, pavot m.
pop-song ['pɔpsɔŋ] n chanson f (à la mode).
populace ['pɔpjuləs] n peuple m, populace f.
popular ['pɔpjulə] a populaire, aimé, couru, à la mode.
popularity [ˌpɔpju'læriti] n popularité f.
popularize ['pɔpjuləraiz] vt populariser, vulgariser.
populate ['pɔpjuleit] vt peupler.
population [ˌpɔpju'leiʃən] n population f.
populous ['pɔpjuləs] a populeux.
porch [pɔːtʃ] n porche m, marquise f.
porcupine ['pɔːkjupain] n porc-épic m.
pore [pɔː] n pore m; vi to — over s'absorber dans.
pork [pɔːk] n porc m; —butcher n charcutier m.
porous ['pɔːrəs] a poreux, perméable.
porpoise ['pɔːpəs] n marsouin m.
porridge ['pɔridʒ] n bouillie d'avoine f.
porringer ['pɔrindʒə] n écuelle f.
port [pɔːt] n port m; home — port d'attache; sabord m, bâbord m, allure f; (wine) porto m; vt mettre à bâbord, présenter; vi venir sur bâbord.
portable ['pɔːtəbl] a portatif, transportable.
portal ['pɔːtl] n portail m.
portcullis [pɔːt'kʌlis] n herse f.
portend [pɔː'tend] vt présager, faire pressentir, annoncer.
portent ['pɔːtent] n présage m.
portentous [pɔː'tentəs] a formidable, menaçant, de mauvais augure.

porter ['pɔːtə] n portier m, concierge m,porteur m, chasseur m.
porterage ['pɔːtəridʒ] n factage m, transport m.
portfolio [pɔːt'fouliou] n portefeuille m, chemise f, serviette f, carton m.
porthole ['pɔːthoul] n hublot m, sabord m.
portico ['pɔːtikou] n portique m.
portion ['pɔːʃən] n portion f, part f, partie f, dot f; vt partager, doter.
portly ['pɔːtli] a corpulent, imposant.
portmanteau [pɔːt'mæntou] n valise f.
portrait ['pɔːtrit] n portrait m.
portray [pɔː'trei] vt faire le portrait de, (dé)peindre.
Portugal ['pɔːtjugəl] n Portugal m.
Portuguese [ˌpɔːtju'giːz] an Portugais(e).
pose [pouz] n pose f, affectation f; vti poser, (fam) coller; to — as s'ériger en, se faire passer pour.
poser ['pouzə] n question embarrassante f, colle f.
position [pə'ziʃən] n position f, condition f, place f, état m.
positive ['pɔzətiv] a positif, catégorique, formel, authentique.
possess [pə'zes] vt posséder, tenir, s'approprier, avoir.
possession [pə'zeʃən] n possession f.
possessive [pə'zesiv] a possessif.
possibility [ˌpɔsə'biliti] n possibilité f, éventualité f.
possible ['pɔsəbl] an possible m; a éventuel.
possibly ['pɔsəbli] ad peut-être.
post [poust] n poste f, courrier m, levée f, mât m, poteau m, place f, emploi m; vt mettre à la poste, poster, affecter; **first** — appel m; **last** — sonnerie aux morts f, retraite f; — **no bills** défense d'afficher.
postage ['poustidʒ] n affranchissement m; — **stamp** timbre (-poste) m.
postcard ['poustkɑːd] n carte postale f.
post-date ['poust'deit] vt postdater.
poster ['poustə] n affiche f, afficheur m.
posterior [pɔs'tiəriə] an postérieur m.
posterity [pɔs'teriti] n postérité f.
postern ['poustəːn] n poterne f, porte de derrière f.
post-free ['poust'friː] a franco, en franchise.
posthumous ['pɔstjuməs] a posthume.
postman ['poustmən] n facteur m.
postmark ['poustmɑːk] n timbre d'oblitération m; vt timbrer.
postmaster ['poust,mɑːstə] n receveur m, directeur des postes m.
post-mortem ['poust'mɔːtəm] n autopsie f.
post office ['poust ɔfis] n (bureau m de) poste f.

post-paid ['poust'peid] *a* port payé.
postpone [poust'poun] *vt* ajourner, remettre, reculer.
postscript ['pousskript] *n* postscriptum *m*.
postulate ['postjulit] *n* postulat *m*; ['postjuleit] *vt* postuler, demander, stipuler.
posture ['postʃə] *n* posture *f*, état *m*, attitude *f*.
posy ['pouzi] *n* petit bouquet *m*.
pot [pot] *n* pot *m*, marmite *f*.
potash ['potæʃ] *n* potasse *f*.
potato [pə'teitou] *n* pomme de terre *f*.
pot-bellied ['pot.belid] *a* ventru, bedonnant.
pot-boiler ['pot.boilə] *n* besogne *f* alimentaire.
potent ['poutənt] *a* puissant, fort, violent.
potential [pə'tenʃəl] *an* potentiel *m*, possible *m*; *a* en puissance, latent.
potentiality [pə,tenʃi'æliti] *n* virtualité *f*, potentialité *f*, potentiel *m*.
pother ['poðə] *n* nuage *m*, tapage *m*, embarras *m* *pl*.
potion ['pouʃən] *n* potion *f*, sirop *m*, philtre *m*.
pot-luck ['pot'lʌk] *n* fortune du pot *f*.
potter ['potə] *n* potier *m*; *vi* baguenauder, bricoler.
pottery ['potəri] *n* poterie *f*.
pouch [pautʃ] *n* blague *f*, cartouchière *f*, sac *m*, poche *f*, bourse *f*.
poulterer ['poultərə] *n* marchand de volailles *m*.
poultice ['poultis] *n* cataplasme *m*.
poultry ['poultri] *n* volaille *f*; **—yard** *n* basse-cour *f*.
pounce [pauns] *n* serre *f*, attaque *f*; *vt* poncer; **to — on** fondre sur, sauter sur.
pound [paund] *n* livre *f*, fourrière *f*, enclos *m*; *vt* piler, broyer, (*mil*) pilonner.
pour [po:] *n* pluie torrentielle *f*; *vt* verser; *vi* se jeter, pleuvoir à verse.
pout [paut] *n* moue *f*, bouderie *f*; *vi* faire la moue, bouder.
poverty ['povəti] *n* pauvreté *f*, rareté *f*, misère *f*.
powder ['paudə] *n* poudre *f*; *vt* (sau)poudrer, pulvériser.
powdered ['paudəd] *a* en poudre.
powder-magazine ['paudəmægə,zi:n] *n* poudrière *f*.
powder-puff ['paudəpʌf] *n* houppe *f*.
powdery ['paudəri] *a* poudreux, friable.
power ['pauə] *n* pouvoir *m*, puissance *f*, faculté *f*, vigueur *f*, (*el*) force *f*; *vt* actionner.
powerful ['pauəful] *a* puissant, énergique, vigoureux.
powerlessness ['pauəlisnis] *n* impuissance *f*, inefficacité *f*.
practicable ['præktikəbl] *a* praticable, faisable, pratique.
practical ['præktikəl] *a* pratique.

practice ['præktis] *n* pratique *f*, étude *f*, clientèle *f*, usage *m*, habitude *f*, exercice *m*, entraînement *m*.
practice ['præktis] *vt* pratiquer, exercer, s'exercer à, étudier; *vi* s'entraîner, faire des exercices.
practitioner [præk'tiʃnə] *n* praticien *m*; **general —** omnipraticien *m*.
prairie ['preəri] *n* prairie *f*, savane *f*.
praise [preiz] *n* éloge *m*, louange *f*; *vt* louer, glorifier.
praiseworthy ['preiz,wə:ði] *a* louable.
prance [prɑ:ns] *vi* se cabrer, piaffer, se pavaner.
prank [præŋk] *n* farce *f*, niche *f*, fredaine *f*, les cents coups *m* *pl*; *vt* orner, pavoiser.
prate [preit] *n* bavardage *m*; *vi* bavarder.
prattle ['prætl] *n* babil *m*; *vi* babiller, jaser.
prattling ['prætliŋ] *a* jaseur.
prawn [pro:n] *n* crevette rose *f*.
pray [prei] *vti* prier.
prayer [preə] *n* prière *f*.
prayer book ['preəbuk] *n* rituel *m*, livre de messe *m*, paroissien *m*.
preach [pri:tʃ] *vti* prêcher.
preamble [pri:'æmbl] *n* préambule *m*.
precarious [pri'kɛəriəs] *a* précaire, incertain.
precariousness [pri'kɛəriəsnis] *n* précarité *f*.
precaution [pri'ko:ʃən] *n* précaution *f*.
precede [pri(:)'si:d] *vt* précéder, préfacer.
precedence ['presidəns] *n* préséance *f*, pas *m*.
precedent ['presidənt] *n* précédent *m*.
precept ['pri:sept] *n* précepte *m*.
preceptor [pri'septə] *n* précepteur *m*.
precincts ['pri:siŋkts] *n* *pl* enceinte *f*, limites *f* *pl*, circonscription *f* électorale.
precious ['preʃəs] *a* précieux, de grand prix.
preciousness ['preʃəsnis] *n* haute valeur *f*, préciosité *f*.
precipice ['presipis] *n* précipice *m*.
precipitate [pri'sipitit] *n* précipité *m*; [pri'sipiteit] *vt* précipiter, brusquer.
precipitation [pri,sipi'teiʃən] *n* précipitation *f*.
precipitous [pri'sipitəs] *a* à pic, escarpé.
precise [pri'sais] *a* précis, exact, pointilleux.
precisely [pri'saisli] *ad* précisément, avec précision.
precision [pri'siʒən] *n* précision *f*.
preclude [pri'klu:d] *vt* exclure, prévenir, priver.
precocious [pri'kouʃəs] *a* précoce.
precociousness [pri'kouʃəsnis] *n* précocité *f*.

precursor [pri(:)'kəːsə] *n* précurseur *m*, avant-coureur *m*, devancier *m*.

predate [pri'deit] *vt* antidater.

predatory ['predətəri] *a* rapace, de proie, de brigand.

predecessor ['priːdisesə] *n* prédécesseur *m*.

predicament [pri'dikəmənt] *n* difficulté *f*, situation fâcheuse *f*.

predict [pri'dikt] *vt* prédire.

predilection [ˌpriːdi'lekʃən] *n* prédilection *f*.

predispose ['priːdis'pouz] *vt* prédisposer.

predisposition ['priːˌdispə'ziʃən] *n* prédisposition *f*.

predominate [pri'dɔmineit] *vi* prédominer.

pre-eminence [pri(:)'eminəns] *n* prééminence *f*.

preen [priːn] **to — oneself** se bichonner, se faire beau, faire des grâces, se piquer (de **on**).

preface ['prefis] *n* préface *f*; *vt* préfacer, préluder à.

prefect ['priːfekt] *n* préfet *m*.

prefer [pri'fəː] *vt* préférer, aimer mieux, avancer.

preferably ['prefərəbli] *ad* de préférence.

preference ['prefərəns] *n* préférence *f*.

preferential [ˌprefə'renʃəl] *a* préférentiel, de faveur.

preferment [pri'fəːmənt] *n* avancement *m*.

pregnancy ['pregnənsi] *n* grossesse *f*.

pregnant ['pregnənt] *a* enceinte, grosse, fertile, plein.

prejudice ['predʒudis] *n* préjudice *m*, tort *m*, préjugé *m*; *vt* faire tort à, prévenir.

prejudicial [ˌpredʒu'diʃəl] *a* préjudiciable, nuisible.

prelate ['prelit] *n* prélat *m*.

preliminary [pri'liminəri] *an* préliminaire *m*; *a* préalable; *n* prélude *m*; *pl* préliminaires *m pl*.

prelude ['preljuːd] *n* prélude *m*; *vi* préluder (à); *vt* annoncer.

premature [ˌpremə'tjuə] *a* prématuré.

prematurely [ˌpremə'tjuəli] *ad* prématurément.

premeditate [pri(:)'mediteit] *vt* préméditer.

premeditation [pri(:)ˌmedi'teiʃən] *n* préméditation *f*.

premier ['premjə] *a* premier; *n* premier ministre *m*, président du conseil *m*.

premise ['premis] *n* prémisse *f*; *pl* maison *f*, lieux *m pl*, local *m*.

premium ['priːmjem] *n* prime *f*, boni *m*; **to be at a — faire prime.**

preoccupation [pri(:)ˌɔkju'peiʃən] *n* préoccupation *f*.

preoccupied [pri(:)'ɔkjupaid] *a* préoccupé.

preparation [ˌprepə'reiʃən] *n* pré-

paration *f*; *pl* préparatifs *m pl*.

preparatory [pri'pærətəri] *a* préparatoire, préalable.

prepare [pri'pɛə] *vt* préparer, apprêter; *vi* se préparer, se disposer (à).

prepay ['priː'pei] *vt* payer d'avance.

preponderance [pri'pɔndərəns] *n* prépondérance *f*.

preponderate [pri'pɔndəreit] *vi* l'emporter (sur **over**).

preposition [ˌprepə'ziʃən] *n* préposition *f*.

prepossessing [ˌpriːpə'zesiŋ] *a* captivant, prévenant.

preposterous [pri'pɔstərəs] *a* absurde, saugrenu.

prerequisite ['priː'rekwizit] *n* condition préalable *f*; *a* nécessaire.

prerogative [pri'rɔgətiv] *n* prérogative *f*, apanage *m*.

presage ['presidʒ] *n* présage *m*, pressentiment *m*, *vt* présager, annoncer, augurer.

prescribe [pris'kraib] *vt* prescrire, ordonner.

prescription [pris'kripʃən] *n* ordonnance *f*, prescription *f*, ordre *m*.

presence ['prezns] *n* présence *f*, distinction *f*, maintien *m*, prestance *f*.

present ['preznt] *n* cadeau *m*, présent *m*; *a* présent.

present [pri'zent] *vt* présenter, offrir, faire cadeau de, soumettre.

presentation [ˌprezen'teiʃən] *n* présentation *f*, don *m*, remise *f*, cadeau-souvenir *m*.

presentiment [pri'zentimənt] *n* pressentiment *m*.

presently ['prezntli] *ad* avant (sous) peu, tout à l'heure, bientôt.

preservation [ˌprezə(:)'veiʃən] *n* préservation *f*, conservation *f*.

preservative [pri'zəːvətiv] *an* préservatif *m*.

preserve [pri'zəːv] *n* chasse (pêche) gardée *f*; *pl* conserves *f pl*, confiture *f*; *vt* préserver, conserver, confire, maintenir, garder, observer, garantir (de **from**).

preside [pri'zaid] *vi* présider.

presidency ['prezidənsi] *n* présidence *f*.

president ['prezidənt] *n* président(e) *mf*.

press [pres] *n* presse *f*, pressoir *m*, pression *f*, foule *f*, hâte *f*, placard *m*, imprimerie *f*; *vt* appuyer sur, presser, serrer, pressurer, donner un coup de fer à; *vi* appuyer, se serrer, peser.

press-button ['pres'bʌtn] *n* bouton pression *m*.

pressing ['presiŋ] *a* pressant, urgent; *n* pressage *m*, pression *f*.

pressure ['preʃə] *n* pression *f*, poussée *f*, urgence *f*.

pressure-cooker ['preʃəˌkukə] *n* cocotte minute *f*.

prestige [pres'tiːʒ] *n* prestige, embarras *m*, tension *f*.

prestressed ['pri'strest] *a* précontraint.

presume [pri'zju:m] *vt* présumer, supposer, se permettre de croire, aimer à croire; **to — on** se prévaloir de, abuser de.

presumption [pri'zʌmpʃən] *n* présomption *f*.

presumptive [pri'zʌmptiv] *a* présomptif.

presumptuous [pri'zʌmptjuəs] *a* présomptueux.

pretend [pri'tend] *vt* feindre, faire semblant de, simuler, prétendre.

pretender [pri'tendə] *n* prétendant *m*, soupirant *m*.

pretense [pri'tens] *n* prétence *f*, prétexte *m*, (faux) semblant *m*.

pretension [pri'tenʃən] *n* prétention *f*.

pretentious [pri'tenʃəs] *a* prétentieux.

pretext ['pri:tekst] *n* prétexte *m*.

prettiness ['pritinis] *n* joliesse *f*, mignardise *f*.

pretty ['priti] *a* joli, beau, mignon, gentil; *ad* à peu près, assez.

prevail [pri'veil] *vi* l'emporter (sur **over**), prévaloir (contre, sur **over**), régner; **to — upon s.o.** to amener qn à, décider qn à, persuader à qn de.

prevailing [pri'veiliŋ] *a* courant, régnant, général.

prevalent ['prevələnt] *a* prédominant, répandu.

prevaricate [pri'værikeit] *vi* tergiverser, ergoter, mentir.

prevarication [pri,væri'keiʃən] *n* chicane *f*, tergiversation *f*, mensonge *m*.

prevent [pri:'vent] *vt* empêcher, prévenir.

prevention [pri'venʃən] *n* empêchement *m*, protection *f*.

preventive [pri'ventiv] *an* préventif *m*.

preview ['pri:'vju:] *n* exhibition préalable *f*, avant-première *f*.

previous ['pri:viəs] *a* précédent, préalable, antérieur.

previously ['pri:viəsli] *ad* précédemment, auparavant, au préalable.

prey [prei] *n* proie *f*; **to — upon** vivre sur, dévorer.

price [prais] *n* prix *m*; *vt* mettre un prix à, estimer.

priceless ['praislis] *a* sans prix, impayable.

prick [prik] *n* piqûre *f*, remords *m*; *vt* piquer, tendre, dresser.

pricker ['prikə] *n* poinçon *m*.

prickle ['prikl] *n* épine *f*, piquant *m*, picotement *m*; *vti* piquer, picoter.

pride [praid] *n* orgueil *m*, fierté *f*; **to — oneself on** s'enorgueillir de, se piquer de.

priest [pri:st] *n* prêtre *m*, prêtresse *f*.

priesthood ['pri:sthud] *n* prêtrise *f*.

prig [prig] *n* poseur *m*.

priggish ['prigiʃ] *a* pédantesque, poseur, bégueule, suffisant.

priggishness ['prigiʃnis] *n* bégueulerie *f*, suffisance *f*.

prim [prim] *a* affecté, collet monté, compassé.

primary ['praiməri] *a* primaire, premier, primitif, brut.

primate ['praimit] *n* primat *m*.

prime [praim] *n* fleur *f* (de l'âge), force *f*, commencement *m*; *a* premier, primordial, de première qualité; *vt* préparer, (*engine*) amorcer.

primer ['praimə] *n* abécédaire *m*, éléments *m pl*.

primeval [prai'mi:vəl] *a* primordial, primitif, vierge.

primitive ['primitiv] *a* primitif (-ve), primaire.

primness ['primnis] *n* affectation *f*, air pincé *m*, air collet monté *m*.

primrose ['primrouz] *n* primevère *f*.

prince [prins] *n* prince *m*.

princely ['prinsli] *a* princier, royal.

princess ['prinses] *n* princesse *f*.

principal ['prinsəpəl] *an* principal *m*; *n* directeur *m*, chef *m*.

principality [,prinsi'pæliti] *n* principauté *f*.

principle ['prinsəpl] *n* principe *m*.

print [print] *n* empreinte *f*, imprimé *m*, gravure *f*, estampe *f*, impression *f*, épreuve *f*, (tissu *m*) imprimé (*m*).

printer ['printə] *n* imprimeur *m*, typographe *m*.

printing ['printiŋ] *n* impression *f*, imprimerie *f*, tirage *m*, typographie *f*; **— office** *n* imprimerie *f*.

prior ['praiə] *n* prieur *m*; *a* antérieur, préalable; *ad* antérieurement (à **to**).

prism ['prizəm] *n* prisme *m*.

prison ['prizn] *n* prison *f*.

prisoner ['priznə] *n* prisonnier, -ière.

privacy ['privəsi] *n* intimité *f*, solitude *f*, secret *m*.

private ['praivit] *n* soldat *m* sans grade, particulier, -ière; *a* privé, personnel, intime, confidentiel, retiré, particulier.

privately ['praivitli] *ad* en particulier, dans l'intimité, en confidence.

privation [prai'veiʃən] *n* privation *f*, manque *m*.

privet ['privit] *n* troène *m*.

privilege ['privilidʒ] *n* privilège *m*, bonne fortune *f*.

privileged ['privilidʒd] *a* privilégié.

privy ['privi] *n* privé *m*, cabinets *m pl*.

prize [praiz] *n* prix *m*, (*at sea*) prise *f*; *vt* apprécier, évaluer, faire grand cas de.

pro [prou] *prep* pour; *an* professionel, -elle.

probability [,probə'biliti] *n* probabilité *f*, vraisemblance *f*.

probable ['probəbl] *a* probable, vraisemblable.

probation [prə'beiʃən] *n* noviciat *m*,

épreuve *f*, surveillance *f*, stage *m*.
probe [proub] *n* sonde *f*; enquête *f*,sondage *m*; *vt* sonder, examiner, approfondir.
probity ['proubiti] *n* probité *f*.
problem ['problem] *n* problème *m*.
problematic [,probli'mætik] *a* problématique, incertain.
procedure [prə'si:dʒə] *n* procédure *f*, façon d'agir *f*.
proceed [prə'si:d] *vi* continuer, poursuivre, passer, se rendre, venir, procéder, se prendre.
proceeding [prə'si:diŋ] *n* procédé *m*, façon d'agir *f*; *pl* poursuites *f pl*, débats *m pl*, réunion *f*, cérémonie *f*.
proceeds ['prousi:dz] *n pl* produit *m*, recette *f*.
process ['prouses] *n* cours *m*, marche *f*, procédé *m*, processus *m*; *vt* apprêter.
procession [prə'seʃən] *n* procession *f*, défilé *m*, cortège *m*.
proclaim [prə'kleim] *vt* proclamer, déclarer, trahir.
proclamation [,proklə'meiʃən] *n* proclamation *f*.
procrastinate [prou'kræstineit] *vi* temporiser.
procrastination [prou,kræsti'neiʃən] *n* temporisation *f*.
procuration [,prokjuə'reiʃən] *n* procuration *f*, commission *f*, obtention *f*.
procure [prə'kjuə] *vt* obtenir, (se) procurer.
procurement [prə'kjuəmənt] *n* approvisionnement *m* (d'un service).
procurer [prə'kjuərə] *n* proxénète *m*.
prod [prod] *vt* bourrer les côtes à, pousser.
prodigal ['prodigəl] *an* prodigue *mf*.
prodigality [,prodi'gæliti] *n* prodigalité *f*.
prodigious [prə'didʒəs] *a* prodigieux, mirobolant.
prodigy ['prodidʒi] *n* prodige *m*, merveille *f*.
produce ['prodju:s] *n* produit *m*, rendement *m*, fruits *m pl*, denrées *f pl*.
produce [prə'dju:s] *vt* produire, présenter, provoquer, (*theatre*) monter, mettre en scène.
producer [prə'dju:sə] *n* producteur, -trice, metteur en scène *m*.
product ['prodəkt] *n* produit *m*, résultat *m*.
production [prə'dʌkʃən] *n* production *f*, produit *m*, œuvre *f*, (re)présentation *f*, mise en scène *f*, fabrication *f*.
productive [prə'dʌktiv] *a* productif, qui rapporte, fécond.
profane [prə'fein] *a* profane, impie; *vi* profaner, violer.
profanity [prə'fæniti] *n* impiété *f*, blasphème *m*.
profess [prə'fes] *vt* professer, faire profession de, exercer, prétendre; to — to be se faire passer pour.

professed [prə'fest] *a* déclaré, avoué, soi-disant.
profession [prə'feʃən] *n* profession *f*, carrière *f*, métier *m*, déclaration *f*, affirmation *f*.
professional [prə'feʃənl] *an* professionel, -elle; *a* de carrière, de métier.
professor [prə'fesə] *n* professeur *m* (d'université).
proffer ['profə] *vt* offrir, présenter.
proficiency [prə'fiʃənsi] *n* aptitude *f*, compétence *f*.
proficient [prə'fiʃənt] *a* bon, fort, compétent, capable.
profile ['proufail] *n* profil *m*.
profit ['profit] *n* profit *m*, gain *m*, bénéfice(s) *m* (*pl*); *vti* profiter (à, de by).
profitable ['profitəbl] *a* profitable, lucratif, avantageux.
profiteer [,profi'tiə] *n* mercanti *m*, exploitation *f*, mercantilisme *m*.
profligacy ['profligəsi] *n* débauche *f*.
profligate ['profligit] *an* débauché(e) *mf*, libertin(e) *mf*.
profound [prə'faund] *a* profond, approfondi.
profoundly [prə'faundli] *ad* profondément.
profuse [prə'fju:s] *a* prodigue, copieux, excessif.
profusely [prə'fju:sli] abondamment.
profusion [prə'fju:ʒən] *n* profusion *f*, abondance *f*.
progeny ['prodʒini] *n* rejeton *m*, progéniture *f*.
prognostic [prəg'nostik] *n* prognostic *m*.
prognosticate [prəg'nostikeit] *vt* prognostiquer, prédire.
program ['prougræm] *n* programme *m*.
progress ['prougres] *n* progrès *m*, cours *m*.
progress [prə'gres] *vi* (s')avancer, progresser.
progression [prə'greʃən] *n* progression *f*.
progressive [prə'gresiv] *a* progressif, de progrès, progressiste, d'avant-garde.
prohibit [prə'hibit] *vt* défendre, interdire (de).
prohibition [,proui'biʃən] *n* prohibition *f*, défense *f*, interdiction *f*.
prohibitive [prə'hibitiv] *a* prohibitif, inabordable.
project ['prodʒekt] *n* projet *m*.
project [prə'dʒekt] *vt* projeter; *vi* s'avancer, faire saillie.
projectile [prə'dʒektail] *n* projectile *m*.
projection [prə'dʒekʃən] *n* projection *f*, saillie *f*.
projector [prə'dʒektə] *n* lanceur *m*, projecteur *m*.
proletarian [,proule'tɛəriən] *an* prolétaire *mf*.
proletariat [,proule'tɛəriət] *n* prolétariat *m*.

prolific [prə'lifik] *a* prolifique, fécond.

prolix ['prouliks] *a* prolixe.

prolong [prə'lɔŋ] *vt* allonger, prolonger.

prolongation [,proulɔŋ'geiʃən] *n* prolongation *f*, prolongement *m*.

promenade [,prɔmi'nɑːd] *n* promenade *f*, esplanade *f*, promenoir *m*; *vi* se promener.

prominence ['prɔminəns] *n* (pro) éminence *f*, importance *f*.

prominent ['prɔminənt] *a* saillant, éminent, en vue, proéminent.

promiscuity [,prɔmis'kju(ː)iti] *n* promiscuité *f*.

promiscuous [prə'miskjuəs] *a* confus, mêlé, en commun.

promise ['prɔmis] *n* promesse *f*; *vt* promettre.

promising ['prɔmisiŋ] *a* qui promet, prometteur.

promontory ['prɔməntri] *n* promontoire *m*.

promote [prə'mout] *vt* promouvoir, nommer, avancer, encourager, soutenir.

promoter [prə'moutə] *n* promoteur *m*, lanceur *m*, auteur *m*.

promotion [prə'mouʃən] *n* avancement *m*, promotion *f*.

prompt [prɔmpt] *a* actif, prompt; *vt* pousser, inspirer, souffler.

prompter ['prɔmptə] *n* souffleur *m*; —'s box trou du souffleur *m*.

promptitude ['prɔmptitjuːd] *n* promptitude *f*, empressement *m*.

prone [proun] *a* couché sur le ventre, porté (à **to**).

prong [prɔŋ] *n* branche *f*, dent *f*, fourchon *m*.

pronoun ['prounaun] *n* pronom *m*.

pronounce [prə'nauns] *vt* prononcer, déclarer.

pronouncement [prə'naunsmənt] *n* déclaration *f*.

pronunciation [prə,nʌnsi'eiʃən] *n* prononciation *f*.

proof [pruːf] *n* preuve *f*, épreuve *f*; *a* à l'épreuve de, à l'abri (de **against**), imperméable, étanche, insensible; *vt* imperméabiliser.

prop [prɔp] *n* étai *m*, tuteur *m*, soutien *m*; *vt* étayer, soutenir, appuyer.

propaganda [,prɔpə'gændə] *n* propagande *f*.

propagate ['prɔpəgeit] *vt* propager, répandre.

propagation [,prɔpə'geiʃən] *n* propagation *f*, dissémination *f*.

propel [prə'pel] *vt* lancer, propulser.

propeller [prə'pelə] *n* hélice *f*.

propensity [prə'pensiti] *n* penchant *m*, inclination *f*, tendance *f* (à, vers **to**, **toward**).

proper ['prɔpə] *a* propre, approprié, décent, vrai, correct, convenable, bon, opportun.

properly ['prɔpəli] *ad* bien, comme il faut, convenablement, correctement, complètement.

property ['prɔpəti] *n* propriété *f*, biens *m pl*, immeuble *m*; *pl* accessoires *m pl*; —**man** *n* machiniste *m*.

prophecy ['prɔfisi] *n* prophétie *f*.

prophesy ['prɔfisai] *vti* prophétiser; *vt* prédire.

prophet ['prɔfit] *n* prophète *m*.

propinquity [prə'piŋkwiti] *n* voisinage *m*, proche parenté *f*, ressemblance *f*.

propitiate [prə'piʃieit] *vt* apaiser, se concilier.

propitious [prə'piʃəs] *a* propice, favorable.

proportion [prə'pɔːʃən] *n* proportion *f*, rapport *m*, part *f*; *vt* proportionner.

proportional [prə'pɔːʃənl] *a* proportionnel, proportionné.

proposal [prə'pouzəl] *n* offre *f*, proposition *f*, projet *m*, demande en mariage *f*.

propose [prə'pouz] *vt* (se) proposer; *vi* demander en mariage.

proposition [,prɔpə'ziʃən] *n* proposition *f*, affaire *f*, entreprise *f*.

propound [prə'paund] *vt* proposer, produire, exposer, émettre.

proprietary [prə'praiətəri] *a* possédant, de propriétaire, de propriété.

proprietor [prə'praiətə] *n* propriétaire *mf*.

propriety [prə'praiəti] *n* convenances *f pl*, bienséance *f*, propriété *f*, correction *f*.

proscribe [prɔs'kraib] *vt* proscrire, interdire.

proscription [prɔs'kripʃən] *n* proscription *f*, interdiction *f*.

prose [prouz] *n* prose *f*, thème *m*.

prosecute ['prɔsikjuːt] *vt* poursuivre, mener.

prosecution [,prɔsi'kjuːʃən] *n* poursuite(s) *f* (*pl*), accusation *f*, le ministère public *m*, plaignants *m pl*, exercice *m* (d'un métier).

prosecutor ['prɔsikjuːtə] *n* demandeur *m*, le ministère public *m*, (UK) procureur du roi *m*.

prose-writer ['prouz'raitə] *n* prosateur *m*.

prospect ['prɔspekt] *n* vue *f*, perspective *f*, chance *f*; *pl* espérances *f pl*.

prospect [prəs'pekt] *vti* prospecter.

prospective [prəs'pektiv] *a* futur, à venir, éventuel.

prospector [prəs'pektə] *n* prospecteur *m*.

prosper ['prɔspə] *vi* prospérer, réussir.

prosperity [prɔs'periti] *n* prospérité *f*.

prosperous ['prɔspərəs] *a* prospère.

prostitute ['prɔstitjuːt] *n* prostituée *f*; *vt* (se) prostituer, se vendre.

prostrate ['prɔstreit] *a* prosterné, prostré, abattu.

prostrate [prɔs'treit] *vt* abattre, accabler; **to — oneself** se prosterner.
prostration [prɔs'treiʃən] *n* prostration *f*, prosternement *m*, abattement *m*.
prosy ['prouzi] *a* prosaïque, fastidieux.
protect [prə'tekt] *vt* protéger, défendre, sauvegarder.
protection [prə'tekʃən] *n* protection *f*, défense *f*, sauvegarde *f*.
protective [prə'tektiv] *a* protecteur.
protein ['prouti:n] *n* protéine *f*.
protest ['proutest] *n* protestation *f*, protêt *m*.
protest [prə'test] *vti* protester; *vt* protester de.
protestant ['prɔtistənt] *n* protestant (e) *mf*.
protocol ['proutəkɔl] *n* protocole *m*.
prototype ['proutətaip] *n* prototype *m*, archétype *m*.
protract [prə'trækt] *vt* prolonger.
protraction [prə'trækʃən] *n* prolongation *f*.
protrude [prə'tru:d] *vi* faire saillie, s'avancer.
proud [praud] *a* fier, orgueilleux.
prove [pru:v] *vt* prouver, démontrer; *vi* se montrer, s'avérer.
provender ['prɔvində] *n* fourrage *m*.
proverb ['prɔvəb] *n* proverbe *m*.
provide [prə'vaid] *vt* fournir, pourvoir, munir, stipuler; *vi* **to — against** se prémunir contre.
provided [prə'vaidid] *cj* pourvu que.
providence ['prɔvidəns] *n* prévoyance *f*, économie *f*, Providence *f*.
provident ['prɔvidənt] *a* prévoyant, économe.
providential [,prɔvi'denʃəl] *a* providentiel.
province ['prɔvins] *n* province *f*.
provincial [prə'vinʃəl] *an* provincial (e) *mf*.
provision [prə'viʒən] *n* provision *f*, approvisionnement *m*, stipulation *f*.
proviso [prə'vaizou] *n* condition *f*, clause *f*.
provocation [,prɔvə'keiʃən] *n* provocation *f*.
provocative [prə'vɔkətiv] *a* provoquant, provocateur.
provoke [prə'vouk] *vt* provoquer, exciter, exaspérer.
provost ['prɔvəst] *n* prévôt *m*, maire *m*.
prow [prau] *n* proue *f*.
prowess ['prauis] *n* courage *m*, prouesse *f*.
prowl [praul] *vi* rôder.
proximate ['prɔksimit] *a* prochain, proche.
proximity [prɔk'simiti] *n* proximité *f*.
proxy ['prɔksi] *n* procuration *f*, mandataire *mf*, fondé *m* de pouvoir(s).
prudence ['pru:dəns] *n* prudence *f*, sagesse *f*.
prudent ['pru:dənt] *a* prudent, sage.

prudery ['pru:dəri] *n* pruderie *f*, pudibonderie *f*.
prudish ['pru:diʃ] *a* prude, bégueule, pudibond.
prune [pru:n] *n* pruneau *m*; *vt* émonder, tailler, élaguer (de **off**).
pruning ['pru:niŋ] *n* élagage *m*, émondage *m*, taille *f*; **—shears** *n* sécateur *m*.
pry [prai] *vi* fureter, fourrer le nez (dans **into**).
psalm [sɑ:m] *n* psaume *m*.
psalmody ['sælmədi] *n* psalmodie *f*.
pseudonym ['psju:dənim] *n* pseudonyme *m*.
psychiatrist [sai'kaiətrist] *n* psychiatre *m*.
psychoanalysis [,saikouə'nælisis] *n* psychanalyse *f*.
psychologist [sai'kɔlədʒist] *n* psychologue *m*.
psychology [sai'kɔlədʒi] *n* psychologie *f*.
pub [pʌb] *n* bistro *m*, bar *m*.
puberty ['pju:bəti] *n* puberté *f*.
public ['pʌblik] *an* public *m*.
publication [,pʌbli'keiʃən] *n* publication *f*.
publicist ['pʌblisist] *n* publiciste *m*.
publicity [pʌb'lisiti] *n* publicité *f*, réclame *f*.
publish ['pʌbliʃ] *vt* publier, faire paraître.
publisher ['pʌbliʃə] *n* éditeur *m*.
publishing ['pʌbliʃiŋ] *n* publication *f*; **— house** maison *f* d'édition.
puck [pʌk] *n* lutin *m*, palet *m*.
pucker ['pʌkə] *n* ride *f*, pli *m*, fronce *f*; *vt* plisser, rider, froncer; *vi* se froncer.
pudding ['pudiŋ] *n* pudding *m*; **black —** boudin *m*.
puddle ['pʌdl] *n* flaque *f*, gâchis *m*; *vi* barboter; *vt* brasser, corroyer.
puff [pʌf] *n* souffle *m*, bouffée *f*, houppe *f*, bouffant *m*, feuilleté *m*, réclame *f*; *vi* haleter, souffler, lancer des bouffées; *vt* vanter, gonfler, essouffler.
puffed ['pʌft] *a* essoufflé, bouffant.
puffy ['pʌfi] *a* gonflé, bouffi.
pug(-nose) ['pʌgnouz] *n* nez *m* épaté.
pugnacious [pʌg'neiʃəs] *a* batailleur.
pull [pul] *n* tirage *m*, influence *f*, avantage *m*, piston *m*, lampée *f*, effort *m*; *vt* traîner; *vti* tirer; **to — down** démolir, baisser, renverser; **to — off** enlever, gagner; **to — out** *vt* tirer, arracher; *vi* démarrer, sortir; **to — through** *vt* tirer d'affaire; *vi* se tirer d'affaire; **to — up** *vt* arracher, relever, arrêter; *vi* s'arrêter; **to — oneself together** se ressaisir.
pullet ['pulit] *n* poulette *f*.
pulley ['puli] *n* poulie *f*.
pullover ['pul,ouvə] *n* pull-over *m*, tricot *m*.
pulp [pʌlp] *n* pulpe *f*, pâte *f*, chair *f*.
pulpit ['pulpit] *n* chaire *f*.

pulsate [pʌl'seit] *vi* battre, palpiter, vibrer.

pulse [pʌls] *n* pouls *m*, pulsation *f*, battement *m*; *vi* battre, palpiter.

pulverize ['pʌlvəraiz] *vt* pulvériser, broyer.

pumice(-stone) ['pʌmis(stoun)] *n* pierre ponce *f*.

pump [pʌmp] *n* pompe *f*; *vt* pomper, tirer les vers du nez à.

pumpkin ['pʌmpkin] *n* citrouille *f*.

pun [pʌn] *n* jeu de mots *m*, calembour *m*.

punch [pʌntʃ] *n* poinçon *m*, Polichinelle *m*, coup de poing *m*; *vt* poinçonner, trouer, étamper, donner un coup de poing à.

punctilious [pʌŋk'tiliəs] *a* pointilleux, chatouilleux.

punctual ['pʌŋktjuəl] *a* exact, ponctuel.

punctuality [,pʌŋktju'æliti] *n* ponctualité *f*, exactitude *f*.

punctuate ['pʌŋktjueit] *vt* ponctuer.

punctuation [,pʌŋktju'eiʃən] *n* ponctuation *f*.

puncture ['pʌŋktʃə] *n* piqûre *f*, crevaison *f*; *vti* crever.

pundit [pʌndit] *n* pontife *m*.

pungency ['pʌndʒənsi] *n* âcreté *f*, mordant *m*, saveur *f*.

pungent ['pʌndʒənt] *a* aigu, -uë, mordant, piquant, âcre.

punish ['pʌniʃ] *vt* punir, corriger.

punishable ['pʌniʃəbl] *a* punissable, délictueux.

punishment ['pʌniʃmənt] *n* punition *f*.

punt [pʌnt] *n* bachot *m*, coup de volée *m*.

puny ['pjuːni] *a* chétif, mesquin.

pup(py) ['pʌp(i)] *n* chiot *m*, petit chien *m*.

pupil ['pjuːpl] *n* élève *mf*, (eye) pupille *f*.

puppet ['pʌpit] *n* marionnette *f*, pantin *m*.

purblind ['pəːblaind] *a* myope, obtus.

purchase ['pəːtʃəs] *n* achat *m*, acquisition *f*, prise *f*, point d'appui *m*; *vt* acheter.

purchaser ['pəːtʃəsə] *n* acheteur, -euse, acquéreur, -euse.

pure [pjuə] *a* pur.

purgation [pəː'geiʃən] *n* purification *f*, purgation *f*, purge *f*.

purgative ['pəːgətiv] *an* purgatif *m*.

purgatory ['pəːgətəri] *n* purgatoire *m*.

purge [pəːdʒ] *n* purge *f*, épuration *f*; *vt* purger, épurer.

purify ['pjuərifai] *vt* purifier.

Puritan ['pjuəritən] *an* puritain(e) *mf*.

purity ['pjuəriti] *n* pureté *f*.

purl [pəːl] *n* murmure *m*; *vi* murmurer.

purlieu ['pəːljuː] *n* lisière *f*, alentours *m pl*, bornes *f pl*.

purloin ['pəːlɔin] *vt* voler, soustraire.

purple ['pəːpl] *an* violet *m*, cramoisi *m*, pourpre *m*; *n* pourpre *f*.

purport ['pəːpət] *n* sens *m*, teneur *f*.

purport [pəː'pɔːt] *vt* signifier, impliquer.

purpose ['pəːpəs] *n* dessein *m*, intention *f*, objet *m*; *vt* se proposer (de).

purposeful ['pəːpəsful] *a* calculé, réfléchi, énergique, avisé.

purposeless ['pəːpəslis] *a* sans objet, inutile.

purposely ['pəːpəsli] *ad* à dessein.

purr [pəː] *n* ronronnement *m*: *vi* ronronner.

purse [pəːs] *n* porte-monnaie *m*, bourse *f*; *vt* plisser, serrer, froncer.

purser ['pəːsə] *n* commissaire *m*.

pursuance [pə'sju(ː)əns] *n* exécution *f*, conséquence *f*; **in — of** conformément à.

pursue [pə'sjuː] *vti* poursuivre.

pursuit [pə'sjuːt] *n* poursuite *f*, occupation *f*, recherche *f*.

purvey [pəː'vei] *vt* fournir.

purveyor [pəː'veiə] *n* fournisseur, -euse.

purview ['pəːvjuː] *n* teneur *f*, portée *f*.

pus [pʌs] *n* pus *m*.

push [puʃ] *n* poussée *f*, coup *m* (d'épaule), effort *m*, pression *f*, crise *f*, entregent *m*; *vti* pousser; *vt* presser, appuyer.

pushing ['puʃiŋ] *a* intrigant, entreprenant, débrouillard, ambitieux.

puss [pus] *n* minet, -ette, minou *m*.

put [put] *vt* mettre, remettre, placer, estimer, lancer, verser; **to — back** retarder, remettre à sa place; **to — by** mettre de côté; **to — down** (dé) poser, réprimer, supprimer, noter, attribuer, rabattre; **to — in** *vt* installer, introduire, glisser, passer; *vi* **to — in at** faire escale à; **to — off** *vt* ajourner, remettre, ôter, dérouter; *vi* démarrer; **to — on** mettre, passer, revêtir, feindre; **to — out** éteindre, tendre, déconcerter, mettre à la porte, sortir, démettre, publier; **to — through** exécuter, mettre en communication; **to — up** *vt* (faire) dresser, construire, monter, hausser, lever, apposer, présenter, loger, héberger, proposer; *vi* descendre, loger; **to — up with** s'accommoder de, supporter.

putrefy ['pjuːtrifai] *vi* pourrir, se putréfier.

putrid ['pjuːtrid] *a* putride, infect.

putty ['pʌti] *n* mastic *m*.

puzzle ['pʌzl] *n* enigme *f*, devinette *f*, embarras *m*; **jigsaw —** puzzle *m*; *vt* intriguer, embarrasser; *vi* se creuser la tête.

puzzling ['pʌzliŋ] *a* embarrassant, intrigant.

pygmy ['pigmi] *n* pygmée *m*.

pylon ['pailən] *n* pylône *m*.

pyramid ['pirəmid] *n* pyramide *f.*
pyre ['paiə] *n* bûcher *m.*
pyx [piks] *n* ciboire *m.*

Q

quack [kwæk] *n* charlatan *m,*
couin-couin *m.*
quackery ['kwækəri] *n* charlatanisme
m.
quadrangle ['kwɔˌdræŋgl] *n* quadri-
latère *m,* cour *f.*
quadruple ['kwɔdrupl] *an* quadruple
m.
quaff [kwɑːf] *vt* lamper, vider d'un
seul trait.
quagmire ['kwægmaiə] *n* fondrière *f.*
quail [kweil] *n* caille *f; vi* flancher,
défaillir.
quaint [kweint] *a* désuet, délicat,
étrange, archaïque, fantasque, vieux
jeu.
quake [kweik] *vi* trembler.
qualification [ˌkwɔlifi'keiʃən] *n* réserve *f,* atténuation *f,* condition *f,*
nom *m; pl* titres *m.*
qualify ['kwɔlifai] *vt* qualifier, traiter
(de), atténuer, modifier, modérer;
vi acquérir les titres, se qualifier.
quality ['kwɔliti] *n* qualité *f.*
qualm [kwɔːm] *n* scrupule *m,*
remords *m.*
quandary ['kwɔndəri] *n* embarras
m, impasse *f.*
quantity ['kwɔntiti] *n* quantité *f.*
quarantine ['kwɔrəntiːn] *n* quarantaine *f.*
quarrel ['kwɔrəl] *n* querelle *f,*
dispute *f; vi* se quereller, se disputer.
quarrelsome ['kwɔrəlsəm] *a* querelleur.
quarry ['kwɔri] *n* proie *f,* carrière *f;
vt* extraire.
quarter ['kwɔːtə] *n* quart *m,* trimestre *m,* région *f,* fogement *m,*
quartier *m,* pièce d'¼ dollar;
vt couper en quatre, loger, équarrir,
écarteler; — **of an hour** quart
d'heure *m;* a — **to** moins le quart;
a — **past** et quart; —**deck** *n*
gaillard d'arrière *m;* —**master-
sergeant** *n* maréchal des logis *m.*
quarterly ['kwɔːtəli] *a* trimestriel.
quartet [kwɔːˈtet] *n* quatuor *m.*
quarto ['kwɔːtou] *n* inquarto *m.*
quash [kwɔʃ] *vt* casser, annuler.
quaver ['kweivə] *n* chevrotement *m,*
trille *m,* croche *f; vi* faire des trilles,
trembloter, chevroter.
quay [kiː] *n* quai *m.*
queasy ['kwiːzi] *a* barbouillé, scrupuleux.
queen ['kwiːn] *n* reine *f,* (*cards*)
dame *f.*
queer ['kwiə] *a* étrange, bizarre,
louche.
quell [kwel] *vt* réprimer, écraser,
apaiser.

quench [kwentʃ] *vt* éteindre, étancher.
querulous ['kweruləs] *a* plaintif,
grognon.
query ['kwiəri] *n* question *f,* (point
m d')interrogation *f; vt* demander,
mettre en question.
quest [kwest] *n* quête *f,* recherche *f.*
question ['kwestʃən] *n* question *f,*
hésitation *f,* doute *m; excl* c'est à
savoir! *vt* interroger, questionner,
mettre en doute, contester; — **mark**
n point d'interrogation *m.*
questionable ['kwestʃənəbl] *a* douteux, contestable.
queue [kjuː] *n* queue *f; vi* faire la
queue.
quibble ['kwibl] *n* jeu *m* de mots,
faux-fuyant *m,* équivoque *f; vi*
ergoter.
quibbler ['kwiblə] *n* ergoteur, -euse.
quick [kwik] *n* vif *m,* fond *m,* moelle
f; a vif, éveillé, rapide, fin; *ad*
rapidement, vite; —**tempered** emporté; —**witted** vif.
quicken ['kwikən] *vt* hâter, exciter,
animer; *vi* s'animer, s'accélérer.
quicklime ['kwiklaim] *n* chaux vive
f.
quickly ['kwikli] *ad* vite.
quickness ['kwiknis] *n* vivacité *f,*
promptitude *f,* rapidité *f,* acuité *f.*
quicksand ['kwikˌsænd] *n* sable
mouvant *m.*
quicksilver ['kwikˌsilvə] *n* mercure
m, vif-argent *m.*
quiet ['kwaiət] *n* calme *m;* paix *f;
a* tranquille, en paix; *vt* apaiser,
calmer.
quietly ['kwaiətli] *ad* doucement,
silencieusement.
quietness ['kwaiətnis] *n* tranquillité
f, repos *m,* quiétude *f,* sagesse *f.*
quill [kwil] *n* plume *f* (d'oie), cure-
dent *m,* bobine *f; vt* gaufrer,
enrouler, rucher.
quilt [kwilt] *n* couverture piquée *f,*
édredon *m; vt* piquer, ouater.
quince [kwins] *n* coing *m.*
quinine [kwi'niːn] *n* quinine.
quinsy ['kwinzi] *n* angine *f.*
quip [kwip] *n* sarcasme *m,* mot fin *m,*
pointe *f.*
quire ['kwaiə] *n* main *f* (de papier).
quirk [kwəːk] *n* argutie *f,* méchant
tour *m,* fioriture *f.*
quit [kwit] *a* libre, quitte, débarrassé;
vt quitter; *vi* démissionner, abandonner la partie.
quite ['kwait] *ad* tout (à fait), bien.
quits [kwits] *n ad* quitte(s).
quiver ['kwivə] *n* carquois *m,*
tremblement *m; vi* trembler, frémir.
quiz [kwiz] *n* jeu *m,* colle *f,* mystification *f,* original *m; vt* dévisager,
lorgner, railler.
quizzical ['kwizikəl] *a* ironique,
railleur.
quoit [kɔit] *n* anneau *m,* palet *m.*
quota ['kwoutə] *n* quotepart *f.*

quotation [kwou'teiʃən] n citation f,
cote f, cours m; — **marks** n pl
guillemets m pl.
quote [kwout] vt citer, coter; n
citation f.
quotient ['kwouʃənt] n quotient m.

R

rabbi ['ræbai] n rabbin m.
rabbit ['ræbit] n lapin m.
rabble ['ræbl] n canaille f.
rabid ['ræbid] a enragé, acharné,
fanatique.
rabies ['reibiz] n rage f.
race [reis] n race f, course f, courant
m, cours m; vi faire une course,
lutter de vitesse, courir; vt faire
courir, (engine) emballer; —**course**
n champ de course m; —**horse** n
cheval de course m.
raciness ['reisinis] n verve f, saveur
f, goût de terroir m.
rack [ræk] n râtelier m, filet m,
égouttoir m, étagère f, chevalet m;
vt torturer, pressurer; **to** — **one's**
brains se creuser la cervelle; —**ed**
by hunger tenaillé par la faim.
racket ['rækit] n raquette f, vacarme
m, vie joyeuse f, affaire véreuse f,
combine f.
racketeer [ˌræki'tiə] n gangster m,
combinard m.
racy ['reisi] a de terroir, savoureux,
piquant, salé.
radiance ['reidiəns] n rayonnement
m, éclat m.
radiant ['reidiənt] a rayonnant,
radieux, resplendissant.
radiate ['reidieit] vi rayonner, irradier; vt dégager, émettre.
radiator ['reidieitə] n radiateur m.
radical ['rædikəl] a radical, foncier.
radicalism ['rædikəlizəm] n radica-
lisme m.
radio ['reidiou] n radio f; vt émettre
par la radio; — **control** téléguidage;
vt téléguider.
radioactive ['reidiou'æktiv] a radio-
actif; — **material** matière f rayon-
nante.
radiograph ['reidiougraːf] vt radiographier; n radio(graphie) f.
radiography [reidi'ɔgrəfi] n radiographie f.
radish ['rædiʃ] n radis m.
radius ['reidiəs] n rayon m.
raffle ['ræfl] n loterie f, tombola f;
vt mettre en loterie, en tombola.
raft [raːft] n radeau m, train de bois
m.
rafter ['raːftə] n chevron m.
rag [ræg] n chiffon m, haillon m,
chahut m, monôme m, brimade f;
vt chahuter, brimer.
ragamuffin ['rægəˌmʌfin] n loqueteux, -euse, va-nu-pieds m.
rage [reidʒ] n rage f, fureur f; vi

rager, faire rage; **to be all the** —
faire fureur.
ragged ['rægid] a en loques, déchiqueté, désordonné.
raging ['reidʒiŋ] a furieux, démonté,
fou, brûlant.
ragman ['rægmæn] n chiffonnier m.
raid [reid] n raid m, rafle f; vt
razzier, faire une rafle dans, bombarder.
rail [reil] n rail m, rampe f, balustrade f, barrière f, parapet m,
garde-fou m; vt bastingages m pl;
vi se déchaîner (contre **at**).
railhead ['reilhed] n tête f de ligne.
railing(s) ['reiliŋ(z)] n grille f,
clôture f.
railroad ['reilroud] n chemin m
de fer; vt faire voter en vitesse un
projet de loi.
railway ['reilwei] n chemin de fer m;
— **line** n voie ferrée f; — **station** n
gare f, station f.
rain [rein] n pluie f; vi pleuvoir.
rainbow ['reinbou] n arc-en-ciel m.
raincoat ['reinkout] n imperméable
m.
rainfall ['reinfɔːl] n précipitation f.
rain-pipe ['rein.paip] n (tuyeau m
de) descente f.
rainy ['reini] a pluvieux.
raise [reiz] vt (é-, sou-, re-)lever,
faire pousser, cultiver, (res)susciter,
provoquer, dresser, hausser, augmenter; n augmentation f (de
salaire).
raisin ['reizn] n raisin sec m.
rake [reik] n râteau m, roué m; vt
ratisser, râcler, balayer; — **off** gratte
f; **to** — **up** vt attiser, raviver.
rakish ['reikiʃ] a coquin, dissolu,
désinvolte, bravache.
rally ['ræli] n ralliement m, réunion
f, rallye m, rétablissement m,
dernier effort m; vt rallier, rétablir;
vi se rallier, se reformer, retrouver
des forces, se reprendre.
Ralph [rælf] Raoul m.
ram [ræm] n bélier m, éperon m,
marteau-pilon m; vt éperonner,
pilonner, tasser, bourrer, enfoncer,
tamponner.
ramble ['ræmbl] n flânerie f,
promenade f, divagation f; vi
errer, flâner, divaguer.
rambler ['ræmblə] n flâneur, -euse,
plante grimpante f.
rambling ['ræmbliŋ] a errant, vagabond, décousu; n pl promenades
f pl, divagations f pl.
ramp [ræmp] n rampe f, pente f,
scandale m, affaire véreuse f,
supercherie f, coup monté m.
rampant ['ræmpənt] a forcené,
répandu, envahissant, rampant.
rampart ['ræmpaːt] n rempart m.
ramshackle ['ræm.ʃækl] a branlant,
délabré.
ran [ræn] pt of **run**.
ranch [raːntʃ] n ranch m, prairie f

d'élevage; *vi* faire de l'élevage.
rancid ['rænsid] *a* rance.
rancidness ['rænsidnis] *n* rancidité *f*.
rancor ['ræŋkə] *n* rancœur *f*, rancune *f*.
rancorous ['ræŋkərəs] *a* rancunier.
random ['rændəm] *n* **at** — à l'aventure, au hasard.
rang [ræŋ] *pt of* **ring**.
range ['reindʒ] *n* rangée *f*, étendue *f*, gamme *f*, rang *m*, direction *f*, portée *f*, fourneau *m* de cuisine, champ de tir *m*, grand pâturage *m*; *vt* ranger, (*gun*) porter, braquer; *vi* s'étendre, errer.
rank ['ræŋk] *n* rang *m*, classe *f*, grade *m*; *vt* ranger; *vi* se ranger, compter; *a* luxuriant, rance, fort, absolu, flagrant, criant, pur.
rankle ['ræŋkl] *vi* s'envenimer, laisser une rancœur.
ransack ['rænsæk] *vt* fouiller, piller.
ransom ['rænsəm] *n* rançon *f*; *vt* rançonner, racheter.
rant [rænt] *n* tirade enflammée *f*, rodomontades *f pl*; *vi* pérorer.
rap [ræp] *n* tape *f*, coup sec *m*, (*fig*) pomme *f*; *vt* donner sur les doigts à; *vti* frapper.
rapacious [rə'peiʃəs] *a* rapace.
rape [reip] *n* viol *m*, (*bot*) colza *m*; *vt* violer.
rapid ['ræpid] *a* rapide.
rapt [ræpt] *a* ravi, recueilli.
rapture ['ræptʃə] *n* ravissement *m*, ivresse *f*.
rapturous ['ræptʃərəs] *a* ravissant, frénétique, extasié.
rare [reə] *a* rare.
rarefaction [ˌreəri'fækʃən] *n* raréfaction *f*.
rarefy ['reərifai] *vt* raréfier.
rarity ['reəriti] *n* rareté *f*.
rascal ['rɑːskəl] *n* gredin *m*, fripon *m*, coquin *m*.
rash [ræʃ] *n* éruption *f*; *a* impulsif, casse-cou, irréfléchi.
rasher ['ræʃə] *n* tranche de lard *f*.
rashness ['ræʃnis] *n* impulsivité *f*, témérité *f*.
rasp [rɑːsp] *n* râpe *f*; *vt* râper, racler; *vi* grincer.
raspberry ['rɑːzbəri] *n* framboise *f*.
rat [ræt] *n* rat *m*, faux frère *m*, mouchard *n*; **to smell a** — soupçonner anguille sous roche; *vi* tourner casaque.
ratchet ['rætʃit] *n* cliquet *m*, rochet *m*.
rate [reit] *n* taux *m*, prix *m*, raison *f*, vitesse *f*, impôt municipal *m*, cas *m*; **at any** — en tout cas; *vt* estimer, compter, considérer, classer, imposer; *vi* passer, être classé.
ratepayer ['reitˌpeiə] *n* contribuable *mf*.
rather ['rɑːðə] *ad* plutôt, assez.
ratification [ˌrætifi'keiʃən] *n* ratification *f*.
ratify ['rætifai] *vt* ratifier, approuver.

ratio ['reiʃiou] *n* proportion *f*, raison *f*.
ration ['ræʃən] *n* ration *f*; *vt* rationner.
rational ['ræʃənl] *a* raisonnable, raisonné, rationnel.
rationalist ['ræʃnəlist] *an* rationaliste *mf*.
rationing ['ræʃniŋ] *n* rationnement *m*.
rat-race ['rætreis] *n* course *f* aux sous.
rattle ['rætl] *n* (bruit de) crécelle *f*, hochet *m*, râle *m*, cliquetis *m*, tintamarre *m*, fracas *m*, crépitement *m*; *vt* faire cliqueter, faire sonner, bouleverser; *vi* ferrailler, cliqueter, crépiter, trembler; **—snake** *n* serpent *m* à sonnettes.
raucous ['rɔːkəs] *a* rauque.
ravage ['rævidʒ] *n* ravage *m*; *vt* ravager, dévaster.
rave [reiv] *vi* hurler, délirer, radoter, s'extasier (sur **about**), raffoler (de **about**).
ravel ['rævəl] *vt* embrouiller; **to — out** débrouiller, effilocher.
raven ['reivn] *n* corbeau *m*.
ravenous ['rævinəs] *a* dévorant, vorace, affamé.
ravine [rə'viːn] *n* ravin *m*.
raving ['reiviŋ] *n* hurlement *m*, délire *m*, *a* délirant; **— mad** fou à lier.
ravish ['ræviʃ] *vt* ravir, violer.
raw [rɔː] *n* vif *m*; *a* cru, (*oil*) brut, âpre, mal dégrossi, inexpérimenté; **— materials** matières premières *f pl*.
rawness ['rɔːnis] *n* crudité *f*, âpreté *f*, inexpérience *f*.
ray [rei] *n* rayon *m*, (*fish*) raie *f*.
rayon ['reiɔn] *n* soie artificielle *f*, rayonne *f*.
raze [reiz] *vt* raser.
razor ['reizə] *n* rasoir *m*.
reach [riːtʃ] *n* portée *f*, (*sport*) allonge *f*, brief *m*; *vt* atteindre, arriver à, parvenir à, (é)tendre; *vi* s'étendre.
react [riː'ækt] *vi* réagir.
reaction [riː'ækʃən] *n* réaction *f*, contre-coup *m*.
reactor [riː'æktə] *n* réacteur *m* atomique; **breeder** — pile couveuse.
read [riːd] *pp* red] *vt* lire, étudier; **to — through** parcourir.
readable ['riːdəbl] *a* lisible, d'une lecture facile.
reader ['riːdə] *n* lecteur, -trice, liseur, -euse, professeur adjoint *m*, livre de lecture *m*.
readily ['redili] *ad* volontiers, facilement.
readiness ['redinis] *n* empressement *m*, alacrité *f*, facilité *f*.
reading ['riːdiŋ] *n* lecture *f*, interprétation *f*.
readjust ['riːə'dʒʌst] *vt* rajuster, rectifier.

ready ['redi] *a* prêt, facile, prompt;
—**made** *a* prêt à porter, tout fait;
— **reckoner** *n* barême *m*.
real [riəl] *n* réel *m*; *a* vrai, naturel,
réel, foncier.
reality [ri'æliti] *n* réalité *f*.
realization [ˌriəlai'zeiʃən] *n* réalisation *f*.
realize ['riəlaiz] *vt* comprendre, se
rendre compte de, réaliser.
really ['riəli] *ad* vraiment, en effet.
realm [relm] *n* royaume *m*, domaine
m.
realtor ['riːəltə] *n* agent *m* immobilier.
ream [riːm] *n* rame *f*.
reap [riːp] *vt* moissonner, récolter.
reaper ['riːpə] *n* moissonneur, -euse,
(machine *f*) moissonneuse *f*.
reaping-hook ['riːpiŋhuk] *n* faucille
f.
reappear ['riːə'piə] *vi* réapparaître.
rear [riə] *n* arrière(s) *m* (*pl*), derrière
m, queue *f*, dernier rang *m*; *a* (d')
arrière, de queue; *vt* élever, dresser, ériger; *vi* se cabrer, s'élever, dresser; —**guard** *n* arrière-garde *f*.
reason ['riːzn] *n* raison *f*, motif *m*;
vi raisonner.
reasonable ['riːznəbl] *a* raisonnable.
reassemble ['riːə'sembl] *vt* rassembler, remonter.
rebate ['riːbeit] *n* rabais *m*, ristourne
f, escompte *m*.
rebel ['rebl] *n* rebelle *mf*; *a* insurgé.
rebel [ri'bel] *vi* se révolter.
rebellion [ri'beljən] *n* rébellion *f*,
révolte *f*.
rebellious [ri'beljəs] *a* rebelle.
rebound [ri'baund] *n* recul *m*,
ricochet *m*, réaction *f*; *vi* rebondir,
ricocher.
rebuff [ri'bʌf] *n* rebuffade *f*, échec
m; *vt* rabrouer, repousser.
rebuke [ri'bjuːk] *n* semonce *f*,
réprimande *f*; *vt* rembarrer, réprimander.
rebut [ri'bʌt] *vt* repousser, réfuter.
recall [ri'kɔːl] *n* rappel *m*, annulation
f; *vt* (se) rappeler, révoquer, reprendre.
recant [ri'kænt] *vt* retirer, rétracter;
vi se rétracter.
recapitulate [ˌriːkə'pitjuleit] *vt* récapituler.
recede [ri'siːd] *vi* reculer, se retirer,
baisser, s'enfuir, fuir.
receipt [ri'siːt] *n* réception *f*,
recette *f*, reçu *m*, récepissé *m*,
quittance *f*; *vt* acquitter.
receive [ri'siːv] *vt* recevoir, admettre,
accueillir.
receiver [ri'siːvə] *n* receleur, -euse,
recepteur *m*, destinataire *mf*; **official**
— syndic.
recent ['riːsnt] *a* récent.
recently ['riːsntli] *ad* récemment,
dernièrement.
receptacle [ri'septəkl] *n* réceptacle
m, récipient *m*.

reception [ri'sepʃən] *n* réception *f*,
accueil *m*.
recess [ri'ses] *n* vacances parlementaires *f pl*, repli *m*, recoin *m*, alcôve *f*.
recipe ['resipi] *n* recette *f*, ordonnance *f*, formule *f*.
reciprocal [ri'siprəkəl] *a* réciproque.
reciprocate [ri'siprəkeit] *vt* (se)
rendre, payer de retour; *vi* rendre la
pareille.
recital [ri'saitl] *n* exposé *m*, recitation *f*, récital *m*.
recite [ri'sait] *vt* réciter, énumérer.
reckless ['reklis] *a* imprudent,
forcené, casse-cou.
recklessness ['reklisnis] *n* imprudence *f*, témérité *f*.
reckon ['rekən] *vt* calculer, compter;
vi estimer.
reckoning ['rekniŋ] *n* règlement de
comptes *m*, calcul *m*, compte *m*.
reclaim [ri'kleim] *vt* reprendre,
réformer, récupérer.
recline [ri'klain] *vt* pencher, étendre,
reposer; *vi* (se) reposer, être appuyé.
recluse [ri'kluːs] *an* reclus(e) *mf*; *n*
anachorète *m*.
recognition [ˌrekəg'niʃən] *n* reconnaissance *f*.
recognizable [ˌrekəg'naizəbl] *a* reconnaissable.
recognizance [ri'kognizəns] *n* engagement *m*, caution *f*.
recognize ['rekəgnaiz] *vt* reconnaître,
avouer.
recoil [ri'kɔil] *n* recul *m*, rebondissement *m*; *vi* reculer, retomber,
rejaillir, se détendre.
recollect [ˌrekə'lekt] *vt* se rappeler,
se souvenir de.
recollection [ˌrekə'lekʃən] *n* mémoire *f*, souvenir *m*.
recommend [ˌrekə'mend] *vt* confier,
recommander, conseiller.
recompense ['rekəmpens] *n* récompense *f*, compensation *f*; *vt* récompenser, dédommager.
reconcilable ['rekənsailəbl] *a* conciliable.
reconcile ['rekənsail] *vt* (ré)concilier
(à, avec).
reconciliation [ˌrekənsili'eiʃən] *n*
(ré)conciliation *f*.
recondite [ri'kɔndait] *a* abstrus,
obscur.
recondition [ˌriːkən'diʃən] *vt* remettre en état, à neuf.
reconnoiter [ˌrekə'nɔitə] *vt* reconnaître; *vi* faire une reconnaissance.
record ['rekɔːd] *n* document *m*,
dossier *m*, casier *m*, record *m*,
disque *m*, enregistrement *m*, passé
m; — **player** tourne-disques *m inv*.
record [ri'kɔːd] *vt* rapporter, enregistrer, prendre acte de.
recorder [ri'kɔːdə] *n* archiviste *m*,
greffier, appareil enregistreur *m*,
flûte à bec *f*.
recount ['riː'kaunt] *vt* raconter.
recoup [ri'kuːp] *vt* défalquer, dé-

dommager; to — one's losses se rattraper de ses pertes.
recourse [ri'kɔːs] *n* recours *m*.
recover [ri'kʌvə] *vt* recouvrer, récupérer, reprendre, rattraper; *vi* se rétablir, se remettre, se ressaisir.
recovery [ri'kʌvəri] *n* recouvrement *m*, récupération *f*, rétablissement *m*, relèvement *m*.
recreation [‚rekri'eiʃən] *n* délassement *m*, divertissement *m*.
recriminate [ri'krimineit] *vi* récriminer.
recruit [ri'kruːt] *n* recrue *f*; *vt* recruter, racoler.
recruiting [ri'kruːtiŋ] *n* recrutement *m*.
rectangle ['rek‚tæŋgl] *an* rectangle *m*.
rectification [‚rektifi'keiʃən] *n* rectification *f*, redressement *m*.
rectify ['rektifai] *vt* rectifier, réparer, redresser.
rector ['rektə] *n* recteur *m*.
recumbent [ri'kʌmbənt] *a* couché.
recuperate [ri'kjuːpəreit] *vt* récupérer; *vi* se rétablir.
recur [ri'kəː] *vi* revenir, se reproduire.
red [red] *a* rouge, roux; **—handed** *a* pris sur le fait; **— herring** *n* hareng saur *m*, diversion *f*; **—hot** chauffé au rouge; **—letter** *a* heureux, mémorable; **— tape** *n* paperasserie *f*, bureaucratie *f*.
redbreast ['redbrest] *n* rouge-gorge *m*.
Red Cross ['red'krɔs] *n* Croix-Rouge *f*.
redden ['redn] *vti* rougir.
reddish ['rediʃ] *a* rougeâtre.
redeem [ri'diːm] *vt* racheter, sauver.
redeemer [ri'diːmə] *n* sauveur *m*, rédempteur *m*.
redemption [ri'dempʃən] *n* rédemption *f*, salut *m*, rachat *m*.
redness ['rednis] *n* rougeur *f*, rousseur *f*.
redolent ['redələnt] *a* qui sent, parfumé.
redouble [ri'dʌbl] *vti* redoubler; *vt* plier en quatre, (*bridge*) surcontrer.
redoubt [ri'daut] *n* redoute *f*.
redoubtable [ri'dautəbl] *a* redoutable.
redress [riː'dres] *n* réparation *f*; *vt* redresser, réparer.
reduce [ri'djuːs] *vt* réduire, diminuer, ravaler, ramener; *vi* maigrir.
reduced [ri'djuːst] *a* diminué, appauvri.
reducible [ri'djuːsəbl] *a* réductible.
reduction [ri'dʌkʃən] *n* réduction *f*, baisse *f*, rabais *m*.
redundant [ri'dʌndənt] *a* redondant, superflu.
reed [riːd] *n* roseau *m*, pipeau *m*, anche *f*.
reef [riːf] *n* récif *m*, écueil *m*, filon *m*, ris *m*.
reek [riːk] *n* fumée *f*, vapeur *f*,

relent *m*; *vi* fumer; **to — of** empester.
reel ['riːl] *n* bobine *f*, dévidoir *m*, moulinet *m*; *vt* enrouler, dévider; *vi* tituber, tourner, être ébranlé.
re-elect ['riːi'lekt] *vt* réélire.
re-embark ['riːim'baːk] *vti* rembarquer.
re-embarkation ['riː‚embaː'keiʃən] *n* rembarquement *m*.
re-enter ['riː'entə] *vi* rentrer, se présenter de nouveau.
re-establish ['riːis'tæbliʃ] *vt* rétablir.
re-establishment ['riːis'tæbliʃmənt] *n* rétablissement *m*.
refection [ri'fekʃən] *n* réfection *f*, collation *f*.
refectory [ri'fektəri] *n* réfectoire *m*.
refer [ri'fəː] *vt* rapporter, référer, renvoyer, attribuer; *vi* se reporter, se rapporter, se référer, avoir trait (à to), faire allusion (à to).
referee [‚refə'riː] *n* arbitre *m*, répondant *m*; *vti* arbitrer.
reference ['refrəns] *n* référence *f*, renvoi *m*, rapport *m*, allusion *f*, mention *f*.
refine [ri'fain] *vt* purifier, (r)affiner.
refinement [ri'fainmənt] *n* (r)affinage *m*, finesse *f*, raffinement *m*.
refinery [ri'fainəri] *n* raffinerie *f*.
refit ['riːfit] *vt* radouber, rééquiper, réarmer, rajuster, remonter.
reflect [ri'flekt] *vti* réfléchir; *vt* refléter, renvoyer; *vi* méditer, rejaillir, faire du tort (à **upon**).
reflection [ri'flekʃən] *n* réflexion *f*, reflet *m*, image *f*, critique *f*, atteinte *f*.
reflector [ri'flektə] *n* réflecteur *m*, cabochon *m*.
reflex ['riːfleks] *n* réflexe *m*, reflet *m*.
reflexive [ri'fleksiv] *a* réfléchi.
reform [ri'fɔːm] *n* réforme *f*; *vt* réformer; *vi* se reformer.
reformation [‚refə'meiʃən] *n* réforme *f*, réformation *f*.
reformer [ri'fɔːmə] *n* réformateur, -trice.
refract [ri'frækt] *vt* réfracter.
refraction [ri'frækʃən] *n* réfraction *f*.
refractory [ri'fræktəri] *a* réfractaire, insoumis.
refrain [ri'frein] *n* refrain *m*; *vi* s'abstenir, s'empêcher.
refresh [ri'freʃ] *vt* rafraîchir, ranimer.
refreshment [ri'freʃmənt] *n* rafraîchissement *m*; **— room** *n* buffet *m*, buvette *f*.
refrigerator [ri'fridʒəreitə] *n* réfrigérateur *m*, glacière *f*.
refuel [ri'fjuəl] *vt* ravitailler en combustible; *vi* se ravitailler en combustible, faire le plein (d'essence).
refuge ['refjuːdʒ] *n* refuge *m*, abri *m*.
refugee ['refjuː'dʒiː] *n* réfugié(e) *mf*.
refund ['riːfʌnd] *n* remboursement *m*; ['riː'fʌnd] *vt* rembourser.

refusal [ri'fjuːzəl] n refus m.
refuse ['refjuːs] n rebut m, ordures f pl, déchets m pl, détritus m.
refuse [ri'fjuːz] vt refuser, repousser.
refutation [,refjuː'teiʃən] n réfutation f.
refute [ri'fjuːt] vt réfuter.
regain [ri'gein] vt regagner, reprendre, recouvrer.
regal ['riːgəl] a royal.
regale [ri'geil] vt régaler.
regalia [ri'geiliə] n joyaux m pl, insignes m pl.
regard [ri'gaːd] vt regarder, considérer, concerner, tenir compte de; n égard m, attention f, estime f; pl compliments m pl; with — to quant à, en égard à.
regardless [ri'gaːdlis] a inattentif; — of sans égard à, sans regarder à.
regency ['riːdʒənsi] n régence f.
regenerate [ri'dʒenəreit] vt régénérer.
regent ['riːdʒənt] n régent(e) mf.
regiment [,redʒiment] n régiment m; vt enrégimenter.
regimentals [,redʒi'mentlz] n uniforme m.
region ['riːdʒən] n région f.
register ['redʒistə] n registre m; vt enregistrer, inscrire, (post) recommander, immatriculer.
registrar [,redʒis'traː] n secrétaire m, greffier m, officier de l'état civil m.
registry ['redʒistri] n mairie f, bureau de l'état civil m, bureau de placement m.
regret [ri'gret] n regret m; vt regretter.
regretful [ri'gretful] a désolé.
regretfully [ri'gretfuli] ad à (avec) regret.
regular ['regjulə] a régulier, habituel, réglé, rangé, normal, réglementaire, permanent.
regularity [,regju'læriti] n régularité f.
regularize ['regjuləraiz] vt régulariser.
regulate ['regjuleit] vt régler, ajuster, réglementer.
regulation [,regju'leiʃən] n règlement m, réglementation f, réglage m; a réglementaire, d'ordonnance.
rehearsal [ri'həːsəl] n répétition f, dress — répétition générale.
rehearse [ri'həːs] vt répéter, énumérer.
reign [rein] n règne m; vi régner.
rein [rein] n rêne f, guide f.
reindeer ['reindiə] n renne m.
reinforce [,riːin'fɔːs] vt renforcer, appuyer.
reinforced [,riːin'fɔːst] a renforcé, armé.
reinforcement [,riːin'fɔːsmənt] n renforcement m.
reinstate ['riːin'steit] vt rétablir, réintégrer.
reinstatement ['riːin'steitmənt] n rétablissement m, réintégration f.

reinvest ['riːin'vest] vt replacer.
reiterate [riː'itəreit] vt réitérer.
reiteration [,riːitə'reiʃən] n réitération f.
reject [ri'dʒekt] vt rejeter, refuser, repousser; ['riːdʒekt] n rebut m, article de rebut m.
rejection [ri'dʒekʃən] n rejet m, refus m, rebut m.
rejoice [ri'dʒɔis] vt réjouir; vi se réjouir.
rejoicing [ri'dʒɔisiŋ] n réjouissance f, allégresse f.
rejoin ['riː'dʒɔin] vi riposter, répliquer.
rejoin ['riː'dʒɔin] vt rejoindre, rallier; vi se rejoindre, se réunir.
rejoinder [ri'dʒɔində] n riposte f, réplique f.
relapse [ri'læps] n rechute f; vi retomber, avoir une rechute.
relate [ri'leit] vt (ra)conter, relater, rapporter, rattacher; vi avoir rapport (à to), se rapporter (à to).
related [ri'leitid] a apparenté, connexe, parent.
relation [ri'leiʃən] n relation f, rapport m, récit m, parent(e) m(f).
relationship [ri'leiʃənʃip] n parenté f, connexion f, rapport m.
relative ['relətiv] n parent(e) m(f); a relatif.
relax [ri'læks] vt détendre, relâcher, délasser, adoucir; vi se détendre, se relâcher, s'adoucir.
relaxation [,riːlæk'seiʃən] n distraction f, détente f, adoucissement m.
relaxing [riː'læksiŋ] a apaisant, reposant, énervant.
relay [ri'lei] vt relayer; n relais m, relève f.
release [ri'liːs] n délivrance f, élargissement m, décharge f, déclenchement m, lancement m, reçu m, transfert m; vt remettre, déclencher, lâcher, dégager, desserrer, faire jouer.
relegate ['religeit] vt reléguer, confier.
relent [ri'lent] vi se radoucir.
relentless [ri'lentlis] a inexorable, implacable, acharné.
relentlessness [ri'lentlisnis] n inflexibilité f, acharnement m.
relevant ['relivənt] a pertinent, qui a rapport (à to).
reliability [ri,laiə'biliti] n sûreté f, régularité f.
reliable [ri'laiəbl] a sûr, de confiance, sérieux, solide, digne de foi.
reliance [ri'laiəns] n confiance f.
relic ['relik] n relique f; pl restes m pl, souvenirs m pl.
relief [ri'liːf] n soulagement m, secours m, délivrance f, relève f, relief m.
relieve [ri'liːv] vt soulager, secourir, délivrer, relever, mettre en relief.
religion [ri'lidʒən] n religion f, culte m.

religious [ri'lidʒəs] *a* religieux, pieux, dévot.
relinquish [ri'liŋkwiʃ] *vt* abandonner, renoncer à.
relinquishment [ri'liŋkwiʃmənt] *n* abandon *m*, renonciation *f*.
relish ['reliʃ] *n* saveur *f*, goût *m*, assaisonnement *m*; *vt* relever, aimer, goûter.
reluctance [ri'lʌktəns] *n* répugnance *f*.
reluctantly [ri'lʌktəntli] *ad* à contre-cœur, à regret.
rely [ri'lai] *vi* s'appuyer (sur **on**), compter (sur **on**).
remain [ri'mein] *vi* rester, demeurer.
remainder [ri'meində] *n* reste *m*, restant *m*.
remains [ri'meinz] *n* restes *m pl*, dépouille mortelle *f*.
remand [ri'mɑːnd] *n* renvoi *m*; *vt* renvoyer en prison.
remark [ri'mɑːk] *n* attention *f*, remarque *f*, observation *f*; *vt* remarquer, (faire) observer.
remarkable [ri'mɑːkəbl] *a* remarquable, frappant.
remedy ['remidi] *n* remède *m*; *vt* remédier à.
remember [ri'membə] *vt* se souvenir de, se rappeler, penser à.
remembrance [ri'membrəns] *n* mémoire *f*, souvenir *m*.
remind [ri'maind] *vt* rappeler, faire penser.
reminder [ri'maində] *n* agenda *m*, rappel *m*.
remiss [ri'mis] *a* négligent, lent, apathique.
remission [ri'miʃən] *n* rémission *f*, remise *f*, relâchement *m*, pardon *m*.
remit [ri'mit] *vt* remettre, relâcher, (r)envoyer.
remittance [ri'mitəns] *n* envoi de fonds *m*.
remnant ['remnənt] *n* reste *m*, (*cloth*) coupon *m*.
remonstrance [ri'mɔnstrəns] *n* remontrance *f*.
remonstrate [ri'mɔnstreit] *to* — **with** faire des représentations à.
remorse [ri'mɔːs] *n* remords *m*.
remorseful [ri'mɔːsful] *a* plein de remords.
remorseless [ri'mɔːslis] *a* sans remords, implacable.
remote [ri'mout] *a* lointain, reculé, écarté, vague, peu probable, distant.
remoteness [ri'moutnis] *n* éloignement *m*.
removable [ri'muːvəbl] *a* amovible, détachable.
removal [ri'muːvəl] *n* déménagement *m*, enlèvement *m*, suppression *f*.
remove [ri'muːv] *vt* enlever, supprimer, déplacer, effacer, révoquer, retirer, écarter, déménager.
remunerate [ri'mjuːnəreit] *vt* rémunérer.

remuneration [ri,mjuːnə'reiʃən] *n* rémunération *f*.
remunerative [ri'mjuːnərətiv] *a* rémunérateur.
rend [rend] *vt* déchirer, arracher, fendre.
render ['rendə] *vt* rendre, remettre, fondre.
renegade ['renəgeid] *n* renégat *m*.
renew [ri'njuː] *vt* renouveler, rafraîchir.
renewal [ri'njuːəl] *n* renouvellement *m*, reprise *f*.
renounce [ri'nauns] *vt* renoncer à, dénoncer, répudier, renier.
renouncement [ri'naunsmənt] *n* renoncement *m*.
renovate ['renəveit] *vt* rénover, remettre à neuf.
renovation [,renə'veiʃən] *n* rénovation *f*, remise à neuf *f*.
renown [ri'naun] *n* renom *m*, renommée *f*.
renowned [ri'naund] *a* célèbre, illustre.
rent [rent] *n* déchirure *f*, accroc *m*, loyer *m*; *vt* louer, affermer.
renunciation [ri,nʌnsi'eiʃən] *n* renoncement *m*, renonciation *f*, reniement *m*.
reopen ['riː'oupən] *vti* rouvrir; *vi* se rouvrir, rentrer.
reopening ['riː'oupniŋ] *n* rentrée *f*, réouverture *f*.
repair [ri'pεə] *n* (état de) réparation *f*, radoub *m*; *vt* réparer, raccommoder; *vi* se rendre.
repartee [,repɑː'tiː] *n* repartie *f*.
repast [ri'pɑːst] *n* repas *m*.
repatriate [riː'pætrieit] *vt* rapatrier.
repatriation ['riːpætri'eiʃən] *n* rapatriement *m*.
repay [riː'pei] *vt* rembourser, rendre, s'acquitter envers.
repayment [riː'peimənt] *n* remboursement *m*, récompense *f*.
repeal [ri'piːl] *n* abrogation *f*; *vt* abroger, révoquer.
repeat [ri'piːt] *vt* répéter, rapporter, renouveler.
repeatedly [ri'piːtidli] *ad* à mainte reprise.
repeating [ri'piːtiŋ] *a* à répétition.
repel [ri'pel] *vt* repousser, répugner à.
repellent [ri'pelənt] *a* répugnant, repoussant.
repent [ri'pent] *vt* regretter, se repentir de; *vi* se repentir.
repentance [ri'pentəns] *n* repentir *m*.
repertory ['repətəri] *n* répertoire *m*.
repetition [,repi'tiʃən] *n* répétition *f*, reprise *f*, récitation *f*.
replace [ri'pleis] *vt* remplacer, replacer, remettre en place.
replaceable [ri'pleisəbl] *a* remplaçable.
replacement [ri'pleismənt] *n* remplacement *m*, pièce de rechange *f*.
replenish [ri'pleniʃ] *vt* remplir de nouveau, regarnir, remonter.

replete [ri'pliːt] *a* plein, bondé, rassasié.

reply [ri'plai] *n* réponse *f*; *vi* répondre.

report [ri'pɔːt] *n* bruit *m*, nouvelle *f*, compte-rendu *m*, bulletin *m*, rapport *m*, réputation *f*, détonation *f*; *vt* faire un rapport sur, rendre compte de, signaler, faire le reportage de; *vi* se présenter, dénoncer.

reporter [ri'pɔːtə] *n* reporter *m*, journaliste *mf*, rapporteur *m*.

repose [ri'pouz] *n* repos *m*; *vi* (se) reposer.

reposeful [ri'pouzful] *a* reposant.

reprehend [ˌrepri'hend] *vt* blâmer, reprendre.

reprehensible [repri'hensəbl] *a* répréhensible.

represent [ˌrepri'zent] *vt* représenter.

representative [ˌrepri'zentətiv] *n* représentant(e) *mf*; *a* représentatif.

repress [ri'pres] *vt* réprimer, refouler, étouffer.

repression [ri'preʃən] *n* répression *f*.

reprieve [ri'priːv] *n* sursis *m*, grâce *f*, répit *m*; *vt* surseoir à, grâcier.

reprimand ['reprimɑːnd] *n* réprimande *f*; *vt* réprimander.

reprint ['riː'print] *n* réimpression *f*; *vt* réimprimer.

reprisal [ri'praizəl] *n* représaille(s) *f* (*pl*).

reproach [ri'proutʃ] *n* honte *f*, reproche *m*; *vt* reprocher, faire des reproches à.

reproachfully [ri'proutʃfuli] *ad* sur un ton de reproche.

reprobate ['reproubeit] *n* réprouvé(e) *mf*, scélérat *m*.

reproduce [ˌriːprə'djuːs] *vt* reproduire.

reproduction [ˌriːprə'dʌkʃən] *n* reproduction *f*.

reproof [ri'pruːf] *n* blâme *m*, reproche *m*, rebuffade *f*.

reprove [ri'pruːv] *vt* blâmer, réprouver, réprimander, reprendre, condamner.

reptile ['reptail] *n* reptile *m*.

republic [ri'pʌblik] *n* république *f*.

republican [ri'pʌblikən] *an* républicain(e) *mf*.

repudiate [ri'pjuːdieit] *vt* répudier, désavouer, renier.

repudiation [riˌpjuːdi'eiʃən] *n* répudiation *f*, reniement *m*.

repugnance [ri'pʌgnəns] *n* répugnance *f*, antipathie *f*.

repugnant [ri'pʌgnənt] *a* répugnant, incompatible.

repulse [ri'pʌls] *n* échec *m*, rebuffade *f*; *vt* repousser.

repulsion [ri'pʌlʃən] *n* répulsion *f*, aversion *f*.

repulsive [ri'pʌlsiv] *a* répulsif, repoussant.

reputable ['repjutəbl] *a* honorable, estimable.

reputation [ˌrepju'teiʃən] *n* réputation *f*, renom *m*.

repute [ri'pjuːt] *n* réputation *f*, renommée *f*, renom *m*.

reputed [ri'pjuːtəd] *a* réputé, censé, putatif.

request [ri'kwest] *n* requête *f*, prière *f*; *vt* demander, prier.

require [ri'kwaiə] *vt* requérir, exiger, réclamer, avoir besoin de, falloir.

requirement [ri'kwaiəmənt] *n* exigence *f*, besoin *m*, demande *f*.

requisite ['rekwizit] *n* condition *f*; *pl* articles *m pl*, accessoires *m pl*; *a* requis, voulu, indispensable.

requisition [ˌrekwi'ziʃən] *n* requête *f*, réquisition(s) *f* (*pl*), commande *f*; *vt* réquisitionner.

requital [ri'kwaitl] *n* revanche *f*, monnaie de sa pièce *f*, retour *m*.

requite [ri'kwait] *vt* recompenser, rendre, payer de retour.

rescind [ri'sind] *vt* annuler.

rescission [ri'siʒən] *n* annulation *f*, abrogation *f*.

rescue ['reskjuː] *n* délivrance *f*, sauvetage *m*; *vt* délivrer, sauver.

rescuer ['reskjuːə] *n* sauveteur *m*, libérateur, -trice.

research [ri'səːtʃ] *n* recherche(s) *f* (*pl*).

resemblance [ri'zembləns] *n* ressemblance *f*, image *f*.

resemble [ri'zembl] *vt* ressembler à.

resent [ri'zent] *vt* ressentir, s'offenser de.

resentful [ri'zentful] *a* plein de ressentiment, rancunier.

resentment [ri'zentmənt] *n* ressentiment *m*, dépit *m*.

reservation [ˌrezə'veiʃən] *n* réservation *f*, réserve *f*, place retenue *f*.

reserve [ri'zəːv] *n* réserve *f*; *vt* réserver, retenir, louer.

reservoir ['rezəvwaː] *n* réservoir *m*.

reshuffle ['riː'ʃʌfl] *n* refonte *f*, remaniement *m*; *vt* rc⁀ondre, remanier, rebattre.

reside [ri'zaid] *vi* résider.

residence ['rezidəns] *n* résidence *f*, séjour *m*.

resident ['rezidənt] *a* résident; *n* habitant(e) *mf*.

residue ['rezidjuː] *n* reste *m*, reliquat *m*, résidu *m*.

resign [ri'zain] *vt* résigner; *vi* démissionner.

resignation [ˌrezig'neiʃən] *n* résignation *f*, démission *f*, abandon *m*.

resilience [ri'ziliəns] *n* élasticité *f*, ressort *m*.

resilient [ri'ziliənt] *a* élastique, rebondissant, qui a du ressort.

resin ['rezin] *n* résine *f*.

resist [ri'zist] *vt* résister à; *vi* résister.

resistance [ri'zistəns] *n* résistance *f*.

resolute ['rezəluːt] *a* résolu.

resolutely ['rezəluːtli] *ad* résolument, avec fermeté.

resolution [ˌrezə'luːʃən] *n* résolution *f.*

resolve [ri'zɔlv] *vt* résoudre; *vi* se résoudre.

resort [ri'zɔːt] *n* recours *m*, ressort *m*, séjour *m*, station (balnéaire) *f*; *vi* recourir (à **to**), se rendre (à **to**).

resound [ri'zaund] *vi* retentir, résonner.

resource [ri'sɔːs] *n* ressource *f.*

resourceful [ri'sɔːsful] *a* débrouillard, ingénieux.

resourcefulness [ri'sɔːsfulnis] *n* ingéniosité *f.*

respect [ris'pekt] *n* respect *m*, égard *m*, rapport *m*; *vt* respecter.

respectability [risˌpektə'biliti] *n* respectabilité *f.*

respectable [ris'pektəbl] *a* respectable.

respectful [ris'pektful] *a* respectueux.

respecting [ris'pektiŋ] *prep* relativement à, quant à.

respective [ris'pektiv] *a* respectif.

respiration [ˌrespə'reiʃən] *n* respiration *f.*

respiratory [ris'paiərətəri] *a* respiratoire.

respite ['respait] *n* répit *m*, sursis *m*; soulager, différer.

resplendent [ris'plendənt] *a* resplendissant.

respond [ris'pɔnd] *vi* répondre, obéir, réagir.

response [ris'pɔns] *n* réponse *f*, réaction *f.*

responsibility [risˌpɔnsəbiliti] *n* responsabilité *f.*

responsible [ris'pɔnsəbl] *a* responsable (devant **to**); **to be — for** répondre de.

responsive [ris'pɔnsiv] *a* sympathique, sensible, souple.

rest [rest] *n* repos *m*, appui *f*, reste *m*, réserves *f pl*; *vt* (faire) reposer, appuyer; *vi* se reposer, s'appuyer.

restaurant ['restərɔ̃ːŋ] *n* restaurant *m.*

restful ['restful] *a* reposant, paisible.

restitution [ˌresti'tjuːʃən] *n* restitution *f.*

restive ['restiv] *a* rétif, nerveux, impatient.

restless ['restlis] *a* agité.

restlessness ['restlisnis] *n* agitation *f*, impatience *f.*

restoration [ˌrestə'reiʃən] *n* restitution *f*, restauration *f*, rétablissement *m.*

restorative [ris'tɔrətiv] *an* fortifiant *m.*

restore [ris'tɔː] *vt* restituer, restaurer, rétablir.

restrain [ris'trein] *vt* réprimer, retenir, contenir, empêcher.

restraint [ris'treint] *n* discrétion *f*, contrôle *m*, sobriété *f*, contrainte *f.*

restrict [ris'trikt] *vt* réduire, limiter, restreindre.

restriction [ris'trikʃən] *n* restriction *f*, réduction *f.*

result [ri'zʌlt] *n* résultat *m*; *vi* résulter, aboutir (à **in**).

resume [ri'zjuːm] *vt* reprendre, résumer.

resumption [ri'zʌmpʃən] *n* reprise *f.*

resurrection [ˌrezə'rekʃən] *n* résurrection *f.*

resuscitate [ri'sʌsiteit] *vt* ressusciter.

retail ['riːteil] *n* vente au détail *f.*

retail [riː'teil] *vt* vendre au détail.

retailer [riː'teilə] *n* détaillant *m.*

retain [ri'tein] *vt* (con-, sou-, re-) tenir, conserver.

retainer [ri'teinə] *n* provision *f*, honoraires *m pl*, suivant *m*; *pl* suite *f.*

retaliate [ri'tælieit] *vi* rendre la pareille (à **on**), riposter.

retaliation [riˌtæli'eiʃən] *n* représailles *f pl*, revanche *f.*

retard [ri'taːd] *vt* retarder.

retch ['riːtʃ] *n* haut-le-cœur *m*; *vi* avoir des haut-le-cœur.

retentive [ri'tentiv] *a* fidèle.

retina ['retinə] *n* rétine *f.*

retinue ['retinjuː] *n* suite *f.*

retire [ri'taiə] *vt* mettre à la retraite, retirer; *vi* se retirer, reculer, battre en retraite, prendre sa retraite.

retirement [ri'taiəmənt] *n* retraite *f*, retrait *m.*

retort [ri'tɔːt] *n* riposte *f*, cornue *f*; *vi* riposter, rétorquer.

retrace [ri'treis] *vt* reconstituer, revenir sur.

retract [ri'trækt] *vt* rétracter, rentrer, escamoter; *vi* se rétracter.

retreat [ri'triːt] *n* retraite *f*, abri *m*; *vi* battre en retraite.

retrench [riː'trentʃ] *vt* retrancher; *vi* faire des économies; **—ment** *n* retranchement *m.*

retribution [ˌretri'bjuːʃən] *n* juste récompense *f.*

retrieve [ri'triːv] *vt* rapporter, retrouver, réparer, rétablir.

retrograde ['retrougreid] *vi* rétrograder; *a* rétrograde.

retrospect ['retrouspekt] *n* regard *m* en arrière.

retrospective [ˌretrou'spektiv] *a* rétrospectif.

return [ri'təːn] *n* retour *m*, restitution *f*, rendement *m*, échange *m*, revanche *f*, rapport *m*; *pl* recettes *f pl*, profit *m*; **— ticket** (billet *m* d') aller et retour *m*; *vi* retourner, revenir, rentrer; *vt* rendre, renvoyer, répliquer, élire.

reunion ['riːjuːnjən] *n* réunion *f.*

reunite ['riːjuːnait] *vt* réunir; *vi* se réunir.

reveal [ri'viːl] *vt* révéler, découvrir, faire voir.

reveille [ri'væli] *n* réveil *m*, diane *f.*

revel ['revl] *n* fête *f*, orgie *f*; *pl* réjouissances *f pl*; *vi* faire la fête, se délecter (à **in**).

revelation [,revi'leiʃən] n révélation f.

reveler ['revlə] n noceur, -euse, fêtard(e) mf.

revenge [ri'vendʒ] n revanche f, vengeance f; vt venger; **to — oneself** se venger.

revengeful [ri'vendʒful] a vindicatif, vengeur, -eresse.

revenue ['revinjuː] n revenu m.

reverberate [ri'vəːbəreit] vt réfléchir, renvoyer; vti réverbérer; vi se réfléchir.

reverberation [ri,vəːbə'reiʃən] n réverbération f, répercussion f.

revere [ri'viə] vt révérer.

reverence ['revərəns] n révérence f.

reverend ['revərənd] a révérend, vénérable.

reverent ['revərənt] a respectueux.

reverse [ri'vəːs] n revers m, envers m, marche arrière f, contraire m; a contraire, opposé; vt renverser, faire reculer, annuler; vi faire machine arrière.

review [ri'vjuː] n revue f, révision f, compte-rendu m; vt revoir, passer en revue, admettre à révision, faire le compte-rendu de.

reviewer [ri'vjuːə] n critique m.

revile [ri'vail] vt vilipender, injurier.

revise [ri'vaiz] vt réviser, revoir, corriger.

revision [ri'viʒən] n révision f.

revival [ri'vaivəl] n renaissance f, renouveau m, reprise f.

revive [ri'vaiv] vt ranimer, renouveler, remonter; vi revivre, renaître, reprendre connaissance, se ranimer.

revocation [,revə'keiʃən] n révocation f, annulation f.

revoke [ri'vouk] vt annuler, révoquer.

revolt [ri'voult] n révolte f; vt révolter; vi se révolter.

revolution [,revə'luːʃən] n révolution f.

revolutionary [,revə'luːʃnəri] an révolutionnaire mf.

revolutionize [,revə'luːʃnaiz] vt révolutionner.

revolve [ri'vɔlv] vt faire tourner, retourner; vi rouler, tourner.

reward [ri'wɔːd] n récompense f; vt récompenser, payer (de retour).

rhetoric ['retərik] n éloquence f, rhétorique f.

rheumatic [ruː'mætik] an rhumatisant(e) mf.

rheumatism ['ruːmətizəm] n rhumatisme m.

rhubarb ['ruːbɑːb] n rhubarbe f.

rhyme [raim] n rime f; vi rimer; vt faire rimer.

rhythm ['riðəm] n rythme m.

rib [rib] n côte f, nervure f, baleine f.

ribald ['ribəld] a paillard, graveleux.

ribaldry ['ribəldri] n obscénité f, paillardises f pl.

ribbon ['ribən] n ruban m, cordon m.

rice [rais] n riz m.

rich [ritʃ] a riche, somptueux, magnifique.

riches ['ritʃiz] n pl richesses f pl.

rick [rik] n meule f.

rickets ['rikits] n rachitisme m.

rickety ['rikiti] a rachitique, branlant.

rid [rid] inf pt pp of **rid**; vt débarrasser; **to get — of** se débarrasser de.

riddance ['ridəns] n débarras m.

ridden ['ridn] pp of **ride**.

riddle ['ridl] n crible m, énigme f, devinette f; vt cribler.

ride [raid] n promenade à cheval f, en auto, tour m; vi monter (aller) à cheval (à bicyclette), chevaucher, flotter, voguer, être mouillé; vt monter.

rider ['raidə] n cavalier, -ière, amazone f, écuyer, -ère, jockey m, annexe f, recommandation f.

ridge [ridʒ] n arête f, crête f, faîte f, ride f.

ridicule ['ridikjuːl] n ridicule m, raillerie f; vt ridiculiser, se moquer de.

ridiculous [ri'dikjuləs] a ridicule, absurde.

riding-school ['raidiŋ,skuːl] n manège m, école f d'équitation.

rife [raif] a commun, courant, fourmillant; **to be —** sévir.

rifle ['raifl] n carabine f; vt dévaliser, vider, fouiller, rayer.

rift [rift] n fente f, fêlure f.

rig [rig] n gréement m, accoutrement m, tenue f; vt gréer, accoutrer, truquer; **to — up** installer, monter.

rigging ['rigiŋ] n agrès m pl, équipement m.

right [rait] n droite f, droit m, dû m; a juste, exact, droit; **to be —** avoir raison; ad droit, juste, très bien; vt redresser, réparer, corriger.

righteous ['raitʃəs] a pur, juste, sans faute, vertueux.

righteousness ['raitʃəsnis] n impeccabilité f, rectitude f, vertu f.

rightful ['raitful] a légitime, équitable.

right-handed ['rait'hændid] a droitier.

rightness ['raitnis] n justesse f.

rigid ['ridʒid] a rigide, raide, strict, inflexible.

rigidity [ri'dʒiditi] n rigidité f, sévérité f.

rigmarole ['rigməroul] n calembredaine f.

rigor ['rigə] n rigueur f, sévérité f.

rigorous ['rigərəs] a rigoureux.

rim [rim] n bord m, cercle m, jante f.

rime [raim] n rime f, givre m; vi rimer.

rimmed [rimd] a cerclé, bordé, cerné, à bord.

rind [raind] n peau f, croûte f, écorce f, couenne f.

ring [riŋ] n anneau m, bague f, cercle m, cerne f, bande f, piste f,

sonnerie *f*, coup *m* de sonnette; *vti* sonner; **to — off** couper; **— finger** *n* annulaire *m*.
ringleader ['riŋ,liːdə] *n* meneur *m*.
ringworm ['riŋ,wəːm] *n* pelade *f*, teigne *f*.
rink [riŋk] *n* patinoire *f*.
rinse [rins] *vt* rincer; *n* rinçage *m*.
riot ['raiət] *n* émeute *f*, orgie *f*; *vi* s'ameuter.
rioter ['raiətə] *n* émeutier *m*.
riotous ['raiətəs] *a* turbulent, tapageur.
rip [rip] *n* déchirure *f*; *vt* déchirer, fendre; *vi* se déchirer, se fendre.
ripe [raip] *a* mûr.
ripen ['raipən] *vti* mûrir.
ripping ['ripiŋ] *a* épatant.
ripple ['ripl] *n* ride *f*, murmure *m*; *vi* se rider, onduler, perler; *vt* rider.
rise [raiz] *n* montée *f*, éminence *f*, avancement *m*, augmentation *f*, hausse *f*, source *f*, naissance *f*, essor *m*; *vi* se lever, s'élever, se soulever, monter, naître.
risen ['rizn] *pp of* **rise**.
rising ['raiziŋ] *n* lever *m*, crue *f*, soulèvement *m*, résurrection *f*, hausse *f*.
risk [risk] *n* risque *m*, péril *m*; *vt* risquer.
risky ['riski] *a* risqué, hasardeux.
rite [rait] *n* rite *m*.
ritual ['ritjuəl] *an* rituel *m*.
rival ['raivəl] *an* rival(e) *mf*; *n* émule *mf*; *vt* rivaliser avec.
rivalry ['raivəlri] *n* rivalité *f*.
rive [raiv] *vt* fendre.
riven ['rivən] *pp of* **rive**.
river ['rivə] *n* rivière *f*, fleuve *m*.
rivet ['rivit] *n* rivet *m*; *vt* river.
rivulet ['rivjulit] *n* ruisselet *m*.
roach [routʃ] *n* gardon *m*.
road [roud] *n* route *f*, rue *f*, rade *f*.
roadside ['roud,said] *n* bas-côté *m*; **— repairs** dépannage *m*.
roadway ['roudwei] *n* chaussée *f*.
roam [roum] *vi* rôder, errer.
roar [rɔː] *n* mugissement *m*, rugissement *m*, grondement *m*, vrombissement *m*, gros éclat de rire *m*; *vi* rugir, mugir, vrombir, hurler, s'esclaffer.
roast [roust] *n* rôti *m*, rosbif *m*; *vt* rôtir, griller.
rob [rɔb] *vt* dérober, voler, piller, détrousser.
robber ['rɔbə] *n* voleur, -euse.
robbery ['rɔbəri] *n* vol *m*, brigandage *m*.
robe [roub] *n* robe *f*.
Robert ['rɔbət] Robert *m*.
robin ['rɔbin] *n* rouge-gorge *m*.
robot ['roubɔt] *n* automate *m*; *a* automatique.
robust [rə'bʌst] *a* robuste, vigoureux.
rock [rɔk] *n* roc *m*, rocher *m*, roche, *f*; *vt* bercer, balancer, (é)branler, basculer; *vi* osciller, (se) balancer.

rocket ['rɔkit] *n* fusée *f*; *a* à fusée.
rocking ['rɔkiŋ] *a* à bascule.
rocky ['rɔki] *a* rocheux, rocailleux, instable.
rod [rɔd] *n* baguette *f*, tringle *f*, perche *f*, gaule *f*, canne à pêche *f*, verge(s) *f* (*pl*), piston *m*.
rode [roud] *pt of* **ride**.
rodent ['roudənt] *an* rongeur *m*.
roe [rou] *n* **hard — ** œufs *m pl*; **soft — ** laitance *f*.
roe(buck) ['rou(bʌk)] *n* chevreuil *m*.
rogue [roug] *n* coquin(e) *mf*, fripon, -onne, gredin *m*.
roguish ['rougiʃ] *a* fripon, coquin, espiègle, malin, -igne.
roll [roul] *n* rouleau *m*, boudin *m*, petit pain *m*, tableau *m*, roulis *m*, roulement *m*; *vt* rouler, enrouler, laminer; *vi* (se) rouler, s'enrouler.
roller ['roulə] *n* rouleau *m*, bande *f*, laminoir *m*, grosse lame *f*; **— skates** patins à roulettes *m pl*.
Roman ['roumən] *a* romain; *n* Romain(e) *mf*.
romance [rə'mæns] *an* roman *m*; *n* idylle *f*, romanesque *m*; *vi* romancer, faire du roman, exagérer.
romantic [rə'mæntik] *a* romanesque, romantique.
romanticism [rə'mæntisizəm] *n* romantisme *m*.
Romany ['rɔməni] *n* bohémien, -ienne.
romp [rɔmp] *n* petit(e) diable(sse), jeu de vilain *m*, gambades *f pl*; *vi* jouer, s'ébattre, gambader.
rood [ruːd] *n* crucifix *n*, quart d'arpent *m*.
roof [ruːf] *n* toit *m*, toiture *f*, (*mouth*) palais *m*.
rook [ruk] *n* corneille *f*, bonneteur *m*, escroc *m*.
room [rum] *n* chambre *f*, pièce *f*, salle *f*, place *f*, lieu *m*.
roomy ['rumi] *a* spacieux, ample.
roost [ruːst] *n* perchoir *m*; *vi* se percher, se jucher.
root [ruːt] *n* racine *f*, source *f*; *vt* planter, enraciner, clouer; *vi* s'enraciner.
rope [roup] *n* corde *f*, cordage *m*, câble *m*, glane *f*, collier *m*; *vt* corder, lier, hâler.
rosary ['rouzəri] *n* rosaire *m*, chapelet *m*.
rose [rouz] *n* rose *f*, rosace *f*, rosette *f*, pomme d'arrosoir *f*; **—bud** *n* bouton *m* de rose; **—bush** *n* rosier *m*.
rosemary ['rouzməri] *n* romarin *m*.
rosin ['rɔzin] *n* colophane *f*.
roster ['rɔstə] *n* tableau *m*, liste *f*, roulement *m*.
rosy ['rouzi] *a* rose, rosé, attrayant.
rot [rɔt] *n* pourriture *f*, carie *f*, démoralisation *f*, bêtises *f pl*; *vti* pourrir; *vi* se carier, se décomposer.
rota ['routə] *n* liste *f*, roulement *m*.
rotate [rou'teit] *vt* faire tourner, alterner; *vi* tourner, pivoter.

rote [rout] *n* routine *f*; **by —** machinalement.

rotten ['rɔtn] *a* pourri, carié, fichu, moche, patraque.

rotter ['rɔtə] *n* propre à rien *m*, sale type *m*, salaud *m*.

rotund [rou'tʌnd] *a* arrondi, sonore.

rouge [ruːʒ] *n* rouge *m*, fard *m*; *vt* farder.

rough [rʌf] *a* rugueux, grossier, brutal, rude, brut, approximatif; **to — it** vivre à la dure.

roughcast ['rʌfkɑːst] *vt* ébaucher, crépir; *n* crépi *m*.

rough copy ['rʌf'kɔpi] *n* brouillon *m*.

roughen ['rʌfn] *vt* rendre grossier, rude; *vi* grossir.

roughly ['rʌfli] *ad* en gros, brutalement, à peu près.

roughness ['rʌfnis] *n* rugosité *f*, rudesse *f*, grossièreté *f*.

roughshod ['rʌfʃɔd] *a* ferré à glace; **to ride — over s.o.** fouler qn aux pieds.

round [raund] *n* rond *m*, ronde *f*, tournée *f*, tour *m*, échelon *m*, (*sport*) circuit *m*, reprise *f*, série *f*, cartouche *f*, salve *f*; *a* rond; *prep* autour de; *ad* en rond, à la ronde; *vt* arrondir, contourner, doubler; **to — up** rassembler, rafler.

roundabout ['raundəbaut] *n* manège *m* (de chevaux de bois), rondpoint *m*.

roundly ['raundli] *ad* rondement, net.

roundworm ['raund,wəːm] *n* chique *f*.

rouse [rauz] *vt* réveiller, exciter, remuer.

rousing ['rauziŋ] *a* retentissant, vibrant.

rout [raut] *n* bande *f*. déroute *f*; *vt*. mettre en déroute.

route [ruːt] *n* itinéraire *m*, parcours *m*, route *f*.

routine [ruː'tiːn] *n* routine *f*.

rove [rouv] *vi* rôder; *vt* parcourir.

rover ['rouvə] *n* vagabond *m*, coureur *m*, pirate *m*.

row [rou] *n* rang *m*, rangée *f*, file *f*, partie de canotage *f*; *vi* ramer, faire du canotage; *vt* conduire à l'aviron.

row [rau] *n* dispute *f*, bagarre *f*, semonce *f*; *vt* attraper; *vi* se chamailler.

rowdy ['raudi] *n* voyou *m*; *a* violent, turbulent.

rowdyism ['raudiizəm] *n* désordre *m*, chahutage *m*.

rower ['rouə] *n* rameur, -euse, canotier *m*.

rowlock ['rɔlək] *n* tolet *m*

royal ['rɔiəl] *a* royal.

royalist ['rɔiəlist] *n* royaliste *mf*.

royalty ['rɔiəlti] *n* royauté *f*; *pl* droits d'auteur *m pl*.

rub [rʌb] *n* frottement *m*, friction *f*, hauts et bas *m pl*, hic *m*; *vti* frotter; *vt* frictionner, calquer, polir, masser; **to — out** effacer.

rubber ['rʌbə] *n* gomme *f*, caoutchouc *m*, frotteur, -euse; **— tree** *n* hévia *m*.

rubbish ['rʌbiʃ] *n* ordures *f pl*, détritus *m*, décombres *m pl*, niaiseries *f pl*; **— chute** vide-ordures *m*.

rubble ['rʌbl] *n* gravats *m pl*.

rubric ['ruːbrik] *n* rubrique *f*.

ruby ['ruːbi] *n* rubis *m*.

rudder ['rʌdə] *n* gouvernail *m*.

ruddy ['rʌdi] *a* coloré, rougeaud, rougeoyant.

rude [ruːd] *a* grossier, mal élevé, violent, brusque, brut.

rudeness ['ruːdnis] *n* rudesse *f*, grossièreté *f*.

rudiment ['ruːdimənt] *n* rudiment *m*.

rudimentary [,ruːdi'mentəri] *a* rudimentaire.

rue [ruː] *vt* regretter, se repentir de.

rueful ['ruːful] *a* triste.

ruefulness ['ruːfulnis] *n* tristesse *f*, regret *m*.

ruffian ['rʌfiən] *n* bandit *m*, brute *f*, polisson *f*.

ruffle ['rʌfl] *n* ride *f*, manchette *f*, jabot *m*; *vt* hérisser, rider, ébouriffer, émouvoir.

rug [rʌg] *n* couverture *f*, tapis *m*.

rugged ['rʌgid] *a* rugueux, inégal, sauvage, rude.

ruin ['ruin] *n* ruine *f*; *vt* ruiner.

ruinous ['ruinəs] *a* ruineux.

rule [ruːl] *n* règle *f*, règlement *m*, autorité *f*; *vt* régir, gouverner, régler, décider; **to — out** écarter.

ruler ['ruːlə] *n* souverain(e) *mf*, dirigeant(e) *mf*, règle *f*.

ruling ['ruːliŋ] *n* décision *f*.

rum [rʌm] *n* rhum *m*; *a* bizarre, louche.

rumble ['rʌmbl] *n* grondement *m*, roulement *m*; *vi* rouler, gronder.

ruminate ['ruːmineit] *vi* ruminer.

rummage ['rʌmidʒ] *vti* fouiller; *vi* fureter.

rumor ['ruːmə] *n* rumeur *f*, bruit *m*; *vt* **it is —ed** le bruit court.

rump [rʌmp] *n* croupe *f*, croupion *m*, culotte *f*.

rumple ['rʌmpl] *vt* froisser, friper.

run [rʌn] *n* course *f*, marche *f*, promenade *f*, direction *f*, série *f*, demande *f*, ruée *f*, moyenne *f*, enclos *m*, libre usage *m*; *vti* courir; *vi* marcher, fonctionner, couler, s'étendre, passer, déteindre, tenir l'affiche; *vt* diriger, exploiter, tenir, entretenir, promener.

runaway ['rʌnəwei] *a* fugitif, emballé.

rung [rʌŋ] *pp of* **ring**; *n* barreau *m*, échelon *m*.

runner ['rʌnə] *n* coureur, -euse, messager *m*, glissoir *m*, patin *m*.

running ['rʌniŋ] *n* course *f*, marche *f*, direction *f*; *a* courant, coulant, continu, de suite.

running-board ['rʌniŋ bɔːd] *n* marche-pied *m*.

runway ['rʌnwei] n piste f.
rupee [ru:'pi:] roupie f.
rupture ['rʌptʃə] n rupture f, hernie f; vt rompre; vi se rompre.
rural ['ruərəl] a rural, agreste, des champs.
rush [rʌʃ] n jonc m, ruée f, hâte f, presse f, montée f; a de pointe, urgent; vt précipiter, brusquer; expédier, bousculer, envahir; vi s'élancer, se précipiter, se jeter, faire irruption.
rusk [rʌsk] n biscotte f.
russet ['rʌsit] n reinette grise f; a brun-roux.
Russia ['rʌʃə] n Russie f.
Russian ['rʌʃən] an russe m; n Russe mf.
rust [rʌst] n rouille f; vt rouiller; vi se rouiller.
rustic ['rʌstik] n paysan, -anne, campagnard(e) mf, rustre m; a rustique, paysan.
rustle ['rʌsl] n frou-frou m, bruissement m; vi bruire, faire frou-frou; vt froisser.
rustless ['rʌstlis] a inoxydable.
rusty ['rʌsti] a rouillé.
rut [rʌt] n ornière f, rut m.
ruthless ['ru:θlis] a implacable, impitoyable.
ruthlessness ['ru:θlisnis] n férocité f, implacabilité f.
rye [rai] n seigle m.

S

Sabbath ['sæbəθ] n sabbat m, dimanche m.
saber ['seibə] n sabre m.
sable ['seibl] n zibeline f; a noir.
sabotage ['sæbətɑ:ʒ] n sabotage m; vt saboter.
saccharine ['sækərin] n saccharine f.
sack [sæk] n sac m, pillage; vt saccager, renvoyer, mettre en sac.
sacrament ['sækrəmənt] n sacrement m.
sacred ['seikrid] a sacré, saint, religieux, consacré.
sacrifice ['sækrifais] n sacrifice m, victime f; vt sacrifier, immoler.
sacrilege ['sækrilidʒ] n sacrilège m.
sad [sæd] a triste, cruel, lourd, déplorable.
sadden ['sædn] vt attrister.
saddle ['sædl] n selle f; vt seller, mettre sur le dos de.
saddler ['sædlə] n sellier m, bourrelier m.
sadness ['sædnis] n tristesse f.
safe [seif] n garde-manger m, coffre-fort m; a sauf, sûr, prudent, à l'abri, en sûreté.
safe-conduct ['seif'kɔndəkt] n sauf-conduit m.
safeguard ['seifgɑ:d] n sauvegarde f, garantie f.
safely ['seifli] ad sain et sauf, bien.

safety ['seifti] n sûreté f, sécurité f; a de sûreté.
sag [sæg] vi céder, fléchir, se détendre, gondoler, baisser; n fléchissement m, ventre m.
sagacious [sə'geiʃəs] a sagace, perspicace, intelligent.
sagacity [sə'gæsiti] n sagacité f, intelligence f.
sage [seidʒ] n (bot) sauge f; an sage m.
sago ['seigou] n tapioca m.
said [sed] pt pp of **say**.
sail [seil] n voile f, voilure f, aile f, traversée f, promenade en bateau f; vi naviguer, mettre à la voile, planer, voguer; vt conduire, naviguer; —ing n mise à la voile f, départ m, navigation f; **to go sailing** faire du bateau.
sailor ['seilə] n matelot m, marin m; **to be a good** — avoir le pied marin.
saint [seint] an saint(e) mf.
sake [seik] **for the** — **of** par égard pour, pour l'amour de, pour les beaux yeux de, dans l'intérêt de.
salable ['seiləbil] a vendable, de vente courante.
salad ['sæləd] n salade f.
salaried ['sælərid] a rétribué, salarié.
salary ['sæləri] n traitement m, appointements m pl.
sale [seil] n vente f, solde(s) f.
salesman ['seilzmən] n vendeur m, courtier m, commis m.
salient ['seiliənt] an saillant m.
saliva [sə'laivə] n salive f.
sallow ['sælou] a blafard, jaunâtre, olivâtre.
sally ['sæli] n sortie f, saillie f; vi faire une sortie, sortir.
salmon ['sæmən] n saumon m; —-trout n truite saumonée f.
saloon [sə'lu:n] n salon m, salle f, cabaret m; — **car** n (voiture f à) conduite intérieure f.
salt [sɔ:lt] n sel m, loup m de mer; a salé; vt saler; —**cellar** n salière f.
saltpeter ['sɔ:lt,pi:tə] n salpêtre m.
salubrious [sə'lu:briəs] a salubre, sain.
salubrity [sə'lu:briti] n salubrité f.
salutary ['sæljutəri] a salutaire.
salute [sə'lu:t] n salut m, salve f; vt saluer.
salvage ['sælvidʒ] n sauvetage m, matériel récupéré m; vt récupérer.
salvation [sæl'veiʃən] n salut m.
salve [sælv] vt calmer, apaiser; n pommade f, baume m.
salver ['sælvə] n plateau m.
salvo ['sælvou] n salve f.
same [seim] a même, monotone; **to do the** — faire de même.
sameness ['seimnis] n ressemblance f, monotonie f, uniformité f.
sample ['sɑ:mpl] n échantillon m; vt éprouver, tâter de, échantillonner, déguster.
sanctify ['sæŋktifai] vt sanctifier, consacrer.

sanctimonious [‚sæŋkti'mouniəs] *a* papelard, hypocrite.

sanction ['sæŋkʃən] *n* sanction *f*, approbation *f*; *vt* sanctionner, approuver.

sanctity ['sæŋktiti] *n* sainteté *f*, inviolabilité *f*.

sanctuary ['sæŋktjuəri] *n* sanctuaire *m*, asile *m*, réfuge *m*.

sand [sænd] *n* sable *m*; *pl* plage *f*; — **dune** dune *f*; —**paper** papier de verre *m*; —**shoes** souliers *mpl* bains de mer, espadrilles *f pl*.

sandal ['sændl] *n* sandale *f*, samara *m*.

sandalwood ['sændlwud] *n* santal *m*.

sandbag ['sændbæg] *n* sac de terre *m*, assommoir *m*; *vt* protéger avec des sacs de terre, assommer.

sandy ['sændi] *a* sablonneux, blond-roux.

sandwich ['sænwidʒ] *n* sandwich *m*.

sane [sein] *a* sain, sensé.

sang [sæŋ] *pt of* **sing**.

sanguinary ['sæŋgwinəri] *a* sanglant, sanguinaire.

sanguine ['sæŋgwin] *a* sanguin, convaincu, optimiste.

sanitary ['sænitəri] *a* sanitaire, hygiénique.

sanity ['sæniti] *n* raison *f*, santé *f* mentale.

sank [sæŋk] *pt of* **sink**.

sap [sæp] *n* sève *f*, sape *f*; *vt* épuiser, saper, miner.

sapling ['sæpliŋ] *n* plant *m*, baliveau *m*, adolescent(e).

sapper ['sæpə] *n* sapeur *m*.

sapphire ['sæfaiə] *n* saphir *m*.

sarcasm ['saːkæzəm] *n* sarcasme *m*, ironie *f*.

sarcastic [saː'kæstik] *a* sarcastique; —**ally** *ad* d'un ton sarcastique.

sardine [saː'diːn] *n* sardine *f*.

Sardinia [saː'diniə] *n* Sardaigne *f*.

sash [sæʃ] *n* châssis *m*, ceinture *f*, écharpe *f*; — **window** *n* fenêtre à guillotine *f*.

sat [sæt] *pt pp of* **sit**.

satchel ['sætʃəl] *n* sacoche *f*, cartable *m*.

sate [seit] *vt* assouvir, rassasier.

sated ['seitid] *a* repu.

sateen [sæ'tiːn] *n* satinette *f*.

satiate ['seiʃieit] *vt* apaiser, rassasier.

satiety [sə'taiəti] *n* satiété *f*.

satin ['sætin] *n* satin *m*.

satire ['sætaiə] *n* satire *f*.

satirical [sə'tirikl] *a* satirique.

satirist ['sætərist] *n* satirique *m*.

satisfaction [‚sætis'fækʃən] *n* paiement *m*, rachat *m*, satisfaction *f*.

satisfactory [‚sætis'fæktəri] *a* satisfaisant.

satisfy ['sætisfai] *vt* satisfaire, convaincre, remplir.

saturate ['sætʃəreit] *vt* tremper, imprégner, saturer.

Saturday ['sætədi] *n* samedi *m*.

satyr ['sætə] *n* satyre *m*.

sauce [sɔːs] *n* sauce *f*, assaisonnement *m*, insolence *f*; —**boat** *n* saucière *f*; —**pan** *n* casserole *f*.

saucer ['sɔːsə] *n* soucoupe *f*.

sauciness ['sɔːsinis] *n* impertinence *f*.

saucy ['sɔːsi] *a* impertinent, effronté, fripon.

saunter ['sɔːntə] *n* flânerie *f*; *vt* flâner.

sausage ['sɔsidʒ] *n* saucisse *f*, saucisson *m*.

sausage-meat ['sɔsidʒmiːt] *n* chair à saucisse *f*.

savage ['sævidʒ] *n* sauvage *mf*; *a* féroce, brutal, barbare.

savagery ['sævidʒəri] *n* sauvagerie *f*, férocité *f*, barberie *f*.

savanna(h) [sə'vænə] *n* savane *f*.

save [seiv] *vt* sauver, préserver, économiser, épargner, ménager; *prep* sauf, excepté.

saving ['seiviŋ] *n* salut *m*, économie *f*; *a* économe, qui rachète.

savior ['seivjə] *n* sauveur *m*.

savor ['seivə] *n* saveur *f*, goût *m*, pointe *f*; *vi* **to — of** sentir, tenir de.

savory ['seivəri] *a* relevé, savoureux, succulent.

Savoy [sə'vɔi] Savoie *f*.

savvy ['sævi] *n* jugeotte *f*; *vti* piger.

saw [sɔː] *n* scie *f*; adage *m*; maxime *f*, proverbe *m*; *vt* scier.

sawdust ['sɔːdʌst] *n* sciure *f*.

sawmill ['sɔːmil] *n* scierie *f*.

sawyer ['sɔːjə] *n* scieur *m*.

sawn [sɔːn] *pp of* **saw**.

say [sei] *n* mot *m*, voix *f*; *vti* dire.

saying ['seiiŋ] *n* dicton *m*, récitation *f*.

scab [skæb] *n* croûte, gourme *f*, gale *f*, jaune *m*, faux-frère *m*; *vi* se cicatriser.

scabbard ['skæbəd] *n* fourreau *m*, gaine *f*.

scabby ['skæbi] *a* galeux, croûteux, mesquin.

scabies ['skeibiːz] *n* gale *f*.

scabrous ['skeibrəs] *a* scabreux, raboteux.

scaffold ['skæfəld] *n* échafaud *m*.

scaffolding ['skæfəldiŋ] *n* échafaudage *m*.

scald [skɔːld] *n* brûlure *f*; *vt* ébouillanter, échauder.

scale [skeil] *n* plateau *m*, balance *f*, bascule *f*, échelle *f*, gamme *f*, écaille *f*, dépôt *m*, tartre *m*; *vt* écailler, peler, écosser, râcler, décrasser, escalader, graduer; *vi* s'écailler, s'incruster.

scallop ['skɔləp] *n* coquille Saint-Jacques *f*, feston *m*.

scalp [skælp] *n* cuir chevelu *m*, scalpe *m*; *vt* scalper.

scalpel ['skælpəl] *n* scalpel *m*.

scamp [skæmp] *n* vaurien *m*; *vt* bâcler.

scamper ['skæmpə] *vi* détaler.

scan [skæn] *vt* scander, scruter, embrasser du regard, parcourir.

scandal ['skændl] *n* scandale *m*, honte *f*, cancans *m pl*.
scandalize ['skændəlaiz] *vt* scandaliser.
scandalous ['skændələs] *a* scandaleux, honteux.
scansion ['skænʃən] *n* scansion *f*.
scanty ['skænti] *a* mince, rare, insuffisant, étroit, peu de, juste, sommaire.
scapegoat ['skeipgout] *n* bouc émissaire *m*, souffre-douleur *m*.
scapegrace ['skeipgreis] *n* étourneau *m*, mauvais sujet *m*.
scar [skɑː] *n* cicatrice *f*; *vt* balafrer; *vi* se cicatriser.
scarab ['skærəb] *n* scarabée *m*.
scarce [skɛəs] *a* rare.
scarcely ['skɛəsli] *ad* à peine, ne ... guère.
scarcity ['skɛəsiti] *n* rareté *f*, pénurie *f*.
scare [skɛə] *n* panique *f*, alarme *f*; *vt* terrifier, effrayer; —**crow** *n* épouvantail *m*; —**monger** *n* alarmiste *mf*.
scarf [skɑːf] *n* écharpe *f*, foulard *m*, cache-col *m*.
scarlet ['skɑːlit] *an* écarlate *f*; — **fever** *n* (fièvre) scarlatine *f*.
scathing ['skeiðiŋ] *a* mordant, cinglant.
scatter ['skætə] *vt* disperser, éparpiller, semer; *vi* se disperser, s'égailler, se dissiper; —**brain** *n* écervelé(e).
scattered ['skætəd] *a* épars, éparpillé, semé.
scattering ['skætəriŋ] *n* dispersion *f*, éparpillement *m*, poignée *f*.
scavenger ['skævindʒə] *n* balayeur *m*, boueux *m*.
scene [siːn] *n* scène *f*, spectacle *m*, lieu *m*, théâtre *m*.
scenery ['siːnəri] *n* décor(s) *m* (*pl*), paysage *m*.
scenic ['siːnik] *a* scénique, théâtral.
scent [sent] *n* odeur *f*, parfum *m*, piste *f*, flair *m*; *vt* flairer, parfumer, embaumer.
scepter ['septə] *n* sceptre *m*.
schedule ['skedjul] *n* horaire *m*, plan *m*, annexe *f*.
scheme [skiːm] *n* plan *m*, projet *m*, intrigue *f*, combinaison *f*; *vi* comploter, intriguer; *vt* combiner, projeter.
schemer ['skiːmə] *n* homme *m* à projets, intrigant(e) *mf*.
schism ['sizəm] *n* schisme *m*.
scholar ['skɔlə] *n* érudit *m*, savant(e) *mf*, boursier, -ière, écolier, -ière.
scholarship ['skɔləʃip] *n* science *f*, érudition *f*, bourse *f*.
school [skuːl] *n* école *f*, faculté *f*; *vt* instruire, dresser, formerent, raîner; **summer**—cours de vacances; **night** — école, classe, cours du soir; **to go to** —aller en classe.
schoolmaster ['skuːlˌmɑːstə] *n* instituteur *m*, professeur *m*, directeur *m*.
schoolmate ['skuːlmeit] *n* camarade de classe *mf*.
schoolroom ['skuːlrum] *n* (salle de) classe *f*.
schooner ['skuːnə] *n* goélette *f*.
science ['saiəns] *n* science *f*.
scientist ['saiəntist] *n* savant(e) *mf*, homme de science *m*, scientifique *m*.
scion ['saiən] *n* rejeton *m*, bouture *f*.
scissors ['sizəz] *n* ciseaux *m pl*.
scoff [skɔf] *n* raillerie *f*; *vt* railler; *vi* se moquer (de **at**).
scold [skould] *n* mégère *f*; *vti* gronder; *vt* attraper.
scolding ['skouldiŋ] *n* semonce *f*, savon *m*.
sconce [skɔns] *n* applique *f*, bobèche.
scoop ['skuːp] *n* pelle *f*, louche *f*, écope *f*, cuiller *f*, reportage *m* en exclusivité; *vt* creuser, vider, écoper, rafler.
scope [skoup] *n* portée *f*, envergure *f*, champ *m*, carrière *f*, compétence *f*.
scorch [skɔːtʃ] *vt* brûler, roussir, rôtir; *vi* filer à toute vitesse, brûler le pavé.
score [skɔː] *n* marque *f*, score *m*, point *m*, compte *m*, partition *f*, coche *f*, éraflure *f*, vingt; *vt* marquer, remporter, (en)cocher, érafler, orchestrer; *vi* marquer les points, avoir l'avantage; réprimander, censurer.
scorn [skɔːn] *n* mépris *m*; *vt* mépriser.
scornful ['skɔːnful] *a* méprisant.
Scotch ['skɔtʃ] *n* Écossais(e) *mf*; *an* écossais *m*; *n* whisky *m*.
scotfree ['skɔt'friː] *a* indemne, sans rien payer.
Scotland ['skɔtlənd] *n* Écosse *f*.
Scot(sman, -swoman) [skɔt(smən, wumən)] *n* Écossais, Écossaise.
Scots, Scottish [skɔts, 'skɔtiʃ] *a* écossais, d'Écosse.
scoundrel ['skaundrəl] *n* canaille *f*, gredin *m*, coquin *m*.
scour ['skauə] *vt* frotter, récurer, purger, battre, balayer, (par)courir.
scourge [skəːdʒ] *n* fléau *m*; *vt* châtier, flageller.
scout [skaut] *n* éclaireur *m*, scout *m*; *vt* reconnaître, rejeter; *vi* partir en reconnaissance.
scowl [skaul] *n* air renfrogné *m*; *vi* faire la tête, se renfrogner.
scrag [skræg] *n* squelette *m*, cou *m*, collet *m*.
scraggy ['skrægi] *a* décharné.
scramble ['skræmbl] *n* mêlée *f*, lutte *f*; *vt* (eggs) brouiller; *vi* se battre, se bousculer.
scrap [skræp] *n* morceau *m*, chiffon *m*, coupure *f*, bribe *f*, bagarre *f*; *pl* déchets *m pl*, restes *m pl*; *vt* mettre au rebut, réformer; *vi* se battre, se bagarrer.
scrape [skreip] *n* grincement *m*,

grattage *m*, embarras *m*; *vti* gratter, frotter; *vt* râcler, décrotter.

scraper ['skreipǝ] *n* grattoir *m*, décrottoir *m*.

scratch [skrætʃ] *n* égratignure *f*, trait (grincement *m*) de plume *mf*, coup de griffe *m*; — **pad** *n* bloc-notes *m*; *vti* égratigner, gratter, griffonner.

scrawl [skrɔ:l] *n* gribouillage *m*; *vt* gribouiller.

scream [skri:m] *n* cri (perçant) *m*; *vi* pousser un cri, crier, se tordre (de rire).

screaming ['skri:miŋ] *a* désopilant, criard.

screen [skri:n] *n* écran *m*, paravent *m*, rideau *m*, crible *m*, jubé *m*; *vt* couvrir, cacher, protéger, projeter, cribler, mettre à l'écran.

screw [skru:] *n* vis *f*, hélice *f*, écrou *m*, pingre *m*; *vt* visser, (res)serrer, pressurer; **to — up one's courage** prendre son courage à deux mains.

screwdriver ['skru:,draivǝ] *n* tourne-vis *m*.

scribble ['skribl] *see* **scrawl.**

scrimmage ['skrimidʒ] *n* bagarre *f*, mêlée *f*.

scrimp [skrimp] *vti* lésiner (sur), sabo-ter.

scripture ['skriptʃǝ] *n* Écriture *f*.

scroll [skroul] *n* rouleau *m*, volute *f*, fioriture *f*.

scrounge [skraundʒ] *vt* chiper, écor-nifler.

scrounger ['skraundʒǝ] *n* chipeur *m*, pique-assiette *m*.

scrub [skrʌb] *n* broussailles *f pl*, coup de brosse *m*, frottée *f*; *vt* frotter, récurer.

scrubbing ['skrʌbiŋ] *n* frottage *m*, récurage *m*.

scrubby ['skrʌbi] *a* rabougri, chétif.

scruple ['skru:pl] *n* scrupule *m*; *vi* se faire scrupule (de **about**).

scrupulous ['skru:pjulǝs] *a* scrupu-leux, méticuleux.

scrutinize ['skru:tinaiz] *vt* scruter, examiner de près.

scrutiny ['skru:tini] *n* examen serré *m*, second compte *m*.

scuffle ['skʌfl] *n* bousculade *f*; *vi* bousculer.

scull [skʌl] *n* godille *f*; *vi* godiller, ramer.

sculptor ['skʌlptǝ] *n* sculpteur *m*.

sculpture ['skʌlptʃǝ] *n* sculpture *f*; *vt* sculpter.

scum [skʌm] *n* écume *f*, rebut *m*; *vti* écumer.

scurf [skǝ:f] *n* pellicule *f*.

scurrilous ['skʌrilǝs] *a* grossier, ordurier, obscène.

scurvy ['skǝ:vi] *n* scorbut *m*; *a* bas, méprisable.

scuttle ['skʌtl] *n* seau *m*, hublot *m*, fuite *f*; *vt* saborder; *vi* décamper.

scythe [saið] *n* faux *f*; *vt* faucher.

sea [si:] *n* mer *f*; *a* marin, maritime, de mer; **——coast** *n* littoral *m*;

——gull *n* mouette *f*; **——horse** *n* mouton *m*; **——level** *n* niveau de la mer *m*; **——plane** *n* hydravion *m*; **——port** *n* port (maritime) *m*; **——sickness** *n* mal de mer *m*; **——wall** *n* digue *f*.

seal [si:l] *n* (zool) phoque *m*; cachet *m*, sceau *m*; *vt* sceller, cacheter.

sealing-wax ['si:liŋwæks] *n* cire à cacheter *f*.

seam [si:m] *n* couture *f*, suture *f*, cicatrice *f*, veine *f*, filon *m*.

seaman ['si:mǝn] *n* marin *m*, matelot *m*.

seamstress ['semstris] *n* couturière *f*.

seamy side ['si:misaid] *n* envers *m*, les dessous *m pl*.

sear [siǝ] *a* séché, flétri; *vt* brûler au fer rouge, flétrir.

search [sǝ:tʃ] *n* quête *f*, visite *f*, perquisition *f*, recherche(s) *f* (*pl*); *vt* fouiller, inspecter, scruter, sonder, examiner; *vti* chercher.

searching ['sǝ:tʃiŋ] *a* pénétrant, minutieux.

searchlight ['sǝ:tʃlait] *n* projecteur *m*, phare *m*.

season ['si:zn] *n* saison *f*, période *f*, bon moment *m*; *vt* endurcir, aguer-rir, mûrir, assaisonner, tempérer.

seasonable ['si:znǝbl] *a* de saison, saisonnier, opportun.

seasoning ['si:zniŋ] *n* assaisonne-ment *m*.

season-ticket ['si:zn'tikit] *n* abonne-ment *m*.

seat [si:t] *n* siège *m*, selle *f*, centre *m*, foyer *m*, propriété *f*, fond *m* (de culotte); *vt* contenir, faire asseoir, installer.

seaweed ['si:wi:d] *n* goémon *m*, algue *f*, varech *m*.

secede [si'si:d] *vi* se séparer.

secession [si'seʃǝn] *n* sécession *f*.

seclude [si'klu:d] *vt* écarter.

seclusion [si'klu:ʒǝn] *n* retraite *f*, solitude *f*.

second ['sekǝnd] *n* seconde *f*, second *m*; *a* second, deuxième; **— to none** sans égal; *vt* seconder, appuyer, (*mil*) détacher; **——hand** *a* d'occasion. **——rate** *a* médiocre, inférieur.

secrecy ['si:krisi] *n* secret *m*, réserve *f*, dissimulation *f*.

secret ['si:krit] *a* secret, réservé, retiré; *n* secret *m*, confidence *f*.

secretariat [,sekrǝ'tɛǝriǝt] *n* secré-tariat *m*.

secretary ['sekrǝtri] *n* secrétaire *mf*.

secrete [si'kri:t] *vt* cacher, sécréter.

secretion [si'kri:ʃǝn] *n* sécrétion *f*.

secretive ['si:kritiv] *a* secret, réservé, cachottier, renfermé.

sect [sekt] *n* secte *f*.

sectarian [sek'tɛǝriǝn] *n* sectaire *m*.

section ['sekʃǝn] *n* section *f*, coupe *f*, tranche *f*, profil *m*.

sector ['sektǝ] *n* secteur *m*.

secular ['sekjulǝ] *a* séculier, profane, séculaire.

secure [si'kjuə] *a* sûr, assuré, en sûreté, assujetti; *vt* mettre en lieu sûr, fixer, s'assurer, obtenir, assujettir.

security [si'kjuəriti] *n* sécurité *f*, sûreté(s) *f* (*pl*), sauvegarde *f*, garantie *f*, solidité *f*.

sedate [si'deit] *a* posé.

sedentary ['sedntəri] *a* sédentaire.

sedge [sedʒ] *n* jonc *m*, laîche *f*.

sediment ['sedimənt] *n* sédiment *m*, lie *f*, dépôt *m*.

sedition [si'diʃən] *n* sédition *f*.

seditious [si'diʃəs] *a* séditieux.

seduce [si'djuːs] *vt* séduire.

seducer [si'djuːsə] *n* séducteur *m*.

seduction [si'dʌkʃən] *n* séduction *f*.

seductive [si'dʌktiv] *a* séduisant.

seductiveness [si'dʌktivnis] *n* attrait *m*, séduction *f*.

sedulous ['sedjuləs] *a* assidu, empressé.

see [siː] *n* évêché *m*, siège *m*; *vti* voir, saisir, comprendre; — **here!** toi, écoute!

seed [siːd] *n* semence *f*, graine *f*, pépin *m*; *vi* monter en graine; *vt* ensemencer, semer.

seedling ['siːdliŋ] *n* plant *m*, sauvageon *m*.

seedy ['siːdi] *a* monté en graine, râpé, souffreteux, minable.

seek [siːk] *vt* (re)chercher.

seem [siːm] *vi* sembler, paraître.

seeming ['siːmiŋ] *a* apparent, soidisant.

seemingly ['siːmiŋli] *ad* apparemment.

seemly ['siːmli] *a* séant.

seemliness ['siːmlinis] *n* bienséance *f*.

seesaw ['siːsɔː] *n* bascule *f*, balançoire *f*.

seethe [siːð] *vi* bouillonner, grouiller, être en effervescence.

seize [siːz] *vt* saisir, s'emparer de; *vi* se caler, gripper.

seizure ['siːʒə] *n* saisie *f*, attaque *f*.

seldom ['seldəm] *ad* rarement.

select [si'lekt] *a* choisi, de choix, d'élite; *vt* choisir, trier, sélectionner.

selection [si'lekʃən] *n* choix *m*, sélection *f*.

self [self] *n* personnalité *f*, moi *m*, égoïsme *m*; *a* même, monotone, uniforme, auto-; —**conscious** emprunté, gêné, conscient; —**contained** (ren)fermé, indépendant; —**control** maîtrise *f* de soi, sangfroid *m*; —**defence** légitime défense *f*; —**denial** sacrifice *m*, abnégation *f*; —**educated** autodidacte; —**government** autonomie *f*; —**indulgence** *n* complaisance *f* (pour soi-même), faiblesse; —**interest** égoïsme, intérêt personnel *m*; —**respect** amour-propre *m*; —**same** *a* identique.

self-determination ['selfdi.təːmi'neiʃən] *n* autodétermination *f*.

selfish ['selfiʃ] *a* égoïste.

selfishness ['selfiʃnis] *n* égoïsme *m*.

selfless ['selflis] *a* désintéressé.

selflessness ['selflisnis] *n* abnégation *f*.

self-possessed ['selfpə'zəst] *a* maître de soi, qui à de l'aplomb *m*.

self-starter ['self'stɑːtə] *n* démarreur *m*.

self-willed ['self'wild] *a* obstiné, volontaire.

sell [sel] *vt* vendre; *v* ¹se vendre, se placer, popularisér.

seller ['selə] *n* vendeur, -euse, marchand(e) *mf*.

semblance ['sembləns] *n* air *m*, apparence *f*, semblant *m*.

semi-colon ['semi'koulən] *n* pointvirgule *m*.

seminary ['seminəri] *n* séminaire *m*, pépinière *f*.

semi-official ['semiə'fiʃəl] *a* officieux.

semolina [.semə'liːnə] *n* semoule *f*.

senate ['senit] *n* sénat *m*.

send [send] *vt* envoyer, expédier; **to — down** renvoyer; **to — for** faire venir; **to — off** reconduire, expédier.

sender ['sendə] *n* envoyeur, -euse, expéditeur, -trice.

sending ['sendiŋ] *n* envoi *m*, expédition *f*.

senior ['siːnjə] *an* ancien, -ienne, aîné(e) *mf*.

seniority [.siːni'ɔriti] *n* ancienneté *f*, aînesse *f*.

sensation [sen'seiʃən] *n* sentiment *m*, sensation *f*, impression *f*.

sensational [sen'seiʃənl] *a* sensationnel, à sensation.

sense [sens] *n* (bon) sens *m*, sentiment *m*; *vt* sentir, pressentir.

senseless ['senslis] *a* déraisonnable, sans connaissance.

sensibility [.sensi'biliti] *n* sensibilité *f*.

sensible ['sensəbl] *a* raisonnable, sensé, perceptible, sensible.

sensitive ['sensitiv] *a* sensible, impressionable.

sensual ['sensjuəl] *a* sensuel.

sensuality [.sensju'æliti] *n* sensualité *f*.

sent [sent] *pt pp of* **send.**

sentence ['sentəns] *n* phrase *f*, sentence *f*; *vt* condamner.

sententious [sen'tenʃəs] *a* sentencieux.

sentiment ['sentimənt] *n* sentiment *m*, opinion *f*.

sentimentality [.sentimen'tæliti] *n* sentimentalité *f*.

sentry ['sentri] *n* sentinelle *f*, factionnaire *m*.

sentry-box ['sentribɔks] *n* guérite *f*.

separate ['seprit] *a* distinct, détaché, séparé.

separate ['sepəreit] *vt* séparer, détacher, dégager; *vi* se séparer, se détacher.

sepoy ['siːpɔi] *n* cipaye *m*.

September [səp'tembə] n septembre m.

septic ['septik] a septique.

sepulcher ['sepəlkə] n sépulcre m.

sequel ['siːkwəl] n suite f.

sequence ['siːkwəns] n série f, suite f, séquence f.

sequester [si'kwestə] vt séquestrer, enfermer.

seraglio [sə'rɑːliou] n sérail m.

serene [si'riːn] a serein, calme.

serenity [si'reniti] n sérénité f, calme m.

serf [səːf] n serf m.

serfdom ['səːfdəm] n servage m.

serge [səːdʒ] n serge f.

sergeant ['sɑːdʒənt] n sergent m, maréchal des logis m, (police) brigadier m.

serial ['siəriəl] n feuilleton m; a en série.

seriatim [.siəri'eitim] ad point par point.

series ['siəriːz] n série f, suite f.

serious ['siəriəs] a sérieux, grave.

seriousness ['siəriəsnis] n sérieux m, gravité f.

sermon ['səːmən] n sermon m.

sermonize ['səːmənaiz] vt sermonner.

serpent ['səːpənt] n serpent m.

serpentine ['səːpəntain] a serpentin, sinueux.

servant ['səːvənt] n domestique mf, serviteur m, servante f.

serve [səːv] vt servir, être utile à, subir, remettre, desservir, purger.

service ['səːvis] n service m, emploi m, entretien m, office m, culte m; a d'ordonnance, de service.

serviceable ['səːvisəbl] a serviable, de bon usage, pratique, utilisable.

servile ['səːvail] a servile.

servility [səː'viliti] n servilité f.

servitude ['səːvitjuːd] n servitude f, esclavage m.

session ['seʃən] n session f, séance f, classe f, cours m pl

set [set] n (tools etc) jeu m, collection f, (people) groupe m, cercle f, (tea etc) service m, (TV etc) poste m, appareil m, (theatre) décor(s) m (pl), (pearls) rangée f, (linen) parure f, (hair) mise-en-plis f, (idea) direction f; a fixe, pris, stéréotype; vt régler, mettre (à **in**), fixer, (print) composer, (jewels) sertir, (trap) tendre, (blade) aiguiser; vi se mettre (à), prendre, durcir, se fixer, (sun) se coucher; **to — going** commencer; **to — aside** mettre de côté, écarter; **to — forth** exposer, faire valoir; **to — in** vi avancer; **—off** vi partir, vt déclencher; **to — out** vi partir, vt arranger; **to — up** vti monter, s'établir, préparer; **to — upon** attaquer.

set-back ['setbæk] n recul m, échec m.

set-off ['set'ɔf] n contraste m, repoussoir m.

set-to ['set'tuː] n pugilat m, échaufourré m.

settee [se'tiː] n divan m.

setter ['setə] n chien d'arrêt m.

setting ['setiŋ] n monture f, pose f, cadre m, mise f (en scène, en marche etc), coucher m.

settle ['setl] vt établir, installer, fixer, ranger, poser, régler, placer; vi s'établir, s'installer, se poser, déposer, s'arranger; n banc m, canapé m.

settlement ['setlmənt] n établissement m, colonie f, contrat m, règlement m.

settler ['setlə] n colon m, immigrant m.

seven ['sevn] an sept m.

sevenfold ['sevnfould] a septuple; ad sept fois autant.

seventeen ['sevn'tiːn] an dix-sept m.

seventeenth ['sevn'tiːnθ] an dix-septième mf.

seventh ['sevnθ] an septième mf.

seventy ['sevnti] an soixante-dix m.

sever ['sevə] vt séparer, trancher, couper.

several ['sevrəl] a respectif, personnel; a pn plusieurs.

severe [si'viə] a sévère, rigoureux, vif.

severity [si'veriti] n sévérité f, rigueur f, violence f.

sew [sou] vt coudre, suturer.

sewage ['sjuidʒ] n vidanges f pl, eaux f pl d'égout.

sewer ['souə] n couturière, brocheuse f.

sewer ['sjuə] n égout m.

sewing-machine ['souiŋmə.ʃiːn] n machine à coudre f.

sewn [soun] pp of sew.

sex [seks] n sexe m; **—appeal** n sex-appeal m.

sexton ['sekstən] n sacristain m, fossoyeur m.

sexual ['seksjuəl] a sexuel.

sexy ['seksi] a (fam) capiteuse, excitante; **to be —** avoir du sex-appeal.

shabby ['ʃæbi] a pingre, râpé, minable, délabré, mesquin, défraîchi.

shackle ['ʃækl] n chaîne f, maillon m; pl fers m pl, entraves f pl; vt enchaîner, entraver.

shade [ʃeid] n ombre f, retraite f, nuance f, store m; pl lunettes de soleil f pl; vt abriter, ombrager, masquer, assombrir, ombrer; vi dégrader.

shadow ['ʃædou] n ombre f; vt filer.

shadowy ['ʃædoui] a ombrageux, vaseux.

shady ['ʃeidi] a ombragé, ombreux, furtif, louche.

shaft [ʃɑːft] n hampe f, trait m, tige f, fût m, manche m, brancard m, arbre m, puits m.

shaggy ['ʃægi] a hirsute, touffu, en broussailles.

shake [ʃeik] *n* secousse *f*, hochement *m*, tremblement *m*; *vt* secouer, agiter, hocher, ébranler, serrer; *vi* trembler, branler.

shaky ['ʃeiki] *a* branlant, tremblant, chancelant.

shallot [ʃə'lɔt] *n* échalote *f*.

shallow ['ʃælou] *n* bas-fond *m*, haut-fond *m*; *a* peu profond, creux, superficiel.

sham [ʃæm] *n* feinte *f*, trompe-l'œil *m*, faux semblant *m*; *a* faux, simulé, postiche, en toc; *vt* feindre, simuler, faire semblant de.

shamble ['ʃæmbl] *vi* trainer les pieds.

shambles ['ʃæmblz] *n* abattoir *m*, tuerie *f*.

shame [ʃeim] *n* honte *f*, pudeur *f*; *vt* faire honte à, couvrir de honte.

shameful ['ʃeimful] *a* honteux, scandaleux.

shameless ['ʃeimlis] *a* éhonté, effronté.

shampoo [ʃæm'pu:] *n* shampooing *m*; *vt* donner un shampooing à.

shamrock ['ʃæmrɔk] *n* trèfle *m*.

shandy ['ʃændi] *n* bière panachée *f*.

shank [ʃæŋk] *n* jambe *f*, tige *f*, fût *m*, manche *m*, tibia *m*.

shape [ʃeip] *n* forme *f*, tournure *f*, moule *m*; *vt* former, façonner; *vi* prendre forme, prendre tournure.

shapeless ['ʃeiplis] *a* informe.

shapely ['ʃeipli] *a* gracieux, bien fait.

share [ʃɛə] *n* part *f*, action *f*, contribution *f*, soc *m*; *vti* partager; *vt* prendre part à.

shareholder ['ʃɛə,houldə] *n* actionnaire *mf*.

shark [ʃɑːk] *n* requin *m*, *n* fort (en maths).

sharp [ʃɑːp] *a* pointu, aigu, tranchant, aigre, vif, fin, malhonnête, expert; *ad* juste, brusquement; tapant.

sharpen ['ʃɑːpən] *vt* aiguiser, affiler, tailler.

sharper ['ʃɑːpə] *n* tricheur *m*, escroc *m*.

sharply ['ʃɑːpli] *ad* vertement, d'un ton tranchant.

sharpness ['ʃɑːpnis] *n* acuité *f*, netteté *f*, finesse *f*.

sharpshooter ['ʃɑːp,ʃuːtə] *n* bon tireur *m*, tirailleur *m*.

shatter ['ʃætə] *vt* mettre en pièces, fracasser.

shave [ʃeiv] *vt* raser, frôler; *vi* se raser; **to have a —** se (faire) raser; **to have a close —** l'échapper belle.

shaving ['ʃeiviŋ] *n* copeau *m*; **—brush** *n* blaireau *m*.

shawl [ʃɔːl] *n* châle *m*.

she [ʃiː] *pn* elle, (ship) il; *n* femelle *f*.

sheaf [ʃiːf] *n* gerbe *f*, liasse *f*.

shear [ʃiə] *vt* tondre.

shearing ['ʃiəriŋ] *n* tonte *f*.

shears [ʃiəz] *n* cisailles *f pl*.

sheath [ʃiːθ] *n* fourreau *m*, gaine *f*, étui *m*.

sheathe [ʃiːð] *vt* (r)engainer, encaisser, doubler.

shed [ʃed] *n* hangar *m*, remise *f*, étable *f*, appentis *m*; *vt* perdre, mettre au rencart, se dépouiller de, verser.

sheep [ʃiːp] *n* mouton *m*.

sheepdog ['ʃiːpdɔg] *n* chien de berger *m*.

sheepish ['ʃiːpiʃ] *a* gauche, timide, penaud, honteux.

sheer [ʃiə] *a* pur, à pic, transparent.

sheet [ʃiːt] *n* drap *m*, feuille *f*, nappe *f*, tôle *f*.

shelf [ʃelf] *n* rayon *m*, corniche *f*.

shell [ʃel] *n* coquille *f*, coque *f*, cosse *f*, écaille *f*, carapace *f*, douille *f*, obus *m*; *vt* écosser, décortiquer, bombarder.

shellfish ['ʃelfiʃ] *n* coquillage *m*.

shelter ['ʃeltə] *n* abri *m*, couvert *m*, asile *m*; *vt* abriter, couvrir, recueillir; *vi* s'abriter, se mettre à l'abri.

shelve [ʃelv] *vt* mettre à l'écart, (en disponibilité, au panier), ajourner.

shepherd ['ʃepəd] *n* berger *m*; *vt* rassembler, garder, conduire.

sherry ['ʃeri] *n* Xérès *m*.

shield [ʃiːld] *n* bouclier *m*, défense *f*; *vt* protéger, couvrir.

shift [ʃift] *n* changement *m*, équipe *f*, expédient *m*, faux-fuyant *m*; **to work in —s** se relayer; *vti* changer; *vt* déplacer; *vi* se déplacer; **to — for oneself** se débrouiller.

shifty ['ʃifti] *a* fuyant, retors, sournois.

shin(-bone) ['ʃin(boun)] *n* tibia *m*; *vi* grimper.

shine [ʃain] *n* brillant *m*, éclat *m*, beau-temps *m*; *vi* briller, reluire, rayonner.

shingle ['ʃiŋgl] *n* galets *m pl*; *vt* couper court.

shingles ['ʃiŋglz] *n pl* zona *m*.

ship [ʃip] *n* vaisseau *m*, navire *m*, bâtiment *m*; *vt* embarquer, charger, expédier; **—broker** courtier *m* maritime; **—load** chargement *m*, cargaison *f*; **—building** construction *f* navale.

shipping ['ʃipiŋ] *n* marine *f*, tonnage *m*, expédition *f*, navires *m pl*.

shipwreck ['ʃiprek] *n* naufrage *m*; *vi* faire échouer, faire naufrager; **to be —ed** faire naufrage.

shipwright ['ʃiprait] *n* charpentier de navires *m*.

shipyard ['ʃip'jɑːd] *n* chantier maritime *m*.

shirk [ʃəːk] *vt* esquiver, renâcler à, se dérober à.

shirker ['ʃəːkə] *n* tire-au-flanc *m*, renâcleur *m*.

shirt [ʃəːt] *n* chemise *f*.

shirt-front ['ʃəːtfrʌnt] *n* plastron *m*.

shiver ['ʃivə] *n* frisson *m*; *vi* frissonner, grelotter.

shoal [ʃoul] *n* banc *m*, masse *f*, haut-fond *m*.

shock [ʃɔk] *n* secousse *f*, heurt *m*, choc *m*, coup *m*; *vt* choquer, frapper, scandaliser.

shoddy ['ʃɔdi] *n* camelote *f*; *a* de pacotille.

shoe [ʃuː] *n* soulier *m*, chaussure *f*, fer à cheval *m*; *vt* chausser, ferrer, armer; —**black** cireur *m*; —**horn** chausse-pied *m*; —**lace** lacet *m*, cordon *m*; —**maker** cordonnier *m*.

shone [ʃɔn] *pt pp of* **shine**.

shoot [ʃuːt] *n* pousse *f*, sarment *m*, gourmand *m*, rapide *m*, partie de chasse *f*, chasse *f*; *vt* pousser, jaillir, tirer, filer; *vt* tirer, abattre, fusiller, lancer, décocher, darder.

shooting ['ʃuːtiŋ] *n* tir *m*, fusillade *f*, chasse (gardée) *f*; —**box** pavillon de chasse *m*; —**party** partie de chasse *f*; —**range** *n* champ de tir *m*; —**star** *n* étoile filante *f*.

shop [ʃɔp] *n* magasin *m*, boutique *f*, atelier *m*; *vi* faire ses achats; —**assistant** vendeur *m*, vendeuse *f*; —**boy** (**-girl**) garçon (demoiselle *f*) de magasin *m*; —**keeper** boutiquier *m*, marchand *m*; —**lifter** voleur *m* à l'étalage; — **window** vitrine *f*.

shore [ʃɔː] *n* côte *f*, rivage *m*, étai *m*; *vt* étayer.

shorn [ʃɔːn] *pp of* **shear**.

short [ʃɔːt] *n* brève *f*, court-métrage *m*, (*drinks*) alcool *m*; *a* bref, court(aud), concis, à court de, cassant; **in** — bref; —**ly** *ad* brièvement, de court, sous peu.

shortage ['ʃɔːtidʒ] *n* manque *m*, crise *f*, pénurie *f*.

shortbread ['ʃɔːtbred] *n* sablé *m*.

short-circuit ['ʃɔːt'səːkit] *n* court-circuit *m*.

shortcoming [ʃɔːt'kʌmiŋ] *n* défaut *m*, insuffisance *f*, imperfection *f*.

shorten ['ʃɔːtn] *vti* raccourcir, abréger.

shorthand ['ʃɔːthænd] *n* sténographie *f*.

shortness ['ʃɔːtnis] *n* brièveté *f*, manque *m*.

shorts [ʃɔːts] *n* culotte *f*, short *m*.

short-sighted ['ʃɔːt'saitid] *a* myope, imprévoyant, de myope.

short-sightedness ['ʃɔːt'saitidnis] *n* myopie *f*, imprévoyance *f*.

short-tempered ['ʃɔːt'tempəd] *a* irritable.

short-winded ['ʃɔːtwindid] *a* court d'haleine, poussif.

shot [ʃɔt] *pt pp of* **shoot**; *n* balle *f*, boulet *m*; plombs *m pl*, coup *m* (de feu), tireur *m*, tentative *f*, portée *f*, prise de vue *f*; —**gun** fusil *m*.

shoulder ['ʃouldə] *n* épaule *f*; *vt* mettre, charger, porter, sur l'épaule; —**blade** omoplate *f*; —**strap** bretelle *f*, patte d'épaule *f*; — **bag** sac *m* en bandoulière.

shout [ʃaut] *n* cri *m*; *vti* crier; **to** —

down huer.

shove [ʃʌv] *n* coup d'épaule *m*; *vti* pousser; *vt* fourrer.

shovel ['ʃʌvl] *n* pelle *f*.

shovelful ['ʃʌvlful] *n* pelletée *f*.

show [ʃou] *n* spectacle *m*, exposition *f*, montre *f*, étalage *m*, apparence *f*, simulacre *m*, affaire *f*, ostentation *f*; **motor** — salon *m* de l'automobile; *vt* montrer, exposer, exhiber, accuser, indiquer, faire preuve de; *vi* se montrer, paraître; **to** — **in** faire entrer, introduire; **to** — **out** reconduire; **to** — **off** *vt* faire étalage de, mettre en valeur; *vi* faire de l'épate, se faire valoir; **to** — **up** démasquer.

show-case ['ʃoukeis] *n* vitrine *f*.

shower ['ʃauə] *n* ondée *f*, averse *f*, pluie *f*, douche *f*, volée *f*; *vt* faire pleuvoir, arroser, accabler.

showiness ['ʃouinis] *n* ostentation *f*, épate *f*.

showman ['ʃoumən] *n* forain *m*, imprésario *m*.

shown [ʃoun] *pp of* **show**.

showroom ['ʃourum] *n* salon d'exposition *m*.

show-window ['ʃou'windou] *n* étalage *m*.

showy ['ʃoui] *a* voyant, criard, prétentieux.

shrank [ʃræŋk] *pt of* **shrink**.

shred [ʃred] *n* pièce *f*, lambeau *m*, brin *m*; *vt* mettre en pièces, effilocher.

shrew [ʃruː] *n* mégère *f*; (*mouse*) musaraigne *f*.

shrewd [ʃruːd] *a* perspicace, entendu, judicieux.

shrewdness ['ʃruːdnis] *n* sagacité *f*, perspicacité *f*, finesse *f*.

shriek [ʃriːk] *n* cri aigu *m*; *vi* crier, déchirer l'air, pousser un cri.

shrill [ʃril] *a* aigu, -uë, perçant.

shrimp [ʃrimp] *n* crevette (grise) *f*, gringalet *m*.

shrine [ʃrain] *n* châsse *f*, tombeau *m*, sanctuaire *m*.

shrink [ʃriŋk] *vt* rétrécir; *vi* se rétrécir, reculer.

shrinkage ['ʃriŋkidʒ] *n* rétrécissement *m*.

shrivel ['ʃrivl] *vi* se ratatiner, se recroqueviller; *vt* ratatiner, brûler.

shroud [ʃraud] *n* linceul *m*, suaire *m*, hauban *m*, voile *m*; *vt* envelopper, cacher, voiler.

Shrove Tuesday ['ʃrouv'tjuːzdi] *n* mardi gras *m*.

shrub [ʃrʌb] *n* arbrisseau *m*.

shrubbery ['ʃrʌbəri] *n* taillis *m*, bosquet *m*.

shrug [ʃrʌg] *n* haussement d'épaules *m*; **to** — **one's shoulders** hausser les épaules.

shudder ['ʃʌdə] *n* frisson *m*; *vi* frissonner.

shuffle ['ʃʌfl] *vt* brouiller, (*cards*) battre, mêler, traîner; *vi* traîner la jambe, louvoyer, tergiverser.

shun [ʃʌn] *vt* éviter, fuir.

shunt [ʃʌnt] *vt* garer, manœuvrer, écarter.

shunting ['ʃʌntiŋ] *n* garage *m*, manœuvre *f*.

shut [ʃʌt] *vtir* fermer, serrer; *vi* (se) fermer; **to — down** arrêter, fermer; **to — in** enfermer, confiner; **to — off** couper; **to — up** *vt* enfermer; *vi* fermer çà.

shut-out ['ʃʌtaut] *n* lock-out *m*.

shutter ['ʃʌtə] *n* volet *m*, obturateur *m*.

shuttle ['ʃʌtl] *n* navette *f*.

shuttlecock ['ʃʌtlkɔk] *n* volant *m*.

shy [ʃai] *n* sursaut *m*, écart *m*, essai *m*; *a* timide, ombrageux; **to be — of** être à court de; *vi* sursauter, faire un écart; *vt* lancer.

sick [sik] *a* malade, écœuré, dégoûté; **—room** *n* chambre *f* de malade.

sicken ['sikn] *vi* tomber malade; *vt* écœurer.

sickle ['sikl] *n* faucille *f*.

sickly ['sikli] *a* maladif, malsain, fade, pâle.

sickness ['siknis] *n* maladie *f*, mal de cœur *m*.

side ['said] *n* côté *m*, flanc *m*, côte *f*, parti *m*, équipe *f*, chichi *m*; *a* de coté, latéral.

sideboard ['saidbɔːd] *n* dressoir *m*, buffet *m*.

sidecar ['saidkɑː] *n* sidecar *m*.

sidelong ['saidlɔŋ] *a* oblique, de côté, en coulisse.

siding ['saidiŋ] *n* voie de garage *f*.

sidewalk ['saidwɔːk] *n* trottoir *m*.

sideways ['saidweiz] *ad* de côté.

siege [siːdʒ] *n* siège *m*.

sieve [siv] *n* tamis *m*, crible *m*, écumoire *f*.

sift [sift] *vt* cribler, tamiser.

sigh [sai] *n* soupir *m*; *vi* soupirer.

sight [sait] *n* vue *f*, hausse *f*, guidon *m*, spectacle *m*; *vt* apercevoir, aviser; (*gun*) pointer.

sightless ['saitlis] *a* aveugle.

sightly ['saitli] *a* bon à voir, avenant.

sightseeing ['sait.siːiŋ] *n* tourisme *m*, visite *f*.

sign [sain] *n* signe *m*, marque *f*, indication *f*, enseigne *f*; *vt* signer; *vi* faire signe; **—board** enseigne *f*; **—post** poteau indicateur *m*.

signal ['signl] *n* signal *m*, indicatif *m*; *vti* signaler.

signatory ['signətəri] *n* signataire *mf*.

signature ['signitʃə] *n* signature *f*; **— tune** indicatif musical *m*.

significance [sig'nifikəns] *n* sens *m*, importance *f*.

significant [sig'nifikənt] *a* significatif, important.

signification [.signifi'keiʃən] *n* signification *f*.

signify ['signifai] *vt* annoncer, signifier; *vi* importer.

silence ['sailəns] *n* silence *m*; *excl* motus! chut!; *vt* réduire au silence,

faire taire, étouffer.

silencer ['sailənsə] *n* silencieux *m*.

silent ['sailənt] *a* silencieux, muet, taciturne.

silk [silk] *n* soie *f*; *a* de, en, soie; **—worm** ver à soie *m*.

silken ['silkən] *a* soyeux, suave, doucereux.

sill [sil] *n* seuil *m*, rebord *m*.

silliness ['silinis] *n* sottise.

silly ['sili] *a* sot, sotte, bête.

silt [silt] *n* vase *f*; *vt* ensabler, envaser; *vi* s'ensabler.

silver ['silvə] *n* argent *m*, argenterie *f*; *a* d'argent, argenté; *vt* argenter, étamer; **— gilt** vermeil *m*; **—paper** papier d'étain *m*; **—side** gîte à la noix *m*; **—smith** orfèvre *m*.

silvery ['silvəri] *a* argenté, argentin.

similar ['similə] *a* semblable; **—ly** *ad* de même.

similarity [.simi'læriti] *n* similarité *f*, ressemblance *f*.

simile ['simili] *n* comparaison *f*.

similitude [si'militjuːd] *n* ressemblance *f*, apparence *f*, similitude *f*.

simmer ['simə] *vti* mijoter; *vi* frémir, fermenter.

simper ['simpə] *n* sourire *m* apprêté; *vi* minauder.

simple ['simpl] *a* simple.

simpleton ['simplton] *n* niais(e) *mf*.

simplicity [sim'plisiti] *n* simplicité *f*, candeur *f*.

simplify ['simplifai] *vt* simplifier.

simplification [.simplifi'keiʃən] *n* simplification *f*.

simulate ['simjuleit] *vt* simuler, feindre, imiter.

simulation [.simju'leiʃən] *n* simulation *f*.

simulator ['simjuleitə] *n* simulateur, -trice.

simultaneous [.siməl'teiniəs] *a* simultané.

simultaneousness [.siməl'teiniəsnis] *n* simultanéité *f*.

sin [sin] *n* péché *m*; *vi* pécher.

since [sins] *prep* depuis; *ad* depuis; *cj* depuis que, puisque.

sincere [sin'siə] *a* sincère.

sincerely [sin'siəli] *ad* **yours —** recevez l'expression de mes sentiments distingués.

sincerity [sin'seriti] *n* sincérité *f*, bonne foi *f*.

sinecure ['sainikjuə] *n* sinécure *f*.

sinew ['sinjuː] *n* tendon *m*, muscle *m*, force *f*; *pl* nerf(s) *m* (*pl*).

sinewy ['sinjuːi] *a* musclé, musculeux, nerveux.

sinful ['sinful] *a* coupable.

sing [siŋ] *vti* chanter.

singe [sindʒ] *vt* roussir, flamber.

singer ['siŋə] *n* chanteur, -euse, chantre *m*; **praise —** griot *m*.

single ['siŋgl] *a* seul, singulier, pour une personne, célibataire, droit, sincère; *n* (*ticket*) aller *m*, (*tennis*) simple *m*; *vt* **to — out** distinguer, désigner; **—handed** sans aide, d'une seule main.

singleness ['siŋglnis] n unité f, droiture f.

singular ['siŋgjulə] a singulier.

singularity [.siŋgju'læriti] n singularité f.

sinister ['sinistə] a sinistre, mauvais.

sink [siŋk] n évier m, cloaque m, trappe f; vi baisser, tomber, s'abaisser, défaillir, sombrer, couler au fond, s'enfoncer; vt placer à fonds perdus, couler, baisser, forer, abandonner, sacrifier.

sinking ['siŋkiŋ] n coulage m, défaillance f, enfoncement m, abaissement m; **—fund** fonds d'amortissement m.

sinner ['sinə] n pécheur, pécheresse.

sinuous ['sinjuəs] a sinueux, souple.

sip [sip] n gorgée f, goutte f; vt siroter, déguster.

siphon ['saifən] n siphon m.

sir [sə:] n monsieur m.

sire ['saiə] n sire m, père m.

siren ['saiərin] n sirène f.

sirloin ['sə:lɔin] n aloyau m, faux-filet m.

sister ['sistə] n sœur f; **—in-law** belle sœur f.

sisterhood ['sistəhud] n état de sœur m, communauté f.

sisterly ['sistəli] a de sœur.

sit [sit] vi être assis, rester assis, se tenir, (s')asseoir, siéger, couver, poser; **to — in** occuper; vt asseoir.

site [sait] n terrain m, emplacement m.

sitter ['sitə] n couveuse f, modèle m.

sitting ['sitiŋ] n séance f, couvaison f, siège m; a assis.

sitting room ['sitiŋrum] n petit salon m, salle j de séjour.

situated ['sitjueitid] a situé.

situation [.sitju'eiʃən] n situation f, place f.

six [siks] an six m.

sixteen ['siks'ti:n] an seize m.

sixteenth ['siks'ti:nθ] an seizième m.

sixth [siksθ] an sixième mf.

sixty ['siksti] an soixante m.

size [saiz] n taille f, dimension f, grandeur f, pointure f, format m, calibre m; **to — up** mesurer, juger.

skate [skeit] n patin m, (fish) raie f; vi patiner.

skating-rink ['skeitiŋriŋk] n patinoire f.

skein [skein] n écheveau m.

skeleton ['skelitn] n squelette m, charpente f, canevas m; **— in the cupboard** secret m, tare f; **—key** passe-partout m, rossignol m.

skeptical ['skeptikəl] a sceptique.

skepticism ['skeptisizəm] n scepticisme m.

sketch [sketʃ] n croquis m, sketch m; vt esquisser.

skew [skju:] a oblique, de biais.

skewer ['skjuə] n brochette f.

skid [skid] n dérapage m, sabot m, patin m; vi déraper, patiner.

skill [skil] n habileté f, adresse f, tact m.

skilled [skild] a qualifié, expert, habile, versé.

skillful ['skilful] a habile, adroit.

skim [skim] vti écumer, écrémer, effleurer; **to — through** parcourir, feuilleter.

skimmer ['skimə] n écumoire f.

skimp [skimp] vt lésiner sur, mesurer.

skin [skin] n peau f, outre f, robe f, pelure f; **— deep** à fleur de peau; vt écorcher, peler, éplucher, se cicatriser.

skinner ['skinə] n fourreur m.

skinny ['skini] a décharné.

skip [skip] n saut m; vi sauter, gambader.

skipper ['skipə] n patron m.

skirmish ['skə:miʃ] n escarmouche f.

skirt [skə:t] n jupe f, basque f, pan m, lisière f; vt longer, contourner.

skit [skit] n pièce satirique f, charge f.

skittle ['skitl] n quille f; pl jeu de quilles m.

skulk [skʌlk] vi se terrer, tirer au flanc, rôder.

skull [skʌl] n crâne m, tête de mort f.

skull-cap ['skʌlkæp] n calotte f.

skunk [skʌŋk] n sconse m, mouffette f, salaud m.

sky [skai] n ciel m; **—lark** alouette f; **—light** lucarne f; **—line** horizon m; **—scraper** gratte-ciel m.

slab [slæb] n dalle f, plaque f, tablette f, pavé m.

slack [slæk] n poussier m, mou m, jeu m; a mou, flasque, veule, desserré, creux; vi (fam) flemmarder, se relâcher.

slacken ['slækən] vt ralentir, (re)lâcher, détendre, desserrer; vi ralentir, se relâcher.

slacker ['slækə] n flemmard(e) mf.

slackness ['slæknis] n veulerie f, laisser-aller m, relâchement m, marasme m, mollesse f, mou m.

slag [slæg] n scorie f, mâchefer m, crasses f pl.

slain [slein] pp of **slay.**

slake [sleik] vt étancher, assouvir.

slam [slæm] n claquement m, schlem m; vti claquer.

slander ['slɑ:ndə] n calomnie f, diffamation f; vt calomnier, diffamer.

slanderer ['slɑ:ndərə] n diffamateur, -trice, calomniateur, -trice.

slanderous ['slɑ:ndərəs] a diffamatoire, calomnieux.

slang [slæŋ] n argot m.

slant [slɑ:nt] n obliquité f, pente f, biais m, point m de vue; vi diverger, obliquer, s'incliner, être en pente; vt incliner, déverser.

slap [slæp] n gifle f, soufflet m, tape f; vt gifler; ad en plein.

slash [slæʃ] n estafilade f, balafre f, taillade f; vt balafrer, taillader,

fouailler, éreinter, (price) réduire.
slashing ['slæʃiŋ] a cinglant, mordant.
slate [sleit] n ardoise f; vt ardoiser, tancer, éreinter.
slaughter ['slɔ:tə] n abattage m, massacre m, boucherie f; vt massacrer, égorger, abattre; **—house** abattoir m.
slave [sleiv] n esclave mf; vi travailler comme un nègre, s'échiner.
slaver ['sleivə] n bave f, lèche f; vi baver, flagorner.
slave-trade ['sleivtreid] n traite des nègres f.
slavery ['sleivəri] n esclavage m, asservissement m.
slavish ['sleiviʃ] n servile.
slay [slei] vt égorger, tuer.
sledge [sledʒ] n traîneau m.
sledge(-hammer) ['sledʒ(ˌhæmə)] n masse f; (fig) massue f.
sleek [sli:k] a lisse, lustré, onctueux.
sleep [sli:p] n sommeil m; vi dormir, coucher; **to go to —** s'endormir, s'engourdir.
sleeper ['sli:pə] n dormeur, traverse f, wagon-lit m.
sleeping-car ['sli:piŋkɑ:] n wagon-lit m.
sleeping-pill ['sli:piŋpil] n somnifère m.
sleeping-sickness ['sli:piŋˈsiknis] n maladie du sommeil f.
sleeplessness ['sli:plisnis] n insomnie f.
sleepy ['sli:pi] a ensommeillé, endormi.
sleet [sli:t] n neige fondue f, grésil m, giboulée f; vi grésiller.
sleeve [sli:v] n manche f.
sleigh [slei] n traîneau m.
sleight [slait] n **— of hand** adresse f, tour de main m, prestidigitation f.
slender ['slendə] a mince, élancé, svelte, faible, maigre.
slenderness ['slendənis] n sveltesse f, exiguïté f.
slept [slept] pt pp of **sleep**.
slew [slu:] pt of **slay**.
slice [slais] n tranche f, rond m, rondelle f, (fish) truelle f; vt couper (en tranches), trancher.
slid [slid] pt pp of **slide**.
slide [slaid] vti glisser; vi faire des glissades; n glissement m, glissement m, glissade f, glissoire f, coulisse f.
sliding ['slaidiŋ] a à coulisse, à glissières, gradué, mobile.
slight [slait] n affront m; vt manquer d'égards envers; a léger, frêle, peu de.
slightest ['slaitist] a le, la (les) moindre(s).
slim [slim] a mince, svelte, délié, rusé.
slime [slaim] n vase f, limon m, bave f.
slimy ['slaimi] a gluant, visqueux.
sling [sliŋ] n fronde f, bretelle f,

écharpe f; vt lancer, hisser, suspendre.
slink [sliŋk] vi marcher furtivement, raser les murs.
slip [slip] n faux-pas m, lapsus m, peccadille f, erreur f, bouture f, bande f, coulisse f, laisse f, enveloppe f, slip m; vt glisser, filer, échapper à; vi (se) glisser, se tromper; **to — away** se sauver, fuir; **to — off** enlever; **to — on** enfiler, passer.
slipper ['slipə] n pantoufle f, patin m.
slippery ['slipəri] a glissant, fuyant, souple, rusé.
slipshod ['slipʃɔd] a négligé, bâclé.
slit [slit] n incision f, fente f, entre-bâillement m; vt déchirer, couper, fendre; vi se fendre, se déchirer.
slogan ['slougən] n slogan m, mot d'ordre m.
slogger ['slɔgə] n cogneur m, bûcheur m.
slope [sloup] n pente f, rampe f, talus m; vi incliner, pencher, être en pente.
slop [slɔp] vt répandre; vt **to — over** vt s'attendrir sur.
slop-pail ['slɔppeil] n seau m de toilette.
slops [slɔps] n eaux sales f pl, bouillie f.
sloppy ['slɔpi] a détrempé, inondé, sale, pleurard, larmoyant, bâclé.
slot [slɔt] n rainure f, fente f.
slot-machine ['slɔtməˌʃi:n] n distributeur automatique m.
sloth ['slouθ] n paresse f.
slothful ['slouθful] a paresseux, indolent.
slouch [slautʃ] n démarche penchée f; a au bord rabattu; vi pencher, se tenir mal, traîner le pas; vt rabattre le bord de (son chapeau).
slough [slau] n fondrière f.
slough [slʌf] n dépouille f, tissu mort m; vi faire peau neuve, muer; vt jeter.
Slovak ['slouvæk] n Slovaque mf; a slovaque.
sloven ['slʌvn] n souillon f.
slovenly ['slʌvənli] a négligé, sale, désordonné.
slow [slou] a lent, en retard.
slowly ['slouli] ad lentement, au ralenti.
slowness ['slounis] n lenteur f.
slug [slʌg] n limace f, limaçon m, lampée f (d'alcool); (tec) lingot m; vt terrasser.
sluggard ['slʌgəd] n paresseux m, flemmard m.
sluggish ['slʌgiʃ] a paresseux, inerte, endormi, lourd.
sluggishly ['slʌgiʃli] ad indolemment, lentement.
sluggishness ['slʌgiʃnis] n inertie f, paresse f.
sluice [slu:s] n écluse f; vt vanner, laver à grande eau; **—gate** vanne f.

slum [slʌm] *n* taudis *m*.
slumber ['slʌmbə] *n* somme *m*, sommeil *m*; *vt* somnoler, sommeiller.
slump [slʌmp] *n* crise *f*, dégringolade *f*; *vi* baisser, dégringoler, se laisser tomber.
slung [slʌŋ] *pt pp of* **sling.**
slunk [slʌŋk] *pt pp of* **slink.**
slur [sləː] *n* blâme *m*, tache *f*, bredouillement *m*, liaison *f*, macule *f*, griffonnage *m*; *vt* bredouiller, griffonner, couler, passer (sur **over**).
sly [slai] *a* retors, malin, madré, en dessous.
smack [smæk] *n* arrière-goût *m*, teinture *f*, bateau *m* de pêche, claquement *m*, gifle *f*, essai *m*, gros baiser *m*; *vt* gifler, faire claquer, taper; *ad* tout droit, en plein, paf; **to — of** sentir.
small [smɔːl] *a* petit, faible, mesquin, modeste, peu important, peu de.
smallness ['smɔːlnis] *n* petitesse *f*, mesquinerie *f*.
smallpox ['smɔːlpɔks] *n* variole *f*, petite vérole *f*.
smart [smɑːt] *n* douleur cuisante *f*; *vi* faire mal, picoter, en cuire à; *a* vif, débrouillard, fin, malin, chic.
smartness ['smɑːtnis] *n* vivacité *f*, finesse *f*, élégance *f*.
smash [smæʃ] *n* collision *f*, coup de poing *m*, faillite *f*, sinistre *m*, effondrement *m*; *vt* mettre en pièces, écraser, heurter; *vi* faire faillite, se fracasser.
smattering ['smætəriŋ] *n* teinture *f*, notions *f pl*.
smear [smiə] *n* tache *f*, souillure *f*; *vt* graisser, barbouiller, enduire.
smell [smel] *n* odorat *m*, flair *m*, odeur *f*; *vt* flairer; *vti* sentir.
smelled [smeld] *pt pp of* **smell;** *n* éperlan *m*; *vt* fondre.
smile [smail] *nm vi* sourire.
smirch [sməːtʃ] *vt* salir, souiller.
smirk [sməːk] *n* sourire *m* affecté; *vi* minauder.
smite [smait] *vt* punir, frapper.
smitten ['smitn] *pp* atteint, épris.
smith [smiθ] *n* forgeron *m*.
smithereens ['smiðə'riːnz] *n* miettes *f pl*, morceaux *m pl*.
smithy ['smiði] *n* forge *f*.
smock [smɔk] *n* blouse *f*, sarrau *m*.
smoke [smouk] *n* fumée *f*; *vti* fumer; *vi* sentir la fumée; *vt* enfumer.
smoker ['smoukə] *n* fumeur *m*.
smokeless ['smouklis] *a* sans fumée.
smoking-car ['smoukiŋˌkɑː] *n* compartiment pour fumeurs *m*.
smoking-room ['smoukiŋˌrum] *n* fumoir *m*.
smoky ['smouki] *a* fumeux, enfumé, noirci par la fumée.
smolder ['smouldə] *vi* couver, brûler et fumer.
mooth [smuːð] *a* lisse, uni, calme, doux, aisé, flatteur, apaisant, souple;
s **smoothly** doucement; *vt* aplanir,

adoucir, lisser, apaiser, pallier.
smoothness ['smuːðnis] *n* égalité *f*, calme *m*, douceur *f*, souplesse *f*.
smote [smout] *pt of* **smite.**
smother ['smʌðə] *vt* étouffer, couvrir, suffoquer.
smudge [smʌdʒ] *n* barbouillage *m*; *vt* barbouiller, salir.
smug [smʌg] *a* bête et solennel, content de soi, béat.
smuggle ['smʌgl] *vt* passer en fraude.
smuggler ['smʌglə] *n* contrebandier *m*.
smuggling ['smʌgliŋ] *n* contrebande *f*, fraude *f*.
smut [smʌt] *n* (grain *m* de) suie *f*, nielle *f*, obscénités *f pl*.
snack [snæk] *n* casse-croûte *m*.
snail [sneil] *n* escargot *m*, limace *f*.
snake [sneik] *n* serpent *m*.
snap [snæp] *n* claquement *m*, bruit sec *m*, déclic *m*, bouton-pression *m*, fermoir *m*, coup *m* (de froid), instantané *m*; *a* immédiat; *vt* happer, dire aigrement, casser, (faire) claquer, prendre un instantané de; *vi* claquer, se casser.
snappish ['snæpiʃ] *n* hargneux, irritable.
snapshot ['snæpʃɔt] *n* instantané *m*.
snare [snɛə] *n* piège *m*; *vt* prendre au piège.
snarl [snɑːl] *n* grognement *m*; *vi* grogner, gronder.
snatch [snætʃ] *n* geste pour saisir *m*, fragment *m*, à-coup *m*, bribe *f*; *vt* saisir, arracher, enlever.
sneak [sniːk] *n* louche individu *m*, mouchard *m*; *vi* se glisser, cafarder, moucharder.
sneaking ['sniːkiŋ] *a* furtif, inavoué, servile.
sneer [sniə] *n* ricanement *m*; *vt* ricaner; **to — at** bafouer, dénigrer.
sneeze [sniːz] *n* éternuement *m*; *vi* éternuer.
sniff [snif] *n* reniflement *m*; *vt* humer; *vti* renifler.
snipe [snaip] *n* bécassine *f*; **to — at** canarder.
sniper ['snaipə] *n* tireur embusqué *m*, canardeur *m*.
snob [snɔb] *n* snob *m*, prétentieux *m*.
snobbery ['snɔbəri] *n* snobisme *m*, prétention *f*.
snooze [snuːz] *n* somme *m*; *vi* faire un somme.
snore [snɔː] *n* ronflement *m*; *vi* ronfler.
snort [snɔːt] *vi* renâcler, s'ébrouer, ronfler, dédaigner.
snout [snaut] *n* museau *m*, mufle *m*, groin *m*, boutoir *m*.
snow [snou] *n* neige *f*; *vi* neiger; **to — under** accabler; **—drop** perceneige *m or f*; **—flake** flocon *m*; **—-plow** chasse-neige *m*; **—-shoes** raquettes *f pl*; **—storm** tempête *f*, rafale *f* de neige; **—field** champ *m* de neige; **—ball** boule *f* de neige.

snub [snʌb] *n* rebuffade *f*; *vt* rabrouer; *a* camus, retroussé.

snuff [snʌf] *n* tabac à priser *m*, prise *f*; *vi* priser; *vt* moucher, éteindre; —**box** tabatière *f*.

snuffle ['snʌfl] *vi* renifler, nasiller.

snug [snʌg] *a* abrité, douillet, gentil, petit, bien.

so [sou] *ad* si, tellement, ainsi, comme ça, de même, à peu près, le; *cj* donc, si bien que; —**called** soi-disant; — **far** jusqu'ici (là); — **long** à bientôt; — **much** tant, autant de; — **much for** assez; — **on** ainsi de suite; — **and** — un(e) tel(le), machin; **in** — **far as** en tant que, dans la mesure où; — **that** de manière à (que), si bien que; — **as to** de façon à, afin de; **so so** comme ci, comme ça.

soak [souk] *vt* tremper, imbiber, pénétrer, abattre, donner un coup de bambou; *vi* s'imbiber, s'infiltrer, baigner.

soaking ['soukiŋ] *n* trempage *m*, douche *f*.

soap [soup] *n* savon *m*; *vt* savonner.

soapy ['soupi] *a* savonneux, onctueux.

soar [sɔː] *vi* prendre l'essor, monter, planer.

sob [sɔb] *n* sanglot *m*; *vi* sangloter.

sober ['soubə] *a* sobre, sérieux, impartial, non ivre.

soberness ['soubənis] *n* sobriété *f*, modération *f*.

sociable ['souʃəbl] *a* sociable.

sociability [,souʃə'biliti] *n* sociabilité *f*.

social ['souʃəl] *n* réunion *f*; *a* social; — **events** mondanités *f pl*.

socialism ['souʃəlizəm] *n* socialisme *m*.

socialist ['souʃəlist] *n* socialiste *mf*.

socialize ['souʃəlaiz] *vt* socialiser.

society [sə'saiəti] *n* société *f*, monde *m*.

sock [sɔk] *n* chaussette *f*.

socket ['sɔkit] *n* trou *m*, orbite *m*, godet *m*, douille *f*, alvéole *m*.

sod [sɔd] *n* motte de gazon *f*.

soda ['soudə] *n* soude *f*, cristaux *m pl*; —**water** eau de Seltz *f*.

sodden ['sɔdn] *a* (dé)trempé, pâteux, hébété, abruti.

sofa ['soufə] *n* canapé *m*, sofa *m*.

soft [sɔft] *a* mou, tendre, doux, facile, ramolli.

soften ['sɔfn] *vt* amollir, adoucir, attendrir.

softness ['sɔftnis] *n* douceur *f*, mollesse *f*, tendresse *f*.

soil [sɔil] *n* terre *f*, sol *m*; *vt* salir, souiller; *vi* se salir.

sojourn ['sɔdʒəːn] *n* séjour *m*; *vi* séjourner.

solace ['sɔləs] *n* consolation *f*; *vt* consoler.

sold [sould] *pt pp of* **sell**.

solder ['sɔldə] *n* soudure *f*; *vt*

souder; —**ing iron** lampe *f* à souder.

soldier ['souldʒə] *n* soldat *m*.

soldiery ['souldʒəri] *n* troupe *f*, (*pej*) soldatesque *f*.

sole [soul] *n* plante du pied *f*, semelle *f*, sole *f*; *vt* ressemeler; *a* seul, unique.

solemn ['sɔləm] *a* solennel.

solemnity [sə'lemniti] *n* solennité *f*.

solemnize ['sɔləmnaiz] *vt* célébrer, solemniser.

solicit [sə'lisit] *vt* solliciter.

solicitation [sə,lisi'teiʃən] *n* sollicitation *f*.

solicitor [sə'lisitə] *n* avoué *m*.

solicitous [sə'lisitəs] *a* zélé, anxieux, préoccupé.

solicitude [sə'lisitjud] *n* sollicitude *f*, anxiété *f*.

solid ['sɔlid] *an* solide *m*; *a* massif.

solidify [sə'lidifai] *vt* solidifier; *vi* se solidifier, se fixer.

solidity [sə'liditi] *n* solidité *f*.

soliloquy [sə'liləkwi] *n* soliloque *m*, monologue *m*.

solitary ['sɔlitəri] *a* solitaire.

solitude ['sɔlitjuːd] *n* solitude *f*, isolement *m*.

soluble ['sɔljubl] *an* soluble *m*.

solution [sə'luːʃən] *n* solution *f*.

solvability [,sɔlvə'biliti] *n* solvabilité *f*.

solve [sɔlv] *vt* résoudre.

solvency ['sɔlvənsi] *n* solvabilité *f*.

solvent ['sɔlvənt] *an* dissolvant *m*; *a* solvable.

some [sʌm] *a* du, de la, des, un peu de, quelques, certains; *pn* quelques-un(e)s, certains, en; *ad* quelque, environ.

somebody ['sʌmbədi] *pn* quelqu'un(e).

somehow ['sʌmhau] *ad* de manière ou d'autre; — **or other** je ne sais comment.

someone ['sʌmwʌn] *pn* quelqu'un.

somersault ['sʌməsɔːlt] *n* saut périlleux *m*, culbute *f*; *vi* faire la culbute, culbuter, capoter.

something ['sʌmθiŋ] *pn* quelque chose.

sometime ['sʌmtaim] *ad* un de ces jours, autrefois.

sometimes ['sʌmtaimz] *ad* quelquefois.

somewhat ['sʌmwɔt] *ad* quelque peu.

somewhere ['sʌmwɛə] *ad* quelque part.

son [sʌn] *n* fils *m*; —**in-law** gendre *m*, beau-fils *m*.

song [sɔŋ] *n* chant *m*, chanson *f*.

songster ['sɔŋstə] *n* chanteur *m*.

sonority [sə'nɔriti] *n* sonorité *f*.

sonorous ['sɔnərəs] *a* sonore.

soon [suːn] *ad* (bien)tôt; **as** — **as** aussitôt que, dès que.

sooner ['suːnə] *ad* plus tôt, plutôt.

soot [sut] *n* suie *f*.

soothe [suːð] *vt* calmer, apaiser, flatter.

sooty ['suti] *a* noir de (comme) suie, fuligineux.

sop [sɔp] *n* trempette *f*, gâteau *m*; *vt* tremper; *vi* être trempé.

sophisticated [sə'fistikeitid] *a* artificiel, blasé, sophistiqué, frelaté.

soporific [‚sɔpə'rifik] *an* soporifique *m*.

sorcerer ['sɔːsərə] *n* sorcier *m*.

sorcery ['sɔːsəri] *n* sorcellerie *f*.

sordid ['sɔːdid] *a* sordide.

sordidness ['sɔːdidnis] *n* sordidité *f*.

sore [sɔː] *n* mal *m*, plaie *f*, blessure *f*; *a* douloureux, envenimé, sévère, malade.

sorely ['sɔːli] *ad* fâcheusement, cruellement, gravement.

sorrel ['sɔrəl] *n* oseille *f*.

sorrow ['sɔrou] *n* chagrin *m*; *vi* s'affliger.

sorrowful ['sɔrəful] *a* affligé, pénible.

sorry ['sɔri] *a* désolé, fâché, pauvre, pitoyable, triste, méchant; —! pardon! excusez-moi.

sort [sɔːt] *n* sorte *f*, espèce *f*; — of pour ainsi dire; **out of** —s hors de son assiette; *vt* trier, assortir, classifier.

sorting ['sɔːtiŋ] *n* triage *m*, assortiment *m*.

sot [sɔt] *n* ivrogne *m*.

sottish ['sɔtiʃ] *a* abruti par la boisson.

sough [sau] *vi* gémir, siffler, soupirer, susurrer.

sought [sɔːt] *pt pp of* **seek**; — **after** *a* demandé, recherché.

soul [soul] *n* âme *f*; **not a** — pas âme qui vive, pas un chat.

soulful ['soulful] *a* pensif, sentimental, expressif.

sound [saund] *n* son *m*, sonde *f*, détroit *m*, chenal *m*; *vt* sonner, prononcer, sonder, ausculter; *vi* (ré)sonner, retentir; *a* sain, solide.

sounding ['saundiŋ] *n* sondage *m*, auscultation *f*.

soundless ['saundlis] *a* silencieux.

soup [suːp] *n* potage *m*, soupe *f*.

sour ['sauə] *a* aigre, vert; *vti* aigrir; *vi* s'aigrir.

source [sɔːs] *n* source *f*, origine *f*, foyer *m*.

sourish ['sauriʃ] *a* aigrelet.

south [sauθ] *n* sud *m*, midi *m*; *a* du sud.

southern ['sʌðən] *a* méridional, du midi, du sud.

southward ['sauθwəd] *ad* vers le sud, au sud.

sovereign ['sɔvrin] *an* souverain(e) *mf*.

sovereignty ['sɔvrənti] *n* souveraineté *f*.

sow [sau] *n* truie *f*.

sow [sou] *vt* semer, ensemencer.

sower ['souə] *n* semeur, -euse.

sowing ['souiŋ] *n* semailles *f pl*, semis *m*.

sown [soun] *pp of* **sow**.

spa [spɑː] *n* station thermale *f*.

space [speis] *n* espace *m*, place *f*, durée *f*, intervalle *m*, étendue *f*; *vt* espacer.

spacious ['speiʃəs] *a* spacieux, vaste, ample.

spade [speid] *n* bêche *f*, (*cards*) pique *m*.

Spain [spein] *n* Espagne *f*.

span [spæn] *pt of* **spin**; *n* durée *f*, longueur *f*, arche *f*, envergure *f*, écartement *m*; *vt* enjamber, embrasser, mesurer.

spangle ['spæŋgl] *n* paillette *f*.

Spaniard ['spænjəd] *n* Espagnol(e).

spaniel ['spænjəl] *n* épagneul *m*.

Spanish ['spæniʃ] *a* espagnol.

spank [spæŋk] *vt* fesser; **to — along** aller grand trot, filer.

spanking ['spæŋkiŋ] *n* fessée *f*; *a* épatant.

spanner ['spænə] *n* clef *f*; **screw —** clef anglaise *f*.

spar [spɑː] *n* épar *m*, mât *m*, perche *f*; *vi* boxer, se harceler, s'escrimer.

spare [spɛə] *a* frugal, frêle, libre, de reste, de réserve, de rechange, à perdre; *vt* ménager, se passer de, épargner, accorder.

sparing ['spɛəriŋ] *a* économe, avare, chiche.

spark [spɑːk] *n* étincelle *f*; *vi* étinceler, pétiller, mousser; — **plug** *n* bougie *f* (d'allumage).

sparkle ['spɑːkl] *vi* étinceler, pétiller, chatoyer.

sparkling ['spɑːkliŋ] *a* mousseux, brillant.

sparrow ['spærou] *n* moineau *m*.

sparse [spɑːs] *a* clairsemé.

spasm ['spæzəm] *n* spasme *m*, accès *m*, quinte *f*, crampe *f*, à-coup *m*.

spat [spæt] *pt pp of* **spit**.

spat [spæt] *n* guêtre *f*; querelle *f*.

spate [speit] *n* crue *f*, flot *m*.

spatter ['spætə] *n* éclaboussure *f*; *vt* éclabousser.

spawn [spɔːn] *n* frai *m*; *vi* frayer.

speak [spiːk] *vti* parler, dire.

speaker ['spiːkə] *n* parleur, -euse, orateur *m*, président des communes *m*; **loud —** haut-parleur *m*.

spear [spiə] *n* lance *f*, javelot *m*, épieu *m*, harpon *m*, sagaie *f*; **—head** extrême pointe *f*.

special ['speʃəl] *a* spécial, particu r; **— delivery** express *m*, pneumatique *m*.

specialist ['speʃəlist] *n* spécialiste *mf*.

speciality [‚speʃi'æliti] *n* spécialité *f*, particularité *f*.

specialize ['speʃəlaiz] *vt* spécialiser; *vi* se spécialiser.

species ['spiːʃiːz] *n* espèce *f*.

specific [spi'sifik] *a* spécifique, explicite, précis.

specify ['spesifai] *vt* spécifier, déterminer.

specimen ['spesimin] *n* spécimen *m*, échantillon *m*.
specious ['spi:ʃəs] *a* spécieux, captieux.
speck [spek] *n* grain *m*, point *m*, tache *f*.
speckled ['spekld] *a* taché, tacheté, grivelé.
spectacle ['spektəkl] *n* spectacle *m*; *pl* lunettes *f pl*.
spectacular [spek'tækjulə] *a* spectaculaire, à grand spectacle.
spectator [spek'teitə] *n* spectateur, -trice, assistant(e) *mf*.
specter ['spektə] *n* spectre *m*.
spectral ['spektrəl] *a* spectral.
speculate ['spekjuleit] *vi* spéculer.
speculation [,spekju'leiʃən] *n* spéculation *f*.
speculative ['spekjulətiv] *a* spéculatif.
speculator ['spekjuleitə] *n* spéculateur *m*.
speech [spi:tʃ] *n* parole *f*, discours *m*.
speechless ['spi:tʃlis] *a* interdit, interloqué.
sped [sped] *pt pp of* **speed.**
speed [spi:d] *n* vitesse *f*; *vt* activer, hâter, régler; *vi* se presser, se hâter, faire de la vitesse, filer.
speediness ['spi:dinis] *n* promptitude *f*, rapidité *f*.
speedometer [spi'dɔmitə] *n* indicateur de vitesse *m*.
speedy ['spi:di] *a* rapide, prompt.
spell [spel] *n* charme *m*, sort *m*, maléfice *m*, tour *m*, moment *m*, période *f*; *vt* épeler, écrire, signifier.
spellbound ['spelbaund] *a* fasciné, sous le charme.
spelled [speld] *pt pp of* **spell.**
spelling ['speliŋ] *n* orthographe *f*.
spend [spend] *vt* dépenser, passer, épuiser.
spendthrift ['spendθrift] *n* dépensier, -ière, panier percé *m*.
spent [spent] *pt pp of* **spend;** *a* fini, à bout, éteint, mort.
spew [spju:] *vti* vomir; *vt* cracher.
sphere [sfiə] *n* sphère *mf*, domaine *m*, zone *f*, ressort.
spherical ['sferikəl] *a* sphérique.
spice [spais] *n* épice *f*, pointe *f*; *vt* épicer, relever.
spick and span [,spikən'spæn] *a* flambant neuf, tiré à quatre épingles, propret.
spicy ['spaisi] *a* épicé, poivré, relevé, pimenté, criard.
spider ['spaidə] *n* araignée *f*.
spike [spaik] *n* épi *m*, clou *m*, crampon *m*, pointe *f*; *vt* (en)clouer.
spill [spil] *n* chute *f*, bûche *f*, allume-feu *m*; *vt* (ren)verser, jeter bas; *vi* se répandre.
spilt [spilt] *pt pp of* **spill.**
spin [spin] *n* tour *m*, effet *m*, vrille *f*; **—drier** *n* essoreuse *f*; *vt* filer; *vi* tourner, rouler, patiner.
spinach ['spinidʒ] *n* épinards *m pl*.

spindle ['spindl] *n* fuseau *m*, broche *f*, essieu *m*.
spindly ['spindli] *a* fluet, de fuseau.
spine [spain] *n* épine dorsale *f*.
spineless ['spainlis] *a* mou.
spinner ['spinə] *n* métier *m*, tisserand(e) *mf*, filateur *m*.
spinney ['spini] *n* petit bois *m*.
spinning-mill ['spiniŋmil] *n* filature *f*.
spinning-wheel ['spiniŋwi:l] *n* rouet *m*.
spinster ['spinstə] *n* vieille fille *f*, célibataire *f*.
spiny ['spaini] *a* épineux.
spiral ['spaiərəl] *n* spirale *f*; *a* en spirale, en colimaçon, spiral.
spire ['spaiə] *n* flèche *f*, aiguille *f*, pointe *f*.
spirit ['spirit] *n* esprit *m*, âme *f*, humeur *f*, cran *m*, ardeur *f*, feu *m*, alcool *m*; **to — away** escamoter.
spirited ['spiritid] *a* animé, fougueux, vif, hardi.
spiritless ['spiritlis] *a* déprimé, mou, terne.
spiritual ['spiritjuəl] *a* spirituel.
spiritualism ['spiritjuəlizəm] *n* spiritisme *m*, spiritualisme *m*.
spiritualist ['spiritjuəlist] *n* spirite *mf*.
spirituous ['spiritjuəs] *a* spiritueux, alcoolique.
spit [spit] *n* broche *f*, langue *f* (de terre), crachement *m*, crachat *m*; *vt* embrocher, mettre à la broche, cracher; *vi* cracher, bruiner, crachiner.
spite [spait] *n* dépit *m*, rancune *f*; *vt* mortifier, vexer; **in — of** malgré, en dépit de.
spiteful ['spaitful] *a* rancunier, méchant.
spitfire ['spitfaiə] *n* boute-feu *m*, soupe-au-lait *mf*, rageur *m*, rageuse *f*.
spittle ['spitl] *n* crachat *m*.
spittoon [spi'tu:n] *n* crachoir *m*.
splash [splæʃ] *n* éclaboussement *m*, éclaboussure *f*, tache *f*, clapotis *m*, sensation *f*; *vt* éclabousser, asperger; *vi* piquer un plat ventre, clapoter, barboter; **to make a —** faire de l'épate.
splay [splei] *n* ébrasure *f*; *a* plat, large, évasé; *vt* ébraser.
spleen [spli:n] *n* rate *f*, spleen *m*, bile *f*.
splendid ['splendid] *a* splendide, magnifique.
splendor ['splendə] *n* splendeur *f*, éclat *m*.
splint [splint] *n* attelle *f*, éclisse *f*.
splinter ['splintə] *n* éclat *m*, esquille *f*, écharde *f*; *vt* faire voler en éclats; *vi* voler en éclats.
split [split] *n* fente *f*, fissure *f*, scission *f*; *pl* grand écart *m*; *vt* fendre, couper, diviser, partager; *vi* se fendre, se diviser, se briser.

spoil(s) [spɔil(z)] *n* butin *m*; *pl* dépouilles *f pl*, profits *m pl*.

spoil [spɔil] *vt* dépouiller, gâter, abîmer, avarier, déparer; *vi* s'abîmer, se gâter.

spoilsport ['spɔilspɔːt] *n* trouble-fête *m*, rabat-joie *m*.

spoke [spouk] *n* rayon *m*, échelon *m*, bâton *m* (dans les roues).

spoke, -ken [spouk, spoukən] *pt pp of* **speak**.

spokesman ['spouksmən] *n* porte-parole *m*.

spoliation [,spouli'eiʃən] *n* spoliation *f*, pillage *m*.

sponge [spʌndʒ] *n* éponge *f*; *vt* passer l'éponge sur, éponger, effacer; **to — on someone** vivre sur qn, vivre aux crochets de qn.

sponge-cake ['spʌndʒ'keik] *n* gâteau de Savoie *m*.

sponger ['spʌndʒə] *n* parasite *m*, pique-assiette *m*.

spongy ['spʌndʒi] *a* spongieux.

sponsor ['spɔnsə] *n* parrain *m*, marraine *f*, garant *m*.

spontaneity [,spɔntə'niːiti] *n* sponta-néité *f*.

spontaneous [spɔn'teiniəs] *a* spon-tané.

spontaneously [spɔn'teiniəsli] *ad* spontanément.

spool [spuːl] *n* bobine *f*, tambour *m*, rouleau *m*.

spoon [spuːn] *n* cuiller *f*.

spoonful ['spuːnful] *n* cuillerée *f*.

sport ['spɔːt] *n* jeu *m*, jouet *m*, sport *m*, chic type *m*; *vi* s'amuser, se divertir; *vt* arborer.

sporting ['spɔːtiŋ] *a* loyal, de chasse, sport, sportif.

sportive ['spɔːtiv] *a* enjoué, folâtre.

sportsman ['spɔːtsmən] *n* sportif *m*, beau joueur *m*, chasseur *m*.

sportsmanship ['spɔːtsmənʃip] *n* franc jeu *m*, l'esprit sportif *m*.

spot [spɔt] *n* endroit *m*, tache *f*, bouton *m*, pois *m*, marque *f*, goutte *f*; *vt* tacher, marquer, dé-pister, repérer.

spotted ['spɔtid] *a* tacheté, mar-queté, à pois.

spotless ['spɔtlis] *a* sans tache, immaculé.

spouse [spauz] *n* époux *m*, épouse *f*.

spout [spaut] *n* bec *m*, jet *m*, gout-tière *f*, colonne *f*; *vt* lancer, dé-clamer; *vi* jaillir, pérorer.

sprain [sprein] *n* entorse *f*, foulure *f*; *vt* se fouler.

sprang [spræŋ] *pt of* **spring**.

sprawl [sprɔːl] *vi* s'étendre, se vautrer, tomber les quatre pattes en l'air, rouler.

spray [sprei] *n* branche *f*, embrun *m*, vaporisateur *m*, bouquet *m*; *vt* asperger, vaporiser.

spread [spred] *n* envergure *f*, largeur *f*, diffusion *f*, propagation *f*; *vtir* répandre, (é)tendre, déployer;

vi se répandre, s'étendre, se disper-ser.

sprig [sprig] *n* branchette *f*, brin *m*, rejeton *m*.

sprightliness ['spraitlinis] *n* gaîté *f*, vivacité *f*.

sprightly ['spraitli] *a* vif, sémillant, allègre.

spring [spriŋ] *n* printemps *m*, source *f*, saut *m*, bond *m*, ressort *m*, élasticité *f*; *vi* bondir, s'élever, poindre, sortir, (*wood*) jouer, se fendre; *vt* lancer, (*trap*) tendre, suspendre.

spring-board ['spriŋbɔːd] *n* tremplin *m*.

springy ['spriŋi] *a* élastique, flexible.

sprinkle ['spriŋkl] *n* pincée *f*; *vt* asperger, éparpiller, saupoudrer.

sprinkler ['spriŋklə] *n* aspersoir *m*, goupillon *m*.

sprinkling ['spriŋkliŋ] *n* aspersion *f*, saupoudrage *m*.

sprite [sprait] *n* lutin *m*.

sprout [spraut] *n* pousse *f*; **Brussels — chou de Bruxelles** *m*; *vti* pousser.

spruce [spruːs] *n* sapin *m*; *a* net, pimpant, soigné.

sprung [sprʌŋ] *pp of* **spring**.

spun [spʌn] *pp of* **spin**.

spur [spəː] *n* éperon *m*, ergot *m*, coup de fouet *m*; *vt* éperonner, exciter, stimuler.

spurious ['spjuəriəs] *a* faux, con-trouvé, contrefait.

spurn [spəːn] *vt* rejeter, dédaigner, traiter avec dédain.

sputter ['spʌtə] *vti* bredouiller; *vi* grésiller, cracher.

spy [spai] *n* espion; *vt* espionner, épier; **—glass** longue-vue *f*; **—hole** judas *m*.

squabble ['skwɔbl] *n* bisbille *f*; *vi* se chamailler.

squad [skwɔd] *n* escouade *f*, peloton *m*, équipe *f*.

squadron ['skwɔdrən] *n* escadron *m*, escadre *f*.

squalid ['skwɔlid] *a* sordide.

squall [skwɔːl] *n* rafale *f*, grain *m*, cri *m*; *pl* grabuge *m*; *vi* piailler.

squander ['skwɔndə] *vt* gaspiller, dissiper, manger.

squanderer ['skwɔndərə] *n* prodigue *m*, gaspilleur, -euse.

square [skwɛə] *n* carré *m*, équerre *f*, square *m*, place *f*; *a* carré, régulier, loyal, tout net, quitté; *vt* accorder, régler, payer, carrer, équarrir; *vi* s'accorder, cadrer.

squash [skwɔʃ] *n* foule *f*, presse *f*, (*drink*) jus de fruit *m*; bouillie *f*, bruit mou *m*; *vt* écraser, rembarrer; *vi* se serrer, s'écraser.

squat [skwɔt] *vi* s'accroupir; *a* trapu, ramassé.

squeak [skwiːk] *n* cri aigu *m*, grincement *m*, couic *m*; *vi* grincer, crier.

squeal [skwiːl] *n* cri aigu *m*; *vi* crier,

criailler, protester; **to — on** dénoncer, moucharder, vendre.

squeamish ['skwiːmiʃ] *a* dégoûté, scrupuleux, prude.

squeamishness ['skwiːmiʃnis] *n* bégueulerie *f*, délicatesse *f*.

squeeze [skwiːz] *n* pression *f*, presse *f*, écrasement *m*, (*pol*) l'austérité *f*; *vt* presser, serrer, écraser, faire pression sur, extorquer, faire entrer sur, extorquer, faire entrer de force; *vi* **to — up** se serrer.

squint [skwint] *n* strabisme *m*, coup d'œil oblique *m*; *vi* loucher.

squirrel ['skwirəl] *n* écureuil *m*, petit gris *m*.

squirt [skwəːt] *n* seringue *f*, jet *m*; *vt* lancer, injecter; *vi* jaillir, gicler.

stab [stæb] *n* coup *m* de couteau; *vt* poignarder, porter un coup de couteau à.

stability [stə'biliti] *n* stabilité *f*, constance *f*.

stabilize ['steibilaiz] *vt* stabiliser.

stable ['steibl] *n* écurie *f*; *a* stable, consistant, solide.

stack [stæk] *n* meule *f*, pile *f*, cheminée *f*, (*mil*) faisceau *m*; *vt* entasser, empiler.

staff [staːf] *n* bâton *m*, mât *m*, hampe *f*, crosse *f*, état-major *m*, personnel *m*.

stag [stæg] *n* cerf *m*.

stage [steidʒ] *n* scène *f*, estrade *f*, échafaudage *m*, étape *f*, phase *f*, relais *m*, débarcadère *m*; *vt* monter, mettre en scène.

stage-coach ['steidʒkoutʃ] *n* diligence *f*.

stage-fright ['steidʒfrait] *n* trac *m*.

stage-hand ['steidʒhænd] *n* machiniste *m*.

stagger ['stægə] *vt* faire chanceler, ébranler, renverser, échelonner; *vi* chanceler, tituber.

stagnant ['stægnənt] *a* stagnant.

stagnate ['stægneit] *vi* croupir, être stagnant, s'encroûter.

stagnation [stæg'neiʃən] *n* stagnation *f*, marasme *m*.

staid [steid] *a* posé, rangé.

stain [stein] *n* tache *f*, colorant *m*; *vti* tacher, colorer.

stainless ['steinlis] *n* inoxydable, immaculé.

stair [stɛə] *n* marche *f*; *pl* escalier *m*.

staircase ['stɛəkeis] *n* escalier *m*.

stake [steik] *n* poteau *m*, bûcher *m*, pieu *m*, (en)jeu *m*, risque *m*, pari *m*; *vt* parier, risquer, jouer, miser.

stale [steil] *a* rassis, éventé, vicié, rebattu.

stalemate ['steil'meit] *n* point mort *m*, pat *m*.

stalk [stɔːk] *n* tige *f*, pied *m*, trognon *m*, queue *f*.

stall [stɔːl] *n* stalle *f*, banc *m*, baraque *f*, étal *m*, étalage *m*; *vt* bloquer; *vi* se bloquer.

stallion ['stæljən] *n* étalon *m*.

stalwart ['stɔːlwət] *a* solide, résolu, robuste.

stamen ['steimən] *n* étamine *f*.

stamina ['stæminə] *n* vigueur *f*, fond *m*.

stammer ['stæmə] *n* bégaiement *m*; *vti* bégayer.

stammerer ['stæmərə] *n* bègue *mf*.

stamp [stæmp] *n* timbre *m*, cachet *m*, poinçon *m*, coin *m*, estampille *f*, marque *f*, trempe *f*; *vt* timbrer, imprimer, marquer, affranchir; *vi* frapper du pied.

stampede [stæm'piːd] *n* débandade *f*, panique *f*; *vi* se débander, se ruer.

stanch [staːntʃ] *vt* étancher.

stand [stænd] *n* halte *f*, position *f*, station *f*, socle *m*, guéridon *m*, étalage *m*, stand *m*, barre *f*; *vi* se tenir (debout), se dresser, s'arrêter, rester, durer, tenir; *vt* supporter, offrir, payer; **to — for** représenter; **to — out** ressortir.

standard ['stændəd] *n* étendard *m*, étalon *m*, moyenne *f*, niveau *m*, qualité *f*; *a* classique, définitif, standard, courant.

standardize ['stændədaiz] *vt* standardiser, unifier.

standing ['stændiŋ] *n* réputation *f*, situation *f*, ancienneté *f*; *a* établi, permanent.

stand-offish ['stænd'ɔfiʃ] *a* distant.

stand-offishness ['stænd'ɔfiʃnis] *n* réserve *f*, hauteur *f*.

standpoint ['stændpoint] *n* point de vue *m*.

stank [stæŋk] *pt of* **stink**.

stanza ['stænzə] *n* stance *f*, strophe *f*.

staple ['steipl] *n* gâche *f*, crampon *m*, agrafe *f*; *a* principal.

stapler ['steiplə] *n* agrafeuse *f*.

star [staː] *n* étoile *f*, astre *m*, astérisque *m*; *vi* tenir le premier rôle, être en vedette.

starboard ['staːbəd] *n* tribord *m*.

starch [staːtʃ] *n* amidon *m*, raideur *f*; *vt* empeser.

starched [staːtʃt] *a* empesé, gourmé, collet monté.

stare [stɛə] *n* regard fixe *m*; *vi* regarder fixement, s'écarquiller; **to — at** regarder fixement, fixer, dévisager; **it is staring you in the face** cela vous saute aux yeux.

staring ['stɛəriŋ] *a* éclatant, fixe.

stark [staːk] *a* raide, tout pur; *ad* complètement.

start [staːt] *n* sursaut *m*, départ *m*, début *m*, avance *f*; *vi* commencer; *vt* lancer, entamer, mettre en marche, provoquer.

starter ['staːtə] *n* démarreur *m*, starter *m*, partant *m*, auteur *m*.

startle ['staːtl] *vt* faire tressaillir, effarer, effrayer.

startling ['staːtliŋ] *a* saisissant, sensationnel.

starvation [staː'veiʃən] *n* faim *f*, inanition *f*, famine *f*.

starve [stɑːv] *vi* mourir de faim, être transi; *vt* affamer, priver, faire mourir de faim.

state [steit] *n* état *m*, rang *m*, situation *f*, pompe *f*; *a* d'état, d'apparat; *vt* déclarer, prétendre, énoncer, fixer.

stately ['steitli] *a* noble, imposant, princier, majestueux.

statement ['steitmənt] *n* déclaration *f*, énoncé *m*, rapport *m*, expression *f*, relevé *m*.

statesman ['steitsmən] *n* homme d'état *m*.

station ['steiʃən] *n* poste *m*, gare *f*, station *f*, rang *m*; *vt* poster, placer; — **house** poste *m* de police.

stationary ['steiʃnəri] *a* stationnaire, immobile.

stationer ['steiʃnə] *n* papetier *m*.

stationery ['steiʃnəri] *n* papeterie *f*.

stationmaster ['steiʃən‚mɑːstə] *n* chef de gare *m*.

statistics [stə'tistiks] *n* statistique *f*.

statue ['stætjuː] *n* statue *f*.

stature ['stætjə] *n* stature *f*, taille *f*.

status ['steitəs] *n* rang *m*, titre *m*, position *f*, statu quo *m*.

statute ['stætjuːt] *n* statut *m*, ordonnance *f*.

statutory ['stætjutəri] *a* statutaire, réglementaire.

staunch [stɔːntʃ] *a* ferme, loyal, étanche; *vt* étancher.

stave [steiv] *n* douve *f*, barreau *m*, stance *f*, portée *f*; *vt* — **in** défoncer, enfoncer; **to** — **off** détourner, conjurer, écarter.

stay [stei] *n* séjour *m*, sursis *m*, frein *m*, soutien *m*; *vi* rester, séjourner, tenir; *vt* arrêter, ajourner, soutenir.

stay-at-home ['steiəthoum] *an* casanier, -ière.

stays [steiz] *n* corset *m*.

stead [sted] *n* lieu *m*, place *f*; **to stand s.o. in good** — être d'un grand secours à qn.

steadfast ['stedfəst] *a* ferme, constant.

steadfastness ['stedfəstnis] *n* constance *f*, fixité *f*.

steadiness ['stedinis] *n* fermeté *f*, régularité, stabilité *f*.

steady ['stedi] *a* ferme, régulier, constant, tranquille, rangé, continu, persistant; *n* petit(e) ami(e); *vt* assurer, (r)affermir, caler.

steak [steik] *n* tranche *f*, bifteck *m*, entrecôte *f*.

steal [stiːl] *vti* voler; *vt* dérober; **to** — **in** entrer à pas de loup.

stealth [stelθ] *n* secret *m*.

stealthily ['stelθili] *ad* secrètement, à la dérobée.

stealthy ['stelθi] *a* furtif.

steam [stiːm] *n* vapeur *f*, buée *f*; *vt* cuire à l'étuvée, vaporiser; *vi* fumer, marcher à la vapeur.

steamboat, -ship ['stiːmbout, -ʃip] *n* vapeur *m*.

steamer ['stiːmə] *n* steamer *m*; marmite à vapeur *f*.

steaming ['stiːmiŋ] *a* fumant, sous vapeur, tout chaud.

steed [stiːd] *n* étalon *m*.

steel [stiːl] *n* acier *m*, baleine *f*; *vt* tremper, aciérer; **to** — **oneself** se raidir, s'armer de courage.

steep [stiːp] *a* raide, escarpé, fort.

steeple ['stiːpl] *n* clocher *m*, flèche *f*.

steeplechase ['stiːpl'tʃeis] *n* steeple *m*, course d'obstacles *f*.

steer [stiə] *vt* diriger, gouverner, piloter.

steering-wheel ['stiəriŋwiːl] *n* volant *m*.

steersman ['stiəzmən] *n* barreur *m*, timonier *m*.

stem [stem] *n* tige *f*, queue *f*, souche *f*, étrave *f*, branche *f*, pied *m*, tuyau *m*; *vt* arrêter, endiguer, remonter.

stench [stentʃ] *n* puanteur *f*.

stencil ['stensl] *n* pochoir *m*, poncif *m*; *vt* imprimer au pochoir, polycopier.

step [step] *n* pas *m*, marche *f*, marche-pied *m*, échelon *m*, promotion *f*, démarche *f*; *pl* échelle *f*, escalier *m*, mesures *f pl*; — **ladder** escabeau *m*; *vi* échelonner.

stepbrother ['step‚brʌðə] *n* demi-frère *m*; —**daughter** belle-fille *f*; —**father** beau-père *m*; —**mother** belle-mère *f*; —**sister** demi-sœur *f*; —**son** beau-fils *m*.

Stephen ['stiːvn] Étienne *m*.

stepping-stone ['stepiŋstoun] *n* marche-pied *m*, tremplin *m*.

sterile ['sterail] *a* stérile.

sterility [ste'riliti] *n* stérilité *f*.

sterilize ['sterilaiz] *vt* stériliser.

sterling ['stəːliŋ] *a* pur, d'or, de bon aloi, massif.

stern [stəːn] *n* arrière *m*, poupe *f*; *a* sévère, austère.

sternness ['stəːnnis] *n* austérité *f*, sévérité *f*.

stevedore ['stiːvidɔː] *n* débardeur *m*.

stew [stjuː] *n* ragoût *m*, civet *m*; **in a** — sur des charbons ardents; *vt* cuire à la casserole, (faire) mijoter; *vi* mijoter, faire une compote.

steward ['stjuəd] *n* intendant *m*, gérant *m*, économe *m*, garçon *m*, commissaire *m*.

stewardess ['stjuədis] *n* femme de chambre *f*, hôtesse *f* de l'air.

stick [stik] *n* bâton *m*, canne *f*, baguette *f*, manche *m*, crosse *f*; *pl* du petit bois, brindilles *f pl*; *vt* enfoncer, fourrer, piquer, percer, afficher, coller, supporter, tenir; *vi* s'enfoncer, se ficher, se piquer, s'attacher, (s'en) tenir, coller, happer, rester (en panne), persister; **to** — **it** tenir le coup, tenir bon; **to** — **at** repugner à, reculer devant, s'obstiner à; **to** — **out** *vt* passer, bomber, tirer; *vi* faire saillie, saillir; **to** — **to** s'en tenir à,

persister à, adhérer à, rester fidèle à.
sticky ['stiki] *a* collant, visqueux, difficile.
stiff [stif] *a* raide, ardu, (*price*) salé, courbaturé, engourdi, gourmé.
stiffen ['stifn] *vt* raidir; *vi* se raidir.
stiff-necked ['stif'nekt] *a* têtu, intraitable.
stiffness ['stifnis] *n* raideur *f*, contrainte *f*, difficulté *f*, fermeté *f*, courbatures *f pl*.
stifle ['staifl] *vt* étouffer, asphyxier, suffoquer.
stigma ['stigmə] *n* marque *f*, stigmate *m*.
stigmatize ['stigmətaiz] *vt* stigmatiser, flétrir.
stile [stail] *n* échalier *m*.
still [stil] *n* alambic *m*; *a* immobile, tranquille, silencieux; *vt* apaiser, calmer; *ad* encore, toujours, cependant.
still-born ['stilbɔːn] *a* mort-né.
still-life ['stil'laif] *n* nature morte *f*.
stillness ['stilnis] *n* calme *m*, paix *f*.
stilt [stilt] *n* échasse *f*.
stilted ['stiltid] *a* guindé.
stimulate ['stimjuleit] *vt* stimuler, aiguillonner.
stimulant ['stimjulənt] *an* stimulant *m*.
stimulation [,stimju'leiʃən] *n* stimulation *f*.
stimulus ['stimjuləs] *n* stimulant *m*, coup de fouet *m*, aiguillon *m*.
sting [stiŋ] *n* dard *m*, aiguillon *m*, crochet *m*, piqûre *f*, pointe *f*; *vti* piquer, mordre.
stinginess ['stindʒinis] *n* ladrerie *f*, lésine *f*.
stingy ['stindʒi] *a* ladre, chiche, pingre, radin.
stink [stiŋk] *n* puanteur *f*; *vti* puer; *vt* empester.
stint [stint] *n* limite *f*, relâche *f*, tâche *f*; *vt* limiter, regarder à, mesurer.
stipend ['staipend] *n* traitement *m*, appointements *m pl*.
stipulate ['stipjuleit] *vt* stipuler.
stipulation [,stipju'leiʃən] *n* stipulation(s) *f* (*pl*).
stir [stəː] *n* remue-ménage *m*, sensation *f*, émoi *m*; *vt* remuer, secouer, agiter, émouvoir; *vi* remuer, bouger.
stirring ['stəːriŋ] *a* excitant, vibrant, mouvementé, empoignant.
stirrup ['stirəp] *n* étrier *m*.
stitch [stitʃ] *n* point *m*, maille *f*, suture *f*; *vt* coudre, raccommoder, brocher, suturer.
stoat [stout] *n* ermine *f* d'été.
stock [stɔk] *n* tronc *m*, souche *f*, provision *f*, stock *m*, fonds *m pl*, giroflée *f*, bouillon; — **cube** concentré *m*; *pl* rentes *f pl*; *vt* approvisionner, tenir, meubler, garnir, stocker; —**account** inventaire *m*; —**broker** agent de change *m*;

— **exchange** bourse *f*; — **jobber** agioteur *m*.
stocking ['stɔkiŋ] *n* bas *m*.
stock-phrase ['stɔk'freiz] *n* cliché *m*.
stocky ['stɔki] *a* épais, trapu.
stodgy ['stɔdʒi] *a* lourd, indigeste, bourré.
stoker ['stoukə] *n* chauffeur *m*.
stole [stoul] *pt of* **steal**; *n* étole *f*, écharpe *f*.
stolen ['stoulən] *pp of* **steal**.
stolid ['stɔlid] *a* stupide, obstiné, flegmatique.
stolidity [stɔ'liditi] *n* stupidité *f*, flegme *m*.
stomach ['stʌmək] *n* estomac *m*, ventre *m*, bedaine *f*, appétit *m*, courage *m*, patience *f*; *vt* manger, avaler, supporter.
stone [stoun] *n* pierre *f*, caillou *m*, noyau *m*, pépin *m*, calcul *m*, 14 livres; *vt* lapider, empierrer, énoyauter.
stony ['stouni] *a* pierreux, dur, glacial, glacé.
stool [stuːl] *n* tabouret *m*, escabeau *m*, selle *f*.
stoop [stuːp] *vi* se pencher, être voûté, daigner, s'abaisser.
stop [stɔp] *n* arrêt *m*, halte *f*, fin *f*; **full** — point *m*; *vt* arrêter, boucher, (*tooth*) plomber, barrer, mettre fin à, ponctuer, empêcher, bloquer, couper; *vi* s'arrêter, cesser.
stoppage ['stɔpidʒ] *n* arrêt *m*, encombrement *m*, occlusion *f*, obstruction. *f*.
stopper ['stɔpə] *n* bouchon *m*.
storage ['stɔːridʒ] *n* emmagasinage *m*, entrepôts *m pl*.
store [stɔː] *n* dépôt *m*, entrepôt *m*, magasin *m*, provision *f*, réserve *f*; *vt* garnir, rentrer, entreposer, tenir, emmagasiner, meubler, mettre en reserve.
stork [stɔːk] *n* cigogne *f*.
storm [stɔːm] *n* orage *m*, tempête *f*, assaut *m*; *vt* emporter d'assaut; *vi* faire rage, tempêter.
stormy ['stɔːmi] *a* orageux, houleux.
story ['stɔːri] *n* histoire *f*, version *f*, conte *m*, récit *m*, étage *m*; —**teller** raconteur *m*, narrateur *m*, griot *m*.
stout [staut] *a* brave, résolu, fort, gros, vigoureux.
stoutness ['stautnis] *n* courage *m*, grosseur *f*, embonpoint *m*, corpulence *f*.
stove [stouv] *pt pp of* **stave**; *n* poêle *m*.
stow [stou] *vt* bien empaqueter, arrimer.
stowaway ['stouəwei] *n* voyageur de fond de cale *m*.
straddle ['strædl] *vt* enfourcher, enjamber, s'installer sur, (*artillery*) encadrer.
strafe [strɑːf] *vt* (*fam*) punir.
straggle ['strægl] *vi* traîner en arrière, s'écarter.

straggler ['stræglə] *n* retardataire *mf*, attardé *m*, traînard *m*.

straight [streit] *n* ligne droite *f*; *ad* droit, juste, directement; *a* droit, rectiligne, loyal, juste.

straighten ['streitn] *vt* redresser, arranger, défausser.

straightforward [streit'fɔːwəd] *a* loyal, droit.

straightforwardness [streit'fɔːwədnis] *n* droiture *f*, franchise *f*.

strain [strein] *n* tension *f*, effort *m*, ton *m*, veine *f*, entorse *f*; *pl* accents *m pl*; *vt* (é)tendre, tirer (sur), forcer, filtrer, fatiguer, faire violence à, (se) fouler.

strainer ['streinə] *n* passoire *f*, filtre *m*.

strait [streit] *n* détroit *m*.

straits [streits] *n* détroit *m*, gêne *f*.

strait-jacket ['streit'dʒækit] *n* camisole de force *f*.

strand [strænd] *n* rive *f*; *vt* échouer.

stranded ['strændid] *a* perdu, en panne, sans ressources.

strange [streindʒ] *a* étrange, singulier, étranger, dépaysé.

strangeness ['streindʒnis] *n* étrangeté *f*, nouveauté *f*.

stranger ['streindʒə] *n* étranger, inconnu.

strangle ['stræŋgl] *vt* étrangler, étouffer.

strangulation [ˌstræŋgju'leiʃən] *n* strangulation *f*, étranglement *m*.

strap [stræp] *n* courroie *f*, sangle *f*, bande *f*, étrivière *f*; *vt* sangler, attacher, aiguiser, bander, frapper.

strapping ['stræpiŋ] *a* robuste, solide.

stratagem ['strætidʒəm] *n* stratagème *m*, ruse *f*.

strategist ['strætidʒist] *n* stratège *m*.

strategy ['strætidʒi] *n* stratégie *f*.

straw [strɔː] *n* paille *f*, fétu *m*; **it is the last** — il ne manquait plus que cela.

strawberry ['strɔːbəri] *n* fraise *f*, fraisier *m*.

stray [strei] *n* bête perdue *f*; *a* égaré, espacé, épars, perdu; *vi* se perdre, s'égarer.

streak [striːk] *n* raie *f*, bande *f*, veine *f*; *vt* rayer, strier; **to — past** passer en trombe.

streaked ['striːkt] *a* rayé, zébré.

stream [striːm] *n* cours d'eau *m*, courant *m*, ruisseau *m*, flot *m*, (*Africa*) marigot *m*; **down—, up—** en aval, en amont; *vi* couler, ruisseler, flotter.

street [striːt] *n* rue *f*.

street-arab ['striːtˌærəb] *n* gavroche *m*, voyou *m*.

strength [streŋθ] *n* force(s) *f* (*pl*), solidité *f*, complet *m*, effectifs *m pl*.

strengthen ['streŋθən] *vt* renforcer, fortifier, (r)affermir.

strenuous ['strenjuəs] *a* énergique, appliqué, ardu.

strenuousness ['strenjuəsnis] *n* vigueur *f*, ardeur *f*.

stress [stres] *n* accent *m*, force *f*, pression *f*, tension *f*; *vt* accentuer, insister sur, souligner, fatiguer.

stretch [stretʃ] *n* étendue *f*, extension *f*, envergure *f*, élasticité *f*; *vt* (é)tendre, étirer, exagérer, élargir, bander; *vi* s'étendre, s'étirer, s'élargir.

stretcher ['stretʃə] *n* civière *f*, brancard *m*.

strew [struː] *vt* semer, joncher.

strict [strikt] *a* strict, sévère, rigoureux, formel.

strictures ['striktʃəz] *n* critiques *f pl*.

stride [straid] *n* enjambée *f*; *vi* marcher à grands pas.

strife [straif] *n* conflit *m*.

strike [straik] *n* grève *f*; *vt* frapper, heurter contre, sonner, trouver, frotter, conclure, (*flag*) amener; *vi* faire grève, porter coup.

striker ['straikə] *n* gréviste *mf*, marteau *m*.

striking ['straikiŋ] *a* frappant, saisissant.

string [striŋ] *n* ficelle *f*, corde *f*, chapelet *m*, enfilade *f*, cordon *m*, fil *m*, lacet *m*, file *f*, (*journal*) série *f*; *pl* instruments à cordes *m*; *vt* ficeler, enfiler.

stringent ['strindʒənt] *a* strict, rigoureux, étroit, serré.

strip [strip] *n* bande *f*, langue *f*; *vt* dépouiller, dégarnir, vider, écorcer; *vi* se déshabiller, se dévêtir.

stripe [straip] *n* bande *f*, barre *f*, raie *f*, (*mil*) galon *m*, chevron *m*; *vt* barrer, rayer.

strive [straiv] *vi* s'efforcer, lutter, rivaliser.

strode [stroud] *pt of* **stride**.

stroke [strouk] *n* coup *m*, attaque *f*, trait *m*, brassée *f*, caresse *f*; *vt* caresser, flatter.

stroll [stroul] *vi* flâner, faire un tour; *n* tour *m*, balade *f*.

strolling ['strouliŋ] *a* ambulant, forain, vagabond.

strong [strɔŋ] *a* fort, robuste, vigoureux, ferme, accusé, puissant, énergique.

strong-box ['strɔŋbɔks] *n* coffre fort *m*.

stronghold ['strɔŋhould] *n* forteresse *f*.

strong-minded ['strɔŋ'maindid] *a* volontaire, décidé.

strop [strɔp] *n* cuir *m*; *vt* affiler, repasser.

structure ['strʌktʃə] *n* structure *f*, construction *f*, édifice *m*, bâtiment *m*.

struck [strʌk] *pt pp of* **strike**.

struggle ['strʌgl] *n* lutte *f*; *vi* lutter, se démener.

strung [strʌŋ] *pt pp of* **string**.

strut [strʌt] *n* étai *m*, traverse *f*; *vi*

se pavaner; *vt* étayer, entretoiser.
stub [stʌb] *n* bout *m*, mégot *m*, chicot *m*, tronçon *m*, souche *f*, talon *m* de chèque; *vt* déraciner, heurter; — out éteindre.
stubble ['stʌbl] *n* chaume *m*.
stubbly ['stʌbli] *a* hérissé, couvert de chaume.
stubborn ['stʌbən] *a* têtu, obstiné.
stubbornness ['stʌbənnis] *n* entêtement *m*, ténacité *f*.
stuck [stʌk] *pt pp of* **stick**.
stud [stʌd] *n* bouton *m*, clou *m*, rivet *m*, écurie *f*, haras *m*.
studded ['stʌdid] *a* semé, orné, clouté.
student ['stjuːdənt] *n* étudiant(e) *mf*, homme *m* qui étudie.
studied ['stʌdid] *a* étudié, délibéré, recherché.
studio ['stjuːdiou] *n* atelier *m*, studio *m*.
studious ['stjuːdiəs] *a* studieux, étudié.
study ['stʌdi] *n* étude *f*, cabinet de travail *m*; *vti* étudier; *vi* faire ses études, apprendre (à).
stuff [stʌf] *n* étoffe *f*, marchandise *f*, camelote *f*, substance *f*, sottise *f*; *vt* bourrer, empiler, empailler, farcir, fourrer, boucher.
stuffy ['stʌfi] *a* étouffant, mal aéré, guindé.
stultify ['stʌltifai] *vt* rendre ridicule, infirmer, ruiner.
stumble ['stʌmbl] *n* faux-pas *m*; *vi* trébucher, se fourvoyer.
stumbling-block ['stʌmbliŋblɔk] *n* pierre d'achoppement *f*.
stump [stʌmp] *n* souche *f*, tronçon *m*, chicot *m*, moignon *m*, bout *m*, (*cricket*) piquet *m*; *vt* estomper, coller; **to — in** entrer clopin-clopant.
stumpy ['stʌmpi] *a* trapu, ramassé.
stung [stʌŋ] *pt pp of* **sting**.
stun [stʌn] *vt* étourdir, assommer, assourdir, renverser.
stunk [stʌŋk] *pp of* **stink**.
stupefaction [ˌstjuːpiˈfækʃən] *n* stupéfaction *f*.
stupefy ['stjuːpifai] *vt* hébéter, stupéfier, engourdir.
stupefying ['stjuːpifaiiŋ] *a* stupéfiant.
stupendous [stjuːˈpendəs] *a* prodigieux, formidable.
stupid ['stjuːpid] *a* stupide, bête.
stupidity [stjuːˈpiditi] *n* stupidité *f*, bêtise *f*.
sturdy ['stəːdi] *a* robuste, vigoureux.
sturgeon ['stəːdʒən] *n* esturgeon *m*.
stutter ['stʌtə] *vti* bredouiller, bégayer.
sty [stai] *n* porcherie *f*, bouge *m*, orgelet *m*.
style [stail] *n* style *m*, genre *m*, titre *m*, espèce *f*; *vt* appeler.
stylish ['stailiʃ] *a* qui a du style, chic, élégant.

subaltern ['sʌbltən] *an* subalterne *m*.
subdue [səbˈdjuː] *vt* soumettre, maîtriser, dompter, adoucir, tamiser.
subdued [səbˈdjuːd] *a* vaincu, tamisé, étouffé.
subject ['sʌbdʒikt] *n* sujet *m*; matière *f*, objet *m*; *an* sujet, -ette; *a* soumis, assujetti, passible; *ad* sous réserve (de to).
subject [səbˈdʒekt] *vt* soumettre, subjuguer, exposer.
subjection [səbˈdʒekʃən] *n* sujétion *f*, assujettissement *m*, soumission *f*.
subjugation [ˌsʌbdʒuˈgeiʃən] *n* soumission *f*, assujettissement *m*.
subjugate ['sʌbdʒugeit] *vt* subjuguer.
sublime [səˈblaim] *a* sublime, suprême.
sublimity [səˈblimiti] *n* sublimité *f*.
submarine ['sʌbməriːn] *an* sous-marin *m*.
submerge [səbˈməːdʒ] *vt* submerger; *vi* plonger.
submersion [səbˈməːʃən] *n* submersion *f*.
submission [səbˈmiʃən] *n* soumission *f*.
submit [səbˈmit] *vt* soumettre; *vi* se soumettre.
subordinate [səˈbɔːdənit] *an* inférieur(e) *mf*, subordonné(e) *mf*; *vt* subordonner.
subordination [səˌbɔːdiˈneiʃən] *n* subordination *f*.
suborn [sʌˈbɔːn] *vt* suborner.
subpoena [səbˈpiːnə] *n* assignation *f*; *vt* citer.
subscribe [səbˈskraib] *vt* souscrire (pour); **to — to** s'abonner à, être abonné à.
subscriber [səbˈskraibə] *n* souscripteur *m*, abonné(e) *mf*.
subscription [səbˈskripʃən] *n* souscription *f*.
subsequent ['sʌbsikwənt] *a* subséquent, ultérieur.
subsequently ['sʌbsikwəntli] *ad* subséquemment, dans la suite.
subservience [səbˈsəːvjəns] *n* soumission *f*, obséquiosité *f*.
subservient [səbˈsəːvjənt] *a* utile, obséquieux.
subside [səbˈsaid] *vi* s'affaisser, déposer, s'apaiser.
subsidence [səbˈsaidəns] *n* affaissement *m*, baisse *f*.
subsidize ['sʌbsidaiz] *vt* subventionner, primer.
subsidy ['sʌbsidi] *n* subvention *f*, prime *f*.
subsist [səbˈsist] *vi* subsister, persister, vivre.
substance ['sʌbstəns] *n* substance *f*, matière *f*, fond *m*, fortune *f*.
substantial [səbˈstænʃəl] *a* matériel, substantiel, solide, riche, important, copieux.
substantiate [səbˈstænʃieit] *vt* fonder, justifier.
substitute ['sʌbstitjuːt] *n* substitut

m, équivalent *m*, doublure *f*, suppléant(e) *mf*, remplaçant(e) *mf*; *vt* substituer; **to — for** remplacer.

substitution [ˌsʌbsti'tjuːʃən] *n* substitution *f*, remplacement *m*.

subterfuge ['sʌbtəfjuːdʒ] *n* subterfuge *m*, faux-fuyant *m*.

subtle ['sʌtl] *a* subtil, fin, astucieux.

subtlety ['sʌtlti] *n* subtilité *f*, finesse *f*.

subtract [səb'trækt] *vt* retrancher, soustraire.

subtraction [səb'trækʃən] *n* soustraction *f*.

suburb ['sʌbəːb] *n* faubourg *m*, banlieue *f*; *a* suburbain, de banlieue.

subvention [səb'venʃən] *n* subvention *f*.

subversion [səb'vəːʃən] *n* subversion *f*.

subversive [səb'vəːsiv] *a* subversif.

subvert [sʌb'vəːt] *vt* renverser.

subway ['sʌbwei] *n* passage souterrain *m*; métro *m*.

succeed [sək'siːd] *vti* succéder (à), réussir.

success [sək'ses] *n* succès *m*, réussite *f*, suite *f*.

successful [sək'sesful] *a* heureux, réussi, reçu, qui a du succès.

succession [sək'seʃən] *n* succession *f*, suite *f*, série *f*.

successive [sək'sesiv] *a* successif, consécutif, de suite.

successor [sək'sesə] *n* successeur *m*.

succinct [sək'siŋkt] *n* succinct, concis.

succor ['sʌkə] *n* secours *m*; *vt* secourir.

succumb [sə'kʌm] *vi* succomber.

such [sʌtʃ] *a* tel, pareil, le même; *pn* tel, celui (qui), en qualité de; **—as** tel que, comme.

suchlike ['sʌtʃlaik] *a* analogue, de la sorte.

suck [sʌk] *n* tétée *f*, succion *f*, sucée *f*; *vti* sucer; *vt* téter.

sucking ['sʌkiŋ] *a* à la mamelle, de lait, en herbe.

suckle ['sʌkl] *vt* allaiter.

suckling ['sʌkliŋ] *n* nourisson *m*, allaitement *m*.

sudden ['sʌdn] *a* soudain, brusque, subit; **—ly** *adv* tout à coup.

suddenness ['sʌdnnis] *n* soudaineté *f*, brusquerie *f*.

sue [suː] *vt* poursuivre, demander.

suet [suit] *n* graisse de rognon *f*.

suffer ['sʌfə] *vti* souffrir; *vt* subir, éprouver, supporter.

sufferance ['sʌfərəns] *n* tolérance *f*.

sufferer ['sʌfərə] *n* patient(e) *mf*, victime *f*.

suffering ['sʌfəriŋ] *n* souffrance *f*.

suffice [sə'fais] *vi* suffire.

sufficiency [sə'fiʃənsi] *n* fortune suffisante *f*, suffisance *f*, aisance *f*.

sufficient [sə'fiʃənt] *a* suffisant, assez de.

sufficiently [sə'fiʃəntli] *ad* suffisamment, assez.

suffocate ['sʌfəkeit] *vti* étouffer, suffoquer.

suffocation [ˌsʌfə'keiʃən] *n* suffocation *f*, asphyxie *f*.

suffrage ['sʌfridʒ] *n* suffrage *m*, droit de vote *m*.

suffuse [sə'fjuːz] *vt* colorer, humecter, se répandre sur.

sugar ['ʃugə] *n* sucre *m*; **castor —** sucre en poudre; **loaf —** sucre en pain; *vt* sucrer; **—bowl** sucrier *m*; **—-beet** betterave à sucre *f*; **—-cane** canne à sucre *f*; **—tongs** pince *f*.

sugary ['ʃugəri] *a* sucré, mielleux, doucereux, mièvre.

suggest [sə'dʒest] *vt* suggérer, inspirer, proposer.

suggestion [sə'dʒestʃən] *n* suggestion *f*, nuance *f*.

suggestive [sə'dʒestiv] *a* suggestif, équivoque.

suicide ['sjuisaid] *n* suicide *m*, suicidé(e) *mf*.

suit [sjuːt] *n* requête *f*, demande *f*, procès *m*, (*cards*) couleur *f*, complet *m*, tailleur *m*; *vt* adapter, accommoder, arranger, convenir à, aller à.

suitable ['sjuːtəbl] *a* approprié, convenable, assorti, qui convient.

suite [swiːt] *n* suite *f*, appartement *m*, mobilier *m*.

suitor ['sjuːtə] *n* plaignant *m*, solliciteur *m*, prétendant *m*, soupirant *m*.

sulk [sʌlk] *vi* bouder; **—s** *n* *pl* bouderie *f*; **—** y *a* bouder.

sullen ['sʌlən] *a* rancunier, maussade, renfrogné.

sullenness ['sʌlənnis] *n* maussaderie *f*, air renfrogné *m*.

sully ['sʌli] *vt* salir, souiller.

sulphur ['sʌlfə] *n* soufre *m*.

sultan ['sʌltən] *n* sultan *m*.

sultana [səl'tɑːnə] *n* raisin de Smyrne *m*; sultane *f*.

sultriness ['sʌltrinis] *n* lourdeur *f*.

sultry ['sʌltri] *a* étouffant, lourd.

sum [sʌm] *n* somme *f*, calcul *m*; **to — up** calculer, récapituler, resumer.

summary ['sʌməri] *n* sommaire *m*, résumé *m*; *a* sommaire, récapitulatif.

summer ['sʌmə] *n* été *m*; *a* estival, d'été.

summing-up ['sʌmiŋ'ʌp] *n* résumé *m*.

summit ['sʌmit] *n* sommet *m*, cîme *f*, comble *m*.

summon ['sʌmən] *vt* citer, convoquer.

summons ['sʌmənz] *n* citation *f*, convocation *f*, procès-verbal *m*.

sumptuous ['sʌmptjuəs] *a* somptueux, fastueux.

sumptuousness ['sʌmptjuəsnis] *n* somptuosité *f*.

sun [sʌn] *n* soleil *m*; *vt* exposer (chauffer) au soleil; **—burn** hâle *m*; **—burnt** *a* hâlé, basané, bronzé; **—glasses** lunettes *f pl* de soleil.

Sunday ['sʌndi] *n* dimanche *m*.

sundial ['sʌndaiəl] *n* cadran solaire *m*.

sunder ['sʌndə] *vt* séparer.

sundry ['sʌndri] *a* chacun à part, divers, différent; *n pl* faux frais *m pl*.

sung [sʌŋ] *pp of* **sing.**

sunk [suŋk] *pp of* **sink.**

sunny ['sʌni] *a* ensoleillé, de soleil.

sunrise ['sʌnraiz] *n* lever du soleil *m*.

sunset ['sʌnset] *n* coucher du soleil *m*.

sunshade ['sʌnʃeid] *n* ombrelle *f*, parasol *m*.

sunshine ['sʌnʃain] *n* (lumière *f* du) soleil, grand jour *m*.

sunstroke ['sʌnstrouk] *n* coup de soleil *m*, insclation *f*.

sup [sʌp] *n* gorgée *f*; *vt* boire à petites gorgées; *vi* souper.

superabundance [ˌsju:pərə'bʌndəns] *n* surabondance *f*.

superabundant [ˌsju:pərə'bʌndənt] *a* surabondant.

superannuated [ˌsju:pə'rænjueitid] *a* en (à la) retraite, suranné.

superb [sju:'pə:b] *a* superbe, magnifique, sensationel.

supercilious [ˌsju:pə'siliəs] *a* dédaigneux, pincé.

superficial [ˌsju:pə'fiʃəl] *a* superficiel.

superficiality [ˌsju:pə.fiʃi:'æliti] *n* superficialité *f*.

superfluous [sju:'pə:fluəs] *a* superflu, de trop.

superfluity [ˌsju:pə'flu:iti] *n* superfluité *f*, embarras *m*, excédent *m*.

superhuman [ˌsju:pə'hju:mən] *a* surhumain.

superintend [ˌsju:prin'tend] *vt* contrôler, surveiller.

superintendence [ˌsju:prin'tendəns] *n* surintendance *f*, surveillance *f*.

superintendent [ˌsju:prin'tendənt] *n* surintendant *m*, surveillant(e) *mf*.

superior [sju:'piəriə] *an* supérieur(e) *mf*.

superiority [sju:.piəri'ɔriti] *n* supériorité *f*.

superlative [sju:'pə:lətiv] *an* superlatif *m*; *a* suprême.

superman ['sju:pəmæn] *n* surhomme *m*.

supernatural [ˌsju:pə'nætʃrəl] *an* surnaturel *m*.

superpose [ˌsju:pə'pouz] *vt* superposer.

supersede [ˌsju:pə'si:d] *vt* supplanter, écarter, remplacer.

superstition [ˌsju:pə'stiʃən] *n* superstition *f*.

superstitious [ˌsju:pə'stiʃəs] *a* superstitieux.

superstructure ['sju:pə.strʌktʃə] *n* superstructure *f*, tablier *m*.

supertax ['sju:pətæks] *n* surtaxe *f*.

supervise ['sju:pəvaiz] *vt* surveiller, contrôler.

supervision [ˌsju:pə'viʒən] *n* surveillance *f*, contrôle *m*.

supervisor ['sju:pəvaizə] *n* surveillant(e) *mf*.

supine ['sju:pain] *a* couché sur le dos, indolent.

supper ['sʌpə] *n* souper *m*.

supplant [sə'plɑ:nt] *vt* supplanter, évincer.

supple ['sʌpl] *a* souple, flexible.

supplement ['sʌplimənt] *n* supplément *m*.

supplement ['sʌpliment] *vt* ajouter à, augmenter.

suppleness ['sʌplnis] *n* souplesse *f*.

supplicate ['sʌplikeit] *vti* supplier.

supplication [ˌsʌpli'keiʃən] *n* supplication *f*.

supplier [sə'plaiə] *n* fournisseur, -euse.

supply [sə'plai] *n* offre *f*, fourniture *f*, provision *f*; *pl* vivres *m pl*; fournitures *f pl*, intendance *f*; *vt* fournir, munir.

support [sə'pɔ:t] *n* support *m*, soutien *m*, appui *m*; *vt* supporter, appuyer, soutenir.

supporter [sə'pɔ:tə] *n* soutien *m*, partisan *m*, supporter *m*.

suppose [sə'pouz] *vt* supposer, s'imaginer.

supposing [sə'pouziŋ] *cj* à supposer que.

supposition [ˌsʌpə'ziʃən] *n* supposition *f*.

suppress [sə'pres] *vt* supprimer, réprimer, étouffer, refouler.

suppression [sə'preʃən] *n* suppression *f*, répression *f*.

suppurate ['sʌpjuəreit] *vi* suppurer.

supremacy [sju'preməsi] *n* suprématie *f*.

supreme [sju:'pri:m] *a* suprême.

sura, surat ['suərə, su'ræt] *n* sourate *f*.

surcharge ['sə:tʃɑ:dʒ] *n* surcharge *f*, surtaxe *f*; *vt* surcharger, surtaxer.

sure [ʃuə] *a* sûr, assuré, certain; **to be — ad** sûrement.

surety ['ʃuəti] *n* garant(e) *mf*, caution *f*.

surf [sə:f] *n* ressac *m*, surf *m*, barre *f*.

surface ['sə:fis] *n* surface *f*, apparence *f*.

surfboard ['sə:fbɔ:d] *n* aquaplane *m*.

surfboat ['sə:fbout] *n* pirogue *f*.

surfing ['sə:fiŋ] *n* planking *m*.

surfeit ['sə:fit] *n* excès *m*, satieté *f*, indigestion *f*, écœurement *m*; *vt* gaver, rassasier.

surge [sə:dʒ] *n* lame *f*, houle *f*, soulèvement *m*; *vi* se soulever, onduler, se répandre en flots.

surgeon ['sə:dʒən] *n* chirurgien *m*.

surgery ['sə:dʒəri] *n* chirurgie *f*, clinique *f*.

surgical ['sə:dʒikəl] *a* chirurgical.

surliness ['sə:linis] *n* morosité *f*, air bourru *m*.

surly ['sə:li] *a* revêche, bourru, morose.

surmise ['sə:maiz] *n* soupçon *m*,

conjecture *f*; [sə:'maiz] *vt* soupçonner, conjecturer.
surmount [sə:'maunt] *vt* surmonter,
triompher de.
surname ['sə:neim] *n* nom *m* de
famille; *vt* nommer.
surpass [sə:'pɑːs] *vt* surpasser, dépasser, excéder.
surplice ['sə:pləs] *n* surplis *m*.
surplus ['sə:pləs] *n* surplus *m*,
excédent *m*, boni *m*, rabiot *m*.
surprise [sə'praiz] *n* surprise *f*; *vt*
surprendre; **by** — à l'improviste.
surprising [sə'praiziŋ] *a* surprenant,
étonnant.
surrealism [sə'riːalizm] *n* sur-
réalisme *m*.
surrender [sə'rendə] *n* reddition *f*,
capitulation *f*; *vt* rendre, renoncer à,
livrer; *vi* se rendre, se livrer.
surreptitious [ˌsʌrəp'tiʃəs] *a* subreptice, clandestin.
surround [sə'raund] *vt* entourer,
cerner.
surrounding [sə'raundiŋ] *a* environ-
nant.
surroundings [sə'raundiŋs] *n pl*
environs *m pl*, ambiance *f*, alentours
m pl.
surtax ['sə:tæks] *n* surtaxe *f*.
survey ['sə:vei] *n* coup d'œil *m*,
examen *m*, arpentage *m*, cadastre
m, aperçu *m*, expertise *f*, plan *m*.
survey [sə:'vei] *vt* examiner, relever,
arpenter, embrasser du regard,
contempler.
surveyor [sə:'veiə] *n* arpenteur *m*,
inspecteur *m*, ingénieur *m* du service
vicinal.
survival [sə'vaivəl] *n* survivance *f*.
survive [sə'vaiv] *vi* survivre; *vt*
survivre à.
Susan ['suːzn] Suzanne *f*.
susceptibility [səˌseptə'biliti] *n* susceptibilité *f*, sensibilité *f*.
susceptible [sə'septəbl] *a* susceptible,
sensible, impressionnable.
suspect [səs'pekt] *vt* soupçonner,
suspecter, se douter de.
suspect ['sʌspekt] *a* suspect.
suspend [səs'pend] *vt* (sus)pendre,
mettre à pied, surseoir à.
suspenders [səs'pendəz] *n* jarretelles
f pl, fixe-chaussettes *n pl*,
bretelles *f pl*.
suspense [səs'pens] *n* attente *f*,
inquiétude *f*, suspens *m*.
suspension [səs'penʃən] *n* suspension
f, mise à pied *f*, retrait *m*.
suspicion [səs'piʃən] *n* suspicion *f*,
soupçon *m*.
suspicious [səs'piʃəs] *a* soupçonneux,
suspect, méfiant, louche.
sustain [səs'tein] *vt* soutenir, sustenter, souffrir, subir.
sustenance ['sʌstinəns] *n* moyens de
se soutenir *m pl*, nourriture *f*.
swab [swɔb] *n* faubert *m*, tampon *m*;
vt balayer, nettoyer, laver à grande
eau.

swaddle ['swɔdl] *vt* emmailloter.
swaddling-clothes ['swɔdliŋklouðz]
n langes *m pl*.
swagger ['swægə] *n* suffisance *f*,
rodomontades *f pl*; *vi* se gober, se
pavaner, crâner.
swain [swein] *n* berger *m*, amoureux
m, tourtereau *m*.
swallow ['swɔlou] *n* hirondelle *f*,
gosier *m*, gorgée *f*; *vt* avaler, engloutir.
swam [swæm] *pt of* **swim**.
swamp ['swɔmp] *n* marais *m*; *vt*
inonder, déborder.
swan [swɔn] *n* cygne *m*.
swank [swæŋk] *vi* faire de l'épate,
se donner des airs.
swap [swɔp] *vt* troquer, échanger.
sward [swɔːd] *n* gazon *m*.
swarm [swɔːm] *n* essaim *m*, nuée *f*;
vi essaimer, fourmiller, grimper.
swarthy ['swɔːði] *a* hâlé, boucané.
swash [swɔʃ] *n* clapotis *m*; *vi*
clapoter.
swastika ['swɔstikə] *n* croix gammée
f.
swath [swɔːθ] *n* andain *m*.
swathe [sweið] *vt* emmailloter, emmitoufler.
sway [swei] *n* balancement *m*,
pouvoir *m*, gouvernement *m*; *vi* se
balancer, vaciller, incliner; *vt* balancer, courber, porter, faire pencher,
gouverner.
swear [sweə] *n* — **word** juron *m*; *vti*
jurer; *vt* assermenter.
sweat [swet] *n* sueur *f*, transpiration
f; *vti* suer; *vi* transpirer, peiner; *vt*
exploiter.
sweater ['swetə] *n* sweater *m*, pull-
over *m*, chandail *m*, exploiteur *m*.
sweating ['swetiŋ] *n* suée *f*, transpiration *f*.
swede [swiːd] *n* rutabaga *m*.
Swede [swiːd] *n* Suédois(e) *mf*.
Sweden ['swiːdn] *n* Suède *f*.
Swedish ['swiːdiʃ] *an* suédois *m*.
sweep [swiːp] *n* mouvement *m*,
large courbe *f*, allée *f*, portée *f*, coup
de balai *m*, godille *f*, ramoneur *m*;
vt balayer, emporter, ramoner,
draguer; *vi* s'élancer, fondre,
s'étendre; **to** — **aside** écarter; **to** —
down *vt* charrier, emporter; *vi*
dévaler.
sweeper ['swiːpə] *n* balayeur *m*,
balai *m* mécanique, balayeuse *f*;
mine— dragueur *m* de mines.
sweeping ['swiːpiŋ] *n* balayage *m*,
dragage *m*, ramonage *m*; *a* excessif,
radical, impétueux, large.
swept [swept] *pt pp of* **sweep**.
sweet [swiːt] *a* doux, sucré, gentil; *n*
bonbon *m*; *pl* sucreries *f pl*, bonbons
m pl, douceurs *f pl*.
sweetbread ['swiːtbred] *n* ris de
veau *m*.
sweeten ['swiːtn] *vt* sucrer, adoucir.
sweetheart ['swiːthɑːt] *n* ami(e) *mf*,
fiancé(e) *mf*, chéri(e) *mf*.

sweetish ['swi:tiʃ] *a* douceâtre.
sweetmeat ['swi:tmi:t] *n* bonbon *m*; *pl* sucreries *f pl*.
sweetness ['swi:tnis] *n* douceur *f*, charme *m*.
sweet-pea ['swi:t'pi:] *n* pois de senteur *m*.
swell [swel] *n* enflure *f*, houle *f*; *pl* (*fam*) élégants *m pl*, gens de la haute *m pl*; *a* (*fam*) chic, épatant; *vt* enfler, gonfler; *vi* se gonfler, (s')enfler, se soulever.
swelter ['sweltə] *n* fournaise *f*; *vi* étouffer de chaleur, être en nage.
swerve [swə:v] *vi* faire un écart, une embardée, donner un coup de volant.
swift [swift] *n* martinet *m*; *a* rapide, prompt.
swiftness ['swiftnis] *n* rapidité *f*, vitesse *f*, promptitude *f*.
swill [swil] *n* rinçage *m*, lavasse *f*, pâtée *f*; *vt* rincer, boire goulûment, lamper.
swim [swim] *vi* nager, flotter, tourner; *vt* traverser à la nage.
swimmer ['swimə] *n* nageur, -euse.
swimming ['swimiŋ] *n* natation *f*, nage *f*.
swindle ['swindl] *n* escroquérie *f*; *vt* escroquer.
swindler ['swindlə] *n* escroc *m*.
swine [swain] *n* cochon *m*, porc *m*, pourceau *m*, salaud *m*.
swing [swiŋ] *n* oscillation *f*, balancement *m*, balançoire *f*, cours *m*, courant *m*, entrain *m*, revirement *m*; *vi* se balancer, tourner, ballotter, danser; *vt* balancer, faire osciller, tourner.
swirl [swə:l] *n* tourbillon *m*, remous *m*; *vi* tourbillonner.
swish [swiʃ] *n* banco *m*; latérite *f*; *vi* bruire.
Swiss [swis] *a* suisse; *n* Suisse, -esse.
switch [switʃ] *n* baguette *f*, badine *f*, (*rails*) aiguille *f*, commutateur *m*, bouton *m*; *vt* cingler, remuer, aiguiller; **to — on (off)** donner (couper) le courant.
switchboard ['switʃbɔ:d] *n* tableau *m*.
Switzerland ['switsələnd] la Suisse *f*.
swivel ['swivl] *n* pivot *m*; *vi* pivoter, tourner.
swoon [swu:n] *n* syncope *f*, défaillance *f*; *vi* s'évanouir.
swoop [swu:p] *n* descente *f*, attaque foudroyante *f*, rafle *f*; *vi* fondre, s'abattre.
sword [sɔ:d] *n* sabre *m*, épée *f*, glaive *m*.
swore [swɔ:] *pt of* **swear.**
sworn [swɔ:n] *pp of* **swear;** *a* assermenté, intimé, juré.
swung [swʌŋ] *pt pp of* **swing.**
syllable ['siləbl] *n* syllabe *f*, mot *m*.
syllabus ['siləbəs] *n* programme *m*, ordre du jour *m*.

symbol ['simbəl] *n* symbole *m*, emblème *m*.
symbolic(al) [sim'bɔlik(əl)] *a* symbolique.
symbolism ['simbəlizəm] *n* symbolisme *f*.
symbolize ['simbəlaiz] *vt* symboliser.
symmetrical [si'metrikəl] *a* symétrique.
symmetry ['simitri] *n* symétrie *f*.
sympathetic [ˌsimpə'θetic] *a* compatissant, de sympathie, sympathique.
sympathize ['simpəθaiz] *vi* compatir, partager la douleur (de), comprendre.
sympathy ['simpəθi] *n* compassion *f*, sympathie *f*.
symphony ['simfəni] *n* symphonie *f*.
symptom ['simptəm] *n* symptôme *m*.
synagogue ['sinəgɔg] *n* synagogue *f*.
syndicate ['sindikit] *n* syndicat *m*; ['sindikeit] *vt* syndiquer.
synod ['sinəd] *n* synode *m*.
synonym ['sinənim] *n* synonyme *m*.
synonymous [si'nɔniməs] *a* synonyme.
synopsis [si'nɔpsis] *n* vue d'ensemble *f*, résumé *m*, mémento *m*.
synoptic(al) [si'nɔptik(əl)] *a* synoptique.
syntax ['sintæks] *n* syntaxe *f*.
synthesis ['sinθisis] *n* synthèse *f*.
synthetic(al) [sin'θetik(əl)] *a* synthétique.
Syria ['siriə] *n* Syrie *f*.
Syrian ['siriən] *a* syrien; *n* Syrien, -ienne.
syringe ['sirindʒ] *n* seringue *f*.
syrup ['sirəp] *n* sirop *m*.
syrupy ['sirəpi] *a* sirupeux.
system ['sistim] *n* système *m*.
systematic [ˌsisti'mætik] *a* systématique.
systematize ['sistimətaiz] *vt* systématiser.

T

tab [tæb] *n* étiquette *f*, oreille *f*, patte *f*, ferret *m*, touche *f*.
table ['teibl] *n* table *f*, tablier *m*, plaque *f*, tablée *f*.
tablecloth ['teiblklɔθ] *n* nappe *f*.
tableland ['teibllænd] *n* plateau *m*.
table-leaf ['teibli:f] *n* rallonge *f*.
tablespoon ['teiblspu:n] *n* cuiller à bouche *f*.
tablet ['tæblit] *n* tablette *f*, cachet *m*, comprimé *m*, plaque *f*, commémorative *f*.
tabloid ['tæblɔid] *n* journal *m* à sensation.
taboo [tə'bu:] *n* tabou *m*; *vt* interdire.
tabulate ['tæbjuleit] *vt* cataloguer, classifier.
tacit ['tæsit] *a* tacite.
taciturn ['tæsitə:n] *a* taciturne.

taciturnity [ˌtæsi'təːniti] *n* taciturnité *f*.

tack [tæk] *n* faufil *m*, (*nail*) semence *f*, bordée *f*, voie *f*; *vt* clouer, faufiler; *vi* louvoyer, tirer des bordées, virer.

tackle ['tækl] *n* poulie *f*, attirail *m*, palan *m*, engins *m pl*; *vt* empoigner, aborder, s'attaquer à, plaquer.

tact [tækt] *n* tact *m*, savoir-faire *m*, doigté *m*.

tactful ['tæktful] *a* de tact, délicat.

tactician [tæk'tiʃən] *n* tacticien *m*.

tactics ['tæktiks] *n* tactique *f*.

tactless ['tæktlis] *a* sans tact, indiscret.

tactlessness ['tæktlisnis] *n* manque de tact *m*.

tadpole ['tædpoul] *n* têtard *m*.

tag [tæg] *n* aiguillette *f*, bout *m*, appendice *m*, cliché *m*, refrain *m*; fiche *f*.

tail [teil] *n* queue *f*, basque *f*, pan *m*, (*tossing*) pile *m*; **to — off** s'éteindre; *vt* suivre, pister.

tail-light [ˈteil'lait] *n* feu arrière *m*.

tailor ['teilə] *n* tailleur *m*; **— made** *a* tailleur, fait sur mesure.

taint [teint] *n* grain *m*, touche *f*, trace *f*, corruption *f*, tare *f*; *vt* corrompre, vicier, gâter.

take [teik] *vti* prendre; *vt* gagner, captiver, tenir (pour), falloir, mettre, demander, vouloir; **to — off** décoller; **to — out** (faire) sortir, tirer, emmener; **to — to** prendre goût à, se prendre d'amitié pour; **to — up** monter, relever, ramasser, occuper.

take in ['teik'in] *vt* tromper.

take-off ['teikɔf] *n* départ *m*, décollage *m*.

taking ['teikiŋ] *a* attrayant; *n* prise *f*.

takings ['teikiŋz] *n pl* recette *f*.

taken ['teikən] *pp of* **take**.

tale [teil] *n* conte *m*, raconter *m*.

tale-teller ['teil,telə] *n* conteur *m*, cancanier *m*, rapporteur, -euse, cafard(e) *mf*.

talent ['tælənt] *n* talent *m*.

talented ['tæləntid] *a* de talent, doué.

talk [tɔːk] *n* conversation *f*, parole *f*, causerie *f*, fable *f*; *vi* causer; *vti* parler.

talkative ['tɔːkətiv] *a* bavard, loquace.

talking of [tɔːkiŋəv] *prep* à propos de.

tall [tɔːl] *a* très grand, haut, raide, fort, extravagant.

tallow ['tælou] *n* suif *m*; **— candle** chandelle *f*.

tally ['tæli] *n* taille *f*, coche *f*, étiquette *f*; *vt* compter, concorder; *vi* s'accorder, cadrer.

talon ['tælən] *n* serre *f*.

tame [teim] *a* apprivoisé, domestique, banal, plat; *vt* apprivoiser, aplatir.

tameness ['teimnis] *n* soumission *f*, banalité *f*, fadeur *f*.

tamper ['tæmpə] *vi* se mêler; **to —**

with se mêler de, toucher à, falsifier, altérer.

tan [tæn] *n* tan *m*, hâle *m*; *vt* tanner, hâler, bronzer; *vi* brunir, se basaner.

tandem ['tændəm] *n* tandem *m*.

tang [tæŋ] *n* saveur *f*, piquant *m*, goût *m*.

tangent ['tændʒənt] *n* tangente *f*; *a* tangent.

tangerine [ˌtændʒə'riːn] *n* mandarine *f*.

tangible ['tændʒəbl] *a* tangible, sensible, réel, palpable.

tangle ['tæŋgl] *n* confusion *f*, enchevêtrement *m*, fouillis *m*; *vt* embrouiller; *vi* s'embrouiller, s'emmêler.

tank [tæŋk] *n* réservoir *m*, citerne *f*, cuve *f*, tank *m*, char d'assaut *m*.

tankard ['tæŋkəd] *n* pot *m*, chope *f*.

tanner ['tænə] *n* tanneur *m*, pièce de sixpence *f*.

tannery ['tænəri] *n* tannerie *f*.

tantalize ['tæntəlaiz] *vt* tantaliser, tourmenter.

tantalizing ['tæntəlaiziŋ] *a* provoquant, décevant.

tantamount ['tæntəmaunt] *a* équivalent, qui revient à.

tantrum ['tæntrəm] *n* accès de colère *m*.

tap [tæp] *n* robinet *m*, tape *f*; *vt* mettre en perce, inciser, ponctionner, intercepter, taper, tapoter.

tape [teip] *n* ruban *m*, ganse *f*, bande *f*; *vt* attacher, border, brocher.

tape-measure ['teip,meʒə] *n* mètre ruban *m*.

taper ['teipə] *n* cierge *m*, bougie *f*, rat de cave *m*; *vt* effiler; *vi* amincir, s'effiler.

tape-recorder ['teipri,kɔːdə] *n* magnétophone *m*.

tapestry ['tæpistri] *n* tapiserie *f*.

tapeworm ['teipwəːm] *n* ver solitaire *m*, ténia *m*.

tapioca [ˌtæpi'oukə] *n* tapioca *m*.

tar [taː] *n* goudron *m*, (*fam*) loup *m* de mer; *vt* goudronner.

tardiness ['taːdinis] *n* lenteur *f*, tardivité *f*, retard *m*.

tardy ['taːdi] *a* lent, tardif.

tare [tɛə] *n* tare *f*, ivraie *f*.

target ['taːgit] *n* cible *f*, disque *m*, objectif *m*.

tariff ['tærif] *n* tarif *m*.

tarmac ['taːmæk] *n* macadam *m*, piste de décollage *f*.

tarnish ['taːniʃ] *n* ternissure *f*; *vt* ternir; *vi* se ternir.

tarpaulin [taː'pɔːlin] *n* bâche (goudronnée) *f*.

tarragon ['tærəgən] *n* estragon *m*.

tarry ['tæri] *vi* rester, attendre, s'attarder.

tart [taːt] *n* tarte *f*, fourte *f*; (*fam*) putain *f*; *a* acide, âpre, piquant, aigre.

tartness ['taːtnis] *n* aigreur *f*, verdeur *f*, acidité *f*.

task [tɑːsk] *n* tâche *f*, devoir *m*, besogne *f*; **to take to —** prendre à partie.

tassel ['tæsəl] *n* gland *m*, signet *m*.

taste [teist] *n* goût *m*, saveur *f*; *vt* goûter (à), sentir, toucher à, déguster.

tasteful ['teistful] *a* qui a du goût, de bon goût.

tasteless ['teistlis] *a* insipide, fade, sans goût.

taster ['teistə] *n* dégustateur *m*.

tasty ['teisti] *a* savoureux.

tatter ['tætə] *n* chiffon *m*; *pl* loques *f pl*, guenilles *f pl*.

tattle ['tætl] *n* bavardage *m*, commérages *m pl*; *vi* bavarder.

tattler ['tætlə] *n* bavard(e) *mf*, cancanier, -ière.

tattoo [tə'tuː] *n* (*mil*) retraite *f*, tatouage *m*; *vi* tambouriner; *vt* tatouer.

taught [tɔːt] *pt pp of* **teach**.

taunt [tɔːnt] *n* reproche *m*, quolibet *m*; *vt* reprocher (à), accabler de quolibets, se moquer de, se gausser de.

taut [tɔːt] *a* tendu, raide.

tavern ['tævən] *n* taverne *f*, cabaret *m*.

tawdriness ['tɔːdrinis] *n* clinquant *m*, faux luxe *m*.

tawdry ['tɔːdri] *a* criard.

tawny ['tɔːni] *a* fauve, basané.

tax [tæks] *n* impôt *m*, taxe *f*, contribution *f*; *vt* taxer, imposer, frapper d'un impôt.

taxation [tæk'seiʃən] *n* imposition *f*, taxation *f*.

tax-collector ['tækskə‚lektə] *n* percepteur *m*.

taxi ['tæksi] *n* taxi *m*.

taxpayer ['tæks‚peiə] *n* contribuable *mf*.

tea [tiː] *n* thé *m*; **—caddy** boîte *f* à thé; **—cloth** napperon *m*; **—pot** théière *f*; **—spoon** cuiller *f* à thé; **— chest** caisse *f* à thé.

teach [tiːtʃ] *vt* enseigner, apprendre (à), instruire.

teacher ['tiːtʃə] *n* professeur *m*, (*primary*) instituteur *m*, institutrice *f*, maître *m*, maîtresse *f*.

teaching ['tiːtʃiŋ] *n* enseignement *m*, doctrine *f*, leçons *f pl*.

teak [tiːk] *n* tek *m*.

team [tiːm] *n* équipe *f*, attelage *m*; *vt* atteler.

tear [tiə] *n* larme *f*, goutte *f*, bulle *f*.

tear [tɛə] *n* déchirure *f*, accroc *m*; *vt* déchirer, arracher.

tearful ['tiəful] *a* larmoyant, en larmes, éploré.

tease [tiːz] *vt* taquiner, effilocher, démêler; *n* taquin(e) *mf*.

teasel ['tiːzl] *n* chardon *m*, carde *f*.

teaser ['tiːzə] *n* problème *m*, colle *f*.

teasing ['tiːziŋ] *n* taquinerie *f*, effilochage *m*; *a* taquin.

teat [tiːt] *n* tétin *m*, tétine *f*, tette *f*.

technical ['teknikəl] *a* technique.

technicality [‚tekni'kæliti] *n* technicité *f*, détail *m* d'ordre technique.

technique [tek'niːk] *n* technique *f*.

tedious ['tiːdjəs] *a* ennuyeux, fastidieux.

teem [tiːm] *vi* pulluler, abonder, fourmiller, grouiller.

teeth [tiːθ] *n pl of* **tooth**.

teethe [tiːð] *vi* faire ses dents.

teething ['tiːðiŋ] *n* dentition *f*.

teetotal [tiː'toutl] *a* de tempérance, antialcoolique.

teetotaler [tiː'toutlə] *n* abstinent(e) *mf*.

telegram ['teligræm] *n* télégramme *m*, dépêche *f*.

telegraph ['teligrɑːf] *n* télégraphe *m*; *vt* télégraphier.

telegraphic [‚teli'græfik] *a* télégraphique.

telegraphist [ti'legrəfist] *n* télégraphiste *mf*.

telepathy [ti'lepəθi] *n* télépathie *f*.

telephone ['telifoun] *n* téléphone *m*; *vt* téléphoner.

telescope ['teliskoup] *n* télescope *f*, longue-vue *f*; *vt* télescoper; *vi* se télescoper.

television ['teli‚viʒən] *n* télévision *f*.

tell [tel] *vt* dire, conter, parler de, distinguer; *vi* porter, compter, militer; **all told** tout compris.

teller ['telə] *n* caissier *m*, conteur, -euse, recenseur *m*.

telltale ['telteil] *n* rapporteur, cafard (e) *mf*; *a* révélateur.

temerity [ti'meriti] *n* témérité *f*.

temper ['tempə] *n* humeur *f*, colère *f*, sang-froid *m*, mélange *m*, trempe *f*; *vt* mêler, tremper, tempérer.

temperament ['tempərəmənt] *n* tempérament *m*.

temperamental [‚tempərə'mentl] *a* inégal, capricieux, nerveux, quinteux.

temperance ['tempərəns] *n* tempérance *f*, sobriété *f*, retenue *f*.

temperate ['tempərit] *a* tempéré, modéré, tempérant, sobre.

temperature ['tempritʃə] *n* température *f*, fièvre *f*.

tempest ['tempist] *n* tempête *f*.

tempestuous [tem'pestjuəs] *a* tempétueux, orageux, violent.

temple ['templ] *n* temple *m*, tempe *f*.

tempo ['tempou] *n* rythme *m*.

temporal ['tempərəl] *a* temporel.

temporary ['tempərəri] *a* temporaire, provisoire.

temporize ['tempəraiz] *vi* temporiser.

temporizer ['tempəraizə] *n* temporisateur *m*.

tempt [tempt] *vt* tenter.

temptation [temp'teiʃən] *n* tentation *f*.

tempter ['temptə] *n* tentateur *m*, séducteur *m*.

ten [ten] *ad* dix.

tenable ['tenəbl] *a* (sou)tenable, défendable.

tenacious [ti'neiʃəs] *a* tenace.

tenacity [ti'næsiti] *n* ténacité *f*.

tenancy ['tenənsi] *n* location *f*.

tenant ['tenənt] *n* locataire *mf*.

tench [tenʃ] *n* tanche *f*.

tend [tend] *vi* tendre (à), se diriger (vers); *vt* soigner, veiller sur, servir.

tendency ['tendənsi] *n* tendance *f*, disposition *f*.

tendentious [ten'denʃəs] *a* tendancieux.

tender ['tendə] *n* devis *m*, offre *f*, monnaie *f*, tender *m*; *vt* offrir; *vi* soumissionner; *a* tendre, délicat, sensible, fragile.

tenderness ['tendənis] *n* tendresse *f*, sensibilité *f*.

tendril ['tendril] *n* vrille *f*.

tenement ['tenimənt] *n* propriété *f*, appartement *m*, maison de rapport *f*.

tenet ['tenit] *n* doctrine *f*, opinion *f*, article de foi *m*.

tenfold ['tenfould] *a* décuple; *ad* dix fois.

tennis ['tenis] *n* tennis *m*; —**court** tennis *m*, court *m*.

tenor ['tenə] *n* teneur *f*, cours *m*, ténor *m*.

tense [tens] *n* temps *m*; *a* tendu, raide.

tension ['tenʃən] *n* tension *f*.

tent [tent] *n* tente *f*.

tentacle ['tentəkl] *n* tentacule *m*.

tentative ['tentətiv] *a* d'essai, expérimental.

tentatively ['tentətivli] *ad* à titre d'essai.

tenth [tenθ] *an* dixième *mf*, dix *m*.

tenuity [te'njuːiti] *n* rareté *f*, ténuité *f*.

tenuous ['tenjuəs] *a* délié, ténu, mince.

tenure ['tenjuə] *n* exercice de fonctions *m*, occupation *f*, tenure *f*.

tepid ['tepid] *a* tiède.

term [təːm] *n* durée *f*, fin *f*, trimestre *m*, terme *m*; *pl* conditions *f pl*; *vt* nommer, désigner.

terminate ['təːmineit] *vt* terminer; *vi* se terminer.

termination [ˌtəːmi'neiʃən] *n* terminaison *f*, conclusion *f*, fin *f*.

terminus ['təːminəs] *n* terminus *m*, tête de ligne *f*.

terrace ['terəs] *n* terrasse *f*.

terrestrial [ti'restriəl] *a* terrestre.

terrible ['terəbl] *a* terrible, atroce, affreux.

terrific [tə'rifik] *a* terrifiant, terrible, formidable.

terrify ['terifai] *vt* terrifier, effrayer.

territorial [ˌteri'tɔːriəl] *a* territorial, terrien.

territory ['teritəri] *n* territoire *m*.

terror ['terə] *n* terreur *f*.

terrorism ['terərizəm] *n* terrorisme *m*.

terrorize ['terəraiz] *vt* terroriser.

terse [təːs] *a* net, délié, sobre, concis.

terseness ['təːsnis] *n* netteté *f*, concision *f*.

test [test] *n* pierre de touche *f*, épreuve *f*, test *m*, réactif *m*; *vt* éprouver, essayer, mettre à l'épreuve, vérifier.

testament ['testəmənt] *n* testament *m*.

testamentary [ˌtestə'mentəri] *a* testamentaire.

testify ['testifai] *vt* attester, témoigner; *vi* déposer.

testily ['testili] *ad* en bougonnant, avec humeur.

testimonial [ˌtesti'mouniəl] *n* recommandation *f*, certificat *m*.

testimony ['testiməni] *n* déposition *f*, témoignage *m*.

testiness ['testinis] *n* irascibilité *f*, susceptibilité *f*.

testy ['testi] *a* chatouilleux, irascible.

tetanus ['tetənəs] *n* tétanos *m*.

tether ['teðə] *n* longe *f*, attache *f*, moyens *m pl*, rouleau *m*; *vt* attacher.

text [tekst] *n* texte *m*.

text-book ['tekstbuk] *n* manuel *m*.

textile ['tekstail] *an* textile *m*; *n* tissu *m*.

textual ['tekstjuəl] *a* textuel, de texte.

texture ['tekstʃə] *n* (con)texture *f*, structure *f*, grain *m*, trace *f*.

Thames [temz] *n* la Tamise *f*.

than [ðən] *cj* que, de.

thank [θæŋk] *vt* remercier, rendre grâce(s) à.

thanks [θæŋks] *n pl* remerciements *m pl*, grâces *f pl*; — **to** grâce à.

thankful ['θæŋkful] *a* reconnaissant.

thankfulness ['θæŋkfulnis] *n* reconnaissance *f*.

thankless ['θæŋklis] *a* ingrat.

thanklessness ['θæŋklisnis] *n* ingratitude *f*.

thanksgiving ['θæŋks'giviŋ] *n* action de grâces *f*; fête *f* d'action de grâces.

that [ðæt] *a* ce, cet, cette; *pn* celui, celle (-là), cela, ça, qui, que, tant de; *cj* que, pour que, si seulement, plaise à Dieu que, dire que.

thatch [θætʃ] *n* chaume *m*; *vt* couvrir de chaume.

thatched [θætʃt] *a* (couvert) de chaume.

thaw [θɔː] *n* dégel *m*; *vi* dégeler.

the [ðə] *def art* le, la, l', les, ce, cet, cette, ces, quel(s), quelle(s); *ad* d'autant; — **more** plus.

theater ['θiətə] *n* théâtre *m*.

theatrical [θi'ætrikəl] *a* théâtral, scénique.

thee [ðiː] *pn* te, toi.

theft [θeft] *n* vol *m*.

their [ðeə] *a* leur(s).

theirs [ðeəz] *pn* le (la) leur, les leurs, à eux (elles).

them [ðem] *pn* les, eux, elles, leur.

theme [θiːm] *n* thème *m*, motif *m*.

themselves [ðəm'selvz] *pn* se, eux-(elles)-mêmes.

then [ðen] *ad* alors, puis, ensuite, donc.

thence [ðens] *ad* de là, par conséquent.

thenceforth ['ðens'fɔːθ] *ad* dès (depuis) lors, désormais.

theologian [θiə'loudʒjən] *n* théologien *m*.

theological [θiə'lɔdʒikəl] *a* théologique.

theology [θi'ɔlədʒi] *n* théologie *f*.

theorem ['θiərəm] *n* théorème *m*.

theoretic(al) [θiə'retikəl] *a* théorique.

theory ['θiəri] *n* théorie *f*.

there [ðɛə] *ad* là, y, il; *excl* voilà.

thereabout(s) ['ðɛərəbauts] *ad* par là, environ.

thereby ['ðɛə'bai] *ad* de ce fait, par là, par ce moyen.

therefore [ðɛə'fɔː] *ad* donc.

thereupon ['ðɛərə'pɔn] *ad* sur quoi, en conséquence, là-dessus.

thermometer [θə'mɔmitə] *n* thermomètre *m*.

these [ðiːz] *a* ces; *pn* ceux, celles(-ci).

thesis ['θiːsis] *n* thèse *f*.

they [ðei] *pn* ils, elles, on, eux, elles, ceux, celles.

thick [θik] *a* épais, touffu, dur, gros, fort, obtus; *ad* dur; *n* plus fort *m*.

thicken ['θikən] *vt* épaissir, lier; *vi* s'épaissir, se lier.

thicket ['θikit] *n* fourré *m*, bosquet *m*.

thickness ['θiknis] *n* épaisseur *f*.

thief [θiːf] *n* voleur, -euse.

thieve [θiːv] *vti* voler.

thigh [θai] *n* cuisse *f*; ——**bone** fémur *m*.

thimble ['θimbl] *n* dé *m*.

thimbleful ['θimblful] *n* dé *m*, doigt *m*.

thin [θin] *a* mince, faible, fin, léger, grêle, clair(semé); *vt* éclaircir, amincir; *vi* s'éclaircir, maigrir, s'amincir.

thine [ðain] *pn* à toi, le (les) tien(s), la (les) tienne(s).

thing [θiŋ] *n* chose *f*, objet *m*, machin *m*, être *m*; *pl* affaires *f pl*, effets *m pl*.

thingummy ['θiŋəmi] *n* chose *m*, machin *m*, truc *m*.

think [θiŋk] *vti* penser, réfléchir; *vt* trouver, juger, s'imaginer; **to —— about** penser à, songer à; **to —— of** penser de, (à), avoir égard à.

thinker ['θiŋkə] *n* penseur *mf*.

thinness ['θinnis] *n* minceur *f*, maigreur *f*, fluidité *f*.

third [θəːd] *n* tiers *m*, tierce *f*; *a* troisième, tiers.

thirdly ['θəːdli] *ad* tertio, en troisième lieu, troisièmement.

thirst [θəːst] *n* soif *f*; *vi* avoir soif (de for).

thirsty ['θəːsti] *a* altéré, assoiffé.

thirteen ['θəː'tiːn] *an* treize *m*.

thirteenth ['θəː'tiːnθ] *an* treizième *mf*, treize *m*.

thirtieth ['θəːtiiθ] *an* trentième *mf*, trente *m*.

thirty ['θəːti] *an* trente *m*.

this [ðis] *a* ce, cet(te); *pn* ceci, ce, celui-ci, ceux-ci, celle(s)-ci.

thistle ['θisl] *n* chardon *m*.

thither ['ðiðə] *ad* y, là.

thong [θɔŋ] *n* courroie *f*, lanière *f*.

thorn [θɔːn] *n* épine *f*.

thorny ['θɔːni] *a* épineux.

thorough ['θʌrə] *a* soigné, minutieux, complet, achevé.

thoroughbred ['θʌrəbred] *an* pur-sang *m*.

thoroughfare ['θʌrefɛə] *n* rue *f*, voie *f*, passage *m*; **no —— entrée** interdite.

thoroughly ['θʌrəli] *ad* à fond, complètement, parfaitement.

thou [ðau] *pn* tu, toi.

though [ðou] *cj* bien que, quoique, même si; *ad* cependant, mais.

thought [θɔːt] *pt pp* of **think**; *n* pensée *f*, considération *f*, idée *f*, réflexion *f*.

thoughtful ['θɔːtful] *a* réfléchi, pensif, rêveur, attentionné, plein de prévenance.

thoughtfulness ['θɔːtfulnis] *n* réflexion *f*, méditation *f*, égards *m pl*, prévenance *f*.

thoughtless ['θɔːtlis] *a* étourdi, mal avisé.

thoughtlessness ['θɔːtlisnis] *n* étourderie *f*, manque d'égards *m*, imprévoyance *f*.

thousand ['θauzənd] *an* mille *m*.

thralldom ['θrɔːldəm] *n* esclavage *m*, servitude *f*.

thrash [θræʃ] *vt* battre, rosser.

thrashing ['θræʃiŋ] *n* battage *m*, correction *f*, raclée *f*.

thread [θred] *n* fil *m*, filet *m*, filon *m*; *vt* enfiler; **to —— one's way** se faufiler.

threadbare ['θredbɛə] *a* usé jusqu'à la corde, râpé.

threat [θret] *n* menace *f*.

threaten ['θretn] *vti* menacer.

threefold ['θriːfould] *a* triple; *ad* trois fois autant.

thresh [θreʃ] *vt* battre.

threshing ['θreʃiŋ] *n* battage *m*.

threshing-machine ['θreʃiŋmə͵ʃin] *n* batteuse *f*.

threshold ['θreʃhould] *n* seuil *m*.

threw [θruː] *pt* of **throw**.

thrice [θrais] *ad* trois fois.

thrift [θrift] *n* frugalité *f*, économie *f*.

thriftless ['θriftlis] *a* dépensier, prodigue.

thriftlessness ['θriftlisnis] *n* prodigalité *f*.

thrifty ['θrifti] *a* frugal, économe, ménager.

thrill [θril] *n* frisson *m*, émotion *f*; *vt* émouvoir, électriser, faire frémir; *vi* frémir, frissonner; tressaillir (de).

thriller ['θrilə] *n* roman à sensation *m*; roman série noire.
thrilling ['θriliŋ] *a* émouvant, empoignant, palpitant, sensationnel.
thrive [θraiv] *vi* prospérer, pousser dru, bien marcher.
thriving ['θraiviŋ] *a* prospère, vigoureux.
throat [θrout] *n* gorge *f*.
throaty ['θrouti] *a* guttural, rauque.
throb [θrɔb] *n* battement *m*, pulsation *f*, palpitation *f*, vrombissement *m*; *vi* battre, vibrer, vrombir.
throes [θrouz] *n pl* douleurs *f pl*, affres *f pl*, agonie *f*.
throne [θroun] *n* trône *m*.
throng [θrɔŋ] *n* foule *f*, cohue *f*; *vt* encombrer, remplir; *vi* affluer, se presser.
throttle ['θrɔtl] *n* régulateur *m*, obturateur *m*; *vt* étrangler.
through [θru:] *a* direct; *prep* à travers, par, au travers de, pendant, dans, à cause de, faute de; *ad* à travers, en communication, jusqu'au bout, à bonne fin, hors d'affaire; **I am — with you** j'en ai fini avec toi.
throughout [θru:'aut] *ad* de fond en comble, d'un bout à l'autre; *prep* d'un bout à l'autre de, partout dans.
throw [θrou] *n* lancement *m*, jet *m*, distance *f*, portée *f*; *vt* (re)jeter (bas, dehors *etc*), lancer, projeter, désarçonner; piquer; **to — away** (re)jeter, gaspiller; **to — back** renvoyer, réverbérer; **to — off** secouer, abandonner, quitter, dégager; **to — out** chasser, mettre à la porte, rejeter, lancer; **to — over** abandonner, plaquer; **to — up** abandonner, rendre, jeter en l'air.
thrown [θroun] *pp of* **throw**.
thrush [θrʌʃ] *n* grive *f*.
thrust [θrʌst] *n* coup de pointe *m*, coup d'estoc *m*, attaque *f*, trait *m*, poussée *f*, botte *f*; *vt* pousser, imposer, enfoncer.
thug [θʌg] *n* assassin *m*, bandit *m*, voyou *m*.
thumb [θʌm] *n* pouce *m*, influence *f*; **—tack** punaise *f*; *vt* feuilleter, manier; (*fam*) **to — a lift** faire de l'autostop.
thump [θʌmp] *n* coup de poing *m*, bruit sourd *m*; *vt* frapper à bras raccourcis, cogner sur.
thunder ['θʌndə] *n* tonnerre *m*; *vti* tonner, fulminer; **—bolt** foudre *f*; **—clap** coup de tonnerre *m*; **—storm** orage *m*; **—struck** foudroyé, renversé, sidéré.
Thursday ['θə:zdi] *n* jeudi *m*.
thus [ðʌs] *ad* ainsi, de cette façon, donc.
thwart [θwɔ:t] *vt* déjouer, contrecarrer.
thy [ðai] *a* ton, ta, tes.
thyme [taim] *n* thym *m*; **wild —** serpolet *m*.
thyself [ðai'self] *pn* te, toi-même.

tiara [ti'ɑ:rə] *n* tiare *f*.
tick [tik] *n* déclic *m*, tic-tac *m*, marque *f*, coche *f*, toile *f*, tique *f*, crédit *m*, instant *m*; *vi* faire tic-tac; **to — off** pointer, (*fam*) rembarrer.
ticket ['tikit] *n* billet *m*, ticket *m*, bulletin *m*, étiquette *f*, programme *m*; *vt* étiqueter; **—collector** contrôleur *m*; **—punch** poinçon *m*.
tickle ['tikl] *n* chatouillement *m*; *vt* chatouiller, amuser.
ticklish ['tikliʃ] *a* chatouilleux, délicat.
tidal wave ['taidl'weiv] *n* ras de marée *m*.
tide [taid] *n* marée *f*, courant *m*.
tidings ['taidiŋz] *n* nouvelles *f pl*.
tidy ['taidi] *a* bien rangé, ordonné, bien tenu, qui a de l'ordre, coquet; *vt* ranger, arranger, mettre de l'ordre dans.
tie [tai] *n* cravate *f*, lien *m*, match nul *m*; *vt* attacher, lier, nouer; *vi* faire match nul, être premier ex aequo.
tier [tiə] *n* gradin *m*, étage *m*.
tiff [tif] *n* pique *f*, petite querelle *f* bisbille *f*.
tiger ['taigə] *n* tigre *m*.
tight [tait] *a* compact, étroit, serré, tendu, étanche, ivre.
tighten ['taitn] *vt* (re)serrer, rétrécir, renforcer.
tight-fisted ['tait'fistid] *a* avare, pingre, radin.
tight-fitting ['tait'fitiŋ] *a* collant, bien ajusté.
tightly ['taitli] *ad* ferme, dur, bien, hermétiquement.
tightness ['taitnis] *n* compacité *f*, étanchéité *f*, étroitesse *f*, tension *f*.
tights [taits] *n* (maillot) collant *m*.
tigress ['taigris] *n* tigresse *f*.
tile [tail] *n* tuile *f*, carreau *m*; *vt* couvrir de tuiles, carreler.
till [til] *n* caisse *f*; *vt* labourer; *prep* jusqu'à; *cj* jusqu'à ce que.
tillage ['tilidʒ] *n* culture *f*, labourage *m*.
tiller ['tilə] *n* cultivateur *m*, laboureur *m*.
tiller ['tilə] *n* barre *f*.
tilt [tilt] *n* bâche *f*, pente *f*, joute *f*; *vt* bâcher, incliner, faire basculer, (faire) pencher; *vi* jouter, pencher, s'incliner, basculer.
timber ['timbə] *n* bois de charpente *m*, poutre *f*, calibre *m*, envergure *f*.
timbrel ['timbrəl] *n* tambourin *m*.
time [taim] *n* temps *m*, fois *f*, époque *f*, moment *m*, cadence *f*, mesure *f*; *vt* choisir le temps de, fixer l'heure de, noter la durée de, chronométrer, régler, juger, mesurer; **—server** opportuniste *mf*; **—table** horaire *m*, emploi du temps *m*.
timeless ['taimlis] *a* éternel, sans fin.
timely ['taimli] *a* opportun.
timid ['timid] *a* timide.

timorous ['timərəs] *a* peureux, timore.

Timothy ['timəθi] Timothé *m.*

tin [tin] *n* étain *m,* fer-blanc *m, vt* étamer; — **can** bidon en fer-blanc.

tinfoil ['tinfɔil] *n* papier d'étain *m,* tain *m.*

tinned [tind] *a* en boîte, de conserve.

tin-hat ['tin'hæt] *n* casque *m.*

tin-opener ['tinoupənə] *n* ouvre-boîte *m.*

tinplate ['tinpleit] *vt* étamer; *n* ferblanterie *f.*

tinware ['tinwɛə] *n* vaisselle d'étain *f.*

tincture ['tiŋktʃə] *n* teinture *f,* saveur *f,* teinte *f; vt* colorer, relever, teinter.

tinder ['tində] *n* amadou *m.*

tinge [tindʒ] *n* teinte *f,* nuance *f,* saveur *f,* point *f; vt* colorer, teinter, nuancer.

tingle ['tiŋgl] *n* foúrmillement *m,* picotement *m,* tintement *m;* four-miller, cuire, picoter, tinter.

tinker ['tiŋkə] *n* rétameur *m; vt* rétamer, retaper; *vi* toucher, brico-ler, tripoter.

tinkle ['tiŋkl] *n* tintement *m,* drelin *m; vi* tinter; *vt* faire tinter.

tinsel ['tinsəl] *n* paillette *f,* clinquant *m; vt* pailleter.

tint [tint] *n* teinte *f,* nuance *f; vt* teinter, colorer.

tiny ['taini] *a* tout petit, minuscule.

tip [tip] *n* bout *m,* pointe *f,* pour-boire *m,* tuyau *m; vt* donner un pourboire à, graisser la patte à, donner un tuyau à, faire basculer, faire pencher, renverser, effleurer.

tippet ['tipit] *n* pèlerine *f.*

tipple ['tipl] *vt* boire sec.

tipsy ['tipsi] *a* ivre, gris.

tiptoe ['tiptou] *n* pointe des pieds *f.*

tiptop ['tip'tɔp] *n* le nec plus ultra; *a* de premier ordre.

tirade [tai'reid] *n* tirade *f,* diatribe *f.*

tire ['taiə] *vt* fatiguer; *vi* se fatiguer, se lasser; *n* pneu *m.*

tired ['taiəd] *a* fatigué, las, dégouté, contrarié.

tireless ['taiəlis] *a* infatigable.

tiresome ['taiəsəm] *a* fatigant, en-nuyeux.

tissue ['tisjuː] *n* tissu *m,* étoffe *f.*

tissue-paper ['tisjuːpeipə] *n* papier de soie *m.*

tit [tit] *n* mésange *f.*

titbit ['titbit] *n* morceau de choix *m,* friandise *f.*

tithe [taið] *n* dîme *f.*

titillate ['titileit] *vt* chatouiller, émoustiller, titiller.

titillation [‚titi'leiʃən] *n* titillation *f,* chatouillement *m,* émoustillement *m.*

title ['taitl] *n* titre *m,* droit *m.*

titled ['taitld] *a* titré.

titter ['titə] *n* rire étouffé *m; vi* rire sous cape.

tittle ['titl] *n* fétu *m.*

tittle-tattle ['titl‚tætl] *n* cancans *m pl,* potins *m pl; vi* cancaner.

titular ['titjulə] *a* titulaire.

to [tuː] *prep* à, de, pour, jusqu'à, (en)vers, contre, à côté de, à l'égard de.

toad [toud] *n* crapaud *m.*

toady ['toudi] *n* parasite *m,* flagor-neur *m;* **to** — **to** faire du plat à, flagorner.

toast [toust] *n* rôtie *f,* pain grillé *m,* toast *m,* canapé *m; vti* griller, rôtir; *vt* boire à la santé de, porter un toast à.

tobacco [tə'bækou] *n* tabac *m;* — **pouch** blague à tabac *f.*

tobacconist [tə'bækənist] *n* mar-chand de tabac *m.*

tobacconist's [tə'bækənists] *n* bu-reau (débit *m*) de tabac *m.*

today [tə'dei] *n ad* aujourd'hui *m;* — **week** d'aujourd'hui en huit.

toddle ['tɔdl] *vt* trottiner, flâner.

to-do [tə'duː] *n* grabuge *m,* scène *f.*

toe [tou] *n* doigt de pied *m,* orteil *m.*

toffee ['tɔfi] *n* caramel *m.*

tog [tɔg] **to** — **oneself up** se faire beau.

together [tə'geðə] *ad* ensemble, à la fois.

toil [tɔil] *n* peine *f,* tâche *f; vi* peiner.

toilet ['tɔilit] *n* toilette *f.*

toilsome ['tɔilsəm] *a* pénible, fati-gant.

token ['toukən] *n* signe *m,* gage *m,* jeton *m,* bou *m.*

told [tould] *pt pp of* **tell.**

tolerable ['tɔlərəbl] *a* tolérable, passable.

tolerance ['tɔlərəns] *n* tolérance *f.*

tolerant ['tɔlərənt] *a* tolérant.

tolerate ['tɔləreit] *vt* tolérer.

toll [toul] *n* droit *m,* péage *m,* octroi *m; vi* tinter, sonner le glas.

tolling ['touliŋ] *n* tintement *m,* glas *m.*

tomato [tə'mɑːtou] *n* tomate *f.*

tomb [tuːm] *n* tombe *f,* tombeau *m,* fosse *f.*

tombstone ['tuːmstoun] *n* pierre tombale *f.*

tomboy ['tɔmbɔi] *n* garçon manqué *m,* luronne *f.*

tomcat ['tɔm'kæt] *n* matou *m.*

tome [toum] *n* tome *m.*

tomfool ['tɔm'fuːl] *n* nigaud *m.*

tomfoolery ['tɔm'fuːləri] *n* pasqui-nade *f,* niaiseries *f pl.*

tomtit ['tɔm'tit] *n* mésange *f.*

tomorrow [tə'mɔrou] *n* demain *m;* — **week** demain en huit.

ton [tʌn] *n* tonne *f,* (*ship*) tonneau *m.*

tone [toun] *n* son *m,* bruit *m,* ton *m,* accent *m; vt* aviver, accorder; **to** — **down** dégrader, adoucir; **to** — **up** tonifier, ravigoter, remonter.

tongs [tɔŋz] *n* pincettes *f pl,* tenailles *f pl.*

tongue [tʌŋ] *n* langue *f,* languette *f.*

tonic ['tɔnik] *an* tonique *m*; *n* fortifiant *m*.

tonight [tə'nait] *ad* ce soir *m*, cette nuit *f*.

tonnage ['tʌnidʒ] *n* tonnage *m*.

tonsil ['tɔnsl] *n* amygdale *f*.

tonsilitis [ˌtɔnsi'laitis] *n* amygdalite *f*, angine *f*.

tonsure ['tɔnʃə] *n* tonsure *f*; *vt* tonsurer.

too [tuː] *ad* trop (de), aussi, et de plus.

took [tuk] *pt of* take.

tool [tuːl] *n* outil *m*, instrument *m*.

tooth [tuːθ] *n* dent *f*; **milk** — dent de lait; **molar** — molaire *f*; **wisdom** — dent de sagesse; **false** — fausse dent; —**ache** mal de dents *m*; —**brush** brosse à dents *f*; —**paste** pâte dentifrice *f*; —**pick** cure-dents *m*.

toothless ['tuːθlis] *a* édenté, sans dents.

toothsome ['tuːθsəm] *a* succulent, friand.

top [tɔp] *n* haut *m*, sommet *m*, premier *m*, tête *f*, toupie *f*, impériale *f*, dessus *m*, haut bout *m*, prise directe *f*, hune *f*; *a* supérieur, plus haut, dernier, du (de) dessus, du haut, premier; *vt* couvrir, éteter, atteindre, dominer, couronner, dé(sur)passer, surmonter, être à la tête de.

top coat ['tɔp'kout] *n* pardessus *m*.

top hat ['tɔp'hæt] *n* chapeau haut de forme *m*.

top-heavy ['tɔp'hevi] *a* trop lourd par le haut.

topaz ['toupæz] *n* topaze *f*.

toper ['toupə] *n* ivrogne *m*.

topic ['tɔpik] *n* sujet *m*, thème *m*, question *f*.

topical ['tɔpikəl] *a* d'actualité, local, topique.

topmost ['tɔpmoust] *a* le plus haut.

topple ['tɔpl] *vi* culbuter, s'écrouler, trébucher; **to — over** *vt* faire tomber, *vi* tomber.

topsy-turvy ['tɔpsi'təːvi] *a* sens dessus dessous, en désordre.

torch [tɔːtʃ] *n* torche *f*, flambeau *m*, lampe électrique *f*.

tore [tɔː] *pt of* tear.

torment ['tɔːmənt] *n* souffrance atroce *f*, supplice *m*, tourment *m*.

torment [tɔː'ment] *vt* tourmenter, torturer.

torn [tɔːn] *pp of* tear.

tornado [tɔː'neidou] *n* tornade *f*, ouragan *m*.

torpedo [tɔː'piːdou] *n* torpille *f*; —**boat** torpilleur *m*; —**tube** lance-torpilles *m*.

torpid ['tɔːpid] *a* engourdi, paresseux, inerte.

torrent ['tɔrənt] *n* torrent *m*.

torrential [tə'renʃəl] *a* torrentiel.

torrid ['tɔrid] *a* torride.

torridity [tə'riditi] *n* chaleur torride *f*.

tortoise ['tɔːtəs] *n* tortue *f*; —**shell** écaille *f*.

tortuous ['tɔːtjuəs] *a* tortueux, sinueux, enchevêtré.

torture ['tɔːtʃə] *n* torture *f*, supplice *m*; *vt* torturer, mettre au supplice.

toss [tɔs] *vt* lancer (en l'air), jeter, ballotter, secouer; *vi* s'agiter, être ballotté, se tourner et se retourner, jouer à pile ou face.

tossing ['tɔsiŋ] *n* ballottement *m*.

total ['toutl] *an* total *m*; *n* montant *m*; *vt* totaliser, additionner; *vi* se monter à.

totalizator ['toutəlaiˌzeitə] *n* totalisateur *m*, pari-mutuel *m*.

totter ['tɔtə] *vi* chanceler, tituber.

touch [tʌtʃ] *n* toucher *m*, touche *f*, attouchement *m*, brin *m*, soupçon *m*, contact *m*, communication *f*, courant *m*; *vt* toucher, effleurer, égaler; *vi* se toucher.

touchiness ['tʌtʃinis] *n* susceptibilité *f*, irascibilité *f*.

touchstone ['tʌtʃstoun] *n* pierre de touche *f*.

touchy ['tʌtʃi] *a* chatouilleux, susceptible.

tough [tʌf] *a* dur, coriace, tenace, ardu, solide; *n* apache *m*; — **guy** dur à cuire *m*.

toughness ['tʌfnis] *n* dureté *f*, ténacité *f*, coriacité *f*.

tour [tuə] *n* tour *m*, tournée *f*, voyage *m*, excursion *f*; *vt* faire le tour de, parcourir; *vi* être en voyage, être en tournée.

touring ['tuəriŋ] *n* tourisme *f*.

tourist ['tuərist] *n* touriste *mf*.

tournament ['tuənəmənt] *n* tournoi *m*, concours *m*.

tousle ['tauzl] *vt* tirer, emmêler, ébouriffer.

tout [taut] *n* démarcheur *m*, racoleur *m*, pisteur *m*, espion *m*; **to — for** relancer (les clients), pister, solliciter.

tow [tou] *n* filasse *f*, étoupe *f*, remorque *f*; *vt* haler, remorquer, prendre à la remorque; —**path** chemin *m* de halage.

toward(s) [tə'wɔːd(z)] *prep* vers, envers, en vue de, pour, à l'égard de.

towel ['tauəl] *n* essuie-mains *m*, serviette (de toilette) *f*; *vt* essuyer avec une serviette; —**rail** porte-serviettes *m* *inv*.

tower ['tauə] *n* tour *f*; *vi* planer, dominer; **church** — clocher *m*; **water** — château *m* d'eau.

towing ['touiŋ] *n* halage *m*, remorquage *m*, remorque *f*.

town [taun] *n* ville *f*.

town council ['taun'kaunsl] *n* conseil municipal *m*.

town councillor ['taun'kaunsilə] *n* conseiller (-ère) municipal(e) *mf*.

town hall ['taun'hɔːl] *n* hôtel de ville *m*, mairie *f*.

town-planning ['taun'plæniŋ] *n* urbanisme *m*.

townsman ['taunzmən] n citadin m, concitoyen m.

toy [tɔi] n jouet m, joujou m, jeu m; vi jouer, s'amuser.

trace [treis] n trace f, vestige m, trait m; vt tracer, calquer, suivre, trouver trace de, suivre la piste de; **to — back to** faire remonter à.

tracer ['treisə] n obus traceur m, balle traceuse f.

track [træk] n trace f; piste f, sillage m, sens m, sentier m, (rails) voie f, chenille f; vt suivre à la piste, traquer.

trackage ['trækidʒ] n (rails) réseau m.

tracing paper ['treisiŋ peipə] n papier-calque m.

tract [trækt] n étendue f, tract m.

tractable ['træktəbl] a traitable, maniable, arrangeant.

traction ['trækʃən] n traction f; a moteur.

tractor ['træktə] n tracteur m.

trade [treid] n commerce m, métier m, échange m, affaires f pl; vi être dans le commerce, faire le commerce (de in); **to — on** abuser de, exploiter.

trader ['treidə] n négociant(e) mf, commerçant(e) mf, navire marchand m.

trade-mark ['treidmɑːk] n marque de fabrique f.

tradesman ['treidzmən] n commerçant m.

trade-union [ˌtreid'juːnjən] n syndicat m (ouvrier).

trade-unionism [ˌtreid'juːnjənizəm] n syndicalisme m.

trade-unionist [ˌtreid'juːnjənist] n syndicaliste mf.

trade wind ['treidwind] n (vent) alizé m.

trading ['treidiŋ] n commerce m; **— in reprise** f (en compte); **— station** n factorerie f.

tradition [trə'diʃən] n tradition f.

traditional [trə'diʃənl] a traditionnel.

traditionalist [trə'diʃnəlist] n traditionaliste mf.

traduce [trə'djuːs] vt calomnier, diffamer.

traducer [trə'djuːsə] n calomniateur, -trice.

traffic ['træfik] n trafic m, circulation f, traite f.

traffic indicator ['træfik'indikeitə] n indicateur m (de direction), flèche f.

traffic jam ['træfikdʒæm] n embouteillage m.

trafficker ['træfikə] n trafiquant m, trafiqueur m.

traffic-light ['træfiklait] n feu m, signal m.

tragedian [trə'dʒiːdjən] n poète mf, (acteur, -trice) tragique.

tragedy ['trædʒidi] n tragédie f, drame m.

tragic ['trædʒik] a tragique.

trail [treil] n traînée f, trace f, piste f, sillon m; vti traîner; vt remorquer, traquer, filer; **to — off** s'éteindre, se perdre.

trailer ['treilə] n baladeuse f, remorque f.

train [trein] n traîne f, suite f, file f, série f, convoi m, train m; **express — rapide** m; **slow — omnibus** m; **through — train direct** m; **corridor — train à couloirs** m; vt former, dresser, entraîner, élever, exercer, préparer, braquer; vi s'entraîner.

trainer ['treinə] n entraîneur m, dresseur m.

training ['treiniŋ] n éducation f, instruction f, formation f, entraînement m; **— ship** vaisseau école m.

traitor ['treitə] n traître m.

trajectory ['trædʒiktəri] n trajectoire f.

tramcar ['træmkɑː] n tramway m, tram m.

trammel ['træməl] n entrave f, crémaillère f.

tramp [træmp] n bruit de pas m, marche f, chemineau m; vi marcher (lourdement), trimarder; vt parcourir à pied, faire à pied.

trample ['træmpl] vt fouler aux pieds, piétiner.

trampoline ['træmpouliːn] n matelas m élastique.

trance [trɑːns] n transe f, hypnose f, catalepsie f, extase f.

tranquil ['træŋkwil] a tranquille.

tranquilizer ['træŋkwilaizə] n tranquillisant, calmant.

tranquillity [træŋ'kwiliti] n tranquillité f, calme m.

transact [træn'zækt] vt passer, traiter.

transaction [træn'zækʃən] n conduite f; pl transactions f pl, rapports m pl.

transcend [træn'send] vt dépasser, exceller, surpasser.

transcribe [træns'kraib] vt transcrire.

transcription [træns'kripʃən] n transcription f.

transept ['trænsept] n transept m.

transfer [træns'fəː] vt transférer, déplacer, calquer.

transfer ['trænsfə] n transfert m, déplacement m, transport m.

transfigure [træns'figə] vt transfigurer.

transfix [træns'fiks] vt transpercer, (fig) pétrifier.

transform [træns'fɔːm] vt transformer, convertir.

transformer [træns'fɔːmə] n transformateur m.

transfuse [træns'fjuːz] vt transfuser.

transfusion [træns'fjuːʒən] n transfusion f.

transgress [træns'gres] vt transgresser, violer.

transgressor [træns'gresə] *n* transgresseur *m*, pécheur *m*.

tranship [træn'ʃip] *vt* transborder; *vi* changer de vaisseau.

transient ['trænziənt] *a* passager, éphémère.

transistor [træn'sistə] *n* transistor *m*.

transit ['trænsit] *n* traversée *f*, passage *m*, transit *m*.

transition [træn'siʒən] *n* transition *f*, passage *m*.

transitory ['trænsitəri] *a* transitoire, fugitif.

translatable [træns'leitəbl] *a* traduisible.

translate [træns'leit] *vt* traduire, interpréter, transférer.

translation [træns'leiʃən] *n* traduction *f*.

translator [træns'leitə] *n* traducteur *m*.

transmission [trænz'miʃən] *n* transmission *f*.

transmit [træns'mit] *vt* transmettre; —**ter** *n* émmetteur *m*, transmetteur.

transmute [trænz'mjuːt] *vt* transmuer.

transparency [træns'pɛərənsi] *n* transparence *f*.

transparent [træns'pɛərənt] *a* transparent.

transpire [træns'paiə] *vi* transpirer.

transplant [træns'plɑːnt] *vt* transplanter, repiquer, greffer.

transport ['trænspɔːt] *n* transport *m*.

transport [træns'pɔːt] *vt* transporter.

transposable [træns'pouzəbl] *a* transposable.

transpose [træns'pouz] *vt* transposer.

trap [træp] *n* trappe *f*, piège *m*, traquenard *m*, cabriolet *m*; *vt* attraper, tendre un piège à, prendre; *vi* trapper.

trapdoor ['træp,dɔː] *n* trappe *f*.

trapper ['træpə] *n* trappeur *m*.

trappings ['træpiŋz] *n* harnachement *m*, falbalas *m*, atours *m pl*, apparat *m*.

trash [træʃ] *n* camelote *f*, fatras *m*, niaiserie *f*, racaille *f*.

trashy ['træʃi] *a* de camelote, sans valeur.

trauma ['trɔːmə] *n* traumatisme *m*.

travel ['trævl] *n* voyage(s) *m pl*; *vi* voyager, être en voyage, marcher, aller; *vt* parcourir.

travel agency ['trævl'eidʒinsi] *n* agence *f* de voyages.

traveler ['trævlə] *n* voyageur, -euse; **commercial** — commis voyageur *m*.

traveling ['trævliŋ] *a* de voyage, ambulant; *n* voyages *m pl*.

traverse ['trævəs] *n* traverse *f*, bordée *f*, plaque tournante *f*; *vt* traverser.

travesty ['trævisti] *n* travestissement *m*; *vt* travestir, parodier.

trawl [trɔːl] *n* chalut *m*; *vi* pêcher au chalut.

trawler ['trɔːlə] *n* chalutier *m*.

tray ['trei] *n* plateau *m*, (*trunk*) compartiment *m*, éventaire *m*.

treacherous ['tretʃərəs] *a* traître, infidèle.

treachery ['tretʃəri] *n* traîtrise *f*, perfidie *f*.

treacle ['triːkl] *n* mélasse *f*.

tread [tred] *n* pas *m*, allure *f*, (*of tire*) chape *f*; *vi* marcher; *vt* fouler, écraser.

treadle ['tredl] *n* pédale *f*.

treason ['triːzn] *n* trahison *f*; **high** — lèse-majesté *f*.

treasure ['treʒə] *n* trésor *m*; *vt* garder précieusement, priser.

treasurer ['treʒərə] *n* trésorier, -ière, econome *mf*.

treasury ['treʒəri] *n* trésor *m*, trésorerie *f*.

treat [triːt] *n* plaisir *m*, fête *f*, régal *m*; *vti* traiter; *vt* régaler, payer.

treatise ['triːtiz] *n* traité *m*.

treatment ['triːtmənt] *n* traitement *m*, cure *f*.

treaty ['triːti] *n* traité *m*, accord *m*.

treble ['trebl] *n* triple *m*, soprano *m*; *a* triple, trois fois.

tree [triː] *n* arbre *m*.

trefoil ['trefɔil] *n* trèfle *m*.

trellis ['trelis] *n* treillis *m*, treillage *m*.

tremble ['trembl] *n* tremblement *m*; *vi* trembler.

tremendous [tri'mendəs] *a* énorme, formidable.

tremor ['tremə] *n* tremblement *m*, frisson *m*, secousse *f*.

tremulous ['tremjuləs] *a* tremblant, craintif, tremblotant.

trench [trentʃ] *n* tranchée *f*, fossé *m*; *vt* creuser.

trencher ['trentʃə] *n* trenchoir *m*.

trend [trend] *n* direction *f*, tendance *f*; *vi* se diriger, tendre.

trepan [tri'pæn] *n* trépan *m*; *vt* trépaner.

trepanning [tri'pæniŋ] *n* trépanation *f*.

trepidation [,trepi'deiʃən] *n* tremblement *m*, trépidation *f*.

trespass ['trespəs] *n* délit *m*, péché *m*, intrusion *f*, offense *f*; *vi* entrer sans permission; **to** — **upon** empiéter sur, abuser de, offenser.

trespasser ['trespəsə] *n* délinquant *m*, intrus *m*, transgresseur *m*.

tress [tres] *n* tresse *f*, natte *f*; *vt* natter, tresser.

trestle ['tresl] *n* tréteau *m*, chevalet *m*.

trial ['traiəl] *n* épreuve *f*, essai *m*, procès *m*, jugement *m*, ennui *m*.

triangle ['traiæŋgl] *n* triangle *m*.

triangular [trai'æŋgjulə] *a* triangulaire.

tribal ['traibəl] *a* de la tribu, tribal.

tribe [traib] *n* tribu *f*.

tribulation [,tribju'leiʃən] *n* tribulation *f*, affliction *f*.

tribunal [trai'bjuːnl] *n* tribunal *m*, cour *f*.

tribune ['tribjuːn] *n* tribun *m*, tribune *f*.

tributary ['tribjutəri] *an* tributaire *m*; *n* affluent *m*.

tribute ['tribjuːt] *n* tribut *m*, hommage *m*.

trick [trik] *n* tour *m*, farce *f*, ruse *f*, truc *m*, levée *f*; *vt* tromper, (dé)jouer.

trickery ['trikəri] *n* tromperie *f*, fourberie *f*.

trickle ['trikl] *vi* couler goutte à goutte, dégouliner; *n* filet *m*.

trickster ['trikstə] *n* escroc *m*, fourbe *m*.

tricky ['triki] *a* rusé, épineux.

tricycle ['traisikl] *n* tricycle *m*.

trifle ['traifl] *n* bagatelle *f*, (cook) diplomate *m*; *vi* badiner, jouer.

trifling ['traifliŋ] *a* insignifiant, futile, minime.

trigger ['trigə] *n* détente *f*, gâchette *f*, manette *f*.

trill [tril] *n* trille *m*, chant perlé *m*; *vi* vibrer, trembler; *vt* rouler, triller.

trim [trim] *n* ordre *m*, état *m*; *a* net, soigné, propret, en ordre; *vt* arranger, tailler, rafraîchir, soigner, orner, arrimer.

trimming ['trimiŋ] *n* mise en état *f*, arrangement *m*, taille *f*; *pl* fournitures *f pl*, garniture *f*, passementerie *f*, rognures *f pl*.

trinity ['triniti] *n* trinité *f*.

trinket ['triŋkit] *n* babiole *f*, bibelot *m*.

trip [trip] *n* excursion *f*, faux-pas *m*, croc-en-jambe *m*; *vi* marcher légèrement, trébucher, déraper, se tromper; *vt* pincer, faire trébucher, faucher les jambes à.

tripe [traip] *n* tripes *f pl*, bêtises *f pl*.

triple ['tripl] *a* triple; *vti* tripler.

triplet ['triplit] *n* trio *m*, tercet *m*, l'un de trois jumeaux.

triplicate ['triplikit] *a* triple, triplé; **in** — en trois exemplaires; *vt* tripler.

tripod ['traipəd] *n* trépied *m*.

trite [trait] *a* banal, usé, rebattu.

triteness ['traitnis] *n* banalité *f*.

triumph ['traiəmf] *n* triomphe *m*, miracle *m*; *vi* triompher, exulter.

triumphal [trai'ʌmfəl] *a* triomphal, de triomphe.

triumphant [trai'ʌmfənt] *a* triomphant, de triomphe.

trivial ['triviəl] *a* trivial, banal, futile.

triviality [ˌtrivi'æliti] *n* trivialité *f*, futilité *f*, insignifiance *f*.

trod, trodden [trɔd, 'trɔdn] *pp* of **tread.**

trolley ['trɔli] *n* tramway *m*, chariot *m*, diable *m*, serveuse *f*, trolley *m*.

trombone [trɔm'boun] *n* trombone *m*.

troop [truːp] *n* troupe(s) *f* (*pl*), bande *f*; *vi* s'attrouper, marcher en troupe.

trooper ['truːpə] *n* cavalier *m*.

troop-ship ['truːpʃip] *n* transport *m*.

trophy ['troufi] *n* trophée *m*.

tropic ['trɔpik] *an* tropique *m*; *a* tropical.

tropical ['trɔpikəl] *a* tropical.

trot [trɔt] *n* trot *m*; *vi* trotter; *vt* faire trotter.

trotter ['trɔtə] *n* (bon) trotteur *m*.

trouble ['trʌbl] *n* difficulté *f*, trouble *m*, ennui *m*, peine *f*, affection *f*, panne *f*, conflits *m pl*, discorde *f*; *vt* inquiéter, affliger, soucier, déranger, embarrasser, troubler, prier; *vi* s'inquiéter, se déranger, se donner la peine (de **to**).

troublemaker ['trʌblˌmeikə] *n* trublion *m*.

troublesome ['trʌblsəm] *a* ennuyeux, gênant, fatigant, énervant.

trough [trɔf] *n* auge *f*, cuve *f*, pétrin *m*, creux *m*.

trounce [trauns] *vt* rouer de coups, rosser, battre à plates coutures, écraser.

trousers ['trauzəz] *n* pantalon *m*.

trout [traut] *n* truite *f*.

trowel ['trauəl] *n* truelle *f*, déplantoir *m*.

truant ['truənt] *a* fainéant *m*, vagabond(e) *mf*; **to play** — faire l'école buissonnière.

truce [truːs] *n* trêve *f*.

truck [trʌk] *n* camion *m*, chariot *m*, troc *m*, camelote *f*.

trudge [trʌdʒ] *vi* traîner la jambe, clopiner.

true [truː] *a* vrai, loyal, sincère.

truffle ['trʌfl] *n* truffe *f*.

truly ['truːli] *ad* à vrai dire, sincèrement.

trump [trʌmp] *n* atout *m*, trompette *f*; *vt* couper; **to** — **up** inventer.

trumpet ['trʌmpit] *n* trompette *f*, cornet acoustique *m*; *vi* trompeter, barir; *vt* proclamer.

trumpeter ['trʌmpitə] *n* trompette *m*, trompettiste *m*.

truncate ['trʌŋkeit] *vt* tronquer.

truncheon ['trʌntʃən] *n* matraque *f*, bâton *m*.

trundle ['trʌndl] *n* roulette *f*; *vti* rouler; *vt* pousser, trimbaler.

trunk [trʌŋk] *n* tronc *m*, malle *f*, trompe *f*; — **call** appel interurbain *m*; — **line** grande ligne *f*; — **road** grand-route *f*, artère *f*.

truss [trʌs] *n* trousse *f*, botte *f*, cintre *m*, bandage *m*; *vt* botteler, renforcer, soutenir, trousser, ligoter.

trust [trʌst] *n* confiance *f*, espoir *m*, parole *f*, dépôt *m*, charge *f*, trust *m*; *vt* confier, en croire, se fier à, faire crédit à; *vi* espérer, mettre son espoir (en **in**).

trustee [trʌs'tiː] *n* administrateur *m*, curateur, -trice.

trusteeship [trʌs'tiːʃip] *n* administration *f*, curatelle *f*.

trustful ['trʌstful] *a* confiant.

trustworthiness ['trʌstˌwəːðinis] *n* loyauté *f*, exactitude *f*.

trustworthy ['trʌst,wəːði] *a* sûr, fidèle, digne de foi.
trusty ['trʌsti] *a* sûr, loyal.
truth [truːθ] *n* vérité *f*; **the — is, to tell the —** à vrai dire.
truthful ['truːθful] *a* véridique, fidèle.
truthfulness ['truːθfulnis] *n* véracité *f*, fidélité *f*.
try [trai] *vt* essayer, mettre à l'épreuve, juger; *n* tentative *f*, essai *m*, coup *m*.
trying ['traiiŋ] *a* fatigant, pénible.
try-on ['trai'ɔn] *n* bluff *m*.
tsetse fly ['tsetsiflai] *n* tsé-tsé *f*.
tub [tʌb] *n* cuve *f*, baquet *m*, caisse *f*, tub *m*, bain *m*.
tube [tjuːb] *n* tube *m*, tuyau *m*, métro *m*, chambre à air *f*.
tubercle ['tjuːbəːkl] *n* tubercule *m*.
tuberculosis [tjuː,bəːkju'lousis] *n* tuberculose *f*.
tuck [tʌk] *n* pli *m*, rempli *m*, pâtisserie *f*; *vt* (re)plier, remplier, plisser, border; **to — in** *vi* bouffer; *vt* border, retrousser.
Tuesday ['tjuːzdi] *n* mardi *m*.
tuft [tʌft] *n* touffe *f*, houpe *f*, huppe *f*, flocon *m*, mèche *f*.
tug [tʌg] *n* effort *m*, secousse *f*, remorqueur *m*; *vti* tirer fort; *vt* remorquer, tirer; **to — at** tirer sur.
tuition [tju'iʃən] *n* leçons *f pl*, instruction *f*.
tulip ['tjuːlip] *n* tulipe *f*.
tumble ['tʌmbl] *n* chute *f*, culbute *f*, désordre *m*; *vi* dégringoler, tomber, faire des culbutes; *vt* déranger, bouleverser, ébouriffer.
tumbledown ['tʌmbldaun] *a* délabré, croulant.
tumbler ['tʌmblə] *n* acrobate *mf*, gobelet *m*.
tumbrel ['tʌmbrəl] *n* caisson *m*, tombereau *m*.
tumor ['tjuːmə] *n* tumeur *f*.
tumult ['tjuːmʌlt] *n* tumulte *m*, agitation *f*, émoi *m*.
tun [tʌn] *n* tonneau *m*.
tune [tjuːn] *n* air *m*, ton *m*, note *f*, accord *m*; *vt* accorder, adapter; **to — in** régler.
tuneful ['tjuːnful] *a* harmonieux.
tuneless ['tjuːnlis] *a* discordant.
tuner ['tjuːnə] *n* accordeur *m*.
tuning-fork ['tjuːniŋfɔːk] *n* diapason *m*.
tunic ['tjuːnik] *n* tunique *f*.
tunnel ['tʌnl] *n* tunnel *m*.
tunny ['tʌni] *n* thon *m*.
turbid ['təːbid] *a* trouble.
turbine ['təːbin] *n* turbine *f*.
turbot ['təːbət] *n* turbot *m*.
turbulent ['təːbjulənt] *a* turbulent.
tureen [tə'riːn] *n* soupière *f*.
turf [təːf] *n* gazon *m*, motte *f*, turf *m*.
turgid ['təːdʒid] *a* boursouflé, enflé, ampoulé.
Turk [təːk] *n* Turc, Turque.
Turkey ['təːki] *n* Turquie *f*.

turkey ['təːki] *n* dinde *f*; **—cock** dindon *m*.
Turkish ['təːkiʃ] *an* turc *m*.
turmoil ['təːmɔil] *n* effervescence *f*, remous *m*.
turn [təːn] *n* tour *m*, tournant *m*, virage *m*, tournure *f*, numéro *m*, crise *f*, service *m*; **in —** à tour de rôle; **to a —** à point; *vti* tourner; *vt* retourner, changer, faire tourner, diriger; *vi* prendre, se tourner, se transformer, recourir (à **to**); **to — down** baisser, refuser, rabattre; **to — off** fermer, couper, renvoyer; **to — on** *vt* ouvrir, donner; *vi* dépendre de; **to — out** *vt* mettre dehors, à la porte, faire sortir, éteindre, retourner, produire; *vi* tourner, arriver, s'arranger; **to — up** *vt* relever, retrousser, déterrer, retourner, remonter; *vi* se présenter, se retrousser.
turncoat ['təːnkout] *n* renégat *m*, girouette *f*.
turner ['təːnə] *n* tourneur *m*.
turning ['təːniŋ] *n* tournant *m*.
turning-lathe ['təːniŋleið] *n* tour *m*.
turning point ['təːniŋpɔint] *n* tournant *m*.
turnip ['təːnip] *n* navet *m*.
turn-out ['təːn,aut] *n* assistance *f*, grève *f*, équipage *m*, tenue *f*, production *f*.
turnover ['təːn,ouvə] *n* chiffre d'affaires *m*, (cook) chausson *m*.
turnpike ['təːnpaik] *n* barrière *f*.
turnspit ['təːnspit] *n* tournebroche *m*.
turnstile ['təːnstail] *n* tourniquet *m*.
turntable ['təːn,teibl] *n* plaque tournante *f*.
turpentine ['təːpəntain] *n* térébenthine *f*.
turret ['tʌrit] *n* tourelle *f*.
turtle ['təːtl] *n* tortue *f*.
turtle-dove ['təːtldʌv] *n* tourterelle *f*.
tusk [tʌsk] *n* défense *f*.
tussle ['tʌsl] *n* lutte *f*; *vi* se battre, s'escrimer.
tutelage ['tjuːtilidʒ] *n* tutelle *f*.
tutor ['tjuːtə] *n* précepteur *m*, directeur d'études *m*, méthode *f*.
twaddle ['twɔdl] *n* verbiage *m*, balivernes *f pl*; *vi* bavasser, radoter.
twain [twein] *an* (*old*) deux.
twang [twæŋ] *n* grincement *m*, nasillement *m*; *vi* grincer, nasiller, vibrer; *vt* pincer.
tweed [twiːd] *n* tweed *m*.
tweezers ['twiːzəz] *n* pince *f*.
twelfth [twelfθ] *an* douzième *mf*; *a* douze.
twelve [twelv] *an* douze *m*.
twentieth ['twentiiθ] *an* vingtième *mf*; *a* vingt.
twenty ['twenti] *an* vingt *m*.
twice [twais] *ad* deux fois.
twig [twig] *n* branchette *f*, brindille *f*.
twilight ['twailait] *n* crépuscule *m*, petit jour *m*.

twin [twin] *n* jumeau *m*, jumelle *f*; *a* accouplé, jumeau, jumelé.

twine [twain] *n* ficelle *f*; *vt* tordre, entrelacer, enrouler.

twinge [twindʒ] *n* élancement *m*, lancinement *m*.

twinkle ['twiŋkl] *n* clignement *m*, scintillement *m*, lueur *f*; *vi* cligner, scintiller.

twinkling ['twiŋkliŋ] *n* clin d'œil *m*, scintillement *m*.

twirl [twəːl] *n* tournoiement *m*, fioriture *f*, pirouette *f*; *vi* tournoyer, tourbillonner, pirouetter; *vt* (*moustache*) tortiller.

twist [twist] *n* cordonnet *m*, torsion *f*, papillote *f*, rouleau *m*, torsade *f*, tour *m*; *vt* tortiller, tordre, entrelacer, se fouler, fausser; *vi* se tordre, tourner, vriller.

twit [twit] *vt* reprocher, railler.

twitch [twitʃ] *n* secousse *f*, tic *m*, contraction *f*, crispation *f*; *vt* crisper, tirer, contracter; *vi* se crisper, se contracter.

twitter ['twitə] *n* gazouillement *m*; *vi* gazouiller.

two [tuː] *an* deux.

two-edged ['tuːʼedʒd] *a* à double tranchant.

twofold ['tuːfould] *a* double; *ad* deux fois.

tympan ['timpæn] *n* tympan *m*.

type [taip] *n* type *m*, modèie *m*, caractère d'imprimerie *m*; *vt* taper à la machine, dactylographier.

typescript ['taipskript] *n* texte *m* dactylographié.

typewriter ['taip͵raitə] *n* machine à écrire *f*.

typhoid ['taifɔid] *n* typhoïde *f*.

typhus ['taifəs] *n* typhus *m*.

typhoon [tai'fuːn] *n* typhon *m*.

typical ['tipikəl] *a* caractéristique, typique.

typify ['tipifai] *vt* incarner, représenter, être caractérisque de.

typist ['taipist] *n* dactylo(graphe) *mf*.

typographer [tai'pɔgrəfə] *n* typographe *m*.

typography [tai'pɔgrəfi] *n* typographie *f*.

tyrannical [ti'rænikəl] *a* tyrannique.

tyrannize ['tirənaiz] *vt* tyranniser.

tyranny ['tirəni] *n* tyrannie *f*.

tyrant ['taiərənt] *n* tyran *m*.

U

U-boat ['juːbout] *n* sous-marin *m* allemand.

udder ['ʌdə] *n* pis *m*, mamelle *f*, tétine *f*.

ugliness ['ʌglinis] *n* laideur *f*.

ugly ['ʌgli] *a* laid.

ulcer ['ʌlsə] *n* ulcère *m*.

ulcerate ['ʌlsəreit] *vt* ulcérer; *vi* s'ulcérer.

ulterior [ʌl'tiəriə] *a* ultérieur, caché.

ultimate ['ʌltimit] *a* dernier, définitif, fondamental.

ultimately ['ʌltimitli] *ad* en fin de compte.

ultimatum [͵ʌlti'meitəm] *n* ultimatum *m*.

ultimo ['ʌltimou] *a* du mois dernier.

umbrage ['ʌmbridʒ] *n* ombrage *m*.

umbrella [ʌm'brelə] *n* parapluie *m*.

umbrella-stand [ʌm'breləstænd] *n* porte-parapluies *m* inv.

umpire ['ʌmpaiə] *n* arbitre *m*; *vt* arbitrer.

umpiring ['ʌmpaiəriŋ] *n* arbitrage *m*.

unabated ['ʌnə'beitid] *a* dans toute sa force, non diminué.

unable ['ʌn'eibl] *a* incapable, hors d'état (de to).

unabridged ['ʌnə'bridʒd] *a* intégral, non abrégé.

unaccomplished ['ʌnə'kʌmpliʃd] *a* inachevé, inaccompli.

unaccountable ['ʌnə'kauntəbl] *a* inexplicable.

unaccustomed ['ʌnə'kʌstəmd] *a* inaccoutumé.

unacknowledged ['ʌnək'nɔlidʒd] *a* sans réponse, non reconnu.

unacquainted ['ʌnə'kweintid] *a* to be — with ne pas connaître.

unadorned ['ʌnə'dɔːnd] *a* simple, nu, pur.

unadulterated [͵ʌnə'dʌltəreitid] *a* non frelaté, pur.

unadvisable ['ʌnəd'vaizəbl] *a* malavisé, imprudent.

unaffected ['ʌnə'fektid] *a* naturel, sincère, insensible.

unaffectedly [͵ʌnə'fektidli] *ad* sans affectation.

unalleviated [͵ʌnə'liːvieitid] *a* sans soulagement.

unalloyed ['ʌnə'lɔid] *a* pur, sans alliage (mélange).

unambiguous ['ʌnæm'bigjuəs] *a* catégorique, clair.

unambitious [͵ʌnæm'biʃəs] *a* sans ambition.

unanimous [ju'næniməs] *n* unanime.

unanimity [͵juːnə'nimiti] *n* unanimité *f*.

unanswerable [ʌn'ɑːnsərəbl] *a* sans réplique.

unanswered ['ʌn'ɑːnsəd] *a* sans réponse, irréfuté.

unarmed ['ʌn'ɑːmd] *a* sans arme.

unassailable [͵ʌnə'seiləbl] *a* inattaquable, indiscutable.

unassisted ['ʌnə'sistid] *a* sans aide, tout seul.

unassuming ['ʌnə'sjuːmiŋ] *a* sans prétention(s), modeste.

unattainable ['ʌnə'teinəbl] *a* hors d'atteinte, inaccessible.

unattractive [͵ʌnə'træktiv] *a* peu attrayant.

unavailable [ʌnə'veiləbl] *a* inaccessible, impossible à obtenir, indisponible.

unavailing ['ʌnə'veiliŋ] *a* inutile, vain.

unavoidable [ˌʌnə'vɔidəbl] *a* inévitable.

unaware ['ʌnə'wɛə] *a* **to be — of** ignorer, ne pas avoir conscience de.

unawares ['ʌnə'wɛəz] *ad* à l'improviste, au dépourvu.

unbalanced ['ʌn'bælənst] *a* déséquilibré, instable.

unbearable [ʌn'bɛərəbl] *a* intolérable.

unbecoming [ˌʌnbi'kʌmiŋ] *a* malséant.

unbeknown ['ʌnbi'noun] *ad* — **to à** l'insu de.

unbelief ['ʌnbi'liːf] *n* incrédulité *f*.

unbelievable [ˌʌnbi'liːvəbl] *a* incroyable.

unbeliever ['ʌnbi'liːvə] *n* incrédule *mf*, incroyant(e) *mf*.

unbend ['ʌn'bend] *vt* détendre; *vi* se dérider, se détendre.

unbending ['ʌn'bendiŋ] *a* raide, inflexible.

unbiased ['ʌn'baiəst] *a* impartial, objectif, sans parti pris.

unbind ['ʌn'baind] *vt* délier, dénouer.

unbleached ['ʌn'bliːtʃt] *a* non blanchi, écru.

unblemished [ʌn'blemiʃt] *a* sans tache, immaculé.

unblended [ʌn'blendid] *a* pur.

unblushing [ʌn'blʌʃiŋ] *a* effronté, éhonté.

unbolt ['ʌn'boult] *vt* déverrouiller.

unborn ['ʌn'bɔːn] *a* encore à naître, futur.

unbosom [ʌn'buzəm] *vt* révéler; **to — oneself** ouvrir son cœur.

unbound ['ʌn'baund] *a* délié, broché.

unbounded [ʌn'baundid] *a* illimité, sans bornes.

unbreakable [ʌn'breikəbl] *n* incassable.

unbreathable ['ʌn'briːðəbl] *a* irrespirable.

unbroken ['ʌn'broukən] *a* intact, ininterrompu, continu.

unburden [ʌn'bɔːdn] *vt* décharger, alléger, épancher.

unburied ['ʌn'berid] *a* sans sépulture.

unbusinesslike [ʌn'biznislaik] *a* peu pratique, sans méthode.

unbutton ['ʌn'bʌtn] *vt* déboutonner.

uncalled-for [ʌn'kɔːldfɔː] *a* non désiré, indiscret, déplacé, immérité.

uncanny [ʌn'kæni] *a* fantastique, inquiétant, mystérieux.

uncared-for ['ʌn'kɛədfɔː] *a* négligé.

uncaring [ʌn'kɛəriŋ] *a* insouciant.

unceasing [ʌn'siːsiŋ] *a* incessant, soutenu.

unceasingly [ʌn'siːsiŋli] *ad* sans cesse.

unceremoniously ['ʌnˌseri'mouniəs-li] *ad* sans cérémonie, sans gêne, sans façons.

uncertain [ʌn'sɔːtn] *a* incertain, inégal, douteux.

unchallenged ['ʌn'tʃælindʒd] *a* sans provocation, indisputé.

unchangeable [ʌn'tʃeindʒəbl] *a* immuable.

uncharitable [ʌn'tʃæritəbl] *a* peu charitable.

unchaste ['ʌn'tʃeist] *a* impudique.

unchecked ['ʌn'tʃekt] *a* sans opposition, non maîtrisé.

uncivil ['ʌn'sivl] *a* impoli.

unclasp ['ʌn'klɑːsp] *vt* dégrafer, desserrer.

uncle ['ʌnkl] *n* oncle *m*; (*pawnbroker*) tante *f*.

unclean ['ʌn'kliːn] *a* malpropre, impur.

unclothe ['ʌn'klouð] *vt* dévêtir.

unclouded ['ʌn'klaudid] *a* sans nuage, limpide, pur.

uncomfortable [ʌn'kʌmfətəbl] *a* mal à l'aise, incommode, peu confortable.

uncommon [ʌn'kɔmən] *a* peu commun, rare, singulier.

uncommonly [ʌn'kɔmənli] *ad* singulièrement.

uncomplimentary ['ʌnˌkɔmpli'mentəri] *a* peu flatteur.

uncompromising [ʌn'kɔmprəmaiziŋ] *a* intransigeant, intraitable.

unconcern ['ʌnkən'sɔːn] *n* indifférence *f*, détachement *m*.

unconcerned ['ʌnkən'sɔːnd] *a* comme étranger, indifférent, dégagé.

unconcernedly ['ʌnkən'sɔːnidli] *ad* d'un air détaché.

unconditional ['ʌnkən'diʃnəl] *a* sans conditions, absolu.

uncongenial ['ʌnkən'dʒiːnjəl] *a* antipathique, ingrat.

unconquerable [ʌn'kɔŋkərəbl] *a* invincible.

unconquered ['ʌn'kɔŋkəd] *a* invaincu.

unconscionable [ʌn'kɔnʃnəbl] *a* inconcevable, sans conscience.

unconscious [ʌn'kɔnʃəs] *a* inconscient, sans connaissance.

unconsciousness [ʌn'kɔnʃəsnis] *n* inconscience *f*, évanouissement *m*.

unconstitutional ['ʌnˌkɔnsti'tjuːʃənl] *a* inconstitutionnel.

uncontrollable [ˌʌnkən'trouləbl] *a* incontrôlable, irrésistible, ingouvernable.

unconventional ['ʌnkən'venʃənl] *a* original.

unconvinced ['ʌnkən'vinst] *a* sceptique.

uncooked ['ʌn'kukt] *a* mal cuit, cru.

uncork ['ʌn'kɔːk] *vt* déboucher.

uncouth [ʌn'kuːθ] *a* rude, grossier, gauche, négligé.

uncover [ʌn'kʌvə] *vt* découvrir, dévoiler.

uncrossed ['ʌn'krɔst] *a* non barré.

unction ['ʌŋkʃən] *n* onction *f*.
unctuous ['ʌŋktjuəs] *a* onctueux, huileux.
undaunted [ʌn'dɔːntid] *a* indompté, intrépide.
undeceive ['ʌndi'siːv] *vt* détromper.
undecided ['ʌndi'saidid] *a* indécis, irrésolu, mal défini.
undecipherable ['ʌndi'saifərəbl] *a* indéchiffrable.
undefiled ['ʌndi'faild] *a* sans tache, pur.
undeniable [ˌʌndi'naiəbl] *a* indéniable, incontestable.
under ['ʌndə] *prep* sous, au-dessous de; *a* de dessous, inférieur, subalterne.
underclothes ['ʌndəklouðz] *n pl* sous-vêtements *m pl*, linge de corps *m*.
underdeveloped ['ʌndədi'veləpt] *a* sous-développé.
underdog ['ʌndədɔg] *n* (*fam*) lampiste *m*, faible *m*.
underdone ['ʌndə'dʌn] *a* saignant.
underfed ['ʌndə'fed] *a* sous-alimenté.
undergo [ˌʌndə'gou] *vt* souffrir, subir.
undergraduate [ˌʌndə'grædjuit] *n* étudiant(e) *mf*.
underground ['ʌndəgraund] *n* métro *m*; *a* souterrain, clandestin; *ad* sous terre.
undergrowth ['ʌndəgrouθ] *n* taillis *m*, fourré *m*.
underhand ['ʌndəhænd] *a* souterrain, sournois, clandestin; *ad* par dessous main, en dessous.
underline ['ʌndəlain] *vt* souligner.
underling ['ʌndəliŋ] *n* sous-ordre *m*, barbin *m*, subordonné(e) *mf*.
undermine [ˌʌndə'main] *vt* miner, saper.
underneath [ˌʌndə'niːθ] *prep* au-dessous de, sous; *ad* dessous, par-dessous, au-dessous; *a* de dessous.
underrate [ˌʌndə'reit] *vt* sous-estimer.
under-secretary ['ʌndə'sekrətəri] *n* sous-secrétaire *mf*.
undersell ['ʌndə'sel] *vt* vendre moins cher que.
undershirt ['ʌndəʃəːt] *n* tricot *m*, gilet *m* (de corps).
undersigned [ˌʌndə'saind] *a* soussigné.
understand [ˌʌndə'stænd] *vt* comprendre, s'entendre à, sous-entendre.
understandable [ˌʌndə'stændəbl] *a* intelligible, compréhensible.
understanding [ˌʌndə'stændiŋ] *n* entendement *m*, intelligence *f*, compréhension *f*.
understatement ['ʌndə'steitmənt] *n* atténuation *f*, amoindrissement *m*.
understood [ˌʌndə'stud] *pp of* **understand** compris.
understudy ['ʌndə'stʌdi] *n* doublure *f*; *vt* doubler.

undertake [ˌʌndə'teik] *vt* entreprendre, s'engager à, se charger de.
undertaker ['ʌndə,teikə] *n* entrepreneur de pompes funèbres *m*.
undertaking [ˌʌndə'teikiŋ] *n* entreprise *f*, engagement *m*.
undertook [ˌʌndə'tuk] *pp of* **undertake.**
undertow ['ʌndətou] *n* ressac *m*, barre *f*.
underwear ['ʌndəwɛə] *n* sous-vêtements *m pl*, dessous *m pl*, lingerie *f*.
underwood ['ʌndəwud] *n* sous-bois *m*.
underworld ['ʌndəwəːld] *n* pègre *f*, bas fonds *m pl*, enfers *m pl*.
underwrite ['ʌndərait] *vt* souscrire, assurer.
underwriter ['ʌndə,raitə] *n* assureur maritime *m*.
undeserved ['ʌndi'zəːvd] *a* immérité.
undeserving ['ʌndi'zəːviŋ] *a* indigne.
undesignedly ['ʌndi'zainidli] *ad* sans intention, innocemment.
undesirable ['ʌndi'zaiərəbl] *a* indésirable.
undigested ['ʌndi'dʒestid] *a* mal digéré, indigeste.
undignified [ʌn'dignifaid] *a* sans dignité.
undiluted ['ʌndai'ljuːtid] *a* pur, non dilué.
undimmed ['ʌn'dimd] *a* non voilé, brillant.
undiscernible ['ʌndi'səːnəbl] *a* indiscernable, imperceptible.
undiscerning ['ʌndi'səːniŋ] *a* sans discernement.
undischarged ['ʌndis'tʃɑːdʒd] *a* non libéré, inacquitté, inaccompli.
undisguised ['ʌndis'gaizd] *a* sans déguisement, évident, franc.
undismayed ['ʌndis'meid] *a* imperturbable.
undisputed ['ʌndis'pjuːtid] *a* incontesté.
undistinguished ['ʌndis'tiŋgwiʃt] *a* commun, médiocre, banal.
undisturbed ['ʌndis'təːbd] *a* non dérangé, non troublé, paisible.
undivided ['ʌndi'vaidid] *a* entier, indivisé, unanime.
undo ['ʌn'duː] *vt* défaire, dénouer, dégrafer, ruiner, annuler.
undoing ['ʌn'duiŋ] *n* perte *f*, ruine *f*.
undone ['ʌn'dʌn] *a* défait, inachevé, perdu.
undoubted [ʌn'dautid] *a* certain, incontestable.
undoubtedly [ʌn'dautidli] *ad* sans aucun doute.
undreamt [ʌn'dremt] *a* dont on n'osait rêver, merveilleux.
undress [ʌn'dres] *n* petite tenue *f*, négligé *m*; *vt* déshabiller; *vi* se déshabiller.
undrinkable ['ʌn'driŋkəbl] *a* imbuvable, non potable.
undue ['ʌn'djuː] *a* excessif, indu.
undulate ['ʌndjuleit] *vti* onduler.

undulating ['ʌndjuleitiŋ] *a* vallonné, ondoyant, onduleux.
unduly ['ʌn'dju:li] *ad* indûment, à l'excès.
undying [ʌn'daiiŋ] *a* immortel, impérissable.
unearned ['ʌn'ə:nd] *a* — income plus-value *f.*
unearth ['ʌn'ə:θ] *vt* déterrer, exhumer.
unearthly [ʌn'ə:θli] *a* qui n'est pas de ce monde, surnaturel.
uneasiness [ʌn'i:zinis] *a* inquiétude *f*, gêne *f.*
uneasy [ʌn'i:zi] *a* mal à l'aise, inquiet, gêné.
uneatable ['ʌn'i:təbl] *a* immangeable.
uneducated ['ʌn'edjukeitid] *a* inculte, sans éducation.
unemployable ['ʌnim'plɔiəbl] *a* bon à rien.
unemployed ['ʌnim'plɔid] *a* désœuvré, sans travail; **the** — les chômeurs *m pl.*
unemployment ['ʌnim'plɔimənt] *n* chômage *m.*
unending [ʌn'endiŋ] *a* interminable, sans fin.
unequal ['ʌn'i:kwəl] *a* inégal; **to be** — **to** ne pas être à la hauteur de, ne pas être de force à.
unequaled ['ʌn'i:kwəld] *a* sans égal, inégalé.
unessential ['ʌni'senʃəl] *a* secondaire.
uneven ['ʌn'i:vən] *a* inégal, irrégulier, rugueux.
uneventful ['ʌni'ventful] *a* sans incident, terne, monotone.
unexceptionable [,ʌnik'sepʃnəbl] *a* irréprochable.
unexpected ['ʌniks'pektid] *a* inattendu, inespéré, imprévu.
unexpectedly ['ʌniks'pektidli] *ad* à l'improviste.
unexpectedness ['ʌniks'pektidnis] *n* soudaineté *f*, caractère imprévu *m.*
unexplored ['ʌniks'plɔ:d] *a* inexploré.
unfailing [ʌn'feiliŋ] *a* immanquable, impeccable, inaltérable.
unfair ['ʌn'fɛə] *a* injuste, déloyal.
unfairness ['ʌn'fɛənis] *n* injustice *f*, déloyauté *f*, mauvaise foi *f.*
unfaithful ['ʌn'feiθful] *a* infidèle; — **ness** *n* infidélité.
unfamiliar ['ʌnfə'miliə] *a* peu familier, étranger.
unfashionable ['ʌn'fæʃnəbl] *a* pas à la mode, démodé.
unfasten ['ʌn'fɑ:sn] *vt* détacher, dégrafer, déverrouiller.
unfathomable [ʌn'fæðəməbl] *a* insondable, impénétrable.
unfavorable ['ʌn'feivərəbl] *a* défavorable, impropice, desavantageux.
unfeasible ['ʌn'fi:zəbl] *a* infaisable, irréalisable.

unfeeling [ʌn'fi:liŋ] *a* insensible, froid, sec.
unfettered ['ʌn'fetəd] *a* sans entraves, libre.
unfinished ['ʌn'finiʃt] *a* inachevé.
unfit ['ʌn'fit] *a* inapte, en mauvaise santé.
unflagging [ʌn'flægiŋ] *a* sans défaillance, soutenu.
unfledged ['ʌn'fledʒd] *a* sans plumes, novice.
unflinchingly [ʌn'flintʃiŋli] *ad* sans fléchir, de pied ferme.
unfold ['ʌn'fould] *vt* déplier, dérouler, révéler; *vi* se dérouler, se déployer.
unforeseeable ['ʌnfɔ:'siəbl] *a* imprévisible.
unforeseen ['ʌnfɔ:'si:n] *a* imprévu.
unforgettable ['ʌnfə'getəbl] *a* inoubliable.
unforgivable ['ʌnfə'givəbl] *a* impardonnable.
unforgiving ['ʌnfə'giviŋ] *a* implacable.
unforgotten ['ʌnfə'gɔtn] *a* inoublié.
unfortunate [ʌn'fɔ:tʃnit] *a* malheureux.
unfortunately [ʌn'fɔ:tʃnitli] *ad* malheureusement.
unfounded ['ʌn'faundid] *a* sans fondement.
unfrequented ['ʌnfri'kwentid] *a* solitaire, écarté.
unfriendly ['ʌn'frendli] *a* inamical, hostile.
unfruitful ['ʌn'fru:tful] *a* infructueux, stérile.
unfulfilled ['ʌnful'fild] *a* irréalisé, inexaucé, inachevé.
unfurl [ʌn'fɔ:l] *vt* dérouler, déployer, déferler.
unfurnished ['ʌn'fə:niʃt] *a* non meublé.
ungainly [ʌn'geinli] *a* gauche, (*fam*) mastoc, dégingandé.
ungentlemanly [ʌn'dʒentlmənli] *a* indigne d'un galant homme, impoli.
ungovernable [ʌn'gʌvənəbl] *a* ingouvernable, irrésistible.
ungracious ['ʌn'greiʃəs] *a* sans grâce, désagréable.
ungrateful [ʌn'greitful] *a* ingrat.
ungratefulness [ʌn'greitfulnis] *n* ingratitude *f.*
ungrudgingly [ʌn'grʌdʒiŋli] *ad* sans grogner, de bon cœur, sans compter.
unguarded ['ʌn'gɑ:did] *a* sans défense, non gardé, inconsidéré.
unhallowed [ʌn'hæloud] *a* profane, impie.
unhandy [ʌn'hændi] *a* difficile à manier, incommode, gauche.
unhappiness [ʌn'hæpinis] *n* malheur *m.*
unhappy [ʌn'hæpi] *a* malheureux, infortuné.
unharmed ['ʌn'hɑ:md] *a* indemne, sain et sauf.
unharness ['ʌn'hɑ:nis] *vt* dételer.

unhealthiness [ʌn'helθinis] *n* état malsain *m*, insalubrité *f*.
unhealthy [ʌn'helθi] *a* malsain, insalubre, maladif.
unheard of [ʌn'həːdɔv] *a* inouï, inconnu.
unheeded ['ʌn'hiːdid] *a* inaperçu, négligé.
unhelpful ['ʌn'helpful] *a* peu serviable, de pauvre secours, inutile.
unhesitatingly [ʌn'heziteitiŋli] *ad* sans hésitation.
unhinge [ʌn'hindʒ] *vt* faire sortir des gonds, déranger.
unholy [ʌn'houli] *a* impie, impur, *(fam)* du diable, affreux.
unhonored [ʌn'ɔnəd] *a* sans honneur, dédaigné.
unhook ['ʌn'huk] *vt* décrocher, dégrafer.
unhoped for [ʌn'houptfɔː] *n* inespéré.
unhurt ['ʌn'həːt] *a* sans mal, indemne.
unicorn ['juːnikɔːn] *n* licorne *f*.
unification [ˌjuːnifi'keiʃən] *n* unification *f*.
uniform ['juːnifɔːm] *an* uniforme *m*.
uniformly ['juːnifɔːmli] *ad* uniformément.
unify ['juːnifai] *vt* unifier.
unilateral ['juːni'lætərəl] *a* unilatéral.
unimaginable [ˌʌni'mædʒinəbl] *a* inimaginable.
unimaginative ['ʌni'mædʒinətiv] *a* sans imagination.
unimpaired ['ʌnim'pɛəd] *a* dans toute sa force, intact.
unimpeachable [ˌʌnim'piːtʃəbl] *a* irréprochable, irrécusable.
unimportant ['ʌnim'pɔːtənt] *a* sans importance.
unimpressed ['ʌnim'prest] *a* non impressionné, froid.
unimpressive [ʌn'impresiv] *a* peu impressionnant.
uninhabitable ['ʌnin'hæbitəbl] *a* inhabitable.
uninhabited ['ʌnin'hæbitid] *a* inhabité.
unintelligent ['ʌnin'telidʒənt] *a* inintelligent.
unintentional ['ʌnin'tenʃənl] *a* sans (mauvaise) intention, involontaire.
uninteresting ['ʌn'intristiŋ] *a* sans intérêt.
uninterrupted ['ʌnˌintə'rʌptid] *a* ininterrompu.
union ['juːnjən] *n* union *f*, accord *m*, syndicat ouvrier *m*.
unionist ['juːnjənist] *n* syndiqué(e) *mf*, syndicaliste *mf*, unioniste *mf*.
Union Jack ['juːnjən'jæk] *n* pavillon britannique *m*.
unique [juː'niːk] *a* unique.
unison ['juːnizn] *n* unisson *m*.
unit ['juːnit] *n* unité *f*.
unite [juː'nait] *vt* unir, unifier; *vi* s'unir.

unity ['juːniti] *n* unité *f*, union *f*.
universal [ˌjuːni'vəːsəl] *a* universel.
universe ['juːnivəːs] *n* univers *m*.
university [ˌjuːni'vəːsiti] *n* université *f*.
unjust ['ʌn'dʒʌst] *a* injuste
unjustifiable [ʌn'dʒʌstifaiəbl] *a* injustifiable.
unkempt ['ʌn'kempt] *a* mal peigné, dépeigné, mal tenu.
unkind [ʌn'kaind] *a* peu aimable, désobligeant, dur.
unkindness [ʌn'kaindnis] *n* méchanceté *f*, désobligeance *f*.
unknowingly ['ʌn'nouiŋli] *ad* sans le savoir (vouloir).
unknown to ['ʌn'nountuː] *ad* à l'insu de.
unlamented ['ʌnlə'mentid] *a* non pleuré.
unlatch ['ʌnlætʃ] *vt* ouvrir.
unlawful ['ʌn'lɔːful] *a* illégal, illicite.
unlawfulness ['ʌn'lɔːfulnis] *n* illégalité *f*.
unlearn ['ʌn'ləːn] *vt* désapprendre, oublier.
unleash [ʌn'liːʃ] *vt* détacher, déchaîner, lâcher.
unleavened ['ʌn'levnd] *a* sans levain, azyme.
unless [ən'les] *cj* à moins que (de), si . . . ne pas.
unlike ['ʌn'laik] *a* différent; *ad* à la différence de.
unlikely [ʌn'laikli] *a* improbable.
unlimited [ʌn'limitid] *a* illimité.
unload ['ʌn'loud] *vt* décharger.
unlock ['ʌn'lɔk] *vt* ouvrir.
unlooked for [ʌn'luktfɔː] *a* inattendu, inespéré.
unlucky [ʌn'lʌki] *a* malchanceux, malheureux, maléfique.
unmanageable [ʌn'mænidʒəbl] *a* intraitable, impossible, difficile à manœuvrer.
unmanly ['ʌn'mænli] *a* peu viril, efféminé.
unmannerliness [ʌn'mænəlinis] *n* manque d'éducation *m*, impolitesse *f*.
unmannerly [ʌn'mænəli] *a* mal élevé, malappris.
unmarketable [ʌn'maːkitəbl] *a* sans marché (demande), invendable.
unmarried ['ʌn'mærid] *a* célibataire, non marié.
unmask ['ʌn'maːsk] *vt* démasquer, dévoiler.
unmentionable [ʌn'menʃnəbl] *a* innommable, dont on ne peut parler.
unmerciful [ʌn'məːsiful] *a* sans pitié, impitoyable.
unmerited ['ʌn'meritid] *a* immérité.
unmindful [ʌn'maindful] *a* oublieux, insouciant.
unmistakable ['ʌnmis'teikəbl] *a* impossible à méconnaître.
unmistakably ['ʌnmis'teikəbli] *ad* à n'en pas douter, à ne pas s'y méprendre.

unmitigated [ʌn'mitigeited] *a* pur, complet, fieffé, parfait.

unmoor ['ʌn'muə] *vt* démarrer.

unmoved ['ʌn'muːvd] *a* indifférent, impassible.

unnamed ['ʌn'neimd] *a* sans nom, innomé, anonyme.

unnatural [ʌn'nætʃrəl] *a* pas naturel, dénaturé, anormal.

unnecessary [ʌn'nesisəri] *a* pas nécessaire, inutile, gratuit.

unneighborly ['ʌn'neibəli] *a* de mauvais voisin.

unnerve ['ʌn'nəːv] *vt* énerver, faire perdre son sang-froid à.

unnoticed ['ʌn'noutist] *a* inaperçu.

unnumbered ['ʌn'nʌmbəd] *a* innombrable, non-numéroté.

unobjectionable ['ʌnəb'dʒekʃnəbl] *a* qui défie toute objection.

unobliging ['ʌnə'blaidʒiŋ] *a* désobligeant, peu obligeant.

unobservant ['ʌnəb'zəːvənt] *a* peu observateur.

unobtainable ['ʌnəb'teinəbl] *a* introuvable.

unobtrusive ['ʌnəb'truːsiv] *a* effacé, discret, pas gênant.

unoccupied ['ʌn'ɔkjupaid] *a* inoccupé.

unoffending ['ʌnə'fendiŋ] *a* qui n'a rien de blessant, innocent.

unofficial ['ʌnə'fiʃəl] *a* officieux, inofficiel.

unostentatious ['ʌn,ɔsten'teiʃəs] *a* sans ostentation, simple.

unpack ['ʌn'pæk] *vt* dépaqueter, déballer, défaire; *vi* défaire sa malle.

unpalatable [ʌn'pælətəbl] *a* dur à avaler, amer, désagréable.

unparalleled [ʌn'pærəleld] *a* incomparable, sans précédent.

unpardonable [ʌn'pɑːdnəbl] *a* impardonnable.

unperceived ['ʌnpə'siːvd] *a* inaperçu.

unperturbed ['ʌnpə'təːbd] *a* imperturbable, peu ému, impassible.

unpleasant [ʌn'pleznt] *a* déplaisant, désagréable.

unpleasantness [ʌn'plezntnis] *n* désagrément *m*, ennui *m*.

unpolished ['ʌn'pɔliʃt] *a* terne, brut, mat, fruste, grossier.

unpopular ['ʌn'pɔpjulə] *a* impopulaire.

unpopularity ['ʌn,pɔpju'læriti] *n* impopularité *f*.

unpractical ['ʌn'præktikəl] *a* peu pratique, chimérique.

npracticed [ʌn'præktist] *a* mal entraîné, novice, inexpérimenté.

unprecedented [ʌn'presidəntid] *a* sans précédent.

unpredictable ['ʌnpri'diktəbl] *a* imprévisible.

unprejudiced [ʌn'predʒudist] *a* impartial.

unpremeditated ['ʌnpri'mediteitid] *a* sans préméditation, inopiné.

unprepared ['ʌnpri'pɛəd] *a* pas préparé, inapprêté, improvisé.

unprepossessing ['ʌn,priːpə'zesiŋ] *a* peu engageant, de mauvaise mine.

unprincipled [ʌn'prinsəpld] *a* sans principes.

unproductive ['ʌnprə'dʌktiv] *a* improductif, stérile.

unprofitable [ʌn'prɔfitəbl] *a* sans profit, ingrat, peu lucratif.

unprogressive ['ʌnprə'gresiv] *a* stagnant, rétrograde.

unprompted [ʌn'prɔmptid] *a* spontané.

unpropitious ['ʌnprə'piʃəs] *a* de mauvais augure, impropice.

unprotected ['ʌnprə'tektid] *a* sans protection, exposé, inabrité.

unprovided ['ʌnprə'vaidid] *a* sans ressources, démuni.

unpublished ['ʌn'pʌbliʃt] *a* inédit, non publié.

unqualified ['ʌn'kwɔlifaid] *a* incompétent, sans titres, sans réserve, absolu, catégorique.

unquestionable [ʌn'kwestʃənəbl] *a* indiscutable.

unravel [ʌn'rævəl] *vt* démêler, affiler.

unreasonable [ʌn'riːznəbl] *a* déraisonnable, exorbitant, extravagant.

unreasonableness [ʌn'riːznəblnis] *n* déraison *f*, extravagance *f*.

unreciprocated ['ʌnri'siprəkeitid] *a* non payé de retour.

unrecognizable ['ʌn'rekəgnaizəbl] *a* méconnaissable.

unreconcilable ['ʌn'rekənsailəbl] *a* irréconciliable.

unredeemed ['ʌnri'diːmd] *a* non racheté, inaccompli, sans compensation.

unrelated ['ʌnri'leitid] *a* étranger, sans rapport.

unrelenting ['ʌnri'lentiŋ] *a* inexorable, acharné.

unreliable ['ʌnri'laiəbl] *a* peu sûr, incertain.

unremitting [,ʌnri'mitiŋ] *a* incessant, acharné; — **efforts** efforts soutenus.

unrepentant ['ʌnri'pentənt] *a* impénitent.

unreservedly [,ʌnri'zəːvidli] *ad* sans réserve.

unresponsive ['ʌnris'pɔnsiv] *a* renfermé, réservé, froid.

unrest ['ʌn'rest] *n* inquiétude *f*, agitation *f*, malaise *m*.

unrestrained ['ʌnris'treind] *a* déréglé, déchaîné, immodéré.

unrestricted ['ʌnris'triktid] *a* sans restriction, absolu.

unripe ['ʌn'raip] *a* pas mûr, vert.

unrivaled [ʌn'raivəld] *a* inégalé, sans rival.

unroll ['ʌn'roul] *vt* dérouler; *vi* se dérouler.

unruffled ['ʌn'rʌfld] *a* imperturbable, serein, calme.

unruly [ʌn'ruːli] *a* indiscipliné, turbulent, déréglé.

unsafe [ʌn'seif] *a* dangereux, hasardeux.

unsalable ['ʌn'seiləbl] *a* invendable.

unsavory ['ʌn'seivəri] *a* fade, nauséabond, repugnant, vilain.

unsay ['ʌn'sei] *vt* retirer, rétracter, se dédire de.

unscathed ['ʌn'skeiðd] *a* sans une égratignure, indemne.

unscrew ['ʌn'skruː] *vt* dévisser.

unscripted ['ʌn'skriptəd] *a* en direct.

unscrupulous [ʌn'skruːpjuləs] *a* sans scrupules, indélicat.

unseal ['ʌn'siːl] *vt* décacheter, desceller.

unseasonable [ʌn'siːznəbl] *a* hors de saison, inopportun, déplacé.

unseat ['ʌn'siːt] *vt* démonter, désarçonner, invalider, faire perdre son siège à.

unseemly [ʌn'siːmli] *ad* inconvenant.

unseen ['ʌn'siːn] *a* inaperçu, invisible.

unselfish ['ʌn'selfiʃ] *a* désintéressé, généreux.

unserviceable ['ʌn'səːvisəbl] *a* hors de service, usé, inutilisable.

unsettled ['ʌn'setld] *a* indécis, variable, impayé.

unshaken ['ʌn'ʃeikən] *a* inébranlable.

unsheathe ['ʌn'ʃiːð] *vt* dégainer.

unship ['ʌn'ʃip] *vt* décharger, débarquer.

unshrinkable ['ʌn'ʃrinkəbl] *a* irrétrécissable.

unsightly [ʌn'saitli] *a* laid, vilain.

unskilled ['ʌn'skild] *a* inexpert.

unsociable [ʌn'souʃəbl] *a* insociable, farouche.

unsoiled [ʌn'sɔild] *a* sans tache.

unsold ['ʌn'sould] *a* invendu.

unsolicited ['ʌnsə'lisitid] *a* spontané.

unsophisticated ['ʌnsə'fistikeitid] *a* naturel, nature, ingénu.

unsound ['ʌn'saund] *a* malsain, dérangé, erroné.

unsparing [ʌn'spɛəriŋ] *a* prodigue, infatigable.

unspeakable [ʌn'spiːkəbl] *a* indicible, innommable.

unspoiled ['ʌn'spɔild] *a* non gâté vierge, ᴅien élevé.

unstable ['ʌn'steibl] *a* instable.

unstamped ['ʌn'stæmpt] *a* non affranchi, non estampillé.

unsteadiness ['ʌn'stedinis] *n* instabilité *f*, indécision *f*, variabilité *f*, irrégularité *f*.

unsteady ['ʌn'stedi] *a* instable, mal assuré, irrésolu, irrégulier, chancelant, variable.

unstuck ['ʌn'stʌk] *a* **to come** — se décoller, se dégommer, (*fig*) s'effondrer.

unsuccessful ['ʌnsək'sesful] *a* malheureux, manqué, raté, vain.

unsuccessfully ['ʌnsək'sesfuli] *ad* sans succès.

unsuitable ['ʌn'sjuːtəbl] *a* inapproprié, impropre, inapte, inopportun.

unsuited ['ʌn'sjuːtid] *a* impropre (à **for**), mal fait (pour **for**).

unsullied ['ʌn'sʌlid] *a* sans tache.

unsurpassable ['ʌnsə'pɑːsəbl] *a* impossible à surpasser.

unsurpassed ['ʌnsə'pɑːst] *a* sans égal.

unsuspected ['ʌnsəs'pektid] *a* insoupçonné.

unsuspicious ['ʌnsəs'piʃəs] *a* confiant, qui ne se doute de rien.

untamable ['ʌn'teiməbl] *a* indomptable.

untaught ['ʌn'tɔːt] *a* ignorant, illettré.

untenanted ['ʌn'tenəntid] *a* vacant, inoccupé.

unthankful ['ʌn'θæŋkful] *a* ingrat.

unthankfulness ['ʌn'θæŋkfulnis] *n* ingratitude *f*.

unthinkable [ʌn'θiŋkəbl] *a* inconcevable.

unthoughtful ['ʌn'θɔːtful] *a* irréfléchi.

untidy [ʌn'taidi] *a* négligé, débraillé, en désordre, mal tenu, mal peigné.

untie ['ʌn'tai] *vt* délier, détacher, défaire.

until [ən'til] *prep* jusqu'à, avant, ne . . . que; *cj* jusqu'à ce que, avant que, ne . . . que quand.

untimely [ʌn'taimli] *a* prématuré, intempestif, mal à propos.

untiring [ʌn'taiəriŋ] *a* infatigable.

untold ['ʌn'tould] *a* tu, passé sous silence, inouï, incalculable.

untoward [ʌn'touəd] *a* fâcheux, malencontreux.

untrammeled [ʌn'træməld] *a* sans entraves, libre.

untranslatable ['ʌntræns'leitəbl] *a* intraduisible.

untried ['ʌn'traid] *a* neuf, qui n'a pas été mis à l'épreuve.

untrodden ['ʌn'trɔdn] *a* vierge, inexploré.

untrue ['ʌn'truː] *a* faux, infidèle, déloyal.

untrustworthy ['ʌn'trʌst wəːði] *a* indigne de confiance.

untruth ['ʌn'truːθ] *n* mensonge m.

untruthful ['ʌn'truːθful] *a* menteur, mensonger, faux.

unusual [ʌn'juːʒuəl] *a* insolite, rare.

unutterable [ʌn'ʌtərəbl] *a* inexprimable, parfait.

unveil [ʌn'veil] *vt* dévoiler, inaugurer.

unveiling [ʌn'veiliŋ] *n* inauguration *f*.

unwarranted ['ʌn'wɔrəntid] *a* injustifié, déplacé, gratuit.

unwary [ʌn'wɛəri] *a* imprudent.

unwavering [ʌn'weivəriŋ] *a* constant, inaltérable, résolu.

unwaveringly [ʌn'weivəriŋli] *ad* de pied ferme, résolument.

unwearying [ʌn'wiəriiŋ] *a* infatigable.

unwelcome [ʌn'welkəm] *a* mal venu, importun, désagréable.

unwell ['ʌn'wel] *a* indisposé, mal en train, souffrant.

unwholesome ['ʌn'houlsəm] *a* malsain, insalubre.

unwieldy [ʌn'wiːldi] *a* difficile à manier, encombrant.

unwilling ['ʌn'wiliŋ] *a* malgré soi, de mauvaise volonté.

unwillingly [ʌn'wiliŋli] *ad* à contre cœur.

unwind ['ʌn'waind] *vt* dérouler, dévider, débobiner.

unwise ['ʌn'waiz] *a* malavisé, imprudent.

unwittingly [ʌn'witiŋli] *ad* sans y penser, étourdiment, sans le savoir.

unwonted [ʌn'wountid] *a* rare, inaccoutumé.

unworkable ['ʌn'wəːkəbl] *a* impraticable, inexploitable.

unworthiness [ʌn'wəːðinis] *a* indignité *f*, peu de mérite *m*.

unworthy [ʌn'wəːði] *a* indigne.

unwrap ['ʌn'ræp] *vt* déballer, défaire.

unwritten ['ʌn'ritn] *a* tacite, oral, non écrit.

unyielding [ʌn'jiːldiŋ] *a* inflexible, intransigeant.

up [ʌp] *a* debout, levé, droit, fini, expiré; *ad* en dessus, plus fort, en montant, en l'air, en avance; — to jusque, jusqu'à; it is all — with him il est fichu, perdu; — there là-haut; to be — to sth. mijoter qch, être à la hauteur de qch; the —s and downs les vicissitudes *f pl*, accidents *m pl*; to walk — and down marcher de long en large.

upbraid [ʌp'breid] *vt* morigéner, faire des reproches à.

upbraiding [ʌp'breidiŋ] *n* réprimande *f*.

upbringing ['ʌp‚briŋiŋ] *n* éducation *f*.

upheaval [ʌp'hiːvəl] *n* soulèvement *m*, convulsion *f*.

uphill ['ʌp'hil] *a* ardu, montant; *ad* en montant.

uphold [ʌp'hould] *vt* soutenir.

upholder [ʌp'houldə] *n* partisan *m*, soutien *m*.

upholster [ʌp'houlstə] *vt* tapisser.

upholsterer [ʌp'houlstərə] *n* tapissier *m*.

upholstery [ʌp'houlstəri] *n* tapisserie *f*, garniture *f*, capitonnage *m*.

upkeep ['ʌpkiːp] *n* entretien *m*.

uplift ['ʌplift] *n* inspiration *f*, prêchi-prêcha *m*; [ʌp'lift] *vt* élever, exalter.

upon [ə'pɔn] *prep* sur; *see* on.

upper ['ʌpə] *n* empeigne *f*; *a* supérieur, de dessus, haut.

uppermost ['ʌpəmoust] *a* le plus haut, premier, du premier rang; *ad* en dessus.

uppish ['ʌpiʃ] *a* hautain, présomptueux.

upright ['ʌprait] *a* vertical, droit, debout, juste, honnête.

uprightness ['ʌp‚raitnis] *n* droiture *f*.

uprising [ʌp'raiziŋ] *n* soulèvement *m*, lever *m*.

uproar ['ʌp‚rɔː] *n* tumulte *m*, brouhaha *m*.

uproarious [ʌp'rɔːriəs] *a* bruyant, tapageur.

uproot [ʌp'ruːt] *vt* déraciner, extirper, arracher.

upset [ʌp'set] *n* bouleversement *m*, renversement *m*, dérangement *m*; *vt* bouleverser, renverser, déranger, indisposer.

upshot ['ʌpʃɔt] *n* conclusion *f*, issue *f*, fin mot *m*.

upside-down ['ʌpsaid'daun] *ad* sens dessus dessous, à l'envers, la tête en bas.

upstairs ['ʌp'stɛəz] *ad* en haut.

upstart ['ʌpstɑːt] *n* parvenu(e) *mf*.

up-to-date ['ʌptu'deit] *a* à la page, au courant.

upturn [ʌp'təːn] *vt* retourner, (re)lever.

upward ['ʌpwəd] *a* montant, ascendant; *ad* en montant, en-(au-)dessus; *ad* en haut, au-dessus, plus de.

urban ['əːbən] *a* urbain.

urbane [əː'bein] *a* affable, suave, courtois.

urbanity [əː'bæniti] *n* urbanité *f*.

urchin ['əːtʃin] *n* oursin *m*, gosse *mf*, gamin(e) *mf*.

urge [əːdʒ] *n* impulsion *f*, besoin *m*; *vt* presser, talonner, alléguer, pousser, recommander.

urgency ['əːdʒənsi] *n* urgence *f*.

urgent ['əːdʒənt] *a* urgent, pressant, instant.

urgently ['əːdʒəntli] *ad* instamment, avec urgence.

urn [əːn] *n* urne *f*.

us [ʌs] *pn* nous.

usable ['juːzəbl] *a* utilisable.

usage ['juːzidʒ] *n* traitement *m*, usage *m*, emploi *m*.

use [juːs] *n* usage *m*, emploi *m*; it is no — il ne sert à rien; what is the —? à quoi bon?

use [juːz] *vt* employer, se servir de, traiter, avoir l'habitude de; to — up consommer, épuiser; to get —d to s'habituer, s'accoutumer à.

useful ['juːsful] *a* utile, pratique.

usefulness ['juːsfulnis] *n* utilité *f*.

useless ['juːslis] *a* inutile.

user ['juːzə] *n* usager, -ère.

usher ['ʌʃə] *n* huissier *m*, répétiteur *m*, pion *m*; ouvreuse *f*; to — in inaugurer, annoncer, introduire, faire entrer; to — out reconduire.

usual ['juːʒuəl] *a* usuel, courant, d'usage.

usually ['juːʒuəli] *ad* d'habitude, d'ordinaire.

usufruct ['juːsjufrʌkt] *n* usufruit *m*.

usurer ['juːʒərə] *n* usurier *m*.

usurp [juːˈzəːp] vt usurper, empiéter sur.

usurpation [ˌjuːzəːˈpeiʃən] n usurpation f.

usury [ˈjuːʒuri] n usure f.

utensil [juˈtensl] n ustensile m, attirail m, outil m.

utilitarian [ˌjuːtiliˈtɛəriən] a utilitaire.

utilitarianism [ˌjuːtiliˈtɛəriənizəm] n utilitarisme m.

utility [juˈtiliti] n utilité f.

utilization [ˌjuːtilaiˈzeiʃən] n utilisation f.

utilize [ˈjuːtilaiz] vt utiliser, tirer parti de.

utmost [ˈʌtmoust] n tout le possible; a extrême, dernier, le plus grand.

utopia [juːˈtoupiə] n utopie f.

utopian [juːˈtoupiən] a utopique.

utter [ˈʌtə] a extrême, absolu, achevé; vt émettre, exprimer, dire, pousser.

utterance [ˈʌtərəns] n voix f, parole f, expression f, articulation f.

utterly [ˈʌtəli] ad absolument.

V

vacancy [ˈveikənsi] n vacance f, vide m.

vacant [ˈveikənt] a vacant, vide, absent, hébété.

vacate [vəˈkeit] vt vider, évacuer, quitter, annuler.

vacation [vəˈkeiʃən] n vacances f pl.

vaccinate [ˈvæksineit] vt vacciner.

vaccination [ˌvæksiˈneiʃən] n vaccination f.

vaccine [ˈvæksiːn] n vaccin m.

vacillate [ˈvæsileit] vi vaciller, hésiter.

vacuous [ˈvækjuəs] a vide, hébété, niais.

vacuum [ˈvækjuəm] n vide m.

vagabond [ˈvægəbɔnd] n vagabond(e) mf, chemineau m.

vagabondage [ˈvægəbɔndidʒ] n vagabondage m.

vagary [ˈveigəri] n lubie f, chimère f, fantaisie f.

vagrancy [ˈveigrənsi] n vagabondage m.

vagrant [ˈveigrənt] n vagabond(e) mf, chemineau m; a errant, vagabond.

vague [veig] a vague, estompé, indécis.

vagueness [ˈveignis] n vague m, imprécision f.

vain [vein] a vain, inutile, vaniteux.

vainglorious [veinˈglɔːriəs] a fier, glorieux.

vainglory [veinˈglɔːri] n gloriole f.

vainly [ˈveinli] ad en vain, avec vanité.

vale [veil] n val m.

valiant [ˈvæljənt] a vaillant.

valiantly [ˈvæljəntli] ad vaillamment.

valid [ˈvælid] a valide, valable, solide.

validate [ˈvælideit] vt rendre valide, ratifier.

validity [vəˈliditi] n validité f.

valley [ˈvæli] n vallée f.

valor [ˈvælə] n valeur f.

valorous [ˈvælərəs] a valeureux.

valuable [ˈvæljuəbl] a de grande valeur, de prix, précieux; n objet de prix m.

valuation [ˌvæljuˈeiʃən] n évaluation f, prix m, expertise f.

value [ˈvæljuː] n valeur f, prix m; vt évaluer, apprécier, estimer.

valve [vælv] n soupape f, valve f, valvule f, lampe f.

vamp [væmp] n femme fatale f, vamp f, empeigne f; vt flirter avec, rapiécer, (fam) retaper, improviser.

vampire [ˈvæmpaiə] n vampire m.

van [væn] n camion m, fourgon m, avant-garde f.

vane [vein] n girouette f, aile f, pale(tte) f.

vanilla [vəˈnilə] n vanille f.

vanish [ˈvæniʃ] vi disparaître, s'évanouir.

vanity [ˈvæniti] n vanité f.

vanquish [ˈvæŋkwiʃ] vt vaincre, venir à bout de.

vantage [ˈvɑːntidʒ] n avantage m.

vapid [ˈvæpid] a fade, plat.

vapor [ˈveipə] n vapeur f, buée f.

vaporization [ˌveipəraiˈzeiʃən] n vaporisation f.

vaporize [ˈveipəraiz] vt vaporiser; vi se vaporiser.

vaporizer [ˈveipəraizə] n vaporisateur m, atomiseur m.

variable [ˈvɛəriəbl] a variable, inconstant.

variance [ˈvɛəriəns] n désaccord m, discorde f.

variant [ˈvɛəriənt] n variante f.

variation [ˌvɛəriˈeiʃən] n variation f, écart m.

varicose [ˈværikous] a variqueux; — vein varice f.

varied [ˈvɛərid] a varié.

variegated [ˈvɛərigeitid] a bigarré, panaché, diapré.

variety [vəˈraiəti] n variété f, diversité f.

various [ˈvɛəriəs] a varié, divers, plusieurs.

variously [ˈvɛəriəsli] ad diversement.

varnish [ˈvɑːniʃ] n vernis m; vt vernir.

varnishing [ˈvɑːniʃiŋ] n vernissage m.

vary [ˈvɛəri] vti varier; vi différer, ne pas être d'accord.

vase [vɑːz] n vase m.

vast [vɑːst] a vaste, énorme.

vat [væt] n cuve f.

vault [vɔːlt] n voûte f, cave f,

caveau *m*, saut *m*; *vt* voûter; *vti* sauter.

vaunt [vɔːnt] *n* vantardise *f*; *vt* se vanter de.

vcal [viːll] *n* veau *m*.

veer [viəl] *vi* tourner, virer, sauter.

vegetable ['vedʒitəbl] *n* légume *m*; *a* végétal.

vegetarian [ˌvedʒi'tɛəriən] *an* végétarien, -ienne.

vegetate ['vedʒiteit] *vi* végéter.

vegetation [ˌvedʒi'teiʃən] *n* végétation *f*.

vehemence ['viːiməns] *n* véhémence *f*.

vehement ['viːimənt] *a* véhément.

vehicle ['viːikl] *n* véhicule *m*, voiture *f*.

veil [veil] *n* voile *m*, voilette *f*; *vt* voiler, masquer.

vein [vein] *n* veine *f*, humeur *f*.

veined [veind] *a* veiné.

vellum ['veləm] *n* vélin *m*.

velocity [vi'lɔsiti] *n* vélocité *f*, rapidité *f*.

velvet ['velvit] *n* velours *m*; *a* de velours, velouté.

velveteen ['velvi'tiːn] *n* velours de coton *m*.

venal ['viːnl] *a* vénal.

venality [viː'næliti] *n* vénalité *f*.

vendor ['vendɔ:] *n* vendeur, -euse, marchand(e) *mf*.

veneer [və'niə] *n* placage *m*, glacis *m*, vernis *m*, mince couche *f*; *vt* plaquer.

venerable ['venərəbl] *a* vénérable.

venerate ['venəreit] *vt* vénérer.

veneration [ˌvenə'reiʃən] *n* vénération *f*.

venereal [vi'niəriəl] *a* vénérien.

venetian blind [vi'niːʃən'blaind] *n* jalousie *f*.

vengeance ['vendʒəns] *n* vengeance *f*.

vengeful ['vendʒful] *a* vindicatif.

venial ['viːniəl] *a* véniel.

venison ['venzn] *n* venaison *f*.

venom ['venəm] *n* venin *m*.

venomous ['venəməs] *a* venimeux, méchant.

vent [vent] *n* trou *m*, passage *m*, cours *m*, carrière *f*, fente *f*; *vt* décharger.

ventilate ['ventileit] *vt* aérer, produire en public.

ventilation [ˌventi'leiʃən] *n* ventilation *f*, aération *f*.

ventilator ['ventileitə] *n* ventilateur *m*, soupirail *m*.

ventriloquist [ven'triləkwist] *n* ventriloque *mf*.

venture ['ventʃə] *n* risque *m*, entreprise *f*; *vt* s'aventurer à, oser, hasarder.

venturesome ['ventʃəsəm] *a* aventureux, risqué.

veracious [və'reiʃəs] *a* véridique.

veracity [ve'ræsiti] *n* véracité *f*.

verb [vəːb] *n* verbe *m*.

verbal ['vəːbəl] *a* verbal, oral.

verbally ['vəːbəli] *ad* de vive voix.

verbatim [vəː'beitim] *ad* mot pour mot.

verbena [və(ː)'biːnə] *n* verveine *f*.

verbose [vəː'bous] *a* verbeux.

verbosity [vəː'bɔsiti] *n* verbosité *f*.

verdant ['vəːdənt] *a* verdoyant.

verdict ['vəːdikt] *n* verdict *m*, jugement *m*.

verge [vəːdʒ] *n* bord *m*, bordure *f*, point *m*, verge *f*, lisière *f*; **to — on** longer, côtoyer, friser.

verger ['vəːdʒə] *n* bedeau *m*, huissier *m*.

verifiable ['verifaiəbl] *a* vérifiable.

verification [ˌverifi'keiʃən] *n* vérification *f*, contrôle *m*.

verify ['verifai] *vt* vérifier, confirmer, justifier.

verisimilitude [ˌverisi'miiitjuːd] *n* vraisemblance *f*.

veritable ['veritəbl] *a* véritable.

vermicelli [ˌvəːmi'seli] *n* vermicelle *m*.

vermin ['vəːmin] *n* vermine *f*.

versatile ['vəːsətail] *a* aux talents variés, universel, souple, étendu.

versatility [ˌvəːsə'tiliti] *n* diversité *f*, universalité *f*, souplesse *f*.

verse [vəːs] *n* vers *m*, strophe *f*, verset *m*, poésie *f*.

versed [vəːst] *a* instruit (de **in**), rompu (à **in**), fort (en **in**), versé (en **in**).

versification [ˌvəːsifi'keiʃən] *n* versification *f*.

versify ['vəːsifai] *vti* versifier, écrire en vers.

version ['vəːʃən] *n* version *f*, interprétation *f*.

vertebra ['vəːtibrə] *n* vertèbre *f*.

vertical ['vəːtikəl] *a* vertical.

very ['veri] *a* vrai, même, seul, propre; *ad* très, fort, bien, tout.

vespers ['vespəz] *n* vêpres *f pl*.

vessel ['vesl] *n* vaisseau *m*, vase *m*, récipient *m*.

vest [vest] *n* gilet *m*, maillot *m* (de corps); *vt* investir (de **with**), conférer (à **with**).

vested ['vestid] *a* acquis.

vestibule ['vestibjuːl] *n* vestibule *m*.

vestige ['vestidʒ] *n* vestige *m*, trace *f*, ombre *f*.

vestment ['vestmənt] *n* vêtement *m*.

vestry ['vestri] *n* sacristie *f*, conseil de fabrique *m*.

veteran ['vetərən] *n* vétéran *m*.

veterinary ['vetərinəri] *an* vétérinaire *m*.

veto ['viːtou] *n* veto; *vt* mettre son veto (à, sur).

vex [veks] *vt* irriter, vexer.

vexation [vek'seiʃən] *n* dépit *m*, colère *f*, ennui *m*.

vexatious [vek'seiʃəs] *a* vexant, fâcheux, vexatoire.

vexed [vekst] *a* très discuté, vexé.

via ['vaiə] *prep* par, via.

viaduct ['vaiədʌkt] *n* viaduc *m*.

vial ['vaiəl] *n* fiole *f*.

viands ['vaiəndz] *n pl* victuailles *f pl.*
viaticum [vai'ætikəm] *n* viatique *m.*
vibrate [vai'breit] *vi* osciller, vibrer.
vibration [vai'breiʃən] *n* vibration *f.*
vicar ['vikə] *n* curé *m,* vicaire *m.*
vice [vais] *n* vice *m,* étau *m; prep* à la place de; *prefix* vice-.
vicinity [vi'siniti] *n* voisinage *m,* alentours *m pl.*
vicious ['viʃəs] *a* vicieux, pervers, méchant.
viciousness ['viʃəsnis] *n* perversité *f,* méchanceté *f.*
vicissitude [vi'sisitjuːd] *n* vicissitude *f,* péripétie *f.*
victim ['viktim] *n* victime *f.*
victimize ['viktimaiz] *vt* persécuter, tromper.
victor ['viktə] *n* vainqueur *m.*
victorious [vik'tɔːriəs] *a* victorieux.
victory ['viktəri] *n* victoire *f.*
victuals ['vitlz] *n pl* comestibles *m pl,* vivres *m pl.*
vie [vai] *vi* rivaliser, le disputer (à **with**).
view [vjuː] *n* (point *m* de) vue *f,* perspective *f,* panorama *m,* regard *m,* opinion *f; vt* voir, regarder; **with a — to** dans l'intention de; **bird's eye — vue** *f* à vol d'oiseau.
viewer ['vjuːə] *n* téléspectateur, -trice, visionneuse *f,* viseur *m,* inspecteur, -trice.
view-finder ['vjuː,faində] *n* viseur *m.*
vigil ['vidʒil] *n* veille *f,* vigile *f.*
vigilance ['vidʒiləns] *n* vigilance *f.*
vigilant ['vidʒilənt] *a* vigilant, alerte.
vigor ['vigə] *n* vigueur *m,* énergie *f.*
vigorous ['vigərəs] *a* vigoureux, solide.
vile [vail] *a* vil, infâme, abominable.
vileness ['vailnis] *n* bassesse *f.*
vilify ['vilifai] *vt* vilipender.
village ['vilidʒ] *n* village *m.*
villager ['vilidʒə] *n* villageois(e) *mf.*
villain ['vilən] *n* scélérat *m,* coquin(e) *mf.*
villainous ['vilənəs] *a* vil, infâme.
villainy ['viləni] *n* scélératesse *f,* infamie *f.*
vindicate ['vindikeit] *vt* défendre, justifier.
vindication [,vindi'keiʃən] *n* défense *f,* justification *f.*
vindicator ['vindikeitə] *n* vengeur *m,* défenseur *m.*
vindictive [vin'diktiv] *a* vindicatif.
vindictiveness [vin'diktivnis] *n* esprit vindicatif *m.*
vine [vain] *n* vigne *f.*
vinegar ['vinigə] *n* vinaigre *m.*
vineyard ['vinjəd] *n* vignoble *m.*
vintage ['vintidʒ] *n* vendange *f,* cru *m,* année *f.*
vintner ['vintnə] *n* marchand de vins *m.*
viol ['vaiəl] *n* viole *f.*
violate ['vaiəleit] *vt* violer.
violation [,vaiə'leiʃən] *n* viol *m,* violation *f,* infraction *f.*

violator ['vaiəleitə] *n* violateur, -trice, ravisseur *m.*
violence ['vaiələns] *n* violence *f.*
violent ['vaiələnt] *a* violent.
violently ['vaiələntli] *ad* violemment.
violet ['vaiələt] *n* violette *f; a* violet.
violin [,vaiə'lin] *n* violon *m.*
violinist ['vaiəlinist] *n* violoniste *mf.*
violoncello [,vaiələn'tʃelou] *n* violoncelle *m.*
viper ['vaipə] *n* vipère *f.*
virago [vi'raːgou] *n* mégère *f.*
virgin ['vəːdʒin] *n* vierge *f.*
virginal ['vəːdʒinl] *a* virginal.
virginity [vəː'dʒiniti] *n* virginité *f.*
virile ['virail] *a* viril, mâle.
virility [vi'riliti] *n* virilité *f.*
virtual ['vəːtjuəl] *a* virtuel, de fait, vrai.
virtue ['vəːtjuː] *n* vertu *f,* qualité *f.*
virtuoso [,vəːtju'ouzou] *n* virtuose *mf.*
virtuous ['vəːtjuəs] *a* vertueux.
virulence ['virjuləns] *n* virulence *f.*
virulent ['virjulənt] *a* virulent.
virus ['vaiərəs] *n* virus *m.*
visa ['viːzə] *n* visa *m.*
viscount ['vaikaunt] *n* vicomte *m.*
viscountess ['vaikauntis] *n* vicomtesse *f.*
viscous ['viskəs] *a* visqueux.
visibility [vizi'biliti] *n* visibilité *f.*
visible ['vizəbl] *a* visible.
vision ['viʒən] *n* vision *f,* vue *f.*
visionary ['viʒnəri] *an* visionnaire *mf; a* chimérique.
visit ['vizit] *n* visite *f; vt* rendre visite à, visiter.
visitation [,vizi'teiʃən] *n* tournée d'inspection *f,* épreuve *f,* calamité *f,* (*fam*) visite fâcheuse *f,* (*eccl*) visitation.
visiting ['vizitiŋ] *a* en (termes de) visite; **— card** carte de visite *f.*
visitor ['vizitə] *n* visiteur, -euse, visite *f,* voyageur, -euse, estivant, -ante.
visor ['vaizə] *n* visière *f.*
vista ['vistə] *n* perspective *f,* percée *f,* échappée *f.*
visual ['vizjuəl] *a* visuel.
visualize ['vizjuəlaiz] *vt* se représenter, envisager.
vital ['vaitl] *a* vital, mortel, capital, essentiel; **— statistics** statistiques démographiques *f pl,* (*fam*) mensurations *f pl.*
vitality [vai'tæliti] *n* vitalité *f,* vigueur *f.*
vitamin ['vitəmin] *n* vitamine *f.*
vitiate ['viʃieit] *vt* vicier, corrompre.
vituperate [vi'tjuːpəreit] *vt* injurier, vilipender.
vituperation [vi,tjuːpə'reiʃən] *n* injures *f pl.*
vivacious [vi'veiʃəs] *a* vif, vivace.
vivacity [vi'væsiti] *n* vivacité *f,* animation *f.*
viva voce ['vaivə'vousi] *an* oral *m;* *ad* de vive voix.

Vivian ['viviən] Vivianne, Vivienne f.
vivid ['vivid] a vif, éclatant.
vividness ['vividnis] n éclat m.
vivify ['vivifai] vt vivifier, animer.
vivisect [,vivi'sekt] vt disséquer à vif.
vivisection [,vivi'sekʃən] n vivisection f.
vixen ['viksn] n renarde f, mégère f.
viz [viz] ad c'est à dire.
vocable ['voukəbl] n vocable m.
vocabulary [və'kæbjuləri] n vocabulaire m.
vocal ['voukəl] a vocal.
vocation [vou'keiʃən] n vocation f, carrière f.
vocational [vou'keiʃənl] a professionnel.
vociferate [vou'sifəreit] vti vociférer.
vociferation [vou,sifə'reiʃən] n vocifération f, clameurs f pl.
vogue [voug] n vogue f.
voice [vɔis] n voix f; vt exprimer, énoncer.
voiceless ['vɔislis] a aphone, muet.
void [vɔid] n vide m; a vide, vacant, dénué, non avenu.
volatile ['vɔlətail] a volatil, vif, gai, volage.
volcanic [vɔl'kænik] a volcanique.
volcano [vɔl'keinou] n volcan m.
volley ['vɔli] n volée f, décharge f, salve f; vi tirer à toute volée; vt reprendre de volée, lâcher.
volt [voult] n volte f, volt m.
volubility [,vɔlju'biliti] n volubilité f.
voluble ['vɔljubl] a volubile, facile, coulant.
volume ['vɔljum] n volume m, tome m, livre m.
voluminous [və'ljuːminəs] a volumineux, ample.
voluntary ['vɔləntəri] an volontaire mf; a spontané.
volunteer [,vɔlən'tiə] n volontaire m, homme de bonne volonté m; vt offrir spontanément; vi s'offrir, s'engager comme volontaire.
voluptuous [və'lʌptjuəs] a voluptueux.
voluptuousness [və'lʌptjuəsnis] n volupté f, sensualité f.
vomit ['vɔmit] vti vomir, rendre.
vomiting ['vɔmitiŋ] n vomissement m.
voracious [və'reiʃəs] a vorace.
voracity [vɔ'ræsiti] n voracité f.
vortex ['vɔːteks] n tourbillon m.
vote [vout] n vote m, voix f; vti voter; vt proposer.
voter ['voutə] n votant m, électeur, -trice.
voting ['voutiŋ] n scrutin m; — **paper** bulletin de vote m.
vouch [vautʃ] vt attester, garantir; **to — for** répondre de.
voucher ['vautʃə] n garantie f, attestation f, reçu m, bon m.
vouchsafe [vautʃ'seif] vt daigner, accorder.

vow [vau] n serment m, vœu m; vt vouer, jurer.
vowel ['vauəl] n voyelle f.
voyage [vɔiidʒ] n voyage m (par eau).
vulgar ['vʌlgə] a vulgaire.
vulgarity [vʌl'gæriti] n vulgarité f.
vulgarization [,vʌlgərai'zeiʃən] n vulgarisation f.
vulgarize ['vʌlgəraiz] vt vulgariser.
vulnerability [,vʌlnərə'biliti] n vulnérabilité f.
vulnerable ['vʌlnərəbl] a vulnérable.
vulture ['vʌltʃə] n vautour m, charognard m.

W

wad [wɔd] n bourre f, liasse f, tampon m; vt (rem)bourrer, ouater.
waddle ['wɔdl] n dandinement m; vi marcher comme un canard, se dandiner.
wade [weid] vi patauger; vti passer à gué.
wadi ['wɔdi] n oued m.
wafer ['weifə] n oublie f, gaufrette f, hostie f, pain à cacheter m.
waffle ['wɔfl] n gaufre f, (fam) radotages m pl; vi parloter, radoter.
waft [wɑːft] n bouffée f, souffle m, coup d'aile m; vt glisser, porter; vi flotter.
wag [wæg] n hochement m, branlement m, mouvement m, farceur m; vt remuer, hocher, lever; vi se remuer, aller.
wage(s) ['weidʒ(iz)] n salaire m, gages m pl; — **freeze** n blocage m des salaires.
wager ['weidʒə] n pari m, gageure f; vt parier.
waggish ['wægiʃ] a facétieux, blagueur, fumiste.
waggishness ['wægiʃnis] n espièglerie f.
waggle ['wægl] vti remuer.
wagon ['wægən] n camion m, chariot m, fourgon m, wagon m, voiture f.
wagoner ['wægənə] n camionneur m, charretier m, roulier m.
wagtail ['wægteil] n bergeronnette f, hochequeue m.
waif [weif] n enfant abandonné m, épave f.
wail [weil] n lamentation f, plainte f; vi se lamenter, vagir.
wainscot ['weinskət] n boiserie f, lambris m; vt lambrisser.
waist [weist] n taille f, ceinture f.
waistband ['weistbænd] n ceinture f, ceinturon m.
waistcoat ['weiskout] n gilet m.
wait [weit] n attente f, embuscade f, battement m; pl chanteurs de Noël m pl; vti attendre; vi servir à table.
waiter ['weitə] n garçon m.
waiting-room ['weitiŋrum] n salle d'attente f.

waitress ['weitris] n serveuse f, **waitress!** mademoiselle!

waive [weiv] vt écarter, renoncer à, lever.

wake [weik] n veillée f, sillage m; vi s'éveiller; vt réveiller.

wakeful ['weikful] a éveillé, vigilant.

wakefulness ['weikfulnis] n insomnie f, vigilance f.

waken ['weikən] vi s'éveiller, se réveiller; vt (r)éveiller.

Wales [weilz] n pays de Galles m.

walk [wɔːk] n (dé)marche f, promenade f, allée f, promenoir m; vi se promener, marcher, aller à pied; vt promener, faire à pied, faire marcher; **to — in** entrer; **to — off** vi s'en aller; vt emmener.

walker ['wɔːkə] n marcheur, -euse, piéton m, promeneur, -euse.

walking ['wɔːkiŋ] a ambulant; n marche f; **— stick** canne f.

walk-out ['wɔːk'aut] n grève f (spontanée).

walk-over ['wɔːk'ouvə] n victoire f par forfait, jeu d'enfant m.

wall [wɔːl] n mur m, muraille f, paroi f.

wallet ['wɔlit] n porte-feuille m, besace f, sacoche f.

wallflower ['wɔːl,flauə] n giroflée f; **to be a —** faire tapisserie.

wallop ['wɔləp] n coup vigoureux m; vt rosser, fesser.

walloping ['wɔləpiŋ] n rossée f, fessée f, raclée f.

wallow ['wɔlou] vi rouler, se vautrer, se baigner.

wallpaper ['wɔːl,peipə] n papier peint m, tenture f.

walnut ['wɔːlnət] n noix f; **— tree** noyer m.

walrus ['wɔːlrəs] n morse m.

waltz [wɔːls] n valse f; vi valser.

wan [wɔn] a blafard, pâle.

wand [wɔnd] n baguette f, bâton m.

wander ['wɔndə] vi errer, se perdre, divaguer; vt (par)courir.

wanderer ['wɔndərə] n voyageur, -euse, promeneur, -euse.

wandering ['wɔndəriŋ] a errant, vagabond, distrait, égaré; n vagabondage m; pl divagations f pl.

wane [wein] n déclin m; vi décliner, décroître.

wanness ['wɔnnis] n pâleur f, lividité f.

want [wɔnt] n manque m, défaut m, gêne f, besoin m; **for — of** faute de; vt manquer de, avoir besoin de, demander, réclamer.

wanted ['wɔntid] a on demande, recherché (par la police).

wanton ['wɔntən] n gourgandine f, femme impudique f; a joueur, capricieux, impudique, débauché, gratuit.

war [wɔː] n guerre f.

warble ['wɔːbl] n gazouillement m; vi gazouiller.

warbler ['wɔːblə] n fauvette f.

ward [wɔːd] n garde f, tutelle f, pupille mf, arrondissement m, division f, cellule f, salle f (d'hôpital); vt garder; **to — off** écarter, parer.

warden ['wɔːdn] n directeur m (d'une institution, d'une prison) f recteur m; gardien m, conservateur m; **game —** garde-chasse m.

warder ['wɔːdə] n gardien m.

wardrobe ['wɔːdroub] n armoire f, garde-robe f.

wardroom ['wɔːdrum] n carré des officiers m.

ware [wɛə] n vaisselle f; pl marchandises f pl.

warehouse ['wɛəhaus] n entrepôt m, magasin m; vt entreposer, emmagasiner.

warfare ['wɔːfɛə] n guerre f.

wariness ['wɛərinis] n prudence , méfiance f.

warlike ['wɔːlaik] a belliqueux.

warm [wɔːm] a chaud, chaleureux, pimenté, vif, échauffé, au chaud; vt (ré)chauffer; vi se (ré)chauffer, s'animer, s'échauffer.

warming ['wɔːmiŋ] n chauffage m.

warming-pan ['wɔːmiŋpæn] n bassinoire f.

warmth [wɔːmθ] n chaleur f, ardeur f.

warn [wɔːn] vt avertir, mettre en garde, prévenir.

warning ['wɔːniŋ] n avertissement m, congé m.

warp [wɔːp] n chaîne f, corde f, (wood) jeu m, gauchissement m, dépôt m; vt ourdir, remorquer, jouer, gauchir, fausser; vi gauchir, se voiler, se déformer.

warrant ['wɔrənt] n autorité f, garantie f, bon m, brevet m, mandat m (d'amener), pouvoir m; vt autoriser, garantir, justifier.

warrantable ['wɔrəntəbl] a justifiable.

warrantor ['wɔrəntɔː] n garant m, répondant m.

warren ['wɔrin] n garenne f.

warrior ['wɔriə] n guerrier m, soldat m; a martial, guerrier.

wart [wɔːt] n verrue f.

wart-hog ['wɔːt'hɔg] n phacochère m.

wary ['wɛəri] a prudent, méfiant, avisé.

wash [wɔʃ] n lavage m, lessive f, lavasse f, lotion f, remous m, sillage m, couche f, lavis m; vt laver, blanchir, badigeonner; vi se laver; **to — away** emporter; **to — down** arroser, laver à grande eau; **to — out** rincer, passer l'éponge sur, supprimer; **to — up** faire la vaisselle.

washable ['wɔʃəbl] a lavable.

wash-basin ['wɔʃ,beisn] n cuvette f.

washed-out ['wɔʃt'aut] a (fam) lessivé; délavé, (fam) flapi.

washer ['wɔʃə] n laveur, -euse, rondelle f; **—up** plongeur m.

washerwoman ['wɔʃə,wumən] *n* blanchisseuse *f*, lavandière *f*.

wash-house ['wɔʃhaus] *n* buanderie *f*, lavoir *m*.

washing ['wɔʃiŋ] *n* lavage *m*, linge *m*, vaisselle *f*, lessive *f*, blanchissage *m*.

wash-out ['wɔʃaut] *n* fiasco *m*, four *m*, débâcle *f*, raté(e).

washstand ['wɔʃstænd] *n* lavabo *m*.

washy ['wɔʃi] *a* insipide, fade.

wasp [wɔsp] *n* guêpe *f*; —'s **nest** guêpier *m*; **mason** — guêpe maçonne *f*.

waspish ['wɔspiʃ] *a* venimeux, méchant, de guêpe.

waste [weist] *n* désert *m*, usure *f*, déchets *m pl*, gaspillage *m*, perte *f*; *a* inculte, désert, de rebut; *v.* gaspiller, épuiser, perdre, rater, gâcher; *vi* s'user, se perdre, s'épuiser.

wasteful ['weistful] *a* ruineux, prodigue, gaspilleur.

waste-paper basket [weist'peipə,baːskit] *n* corbeille à papier *f*.

waster ['weistə] *n* vaurien *m*, gaspilleur, -euse.

watch [wɔtʃ] *n* garde *f*, guet *m*, quart *m*, montre *f*; *vt* (sur)veiller, observer, regarder, guetter; *vi* prendre garde, veiller, faire attention.

watchdog ['wɔtʃdɔg] *n* chien *m* de garde; — **committee** comité *f* de surveillance.

watchful ['wɔtʃful] *a* attentif, vigilant.

watchfulness ['wɔtʃfulnis] *n* vigilance *f*.

watchmaker ['wɔtʃ,meikə] *n* horloger *m*.

watchman ['wɔtʃmən] *n* veilleur de nuit *m*, guetteur *m*.

watchword ['wɔtʃwəːd] *n* mot d'ordre *m*.

water ['wɔːtə] *n* eau *f*; *vt* arroser, abreuver; *vi* faire de l'eau, (*eyes*) se mouiller; **to — down** affaiblir, diluer, atténuer, frelater.

water bottle ['wɔːtə,bɔtl] *n* bidon *m*, gourde *f*; **hot—** bouillotte *f*.

water-closet ['wɔːtə,klɔzit] *n* cabinets *m pl*.

water-color ['wɔːtə,kʌlə] *n* aquarelle *f*.

watercress ['wɔːtəkres] *n* cresson *m*.

waterfall ['wɔːtəfɔːl] *n* cascade *f*.

watering ['wɔːtəriŋ] *n* arrosage *m*, dilution *f*.

watering-can ['wɔːtəriŋkæn] *n* arrosoir *m*.

watering-place ['wɔːtəriŋpleis] *n* abreuvoir *m*, ville d'eau *f*, plage *f*.

water-lily ['wɔːtə,lili] *n* nénuphar *m*.

waterline ['wɔːtəlain] *n* ligne de flottaison *f*.

waterlogged ['wɔːtəlɔgd] *a* plein d'eau, détrempé.

watermark ['wɔːtəmaːk] *n* filigrane *m*.

water-melon ['wɔːtə'melən] *n* pastèque *f*.

water-pipe ['wɔːtəpaip] *n* conduite *f* d'eau.

water-power ['wɔːtə,pauə] *n* force hydraulique *f*.

waterproof ['wɔːtəpruːf] *an* imperméable *m*.

watershed ['wɔːtəʃed] *n* ligne de partage des eaux *f*.

waterskiing ['wɔːtə'skiːiŋ] *n* ski nautique *m*.

waterspout ['wɔːtəspaut] *n* trombe *f*.

watertight ['wɔːtətait] *a* étanche.

waterway ['wɔːtəwei] *n* voie navigable *f*.

waterworks ['wɔːtəwəːks] *n pl* canalisations *f pl*, usine hydraulique *f*.

watery ['wɔːtəri] *a* aqueux, humide, dilué, déteint, chargé de pluie, insipide.

wattle ['wɔtl] *n* claie *f*, fanon *m*, barbe *f*.

wave [weiv] *n* vague *f*, ondulation *f*, (*radio*) onde *f*, signe *m*; *vt* brandir, agiter; *vti* onduler, ondoyer; *vi* s'agiter, flotter, faire signe (de la main).

wavelength ['weivleŋθ] *n* longueur *f* d'onde.

waver ['weivə] *vi* hésiter, défaillir, fléchir, vaciller, trembler.

wavy ['weivi] *a* ondulé, onduleux, tremblé.

wax [wæks] *n* cire *f*, (*cobbler's*) poix *f*; *vt* cirer, encaustiquer; *vi* croître, devenir.

waxwork ['wækswəːk] *n* figure de cire *f*, modelage en cire *m*; *pl* musée des figures de cire *m*.

waxy ['wæksi] *a* de cire, cireux, plastique.

way [wei] *n* chemin *m*, voie *f*, distance *f*, côté *m*, sens *m*, habitude *f*, manière *f*, point de vue *m*, état *m*; **by the —** à propos; **by — of** par manière de, en guise de; **this —** par ici; **under —** en train; **out of the —** insolite, écarté.

wayfarer ['wei,feərə] *n* voyageur, -euse.

waylay [wei'lei] *vt* dresser un guet-apens à.

way-out ['wei'aut] *n* sortie *f*, échappatoire *f*.

wayside ['weisaid] *n* bord *m* de route, bas côté *m*; *a* du bord de la route.

way train ['wei,trein] *n* train *m* omnibus.

wayward ['weiwəd] *a* entêté, capricieux.

waywardness ['weiwədnis] *n* humeur fantasque *f*.

we [wiː] *pn* nous.

weak [wiːk] *a* faible, chétif, léger, doux.

weaken ['wiːkən] *vt* affaiblir; *vi* s'affaiblir, fléchir.

weakish ['wiːkiʃ] *a* faiblard.

weakness ['wiːknis] *n* faiblesse *f*, faible *m*.
weal [wiːl] *n* bien *m*, zébrure *f*.
wealth [welθ] *n* richesse(s) *f* (*pl*), profusion *f*.
wealthy ['welθi] *a* riche.
wean [wiːn] *vt* sevrer, guérir.
weaning ['wiːniŋ] *n* sevrage *m*.
weapon ['wepən] *n* arme *f*.
wear [wɛə] *n* usage *m*, usure *f*; *vt* porter, mettre, user; *vi* s'user, tirer.
weariness ['wiərinis] *n* fatigue *f*, lassitude *f*.
wearisome ['wiərisəm] *a* ennuyeux, fastidieux.
weary ['wiəri] *a* fatigué, assommant; *vt* ennuyer, fatiguer; *vi* s'ennuyer, languir.
weasel ['wiːzl] *n* belette *f*.
weather ['weðə] *n* temps *m*; *vt* exposer aux intempéries, échapper à, survivre à, (*cape*) doubler.
weather-beaten ['weðəˌbiːtn] *a* battu par la tempête, hâlé.
weather-bound ['weðəbaund] *a* retenu par le mauvais temps.
weathercock ['weðəkɔk] *n* girouette *f*.
weathered ['weðəd] *a* décoloré, rongé, patiné.
weather forecast ['weðə'fɔːkɑːst] *n* bulletin météorologique *m*.
weather station ['weðə'steiʃən] *n* station météorologique *f*.
weave [wiːv] *vt* tisser, tramer.
weaver ['wiːvə] *n* tisserand *m*.
weaving ['wiːviŋ] *n* tissage *m*.
web [web] *n* tissu *m*, toile *f*.
webbing ['webiŋ] *n* sangles *f* *pl*, ceinture *f*.
web-footed ['web.futid] *a* palmé.
wed [wed] *vt* marier, se marier avec, épouser.
wedded ['wedid] *a* conjugal, marié.
wedding ['wediŋ] *n* mariage *m*, noce(s) *f* (*pl*).
wedding breakfast ['wediŋ'brekfəst] *n* repas de noces *m*.
wedge [wedʒ] *n* coin *m*, cale *f*, part *f*; *vt* coincer, presser, caler.
wedlock ['wedlɔk] *n* (état *m* de) mariage *m*, vie conjugale *f*.
Wednesday ['wenzdi] *n* mercredi *m*.
wee [wiː] *a* tout petit; *vi* faire pipi.
weed [wiːd] *n* mauvaise herbe *f*, tabac *m*; *vt* sarcler; **to — out** trier, éliminer.
weeds [wiːdz] *n* *pl* deuil de veuve *m*.
week [wiːk] *n* semaine *f*; **today —** d'aujourd'hui en huit.
weekday ['wiːkdei] *n* jour *m* de semaine.
weekend ['wiːk'end] *n* weekend *m*.
weekly ['wiːkli] *a* hebdomadaire; *ad* tous les huit jours.
weep [wiːp] *vi* pleurer, suinter.
weeping willow ['wiːpiŋ'wilou] *n* saule pleureur *m*.
weft [weft] *n* trame *f*.
weigh [wei] *vti* peser; *vt* (*anchor*)

lever, calculer; **to — down** courber, accabler.
weight [weit] *n* poids *m*, pesanteur *f*, gravité *f*.
weighty ['weiti] *a* pesant, de poids, puissant.
weir [wiə] *n* barrage *m*.
weird [wiəd] *a* fantastique, bizarre, mystérieux.
welcome ['welkəm] *n* bienvenue *f*, accueil *m*; *a* bienvenu, acceptable; *vt* (bien) accueillir, souhaiter la bienvenue à.
weld [weld] *vt* souder, unir.
welding ['weldiŋ] *n* soudure *f*, soudage *m*.
welfare ['welfɛə] *n* bien-être *m*, bonheur *m*.
well [wel] *n* puits *m*, source *f*, fontaine *f*, cage d'escalier *f*, godet *m*; *vi* jaillir, sourdre; *a* bien portant; *ad* bien; **— enough** pas mal; **all very — bel** et bien; *excl* eh bien!
wellbeing ['wel'biːiŋ] *n* bien-être *m*.
well-bred ['wel'bred] *a* bien élevé, (*horse*) racé.
well-built ['wel'bilt] *a* bien bâti.
well-done ['wel'dʌn] *a* bien fait, (*cook*) bien cuit; *excl* bravo!
well-meaning ['wel'miːniŋ] *a* bien intentionné.
well-off ['wel'ɔf] *a* cossu, à l'aise.
Welsh [welʃ] *an* gallois *m*.
Welshman ['welʃmən] *n* Gallois(e) *mf*.
welter ['weltə] *n* confusion *f*, fatras *m*; *vi* baigner, se vautrer.
wen [wen] *n* loupe *f*, goître *m*.
wench [wentʃ] *n* fille *f*, gaillarde *f*.
went [went] *pt of* **go**.
wept [wept] *pt pp of* **weep**.
west [west] *n* ouest *m*, occident *m*; *a* à (de, vers) l'ouest, ouest, occidental.
western ['westən] *a see* **west**.
westward ['westwəd] *ad* vers l'ouest.
wet [wet] *n* humidité *f*, pluie *f*; *a* humide, mouillé, trempé; **— blanket** rabat-joie *m*; *vt* mouiller, humecter.
wet-nurse ['wetnəːs] *n* nourrice *f*.
wetting ['wetiŋ] *n* douche *f*; **to get a — se faire tremper.
whack [wæk] *n* coup de bâton *m*, essai *m*, part *f*; *vt* bâtonner, rosser, écraser; *excl* vlan!
whacking ['wækiŋ] *n* rossée *f*, raclée *f*.
whale [weil] *n* baleine *f*.
whaleboat ['weilbout] *n* baleinière *f*.
whalebone ['weilboun] *n* fanon *m*, baleine *f*.
wharf [wɔːf] *n* quai *m*.
what [wɔt] *rel pn* ce qui, ce que, ce dont; *inter pn* qu'est-ce qui?, qu'est ce que?, que?, quoi?, combien?; *a inter excl* quel(s)?, quelle(s); *excl* quoi! comment!
what(so)ever [ˌwɔt(sou)'evə] *pn* tout ce qui, tout ce que, quoi qui, quoi,

que, n'importe quoi; *a* quel que, quelque ... qui (que), quelconque.
wheat [wi:t] *n* blé *m*, froment *m*.
wheatear ['wi:tiər] *n* traquet *m*.
wheedle ['wi:dl] *vt* cajoler, engager; **to — out of** soutirer par cajolerie.
wheedler ['wi:dlə] *n* enjôleur, -euse.
wheel [wi:l] *n* roue *f*, tour *m*, cercle *m*, vélo *m*; *vt* rouler, tourner; *vi* tournoyer; **to — around** se retourner, faire volte-face, demi-tour.
wheelbarrow ['wi:l‚bærou] *n* brouette *f*.
wheelwright ['wi:lrait] *n* charron *m*.
wheeze [wi:z] *n* respiration asthmatique *f*; *vi* respirer péniblement.
wheezing ['wi:ziŋ] *n* sifflement *m*, râle *m*.
wheezy ['wi:zi] *a* asthmatique, poussif.
whelp [welp] *n* jeune chien *etc*, petit *m*, drôle *m*; *vi* mettre bas.
when [wen] *cj* quand, lorsque, où, que; *inter ad* quand?
whence [wens] *ad* d'où.
whenever [wen'evə] *cj* toutes les fois que.
where [wεə] *ad* où, là où, (à) l'endroit où.
whereabouts ['wεərəbauts] *ad* où (donc); *n* lieu *m* où on est; **his —** où il est.
whereas [wεər'æz] *cj* vu que, tandis que, alors que.
whereby [wεə'bai] *ad* par quoi? par lequel.
wherefore ['wεəfɔ:] *ad* en raison de quoi, donc, pourquoi.
wherein [wεər'in] *ad* en quoi, où.
whereupon [‚wεərə'pɔn] *ad* sur quoi.
wherever [wεər'evə] *ad* partout où, où que.
wherewithal ['wεəwi'ðɔ:l] *n* moyen(s) de quoi *m* (*pl*).
whet [wet] *vt* aiguiser, repasser, affiler, exciter.
whether ['weðə] *cj* si; **— ... or** soit (que) ... soit (que).
whetstone ['wetstoun] *n* pierre à aiguiser *f*.
whey [wei] *n* petit lait *m*.
which [witʃ] *a* quel(s), quelle(s); *rel pn* qui, que, lequel, laquelle, lesquels, lesquelles, ce qui, ce que, ce dont; *inter pn* lequel *etc*.
whichever [witʃ'evə] *rel pn* celui qui, celui que, n'importe lequel; *a* que que, quelque ... que, n'importe quel.
whiff [wif] *n* bouffée *f*.
while [wail] *n* temps *m*, instant *m*; *cj* pendant que, tandis que, tout en; **once in a —** à l'occasion; **to — away** passer, tuer, tromper.
whim [wim] *n* caprice *m*, toquade *f*, fantaisie *f*.
whimper ['wimpə] *n* geignement *m*, pleurnichement *m*; *vi* geindre, pleurnicher.

whimsical ['wimzikəl] *a* fantasque, bizarre.
whimsicality [‚wimzi'kæliti] *n* bizarrerie *f*, humeur *f* fantasque.
whine [wain] *n* gémissement *m*, jérémiade *f*; *vi* gémir, pleurnicher, se plaindre.
whinny ['wini] *n* hennissement *m*; *vi* hennir.
whip [wip] *n* fouet *m*, cravache *f*, cocher *m*, piqueur *m*, chef de file *m*, convocation urgente *f*; *vti* fouetter; *vt* battre; **to — off** enlever vivement; **to — around** se retourner brusquement, faire un tête à queue; **to — up** fouetter, activer.
whipcord ['wipkɔ:d] *n* corde *f*.
whiphand ['wip'hænd] *n* haute main *f*, avantage *m*.
whiplash ['wip:læʃ] *n* mèche de fouet *f*.
whipping ['wipiŋ] *n* fouettée *f*; **to give a — to** donner le fouet à.
whir(r) [wə:] *n* bourdonnement *m*, battement d'ailes *m*, ronronnement *m*, ronflement *m*; *vi* bourdonner, ronfler, ronronner.
whirl [wə:l] *n* tourbillon *m*, tournoiement *m*; **to be in a —** avoir la tête à l'envers; *vi* tournoyer, tourbillonner, pirouetter, tourner, virevolter.
whirlpool ['wə:lpu:l] *n* tourbillon *m*, remous *m*.
whirlwind ['wə:lwind] *n* trombe *f*, tourbillon *m*.
whisk [wisk] *n* fouet *m* (à crème), frétillement *m*; plumeau *m*, époussette *f*; *vt* fouetter, battre, remuer; **to — away** enlever vivement, escamoter, chasser.
whisker(s) ['wiskə(z)] *n* (*of cat*) moustache(s) *f* (*pl*), favoris *m pl*.
whisper ['wispə] *n* murmure *m*, chuchotement *m*, bruissement *m*; *vti* murmurer, chuchoter.
whistle ['wisl] *n* sifflet *m*, sifflement *m*; *vt* siffler; **to — for** siffler.
whistler ['wislə] *n* siffleur, -euse.
white [wait] *a* blanc, à blanc; *n* blanc *m*; **— heat** incandescence *f*; **— caps** moutons *m pl*; **— hot** chauffé à blanc; **— lead** céruse *f*; **— paper** rapport ministériel *m*; **— slavery** traite des blanches *f*.
whiten ['waitn] *vt* blanchir; *vi* pâlir.
whiteness ['waitnis] *n* blancheur *f*, pâleur *f*.
whitening ['waitniŋ] *n* blanchiment *m*, blanchissement *m*.
whitewash ['waitwɔʃ] *n* lait de chaux *m*, badigeon *m*, poudre aux yeux *f*; *vt* blanchir, badigeonner en blanc.
whither ['wiðə] *ad* où, là où.
whiting ['waitiŋ] *n* merlan *m*.
whitish ['waitiʃ] *a* blanchâtre.
whitlow ['witlou] *n* panaris *m*, mal blanc *m*.
Whitsun ['witsn] *n* Pentecôte *f*.
whittle ['witl] *vt* (dé)couper, amenui-

ser, amincir, diminuer, rogner.
whizz [wiz] *n* sifflement *m*; *vi* siffler;
to — along filer à toute vitesse.
who [hu:] *rel pn* qui, lequel *etc*;
inter pn qui? qui est-ce qui? quel?
who(so)ever [‚hu:(sou)'evə] *pn* quiconque, toute personne qui.
whole [houl] *n* tout *m*, ensemble *m*,
totalité *f*; **on the — en somme, à
tout prendre, dans l'ensemble; *a*
tout, entier, complet, intégral,
intact.
wholeheartedly ['houl'hɑ:tidli] *ad*
de grand (tout) cœur.
wholeheartedness ['houl'hɑ:tidnis]
n cordialité *f*, ardeur *f*, ferveur *f*.
wholesale ['houlseil] *n* vente en
gros *f*; *a* général, en masse; *ad* en
gros.
wholesome ['houlsəm] *a* salubre,
sain, salutaire.
wholesomeness ['houlsəmnis] *n*
santé *f*, salubrité *f*.
wholly ['houlli] *ad* sans réserve,
intégralement, entièrement, tout à
fait.
whom [hu:m] *rel pn* que, lequel *etc*;
inter pn qui? qui est-ce que?
whoop [hu:p] *vi* huer.
whooping-cough ['hu:piŋkɔf] *n*
coqueluche *f*.
whore [hɔ:] *n* prostituée *f*.
whose [hu:z] *rel pn* dont, de qui,
duquel *etc*; *poss pn* à qui? de qui?
why [wai] *nm ad* pourquoi; *excl*
allons! mais! tiens! voyons!
wick [wik] *n* mèche *f*.
wicked ['wikid] *a* méchant, vicieux,
pervers, inique.
wickedly ['wikidli] *ad* méchamment.
wickedness ['wikidnis] *n* méchanceté
f.
wicker ['wikə] *n* osier *m*.
wicket ['wikit] *n* guichet *m*, tourniquet *m*, barrière *f*, portillon *m*.
wide [waid] *a* large, vaste, (tout)
grand; **— of** *prep* loin de, au large de.
wide awake ['waidə'weik] *a* bien
éveillé, (*fam*) déluré.
widely ['waidli] *ad* grandement, très,
largement.
widen ['waidn] *vt* élargir, étendre;
vi s'élargir.
widening ['waidniŋ] *n* élargissement
m, extension *f*.
widespread ['waidspred] *a* très
répandu.
widow ['widou] *n* veuve *f*.
widowed ['widoud] *a* (devenu(e))
veuf, veuve.
widower ['widouə] *n* veuf *m*.
width [widθ] *n* largeur *f*.
wield [wi:ld] *vt* (dé)manier, tenir,
exercer.
wife [waif] *n* femme *f*, épouse *f*.
wig [wig] *n* perruque *f*.
wild [waild] *a* sauvage, fou, égaré,
violent, farouche, déréglé.
wilderness ['wildənis] *n* déser. *m*,
pays inculte *m*.

wildfire ['waild‚faiə] *n* feu grégeois
m, (*fig*) poudre *f*; **like — comme une
traînée de poudre.
wildly ['waildli] *ad* sauvagement, à
l'aveugle, d'une façon extravagante.
wilds [waildz] *n pl* désert *m*, solitude
f, brousse *f*, bled *m*, pays sauvage *m*.
wile [wail] *n* astuce *f*, ruse *f*.
will [wil] *n* volonté *f*, vouloir *m*, (*free*)
arbitre *m*, testament *m*; *vt* vouloir,
ordonner, léguer.
willful ['wilful] *a* volontaire, obstiné,
prémédité.
willfulness ['wilfulnis] *n* opiniâtreté
f, obstination *f*.
William ['wiljəm] Guillaume *m*.
willing ['wiliŋ] *a* tout disposé, de
bonne volonté.
willingly ['wiliŋli] *ad* volontiers.
willingness ['wiliŋnis] *n* empressement *m*, bonne volonté *f*.
will-o'-the-wisp ['wiləðə'wisp] *n* feu
follet *m*, chimère *f*.
willow ['wilou] *n* saule *m*.
willy-nilly ['wili'nili] *ad* bon gré mal
gré.
wilt [wilt] *vi* dépérir, se flétrir, se
dégonfler.
wily ['waili] *a* retors, rusé.
win [win] *vt* gagner, remporter,
vaincre; **to — over** gagner.
wince [wins] *n* haut-le-corps *m*,
tressaillement *m*; *vi* tressaillir,
broncher.
winch [wintʃ] *n* treuil *m*, manivelle *f*.
wind [wind] *n* vent *m*, instruments à
vent *m pl*, souffle *m*, haleine *f*; **to
have the — up** avoir la trouille; *vt*
essouffler.
wind [waind] *vt* enrouler, remonter,
sonner; *vi* serpenter, tourner, s'enrouler; **to — up** remonter, liquider,
régler.
windbag ['windbæg] *n* moulin à
paroles *m*.
winded ['windid] *a* essoufflé, hors
d'haleine.
windfall ['windfɔ:l] *n* aubaine *f*,
fruit tombé *m*.
winding ['waindiŋ] *a* sinueux, tortueux, tournant; *n* enroulement *m*,
cours sinueux *m*; *pl* méandres *m pl*,
sinuosités *f pl*, lacets *m pl*.
winding-sheet ['waindiŋʃi:t] *n* linceul *m*.
winding-up ['waindiŋ'ʌp] *n* conclusion *f*, liquidation *f*, remontage *m*.
windlass ['windləs] *n* cabestan *m*,
treuil *m*.
windmill ['winmil] *n* moulin à vent
m.
window ['windou] *n* fenêtre *f*,
croisée *f*, (*shop*) vitrine *f*; **stained-
glass — verrière *f*.
window-dressing ['windou‚dresiŋ] *n*
art de l'étalage *m*, trompe-l'œil *m*.
window fastening ['windou'fɑ:sniŋ]
n espagnolette *f*.
window frame ['windou'freim] *n*
châssis *m* de fenêtre.

window pane ['windoupein] *n* carreau *m*, vitre *f*, glace *f*.
window-shopping ['windou'ʃɔpiŋ] *n* lèche-vitrine *m*.
windscreen ['windskri:n] *n* paravent *m*, pare-brise *m*.
windshield ['windʃi:ld] *n* parebrise *m*; — **wiper** *n* essuie-glace *m*.
windswept ['windswept] *a* (*hair style*) en coup de vent, (*place*) venteux.
windy ['windi] *a* venteux, balayé par le vent, agité, creux, verbeux, vide, qui a la frousse.
wine [wain] *n* vin *m*.
wine-merchant ['wain'mə:tʃənt] *n* négociant en vins *m*.
wine-press ['wainpres] *n* pressoir *m*.
wing [wiŋ] *n* aile *f*, essor *m*, vol *m*; *vt* donner des ailes à, empenner, blesser à l'aile.
winged [wiŋd] *a* ailé.
winger ['wiŋə] *n* ailier *m*.
wink [wiŋk] *n* clin d'œil *m*; *vi* cligner, clignoter, faire de l'œil (à **at**); **to** — **at** fermer les yeux sur.
winker ['wiŋkə] *n* (*aut*) clignotant *m*.
winner ['winə] *n* gagnant(e) *mf*, vainqueur *m*, grand succès *m*.
winning ['winiŋ] *a* gagnant, engageant, décisif; —**post** *n* poteau d'arrivée *m*.
winnow ['winou] *vt* vanner, trier.
winnower ['winouə] *n* vanneur, -euse, (*machine*) vanneuse *f*.
winsome ['winsəm] *a* charmant, séduisant.
winter ['wintə] *n* hiver *m*; *vi* passer l'hiver, hiverner.
wintry ['wintri] *a* d'hiver, hivernal, glacial.
wipe [waip] *n* coup de balai *m*, de torchon, d'éponge; *vt* balayer, essuyer; **to** — **out** effacer, liquider, anéantir.
wire ['waiə] *n* fil de fer *m*, dépêche *f*, télégramme *m*; *vt* grill(ag)er, rattacher avec du fil de fer; *vti* télégraphier.
wire-cutter ['waiə,kʌtə] *n* cisailles *f pl*.
wire-haired ['waiəhεəd] *a* à poil rêche.
wireless ['waiəlis] *n* radio *f*, télégraphie sans fil *f*; *vt* envoyer par la radio; *vi* envoyer un sans-fil; *a* sans-fil.
wire-netting ['waiə'netiŋ] *n* treillis (métallique) *m*.
wire-puller ['waiə,pulə] *n* combinard *m*, intrigant(e) *mf*.
wire-pulling ['waiə,puliŋ] *n* manipulation *f*, intrigues *f pl*, manigances *f pl*.
wiry ['waiəri] *a* tout nerfs, sec, nerveux, en fil de fer.
wisdom ['wizdəm] *n* sagesse *f*, prudence *f*.
wise [waiz] *n* manière *f*; *a* sage,

savant, prudent, informé, averti.
wiseacre ['waiz,eikə] *n* gros bêta *m*, faux sage *m*.
wisecrack ['waizkræk] *n* bon mot *m*; *vi* faire de l'esprit.
wish [wiʃ] *n* souhait *m*, désir *m*, vœu *m*; *vt* souhaiter, désirer, vouloir.
wishful ['wiʃful] *a* désireux, d'envie; — **thinking** optimisme béat *m*.
wisp [wisp] *n* bouchon *m* (de paille), petit bout *m*, mèche folle *f*, traînée *f* (de fumée).
wistful ['wistful] *a* pensif, plein de regret, insatisfait, d'envie.
wistfully ['wistfuli] *ad* d'un air pensif, avec envie.
wit [wit] *n* esprit *m*, homme d'esprit *m* (de ressource); **to** — à savoir.
witch [witʃ] *n* sorcière *f*, ensorceleuse *f*; *vt* ensorceler.
witchcraft ['witʃkra:ft] *n* sorcellerie *f*, magie noire *f*.
witch-doctor ['witʃ,dɔktə] *n* sorcier *m*.
with [wið] *prep* avec, à, au, à la, aux, chez, auprès de, envers, pour ce qui est de; **to be** — **it** être dans le vent.
withal [wi'ðɔ:l] *ad* avec cela, d'ailleurs, en même temps.
withdraw [wið'drɔ:] *vt* (re)tirer, reprendre, annuler, soustraire; *vi* se retirer, se replier, se rétracter.
withdrawal [wið'drɔ:əl] *n* retrait *m*, retraite *f*, rétraction *f*, repliement *m*, rappel *m*.
wither ['wiðə] *vt* dessécher, flétrir; *vi* se flétrir, se faner, dépérir.
withhold [wið'hould] *vt* retenir, refuser, cacher.
within [wi'ðin] *prep* dans, en dedans de, à l'intérieur de, en, entre, en moins de, à . . . près; *ad* au (en) dedans, à l'intérieur.
without [wi'ðaut] *prep* sans, hors de, en (au) dehors de; *ad* en (au) dehors, à l'extérieur.
withstand [wið'stænd] *vt* résister à, soutenir.
witness ['witnis] *n* témoin *m*, témoignage *m*; *vi* témoigner; *vt* attester, certifier, assister à, être témoin de.
witness-box ['witnis,bɔks] *n* banc *m*, barre des témoins *f*.
witticism ['witisizəm] *n* mot (trait *m*) d'esprit *m*, bon mot *m*.
wittingly ['witiŋli] *ad* à dessein, sciemment.
witty ['witi] *a* spirituel.
wizard ['wizəd] *n* magicien *m*, sorcier *m*, escamoteur *m*.
wizened ['wiznd] *a* ratatiné, desséché.
wobble ['wɔbl] *n* vacillation *f*, dandinement *m*; *vi* aller de travers, vaciller, trembler, branler, tituber, zigzaguer.
woe [wou] *n* malheur *m*.
woebegone ['woubi,gɔn] *a* lamentable, désolé.

woeful ['wouful] *a* triste, atroce, déplorable, affligé.
wold [would] *n* lande *f.*
wolf [wulf] *n* loup *m;* — **whistle** (*fam*) sifflement admiratif *m.*
wolf-cub ['wulfkʌb] *n* louveteau *m.*
woman ['wumən] *n* femme *f.*
womanhood ['wumənhud] *n* âge de femme *m,* fémininité *f.*
womanish ['wuməniʃ] *a* efféminé.
womanly ['wumənli] *a* féminin, de femme.
womb [wu:m] *n* matrice *f,* sein *m.*
won [wʌn] *pt pp of* **win.**
wonder ['wʌndə] *n* merveille *f,* prodige *m,* émerveillement *m;* **no** — rien d'étonnant, (*fam*) bien entendu; *vi* s'étonner; *vt* se demander; **to** — **at** admirer, s'étonner de.
wonderful ['wʌndəful] *a* étonnant, merveilleux.
wonderingly ['wʌndəriŋli] *ad* d'un air étonné.
wonderment ['wʌndəmənt] *n* étonnement *m,* émerveillement *m*
wont [wount] *n* habitude *f;* **to be** — **to** avoid l'habitude de.
wonted ['wountid] *a* habituel, coutumier.
woo [wu:] *vt* courtiser, faire la cour à.
wood [wud] *n* bois *m,* forêt *f.*
woodcock ['wudkɔk] *n* bécasse *f.*
woodcut ['wudkʌt] *m* gravure sur bois *f.*
woodcutter ['wudkʌtə] *n* bûcheron *m,* graveur sur bois *m.*
wooden ['wudn] *a* de (en) bois.
woodland ['wudlənd] *n* pays boisé *m.*
woodman ['wudmən] *n* garde forestier *m,* bûcheron *m.*
woodpecker ['wud,pekə] *n* pic *m,* pivert *m.*
woodwork ['wudwə:k] *n* boisage *m,* boiserie *f,* menuiserie *f,* charpenterie *f.*
wool [wul] *n* laine *f.*
woolen ['wulin] *n* lainage *m; a* de laine, laineux.
woolly ['wuli] *a* de laine, laineux, ouaté, flou, cotonneux, (*fig*) confus, vaseux; *n* vêtement de laine *m,* pull-over *m.*
word [wə:d] *n* mot *m,* parole *f; vt* exprimer, rédiger, formuler, énoncer.
wordiness ['wə:dinis] *n* verbosité *f.*
wording ['wə:diŋ] *n* expression *f,* rédaction *f,* énoncé *m,* libellé *m.*
wordy ['wə:di] *a* verbeux, diffus, prolixe.
wore [wɔ:] *pt of* **wear.**
work [wə:k] *n* travail *m* (*pl* travaux), ouvrage *m,* œuvre *f; pl* usine *f,* atelier *m,* chantier *m,* mécanisme *m; vti* travailler; *vi* marcher, fonctionner, agir; *vt* faire travailler, faire marcher, actionner, exploiter, diriger, opérer, façonner; **to** — **out** *vt* élaborer, calculer; *vi* se monter (à at); **to** — **up** *vt* perfectionner, développer, préparer, exciter; *vi* se développer, se préparer, remonter.
workable ['wə:kəbl] *a* faisable, réalisable, exploitable.
work-basket ['wə:k,ba:skit] *n* corbeille à ouvrage *f.*
workday ['wə:kdei] *n* jour ouvrable *m.*
worker ['wə:kə] *n* ouvrier, -ière.
workhouse ['wə:khaus] *n* asile *m,* hospice *m.*
working ['wə:kiŋ] *n* travail *m,* (*wine*) fermentation *f,* fonctionnement *m; a* — **class** classe ouvrière *f,* prolétariat *m;* — **majority** majorité suffisante *f.*
workmanlike ['wə:kmənlaik] *a* bien fait, pratique, en bon ouvrier.
workmanship ['wə:kmənʃip] *n* habileté manuelle *f,* fin travail *m,* façon *f.*
workshop ['wə:kʃɔp] *n* atelier *m,* usine *f.*
work-table ['wə:k,teibl] *n* table à ouvrage *f.*
world [wə:ld] *n* monde *m.*
worldliness ['wə:ldlinis] *n* mondanité *f.*
worldly ['wə:ldli] *a* de ce monde, matériel, du siècle.
worldwide ['wə:ldwaid] *a* mondial, universel.
worm [wə:m] *n* ver *m; vi* ramper, se glisser; **to** — **it out of s.o.** tirer les vers du nez à qn; **to** — **one's way into** se faufiler dans, s'insinuer dans.
worm-eaten ['wə:m,i:tn] *a* mangé des vers, vermoulu.
wormwood ['wə:mwud] *n* absinthe *f.*
worn [wɔ:n] *pp of* **wear.**
worn-out ['wɔ:n'aut] *a* épuisé, usé.
worried ['wʌrid] *a* soucieux.
worry ['wʌri] *n* souci *m,* tracas *m,* ennui *m; vt* tourmenter, inquiéter; *vi* se tourmenter, s'inquiéter.
worse [wə:s] *n* pis; *an* pire *m; ad* pis, moins bien, plus mal.
worsen ['wə:sn] *vti* empirer; *vt* aggraver; (*fam*) avoir le dessus sur; *vi* s'aggraver.
worship ['wə:ʃip] *n* culte *m,* adoration *f,* Honneur *m; vt* adorer, rendre un culte à.
worshipper ['wə:ʃipə] *n* fidèle *mf,* adorateur, -trice.
worst [wə:st] *n* le pis *m,* le pire *m,* le dessous *m,* désavantage *m; a* le pire; *ad* au pis, le pis, le plus mal; *vt* battre.
worsted ['wustid] *n* laine *f,* peigné *m.*
worth [wə:θ] *n* valeur *f,* mérite *m; a* qui vaut (la peine de), de la valeur de; **to be** — valoir.
worthiness ['wə:ðinis] *n* mérite *m,* justice *f.*
worthless ['wə:θlis] *a* sans valeur, bon à rien.
worthwhile ['wə:θ'wail] *a* de valeur, qui en vaut la peine.
worthy ['wə:ði] *a* digne, respectable; *n* personnage (notable) *m.*

would [wud] *part. of* **will.**
would-be ['wudbiː] *a* soi-disant, prétendu.
wound [waund] *pt pp of* **wind.**
wound [wuːnd] *n* blessure *f*, plaie *f*; *vt* blesser, atteindre.
wove, woven [wouv, 'wouvən] *pt pp of* **weave.**
wrack [ræk] *n* varech *m.*
wraith [reiθ] *n* fantôme *m*, apparition *f.*
wrangle ['ræŋgl] *n* dispute *f*; *vi* se disputer.
wrap [ræp] *vt* envelopper.
wrapped [ræpt] *a* enveloppé, absorbé.
wrapper ['ræpə] *n* bande *f*, couverture *f*, écharpe *f.*
wrath [rɔθ] *n* courroux *m.*
wreak [riːk] *vt* assouvir, décharger.
wreath [riːθ] *n* couronne *f*, volute *f.*
wreathe [riːð] *vt* couronner de fleurs, tresser, entourer, enrouler.
wreathed [riːðd] *a* enveloppé, baigné; **— in smiles** épanoui, rayonnant.
wreck [rek] *n* ruine *f*, naufrage *m*, épave(s) *f* (*pl*); *vt* perdre, ruiner, saboter, démolir, faire dérailler.
wreckage ['rekidʒ] *n* débris *m pl*; **piece of —** épave *f.*
wrecked [rekt] *a* jeté à la côte, naufragé, ruiné; **to be —** faire naufrage.
wrecker ['rekə] *n* naufrageur *m*, pilleur d'épaves *m*, dérailleur *m*, dépanneur *m* (*aut*), récupérateur *m* (d'épaves).
wrecking ['rekiŋ] *n* sauvetage *m*, renflouage *m* (de navire); **— train** carvée *f* de secours; **— lorry** dépanneuse *f.*
wren [ren] *n* roitelet *m.*
wrench [rentʃ] *n* torsion *f*, tour *m*, secousse *f*, coup *m*, clé *f*, entorse *f*; *vt* tordre, arracher; **to — open** ouvrir violemment, forcer.
wrest [rest] *vt* tourner, forcer, arracher.
wrestle ['resl] *n* lutte *f*; *vi* lutter; **to — with** lutter contre, s'attaquer à.
wrestler ['reslə] *n* lutteur *m.*
wrestling ['resliŋ] *n* lutte *f*, catch *m.*
wretch [retʃ] *n* malheureux, -euse, scélérat *m*, pauvre diable *m*, triste sire *m*, fripon(ne).
wretched ['retʃid] *a* misérable, lamentable, minable.
wretchedness ['retʃidnis] *n* état *m* misérable, malheur *m*, misère *f.*
wriggle ['rigl] *n* tortillement; *vt* tortiller, agiter; *vi* se tortiller, s'insinuer, se faufiler, frétiller.
wring [riŋ] *n* torsion *f*, pression *f*; *vt* presser, tordre, détourner, extorquer.
wrinkle ['riŋkl] *n* ride *f*, tuyau *m*; *vt* rider, froncer; *vi* se rider, se plisser.
wrist [rist] *n* poignet *m.*
wrist-watch ['ristwɔtʃ] *n* montre-bracelet *f.*

writ [rit] *n* écriture *f*, assignation *f*, mandat d'arrêt *m.*
write [rait] *vti* écrire; **to — down** noter, coucher par écrit, estimer, décrier; **to — off** réduire, défalquer, déduire, annuler; **to — up** rédiger, faire un éloge exagéré de, faire de la réclame pour, décrire, mettre à jour.
writer ['raitə] *n* écrivain *m*, auteur *m*, commis aux écritures *m.*
writhe [raið] *vi* se tordre, se crisper.
writing ['raitiŋ] *n* écriture *f*, œuvre *f*, écrit *m*, métier d'écrivain *m.*
writing-case ['raitiŋkeis] *n* nécessaire à écrire *m.*
writing-desk ['raitiŋdesk] *n* bureau *m.*
writing-pad ['raitiŋpæd] *n* sous-main *m*, bloc *m* de papier à lettres.
writing-paper ['raitiŋˌpeipə] *n* papier à lettres *m.*
written ['ritn] *pp of* **write.**
wrong [rɔŋ] *n* tort *m*, mal *m*, injustice *f*, préjudice *m*; *a* dérangé, mauvais, faux, inexact; *ad* mal, à tort, de travers; *vt* léser, faire tort à; **to be —** se tromper, avoir tort.
wrongdoer ['rɔŋˌduə] *n* malfaiteur, -trice, coupable *mf.*
wrongdoing ['rɔŋˈdu(ː)iŋ] *n* méfaits *m pl*, mauvaises actions *f pl.*
wrongful ['rɔŋful] *a* injuste, faux.
wrongfully ['rɔŋfuli] *ad* à tort, de travers.
wrote [rout] *pt of* **write.**
wroth [rouθ] *a* en colère.
wrung [rʌŋ] *pt pp of* **wring.**
wrought [rɔːt] *pt pp of* **work;** *a* travaillé, forgé, excité.
wry [rai] *a* tors, tordu, de travers.

X

X-ray ['eks'rei] *n pl* rayons X *m pl*; *vt* radiographier, passer aux rayons X; **— treatment** radiothérapie.

Y

yacht [jɔt] *n* yacht *m.*
yam [jæm] *n* igname *f.*
yank [jæŋk] *vt* tirer brusquement; *n* coup sec *m.*
yap [jæp] *n* jappement *m*; *vi* japper.
yard [jɑːd] *n* mètre *m*, cour *f*, chantier *m*, vergue *f*; **—stick** mètre *m*, aune *f.*
yarn [jɑːn] *n* fil *m*, conte *m*, histoire *f.*
yaw [jɔː] *n* embardée *f*; *vi* embarder.
yawl [jɔːl] *n* yole *f.*
yawn [jɔːn] *n* bâillement *m*; *vi* bâiller, béer.
ye [jiː] *pn* vous.
yea [jei] *ad* oui, voire.
year [jəː] *n* an *m*, année *f.*

year-book ['jəːbuk] n annuaire m.
yearling ['jəːliŋ] a d'un an.
yearly ['jəːli] a annuel; ad annuellement.
yearn [jəːn] vi aspirer (à **after**), soupirer (après **after**).
yearning ['jəːniŋ] n aspiration f, désir passionné m; a ardent.
yeast [jiːst] n levure f, levain m.
yell [jel] n hurlement m; vti hurler.
yellow ['jelou] an jaune m; a lâche.
yellowish ['jelouiʃ] a jaunâtre.
yellowness ['jelounis] n couleur jaune f.
yelp [jelp] n jappement m, glapissement m; vi japper, gémir, glapir.
yes [jes] n oui m; ad oui, si.
yes-man ['jesmæn] n qui dit amen à tout, béni-oui-oui m.
yesterday ['jestədi] n ad hier m; **the day before** — avant-hier.
yet [jet] ad encore, de plus, jusqu'ici, déjà; cj pourtant, tout de même.
yew [juː] n if m.
yield [jiːld] n produit m, rendement m, rapport m, revenu m, production f; vt rendre, rapporter, donner; vti céder; vi se rendre, succomber, plier, fléchir.
yielding ['jiːldiŋ] a arrangeant, faible, mou.
yoke [jouk] n joug m, paire (de bœufs) f; vt atteler, lier, unir.
yolk [jouk] n jaune d'œuf m, suint m.
yonder ['jɔndə] ad là-bas.
yore [jɔː] n of — d'antan, du temps jadis.
you [juː] pn vous.
young [jʌŋ] n petit, jeune; a jeune.
younger ['jʌŋgə] a jeune, cadet, puîné.

youngish ['jʌŋiʃ] a jeunet.
youngster ['jʌŋstə] n enfant mf, gosse mf.
your [jɔː] a votre, vos, ton, ta, tes.
yours [jɔːz] pn vôtre(s), à vous; le, la, (les) vôtre(s); tien(s), tienne(s), à toi; le(s) tien(s), la tienne, les tiennes.
yourself, -selves [jɔːˈself, selvz] pn vous-même(s).
youth [juːθ] n jeunesse f, jeune homme m.
youthful ['juːθful] a jeune, juvénile.

Z

zeal [ziːl] n zèle m, empressement m.
zealous ['zeləs] a zélé, empressé.
zealously ['zeləsli] ad avec empressement.
zebra ['ziːbrə] n zèbre m.
zebu ['ziːbu] n zébu m.
zenith ['zeniθ] n zénith m.
zero ['ziərou] n zéro m.
zest [zest] n piquant m, enthousiasme m, entrain m.
zigzag ['zigzæg] n zigzag m; vi zigzaguer.
zinc [ziŋk] n zinc m.
zip [zip] n sifflement m: — **fastener** fermeture éclair f.
zither ['ziðə] n cithare f.
zone [zoun] n zone f, ceinture f.
zoo [zuː] n jardin d'acclimatation m, jardin zoologique m.
zoological [ˌzouəˈlɔdʒikəl] a zoologique.
zoologist [zouˈɔlədʒist] n zoologiste m.
zoology [zouˈɔlədʒi] n zoologie f.

Mesures et monnaies françaises
French measures, weights and money

MESURES DE LONGUEUR—LENGTH
1 millimètre = ·001 mètre = ·0394 inch.
1 centimètre = ·01 mètre = ·394 inch.
1 mètre = 39·4 inches = *1 yard.
1 kilomètre = 1000 mètres = *1094 yards or ⅝ mile.
8 kilomètres = 5 miles.

MESURES DE SURFACE—AREA
1 are = *120 square yards.
1 hectare = 100 ares = *2½ acres.

MESURES DE CAPACITÉ—CAPACITY (FLUIDS AND GRAIN)
1 centilitre = ·01 litre = ·0176 pint.
1 litre = *1¾ pints = ·2201 gallon.
1 hectolitre = 100 litres = *22 gallons = 2¾ bushels.
1 kilolitre = 1000 litres = *220 gallons = 27½ bushels.

MESURES DE POIDS—WEIGHTS
1 milligramme = ·001 gramme = ·0154 grain.
1 centigramme = ·01 gramme = ·1543 grain.
1 gramme = 15·43 grains.
1 hectogramme = 100 grammes = *3½ oz.
1 livre = 500 grammes = 1 lb. 1½ oz.
1 kilogramme = 1000 grammes = *2 lbs. 3 oz.
1 quintal = 100 kilogrammes = *2 cwts.
1 tonne = 1000 kilogrammes = *1 ton.

MESURES THERMOMÉTRIQUES—THE THERMOMETER
Point de congélation⎫ —Centigrade 0°
Freezing point ⎭ —Fahrenheit 32°
Point d'ébullition ⎫ —Centigrade 100°
Boiling point ⎭ —Fahrenheit 212°
    To convert Centigrade to Fahrenheit degrees, divide by 5, multiply by 9 and add 32.

MONNAIES—MONEY
100 centimes = 1 franc.
* roughly.

Notes on French Grammar

A. THE ARTICLE

(i) The *definite article* is **le** (*m*), **la** (*f*), and **les** (*mf pl*). **Le** and **la** are shortened to **l'** before a vowel or H-mute.

(ii) The *indefinite article* is **un** (*m*), **une** (*f*).

(iii) When the prepositions **à** or **de** are used before the definite article they combine with **le** to form **au** and **du** respectively. They combine with **les** to form **aux** and **des**. They make no change before **la** or **l'**.

(iv) The partitive article, **du** (*m*), **de la** (*f*), **des** (*mf pl*), corresponds to the English *some* or *any* when the latter denotes an indefinite quantity. e.g. Have you any milk? **Avez-vous du lait?**

B. THE NOUN

(i) The plural is usually formed in **s**. Nouns ending in **s, x, z** have the same form in the plural. Those ending in **au**, and **eu** (except **bleu**) and some in **ou (bijou, caillou, hibou, genou, chou, pou, joujou)** form their plural in **x**. Those ending in **al** and **ail** form their plural in **aux**. **Aïeul, ciel, œil** become **aïeux, cieux** and **yeux**.

(ii) All French nouns are either masculine or feminine in gender. Most nouns ending in mute **e** are feminine, except those in **isme, age (image, rage, nage** are *f*) and **iste** (often either *m* or *f*). Most nouns ending in a consonant or a vowel other than mute **e** are masculine, but nouns ending in **tion** and **té (été, pâté** are *m*) are feminine.

iii) The feminine is usually formed by adding **e** to the masculine. Nouns ending in **er** have a femine in **ère**, and those ending in **en, on** have a feminine in **enne, onne**. Nouns ending in **eur** have a feminine in **euse**, except those ending in **ateur** which give **atrice**. A few words ending in **e** have a feminine in **esse**.

C. THE ADJECTIVE

i) The plural is usually formed by adding an **s**. Adjectives ending in **s, x** are the same in the plural. Those ending in **al** have a plural in **aux**, but the following take an **s: bancal, fatal, final, glacial, natal, naval.**

ii) The feminine is usually formed by adding **e** to the masculine form. Adjectives ending in **f** change **f** into **ve**, and those ending in **x** change **x** into **se**. Adjectives ending in **er** have **ère** in the feminine form. To form the feminine of adjectives ending in **el, eil, en, et, on**, the final consonant must be doubled before adding an **e**.

(iii) Comparison of adjectives. The Comparative is formed regularly by adding **plus** to the ordinary form, and the Superlative by adding **le, la,** or **les,** as required, to the Comparative form. **Moins** (= less) is employed in the same way as **plus,** giving, for example, **moins long**—less long, **les moins récentes**—the least recent. Irregular forms are: **bon, meilleur, le meilleur; mauvais, pire** or **plus mauvais, le pire** or **le plus mauvais; petit, moindre** or **plus petit, le moindre** or **le plus petit.** 'Than' is always rendered by **que.** Other expressions of comparison are: **aussi . . . que,** as . . . as; **pas si . . . que,** not so (as) . . . as; **autant (de) . . . que,** as much (or many) . . . as; **pas tant (de) . . . que,** not so much (or many) . . . as.

(iv) The demonstrative adjectives 'this' and 'that' and their plural 'these' or 'those' are in French **ce, cet** (*m*), **cette** (*f*) and **ces** (*pl*). **Ce** is used with all masculine words except before those beginning with a vowel or an H-mute, in which case **cet** is used. The opposition between 'this' and 'that' may be emphasized by adding the suffix **-ci** or **-là** to the noun concerned. 'That' is in French **celui** (*f* **celle,** *pl* **ceux, celles**) **de.** Expressions such as 'he who', 'the one which', 'those or they who' should be translated by **celui (celle, ceux, celles) qui.**

(v) Possessive adjectives.

my	**mon** (*m*)	**ma** (*f*)	**mes** (*pl*)
your	**ton**	**ta**	**tes**
his	**son**	**sa**	**ses**
our	**notre**	**notre**	**nos**
your	**votre**	**votre**	**vos**
their	**leur**	**leur**	**leurs**

All of these agree in gender with the following noun.

D. THE PRONOUN

I. (i) Unstressed forms.

	Nom.	*Acc.*	*Dat.*	*Gen.*
1*st sing.*	**je**	**me**	**me**	
2*nd sing.*	**tu**	**te**	**te**	
3*rd sing.*	**il, elle**	**le, la (se)**	**lui, y**	**en**
	Nom.	*Acc.*	*Dat.*	*Gen.*
1*st plur.*	**nous**	**nous**	**nous**	
2*nd plur.*	**vous**	**vous**	**vous**	
3*rd plur.*	**ils, elles**	**les (se)**	**leur, y (se)**	**en**

(i) **Tu** and **te** are normally used when speaking to one person who is a close relative or an intimate friend. They

are also used to any child or an animal. Otherwise the 2nd
plural **vous** is normally used to address single persons. In
this use it retains a plural verb, but its other agreements
(with adjectives, participles etc.) are singular, provided it
refers to a single person.

(ii) The forms **me, te, se, nous, vous, se** may be used in
reflexive verbs, and also to denote mutual participation in
an action. E.g. they looked at each other, **ils se regar-
daient.**

II. Stressed forms.

	Singular	*Plural*
1st Person	**moi**	**nous**
2nd Person	**toi**	**vous**
3rd Person m	**lui**	**eux**
f	**elle**	**elles**
Reflexive	**soi**	

(i) This form is used when the pronoun is governed by a
preposition.

(ii) It is used where people are singled out or contrasted,
i.e. for emphasis.

(iii) It is also used when a pronoun stands as the sole word
in a sentence, stands as the antecedent of a relative, forms
part of a double subject or object of a verb, is the complement of **être** or when it stands after **que** in comparative
sentences.

III. When used together, personal pronouns are positioned according to the following scheme.

me	le	lui	y	en
te	la	leur		
nous	les			
vous				
se				

IV. Possessive pronouns.

	Singular	*Plural*
1st sing. m	**le mien**	**les miens**
f	**la mienne**	**les miennes**
2nd sing. m	**le tien**	**les tiens**
f	**la tienne**	**les tiennes**
3rd sing. m	**le sien**	**les siens**
f	**la sienne**	**les siennes**
1st plur.	**le (la) nôtre**	**les nôtres**
2nd plur.	**le (la) vôtre**	**les vôtres**
3rd plur.	**le (la) leur**	**les leurs**

482

E.g. I have lost my pen; lend me yours = **j'ai perdue ma plume, prêtez-moi la vôtre.**

V. Relative pronouns. 'Who' is translated by **qui**; 'whom' by **que** (or by **qui** after a preposition); 'whose' by **dont**; 'which' by **qui** (subject) or **que** (object). After a preposition 'which' is translated by **lequel** (*m*), **laquelle** (*f*), **lesquels** (*m pl*) and **lesquelles** (*f pl*). With the prepositions **à** and **de** the following contractions take place: **auquel** (but **à laquelle**), **auxquels, auxquelles; duquel** (but **de laquelle**), **desquels, desquelles.**

VI. Interrogative pronouns. 'Who' and 'whom' are both **qui**. 'What', when object, is **que** and when subject is **qu'est-ce qui**. When 'what' is used adjectivally it should be translated by **quel, quelle, quels, quelles.**

E. ADVERBS

Most French adverbs are formed by adding **ment** to the feminine form of the corresponding adjective. Adjectives ending in **ant** and **ent** have adverbial endings in **amment** and **emment** respectively.

Negative forms. 'Not' is **ne . . . pas**, 'nobody' **ne . . . personne**, 'nothing' **ne . . . rien** and 'never' is **ne . . . jamais.**

Examples. I do not know, **je ne sais pas.** I know nothing, **je ne sais rien.**

'Nobody and 'nothing' when subject are rendered by **personne ne . . ., rien ne . . .**

F. VERBS

I. Regular verbs.

There are three principal types of regular conjugation of French verbs, corresponding to the three infinitive endings: **-er, -ir, -re.** They provide patterns for conjugating large numbers of verbs which have one or other of these infinitive endings. As a convenient simplification, each part of a verb may be stated to consist of a basic stem and a characteristic ending. From the stem and ending of the present infinitive and of the present participle, all parts of a regular verb may be built up.

Examples. **parler, finir, vendre.**

Present infinitive	**parl/er**	**fin/ir**	**vend/re**
Present participle	**parl/ant**	**finiss/ant**	**vend/ant**
Past participle	stem+**-é**	stem+**-i**	stem+**-u**

Present indicative	stem+-e,	stem+-is,	stem+-s,
	-es, -e,	-is, -it,	-s, -,
	-ons, -ez,	-issons,	-ons, -ez,
	-ent	-issez,	-ent
		-issent	

Imperative   2nd singular, 1st plural and 2nd plural of present indicative, without subject pronouns. First conjugation drops final **s** of 2nd singular, except before **y, en.**

Imperfect   stem of present participle+**-ais, -ais, -ait, -ions, -iez, -aient.**

Past historic	stem+-ai, -as,	stem+-is, -is,
	-a, -âmes, -âtes,	-it, -îmes, -îtes,
	-èrent	-irent

Future   infinitive+**-ai, -as, -a, -ons, -ez, -ont.** Third conjugation drops final **e** of infinitive.

Conditional   infinitive+**-ais, -ais, -ait, -ions, -iez, -aient.** Third conjugation drops final **e** of infinitive.

Present subjunctive   stem of present participle+ **-e, -es, -e, -ions, -iez, -ent.**

Imperfect subjunctive   remove final **e** from 2nd singular of past historic and add **-sse, -sses, ît, -ssions, -ssiez, -ssent.**

Compound tenses are formed with the auxiliary **avoir** and the past participle, except reflexive verbs and some common intransitive verbs (like **aller, arriver, devenir, partir, rester, retourner, sortir, tomber, venir** etc.) which are conjugated with **être.** The following scheme is applicable to all three conjugations.

Perfect   present indicative of **avoir** (or **être**)+past participle.

Pluperfect   imperfect of **avoir** (or **être**)+ past participle.

Future perfect   future of **avoir** (or **être**)+past participle.

Conditional perfect   conditional of **avoir** (or **être**)+ past participle.

Perfect infinitive   infinitive of **avoir** (or **être**)+ past participle.

Note on agreement. The French past participle always agrees with the noun to which it is either an attribute or an adjective. It agrees with the object of a verb conjugated with **avoir** only when the object comes before it. E.g. I loved that woman, **j'ai aimé cette femme**; the women I have loved, **les femmes que j'ai aimées**.

For the conjugation of the auxiliaries **avoir** and **être** consult the list of irregular verbs.

G. MISCELLANEOUS NOTES

(i) Verbs having a mute **e** or closed **é** in the last syllable but one of the present infinitive, change the mute **e** or closed **é** to open **è** before a mute syllable (except in the future and conditional tenses). E.g. **espérer, j'espère, il espérera, il espérerait.**

(ii) Verbs with infinitive endings in -**cer** have **ç** before endings in **a, o.** E.g. **commencer, je commençais, nous commençons.**

(iii) Verbs with infinitive endings in -**ger** have an additional **e** before endings in **a, o.** E.g. **manger, je mangeais, nous mangeons.**

(iv) Verbs ending in -**eler**, -**eter** double the **l** or **t** before a mute **e.** E.g. **appeler, j'appelle; jeter, je jette.** The following words do not obey this rule and take only **è**: **acheter, agneler, bégueter, celer, ciseler, congeler, corseter, crocheter, déceler, dégeler, démanteler, écarteler, fureter, geler, harceler, marteler, modeler, peler, racheter, receler, regeler.**

(v) Verbs with infinitive endings in -**yer** change **y** into **i** before a mute **e.** They require a **y** and an **i** in the first two persons plural of the imperfect indicative and of the present subjunctive. Verbs with infinitive endings in -**ayer** may keep the **y** or change it to **i** before a mute **e.** Verbs with infinitive endings in -**eyer** keep the **y** throughout the conjugation.

IRREGULAR VERBS

Order of principal tenses and essential parts of the French irregular verbs in most frequent use. (1) Present Participle; (2) Past Participle; (3) Present Indicative; (4) Imperfect Indicative; (5) Preterite; (6) Future; (7) Present Subjunctive.

Prefixed verbs not included in this list follow the root verb, e.g., sourire—rire: abattre—battre.

acquérir (1) acquérant; (2) acquis; (3) acquiers, acquiers, acquiert, acquérons, acquérez, acquièrent; (4) acquérais; (5) acquis; (6) acquerrai; (7) acquière.

aller (1) allant; (2) allé; (3) vais, vas, va, allons, allez, vont; (4) allais; (5) allai; (6) irai; (7) aille.

485

asseoir (1) asseyant; (2) assis; (3) assieds, assieds, assied, asseyons, asseyez, asseyent; (4) asseyais; (5) assis; (6) assiérai or asseyerai; (7) asseye.

atteindre (1) atteignant; (2) atteint; (3) atteins, atteins, atteint, atteignons, atteignez, atteignent; (4) atteignais; (5) atteignis; (6) atteindrai; (7) atteigne.

avoir (1) ayant; (2) eu; (3) ai, as, a, avons, avez, ont; (4) avais; (5) eus; (6) aurai; (7) aie. *N.B.*—Imperative aie, ayons, ayez.

battre (1) battant; (2) battu; (3) bats, bats, bat, battons, battez, battent; (4) battais; (5) battis; (6) battrai; (7) batte.

boire (1) buvant; (2) bu; (3) bois, bois, boit, buvons, buvez, boivent; (4) buvais; (5) bus; (6) boirai; (7) boive.

bouillir (1) bouillant; (2) bouilli; (3) bous, bous, bout, bouillons, bouillez, bouillent; (4) bouillais; (5) bouillis; (6) bouillirai; (7) bouille.

conclure (1) concluant; (2) conclu; (3) conclus, conclus, conclut, concluons, concluez, concluent; (4) concluais; (5) conclus; (6) conclurai; (7) conclue.

conduire (1) conduisant; (2) conduit; (3) conduis, conduis, conduit, conduisons, conduisez, conduisent; (4) conduisais; (5) conduisis; (6) conduirai; (7) conduise.

connaître (1) connaissant; (2) connu; (3) connais, connais, connaît, connaissons, connaissez, connaissent; (4) connaissais; (5) connus; (6) connaîtrai; (7) connaisse.

coudre (1) cousant; (2) cousu; (3) couds, couds, coud, cousons, cousez, cousent; (4) cousais; (5) cousis; (6) coudrai; (7) couse.

courir (1) courant; (2) couru; (3) cours, cours, court, courons, courez, courent; (4) courais; (5) courus; (6) courrai; (7) coure.

couvrir (1) couvrant; (2) couvert; (3) couvre, couvres, couvre, couvrons, couvrez, couvrent; (4) couvrais; (5) couvris; (6) couvrirai; (7) couvre.

craindre (1) craignant; (2) craint; (3) crains, crains, craint, craignons, craignez, craignent; (4) craignais; (5) craignis; (6) craindrai; (7) craigne.

croire (1) croyant; (2) cru; (3) crois, crois, croit, croyons, croyez, croient; (4) croyais; (5) crus; (6) croirai; (7) croie.

croître (1) croissant; (2) crû, crue (*pl* crus, crues); (3) croîs, croîs, croît, croissons, croissez, croissent; (4) croissais; (5) crûs; (6) croîtrai; (7) croisse.

cueillir (1) cueillant; (2) cueilli; (3) cueille, cueilles, cueille, cueillons, cueillez, cueillent; (4) cueillais; (5) cueillis; (6) cueillerai; (7) cueille.

devoir (1) devant; (2) dû, due (*pl* dus, dues); (3) dois, dois, doit, devons, devez, doivent; (4) devais; (5) dus; (6) devrai; (7) doive.

dire (1) disant; (2) dit; (3) dis, dis, dit, disons, dites, disent; (4) disais; (5) dis; (6) dirai; (7) dise.

dormir (1) dormant; (2) dormi; (3) dors, dors, dort, dormons, dormez, dorment; (4) dormais; (5) dormis; (6) dormirai; (7) dorme.

écrire (1) écrivant; (2) écrit; (3) écris, écris, écrit, écrivons, écrivez, écrivent; (4) écrivais; (5) écrivis; (6) écrirai; (7) écrive.

être (1) étant; (2) été; (3) suis, es, est, sommes, êtes, sont; (4) étais; (5) fus; (6) serai; (7) sois. *N.B.*—Imperative sois, soyons, soyez.

faire (1) faisant; (2) fait; (3) fais, fais, fait, faisons, faites, font; (4) faisais; (5) fis; (6) ferai; (7) fasse.

falloir (2) fallu; (3) faut; (4) fallait; (5) fallut; (6) faudra; (7) faille.

fuir (1) fuyant; (2) fui; (3) fuis, fuis, fuit, fuyons, fuyez, fuient; (4) fuyais; (5) fuis; (6) fuirai; (7) fuie.

joindre (1) joignant; (2) joint; (3) joins, joins, joint, joignons, joignez, joignent; (4) joignais; (5) joignis; (6) joindrai; (7) joigne.

lire (1) lisant; (2) lu; (3) lis, lis, lit, lisons, lisez, lisent; (4) lisais; (5) lus; (6) lirai; (7) lise.

luire (1) luisant; (2) lui; (3) luis, luis, luit, luisons, luisez, luisent; (4) luisais; (5) luisis; (6) luirai; (7) luise.

maudire (1) maudissant; (2) maudit; (3) maudis, maudis, maudit, maudissons, maudissez, maudissent; (4) maudissait; (5) maudis; (6) maudirai; (7) maudisse.

mentir (1) mentant; (2) menti; (3) mens, mens, ment, mentons, mentez, mentent; (4) mentais; (5) mentis; (6) mentirai; (7) mente.

mettre (1) mettant; (2) mis; (3) mets, mets, met, mettons, mettez, mettent; (4) mettais; (5) mis; (6) mettrai; (7) mette.

mourir (1) mourant; (2) mort; (3) meurs, meurs, meurt, mourons, mourez, meurent; (4) mourais; (5) mourus; (6) mourrai; (7) meure.

naître (1) naissant; (2) né; (3) nais, nais, naît, naissons, naissez, naissent; (4) naissais; (5) naquis; (6) naîtrai; (7) naisse.

offrir (1) offrant; (2) offert; (3) offre, offres, offre, offrons, offrez, offrent; (4) offrais; (5) offris; (6) offrirai; (7) offre.

partir (1) partant; (2) parti; (3) pars, pars, part, partons, partez, partent; (4) partais; (5) partis; (6) partirai; (7) parte.

plaire (1) plaisant; (2) plu; (3) plais, plais, plaît, plaisons, plaisez, plaisent; (4) plaisais; (5) plus; (6) plairai; (7) plaise.

pleuvoir (1) pleuvant; (2) plu; (3) pleut, pleuvent; (4) pleuvait; (5) plut; (6) pleuvra; (7) pleuve.

pourvoir (1) pourvoyant; (2) pourvu; (3) pourvois, pourvois, pourvoit, pourvoyons, pourvoyez, pourvoient; (4) pourvoyais; (5) pourvus; (6) pourvoirai; (7) pourvoie.

pouvoir (1) pouvant; (2) pu; (3) puis or peux, peux, peut, pouvons, pouvez, peuvent; (4) pouvais; (5) pus; (6) pourrai; (7) puisse.

prendre (1) prenant; (2) pris; (3) prends, prends, prend, prenons, prenez, prennent; (4) prenais; (5) pris; (6) prendrai; (7) prenne.

prévoir like voir. *N.B.*—(7) prévoirai.

recevoir (1) recevant; (2) reçu; (3) reçois, reçois, reçoit, recevons, recevez, reçoivent; (4) recevais; (5) reçus; (6) recevrai; (7) reçoive.

résoudre (1) résolvant; (2) résolu; (3) résous, résous, résout, résolvons, résolvez, résolvent; (4) résolvais; (5) résolus; (6) résoudrai; (7) résolve.

rire (1) riant; (2) ri; (3) ris, ris, rit, rions, riez, rient; (4) riais; (5) ris; (6) rirai; (7) rie.

savoir (1) sachant; (2) su; (3) sais, sais, sait, savons, savez, savent; (4) savais; (5) sus; (6) saurai; (7) sache. *N.B.*— Imperative sache, sachons, sachez.

servir (1) servant; (2) servi; (3) sers, sers, sert, servons, servez, servent; (4) servais; (5) servis; (6) servirai; (7) serve.

sortir (1) sortant; (2) sorti; (3) sors, sors, sort, sortons, sortez, sortent; (4) sortais; (5) sortis; (6) sortirai; (7) sorte.

souffrir (1) souffrant; (2) souffert; (3) souffre, souffres, souffre, souffrons, souffrez, souffrent; (4) souffrais; (5) souffris; (6) souffrirai; (7) souffre.

suffire (1) suffisant; (2) suffi; (3) suffis, suffis, suffit, suffisons, suffisez, suffisent; (4) suffisais; (5) suffis; (6) suffirai; (7) suffise.

suivre (1) suivant; (2) suivi; (3) suis, suis, suit, suivons, suivez, suivent; (4) suivais; (5) suivis; (6) suivrai; (7) suive.

taire (1) taisant; (2) tu; (3) tais, tais, tait, taisons, taisez, taisent; (4) taisais; (5) tus; (6) tairai; (7) taise.

tenir (1) tenant; (2) tenu; (3) tiens, tiens, tient, tenons, tenez, tiennent; (4) tenais; (5) tins; (6) tiendrai; (7) tienne.

vaincre (1) vainquant; (2) vaincu; (3) vaincs, vaincs, vainc, vainquons, vainquez, vainquent; (4) vainquais; (5) vainquis; (6) vaincrai; (7) vainque.

valoir (1) valant; (2) valu; (3) vaux, vaux, vaut, valons, valez, valent; **(4** valais; (5) valus; (6) vaudrai; (7) vaille.

venir (1) venant; (2) venu; (3) viens, viens, vient, venons,

venez, viennent; (4) venais; (5) vins; (6) viendrai; (7) vienne.
vivre (1) vivant; (2) vécu; (3) vis, vis, vit, vivons, vivez,
vivent; (4) vivais; (5) vécus; (6) vivrai; (7) vive.
voir (1) voyant; (2) vu; (3) vois, vois, voit, voyons, voyez,
voient; (4) voyais; (5) vis; (6) verrai; (7) voie.
vouloir (1) voulant; (2) voulu; (3) veux, veux, veut,
voulons, voulez, veulent; (4) voulais; (5) voulus; (6)
voudrai; (7) veuille. *N.B.*—Imperative veuille, veuillons,
veuillez.

U.S. and U.K. measures, weights and money
Mesures et monnaies anglaises

LENGTH—MESURES DE LONGUEUR
Inch (in.) = 25 millimètres.
Foot (ft.) (12 in.) = 304 mm.
Yard (yd.) (3 ft.) = 914 mm. (approximativement 1 mètre).
Fathom (fthm.) (2 yds.) = 1 mètre 828 mm.
Mile (8 furlongs, 1760 yds.) = 1609 mètres
    (approximativement 1 kilomètre et demi).
Nautical mile, knot = 1853 mètres.
5 miles = 8 kilomètres.

AREA—MESURES DE SURFACE
Square inch = 6 centimètres carrés.
Square foot = 929 centimètres carrés.
Square yard = 0·8360 mètre carré.
Acre   = 4047 mètres carrés.

CAPACITY (FLUIDS AND GRAIN)—MESURES DE CAPACITÉ
Pint = 0·567 litre (approximativement ½ litre).
Quart (2 pints) = 1·135 litre.
Gallon (4 quarts) = 4·543 litres.
Peck (2 gallons) = 9·086 litres.
Bushel (8 gallons) = 36·348 litres.
Quarter (8 bushels) = 290·781 litres.

WEIGHTS (AVOIRDUPOIS)—MESURES DE POIDS
Ounce (oz.) = 28·35 grammes.
Pound (lb.—16 oz.) = 453·59 grammes.
Stone (st.—14 lb.) = 6 kilos 350 grammes.
Quarter (qr.—28 lb.) = 12·7 kilos.
Hundredweight (cwt.—112 lb.) = 50·8 kilos.
Ton (T.—20 cwts.) = 1016 kilos.

THE THERMOMETER—MESURES THERMOMÉTRIQUES

Freezing point ⎫ — Fahrenheit 32°
Point de congélation ⎭ — Centigrade 0°
Boiling point ⎫ — Fahrenheit 212°
Point d'ébullition ⎭ — Centigrade 100°

    Pour convertir les mesures Fahrenheit en mesures Centigrade soustraire 32, multiplier par 5 et diviser par 9

MONEY—MONNAIES

USA

100 cents = 1 dollar

UK

A partir de 1971:
100 pence = 1 pound

Verbes forts et irréguliers anglais

PRÉSENT	PRÉTÉRIT	PARTICIPE PASSÉ
abide	abode	abode
arise	arose	arisen
awake	awoke, awaked	awaked, awoke
be	was	been
bear	bore	born(e)
beat	beat	beaten
become	became	become
befall	befell	befallen
begin	began	begun
behold	beheld	beheld
bend	bent	bent
bereave	bereft	bereft
beseech	besought	besought
bespeak	bespoke	bespoke(n)
bet	bet	bet
bid	bade, bid	bidden
bid	bid	bid
bind	bound	bound
bite	bit	bitten
bleed	bled	bled
blow	blew	blown
break	broke	broken
breed	bred	bred
bring	brought	brought
build	built	built
burn	burnt, burned	burnt, burned
burst	burst	burst
buy	bought	bought
cast	cast	cast
catch	caught	caught
chide	chid	chid(den)
choose	chose	chosen
cling	clung	clung
come	came	come

490

cost	cost	cost
creep	crept	crept
cut	cut	cut
deal	dealt	dealt
dig	dug	dug
do	did	done
draw	drew	drawn
dream	dreamt, dreamed	dreamt, dreamed
drink	drank	drunk
drive	drove	driven
dwell	dwelt	dwelt
eat	ate	eaten
fall	fell	fallen
feed	fed	fed
feel	felt	felt
fight	fought	fought
find	found	found
flee, fly	fled	fled
fling	flung	flung
fly	flew	flown
forbid	forbade	forbidden
forget	forgot	forgotten
forgive	forgave	forgiven
forsake	forsook	forsaken
freeze	froze	frozen
get	got	got
give	gave	given
go	went	gone
grind	ground	ground
grow	grew	grown
hang	hung	hung
have	had	had
hear	heard	heard
hew	hewed	hewn
hide	hid	hid(den)
hit	hit	hit
hold	held	held
hurt	hurt	hurt
keep	kept	kept
kneel	knelt	knelt
know	knew	known
lay	laid	laid
lead	led	led
lean	leaned, leant	leaned, leant
leap	leapt, leaped	leapt, leaped
learn	learned, learnt	learned, learnt
leave	left	left
lend	lent	lent
let	let	let
lie	lay	lain
light	lit	lit
lose	lost	lost
make	made	made
mean	meant	meant
meet	met	met
mow	mowed	mown
pay	paid	paid
put	put	put
quit	quit	quit

PRÉSENT	PRÉTÉRIT	PARTICIPE PASSÉ
read	read	read
rend	rent	rent
rid	rid	rid
ride	rode	ridden
ring	rang	rung
rise	rose	risen
run	ran	run
saw	sawed	sawn
say	said	said
see	saw	seen
seek	sought	sought
sell	sold	sold
send	sent	sent
set	set	set
sew	sewed	sewn
shake	shook	shaken
shed	shed	shed
shine	shone	shone
shoe	shod	shod
shoot	shot	shot
show	showed	shown
shrink	shrank	shrunk
shrive	shrove	shriven
shut	shut	shut
sing	sang, sung	sung
sink	sank, sunk	sunk
sit	sat	sat
slay	slew	slain
sleep	slept	slept
slide	slid	slid
sling	slung	slung
slink	slunk	slunk
slit	slit	slit
smell	smelled, smelt	smelled, smelt
smite	smote, smit	smitten, smit
sow	sowed	sówn
speak	spoke	spoken
speed	sped	sped
spend	spent	spent
spill	spilt	spilt
spin	spun, span	spun
spit	spat, spit	spat, spit
split	split	split
spoil	spoiled, spoilt	spoiled, spoilt
spread	spread	spread
spring	sprang	sprung
stand	stood	stood
steal	stole	stolen
stick	stuck	stuck
sting	stung	stung
stink	stank, stunk	stunk
strew	strewed	strewn, strewed
stride	strode	stridden, strid
strike	struck	struck
string	strung	strung
strive	strove	striven
swear	swore	sworn

sweep	swept	swept
swell	swelled	swollen
swim	swam	swum
swing	swung	swung
take	took	taken
teach	taught	taught
tear	tore	torn
tell	told	told
think	thought	thought
thrive	throve	thriven
throw	threw	thrown
thrust	thrust	thrust
tread	trod	trodden
wake	woke	woken
wear	wore	worn
weave	wove	woven, wove
weep	wept	wept
wet	wet	wet
win	won	won
wind	wound	wound
wring	wrung	wrung
write	wrote	written

English Abbreviations

ABRÉVIATIONS ANGLAISES

A	adults (*adultes*)
AAA	American Automobile Association (*association américaine d'automobilistes*)
AA	Alcoholics Anonymous (*société antialcoolique*)
a/c	account (current) (*compte courant*)
AC	alternating current (*current alternatif*)
AF of L	American Federation of Labor (*fédération américaine du travail*)
am	before noon (L. *ante meridiem*) (*avant midi*)
AMA	American Medical Association (*conseil de l'ordre de médecins américains*)
approx	approximately (*approximativement*)
assn	association (*association*)
asst	assistant (*auxiliaire ou aide*)
av	average (*moyen*)
b	born (*né*)
BA	Bachelor of Arts (*Licencié ès Lettres*)
BC	Before Christ (*avant Christ*); British Columbia (*Colombie Britannique*)
BD	Bachelor of Divinity (*diplôme d'études théologiques*)
Bd	Board (*conseil d'administration*)
BDS	Bachelor of Dental Surgery (*diplôme sanctionnant les études dentaires*)
B/E	Bill of exchange (*lettre de change, bon*)
BEA	British European Airways (*compagnie aérienne qui dessert l'Europe*)
B. Litt.	Bachelor of Letters (*diplôme d'études littéraires, diplôme d'études supérieures*)
B. Mus.	Bachelor of Music (*diplôme des études musicales*)
BOAC	British Overseas Airways Corporation (*compagnie aérienne qui dessert le monde entier*)

Brit	Britain (*Bretagne*); British (*Britannique*)
Bros	Brothers (*Frères*)
B/S	Bill of Sale (*acte de vente, reçu*)
BSc	Bachelor of Science (*diplôme de sciences*)
C	Cape (*cap*); centigrade (*centigrade*); central (*central*)
c	cent (*cent*); centime (*centime*); century (*siècle*); chapter (*chapitre*); about (*L. circa*) (*vers*)
CIA	Central Intelligence Agency (*agence américaine de contre-espionnage*)
CID	Criminal Investigation Department (*section de la police anglaise qui s'occupe de l'investigation des actes criminels*)
cif	Cost, Insurance and Freight (*coût, assurance et fret*)
CO	Commanding Officer (*commandant*); conscientious objector (*objecteur de conscience*)
Co	Company (*Cie, compagnie*)
c/o	care of (*aux bons soins de, chez*)
COD	cash on delivery (*payable à la livraison, livraison contre remboursement*)
CP	Communist Party (*parti communiste*)
cwt	hundredweight (*quintal*)
d	died (*mort*); date (*date*); daughter (*fille*); penny
DA	district attorney (*procureur de l'état*)
DC	District of Columbia (*district fédéral de Columbia*); direct current (*courant continu*)
DD	Doctor of Divinity (*docteur en théologie*)
doz	dozen (*douzaine*)
EEC	European Economic Community—Common Market (*Communauté économique européenne—Marché commun*)
EFTA	European Free Trade Association (*Association européenne pour le libre échange*)
eg	for example ((*L. exampli gratia*) *par exemple*)
esp	especially (*spécialement*)
est	established (*établi*)
FBI	Federal Bureau of Investigation (*police fédérale américaine*)
fob	free on board (*franco à bord*)
ft	foot (*pied*); feet (*pieds*); fort (*fort*)
gal	gallon(s) (*gallon(s)*—5 *litres*=1.1 gallons)
GB	Great Britain (*Grande Bretagne*)
GI	Government issue (American private soldier) (*nom donné au simple soldat américain*)
GMT	Greenwich mean time (*l'heure de Greenwich*)
GOP	Republican Party (*parti républicain*)
Govt	government (*gouvernement*)
GP	General practitioner (*médecin de médecine générale, omnipraticien*)
GPO	General Post Office (=*P et T*)
h & c	hot and cold (*chaud et froid*)
HM(S)	Her Majesty('s Service, Her Majesty's Ship) (*Le Service de Sa Majesté, Le Bateau de Sa Majesté*)
Hon.	Honorary (*Honoraire*); Honourable (*Honorable*)
hp	Horse-power (*cheval-vapeur*)
HQ	Headquarters (*quartier général*)
HRH	His (Her) Royal Highness (*Son Altesse Royale*)
I, Is	islands (*îles*)
ICBM	Inter-Continental Ballistic Missile (*missile intercontinental*)
i.e.	that is; namely (*L. id est*) (*c'est-à-dire*)

ILO	International Labour Organization (*Bureau international du travail*)
IMF	International Monetary Fund (*Fond monétaire international*)
in	inch(es) (*pouce(s)*)
Inc, Incorp	Incorporated (*incorporé*)
incl	included; including; inclusive (*ci-joint, ci-inclus*)
IOU	I owe you (*traite*)
IQ	Intelligence Quotient (*quotient intellectuel, coefficient de l'âge mental*)
JP	Justice of the Peace (*juge de paix*)
jr	junior (*cadet, subalterne*)
L	Latin (*latin*); law (*le Droit*)
l	lake (*lac*); left (*gauche*); lira (*lire*)
lb	pound (*livre (poids)*)
LLB	Bachelor of Law (*licencié en droit*)
LP	Long-Playing (record) (*longue durée*); Labour Party (*le parti travailliste*)
LSD	lysergic acid diethylamide (*stupéfiant*); (also £sd) pounds, shillings and pence (*monnaie anglaise*)
Ltd	Limited (*Limité*)
m	male (*mâle*); married (*marié*); meter (*mètre*); mile (*mille*) minute (*minute*); month (*mois*)
MA	Master of Arts (*Licencié ès Lettres*)
MB, ChB	Bachelor of Medicine (*docteur en médecine*); Bachelor of Surgery (*docteur en chirurgie*)
MC	Master of Ceremonies (*maître de cérémonies*); Member of Congress (*député*); Military Cross (*croix militaire*)
MD	Doctor of Medicine (*docteur en médecine, médecin*)
Messrs	the plural of Mr. (*le pluriel de M. (MM), employé avec le nom d'une maison commerciale ou en tête d'une liste de plusieurs noms*)
MI	Military Intelligence (*service du contre-espionnage*)
MP	Member of Parliament (*membre de la chambre des communes, député*); Military Police (*police militaire*); Metropolitan Police (*police métropolitain*)
mph	miles per hour (*milles à l'heure*)
Mr.	Mister (*monsieur*)
Mrs.	Mistress (*madame*)
Mt	mount (*mont*); mountain (*montagne*)
n	name (*nom*); noun (*nom*); neuter (*neutre*); noon (*midi*); nephew (*neveu*); born (*L. natus*) (*né*)
NAM	National Association of Manufacturers (*association nationale de fabricants*)
Nat	National (*national*); Nationalist (*nationaliste*)
NATO	North Atlantic Treaty Organization (*l'Organisation du traité de l'Atlantique Nord*)
NCO	Non-commissioned officer (*sous-officier*)
NHS	National Health Service (*service de santé nationale— sécurité sociale*)
no(s)	number(s) (*L. numero*) (*numéro(s)*)
NW	nord-west (*nord-ouest*)
NY	New York
NZ	New Zealand (*Nouvelle Zélande*)
OAS	Organization of American States (*Organisation d'etats américains*); (*Organisation de l'armée secrète*)
OK	all correct (*correct*); all right (*d'accord*)

495

OM	Order of Merit (*décoration civile accordée à certaines personnes en récompense de leur mérite particulier*)
PhD	Doctor of Philosophy (*docteur en philosophie*)
PM	Prime Minister (*premier ministre*); Past Master (*ancien maître*)
pm	afternoon (*L. post meridiem*) (*après-midi*); after death (*L. post mortem*) (*après décès*)
PO	Post office (*bureau de poste*)
POB	Post Office Box (*boîte postale*)
POW	Prisoner of War (*prisonnier de guerre*)
pp	on behalf of (*pour le compte de*); pages (*pages*)
Pres	President (*président*)
PRO	Public Relations Officer (*un agent de Public Relations*)
PTO	Please Turn Over (*tournez s'il vous plaît*)
QED	quod erat demonstrandum (*C.Q.F.D.*)
qt	quart (*quart de gallon*)
qv	which see (*L. quod vide*)
RA	Royal Academy (*académie royale*)
RAF	Royal Air Force (*forces aériennes royales*); Royal Air Factory (*camp de RAF*)
RC	Roman Catholic (*catholique romain*); Red Cross (*Croix-Rouge*)
regd	registered (*recommandé, enregistré, inscrit*)
Rep	Representative (*reps*); Republic (*république*); Republican (*républicain*); Repertory (*répertoire, compagnie en tournée ou compagnie provinciale*); Reporter (*journaliste, correspondant*)
Rev	Reverend (*révérend*); Revelations (*Apocalypse*)
RN	Registered nurse (*infirmière diplômée*)
Rt. Hon.	Right Honorable (*très honorable—titre accordé à un ministre ou ancien ministre du gouvernement britannique*)
s	second (*deuxième*); shilling (*shilling*); son (*fils*); singular (*singulier*); substantive (*substantif*); solubility (*solubilité*)
Sch	School (*école*)
Sec, Secy	Secretary (*secrétaire*)
SHAPE	Supreme Headquarters Allied Powers Europe (*Quartier général des alliés en Europe*
St	Saint (*saint*); Strait (*détroit*); street (*rue*)
SW	South-west (*sud-ouest*))
TB	Tuberculosis (*tuberculose*)
TNT	trinitrotoluene (explosive) (*explosif*)
TT	total abstainer (teetotal) (*abstinent, antialcoolique*)
TV	Television (*télévision, téléviseur*)
TWA	Trans World Airlines (*compagnie aérienne américaine*)
UK	United Kingdom (*royaume uni*)
UN(O)	United Nations (Organization) (*Organisation des Nations Unies*)
UNESCO	United Nations Educational, Scientific and Cultural Organization (*Organisation des Nations Unies pour l'Education, la Science et la Culture*) *qui s'occupe de l'éducation et de la vie scientifique et culturelle des pays sous-développés*)
UNICEF	UN International Children's Emergency Fund (*fonds spécial pour l'assistance des enfants réfugiés*)
US(A)	United States (of America) (*États-Unis*)
USAF	United States Air Force (*forces aériennes des États-Unis*)
USN	United States Navy (*la marine américaine*)
USSR	Union of Socialist Soviet Republics (*URSS*)

VD	Veneral Disease (*maladie venérienne*)
VHF	very high frequency (*très haute fréquence*)
VIP	(*fam*) very important person (*fam—personnage très important*)
viz	namely (*L. videlicet*) (*nommément*)
W	West (*ouest*); Western (*de l'ouest*)
wc	water closet (*W.C., toilet*)
WHO	World Health Organization (*Organisation mondiale de la santé*)
wk	week (*semaine*)
wp	weather permitting (*si le temps le permet*)
yd	yard(s) (*yard=approx. 1 mètre*)
YHA	Youth Hostels Association (*les Auberges de jeunesse*)
YMCA	Young Men's Christian Association (*association de jeunes chrétiens*)
yr	year (*an*); younger (*cadet*); your (*ton, votre*)
YWCA	Young Women's Christian Association (*association de jeunes chrétiennes*)

Abréviations Françaises

FRENCH ABBREVIATIONS

a.b.s.	aux bon soins de (*c/o*)
AC	Avant Christ (*before Christ*)
a.c.	argent comptant (*ready money*)
ACF	Automobile Club de France (*French automobile club*)
AEF	Afrique Equatoriale Française (*French Equatorial Africa*)
AF	Air France (*French airline company*)
AFP	Agence France Presse (*French Press Agency*)
AM	Assurance mutuelle (*mutual assurance*)
Amal	Amiral (*Admiral*)
anme	Anonyme (*limited liability company*)
AOF	Afrique Occidentale Française (*French West Africa*)
AP	Assistance publique (*public assistance*)
AR	Arrière (*rear*)
arr.	arrondissement (*district*)
AS	Assurance sociale (*social security*)
ASLV	Assurance sur la vie (*life assurance*)
asse	Assurance (*insurance*)
AT	Ancien Testament (*Old Testament*)
à t.p.	à tout prix (*at any cost*)
auj.	aujourd'hui (*today*)
av.	avenue (*avenue*)
AV	avant (*front*)
Bac	Baccalauréat (*certificate of secondary education*)
b à p	billet à payer (*bill payable*)
b à r	billet à recevoir (*bill receivable*)
bd	boulevard (*boulevard*)
BF	Banque de France (*Bank of France*)
Bib	Bible (*Bible*), Bibliothèque (*library*)
BIT	Bureau international du travail (*International Labor Office*)
BN	Bibliothèque Nationale (*national library*)
BO	Bulletin officiel (*official bulletin*)
BNP	Banque Nationale de Paris (*large banking house*)
BP	Boîte postale (*Post Office Box*)

BSGDC	Breveté sans garantie du gouvernement (*patent without government guarantee of quality*)
bté	breveté (*patented*)
ca	courant alternatif (*alternating current*)
c-à-d	c'est-à-dire (*that is*)
CAF	Coût, assurance, fret (*cost, insurance, freight*)
CAP	Certificat d'aptitude professionelle (*certificate of general proficiency in industry*)
	Certificat d'aptitude pédagogique (*teaching certificate*)
Cap.	capitaine (*captain*)
CAPES	Certificat d'aptitude au professorat de l'enseignement secondaire (*certificate for teaching in secondary schools*)
cc	courant continu (*direct current*)
c/c	compte courant (*current account*)
CCP	Compte chèques postaux (*Post Office Account*)
CD	Corps diplomatique (*Diplomatic Corps*)
CEE	Communauté économique européenne—Marché commun (*European Economic Community—Common Market*)
CEG	Collège d'enseignement général (*Secondary Modern School*)
CEI	Commission Electro-technique international (*International electro-technical commission*)
CEP	Certificat d'études primaires (*certificate for primary studies*)
CES	College d'enseignement secondaire (*Secondary School*)
CFDT	Confédération française démocratique de travail (*Catholic trade union—branch of CFTC*)
CFTC	Confédération française de travailleurs chrétiens (*union of Catholic workers*)
cg	centigramme (*centigram*)
CGC	Confédération générale des cadres (*communist white collar union*)
CGE	Compagnie générale d'électricité (*large electronics company*)
CGT	Confédération générale du travail (*communist trade union*)
ch-l	chef-lieu (=*county seat*)
CICR	Commission internationale de la Croix-Rouge (*International Commission of the Red Cross Organization*)
CM	Croix Militaire (*Military Cross*)
CNI	Centre National d'Information (*official government information department*)
CNRS	Centre national de la recherche scientifique (*national research board*)
CQFD	ce qu'il fallait démontré (*QED*)
CR	Croix-Rouge (*Red Cross*)
CRS	Compagnie républicaine de sécurité (*State Security Police*)
CT	Cabine téléphonique (*telephone booth*)
c.v.	cheval-vapeur (*horse-power*)
cv	chevaux (*horses*); curriculum vitae
d	diamètre (*diameter*)
DCA	Défense contre avions (*anti-aircraft defense*)
déb	débit (*debit*)
déc	décédé (*deceased*); décembre (*December*)
dép	département (*administrative department*)
DM	Docteur Médecin (*Doctor of Medicine*)
DP	défense passive (*civil defense*)

EC	École centrale (*Central School of Engineering at Paris*)
éd(it)	édition (*edition*)
ÉLO	École des langues orientales (*School of Oriental Languages*)
É-M	État-major (*headquarters*)
ÉNA	École nationale d'administration (*national administrative school*)
env	environ (*about*)
et Cie	et Compagnie (*and Company, & Co.*)
Éts	Établissements (*establishments*)
EV	en ville (*Post. local*)
ex	exemple (*example*)
exempl.	exemplaire (*copy*)
F	Franc : NF Nouveau France (*new franc*) AF Ancien Franc (*old franc*)
fàb	franco à bord (*free on board, fob*)
fab	fabrication (*make*)
FEN	Fédération de l'éducation nationale (*University teachers' union*); Fédération des étudiants nationalistes (*extreme right union of student*)
FFI	Forces françaises de l'intérieur (*internal security forces*)
FFLT	Fédération française de Lawn-Tennis (*French Lawn Tennis Federation*)
FGDS	Fédération de la gauche démocratique et socialiste (*left-wing political grouping*)
FIFA	Fédération Internationale de Football Association (*body governing international football*)
FLN	Front de libération nationale (*nationalist movement in Algerian War*)
FMI	Fond monétaire international (*International Monetary Fund*)
FO	Fédération ouvrière (*left-wing trade union*)
fo(l)	folio (*folio*)
FS	faire suivre (*please forward*)
g	gramme (*gram*)
GC	Grand-Croix (*Grand cross of Legion of Honour*)
GQG	Grand quartier général (*General Headquarters*)
h	heure (*hour*)
HC	hors concours (*not competing*); hors cadre (*not on the strength*)
HÉC	Hautes études commerciales (*business school*)
HLM	Habitations à loyer modéré (*accommodation at reasonable rents*)
hp	haute pression (*high pressure*)
HS	hors de service (*unfit for service*)
inéd	inédit (*unpublished*)
inf	infanterie (*infantry*); faites infuser (*infuse*)
in-f(o), infol	in-folio (*folio*)
IDHÉC	Institut des hautes études cinématographiques (*school for cinema-arts*)
in-pl	in plano (*broadsheet*)
JÉC	Jeunesse étudiante catholique (*catholic student association*)
JOC	Jeunesse ouvrière catholique (*young catholic workers*)
kil(o)	kilogramme (*kilogram*)
km/h	kilomètres par heure (*kilometers per hour*)
labo	laboratoire (*laboratory*)
l.c. or loc. cit.	L. loco citato (*at the place cited*)

499

liv(r)	livraison (*delivery*)
liv. st.	livre sterling (*pound sterling*)
M	Monsieur (*Mister, Mr.*)
MA	Moyen Age (*Middle Ages*)
Me	Maître (*Master—title given to some lawyers*)
Mgr	Monseigneur (*monsignor*)
Mlle	Mademoiselle (*miss*)
MM	Messieurs (*Messrs.*)
Mme	Madame (*Mistress, Mrs.*)
Mon	Maison (*Firm*)
M-P	Mandat-poste (*post-office order*)
MRP	Mouvement républicain populaire (*Catholic center party*)
n/c	notre compte (*our account*)
NDÉ	note de l'éditeur (*editor's note*)
négt	négotiant (*wholesaler*)
N du T	note du traducteur (*translator's note*)
NRF	Nouvelle Revue Française (*editions of Gallimard publishing house*)
O	à l'ordre de (*to the order of*)
OAS	Organisation de l'armée secrète (*extreme right army group during Algerian War*)
OCDE	Organisation de coopération et de développement économique (*Organization for Economic Co-operation and Development*)
OER	Officiers élèves de la réserve (*officer cadets*)
ONU	Organisation des Nations Unies (*United Nations Organization*)
ORTF	Office de radiodiffusion et télévision françaises (*national broadcasting body*)
OTAN	Organisation du traité de l'Atlantique Nord (*North Atlantic Treaty Organization*)
p	page (*page*); par (*per*); pour (*per*); poids (*weight*)
pass	passim (*in various places*)
P-B	Pays-Bas (*Netherlands*)
p/c	pour compte (*on account*)
PC	Parti communiste (*Communist Party*); poste de commandement (*command post*)
PCC	pour copie conforme (*true copy*)
PG	prisonnier de guerre (*prisoner of war*)
p.ex.	par exemple (*for example*)
p.g.	pour garder (*to be called for, poste restante*)
PJ	Police judiciaire
PMU	Pari mutuel urbain (*licensed betting shop*)
PN	passage à niveau (*level crossing*)
pp	port payé (*carriage paid*)
PSU	Parti socialiste unifié (*left-wing party formed in 1960*)
PSV	Pilotage sans visibilité (*automatic pilot*)
P et T	Postes et Télécommunications (*=GPO*)
PV	procès-verbal (*parking ticket, etc*)
QG	Quartier général (*headquarters*)
QM	Quotient mental (*intelligence quotient*)
qq	quelques (*some*); quelqu'un (*someone*)
qqf	quelquefois (*sometimes*)
r	rue (*road, street*); recommandé (*registered*)
RATP	Régie autonome des transports parisiens (*body which runs Paris transport*)
RAU	République Arabe Unie (*United Arab Republic*)
RDF	Rassemblement démocratique français (*political grouping of center parties*)

rd-vs	rendez-vous (*meeting place*)
rel	relié (*bound*)
Rép	République (*republic*)
RF	République française (*French Republic*)
le RP	le Révérend père (*the Reverend Father*)
RSVP	Répondez s'il vous plaît (*please reply*);
SA	Son Altesse (*His (Her) Highness*);
	Société anonyme (*limited company*)
SAR	Son Altesse Royale (*His (Her) Royal Highness*)
SARL	Société anonyme à responsabilité limitée (*limited liability company*)
s/c	son compte (*his account*);
	sous le couvert (*under (plain) cover*)
SE	Son Excellence (*His (Her) Excellency*);
	Son Eminence (*His Eminence*)
sept	Septentrional (*northern*)
SFIO	Section française de l'Internationale ouvrière (*French Socialist party*)
SI	Syndicat d'initiative (*tourist information bureau*)
slnd	sans lieu ni date (*of no place and no date*)
SM	Sa Majesté (*His (Her) Majesty*)
SMAG	Salaire minimum agricole garanti (*minimum agricultural wage*)
SMIG	Salaire minimum interprofessionnel garanti (*guaranteed minimum wage*)
SNCF	Société nationale des chemins de fer français (*French government railways*)
SNES	Syndicat national de l'enseignement secondaire (*teachers' union*)
SS	Sécurité sociale (*social security*);
	Sa Sainteté (*His Holiness*)
Sté	Société (*society*)
suiv.	suivant (*following*)
svp	s'il vous plaît (*please*)
tàv	tout à vous (*ever yours*)
TEP	Théâtre de l'Est Parisien (*Parisian theater*)
TNP	Théâtre national populaire (*Parisian theater company*)
t-p	timbre-poste (*stamp*)
tpm	tours par minute (*revolutions per minute*)
TSF	télégraphie sans fil (*wireless telegraphy*)
TSVP	tournez s'il vous plaît (*please turn over*)
TVA	taxe à la valeur ajoutée (*sales tax*)
UD	Union démocratique (*political grouping*)
UFF	Union familiale française (*Family association*)
UNAF	Union nationale des associations familiales (*Family association*)
UNEF	Union nationale des etudiants de France (*left-wing union of students*)
UNR	Union pour la Nouvelle République (*Gaullist political party*)
UP	Union postale (*Postal Union*)
URSS	Union de Républiques Socialistes Soviétiques (*USSR*)
UTA	Union de transports aériens (*united transport airline*)
v/c	votre compte (*your account*)
V-C	Vice-Consul (*Vice Consul*)
vo	verso (*back of page*)
Vte	Vicomte (*Viscount*)
WL	Wagons-lits (*sleeping cars*)
WR	Wagons-restaurants (*dining cars*)
XP	Exprès payé (*express paid*)